S0-AFD-947

ANDERSON'S
Law School Publications

Administrative Law Anthology
Thomas O. Sargentich

Administrative Law: Cases and Materials
Daniel J. Gifford

An Admiralty Law Anthology
Robert M. Jarvis

Alternative Dispute Resolution: Strategies for Law and Business
E. Wendy Trachte-Huber and Stephen K. Huber

The American Constitutional Order: History, Cases, and Philosophy
Douglas W. Kmiec and Stephen B. Presser

American Legal Systems: A Resource and Reference Guide
Toni M. Fine

Analytic Jurisprudence Anthology
Anthony D'Amato

An Antitrust Anthology
Andrew I. Gavil

Appellate Advocacy: Principles and Practice, *Third Edition*
Ursula Bentele and Eve Cary

Arbitration: Cases and Materials
Stephen K. Huber and E. Wendy Trachte-Huber

Basic Accounting Principles for Lawyers: With Present Value and Expected Value
C. Steven Bradford and Gary A. Ames

Basic Themes in Law and Jurisprudence
Charles W. Collier

The Best-Kept Secrets of Evidence Law: 101 Principles, Practices, and Pitfalls
Paul R. Rice

A Capital Punishment Anthology (and Electronic Caselaw Appendix)
Victor L. Streib

Cases and Materials in Juvenile Law
J. Eric Smithburn

Cases and Materials on Corporations
Thomas R. Hurst and William A. Gregory

Cases and Materials on the Law Governing Lawyers
James E. Moliterno

Cases and Problems in California Criminal Law
Myron Moskovitz

Cases and Problems in Criminal Law, *Fourth Edition*
Myron Moskovitz

The Citation Workbook: How to Beat the Citation Blues, *Second Edition*
Maria L. Ciampi, Rivka Widerman, and Vicki Lutz

Civil Procedure Anthology
David I. Levine, Donald L. Doernberg, and Melissa L. Nelken

Civil Procedure: Cases, Materials, and Questions, *Third Edition*
Richard D. Freer and Wendy Collins Perdue

Civil Procedure for Federal and State Courts
Jeffrey A. Parness

Clinical Anthology: Readings for Live-Client Clinics
Alex J. Hurder, Frank S. Bloch, Susan L. Brooks, and Susan L. Kay

Commercial Transactions Series: Problems and Materials
Louis F. Del Duca, Egon Guttman, Alphonse M. Squillante, Fred H. Miller, Linda Rusch, and Peter Winship
Vol. 1: Secured Transactions Under the UCC
Vol. 2: Sales Under the UCC and the CISG
Vol. 3: Negotiable Instruments Under the UCC and the CIBN

Communications Law: Media, Entertainment, and Regulation
Donald E. Lively, Allen S. Hammond, Blake D. Morant, and Russell L. Weaver

A Conflict-of-Laws Anthology
Gene R. Shreve

Constitutional Conflicts
Derrick A. Bell, Jr.

A Constitutional Law Anthology, *Second Edition*
Michael J. Glennon, Donald E. Lively, Phoebe A. Haddon, Dorothy E. Roberts, and Russell L. Weaver

Constitutional Law: Cases, History, and Dialogues, *Second Edition*
Donald E. Lively, Phoebe A. Haddon, Dorothy E. Roberts, Russell L. Weaver, and William D. Araiza

The Constitutional Law of the European Union
James D. Dinnage and John F. Murphy

The Constitutional Law of the European Union: Documentary Supplement
James D. Dinnage and John F. Murphy

Constitutional Torts
Sheldon H. Nahmod, Michael L. Wells, and Thomas A. Eaton

A Contracts Anthology, *Second Edition*
Peter Linzer

Contract Law and Practice
Gerald E. Berendt, Michael L. Closen, Doris Estelle Long, Marie A. Monahan, Robert J. Nye, and John H. Scheid

Contracts: Contemporary Cases, Comments, and Problems
Michael L. Closen, Richard M. Perlmutter, and Jeffrey D. Wittenberg

A Copyright Anthology: The Technology Frontier
Richard H. Chused

Corporate Law Anthology
Franklin A. Gevurtz

Corporate and White Collar Crime: An Anthology
Leonard Orland

Criminal Law: Cases and Materials, *Second Edition*
Arnold H. Loewy

A Criminal Procedure Anthology
Silas J. Wasserstrom and Christie L. Snyder

Criminal Procedure: Arrest and Investigation
Arnold H. Loewy and Arthur B. LaFrance

Criminal Procedure: Trial and Sentencing
Arthur B. LaFrance and Arnold H. Loewy

Economic Regulation: Cases and Materials
Richard J. Pierce, Jr.

Elder Law: Readings, Cases, and Materials
Thomas P. Gallanis, A. Kimberley Dayton, and Molly M. Wood

Elder Law: Statutes and Regulations
Thomas P. Gallanis, A. Kimberley Dayton, and Molly M. Wood

Elements of Law
Eva H. Hanks, Michael E. Herz, and Steven S. Nemerson

Ending It: Dispute Resolution in America
Descriptions, Examples, Cases and Questions
Susan M. Leeson and Bryan M. Johnston

An Environmental Law Anthology
Robert L. Fischman, Maxine I. Lipeles, and Mark S. Squillace

Environmental Law Series
Environmental Decisionmaking, *Third Edition*
Robert L. Fischman and Mark S. Squillace

Water Pollution, *Third Edition*
Jackson B. Battle and Maxine I. Lipeles

Air Pollution, *Third Edition*
Mark S. Squillace and David R. Wooley

Hazardous Waste, *Third Edition*
Maxine I. Lipeles

Environmental Protection and Justice
Readings and Commentary on Environmental Law and Practice, *Second Edition*
Kenneth A. Manaster

European Union Law Anthology
Karen V. Kole and Anthony D'Amato

An Evidence Anthology
Edward J. Imwinkelried and Glen Weissenberger

Family Law in Action: A Reader
Margaret F. Brinig, Carl E. Schneider, and Lee E. Teitelbaum

Federal Antitrust Law: Cases and Materials
Daniel J. Gifford and Leo J. Raskind

Federal Income Tax Anthology
Paul L. Caron, Karen C. Burke, and Grayson M.P. McCouch

Federal Rules of Civil Procedure
Publisher's Staff

Federal Rules of Evidence Handbook
Publisher's Staff

Federal Rules of Evidence: Rules, Legislative History, Commentary and Authority
Glen Weissenberger and James J. Duane

Federal and State Civil Procedure Handbook, *Second Edition*
Jeffrey A. Parness

Federal Wealth Transfer Tax Anthology
Paul L. Caron, Grayson M.P. McCouch, Karen C. Burke

First Amendment Anthology
Donald E. Lively, Dorothy E. Roberts, and Russell L. Weaver

The History, Philosophy, and Structure of the American Constitution
Douglas W. Kmiec and Stephen B. Presser

Individual Rights and the American Constitution
Douglas W. Kmiec and Stephen B. Presser

International Environmental Law Anthology
Anthony D'Amato and Kirsten Engel

International Human Rights: Law, Policy, and Process, *Third Edition*
David Weissbrodt, Joan Fitzpatrick, and Frank Newman

Selected International Human Rights Instruments and Bibliography for Research on International Human Rights Law, *Third Edition*
David Weissbrodt, Joan Fitzpatrick, Frank Newman, Marci Hoffman, and Mary Rumsey

International Intellectual Property Anthology
Anthony D'Amato and Doris Estelle Long

International Law Anthology
Anthony D'Amato

International Taxation: Cases, Materials, and Problems
Philip F. Postlewaite

Introduction to the Study of Law: Cases and Materials, *Second Edition*
John Makdisi

Judicial Externships: The Clinic Inside the Courthouse, *Second Edition*
Rebecca A. Cochran

A Land Use Anthology
Jon W. Bruce

Law and Economics Anthology
Kenneth G. Dau-Schmidt and Thomas S. Ulen

The Law of Disability Discrimination, *Third Edition*
Ruth Colker and Bonnie Poitras Tucker

The Law of Disability Discrimination Handbook: Statutes and Regulatory Guidance *Third Edition*
Ruth Colker and Bonnie Poitras Tucker

Lawyers and Fundamental Moral Responsibility
Daniel R. Coquillette

Mediation and Negotiation: Reaching Agreement in Law and Business
E. Wendy Trachte-Huber and Stephen K. Huber

Microeconomic Predicates to Law and Economics
Mark Seidenfeld

Natural Resources: Cases and Materials
Barlow Burke

Patients, Psychiatrists and Lawyers: Law and the Mental Health System, *Second Edition*
Raymond L. Spring, Roy B. Lacoursiere, and Glen Weissenberger

Preventive Law: Materials on a Non Adversarial Legal Process
Robert M. Hardaway

Principles of Evidence, *Fourth Edition*
Irving Younger, Michael Goldsmith, and David A. Sonenshein

Problems and Simulations in Evidence, *Second Edition*
Thomas F. Guernsey

A Products Liability Anthology
Anita Bernstein

Professional Responsibility Anthology
Thomas B. Metzloff

A Property Anthology, *Second Edition*
Richard H. Chused

Property Law: Cases, Materials, and Questions
Edward E. Chase

Public Choice and Public Law: Readings and Commentary
Maxwell L. Stearns

The Question Presented: Model Appellate Briefs
Maria L. Ciampi and William H. Manz

Readings in Criminal Law
Russell L. Weaver, John M. Burkoff, Catherine Hancock, Alan Reed, and Peter J. Seago

Science in Evidence
D.H. Kaye

A Section 1983 Civil Rights Anthology
Sheldon H. Nahmod

Sports Law: Cases and Materials, *Fourth Edition*
Ray L. Yasser, James R. McCurdy, C. Peter Goplerud, and Maureen A. Weston

State and Local Government Law: A Transactional Approach
John Martinez and Michael E. Libonati

A Torts Anthology, *Second Edition*
Julie A. Davies, Lawrence C. Levine, and Edward J. Kionka

Trial Practice
Lawrence A. Dubin and Thomas F. Guernsey

Understanding Negotiation
Melissa L. Nelken

Unincorporated Business Entities, *Second Edition*
Larry E. Ribstein

FORTHCOMING PUBLICATIONS

First Amendment Law: Cases, Comparative Perspectives, and Dialogues
Donald E. Lively, William D. Araiza, Phoebe A. Haddon, John C. Knechtle, and Dorothy E. Roberts

The Lawyer's Craft: An Introduction to Legal Reasoning, Writing, Research, and Advocacy
Cathy Glaser, Jethro K. Lieberman, Robert A. Ruescher, and Lynn Boepple Sue

CASES AND MATERIALS IN JUVENILE LAW

CASES AND MATERIALS IN JUVENILE LAW

J. ERIC SMITHBURN

Professor of Law
Notre Dame Law School

ANDERSON PUBLISHING CO.
CINCINNATI, OHIO

NOTE TO USERS

To ensure that you are using the latest materials available in this area, please be sure to periodically check Anderson Publishing's web site for downloadable updates and supplements at www.andersonpublishing.com

CASES AND MATERIALS IN JUVENILE LAW
J. ERIC SMITHBURN

Anderson Publishing Co.
2035 Reading Road / Cincinnati, Ohio 45202
800-582-7295 / e-mail lawschool@andersonpublishing.com / Fax 513-562-5430
www.andersonpublishing.com

ISBN: 0-87084-318-4

Dedication

Dedicated to child welfare caseworkers and probation officers everywhere.

Table of Contents

Preface xxv
Foreword xxvii
Table of Cases xxix
Table of Statutes and Rules xlix

CHAPTER 1: History and Philosophy of the Juvenile Justice System 1
A. Children in Criminal Court 1
1. England 1
2. United States 2
B. The Reform Movement 4
1. England 4
2. United States 5
Ex Parte Crouse (Pa. 1839) 6
People ex rel. O'Connell v. Turner (Ill. 1870) 8
C. Rise of the Juvenile Court 11
1. Doctrine of *Parens Patriae* 11
2. Philosophy of a Separate Juvenile Court 13
3. The Illinois Juvenile Court Act of 1899 15
Illinois Juvenile Court Act of 1899 16

CHAPTER 2: Juvenile Delinquency: The Child as Respondent 23
A. Jurisdiction 24
California Welfare and Institutions Code §§ 601-602 (West Supp. 2001) 24
B. Substantive Requirements 24
1. Status Offenses 24
a. Sample Status Offense Statute 24
Georgia Code Annotated §§ 15-11-2(11) & 2(12) (Lexis Supp. 2000) 24
b. Runaway 25
In re Darlene C. (S.C. 1983) 25
c. Incorrigibility 28
In re Welfare of Snyder (Wash.1975) 28

d. Curfew 31
Qutb v. Strauss (5th Cir. 1993) 31
e. Truancy 37
In re E.B. (N.D. 1980) 37
2. Crime Delinquency 42
a. Sample Delinquency Statute 42
New Jersey Statutes Annotated § 2A:4A-23 (West Supp. 2001) 42
b. Civil Label 42
K.M.S. v. State (Ga. Ct. App. 1973) 42
c. Defenses 45
(1) Infancy 45
In re Robert M. (N.Y. Fam. Ct. 1981) 45
(2) Insanity 49
Commonwealth v. Chatman (Va. 2000) 49
3. Street Gangs 53
a. Sample Street Gang Statute 53
Texas Penal Code Annotated § 71.02 (West Supp. 2001) 53
b. Cases 53
In re Alberto R. (Cal. Ct. App. 1991) 53
People ex rel. Gallo v. Acuna (Cal. Ct. App. 1977) 58
4. Excluded Offenses 63
California Welfare and Institutions Code § 603.5 (West Supp. 2001) 63

CHAPTER 3: Delinquency Intake Process 65
A. IJA-ABA Standards On Intake 65
IJA-ABA Standards Relating to the Juvenile Probation Function: Intake and Predisposition Investigative Services, Juvenile Justice Standards Annotated 155, 161-64 (Robert E. Shepherd, Jr., ed., 1996) 65
B. Arrest 70
1. IJA-ABA Standards on Arrest
IJA-ABA Standards Relating to Police Handling of Juvenile Problems, Juvenile Justice Standards Annotated 233, 235-36 (Robert E. Shepherd, Jr., ed., 1996) 70
IJA-ABA Standards Relating to Interim Status: The Release, Control and Detention of Accused Juvenile Offenders Between Arrest and Disposition, Juvenile Justice Standards Annotated 119, 133-34 (Robert E. Shepherd, Jr., ed., 1996) 71
2. Search and Seizure 72
State v. Lowry (N.J. Super. Ct. 1967) 72

C. Detention 78
Schall v. Martin (U.S. 1984) 78
IJA-ABA Standards Relating to Interim Status: The Release, Control and Detention of Accused Juvenile Offenders Between Arrest and Disposition, Juvenile Justice Standards Annotated 119-21, 123-34 (Robert E. Shepherd, Jr., ed., 1996) 89
D. Investigation and Interrogation 91
Fare v. Michael C. (U.S. 1979) 93
E. Diversion 105
State v. Quiroz (Wash. 1987) 105
IJA-ABA Standards Relating to Youth Service Agencies, Juvenile Justice Standards Annotated 293, 293-97 (Robert E. Shepherd, Jr., ed., 1996) 108
F. Charging the Juvenile: Prosecutorial Discretion 111
State v. McDowell (Wash. 1984) 111
G. Interface with Child Welfare Proceedings 115
Burns Indiana Statutes Annotated §§ 31-33-13-5, 31-33-14-1, 31-33-14-2, 31-33-18-2, 31-39-2-5, 31-39-2-6, 31-39-2-9, 31-39-4-6 & 31-39-4-7 (Michie 2000) 115

CHAPTER 4: Children's Rights in Public Schools 117
A. First Amendment Freedoms 117
1. Speech 117
Tinker v. Des Moines Independent Community School District (U.S. 1969) 117
2. Religion 126
School District of Abington Township Pennsylvania v. Schempp (U.S. 1963) 126
B. School Suspension 135
Goss v. Lopez (U.S. 1975) 135
C. Corporal Punishment 143
Ingraham v. Wright (U.S. 1977) 143
D. Fourth Amendment: Search and Seizure 153
New Jersey v. T.L.O. (U.S. 1985) 153
Isiah B. v. State (Wis. 1993) 158
Vernonia School District 47J v. Acton (U.S. 1995) 161

CHAPTER 5: The Waiver Decision: Whether to Charge the Juvenile as an Adult 173
A. Due Process and the Waiver Hearing 174
Kent v. United States (U.S. 1966) 174
Standards Relating to Transfer Between Courts, Juvenile Justice Standards Annotated 285, 285-92 (Robert E. Sheperd, Jr., ed. 1996) 184

B. Criteria for Waiver of Juvenile Court Jurisdiction 187
Connecticut General Statutes Annotated § 46b-127 (West Supp. 2001) 187
United States v. K.J.C. (N.D. Iowa 1997) 187
C. Reverse Waiver 197
State v. Verhagen (Wis. Ct. App. 1995) 197

CHAPTER 6: Adjudication in Delinquency Proceedings 205
A. Competency of Juvenile to Stand Trial 205
In re Carey (Mich. Ct. App. 2000) 205
B. The Adjudication Hearing 212
1. Due Process Framework 212
In re Gault (U.S. 1967) 212
2. Burden of Proof 232
In re Winship (U.S. 1970) 232
3. Jury Trial 238
McKeiver v. Pennsylvania (U.S. 1971) 238
4. Public Trial 244
IJA-ABA Standards Relating to Adjudication, Juvenile Justice Standards Annotated 1, 11-12 (Robert E. Shepherd, Jr., ed. 1996) 244
Alabama Code § 12-15-65 (Lexis Supp. 2000) 245
In re Jesse McM. (Cal. Ct. App. 1980) 245
5. Speedy Trial 248
In re C.T.F. (Iowa 1982) 248
6. Double Jeopardy 253
Breed v. Jones (U.S. 1975) 253
7. Sealing and Expungement of Juvenile Records 260
Kentucky Bar Association v. Guidugli (Ky. 1998) 260
Doe v. United States (S.D. Cal. 1997) 262

CHAPTER 7: Dispositions in Delinquency Proceedings 267
A. Treatment and Rehabilitation 268
1. Right to Treatment 268
Martarella v. Kelley (S.D.N.Y. 1972) 268
Whatever Happened to the Right to Treatment?: The Modern Quest for a Historical Promise, Paul Holland & Wallace J. Mlyniec, 68 Temp. L. Rev. 1791 (1995) 270
2. Least Restrictive Alternative 278
State ex rel. R.S. v. Trent (W. Va 1982) 278
3. Use of Predispositional Reports 282

In re B.B. (Fla. Dis. Ct. App. 1994) 282
In re Pima County Delinquency Action No. 90101-1 (Ariz. Ct. App. 1987) 283
B. Probation: Conditions and Challenges 285
1. Restitution 285
P.R. v. State (Ga. Ct. App. 1974) 285
2. Community Service 289
M.J.W. v. State (Ga. Ct. App. 1974) 289
3. Curfew 292
In re Rodriguez (Tex. App. 1985) 292
4. Association 294
In re Babak S. (Cal. Ct. App. 1993) 294
5. Home Supervision 300
In re Curtis T. (Cal. Ct. App 1989) 300
6. Drug Testing 305
In re Kacy S. (Cal. Ct. App. 1998) 305
7. Church Attendance 310
L.M. v. State (Fla. Dist. Ct. App. 1992) 310
8. Restrictions on Travel 316
In re Pedro Q. (Cal. Ct. App. 1989) 316
9. Implied Conditions 319
In re Litdell (Miss. 1970) 319
C. Movement of Juveniles Across State Lines 321
Interstate Compact on Juveniles 321
D. Institutional Confinement 327
1. Deterrence 327
Scott L. v. State (Nev. 1988) 327
2. Protection of Society 330
In re Michael D. (Cal. Ct. App. 1987) 330
3. Punishment 333
Scott L. v. State (Nev. 1988) 333
4. No Confinement for Status Offenders 336
In re Ellery C. (N.Y. 1973) 336
5. Education Rights of Incarcerated Juveniles 338
Tunstall ex rel. Tunstall v. Bergeson (Wash. 2000) 338
E. Community Based Programs 345
State v. J.D.G. (Wash. Ct. App. 1997) 345
In re Groves (N.C. App. 1989) 347
F. Blended Sentencing 351
In re L.J.S. (Minn. Ct. App. 1995) 352
G. Death Penalty for Children 356
Thompson v. Oklahoma (U.S. 1988) 356
Stanford v. Kentucky (U.S. 1989) 365

CHAPTER 8: Dependency, Abuse, and Neglect: The Child as Victim 377
A. Jurisdiction—General 378
Idaho Code § 16-1603 (Michie 2001) 378
B. Duty to Report 379
Florida Statues Annotated § 39.201 (West Supp. 2001) 379
State v. Snell (N.J. Super. Ct. App. Div. 1998) 380
C. Substantive Requirements 385
1. Dependency 385
General Statutes of North Carolina § 7B-101(9) (Lexis 1999) 385
In re Tikyra A. (Ohio Ct. App. 1995) 386
2. Abuse—Generally 389
General Statutes of North Carolina § 7B-101(1) (Lexis 1999) 389
a. Physical Abuse 390
Utah Code Annotated § 76-5-109 (Lexis Supp. 2000) 390
In re Ethan H. (N.H. 1992) 391
Hawaii v. Kaimimoku (Haw. Ct. App. 1992) 394
b. Sexual Abuse 399
West Virginia Code § 49-1-3 (Lexis 1999) 399
Alaska v. Jackson (Alaska Ct. App. 1989) 400
c. Mental Abuse 406
23 Pennsylvania Consolidated Statutes Annotated § 6303 (West Supp. 2001) 406
T.S. v. Department of Health and Rehabilitative Services (Fla. Dist. Ct. App. 1995) 407
d. Fetal Abuse 410
State ex rel. Angela M.W. v. Kruzicki (Wis. 1997) 410
3. Neglect 420
General Statutes of North Carolina § 7B-101(15) (Lexis 1999) 420
a. Nutritional Neglect 420
In re Mendez (Or. Ct. App. 1999) 420
b. Housing Neglect 425
In re E.R. (Neb. 1988) 425
c. Medical Neglect 428
In re E.G. (Ill. 1989) 428
d. Educational Neglect 434
In re B.A.B. (Minn. Ct. App. 1998) 434
e. Lack of Supervision 437
In re Zeiser (Ohio Ct. App. 1999) 437
f. Domestic Violence 443

Delaware Code Annotated tit. 13, § 705A (Michie Supp. 2000) 443
In re Lonell J. (N.Y. App. Div. 1998) 444

CHAPTER 9: The Child's Right to State Protection 449
A. Constitutional Protections: Parental Authority and Family Privacy 450
Meyer v. Nebraska (U.S. 1923) 450
Pierce v. Society of Sisters (U.S. 1925) 452
B. Compelling State Interest of Child Protection 454
1. Intervention in Family Life 454
Prince v. Massachusetts (U.S. 1944) 454
2. Removal of Child from Home 458
In the Matter of the Appeal in Cochise County Juvenile Action No. 5666-J (Ariz. 1982) 458
C. Duty of State to Protect Child 462
DeShaney v. Winnebago Department of Social Services (U.S. 1989) 462
Nicini v. Morra (3d Cir. 2000) 468

CHAPTER 10: The Child Welfare Process 477
A. Emergency Removal of Children 479
1. Due Process 479
Tenenbaum v. Williams (2d Cir. 1999) 479
2. Detention Hearing 487
Washington Revised Code Annotated § 13.40.050 (West Supp. 2001) 487
3. Reasonable Efforts to Reunify 488
Title I—Reasonable Efforts And Safety Requirements for Foster Care and Adoption Placements 489
B. Initial Hearing 492
1. Superseding Public Law Jurisdiction 492
Alexander v. Cole (Ind. Ct. App. 1980) 492
2. Due Process Framework 495
Arizona Revised Statutes Annotated § 8-843 (West Supp. 2000) 495
In re E.P. (Ind. Ct. App. 1995) 496
New Mexico v. Lili L. (N.M. Ct. App. 1995) 500
C. Factfinding Hearing 506
Wisconsin Statutes Annotated § 48.31 (West Supp. 2000) 506
1. Burden of Proof 507
In re N.H. (D.C. 1990) 507
2. Need for Coercive Court Intervention 511
Indiana Code Annotated § 31-34-1-1 (Lexis 1997) 511

In re Juvenile Appeal (83-CD) (Conn. 1983) 511

D. Permanency Hearings 515

1. Permanency Plan 515

Iowa Code Annotated § 232.104 (West Supp. 2001) 515

Adoption and Safe Families Act (1997), 42 U.S.C. § 675(5)(C) (West Supp. 2001) 516

In re Scott Y. (Wis. Ct. App. 1993) 517

2. Reunification Services 520

In re Angel N. (N.H. 1996) 520

In re Joshua H. (Cal. Ct. App. 1993) 523

3. Reunification Versus Child Protection 529

In re Edward C. (Cal. Ct. App. 1981) 529

E. Dispositional Orders 534

1. Child Placement—Interstate Dimension 534

Interstate Compact on the Placement of Children (1961) 534

In re Adoption of A.M.M. (Kan. Ct. App. 1997) 537

2. Visitation 543

Troxel v. Granville (U.S. 2000) 543

F. Post-Disposition Proceedings 555

1. Court's Use of Contempt Power 555

Baltimore Department of Social Services v. Bouknight (U.S. 1990) 555

2. Protective Orders 562

California Welfare and Institutions Code § 213.5(a) (West Supp. 2001) 562

3. Administrative Review Process 563

Ohio Revised Code Annotated § 2151.416 (Anderson Supp. 2000) 563

G. Native American Children: The Indian Child Welfare Act 565

House of Representatives Report No. 95-1386 (1978 U.S.C.C.A.N. 7530) 565

The Indian Child Welfare Act, Subchapter I—Child Custody Proceedings, 25 U.S.C.A. §§ 1911 et seq. (West Supp. 2000) 568

Mississippi Band of Choctaw Indians v. Holyfield (U.S. 1989) 573

CHAPTER 11: Special Advocacy for Children 583

A. The Child's Legal Status in Child Protection Proceedings 584

1. Party Status 584

Indiana Code Annotated § 31-34-9-7 (Lexis 1997) 584

2. Standing 584
Kingsley v. Kingsley (Fla. Dist. Ct. App. 1993) 584
In re Pima County Juvenile Severance Action No. S-113432 (Ariz. Ct. App. 1993) 586
B. Nature of Special Advocacy for Children 590
1. Role of Special Advocate 590
Alaska Code § 25.24.310 (Lexis 2000) 590
New Mexico ex rel. Children, Youth and Families Department v. George F. (N.M. Ct. App. 1998) 590
2. Child Protection Proceedings 596
In re Esperanza M. (N.M. Ct. App. 1998) 596
3. Termination of Parental Rights Proceedings 602
Mississippi Code Annotated § 93-15-107(1) (Lexis Supp. 2000) 602
Stanley v. Fairfax County Department of Social Services (Va. 1991) 602
C. Immunity and Liability of Special Advocates 606
Kansas Supreme Court Rule 110 606
Louisiana Revised Statutes Annotated, Children's Code § 424.10 (West Supp. 2001) 607
Tara M. v. City of Philadelphia (3d Cir. 1998) 608

CHAPTER 12: The Special Role of Foster Parents 613
A. Standing 614
Maine Revised Statutes Annotated title 22, § 4005-A (West Supp. 2000) 614
Rhode Island General Laws § 14-1-30.2 (Lexis 2000) 614
Worrell v. Elkhart County Office of Family and Children (Ind. 1998) 615
In re Michael Ray T. (W. Va. 1999) 616
B. Rights of Foster Parents 622
20 Illinois Compiled Statutes Annotated § 520/1-15 (West Supp. 2001) 622
Smith v. Organization of Foster Families (U.S. 1977) 624
C. Authority of Foster Parents 632
J.M.A. v. State (Alaska 1975) 632
D. Adoption By Foster Parents 636
C.S. v. S.H. (Fla. Dist. Ct. App. 1996) 636
E. Foster Parent Liability 645
1. Liability to the Foster Child 645
Washington Revised Code Annotated § 4.24.590 (West Supp. 2001) 645
Mayberry v. Pryor (Mich. 1985) 645
2. Liability to Third Parties 650

Missouri Annotated Statutes § 537.045 (West 2000) 650
Kerins v. Lima (Mass. 1997) 651

CHAPTER 13: Medical and Psychological Issues 655
A. Medical Issues 657
1. Maternal Deprivation Syndrome (Failure to Thrive) 657
In re Riffe (Mich. Ct. App. 1985) 657
2. Shaken Baby Syndrome 663
People v. Ripley (Ill. App. Ct. 1997) 663
3. The Cocaine Baby 668
In re Valerie D. (Conn. 1992) 668
4. Fetal Alcohol Syndrome 675
Adoption of Oliver (Mass. App. Ct. 1990) 675
5. Battered Child Syndrome 681
State v. Tanner (Utah 1983) 681
B. Psychological Evidence 689
1. Child Sexual Abuse Accommodation Syndrome 689
State v. J.Q. (N.J. 1993) 689
2. Anatomically Correct Dolls 699
In re Amber B. (Cal. Ct. App. 1987) 699
3. Battering Parent Syndrome 707
Sanders v. State (Ga. 1983) 707
4. Munchausen Syndrome by Proxy 711
In re Jessica Z. (N.Y. Fam. Ct. 1987) 711
5. Parent Alienation Syndrome 721
Karen B. v. Clyde M. (N.Y. Fam. Ct. 1991) 721

CHAPTER 14: Termination of Parental Rights 729
A. Substantive Due Process Rights—Parents 731
Meyer v. Nebraska (U.S. 1923) 731
Pierce v. Society of Sisters (U.S. 1925) 731
Prince v. Massachusetts (U.S. 1944) 731
Stanley v. Illinois (U.S. 1972) 731
B. Procedural Due Process 736
1. Notice and Hearing 736
a. Basic Requirements 736
Delaware Code Annotated tit. 13, § 1107 (Michie Supp. 2000) 736
b. The Incarcerated Parent 740
California Penal Code § 2625 (West Supp. 2001) 740
In re Ruth Anne E. (N.M. Ct. App. 1999) 741
2. Right to Counsel 747
Georgia Code Annotated § 17-12-38.1 (Lexis 1997) 747

Lassiter v. Department of Social Services of Durham County, North Carolina (U.S. 1981) 748
3. Exclusion of Public 756
Arizona Revised Statutes Annotated § 8-537(A) (West Supp. 2000) 756
4. Burden of Proof 756
Santosky v. Kramer (U.S. 1982) 756
Arizona Revised Statutes Annotated § 8-537(B) (West Supp. 2000) 762
The Indian Child Welfare Act, Subchapter I—Child Custody Proceedings, 25 U.S.C.A. § 1912(f) (West 2000) 763
In re D.S.P. (Wis. 1992) 763
5. Confrontation 768
In Interest of M.S. et al. (Ga. Ct. App. 1986) 768
In re E.D. (Utah Ct. App. 1994) 770

C. Grounds for Termination 776
1. Basic Requirements 776
Montana Code Annotated § 41-3-609 (1999) 776
a. Best Interests of the Child 778
In re Justin T. (Me. 1994) 778
b. Reconciling Child's Best Interests and Parents' Rights 782
In re Dallas M. (Wis. Ct. App. 1998) 782
2. Special Grounds 787
a. Mother's Prenatal Conduct 787
Adoption of Oliver (Mass. App. Ct. 1990) 787
In re Valerie D. (Conn. 1991) 787
b. Mental Status of Parents 790
In re Welfare of P.J.K. (Minn. 1985) 790
c. Incarceration of Parent 797
Florida Statutes Annotated § 39.806(1)(d) (West Supp. 2001) 797
In the Matter of the Adoption of C.A.W. (Pa. Super. Ct. 1996) 797
d. Terminal Illness of Parent 804
Micah Alyn R. (W. Va. 1998) 804

D. Application of Americans with Disabilities Act 813
In re B.S. (Vt. 1997) 813

E. Application of Uniform Child Custody Jurisdiction Act 818
In re M.C.S. (S.D. 1993) 818
Uniform Child-Custody Jurisdiction and Enforcement Act §§ 201-201, 206-207 9 U.L.A. 671 (1997) 822

F. Who May File Termination Petitions 826
23 Pennsylvania Consolidated Statutes Annotated § 2512 (West Supp. 2001) 826
Kingsley v. Kingsley (Fla. Dist. Ct. App. 1993) 827
In re Pima County Juvenile Severance, Action No. S-113432 (Ariz. Ct. App. 1993) 827
G. Termination of Parental Rights and Adoption 827
1. Adoption and Safe Families Act (1997) 827
The Adoption and Safe Families Act of 1997, 42 U.S.C.S. § 675(5) (Lexis 1998) 827
The Adoption and Safe Families Act of 1997, 42 U.S.C.S. § 673b (Lexis 1998) 828
2. Constitutional Considerations 831
Stanley v. Illinois (U.S. 1972) 831
Lehr v. Robertson (U.S. 1983) 831

CHAPTER 15: Mental Health Commitment of Children 843
A. Mental Health Classifications 844
The Book of Names: DSM-IV in Context, Peter S. Jensen & Kimberly Hoagwood, 9 Development and Psychopathology 231 (1997) 844
B. Substantive Requirements 847
New Mexico Statutes Annotated § 32A-6-13 (Michie 1999) 847
C. Due Process Framework 849
New Mexico Statutes Annotated § 32A-6-13(E), (F) & (G) (Michie 1999) 849
Kentucky Revised Statute Annotated § 645.230 (West 2000) 849
Parham v. J.R. (U.S. 1979) 850
M.W. v. Davis (Fla. 2000) 859

CHAPTER 16: The Future of the Juvenile Court 865
A. Maintain a Rehabilitative Approach 865
1. Rehabilitation Generally 865
2. Restorative Justice 867
B. Abolition of the Juvenile Court? 868
C. Specialization: Different Kinds of Juvenile Courts 870
1. Juvenile Drug Courts 870
2. Family Drug Courts 871
3. Youth Courts 871

Index of Authorities 873

Preface

The juvenile court in this country began as a social welfare institution to provide appropriate remedial care for juvenile offenders and children at risk. The Illinois Juvenile Court Act of 1899 signaled that juvenile delinquency and child protection proceedings were to be handled under one statutory umbrella. During the first half of the last century, however, while continuing to trumpet parens patriae, juvenile courts began to emphasize the importance of a child's rights in delinquency cases. The view emerged that the child who had no rights and who received no paternal care from the court needed the law's protection. The due process landscape of delinquency proceedings was radically changed by the *In re Gault,* 387 U.S. 1 (1967), decision and other cases which followed, together with federal legislation focused on the rights of status offenders. The juvenile court of the post-*Gault* era, which insured the child with most of the rights of an adult defendant in criminal court, was a far cry from the first juvenile court in Cook County, Illinois.

Understandably, most of the juvenile law and juvenile justice process books written in the wake of *Gault* focused primarily upon procedural due process in delinquency proceedings and other emerging issues concerning the increase in violence among juvenile offenders, e.g., new approaches to waiver of juvenile court jurisdiction, special laws for juvenile gang members, blended sentencing schemes and the death penalty for children. These course materials devoted less attention to the child welfare side of the juvenile justice system, which developed its own branch of law concerned with the balance between parents' fundamental rights of autonomy and privacy in making decisions about their children and the state's compelling interest in protecting children. With increasing frequency, the courts relied upon federal and state constitutional law in child welfare cases, particularly in termination of parental rights proceedings. Also, we witnessed a shift in emphasis from family preservation to protection of the child's health and safety and earlier permanency decisions. Guidelines for courts and state agencies were provided by the Adoption Assistance and Child Welfare Act of 1980 and the Adoption and Safe Families Act of 1997.

The purpose of this book is to provide teachers of juvenile law and process with a comprehensive set of course materials to examine both the delinquency and child welfare systems. Arranged in sixteen chapters, the book is roughly divided equally between delinquency and child welfare. Most footnotes have been removed from the cases and those retained have the original footnote numbers. There are separate chapters on children's rights in public schools, special advocacy for children and mental health commitment of children. Each chapter contains notes and questions, which follow the case opinions and statutes, intended to supplement this material and stimulate discussion. Some chapters contain problems, which put the student in a practical setting to analyze possible legal solutions. The first and last chapters of the book contain material which encourages an examination of the history and philosophical underpinnings of the juvenile court and a critical analysis of the future of the juvenile court. No attempt is made to advocate a blueprint for the juvenile court in the new millennium; rather various possibilities are offered for discussion at the end of term.

I'm most grateful to my juvenile law students who over the years have provided thoughtful insights, which prompted my further investigation of the ever-changing juvenile justice system. In particular, I thank former students Phylip Divine, Jennifer Gardiner, Carrie Strobel and Kristy Hiebert for their assistance. Special thanks go to my research assistant, Tony Fehrenbacher, and my secretary, Jacqueline Weiler, for their help on the book.

J. Eric Smithburn

Foreword

Juvenile law came of age during the last half of the twentieth century. With the United States Supreme Court cases of *Kent v. United States* (1966) and *In re Gault* (1967), American law recognized that children charged with criminal conduct were protected by certain rights guaranteed under the United States Constitution. Since then a large body of law has been developed by the United States Supreme Court, state supreme courts and state legislatures clarifying and expanding rights for children, not only in courts, but in a variety of other settings like schools and hospitals. Because of the extent of these laws, which normally would be included in courses like Constitutional Law and Criminal Law, a new area of law developed under the heading of Juvenile Law, and only a handful of law schools offered courses in that specialty. It took almost a decade for Juvenile Law to be an integral part of the law school curriculum. This was not because students had no interest in the area, but because of the lack of teaching materials and law professors who had the practical experience necessary or the interdisciplinary background and education so necessary for the full exploration of the issues in Juvenile Law.

At the same time as Juvenile Law was developing as an outgrowth of Constitutional Law and Criminal Law, another area, laws and cases dealing with child abuse and neglect, foster care and adoption, and the mental health of children were becoming so vast that they could no longer be covered in Family Law courses. Thus, another specialty called Child Welfare Law was created. By the end of the century, two parallel courses, one in Juvenile Law and the other in Child Welfare Law, had become part of some law school curriculums. The core of Child Welfare Law courses concerns the realm of legal problems associated with the administrative and judicial procedures by which children are removed from their homes because of abuse or neglect and are either reunited with their parents after the parents have been rehabilitated or are placed in foster care or in adoptive homes. An extraordinary amount of new case law and federal and state statutory law has been developed with attempts to balance parental rights with the best interests of the child in this process.

This book is the first successful attempt to combine Juvenile Law and the legal and social problems associated with juvenile delinquency and the juvenile court with Child Welfare Law and the issues of child protection. By uniting both areas in a single volume, Professor Smithburn has provided law students, legislators and judges with a holistic approach to the study of children in the judicial system. For that achievement, we who work and study in both fields are in his debt.

Sanford N. Katz
Boston College School of Law

Table of Cases

A.A., In re (Wash. App. Ct. 2001) 527-28
A.B., In the Interest of (Wyo. 1992) 427
A.B.M., In re (Mo. Ct. App. 2000) 802
A.C., M.C., and J.C., In the Interest of (Iowa Ct. App. 1999) 442
A.D., State ex rel. (Utah Ct. App. 2000) 589
A.D.J., United States v. (8th Cir. 1997) 182, 194
A.D.R., In re (Tex. Ct. App. 2000) 594
A.E.H., In re (Wis. 1991) 824
A.H., In the Matter of (D.C. 1983) 299
A.J.D., In the Interest of (Ill. App. Ct. 1987) 351
A.J.R., In re Welfare of (Wash. Ct. App. 1995) 818
A.M., In re (Ohio Ct. App. 2000) 184
A.M.D., In re (Colo. 1982) 514
A.M.M., In re Adoption of (Kan. Ct. App. 1997) *537*
A.O. v. State (Fla. Dist. Ct. App. 1983) 41
A.S.A., In re (Mont. 1993) 754
A.S.B., In re (Ill. App. Ct. 1997) 840
A.W., In re Dependency of (Wash. Ct. App. 1988) 514
Aaron S., In Matter of (N.Y. Fam. Ct. 1993) 719
Abdul Kaheem Unique Mohammed Jewel Cameron C., aka David C., In re Custody of (N.Y. 1994) 746
Adoption of K.A.S., In re (N.D. 1992) 754-55
Adoption/Guardianship No. A91-71A, In re (Md. 1994) 543
Alaska v. Jackson (Alaska Ct. App. 1989) *400*
Alberto R., In re (Cal. Ct. App. 1991) *53*, 61, 63
Alexander S. by and Through Bowers v. Boyd (D.S.C. 1995) 344
Alexander v. Cole (Ind. Ct. App. 1980) *492*, 495
Alexander, In re Adoption of (Fla. Dist. Ct. App. 1968) 644
Alexander V., In re (Conn. 1992) 738
Alford v. Carter (Okla. Crim. App. 1972) 244
Alfredo A. v. Superior Court (Cal. 1994) 85-86
Aline D., In re (Cal. 1975) 281, 350
Allen, People v. (N.Y. 1968) 338
Allen, In re (Cal. Ct. App. 1969) 315
Alpha J., In re (Conn. Super. Ct. 2000) 514-15
Amber B., In re (Cal. Ct. App. 1987) *699*, 705
Amber D., In re (Cal. Ct. App. 1991) 774
American Civil Liberties Union of New Jersey v. Black Horse Pike Regional Board of Education (3d Cir. 1996) 132
Anders v. California (U.S. 1967) 230-31

Anderson v. Anderson (Utah 1966) 494
Anderson v. State (Ala. Crim. App. 1998) 102
Andrew M.M., In re (N.Y. App. Div. 1992) 351
Andrews v. County of Ostego (N.Y. Sup. Ct. 1982) 649
Angel N., In re (N.H. 1996) *520*
Angela M.W. v. Kruzicki, State ex rel. (Wis. 1997) *410*
Anjelica A., In re (Conn. Super. Ct. 1997) 661
Anthony B., In re (Conn. Super. Ct. 1999) 817
Anthony P., In re (N.Y. Fam. Ct. 1980) 252
Anton v. State (Ind. Ct. App. 1967) 284
Appeal No. 544, In re (Md. Ct. Spec. App. 1975) 230
Appellate Defenders v. Cheri S. (Cal. Ct. App. 1995) 755
Ariel C., Matter of (N.Y. App. Div. 1998) 802
Arkansas Department of Human Services v. Caldwell (Ark. Ct. App. 1992) 151
Armstead v. Lima City Board of Education (Ohio Ct. App. 1991) 141
Arteaga v. Texas Dep't of Protective and Regulatory Services (Tex. App. Ct. 1996) 487
Ashley M., In re (Me. 2000) 528
Ashley Elizabeth R., Matter of Guardianship of (N.M. Ct. App. 1993) 581
Athena M., In re (N.Y. App. Div. 1998) 446

B.A.B., In re (Minn. Ct. App. 1998) *433*
B.B., In re (Fla. Dist. Ct. App. 1994) *282*, 285
B.B., In the Interest of (Iowa 1993) 409, 720
B.J.B., In re (Tex. Civ. App. 1977) 446
B.L.S., In re (Okla. Civ. App. 2000) 735
B.M., In Interest of (Wis. 1981) 281
B.M.H., In re (Ga. Ct. App. 1986) 230
B.S., In re (Vt. 1997) *813*
B.S., In re (Ill. App. Ct. 1989) 281
B.W., In re (Ind. Ct. App. 1999) 494
Babak S., In re (Cal. Ct. App. 1993) *294*, 299-300, 318
Baby K., In re (N.H. 1998) 747
Baby Boy N., In re (Kan. Ct. App. 1994) 735
Baby Girl D., In re (Cal. Ct. App. 1989) 644
Baby Boy L., In re (Kan. 1982) 581
Baltimore Department of Social Services v. Bouknight (U.S. 1990) *555*, 561-62
Barrett, State v. (La. Ct. App. 1996) 170
Bartell v. Lohiser (6th Cir. 2000) 817
Bates v. Wells (Mich. 1993) 631
Baxley, In re (N.C. Ct. App. 1985) 278
Behl, State v. (Minn. 1997) 182
Bell, State v. (Iowa 1974) 397
Bell v. Superior Court (Ariz. 1977) 85
Bell, People v. (Ill. 1974) 398
Bell, State v. (Utah 1989) 182

Bellotti v. Baird (U.S. 1979) 35
Benoit, State v. (N.H. 1985) 102
Berg v. Glen Cove City School District (E.D.N.Y. 1994) 433
Bessette v. Saratoga (N.Y. App. Div. 1994) 621
Bethel School District No. 403 v. Fraser (U.S. 1986) 123-24
Bettye K., In re (Cal. Ct. App. 1991) 31
Beulow, State v. (Vt. 1990) 203
Biancamano, State v. (N.J. Super. Ct. 1995) 100
Bivens v. Albuquerque Public Schools (D.N.M. 1995) 124
Bland, United States v. (D.C. Cir. 1972) 181, 183-84
Blondheim v. State (Wash. 1975) 31
Bluebird, In re (N.C. Ct. App. 1992) 755
Board of Education of Westside Community Schools v. Mergens (U.S. 1990) 134
Board of Education, Island Trees Union Free School District No. 26 v. Pico (U.S. 1982) 123
Board of Education v. Rowley (U.S. 1982) 344-45
Boddie v. Connecticut (U.S. 1971) 485
Boykins v. Fairfield Board of Education (5th Cir. 1974) 142
Bracewell, In re (Ohio Ct. App. 1998) 44
Brandon S.S., In Interest of (Wis. Ct. App. 1993) 589
Breed v. Jones (U.S. 1975) *253*, 259-60
Bridget, In re (Cal. Ct. App. 1996) 581
Briscoe v. Lathe (U.S. 1983) 607
Brodbeck, In re (Ohio Ct. App. 1994) 505
Brokaw v. Mercer County (7th Cir. 2000) 462
Brooks v. State (Ark. 1996) 196
Brown v. County of San Joaquin (E.D. Cal. 1985) 631
Brown v. Gwinnett County School District (11th Cir. 1997) 133
Brown v. Phillips (Ga. Ct. App. 1986) 649
Burrus, In re (N.C. Ct. App. 1969) 247
Burt, State v. (La. Ct. App. 1989) 281
Burton, People v. (Cal. 1971) 101
Bykofsky v. Middletown (3d Cir. 1976) 36

C.A.J. v. State (Ga. Ct. App. 1973) 231
C.A.W., In the Welfare of (Minn. Ct. App. 1998) 328
C.A.W., In the Matter of the Adoption of (Pa. Super. Ct. 1996) *797*
C.D., In re (Mo. Ct. App. 2000) 605
C.H., In re (Mont. 1984) 337
C.J., In re (Ill. App. Ct. 1995) 746
C.O.S., In re (Tex. 1999) 44
C.R.M., In re (N.D. 1996) 183
C.S. v. S.H. (Fla. Dist. Ct. App. 1996) *636*
C.T.F., In re (Iowa 1982) *248*, 252-53
Caban v. Mohammed (U.S. 1979) 839
Cabrera, In re (Pa. Super. Ct. 1989) 433
Caldwell, In the Matter of (Or. Ct. App. 2000) 827

Cales v. Howell Public Schools (E.D. Mich. 1985) 170
Callender v. Skiles (Iowa 1999) 735
Calynn, In Adoption of (N.Y. Fam. Ct. 1987) 543
Campbel, State v. (Conn. 1992) 277-78
Carey, In re (Mich. Ct. App. 2000) *205*
Carmen G., In Interest of (Conn. Super. Ct. 1998) 803
Carney, In re (Cal. 1979) 810
Carswell v. State (Ind. Ct. App. 1999) 308
Carter, In re (Md. Ct. Spec. App. 1974) 104
Cass, Commonwealth v. (Pa. 1998) 170-71
Causey, State v. (La. 1978) 52, 211
Charles S. v. Board of Education, San Francisco Unified School District (Cal. Ct. App. 1971) 141
Charles S. v. Superior Court of Los Angeles (Cal. 1982) 287
Chase, In re (N.Y. Fam. Ct. 1982) 247
Chatham, State v. (Wash. Ct. App. 1981) 111
Chatman, Commonwealth v. (Va. 2000) *49*, 52
Child v. Beame (S.D.N.Y. 1976) 594
Christina D., In re (R.I. 1987) 589
Christina H., In re (Me. 1992) 786
Christopher B., In re (Cal. Ct. App. 1978) 387, 510
Clark v. Alexander (Wyo. 1998) 610
Clements v. Phillips (Ga. Ct. App. 1998) 589
Clemons v. State (Ind. Ct. App. 1974) 183
Cleveland Protestant Orphan Asylum v. Soule (Ohio Ct. App. 1915) 494-95
Cochise County Juvenile Action No. 5666-J, In the Matter of the Appeal In (Ariz. 1982) *458*, 461
Colin, In re (Md. Ct. Spec. App. 1985) 720
Colquitt v. Rich Township High School District No. 227 (Ill. App. Ct. 1998) 142
Columbia Newspapers, Inc., Ex parte (S.C. 1985) 247
Conlogue, State v. (Me. 1984) 711
Connick v. Myers (U.S. 1983) 384
Consuelo-Gonzalez, United States v. (9th Cir. 1975) 308
Coplin v. Conejo Valley Unified School District (5th Cir. 1985) 141-42
Cornfield v. Consolidated High School District (7th Cir. 1993) 170
Cotto, Commonwealth v. (Pa. Super. Ct. 1998) 64, 277-78
Country Mut. Ins. Co. v. Peoples Bank (Ill. App. Ct. 1997) 635
County of Allegheny v. American Civil Liberties Union (U.S. 1989) 132
County of Sacramento v. Lewis (U.S. 1998) 474
Cox v. Turley (6th Cir. 1974) 85-86
Cox v. Court of Common Pleas of Franklin County (Ohio Ct. App. 1988) 419
Coy v. Iowa (U.S. 1987) 774
Crabtree, State v. (Kan. 1991) 688
Craven M., In re Matter of the Adoption of (Idaho 1996) 802
Creek v. Stone (D.C. Cir. 1967) 277

Crews, In re Adoption of (Wash. 1992) 581
Crosby v. Holsinger (4th Cir. 1988) 124
Crouse, Ex parte (Pa. 1839) *6*, 7, 10-11
Cruse v. State (Ala. Crim. App. 1986) 260
Crystal R. v. Superior Court of Santa Cruz County (Cal. Ct. App. 1997) 581
Currence, In re (N.Y. Fam. Ct. 1963) 437
Currier v. Doran (D.N.M. 1998) 476
Curtis S., In re (Cal. Ct. App. 1994) 755
Curtis T., In re (Cal. Ct. App. 1989) *300*
Custody of Minor, In re (Mass. 1979) 433
Cynthia D. v. San Diego County (Cal. 1993) 767

D.A.S., In re (Tex. 1998) 230-31
D.D.A. v. State (Ala. Crim. App. 1994) 183
D.D.F., In re (Okla. 1990) 754
D.D.P., Jr., T.P., and B.J.P., In the Interest of (Kan. 1991) 595, 606
D.H., In re (D.C. 1995) 43
D.S.P., In re (Wis. 1992) *763*
Dallas M., In re (Wis. Ct. App. 1998) *782*
Dandoy v. Superior Court, State ex rel. (Ariz. 1980) 210-11
Daniel, People v. (Ill. App. Ct. 1992) 76
Danielle D., In re (Neb. 1999) 774
Darlene C., In re (S.C. 1983) *25*, 27, 560
Daubert v. Merrell Dow Pharmaceuticals, Inc. (U.S. 1993) 656
Daubert v. Merrell Dow Pharmaceuticals, Inc. (9th Cir. 1995) 656
Davis v. State (Fla. 1974) 195
Deborah T., In re (N.Y. App. Div. 1998) 446
Deborah C., In re (Cal. 1981) 100
Deerfield v. Greenberg (Ill. App. Ct. 1990) 36
Delcourt v. Silverman (Tex. App. 1996) 610
Denice F., In re (Me. 1995) 442
Dennis, In re (Miss. 1974) 229, 231
DeShaney v. Winnebago Department of Social Services (U.S. 1989) 449, *462*, 474-75
Detrick, State v. (Wash. Ct. App. 1998) 44
DeWater v. Washington (Wash. 1996) 636
Dietrich v. Anderson (Md. 1945) 543
Dino, In re (La. 1978) 103-04
Dino E., In re (Cal. Ct. App. 1992) 527
Dinson, In re (Haw. 1978) 183
Dixon, State v. (Wash. 1990) 114, 253
Dixon v. Alabama State Board of Education (5th Cir. 1961) 141
Doe, United States v. (9th Cir. 1988) 229
Doe v. Aldine Independent School District (S.D. Tex. 1982) 132
Doe v. Duncanville Independent School District (5th Cir. 1995) 132
Doe v. Shenandoa County School Board (W.D. Va. 1990) 133
Doe v. United States (S.D. Cal. 1997) *262*

Doe, United States v. (2d Cir. 1995) 193, 195
Doe, State v. (Idaho Ct. App. 1993) 505
Doe v. Superintendent of Schools of Worcester (Mass. 1995) 142
Doe, United States v. (D. Ariz. 1974) 247
Donaldson v. Board of Education for Danville School District No. 118 (Ill. App. Ct. 1981) 150
Dornes v. Lindsey (C.D. Cal. 1998) 142
Dow, In re (Ill. App. Ct. 1979) 47
Drakeford, In re (N.C. Ct. App. 1977) 259
Draper v. Columbus Public Schools (S.D. Ohio 1991) 142
Dryden v. Commonwealth (Ky. 1968) 243
Dubinsky, State ex rel. v. Weinstein (Mo. 1967) 494-95
Duchesne v. Sugarman (2d Cir. 1977) 735
Duley v. State (Md. Ct. Spec. App. 1983) 711
Dumlao, State v. (Conn. App. Ct. 1985) 688
Durfee, State v. (Minn. 1982) 688
Durham, Commonwealth v. (Pa. Super. Ct. 1978) 48

E.B., In re (N.D. 1980) *37*
E.C., State v. (Wash. Ct. App. 1996) 211
E.D., In re (Utah Ct. App. 1994) *770*
E.D.M., In re (Tex. Ct. App. 1995) 244
E.E., In re (Ind. Ct. App. 2000) 817
E.G., In re (Ill. 1989) *428*
E.P., In re (Ind. Ct. App. 1995) *496*, 505
E.P. v. District Court of Garfield County (Colo. 1985) 486
E.R., In re (Neb. 1988) *425*, 428
E.R. v. Marion County Office of Family and Children (Ind. Ct. App. 2000) 487
E.S., In re (Cal. Ct. App. 1985) 796
E.S. v. State (Ga. Ct. App. 1975) 253
E.T.C., In re (Vt. 1982) 103
Eddie K., State v. (W. Va. 1995) 247
Edison v. State (Alaska 1983) 318
Edward C., In re (Cal. Ct. App. 1981) *529*
Egly v. Blackford County Department of Public Welfare (Ind. 1992) 795
Egly v. Blackford County Dept. of Public Welfare (Ind. Ct. App. 1991) 534
Ellery C., In re (N.Y. 1973) *336*
Elliot, State v. (N.C. 1996) 687
Engel v. Vitale (U.S. 1962) 132
Eslava v. State (Ala. Crim. App. 1985) 687
Esperanza M., In re (N.M. Ct. App. 1998) *596*
Estelle v. McGuire (U.S. 1991) 687-88
Ethan H., In re (N.H. 1992) *391*
Eugene, Adoption of (Mass. 1993) 840
Everett S., In re (N.Y. App. Div. 1978) 795

F.S., In re (Alaska 1978) 195

Fare v. Michael C. (U.S. 1979) 92, *93*, 100-02, 104, 230-31
Farrell, State v. (N.H. 2001) 102
Fathima Ashanti K.J., In re (N.Y. Fam. Ct. 1990) 674
Fernandez, State v. (La. 1998) 103
Ferrier, In re (Ill. 1882) 11
Fetterkoff, State v. (Mo. Ct. App. 1989) 308
Foley, State v. (Wash. Ct. App. 1992) 110
Foster v. Stein (Mich. Ct. App. 1990) 825
Foster v. Washoe County (Nev. 1998) 606
Fox v. Arthur (Ind. Ct. App. 1999) 494
Francis v. Keane (S.D.N.Y. 1995) 436
Frank, In re (Wash. 1952) 433
Franklin, State v. (La. 1943) 86
Fricke v. Lynch (D.R.I. 1980) 124
Frye v. United States (D.C. Cir. 1923) 655, 711, 719
Fucini, In re (Ill. 1970) 243

G.B., In re (Ill. 1981) 27
G.D.M., Florida v. (Fla. 1981) 64
G.J.I. v. State (Okla. Crim. App. 1989) 210
G.M., In re (Minn. 1997) 75
G.S., People in Interest of (Colo. Ct. App. 1991) 589
G.W.H. v. D.A.H. (Tex. Civ. App. 1983) 446
Gainey v. Olivo (Ga. 1998) 825
Gallegos v. Colorado (U.S. 1962) 92
Gallo, People ex rel. v. Acuna (Cal. Ct. App. 1997) *58*, 63
Garcia v. Miera (10th Cir. 1987) 151
Garcia, Commonwealth v. (Pa. Super. Ct. 1997) 698
Gardner v. Parson (3d Cir. 1989) 607, 610
Gault, In re (U.S. 1967) 21, 43-44, 69, 75, 91, 181, 205, 210, *212*, 228-31, 236-37, 252, 377
Germaine v. State (Ind. App. Ct. 1999) 427
Gerrick v. State (Ind. 1983) 195
Gerstein v. Pugh (U.S. 1974) 85
Gibbs, State v. (Idaho 1972) 195
Gibson, In re (Or. Ct. App. 1986) 101
Gibson v. Merced County Department of Human Resources (9th Cir. 1986) 631
Ginsberg v. New York (U.S. 1968) 405
Gladys R., In re (Cal. 1970) 211
Golden v. State (Ark. 2000) 52
Golding v. Golding (Fla. Dist. Ct. App. 1995) 825
Gonzales v. McEuen (C.D. Cal. 1977) 141
Gordon v. Santa Ana Unified School District (Cal. Ct. App. 1985) 170
Goss v. Lopez (U.S. 1975) *135*, 141-42, 152
Gray, State v. (Ohio Ct. App. 1990) 674-75
Green, In re (Pa. 1972) 433

Green, State v. (Kan. 1975) 195
Griffin v. Wisconsin (U.S. 1987) 308
Griswold v. Connecticut (U.S. 1965) 735
Groves, In re (N.C. App. 1989) *347*, 351
Guardianship of B.L.N., In re (N.J. Super. Ct. Ch. Div. 1991) 754
Gullings, State v. (Or. 1966) 183

H., In re (N.Y. Fam. Ct. 1972) 69
H.B.E., III v. State (Fla. Dist. Ct. App. 1986) 291
H.J., In re Dependency of (Wash. 1991) 631
H.J.P., In re (Wash. 1990) 785
Haaby, State v. (Wash. Ct. App. 1988) 110
Haley v. Ohio (U.S. 1948) 91-92
Hana, People v. (Mich. 1993) 183
Hans v. State (Mont. 1997) 231
Hardy, State v. (Mich. Ct. App. 1991) 674-75
Harris, State ex rel. v. Calendine (W. Va. 1977) 337
Hartman, In re (Neb. 1972) 427
Hassan v. Lubbock Independent School District (5th Cir. 1995) 151
Hawaii v. Kaimimoku (Haw. Ct. App. 1992) *394*
Hazelwood School District v. Kuhlmeier (U.S. 1988) 124
Heitzman, People v. (Cal. 1994) 427
Henry, State v. (N.M. 1967) 252
Herman S., In re (N.Y. Fam. Ct. 1974) 75
Herron v. State (Ind. Ct. App. 2000) 674
Higby, In re (Ohio Ct. App. 1992) 786
Hill v. State (Ala. Crim. App. 1981) 436
Hirenia C., In re (Cal. Ct. App. 1993) 589
Hobson, In re (Miss. 1976) 86
Hoener v. Bertinato (N.J. Super. Ct. App. Div. 1961) 433
Hogan, People ex rel. v. Newton (N.Y. 1945) 151
Hogenson v. Williams (Tex. Civ. App. 1976) 151
Holmes, In re (Pa. 1954) 229
Horton v. Goose Creek Independent School District (5th Cir. 1982) 170
Howard v. Howard (Neb. App. 1995) 427
Huey v. Lente (N.M. Ct. App. 1973) 644
Hughes, People v. (Colo. Ct. App. 1997) 114
Hunt, State v. (Utah 1980) 101
Hunte v. Blumenthal (Conn. 1996) 635-36
Hurlman v. Rice (2d Cir. 1991) 485
Hutchins v. District of Columbia (D.C. Cir. 1999) 36

I.D.P., United States v. (11th Cir. 1996) 193, 195
I.Q.S., In re Welfare of (Minn. 1976) 195
I.V., In Interest of (Wis. Ct. App. 1982) 287
Imel v. State (Ind. Ct. App. 1976) 195
Ingebretsen v. Jackson Public School District (5th Cir. 1996) 132
Ingraham v. Wright (U.S. 1977) *143*, 151-52

Inmates of Boys' School v. Affleck (D.R.I. 1972) 277
Isiah B. v. State (Wis. 1993) *158*, 169-71
Ivy v. Gladney Home (Tex. App. 1990) 840

J.A.T., In the Interest of (Fla. Dist. Ct. App. 1991) 736
J.B., People in Interest of (Colo. Ct. App. 1985) 755
J.B. v. Florida Dep't of Children and Family Serv. (Fla. 2000) 740
J.B., In re (N.J. Super. Ct. 1974) 75
J.C., In Matter of (N.J. 1992) 785
J.D., State v. (Ind. Ct. App. 1998) 405
J.D.G., State v. (Wash. Ct. App. 1997) *345*
J.E.S. v. State (Fla. Dist. Ct. App. 1979) 103
J.F., In re (Mont. 1990) 351
J.G., In Interest of (Fla. Dist. Ct. App. 1991) 755
J.G., In re (Wis. 1984) 183
J.H., State v. (Fla. Dist. Ct. App. 1974) 252
J.J.M., In re (Ill. App. Ct. 1998) 43
J.L.P., People in Interest of (Colo. Ct. App. 1994) 581
J.M., In re (D.C. 1992) 76
J.M., In re (Ill. App. Ct. 1998) 486
J.M., In re (Fla. Dist. Ct. App. 1985) 409
J.M. v. Taylor, State ex rel. (W. Va. 1981) 230
J.M., In re (Colo. 1989) 36
J.M.A. v. State (Alaska 1975) *632*
J.M.J. v. State (Fla. Dist. Ct. App. 1980) 27
J.P.S., State v. (Wash. 1998) 48
J.Q., State v. (N.J. 1993) 405, *689*, 699
J.S., In re (Vt. 1981) 248
J.S.P.L., In re (N.D. 1995) 505, 755
J.T. v. Arkansas Dep't of Human Serv. (Ark. 1997) 817
Jackson v. State (Miss. 1975) 182
Jackson v. Commonwealth (Va. 1998) 253
Jacqueline H., In re (Cal. 1978) 755
Jager v. Douglas County School District (11th Cir. 1989) 132
James H. v. Superior Court (Cal. Ct. App. 1978) 211, 230
James D., In re (Cal. 1987) 75
James W.H., In re (N.M. Ct. App. 1993) 755
James, State v. (Wash. 1993) 688
James B., In re (N.Y. App. Div. 1980) 86
Jane, State v. (Wash. 1993) 409
Jason J., In re (Cal. Ct. App. 1991) 294
Jeanette H., State ex rel. v. Pancake (W. Va. 2000) 746
Jeannette P., In re (N.Y. App. Div. 1970) 277
Jefferson v. Griffin Spaulding County Hospital Authority (Ga. 1981) 419
Jeffrey R.L., In re (W. Va. 1993) 595
Jeffs v. Stubbs (Utah 1998) 436
Jegin v. Jacinto Unified School District (C.D. Cal. 1993) 124
Jenkins v. Talladega City Board of Education (11th Cir. 1997) 170

Jennifer P., In re (Conn. App. Ct. 1989) 621
Jennings v. State (Ala. 1980) 47
Jensen, State v. (S.D. 1998) 195
Jermaine, In re (Pa. Super. Ct. 1990) 75
Jesse W. v. Superior Court (Cal. 1979) 260
Jesse McM., In re (Cal. Ct. App. 1980) *245*, 247
Jessica Z., In re (N.Y. Fam. Ct. 1987) *711*, 720
Jimi A., In re (Cal. Ct. App. 1989) 308-09
John H., In re (N.Y. App. Div. 1995) 350
John D. v. Department of Social Services (Mass. 2001) 405
John A. v. San Bernadino City Unified School District (Cal. 1983) 142
Johnson v. State (Fla. 1992) 420, 674-75
Johnson v. Opelousas (5th Cir. 1981) 36
Johnson, In re (Neb. 1972) 427
Joiner ex rel. Rivas v. Rivas (S.C. 2000) 595, 606
Jones v. Commonwealth (Va. 1946) 314-15
Jones v. Cedar Creek Independent School District (5th Cir. 1992) 132
Jones, Interest of (Pa. Super. Ct. 1981) 510
Jordan, In re (Ind. Ct. App. 1993) 486
Jose R., In re (Cal. Ct. App. 1982) 309
Jose P., In re (Cal. Ct. App. 1980) 281
Joseph T., State v. (W. Va. 1985) 171
Joseph L., In re Interest of (Neb. Ct. App. 1999) 737-38
Joseph Eugene M., In Interest of (S.C. 1985) 287
Joshua, In re (La. Ct. App. 1976) 85
Joshua H., In re (Cal. Ct. App. 1993) *520*
Joshua S., In re (Cal. Ct. App. 1988) 514
Juan C. v. Cortines (N.Y. 1997) 170
Justin T., In re (Me. 1994) *778*
Juvenile Department, Oregon ex rel. v. Geist (Ore. 1990) 755
Juvenile Appeal (83-CD), In re (Conn. 1983) 486, *511*
Juvenile, A, Commonwealth v. (No. 1) (Mass. 1983) 103
Juvenile Department v. Reynolds, State ex rel. (Or. 1993) 244
Juvenile Male J.A.J., United States v. (8th Cir. 1998) 114, 193, 195
Juvenile Male No. 1, United States v. (4th Cir. 1996) 193-94

K.B.S. v. State (Fla. Dist. Ct. App. 1999) 405
K.H. v. Morgan (7th Cir. 1990) 649
K.J.C., United States v. (N.D. Iowa 1997) *187*, 193-95, 236
K.K.B. v. State (Tex. Civ. App. 1980) 316
K.L.J., In the Matter of (Alaska 1991) 505, 754
K.M. v. State (Ark. 1998) 52
K.M.H., In Interest of (Ga. Ct. App. 1993) 802
K.M.S. v. State (Ga. Ct. App. 1973) *42*, 44, 47
K.P., In re (N.J. Ch. 1997) 248
K.P.B. v. D.C.A. (Ala. Civ. App. 1996) 505
K.R.C., In re (Ga. Ct. App. 1998) 595
Kacy S., In re (Cal. Ct. App. 1998) *305*

Kalie W., In re Interest of (Neb. 1999) 802
Karen B. v. Clyde M. (N.Y. Fam. Ct. 1991) *721*, 726
Karow, State v. (Wis. Ct. App. 1990) 69
Karwath, In re (Iowa 1977) 433
Keijam T., In re (Conn. 1992) 183
Keith G. v. Bilbray (Cal. Ct. App. 1995) 277
Keller, People v. (Cal. Ct. App. 1978) 308
Kelsey S., Adoption of (Cal. 1992) 841
Kempf, State v. (Iowa 1979) 210
Kennedy v. Dexter Consolidated Schools (N.M. 1998) 170
Kent v. United States (U.S. 1966) *174*, 181-82, 184, 186-87, 194-95, 203, 229
Kentucky Bar Association v. Guidugli (Ky. 1998) 260
Kerins v. Lima (Mass. 1997) *651*
Keyes v. County Department of Public Welfare (7th Cir. 1979) 631
Kia P. v. McIntyre (2d Cir. 2000) 419
Kimberly, Adoption of (Mass. 1993) 774
King v. Department of Social Services (Wash. Ct. App. 1987) 561
King v. State (Ala. Crim. App. 1990) 319
King v. State (Md. Ct. Spec. App. 1977) 203
Kingsley v. Kingsley (Fla. Dist. Ct. App. 1993) *584*, *827*
Kirby v. Illinois (U.S. 1972) 229
Knight v. Deavers (Ark. 1976) 643
Konop v. Northwestern School District (D.S.D. 1998) 170
Kristin H., In re (Cal. Ct. App. 1996) 505
Kumho Tire Co. v. Carmichael (U.S. 1999) 656
Kyle S.G. v. Carolyn S.G. (Wis. 1995) 767-68

L. v. A.S. (La. Ct. App. 1995) 427
L.A.M. v. State (Alaska 1976) 27-28
L.A.M., In re (Kan. 2000) 487
L.A.V., State in Interest of (La. Ct. App. 1987) 427
L.B. v. State (Ind. Ct. App. 1996) 589
L.C., In the Interest of (Kan. Ct. App. 1993) 825
L.E.A. v. Hammergren (Minn. 1980) 28
L.H. v. Arkansas (Ark. 1998) 264
L.H., In re (D.C. 1993) 827
L.J.S., In re (Minn. Ct. App. 1995) *352*
L.M., In the Interest of (Fla. Dist. Ct. App. 1991) 315-16
L.M. v. State (Fla. Dist. Ct. App. 1992) *310*, 315-16
L.V.A., In re (S.D. 1976) 260
L.Z., In re (Minn. 1986) 231
Laasch v. State (Wis. 1978) 76-77
Lakeside Family and Children's Services on Behalf of Angel Takima C., Matter of (N.Y. App. Div. 1997) 802
LaMunyon, State v. (Kan. 1996) 244
Landeros v. Flood (Cal. 1976) 384
Lanes v. State (Tex. Crim. App. 1989) 75

Lang, Matter of (N.Y. Fam. Ct. 1969) 44
Lang, In re (N.Y. Fam. Ct. 1965) 75
Lantrip v. Kentucky (Ky. 1986) 698
Laramire v. Hysong (Wyo. 1991) 486
Lassiter v. Department of Social Services of Durham County, North Carolina (U.S. 1981) *748*, 754
Lawley, State v. (Wash. 1979) 244
Laylah K., In re (Cal. Ct. App. 1991) 293-94
Leal v. Texas Dept. of Protective and Regulatory Services (Tex. App. 2000) 427
LeBay v. Jenkins (La. Ct. App. 1980) 151
Lee v. Weisman (U.S. 1982) 132
Lee, People v. (N.Y. Crim. Ct. 1992) 103
Lehr v. Robertson (U.S. 1983) *831*
Leif A., In re (N.Y. Fam. Ct. 1980) 409
Lemon v. Kurtzman (U.S. 1970) 131-33
Lewis v. State (Ind. 1972) 102-03
Lincoln v. State (Ga. Ct. App. 1976) 259
Lindsey C., In re (W. Va. 1995) 505
Litdell, In re (Miss. 1970) *319*
Little Flower Children's Services v. Andrew C. (N.Y. Fam. Ct. 1989) 644
Loebach, State v. (Minn. 1981) 710
Lonell J., In re (N.Y. App. Div. 1998) *444*
Los Angeles County Department of Children's Services v. Superior Court (Cal. Ct. App. 1988) 486
Lossman v. Pekarski (7th Cir. 1983) 485
Lowe, United States v. (9th Cir. 1981) 318
Lowry, State v. (N.J. Super. Ct. 1967) *72*, 75, 85

M.A.V., In re Interest of (Ga. Ct. App. 1992) 720
M.B., In re (Wash. Ct. App. 2000) 561
M.B., In the Matter of (Ind. Ct. App. 1993) 774
M.C. v. Department of Children and Families (Fla. Dist. Ct. App. 2000) 817
M.C.S., In re (S.D. 1993) *818*
M.D.S., In re (Wis. 1992) 755
M.E.C. v. State (Ala. Crim. App. 1992) 231
M.G. v. State (Fla. Dist. Ct. App. 1990) 291
M.G.S., In re (Cal. Ct. App. 1968) 52
M.H., In re (Tex. Ct. App. 1988) 661
M.H.J. v. State Dept. of Human Resources (Ala. Civ. App. 2000) 735
M.J.W. v. State (Ga. Ct. App. 1974) *289*, 291
M.K.K. v. State (Okla. Crim. App. 1997) 203
M.L.C., State v. (Utah 1997) 86
M.L.M., Matter of (Wyo. 1984) 427
M.M., In re (Ill. App. Ct. 1999) 795
M.N.M., In re (D.C. 1992) 840
M.N.W., In re (Iowa Ct. App. 1990) 427

M.S. et al., In Interest of (Ga. Ct. App. 1986) *768*, 773-74
M.W. v. Davis (Fla. 2000) *859*
Madyun v. Franzen (7th Cir. 1983) 436
Mafnas v. Owen County Office of Family and Children (Ind. Ct. App. 1998) 494
Maine v. Williamson (Me. 1979) 64
Maricopa County Juvenile Action No. 7499, In the Matter of the Appeal in (Ariz. Ct. App. 1989) 773
Mark E.P., In re (W. Va. 1987) 183
Markle, Commonwealth v. (Pa. 1977) 103
Marsh, In re (Pa. Super. Ct. 1940) 41
Martarella v. Kelley (S.D.N.Y. 1972) *268*, 277
Martin v. State (Nev. 1979) 183
Maryland v. Craig (U.S. 1990) 774
Massiah v. United States (U.S. 1964) 104
Mathews v. Eldridge (U.S. 1976) 740, 773-74
Matthew YY, In re (N.Y. App. Div. 2000) 802
Matthew S., In re (Conn. Super. Ct. 1999) 817
Matzen, In re Marriage of (Fla. Dist. Ct. App. 1992) 785
Maximo, State v. (Ariz. Ct. App. 1991) 76
May v. Cooperman (3d Cir. 1984) 133
Mayberry v. Pryor (Mich. 1985) *645*, 649-50
Mazanec v. North Judson-San Pierre School corp. (N.D. Ind. 1985) 437
McCauley, In re (Mass. 1991) 433
McCollester v. Keene (D.N.H. 1984) 36
McCollum, People ex rel. v. Board of Education (U.S. 1948) 133
McDowell, State v. (Wash. 1984) *111*, 114-15
McKay v. Owens (Idaho 1997) 610
McKeiver v. Pennsylvania (U.S. 1971) 43, *238*, 243-44, 247
McKenzie v. Department of Health and Rehabilitative Services (Fla. Dist. Ct. App. 1995) 505
Mendez, In re (Or. Ct. App. 1999) *420*, 423-24
Metzger v. Osbeck (3d Cir. 1988) 151
Meyer, In re (Ohio Ct. App. 1994) 442
Meyer v. Nebraska (U.S. 1923) 449, *450*, *731*, 735, 785
Micah Alyn R. (W. Va. 1998) *804*
Michael, In re (Ohio Ct. App. 1997) 231
Michael B., In re Interest of (Neb. 2000) 794
Michael B., In re (N.Y. 1992) 644
Michael D., In re (Cal. Ct. App. 1987) *330*
Michael D., In re (Cal. Ct. App. 1989) 294
Michael G., State v. (N.M. 1987) 171
Michael J., In re (N.Y. Fam. Ct. 1999) 44
Michael Ray T., In re (W. Va. 1999) *616*, 622
Michael W., In re (N.Y. App. Div. 1986) 621-22
Michigan v. Smith (Mich. 1991) 264
Milburn v. Anne Arundel County Department of Social Services (4th Cir. 1989) 649

Miller, In re (Ohio Ct. App. 1992) 318
Miller v. Miller (Me. 1996) 589
Miller, In re (Mich. Ct. App. 1989) 244
Minor, Custody of (Mass. 1979) 514
Miranda v. Arizona (U.S. 1966) 91-92, 100-04
Mississippi Band of Choctaw Indians v. Holyfield (U.S. 1989) *573*, 581
Mitchell v. Davis (Ala. 1992) 649
Mitchell v. Davis (Tex. Civ. App. 1947) 433
Moore v. State (Md. Ct. Spec. App. 1972) 397
Morgan v. Sproat (S.D. Miss. 1977) 344
Morris v. D'Amario (R.I. 1980) 85-86
Morrow v. United States (D.C. 1991) 182
Mosier, In re (59 Ohio Misc. 83 1978) 36
Moss v. Weaver (5th Cir. 1976) 85
Moyer, State v. (Ariz. Ct. App. 1986) 688
Mucci, People ex rel. (N.Y. App. Div. 1974) 231
Myatt, People v. (N.Y. App. Div. 1998) 318
Myers v. Collett (Utah 1954) 86

N.E., In re (Wis. 1985) 243
N.H., In re (D.C. 1990) *507*
N.H.B., In re (Utah Ct. App. 1989) 203
Naprstek v. City of Norwich (2d Cir. 1976) 36
New Jersey Division of Youth and Family Services v. A.W. (N.J. 1986) 532
New Mexico v. Lili L. (N.M. Ct. App. 1995) *500*
New Mexico ex rel. Children, Youth and Families Department v. George F. (N.M. Ct. App. 1998) *590*
New York v. Coulter (N.Y. Dist. Ct. 1999) 719
New York State National Organization for Women v. Terry (2d Cir. 1989) 561
New Jersey v. T.L.O. (U.S. 1985) *153*, 169, 171, 308
Newman v. Newman (Conn. 1995) 589
Newsome v. Batavia Local School District (6th Cir. 1988) 141-42
Nichol v. Stass (Ill. 2000) 649
Nicini v. Morra (3d Cir. 2000) *468*, 474
Nieves v. United States (S.D.N.Y. 1968) 247
Norlund, State v. (Wash. Ct. App. 1982) 27
Norman, State v. (Wash. Ct. App. 1991) 432
Norwood, In Interest of (Neb. 1975) 427
Nunez v. City of San Diego (9th Cir. 1997) 36

O.C., State v. (Fla. 1999) 61, 63
O.M. v. State (Ala. Crim. App. 1991) 229, 231
O'Connell, People ex rel. v. Turner (Ill. 1870) *8*, 10-11
Oklahoma v. Walker (Okla. 2000) 773-74
Oliver, Adoption of (Mass. App. Ct. 1990) *675*, *787*
Orville v. Division of Family Services (Del. Super. Ct. 2000) 746

Ostrum v. Department of Health and Rehabilitative Services
(Fla. Dist. Ct. App. 1995) 505
Oxendine v. Catawba Department of Social Services (N.C. 1982) 643
Oyoghok v. Anchorage (Alaska 1982) 318

P.B. v. Koch (9th Cir. 1996) 151
P.J.K., In re Welfare of (Minn. 1985) *790*
P.K. v. Polk County (Iowa Ct. App. 2000) 486
P.L.F., In re (Neb. 1984) 265
P.R. v. State (Ga. Ct. App. 1974) *285*
P.R.J. v. State (Alaska Ct. App. 1990) 281
Palmer v. Merluzzi (3d Cir. 1989) 141
Palmer v. State (Del. 1993) 86
Parham v. J.R. (U.S. 1979) 844, *850*, 861-62
Parker, United States v. (8th Cir. 1992) 183
Parker v. Monroe County Department of Public Welfare
(Ind. Ct. App. 1989) 461-62
Pauley v. Gross (Kan. Ct. App. 1977) 86
Pedro Q., In re (Cal. Ct. App. 1989) *316*, 318
Peery v. Hanley (Or. Ct. App. 1995) 486
Penny J., State v. (N.M. Ct. App. 1994) 817
Perkins, Matter of (Ind. Ct. App. 1976) 397
Pernishek, In re (Pa. Super. Ct. 1979) 662
Perry v. State (Ind. 1989) 76
Pesce v. J. Sterling Morton High School District 302
(N.D. Ill. 1986) 384-85
Picha v. Wielgos (N.D. Ill. 1976) 170
Pickens, State v. (Ohio Ct. App. 1996) 110
Pickens, People v. (Ill. App. Ct. 1989) 319
Pierce v. Society of Sisters (U.S. 1925) *452*, *731*, 735
Piland v. Clark County Juvenile Court Services (Nev. 1969) 252
Pima County Delinquency Action No. 90101-1, In re
(Ariz. Ct. App. 1987) *283*, 285
Pima County Juvenile Severance Action No. S-113432, In re
(Ariz. Ct. App. 1993) *586*, *827*
Plain Dealer Publishing Co. v. Geauga County Court of Common
Pleas, Juvenile Division, Ohio, State ex rel. (Ohio 2000) 248
Planned Parenthood of Southern Nevada, Inc. v. Clark County
School District (9th Cir. 1991) 124
Planned Parenthood v. Casey (U.S. 1992) 735
Plotkin v. Department of Health and Social Services, State ex rel.
(Wis. 1974) 318
Pointer, People v. (Cal. Ct. App. 1984) 420
Poling v. Murphy (6th Cir. 1989) 124
Prince v. Massachusetts (U.S. 1944) *454*, *731*, 785

Q.D., State v. (Wash. 1984) 48
Quilloin v. Walcott (U.S. 1978) 839

Quiroz, State v. (Wash. 1987) *105*, 110
Qutb v. Strauss (5th Cir. 1993) *31*, 36-37

R., In re (Cal. 1970) 48
R.A., In Interest of (Ga. Ct. App. 1997) 802
R.G.S. v. District Court (Okla. Crim. App. 1981) 260
R.H.N., In the Matter of (Colo. 1985) 786
R.L.K., In re (Ill. App. Ct. 1978) 259
R.L.R. v. State (Alaska 1971) 243, 247
R.S. v. Trent, State ex rel. (W. Va. 1982) *278*, 281
R.T., In Interest of (Pa. Super. Ct. 1991) 589
Racine Unified School Districts v. Thompson (Wis. Ct. App. 1982) 142
Ramos, Commonwealth v. (Pa. Super. Ct. 1990) 351
Randolph T., In re (Md. 1981) 195
Rayes, State v. (N.H. 1997) 114
Reid v. Texas (Tex. Ct. App. 1998) 719
Rejda v. Rejda (Neb. 1977) 427
Richards, In re (N.Y. Fam. Ct. 1938) 436
Richie v. Board of Education of Lead Hill School District (Ark. 1996) 141
Ricky H., In re (Cal. 1970) 104
Riddle, State v. (W. Va. 1981) 437
Ridgley, State v. (Alaska 1987) 103
Riffe, In re (Mich. Ct. App. 1985) *657*, 662
Ripley, People v. (Ill. App. Ct. 1997) *663*
Rivera v. Marcus (2d Cir. 1982) 631
Robert M., In re (N.Y. Fam. Ct. 1981) *45*, 48
Robert H., State v. (N.H. 1978) 767
Robertson, In Interest of (Ill. App. Ct. 1977) 505
Robinson, Commonwealth v. (Mass. App. Ct. 1991) 661
Rodarte v. Cox (Tex. Ct. App. 1991) 631
Rodgers, Commonwealth v. (Pa. Super. Ct. 1987) 687
Rodriguez, In re (Tex. App. 1985) *292*
Rodriquez v. McLoughlin (2d Cir. 2000) 631
Roe v. Wade (U.S. 1973) 735
Roe v. Conn (M.D. Ala. 1976) 514, 735
Rogers, State v. (N.C. Ct. App. 1974) 103
Ronald S., In re (Cal. Ct. App. 1977) 27
Rosado v. Corrections (1st Cir. 1997) 195
Rouw v. State (Ark. 1979) 101
Ruth Anne E., In re (N.M. Ct. App. 1999) *741*, 746

S.B., In re (Mont. 1986) 661
S.C., In re (Miss. 1991) 171
S.C., State in the Interest of v. D.N.C. (La. Ct. App. 1994) 505, 755
S.E., In Interest of (Ill. App. Ct. 1998) 802
S.H., In re (Tex. Ct. App. 1992) 243-44
S.H., In re (Ga. Ct. App. 1996) 210
S.H., State v. (Wash. Ct. App. 1994) 278

S.H., In re (N.J. 1972) 101
S.M. v. Elkhart County Office of Family and Children (Ind. Ct. App. 1999) 774
S.M., In re (Pa. Super. Ct. 1992) 505
S.R., In re (Vt. 1991) 720
S.S., In Interest of (Ga. Ct. App. 1998) 427
S.W.T., In re Welfare of (Minn. 1979) 210
Samantha D., In re (N.M. Ct. App. 1987) 785
Sampson, In re (N.Y. Fam. Ct. 1970) 433
Sanders v. State (Ga. 1983) *707*
Santana v. Collazo (1st Cir. 1986) 277
Santosky v. Kramer (U.S. 1982) 477, 730, 735-36, 746, *756*, 766-67
Schall v. Martin (U.S. 1984) *78*, 84-87, 91
Schauer, Matter of (Minn. Ct. App. 1990) 862
Schmidt, State v. (Ohio 1987) 437
Schneckloth v. Bustamonte (U.S. 1973) 76
School District of Abington Township Pennsylvania v. Schempp (U.S. 1963) *126*, 131, 133
Scott Y., In re (Wis. Ct. App. 1993) *517*
Scott L. v. State (Nev. 1988) *327*, 328, *333*
Seattle v. Pullman (Wash. 1973) 36
Shane T., In re (N.Y. Fam. Ct. 1982) 409
Sharon K., In re (W. Va. 1989) 862
Sherrard v. Owens (W.D. Mich. 1980) 631
Short v. Short (D. Colo. 1990) 610
Sims v. State Department of Public Welfare (S.D. Tex. 1977) 485
Sims v. Waln (6th Cir. 1976) 151
Singleton v. State (Ga. Ct. App. 1973) 397
Skinner v. Oklahoma (U.S. 1942) 735
Skipwith, In re (N.Y. Fam. Ct. 1958) 436
Smagula, State v. (N.H. 1977) 195
Smith v. State (Fla. 1975) 259
Smith, Commonwealth v. (Pa. 1977) 103-04
Smith, In re (La. Ct. App. 1992) 231
Smith v. Organization of Foster Families (U.S. 1977) 613, *624*, 631
Snell, State v. (N.J. Super. Ct. App. Div. 1998) *380*, 385
Snyder, Commonwealth v. (Mass. 1992) 171
Sosa by and through Grant v. Koshy (Tex. Ct. App. 1997) 595
Souza v. Superior Court (Cal. Ct. App. 1987) 824
Spaulding, In re (Md. 1975) 75
Spencer, Commonwealth v. (Mass. App. Ct. 1998) 195
Spikes v. Banks (Mich. Ct. App. 1998) 649
Stacey R., In re (S.C. 1993) 231
Stanford v. Kentucky (U.S. 1989) *365*, 375
Stanley v. Fairfax County Department of Social Services (Va. 1991) *602*
Stanley v. Illinois (U.S. 1972) 399, *731*, 785, *831*, 839
Stapelkemper, Matter of (Mont. 1977) 52
Stephanie M., In re (Cal. 1994) 487

Stephens, In re (Pa. 1983) 260
Steven G., In re (Conn. 1989) 229
Steven J., In Interest of (Pa. Super. Ct. 1985) 287
Steven A., In re Interest of (Neb. Ct. App. 1994) 442
Steven S., In re (Cal. Ct. App. 1981) 419
Stokes v. Commonwealth (Mass. 1975) 260
Stone, United States v. (7th Cir. 1968) 76
Stremski v. Owens (Kan. 1987) 486
Summers v. State (Ind. 1967) 195
Swisher v. Brady (U.S. 1978) 259-60

T.D.W., In re (Ill. App. Ct. 1982) 210-11
T.F.F., United States v. (6th Cir. 1995) 194-95
T.L.B., In Interest of (Ill. App. Ct. 1989) 281
T.M.B., In re (N.J. Super. Ct. Ch. Div. 1993) 827
T.M.W., In the Interest of (Fla. Dist. Ct. App. 1989) 726
T.O., In Interest of (Iowa 1991) 534
T.S. v. Department of Health and Rehabilitative Services
(Fla. Dist. Ct. App. 1995) *407*
Taft v. Taft (Mass. 1983) 419
Tamara R., In re (Md. Ct. App. 2000) 554
Tanner, State v. (Utah 1983) *681*
Tara M. v. City of Philadelphia (3d Cir. 1998) *608*
Tasseing H., In re (Pa. Super. Ct. 1980) 27
Taylor v. State (Ala. Crim. App. 1986) 76
Tenenbaum v. Williams (2d Cir. 1999) 462, *479*, 487
Terry, State v. (Iowa 1997) 203
Thompson v. State (Ind. Ct. App. 1998) 100
Thompson, In re (Iowa 1976) 101
Thompson v. Carthage School District (8th Cir. 1996) 170
Thompson v. Oklahoma (U.S. 1988) *356*, 375
Thorpe, People v. (Colo. 1982) 182
Tibbs, In the Interest of (Neb. 1976) 427
Tibbs v. Board of Education of Franklin Township (N.J. Super.
1971) 141-42
Tikyra A., In re (Ohio Ct. App. 1995) *386*
Tinker v. Des Moines Independent Community School District
(U.S. 1969) *117*, 123-25, 134
Todd v. Rush County Schools (7th Cir. 1998) 171
Toennis, State v. (Wash. Ct. App. 1988) 688
Tonry, United States v. (5th Cir. 1979) 308
Torrance P. v. Raymond C. (Wis. Ct. App. 1994) 817
Trimble v. Stone (D.D.C. 1960) 86
Trinidad School District No. 1 v. Lopez (Colo. 1998) 171
Trowbridge, Matter of (Mich. Ct. App. 1986) 505
Troxel v. Granville (U.S. 2000) *543*, 554-55, 621
Trujillo v. Taos Municipal Schools (D.N.M. 1995) 142
Tunstall ex rel. Tunstall v. Bergeson (Wash. 2000) *338*

Turner, State v. (Or. 1969) 243
Two Minor Children, Matter of (Nev. 1979) 52, 211
Tyvonne, In re (Conn. 1989) 47-48

Unrue, In re (Ohio Ct. App. 1996) 231

Valencia, State v. (Ariz. 1979) 101
Valerie D., In re (Conn. 1992) *668*, 674-75
Valerie D., In re (Conn. 1991) *787*
Valmonte v. Bane (2d Cir. 1994) 384
Van Lue v. Collins (Or. Ct. App. 1989) 840
Vanessa C., In re (Md. Ct. Spec. App. 1995) 486
Vasquez v. Hillary (U.S. 1986) 738
Vento v. State (Tex. Ct. App. 1987) 308
Verhagen, State v. (Wis. Ct. App. 1995) *196*
Vernonia School District 47J v. Acton (U.S. 1995) *161*, 171-72

W.A.F., In re (D.C. 1990) 211
W.L.W. III, In re (Ill. App. Ct. 1998) 505
W.M. v. State (Ind. Ct. App. 1982) 27-28, 337
Wade v. Green (Okla. 1987) 785
Wallace v. Smyth (Ill. App. Ct. 1998) 649
Wallace v. Jaffree (U.S. 1985) 133
Walter v. State (N.D. 1969) 328
Walz v. Tax Commission (U.S. 1970) 131
Ward, People v. (N.Y. App. Div. 1983) 101
Washington v. Glucksberg (U.S. 1997) 477
Waters v. Barry (D.D.C. 1989) 36
Watts, United States v. (10th Cir. 1975) 229
Webster, Commonwealth v. (Pa. 1974) 101
Weiss, In re (Mich. Ct. App. 1997) 31
Welfare of Snyder, In re (Wash. 1975) *28*, 31, 87
Wellington, United States v. (11th Cir. 1996) 194
West v. United States (5th Cir. 1968) 101
West, State v. (Wis. Ct. App. 1994) 397
West v. Derby Unified School District No. 260 (D. Kan. 1998) 142
White, In re (Cal. Ct. App. 1979) 319
White, United States v. (4th Cir. 1998) 193
White Bear, United States v. (8th Cir. 1982) 229
Whitner v. State (S.C. 1997) 674-75
Wiley v. Franklin (D. Tenn. 1980) 133
William A., In re (Md. 1988) 48
Williams v. Coleman (Mich. Ct. App. 1992) 384
Williams v. Colton (Fla. Ct. App. 1977) 151
Willis v. Anderson Community School Corporation (7th Cir. 1998) 171
Wilson v. Georgia Dept. of Human Resources (Ga. Ct. App. 1984) 802
Winburn v. State (Wis. 1966) 52
Winship, In re (U.S. 1970) *232*, 236-37

Wisconsin v. Yoder (U.S. 1972) 436
Wise v. Pea Ridge School District (8th Cir. 1988) 151
Wolf v. State (Idaho 1978) 183
Woodard v. Los Fresnos Independent School District (5th Cir. 1984) 151
Worrell v. Elkhart County Office of Family and Children (Ind. 1998) *615*, 621

Ybarra v. Texas Dep't of Human Services (Tex. Ct. App. 1993) 505, 755
Young v. Young (N.Y. App. Div. 1987) 561
Young, State v. (Ohio Ct. App. 1991) 688
Young, State v. (Ohio Ct. App. 1975) 252
Youngberg v. Romeo (U.S. 1982) 862

Zachariah K., Adoption of (Cal. 1992) 825
Zamora v. Pomeroy (10th Cir. 1981) 170
Zanica C., Termination of Parental Rights of (Wis. App. Ct. 1998) 767
Zeiser, In re (Ohio Ct. App. 1999) *437*, 442
Zorach v. Clauson (U.S. 1952) 133

Table of Statutes and Rules

Federal

18 U.S.C. § 5032 193-94
18 U.S.C. § 5033 229
18 U.S.C. § 5036 253
The Equal Access Act of 1984
  20 U.S.C. § 4071 133-34
The Indian Child Welfare Act
  25 U.S.C. §§ 1911 et seq. *568*
  25 U.S.C. § 1911(a) 580-81
  25 U.S.C. § 1911(b) 581
  25 U.S.C. § 1911(d) 582
  25 U.S.C. § 1912(f) *763*
Adoption Assistance and Child Welfare Act of 1980
  42 U.S.C. §§ 620-628, 670-679 ....488, 564-65
  42 U.S.C. § 670 830
  42 U.S.C. § 671(a)(15) 488-89, 490
Adoption and Safe Families Act of 1997
  42 U.S.C. § 673b *828*, 830
  42 U.S.C. § 675(5) *827*
  42 U.S.C. § 675(5)(C)....................516-17, 519, 533, 621, 829
Title I—Reasonable Efforts and Safety Requirements for Foster Care and Adoption Placements, § 101 ....*489-91*
42 U.S.C. § 1786 424
42 U.S.C. § 1983 ....170, 462, 476, 649
Child Abuse Prevention and Treatment Act
  42 U.S.C. §§ 5101-5107 600
Juvenile Justice and Delinquency Prevention Act of 1974
  42 U.S.C. §§ 5601-5778 110
  42 U.S.C. § 5601 337
  42 U.S.C. § 5633(a)(12)(A) 337
  42 U.S.C. §§ 5667e et seq. 866
42 U.S.C. § 12132 817
Uniform Child-Custody Jurisdiction and Enforcement Act §§ 201-204, 206-207, 9 U.L.A. 671 (1997) *822*
Uniform Juvenile Court Act
  § 30(a)....................532-33
  § 47(a) 533
  § 58....................561
Interstate Compact on the Placement of Children (1961) *534*

U.S. Const. Amend. XIII 291
Federal Rule of Civil Procedure 17(c) 589
Model Penal Code
§ 3.08 398
§ 210.6 374
§ 213.4 404
§ 301.1(2)(1) 315

Alabama
Ala. Code § 12-15-1.1 281
Ala. Code § 12-15-34(a) 182
Ala. Code § 12-15-63(b) 755
Ala. Code § 12-15-65 ....*245*, 247, 491, 510, 766
Ala. Code § 15-25-5 706
Ala. Code § 26-18-7 ....766, 803
Ala. Code § 26-18-7(a)(2) 795

Alaska
Alaska Stat. § 25.24.310 ....*590*
Alaska Stat. § 34.50.020 636
Alaska Stat. § 47.10.080 ....281, 766
Alaska Stat. § 47.10.086 491
Alaska Stat. § 47.12.100(b) 195
Alaska Stat. § 47.30-735(d) 862
Alaska Admin. Code tit. 7, § 53.100 636

Arizona
Ariz. Rev. Stat. Ann. § 8-221 755
Ariz. Rev. Stat. Ann. § 8-247 560
Ariz. Rev. Stat. Ann. § 8-523(C) 607
Ariz. Rev. Stat. Ann. § 8-533 766
Ariz. Rev. Stat. Ann. § 8-535 605
Ariz. Rev. Stat. Ann. § 8-537 739
Ariz. Rev. Stat. Ann. § 8-537(A) *756*
Ariz. Rev. Stat. Ann. § 8-537(B) *762*
Ariz. Rev. Stat. Ann. § 8-843 ....*495*
Ariz. Rev. Stat. Ann. § 8-844 510
Ariz. Rev. Stat. Ann. § 8-846(C) 796
Ariz. Rev. Stat. Ann. § 8-863 ....739, 766
Ariz. Rev. Stat. Ann. § 8-871 491
Ariz. Rev. Stat. Ann. § 13-1416 404
Ariz. Rev. Stat. Ann. § 36-518 861

Arkansas
Ark. Code Ann. § 9-9-201 491
Ark. Code Ann. § 9-27-316 607
Ark. Code Ann. § 9-27-317(a) 230
Ark. Code Ann. § 9-27-318(b) 183

Ark. Code Ann. § 9-27-319 259
Ark. Code Ann. § 9-27-327(b) 252
Ark. Code Ann. § 9-27-329(d) 281
Ark. Code Ann. § 9-27-338 519
Ark. Code Ann. § 9-27-341 739
Ark. Code Ann. § 16-6-105 607

California
Cal. Health & Safety Code § 24520(a) 667
Cal. Health & Safety Code § 24520(b) 666
Cal. Health & Safety Code § 24520(c) 667
Cal. Health & Safety Code § 24522 667
Cal. Penal Code §§ 11161.8, 11166 384
Cal. Penal Code § 2625 ....*740*
Cal. Prob. Code § 2105 812
Cal. Welf. & Inst. Code § 202 290
Cal. Welf. & Inst. Code § 213.5(a) 379, *562*
Cal. Welf. & Inst. Code § 300 387-88
Cal. Welf. & Inst. Code § 317 ....596, 755
Cal. Welf. & Inst. Code § 346 247
Cal. Welf. & Inst. Code § 361 491
Cal. Welf. & Inst. Code § 366.23(b) 739
Cal. Welf. & Inst. Code §§ 601-602 ....*24*
Cal. Welf. & Inst. Code § 603.5 ....*63*
Cal. Welf. & Inst. Code § 626 281
Cal. Welf. & Inst. Code § 701 237
Cal. Welf. & Inst. Code § 729.3(c) 294
Cal. Welf. & Inst. Code § 6000 861

Colorado
Colo. Rev. Stat. § 19-2-107 243
Colo. Rev. Stat. § 19-3-203(3) 596
Colo. Rev. Stat. § 19-3-505 510
Colo. Rev. Stat. § 19-3-602 ....605, 739, 755
Colo. Rev. Stat. § 19-3-604 491
Colo. Rev. Stat. § 19-3-702 519
Colo. Rev. Stat. § 19-5-105 766

Connecticut
Conn. Gen. Stat. Ann. § 17a-112 (West 1998 & Supp. 2001)
Conn. Gen. Stat. Ann. § 45a-624 811
Conn. Gen. Stat. Ann. § 45a-716 755
Conn. Gen. Stat. Ann. § 45a-717 766
Conn. Gen. Stat. Ann. § 46b-127 ....*187*
Conn. Gen. Stat. Ann. § 46b-135(a) 231
Conn. Gen. Stat. Ann. § 46b-137 102
Conn. Gen. Stat. Ann. § 54-86g(b) 706

Delaware
Del. Code Ann. tit. 10, § 901(11) 432
Del. Code Ann. tit. 10, § 1007(g) 252
Del. Code Ann. tit. 13, § 705A *443*
Del. Code Ann. tit. 13, § 1107 ....*736*, 739
Del. Code Ann. tit. 13, § 722(a) 781
Del. Code Ann. tit. 16, § 5010(2) 862
Del. Code Ann. tit. 31, § 3605(d) 595

District of Columbia
D.C. Code Ann. § 16-2307(e) 195
D.C. Code Ann. § 16-2316(a) 243
D.C. Code Ann. § 16-2353 781
D.C. Code Ann. § 16-2354 605
D.C. Code Ann. § 16-2358 738
D.C. Code Ann. § 16-2359 738
D.C. Code Ann. § 16-2372 607
D.C. Code Ann. § 21-511 861

Florida
Fla. Stat. Ann. §§ 39.001- .002 329
Fla. Stat. Ann. § 39.01(70) 605
Fla. Stat. Ann. § 39.201 ....*379*
Fla. Stat. Ann. § 39.704 491
Fla. Stat. Ann. § 39.801 739
Fla. Stat. Ann. § 39.802 766
Fla. Stat. Ann. § 39.806(1)(d) *797*
Fla. Stat. Ann. § 39.807 605
Fla. Stat. Ann. § 39.807(2)(d) 605
Fla. Stat. Ann. § 39.809 739
Fla. Stat. Ann. § 39.809 803
Fla. Stat. Ann. § 394.467 862
Fla. Stat. Ann. § 744.304 811
Fla. Stat. Ann. § 948.04 291
Fla. Stat. Ann. § 985.226(3)(c) 195

Georgia
Ga. Code Ann. § 15-11-1 329
Ga. Code Ann. §§ 15-11-2(11), 2(12) *24-25*
Ga. Code Ann. § 15-11-2(12)(E) 41
Ga. Code Ann. § 15-11-5(b) 562
Ga. Code Ann. § 15-11-28(c.1) 247
Ga. Code Ann. § 15-11-30(b) 230
Ga. Code Ann. § 15-11-31(b) 231
Ga. Code Ann. § 15-11-100 738
Ga. Code Ann. § 17-12-38.1 ....*747*
Ga. Code Ann. § 19-8-10 766
Ga. Code Ann. § 24A-1603(a) 44

Ga. Code Ann. § 42-2-5.1 344

Hawaii
Haw. Rev. Stat. § 571-41(a) 243
Haw. Rev. Stat. § 571-62 739

Idaho
Idaho Code § 16-1603 378
Idaho Code § 66-329(k)(2) 862

Illinois
5 Ill. Comp. Stat. Ann. 350/1 636
20 Ill. Comp. Stat. Ann. 505/7 519
20 Ill. Comp. Stat. Ann. 520/1-15 622
235 Ill. Comp. Stat. Ann. 5/6-24a(b) 679
705 Ill. Comp. Stat. Ann. 405/1-5(1) 230
705 Ill. Comp. Stat. Ann. 405/2-13.1 491
705 Ill. Comp. Stat. Ann. 405/2-13.1(1)(a) 595
705 Ill. Comp. Stat. Ann. 405/2-16 739
705 Ill. Comp. Stat. Ann. 405/2-17.1(8) 607
705 Ill. Comp. Stat. Ann. 405/2-18 679
705 Ill. Comp. Stat. Ann. 405/2-18(1) & 405/3-20 237
705 Ill. Comp. Stat. Ann. 405/2-21 510
705 Ill. Comp. Stat. Ann. 405/2-29 766
705 Ill. Comp. Stat. Ann. 405/5-605 52
705 Ill. Comp. Stat. Ann. 405/5-750 281
705 Ill. Comp. Stat. Ann. 405/5-805(2)(b) 195
735 Ill. Comp. Stat. Ann. 5/8-2601 404
750 Ill. Comp. Stat. Ann. 5/203 679
755 Ill. Comp. Stat. Ann. 5/11-5.3 811
Illinois Juvenile Court Act of 1899 ....15, *16-19*, 20

Indiana
Ind. Code Ann. § 16-41-40-2 666
Ind. Code Ann. § 16-41-40-5 667
Ind. Code Ann. § 31-15-6-9 607
Ind. Code Ann. § 31-30-2-1 494
Ind. Code Ann. §§ 31-30-3-2 & -3 195
Ind. Code Ann. § 31-32-5-1 103
Ind. Code Ann. §§ 31-33-13-5, 31-33-14-1, 31-33-14- 2 & 31-33-18-2 115-16
Ind. Code Ann. § 31-34-1-1 511
Ind. Code Ann. § 31-34-9-7 584
Ind. Code Ann. § 31-34-12-4 397
Ind. Code Ann. § 31-34-18-1(a) 284
Ind. Code Ann. § 31-34-18-1.1 284
Ind. Code Ann. § 31-34-18-2 284
Ind. Code Ann. § 31-34-18-3 284
Ind. Code Ann. § 31-34-18-4 284

Ind. Code Ann. § 31-34-18-6.1 284
Ind. Code Ann. § 31-34-21-5.6 491
Ind. Code Ann. § 31-35-3-4 803
Ind. Code Ann. § 31-35-4-3 775
Ind. Code Ann. §§ 31-39-2-5, 31-39-2-6, 31-39-2-9, 31-39-4-6 & 31-39-4-7 116

Iowa
Iowa Code Ann. § 232.8(1)(c) 203
Iowa Code Ann. § 232.104 515-16
Iowa Code Ann. § 232.116 ....491, 803
Iowa Code Ann. § 600A.6 739

Kansas
Kan. Stat. Ann. § 38-1505a 607
Kan. Stat. Ann. § 38-1583 ....766, 795
Kan. Stat. Ann. § 38-1656 243
Kan. Stat. Ann. § 59-2136 491
Kansas Supreme Court Rules, Rule 110 606

Kentucky
Ky. Rev. Stat. Ann. § 202A.026 862
Ky. Rev. Stat. Ann. § 605.090(1)(c) 27
Ky. Rev. Stat. Ann. § 620.060 486
Ky. Rev. Stat. Ann. § 620.100 510
Ky. Rev. Stat. Ann. § 620.230 519
Ky. Rev. Stat. Ann. §§ 620.230(1), .230(2)(e) 519
Ky. Rev. Stat. Ann. § 625.041 605
Ky. Rev. Stat. Ann. § 625.042 739
Ky. Rev. Stat. Ann. § 625.090 .... 766, 781, 794
Ky. Rev. Stat. Ann. § 645.230 849
Kentucky Rules of Jefferson Family Court § 403 739

Louisiana
La. Rev. Stat. Ann., Ch. C. § 424.10 607
La. Rev. Stat. Ann., Ch. C. § 682 491
La. Rev. Stat. Ann., Ch. C. § 1509.1 561

Maine
Me. Rev. Stat. Ann. tit. 15, § 3101.4.E-2 195
Me. Rev. Stat. Ann. tit. 15, § 3315 281
Me. Rev. Stat. Ann. tit. 22, § 4005-A 614
Me. Rev. Stat. Ann. tit. 34-B, § 3851 861-62

Maryland
Md. Code Ann., Cts. & Jud. Proc. § 3-819(b) 237
Md. Code Ann., Cts. & Jud. Proc. § 3-819(d) 237
Md. Code Ann., Cts. & Jud. Proc. § 3-286.1(d)(2)-(3) 519
Md. Code Ann., Fam. Law § 5-313 ....766, 781

Massachusetts
Mass. Gen. Laws Ann. ch. 119, § 67 86
Mass. Gen. Laws Ann. ch. 119, § 29C 491
Mass. Gen. Laws Ann. ch. 123, § 8 862
Mass. Gen. Laws Ann. ch. 201, § 2D 811

Michigan
Mich. Comp. Laws Ann. § 24.275a 706
Mich. Comp. Laws Ann. § 600.2163a 706
Mich. Comp. Laws Ann. § 712A.4(4) 195
Mich. Comp. Laws Ann. § 712A.12 229
Mich. Comp. Laws Ann. § 712A.18f 491
Mich. Comp. Laws Ann. § 722.25 766

Minnesota
Minn. Stat. Ann. § 145.9265 680
Minn. Stat. Ann. § 145.9266 679
Minn. Stat. Ann. § 260B.001(2) 45
Minn. Stat. Ann. § 260.012 ....329, 491
Minn. Stat. Ann. § 260B.125(2)(6) 195-96
Minn. Stat. Ann. §§ 260B.143 & 260C.143 229

Mississippi
Miss. Code Ann. § 93-15-103 794
Miss. Code Ann. § 93-15-107(1) 602
Miss. Code Ann. § 93-15-109 766

Missouri
Mo. Ann. Stat. § 211.071(6) 284
Mo. Ann. Stat. § 211.447 ....766-67, 803
Mo. Ann. Stat. § 537.045 650
Mo. Ann. Stat. § 632.110 862

Montana
Mont. Code Ann. § 41-3-607 605
Mont. Code Ann. § 41-3-609 ....776, 794
Mont. Code Ann. § 41-3-609(4)(b) 796
Mont. Code Ann. § 41-5-1502(1) 243
Mont. Code Ann. § 40-7-103 824

Nebraska
Neb. Rev. Stat. § 43-247 183
Neb. Rev. Stat. § 43-272(1) 230
Neb. Rev. Stat. § 43-279.01 773
Neb. Rev. Stat. § 43-283.01 491
Neb. Rev. Stat. § 43-286(1)(a) 288
Neb. Rev. Stat. § 43-291 739

Nevada

Nev. Rev. Stat. § 62.080 182
Nev. Rev. Stat. § 128.100 755
Nev. Rev. Stat. § 128.106 803
Nev. Rev. Stat. § 432B.393 491

New Hampshire

N.H. Rev. Stat. Ann. § 169-B:1 329
N.H. Rev. Stat. Ann. § 169-C:24-a 491
N.H. Rev. Stat. Ann. § 170-C:7 739
N.H. Rev. Stat. Ann. § 170-C:5 795
1997 N.H. Laws 93-A 706

New Jersey

N.J. Stat. Ann. § 2A:4A-21 329
N.J. Stat. Ann. § 2A:4A-23 42
N.J. Stat. Ann. §2A:4A-26(a)(3) 195
N.J. Stat. Ann. § 2A:4A-34(e) 85, 91
N.J. Stat. Ann. § 2A:4A-40 243
N.J. Stat. Ann. § 3B:12-69 811
N.J. Stat. Ann. § 3B:12-72 811
N.J. Stat. Ann. § 30:4-123.59 281
N.J. Stat. Ann. § 30:4C-11.3 491

New Mexico

N.M. Stat. Ann. § 32A-2-14(E) 102
N.M. Stat. Ann. § 32A-2-14(H) 230
N.M. Stat. Ann. § 32A-2-16(E) 237
N.M. Stat. Ann. §§ 32A-3B-14(b) & -4-20(H) 237
N.M. Stat. Ann. § 32A-4-29(G) 605
N.M. Stat. Ann. § 32A-4-29(F) 755
N.M. Stat. Ann. § 32A-6-13 847
N.M. Stat. Ann. § 32A-6-13(E)-(G) 849

New York

N.Y. Crim. Proc. Law § 60.44 706
N.Y. Exec. Law § 642-a 706
N.Y. Fam. Ct. Act § 341.1 247
N.Y. Fam. Ct. Act § 342.2(2) 237
N.Y. Fam. Ct. Act § 352.2 281
N.Y. Fam. Ct. Act § 352.2(2)(a) 332
N.Y. Fam. Ct. Act § 353.6(1)(a) 287
N.Y. Fam. Ct. Act § 744(b) 237
N.Y. Fam. Ct. Act § 1012(f) 378
N.Y. Surr. Ct. Proc. Act § 1726(3) 811

North Carolina

N.C. Gen. Stat. Ann. § 7A-608 182
N.C. Gen. Stat. § 7A-628 210
N.C. Gen. Stat. § 7B-101(9) *385*, 388
N.C. Gen. Stat. § 7B-101(1) *389*
N.C. Gen. Stat. § 7B-101(15) *420*
N.C. Gen. Stat. § 7B-507 491
N.C. Gen. Stat. § 35A-1373 811
1998 N.C. Sess. Laws 202 294

North Dakota

N.D. Cent. Code § 14-15-19(6) 755
N.D. Cen. Code §§ 15-11-35, 15-11-36 680
N.D. Cent. Code § 27-20-23 229
N.D. Cent. Code § 27-20-29(2) 237
N.D. Cent. Code § 27-20-32.2 491

Ohio

Ohio Rev. Code Ann. § 2151.01 329
Ohio Rev. Code Ann. § 2151.26(C)(1)(c) 195
Ohio Rev. Code Ann. § 2151.35 510
Ohio Rev. Code Ann. § 2151.414 ....767, 781
Ohio Rev. Code Ann. § 2151.416 ....*563*
Ohio Rev. Code Ann. § 2151.419 491

Oklahoma

Okla. Stat. Ann. tit. 10, § 7003-4.3 774
Okla. Stat. Ann. tit. 43A, § 5-505(B)(2)(b) 862

Oregon

Or. Rev. Stat. § 106.081 679
Or. Rev. Stat. § 109.119 621
Or. Rev. Stat. § 426.220 862

Pennsylvania

23 Pa. Cons. Stat. Ann. § 2512 ....*826*
23 Pa. Cons. Stat. Ann. § 6303 ....*406*
42 Pa. Cons. Stat. Ann. § 6340(e) 259
42 Pa. Cons. Stat. Ann. § 6341 510
42 Pa. Cons. Stat. Ann. § 6342(b) 607
42 Pa. Cons. Stat. Ann. § 6351 491
42 Pa. Cons. Stat. Ann. § 5984 776
42 Pa. Cons. Stat. Ann. § 5987 706

Rhode Island

R.I. Gen. Laws § 9-1-27.2 608

R.I. Gen. Laws § 14-1-30.2 .... *614*
R.I. Gen. Laws § 15-2-3.1 679
R.I. Gen. Laws § 15-7-7 767
R.I. Gen. Laws § 15-7-7(a) 766
R.I. Gen. Laws § 40-11-6.1 384

South Carolina
S.C. Code Ann. § 20-7-736(G) 679
S.C. Code Ann. § 20-7-763 491
S.C. Code Ann. § 20-7-1570 605

South Dakota
S.D. Codified Laws § 26-7A-56 281
S.D. Codified Laws §§ 26-7A-86 & -87 237
S.D. Codified Laws § 26-8A-26 491
S.D. Codified Laws § 26-8A-27 767
S.D. Codified Laws § 34-20A-63(3) 420

Tennessee
Tenn. Code Ann. § 37-1-101 329
Tenn. Code Ann. § 37-1-124(a) 243
Tenn. Code Ann. § 37-1-127(a) 231
Tenn. Code Ann. § 37-1-127(b) 231
Tenn. Code Ann. § 37-1-129 510
Tenn. Code Ann. § 37-1-129(b) 237
Tenn. Code Ann. § 37-1-129(c) 237
Tenn. Code Ann. § 57-1-211 679
Tenn. Code Ann. § 68-143-103 667

Texas
Tex. Fam. Code Ann. § 39.401(1)(3) 486
Tex. Fam. Code Ann. § 51.10(b) 230
Tex. Fam. Code Ann. § 53.02(b) 85, 91
Tex. Fam. Code Ann. § 53.04(d)(1) 229
Tex. Fam. Code Ann. § 54.02(f) 195
Tex. Fam. Code Ann. § 54.03(f) 237
Tex. Fam. Code Ann. § 59.005(a)(2), (6) & (7) 290
Tex. Fam. Code Ann. § 107.001 605
Tex. Fam. Code Ann. § 262.201 491
Tex. Hum. Res. Ann. § 42-0421 667
Tex. Penal Code Ann. § 71.02 .... *53*, 63

Utah
Utah Code Ann. § 76-5-109 .... *390*
Utah Code Ann. § 78-3a-117(3) 259
Utah Code Ann. § 78-3a-305.1 397
Utah Code Ann. § 78-3a-404 827
Utah Code Ann. § 78-3a-406 767

Utah Code Ann. § 78-3a-602 182
Utah Code Ann. § 62A-4a-404 679

Vermont
Vt. Stat. Ann. tit. 18, § 7617(c) 862
Vt. Stat. Ann. tit. 33, § 5501 329
Vt. Stat. Ann. tit. 33, § 5540 781

Virginia
Va. Code Ann. §§ 16.1-266(B) & -268 230
Va. Code Ann. § 16.1-277.1 252
Va. Code Ann. § 16.1-277.02(B) 773
Va. Code Ann. § 16.1-283 767
Va. Code Ann. § 16.1-349 811

Washington
Wash. Rev. Code Ann. § 4.24.590 645
Wash. Rev. Code Ann. § 9A-44.120 404
Wash. Rev. Code Ann. § 13.34.090 755
Wash. Rev. Code Ann. § 13.40.050 487-88
Wash. Rev. Code Ann. § 13-40-100(2) 229
Wash. Rev. Code Ann. § 26.44.053 596
Wash. Rev. Code Ann. § 43.121.140 667
Wash. Rev. Code Ann. § 66.16.110 679
Wash. Rev. Code Ann. §§ 70.83C.020, 70.96A.500 680

West Virginia
W. Va. Code § 18-8-1 436-37
W. Va. Code § 49-1-1 329
W. Va. Code § 49-1-3 399
W. Va. Code § 49-5-6 243
W. Va. Code § 49-6-2 767
W. Va. Code § 49-6-2(a) 596
W. Va. Code § 61-8-13 706
W. Va. Code §§ 61-8B-11(d), 61-8C-5(b) 706

Wisconsin
Wis. Stat. Ann. § 48.13 767
Wis. Stat. Ann. § 48.31 506-07
Wis. Stat. Ann. § 48.426 780
Wis. Stat. Ann. § 765.12(1) 679
Wis. Stat. Ann. § 767.045(5) 595
Wis. Stat. Ann. § 880.36 811
Wis. Stat. Ann. § 938.18(6) 196

Wyoming
Wyo. Stat. Ann. § 7-11-408(f) 706
Wyo. Stat. Ann. § 14-3-211(a) 610

Wyo. Stat. Ann. § 14-6-223(a) 231
Wyo. Stat. Ann. § 14-6-223(b) 231
Wyo. Stat. Ann. § 14-6-244 294
Wyo. Stat. Ann. § 25-10-106 862

Chapter 1

History and Philosophy of the Juvenile Justice System

A. Children in Criminal Court

1. England

Under the common law of England in the Fifteenth Century, children under the age of seven were conclusively presumed incapable of forming criminal intent, and thus could not be found guilty of crimes.[1] Children between the ages of seven and fourteen were also presumed incapable of forming criminal intent; however, a showing that the child could distinguish between right and wrong would rebut this presumption. A child over the age of fourteen was presumed to be able to form criminal intent and was held to the same level of responsibility for criminal wrongdoing as an adult.[2] During this period, there were no juvenile courts in England. Thus, a child between the ages of seven and fourteen who was accused of a crime (and found fit for trial) would be tried in an adult criminal court. If convicted, the child would receive the same sentence as an adult convicted of the same crime. Since there were no separate facilities for the incarceration of juvenile offenders, children were sent to adult jails. Within the prison, children received no special treatment and were housed alongside their adult counterparts.

As an alternative to incarceration, England tried various methods for dealing with delinquents or vagrant youths. The Marine Society, established in 1756, was one of the earliest private agencies in London interested in reclaiming delinquent boys. However, the Society's interests were not purely philanthropic. The Marine Society's main objective was to encourage recruits for the Royal Navy. In 1758, a House of Refuge for Orphan Girls opened with the purpose of rescuing destitute girls

---

1 From the Tenth Century until the reign of Henry VIII very little is known about England's laws affecting children.

2 *See* STEVEN M. COX & JOHN J. CONRAD, JUVENILE JUSTICE: A GUIDE TO PRACTICE AND THEORY 2 (1987).

from lives of prostitution. By the late 1700s, England even transported delinquent children out of the country. The Report of the Select Committee appointed by the House of Commons states that between 1787 and 1797 ninety-three delinquent children were transported from England to Australia due to crimes committed. This practice continued into the early 1800s when transportation for life was actually recommended for juvenile delinquents.[3]

Offending children were treated with severity throughout the Middle Ages in England. This harshness climaxed in the Seventeenth and Eighteenth Centuries with capital punishment being exercised against children for rather minor offenses. There were at times more than 300 offenses punishable by death.[4] The laws affecting juveniles were in desperate need of reform.[5]

2. United States

The American Colonies inherited this "juvenile justice system" from England, with a few modifications. In the Massachusetts Bay Colony, for example, there was no exemption from criminal culpability for children under the age of seven. While there were fewer death penalty offenses in colonial America, such penalties still existed, as evidenced by the 1650 Code of the Connecticut General Court (known as the "Connecticut Blue Laws").[6] Some of the capital offenses included offenses for which no adult would be liable. Among such capital offenses were the following:

* * *

> 13. If any child or children above sixteen years old and of sufficient understanding shall curse or smite their natural father or mother, he or they shall be put to death; unless it can be sufficiently testified that the parents have been very unchristianly negligent in the education of such children, or so provoke them by extreme and cruel correction that they have been forced thereunto to preserve themselves from death [or] maiming. Ex[odus] 21:15, 17; Lev[iticus] 20.

---

[3] *See* CLIFFORD E. SIMONSEN, JUVENILE JUSTICE IN AMERICA 10-11 (Collier Macmillan ed., Macmillan Publishing Company, 1991).

[4] *See* HERBERT H. LOU, PH.D., JUVENILE COURTS IN THE UNITED STATES 13-14 (1927).

[5] *See generally* WILEY B. SANDERS, JUVENILE OFFENDERS FOR A THOUSAND YEARS 3-91 (1970); Marvin Ventrell, *Evolution of the Dependency Component of the Juvenile Court,* 19 CHILDREN'S LEGAL RTS. J. 1, 3-5 (Winter 1999-2000).

[6] Between 1642 and the present, at least 287 juveniles were executed. Twelve of these executions involved children under fourteen years of age. Interestingly, 66.9 percent of the juvenile executions took place after a separate juvenile system was developed in 1899. *See* Victor L. Streib, *Death Penalty for Children: The American Experience with Capital Punishment for Crimes Committed While Under Age Eighteen,* 36 OKLA. L. REV. 613, 619 (1983).

> 14. If any man have a stubborn or rebellious son of sufficient years and understanding, viz., sixteen years of age, which will not obey the voice of his father or the voice of his mother, and that when they have chastened him will not hearken unto them, then may his father and mother, being his natural parents, lay hold on him and bring him to the magistrates assembled in Court, and testify unto them that their son is stubborn and rebellious and will not obey their voice and chastisement, but lives in sundry notorious crimes, such son shall be put to death. Deut[eronomy] 21:20, 21.

Other American Colonies had similar laws which, like the Connecticut Blue Laws, reflect the ecclesiastical underpinnings of colonial law.[7] As in England, the law treated children most severely in the Seventeenth and Eighteenth Centuries when minor offenses could result in capital punishment. For example, a child of eight was convicted of a felony and hanged for setting fire to a barn "with malice, revenge, craft and cunning" during this period.[8] Some early American reformers believed capital punishment and even physical punishments were too harsh for this new nation. Colonies such as New York and Pennsylvania began imprisoning the juvenile offenders in adult jails instead. However, imprisoning juveniles in adult jails was not the ideal solution either.[9]

In addition to a system for dealing with juvenile offenders, the Colonies also took from their forebears the English Poor Laws.[10] The colonists viewed poverty as a vice, a personal rather than a social problem. People were poor because they were lazy, idle, or dissolute. Thus, rather than providing outdoor aid,[11] the colonies, and later the states, set up programs of indoor aid in the form of poorhouses, almshouses, and workhouses. These institutions were touted as places where the poor could, through proper instruction and training, be cured of their mendicancy. In reality, these places were little more than pauper prisons.

---

[7] *See, e.g.,* the New Hampshire Province Laws of the First General Assembly and the Charters and General Laws of the Colony and Province of Massachusetts Bay.

[8] HERBERT H. LOU, PH.D., JUVENILE COURTS IN THE UNITED STATES 13 (1927).

[9] *See* Sanford J. Fox, *A Contribution to the History of the American Juvenile Court,* 49 JUV. & FAM. CT. J. 7 (1998).

[10] In England, Parliament passed the "Statute of Artificers" in 1562 which allowed the children of paupers to be involuntarily removed from their parents and apprenticed to others. In 1601, England passed the Poor Law Act that allowed children to be involuntarily separated from their poor parents and apprenticed to local residents. *See* STEVEN M. COX & JOHN J. CONRAD, JUVENILE JUSTICE: A GUIDE TO PRACTICE AND THEORY 3 (1987).

[11] "Outdoor aid" refers to cash payments to support the poor, the forerunner of the modern welfare system.

Because poverty was seen as a vice, poor parents were seen as unfit to raise their children. Many pauper children were removed from their homes and placed in apprenticeships or poorhouses. As with the prisons of the time, the poorhouses did not attempt to segregate children from adults. Thus, pauper children were, in essence, incarcerated along with older youths and adults, many of whom were beggars, thieves, and common criminals.[12]

A number of factors led to an increase in crime in the late Eighteenth Century. First, the Industrial Revolution caused poverty to become a larger problem as the gap in wealth between the rich and poor increased. Second, crimes involving property increased as more transportable goods existed. The Reform Movement began in response to this increase in juvenile crimes as the current juvenile system was not working.[13]

B. The Reform Movement

1. England

In the beginning of the Nineteenth Century, English law slowly began to change the way it viewed a child's capacity for criminal responsibility.[14] Societal views suggested that children older than seven were not fully responsible for their actions given their immaturity and inexperience. As a result, it was proposed that a separate tribunal be established specifically for the treatment of delinquent children. Such a system would benefit young offenders, as they would be spared the stigma of a public prison, the publicity of a trial, and all of the disadvantages and entrapments of early imprisonment. In addition, treating juveniles separately from adult criminals would provide an opportunity for the child to avoid the unwanted education of adult prison, increasing the chances that the child could become a productive member of society. As a result, an act was proposed to create a separate system designed for cases of larceny committed by persons under the age of twenty-one. Also, a suggestion was made that dependent or neglected children be appointed legal guardians to aid the children through care and education. These propositions were rejected due to opposition to the magis-

---

[12] *See* Douglas R. Rendleman, *Parens Patriae: From Chancery to the Juvenile Court,* 23 S.C. L. REV. 205, 213-23 (1971).

[13] *See* MARGARET C. JASPER, JUVENILE JUSTICE AND CHILDREN'S LAW 4-5 (1994); *see generally* Marvin Ventrell, *Evolution of the Dependency Component of the Juvenile Court,* 19 CHILDREN'S LEGAL RTS. J. 1, 6-7 (Winter 1999-2000).

[14] *See* Candace Zierdt, *The Little Engine that Arrived at the Wrong Station: How to Get Juvenile Justice Back on the Right Track,* 33 U.S.F. L. REV. 401 (1999), for a discussion of the early developments in English juvenile law.

trates becoming "judges, juries, and executioners" and because the people were suspicious of the proceedings being confidential.[15] In the early Nineteenth Century, England began to realize that juveniles could not be treated in the same manner as adults. However, England was not yet comfortable with the procedural issues surrounding the changes. Therefore, the positive changes were rejected.

During this era, the philosophies of the English reformers included explanations for the causes of juvenile delinquency. It was determined that poverty and neglect of the child were primarily responsible for aberrant behavior. This link between parental irresponsibility and juvenile delinquency introduced the concept of holding the parent responsible for the child's acts. In determining how best to address juvenile crime, the reformers eventually concluded that it was more efficient to rehabilitate juvenile delinquents than to incarcerate them.[16]

2. United States

Reformers in the United States were contemplating similar concerns, and this new awareness in the Nineteenth Century introduced a new era in the treatment of children.

Reformers began to speak out against the problems inherent in the system, especially the evils associated with housing pauper and delinquent children with their adult counterparts, while offering children no protection from the influences of these adults. Humanitarian reformers sought to divert children from the criminal justice system. They believed that children were especially amenable to treatment and rehabilitation and sought to institute these ideals in place of the prevailing notions of punishment and incarceration.

The reformers' voices were eventually heard, and several states established Houses of Refuge to replace the workhouses, poorhouses, apprenticeships, and, in some cases, incarceration in adult prisons for children.[17] The New York House of Refuge, established in 1824, was the first institution founded for the exclusive treatment of children. Several other cities soon followed suit; for example, Boston in 1826 and Philadelphia in 1828. By 1850, eight cities had established Houses of Refuge and more were established throughout the latter half of the century.

---

15 *See* STEVEN M. COX & JOHN CONRAD, JUVENILE JUSTICE: A GUIDE TO PRACTICE AND THEORY 4 (1987).

16 *See generally* WILEY B. SANDERS, JUVENILE OFFENDERS FOR A THOUSAND YEARS 96-313 (1970) (discussing English juvenile law in the Nineteenth Century).

17 *See* HERBERT H. LOU, PH.D., JUVENILE COURTS IN THE UNITED STATES 15-16 (1927), for a discussion of the Houses of Refuge.

Although they differed in some respects from each other, these institutions all shared several basic principles.[18] First and foremost, the Houses of Refuge segregated children from adults. It was recognized that children required special protections and merited special treatment, neither of which could be provided in an adult institution. The Houses of Refuge also sought to implement the reformers' goal of rehabilitation. In keeping with this goal, the institutions were limited to those children deemed amenable to rehabilitation. Those judged to be inappropriate candidates for rehabilitation and training were still handled in the adult system.[19]

While these reforms were a marked improvement over the previous system, serious problems continued to exist. For example, although children were housed separately from adults, no attempt was made within the Houses of Refuge to segregate juvenile delinquents from neglected or dependent children (those removed from their homes for lack of proper parental care). Thus, the problems associated with housing needy children alongside the criminally culpable continued to exist, albeit to a lesser degree. In addition, the custody rights of parents were ignored. The state was able, for class and economic reasons, to remove children permanently from the custody of their parents. Indeed, many children remained in the Houses of Refuge until they reached majority or were adopted out to unrelated third parties who were viewed as "more suitable" parents in the state's eyes.[20]

Ex parte Crouse

4 Whart. 9 (Pa. 1839)

This was a *habeas corpus* directed to the keeper and managers of the "House of Refuge," in the county of Philadelphia, requiring them to produce before the Court one Mary Ann Crouse, an infant, detained in that institution. The petition for the *habeas corpus* was in the name of her father.

[T]he girl had been committed to the custody of the managers by virtue of a warrant, . . . which recited that complaint and due proof had been made before [a justice of the peace] by Mary Crouse, the mother of the said Mary Ann Crouse, "that the said infant by reason of vicious conduct, has rendered her control beyond the power of the said complainant, and made it manifestly requisite that from regard to the moral and future welfare of the said infant she should be placed under the guardianship of the managers of the House of Refuge;"

---

[18] *See* Sanford J. Fox, *The Early History of the Court*, FUTURE OF CHILDREN, Winter 1996, 29, 30.

[19] *See id.*

[20] *See generally* WILEY B. SANDERS, JUVENILE OFFENDERS FOR A THOUSAND YEARS 331-453 (1970); Marvin Ventrell, *Evolution of the Dependency Component of the Juvenile Court,* 19 CHILDREN'S LEGAL RTS. J. 1, 7-9 (Winter 1999-2000).

and the said alderman certified that in his opinion the said infant was "a proper subject for the said House of Refuge." Appended to the warrant of commitment were the names and places of residence of the witnesses examined, and the substance of the testimony given by them respectively, upon which the adjudication of the magistrate was founded.

* * *

The House of Refuge is not a prison, but a school. Where reformation, and not punishment is the end, it may indeed be used as a prison for juvenile convicts who would else be committed to a common goal; and in respect to these, the constitutionality of the act which incorporated it, stands clear of controversy. . . . The object of the charity is reformation, by training its inmates to industry; by imbuing their minds with principles of morality and religion; by furnishing them with means to earn a living; and, above all, by separating them from the corrupting influence of improper associates. To this end, may not the natural parents, when unequal to the task of education, or unworthy of it, be superseded by the *parens patriae*, or common guardian of the community? It is to be remembered that the public has a paramount interest in the virtue and knowledge of its members, and that, of strict right, the business of education belongs to it. That parents are ordinarily entrusted with it, is because it can seldom be put into better hands; but where they are incompetent or corrupt, what is there to prevent the public from withdrawing their faculties, held, as they obviously are, at its sufferance? The right of parental control is a natural, but not an unalienable one. . . . As to abridgment of indefeasible rights by confinement of the person, it is no more than what is borne, to a greater or less extent, in every school; and we know of no natural right to exemption from restraints which conduce to an infant's welfare. Nor is there a doubt of the propriety of their application in the particular instance. The infant has been snatched from a course which must have ended in confirmed depravity; and, not only is the restraint of her person lawful, but it would be an act of extreme cruelty to release her from it.

Notes

1. The doctrine of *parens patriae* is discussed in the next section. At this point, however, note that *Ex parte Crouse* is the first published opinion upholding the state's *parens patriae* right to "protect" children by removing them from their parents and granting custody to the state.

2. As evidenced by the *Crouse* opinion, children continued to be treated harshly, even during the reform era of the Nineteenth Century. The reformers continued to fight the wrongs they saw in the system, and, slowly but steadily, attitudes toward children, both delinquents and those who were neglected, began to undergo drastic changes. This change in attitude can be seen in the following case, decided thirty-one years after *Crouse*.

People ex rel. O'Connell v. Turner
55 Ill. 280 (1870)

Mr. Justice THORNTON delivered the opinion of the Court:

By the order of this court, the writ of *habeas corpus* was issued, commanding Robert Turner, superintendent of the reform school of the city of Chicago, to show cause for the caption and detention of Daniel O'Connell.

The petition of Michael O'Connell represents that he is the father of Daniel, a boy between fourteen and fifteen years of age, and that he is restrained of his liberty contrary to the law, without conviction of crime. . . .

* * *

The only question for determination, is the power of the legislature to pass the laws, under which this boy was arrested and confined.

The first act, in relation to this "reform school," is a part of the charter of the city of Chicago, approved February 13, 1863, and the second is entitled, "an act in reference to the reform school of the city of Chicago," approved March 5, 1867.

The first section establishes "a school for the safe keeping, education, employment and reformation of all children between the ages of six and sixteen years, who are destitute of proper parental care, and growing up in mendicancy, ignorance, idleness or vice."

Section four, of the act of 1867, provides, that "whenever any police magistrate, or justice of the peace, shall have brought before him any boy or girl, within the ages of six or sixteen years, who he has reason to believe is a vagrant, or is destitute of proper parental care, or is growing up in mendicancy, ignorance, idleness or vice," he shall cause such boy or girl to be arrested, and, together with the witnesses, taken before one of the judges of the superior or circuit court of Cook County. . . . The section then directs, "if, upon . . . examination, such judge shall be of opinion that said boy or girl is a proper subject for commitment to the reform school, and that his or her moral welfare, and the good of society, require that he or she should be sent to said school for employment, instruction and reformation, he shall so decide, and direct the clerk of the court of which he is judge, to make out a warrant of commitment to said reform school; and such child shall thereupon be committed."

Section nine, of the act of 1863, directs, that all persons between six and sixteen years of age, convicted of crime punishable by fine or imprisonment, who, in the opinion of the court, would be proper subjects for commitment, shall be committed to said school.

Section ten authorizes the confinement of the children, and that they "shall be kept, disciplined, instructed, employed and governed," until they shall be reformed and discharged, or shall have arrived at the age of twenty-one years; and that the sole authority to discharge shall be in the board of guardians.

The warrant of commitment does not indicate that the arrest was made for a criminal offense. Hence, we conclude that it was issued under the general grant of power, to arrest and confine for misfortune.

The contingencies enumerated, upon the happening of [any] of which the power may be exercised, are vagrancy, destitution of proper parental care, mendicancy, ignorance, idleness or vice. Upon proof of any one, the child is deprived of home, and parents, and friends, and confined for more than half of an ordinary life. . . .

What is proper parental care? The best and kindest parents would differ, in the attempt to solve the question. No two scarcely agree; and when we consider the watchful supervision, which is so unremitting over the domestic affairs of others, the conclusion is forced upon us, that there is not a child in the land who could not be proved, by two or more witnesses, to be in this sad condition. Ignorance, idleness, vice, are relative terms. . . . What is the standard to be? What extent of enlightenment, what amount of industry, what degree of virtue, will save from the threatened imprisonment? In our solicitude to form youth for the duties of civil life, we should not forget the rights which inhere both in parents and children. The principle of the absorption of the child in, and its complete subjection to the despotism of, the State is wholly inadmissible in the modern civilized world.

The parent has the right to the care, custody and assistance of his child. The duty to maintain and protect it, is a principle of natural law. . . . Another branch of parental duty, strongly inculcated by writers on natural law, is the education of children. To aid in the performance of these duties, and enforce obedience, parents have authority over them. The municipal law should not disturb this relation, except for the strongest reasons. The ease with which it may be disrupted under the laws in question, the slight evidence required, and the informal mode of procedure, make them conflict with the natural right of the parent. Before any abridgment of the right, gross misconduct or almost total unfitness on the part of the parent, should be clearly proved. This power is an emanation from God, and every attempt to infringe upon it, except from dire necessity, should be resisted in all well governed States. "In this country, the hope of the child, in respect to its education and future advancement, is mainly dependent upon the father. . . . The violent abruption of this relation would not only tend to wither these motives to action, but necessarily, in time, alienate the father's natural affections."

But even the power of the parent must be exercised with moderation. He may use correction and restraint, but in a reasonable manner. He has the right to enforce only such discipline, as may be necessary to the discharge of his sacred trust; only moderate correction and temporary confinement. . . . Can the State, as *parens patriae*, exceed the power of the natural parent, except in punishing crime?

. . . The confinement [under the statute] may be from one to fifteen years, according to the age of the child. . . . Such a restraint upon natural liberty is tyranny and oppression. If, without crime, without the conviction of any offense, the children of the State are to be thus confined for the "good of society," then society had better be reduced to its original elements, and free government acknowledged a failure.

* * *

Can we hold children responsible for crime, liable for their torts, impose onerous burdens upon them, and yet deprive them of the enjoyment of liberty, without charge or conviction of crime? The Bill of Rights declares, that "all men are, by nature, free and independent, and have certain inherent and inalienable rights—among these are life, liberty, and the pursuit of happiness." This language is not restrictive; it is broad and comprehensive, and declares a grand truth, that "all men," all people, everywhere, have the inherent and inalienable right to liberty. Shall we say to the children of the State, you shall not enjoy this right—a right independent of all human laws and regulations? It is declared in the Constitution; is higher than Constitution and law, and should be held forever sacred.

Even criminals cannot be convicted and imprisoned without due process of law—without a regular trial, according to the course of the common law. Why should minors be imprisoned for misfortune? Destitution of proper parental care, ignorance, idleness and vice, are misfortunes, not crimes. . . . Why should children, only guilty of misfortune, be deprived of liberty without "due process of law?"

It cannot be said that in this case there is no imprisonment. This boy is deprived of a father's care; benefit of home influences; has no freedom of action; is committed for an uncertain time; is branded as a prisoner; made subject to the will of others, and thus feels that he is a slave. Nothing could more contribute to paralyze the youthful energies, crush all noble aspirations, and unfit him for the duties of manhood. . . .

It is a grave responsibility to pronounce upon the acts of the legislative department. It is, however, the solemn duty of the courts to adjudge the law, and guard, when assailed, the liberty of the citizen. The Constitution is the highest law; it commands and protects all. Its declaration of rights is an express limitation of legislative power, and as the laws under which the detention is had are in conflict with its provisions, we must so declare.

It is therefore ordered, that Daniel O'Connell be discharged from custody.

Notes

1. According to Fox, reform houses such as those at issue in *Crouse* and *O'Connell* were originally intended to save children who were "not yet truly criminal" from a life of delinquency. Sanford J. Fox, *Juvenile Justice Reform: An Historical Perspective*, 22 STAN. L. REV. 1187, 1190 (1970). These "predelinquents" were mainly those accused of idleness, begging, and wandering the streets. As Fox states, they "were guilty of little more than being poor and neglected." *Id.* at 1191. Serious offenders were from the beginning dealt with in adult criminal courts. *Id.* Thus, one can see early in the development of the juvenile justice system a recognition of two often-conflicting ideas which underlie much of juvenile law: first, the notion that children generally require more protection than adults; and second, the belief that it is sometimes necessary to deal with children as though they were adults.

2. The court in *O'Connell* implicitly rejected *Crouse*'s holding that the right of parents to educate their children is granted by the state (and may therefore be withdrawn by the state). Justice Thornton, writing for the court in *O'Connell,* made much of the rights of parents to raise their children free of government intervention. The state, he believed, should not interfere with the parents' authority for the education and upbringing of their children "except for the strongest reasons."

Twelve years after its ruling in *O'Connell*, however, the Illinois Supreme Court handed down another ruling which, while not specifically overruling *O'Connell*, limited its holding to the statute at issue in that case. In *In re Ferrier*, 103 Ill. 367 (1882), the court upheld a statute under which Winifred Breen, a nine-year-old girl, was sent to the Industrial School for Girls in Evanston. The court distinguished the Industrial School in *Ferrier* from the reform school in *O'Connell*, referring to the latter as a "place of confinement" for the "imprisonment" and "punishment" of adjudged youthful criminals. 103 Ill. at 371. The court found that the Industrial School, on the other hand, was a school not a prison.

The *Ferrier* court also pointed out that the statute at issue in *O'Connell* was much more broadly written and did not adequately protect the child's rights to procedural fairness. In *Ferrier*, by contrast, the procedures for an adjudication of dependency were sufficiently detailed in the statute, and girls were only sent to the Industrial School after proceedings that, in the opinion of the court, adequately protected the girls' rights.

Questions

1. Would the ruling in either *Crouse* or *O'Connell* have been different if the child had been convicted of a crime? Would the court in *Crouse* have required a greater showing of necessity before confining Mary Ann if she had been accused of thievery rather than "vicious conduct"? Would Daniel O'Connell's confinement in reform school have been upheld had he been convicted of something other than idleness, ignorance, or vice?

2. Would you expect the court to reach the same result in each case if the child had been placed in state custody because of abuse at the hands of an alcoholic father?

C. Rise of the Juvenile Court

1. Doctrine of *Parens Patriae*

BLACK'S LAW DICTIONARY defines *parens patriae* as follows:

> *"Parens patriae,"* literally, "parent of the country," refers to [the] role of [the] state as sovereign and guardian of persons under legal disability, such as juveniles or the insane, and in child custody determinations, when acting on behalf of the

> state to protect the interests of the child (citation omitted). It is the principle that the state must care for those who cannot take care of themselves, such as minors who lack proper care and custody from their parents. . . .
>
> *Parens patriae* originates from the English common law where the King had a royal prerogative to act as guardian to persons with legal disabilities such as infants. In the United States, the *parens patriae* function belongs with the states. . . .[21]

Professor Rendleman has traced the development of the doctrine of *parens patriae* from the chancery courts of England[22] to its use in the United States.[23] As the doctrine was imported into the United States, it was used to remove poor children from their parents, initially by placing them into apprenticeships, and later through the commitment of poor children to almshouses. Eventually, the *parens patriae* concept extended to the protection of children and to juvenile delinquency cases.

In the following excerpt from *Parens Patriae: From Chancery to the Juvenile Court*, Professor Rendleman summarizes the development of the doctrine of *parens patriae* in the Nineteenth and Twentieth Centuries:

> The *parens patriae* approach appealed to the judicial and social conservatism of the [Nineteenth Century]. In a time of limited government the idea of state interference in family life was viewed with skepticism. A parent, the state courts held, had some sort of variously stated right to the custody of his children and the child had some right to liberty. However, the state had a protective power either by analogy to the chancery power of *parens patriae* or inherent in its sovereignty or by a simple recitation that the state was *parens patriae*. Statutes which carried out this state interest were valid; and because the institutions were schools and not prisons, no more liberty than necessary was taken when the children were placed there. Nor could the parent complain: "when a parent is unable or unwilling to provide for his child, and leaves the child dependent on the charity of the state, we are at a loss to comprehend the right of the parent to object to the form which the state gives to its charity, with intelligent regard for the welfare of the child." [*Milwaukee Industrial School v. Supervisors of Milwaukee County*, 40 Wisc. 328, 337 (1876).] Even so, the

---

21 BLACK'S LAW DICTIONARY 1114 (6th ed. 1990).

22 *See* STEVEN M. COX & JOHN J. CONRAD, JUVENILE JUSTICE: A GUIDE TO PRACTICE AND THEORY 2 (1987), for a discussion of parens patriae's birth in the English chancery courts.

23 *See* Douglas R. Rendleman, *Parens Patriae: From Chancery to the Juvenile Court,* 23 S.C. L. REV. 205 (1971).

courts, at the peril of reversal, required the government to follow the statute with care.

The courts realized that they were dealing with statutes which descended from the poor laws. The judges, however, were not sure whether the legislation was criminal or civil. Statutes depriving pauper parents of their children were old and familiar, but these statutes which allowed the state to intercalate [sic] on behalf of endangered children and to place the children in an institution were new: the schemes were protective of the child and humane in application. . . .

There were, among the appealed cases, only a few crimes. . . . Many, if not most of the institutional commitments under the protective statutes were for simple poverty. Others were for "poverty plus" such as begging, poverty destitution and neglect, and dependency. And in some cases it is impossible to tell from the decision why the child was separated from his parents. Even so, it is evident from the decisions that small children were being taken from their parents not because there was any breach of the criminal law by either the parents or the children and not because of any intentional failing of the parents, but simply because the parents were poor and behaved as poor people always have. In addition it is also evident that, once made, the institutional commitments were potentially almost permanent and difficult to attack.

* * *

The concept of *parens patriae* was borrowed from equity and misapplied in statutory poverty and protective proceedings. In the process, it took on a new meaning which was nearly synonymous with the general power of government to regulate. Thus, in analyzing state power over minors and inter-family relationships today, *parens patriae* adds nothing, except that in the twentieth century it is a nice way to beg a question. (Footnotes omitted throughout).[24]

2. Philosophy of a Separate Juvenile Court

The juvenile court originated at the end of the Nineteenth Century with the creation of a separate juvenile system in Cook County, Illinois. Its founding was rooted in the changing intellectual understandings of childhood and the emergence of criminology and child development as

---

24 *Id.* at 239-58. Reprinted with permission.

influential disciplines.[25] These new fields of thought suggested that human behavior can be modified, especially in young, vulnerable children. More particularly, a radical shift in the philosophy of crime contributed to the philosophical foundations of the juvenile justice system.

During the Nineteenth Century, the classical theory of criminal accountability was replaced with the positivist theory. The classical theory blames the criminal, while the positivist theory looks to external determinants that are beyond the control of the criminal. Applying this determinism to juvenile crime, revolutionists argued that children who commit crimes are not criminals because they are incapable of voluntary acts. Accordingly, the three major determinants of criminal action, according to the positivist theory, are (1) defects in the criminal's environment, (2) defects in his physical makeup, and (3) defects in his psychological condition.[26] Translated for the juvenile context, the causes of juvenile criminal action are (1) defects or disorders in family life or struggles due to his or her social or economic class, (2) defects in his or her physical condition, and (3) defects in his or her psychological condition. These forces act to push the child into delinquency, which led the reformers to endorse the philosophy that the young offender should not be punished. This determinism allowed early reformers to absolve juvenile offenders from moral culpability.

This philosophy also had the benefit of providing explanations for the foundation of juvenile crime and therefore offered strategies to address the causes. For example, if being a member of an oppressed social or economic class pushed a juvenile into delinquency, reformers believed they could cure the delinquent behavior by alleviating the effects of that oppression. This rehabilitative ideal became the impetus for the development of a separate juvenile system whose goal was to rehabilitate and reform juvenile offenders into law-abiding citizens.

Within this new framework, the court itself was to play an integral role in the rehabilitative process.[27] The reformers were confident they understood the causes of juvenile crime and were insistent that the conduct of the offenders could be influenced with the appropriate treatment by and intervention of the juvenile court. One such example of the perceived cause of youth crime was the above-stated evolution of a new social theory that stressed the importance of environmental factors on the development of delinquent behavior. These theories of crime

---

[25] For a discussion of the philosophy underlying the juvenile court's creation, see Marygold S. Melli, *Juvenile Justice Reform in Context,* 1996 WIS. L. REV. 375 (1996).

[26] See Arthur R. Blum, *Disclosing the Identities of Juvenile Felons: Introducing Accountability to Juvenile Justice,* 27 LOY. U. CHI. L.J. 349 (1996), for a discussion on the developments of the juvenile court within the context of changing philosophies.

[27] For a discussion of the original framework of the court, see Marygold S. Melli, *Juvenile Justice Reform in Context,* 1996 WIS. L. REV. 375 (1996).

causation led to a focus on early intervention, not only with regard to criminal conduct, but also in what the founders considered to be precursors to delinquent behavior (such as patronizing pool halls, running away, truancy, or lack of parental supervision). In this way, the juvenile court was an innovation for all problem children.

This new court was based on a non-adversarial clinical therapeutic model. Attorneys were discouraged from the process, as the judge was to offer guidance to the juvenile while serving as his or her defender as well. The primary role of the court was to determine the most appropriate path for rehabilitation of the child, absent a punitive or adversarial component.

In order to successfully assess the juvenile and his or her circumstances, the judge was not limited by the rules of evidence in determining what information was relevant. Instead, the judge was encouraged to consider all relevant information in addressing the problem at issue. In devising a treatment plan, the judge was afforded broad discretion, limited only by the available resources. The statute that began this evolution was the Illinois Juvenile Court Act of 1899.

3. The Illinois Juvenile Court Act of 1899

Illinois was the first state to enact legislation creating a separate juvenile court. The Illinois Juvenile Court Act of 1899, reprinted in part below, was passed on April 21, 1899. The Juvenile Court of Cook County, established by the Act, began operation on July 1, 1899, Judge Richard S. Tuthill presiding, in a courtroom provided by Cook County. The County also provided offices, a court clerk, and a prosecutor. The City of Chicago assigned sixteen police officers as probation officers to handle juvenile delinquency cases. Private institutions and associations provided fourteen probation officers to deal with neglected and dependent children. Twenty-one truant officers were provided by the public school system. All actions of the Juvenile Court were preceded by investigations into the child's home environment, generally conducted by the probation officer assigned to the case. Dispositions in both delinquency and dependency cases were to be based on findings relating to the child's home environment (i.e., parental fitness) and the child's rehabilitative potential.[28]

---

[28] *See* 49 JUV. & FAM. CT. J. i, iv (1998).

Illinois Juvenile Court Act of 1899

An Act to regulate the treatment and control of dependent, neglected and delinquent children.

Section 1. *Be it enacted by the People of the State of Illinois, represented in the General Assembly:*

DEFINITIONS: This act shall apply only to children under the age of 16 years not now or hereafter inmates of a State institution, or any training school for boys or industrial school for girls or some institution incorporated under the laws of this State . . . . For the purposes of this act the words dependent child and neglected child shall mean any child who for any reason is destitute or homeless or abandoned; or dependent upon the public for support; or has not proper parental care or guardianship; or who habitually begs or receives alms; or who is found living in any house of ill fame or with any vicious or disreputable person; or whose home, by reason of neglect, cruelty or depravity on the part of its parents, guardian or other person in whose care it may be, is an unfit place for such a child; and any child under the age of 8 years who is found peddling or selling any article or singing or playing any musical instrument upon the streets or giving any public entertainment. The words delinquent child shall include any child under the age of 16 years who violates any law of this State or any city or village ordinance. . . .

§ 2. JURISDICTION. The circuit and county courts of the several counties in this State shall have original jurisdiction in all cases coming within the terms of this act. In all trials under this act any person interested therein may demand a jury of six, or the judge of his own motion may order a jury of the same number, to try the case.

§ 3. JUVENILE COURT. In countries having over 500,000 population the judges of the circuit court shall, at such times as they shall determine, designate one or more of their number whose duty it shall be to hear all cases coming under this act. A special court room, to be designated as the juvenile court room, shall be provided for the hearing of such cases, and the findings of the court shall be entered in a book or books to be kept for that purpose and known as the "Juvenile Record," and the court may, for convenience, be called the "Juvenile Court."

§ 4. PETITION TO THE COURT. Any reputable person being resident in the county, having knowledge of a child in his county who appears to be either neglected, dependent or delinquent, may file with the clerk of a court having jurisdiction in the matter a petition in writing, setting forth the facts, verified by affidavit. It shall be sufficient that the affidavit is upon information and belief.

§ 5. SUMMONS. Upon the filing of the petition a summons shall issue requiring the person having custody or control of the child, or with whom the child may be, to appear with the child at a place and time stated in the summons, which time shall be not less than 24 hours after service. The parents of the child . . . or its legal guardian . . . shall be notified of the proceedings, and in any case the judge may appoint some suitable person to act in behalf of the child. If the person summoned as herein provided shall fail, without reasonable cause, to appear and abide the order of the court, or to bring the child, he may be proceeded against as in the case of contempt of court. In case the summons cannot be served or the party served fails to obey the same, and in any case when it shall be made to appear to the court that such summons will be ineffectual, a warrant may issue on the order of the court, either against the parent or guardian or the person having custody of the child or with whom the child may be, or against the child itself. On the return of the summons or other process, or as soon thereafter as may be, the court shall proceed to hear and dispose of the case in a summary manner. Pending the final disposition of any case the child may be retained in the possession of the person having the charge of same, or may be kept in some suitable place provided by the city or county authorities.

§ **6. PROBATION OFFICERS.** The court shall have authority to appoint or designate one or more discreet persons of good character to serve as probation officers during the pleasure of the court: said probation officers to receive no compensation from the public treasury. In case a probation officer shall be appointed by any court, it shall be the duty of the clerk of the court, if practicable, to notify the said probation officer in advance when any child is to be brought before the said court: it shall be the duty of the said probation officer to make such investigation as may be required by the court; to be present in court in order to represent the interests of the child when the case is heard; to furnish to the court such information and assistance as the judge may require; and to take such charge of any child before and after trial as may be directed by the court.

§ **7. DEPENDENT AND NEGLECTED CHILDREN.** When any child under the age of sixteen (16) years shall be found to be dependent or neglected within the meaning of this act, the court may make an order committing the child to the care of some suitable State institution, or to the care of some reputable citizen of good moral character, or to the care of some training school or an industrial school, as provided by law, or to the care of some association willing to receive it embracing in its objects the purpose of caring or obtaining homes for dependent or neglected children, which association shall have been accredited as hereinafter provided.

§ **8. GUARDIANSHIP.** In any case where the court shall award a child to the care of any association or individual in accordance with the provisions of this act the child shall, unless otherwise ordered, become a ward and be subject to the guardianship of the association or individual to whose care it is committed. Such association or individual shall have authority to place such child in a family home, with or without indenture, and may be made party to any proceeding for the legal adoption of the child, and may by its or his attorney or agent appear in any court where such proceedings are pending and assent to such adoption. And such assent shall be sufficient to authorize the court to enter the proper order or decree of adoption. Such guardianship shall not include the guardianship of any estate of the child.

§ 9. DISPOSITION OF DELINQUENT CHILDREN. In the case of a delinquent child the court may continue the hearing from time to time, and may commit the child to the care and guardianship of a probation officer duly appointed by the court, and may allow said child to remain in its own home, subject to the visitation of the probation officer; such child to report to the probation officer as often as may be required and subject to be returned to the court for further proceedings whenever such action may appear to be necessary; or the court may commit the child to the care and guardianship of the probation officer, to be placed in a suitable home, subject to the friendly supervision of such probation officer; or it may authorize the said probation officer to board out the said child in some suitable family home, in case provision is made by voluntary contribution or otherwise for the payment of the board of such child, until a suitable provision may be made for the child in a home without such payment; or the court may commit the child, if a boy, to a training school for boys, or if a girl, to an industrial school for girls. Or, if the child is found guilty of any criminal offense, and the judge is of the opinion that the best interest requires it, the court may commit the child to any institution within said county incorporated under the laws of this State for the care of delinquent children, or provided by a city for the care of such offenders, or may commit the child, if a boy over the age of ten years, to the State reformatory, or if a girl over the age of ten years, to the State Home for Juvenile Female Offenders. In no case shall a child be committed beyond his or her minority. . . .

* * *

§ 11. CHILDREN UNDER TWELVE YEARS NOT TO BE COMMITTED TO JAIL. No court or magistrate shall commit a child under twelve (12) years of age to a jail or police station, but if such child is unable to give bail it may be committed to the care of the sheriff, police officer or probation officer, who shall keep such child in some suitable place provided by the city or county outside of the inclosure of any jail or police station. When any child shall be sentenced to confinement in any institution to which adult convicts are sentenced it shall be unlawful to confine such child in the same building with such adult convicts or to confine such child in the same yard or inclosure with such adult convicts, or to bring such child into any yard or building in which such adult convicts may be present.

* * *

§ 15. SURRENDER OF DEPENDENT CHILDREN—ADOPTION. It shall be lawful for the parents, parent, guardian or other person having the right to dispose of a dependent or neglected child to enter into an agreement with any association or institution incorporated under any public or private law of this state for the purpose of aiding, caring for or placing in homes such children, and being approved as herein provided, for the surrender of such child to such association or institution, to be taken and cared for by such association or institution or put into a family home. . . .

* * *

§ 17. RELIGIOUS PREFERENCES. The court in committing children shall place them as far as practicable in the care and custody of some individual holding the same religious belief as the parents of said child, or with some association which is controlled by persons of like religious faith of the parents of the said child.

* * *

§ 21. CONSTRUCTION OF THE ACT. This act shall be liberally construed, to the end that its purpose may be carried out, to-wit: That the care, custody and discipline of a child shall approximate as nearly as may be that which should be given by its parents, and in all cases where it can properly be done the child be placed in an improved family home and become a member of the family by legal adoption or otherwise.

Notes

1. The Illinois Juvenile Court Act of 1899 codified many of the philosophical underpinnings that emerged during the Nineteenth Century reform of the treatment of juveniles. The statute was created in response to the growing concern that the criminal court system was unable to adequately respond to the problems unique to young offenders. For example, the reformers called for the physical separation of juveniles from adult offenders, explaining that children required special treatment. Section 7 of the statute responded by placing dependent and neglected children in any "suitable State institution," training or industrial school, or association geared towards placing these children in homes. Likewise, delinquent children were allowed a number of options as to placement, none of which included buildings that housed adult offenders (§§ 9 and 11). Rather than relying upon incarceration as the previous system had done, the statute focused on schools and institutions as a way to care for, protect and rehabilitate the child. In fact, in enumerating the guidelines to be followed by the probation officers of the new court, Judge Tuthill emphasized that one of the most important sections of the Act was a requirement that the court strive to place children in a family environment. Justice Tuthill went on to note that the welfare of the child was listed as the foremost priority and was to be considered paramount to the welfare of the community or the concerns of the family (§ 21). For a discussion of the Illinois Juvenile Court Act, see Candace Zierdt, *The Little Engine that Arrived at the Wrong Station: How to Get Juvenile Justice Back on the Right Track,* 33 U.S.F. L. REV. 401 (1999). For an interesting discussion of the development of the juvenile court system, see Robert E. Shepherd, Jr., *The Juvenile Court at 100: Birthday Cake or Funeral Pyre?,* 13 CRIM. JUST. 47 (1999).

2. The statute also contains a unique perspective on what conditions fall within the definition of dependent and neglected children. The Act includes those children who "habitually beg or receive alms" as well as "any child under the age of 8 years who is found peddling or selling any article or singing or playing any musical instrument upon the streets or giving any public entertainment." The inclusion in the Act of this class of children is a remnant of the belief that poor parents were unfit and that the State, in its role as *parens patriae,* was afforded the legal power to remove these children from this lifestyle and rehabilitate them in a training school or the home of a "reputable citizen of good moral character" (§ 7).

3. Dependent, neglected, and delinquent children were all under the purview of the Illinois Court Act of 1899. As such, all of the problems and issues specific to each child, be he delinquent or dependent, were supposedly addressed by the same statutory regime. For example, certain provisions of the Act refer to "child" without modification; presumably, therefore, dependent, neglected, and delinquent children were all governed by the same rules as to jurisdiction, procedure, and guardianship. An examination of the treatment of children found to be dependent, neglected, or delinquent also bears similarities. Dependent and neglected children, in § 7 of the Act, were committed to institutions, citizen care, training or industrial schools, or associations accredited with finding them homes. A child found delinquent was faced with parallel consequences in that the child could remain in his own home, be committed to the care of his parole officer, or be placed in a home, a training school, or an industrial school (§ 9). The court in every instance was entitled to exercise discretion as to placement.

By 1910, thirty-two states responded to the example set by Illinois and created separate juvenile courts or probation systems. By 1925, all but two states had adopted a juvenile justice framework. These new courts shared the rehabilitative ideal of the first court of 1899 by maintaining a focus on the treatment of juveniles, with the goal of turning delinquents into law-abiding citizens. The statutes that created these courts reflected their mission and purpose as one of rehabilitation and not punishment.

These new courts differed from traditional courts and succeeded in developing a new approach to the judicial handling of juveniles. For an interesting discussion on the format and characteristics of the early juvenile court, see Marygold S. Melli, *Juvenile Justice Reform in Context,* 1996 WIS. L. REV. 375 (1996). The first juvenile courts' structure resembled a social agency more than a court. An intake department effectively screened incoming cases and could divert certain juveniles from the formal court process. In this way, the juvenile court was able to control its own intake by considering extra-legal and legal factors in deciding how to handle each individual case, with the option of bypassing judicial action altogether.

The format of these early hearings also incorporated concern for the child as the founding principle and avoided accusatory undertones. Therefore, the judge, the child, the parents and the probation officer convened in the judge's chambers or around a conference table to consider what would be best for the child. Within this early framework, attorneys were viewed as unnecessary for the successful operation of the system.

The dispositional alternatives that resulted from these informal hearings were varied, as the judge had the discretion to formulate a treatment plan tailored to the child's needs. The chosen treatment lasted until the child was rehabilitated, or "cured," or reached the age where they could no longer be kept in custody.

This new framework was accompanied by a special vocabulary that embodied the ideals of the juvenile court. There was no complaint or charge that initiated proceedings, but instead a petition. People were ordered to court by a summons and not a warrant. Also, juveniles were taken into custody and held in detention, instead of being arrested and held in jail. Finally, juveniles were not convicted of crimes, but were instead found to be delinquent and were addressed with dispositions instead of sentences. In this way, the juvenile court attempted to further distance itself from the criminal courts by adopting specifically non-criminal definitional terms.

The evolution of the juvenile system has effectively divided the treatment of dependent, neglected, and delinquent children into different subsystems, yet these components continue to exist under the same umbrella. The delinquency intake process, as described in Chapter 3, represents a subsystem specific to juvenile offenders, as does the adjudicatory phase described in Chapter 6. A major alteration, and the beginning of the juvenile court's constitutionalization, came with the recognition of the applicability of the Fourteenth Amendment due process rights in *In re Gault,* 387 U.S. 1 (1967), as examined in Chapter 6. This energized a transformation of the court, as juvenile offenders were afforded numerous protections previously reserved for the adult criminal system. These developments resulted in a system that is more specialized in its assessment and treatment of the juvenile offender than the system originally envisioned under the 1899 Act.

4. As discussed above, the goals and ideals underlying the juvenile justice system focus on rehabilitation and treatment. This is evidenced by the Illinois Juvenile Court Act of 1899's stated purpose: "That the care, custody and discipline of a child shall approximate as nearly as may be that which should be given by its parents, and in all cases where it can properly be done the child will be placed in an improved family home and become a member of the family by legal adoption or otherwise." Nowhere does the Act advise as to the treatment of violent juvenile offenders, a circumstance not of apparent concern given the state of society at the time of the Act's passage.

However, the rise in the incidence of violent juvenile crime has focused legal and political attention on the capabilities of the existing system to effectively manage these offenders while maintaining a case of rehabilitation. For an interesting discussion of the history of the juvenile justice system and the necessity of combining punitive and rehabilitative philosophies, see Brian R. Suffredini, Note, *Juvenile Gunslingers: A Place for Punitive Philosophy in Rehabilitative Juvenile Justice*, 35 B.C. L. REV. 885 (1994) (suggesting that society's call for a more punitive system that deters youths with appropriate punishment is addressing the needs of the state at the expense of the rehabilitative needs of the juvenile). For an argument that the federal government should intervene in the treatment of juvenile offenders due to the perceived inadequacies of the state systems, see Joseph F. Yeckel, Note, *Violent Juvenile Offenders: Rethinking Federal Intervention in Juvenile Justice*, 51 WASH. U. J. URB. & CONTEMP. L. 331 (1997).

It has also been suggested that the existing juvenile justice system was developed with a focus on the male juvenile offender and, with an influx of female offenders, is currently unable to effectively address the unique needs of these female delinquents. *See* Laurie Schaffner, *Violence and Female Delinquency: Gender Transgressions and Gender Invisibility*, 14 BERKELEY WOMEN'S L.J. 40 (1999).

Chapter 2

Juvenile Delinquency: The Child as Respondent

Following the Reform Movement of the Nineteenth Century and establishment of new juvenile courts early in the last century, the United States no longer treated minors within the adult court system. Currently, all states have statutes giving juvenile courts jurisdiction over designated minors. If the juvenile court has jurisdiction, a juvenile offender will be judged within the civil system by juvenile laws and he or she will receive treatment or punishment that the state deems appropriate for a juvenile. A juvenile court has jurisdiction over a minor if that minor is found to be a status offender or a juvenile delinquent. A juvenile will be labeled a status offender if he or she commits an act which is an offense if committed by a juvenile, but not a crime when committed by an adult. This chapter discusses four acts that are commonly status offenses:[1] (1) a child runs away from home, (2) a child is found to be incorrigible, (3) a child is found in public after expiration of a curfew, and (4) a child is habitually and without justification truant from school. A juvenile is considered delinquent if he or she commits an act that would be a crime if done by an adult and there is no defense available to the minor. This chapter will also examine the statutes enacted by some states that increase the level of an offense if the crime is committed by a gang member.

---

1 There are a number of other behaviors that may be considered status offenses such as underage liquor law violations and tobacco offenses.

A. Jurisdiction

California Welfare and Institutions Code
§§ 601-602 (West Supp. 2001)

§ 601. Minors habitually disobedient or truant

(a) Any person under the age of 18 years who persistently or habitually refuses to obey the reasonable and proper orders or directions of his or her parents, guardian, or custodian, or who is beyond the control of that person, or who is under the age of 18 years when he or she violated [sic] any ordinance of any city or county of this state establishing a curfew based solely on age is within the jurisdiction of the juvenile court which may adjudge the minor to be a ward of the court.

(b) If a minor has four or more truancies within one school year . . . , the minor is then within the jurisdiction of the juvenile court which may adjudge the minor to be a ward of the court. . . .

§ 602. Minors violating laws defining crime; ward of court

(a) . . . [A]ny person who is under the age of 18 years when he violates any law of this state or of the United States or any ordinance of any city or county of this state defining crime other than an ordinance establishing a curfew based solely on age, is within the jurisdiction of the juvenile court, which may adjudge such person to be a ward of the court.

B. Substantive Requirements

1. Status Offenses

a. Sample Status Offense Statute

Georgia Code Annotated
§§ 15-11-2(11) & 2(12) (Lexis Supp. 2000)

§§ 15-11-2 Definitions

(11) "Status offender" means a child who is charged with or adjudicated of an offense which would not be a crime if it were committed by an adult, in other words, an act which is only an offense because of the perpetrator's status as a child. Such offenses shall include, but are not limited to, truancy, running away from home, incorrigibility, and unruly behavior.

(12) "Unruly child" means a child who:

(A) While subject to compulsory school attendance is habitually and without justification truant from school;

(B) Is habitually disobedient of the reasonable and lawful commands of his or her parent, guardian, or other custodian and is ungovernable;

(C) Has committed an offense applicable only to a child;

(D) Without just cause and without the consent of his or her parent or legal custodian deserts his or her home or place of abode;

(E) Wanders or loiters about the streets of any city, or in or about any highway or any public place, between the hours of 12:00 Midnight and 5:00 A.M.;

(F) Disobeys the terms of supervision contained in a court order which has been directed to such child, who has been adjudicated unruly; or

(G) Patronizes any bar where alcoholic beverages are being sold, unaccompanied by such child's parents, guardian, or custodian, or possesses alcoholic beverages; and

(H) In any of the foregoing, is in need of supervision, treatment, or rehabilitation; or

(I) Has committed a delinquent act and is in need of supervision, but not of treatment or rehabilitation.

b. Runaway

In re Darlene C.

301 S.E.2d 136 (S.C. 1983)

HARWELL, Justice:

This is an appeal from a juvenile proceeding in family court. Appellant alleges the court erred in adjudicating her delinquent and committing her to the Department of Youth Services for an indeterminate period not exceeding her twenty-first birthday. We remand for resentencing.

During oral argument appellant's counsel stated that appellant served several months in the detention center and is presently on probation. Normally, this would render the case moot, but we find the issue raised is "capable of repetition but evading review" and, therefore, take jurisdiction. *Roe v. Wade*, 410 U.S. 113, 93 S.Ct. 705, 35 L.Ed.2d 147 (1973).

On February 9, 1982, the family court found appellant, a sixteen year old, to be a runaway child. It ordered her to be placed in the North Augusta Girls' Home and to receive counseling from the Mental Health Center. Further, the order stated that if appellant failed to abide by its mandate, the court would find her in contempt. Two days later, appellant promptly ran away again. Consequently, the family court issued a Rule to Show Cause as to why appellant should not be held in contempt of court for violating the previous court order. Appellant appeared at the Rule to Show Cause hearing but offered no defense. Thereafter, the judge ruled her in contempt of his February 9 order. The judge acknowledged that appellant had appeared before him on several occasions as a truant and runaway, a status offender. A status offense is one which, if committed by an adult would not be a crime. S.C. Code Ann. § 20-7-30(6) (1981 Cum. Supp.). The legislature has mandated that a status offender not be placed in a detention facility. S.C. Code Ann. § 20-7-600 (1981 Cum. Supp.). Nevertheless, the court concluded that by violating the previous order, appellant elevated her status to one of a delinquent. The court sentenced her as a delinquent to commitment in a detention center for an indeterminate period not to exceed her twenty-first birthday.

The issue is whether a juvenile who commits criminal contempt by running away in violation of a court order may be given a disposition reserved for delinquents who have committed offenses which would be crimes if committed by an adult. We conclude that, under the most egregious circumstances as we have here, family courts may exercise their contempt power in such a manner that a status offender will be incarcerated in a secure facility.

Although we have held that juvenile offenders may be punished only as prescribed by the South Carolina Children's Code, *Matter of Westbrooks*, S.C., 288 S.E.2d 395 (1982), the Code specifically provides that it shall be interpreted in conjunction with all relevant laws and regulations. S.C. Code Ann. § 20-7-20 (1981 Cum. Supp.). Therefore, when dealing with juveniles, family courts may look to their inherent powers as well as to the Children's Code. All courts possess the inherent power to punish contemnors. That power is essential to the preservation of order in judicial proceedings, and to the enforcement of the courts' judgments, orders and writs and consequently to the due administration of justice. We conclude the family court properly held appellant in contempt. In this case the record reflects that appellant had appeared in family court for the status offenses of running away and truancy. She appeared in court fourteen different times over a two and a half year span. In this particular instance, she ran away from the very home in which she asked to be placed.

We acknowledge the legislature's concern with the effects of commingling disobedient children with juveniles who have allegedly committed more serious crimes. However, the legislature has not dealt adequately with the problem of chronic runaways. By enacting S.C. Code Ann. § 20-7-600, the legislature requires the family court to perform an exercise in futility by requiring the court to place a runaway in a nonsecure environment. We believe that if family courts are to retain jurisdiction of runaways, they must have the authority to handle them. Their inherent contempt powers provide such tools.

Nevertheless, we hold that *only* under the most egregious circumstances should family courts exercise their contempt power in such a manner that a status offender will be incarcerated in a secure facility. Before a chronic status offender is placed in a secure facility, the record must show that all less restrictive alternatives have failed in the past. Additionally the following elements should exist: (1) the existence of a valid order directing the alleged contemnor to do or refrain from doing something and the court's jurisdiction to enter that order; (2) the contemnor's notice of the order with sufficient time to comply with it; and in most cases, (3) the contemnor's ability to comply with the order; and (4) the contemnor's willful failure to comply with the order. *L.A.M. v. State*, 547 P.2d 827 (Alaska 1976). Furthermore, the record must reflect the juvenile understood that disobedience would result in incarceration in a secure facility. Recently, Indiana's legislature has provided by statute similar dispositions for its chronic status offenders. *See W.M. v. State*, 437 N.E.2d 1028 (Ind. App. 1982).

In this case, the family court adjudicated appellant a delinquent before sentencing her under the provisions of the Children's Code. We think that procedure is unnecessary, if not improper. Today we have held that family courts possess the inherent power to punish contemnors. Therefore, we remand for resentencing appellant as a contemnor, not as a delinquent. Upon resentencing, appellant may be committed to a secured facility for no more than six months. Additionally, appellant should receive credit for the time she already has served.

We conclude that the family court may punish appellant as a contemnor under its inherent powers. However, under the Children's Code, it may not sentence appellant as a delinquent when she is, in fact, merely a chronic status offender.

Remanded.

Notes

1. As evidenced in this case, courts generally cannot label truants or other status offenders "delinquent." In many jurisdictions, the legislature has determined that delinquents and dependents (the label often given to status offenders) are to be treated separately. *See J.M.J. v. State*, 389 So. 2d 1208, 1210 (Fla. Dist. Ct. App. 1980) ("The legislature, in deliberate wisdom, chose to classify persistent runaways and habitual truants only as dependent children"); Harry J. Rothgerber, Jr., *The Bootstrapping of Status Offenders: A Vicious Practice,* KY. CHILDREN'S RTS. J. 1, 3 (July 1991) ("Federal and state policies mandate that status offenders be treated differently than public offenders (delinquents)"). Furthermore, status offenders generally cannot be confined with delinquents. *See, e.g.,* KY. REV. STAT. ANN. § 605.090(1)(c) (West 2000). This creates a problem for juvenile courts and law enforcement officers: runaways must often be "held" in a nonsecure environment that they can easily leave. As the court in *In re Ronald S.* stated, "[w]hile it may seem ridiculous to place a runaway in a nonsecure setting, nevertheless, that is what the Legislature has ordained." 138 Cal. Rptr. 387, 392 (Ct. App. 1977).

2. Courts have attempted to solve this dilemma using one of their inherent powers—the power of contempt. *Darlene C.* presents the typical scenario: (1) a child runs away from home; (2) the child is adjudged a runaway and ordered not to run away again; (3) the child runs away again; and (4) the court finds the child in contempt of court and orders her confined to a secure environment, such as a reform school. While this solution addresses the problem of how to deal with persistent runaways, it has not received universal acceptance in appellate courts. *See, e.g., W.M. v. State*, 437 N.E.2d 1028, 1034 (Ind. Ct. App. 1982) ("Juvenile courts cannot be permitted to accomplish indirectly that which they could not accomplish directly"). For additional cases rejecting the use of contempt in status offense adjudications, see *J.M.J. v. State,* 389 So. 2d 1208 (Fla. Dist. Ct. App. 1980); *In re Tasseing H.*, 422 A.2d 530 (Pa. Super. Ct. 1980). For cases upholding adjudications of contempt, see *In re G.B.*, 430 N.E.2d 1096 (Ill. 1981); *State v. Norlund*, 644 P.2d 724 (Wash. Ct. App. 1982).

3. Like the Supreme Court of South Carolina in *Darlene C.,* other courts have also relied on the four elements from *L.A.M. v. State* that must be met before a habitual status offender may be held in a secure facility. *See, e.g., W.M. v. State,* 437 N.E.2d 1028 (Ind. Ct. App. 1982); *State ex rel. L.E.A. v. Hammergren,* 294 N.W.2d 705 (Minn. 1980).

Questions

1. What policies are served by the notion that runaways should not be locked up in secure facilities? Should persistent status offenders be kept separate from delinquent offenders? How might the child's lawyer utilize expert psychological evidence on this issue?

2. Is the use of the court's inherent power of contempt a good solution to the problem of how best to deal with repeat status offenders? Why or why not?

3. Is there merit to the judicial complaint that the legislature has, in essence, tied the hands of the courts by disallowing incarceration of persistent runaways? What could the legislative branch do to give the courts more power to deal effectively with habitual status offenders while maintaining separate systems for handling status offenders and delinquents?

c. Incorrigibility

In re Welfare of Snyder
532 P.2d 278 (Wash. 1975)

Paul Snyder and Nell Snyder, petitioners, seek review of the King County Juvenile Court's finding that their daughter, Cynthia Nell Snyder, respondent, was an incorrigible child as defined under RCW 13.04.010(7). The issue before this court is whether the juvenile court's determination is supported by substantial evidence.

Cynthia Nell Snyder is 16 years old, attends high school, and has consistently received above average grades. Prior to the occurrences which led to this action, she resided with her parents in their North Seattle home. The record shows that as Cynthia entered her teen years, a hostility began to develop between herself and her parents. This environment within the family home worsened due to a total breakdown in the lines of communication between Cynthia and her parents. Cynthia's parents, being strict disciplinarians, placed numerous limitations on their daughter's activities, such as restricting her choice of friends, and refusing to let her smoke, date, or participate in certain extra-curricular activities within the school, all of which caused Cynthia to rebel against their authority. These hostilities culminated in a total collapse of the parent-child relationship. This atmosphere resulted in extreme mental abuse to all parties concerned.

On June 18, 1973, Mr. Snyder, having concluded that the juvenile court might be able to assist him in controlling his daughter, removed Cynthia from the family home and delivered her to the Youth Service Center. As a result, Cynthia was placed in a receiving home. On July 19, 1973, in an attempt to avoid returning home, Cynthia filed a petition in the Juvenile Department of the Superior Court for King County, alleging that she was a dependent child as defined by RCW 13.04.010(2) and (3), which provide:

> For the purpose of this chapter the words "dependent child" shall mean any child under the age of eighteen years: . . .
>
> (2) Who has no parent, guardian or other responsible person; or who has no parent or guardian willing to exercise, or capable of exercising, proper parental control; or
>
> (3) Whose home by reason of neglect, cruelty or depravity of his parents or either of them, or on the part of his guardian, or on the part of the person in whose custody or care he may be, or for any other reason, is an unfit place for such child; . . .

On July 23, 1973, Cynthia was placed in the temporary custody of the Department of Social and Health Services and an attorney was appointed to be her guardian ad litem. On October 12, 1973, the juvenile court held that the allegations attacking the fitness of Cynthia's parents were incorrect, at least to the extent that they alleged dependency, and that Cynthia should be returned to the custody of her parents. Cynthia did return to the family residence, where she remained until November 16, 1973. . . . On November 21, 1973, Margaret Rozmyn, who was in charge of the intake program at the [Youth Services] center, filed a petition alleging that Cynthia was incorrigible as defined under RCW 13.04.010(7), which provides:

> For the purpose of this chapter the words "dependent child" shall mean any child under the age of eighteen years:
>
> (7) Who is incorrigible; that is, who is beyond the control and power of his parents, guardian, or custodian by reason of the conduct or nature of said child. . . .

A hearing . . . was held on December 10 and 11, 1973. At that time, Commissioner Quinn found that Cynthia was incorrigible and continued that matter for one week in order for the entire family to meet with a counselor. . . . [O]n December 18, 1973, Commissioner Quinn, upon hearing the comments and conclusions of the counseling psychiatrists chosen by the parents, decided that Cynthia was to be placed in a foster home. . . .

This court assumed jurisdiction of the case upon our issuance of the requested writ of certiorari.

The sole issue presented by these facts is whether there is substantial evidence in the record, taken as a whole, to support the juvenile court's determination that Cynthia Nell Snyder is incorrigible. Her parents contend that Cynthia is not incorrigible, as a matter of law, since the only evidence to support such a finding is their daughter's own statements. We disagree.

A child is incorrigible when she is beyond the power and control of her parents by reason of her own conduct. RCW 13.04.010(7). In reviewing the record in search of substantial evidence, we must find "evidence in sufficient quantum to persuade a fair-minded, rational person of the truth of a declared premise." *Helman v. Sacred Heart Hospital*, 62 Wash.2d 136, 147, 381 P.2d 605, 612 (1963). In applying this criteria for review, we are mindful that our paramount consideration, irrespective of the natural emotions in cases of this nature, must be the welfare of the child. When the questions of dependency and incorrigibility arise, "we have often noted what we think is a realistic and rational appellate policy of placing *very strong* reliance on trial court determinations of what course of action will be in the best interests of the child." *In re Todd*, 68 Wash.2d 587, 591, 414 P.2d 605, 608 (1966). In reviewing the record, we find no evidence which would indicate that Commissioner Quinn acted unfairly, irrationally, or in a prejudicial manner in reaching his conclusion. Therefore, we must give "very strong" credence to his determinations. . . . The issue is whether there is substantial evidence to support a finding that the parent-child relationship has dissipated to the point where parental control is lost and, therefore, Cynthia is incorrigible. . . . This child has established a pattern of refusing to obey her parents and, on two occasions, has, in effect, fled her home by filing petitions in the juvenile court in order that she might be made a ward of the court. . . .

In addition, the parents and the older sister, by their testimony, admitted that a difficult situation existed in the home. . . . Finally, the court considered the opinion of Dr. Gallagher, who met with Cynthia and her parents, and reported that counseling would not be beneficial until all of the individuals concerned backed away from the hard and fast positions they now held in regard to this matter which, in his opinion, was the cause of the tension which resulted in overt hostility. In other words, the finding of incorrigibility is not supported solely by Cynthia's testimony and her refusal to return home. But in addition thereto, the commissioner's opinion finds support in the testimony of other individuals who are familiar with the situation, either from a personal or a professional standpoint. . . .

Having found the juvenile court's finding of incorrigibility . . . to be supported by substantial evidence within the entire record, we are constitutionally bound to affirm the juvenile court's decision. *Thorndike v. Hesperian Orchards, Inc.*, 54 Wash.2d 570, 343 P.2d 183 (1959).

* * *

The record clearly shows that numerous attempts were made by the juvenile court commissioner to reconcile the family differences. . . . In view of our disposition of this case, we are satisfied that the juvenile court, in exercising its continuing jurisdiction, will continue to review the progress of the parties to the end of a hoped for reconciliation.

The decision of the juvenile court for King County is affirmed.

Notes

1. Courts often base a finding of incorrigibility on numerous occurrences of some other status offense which, in effect, establish that the juvenile is beyond parental control. For example, in *Snyder* the court found Cynthia incorrigible after concluding that she had "on two occasions . . . fled her home." *See also Blondheim v. State*, 529 P.2d 1096 (Wash. 1975) (habitual runaway adjudged incorrigible); *In re Weiss*, 568 N.W.2d 336 (Mich. Ct. App. 1997) (incorrigibility based on repeated truancy).

2. Cynthia Nell Snyder declared herself incorrigible in order to obtain placement in a foster home after she decided she no longer wished to live with her parents. For a case in which a juvenile "declared" herself a runaway for similar reasons, see *In re Bettye K.*, 285 Cal. Rptr. 633 (Ct. App. 1991) (child ran away from home and refused to return, claiming she would run again due to "irreconcilable differences" with her father).

Questions

1. Did the court really base its holding on the breakdown of communication between a teenager and her parents? If so, does this create a dangerous precedent?

2. As a matter of public policy, should a juvenile be permitted to declare himself or herself incorrigible in order to get away from parents who have not been judicially determined to be unfit?

d. Curfew

Qutb v. Strauss
11 F.3d 488 (5th Cir. 1993)

E. Grady JOLLY, Circuit Judge:

This appeal presents a challenge to the constitutionality of a nocturnal juvenile curfew ordinance enacted by Dallas, Texas. The ordinance makes it a misdemeanor for persons under the age of seventeen to use the city streets or to be present at other public places within the city between certain hours. Several plaintiffs brought suit against the city to strike down the ordinance. The district court ruled for the plaintiffs, holding that the ordinance violated both the United States and the Texas Constitutions, and permanently enjoined enforcement of the ordinance. The city appeals. Because we conclude that this ordinance does not violate the Untied States or Texas Constitutions, we reverse the district court.

I

On June 12, 1991, in response to citizens' demands for protection of the city's youth, the Dallas City Council enacted a juvenile curfew ordinance. This ordinance prohibits persons under seventeen years of age from remaining in a public place or establishment from 11 p.m. until 6 a.m. on week nights, and from 12 midnight until 6 a.m. on weekends. . . .

Although the ordinance restricts the hours when minors are allowed in public areas, the ordinance also contains a number of exceptions, or defenses. A person under the age of seventeen in a public place during curfew hours does not violate the ordinance if he or she is accompanied by a parent or guardian, or is on an errand for a parent or guardian. Likewise, minors would be allowed in public places if they are in a motor vehicle traveling to or from a place of employment, or if they are involved in employment related activities. Affected minors could attend school, religious, or civic organizational functions—or generally exercise their First Amendment speech and associational rights—without violating the ordinance. Nor is it a violation to engage in interstate travel, or remain on a sidewalk in front of the minor's home, or the home of a neighbor. And finally, the ordinance places no restrictions on a minor's ability to move about during curfew hours in the case of an emergency.

. . . If a minor is apparently violating the ordinance, the ordinance requires police officers to ask the age of the apparent offender, and to inquire into the reasons for being in a public place during curfew hours before taking any enforcement action. An officer may issue a citation or arrest the apparent offender only if the officer reasonably believes that the person has violated the ordinance and that no defenses apply. If convicted, an offending party is subject to a fine not to exceed $500 for each separate offense.

Like minors who have violated the offense, a parent of a minor, or an owner, operator, or employee of a business establishment is also subject to a fine not to exceed $500 for each separate offense. A parent or guardian of a minor violates the ordinance if he or she knowingly permits, or by insufficient control allows, a minor child to remain in any public place or on the premises of any establishment during curfew hours. An owner, operator, or employee of a business establishment commits an offense by knowingly allowing a minor to remain upon the premises of the establishment during curfew hours.

II

On July 3, 1991, two weeks after the ordinance was enacted, Elizabeth Qutb and three other parents filed suit—both individually and as next friends of their teenage children—seeking a temporary restraining order and a permanent injunction against the enforcement of the juvenile curfew ordinance on the basis that the ordinance is unconstitutional. The district court certified the plaintiffs as a class that consisted of two sub-classes: persons under the age of seventeen, and parents of persons under the age of seventeen. . . . The case was tried on July 22-23, and the district court denied the plaintiffs' request for a temporary injunction. The city, however, voluntarily delayed enforcement of the curfew pending the district court's decision on the merits.

. . . On August 10, 1992, the district court held that the curfew impermissibly restricted minors' First Amendment right to associate, and that it created classifications that could not withstand constitutional scrutiny. Accordingly, the district court permanently enjoined enforcement of the curfew, and the city now appeals.

III

A

* * *

The minor plaintiffs . . . have argued that the curfew ordinance impinges upon their "fundamental right" to move about freely in public. For purposes of our analysis, we assume without deciding that the right to move about freely is a fundamental right. We are mindful, however, that this ordinance is directed solely at the activities of juveniles and, under certain circumstances, minors may be treated differently from adults.

B

Because we assume that the curfew impinges upon a fundamental right, we will now subject the ordinance to strict scrutiny review. [T]o survive strict scrutiny, a classification created by the ordinance must promote a compelling governmental interest, and it must be narrowly tailored to achieve this interest. The city's stated interest in enacting the ordinance is to reduce juvenile crime and victimization, while promoting juvenile safety and well-being. The Supreme Court has recognized that the state "has a strong and legitimate interest in the welfare of its young citizens, whose immaturity, inexperience, and lack of judgment may sometimes impair their ability to exercise their rights wisely." *Hodgson v. Minnesota*, 497 U.S. 417, 444, 110 S.Ct. 2926, 2942, 111 L.Ed.2d 344 (1990). In this case, the plaintiffs concede and the district court held that the state's interest in this case is compelling. Given the fact that the state's interest is elevated by the minority status of the affected persons, we have no difficulty agreeing with the parties and with the district court.

C

In the light of the state's compelling interest in increasing juvenile safety and decreasing juvenile crime, we must now determine whether the curfew ordinance is narrowly tailored to achieve that interest. The district court held that the city "totally failed to establish that the Ordinance's classification between minors and non-minors is narrowly tailored to achieve the stated goals of the curfew." We disagree.

To be narrowly tailored, there must be a nexus between the stated government interest and the classification created by the ordinance. . . . The articulated purpose of the curfew ordinance enacted by the city of Dallas is to protect juveniles from harm, and to reduce juvenile crime and violence occurring in the city. The ordinance's distinction based upon age furthers these objectives. Before the district court, the city presented the following statistical information:

1. Juvenile crime increases proportionally with age between ten years old and sixteen years old.
2. In 1989, Dallas recorded 5,160 juvenile arrests, while in 1990 there were 5,425 juvenile arrests. . . .

3. Murders are most likely to occur between 10:00 p.m. and 1:00 a.m. and most likely to occur in apartments and apartment parking lots and streets and highways.
4. Aggravated assaults are most likely to occur between 11:00 p.m. and 1:00 a.m.
5. Rapes are most likely to occur between 1:00 a.m. and 3:00 a.m. and sixteen percent of rapes occur on public streets and highways.
6. Thirty-one percent of robberies occur on streets and highways.

Although the city was unable to provide precise data concerning the number of juveniles who commit crimes during the curfew hours, or the number of juvenile victims of crimes committed during the curfew, the city nonetheless provided sufficient data to demonstrate that the classification created by the ordinance "fits" the state's compelling interest.

Furthermore, we are convinced that this curfew also employs the least restrictive means of accomplishing its goals. The ordinance contains various "defenses" that allow affected minors to remain in public areas during curfew hours. . . . To be sure, the defenses are the most important consideration in determining whether this ordinance is narrowly tailored.

* * *

With the ordinance before us today, the city of Dallas has created a nocturnal juvenile curfew that satisfies strict scrutiny. By including the defenses to a violation of the ordinance, the city has enacted a narrowly drawn ordinance that allows the city to meet its stated goals while respecting the rights of the affected minors. As the city points out, a juvenile may move about freely in Dallas if accompanied by a parent or a guardian, or a person at least eighteen years of age who is authorized by a parent or guardian to have custody of the minor. If the juvenile is traveling interstate, returning from a school-sponsored function, a civic organization-sponsored function, or a religious function, or going home after work, the ordinance does not apply. If the juvenile is on an errand for his or her parent or guardian, the ordinance does not apply. If the juvenile is involved in an emergency, the ordinance does not apply. If the juvenile is on a sidewalk in front of his or her home *or* the home of a neighbor, the ordinance does not apply. Most notably, if the juvenile is exercising his or her First Amendment rights, the curfew ordinance does not apply.

* * *

Thus, after carefully examining the juvenile curfew ordinance enacted by the city of Dallas, we conclude that it is narrowly tailored to address the city's compelling interest and any burden this ordinance places upon minors' constitutional rights will be minimal.

D

In addition to the claims presented by the minor plaintiffs, the parental plaintiffs argue that the curfew ordinance violates their fundamental right of privacy because it dictates the manner in which their children must be raised.

Although we recognize that a parent's right to rear their [sic] children without undue governmental interference is a fundamental component of due process, we are convinced that this ordinance presents only a minimal intrusion into the parents' rights. In fact, the only aspect of parenting that this ordinance bears upon is the parents' right to allow the minor to remain in public places, unaccompanied by a parent or guardian or other authorized person, during the hours restricted by the curfew ordinance. Because of the broad exemptions included in the curfew ordinance, the parent retains the right to make decisions regarding his or her child in all other areas: the parent may allow the minor to remain in public so long as the minor is accompanied by a parent or guardian, or a person at least eighteen years of age who is authorized by a parent or guardian to have custody of the minor. The parent may allow the minor to attend all activities organized by groups such as church groups, civic organizations, schools, or the city of Dallas. The parent may still allow the child to hold a job, to perform an errand for the parent, and to seek help in emergency situations.

In this case, the parents have failed to convince us that the ordinance will impermissibly impinge on their rights as parents. . . .

IV

In conclusion, we find that the state has demonstrated that the curfew ordinance furthers a compelling state interest, *i.e.*, protecting juveniles from crime on the streets. We further conclude that the ordinance is narrowly tailored to achieve this compelling state interest. Accordingly, we hold that the nocturnal juvenile curfew ordinance enacted by the city of Dallas is constitutional. The judgment of the district court is therefore reversed.

Notes

1. Many jurisdictions, especially large municipalities, have enacted juvenile curfews. In fact, it is estimated that over half of all cities with populations over 100,000 have curfews on their books. *See* Note, *Assessing the Scope of Minors' Fundamental Rights: Juvenile Curfews and the Constitution*, 97 HARV. L. REV. 1163, 1164 n.9 (1984). Despite their popularity among legislatures and municipal government authorities, however, juvenile curfews have met with mixed and often inconsistent responses from the judiciary. The courts differ in their view of what a curfew law must (and must not) contain in order to pass constitutional muster. *See generally* Martine E. Mooney, Note, *Assessing the Constitutional Validity of Juvenile Curfew Statutes*, 52 NOTRE DAME L. REV. 858 (1977) (discussing the lack of consensus among courts and the fact that some courts reject curfew laws nearly identical to those upheld in other jurisdictions).

2. Courts analyzing the validity of juvenile curfew laws often refer to the three factors outlined by the plurality in *Bellotti v. Baird* to determine when the rights of children do not equal those of adults. 443 U.S. 622 (1979). These factors include (1) "the peculiar vulnerability of children"; (2) children's "inability to make critical decisions in an informed, mature manner"; and (3) "the importance of the parental role in child rearing." *Id.* at 634. However, courts cite *Bellotti* both to uphold juvenile curfew laws (*see, e.g., Deerfield v. Greenberg*, 550 N.E.2d 12 (Ill. App. Ct. 1990); *In re J.M.*, 768 P.2d 219 (Colo. 1989)) and to strike them down (*see, e.g., Johnson v. Opelousas*, 658 F.2d 1065 (5th Cir. 1981); *McCollester v. Keene*, 586 F. Supp. 1381 (D.N.H. 1984); *Waters v. Barry*, 711 F. Supp. 1125 (D.D.C. 1989)).

3. As evidenced in *Strauss*, challenges to juvenile curfews generally focus on the constitutionality of the statute or ordinance. These cases tend to concentrate on several issues:

a. First Amendment free speech issues (*see, e.g., Waters v. Barry*, 711 F. Supp. 1125 (D.D.C. 1989));
b. due process issues under the Fifth and Fourteenth Amendments (*see, e.g., In re Mosier*, 59 Ohio Misc. 83 (1978));
c. parents' rights under the Fifth Amendment to raise their children as they see fit (*see, e.g., Hutchins v. District of Columbia*, 188 F.3d 531 (D.C. Cir. 1999); and
d. challenges based on the Fourteenth Amendment guarantee of equal protection of the law (*see, e.g., Seattle v. Pullman*, 514 P.2d 1059 (Wash. 1973)).

As noted above, these challenges have met with mixed reactions from courts, with some overturning ordinances strikingly similar to those upheld by other courts.

4. The Supreme Court has not ruled on the constitutionality of juvenile curfew laws, and only a few circuit courts have addressed the issue. As discussed in the following note, the Fifth Circuit, which upheld the Dallas curfew ordinance in *Strauss*, had previously struck down a curfew law as overly broad. The Third Circuit upheld a Pennsylvania town's curfew ordinance in *Bykofsky v. Middletown*, 535 F.2d 1245 (3d Cir. 1976); the D.C. Circuit similarly upheld the District's curfew ordinance in *Hutchins v. District of Columbia,* 188 F.3d 531 (D.C. Cir. 1999). However both the Ninth and Second Circuits have held juvenile curfews unconstitutional (*see Nunez v. City of San Diego*, 114 F.3d 935 (9th Cir. 1997); *Naprstek v. City of Norwich*, 545 F.2d 815 (2d Cir. 1976)).

5. Although there is no consensus among the courts regarding the validity of juvenile curfew statutes and ordinances, as a general proposition it can be said that the less restrictive the curfew (e.g., the more exceptions it has), the greater the chance it will be upheld. For example, the Fifth Circuit, which upheld the ordinance in *Strauss*, overturned a juvenile curfew ordinance in *Johnson v. Opelousas*, finding it unconstitutionally overbroad. 658 F.2d 1065 (5th Cir. 1981). In fact, the ordinance at issue in *Strauss* seems to have been written in an attempt to address the concerns that led the court to strike down the curfew in *Opelousas*. For example, the court in *Opelousas* overturned the curfew ordinance in part because the only exceptions allowed were if the child was accompanied by a parent or responsible adult or was on an emergency errand. By contrast, in *Strauss* the court upheld the curfew stating that by including more exceptions for legitimate night time use of the streets by juveniles, it accomplished its goals of protecting juveniles and reducing juvenile crime while employing "the least restrictive means."

6. For a discussion of various curfew regulations and decisional law regarding their validity, see Danny R. Veilleux, Annotation, *Validity, Construction, and Effect of Juvenile Curfew Regulations*, 83 A.L.R. 4TH 1056 (1991).

Questions

1. *Strauss* lists several "defenses" to a curfew violation. One of these defenses is the exercise by minors of "their First Amendment speech and association rights." This exception to the curfew law seems to have been included to meet one of the main constitutional objections to curfew ordinances—the contention that curfew laws unduly impinge upon the rights of minors to move about and speak freely. Does the inclusion of this defense to a curfew violation adequately address this concern? Does it go too far, opening the door to the type of late-night gatherings the regulation was enacted to curtail? For example, would a group of juveniles gathered in the city park at 3:00 a.m. to protest the curfew be violating the curfew ordinance or exercising their rights of free speech and association?

2. Imagine that a member of the municipal board has approached you for advice on drafting a juvenile curfew ordinance that the board is considering. Given the inconsistent treatment curfew laws have received from the courts, how would you advise the board member? What language would you suggest the ordinance contain? What should be left out? What exceptions or defenses to a violation would you recommend? In the end, how confident would you be that the ordinance you propose would withstand a constitutional challenge?

e. Truancy

In re E.B.

287 N.W.2d 462 (N.D. 1980)

PEDERSON, Justice.

E.B., a juvenile, appeals from a decision of the juvenile court entered May 16, 1979, finding him to be an unruly child in that he was "habitually and without justification truant from school" in violation of § 27-20-02(4)(a), NDCC. We find that § 27-20-02(4)(a) is not unconstitutionally vague, and affirm the holding that E.B. is an unruly child.

* * *

E.B. is fifteen years old and lives with his mother. He was involved in an informal adjustment before a juvenile supervisor in May of 1978, at which time he admitted committing the unruly act of truancy during the 1977-78 school year, and was placed on probation.

The problem reoccurred the following year and on January 30, 1979, a petition was filed alleging that E.B. was an unruly child in that he was habitually truant from school. He missed a total of eighteen days of school, six and one-half of which were unexcused, between September 5, 1978, and January 30, 1979.

E.B.'s attorney moved to dismiss the petition on the ground that § 27-20-02(4)(a) was unconstitutionally vague. The juvenile supervisor denied the motion and found that E.B. was an unruly child. The district court confirmed the supervisor's finding.

As grounds for reversal, E.B. contends that the terms "habitually" and "without justification" are too vague for the fair administration of justice; secondly, that the State must prove that the child's absences from school were willful and that there was no justification for them; and, lastly, that six and one-half days of unexcused absences do not constitute habitual truancy.

Section 27-20-02(4) provides as follows:

"4. 'Unruly child' means a child who:
b. is habitually and without justification truant from school. . . ."

E.B. asserts that the terms "habitually" and "without justification" do not provide adequate standards for the juvenile court in applying the statute so that § 27-20-02(4)(a) violates the due process clause of the Fourteenth Amendment to the United States Constitution and Section 13 of the North Dakota Constitution. . . .

In *United States v. Harriss*, 347 U.S. 612, 74 S.Ct. 808, 98 L.Ed. 989 (1954), the Supreme Court set forth applicable principles for determining whether a statute is void for vagueness:

> "The underlying principle is that no man shall be held criminally responsible for conduct which he could not reasonably understand to be proscribed. [Footnote omitted.]" *Id.* at 617, 74 S.Ct. at 812.

This guarantee of due process is applicable to civil statutes as well as criminal. In *In re J.Z.*, 190 N.W.2d 27 (N.D. 1971), this court considered a vagueness challenge to a portion of the Uniform Juvenile Court Act and stated:

> "A statute which either forbids or requires the doing of an act in terms so vague that men of common intelligence must necessarily guess at its meaning and differ as to its application violates the first essential of due process of law. On the other hand, where the words assailed, taken in connection with the context, are commonly understood, their use does not render a statute invalid. . . . [Footnotes omitted.]" *Id.* at 35.

* * *

We find the argument less than persuasive that the words "habitually" and "without justification" are too vague to provide adequate standards. Statutory draftsmen often use these words and the courts have construed them without apparent difficulty. For example, in *State v. Harm*, 200 N.W.2d 387 (N.D. 1972), this court declined to hold that § 39-06-32(3), NDCC, was invalid on the basis that the words "habitually reckless or negligent driver" were unconstitutionally vague:

"It has been said that the terms 'habitual,' 'reckless,' and 'negligent' are well known to all and the suspending or revoking officials have thereby a definite and tangible standard to guide them in their determination." *Id.* at 392.

Mere use of general language does not support a vagueness challenge. *State v. Woodworth*, 234 N.W.2d 243, 245 (N.D. 1975).

. . . In *Sheehan v. Scott*, 520 F.2d 825 (7th Cir. 1975), the court held that the words "habitually truant" were not unconstitutionally vague. The plaintiff in that case complained that he was unaware of what actions he must take in order to comply with the law. "The simple answer is to comply with the law which requires compulsory attendance at school by going to school." *Id.* at 830.

* * *

It appears that the phrase "habitually truant" has been used in numerous statutes and courts have uniformly upheld them. Although the phrase may lack mathematical precision, it has a common-sense meaning which provides adequate standards for the guidance of the court. . . . As the Seventh Circuit said in *Sheehan v. Scott, supra*, we decline to interfere with the reasonable discretion to be exercised by school authorities in defining exactly where the thin ice ends.

We also decline to hold that the words "without justification" are unconstitutionally vague. These words are not ambiguous and have a meaning well understood in common language. These are also terms which have withstood previous vagueness challenges. *See Ex parte Strong*, 95 Tex. Cr. R. 250, 252 S.W. 767 (Texas 1923); *State v. Gardner*, 51 N.J. 444, 242 A.2d 1 (1968); *State v. Norflett*, 67 N.J. 268, 337 A.2d 609 (1975).

E.B. asserts that the State must prove that the child's absences were at least "voluntary" and perhaps "willful," and he asserts that oversleeping is not the kind of conduct the statute meant to proscribe. Our state requires each child to attend school every day. If the child does not attend, and his or her parent did not give permission for the absence—the child's absence is marked unexcused. This is the exact conduct meant to be proscribed, whether the reason for the absence was oversleeping or something else. We are hard-pressed to see how oversleeping is not volitional conduct, unless the fatigue producing the oversleeping is due to illness or other conditions beyond the juvenile's control.

* * *

The State does not have to prove there was no justification for the absences. The Compulsory School Attendance chapter, 15-34.1, provides several exceptions to compulsory attendance and places the burden of proving them on the parent. *See* § 15-34-1-03, NDCC. We see no reason why a child charged with habitual truancy should not have the same burden.

Lastly, E.B. contends that six and one-half days of unexcused absences do not constitute habitual truancy.

* * *

The findings of the juvenile referee and the record below indicate that E.B. admitted committing the act of truancy for the previous school year (1977-78). There is a separate finding of fact that E.B.'s mother had difficulty controlling the child and that he did not submit to her reasonable wishes. The transcript indicates that she had not given E.B. permission to miss school on the days he was marked unexcused. E.B. was absent from school a total of 18 times during the five months in question, not just the six and one-half days marked unexcused. Viewing the total picture, school authorities were able to detect a developing, consistent pattern of truancy in E.B. for the 1978-79 school year. With this conclusion we agree.

The Uniform Juvenile Court Act has separate provisions for the "unruly child" to remove any taint of criminality and to provide for treatment or rehabilitation. School officials should be encouraged to act upon developing patterns of truancy so that the child can be helped and the problem cured.

Having reviewed the evidence anew, we find that § 27-20-02(4)(a) is not unconstitutionally vague and affirm the district court's holding that E.B. was an unruly child in that he was habitually and without justification truant from school.

Notes

1. The juvenile court system has struggled with how best to respond to status offenders for a long time. Even before the juvenile court system was established, the court intervened in the lives of poor children by removing them from their homes because society believed poverty led to moral turpitude. Society feels justified in intervening in minors' lives where they would not interfere with adults' lives because of two beliefs. First, society believes the state should protect and guide young people. Second, society believes that children's behavior can be shaped and corrected; whereas, adults' behavior cannot easily be changed. However, until the 1960s, status offenders were treated as delinquents.

In the 1960s, a status offense reform movement began in the United States as critics demanded that status offenders be treated differently than delinquents. These critics wanted services, rather than incarceration, for status offenders. In 1961, California created a status offense statute, New York followed in 1962, Illinois in 1965, and Colorado in 1967. In 1974, Congress passed the Juvenile Justice and Delinquency Prevention Act, which is codified as 42 U.S.C.A §§ 5601-5751, and further distinguished status offense cases from delinquency cases. Under this Act, status offenders have essentially the same due process rights as delinquents, but the disposition of the two types of cases is very different. The Juvenile Justice and Delinquency Prevention Act of 1974 discouraged placement of status offenders in secure detention facilities by conditioning the receipt of federal funds on state efforts to deinstitutionalize noncriminal youth. The Act created the Office of Juvenile Justice and Delinquency Prevention to determine what states qualify for these federal funds. The Act also encouraged states to develop service programs for status offenders. *See generally* Carol S.

Stevenson, *et al., The Juvenile Court: Analysis and Recommendations,* 6 FUTURE OF CHILDREN 4, 13-14 (1996) (discussing the status offense reform movement).

In 1980, the Juvenile Justice and Delinquency Prevention Act was amended to allow the secure detention of status offenders who violate valid court orders. Some scholars argue that this is one of a number of indications that there is a trend toward greater control and more punitive responses over status offenders. *See* David J. Steinhart, *Status Offenses,* 6 FUTURE OF CHILDREN 86 (1996), for a discussion of why some believe that the federal and state commitment to a policy of deinstitutionalization is weakening.

Statistics suggest that the reform movement has been successful. The number of status offense cases that were petitioned and formally disposed of in 1997 was 101% more than those handled in 1988. However, the number of petitioned status offense cases handled by juvenile courts that resulted in formal adjudication declined 66% in 1988 to 52% in 1997. *See* U.S. DEP'T OF JUST., *National Estimates of Petitioned Status Offense Cases, in* JUVENILE COURT STATISTICS 37 (1997).

2. Like persistent runaways, habitual truants have often been found in contempt of court and incarcerated in training schools. *See, e.g., In re Marsh*, 14 A.2d 368 (Pa. Super. Ct. 1940); *A.O. v. State*, 433 So. 2d 22 (Fla. Dist. Ct. App. 1983). However, as noted above, the recent trend in both statutory and case law has been away from labeling truants as delinquent. Those found guilty of truancy are more likely to be labeled "dependent" or "in need of supervision." *See generally* Janet Boeth Jones, Annotation, *Truancy as Indicative of Delinquency or Incorrigibility, Justifying Commitment of Infant or Juvenile*, 5 A.L.R.4TH 1211 (1981).

Questions

1. Review the cases in this section. Applying the Georgia Code sections reprinted at the beginning of Chapter 2, which of the juveniles in these cases would be adjudged "unruly children"? What section(s) of the Code would apply in each case?

2. Does the Georgia Code adequately address the concerns noted by the courts in the preceding cases regarding status offense laws?

a. Is the statute vague? Which sections, if any, should be more precise?
b. Would the curfew outlined in § 15-11-2(12)(E) withstand the analysis in *Strauss*?
c. Does the statute adequately equip the court to deal with repeat status offenders, such as habitual truants and persistent runaways?

2. Crime Delinquency

a. Sample Delinquency Statute

New Jersey Statutes Annotated
§ 2A:4A-23 (West Supp. 2001)

§ 2A:4A-23. Definition of delinquency

As used in this act, "delinquency" means the commission of an act by a juvenile which if committed by an adult would constitute:

a. A crime;
b. A disorderly persons offense or petty disorderly persons offense; or
c. A violation of any other penal statute, ordinance or regulation.

b. Civil Label

K.M.S. v. State
200 S.E.2d 916 (Ga. Ct. App. 1973)

STOLZ, Judge.

K.M.S., a juvenile, appeals from an order . . . of the Juvenile Court of DeKalb County denying her motion to dismiss the petition alleging her to be delinquent. The petition in question alleged "that said child is delinquent and is [sic] need of treatment and/or rehabilitation or supervision in the meaning of the law and that said child did on February 1, 1973 . . . commit *murder* when she unlawfully and with malice aforethought caused the death of Michael Anthony Street, a human being, by stabbing him with a knife." The juvenile in question was 12 years old at the time of the fatal stabbing. . . .

* * *

"A person shall not be considered or found guilty of a crime unless he has attained the age of 13 years at the time of the act, omission, or negligence constituting the crime." Code Ann. § 26-701. "A crime is a violation of a statute of this State in which there shall be a union or joint operation of act, or omission to act, and intention, or criminal negligence." Code Ann. § 26-601. Murder, of course, is a crime in Georgia. Code Ann. § 26-1101.

Here, it is contended that, since the juvenile is under age 13, it is impossible for her to have committed the act of murder and that, since the sole delinquent act alleged in the petition was the murder, the juvenile court has no authority to find the child to be a delinquent and in need of treatment and/or rehabilitation or supervision.

The Juvenile Court Code is intended to be "liberally construed to the end that children whose well-being is threatened shall be assisted and protected and restored, if possible, as secure law-abiding members of society; and that each child coming within the jurisdiction of the court shall receive. . . the care, guidance, and control that will conduce to his welfare and the best interest of the State. . . ." Code Ann. § 24A-101. Among the requisite contents of a petition in the juvenile court is that it set forth plainly "(a) the facts which bring the child within the jurisdiction of the court. . . ." Code Ann. § 24A-1603(a). . . .

The juvenile court is a civil court, not a criminal court, and an adjudication of delinquency is not a conviction of a crime. The juvenile court cannot find anyone guilty of a crime. However, the juvenile court might well find that any act which is designated a crime under Georgia law is a delinquent act when committed by a juvenile. In order to do this, it is not necessary that the juvenile be "considered or found guilty of a crime." Thus, one under the prescribed age (13 years) is not prosecuted as a criminal, but is dealt with as the law provides for juveniles who violate the law.

Here, the petition alleged the juvenile to be "delinquent in the meaning of law in that [she] did [in] February 1973 . . ." commit the act heretofore quoted. [Georgia Law] defines a delinquent child as one "who has committed a delinquent act and is in need of treatment or rehabilitation." Code Ann. § 24A-401(e)(1) defines a delinquent act as one "designated a crime by the laws of Georgia. . . ." Moreover, Code Ann. § 26-701 does not provide that a person under 14 years of age is *incapable* of performing an act which is designated a crime under the laws of Georgia; it simply raises a defense for such a person because of the social desirability of protecting those no more than 12 years of age from the consequences of criminal guilt.

The order of the Juvenile Court of DeKalb County was correct and is hereby affirmed.

Notes

1. The civil nature of juvenile delinquency proceedings has been used to explain the absence of various rights that otherwise apply in adult criminal proceedings. For example, the civil label, in combination with the juvenile courts' focus on welfare and rehabilitation, renders the proceedings "non-criminal," and thus there is no Sixth Amendment guarantee to a speedy trial. *In re D.H.,* 666 A.2d 462 (D.C. 1995), *citing McKeiver v. Pennsylvania*, 403 U.S. 528 (1971). Similarly, a juvenile has no right to a jury trial because civil adjudication by a juvenile court is not a criminal conviction; instead the proceedings are "protective" in nature "with a rehabilitative purpose." *In re J.J.M.,* 701 N.E.2d 1170 (Ill. App. Ct. 1998).

2. However, other courts have relied on *In re Gault*, 387 U.S. 1 (1967), to diminish the significance of the "civil label" and its effect on constitutional application to juvenile proceedings. *Gault* determined that the Fifth Amendment privilege against self-incrimination applied to juvenile proceedings irrespective of their civil nature: "juvenile proceedings to determine 'delinquency' which may lead to commitment to a state institution, must be regarded as 'criminal' for purposes of the privilege against self incrimination. To hold otherwise would be to disregard substance because of the feeble enticement of the 'civil' label-of-convenience which has attached to juvenile proceedings." *Id.* at 49-50. The court in *In the Matter of Lang*, 301 N.Y.S.2d 136 (N.Y. Fam. Ct. 1969), noted that "whatever circumvention of constitutional rights and due process could be rationalized from the 'civil' label applied to juvenile delinquency proceedings has been completely swept away by the Supreme Court's decision in *Gault.*" *Id.* at 140. For a discussion on the constitutionalization of the juvenile court and argued demise of its civil label, see Adam D. Kamenstein, Note, *The Inner-Morality of Juvenile Justice: The Case for Consistency and Legality*, 18 CARDOZO L. REV. 2105 (1997).

The court in *K.M.S.* points out that juvenile court proceedings are civil rather than criminal in nature. This is a common theme in juvenile law. *See, e.g., In re Michael J.,* 691 N.Y.S.2d 277, 279 (N.Y. Fam. Ct. 1999) ("juvenile cases . . . are essentially civil in nature"); *State v. Detrick*, 954 P.2d 949, 952 (Wash. Ct. App. 1998) ("juvenile proceeding are civil, not criminal, in nature"); *In re Bracewell*, 709 N.E.2d 938 (Ohio Ct. App. 1998) ("juvenile court proceedings are not criminal but civil in nature, and are designed to provide for the care, protection, and mental and physical development of children who engage in what otherwise would be criminal behavior"). Indeed, the desire to treat children outside of the criminal justice system is the main justification for a separate juvenile court.

However, while courts continue to acknowledge as a goal the separate, benevolent treatment of children, judges also recognize that juvenile adjudicatory hearings have become increasingly like criminal trials. For example, in *In re C.O.S.*, the court stated that "a juvenile proceeding is not purely a civil matter. It is quasi-criminal." 988 S.W.2d 760 (Tex. 1999). The Supreme Court has also recognized the similarity between juvenile proceedings and criminal trials and has extended some of the procedural and due process safeguards present in the criminal justice system to juvenile adjudications. (*See, infra,* Chapter 6, Section B.) This theme will be explored in detail throughout the next five chapters of this book. As you study these materials, notice the tension inherent in a system that attempts to treat delinquent children separately from their adult counterparts but still demands retribution from those it would protect.

3. Despite criticism of the juvenile court system, during the 1970s and 1980s everyone agreed that the purpose of the juvenile court should be to rehabilitate juveniles. Delinquency statutes reflected the belief that the state was *parens patriae.* Hence, the statutes did not discuss the need to protect the community or to punish juveniles at any length. An example of a child friendly statute is the Georgia statute in place in 1973 that is reprinted in part in *K.M.S.* This statute is concerned with protecting and rehabilitating juvenile delinquents. Georgia's statute states that the Juvenile Court Code is intended to be "liberally construed to the end that children whose well-being is threatened shall be assisted and protected and restored, if possible, as secure law-abiding members of society; and that each child coming within the jurisdiction of the court shall receive . . . the care, guidance, and control that will conduce to his welfare and the best interest of the state. . . ." GA. CODE ANN. § 24A-1603(a). However, by the late 1980s to early 1990s the critics and commentators were no longer in agreement. A debate took place between scholars and legislative bodies regarding what should be the priority—rehabilitative objectives or retributive goals. Those in support of retributive goals felt that juvenile crimes were becoming more frequent and more violent because the rehabilitative approach was not deterring juvenile crime. Some states' statutes reflect this concern with public safety and the need to properly punish juvenile delinquency. Minnesota's statute states that the purpose of the delinquency laws "is to promote the public safety and reduce juvenile delinquency by maintaining the integrity of the substantive law prohibiting certain behavior and by developing individual responsibility for lawful behavior. This purpose should be pursued through means that are fair and just, that recognize the unique characteristics and needs of children, and that give children access to opportunities for personal and social growth." MINN. STAT. § 260B.001(2) (West Supp. 2001). This debate has influenced the juvenile delinquency proceedings in some states by either sending more children to adult courts or requiring juvenile judges to punish children more harshly for their crimes. *See* Charles W. Thomas & Shay Bilchik, *Criminal Law: Prosecuting Juveniles in Criminal Courts: A Legal and Empirical Analysis*, 76 J. CRIM. L. & CRIMINOLOGY 439 (1985); Hon. W. Don Reader, *They Grow Up So Fast: When Juveniles Commit Adult Crimes: The Laws of Unintended Results,* 29 AKRON L. REV. 477 (1996); Eric K. Klein, Note, *Dennis the Menace or Billy the Kid: An Analysis of the Role of Transfer to Criminal Court in Juvenile Justice,* 35 AM. CRIM. L. REV. 371 (1998); Candace Zierdt, *The Little Engine that Arrived at the Wrong Station: How to Get Juvenile Justice Back on the Right Track,* 33 U.S.F. L. REV. 401 (1999).

c. Defenses

(1) Infancy

In re Robert M.

441 N.Y.S.2d 860 (N.Y. Fam. Ct. 1981)

Peggy C. DAVIS, Judge.

This case involves a charge of delinquency brought as a result of the robbery of a bank. Evidence has been offered to show that because of his immaturity the Respondent, who was nine years and ten months old at the time of the alleged offense, could not—or did not—have a culpable mental state. The court is urged to apply the common law rebuttable presumption that a child between the ages of seven and fourteen is incapable of *mens rea* or criminal intent, see 4 Blackstone, Commentaries 23 (1769). For reasons set forth below it is held that the presumption of infancy is inapplicable in delinquency cases and found that Respondent committed the acts charged with the requisite state of mind.

In 1968 Sanford Kadish noted that "[t]he term *'mens rea'* is rivaled only by the term 'jurisdiction' for the varieties of senses in which it has been used and for the quantity of obfuscation it has created."[2] He proceeded to set out the helpful distinction between "*mens rea* in its special sense . . . [which] refers only to the mental state required by the definition of the offense"[3] and "*mens rea* in

---

[2] Kadish, *The Decline of Innocence,* 26 CAMBRIDGE L.J. 273 (1968).

[3] *Id.* at 274.

the sense of legal responsibility."[4] If, for example, a person takes something with the mistaken belief that it belongs to him, there is no *mens rea* in the special sense—no obligation to meet the requirements of law—and therefore no crime.

The complete defense of infancy (available at common law to children under seven) and the presumption of infancy . . . concerned both kinds of *mens rea*. For there is reason to question whether the very young are capable of formulating a specific guilty intent and whether the very young should be held to an adult standard of legal accountability.

The latter concern seems to have been fully met by legislation which absolves children under seven of any legal responsibility for violation of the Penal Law and subjects children between the ages of seven and sixteen to the less severe penalties and lesser stigma of delinquency adjudication. . . .[6] Moreover, there is strong evidence that age seven is a significant milestone in physical and psychosocial development.[9] A review of the recent scientific evidence includes reference to

> the remarkable fact that the chronological age of 7 ± 1 is referred to so frequently as to suggest a milestone marking discontinuous development. . . . Indeed, the longer view of history and sociology of childhood . . . indicates that empirically many cultures had already discovered the unique competence of 7-year-olds that permitted them to assume new roles not available when they were younger. Society seemed to know empirically when to begin its push on the child toward greater autonomy. . . . In modern society children are considered to be ready for learning in school at age 7 ± 1. . . . The Roman Church considers age 7 "the age of reason" in that only then can the child differentiate between the bread of everyday life and the "host." . . . Moreover, in English Common Law, children under 7 are deemed incapable of criminal intent.[10]

New York's decision to charge seven, eight and nine year olds with limited legal responsibility is not, therefore, without basis.

The issue of specific intent appears to be more troublesome. The legislative scheme is based on an assumption that a child over seven is capable of forming a specific criminal intent, for surely the legislature did not intend to create a system of strict liability for children. However, there may well be cases in which a child between seven and sixteen who is developmentally slow does in fact lack the capacity to form the requisite specific intent. Appellate courts in at least two jurisdictions have, in the face of such cases, held that the common law presumption of incapacity by reason of infancy is applicable in all delin-

---

4 *Id.* at 275.

6 Penal Law § 30.00; Family Ct. Act § 712.

9 Shapiro and Perry, *Latency Revisited, The Age 7 Plus or Minus 1*, 31 PSYCHOANALYTIC STUDY OF THE CHILD 79-105 (1976). . . .

10 *Id.* at 80-81 (footnotes and citations omitted).

quency trials. . . .[12] It does not, however, seem sensible to give the petitioner in every delinquency case involving a child under fourteen the burden of overcoming a presumption that the respondent could not have had the requisite specific intent, *Commonwealth v. Durham, supra,* 225 Pa. Super. 545, 389 A.2d at 110-111 (dissenting opinion of Price, J.).[14]

The petitioner in a delinquency matter does, however, have the burden of proving, beyond a reasonable doubt, every element of the crime charged, including the element of intent. Moreover, if the Respondent offers evidence that any combination of factors, including immaturity, negatives the requisite specific intent, he will be exonerated unless his evidence is overcome beyond reasonable doubt.

The application of these principles protects against imposition of undeserved punishment upon those who are "developmentally abnormal" or "grossly immature" without imposing a common law presumption which is inappropriate in the usual case and inconsistent with the legislative scheme for the adjudication of juvenile offenses.

The court finds beyond reasonable doubt that Respondent intentionally committed acts which would have been criminal had he been sixteen or older.

Consideration of Respondent's age and mental state does not however end with that finding. A delinquency petition must allege that the Respondent is in need of supervision, treatment or confinement. If this allegation is not proved, the petition should be dismissed. The Department of Probation is directed to investigate and report at a dispositional hearing . . . . At that time the court will consider whether Respondent's violation of the Penal Law signals a need for court intervention and, if such a need is established, the kind of intervention required.

Notes

1. Courts are divided on the issue of whether the infancy defense is available in a juvenile delinquency proceeding. A majority of jurisdictions agree with the reasoning of *K.M.S. v. State*, *supra*, and find a defense of infancy inapplicable to an adjudication of delinquency. *See, e.g., In re Tyvonne,* 558 A.2d 661 (Conn. 1989); *Jennings v. State,* 384 So. 2d 104 (Ala. 1980); *In re Dow,* 393 N.E.2d 1346 (Ill. App. Ct. 1979). These courts generally rely on the belief that juvenile courts are

---

[12] *Commonwealth v. Durham,* 255 Pa. Super. 539, 389 A.2d 108 (1978) (involving an act by a nine year old girl who suffered from borderline retardation, *id.* at 109, 110); *In re Gladys R.,* 83 Cal. Rptr. 671, 464 P.2d 127 (1970) (involving an "emotionally disturbed child of 12 years," *id.* at 138).

[14] ". . . the law is that a child under the age of seven is conclusively presumed to lack the capacity to commit a crime, that a child between ages seven and fourteen is entitled to a rebuttable presumption of incapacity and when the age of fourteen is reached any special immunity or resumption of incapacity ceases. But these presumptions . . . have been applied where the child under discussion is being measured against adult standards. . . . That application I can accept. However, to make the application in juvenile proceedings is, to me, contrary to the whole concept of the creation of juvenile courts, which were created throughout the country in an attempt to depart from the traditional treatment of children as ordinary criminal defendants. Indeed, the use of presumptions concerning a child's capacity to commit crime was earlier born of the same effort. The majority would give . . . [a respondent] the benefit of both these efforts. I would not."

essentially civil in nature to support their position that "the common law infancy defense . . . has no place in delinquency proceedings." *In re Tyvonne,* 558 A.2d at 666.

A number of courts, however, have found that the defense of infancy is available in a delinquency proceeding. *See, e.g., In re William A.,* 548 A.2d 130 (Md. 1988); *Commonwealth v. Durham*, 389 A.2d 108 (Pa. Super. Ct. 1978); *State v. Q.D.,* 685 P.2d 557 (Wash. 1984); *In re R.,* 464 P.2d 127 (Cal. 1970). These courts find that delinquency adjudications are at least partially punitive in character and that the infancy defense "should be available [in] juvenile proceedings that are criminal in nature." Therefore, the infancy defense should be available in delinquency adjudications. *In re William A.*, 548 A.2d 130, 134 (Md. 1988) (internal quotation marks omitted). *See also* Andrew Walkover, *The Infancy Defense in the New Juvenile Court,* 31 UCLA L. REV. 503 (1984); D. Keith Foren, Note, In re Tyvonne M. *Revisited: Criminal Defense in Connecticut,* 18 QUINNIPIAC L. REV. 733 (1999).

2. For an overview of the applicability of the infancy defense in juvenile proceedings as interpreted by the courts of various jurisdictions, see Tim A. Thomas, Annotation, *Defense of Infancy in Juvenile Delinquency Proceedings,* 83 A.L.R. 4TH 1135 (1991).

3. In addition to the court's discussion of infancy as a defense, the court in *Robert M.* alludes to the common law presumptions regarding a child's capacity to commit a crime. Under the common law, a child under seven years of age was conclusively presumed to be incapable of committing a criminal offense. A child over fourteen was presumptively capable of committing a crime and could be tried as an adult. Children between the ages of seven and fourteen were under a rebuttable presumption of incapacity, with the burden on the state to prove criminal capacity.

The Supreme Court of Washington has recently discussed the state's burden in rebutting the presumption of incapacity. In *State v. J.P.S.*, 954 P.2d 894, 896 (Wash. 1998), the court, interpreting a state statute, held that the state must, by clear and convincing evidence, prove that "the child had sufficient capacity to (1) understand the act and (2) know that it was wrong." In determining whether the child knew that the act he or she committed was wrong, the court found the following factors to be relevant:

(1) the nature of the crime;
(2) the child's age and maturity;
(3) whether the child showed a desire for secrecy;
(4) whether the child admonished the victim not to tell;
(5) prior conduct similar to that charged;
(6) any consequences that attached to the conduct; and
(7) acknowledgment that the behavior was wrong and could lead to detention.

954 P.2d at 897.

The court in *J.P.S.* emphasized that the inquiry into the child's knowledge and understanding relates only to the time of the occurrence of the act in question. The child's admission or acknowledgment after the fact that his or her actions were wrong cannot, by itself, overcome the presumption of incapacity.

Questions

1. Is the complete defense of infancy for children under the age of seven applicable in today's society? Is a child under seven years of age incapable of understanding the nature of his or her actions in all cases?

2. Which of the views expressed in Note 1 is correct? Should courts continue to separate juvenile delinquency from criminal adjudication or is it time to concede that juvenile delinquency proceedings are essentially "criminal in nature"?

3. If the majority of courts and legislatures accepted the view that there is, in reality, very little difference between the criminal and juvenile courts, what changes would you expect to see in the juvenile justice system? (Keep this question in mind as you study the subsequent materials on delinquency, especially those relating to the adjudication process (Chapter 6, *infra*).)

(2) Insanity

Commonwealth v. Chatman

2000 WL 1650120, *1 (Va. Nov. 3, 2000)

FACTS

Since the facts of the underlying offense are not essential to the issue on appeal, we will not discuss them in detail. Both Chatman, who was 13 years old at the time of the offense, and the victim were students in a public school special education program. They had exchanged angry words at school on January 22, 1997, and after school rode home together in a school vehicle. When the vehicle stopped at Chatman's house for him to exit, the victim also got out of the vehicle. Chatman then pulled out a knife and stabbed the victim in the shoulder.

ANALYSIS

Although the Court of Appeals based its decision on the Due Process Clause of the Fourteenth Amendment, the Commonwealth argues that Chatman has neither a constitutional nor a statutory right to raise an insanity defense. These are the two sources upon which Chatman relies to assert that he has such a right. Consequently, we will address the arguments seriatim.

* * *

Chatman asserts that he has a right under the Due Process Clause of the Fourteenth Amendment to assert this insanity defense. Relying on the decisions of the Supreme Court in *In re Gault*, 387 U.S. 1, 87 S.Ct. 1428, 18 L.Ed.2d 527 (1967), and *In re Winship*, 397 U.S. 358, 90 S.Ct. 1068, 26 L.Ed.2d 368 (1970), Chatman argues that "the right to present an insanity defense goes to fundamental due process fairness and is not one of those rights that can be withheld from him."

The Commonwealth, however, disagrees and argues that, since the Constitution does not require states to recognize an insanity defense for adults charged with committing criminal acts, see *Medina v. California*, 505 U.S. 437, 112 S.Ct. 2572, 120 L.Ed.2d 353, (1992); *Powell v. Texas*, 392 U.S. 514, 88 S.Ct. 2145, 20 L.Ed.2d 1254, (1968) (plurality opinion), it follows that a juvenile likewise does not have a right under the Due Process Clause to assert such a defense in a delinquency proceeding. The Commonwealth contends that, even if the insanity defense were constitutionally guaranteed in adult criminal trials, the right ro raise the defense would nonetheless still not apply in juvenile delinquency proceedings. Continuing, the Commonwealth asserts that, in contrast to those rights that were afforded to juveniles in *Gault* and *Winship*, the insanity defense is not fundamental to the factfinding process because sanity, unike mens rea, is not an element of the offense. We agree with the Commonwealth's position.

* * *

The Court of Appeals did not discuss the decision in *Powell* or *Medina*. Nor did it acknowledge the fact that the Supreme Court has never held that the Due Process Clause requires states to recognize the defense of insanity for an adult accused of committing a crime. Yet, in *Gault* and *Winship*, the rights that were afforded to juveniles under the Due Process Clause, i.e., adequate written notice; advice concerning the right to counsel, retained or appointed; the right to confront evidence and to cross-examine witnesses; the privilege against self-incrimination; and the requirement of proof beyond a reasonable doubt, were rights that were unquestionably available to adults in criminal proceedings. Neither the Court of Appeals nor Chatman has explained why a 13-year-old juvenile should be granted a right under the Due Process Clause in a proceedings to adjudicate delinquency when that right is not constitutionally mandated for adults in criminal proceedings to adjudicate their guilt or innocence.

The plurality in *Powell* recognized the difficulties in elevating the opportunity to assert an insanity defense to a right of constitutional dimensions. Not all states that allow a defendant to raise an insanity defense utilize the *M'Naghten* test for insanity. . . . Thus, if due process includes the right to assert the defense of insanity, the Supreme Court would "be impelled into defining some sort of insanity test in constitutional terms." *Powell*, 392 U.S. at 536. But, as the plurality said, "formulating a constitutional rule would reduce, if not eliminate, [the] fruitful experimentation [with different standards], and freeze the developing productive dialogue between law and psychiatry into a rigid constitutional mold." *Id.* at 536-37 . . . .

Thus, we conclude that the Court of Appeals erred in holding that the circuit court violated Chatman's due process rights when it denied his motion for a psychiatric evaluation, thereby preventing him from asserting an insanity defense at the adjudicatory proceeding on the petition charging Chatman with delinquency.

Having disposed of Chatman's constitutional claim, we now turn to his argument that he also has a statutory right to raise an insanity defense. With regard to this issue, Chatman first notes that Chapter 11 of Article 16.1, dealing with juvenile and domestic relations district court, does not contain any language prohibiting a juvenile from presenting such a defense. Continuing, he posits that the use of the term "person" in Code §§ 19.2-168 and 16.1-287.11 necessarily includes both adults and juveniles. Otherwise, the General Assembly would have used some term other than "person" in these two provisions. We are not persuaded by Chatman's arguments.

* * *

Notably, in contrast to the specific statutory provisions dealing with a juvenile's incompetence to stand trial, see Code §§ 16.1-356 through -361, the Codes does not contain any provision allowing the use of an insanity defense at the adjudicatory phase of a delinquency proceeding. Instead, the General Assembly elected to make a juvenile's mental illness or insanity a factor to be considered during disposition after the juvenile had been adjudicated delinquent. Code § 16.1-280. "Courts 'cannot read into a statute something that is not within the manifest intention of the legislature as gathered from the statute itself.'" *Jordan v. Town of South Boston*, 138 Va. 838, 844, 122 S.E. 265, 267 (1924) (quoting 25 R.C.L. 963, § 218).

Nevertheless, Chatman contends that the provisions of Chapters 11 (proceedings on questions of insanity) and 11.1 (disposition of persons acquitted by reason of insanity) of Title 19.2 should be interpreted as applying to juveniles during an adjudication of delinquency. In response, the Commonwealth points out that, under the provisions pertaining to the disposition of persons acquitted by reason of insanity, it is possible to have an indeterminate period of commitment for inpatient treatment. Because of this possibility, the Commonwealth reasons that those provisions cannot apply to juveniles because the juvenile and domestic relations district courts do not have jurisdiction over a juvenile beyond the juvenile's 21st birthday. We agree with the Commonwealth.

When a defendant is acquitted by reason of insanity at the time of the offense, the court must place the acquittee in the temporary custody of the Commissioner of Mental Health, Mental Retardation and Substance Abuse Services for an evaluation to determine whether that acquittee can be released or requires commitment. Code § 19.2-182.2. If an acquittee is mentally ill and in need of inpatient hospitalization, the court must commit the acquittee. Code § 19.2-182.3. When an acquittee is committed for inpatient hospitalization, the committing court must conduct periodic assessments of the confined acquittee's continuing need for such treatment. Code § 192.182.5. As the Commonwealth points out, the provisions of the Code dealing with the disposition of persons acquitted by reason of insanity do not, however, limit the length of time that an acquittee could be confined for inpatient treatment. Thus, it is conceivable that an acquittee could be confined for inpatient treatment for many years or for the remainder of his or her life, if the acquittee continues to be mentally ill and in need of inpatient treatment. Code §§ 19.2-182.5(C) and 182.6(C).

However, the juvenile and domestic relations district courts retain jurisdiction over a juvenile only until that juvenile attains the age of 21 years. Code § 16.10242. Thus, if the statutory scheme governing the disposition of persons acquitted by reason if insanity were available to a 13-year-old juvenile, that scheme's indeterminate period of commitment for inpatient hospitalization could run afoul of the limited duration of the juvenile and domestic relations district courts' jurisdiction. If the General Assembly had intended for a juvenile such as Chatman to assert an insanity defense under Chapters 11 and 11.1 of

Title 19.2, we believe that it would have resolved this conflict. Thus, we conclude that Chatman does not have a statutory right to raise the defense of insanity at the adjudicatory phase of his delinquency proceedings.

For these reasons, we will reverse the judgment of the Court of Appeals and reinstate the judgment of the circuit court adjudicating Chatman to be delinquent.

Reversed and final judgment.

[Dissent omitted.]

Notes

1. Some courts agree that juveniles should not be afforded the insanity defense in delinquency cases. The Arkansas Supreme Court ruled in *K.M. v. State,* 983 SW.2d 93 (1998), that the insanity defense should not be allowed in a delinquency hearing if the legislature did not make such a defense available. Ironically, the Arkansas legislature passed legislation the next year giving juveniles the insanity defense as an option at a delinquency hearing. *See* 1999 Ark. Adv. Legis. Serv. 1192(2) (Michie). *See also Golden v. State,* 21 S.W.3d 801 (Ark. 2000) (juvenile has a due process right to have his competency determined before adjudication but does not have a due process or equal protection right to an insanity defense). Other states such as Illinois have also passed statutes making the insanity defense available to juveniles. *See* 705 ILL. COMP. STAT. ANN. 405/5-605 (West 1999).

2. The *Chatman* decision runs contrary to a growing trend in which more courts allow juveniles to assert the insanity defense in delinquency cases. *See, e.g., In re M.G.S.*, 267 Cal. App. 2d 329 (1968); *State v. Causey*, 363 So. 2d 472, 473-74 (La. 1978); *Matter of Two Minor Children*, 592 P.2d 166, 169 (Nev. 1979); *Winburn v. State*, 145 N.W.2d 178, 184 (Wis. 1966); *Matter of Stapelkemper*, 562 P.2d 815, 816 (Mont. 1977).

Questions

1. A growing number of courts have decided that a juvenile should be permitted to use the insanity defense because of the parallels that exist between the delinquency system and the adult criminal system (because the defense is available to the adult defendant). Is this rationale sufficient to justify the allowance of the defense in delinquency hearings? How might the *parens patriae* doctrine support the court allowing the defense?

2. Several state courts agree that the insanity defense should be available to juveniles in delinquency hearings regardless of whether the legislature has created the defense. Do you agree with this argument? Or, do you agree with the *K.M.* court, *supra*, that courts should not allow juveniles to use the defense in delinquency proceedings if the legislature does not create it? How does due process of law affect your answer?

3. Street Gangs

a. Sample Street Gang Statute

Texas Penal Code Annotated

§ 71.02 (West Supp. 2001)

§ 71.02 Engaging in Organized Criminal Activity

(a) A person commits an offense if, with the intent to establish, maintain, or participate in . . . a criminal street gang, he commits or conspires to commit one or more of the following:

(1) murder, capital murder, arson, aggravated robbery, robbery, burglary, theft, aggravated kidnapping, kidnapping, aggravated assault, aggravated sexual assault, sexual assault, forgery, deadly conduct, assault punishable as a Class A misdemeanor, burglary of a motor vehicle, or unauthorized use of a motor vehicle;
(2) any gambling offense punishable as a Class A misdemeanor;
(3) promotion of prostitution . . . ;
(4) unlawful manufacture, transportation, repair, or sale of firearms or prohibited weapons;
(5) unlawful manufacture, delivery, dispensation, or distribution of a controlled substance or dangerous drug . . . ;
(6) any unlawful wholesale promotion or possession of any obscene material or obscene device with the intent to wholesale promote the same;

* * *

(b) [An] offense under this section is one category higher than the most serious offense listed in Subdivisions (1) through (10) of Subsection (a) of this section that was committed, and if the most serious offense is a Class A misdemeanor, the offense is a felony of the third degree, except that if the most serious offense is a felony of the first degree, the offense is a felony of the first degree.

b. Cases

In re Alberto R.

1 Cal. Rptr. 2d 348 (Cal. Ct. App. 1991)

On February 7, 1990, at about 5 p.m., Alberto R., a member of the 38th Street Shelltown Gang (Shelltown), was a passenger, along with three other Shelltown members, in his ex-girlfriend's car, which she was driving at his request through rival gang territory, following another car. As the cars turned the corner, driving in front of La Central Store (La Central), a regular hangout for the Logan Red Steps (Red Steps) across from Chicano Park, a person in the first car threw a bottle out the window and yelled "1920," a known slogan for the Shelltown gang.

A member of the Red Steps, who was standing in front of La Central at the time, bent over while looking toward the first car. Alberto then fired a few shots at that person, hitting him in the leg and lower backside.

Alberto's girlfriend immediately ducked down in the car and sped off. When she stopped for a red light, her car was rammed from behind twice by a large pickup truck which spun her car completely around. Alberto and his friends jumped out of her car and ran. After she drove home, she called the police.

Alberto and six other Shelltown members were charged with various crimes arising out of the drive-by shooting. In an amended petition filed under Welfare and Institutions Code section 602, Alberto was alleged to have conspired to commit murder (§§ 187, 182), to have attempted to commit murder (§§ 187, 664), and to have committed an assault with a firearm (§ 245, subd. (a)(2)). [It was] alleged [that] the attempted murder and the armed assault were committed by Alberto as a gang member under section 186.22, subdivision (b)(2). . . .

[A]t the close of the People's case, the juvenile court granted a motion to dismiss . . . the conspiracy count against Alberto under Welfare and Institutions Code section 701.1. After the defense and rebuttal evidence was heard, the court found the remaining allegations true. . . .

At the dispositional hearing, Alberto was sentenced to the California Youth Authority for a total of seventeen years, consisting of a nine-year upper term for the second degree attempted murder, a five-year consecutive term for the firearm use, and a three-year consecutive term for committing the crimes as a gang member. . . . Alberto has timely appealed, launching a multifaceted constitutional challenge to section 186.22 subdivision (b). . . . We affirm. . . .

* * *

Alberto's major contention on appeal concerns section 186.22, subdivision (b), which allows additional punishment when a person is found to have committed a felony as a "criminal street gang" member. He argues this statute is unconstitutionally vague on its face and its application in his case is overbroad, thereby violating his due process, freedom of association and equal protection rights. Alberto's attack first concentrates on five different phrases within the statute he considers vague and then switches to other constitutional considerations. [I]n holding section 186.22, subdivision (b) is constitutional, we first review the applicable law, the language of the statute, its legislative history, other California cases that have dealt with or construed the statute, and Alberto's specific constitutional complaints.

* * *

Concerning a challenge to a statute on grounds it is overbroad, the United States Supreme Court has "traditionally viewed vagueness and overbreadth as logically related and similar doctrines." *Kolender v. Lawson*, 461 U.S. 352, 359 n.8, 103 S. Ct. 1855, 75 L. Ed. 2d 903 (1983). Thus "a governmental purpose to control or prevent activities constitutionally subject to state regulation may not be achieved by means which sweep unnecessarily broadly and thereby invade the area of protected freedoms." *NAACP v. Alabama*, 377 U.S. 288, 84 S. Ct. 1302, 12 L. Ed 2d (1964). . . .

Section 186.22, subdivision (b) provides:

> (1) Except as provided in paragraph (2), any person who is convicted of a felony which is committed for the benefit of, at the direction of, or in association with any criminal street gang, with the specific intent to promote, further, or assist in any criminal conduct by gang members, shall upon conviction of that felony, in addition, and consecutive to the punishment prescribed for the felony or attempted felony of which he or she has been convicted, be punished by an additional term of one, two, or three years at the court's discretion. The court shall order the imposition of the middle term of the sentence enhancement unless there are circumstances in aggravation or mitigation. The court shall state the reasons for its choice of sentence enhancements on the record at the time of sentencing.
>
> (2) Any person who violates this subdivision in the commission of a felony punishable by imprisonment in the state prison for life, shall not be paroled until a minimum of 15 calendar years have been served.

* * *

The Act in section 186.22, subdivision (a) makes it a criminal offense for any person to actively participate in any criminal street gang "with knowledge that its members engage in or have engaged in a pattern of criminal gang activity," and to willfully promote, further or assist "in any felonious criminal conduct by members of that gang."

A "criminal street gang" is specifically defined under the Act in subdivision (f) of section 186.22, as: "any ongoing organization, association, or group of three or more persons, whether formal or informal, having as one of its primary activities the commission of one or more of the criminal acts enumerated in paragraphs (1) to (8), inclusive, of subdivision (e), which has a common name or common identifying sign or symbol, whose members individually or collectively engage in or have engaged in a pattern of criminal gang activity."

A "pattern of criminal gang activity" is defined in subdivision (e) of section 186.22, as: "the commission, attempted commission, or solicitation of two or more of the following offenses, provided at least one of those offenses occurred after the effective date of this chapter and the last of those offenses occurred within three years after a prior offense, and the offenses are committed on separate occasions, or by two or more persons: (1) Assault with a deadly weapon or by means of force likely to produce great bodily injury; . . . (2) Robbery; . . . (3) Unlawful homicide or manslaughter; . . . (4) The sale, possession for sale, transportation, manufacture, offer for sale, or offer to manufacture controlled substances; . . . (5) Shooting at an inhabited dwelling or occupied motor vehicle; . . . (6) Arson; . . . (7) The intimidation of witnesses and victims; . . . (8) Grand theft of any vehicle, trailer, or vessel. . . ."

The constitutionality of section 186.22, subdivision (a) was upheld earlier this year. *People v. Green*, 227 Cal. App. 3d 692, 278 Cal. Rptr. 140 (1991). The defendant, convicted for his participation in a criminal street gang, brought claims of vagueness and overbreadth similar to those which Alberto now raises, that key words in the statute were undefined, uncertain and were capable of including persons who became members of a gang out of intimidation.

The court in *Green* found the terms "actively participates," "member," "membership," "criminal street gang," "knowledge," "pattern of criminal gang activity," and "willfully promotes, furthers, or assists" to be sufficiently certain to give a defendant "reasonable notice of the conduct which [the statute] prohibits and is no more susceptible to arbitrary enforcement than any other criminal statute." *Green*, 227 Cal. App. 3d at 699-704. Although it found the term "felonious criminal conduct" to impart some uncertainty, it construed the provision as covering "only conduct which is clearly felonious, i.e., conduct which amounts to the commission of an offense punishable by imprisonment in state prison." *Id.* at 704. As the court stated, "Section 186.22 does not prohibit membership; it prohibits the promotion, furtherance or assistance in any felonious criminal conduct by members. That a member may not be a whole-hearted participant in the felonious criminal conduct should have no bearing on the criminal liability of the person who promotes, furthers or assists such conduct." *Id.* at p. 700. The court in *Green* further noted section 186.22 "carefully circumscribes the conduct to which it applies; a person cannot be made criminally liable under it unless he or she acts with the intention of promoting, furthering or assisting the commission of a felony." *Green*, 227 Cal. App. 3d at 704.

* * *

Alberto, like Green, alleges specific terms in the statute make it so uncertain and so broad the statute fails to give fair notice of what conduct it proscribes, thereby inviting arbitrary enforcement by local police, and includes all forms of association in violation of the First Amendment. As discussed above, two of the phrases Alberto challenges, "to promote, further, or assist" and "felonious criminal conduct," were specifically addressed by the court in *Green*. We agree with that court's conclusions, there is nothing unconstitutionally vague or overbroad about the phrase "promote, further, or assist," which has been consistently used by the courts to describe "aiding and abetting" *id., see People v. Beeman*, 35 Cal. 3d 547, 560, 199 Cal. Rptr. 60, 674 P.2d 1318 (1984), and that "felonious criminal conduct" passes constitutional muster when that phrase is narrowly construed to only pertain to conduct which is purely felonious, i.e., punishable in state prison.

Alberto also claims the term "benefit of" contained in the enhancement subsection is impermissibly ambiguous because the Legislature may have only meant for the enhancement to apply when a monetary profit is made by a gang member committing a crime. Because "benefit" may be defined as anything contributing to an improvement in condition, advantage, help, or profit, Alberto argues the phrase "benefit of" makes the statute overbroad, catching within its web those who merely assist gang members and make no monetary profit. Such a narrow construction of the term is unwarranted.

The Legislature used the words "profits" and "proceeds" concerning forfeiture in the findings and declarations of the Act; it knew these words, but chose not to use them in defining the element of the enhancement. Thus it is only common sense the Legislature did not intend such a restricted view as Alberto offers. Alberto takes the word "benefit" out of context and treats it in a vacuum. When it is read in context with the other words in the enhancement subdivision, it becomes clear the Legislature intended "benefits" to be interpreted by the qualifying language of the statute, thereby limiting the scope of such conduct to only those acts committed "with the specific intent to promote, further, or assist in any criminal conduct by gang members. . . ." (§ 186.22, subd. (b)). As so defined, the potential for vagueness or overbreadth is eliminated.

* * *

Alberto's due process argument, [that] there are no standards governing the exercise of the discretion granted by the Act, is likewise invalid. A similar due process argument was raised and rejected in *People v. Green,* 227 Cal. App. 3d at 698-704. We agree with that analysis. Section 186.22, subdivisions (e) and (f), specifically designate what crimes a gang must be involved in before a member who knowingly and willfully "promotes, furthers, or assists in" that conduct can be found guilty of the enhancement. As in all criminal cases, the trier of fact then determines whether there is sufficient evidence to support the allegations. No unfettered discretion is shown.

Further, Alberto's contention the "specific intent" phrase of the statue does not save it from being too vague is specious. The plain language of the statute reflects the "specific intent" necessary is "to promote, further, or assist in any criminal conduct by gang members. . . ." § 186.22, subd. (b). Such is adequate notice of what conduct is proscribed. As Alberto concedes, the inclusion of a "specific intent" in the terms of a statute will generally overcome any potential vagueness problem; persons of ordinary intelligence will not have to guess at the applicability of the statute.

* * *

Moreover, because the plain language of the statute requires "active participation in criminal gang activity," Alberto's assertion [that] section 186.22 is unconstitutionally overbroad is easily rejected. The requirements [that] a person know of the group's criminal activity and intentionally further the group's illegal conduct limit the Act's application to those gang members who actually engage in criminal activity. Alberto's attempt to twist around the terms of the statute to create vagueness and overbreadth is similar to the arguments concerning active participation and membership addressed and rejected in *People v. Green*, 227 Cal. App. 3d at 699-701. For the reasons stated there, and above, we reject Alberto's argument.

People ex rel. Gallo v. Acuna

60 Cal. Rptr. 2d 27 (Cal. Ct. App. 1997)

At the request of the City Attorney of the City of San Jose (hereafter the City), we granted review to resolve an array of challenges to two provisions of a preliminary injunction entered by the Superior Court against individual members of an alleged "criminal street gang." . . .

The 48 declarations submitted by the City in support of its plea for injunctive relief paint a graphic portrait of life in the community of Rocksprings. Rockspings is an urban war zone. The four-square-block neighborhood, claimed as the turf of a gang variously known as Varrio Sureno Town, Varrios Sureno Treces (VST), or Varrios Sureno Locos (VSL), is an occupied territory. Gang members, all of whom live elsewhere, congregate on lawns, on sidewalks, and in front of apartment complexes at all hours of the day and night. They display a casual contempt for notions of law, order, and decency—openly drinking, smoking dope, sniffing tolune, and even snorting cocaine laid out in neat lines on the hoods of residents' cars. The people who live in Rocksprings are subjected to loud talk, loud music, vulgarity, profanity, brutality, fistfights and the sound of gunfire echoing in the streets. Gang members take over sidewalks, driveways, carports, apartment parking areas, and impede traffic on the public thoroughfares to conduct their drive-up bazaar. Murder, attempted murder, drive-by shootings, assault and battery, vandalism, arson, and theft are commonplace. The community has become a staging area for gang-related violence and a dumping ground for the weapons and instrumentalities of crime once the deed is done. Area residents have had their garages used as urinals; their homes commandeered as escape routes; their walls, fences, garage doors, sidewalks, and even their vehicles turned into a sullen canvas of gang graffiti.

The people of this community are prisoners in their own homes. Violence and the threat of violence are constant. Residents remain indoors, especially at night. They do not allow their children to play outside. Strangers wearing the wrong color clothing are at risk. Relatives and friends refuse to visit. The laundry rooms, the trash dumpsters, the residents' vehicles, and their parking spaces are used to deal and stash drugs. Verbal harassment, physical intimidation, threats of retaliation, and retaliation are the likely fate of anyone who complains of the gang's illegal activities or tells police where drugs may be hidden.

Among other allegations, the City's complaint asserted that the named defendants and others "[f]or more than 12 months precedent to the date of [the] complaint, continuing up to the present time [have] occupied [and] used the area commonly known as 'Rocksprings' . . . in such a manner so as to constitute a public nuisance . . . injurious to the health, indecent or offensive to the sense, [and] an obstruction to the free use of property so as to interfere with the comfortable enjoyment of life or property by those persons living in the . . . neighborhood."

After alleging the usual requisites for equitable relief—the prospect of "great and irreparable injury" and the absence of "a plain, adequate and speedy remedy at law"—the complaint prayed for a broad and comprehensive injunction against defendants' alleged activities in Rocksprings. The Superior Court granted an *ex parte* temporary restraining order enjoining all 38 defendants named in the complaint and issued an order to show cause (OSC) why a preliminary injunction should not be entered.

Only five of the named defendants appeared in response to the OSC. Following a hearing, the superior court entered a preliminary injunction against the 33 defendants who had not appeared and continued the matter as to those 5 defendants who opposed entry of a preliminary injunction, leaving the temporary restraining order in force as to them. Eleven of the named defendants (the five who had originally appeared in opposition to the OSC, together with another six of the named defendants) moved to vacate the injunctions. After the matter was briefed and argued, the Superior Court entered a preliminary injunction. The multipart decree, consisting of some 24 paragraphs, was the subject of an interlocutory appeal by these 11 defendants.

The Court of Appeals disagreed with the Superior Court, upholding only provisions of the preliminary injunction enjoining acts or conduct defined as crimes under specific provisions of the Penal Code. [We] now reverse.

* * *

At this initial stage in the proceeding, the scope of our inquiry is narrow. We review an order granting a preliminary injunction under an abuse of discretion standard *King v. Meese*, 43 Cal. 3d 1217, 1227-28, 240 Cal. Rptr. 829, 743 P.2d 889 (1987); *Cohen v. Board of Supervisors*, 40 Cal. 3d 277, 286, 219 Cal. Rptr. 467, 707 P.2d 840 (1985). Review is confined, in other words, to a consideration whether the trial court abused its discretion in "'evaluat[ing] two interrelated factors when deciding whether or not to issue a preliminary injunction. The first is the likelihood that the plaintiff will prevail on the merits at trial. The second is the interim harm that the plaintiff is likely to sustain if the injunction were denied as compared to the harm the defendant is likely to suffer if the preliminary injunction were issued.'" *Cohen*, 40 Cal. 3d at 286. . . .

The Court of Appeals held that paragraph (a) of the preliminary injunction, enjoining defendants from "Standing, sitting, walking, driving, gathering or appearing anywhere in public view with any other defendant . . . or with any other known 'VST' or 'VSL' member" was invalid on associational grounds; that is, the provision infringed defendants' right to associate with fellow gang members, a right protected by the First Amendment. We disagree.

In a series of opinions, the United States Supreme Court has made it clear that, although the Constitution recognizes and shields from government intrusion a limited right of association, it does not recognize "a generalized right of 'social association.'" *Dallas v. Stanglin*, 490 U.S. 19, 25 (1989). [Neither] does the First Amendment protect the collective public activities of the gang members within the four-block precinct of Rocksprings, activities directed in the main at trafficking in illegal drugs and securing control of the community through systematic acts of intimidation and violence.

* * *

Freedom of association, in the sense protected by the First Amendment, "does not extend to joining with others for the purpose of depriving third parties of their lawful rights." *Madsen v. Women's Health Center, Inc.*, 512 U.S. 753 (1994). We do not, in short, believe that the activities of the gang and its members in Rocksprings at issue here are either "private" or "intimate" as constitutionally defined. . . .

The Court of Appeals also invalidated paragraph (a) of the trial court's preliminary decree on the ground that these provisions were "overbroad," as that term has come to be understood and applied in the context of First Amendment litigation. It acknowledged that the reach of the overbreadth doctrine has been cabined in a series of High Court opinions. . . . However, it did not consider one crucial fact: no one, apart from defendants themselves, is or can be subject to the prophylactic relief granted by the trial court.

[As] with any injunction, the preliminary decree here is addressed to identifiable parties and to specific circumstances; the enjoined acts are particularly described in the trial court's order. Unlike the pervasive "chill" of an abstract statutory command that may broadly affect the conduct of an absent class and induce self-censorship, the decree here did not issue until after these defendants had had their day in court, a procedure that assures "'a prompt and carefully circumscribed determination of the issue.'" *Kingsley Books, Inc. v. Brown*, 354 U.S. 436, 442 (1957). . . .

* * *

Having concluded that [the provisions] of the preliminary injunction are not unconstitutionally vague or overbroad and do not infringe defendants' constitutionally protected associational interests, we must complete our inquiry by considering the limitations on the scope of the interlocutory decree as a matter of both public nuisance and constitutional law. . . .

* * *

It is the threat of collective conduct by gang members loitering in a specific and narrowly described neighborhood that the provision is sensibly intended to forestall. Given that overriding purpose, the prohibitions enumerated in provision (a) are not easily divisible. Permitting two or more gang members to drive together but not sit, or to stand together but not walk, would obviously defeat the core purpose behind the proscription. Moreover, given the factual showing made by the City in support of preliminary relief—the carnival-like atmosphere of collective mayhem described above—we cannot say that the ban on any association between gang members within the neighborhood goes beyond what is required to abate the nuisance.

The effect of provision (a)'s ban on defendants' protected speech is minimal. To judge from the evidence placed before the Superior Court, the gangs appear to have had no constitutionally protected or even lawful goals within the limited territory of Rocksprings. So far as the record before the trial court shows, the gangs and their members engaged in no expressive or speech-related activities which were not either criminally or civilly unlawful or inextricably intertwined with unlawful conduct. . . .

[W]e are compelled to defer to the superior knowledge of the trial judge, who is in a better position than we to determine what conditions "on the ground" in Rocksprings will reasonably permit. Outside the perimeter of Rocksprings, the Superior Court's writ does not run; gang members are subject to no special restrictions that do not affect the general population. Given the limited area within which the Superior Court's injunction operates, the absence of any showing of constitutionally protected activity by gang members within that area, the aggravated nature of gang misconduct, the fact that even within Rocksprings gang members may associate freely out of public view, and the kind of narrow yet irreducible arbitrariness that inheres in such line-drawing, we conclude that this aspect of provision (a) passes muster as well under the standard of *Madsen*, 512 U.S. 753.

We reach a similar resolution with respect to provision (k). That provision forbids those subject to the injunction from confronting, intimidating or similarly challenging—including assaulting and battering—residents of Rocksprings, "or any other persons" who gang members know have complained about their conduct within the neighborhood. It has long been the rule, of course, that physical violence and the threat of violence are not constitutionally protected: "The First Amendment does not protect violence." *NAACP v. Claiborne Hardware Co.*, 458 U.S. 886, 916 (1982). Because the conduct proscribed by provision (k) consists of threats of violence and violent acts themselves, it "fall[s] outside the protection of the First Amendment because [such acts] coerce by unlawful conduct, rather than persuade by expression, and thus play no part in the 'marketplace of ideas.' As such, they are punishable because of the state's interest in protecting individuals from the fear of violence, the disruption fear engenders and the possibility the threatened violence will occur." *In re M.S.,* Cal. 4th 698, 714. "[A] physical assault is not by any stretch of the imagination expressive conduct protected by the First Amendment." *Wisconsin v. Mitchell*, 508 U.S. 476, 484. By the same token, "utterance in a context of violence can lose its significance as an appeal to reason and become part of an instrument of force. Such utterance was not meant to be sheltered by the Constitution." *Drivers Union v. Meadowmoor Co.,* 312 U.S. 287 293 (1941).

* * *

The judgment of the Court of Appeals is reversed insofar as it invalidated paragraphs (a) and (k) of the preliminary injunction and concluded that defendant Blanca Gonzalez was not subject to its terms. Because our grant of review encompassed only those two of the fifteen provisions invalidated by the Court of Appeals, we do not address any other aspect of the preliminary injunction entered by the Superior Court.

[Reversed.]

Notes

1. In contrast to the California court's decision in *In re Alberto R.*, the Florida Supreme Court has recently determined that a similar statute violated the Due Process Clause of the Federal and state Constitutions because it did not require that the state establish a nexus between the crime that the juvenile committed and his or her gang membership. *See State v. O.C.*, 748 So. 2d 945 (Fla. 1999).

2. Since 1980, membership in juvenile gangs has grown at an alarming rate. The number of gangs has increased from 2,000 to 31,000 and the number of gang members from 10,000 to 846,000 between 1980 and 1996. *See* JAMES C. HOWELL, U.S. DEP'T OF JUST., YOUTH GANGS: AN OVERVIEW 1 (1988) (citing W.B. MILLER, U.S. DEP'T OF JUST., CRIME BY YOUTH GANGS AND GROUPS IN THE UNITED STATES (1992), and J.P. MOORE & C.P. TERRETT, U.S. DEP'T OF JUST., HIGHLIGHTS OF THE 1996 NATIONAL YOUTH GANG SURVEY (1997)). Children who are susceptible to joining gangs exhibit similar individual and family demographics, personal attributes, peer group relationships, and school and community environments. For further discussion of these gang-related factors, see FINN-AAGE ESBENSEN, U.S. DEP'T OF JUST., PREVENTING ADOLESCENT GANG INVOLVEMENT (2000).

Because jurisdictions disagree about what constitutes a "gang," and because data has not been systematically collected on the county or city level, it is difficult to estimate the scope of the problem. In 1996, the National Youth Gang Center surveyed more than 3,000 law enforcement agencies and reported that 74% of the cities with a population greater than 25,000 and 34% of small cities indicated that there were juvenile gangs in their communities. *See* J.P. MOORE & C.P. TERRETT, U.S. DEP'T OF JUST., HIGHLIGHTS OF THE 1996 NATIONAL YOUTH GANG SURVEY (1997).

Despite the historical trend in the increasing number of gangs in large cities, suburban counties, and small cities reported in the HIGHLIGHTS OF THE 1996 NATIONAL YOUTH GANG SURVEY, recent statistics from the 1999 National Youth Gang Survey report that gang activity, the number of juvenile gangs, and juvenile gang membership decreased since the 1996 survey. ARLEN EGLEY, U.S. DEP'T OF JUST., HIGHLIGHTS OF THE 1999 NATIONAL YOUTH GANG SURVEY (2000). The 1999 survey indicates that juvenile gang activity was reported in 66% of large cities, 47% of suburban communities, and 27% of small cities. According to the 1999 survey, the number of juvenile gang members decreased 8% from 1998, while the number of active gangs also decreased 9% during the same time period. Despite the decreasing numbers of gangs and gang membership, an estimated 26,000 gangs still exist and have an estimated membership of 840,500. Therefore, gang activities and involvement "continue[ ] to be widespread and substantial across the United States." *Id.* For additional information concerning juvenile gangs in the United States, see http://www.iir.com/nygc.

3. Other studies have established that a substantial portion of violent offenses are committed by juveniles who are members of a gang. *See, e.g.,* T.P. Thornberry, *Membership in Youth Gangs and Involvement in Serious and Violent Offending, in* SERIOUS AND VIOLENT OFFENDERS: RISK FACTORS AND SUCCESSFUL INTERVENTIONS 147-66 (R. Loeber & D.P. Farrington eds., 1998) (reporting that juvenile gang members were responsible for 68% of violent crimes in Rochester, New York); S.R. Battin *et al., The Contribution of Gang Membership to Delinquency Beyond Delinquent Friends,* 36 CRIMINOLOGY 93 (1998) (reporting that juvenile gang members were responsible for 85% of the robberies committed in Seattle, Washington); D. Huizinga, The Volume of Crime by Gang and Nongang Members (1997) (unpublished manuscript), *cited in* JAMES C. HOWELL, U.S. DEP'T OF JUST., CRIME BY YOUTH GANGS AND GROUPS IN THE UNITED STATES (1992) (reporting that juvenile gang members were responsible for 89% of violent crimes in Denver, Colorado). For a discussion of the impact of gang-involvement in public and private schools, see JAMES C. HOWELL & JAMES P. LYNCH, U.S. DEP'T OF JUST., YOUTH GANGS IN SCHOOLS (2000).

4. For a discussion of gang-prevention programs used in cities such as Chicago, see PREVENTING ADOLESCENT GANG INVOLVEMENT, *supra.*

Questions

1. *In State v. O.C.,* 748 So. 2d 945 (Fla. 1999), the court required a state to establish a nexus between the delinquent act committed by a juvenile and his or her gang membership. California (*see In re Alberto R.* and *People ex rel. Gallo v. Acuna*) and Texas (*see* § 71.02 of the Texas Penal Code Annotated) require the intent to participate, assist, etc. the felonious conduct of gang membership. Which view is correct? Why?

2. Is adding a consecutive sentence for participation in a gang to the sentences for other delinquent offenses consistent with the traditional belief discussed in Chapter 2 that juvenile law should be rehabilitative rather than punitive in nature? What are the arguments which support contentions that gang-related laws are designed as rehabilitation, deterrence, or for punitive purposes?

3. As courts become more concerned about juvenile gang membership, should legislatures give greater arresting power to police by expanding the number of delinquent acts which may trigger application of gang-related laws (e.g., theft, forgery, etc.) with the purpose of curtailing gang activity? If you were a member of a state legislature, where would you draw the line? What constitutional implications might arise?

4. Excluded Offenses

California Welfare and Institutions Code
§ 603.5 (West Supp. 2001)

§ 603.5 Vehicle Code infractions

(a) Notwithstanding any other provision of law, . . . jurisdiction over the case of a minor alleged to have committed only a violation of the Vehicle Code . . . is with the municipal court or the superior court in a county in which there is no municipal court, except that the court may refer to the juvenile court for adjudication, cases involving a minor who has been adjudicated a ward of the juvenile court, or who has other matters pending in the juvenile court.

(b) The cases specified in subdivision (a) shall not be governed by the procedures set forth in the juvenile court law.

(c) Any provision of juvenile court law requiring that confidentiality be observed as to cases and proceedings, prohibiting or restricting the disclosure of juvenile court records, or restricting attendance by the public a juvenile court proceedings shall not apply. . . .

Notes

1. In establishing a juvenile court, states are free to include or exclude offenses in the creation of that court's jurisdiction. Many courts respond by noting that there is no constitutional guarantee for juvenile offenders to the protection of the juvenile court; as such, statutory law defines any existing rights to treatment as a "juvenile." *See Commonwealth v. Cotto*, 708 A.2d 806 (Pa. Super. Ct. 1998). In so doing, the legislature may expand or narrow the scope of the juvenile court's jurisdiction and exclude certain offenses from the court's province. *See Florida v. G.D.M.*, 394 So. 2d 1017 (Fla. 1981); *State of Maine v. Wilson*, 409 A.2d 226 (Me. 1979).

2. Some commentators argue that offense exclusion is the legislature's response to the public outcry against violent juvenile offenders. *See generally* Eric J. Fritsch & Craig Hemmens, *An Assessment of Legislative Approaches to the Problem of Serious Juvenile Crime: A Case Study of Texas 1973-1995*, 23 AM. J. CRIM. L. 563 (1996) (suggesting that one reason for excluding certain violent offenses from the jurisdiction of the juvenile court is that juvenile courts cannot impose sufficiently severe sanctions; offense exclusion is seen as the best way to prosecute some juveniles as adults. As a result, some legislatures are changing the focus of the juvenile justice system from rehabilitation to restitution).

Chapter 3

Delinquency Intake Process

In this chapter, we are introduced to additional unique terminology that evolved with the juvenile justice system in its attempt to distinguish itself from the criminal justice process. "Delinquency intake," for example, is the juvenile court equivalent of "arrest" in the adult criminal justice system. Similarly, juveniles are not "jailed" pending "trial," they are "detained" pending "adjudication." Even where the terms are similar, the process for handling juvenile cases may differ markedly from that of adults. This chapter will explore the juvenile intake process, highlighting both the terminology unique to the juvenile court system and the methods by which juveniles are processed in the system. Special attention will be given to the differences between adult arrests and pretrial procedures and the juvenile intake, diversion, and detention process.

A. IJA-ABA Standards on Intake

IJA-ABA Standards Relating to the Juvenile Probation Function: Intake and Predisposition Investigative Services

Juvenile Justice Standards Annotated 155, 161-64
(Robert E. Shepherd, Jr., ed., 1996)*

PART I: DEFINITIONS

1.1 Definitions as used herein:

* * *

D. A "complaint" is a report made to a juvenile court that alleges that a juvenile is delinquent and that initiates the intake process.

* * *

---

* Reprinted with permission.

G. "Intake" is a preliminary screening process initiated by the receipt of a complaint, the purpose of which is to determine what action, if any, should be taken upon the complaint.

H. An "Intake officer" is an individual who screens complaints and makes intake dispositional decisions with respect to complaints.

* * *

SECTION IV: INTAKE PROCEDURES

2.9 Necessity for and desirability of written guidelines and rules.

Juvenile probation agencies and other agencies responsible for intake services should develop and publish written guidelines and rules with respect to intake procedures.

2.10 Initiation of intake proceedings and receipt of complaint by intake officer.

A. An intake officer should initiate proceedings upon receipt of a complaint.

B. Any complaint that serves as the basis for the filing of a petition should be sworn to and signed by a person who has personal knowledge of the facts or is informed of them and believes that they are true.

2.11 Intake investigation.

A. Prior to making a dispositional decision, the intake officer should be authorized to conduct a preliminary investigation in order to obtain information essential to the making of the decision.

B. In the course of the investigation the intake officer may:

1. interview or otherwise seek information from the complainant, a victim of, witness to, or coparticipant in the delinquent conduct allegedly engaged in by the juvenile;

2. check existing court records, the records of law enforcement agencies and other public records of a nonprivate nature;

3. conduct interviews with the juvenile and his or her parents or legal guardian in accordance with the requirements set forth in Standard 2.14.

C. If the officer wishes to make any additional inquiries, he or she should do so only with the consent of the juvenile and his or her parents or legal guardian.

D. It is the responsibility of the complainant to furnish the intake officer with information sufficient to establish the jurisdiction of the court over the juvenile and to support the charges against the juvenile. . . .

2.12 Juvenile's privilege against self-incrimination at intake.

A. A juvenile should have a privilege against self-incrimination in connection with questioning by intake personnel during the intake process.

B. Any statement made by a juvenile to an intake officer or other information derived directly or indirectly from such a statement is inadmissible in evidence in any judicial proceeding prior to a formal finding of delinquency unless the statement was made after consultation with and in the presence of counsel.

2.13 Juvenile's right to assistance of counsel at intake.

A juvenile should have an unwaivable right to the assistance of counsel at intake:

A. in connection with any questioning by intake personnel at an intake interview involving questioning in accordance with Standard 2.14 or other questioning by intake personnel; and

B. in connection with any discussions or negotiations regarding a non-judicial disposition, including discussions and negotiations in the course of a dispositional conference in accordance with Standard 2.14.

2.14 Intake interviews and dispositional conferences.

A. If the intake officer deems it advisable, the officer may request and arrange an interview with the juvenile and his or her parents or legal guardian.

B. Participation in an intake interview by the juvenile and his or her parents or legal guardian should be voluntary. . . .

C. At the time the request to attend the interview is made, the intake officer should inform the juvenile and his or her parents or legal guardian either in writing or orally that attendance is voluntary and that the juvenile has the right to be represented by counsel.

D. At the commencement of the interview, the intake officer should:

1. explain to the juvenile and his or her parents or legal guardian that a complaint has been made and explain the allegations of the complaint;

2. explain the function of the intake process, the dispositional powers of the intake officer, and intake procedures;

3. explain that participation in the intake interview is voluntary and that they may refuse to participate; and

4. notify them of the right of the juvenile to remain silent and the right to counsel. . . .

E. Subsequent to the intake interview, the intake officer may schedule one or more dispositional conferences with the juvenile and his or her parents or legal guardian in order to effect a nonjudicial disposition.

F. Participation in a dispositional conference by a juvenile and his or her parents or legal guardian should be voluntary. . . .

* * *

2.15 Length of intake process.

A decision at the intake level as to the disposition of a complaint should be made as expeditiously as possible. The period within which the decision is made should not exceed thirty (30) days from the date the complaint is filed in cases in which the juvenile who is the subject of a complaint has not been placed in detention or shelter care facilities.

SECTION V: SCOPE OF INTAKE OFFICER'S DISPOSITIONAL POWERS

2.16 Role of intake officer and prosecutor in filing of petition; right of complainant to file a petition.

A. If the intake officer determines that a petition should be filed, the officer should submit a written report to the appropriate prosecuting official requesting that a petition should be filed. The officer should also submit a written statement of his or her decision and of the reasons for the decision to the juvenile and his or her parents or legal guardian. . . . The prosecutor may refuse the request of the intake officer to file a petition. Any determination by the prosecutor that a petition should not be filed should be final.

B. If the intake officer determines that a petition should not be filed, the officer should notify the complainant of his or her decision and of the reasons for the decision and should advise the complainant that he or she may submit the complaint to the appropriate prosecuting official for review. Upon receiving a request for review, the prosecutor should consider the facts presented by the complainant, consult with the intake officer who made the initial decision, and then make the final determination as to whether a petition should be filed.

Notes

1. According to Ferster and Courtless, the main function of the juvenile intake officer is to determine which complaints should be referred for a judicial hearing. Elyce Zenoff Ferster & Thomas F. Courtless, *The Intake Process in the Affluent County Juvenile Court,* 22 HASTINGS L.J. 1127, 1128 (1971) [hereinafter Ferster & Courtless]. This assessment is based on what is in the best interest of the child and the community. *Id.* at 1133; *see also* § 2.8(A) *Standards Relating to the Juvenile Probation Function: Intake and Predisposition Investigative Services*, in JUVENILE JUSTICE STANDARDS ANNOTATED 155, 160 (Robert E. Shepherd, Jr., ed., 1996) [hereinafter IJA-ABA *Standards on Intake*].

2. The police generally administer the intake process, often in conjunction with a juvenile intake official. In approximately one-third of the cases, the juvenile is released, usually after a warning, without referral to the juvenile court. Robert E. Shepherd, Jr., *The Juvenile Court Intake Process,* 5 A.B.A. SEC. CRIM. JUST. 26, 26 (Summer 1990). This represents an increase in the number of referred cases: until recently, the number of cases dismissed was consistently around 50%. *Id.; see also* David R. Barrett et al., Note, *Juvenile Delinquents: The Police, State Courts, and Individualized Justice,* 79 HARV. L. REV. 775, 776 (1966) [hereinafter Barrett et al., *Juvenile Delinquents*] (half of all police contacts were settled without referral to the juvenile court). Police have traditionally been encouraged by the courts to make these initial determinations, at least in part because the courts lack the necessary personnel to handle every complaint involving juveniles. *Id.* at 777.

These early contacts, whether with police or with a juvenile intake official, help to eliminate cases which are not appropriate for the juvenile court. Section

2.7 of the IJA-ABA *Standards on Intake* requires the intake officer to make an initial determination of the legal sufficiency of the complaint. The officer must determine whether the juvenile court has jurisdiction over the juvenile and whether there is sufficient evidence to support a charge against the juvenile. The intake officer is required to dismiss the complaint if either of these elements is not met. In addition, some jurisdictions also require dismissal of minor offenses. Ferster & Courtless, *supra,* at 1129.

3. Juveniles generally do not have the right to have counsel present during intake proceedings. Ferster & Courtless, *supra*, at 1145. In *In re Gault,* 387 U.S. 1 (1967) (*see infra* Chapter 6), the Supreme Court held that a child is entitled to have an attorney present during critical stages of the juvenile process. The Court, however, declined to extend its holding to include the pre- and post-adjudicatory phases in juvenile proceedings. Many state courts have held that intake is not a "critical stage" and therefore the juvenile has no right to have an attorney present during intake proceedings. *See, e.g., In re H.,* 337 N.Y.S.2d 118, 122 (Fam. Ct. 1972); *State v. Karow,* 453 N.W.2d 181 (Wis. Ct. App. 1990). Several commentators and the American Bar Association, however, recommend the presence of counsel at intake proceedings, especially when the proceeding could result in pretrial detention, informal probation, or diversion. *See* Shepherd, *The Juvenile Court Intake Process, supra,* at 27; IJA-ABA *Standards on Intake* § 2.13.

4. There are several possible outcomes when a juvenile encounters the police or a juvenile intake officer with regard to a complaint. The police or intake personnel generally have the option of releasing the juvenile, with or without filing a written report, or referring the child to juvenile authorities. Barrett et al., *Juvenile Delinquents, supra*, at 777. However, under certain circumstances—such as when the child is on probation or parole, or where the alleged act was a crime of violence, a felony, or a "serious" misdemeanor—referral may be mandatory. *Id.* at 778. Juvenile authorities also have several choices concerning the disposition of a complaint referred by the police or intake officer. The juvenile authority can dismiss the case, divert the juvenile (*see infra* Part E), refer the case to the appropriate court, or place the juvenile on informal probation. *Id.* at 781; Ferster & Courtless, *supra,* at 1141. The juvenile authority considers several factors when making this determination. As noted above, the disposition chosen should be in the best interest of both the community and the child. Section 2.8(B) of the IJA-ABA *Standards on Intake* recommends consideration of the following factors: (1) the gravity of the offense alleged; (2) the child's previous contacts with the juvenile justice system; (3) the circumstances involved in the alleged offense, including the participation of others; (4) the child's age and maturity level; (5) the child's previous behavior, as evidenced by school attendance, family and other relationships, etc.; (6) the juvenile's attitude toward the alleged delinquency, police, and the juvenile court; and (7) services available to meet the child's needs, whether within or outside the juvenile justice system.

The determination of the juvenile intake official is not necessarily final. The complainant may be able to appeal the intake worker's decision to the prosecutor, who must then make an independent determination regarding the case. *See* Ferster & Courtless, *supra*, at 1131. The prosecutor's office may also file a petition on its own authority, regardless of the recommendation of the intake officer or the complainant. *See* IJA-ABA *Standards on Intake* § 2.16(C).

If the child is referred, the court must decide whether to detain the child pending a fact-finding hearing (*see infra* Part C). As with the intake determination, this decision should be based on the best interests of the child and concern for the protection of the public.

Questions

1. Do the IJA-ABA Standards maintain the flexibility necessary in the juvenile justice system, or are they too stringent, effectively constraining intake personnel in their determinations? Do the Standards threaten the informality of the intake process?

2. Should a juvenile have the right to the assistance of counsel during the intake process? The authors of the IJA-ABA Standards believe that a child has an unwaivable right to counsel at intake. The majority of state courts and legislatures conclude otherwise, finding that intake is not a critical stage requiring counsel and that the child is adequately protected by the fact that statements made during intake are generally inadmissible in later proceedings. Which is the more persuasive argument? Would the presence of counsel during intake lead to increased fairness in the proceedings, or would it destroy the informality crucial to the process? If you believe lawyers should be a part of the process, who is entitled to representation? The child? The parents? The state? (In most intake proceedings, neither the juvenile nor the state is represented by counsel.)

B. Arrest

1. IJA-ABA Standards on Arrest

IJA-ABA Standards Relating to Police Handling of Juvenile Problems

Juvenile Justice Standards Annotated 233, 235-36 (Robert E. Shepherd, Jr., ed., 1996)*

PART III: THE AUTHORITY OF THE POLICE TO HANDLE JUVENILE DELINQUENCY AND CRIMINAL PROBLEMS

3.2 Police investigation into criminal matters should be similar whether the suspect is an adult or a juvenile. Juveniles, therefore, should receive at least the same safeguards available to adults in the criminal justice system. This should apply to:

A. preliminary investigations (e.g., stop and frisk);
B. the arrest process;
C. search and seizure;

---

* Reprinted with permission.

D. questioning;
E. pretrial identifications; and
F. prehearing detention and release.

For some investigative procedures, greater constitutional safeguards are needed because of the vulnerability of juveniles. Juveniles should not be permitted to waive constitutional rights on their own. In certain investigative areas not governed by constitutional guidelines, guidance to police officers should be provided either legislatively or administratively by court rules or through police agency policies.

3.3 Even if a juvenile is taken into custody under authority other than the arrest power . . . , police should be subject to the same investigative restrictions set forth above in the handling of the juvenile.

IJA-ABA Standards Relating to Interim Status: The Release, Control and Detention of Accused Juvenile Offenders Between Arrest and Disposition

Juvenile Justice Standards Annotated 119, 133-34
(Robert E. Shepherd, Jr., ed., 1996)*

PART VII: STANDARDS FOR THE JUVENILE COURT

7.1 Authority to issue summons in lieu of arrest warrant.

Judges should be authorized to issue a summons (which may be served by certified mail or in person) rather than an arrest warrant in every case in which a complaint, information, indictment, or petition is filed or returned against an accused juvenile not already in custody.

7.2 Policy favoring summons over warrant.

In the absence of reasonable grounds indicating that, if an accused juvenile is not promptly taken into custody, he or she will flee to avoid prosecution, the court should prefer the issuance of a summons over the issuance of an arrest warrant.

7.3 Application for summons or warrant.

Whenever an application for a summons or warrant is presented, the court should require all available information relevant to an interim status decision, the reasons why a summons or warrant should be issued, and information concerning the juvenile's schooling or employment that might be affected by service of a summons or warrant at particular times of the day.

7.4 Arrest warrant to specify initial interim status.

A. Every warrant issued by a court for the arrest of a juvenile should specify an interim status for the juvenile. The court may order the arresting

---

* Reprinted with permission.

officer to release the juvenile with a citation, or to place the juvenile in any other interim status permissible under these standards.

B. The warrant should indicate on its face the interim status designated. If any form of detention is ordered, the warrant should indicate the place to which the accused juvenile should be taken, if other than directly to court. In each such case, the court should simultaneously file a written statement indicating the reasons why no measure short of detention would suffice.

7.5 Service of summons or warrant.

In the absence of compelling circumstances that prompt the issuing court to specify to the contrary, a summons or warrant should not be served on an accused juvenile while in school or at a place of employment.

* * *

2. Search and Seizure

State v. Lowry

230 A.2d 907 (N.J. Super. Ct. 1967)

Alan Lowry and Benjamin Ferguson, adults, and B, a juvenile aged 17, move to suppress evidence . . . seized as the result of an allegedly illegal search of a parked car in which they were seated . . . . Juvenile B is charged with an offense under the Juvenile Delinquency Act . . . in the Essex County Juvenile Court, the disposition of which is awaiting the outcome of this motion.

All defendants urge the court to suppress the evidence—marijuana cigarettes and a handkerchief filled with pieces of chopped tobacco leaves, identified as marijuana—because the search of their person and the car was warrantless and not incident to a valid arrest.

The issues presented are (a) whether the Fourth Amendment right is applicable to a juvenile, and (b) if the answer is in the affirmative, is the motion to suppress rule . . . the proper method of implementing that right.

* * *

I

The Fourth Amendment to the United States Constitution provides:

> "The right of the people to be secure in their persons, houses, papers, and effects, against unreasonable searches and seizures, shall not be violated, and no Warrants shall issue, but upon probable cause, supported by Oath or affirmation, and particularly describing the place to be searched, and the persons or things to be seized."
>
> This constitutional mandate is a fundamental right of all *persons* regardless of age.

Urbasek v. People, 76 Ill. App. 2d 375, 222 N.E.2d 233, 238 (App. Ct. 1966).

* * *

[T]he Juvenile Court Act was promulgated, not to deprive a juvenile of his rights but to ameliorate the harshness of the criminal law. True, all the niceties of the evidentiary rules and technicalities of procedure may be relaxed in ascertaining the "truth" in a juvenile hearing, yet substantial rights cannot be so disregarded. As stated in *In re Contreras,* 109 Cal. App. 2d 787, 241 P.2d 631 (D. Ct. App. 1952):

> "[I]t cannot seriously be contended that the constitutional guarantee of due process of law does not extend to minors as well as to adults." (109 Cal. App. 2d, at p. 791, 241 P.2d, at p. 634).

* * *

The constitutional right of privacy should be applicable to the young and old alike. This is especially true when the juvenile is accused of an act which, as here, is equivalent to criminal conduct had it been committed by an adult.

* * *

Although the Juvenile Court Act is intended to be salutary, and every effort should be made to further its purposes, it should not be made an instrument denying to a juvenile constitutional guarantees afforded to all persons, whether accused of crime or not. Our State and Federal Constitutions cannot be nullified by mere nomenclature, the end and substance being the same.

As the Appellate Court of Illinois indicated, the protection against unlawful search and seizure is a fundamental right and should be available to the juvenile, especially when viewed in the spirit of the "laudable purposes of Juvenile Courts." *Urbasek v. People, supra*, 222 N.E.2d at p. 238.

This court, therefore, . . . holds that the right of privacy, security and liberty against unreasonable searches and seizures is applicable to a juvenile in accordance with reason and due process of law.

II

The next issue presented is the manner in which the juvenile can implement his Fourth Amendment right. . . . [I]t is the opinion of this court that a rule presently exists, namely, R.R. 3:2A-6, which would enable the juvenile, as it does an adult, to move to suppress evidence illegally seized. The pertinent part of the rule . . . provides:

> "[A] *person* claiming to be aggrieved by an unlawful search and seizure, and having reasonable grounds to believe that the evidence obtained may be used against him in a penal proceeding, may apply . . . to the Superior Court or County Court for the county in which the evidence was obtained for the return of property seized and to suppress the evidence obtained, even though the offense charged or to be charged may be within the jurisdiction of a municipal court." (Emphasis added).

* * *

[T]he court holds that as with any person claiming to be aggrieved by an unlawful search and seizure, a juvenile, charged with an act of juvenile delinquency that would otherwise be a high misdemeanor, misdemeanor or other offense, or violation of a penal law or municipal ordinance, or an offense which could be prosecuted in a method partaking of the nature of a criminal proceeding, or being a disorderly person, may move to suppress evidence pursuant to R.R. 3:2A-6.

III

The final issue to be resolved in this case is whether the evidence—marijuana cigarettes, a handkerchief filled with chopped up greenish-brown leaves, and a box of paper used for rolling cigarettes—was seized as the result of an unlawful search.

* * *

The testimony adduced was uncontradicted that there were three males sitting in a new Mustang automobile in a deserted area known to the police officers as a drop area for stolen cars, as Lovers Lane, and an area known for criminal activity. It cannot seriously be contended that these officers had no right to investigate this situation and even request the driver's license and registration. R.S. 39:3-29, N.J.S.A.

> "A law enforcement officer has the right to stop and question a person found in circumstances suggestive of the possibility of violation of criminal law. [Citations omitted.] Such investigatory detention is not an arrest, '[a]nd the evidence needed to make the inquiry is not of the same degree or conclusiveness as that required for an arrest.'" *State v. Hope,* 85 N.J. Super. 551, 554, 205 A.2d 457, 459 (App. Div. 1964).

Not only did the police officers have a right to investigate under the aforementioned circumstances, but they had a *duty* to investigate, *State v. Smith,* 37 N.J. 481, 496, 181 A.2d 761 (1962); and in the proper exercise of their responsibility these officers observed through the car windows the crimped cigarettes on the floor of the car and on the lap of defendant Ferguson. Officer Janowski also observed through the window from the passenger's side the handkerchief lying open on the console with the chopped up leaves inside of it. . . .

In the absence of any physical entry into the automobile there is no unreasonable search, for in fact there was no search. Observing this evidence, fully disclosed and in plain view of the police officers, whether or not in artificial light, is not a search. *State v. Griffin,* 84 N.J. Super. 508, 517, 202 A.2d 856 (App. Div. 1964). . . . This was observation of objects in open view to Officers Janowski and Pepe, who were conscientiously performing their duty.

* * *

Defendants' motion for suppression is denied. Submit appropriate order providing, among other things, that the matter before the Juvenile Court proceed in its normal course.

Notes

1. *IJA-ABA Standards on Arrest*

As indicated above, the American Bar Association Standards recommend granting judges the authority to issue a summons rather than an arrest warrant for a suspected juvenile offender. Indeed, § 7.2 expresses a preference toward the use of a summons unless there is a reasonable belief that the juvenile will flee to avoid prosecution. Section 7.5 limits the serving of a summons, urging that, if possible, a summons not be served on a juvenile while she is at school or work.

2. *Search Incident to Arrest*

Courts apply the same standards to the arrest of a juvenile as they do to the arrest of an adult offender. *See, e.g., In re J.B.*, 328 A.2d 46, 51 (N.J. Super. Ct. 1974). Courts also routinely uphold searches incident to a valid arrest for juveniles, just as they do for adults. *Id.* at 50. As with an adult offender, probable cause is required to arrest a juvenile without a warrant. *See, e.g., Lanes v. State,* 767 S.W.2d 789, 800 (Tex. Crim. App. 1989).

The arrest of juveniles does, however, present some unique problems for law enforcement agencies and the courts. For example, because juveniles can be arrested for non-criminal activities such as status offenses (*see supra* Chapter 2, Part B(1)), the question arises whether a search *not* incident to a criminal arrest is also valid. Although there is no clear precedent on this issue, some courts, relying on *In re Gault,* 387 U.S. 1 (1967) (*see infra* Chapter 6), have held that, where the juvenile is charged with a status offense, as opposed to an offense which would be a crime if committed by an adult, due process rules do not apply. *See, e.g., In re Spaulding*, 332 A.2d 246, 257 (Md. 1975) (privilege against self-incrimination does not apply to CHINS proceedings).

3. *Stop and Frisk*

As with arrest standards, courts regularly find that stop and frisk procedures apply to juveniles just as they do to adults. *See* SAMUEL M. DAVIS, RIGHTS OF JUVENILES 3-20 (2d ed. 1996); *In re James D.,* 741 P.2d 161 (Cal. 1987); *In re Lang,* 255 N.Y.S.2d 987 (Fam. Ct. 1965); *In re G.M.,* 560 N.W.2d 687 (Minn. 1997); *In re Jermaine,* 582 A.2d 1058 (Pa. Super. Ct. 1990). In order for a stop and frisk to be valid, the police must have a reasonable suspicion that the juvenile has committed a particular crime. *See, e.g., In re Herman S.,* 359 N.Y.S.2d 645, 647 (Fam. Ct. 1974).

4. *The Exclusionary Rule*

The court in *Lowry* held that the exclusion of improperly seized evidence under the Fourth Amendment applies to juvenile delinquency proceedings. Although the Supreme Court of the United States has never ruled on the matter (*see* Irene Merker Rosenberg, *A Door Left Open: Applicability of the Fourth Amendment Exclusionary Rule to Juvenile Court Delinquency Hearings,* 24 AM. J. CRIM. L. 29, 31 (1996)), the New Jersey Superior Court is not alone in finding that the exclusionary rule applies to juvenile hearings. In fact, "no court considering the question has held the Fourth Amendment to be inapplicable to juvenile proceedings." Davis, *supra*, at 3-17; *see also In re J.B.,* 328 A.2d 46, 50 (N.J. Super. Ct. 1974). Some states have made the exclusionary rule applicable through legislation. *See* Rosenberg, *supra*, at 58 n.180 (citing cases and legislation applying exclusionary rule to delinquency proceedings).

5. *Consent Searches*

(a) Voluntary consent.

Courts take special care when evaluating whether consent to search by a juvenile is voluntary. Although there is no consensus among the courts that have considered the issue, it is generally held that the "totality of the circumstances" approach outlined by the Supreme Court in *Schneckloth v. Bustamonte,* 412 U.S. 218 (1973), is applicable in assessing the voluntariness of consent to search by juveniles. *See* Lourdes M. Rosado, Note, *Minors and the Fourth Amendment: How Juvenile Status Should Invoke Different Standards for Searches and Seizures on the Street,* 71 N.Y.U. L. REV. 762, 767 n.43 (1996), for cases illustrating this approach. Age and maturity are generally among the factors the court will look to in determining the voluntariness of a juvenile's consent. *See, e.g., In re J.M.,* 619 A.2d 497 (D.C. 1992).

One writer recommends a two-part test for assessing the voluntariness of a juvenile's consent to search. *See* Rosado, *supra,* at 791. According to Rosado, the correct analysis would involve: (1) the totality of the circumstances test, as viewed "through the unique lens of a minor" and (2) requiring the state to prove informed consent by showing that the police told the minor of his right to refuse consent or that the minor already knew of this right. *Id.* This test has to date not been widely applied. *Id.* at 768; *but see In re J.M.,* 619 A.2d 497 (D.C. 1992) (applying similar test).

(b) Third party consent, by parent.

Parents generally have the right to consent to a search of their property, including rooms used exclusively by their children, regardless of whether or not those children are minors. Even if the child has an expectation of privacy, so long as the parent has access to the room, she can consent to a search of it. In fact, a parent's consent will generally be found valid even over the objection of a child present at the time of the search. *See* WAYNE R. LAFAVE & JEROLD H. ISRAEL, CRIMINAL PROCEDURE § 3.10(e) (2d ed. 1992). Both federal and state courts have upheld parental consent to search. *See, e.g., United States v. Stone,* 401 F.2d 32 (7th Cir. 1968); *Taylor v. State,* 491 So. 2d 1042 (Ala. Crim. App. 1986); *People v. Daniel,* 606 N.E.2d 94 (Ill. App. Ct. 1992); *State v. Maximo,* 821 P.2d 1379 (Ariz. Ct. App. 1991); *Perry v. State*, 538 N.E.2d 950 (Ind. 1989).

For a thorough analysis of state case law regarding third party consent by parents, see George L. Blum, Annotation, *Admissibility of Evidence Discovered in Search of Defendant's Property or Residence Authorized by Defendant's Adult Relative Other Than Spouse—State Cases,* 55 A.L.R.5TH 125 (1998).

(c) Third party consent, by child.

As with the issue of voluntariness, there is no consensus among courts regarding the admissibility against an adult of evidence seized in a search authorized by a minor child. While some courts have held that children under a certain age are incapable of consenting to a search of their parents' home (*see, e.g., Laasch v. State,* 267 N.W.2d 278 (Wis. 1978) (five-year-old cannot consent to search)), most courts consider the child's age and maturity in determining if the child had authority to consent.

6. For the applicability of search and seizure rules to students in public schools, see Chapter 6, *infra*.

Questions

1. Why do you think the A.B.A. prefers the use of a summons to the arrest of the juvenile? Do you think this is good policy? Is it reasonable to assume that a juvenile will respond to a summons, especially where the juvenile may be adjudicated delinquent and possibly sent to a juvenile detention center? Should the summons be served on the juvenile alone, or also on his parents or guardian?

2. Should the non-criminal nature of the juvenile justice system preclude the use of adult standards of arrest when a juvenile is taken into custody? Does the application of adult standards to a juvenile arrest afford the juvenile necessary protections, or does it serve to abrogate the distinction between the criminal justice process and the juvenile justice system? Should adult standards apply to a juvenile arrested for a status offense? Why or why not? Do you agree with the *Lowry* court in its extension of the exclusionary rule to juvenile delinquency proceedings?

3. Should a juvenile, regardless of age, have the authority to consent to a search of her person? Her parents' house? Her parents' bedroom? Does it matter if the juvenile is not allowed in certain rooms or areas of the house? What affect, if any, should the juvenile's age and level of intelligence or maturity have on the issue?

4. Should a juvenile's parents be able to consent to the search of the juvenile's room in their house? To a search of the juvenile's personal property? To a search of the juvenile's person?

C. Detention

Schall v. Martin

467 U.S. 253, 104 S. Ct. 2403, 81 L. Ed.2d 207 (1984)

Justice REHNQUIST delivered the opinion of the Court.

Section 320.5(3)(b) of the New York Family Court Act authorizes pretrial detention of an accused juvenile delinquent based on a finding that there is a "serious risk" that the child "may before the return date commit an act which if committed by an adult would constitute a crime."[1] Appellees brought suit on behalf of a class of all juveniles detained pursuant to that provision. The District Court struck down § 320.5(3)(b) as permitting detention without due process of law and ordered the immediate release of all class members. The Court of Appeals for the Second Circuit affirmed, holding the provision "unconstitutional as to all juveniles" because the statute is administered in such a way that "the detention period serves as punishment imposed without proof of guilt established according to the requisite constitutional standard." We noted probable jurisdiction and now reverse. We conclude that preventive detention under the FCA serves a legitimate state objective, and that the procedural protections afforded pretrial detainees by the New York statute satisfy the requirements of the Due Process Clause of the Fourteenth Amendment to the United States Constitution.

I

Appellee Gregory Martin was arrested on December 13, 1977, and charged with first-degree robbery, second-degree assault, and criminal possession of a weapon based on an incident in which he, with two others, allegedly hit a youth on the head with a loaded gun and stole his jacket and sneakers. Martin had possession of the gun when he was arrested. He was 14 years old at the time and, therefore, came within the jurisdiction of New York's Family Court. . . .

---

[1] New York Jud. Law § 320.5 (McKinney 1983) (Family Court Act (hereinafter FCA)) provides, in relevant part:

1. At the initial appearance, the court in its discretion may release the respondent or direct his detention.

* * *

3. The court shall not direct detention unless it finds and states the facts and reasons for so finding that unless the respondent is detained:
   (a) there is substantial probability that he will not appear in court on the return date; or
   (b) there is a serious risk that he may before the return date commit an act which if committed by an adult would constitute a crime.

Appellees have only challenged pretrial detention under § 320.05(3)(b). Thus, the propriety of detention to ensure that a juvenile appears in court on the return date, pursuant to § 320.5(3)(a), is not before the Court.

A petition of delinquency was filed,[6] and Martin made his "initial appearance" in Family Court on December 14th, accompanied by his grandmother. The Family Court Judge, citing the possession of the loaded weapon, the false address given to the police, and the lateness of the hour, as evidencing a lack of supervision, ordered Martin detained under § 320.5(3)(b). A probable-cause hearing was held five days later, on December 19th, and probable cause was found to exist for all the crimes charged. At the factfinding hearing held December 27-29, Martin was found guilty on the robbery and criminal possession charges. He was adjudicated a delinquent and placed on two years' probation.[8] He had been detained pursuant to § 320.5(3)(b), between the initial appearance and the completion of the factfinding hearing, for a total of 15 days.

Appellees Luis Rosario and Kenneth Morgan, both age 14, were also ordered detained pending their factfinding hearings. . . .

* * *

On December 21, 1977, while still in preventive detention pending his factfinding hearing, Gregory Martin instituted a habeas corpus class action on behalf of "those persons who are, or during the pendency of this action will be, preventively detained pursuant to" § 320.5(3)(b) of the FCA. Rosario and Morgan were subsequently added as additional named plaintiffs. These three class representatives sought a declaratory judgment that § 320.5(3)(b) violated the Due Process . . . Claus[e] of the Fourteenth Amendment.

* * *

At trial, appellees offered in evidence the case histories of 34 members of the class, including the three named petitioners. Both parties presented some general statistics on the relation between pretrial detention and ultimate disposition. In addition, there was testimony concerning juvenile proceedings from a number of witnesses, including a legal aid attorney specializing in juvenile cases, a probation supervisor, a child psychologist, and a Family Court Judge. On the basis of this evidence, the District Court . . . agreed with appellees that

---

6 A delinquency petition, prepared by the "presentment agency," originates delinquency proceedings. FCA § 310.1. The petition must contain, inter alia, a precise statement of each crime charged and factual allegations which "clearly apprise" the juvenile of the conduct which is the subject of the accusation. § 311.1. A petition is not deemed sufficient unless the allegations of the factual part of the petition, together with those of any supporting depositions which may accompany it, provide reasonable cause to believe that the juvnile committed the crime or crimes charged. . . .

8 The "factfinding" is the juvenile's analogue of a trial. . . . If guilt is established, the court enters an appropriate order and schedules a dispositional hearing. The dispositional hearing is the final and most important proceeding in the Family Court. If the juvenile has committed a designated felony, the court must order a probation investigation and a diagnostic assessment . . . . The court must find, based on a preponderance of the evidence, that the juvenile is delinquent and requires supervision, treatment, or confinement. Otherwise, the petition is dismissed. If the juvenile is found to be delinquent, then the court enters an order of disposition. Possible alternatives include a conditional discharge; probation for up to two years; nonsecure placement with, perhaps, a relative or the Division for Youth; transfer to the Commissioner of Mental Health; or secure placement. Unless the juvenile committed one of the designated felonies, the court must order the least restrictive available alternative consistent with the needs and best interests of the juvenile and the need for protection of the community. § 352.2(2)

pretrial detention under the FCA violates due process. The court ordered that "all class members in custody pursuant to Family Court Act Section [320.5(3)(b)] shall be released forthwith."

The Court of Appeals affirmed. . . . The court concluded . . . that § 320.5(3)(b) "is utilized principally, not for preventive purposes, but to impose punishment for unadjudicated criminal acts. . . ." The court therefore concluded that § 320.5(3)(b) must be declared unconstitutional as to all juveniles. . . .

II

There is no doubt that the Due Process Clause is applicable in juvenile proceedings. "The problem," we have stressed, "is to ascertain the precise impact of the due process requirement upon such proceedings." *In re Gault,* 387 U.S. 1, 13-14 (1967). . . .

The statutory provision at issue in these cases, § 320.5(3)(b), permits a brief pretrial detention based on a finding of a "serious risk" that an arrested juvenile may commit a crime before his return date. The question before us is whether preventive detention of juveniles pursuant to § 320.5(3)(b) is compatible with the "fundamental fairness" required by due process. Two separate inquiries are necessary to answer this question. First, does preventive detention under the New York statute serve a legitimate state objective? *See Bell v. Wolfish,* 441 U.S. 520, 534, n. 15 (1979). . . . And, second, are the procedural safe-guards contained in the FCA adequate to authorize the pretrial detention of a least some juveniles charged with crimes? *See* . . . *Gerstein v. Pugh,* 420 U.S. 103, 114 (1975).

A

Preventive detention under the FCA is purportedly designed to protect the child and society from the potential consequences of his criminal acts. *People ex rel. Wayburn v. Schupf,* 39 N.Y.2d 682, 689-690, 350 N.E.2d 906, 910 (1976). When making any detention decision, the Family Court judge is specifically directed to consider the needs and best interests of the juvenile as well as the need for the protection of the community. . . .

The "legitimate and compelling state interest" in protecting the community from crime cannot be doubted. We have stressed before that crime prevention is "a weighty social objective," *Brown v. Texas,* 443 U.S. 47, 52 (1979), and this interest persists undiluted in the juvenile context. The harm suffered by the victim of a crime is not dependent upon the age of the perpetrator. And the harm to society generally may even be greater in this context given the high rate of recidivism among juveniles.

The juvenile's countervailing interest in freedom from institutional restraints . . . is undoubtedly substantial as well. But that interest must be qualified by the recognition that juveniles, unlike adults, are always in some form of custody. *In re Gault, supra,* at 17. Children, by definition, are not assumed to have the capacity to take care of themselves. They are assumed to be subject to the control of their parents, and if parental control falters, the State must play its part as *parens patriae.* In this respect, the juvenile's liberty interest may, in appropriate circumstances, be subordinated to the State's "*parens patriae* interest in preserving and promoting the welfare of the child." *Santosky v. Kramer,* 455 U.S. 745, 766 (1982).

* * *

The substantiality and legitimacy of the state interest underlying this statute are confirmed by the widespread use and judicial acceptance of preventive detention for juveniles. Every State, as well as . . . the District of Columbia, permits preventive detention of juveniles accused of crime. . . . And the courts of eight States, including the New York Court of Appeals, have upheld their statutes with specific reference to protecting the juvenile and the community from harmful pretrial conduct, including pretrial crime. . . .

. . . In light of the uniform legislative judgment that pretrial detention of juveniles properly promotes the interests both of society and the juvenile, we conclude that the practice serves a legitimate regulatory purpose compatible with the "fundamental fairness" demanded by the Due Process Clause in juvenile proceedings.

Of course, the mere invocation of a legitimate purpose will not justify particular restrictions and conditions of confinement amounting to punishment. . . . Even given, therefore, that pretrial detention may serve legitimate regulatory purposes, it is still necessary to determine whether the terms and conditions of confinement under § 320.5(3)(b) are in fact compatible with those purposes. . . .

There is no indication in the statute itself that preventive detention is used or intended as a punishment. First of all, the detention is strictly limited in time. If a juvenile is detained at his initial appearance and has denied the charges against him, he is entitled to a probable cause hearing to be held not more than three days after the conclusion of the initial appearance or four days after the filing of the petition, whichever is sooner. If the Family Court judge finds probable cause, he must also determine whether continued detention is necessary pursuant to § 320.5(3)(b).

Detained juveniles are also entitled to an expedited factfinding hearing. . . . [T]he maximum possible detention under § 320.5(3)(b) of a youth accused of a serious crime . . . is 17 days. The maximum detention for less serious crimes . . . is six days. These time frames seem suited to the limited purpose of providing the youth with a controlled environment and separating him from improper influences pending the speedy disposition of his case.

The conditions of confinement also appear to reflect the regulatory purposes relied upon by the State. When a juvenile is remanded after his initial appearance, he cannot, absent exceptional circumstances, be sent to a prison or lockup where he would be exposed to adult criminals. . . .

* * *

Pretrial detention need not be considered punitive merely because a juvenile is subsequently discharged subject to conditions or put on probation. In fact, such actions reinforce the original finding that close supervision of the juvenile is required. Lenient but supervised disposition is in keeping with the Act's purpose to promote the welfare and development of the child. As the New York Court of Appeals noted:

> "It should surprise no one that caution and concern for both the juvenile and society may indicate the more conservative decision to detain at the very outset, whereas the later development of very much more relevant information may prove that while a finding of delinquency was warranted, placement may not be indicated." *People ex rel. Wayburn v. Schupf,* 39 N.Y.2d, at 690, 350 N.E.2d, at 910.

* * *

. . . We find no justification for the conclusion that, contrary to the express language of the statute and the judgment of the highest state court, § 320.5(3)(b) is a punitive rather than a regulatory measure. Preventive detention under the FCA serves the legitimate state objective, held in common with every State in the country, of protecting both the juvenile and society from the hazards of pretrial crime.

B

Given the legitimacy of the State's interest in preventive detention, and the nonpunitive nature of that detention, the remaining question is whether the procedures afforded juveniles detained prior to factfinding provide sufficient protection against erroneous and unnecessary deprivations of liberty. . . .

In many respects, the FCA provides far more predetention protection for juveniles than we found to be constitutionally required for a probable-cause determination for adults in *Gerstein v. Pugh.* The initial appearance is informal, but the accused juvenile is given full notice of the charges against him and a complete stenographic record is kept of the hearing. The juvenile appears accompanied by his parent or guardian. He is first informed of his rights, including the right to remain silent and the right to be represented by counsel chosen by him or by a law guardian assigned by the court. . . . When his counsel is present, the juvenile is informed of the charges against him and furnished with a copy of the delinquency petition. A representative from the presentment agency appears in support of the petition.

* * *

At the conclusion of the initial appearance, the presentment agency makes a recommendation regarding detention. . . . Opposing counsel, the juvenile's parents, and the juvenile himself may all speak on his behalf and challenge any information or recommendation. If the judge does decide to detain the juvenile under § 320.5(3)(b), he must state on the record the facts and reasons for the detention.

[A] detained juvenile is entitled to a formal, adversarial probable-cause hearing within three days of his initial appearance. If the court finds probable cause, the court must again decide whether continued detention is necessary under § 320.5(3)(b). Again, the facts and reasons for the detention must be stated on the record.

In sum, notice, a hearing, and a statement of facts and reasons are given prior to any detention under § 320.5(3)(b). A formal probable-cause hearing is then held within a short while thereafter, if the factfinding hearing is not itself scheduled within three days. These flexible procedures have been found constitutionally adequate under the Fourth Amendment, *see Gerstein v. Pugh,* and under the Due Process Clause, *see Kent v. United States,* 383 U.S. 541, 557 (1966). Appellees have failed to note any additional procedures that would significantly improve the accuracy of the determination without unduly impinging on the achievement of legitimate state purposes.

Appellees argue, however, that the risk of erroneous and unnecessary detentions is too high despite these procedures because the standard for detention is fatally vague. Detention under § 320.5(3)(b) is based on a finding that there is a "serious risk" that the juvenile, if released, would commit a crime prior to his next court appearance. . . . [A]ppellees claim . . . that it is virtually impossible to predict future criminal conduct with any degree of accuracy. . . . The procedural protections noted above are thus, in their view, unavailing because the ultimate decision is intrinsically arbitrary and uncontrolled.

* * *

We have . . . recognized that a prediction of future criminal conduct is "an experienced prediction based on a host of variables" which cannot be readily codified. *Greenholtz v. Nebraska Penal Inmates,* 442 U.S. 1, 16 (1979). Judge Quinones of the Family Court testified at trial that he and his colleagues make a determination under § 320.5(3)(b) based on numerous factors including the nature and seriousness of the charges; whether the charges are likely to be proved at trial; the juvenile's prior record; the adequacy and effectiveness of his home supervision; his school situation, if known; the time of day of the alleged crime as evidence of its seriousness and a possible lack of parental control; and any special circumstances that might be brought to his attention by the probation officer, the child's attorney, or any parents, relatives, or other responsible persons accompanying the child. The decision is based on as much information as can reasonably be obtained at the initial appearance.

Given the right to a hearing, to counsel, and to a statement of reasons, there is no reason that the specific factors upon which the Family Court judge might rely must be specified in the statute. As the New York Court of Appeals concluded, *People ex rel. Wayburn v. Schupf,* 39 N.Y.2d, at 690, 350 N.E.2d, at 910, "to a very real extent Family Court must exercise a substitute parental control for which there can be no particularized criteria." There is also no reason, we should add, for a federal court to assume that a state court judge will not strive to apply state law as conscientiously as possible.

* * *

III

The question before us today is . . . whether the preventive detention system chosen by the State of New York and applied by the New York Family Court comports with constitutional standards. Given the regulatory purpose for the detention and the procedural protections that precede its imposition, we conclude that § 320.5(3)(b) of the New York FCA is not invalid under the Due Process Clause of the Fourteenth Amendment.

The judgment of the Court of Appeals is *Reversed.*

Justice MARSHALL, with whom Justice BRENNAN and Justice STEVENS join, dissenting.

* * *

There are few limitations on § 320.5(3)(b). Detention need not be predicated on a finding that there is probable cause to believe the child committed the offense for which he was arrested. The provision applies to all juveniles, regardless of their prior records or the severity of the offenses of which they are accused. The provision is not limited to the prevention of dangerous crimes; a prediction that a juvenile if released may commit a minor misdemeanor is sufficient to justify his detention. Aside from the reference to "serious risk," the requisite likelihood that the juvenile will misbehave before his trial is not specified by the statute.

The Court today holds that preventive detention of a juvenile pursuant to § 320.5(3)(b) does not violate the Due Process Clause. Two rulings are essential to the Court's decision: that the provision promotes legitimate government objective important enough to justify the abridgment of the detained juveniles' liberty interests, and that the provision incorporates procedural safeguards sufficient to prevent unnecessary or arbitrary impairment of constitutionally protected rights. Because I disagree with both of those rulings, I dissent.

* * *

The majority acknowledges—indeed, founds much of its argument upon—the principle that a State has both the power and the responsibility to protect the interests of the children within its jurisdiction. Yet the majority today upholds a statute whose net impact on the juveniles who come within its purview is overwhelmingly detrimental. Most persons detained under the provision reap no benefit and suffer serious injuries thereby. The welfare of only a minority of the detainees is even arguably enhanced. The inequity of this regime, combined with the arbitrariness with which it is administered, is bound to disillusion its victims regarding the virtues of our system of criminal justice. I can see—and the majority has pointed to—no public purpose advanced by the statute sufficient to justify the harm it works.

I respectfully dissent.

Notes

1. The Court's decision in *Schall* has been widely criticized. Many commentators feel that the Supreme Court went too far in upholding the statute at issue in the case and that the opinion served to denigrate the liberty interests of juveniles. *See, e.g.,* Claudia Worrell, Note, *Pretrial Detention of Juveniles: Denial of Equal Protection Masked by the* Parens Patriae *Doctrine,* 95 YALE L.J. 174, 178-79 (1985); Irene Merker Rosenberg, Schall v. Martin: *A Child is a Child is a Child,* 12 AM. J. CRIM. L. 253 (1984); Jean Koh Peters, Schall v. Martin *and the Transformation of Judicial Precedent,* 31 B.C. L. REV. 641, 644 n.12 (1990); *Leading Cases of the 1983 Term, Pretrial Detention of Juveniles,* 98 HARV. L. REV. 87, 130 (1984).

2. As stated in *Schall*, all states and the District of Columbia have statutes permitting the detention of juveniles pending adjudication. *See also* Comment, *The Supreme Court and Pretrial Detention of Juveniles: A Principled Solution to a*

Due Process Dilemma, 132 U. PA. L. REV. 95, 95 (1983); David A. Geller, Note, *Putting the "Parens" Back Into Parens Patriae: Parental Custody of Juveniles as an Alternative to Pretrial Juvenile Detention,* 21 NEW ENG. J. ON CRIM. & CIV. CONFINEMENT 509, 511 (1995) [hereinafter Geller, *Parens Patriae*]. While punishment is *not* an appropriate reason to detain a juvenile pending adjudication (*see Schall;* Geller, *supra,* at 509; Comment, *The Supreme Court and Pretrial Detention of Juveniles: A Principled Solution to a Due Process Dilemma, supra* at 106-07; *Leading Cases of the 1983 Term, Pretrial Detention of Juveniles, supra,* at 132-33), courts and state legislatures find numerous reasons which are.

For example, the Texas Family Code allows the detention of a juvenile if: "(1) he is likely to abscond . . . ; (2) suitable supervision . . . is not being provided by a parent [or] guardian . . . ; (3) he has no parent [or] guardian . . . able to return him to the court when required; (4) he may be dangerous to himself or . . . the public if released; or (5) he has previously been found to be a delinquent child . . . and is likely to commit an offense if released." TEX. FAM. CODE ANN. § 53.02(b) (West Supp. 2001). In addition to the consideration of factors similar to those in the Texas Family Code, the New Jersey statute relating to the preadjudicatory detention of juveniles also requires the judge to consider the nature of the offense charged and the juvenile's age, ties to the community, prior record, and history of appearing (or failing to appear) at court proceedings. N.J. STAT. ANN. § 2A:4A-34(e) (West Supp. 2001). Other jurisdictions have statutes requiring the consideration of some or all of these factors. *See generally* Geller, *supra,* at 511; Worrell, *supra,* at 178; Carol Bombardi, *Juvenile Detention Hearings: A Proposed Model Provision to Limit Discretion During the Preadjudicatory Stage,* 12 FORDHAM URB. L.J. 285, 310 (1984).

3. Just as probable cause is required to arrest a juvenile without a warrant (*see supra,* Note 2 following *Lowry*), a finding of probable cause is also generally required before the detention of a juvenile pending adjudication. However, as evidenced in *Schall*, a juvenile can be detained *before* the detention hearing. Under the New York Family Court Act at issue in *Schall*, for example, a juvenile can be detained for up to six days before a detention hearing is held. *See Pretrial Detention of Juveniles, supra,* at 131.

Courts requiring a probable cause determination prior to preadjudicatory detention often rely on *Gerstein v. Pugh*, 420 U.S. 103 (1974), in which the Supreme Court held that the Fourth Amendment requires a judicial probable cause determination as a prerequisite to the extended pretrial detention of adult defendants. *See, e.g., In re Joshua,* 327 So. 2d 429 (La. Ct. App. 1976); *Moss v. Weaver,* 525 F.2d 1258 (5th Cir. 1976); *Bell v. Superior Court,* 574 P.2d 39 (Ariz. 1977). The court in *Bell,* for example, found that the "pre-trial detention of juveniles without determination of probable cause violates the Fourth Amendment." *Id.* at 41. In *Cox v. Turley,* the Sixth Circuit Court of Appeals found that a prompt probable cause determination was a "constitutional mandate" to protect juveniles. 506 F.2d 1347, 1353 (6th Cir. 1974).

Whether specifically relying on *Gerstein* or not, courts sometimes require a probable cause determination for juveniles wherever an adult suspect would get one under similar circumstances. *See, e.g., In re Joshua, supra; Bell v. Superior Court, supra.* A few courts, however, have held that juveniles are not entitled to the same protections as their adult counterparts vis-à-vis probable cause hearings. *See, e.g., Morris v. D'Amario,* 416 A.2d 137 (R.I. 1980); *Alfredo A. v. Superior*

Court, 865 P.2d 56 (Cal. 1994). Some commentators recommend a probable cause hearing before juveniles are detained for any length of time. *See, e.g.,* Richard S. Baum, Comment, *Denial of Fourth Amendment Protections in the Pretrial Detention of Juveniles,* 35 SANTA CLARA L. REV. 689 (1995); Bombardi, *supra,* at 304.

4. When deciding whether to release a juvenile suspect, courts sometimes encounter the issue of whether bail should be available to juveniles, although juvenile suspects do not have a constitutional right to release on bail. Courts do not face this question very often, however, mainly because the liberal release provisions in most juvenile court rules lead to the discharge of the juvenile before the issue arises. *See* Samuel M. Davis, *Rights of Juveniles* 3-64 (2d ed. 1996). Although some state statutes make bail available to juveniles (*see, e.g.*, MASS. GEN. LAWS ANN. ch. 119 § 67 (Lexis 1994)), courts are split on the issue. *See, e.g., State v. M.L.C.,* 933 P.2d 380 (Utah 1997) (no right to bail for juvenile); *Morris v. D'Amario, supra* (no right to bail); *Pauley v. Gross,* 574 P.2d 234 (Kan. Ct. App. 1977) (no right to bail); *In re Hobson,* 335 So. 2d 763 (Miss. 1976) (right to bail under state statute); *State v. Franklin*, 12 So. 2d 211 (La. 1943) (right to bail under state constitution); *Trimble v. Stone*, 187 F. Supp. 483 (D.D.C. 1960) (right to bail under federal Constitution applicable to juvenile case). A juvenile who is tried as an adult, however, is entitled to the same bond hearing as any other adult defendant. *See, e.g., State v. M.L.C., supra*. For an overview of a juvenile's right to release on bail under various statutes and court rulings, see Davis, *supra,* at 3-64 nn.255-57.

5. A juvenile generally does not have the right to counsel at a detention hearing. The rationale is the same as that used to deny the right to counsel at intake—a detention hearing is not viewed as a "critical stage" in a delinquency proceeding. (*See, supra,* Part A, Note 3.)

6. The police or juvenile authority is generally required to notify the juvenile's parents or guardian when a child is taken into custody. *See, e.g., Cox v. Turley, supra; Palmer v. State,* 626 A.2d 1358 (Del. 1993); *see also* Davis, *supra,* at 3-56. Notice need not be given prior to arrest, or even immediately thereafter, so long as parents are notified within a reasonable amount of time. *See, e.g., Myers v. Collett,* 268 P.2d 432, 434 (Utah 1954). The notice requirement is itself not absolute. Exceptions have been allowed, for example, where a juvenile was arrested and detained without notice to his mother because the juvenile refused to give her name or phone number, so that police could not find her even after "reasonable effort." *See In re James B.,* 433 N.Y.S.2d 21, 22 (App. Div. 1980).

In most cases, a juvenile is released to the custody of her parents pending adjudication, often after the parents promise in writing that the juvenile will appear at the subsequent hearing. *See* Davis, *supra,* at 3-56; Geller, *supra,* at 537. The police, however, are not required to inform the juvenile or her parents of this right. *See, e.g., Myers v. Collett, supra*, at 435.

7. The majority and dissent in *Schall* were sharply split on the issue of the feasibility of predicting the dangerousness of juveniles awaiting adjudication. While the majority believed it was possible to make an "experienced" prediction of future criminal conduct based on a "host of variables," most commentators agree with the dissent that accuracy in such prognostication is nearly impossible to achieve.

See; *e.g.*, *Leading Cases of the 1983 Term, Pretrial Detention of Juveniles, supra*, at 137-38; Geller, *supra*, at 520. Some of the reasons given for the difficulty of making accurate predictions include: (1) the limitations on knowledge of the dynamics of human behavior; (2) the short time frame in which juvenile court judges must make detention determinations; (3) incomplete information relied upon by judge; and (4) the expense involved in acquiring more and better information. *Id.*

Questions

1. Do you agree with the majority in *Schall* that a child is "always in some form of custody" and the state, acting as *parens partriae,* may step in and take over the child's custody when it determines that parental control has faltered? Was the juvenile court's objective in *Schall* really to "preserv[e] and promot[e] the welfare of the child"?

2. The Court's holding in *Schall* relies on two findings. First, the majority found that preventative detention under the New York statute serves a legitimate state objective. Second, the Court held that the procedure under the act adequately protected detainees' Fourth Amendment due process rights.

(a) As noted above, the Court refers to the welfare of the child; but even the majority acknowledges that the "legitimate and compelling state interest" involved is that of protecting the community from crime. Is this interest an adequate justification to detain juveniles before an adjudicatory hearing? Does the Court give proper weight to the juveniles' liberty interests in its decision?

(b) As discussed above, most commentators do not believe it is possible to predict future criminality with any degree of certainty. Assuming this is true, can the holding in *Schall* be correct? Can the Court's ruling stand without the assumption that juvenile court judges *can* predict which juveniles are likely to commit crimes while awaiting adjudication? Do the other protections afforded juveniles in New York Family Courts (notice of charges, record of hearings, presence of parents, availability of counsel, notice of rights) offset the inadequacies of predictions of future criminality in detention decisions? Given that most juveniles are released to parental custody pending a factfinding hearing, should preadjudicatory detention be an area of concern for juvenile court judges?

3. Do you agree with the majority's conclusion that preventative detention is not used as a mode of punishment to teach juveniles a lesson? (*See In re Welfare of Snyder* (*supra* Chapter 2, Part B.1.c), where the child's father originally dropped her off at Children's Services and left her there overnight as punishment.) What additional safeguards, if any, would you recommend to assure that police, juvenile authorities, and parents do not use preadjudicatory detention to punish children who have not yet been found delinquent?

Problem

Jimmy is in the fifth grade. He is ten years old. The police received a call this morning from the principal at Jimmy's school, informing them that Jimmy brought a gun to school today. Officer Scott went to the school, spoke with Jimmy's teacher, the principal, and Jimmy. The teacher told Officer Scott that Jimmy showed the gun to some of his classmates at recess, and one of them told her about it. Jimmy gave her the gun when she asked him for it and said he brought it to school to show it to his friends. The teacher stated that Jimmy is an excellent student and has never been a discipline problem. Officer Scott phoned Jimmy's father at work and informed him that Jimmy was being taken to the Juvenile Justice Center (JJC).

A conversation with Jimmy's father at the JJC revealed the following information: Jimmy's mother died last year after a prolonged battle with cancer. Jimmy's father has been raising Jimmy and his six-year-old sister on his own, although both the father's mother and his late wife's parents help as much as they can. Jimmy misses his mother very much but has offered a lot of emotional support to his father and sister.

Jimmy's father is an avid sportsman and has several rifles, shotguns, and handguns in the rec room of his house. The guns are kept locked in a display case, and Jimmy's father keeps the key with him. No ammunition is stored at the house. Jimmy and his sister know they are not allowed to touch the guns. The gun Jimmy had at school belongs to his father. It was not loaded. Jimmy's father had the gun out last night to clean it. He returned the gun to the cabinet when he was finished. He always locks the cabinet after he removes or replaces a gun, but he cannot specifically recall locking it last night.

Suppose you are the Juvenile Court Judge. Jimmy and his father appear before you, and you must decide whether to detain Jimmy pending his delinquency hearing. The juvenile probation officer has told you privately that, unless something surprising and unexpected turns up during his investigation, he will probably recommend that no formal charges be filed and that Jimmy be released with a warning. He does not think that Jimmy presents a risk of flight or that it is likely that Jimmy will commit another delinquent act before his case is settled. However, the probation officer is concerned about the message that will be sent to Jimmy and other kids if Jimmy "gets off scot-free." He recommends that Jimmy be detained at the JJC overnight. The probation officer assures you that he will complete his investigation by the next morning and that he will make his final recommendation to you before noon.

How would you rule on the issue of preadjudicatory detention? Would your answer change if Jimmy had been causing disruption at school since the death of his mother? Would it make a difference to your decision if Jimmy had been in trouble with the police and juvenile authorities in the past? Is "sending a message," either to the child or to other children who may be watching, ever sufficient justification for a one- or two-day preadjudicatory detention?

IJA-ABA Standards Relating to Interim Status: The Release, Control and Detention of Accused Juvenile Offenders Between Arrest and Disposition

Juvenile Justice Standards Annotated 119-21, 123-24
(Robert E. Shepherd, Jr., ed., 1996)*

PART II: DEFINITIONS

1.1 Scope and overview.

The standards in this volume set out in detail the decision-making process that functions between arrest of a juvenile on criminal charges and final disposition of the case. By limiting the discretion of officials involved in that process, and by imposing affirmative duties on them to release juveniles or bear the burden of justification for not having done so, the standards seek to reduce the volume, duration, and severity of detention, and of other curtailment of liberty during the interim period.

* * *

2.4 Status decision.

A decision made by an official that results in the interim release, control, or detention of an arrested juvenile. In the adult criminal process, it is often referred to as the bail decision.

2.5 Release.

The unconditional and unrestricted interim liberty of a juvenile, limited only by the juvenile's promise [to] appear at judicial proceedings as required. It is sometimes referred to as "release on own recognizance."

2.6 Control.

A restricted or regulated nondetention interim status, including release on conditions or under supervision.

2.7 Release on conditions.

The release of an accused juvenile under written requirements that specify the terms of interim liberty, such as living at home, reporting periodically to a court officer, or refraining from contact with named witnesses.

2.8 Release under supervision.

The release of an accused juvenile to an individual or organization that agrees in writing to assume the responsibility for directing, managing, or overseeing the activities of the juvenile during the interim period.

2.9 Detention.

Placement during the interim period of an accused juvenile in a home or facility other than that of a parent, legal guardian, or relative, including facilities commonly called "detention," "shelter care," "training school," "receiving home," "group home," "foster care," and "temporary care."

---

* Reprinted with permission.

* * *

PART III: BASIC PRINCIPLES

3.1 Policy favoring release.

Restraints on the freedom of accused juveniles pending trial and disposition are generally contrary to public policy. The preferred course in each case should be unconditional release.

3.2 Permissible control or detention.

The imposition of interim control or detention on an accused juvenile may be considered for the purposes of:

A. protecting the jurisdiction and process of the court;
B. reducing the likelihood that the juvenile may inflict serious bodily harm on others during the interim period; or
C. protecting the accused juvenile from imminent bodily harm upon his or her request.

* * *

3.3 Prohibited control or detention.

Interim control or detention should not be imposed on an accused juvenile:

A. to punish, treat, or rehabilitate the juvenile;
B. to allow parents to avoid their legal responsibilities;
C. to satisfy demands by a victim, the police, or the community;
D. to permit more convenient administrative access to the juvenile;
E. to facilitate further interrogation or investigation; or
F. due to a lack of a more appropriate facility or status alternative.

3.4 Least intrusive alternative.

When an accused juvenile cannot be unconditionally released, conditional or supervised release that results in the least necessary interference with the liberty of the juvenile should be favored over more intrusive alternatives.

3.5 Values.

Whenever the interim curtailment of an accused juvenile's freedom is permitted under these standards, the exercise of authority should reflect the following values:

A. respect for the privacy, dignity, and individuality of the accused juvenile and his or her family;
B. protection of the psychological and physical health of the juvenile;
C. tolerance of the diverse values and preferences among different groups and individuals;
D. insurance of equality of treatment by race, class, ethnicity, and sex;
E. avoidance of regimentation and depersonalization of the juvenile;
F. avoidance of stigmatization of the juvenile; and
G. insurance that the juvenile receives adequate legal assistance.

3.6 Availability of adequate resources.

[T]he absence of funds cannot be a justification for resources or procedures that fall below the standards or unnecessarily infringe on individual liberty. Accused juveniles should be released or placed under less restrictive control whenever a form of detention or control otherwise appropriate is unavailable to the decision maker.

Questions

1. Compare the IJA-ABA standards with the statute at issue in *Schall* and with the Texas and New Jersey code sections discussed in the notes following *Schall.* Do the juvenile codes in New York, New Jersey, and Texas meet the standards recommended by the A.B.A.? If not, in what ways do they fall short of the A.B.A. recommendations?

2. Section 3.2A of the IJA-ABA standards allows detention of a juvenile to protect the court's "jurisdiction and process," whereas § 3.3D prohibits detention for the purpose of giving the court "more convenient administrative access to the juvenile." Are these sections compatible? Under a statute codifying both standards, would detention to assure the appearance of a juvenile be appropriate? Would the court be permitted to consider, as Texas juvenile courts do, a juvenile's history of failing to appear for adjudicatory hearings in reaching a decision regarding detention?

3. Do the IJA-ABA standards adequately protect children without placing too many restrictions on the discretion of juvenile authorities? Should juvenile officials "bear the burden of justification" any time a juvenile is detained pending adjudication?

D. Investigation and Interrogation

A juvenile's rights during interrogation predate both *Miranda v. Arizona,* 384 U.S. 436 (1966), and *In re Gault,* 387 U.S. 1 (1967) (*see infra* Chapter 6). In an early case, the United States Supreme Court acknowledged that juveniles were entitled to certain protections under the Fourteenth Amendment. The Court in *Haley v. Ohio*, 332 U.S. 596 (1948), overturned the conviction of a fifteen year old boy whose confession the police obtained after an all-night interrogation session. In an often-quoted passage, Justice Douglas wrote:

> A 15-year-old lad, questioned through the dead of night by relays of police, is a ready victim of the inquisition. Mature men possibly might stand the ordeal from midnight to 5 a.m., but we cannot believe that a lad of tender years is a match for

> the police in such a contest. He needs counsel and support if he is not to become the victim first of fear, then of panic.

Id. at 599-600. The Court thus recognized that a juvenile has at least some rights and protections due under the Constitution. While not specifying what these rights may be, the Supreme Court in *Haley* nonetheless hinted that a child needs someone to protect him from coercion at the hands of the police.

Fourteen years after it decided *Haley*, the Supreme Court revisited the issue of a juvenile's need for extra protection during interrogation. In *Gallegos v. Colorado,* 370 U.S. 49 (1962), the Court overturned the conviction of a fourteen-year-old obtained after the boy had been held incommunicado for five days. Reiterating its condemnation of confessions obtained through "'secret inquisitorial processes,'" *id.* at 50 (citation omitted), Justice Douglas, writing for the majority, found that the defendant's youth and immaturity put him on unequal footing with his interrogators to a constitutionally unacceptable degree. Justice Douglas stated:

> [A] 14-year-old boy, no matter how sophisticated, is unlikely to have any conception of what will confront him when he is made accessible only to the police. That is to say, we deal with a person who is not equal to the police in knowledge and understanding of the consequences of the questions and answers being recorded and who is unable to know how to protect his own interests or how to get the benefits of his constitutional rights.

Id. at 54. Thus, early in the history of modern juvenile law, the Supreme Court recognized that children were different from adults and merited special treatment under certain circumstances.

Although *Gault* is universally viewed as the first case of the modern juvenile court era, the holding in that case dealt with a juvenile's rights during the fact-finding stage in juvenile proceedings and specifically left open the issue of what rights a juvenile has in pre- and post-adjudicatory stages. Thus, although *Miranda* had been decided the year before *Gault*, it was not immediately apparent what effect, if any, the Court's ruling in *Miranda* would have on juveniles. The Supreme Court would, in fact, not address this issue until its decision in *Fare v. Michael C.,* twelve years after *Gault*.

Fare v. Michael C.

442 U.S. 707, 99 S. Ct. 2560, 61 L. Ed. 2d 197 (1979)

Mr. Justice BLACKMUN delivered the opinion of the Court.

In *Miranda v. Arizona,* 384 U.S. 436 (1966), this Court established certain procedural safeguards designed to protect the rights of an accused, under the Fifth and Fourteenth Amendments, to be free from compelled self-incrimination during custodial interrogation. The Court specified, among other things, that if the accused indicates in any manner that he wishes to remain silent or to consult an attorney, interrogation must cease, and any statement obtained from him during interrogation thereafter may not be admitted against him at his trial. *Id.*, at 444-445, 473-474.

In this case, the State of California, in the person of its acting chief probation officer, attacks the conclusion of the Supreme Court of California that a juvenile's request, made while undergoing custodial interrogation, to see his probation officer is *per se* an invocation of the juvenile's Fifth Amendment rights as pronounced in *Miranda.*

I

Respondent Michael C. was implicated in the murder of Robert Yeager. The murder occurred during a robbery of the victim's home on January 19, 1976. A small truck registered in the name of the respondent's mother was identified as having been near the Yeager home at the time of the killing, and a young man answering respondent's description was seen by witnesses near the truck and near the home shortly before Yeager was murdered.

On the basis of this information, Van Nuys, CA., police took respondent into custody at approximately 6:30 p.m. on February 4. Respondent then was 16½ years old and on probation to the Juvenile Court. He had been on probation since the age of 12. Approximately one year earlier he had served a term in a youth corrections camp under the supervision of the Juvenile Court. He had a record of several previous offenses, including burglary of guns and purse snatching, stretching back over several years.

Upon respondent's arrival at the Van Nuys station house two police officers began to interrogate him. . . . One of the officers initiated the interview by informing respondent that he had been brought in for questioning in relation to a murder. The following exchange then occurred as set out in the opinion of the California Supreme Court, *In re Michael C.,* 21 Cal. 3d 471, 473-474, 549 P.2d 7, 8 (1978):

"Q. . . . Do you understand all of these rights as I have explained them to you?

"A. Yeah.

"Q. Okay, do you wish to give up your right to remain silent and talk to us about this murder?

"A. What murder? I don't know about no murder.

"Q. I'll explain to you which one it is if you want to talk to us about it.

"A. Yeah, I might talk to you.

"Q. Do you want to give up your right to have an attorney present here while we talk about it?

"A. Can I have my probation officer here?

"Q. Well I can't get a hold of your probation officer right now. You have the right to an attorney.

"A. How I know you guys won't pull no police officer in and tell me he's an attorney?

"Q. Huh?

"A. [How I know you guys won't pull no police officer in and tell me he's an attorney?]

"Q. Your probation officer is Mr. Christiansen.

"A. Yeah.

"Q. Well, I'm not going to call Mr. Christiansen tonight. There's a good chance we can talk to him later, but I'm not going to call him right now. If you want to talk to us without an attorney present, you can. If you don't want to, you don't have to. But if you want to say something, you can, and if you don't want to say something you don't have to. That's your right. You understand that right?

"A. Yeah.

"Q. Okay, will you talk to us without an attorney present?

"A. Yeah I want to talk to you."

Respondent thereupon proceeded to answer questions put to him by the officers. He made statements and drew sketches that incriminated him in the Yeager murder.

Largely on the basis of respondent's incriminating statements, probation authorities filed a petition in Juvenile Court alleging that respondent had murdered Robert Yeager. . . . Respondent thereupon moved to suppress the statements and sketches he gave the police during the interrogation. He alleged that the statements had been obtained in violation of *Miranda* in that his request to see his probation officer at the outset of the questioning constituted an invocation of his Fifth Amendment right to remain silent, just as if he had requested the assistance of an attorney. Accordingly, respondent argued that since the interrogation did not cease until he had a chance to confer with his probation officer, the statements and sketches could not be admitted against him in the Juvenile Court proceedings. In so arguing, respondent relied by analogy on the decision in *People v. Burton,* 6 Cal. 3d 375, 491 P.2d 793 (1971), where the Supreme Court of California had held that a minor's request, made during custodial interrogation, to see his parents constituted an invocation of the minor's Fifth Amendment rights.

* * *

In a ruling from the bench, the court denied the motion to suppress. It held that the question whether respondent had waived his right to remain silent was one of fact to be determined on a case-by-case basis, and that the facts of this case showed a "clear waiver" by respondent of that right. The court observed that the transcript of the interrogation revealed that respondent specifically had told the officers that he would talk with them, and that this waiver had come at the outset of the interrogation and not after prolonged questioning. The court noted that respondent was a "16 and a half year old minor who has been through the court system before, has been to [probation] camp, has a probation officer, [and is not] a young naive minor with no experience with the courts." *Ibid.* Accordingly, it found that on the facts of the case respondent had waived his Fifth Amendment rights, notwithstanding the request to see his probation officer.

On appeal, the Supreme Court of California . . . by a divided vote, reversed. *In re Michael C.,* 21 Cal. 3d 471, 579 P.2d 7 (1978). The court held that respondent's "request to see his probation officer at the commencement of interrogation negated any possible willingness on his part to discuss his case with the police [and] thereby invoked his Fifth Amendment privilege." *Id.* at 474, 579 P.2d at 8. The court based this conclusion on its view that, because of the juvenile court system's emphasis on the relationship between a probation officer and the probationer, the officer was "a trusted guardian figure who exercises the authority of the state as *parens patriae* and whose duty it is to implement the protective and rehabilitative powers of the juvenile court." *Id.* at 476, 579 P.2d at 10. As a consequence, the court found that a minor's request for his probation officer was the same as a request to see his parents during interrogation, and thus under the rule of *Burton* constituted an invocation of the minor's Fifth Amendment rights.

[Relying] on *Burton*, the court ruled that it would unduly restrict *Miranda* to limit its reach in a case involving a minor to a request by the minor for an attorney, since it would be "'fatuous to assume that a minor in custody will be in a position to call an attorney for assistance and it is unrealistic to attribute no significance to his call for help from the only person to whom he normally looks—a parent or guardian.'" 21 Cal. 3d at 475-476, 579 P.2d at 9, quoting *People v. Burton*, 6 Cal. 3d at 382, 491 P.2d at 797-798. The court dismissed the concern expressed by the State that a request for a probation officer could not be distinguished from a request for one's football coach, music teacher, or clergyman on the ground that the probation officer, unlike those other figures in the juvenile's life, was charged by statute to represent the interests of the juvenile.

The court accordingly held that the probation officer would act to protect the minor's Fifth Amendment rights in precisely the way an attorney would act if called for by the accused. In so holding, the court found the request for a probation officer to be a *per se* invocation of Fifth Amendment rights in the same way the request for an attorney was found in *Miranda* to be, regardless of what the interrogation otherwise might reveal. . . . The court went on to conclude that since the State had not met its "burden of proving that a minor who requests to see his probation officer does not intend to assert his Fifth Amendment privilege," 26 Cal. 3d at 478, 579 P.2d at 11, the trial court should not have admitted the confession obtained after respondent had requested his probation officer.

The State of California petitioned this Court for a writ of certiorari. . . . Because the California judgment extending the *per se* aspects of *Miranda* presents an important question about the reach of that case, we . . . issued the writ.

II

We note at the outset that it is clear that the judgment of the California Supreme Court rests firmly on that court's interpretation of federal law. This Court, however, has not heretofore extended the *per se* aspects of the *Miranda* safeguards beyond the scope of the holding in the *Miranda* case itself.[4] We therefore must examine the California court's decision to determine whether that court's conclusion so to extend *Miranda* is in harmony with *Miranda's* underlying principles. For it is clear that "a State may not impose . . . greater restrictions as a matter of *federal constitutional law* when this Court specifically refrains from imposing them." *Oregon v. Hass*, 420 U.S. 714, 719 (1975) (emphasis in original).

The rule the Court established in *Miranda* is clear. In order to be able to use statements obtained during custodial interrogation of the accused, the State must warn the accused prior to such questioning of his right to remain silent and of his right to have counsel, retained or appointed, present during interrogation. 384 U.S. at 473. "Once [such] warnings have been given, the subsequent procedure is clear." *Ibid.*

> If the individual indicates in any manner, at any time prior to or during questioning, that he wishes to remain silent, the interrogation must cease. At this point he has shown that he intends to exercise his Fifth Amendment privilege; any statement taken after the person invokes his privilege cannot be other than the product of compulsion, subtle or otherwise. . . . If the individual states that he wants an attorney, the interrogation must cease until an attorney is present. At that time, the individual must have an opportunity to confer with the attorney and to have him present during any subsequent questioning. If the individual cannot obtain an attorney and he indicates that he wants one before speaking to police, they must respect his decision to remain silent.

Id. at 473-474 (footnote omitted). Any statements obtained during custodial interrogation conducted in violation of these rules may not be admitted against the accused, at least during the State's case in chief.

* * *

The California court in this case, however, significantly has extended this rule by providing that a request by a juvenile for his probation officer has the same effect as a request for an attorney. [T]he California decision found that consultation with a probation officer fufilled the role for the juvenile that consultation with an attorney does in general, acting as a "'protective [device] . . . to dispel the compulsion inherent in custodial surroundings.'" 21 Cal. 3d at 477, 579 P.2d at 10, quoting *Miranda v. Arizona,* 384 U.S. at 458.

---

[4] Indeed, this Court has not yet held that *Miranda* applies with full force to exclude evidence obtained in violation of its proscriptions from consideration in juvenile proceedings, which for certain purposes have been distinguished from formal criminal prosecutions. We do not decide that issue today. In view of our disposition of this case, we assume without deciding that the Miranda principles were fully applicable to the present proceedings.

* * *

The *per se* aspect of *Miranda* was . . . based on the unique role the lawyer plays in the adversary system of criminal justice in this country. Whether it is a minor or an adult who stands accused, the lawyer is the one person to whom society as a whole looks as the protector of the legal rights of that person in his dealings with the police and the courts. For this reason, the Court fashioned in *Miranda* the rigid rule that an accused's request for an attorney is *per se* an invocation of his Fifth Amendment rights, requiring that all interrogation cease.

A probation officer is not in the same posture with regard to either the accused or the system as a whole. Often he is not trained in the law, and so is not in a position to advise the accused as to his legal rights. . . . He does not assume the power to act on behalf of his client by virtue of his status as adviser, nor are the communications of the accused to the probation officer shielded by the lawyer-client privilege.

Moreover, the probation officer is the employee of the State which seeks to prosecute the alleged offender. He is a peace officer, and as such is allied, to a greater or lesser extent, with his fellow peace officers. He owes an obligation to the State, notwithstanding the obligation he may also owe the juvenile under his supervision. In most cases, the probation officer is duty bound to report wrongdoing by the juvenile when it comes to his attention, even if by communication from the juvenile himself. Indeed, [i]t was respondent's probation officer who filed the petition against him. . . .

* * *

We thus believe it is clear that the probation officer is not in a position to offer the type of legal assistance necessary to protect the Fifth Amendment rights of an accused undergoing custodial interrogation that a lawyer can offer. The Court in *Miranda* recognized that "the attorney plays a vital role in the administration of criminal justice under our Constitution." 384 U.S. at 481. It is this pivotal role of legal counsel that justifies the *per se* rule established in *Miranda*, and that distinguishes the request for counsel from the request for a probation officer, a clergyman, or a close friend. . . .

The California Supreme Court, however, found that the close relationship between juveniles and their probation officers compelled the conclusion that a probation officer, for purposes of *Miranda*, was sufficiently like a lawyer to justify extension of the *per se* rule. The fact that a relationship of trust and cooperation between a probation officer and a juvenile might exist, however, does not indicate that the probation officer is capable of rendering effective legal advice sufficient to protect the juvenile's rights during interrogation by the police, or of providing the other services rendered by a lawyer. . . . If it were otherwise, a juvenile's request for almost anyone he considered trustworthy enough to give him reliable advice would trigger the rigid rule of *Miranda*.

Similarly, the fact that the State has created a statutory duty on the part of the probation officer to protect the interests of the juvenile does not render the probation officer any more capable of rendering legal assistance to the juvenile or of protecting his legal rights, especially in light of the fact that the State has also legislated a duty on the part of the officer to report wrongdoing by the juvenile and serve the ends of the juvenile court system. . . .

Nor do we believe that a request by a juvenile to speak with his probation officer constitutes a *per se* request to remain silent. As indicated, since a probation officer does not fulfill the important role in protecting the rights of the accused juvenile that an attorney plays, we decline to find that the request for the probation officer is tantamount to the request for an attorney. And there is nothing inherent in the request for a probation officer that requires us to find that a juvenile's request to see one necessarily constitutes an expression of the juvenile's right to remain silent. . . .

We hold, therefore, that it was error to find that the request by respondent to speak with his probation officer *per se* constituted an invocation of respondent's Fifth Amendment right to be free from compelled self-incrimination. It therefore was also error to hold that because the police did not then cease interrogating respondent the statements he made during interrogation should have been suppressed.

III

Miranda further recognized that after the required warnings are given the accused, "[i]f the interrogation continues without the presence of an attorney and a statement is taken, a heavy burden rests on the government to demonstrate that the defendant knowingly and intelligently waived his privilege against self-incrimination and his right to retained or appointed counsel." 384 U.S. at 475. . . . [T]he determination whether statements obtained during custodial interrogation are admissible against the accused is to be made upon an inquiry into the totality of the circumstances surrounding the interrogation, to ascertain whether the accused in fact knowingly and voluntarily decided to forego his rights to remain silent and to have the assistance of counsel. *Id.* at 475-477.

This totality-of-the-circumstances approach is adequate to determine whether there has been a waiver even where interrogation of juveniles is involved. We discern no persuasive reasons why any other approach is required where the question is whether a juvenile has waived his rights, as opposed to whether an adult has done so. The totality approach permits—indeed, it mandates—inquiry into all the circumstances surrounding the interrogation. This includes evaluation of the juvenile's age, experience, education, background, and intelligence, and into whether he has the capacity to understand the warnings given him, the nature of his Fifth Amendment rights, and the consequences of waiving those rights.

Courts repeatedly must deal with these issues of waiver with regard to a broad variety of constitutional rights. There is no reason to assume that such courts—especially juvenile courts, with their special expertise in this area—will be unable to apply the totality-of-the-circumstances analysis so as to take into account those special concerns that are present when young persons, often with limited experience and education and with immature judgment, are involved. Where the age and experience of a juvenile indicate that his request for his probation officer or his parents is, in fact, an invocation of his right to remain silent, the totality approach will allow the court the necessary flexibility to take this into account in making a waiver determination. At the same time, that approach refrains from imposing rigid restraints on police and courts in dealing with an experienced older juvenile with an extensive prior record who knowingly and intelligently waives his Fifth Amendment rights and voluntarily consents to interrogation.

In this case, we conclude that the California Supreme Court should have determined the issue of waiver on the basis of all the circumstances surrounding the interrogation of respondent. The Juvenile Court found that under this approach, respondent in fact had waived his Fifth Amendment rights and consented to interrogation by the police after his request to see his probation officer was denied. Given its view of the case, of course, the California Supreme Court did not consider this issue. . . .

We feel that the conclusion of the Juvenile Court was correct. The transcript of the interrogation reveals that the police officers conducting the interrogation took care to ensure that respondent understood his rights. They fully explained to respondent that he was being questioned in connection with a murder. They then informed him of all the rights delineated in *Miranda*, and ascertained that respondent understood those rights. There is no indication in the record that respondent failed to understand what the officers told him. Moreover, after his request to see his probation officer had been denied, and after the police officer once more had explained his rights to him, respondent clearly expressed his willingness to waive his rights and continue the interrogation.

Further, no special factors indicate that respondent was unable to understand the nature of his actions. He was a 16½-year-old juvenile with considerable experience with the police. He had a record of several arrests. He had served time in a youth camp, and he had been on probation for several years. He was under the full-time supervision of probation authorities. There is no indication that he was of insufficient intelligence to understand the rights he was waiving, or what the consequences of that waiver would be. He was not worn down by improper interrogation tactics or lengthy questioning or by trickery or deceit.

On these facts, we think it clear that respondent voluntarily and knowingly waived his Fifth Amendment rights. . . .

* * *

IV

We hold, in short, that the California Supreme Court erred in finding that a juvenile's request for his probation officer was a *per se* invocation of that juvenile's Fifth Amendment rights under *Miranda*. We conclude, rather, that whether the statements obtained during subsequent interrogation of a juvenile who has asked to see his probation officer, but who has not asked to consult an attorney or expressly asserted his right to remain silent, are admissible on the basis of waiver remains a question to be resolved on the totality of the circumstances surrounding the interrogation. On the basis of the record in this case, we hold that the Juvenile Court's findings that respondent voluntarily and knowingly waived his rights and consented to continued interrogation, and that the statements obtained from him were voluntary, were proper, and that the admission of those statements in the proceeding against respondent in Juvenile Court was correct.

The judgment of the Supreme Court of California is reversed, and the case is remanded for further proceedings not inconsistent with this opinion.

Mr. Justice Marshall, with whom Mr. Justice Brennan and Mr. Justice Stevens join, dissenting.

* * *

On my reading of *Miranda*, a California juvenile's request for his probation officer should be treated as a *per se* assertion of Fifth Amendment rights. The California Supreme Court determined that probation officers have a statutory duty to represent minors' interests and, indeed, are "trusted guardian figure[s]" to whom a juvenile would likely turn for assistance. 21 Cal. 3d at 476, 579 P.2d at 10. In addition, the court found, probation officers are particularly well suited to assist a juvenile "on such matters as to whether or not he should obtain an attorney" and "how to conduct himself with police." *Id.* at 476, 477, 579 P.2d at 10. Hence, a juvenile's request for a probation officer may frequently be an attempt to secure protection from the coercive aspects of custodial questioning.

* * *

Thus, given the role of probation officers under California law, a juvenile's request to see his officer may reflect a desire for precisely the kind of assistance *Miranda* guarantees an accused before he waives his Fifth Amendment rights. At the very least, such a request signals a desire to remain silent until contact with the office is made. Because the Court's contrary determination withdraws the safeguards of *Miranda* from those most in need of protection, I respectfully dissent.

[The dissenting opinion of Justice Powell is omitted.]

Notes

1. As noted earlier in this chapter, the Supreme Court had previously recognized a juvenile's need for protection over and above that afforded an adult. The Court in *Fare,* however, declined to require any additional safeguards for juveniles vis-à-vis the invocation of their *Miranda* rights. It should come as no surprise, then, to learn that in many ways a juvenile's rights under *Miranda* mirror those of adults. For example, the Fifth Amendment protections afforded juveniles under *Miranda* and *Fare* do not extend to statements made by the juvenile outside of custodial interrogation. *See, e.g., Thompson v. State*, 692 N.E.2d 474 (Ind. Ct. App. 1998). Similarly, *Miranda* does not apply to voluntary statements made by a juvenile to private citizens. *See, e.g., In re Deborah C.,* 635 P.2d 446 (Cal. 1981) (store detective not required to give *Miranda* warnings to juvenile); *State v. Biancamano,* 666 A.2d 199 (N.J. Super. Ct. 1995) (school official not agent of police for *Miranda* purposes). Further, a juvenile's rights under *Miranda* are the same whether the minor is eventually tried as a juvenile or waived to an adult court (*see infra* Chapter 5).

2. Although the Court in *Fare* held that a request to see one's probation officer did not amount to an invocation of the right to silence under *Miranda*, the Court left open the issue of how a juvenile *could* invoke her *Miranda* rights. In attempting to answer this question, lower courts have generally taken either of two approaches. Some courts have interpreted *Fare* to mean that *Miranda* applies to juveniles in precisely the same way as it does to adults. These courts find that a juvenile effects her *Miranda* rights in the same way an adult suspect does: by invoking the right to silence or by requesting an attorney. *See, e.g., In re Gibson*, 718 P.2d 759 (Or. Ct. App. 1986). Other courts, however, have held that a minor need not necessarily request an attorney or articulate a desire to remain silent in order to invoke the protections afforded by *Miranda*. These courts generally find that a request to speak to a parent or close friend constitutes a valid invocation of the privilege against self-incrimination. *See, e.g., People v. Burton,* 491 P.2d 793 (Cal. 1971); *but see State v. Valencia*, 589 P.2d 434 (Ariz. 1979) (request to speak to mother not equivalent to request for attorney). Furthermore, as discussed below, some courts require the presence of a parent, guardian, or attorney before a child can make a valid waiver of rights.

3. The Supreme Court applied a totality of the circumstances test in *Fare* and found that, under the facts presented in the case, Michael C. had made a valid waiver of his rights. The test is essentially the same as that applied to adults: in order for the waiver to be valid, the juvenile must possess the necessary capacity to make a knowing, intelligent, and voluntary waiver of his rights and must have made such a waiver. The majority of state courts have followed the *Fare* decision in holding that a juvenile's waiver of rights must be analyzed under the totality of the circumstances. *See, e.g., State v. Hunt,* 607 P.2d 297 (Utah 1980); *People v. Ward*, 466 N.Y.S.2d 686 (App. Div. 1983); *Rouw v. State*, 581 S.W.2d 313 (Ark. 1979).

The courts in some jurisdictions have essentially adopted the *Fare* totality test but place special emphasis on the juvenile's age and maturity when analyzing a juvenile's waiver of her rights. *See, e.g., In re S.H.,* 293 A.2d 181 (N.J. 1972); *Commonwealth v. Webster,* 353 A.2d 372 (Pa. 1974). These courts often rely on the factors outlined in *West v. United States,* 399 F.3d 467 (5th Cir. 1968). The *West* court considered the following in determining whether a juvenile's waiver of his privilege against self-incrimination was voluntarily made:

> (1) age of the accused; (2) education of the accused; (3) knowledge of the accused as to both the substance of the charge . . . and the nature of his rights to consult with an attorney and remain silent; (4) whether the accused is held incommunicado or allowed to consult with relatives, friends or an attorney; (5) whether the accused was interrogated before or after formal charges had been filed; (6) methods used in interrogation; (7) length of interrogations; (8) whether *vel non* the accused refused to voluntarily give statements on prior occasions; and (9) whether the accused has repudiated an extra-judicial statement at a later date.

Id. at 469. A number of courts, while applying the totality approach, will closely scrutinize the voluntariness of a waiver made in the absence of a parent or guardian. *See, e.g., In re Thompson*, 241 N.W.2d 2 (Iowa 1976).

In *State v. Farrell*, 2001 WL 65607 (N.H., Jan. 29, 2001), the court held that police must cease interrogating a juvenile when a parent arrives at the police station in order for a juvenile's waiver of his *Miranda* rights to be valid. In *Farrell*, police interrogated a juvenile charged with murder before and after his parent arrived at the police station. The police failed to inform the juvenile that his parent had arrived at the police station. The court held that "when a parent or guardian arrives at a police station or other site of custodial detention and requests to see a child in custody, the police must (1) immediately cease interrogating the juvenile; (2) notify him that his parent or guardian is present at the station; and (3) immediately allow the parent or guardian into the interrogation room." The court, however, failed to adopt a per se rule that a juvenile's waiver of his *Miranda* rights in a parent's absence is invalid.

4. Although most courts apply the totality of the circumstances approach outlined in *Fare*, the courts in a number of jurisdictions have rejected this approach in favor of a *per se* rule. Under the *per se* doctrine, evidence derived from the interrogation of a juvenile is inadmissible absent a showing that the juvenile was questioned in the presence of a parent, guardian, or attorney (often referred to as an "interested adult") or that such an adult was present when the juvenile waived the right to silence. At a minimum, the courts applying the *per se* approach generally require that the juvenile be allowed to consult with an interested adult before waiving her rights. For further discussion of a juvenile's right to consultation, see *infra* Chapter 6, Part B.2.

The courts that accept this doctrine often criticize the totality test as being too speculative and unpredictable in its application. Critics of the totality approach point to the *Fare* decision itself as evidence of the varying interpretations possible under such a test. Although they were applying the same set of facts, the majority and Justice Powell (dissenting) arrived at opposite conclusions concerning the validity of Michael's waiver. *See* Lawrence Schalm, *Police Interrogation of Children and State Constitutions: Why Not Videotape the MTV Generation?*, 26 U. TOL. L. REV. 901, 913 (1995).

5. The legislatures of several states have developed laws regarding a juvenile's ability to waive her *Miranda* rights. Some statutes require the presence of a parent or guardian for the waiver to be effective. *See, e.g.,* CONN. GEN. STAT. ANN. § 46b-137 (West Supp. 2001). Others apply a totality of the circumstances test which takes into account the presence or absence of parents, a guardian, and counsel. *See., e.g.,* N.M. STAT. ANN. § 32A-2-14(E) (Michie 1999).

The Alabama Court of Criminal Appeals recently upheld a provision requiring "Super *Miranda*" rights (specifying the right to consult with a parent or guardian in addition to traditional *Miranda* rights), as outlined in the Alabama Rules of Civil Procedure (Rule 11(B)(4)). *See Anderson v. State*, 729 So. 2d 900 (Ala. Crim. App. 1998). In *State v. Benoit,* 490 A.2d 295 (N.H. 1985), the court recommended the use of a simplified "Juvenile Rights Form," which explains juveniles' rights in words they can understand and includes a section to advise accused felons that they may be tried in an adult court.

6. In *Lewis v. State,* 288 N.E.2d 138 (Ind. 1972), the court created a *per se* requirement for assessing the validity of a juvenile's waiver of the right to counsel, guaranteeing the juvenile the right to consultation. In *Lewis*, two police officers suspected that the seventeen-year-old appellant committed murder during the commission of a robbery. Before the police interrogated him, the juvenile read a paper containing his *Miranda* rights and stated that he understood them. The juvenile immediately confessed to the robbery and the murder before consulting with his mother. Before the police officers could take a written statement, the juvenile invoked his *Miranda* right to speak to an attorney and later refused to provide a written statement only after he spoke with his mother. The trial court later admitted the juvenile's initial confession into the criminal trial. The Indiana Supreme Court, however, held that a child and his parents must be informed of the child's rights and that the child must be given the opportunity to consult with a parent, guardian, or attorney before making a waiver decision. Using this standard, the court decided that the juvenile's initial confession was inadmissible. In its codification of the requirements outlined in *Lewis,* the Indiana Legislature went a step further by requiring that the child's parents, guardian, or attorney join in the waiver decision unless the juvenile is an emancipated minor. *See* IND. CODE ANN. § 31-32-5-1 (Michie 1997).

7. The courts of several other states have established requirements similar to those outlined in *Lewis. See, e.g., Commonwealth v. Markle,* 380 A.2d 346 (Pa. 1977) (confession suppressed where juvenile not informed of right to speak with interested adult); *Commonwealth v. A Juvenile (No. 1),* 449 N.E.2d 654 (Mass. 1983) (waiver by anyone under the age of fourteen cannot be effected without presence of interested adult); *In re E.T.C.,* 449 A.2d 937 (Vt. 1982) (director of group home not "interested adult" for purposes of validating juvenile's waiver decision); *but see State v. Ridgley,* 732 P.2d 550 (Alaska 1987) (presence of father during questioning offered sufficient protection even though father not advised of son's rights).

The State of Louisiana, in contrast, has recently abandoned the *per se* rule it established in *In re Dino,* 359 So. 2d 586 (La. 1978), and returned to the totality of the circumstances test discussed in this chapter. The Supreme Court of Louisiana, in *State v. Fernandez,* 712 So. 2d 485 (La. 1998), overruled *Dino* because it found that the totality of the circumstances standard could best accommodate the interests of the juvenile and society, and that "[t]he Louisiana Constitution requires no more." *Id.* at 487.

8. An issue that sometimes arises regarding parental involvement in a juvenile's waiver of counsel decision is whether the parent can validly invoke a child's rights for her. Several courts have held that a juvenile's parents can invoke the child's rights by requesting to be present during questioning or by asking the police to refrain from interrogating the child until the parents are able to contact the family's attorney. *See e.g., J.E.S. v. State,* 366 So. 2d 538 (Fla. Dist. Ct. App. 1979); *People v. Lee,* 589 N.Y.S.2d 263 (Crim. Ct. 1992). Other courts, however, have held that a parent's indication of an intention to secure counsel for a child does not amount to an invocation of the child's rights. *See, e.g., State v. Rogers,* 208 So. 2d 384 (N.C. Ct. App. 1974).

9. Courts recognizing the right to consultation must at times decide whether a juvenile's parents qualify as "interested adults." The parents may be alleged to be disinterested in the welfare of the child (*see, e.g., Commonwealth v.*

Smith, 372 A.2d 797 (Pa. 1977)), or may be found to have pressured the child into offering incriminating testimony. *See, e.g., In re Carter*, 318 A.2d 269 (Md. Ct. Spec. App. 1974). In one case, the Supreme Court of California overturned a juvenile's confession where it found the child had waived his right to counsel after he and his parents were informed that the father would have to reimburse the county for the child's legal services. *See In re Ricky H.*, 468 P.2d 204 (Cal. 1970).

Questions

1. Do you agree with the Supreme Court's holding in *Fare*? Does the totality of the circumstances test provide sufficient protection to a juvenile offender by considering the child's age and maturity in evaluating the waiver decision? If not, what else should the courts consider? Is a *per se* standard necessary to ensure that the child's waiver is voluntarily, knowingly, and intelligently made? If you prefer a *per se* standard, what should be required for the waiver to be valid? Must the parents be present? Should the parents be read the child's rights? Must the parents sign a waiver form? Should counsel be required even when the parents are present?

2. Should a juvenile's parents be permitted to invoke the child's *Miranda* rights for her? If so, what would be the outcome if the parents and child disagree? Should the court assume that a juvenile's parents or legal guardians are "interested adults"? If the court cannot safely assume this in every case, how can it protect the child's interest as against that of the parents? Should a guardian *ad litem* be appointed in every case in order to assure that the child's best interests are being protected?

3. A possible criticism of the *per se* rule is whether all juveniles are incapable of giving knowing and intelligent waivers of their Fifth or Sixth Amendment rights. Is a person who just turned eighteen years old two weeks ago more capable to giving a knowing and intelligent waiver than a juvenile who is two weeks away from turning eighteen?

Which rule do you find more persuasive, a *per se* rule or a totality of the circumstances rule as adopted by Louisiana in *In re Dino, supra* Note 7? What effect does the per se rule have on the ability of law enforcement officers to question juveniles about possible delinquent behavior?

4. As courts continue to roll back measures designed to protect Fifth and Sixth Amendment rights created by *Miranda, supra,* and *Massiah v. United States*, 377 U.S. 201 (1964), should state courts likewise roll back similar protections offered in delinquency cases? What policy arguments can you make for each side?

5. If the totality of the circumstances test was adopted rather than the *per se* rule for waiving Fifth and Sixth Amendment rights, what factors should be considered to determine whether a juvenile waived his or her rights guaranteed by these Amendments? How much emphasis should be placed on these factors: the age of the juvenile, educational background and level, prior delinquency record, and the ability to comprehend what is going on?

E. Diversion

State v. Quiroz

733 P.2d 963 (Wash. 1987)

Two juvenile offenders challenge the use of a diversion agreement in their criminal history on the basis that the agreement violated their constitutional and statutory rights.

* * *

DIVERSION AGREEMENTS

A diversion agreement is "a contract between a juvenile accused of an offense and a diversionary unit whereby the juvenile agrees to fulfill certain conditions in lieu of prosecution." RCW 13.40.080(1). Typically, for minor offenses the county prosecutor often refers a juvenile to a probation officer who enters into a diversion agreement with the juvenile. A diversion agreement can require community service and supervision, as well as a fine, but the juvenile cannot be sentenced to detention unless after a hearing a judge decides the juvenile has violated the terms of the agreement. RCW 13.40.080(2); 13.40.080(6). Diversion agreements benefit the State and the juvenile. The more informal diversion process is faster than court proceedings. The process also keeps juvenile offenders out of institutions and in the community where the resources to deal with their behavior are better suited to their age. Finally, although the diversion agreement may for a time figure into a juvenile's criminal history and therefore affect a detention sentence for a future offense, the agreement is not the same as a conviction. Thus, the juvenile does not have the same stigma of having been convicted of a crime.

* * *

RIGHT TO COUNSEL

Quiroz and Haas challenge the method the Yakima probation officers used during the diversion process. One of their chief objections is that they did not receive an adequate opportunity to consult with counsel.

In Quiroz's case, he arrived at the diversion unit prior to his appointment and was given a form entitled "Advice About Diversion." He read this form and then discussed it point by point with the probation officer who then entered into the diversion agreement with Quiroz. The advice agreement specifically stated:

> You have the right to talk to a lawyer to help you decide whether or not you should enter into a Diversion Agreement or go to court. If you cannot afford a lawyer, the Court will appoint one at no cost. If you do not believe you committed this offense, you should talk to a lawyer.

. . . Quiroz then signed the diversion agreement and a waiver of counsel form, which specifically stated:

> I know that a lawyer can look at my police reports, tell me about the law, help me understand my rights and help me decide whether I should enter into the diversion process or go to Juvenile Court. I have decided *not* to talk to a lawyer at this time.

The facts surrounding Haas' interview are similar. Haas was in detention at the time of his interview. The probation officer assigned to the case, who had entered into a prior diversion agreement with Haas, gave Haas the same type of form Quiroz received about the diversion agreement and waiver of counsel. The probation officer then explained the forms to Haas, and Haas signed them.

Nevertheless, despite their signatures, the juveniles argue that they did not have an adequate opportunity to consult with counsel, and that any waiver of their rights could not be described as knowing, intelligent and voluntary. . . . However, . . . each court found that the juveniles made knowing and voluntary waivers of their right to counsel. Ample evidence supports the trial judge's conclusion, and we therefore will not overturn on appeal the lower court's determination that the juveniles waived their rights to counsel.

* * *

ADEQUATE NOTICE OF CHARGES

The juveniles also argue that the diversion process did not adequately inform them of the nature of the charges against them. In both cases, the only notice the juveniles received about the nature of the charges was written at the top of the diversion agreement. In Quiroz's case, the agreement stated at the top: "Simple assault, Disorderly conduct, Resisting arrest." In Haas' case, the agreement stated "possession of a dangerous weapon." The probation officers gave no explanation as to what the legal description of the crimes were, nor what defenses or mitigating circumstances might apply. Nevertheless, the waiver of attorney form did state specifically that "a lawyer can . . . tell me about the law. . . ."

The juveniles point to *In re Gault*, 387 U.S. 1, 87 S. Ct. 1428, 18 L. Ed. 2d 527 (1967), for authority that this notice is inadequate. In *Gault*, notice to a juvenile was first given at the initial hearing, which was an adjudication on the merits. The charge against the child was for being a juvenile delinquent, and the juvenile never was informed of the underlying charges on which a delinquency finding was to be based. The United States Supreme Court held that this notice was inadequate. . . .

Both juveniles were notified of the charges against them in writing at the top of the diversion forms. They could have received a detailed explanation of the factual and legal explanations of the charges from lawyers had they chosen to do so. Furthermore, while this notice would not have been sufficient to uphold a criminal conviction by a guilty plea, the less formal nature of the diversion process, coupled with the fact that such an agreement is not the same as a conviction, justifies a less formal notice process. As we said in *Sheppard v. Rhay*, 73 Wash. 2d 734, 737, 440 P.2d 422 (1968), in describing the due process requirements described in *Gault*,

> *In re Gault*, . . . is not to be considered as a mandate to abandon the beneficial aspects of the juvenile court system so long as the essentials of due process and fair play are observed.

In this case, we believe the written notice given to the juveniles prior to their signing the diversion agreement which indicated that they could consult with counsel meets our conceptions of fair play. The juveniles had adequate notice of the charges.

RIGHTS SURROUNDING TRIAL

The juveniles also argue that the diversion process is tantamount to a conviction and does not safeguard basic constitutional rights such as: the right against self-incrimination, the right of confrontation and the right to trial. They also cite in *In re Keene,* 95 Wash. 2d 203, 622 P.2d 360 (1980), which holds that a plea must have a factual basis in the record in order to be valid.

These arguments fail to recognize that a fundamental difference exists between a diversion agreement, which is essentially a contract between the juvenile and the diversion unit, and a guilty plea which results in a criminal conviction. A diversion agreement cannot result in a detention sentence, and requires at most that the juvenile pay a fine of $100 or less and attend community supervision and service activities for a short length of time. We believe the less formal procedure used in this diversion context need not guarantee that the juvenile be informed of the panoply of constitutional rights which the juvenile would have if he or she were pleading guilty. A diversion agreement is not equivalent to a conviction, and there is no necessity to formalize this procedure by a lengthy recitation of rights which attach during criminal proceedings.

FUTURE USE AS A BASIS FOR INCREASING A SENTENCE

* * *

[T]he juveniles also claim that, because the diversion agreement can later be used to increase a detention sentence, additional constitutional rights associated with criminal adjudications apply. In essence, the juveniles attempt "to bootstrap" additional constitutional rights to the initial diversion agreement because the agreement can later have the effect of increasing a detention sentence.

This argument is without merit. In these cases the diversion agreement plainly indicated that it could serve to enhance a future crime's penalty. The agreement warned the juveniles of its effect on their criminal histories, and therefore, the juveniles cannot complain that they were unaware of its consequences. Therefore, because the agreement warned about the possibility of its future use, and because the agreement itself was not the same as a conviction, its future use did not violate their constitutional rights. . . .

CONCLUSION

The diversion process which both juveniles completed was constitutional. . . . The trial courts therefore did not err in denying their motions to void their diversion agreements. . . .

The trial court's orders and sentences are affirmed.

IJA-ABA Standards Relating to Youth Service Agencies

Juvenile Justice Standards Annotated 293-97
(Robert E. Shepherd, Jr., ed., 1996)*

PART I: ESTABLISHMENT OF YOUTH SERVICE AGENCIES

1.1 Enabling legislation.

Jurisdictions should by statute require the development of community-based youth service agencies that would focus on the special problems of juveniles in the community. . . .

PART II: OBJECTIVES

2.1 Service provision.

The primary objective of a youth service agency should be to ensure the delivery of needed services to juveniles in the community and their families, including juveniles diverted to the agency from the formal court system. . . .

PART III: DECISION STRUCTURE

3.1 Control.

. . . [I]n no case should the youth service agency be under the control of any component of the formal juvenile justice system.

PART IV: ACCESS TO THE YOUTH SERVICE AGENCY

* * *

Formal Referrals of Juveniles by Police and Courts

4.4 Police referrals.

The police should become a prime source of formal referrals to the youth service agency in order to ensure early diversion. To encourage such referrals:

* * *

B. Diversion to the youth service agency should be made an official policy of the [police] department.

* * *

D. Every referral to the juvenile court should be accompanied by a written statement of the referring officer explaining why the juvenile was not diverted to the youth service agency.

4.5 Police diversion standards.

Police diversion should be made pursuant to guidelines in order to avoid discrimination based on race, color, religion, national origin, sex, or income. At a minimum, the following standards should be observed:

A. No juvenile who comes to the attention of the police [or court] should be formally referred to the youth service agency if, prior to the existence of the

---

* Reprinted with permission.

diversionary alternative, that juvenile would have been released with a warning. . . .

B. All juveniles accused of class four or five offenses (as defined in standard 5.2 of the *Juvenile Delinquency and Sanctions* volume) who have no prior convictions or formal referrals should be formally referred to the youth service agency rather than to the juvenile court.

C. All other juveniles accused of class four or five offenses who have been free of involvement with the juvenile court for the preceding twelve months should be formally referred to the youth service agency rather than to the juvenile court.

D. Serious consideration should be given to the formal diversion of all other apprehended juveniles, taking into account the following factors:

1. prosecution toward conviction might cause serious harm to the juvenile or exacerbate the social problems that led to his or her criminal acts;
2. services to meet the juvenile's needs and problems may be unavailable within the court system or may be provided more effectively by the youth service agency;
3. the nature of the alleged offense;
4. the age and circumstances of the alleged offender;
5. the alleged offender's record, if any;
6. recommendations for diversion made by the complainant or victim.

* * *

4.8 Court diversion guidelines.

Court intake guidelines, at a minimum, should contain the same diversion standards set forth in Standard 4.5 above. . . .

* * *

4.10 Court review.

Decisions by the court intake official (1) not to divert a juvenile, or (2) in the case of a previously diverted juvenile, to require the signing of a participation agreement . . . as a condition of diversion, or (3) to resume proceedings against a juvenile who has allegedly violated the terms of a participation agreement, may be appealed by motion of the juvenile or by his or her attorney to the juvenile court at any time prior to the fact-finding hearing. A judge who hears such a motion should not also preside at the fact-finding hearings(s) for that juvenile.

4.11 Legal consequences of diversion to YSA.

Formal referral to a youth service agency should represent an alternative to prosecution; such referral therefore should be accompanied by a formal termination of all legal proceedings against the juvenile which were the subject of the referral. . . .

* * *

4.13 Right to refuse diversion.

Any juvenile should have the right at any time to request processing by the juvenile court in lieu of formal diversion to a youth service agency. Before a juvenile can be required to elect diversion to a YSA or to sign a participation agreement as a condition of diversion . . . , the juvenile and his or her parents or guardian should be advised that the juvenile has a right to first consult with an attorney, who, among other things, may appeal the requirement of a participation agreement to the court (*see* Standard 4.10).

Notes

1. Although diversion programs have been around since the 1960s, the idea gained nationwide attention with the passage of the Juvenile Justice and Delinquency Prevention Act of 1974. 42 U.S.C.S. §§ 5601-5785 (Lexis Supp. 2001). One of the Act's stated goals is "to divert juveniles from the traditional juvenile justice system and to provide critically needed alternatives to institutionalization." 42 U.S.C.S. § 5602(b)(2) (Law. Co-op. 1994). Within a few years of the passage of the Act, diversion programs were in place across the country. *See* S'Lee Arthur Hinshaw II, Comment, *Juvenile Diversion: An Alternative to Juvenile Court*, 1993 J. DISP. RESOL. 305, 312.

2. One of the advantages touted by the supporters of diversion is that it provides a method for dealing with juvenile offenders outside of the court system, thereby enabling the juveniles to receive treatment while avoiding the negative stigma associated with an adjudication of delinquency. For example, in *Quiroz,* the court pointed out that a diversion agreement was "not the same as a conviction," and that the existence of a prior diversion agreement can be used as part of the offender's criminal history only for a limited time. *See also State v. Haaby,* 755 P.2d 189 (Wash. Ct. App. 1988).

3. As discussed in *Quiroz*, there are several types of diversion agreements. A typical agreement may contain one or more of the following: community service, supervision (e.g., by a probation officer), a fine, and restitution to the victim. *See, e.g., State v. Foley*, 834 P.2d 1108 (Wash. Ct. App. 1992). Although not discussed in the *Quiroz* opinion, restitution has become increasingly popular, in that it requires accountability of the offender and provides the victim some measure of compensation for her loss. In fact, the majority of jurisdictions include restitution among the dispositional alternatives available in a diversion agreement. *See* Harry Mika et al., *Mediation Interventions and Restorative Potential: A Case Study of Juvenile Restitution*, 1989 J. DISP. RESOL. 89, 90.

All diversion agreements involve the suspension of charges against the juvenile, whether or not the charges have been formally filed. Further, a diversion agreement entered into after the commencement of proceedings against the juvenile supersedes all elements of those proceedings, including release conditions. *See, e.g., State v. Foley, supra.* However, the prosecutor can reinstate the suspended charges if the juvenile violates the conditions of the diversion agreement. *See, e.g., State v. Pickens,* 671 N.E.2d 1116 (Ohio Ct. App. 1996).

4. Diversionary units generally have the authority to set their own standards regarding what types of offenses are suited to diversion. These units may refuse the diversion referral of a juvenile who does not meet these standards. *See, e.g., State v. Chatham,* 624 P.2d 1180 (Wash. Ct. App. 1981) (juvenile had right to have case referred, but unit had right to refuse to enter diversion agreement with him). The juvenile may also refuse to enter into a diversion agreement and instead insist on adjudication of his case in the court system. *State v. McDowell*, 685 P.2d 595 (Wash. 1984).

Questions

1. Given that the diversionary agreement may include community service, fines, or restitution, what is to distinguish diversion from an admission of guilt by the juvenile? Could an innocent juvenile be coerced into participating in a diversion program by the knowledge that even an acquittal in a juvenile court could stigmatize her in the eyes of her community? If so, does the existence of a diversionary program give juveniles an unconstitutionally unfair choice?

2. Should a juvenile be entitled to the assistance of counsel when deciding whether to enter into a diversion agreement? Should a juvenile have the opportunity to review a diversion agreement with a lawyer before signing it?

E. Charging the Juvenile: Prosecutorial Discretion

State v. McDowell
685 P.2d 595 (Wash. 1984)

When a juvenile refuses to enter a diversion program on a complaint alleging a misdemeanor and the case is referred back to the prosecutor for filing, does the prosecutor have discretion to file a felony information? If the juvenile is then found to have committed the felony, is the sentencing court's discretion limited to imposing terms allowed under a diversion program? We hold that, under the circumstances of this case, the prosecutor's discretion was properly exercised. We further find that appellant McDowell's sentence is valid.

In November 1982, the Seattle Police Department received a complaint alleging that McDowell had ordered his father's Doberman pinscher dogs to menace a group of neighborhood children. After investigating the incident, the police sent a report to the King County Prosecutor's Office recommending that McDowell be charged with reckless endangerment. The case was screened and diverted to a diversion unit on the reckless endangerment complaint. McDowell met with a diversion staff member, but decided to reject the diversion program.

The complaint was referred back to the prosecutor's office with notice that McDowell had refused diversion. Several weeks later an information was filed charging second degree assault. Prior to the fact finding hearing on the charge, McDowell moved to dismiss the felony information because of prosecutorial vindictiveness. McDowell's motion was denied and he was found guilty of second degree assault.

During the disposition hearing on the assault conviction, McDowell argued that the sentencing court was limited by statute to a sentence no greater than what he could have received under the diversion program. The trial court ruled otherwise, and sentenced McDowell within the standard range for second degree assault, requiring 2 days of detention time and regular school attendance.

McDowell's appeal was certified to us by the Court of Appeals. He challenges the denial of his motion to dismiss the charge and his sentence.

I

McDowell claims that he is entitled to dismissal of the assault charge because allowing the prosecutor to file a greater charge once a juvenile rejects diversion penalizes that juvenile for exercising his right to take his case to court. He relies on United States Supreme Court cases finding that "while an individual certainly may be penalized for violating the law, he just as certainly may not be punished for exercising a protected statutory or constitutional right." *United States v. Goodwin,* 457 U.S. 368, 372, 102 S. Ct. 2485, 2488, 73 L. Ed. 2d 74 (1982).

In *Blackledge v. Perry,* 417 U.S. 21, 94 S. Ct. 2098, 40 L. Ed. 2d 628 (1974), the Court held that the prosecutor could not "up the ante" by filing felony charges against a defendant convicted of a misdemeanor, who chose to file for a trial de novo in a higher court. . . . In order to free defendants from fearing a prosecutor's retaliatory motivations, the Court held that charging a more serious crime upon retrial raised a realistic likelihood of vindictiveness and justified a presumption of illegal motives.

The *Perry* presumption of vindictiveness was not applied, however, to invalidate increased charges filed pretrial in *United States v. Goodwin, supra.* Goodwin had been originally charged by complaint with several misdemeanors, including assault. Goodwin refused to plead guilty before a magistrate, requesting, instead, a jury trial. His request necessitated a transfer to District Court and assignment of a new prosecutor. The new prosecutor determined that seeking a 4-count indictment, including one felony assault charge, was appropriate based on the evidence.

The Court found no fault with charging felony assault. First, actual vindictiveness in bringing the felony indictment had not been shown. Second, the Court found that *Perry's* presumption of vindictiveness was not appropriate in a pretrial setting. The Court explained that "[t]he possibility that a prosecutor would respond to a defendant's pretrial demand for a jury trial by bringing charges not in the public interest that could be explained only as penalty imposed on the defendant is so *unlikely* that a presumption of vindictiveness certainly is not warranted." (Emphasis in original.) *Goodwin*, 457 U.S. at 384, 102 S. Ct. at 2494.

Washington case law, in accord with *Goodwin,* suggests that actual vindictiveness is required to invalidate the prosecutor's adversarial decisions made prior to trial. *State v. Johnson,* 33 Wash. App. 534, 656 P.2d 1099 (1982); *State v. Penn,* 32 Wash. App. 911, 650 P.2d 1111 (1982); *State v. McKenzie,* 31 Wash. App. 450, 642 P.2d 760 (1981).

McDowell concedes that there is no evidence of actual vindictive motivation on the part of the prosecutor in this case. He does not contend that either *Goodwin* or the Washington rule respecting prosecutorial pretrial discretion in the adult criminal justice system is error. Instead, he argues that the structure of the juvenile diversion system requires a presumption of illegal motive whenever the prosecutor, without justification, increases the charges against a juvenile who refuses diversion. He contends that, unlike other pretrial settings, the system presents a "realistic likelihood" of retaliatory motivation, because the safeguards of the adult criminal justice system are not present to ensure good faith behavior by the prosecutor.

We find no reason to presume that abuse of prosecutorial discretion is more likely when juveniles are brought to justice than when adults are prosecuted. Nor do we conclude that the statutory scheme of the juvenile diversion system presents any special potential for abuse. The prosecutor's charging function under RCW 13.40.070(3), (5)-(7), which delineates circumstances under which filing and diversion are required, does not alter the prosecutor's traditional discretion when making the charging decision. Under the juvenile justice system, it remains a prosecutorial duty to determine the extent of society's interest in prosecuting an offense.

Before an information is filed, however, the prosecutor's statutory duty is simply to screen complaints for legal sufficiency. Complaints are then diverted to community programs or retained for further prosecutorial action depending on whether the complaint alleges a misdemeanor or felony, and on other statutory factors.

Once a legally sufficient complaint is determined to require filing, such as when the juvenile refuses the offer of diversion, the prosecutor's charging discretion must be exercised.* Common sense dictates that the original complaint and screening procedure will be reviewed and evaluated before an information is filed. For any number of reasons, whether it be new evidence or new conclusions about the significance of the allegations in the complaint, the charge actually filed might differ from the offense alleged in the initial complaint. Nothing in this procedure suggests that retaliatory motivation on the part of the prosecutor will underlie the charging decision.

* * *

In summary, we are not persuaded that the juvenile justice system creates a "realistic likelihood" of retaliatory motivation, not present in the adult criminal justice system. Presuming improper motivation for the prosecutor's filing decisions whenever an information differed from the original complaint would restrict the prosecutor's ability to make necessary pretrial adversarial decisions. In McDowell's case . . . the charging discretion was properly exercised.

---

* These are offenses for which the maximum authorized penalty is imprisonment for one year or less.—Ed.

Under these circumstances, and with no evidence of actual vindictiveness in the filing of charges against McDowell, we find no due process violation.

II

McDowell contends that even if he may be prosecuted for a greater offense after he rejects diversion, the Legislature has mandated that he shall receive no greater punishment than he would have received in the diversion program. He cites RCW 13.-40.160(3), which provides:

> Where a respondent is found to have committed an offense for which the respondent declined to enter into a diversion agreement, the court shall impose a term of community supervision limited to the conditions allowed in a diversion agreement as provided [by law].

Community supervision under RCW 13.40.080(2) is limited to community service, restitution, counseling sessions and a fine. McDowell received a sentence, however, requiring 2 days of detention time and regular school attendance.

The State argues that the limitation of RCW 13.40.160(3) literally does not apply when the offense found to be committed is different from the offense for which the juvenile was originally diverted. We agree. We have already determined that the Legislature contemplated prosecutorial discretion to charge a more serious crime in the information than was alleged in the original complaint. It is only reasonable to conclude that the Legislature intended the offender to be punished appropriately for the more serious offense.

* * *

We find no error in petitioner's conviction or sentence.
Affirmed.

Notes

1. *McDowell* supports the long-standing notion of prosecutorial discretion whereby courts grant almost unqualified deference to the state's decisions regarding the filing of charges against a defendant, whether adult or juvenile. The Colorado Court of Appeals articulated this idea in *People v. Hughes*, 946 P.2d 509, 516 (1997), by stating that "prosecutorial discretion is a hallmark of our criminal justice system that flows from the doctrine of the separation of powers." As noted in *McDowell*, courts will not overturn a prosecutor's exercise of discretion in adversarial decisions absent a showing of actual vindictiveness.

2. The idea of prosecutorial discretion has led reviewing courts to uphold decisions by prosecutors leading to the loss of juvenile court jurisdiction and the subsequent trial of the defendant in adult criminal court. *See, e.g., State v. Dixon*, 792 P.2d 137 (Wash. 1990); *United States v. Juvenile Male J.A.J.*, 134 F.3d 905 (8th Cir. 1998). Courts also routinely uphold decisions to bring additional charges against the juvenile subsequent to the original proceedings. *See, e.g., State v. Rayes*, 702 A.2d 1381 (N.H. 1997).

Questions

1. Do you agree with the notion that prosecutors should have the same discretion in filing charges against juveniles as they do with regard to adult defendants? Was the *McDowell* court correct in extending this discretion to bringing additional charges against a juvenile after the child decides to refuse diversion?

2. Should prosecutors be permitted to exercise their discretion in such a way as to deprive a youthful offender of adjudication in a juvenile court?

G. Interface with Child Welfare Proceedings

Burns Indiana Statutes Annotated
(Michie 2000)

§ 31-33-13-5. Court to have access to information.—

The local child protection service shall provide a court with access to information relating to a [child abuse or neglect] services referral agreement whenever the court:

(1) approves a program of informal adjustment; or

(2) presides over a child in need of services proceeding;

involving the same person or family to whom services were recommended under the services referral agreement.

§ 31-33-14-1. Referral to juvenile court or prosecuting attorney.—

If the local child protection service determines [after an investigation for abuse or neglect] that the best interests of the child require action in the juvenile or criminal court, the local child protection service shall:

(1) refer the case to the juvenile court . . . ; or

(2) make a referral to the prosecuting attorney if criminal prosecution is desired.

§ 31-33-14-2. Assistance by local child protection service.—

The local child protection service shall assist the juvenile court or the court having criminal jurisdiction during all stages of the proceedings. . . .

§ 31-33-18-2. Persons to whom material shall be made available.—

The [confidential] reports and other material described in . . . this chapter shall be made available only to the following:

* * *

(3) A police or other law enforcement agency [or] prosecuting attorney . . . who is investigating a report of a child who may be a victim of child abuse or neglect.

* * *

9. A court, upon the court's finding that access to the records may be necessary for determination of an issue before the court. . . .

10. A grand jury upon the grand jury's determination that access to the records is necessary in the conduct of the grand jury's official business. . . .

* * *

§ 31-39-2-5. Access to juvenile court records. Prosecuting attorney and staff.—

The records of the juvenile court are available without a court order to the prosecuting attorney or any authorized staff member.

§ 31-39-2-6. Attorney for county office of family and children or staff members of certain agencies.—

The records of the juvenile court are available without a court order to:

(a) the attorney for the county office of family and children; or

(b) any authorized staff member of:

  (A) the county office of family and children;

  (B) the division of family and children; or

  (C) the department of correction.

§ 31-39-2-9. Persons providing services to child or child's family.—

The juvenile court may grant any person providing services to the child or the child's family access to the records on the child and the child's family.

§ 31-39-4-6. Prosecuting attorney or staff.—

The records of a law enforcement agency are available, without specific permission from the head of the agency, to the prosecuting attorney or any authorized member of the staff of the prosecuting attorney.

§ 31-39-4-7. Attorney for county office of family and children or staff.—

The records of a law enforcement agency are available, without specific permission from the head of the agency, to the attorney for the county office of family and children or any authorized staff member.

Chapter 4

Children's Rights in Public Schools

This chapter addresses the unique problems that face public school administrators when dealing with the children in their schools. The cases in this chapter often refer to school officials as standing *in loco parentis*, that is, in the place of the parents. Courts generally hold that school officials' duties as "substitute parents" require that they be given more latitude than other state actors. However, courts disagree on how much latitude school officials require in order to do their jobs effectively. As you read this chapter, note the tension between two fundamental principles: first, that school students do not enjoy the same level of freedom as their adult counterparts; and, second, that children nonetheless retain some of their rights and liberty interests even while attending public schools.

A. First Amendment Freedoms

1. Speech

Tinker v. Des Moines Independent Community School District

393 U.S. 503, 89 S. Ct. 733, 21 L. Ed. 2d 731 (1969)

Mr. Justice FORTAS delivered the opinion of the Court.

Petitioner John F. Tinker, 15 years old, and petitioner Christopher Eckhardt, 16 years old, attended high schools in Des Moines, Iowa. Petitioner Mary Beth Tinker, John's sister, was a 13 year-old student in junior high school.

In December 1965, a group of adults and students in Des Moines held a meeting at the Eckhardt home. The group determined to publicize their objections to the hostilities in Vietnam and their support for a truce by wearing black armbands during the holiday season and by fasting on December 16 and New Year's Eve. . . .

The principals of the Des Moines schools became aware of the plan to wear armbands. On December 14, 1965, they met and adopted a policy that any student wearing an armband to school would be asked to remove it, and if he refused he would be suspended until he returned without the armband. Petitioners were aware of the regulation that the school authorities adopted.

On December 16, Mary Beth and Christopher wore black armbands to their schools. John Tinker wore his armband the next day. They were all sent home and suspended from school until they would come back without their armbands. They did not return to school until after the planned period for wearing armbands had expired—that is, until after New Year's Day.

This complaint was filed in the United States District Court by petitioners, through their fathers, under § 1983 of Title 42 of the United States Code. It prayed for an injunction restraining the respondent school officials and the respondent members of the board of directors of the school district from disciplining the petitioners, and it sought nominal damages. After an evidentiary hearing the District Court dismissed the complaint. It upheld the constitutionality of the school authorities' action on the ground that it was reasonable in order to prevent disturbance of school discipline. The court referred to but expressly declined to follow the Fifth Circuit's holding in a similar case that the wearing of symbols like the armbands cannot be prohibited unless it "materially and substantially interfere[s] with the requirements of appropriate discipline in the operation of the school." *Burnside v. Byars*, 363 F.2d 744, 749 (1966).

On appeal, the Court of Appeals for the Eighth Circuit . . . affirmed without opinion. We granted certiorari.

* * *

I.

First Amendment rights, applied in light of the special characteristics of the school environment, are available to teachers and students. It can hardly be argued that either students or teachers shed their constitutional rights to freedom of speech or expression at the schoolhouse gate. This has been the unmistakable holding of this Court for almost 50 years. In *Meyer v. Nebraska*, 262 U.S. 390 (1923), and *Bartels v. Iowa*, 262 U.S. 404 (1923), this Court, in opinions by Mr. Justice McReynolds, held that the Due Process Clause of the Fourteenth Amendment prevents States from forbidding the teaching of a foreign language to young students. Statutes to this effect, the Court held, unconstitutionally interfere with the liberty of teacher, student, and parent. *See also Pierce v. Society of Sisters*, 268 U.S. 510 (1925); *West Virginia v. Barnette*, 319 U.S. 624 (1943).

In *West Virginia v. Barnette*, *supra*, this Court held that under the First Amendment, the student in public school may not be compelled to salute the flag. Speaking through Mr. Justice Jackson, the Court said:

> "The Fourteenth Amendment, as now applied to the States, protects the citizen against the State itself and all of its creatures—Boards of Education not excepted. These have, of course, important, delicate, and highly discretionary functions, but none that they may not perform within the limits of the Bill of Rights. That they are educating the young for citizenship is reason for scrupulous protection of Constitutional freedoms of the individual, if we are not to strangle the

free mind at its source and teach youth to discount important principles of our government as mere platitudes."

319 U.S. at 637.

On the other hand, the Court has repeatedly emphasized the need for affirming the comprehensive authority of the States and of school officials, consistent with fundamental constitutional safeguards, to prescribe and control conduct in the schools. Our problem lies in the area where students in the exercise of First Amendment rights collide with the rules of the school authorities.

II.

The problem posed by the present case does not . . . concern aggressive, disruptive action or even group demonstrations. Our problem involves direct, primary First Amendment rights akin to "pure speech."

The School officials banned and sought to punish petitioners for a silent, passive expression of opinion, unaccompanied by any disorder or disturbance on the part of petitioners. There is here no evidence whatever of petitioners' interference, actual or nascent, with the schools' work or of collision with the rights of other students to be secure and to be let alone. Accordingly, this case does not concern speech or action that intrudes upon the work of the schools or the rights of other students.

Only a few of the 18,000 students in the school system wore the black armbands. Only five students were suspended for wearing them. There is no indication that the work of the schools or any class was disrupted. Outside the classrooms, a few students made hostile remarks to the children wearing armbands, but there were no threats or acts of violence on school premises.

The District Court concluded that the action of the school authorities was reasonable because it was based upon their fear of a disturbance from the wearing of the armbands. But, in our system, undifferentiated fear or apprehension of disturbance is not enough to overcome the right to freedom of expression. . . . Any word spoken, in class, in the lunchroom, or on the campus, that deviates from the views of another person may start an argument or cause a disturbance. But our Constitution says we must take this risk, and our history says that it is this sort of hazardous freedom—this kind of openness—that is the basis of our national strength and of the independence and vigor of Americans who grow up and live in this relatively permissive, often disputatious, society.

In order for the State in the person of school officials to justify prohibition of a particular expression of opinion, it must be able to show that its action was caused by something more than a mere desire to avoid the discomfort and unpleasantness that always accompany an unpopular viewpoint. Certainly where there is no finding and no showing that engaging in the forbidden conduct would "materially and substantially interfere with the requirements of appropriate discipline in the operation of the school," the prohibition cannot be sustained. *Burnside v. Byars, supra,* at 749.

In the present case, the District Court made no such finding, and our independent examination of the record fails to yield evidence that the school authorities had reason to anticipate that the wearing of the armbands would substantially interfere with the work of the school or impinge upon the rights of other students. . . . On the contrary, the action of the school authorities appears to have been based upon an urgent wish to avoid the controversy which might result from the expression, even by the silent symbol of armbands, of opposition to this Nation's part in the conflagration in Vietnam. . . .

It is also relevant that the school authorities did not purport to prohibit the wearing of all symbols of political or controversial significance. The record shows that students in some of the schools wore buttons relating to national political campaigns and some even wore the Iron Cross, traditionally a symbol of Nazism. The order prohibiting the wearing of armbands did not extend to these. Instead, a particular symbol—black armbands worn to exhibit opposition to this Nation's involvement in Vietnam—was singled out for prohibition. Clearly, the prohibition of expression of one particular opinion, at least without evidence that it is necessary to avoid material and substantial interference with school work or discipline, is not constitutionally permissible.

In our system, state-operated schools may not be enclaves of totalitarianism. School officials do not possess absolute authority over their students. Students in school as well as out of school are "persons" under our Constitution. . . . In the absence of a specific showing of constitutionally valid reasons to regulate their speech, students are entitled to freedom of expression of their views. As Judge Gewin, speaking for the Fifth Circuit, said, school officials cannot suppress "expressions of feelings with which they do not wish to contend." *Burnside v. Byars, supra,* at 749.

* * *

Under our Constitution, free speech is not a right that is given only to be so circumscribed that it exists in principle but not in fact. . . . The Constitution says that Congress (and the States) may not abridge the right to free speech. This provision means what it says. We properly read it to permit reasonable regulation of speech-connected activities in carefully restricted circumstances. But we do not confine the permissible exercise of First Amendment rights to a telephone booth or the four corners of a pamphlet, or to supervised and ordained discussion in a school classroom.

If a regulation were adopted by school officials forbidding discussion of the Vietnam conflict, or the expression by any student of opposition to it anywhere on school property except as part of a prescribed classroom exercise, it would be obvious that the regulation would violate the constitutional rights of students, at least if it could not be justified by a showing that the students' activities would materially and substantially disrupt the work and discipline of the school. In the circumstances of the present case, the prohibition of the silent, passive "witness of the armbands," as one of the children called it, is no less offensive to the Constitution's guarantees.

As we have discussed, the record does not demonstrate any facts which might reasonably have led school authorities to forecast substantial disruption of or material interference with school activities, and no disturbances or disorders on the school premises in fact occurred. These petitioners merely went about their ordained rounds in school. Their deviation consisted only in wearing on their sleeve a band of black cloth, not more than two inches wide. They wore it to exhibit their disapproval of the Vietnam hostilities and their advocacy of a truce, to make their view known, and, by their example, to influence others to adopt them. They neither interrupted school activities nor sought to intrude in the school affairs or the lives of others. They caused discussion outside of the classrooms, but no interference with work and no disorder. In the circumstances, our Constitution does not permit officials of the State to deny their form of expression. . . .

We reverse and remand for further proceedings consistent with this opinion.

[The concurring opinions of Justices WHITE and STEWART are omitted.]

Mr. Justice BLACK, dissenting.

The Court's holding in this case ushers in what I deem to be an entirely new era in which the power to control pupils by the elected "officials of state supported public schools . . ." in the United States is in ultimate effect transferred to the Supreme Court. . . .

As I read the Court's opinion it relies upon the following grounds for holding unconstitutional the judgment of the Des Moines school officials and the two courts below. First, the Court concludes that the wearing of armbands is "symbolic speech" which is "akin to 'pure speech'" and therefore protected by the First and Fourteenth Amendments. Secondly, the Court decides that the public schools are an appropriate place to exercise "symbolic speech" as long as normal school functions are not "unreasonably" disrupted. Finally, the Court arrogates to itself, rather than to the State's elected officials charged with running the schools, the decision as to which school disciplinary regulations are "reasonable."

Assuming that the Court is correct in holding that the conduct of wearing armbands for the purpose of conveying political ideas is protected by the First Amendment, the crucial remaining questions are whether students and teachers may use the schools at their whim as a platform for the exercise of free speech—"symbolic" or "pure"—and whether the courts will allocate to themselves the function of deciding how the pupils' school day will be spent. While I have always believed that under the First and Fourteenth Amendments neither the State nor the Federal Government has any authority to regulate or censor the content of speech, I have never believed that any person has a right to give speeches or engage in demonstrations where he pleases and when he pleases. This Court has already rejected such a notion. In *Cox v. Louisiana*, 379 U.S. 536, 554 (1965), for example, the Court clearly stated that the rights of free speech and assembly "do not mean that everyone with opinions or beliefs to express may address a group at any public place and at any time."

* * *

I deny . . . that it has been the "unmistakable holding of this Court for almost 50 years" that "students" and "teachers" take with them into the "schoolhouse gate" constitutional rights to "freedom of speech or expression. . . ." The truth is that a teacher of kindergarten, grammar school, or high school pupils no more carries into a school with him a complete right to freedom of speech and expression than an anti-Catholic or anti-Semite carries with him a complete freedom of speech and religion into a Catholic church or Jewish synagogue. Nor does a person carry with him into the United States Senate or House, or into the Supreme Court, or any other court, a complete constitutional right to go into those places contrary to their rules and speak his mind on any subject he pleases. It is a myth to say that any person has a constitutional right to say what he pleases, and when he pleases. . . .

In my view, teachers in state-controlled public schools are hired to teach there. [C]ertainly a teacher is not paid to go into school and teach subjects the State does not hire him to teach as part of its selected curriculum. Nor are public school students sent to the schools at public expense to broadcast political or any other views to educate and inform the public. . . . It may be that the Nation has outworn the old-fashioned slogan that "children are to be seen not heard," but one may, I hope, be permitted to harbor the thought that taxpayers send children to school on the premise that at their age they need to learn, not teach.

[T]he record amply shows that public protest in the school classes against the Vietnam war "distracted from that singleness of purpose which the State desired to exist in its public educational institutions. . . ." Of course students, like other people, cannot concentrate on lesser issues when black armbands are being ostentatiously displayed in their presence to call attention to the wounded and dead of the war, some of the wounded and the dead being their friends and neighbors. It was, of course, to distract the attention of other students that some students insisted up to the very point of their own suspension from school that they were determined to sit in school with their symbolic armbands.

[The] schools of this Nation have undoubtedly contributed to giving us tranquility and to making us a more law-abiding people. Uncontrolled and uncontrollable liberty is an enemy to domestic peace. . . . Here a very small number of students have crisply and summarily refused to obey a school order designed to give pupils who want to learn the opportunity to do so. One does not need to be a prophet or the son of a prophet to know that after the Court's holding today some students in Iowa schools and indeed in all schools will be ready, able, and willing to defy their teachers on practically all orders. This is the more unfortunate for schools since groups of students all over the land are already running loose, conducting break-ins, sit-ins, lie-ins, and smash-ins. . . . Students engaged in such activities are apparently confident that they know far more about how to operate public school systems than do their parents, teachers, and elected school officials. . . . This case, therefore, wholly without constitutional reasons in my judgment, subjects all the public schools in the country to the whims and caprices of their loudest-mouthed, but maybe not their brightest, students. . . . I wish, therefore, wholly to disclaim any purpose on my part to hold that the Federal Constitution compels the teachers, parents, and elected school officials to surrender control of the American public school system to public school students. I dissent.

Mr. Justice HARLAN, dissenting.

I certainly agree that state public school authorities in the discharge of their responsibilities are not wholly exempt from the requirements of the Fourteenth Amendment respecting the freedoms of expression and association. At the same time I am reluctant to believe that there is any disagreement between the majority and myself on the proposition that school officials should be accorded the widest authority in maintaining discipline and good order in their institutions. To translate that proposition into a workable constitutional rule, I would, in cases like this, cast upon those complaining the burden of showing that a particular school measure was motivated by other than legitimate school concerns—for example, a desire to prohibit the expression of an unpopular point of view, while permitting expression of the dominant opinion.

Finding nothing in this record which impugns the good faith of respondents in promulgating the armband regulation, I would affirm the judgment below.

Notes

1. After its decision in *Tinker*, the Court would revisit the issue of school children's First Amendment rights on several occasions. In 1982, the Court decided *Board of Education, Island Trees Union Free School District No. 26 v. Pico*, 457 U.S. 853, in which a group of high school students and their parents sought to enjoin the school board from removing allegedly objectionable books from the school library. The plurality opinion, written by Justice Brennan, upheld the appellate court's decision reversing the district court's grant of summary judgment to the school board. The plurality held that the board could not order the removal of books from the school library simply because the board members objected to the ideas presented in the books. Although the Court recognized that the school board has broad discretion in creating curriculum, the plurality felt that this discretion did not extend "beyond the compulsory environment of the classroom" to include regulation of a student's "voluntary inquiry" in the school library. *Id.* at 869. The board's action in this case was, in the plurality's opinion, a constitutional issue because the removal of books from a school library "may . . . directly and sharply implicate[ ]" students' First Amendment rights. *Id.* at 866. "Our Constitution does not permit the official suppression of ideas." *Id.* at 871.

Four years after its decision in *Pico*, the Supreme Court again considered the scope of free speech rights enjoyed by high school students. In *Bethel School District No. 403 v. Fraser,* 478 U.S. 675 (1986), the Court held that a student did not have the right under the First Amendment to use lewd and indecent language in a speech before a high school assembly. In reversing the appellate court, which had affirmed the district court's holding, the Court reaffirmed its holding in *Tinker* but considered it inapplicable because the majority found the political message at issue in *Tinker* distinguishable from the speech in *Fraser*, which was sexual in nature. The Court said that fundamental rights include the right not to be exposed to offensive materials, especially in the essentially captive audience that exists at a mandatory high school assembly. *Id.* at 681. The Court found it "a highly appropriate function of public discourse." *Id.* at 683. The majority was concerned that the public would view allowing indecent speech at a school-sponsored function as an endorsement of such speech by school officials. The holding in *Fraser* thereby distinguished free speech from school-sponsored speech. The Court left "the determination of what manner of speech in the classroom or in school assembly is inappropriate [to] the school board." *Id.*

Hazelwood School District v. Kuhlmeier, 484 U.S. 260 (1988), represents the Court's most recent foray into the realm of First Amendment free speech rights in the public schools. The *Kuhlmeier* Court upheld the right of school officials to censor articles appearing in the school newspaper, reasoning that publication of the newspaper was part of the school curriculum and was funded largely by the school board. The Court distinguished activities in the public school context from those occurring in a public forum. In so doing, the Court backed further away from its holding in *Tinker*, in essence establishing a new method to test the constitutionality of speech restrictions in a public school. Building on *Fraser*, the new test would determine the reasonableness of the restriction in light of the duty of school officials to maintain order and to establish and preserve an environment conducive to learning.

For further discussion of how this line of cases has affected the First Amendment rights of public school children, see Lisa A. Brown & Christopher Gilbert, *Understanding the Constitutional Rights of School Children,* 34 HOUS. LAW. 40 (1997). For a criticism of the *Kuhlmeier* decision, see Helen Bryks, *A Lesson in School Censorship:* Hazelwood v. Kuhlmeier, 55 BROOK. L. REV. 291 (1989).

2. Lower courts attempting to interpret and apply the rules of *Tinker* and its progency have struggled to distinguish between "free" and "school-sponsored" speech. For example, using a *Tinker* analysis, one court has held that a gay high school student had a First Amendment right to bring a male escort to the senior prom. *See Fricke v. Lynch*, 491 F. Supp. 381 (D.R.I. 1980) (attending prom with same-sex escort amounts to a political statement). Other courts have upheld the right of school officials to reject controversial advertisements in a high school yearbook, *Planned Parenthood of Southern Nevada, Inc. v. Clark County School District,* 941 F.2d 817 (9th Cir. 1991); rejected the claim that students have a First Amendment right to retain a Confederate school mascot, *Crosby v. Holsinger*, 852 F.2d 162 (4th Cir. 1988) ("school officials need not sponsor or promote all student speech"); and held that a student does not have a constitutional right to run for student council office, *Poling v. Murphy*, 872 F.2d 757 (6th Cir. 1989) (upholding disqualification of honor student after he made inappropriate nomination speech).

3. One of the most hotly debated First Amendment issues in recent years has been whether school officials can enact dress codes in public schools. School dress codes have been introduced largely to combat gang-related violence in public schools. Many schools regulate dress by banning certain items or styles of clothing. Uniforms, on the other hand, are generally introduced only at the elementary and middle school levels. *See* Dena M. Sarke, *Coed Naked Constitutional Law: The Benefits and Harms of Uniform Dress Regulations in American Public Schools*, 78 B.U. L. REV. 153, 167 (1998). There is some evidence that the introduction of uniforms and dress codes has had the effect of reducing violence and increasing school spirit and respect. *Id.* at 166.

Judicial reaction to dress codes has been mixed. *See, e.g., Jegin v. Jacinto Unified School District*, 827 F. Supp. 1459 (C.D. Cal. 1993) (upholding ban on clothing with sports insignias in high school; rejecting same ban at elementary and middle school levels); *Bivens v. Albuquerque Public Schools,* 899 F. Supp. 556 (D.N.M. 1995) (upholding ban on baggy pants: "[p]laintiff ha[s] not shown that his wearing of sagging pants was speech protected by the First Amendment"). As a general proposition, it can be said that school dress codes, like curfews (*see, supra*, Chapter 2, Part B.1.d), are more likely to withstand constitutional scrutiny if they are narrowly tailored to meet clearly stated goals.

Questions

1. What test does Justice Harlan propose to analyze the issue in *Tinker*? How does this test differ from the analysis employed by the majority? Applying Justice Harlan's rule, does he reach the correct result?

2. Do students have a First Amendment right to uncensored access to the internet at school? Must school officials choose between offering students no internet connection or letting them view any material available on the internet? If not, how could a school board justify both offering access to the internet and at the same time limiting that access? What would be the argument against such restrictions? Would you expect such a scheme to withstand scrutiny under the First Amendment?

Problem

Mark is a senior at Whitmore High School, a large, suburban high school. He has suspected that he is gay for some time, and last year he came out to his family and friends. Since then, Mark has met several other students at his school who are gay, bisexual, or unsure of their sexual orientation. Mark and several of his friends have decided to start a gay student group at Whitmore. Upon learning of Mark's plans, Mr. Andrews, the school principal, calls Mark into his office to inform him of the school district's policy against allowing any groups dealing primarily with "issues of a sexual nature" from meeting on school property. Mark contends that the group is being formed to offer support for homosexual students, not to discuss sexual issues. Mr. Andrews replies, "Well, I don't see how you can say that a group of gays getting together to talk about being gay is anything *but* 'sexual in nature.' I'm sorry, Mark, but your club will have to meet somewhere else. The school district just can't make school property available for such controversial groups."

Assume that after going through all of the appropriate administrative appeals, Mark and his parents file suit against the school district, alleging that the district has denied Mark and his friends their First Amendment rights by prohibiting the group from meeting at the school. The school district has filed a motion for summary judgment, stating that it has the discretion to monitor organizations using school property and that the school is not a public forum open to everyone. What further arguments would you expect the school district to make to justify its decision to keep gay student groups from meeting on school property? What would Mark argue in reply? How should the court rule on the district's motion for summary judgment?

For a discussion of this issue, see Doni Gewirtzman, *"Make Your Own Kind of Music": Queer Student Groups and the First Amendment*, 86 CAL. L. REV. 1131 (1998).

2. Religion

School District of Abington Township Pennsylvania v. Schempp

374 U.S. 203, 83 S. Ct. 1560, 10 L. Ed. 2d 844 (1963)

Mr. Justice CLARK delivered the opinion of the Court.

[W]e are called upon to consider the scope of the provision of the First Amendment to the United States Constitution which declares that "Congress shall make no law respecting an establishment of religion, or prohibiting the free exercise thereof . . ." in the context of state action requiring that schools begin each day with readings from the Bible. . . . In light of the history of the First Amendment and of our cases interpreting and applying its requirements, we hold that the practices at issue and the laws requiring them are unconstitutional under the Establishment Clause, as applied to the States through the Fourteenth Amendment.

I.

[The] Commonwealth of Pennsylvania by law . . . requires that "[a]t least ten verses from the Holy Bible shall be read, without comment, at the opening of each public school on each school day. Any child shall be excused from such Bible reading, or attending such Bible reading, upon the written request of his parent or guardian." The Schempp family, husband and wife and two of their three children, brought suit to enjoin enforcement of the statute, contending that their rights under the Fourteenth Amendment to the Constitution of the United States are, have been, and will continue to be violated unless this statute be declared unconstitutional as violative of these provisions of the First Amendment. They sought to enjoin the appellant school district . . . from continuing to conduct such readings and recitation of the Lord's Prayer in the public schools of the district pursuant to the statute. A three-judge statutory District Court for the Eastern District of Pennsylvania held that the statute is violative of the Establishment Clause of the First Amendment as applied to the States by the Due Process Clause of the Fourteenth Amendment and directed that appropriate injunctive relief issue. . . .

The appellees . . . are of the Unitarian faith and are members of the Unitarian Church in Germantown, Philadelphia, Pennsylvania, where they . . . regularly attend religious services. . . . The . . . children attend the Abington Senior High School, which is a public school operated by appellant district.

On each school day at the Abington Senior High School between 8:15 and 8:30 a.m., while the pupils are attending their home rooms or advisory sections, opening exercises are conducted pursuant to the statute. The exercises are broadcast into each room in the school building through an intercommunications system and are conducted under the supervision of a teacher by students attending the school's radio and television workshop. Selected students from this course gather each morning in the school's workshop studio for the exercises, which include readings by one of the students of 10 verses of the Holy Bible, broadcast to each room in the building. This is followed by the recitation of the Lord's Prayer, likewise over the intercommunications system, but also by the students in the various classrooms, who are asked to stand and join in repeating the prayer in unison. The exercises are closed with the flag salute and such pertinent announcements as are of interest to the students. Participation in the opening exercises, as directed by the statute, is voluntary. . . . There are no prefatory statements, no questions asked or solicited, no comments or explanations made and no interpretations given at or during the exercises. The students and parents are advised that the student may absent himself from the classroom or, should he elect to remain, not participate in the exercises.

* * *

The trial court, in striking down the practices and the statute requiring them, made specific findings of fact that the children's attendance at Abington Senior High School is compulsory and that the practice of reading 10 verses from the Bible is also compelled by law. It also found that:

> The reading of the verses, even without comment, possesses a devotional and religious character and constitutes in effect a religious observance. The devotional and religious nature of the morning exercises is made all the more apparent by the fact that the Bible reading is followed immediately by a recital in unison by the pupils of the Lord's Prayer. The fact that some pupils, or theoretically all pupils might be excused from attendance at the exercises does not mitigate the obligatory nature of the ceremony. . . . The exercises are held in the school buildings and perforce are conducted by and under the authority of the local school authorities and during school sessions. Since the statute requires the reading of the "Holy Bible," a Christian document, the practice . . . prefers the Christian religion. The record demonstrates that it was the intention of . . . the Commonwealth . . . to introduce a religious ceremony into the public schools of the Commonwealth.

* * *

II

It is true that religion has been closely identified with our history and government. As we said in *Engel v. Vitale*, 370 U.S. 421, 434 (1962), "The history of man is inseparable from the history of religion. And . . . since the beginning of that history many people have devoutly believed that 'More things are wrought by prayer than this world dreams of.'" In *Zorach v. Clauson*, 343 U.S. 306, 313 (1952), we gave specific recognition to the proposition that "[w]e are a religious people whose institutions presuppose a Supreme being. . . ." Indeed, only last year an official survey of the country indicated that 64% of our people have church membership, Bureau of the Census, U.S. Department of Commerce, Statistical Abstract of the United States 48 (83d ed. 1962), while less than 3% profess no religion whatever. *Id.* at p. 46. It can be truly said, therefore, that today, as in the beginning, our national life reflects a religious people. . . .

This is not to say, however, that religion has been so identified with our history and government that religious freedom is not likewise as strongly imbedded in our public and private life [sic]. . . . This freedom to worship was indispensable in a country whose people came from the four quarters of the earth and brought with them a diversity of religious opinion. Today authorities list 83 separate religious bodies, each with membership exceeding 50,000, existing among our people, as well as innumerable smaller groups. Bureau of the Census, *op. cit., supra,* at 46-47.

III

* * *

[T]his Court has decisively settled that the First Amendment's mandate that "Congress shall make no law respecting an establishment of religion, or prohibiting the free exercise thereof" has been made wholly applicable to the States by the Fourteenth Amendment. Twenty-three years ago in *Cantwell v. Connecticut,* 310 U.S. 296, 303 (1940), this Court, through Mr. Justice Roberts, said:

> The fundamental concept of liberty embodied in that [Fourteenth] Amendment embraces the liberties guaranteed by the First Amendment. The First Amendment declares that Congress shall make no law respecting an establishment of religion or prohibiting the free exercise thereof. The Fourteenth Amendment has rendered the legislatures of the states as incompetent as Congress to enact such laws. . . .

In a series of cases since *Cantwell* the Court has repeatedly reaffirmed that doctrine, and we do so now. *Murdock v. Pennsylvania,* 319 U.S. 105, 108 (1943); *Everson v. Board of Education,* 330 U.S. 1 (1947); *Illinois ex rel. McCollum v. Board of Education,* 333 U.S. 203, 210-211 (1948); *Zorach v. Clauson, supra; McGowan v. Maryland,* 366 U.S. 420 (1961); *Torcaso v. Watkins,* 367 U.S. 488 (1961); and *Engel v. Vitale, supra.*

[T]his Court has [also] rejected unequivocally the contention that the Establishment Clause forbids only governmental preference of one religion over another. Almost 30 years ago in *Everson, supra,* at 15, the Court said that "[n]either a state nor the Federal Government can set up a church. Neither can pass laws which aid one religion, aid all religions, or prefer one religion over another. . . ." The same conclusion has been firmly maintained ever since that time, *see Illinois ex rel. McCollum, supra,* at pp. 210-211; *McGowan v. Maryland, supra,* at 442-443; *Torcaso v. Watkins, supra,* at 492-493, and we reaffirm it now.

* * *

IV.

The interrelationship of the Establishment and the Free Exercise Clauses was first touched upon by Mr. Justice Roberts for the Court in *Cantwell v. Connecticut, supra,* at 303-304, where it was said that their "inhibition of legislation" had

> a double aspect. On one hand, it forestalls compulsion by law of the acceptance of any creed or the practice of any form of worship. Freedom of conscience and freedom to adhere to such religious organization or form of worship as the individual may choose cannot be restricted by law. On the other hand, it safeguards the free exercise of the chosen form of religion. Thus the Amendment embraces two concepts, freedom to believe and freedom to act. The first is absolute but, in the nature of things, the second cannot be.

A half dozen years later in *Everson v. Board of Education, supra*, at 14-15, this Court, through Mr. Justice Black, stated that the "scope of the First Amendment . . . was designed forever to suppress" the establishment of religion or the prohibition of the free exercise thereof. . . . And Mr. Justice Jackson, in dissent, declared that public schools are organized

> on the premise that secular education can be isolated from all religious teaching so that the school can inculcate all needed temporal knowledge and also maintain a strict and lofty neutrality as to religion. The assumption is that after the individual has been instructed in worldly wisdom he will be better fitted to choose his religion.

Id. at 23-24. . . .

* * *

In 1952 in *Zorach v. Clauson, supra,* Mr. Justice Douglas for the Court reiterated:

> There cannot be the slightest doubt that the First Amendment reflects the philosophy that Church and State should be separated. And so far as interference with the "free exercise" of religion and an "establishment" of religion are concerned, the separation must be complete and unequivocal. The First Amendment within the scope of its coverage permits no exception; the prohibition is absolute. . . .

343 U.S. at 312.

* * *

Finally, in *Engel v. Vitale*, only last year, these principles were so universally recognized that the Court, without the citation of a single case and over the sole dissent of Mr. Justice Stewart, reaffirmed them. The Court found the 22-word prayer used in "New York's program of daily classroom invocation of God's blessings as prescribed in the Regents' prayer . . . [to be] a religious activity." 370 U.S. at 424. It held that "it is no part of the business of government to compose official prayers for any group of the American people to recite as a part of a religious program carried on by government." *Id.* at 425. . . .

[T]he Establishment Clause has been directly considered by this Court eight times in the past score of years and, with only one Justice dissenting on the point, it has consistently held that the Clause withdrew all legislative power respecting religious belief or the expression thereof. The test may be stated as follows: what are the purpose and the primary effect of the enactment? If either is the advancement or inhibition of religion then the enactment exceeds the scope of legislative power as circumscribed by the Constitution. That is to say that to withstand the strictures of the Establishment Clause there must be a secular legislative purpose and a primary effect that neither advances nor inhibits religion. *Everson v. Board of Education, supra; McGowan v. Maryland, supra,* at 442. The Free Exercise Clause, likewise considered many times here withdraws from legislative power, state and federal, the exertion of any restraint on the free exercise of religion. Its purpose is to secure religious liberty in the individual by prohibiting any invasions thereof by civil authority. Hence it is necessary in a free exercise case for one to show the coercive effect of the enactment as it operates against him in the practice of his religion. The distinction between the two clauses is apparent—a violation of the Free Exercise Clause is predicated on coercion while the Establishment Clause violation need not be so attended.

Applying the Establishment Clause principles to the [case] at bar we find that the [State is] requiring the selection and reading at the opening of the school day of verses from the Holy Bible and the recitation of the Lord's Prayer by the students in unison. These exercises are prescribed as part of the curricular activities of students who are required by law to attend school. They are held in the school buildings under the supervision and with the participation of teachers employed in those schools. . . . The trial court . . . has found that such an opening exercise is a religious ceremony and was intended by the State to be so. We agree with the trial court's finding as to the religious character of the exercises. Given that finding, the exercises and the law requiring them are in violation of the Establishment Clause.

* * *

The conclusion follows that . . . the la[w] require[s] religious exercises and such exercises are being conducted in direct violation of the rights of the appellees. . . . Nor are these required exercises mitigated by the fact that individual students may absent themselves upon parental request, for that fact furnishes no defense to a claim of unconstitutionality under the Establishment Clause. Further, it is no defense to urge that the religious practices here may be relatively minor encroachments on the First Amendment. . . .

It is insisted that unless these religious exercises are permitted a "religion of secularism" is established in the schools. We agree of course that the State may not establish a "religion of secularism" in the sense of affirmatively opposing or showing hostility to religion, thus "preferring those who believe in no religion over those who do believe." *Zorach v. Clauson, supra,* at 314. We do not agree, however, that this decision in any sense has that effect. In addition, it might well be said that one's education is not complete without a study of comparative religion or the history of religion and its relationship to the advancement of civilization. It certainly may be said that the Bible is worthy of study for its literary and historic qualities. Nothing we have said here indicates that such study of the Bible or of religion, when presented objectively as part of a secular program of education, may not be effected consistently with the First Amendment. But the exercises here do not fall into those categories. They are religious exercises, required by the States in violation of the command of the First Amendment that the Government maintain strict neutrality, neither aiding nor opposing religion.

* * *

The place of religion in our society is an exalted one, achieved through a long tradition of reliance on the home, the church and the inviolable citadel of the individual heart and mind. We have come to recognize through bitter experience that it is not within the power of government to invade that citadel, whether its purpose or effect be to aid or oppose, to advance or retard. In the relationship between man and religion, the State is firmly committed to a position of neutrality. Though the application of that rule requires interpretation of a delicate sort, the rule itself is clearly and concisely stated in the words of the First Amendment. Applying that rule . . . , we affirm the judgment. . . .

[The concurring opinions of Justices DOUGLAS, BRENNAN, and GOLDBERG are omitted. In his dissent (also omitted), Justice Stewart expressed his opinion that the law involved would be constitutional as long as the school did not coerce students to participate. He believed the record showed no evidence of such coercion.]

Notes

1. The Supreme Court's analysis of cases regarding religion in public schools, like its handling of free speech rights for public school children, has been mixed and somewhat confusing at times. Eight years after *Schempp*, the Court announced the rule it would use to decide when schools (or other governmental bodies) had become too involved in religious activities and had thus violated the Establishment Clause of the First Amendment. *Lemon v. Kurtzman,* 403 U.S. 602 (1970). The so-called *Lemon* test was announced by the Court as the vehicle for determining the constitutionality of a statute under the Establishment Clause. To pass the test, a challenged statute or regulation must withstand three inquiries. The first two prongs of the *Lemon* test were derived from the *Schempp* decision. First, the statute must have a secular legislative purpose. Next, the primary effect of the statute must not be to advance or inhibit religion. The third prong, and the one that has proved the most problematic for lower courts to apply, was announced by the Court in *Walz v. Tax Commission,* 397 U.S. 664 (1970). In order to pass constitutional muster under this prong, the statute must not lead to excessive governmental entanglement with religion. Lower courts have struggled to determine the meaning of this part of the *Lemon* test, especially since it seems in some ways to do little more than restate the second prong.

The Court has itself apparently recognized the shortcomings of the test it announced in *Lemon,* and has promulgated a number of other tests judges can employ when analyzing claims under the Establishment Clause. The "coercive effect" test, announced in *Lee v. Weisman*, for example, is violated where students are compelled by school officials to participate in religious activities. 505 US. 577 (1982). In *County of Allegheny v. American Civil Liberties Union*, 492 U.S. 573 (1989), the Court analyzed an Establishment Clause case using what has been termed the "apparent endorsement" test. The analysis under this test is accomplished by answering the question: "does the government appear to be endorsing religion?" If so, the challenged regulation violates the Establishment Clause.

Although the *Lemon* test has been widely critized, and the Supreme Court has analyzed claimed Establishment Clause violations using different tests, the Court has never specifically abandoned the *Lemon* test in favor of another test. As discussed above, lower courts have struggled to understand and apply the three prongs of the *Lemon* test. Most courts, however, continue to analyze claims of government sponsoring of religion under the standards set forth in the test.

2. The Supreme Court has long recognized that school-sponsored prayer violates the Establishment Clause of the First Amendment. *See also Engel v. Vitale*, 370 U.S. 421 (1962). The issue of prayer in schools, however, is far from settled. This is true because the definitions of "prayer" and of what events are "school-sponsored" are not always clear-cut.

The issue of invocations at high school graduations has been a particularly contentious one in recent years. For example, the Supreme Court found that the Establishment Clause had been violated in *Lee v. Weisman* because school officials had invited local clergy to offer an invocation at a high school graduation. 505 U.S. 577 (1992). The Fifth Circuit in *Jones v. Cedar Creek Independent School District*, on the other hand, found no violation where the graduation prayer was student led, non-sectarian, and non-proselytizing. 977 F.2d 963 (1992). In an opinion critical of the holding in *Jones*, the Third Circuit held that the Establishment Clause was violated under facts similar to those in the *Jones* case because, while students chose to have prayer at graduation, school officials were still in control of the entire graduation ceremony. *American Civil Liberties Union of New Jersey v. Black Horse Pike Regional Board of Education*, 84 F.3d 1471 (3d Cir. 1996). In a more recent decision from the Fifth Circuit, *Ingebretsen v. Jackson Public School District*, the court again affirmed the propriety of student-led prayer at a high school graduation, although the court struck down an ordinance allowing prayer at scholastic sporting events and lower grade graduation ceremonies. 88 F.3d 274 (1996).

For other cases striking down school ordinances which allowed prayer at school-sponsored sporting events, see *Jager v. Douglas County School District,* 862 F.2d 824 (11th Cir. 1989); *Doe v. Duncanville Independent School District*, 70 F.2d 402 (5th Cir. 1995) (prayer by coach); *Doe v. Aldine Independent School District*, 563 F. Supp. 883 (S.D. Tex. 1982) (school fight song too much like a prayer). For a criticism of the courts' acceptance of student-initiated prayer, see Jessica Smith, *"Student-Initiated" Prayer: Assessing the Newest Initiatives to Return Prayer to the Public Schools*, 18 CAMPBELL L. REV. 303 (1996). For a contrary viewpoint, see Daniel N. McPherson, *Student-Initiated Religious Expression in the Public*

Schools: The Need for a Wider Opening in the Schoolhouse Gate, 30 CREIGHTON L. REV. 393 (1997).

3. Many school children begin the day with the pledge of allegiance to the flag and a moment of silence. While the pledge of allegiance is rarely challenged, it should come as no surprise to learn that the propriety of silent meditation has been disputed numerous times. In *Wallace v. Jaffree,* the Supreme Court held that an Alabama statute calling for a minute of "voluntary prayer" was unconstitutional, as it lacked a "clearly secular purpose." 472 U.S. 38, 38-39 (1985). Using rationale similar to that in *Wallace*, the Third Circuit struck down a statute calling for a "moment of silence" at the beginning of the school day. *May v. Cooperman*, 780 F.2d 240 (1984). Other courts, however, have upheld moment of silence statutes, finding that quiet reflection, even if compulsory, is not the same as prayer. *See, e.g., Brown v. Gwinnett County School District,* 112 F. 3d 1464 (11th Cir. 1997).

4. In 1948, the Supreme Court held in *People ex rel. McCollum v. Board of Education*, 333 U.S. 203, that religious education cannot take place on public school grounds. However, school officials may allow students to leave school grounds during the school day to receive such instructions. *Zorach v. Clauson*, 343 U.S. 306 (1952). In a more recent case, a district court found the religious education release program of a school was constitutional, but the practice of allowing religious instructors to come onto school grounds to "recruit" children was not. *Doe v. Shenandoa County School Board*, 737 F. Supp. 913 (W.D. Va. 1990). Lower courts have also held that Bible classes may be taught as part of the public school curriculum without violating *Schempp*, but only so long as those classes are taught as part of a history or comparative religion regime and thus do not amount to religious instruction. *See, e.g., Wiley v. Franklin*, 497 F. Supp. 390 (D. Tenn. 1980).

Questions

1. As discussed above, the Supreme Court has developed several tests that judges can use to determine whether a law or school policy violates the Establishment Clause. Of these tests—the *Lemon* test, the Apparent Endorsement test, and the Coercive Effect test—which offers a lower court judge the most guidance? Are the three tests distinguishable, or do they, in essence, say the same thing in slightly different ways? Could the Pennsylvania law at issue in the principle case withstand constitutional analysis under any of the three tests?

2. *The Equal Access Act of 1984*

§ 4071. Denial of equal access prohibited

(a) Restriction of limited open forum on basis of religious, political, philosophical, or other speech content prohibited.

It shall be unlawful for any public secondary school which receives Federal financial assistance and which has a limited open forum to deny equal access or a fair opportunity to, or discriminate against, any students who wish to conduct a meeting within that limited open forum on the basis of the religious, political, philosophical, or other content of the speech at such meetings.

(b) "Limited open forum" defined

A public secondary school has a limited open forum whenever such school grants an offering to or opportunity for one or more non-curriculum related student groups to meet on school premises during noninstructional time.

(c) Fair opportunity criteria

Schools shall be deemed to offer a fair opportunity to students who wish to conduct a meeting within its limited open forum if such school uniformly provides that—

(1) the meeting is voluntary and student-initiated;

(2) there is no sponsorship of the meeting by the school . . .;

(3) employees or agents of the school or government are present at religious meetings only in a nonparticipatory capacity;

(4) the meeting does not materially and substantially interfere with the orderly conduct of educational activities within the school; and

(5) nonschool persons may not direct, conduct, control, or regularly attend activities of student groups. . . .

* * *

20 U.S.C.S. § 4071 (Lexis 1997).

What effect does the Equal Access Act of 1989 have on religion in public schools? Does that effect comport with the First Amendment? Under the Act, does a public school have to permit religious groups to meet on school grounds? How could public school officials get around the Act and deny a religious group permission to meet on school grounds?

Would the Act require the principal in the Whitmore High School problem (following *Tinker*, *supra*) to make space available for the proposed gay student group?

Note that the Supreme Court upheld the constitutionality of the Equal Access Act of 1984 in *Board of Education of Westside Community Schools v. Mergens,* 496 U.S. 226 (1990) (allowing noncurriculum-related clubs to meet on school grounds creates a "limited open forum" giving other student-initiated groups a right to equal access).

3. Although the Court's holding is clear that school-sponsored prayer in a public school violates the Establishment Clause of the First Amendment, many public school students continue to start their school day with prayers read over the public address system by school officials or by students under the direction of school officials. Given what you know about public schools and high school students, why do you suppose this practice remains so common?

B. School Suspension

Goss v. Lopez

419 U.S. 565, 95 S. Ct. 729, 42 L. Ed. 2d 725 (1975)

Mr. Justice WHITE delivered the opinion of the Court.

This appeal by various administrators of the Columbus, Ohio, Public School System (CPSS) challenges the judgment of a three-judge federal court, declaring that appellees—various high school students in the CPSS—were denied due process of law contrary to the command of the Fourteenth Amendment in that they were temporarily suspended from their high schools without a hearing either prior to suspension or within a reasonable time thereafter, and enjoining the administrators to remove all references to such suspensions from the students' records.

I

Ohio law, Rev. Code Ann. § 3313.64 (1972), provides for free education to all children between the ages of six and 21. Section 3313.66 of the Code empowers the principal of an Ohio public school to suspend a pupil for misconduct for up to 10 days or to expel him. In either case, he must notify the student's parents within 24 hours and state the reasons for his action. A pupil who is expelled, or his parents, may appeal the decision to the Board of Education and in connection therewith shall be permitted to be heard at the board meeting. The Board may reinstate the pupil following the hearing. No similar procedure is provided in § 3313.66 or any other provision of state law for a suspended student. . . .

The nine . . . appellees, each of whom alleged that he or she had been suspended from public high school in Columbus for up to 10 days without a hearing pursuant to § 3313.66, filed an action under 42 U.S.C. § 1983. . . . The complaint sought a declaration that § 3313.66 was unconstitutional in that it permitted public school administrators to deprive plaintiffs of their rights to an education without a hearing of any kind, in violation of the procedural due process component of the Fourteenth Amendment. It also sought . . . to require [school officials] to remove references to the past suspensions from the records of the students in question.

The proof below established that the suspensions arose out of a period of widespread student unrest in the CPSS during February and March, 1971. Six of the . . . plaintiffs . . . were students at the Marion-Franklin High School and were each suspended for 18 days on account of disruptive or disobedient conduct committed in the presence of the school administrator who ordered the suspension. . . . None was given a hearing to determine the operative facts underlying the suspension, but each, together with his or her parents, was offered the opportunity to attend a conference, subsequent to the effective date of the suspension, to discuss the student's future. [The three remaining plaintiffs were also suspended without a hearing.]

* * *

On the basis of this evidence, the three-judge court declared that plaintiffs were denied due process of law because they were "suspended without hearing prior to suspension or within a reasonable time thereafter," and that Ohio Rev. Code Ann. § 3313.66 (1972) [was] unconstitutional in permitting such suspensions. It was ordered that all references to plaintiffs' suspensions be removed from school files.

Although not imposing upon the Ohio school administrators any particular disciplinary procedures and leaving them "free to adopt regulations providing for fair suspension procedures which are consonant with the educational goals of their schools and reflective of the characteristics of their school and locality," the District Court declared that there were "minimum requirements of notice and a hearing prior to suspension, except in emergency situations." In explication, the court stated that relevant case authority would: (1) permit "[i]mmediate removal of a student whose conduct disrupts the academic atmosphere of the school, endangers fellow students, teachers or school officials, or damages property"; (2) require notice of suspension proceedings to be sent to the student's parents within 24 hours of the decision to conduct them; and (3) require a hearing to be held, with the student present, within 72 hours of his removal. Finally, the court stated that, with respect to the nature of the hearing the relevant cases required that statements in support of the charge be produced, that the student and others be permitted to make statements in defense or mitigation, and that the school need not permit attendance by counsel.

The defendant school administrators have appealed the three-judge court's decision. Because the order below granted plaintiffs' request for an injunction—ordering defendants to expunge their records—this Court has jurisdiction of the appeal pursuant to 28 U.S.C. § 1253. We affirm.

II

[A]ppellants contend that because there is no constitutional right to an education at public expense, the Due Process Clause does not protect against expulsions from the public school system. This position misconceives the nature of the issue. . . . The Fourteenth Amendment forbids the State to deprive any person of life, liberty, or property without due process of law. Protected interests in property are normally . . . created by . . . state statutes or rules entitling the citizen to certain benefits. *Board of Regents v. Roth*, 408 U.S. 564, 577 (1972).

[Here], on the basis of state law, appellees plainly had legitimate claims of entitlement to a public education. . . . It is true that § 3313.66 of the Code permits school principals to suspend students for up to 10 days; but suspensions may not be imposed without any grounds whatsoever. . . . Having chosen to extend the right to an education to people of appellees' class generally, Ohio may not withdraw that right on grounds of misconduct, absent fundamentally fair procedures to determine whether the misconduct has occurred. *Arnett v. Kennedy*, 416 U.S. 134, 164 (1974) (Powell, J., concurring), 171 (White, J., concurring and dissenting), 206 (Marshall, J., dissenting).

Although Ohio may not be constitutionally obligated to establish and maintain a public school system, it has nevertheless done so and has required its children to attend. These young people do not "shed their constitutional rights" at the schoolhouse door. *Tinker v. Des Moines School Dist.*, 393 U.S.

503, 506 (1969). "The Fourteenth Amendment, as now applied to the States, protects the citizen against the State itself and all of its creatures—Boards of Education not excepted." *West Virginia Board of Education v. Barnette,* 319 U.S. 624, 637 (1943). . . . Among other things, the State is constrained to recognize a student's legitimate entitlement to a public education as a property interest which is protected by the Due Process Clause and which may not be taken away for misconduct without adherence to the minimum procedures required by that Clause.

The Due Process Clause also forbids arbitrary deprivations of liberty. "Where a person's good name, reputation, honor, or integrity is at stake because of what the government is doing to him," the minimal requirements of the Clause must be satisfied. *Wisconsin v. Constantineau,* 400 U.S. 433, 437 (1971); *Board of Regents v. Roth, supra,* at 573. School authorities here suspended appellees from school for periods of up to 10 days based on charges of misconduct. If sustained and recorded, those charges could seriously damage the students' standing with their fellow pupils and their teachers as well as interfere with later opportunities for higher education and employment. It is apparent that the claimed right of the State to determine unilaterally and without process whether that misconduct has occurred immediately collides with the requirements of the Constitution.

Appellants proceed to argue that even if there is a right to a public education protected by the Due Process Clause generally, the Clause comes into play only when the state subjects a student to a "severe detriment or grievous loss." The loss of 10 days, it is said, is neither severe nor grievous and the Due Process clause is therefore of no relevance. . . . The Court's view has been that as long as a property deprivation is not *de minimis,* its gravity is irrelevant to the question whether account must be taken of the Due Process Clause. *Sniadach v. Family Finance Corp.,* 395 U.S. 337, 342 (1969) (Harlan, J., concurring); *Boddie v. Connecticut,* 401 U.S. 371, 378-379 (1971); *Board of Regents v. Roth, supra,* at 470 n.8. A 10-day suspension from school is not *de minimis* in our view and may not be imposed in complete disregard of the Due Process Clause. [Neither] the property interest in educational benefits temporarily denied nor the liberty interest in reputation, which is also implicated, is so insubstantial that suspensions may constitutionally be imposed by any procedure the school chooses, no matter how arbitrary.[9]

III

"Once it is determined that due process applies, the question remains what process is due." *Morrissey v. Brewer,* 408 U.S. 471, 481 (1972). We turn to that question, fully realizing as our cases regularly do that the interpretation and application of the Due Process Clause are intensely practical matters and that "[t]he very nature of due process negates any concept of inflexible proce-

---

9 Since the landmark decision of the Court of Appeals for the Fifth Circuit in *Dixon v. Alabama State Board of Education,* 294 F.2d 150, *cert. denied,* 368 U.S. 930 (1961), the lower federal courts have uniformly held the Due Process Clause applicable to decisions made by tax-supported educational institutions to remove a student from the institution long enough for the removal to be classified as an expulsion.

dures universally applicable to every imaginable situation." *Cafeteria Workers v. McElroy,* 367 U.S. 886, 895 (1961). We are also mindful of our own admonition:

> "Judicial interposition in the operation of the public school system of the Nation raises problems requiring care and restraint. . . . By and large, public education in our Nation is committed to the control of state and local authorities." *Epperson v. Arkansas,* 393 U.S. 97, 104 (1968).

There are certain bench marks to guide us, however. *Mullane v. Central Hanover Trust Co.,* 339 U.S. 306 (1950) . . . said that "at a minimum [Due Process] require[s] that deprivation of life, liberty or property by adjudication be preceded by notice and opportunity for hearing appropriate to the nature of the case." *Id.* at 313. "The fundamental requisite of due process of law is the opportunity to be heard." *Grannis v. Ordean,* 234 U.S. 385, 394 (1914), a right that "has little reality or worth unless one is informed that the matter is pending and can chose for himself whether to . . . contest." *Mullane v. Central Hanover Trust Co., supra,* at 314. *See also Armstrong v. Manzo,* 380 U. S. 545, 550 (1965); *Anti-Fascist Committee v. McGrath,* 341 U. S. 123, 168-169 (1951) (Frankfurter, J., concurring). At the very minimum, therefore, students facing suspension and the consequent interference with a protected property interest must be given *some* kind of notice and afforded *some* kind of hearing. . . .

It also appears from our cases that the timing and content of the notice and the nature of the hearing will depend on appropriate accommodation of the competing interests involved. *Cafeteria Workers v. McElroy, supra,* at 895; *Morrissey v. Brewer, supra,* at 481. The student's interest is to avoid unfair or mistaken exclusion from the educational process, with all of its unfortunate consequences. . . . Disciplinarians, although proceeding in utmost good faith, frequently act on the reports and advice of others; and the controlling facts and the nature of the conduct under challenge are often disputed. The risk of error is not at all trivial, and it should be guarded against if that may be done without prohibitive cost or interference with the educational process.

* * *

We do not believe that school authorities must be totally free from notice and hearing requirements if their schools are to operate with acceptable efficiency. Students facing temporary suspension have interests qualifying for protection of the Due Process Clause, and due process requires, in connection with a suspension of 10 days or less, that the student be given oral or written notice of the charges against him and, if he denies them, an explanation of the evidence the authorities have and an opportunity to present his side of the story. . . .

There need be no delay between the time "notice" is given and the time of the hearing. In the great majority of cases the disciplinarian may informally discuss the alleged misconduct with the student minutes after it has occurred. We hold only that in being given an opportunity to explain his version of the facts at this discussion, the student first be told what he is accused of doing and what the basis of the accusation is. . . . Since the hearing may occur almost immediately following the misconduct, it follows that as a general rule notice and hearing should precede removal of the student from school. We agree with the District Court, however, that there are recurring situations in which prior notice and hearing cannot be insisted upon. Students whose presence poses a continuing danger to persons or property or an ongoing threat of disrupting the academic process may be immediately removed from school. In such cases, the necessary notice and rudimentary hearing should follow as soon as practicable, as the District Court indicated.

* * *

We stop short of construing the Due Process Clause to require, countrywide, that hearings in connection with short suspensions must afford the student the opportunity to secure counsel, to confront and cross-examine witnesses supporting the charge, or to call his own witnesses to verify his version of the incident. . . . On the other hand, requiring effective notice and informal hearing permitting the student to give his version of the events will provide a meaningful hedge against erroneous action. . . .

* * *

We should also make it clear that we have addressed ourselves solely to the short suspension, not exceeding 10 days. Longer suspensions or expulsions for the remainder of the school term, or permanently may require more formal procedures. Nor do we put aside the possibility that in unusual situations, although involving only a short suspension, something more than the rudimentary procedures will be required.

IV

The District Court found each of the suspensions involved here to have occurred without a hearing, either before or after the suspension, and that each suspension was therefore invalid and the statute unconstitutional insofar as it permits such suspensions without notice or hearing. Accordingly, the judgment is affirmed.

Mr. Justice POWELL, with whom THE CHIEF JUSTICE, Mr. Justice BLACKMUN, and Mr. Justice REHNQUIST join, dissenting.

* * *

The Court's decision rests on the premise that, under Ohio law, education is a property interest protected by the Fourteenth Amendment's Due Process Clause and therefore that any suspension requires notice and a hearing. In my view, a student's interest in education is not infringed by a suspension within the limited period prescribed by Ohio law. Moreover, to the extent that there may be some arguable infringement, it is too speculative, transitory, and insubstantial to justify imposition of a *constitutional* rule.

. . . The Court . . . disregards the basic structure of Ohio law in posturing this case as if Ohio had conferred an unqualified right to education, thereby compelling the school authorities to conform to due process procedures in imposing the most routine discipline. But however one may define the entitlement to education provided by Ohio law, I would conclude that a deprivation of not more than 10 days' suspension from school, imposed as a routine disciplinary measure, does not assume constitutional dimensions. . . .

The Ohio suspension statute allows no serious or significant infringement of education. It authorizes only a maximum suspension of eight school days, less than 5% of the normal 180-day school year. Absences of such limited duration will rarely affect a pupil's opportunity to learn or his scholastic performance. . . .

* * *

II

In prior decisions, this Court has explicitly recognized that school authorities must have broad discretionary authority in the daily operation of public schools. This includes wide latitude with respect to maintaining discipline and good order. Addressing this point specifically, the Court stated in *Tinker v. Des Moines School Dist.,* 393 U.S. 503, 507 (1969):

> [T]he Court has repeatedly emphasized the need for affirming the comprehensive authority of the States and of school officials, consistent with fundamental constitutional safeguards, to prescribe and control conduct in the schools.

Such an approach properly recognizes the unique nature of public education and the correspondingly limited role of the judiciary in its supervision. In *Epperson v. Arkansas,* 393 U. S. 97, 104 (1968), the Court stated:

> By and large, public education in our Nation is committed to the control of state and local authorities. Courts do not and cannot intervene in the resolution of conflicts which arise in the daily operation of school systems and which do not directly and sharply implicate basic constitutional values.

The Court today turns its back on these precedents. It can hardly seriously be claimed that a school principal's decision to suspend a pupil for a single day would "directly and sharply implicate basic constitutional values." *Ibid.*

Moreover, the Court ignores the experience of mankind, as well as the long history of our law, recognizing that there *are* differences which must be accommodated in determining the rights and duties of children as compared with those of adults. Examples of this distinction abound in our law: in contracts, in torts, in criminal law and procedure, in criminal sanctions and rehabilitation, and in the right to vote and to hold office. Until today, and except in the special context of the First Amendment issue in *Tinker*, the educational rights of children and teenagers in the elementary and secondary schools have not been analogized to the rights of adults or to those accorded college students. Even with respect to the First Amendment, the rights of children have not been regarded as "co-extensive with those of adults." *Tinker, supra,* at 515 (Stewart, J., concurring).

* * *

IV

Not so long ago, state deprivations of the most significant forms of state largesse were not thought to require due process protection on the ground that the deprivation resulted only in the loss of a state-provided "benefit." In recent years the Court, wisely in my view, has rejected the "wooden distinction between 'rights' and 'privileges,'" *Board of Regents v. Roth,* 408 U.S. 564, 571 (1972), and looked instead to the significance of the state-created or state-enforced right and to the substantiality of the alleged deprivation. Today's opinion appears to abandon this reasonable approach by holding in effect that government infringement of any interest to which a person is entitled, no matter what the interest or how inconsequential the infringement, requires *constitutional* protection. As it is difficult to think of any less consequential infringement than suspension of a junior high school student for a single day, it is equally difficult to perceive any principled limit to the new reach of procedural due process.

Notes

1. As indicated in the principal case, school officials must notify a student (and often her parents) before considering a suspension or expulsion of the student. *See also Armstead v. Lima City Board of Education*, 600 N.E.2d 1085 (Ohio Ct. App. 1991) (student may request public hearing). Courts generally require that the notice include the specific ground or grounds for action. *See, e.g., Dixon v. Alabama State Board of Education,* 294 F.2d 150 (5th Cir. 1961). This requirement may also direct school officials to provide the student access to evidence, such as records or reports, which the officials may rely on at the suspension hearing. *See Dixon, supra; Gonzales v. McEuen,* 435 F. Supp. 460 (C.D. Cal. 1977) (deficient notice corrected by school district). At least one circuit, however, has held that notice is not required if the school's action involves only suspending the student from extracurricular activities. *See Palmer v. Merluzzi,* 868 F.2d 90 (3d Cir. 1989).

2. When school officials are considering suspending or expelling a student, the student must be afforded the opportunity to be heard. This includes the opportunity for the student to present evidence on his own behalf. *See, e.g., Charles S. v. Board of Education, San Francisco Unified School District,* 97 Cal. Rptr. 422 (Ct. App. 1971); *Richie v. Board of Education of Lead Hill School District*, 933 S.W.2d 375 (Ark. 1996). Note, however, that the court in *Gonzales, supra*, held that the student or her parents may waive the student's right to a hearing.

The Court in *Goss* declined to extend the rights of students to include the right to cross-examine adverse witnesses at a suspension hearing. Similarly, most lower courts to consider the issue have held that students enjoy no right to examine adverse witnesses. *See, e.g., Newsome v. Batavia Local School District,* 842 F.2d 920 (6th Cir. 1988); *Coplin v. Conejo Valley Unified School District*, 779 F.2d 260 (5th Cir. 1985). At least one lower court, however, has held that a student might have a right to cross-examine adverse witnesses where the hearing may result in the student's expulsion. *See Tibbs v. Board of Education of Franklin Town-*

ship, 276 A.2d 165 (N.J. Super. 1971). Such a holding may be complicated by the fact that, unlike courts, school boards generally do not have the power to subpoena witnesses. Furthermore, students generally do not enjoy the right to know the identity of their accusers. *See Coplin, supra; Newsome, supra.*

An issue arising less frequently is the right of a student to be represented by counsel at a suspension or expulsion hearing, or at an appeal therefrom. Courts generally do not require legal representation at a suspension hearing. *See, e.g., Coplin, supra; Doe v. Superintendent of Schools of Worcester*, 653 N.E.2d 1088 (Mass. 1995); *Trujillo v. Taos Municipal Schools,* No. CIV-94-1350, 1995 WL 868603 at *1 (D.N.M. Aug. 10, 1995). A few courts recognize the right to counsel if the hearing could result in the student's expulsion. *See, e.g., Trujillo, supra.* Other courts recognize the right to counsel, not at the original hearing, but only where the student appeals the school board's ruling. *See, e.g., Doe v. Superintendent of Schools of Worcester, supra.* Those courts that extend the right to counsel to students generally do so under state law. *See, e.g., Draper v. Columbus Public Schools,* 760 F. Supp. 131 (S.D. Ohio 1991) (right to counsel arose, not from *Goss*, but from local law); *John A. v. San Bernadino City Unified School District,* 187 Cal. Rptr. 472 (Cal. 1983). Note that the *John A.* court held that the student's right to counsel did not include the right to the appointment of counsel for an indigent student.

3. The information available to school officials during a suspension hearing is often secondhand. Decisions are routinely based on written reports, prepared by teachers who witnessed the alleged wrong or by school officials who interviewed student and faculty witnesses. As discussed above, a student at such a hearing generally does not have the right to confront her accusers. While such laxity would bring many evidence scholars immediately to their feet, the majority of courts find no fault in school suspensions based on hearsay evidence. These courts generally rely, as did the Supreme Court in *Goss,* upon the fundamental differences between a school suspension hearing and a trial. If school officials are to do their job, it is reasoned, they must be able to act swiftly and by their own best judgment, free from many of the formalities of the legal system. Many courts agree with the Fifth Circuit, which said in *Boykins v. Fairfield Board of Education:* "We decline to place upon a board of laymen the duty of observing and applying the . . . rules of evidence." 492 F.2d 697, 701 (1974). *See also Racine Unified School Districts v. Thompson*, 321 N.W.2d 334 (Wis. Ct. App. 1982); *Dornes v. Lindsey*, 18 F. Supp. 2d 1086 (C.D. Cal. 1998); *West v. Derby Unified School District No. 260*, 23 F. Supp. 2d 1223 (D. Kan. 1998) (rules of evidence apply, but written statements of other students fall under hearsay exception). For a contrary holding, see *Colquitt v. Rich Townhip High School District No. 227,* 699 N.E.2d 1109 (Ill. App. Ct. 1998) (student denied due process of law where hearsay used to expel without right to cross-examine).

Questions

1. Assuming that the Court was correct in holding that a school student facing a possible suspension is entitled to some level of due process protection, did the Court go too far in extending that protection to include minor suspensions? Did the Court go far enough? As between the majority and the dissent, who has the better argument where the maximum penalty the student could face is a one-day suspension? Is a short suspension *de minimis*? In whose view?

2. Is "notice" given immediately before a hearing adequate and timely? If not, how much notice should a student receive? Should the student at least be given time to contact her parents? Should the parents have the right to be present at a suspension hearing?

3. Should a student be suspended from school on hearsay evidence with no right of cross-examination? Would allowing a student to confront his accusers make the process fairer, or would it make disciplinary hearings too cumbersome?

C. Corporal Punishment

Ingraham v. Wright

430 U.S. 651, 97 S. Ct. 1401, 51 L. Ed. 2d 711 (1977)

Mr. Justice POWELL delivered the opinion of the Court.

This case presents questions concerning the use of corporal punishment in public schools: first, whether the paddling of students as a means of maintaining school discipline constitutes cruel and unusual punishment in violation of the Eighth Amendment; and, second, to the extent that paddling is constitutionally permissible, whether the Due Process Clause of the Fourteenth Amendment requires prior notice and an opportunity to be heard.

I

Petitioners James Ingraham and Roosevelt Andrews filed the complaint in this case on January 7, 1971, in the United States District Court for the Southern District of Florida. . . . The complaint contained three counts, each alleging a separate cause of action for deprivation of constitutional rights, under 42 U.S.C. §§ 1981-1988. Counts one and two were individual actions for damages by Ingraham and Andrews based on paddling incidents that allegedly occurred in October, 1970, at Drew Junior High School. Count three was a class action for declaratory and injunctive relief filed on behalf of all students in the Dade County schools. . . .

* * *

In the 1970-1971 school year, many of the 237 schools in Dade County used corporal punishment as a means of maintaining discipline pursuant to Florida legislation and a local School Board regulation. The statute . . . authorized limited corporal punishment by negative inference, proscribing punishment which was "degrading or unduly severe" or which was inflicted without prior consultation with the principal or the teacher in charge of the school. Fla. Stat. Ann. § 232.27 (1961). The regulation . . . contained explicit directions and limitations. The authorized punishment consisted of paddling the recalcitrant student on the buttocks. . . . School authorities viewed corporal punishment as a less drastic means of discipline than suspension or expulsion.

Petitioners focused on Drew Junior High School, the school in which both Ingraham and Andrews were enrolled in the fall of 1970. The evidence, consisting mainly of the testimony of 16 students, suggests that the regime at Drew was exceptionally harsh. . . .

The District Court made no findings on the credibility of the students' testimony. Rather, assuming their testimony to be credible, the court found no constitutional basis for relief. With respect to count three, the class action, the court concluded that the punishment authorized and practiced generally in the county schools violated no constitutional right. With respect to counts one and two, the individual damages actions, the court concluded that while corporal punishment could in some cases violate the Eighth Amendment, in this case a jury could not lawfully find "the elements of severity, arbitrary infliction, unacceptability in terms of contemporary standards, or gross disproportion which are necessary to bring 'punishment' to the constitutional level of 'cruel and unusual punishment.'"

[T]he Court of Appeals . . . affirmed the judgment of the District Court. 525 F.2d 909 (1976). The full court held that the Due Process Clause did not require notice or an opportunity to be heard. . . . The court also rejected the petitioners' substantive contentions. The Eighth Amendment, in the court's view, was simply inapplicable to corporal punishment in public schools. . . . Nor was there any substantive violation of the Due Process Clause. The court noted that "[p]addling of recalcitrant children has long been an accepted method of promoting good behavior and instilling notions of responsibility and decorum into the mischievous heads of school children." *Id.* at 917. . . .

We granted certiorari, limited to the questions of cruel and unusual punishment and procedural due process.

II

In addressing the scope of the Eighth Amendment's prohibition on cruel and unusual punishment, this Court has found it useful to refer to "[t]raditional common-law concepts," *Powell v. Texas,* 392 U.S. 514, 535 (1968) (plurality opinion), and to the "attitude[s] which our society has traditionally taken." *Id.* at 531. So, too, in defining the requirements of procedural due process under the Fifth and Fourteenth Amendments, the Court has been attuned to what "has always been the law of the land," *United States v. Barnett,* 376 U.S. 681, 692 (1964), and to "traditional ideas of fair procedure." *Greene v. McElroy,* 360 U.S. 474, 508 (1959). . . .

* * *

At common law a single principle has governed the use of corporal punishment since before the American Revolution: Teachers may impose reasonable but not excessive force to discipline a child. . . .[19] The prevalent rule in this country today privileges such force as a teacher or administrator "reasonably believes to be necessary for [the child's] proper control, training, or education."

---

[19] *See* 1 F. HARPER & F. JAMES, LAW OF TORTS § 3.20, pp. 288-292 (1956); Proehl, *Tort Liability of Teachers,* 12 VAND. L. REV. 723, 734-738 (1959); W. PROSSER, LAW OF TORTS 136-137 (4th ed. 1971).

RESTATEMENT (SECOND) OF TORTS § 147 (2) (1965); *see id.,* § 153 (2). To the extent that the force is excessive or unreasonable, the educator in virtually all States is subject to possible civil and criminal liability.

[All] of the circumstances are to be taken into account in determining whether the punishment is reasonable in a particular case. Among the most important considerations are the seriousness of the offense, the attitude and past behavior of the child, the nature and severity of the punishment, the age and strength of the child, and the availability of less severe but equally effective means of discipline. RESTATEMENT (SECOND) OF TORTS § 150, comments *c-e*, p. 268 (1965).

Of the 23 States that have addressed the problem through legislation, 21 have authorized the moderate use of corporal punishment in public schools. . . . Only two States, Massachusetts and New Jersey, have prohibited all corporal punishment in their public schools. Where the legislatures have not acted, the state courts have uniformly preserved the common-law rule permitting teachers to use reasonable force in disciplining children in their charge.

Against this background of historical and contemporary approval of reasonable corporal punishment, we turn to the constitutional questions before us.

III

The Eighth Amendment provides: "Excessive bail shall not be required, nor excessive fines imposed, nor cruel and unusual punishments inflicted." Bail, fines, and punishment traditionally have been associated with the criminal process, and by subjecting the three to parallel limitations the text of the Amendment suggests an intention to limit the power of those entrusted with the criminal-law function of government. An examination of the history of the Amendment and the decisions of this Court construing the proscription against cruel and unusual punishment confirms that it was designed to protect those convicted of crimes. We adhere to this long-standing limitation and hold that the Eighth Amendment does not apply to the paddling of children as a means of maintaining discipline in public schools.

* * *

Petitioners acknowledge that the original design of the Cruel and Unusual Punishments Clause was to limit criminal punishments, but urge nonetheless that the prohibition should be extended to ban the paddling of schoolchildren. [P]etitioners contend that extension of the prohibition against cruel punishments is necessary lest we afford greater protection to criminals than to schoolchildren. It would be anomalous, they say, if schoolchildren could be beaten without constitutional redress, while hardened criminals suffering the same beatings at the hands of their jailers might have a valid claim under the Eighth Amendment. Whatever force this logic may have in other settings, we find it an inadequate basis for wrenching the Eighth Amendment from its historical context and extending it to traditional disciplinary practices in the public schools.

* * *

The openness of the public school and its supervision by the community afford significant safeguards against the kinds of abuses from which the Eighth Amendment protects the prisoner. . . . Public school teachers and administrators are privileged at common law to inflict only such corporal punishment as is reasonably necessary for the proper education and discipline of the child; any punishment going beyond the privilege may result in both civil and criminal liability. As long as the schools are open to public scrutiny, there is no reason to believe that the common-law constraints will not effectively remedy and deter excesses such as those alleged in this case.

We conclude that when public school teachers or administrators impose disciplinary corporal punishment, the Eight Amendment is inapplicable. The pertinent constitutional question is whether the imposition is consonant with the requirements of due process.

IV

The Fourteenth Amendment prohibits any state deprivation of life, liberty or property without due process of law. Application of this prohibition requires the familiar two-stage analysis: We must first ask whether the asserted individual interests are encompassed within the Fourteenth Amendment's protection of "life, liberty or property"; if protected interests are implicated, we then must decide what procedures constitute "due process of law." *Morrissey v. Brewer*, 408 U.S. 471, 481 (1972); *Board of Regents v. Roth*, 408 U.S. 564, 569-572 (1972). *See* Friendly, *Some Kind of Hearing*, 123 U. PA. L. REV. 1267 (1975). Following that analysis here, we find that corporal punishment in public schools implicates a constitutionally protected liberty interest, but we hold that the traditional common-law remedies are fully adequate to afford due process.

A

"[T]he range of interests protected by procedural due process is not infinite." *Board of Regents v. Roth, supra*, at 570. . . . Due process is required only when a decision of the State implicates an interest within the protection of the Fourteenth Amendment. And "to determine whether due process requirements apply in the first place, we must look not to the 'weight' but to the *nature* of the interest at stake." *Roth, supra,* at 570-571.

The Due Process Clause of the Fifth Amendment, later incorporated into the Fourteenth, was intended to give Americans at least the protection against governmental power that they had enjoyed as Englishmen against the power of the Crown. The liberty preserved from deprivation without the process included the right "generally to enjoy those privileges long recognized at common law as essential to the orderly pursuit of happiness by free men." *Meyer v. Nebraska*, 262 U.S. 390, 399 (1923). . . .

While the contours of this historic liberty interest in the context of our federal system of government have not been defined precisely, they always have been thought to encompass freedom from bodily restraint and punishment. It is fundamental that the state cannot hold and physically punish an individual except in accordance with due process of law.

This constitutionally protected liberty interest is at stake in this case. There is, of course, a *de minimis* level of imposition with which the Constitution is not concerned. But at least where school authorities, acting under color of state law, deliberately decide to punish a child for misconduct by restraining the child and inflicting appreciable physical pain, we hold that Fourteenth Amendment liberty interests are implicated.

B

"[T]he question remains what process is due." *Morrissey v. Brewer, supra,* at 481. . . . .

> "[D]ue process," unlike some legal rules, is not a technical conception with a fixed content unrelated to time, place and circumstances. . . . Representing a profound attitude of fairness . . . "due process" is compounded of history, reason, the past course of decisions, and stout confidence in the strength of the democratic faith which we profess. . . .

Anti-Fascist Comm. v. McGrath, 341 U.S. 123, 162-163 (1951) (Frankfurter, J., concurring).

Whether in this case the common-law remedies for excessive corporal punishment constitute due process of law must turn on an analysis of the competing interests at stake, viewed against the background of "history, reason, [and] the past course of decisions." The analysis requires consideration of three distinct factors: "First, the private interest that will be affected . . .; second, the risk of an erroneous deprivation of such interest . . . and the probable value, if any, of additional or substitute procedural safeguards; and finally, the [State] interest, including the function involved and the fiscal and administrative burdens that the additional or substitute procedural requirement would entail." *Mathews v. Eldridge*, 424 U.S. 319, 335 (1976).

1

Because it is rooted in history, the child's liberty interest in avoiding corporal punishment while in the care of public school authorities is subject to historical limitations. Under the common law, an invasion of personal security gave rise to a right to recover damages in a subsequent judicial proceeding. 3 W. BLACKSTONE, COMMENTARIES *120-121. But the right of recovery was qualified by the concept of justification. Thus, there could be no recovery against a teacher who gave only "moderate correction" to a child. *Id.* at *120. To the extent that the force used was reasonable in light of its purpose, it was not wrongful, but rather "justifiable or lawful." *Ibid.*

The concept that reasonable corporal punishment in school is justifiable continues to be recognized in the laws of most States. It represents "the balance struck by this country," *Poe v. Ullman*, 367 U.S. 497, 542 (1961) (Harlan, J., dissenting), between the child's interest in personal security and the traditional view that some limited corporal punishment may be necessary in the course of a child's education. Under that longstanding accommodation of interests, there can be no deprivation of substantive rights as long as disciplinary corporal punishment is within the limits of the common-law privilege.

This is not to say that the child's interest in procedural safeguards is insubstantial. The school disciplinary process is not "a totally accurate, unerring process, never mistaken and never unfair. . . ." *Goss v. Lopez,* 419 U.S. 565, 579-580 (1975). In any deliberate infliction of corporal punishment on a child who is restrained for that purpose, there is some risk that the intrusion on the child's liberty will be unjustified and therefore unlawful. In these circumstances the child has a strong interest in procedural safeguards that minimize the risk of wrongful punishment and provide for the resolution of disputed questions of justification.

We turn now to a consideration of the safeguards that are available under applicable Florida law.

2

Florida has continued to recognize, and indeed has strengthened by statute, the common-law right of a child not to be subjected to excessive corporal punishment in school. Under Florida law the teacher and principal of the school decide in the first instance whether corporal punishment is reasonably necessary under the circumstances in order to discipline a child who has misbehaved. . . . If the punishment inflicted is later found to have been excessive—not reasonably believed at the time to be necessary for the child's discipline or training—the school authorities inflicting it may be held liable in damages to the child and, if malice is shown, they may be subject to criminal penalties.

[The] uncontradicted evidence suggests that corporal punishment in the Dade County schools was, "[w]ith the exception of a few cases, . . . unremarkable in physical severity." Moreover, because paddlings are usually inflicted in response to conduct directly observed by teachers in their presence, the risk that a child will be paddled without cause is typically insignificant. In the ordinary case, a disciplinary paddling neither threatens seriously to violate any substantive rights nor condemns the child "to suffer grievous loss of any kind." *Anti-Fascist Comm. v. McGrath,* 341 U.S. at 168 (Frankfurter, J., concurring).

* * *

It still may be argued, of course, that the child's liberty interest would be better protected if the common-law remedies were supplemented by the administrative safeguards of prior notice and a hearing. We have found frequently that some kind of prior hearing is necessary to guard against arbitrary impositions on interests protected by the Fourteenth Amendment. But where the State has preserved what "has always been the law of the land," *United States v. Barnett,* 376 U.S. 681, 692 (1964), the case for administrative safeguards is significantly less compelling.

* * *

3

But even if the need for advance procedural safeguards were clear, the question would remain whether the incremental benefit could justify the cost. Acceptance of petitioners' claims would work a transformation in the law governing corporal punishment in Florida and most other States. Given the impracticability of formulating a rule of procedural due process that varies with the severity of the particular imposition, the prior hearing petitioners seek would have to precede *any* paddling, however moderate or trivial.

Such a universal constitutional requirement would significantly burden the use of corporal punishment as a disciplinary measure. Hearings—even informal hearings—require time, personnel, and a diversion of attention from normal school pursuits. School authorities may well choose to abandon corporal punishment rather than incur the burdens of complying with the procedural requirements. Teachers, properly concerned with maintaining authority in the classroom, may well prefer to rely on other disciplinary measures—which they may view as less effective—rather than confront the possible disruption that prior notice and a hearing may entail. . . .

* * *

"At some point the benefit of an additional safeguard to the individual affected . . . and to society in terms of increased assurance that the action is just, may be outweighed by the cost." *Mathews v. Eldridge,* 424 U.S. at 348. We think that point has been reached in this case. In view of the low incidence of abuse, the openness of our schools, and the common-law safeguards that already exist, the risk of error that may result in violation of a schoolchild's substantive rights can only be regarded as minimal. Imposing additional administrative safeguards as a constitutional requirement might reduce that risk marginally, but would also entail a significant intrusion into an area of primary educational responsibility. We conclude that the Due Process Clause does not require notice and a hearing prior to the imposition of corporal punishment in the public schools, as that practice is authorized and limited by the common law.

V

Petitioners cannot prevail on either of the theories before us in this case. The Eighth Amendment's prohibition against cruel and unusual punishment is inapplicable to school paddlings, and the Fourteenth Amendment's requirement of procedural due process is satisfied by Florida's preservation of common-law constraints and remedies. We therefore agree with the Court of Appeals that petitioners' evidence affords no basis for injunctive relief, and that petitioners cannot recover damages on the basis of any Eighth Amendment or procedural due process violation.

Affirmed.

Mr. Justice WHITE, with whom Mr. Justice BRENNAN, Mr. Justice MARSHALL, and Mr. Justice STEVENS join, dissenting.

Today the Court holds that corporal punishment in public schools, no matter how severe, can never be the subject of protections afforded by the Eighth Amendment. It also holds that students in the public school systems are not constitutionally entitled to a hearing of any sort before beatings can be inflicted on them. Because I believe that these holdings are inconsistent with the prior decisions of this Court and are contrary to a reasoned analysis of the constitutional provisions involved, I respectfully dissent.

* * *

[T]he majority holds that the Eighth Amendment "was designed to protect [only] those convicted of crimes. . . ." Certainly, the fact that the Framers did not choose to insert the word "criminal" into the language of the Eighth Amendment is strong evidence that the Amendment was designed to prohibit all inhumane or barbaric punishments, no matter what the nature of the offense for which the punishment is imposed.

No one can deny that spanking of schoolchildren is "punishment" under any reasonable reading of the word. . . . Like other forms of punishment, spanking of schoolchildren involves an institutionalized response to the violation of some official rule or regulation proscribing certain conduct and is imposed for the purpose of rehabilitating the offender, deterring the offender and others like him from committing the violation in the future, and inflicting some measure of social retribution for the harm that has been done.

* * *

In fact, as the Court recognizes, the Eighth Amendment has never been confined to criminal punishments. Nevertheless, the majority adheres to its view that any protections afforded by the Eighth Amendment must have something to do with criminals, and it would therefore confine any exceptions to its general rule that only criminal punishments are covered by the Eighth Amendment to abuses inflicted on prisoners. Thus, if a prisoner is beaten mercilessly for a breach of discipline, he is entitled to the protection of the Eighth Amendment, while a schoolchild who commits the same breach of discipline and is similarly beaten is simply not covered. . . .

[The dissenting opinion of Justice STEVENS is omitted.]

Notes

1. School officials enjoy wide discretion in disciplining students, and courts generally do not like to involve themselves in the day-to-day operation of school systems. This is due in part to the continuing recognition that teachers and other school officials act *in loco parentis* toward school children. The Appellate Court of Illinois explained the court's unwillingness to supervise school officials in *Donaldson v. Board of Education for Danville School District No. 118.* The court said:

> School discipline is an area which courts enter with great hesitation and reluctance, and rightly so. School officials are trained and paid to determine what form of punishment best addresses a particular student's transgression. They are in a better position than is a black-robed judge to decide what to do with a disobedient child at school. . . . Because of their expertise and their closeness to the situation and because we do not want them to fear court challenges to their every act, school officials are given wide discretion in their disciplinary actions.

424 N.E.2d 737, 738-39 (Ill. App. Ct. 1981).

As recalcitrant students know all too well, many schools still authorize corporal punishment. *See, e.g., Hassan v. Lubbock Independent School District,* 55 F.3d 1075 (5th Cir. 1995); *Sims v. Waln,* 536 F.2d 686 (6th Cir. 1976). However, the fear of litigation has led some districts to abandon the practice. A number of schools that allow corporal punishment require prior written consent from parents before a student may be paddled. *See* Lisa A. Brown & Christopher Gilbert, *Understanding the Constitutional Rights of School Children,* 34 HOUS. LAW. 40, 41 (1997).

2. The Court in *Ingraham* held that corporal punishment of school children does not violate the Eighth Amendment. Lower courts, however, have found other violations, especially where the punishment goes beyond the traditional paddling. For example, the Tenth Circuit, in *Garcia v. Miera,* found that the excessive punishment of a student violated the student's due process rights. 817 F.2d 650 (10th Cir. 1987). For similar reasons, the court in *Metzger v. Osbeck*, reversed a district court order granting summary judgment to a gym teacher whose discipline of a student resulted in a broken nose and other injuries to the student. 841 F.2d 518 (3d Cir. 1988). Excessive punishment may also rise to the level of child abuse. *See, e.g., Arkansas Department of Human Services v. Caldwell*, 832 S.W.2d 510 (Ark. Ct. App. 1992).

In determining whether a specific instance of corporal punishment is acceptable in the context of school discipline, courts generally focus on the reasonableness of the punishment. Paddling, for example, is widely accepted as reasonable in most circumstances. *See, e.g., Ingraham, supra*; *Woodard v. Los Fresnos Independent School District*, 732 F.2d 1243 (5th Cir. 1984); *Sims v. Waln, supra; Wise v. Pea Ridge School District,* 855 F.2d 560 (8th Cir. 1988) (summary judgment for defendant teacher where student received two "swats"). Other forms of discipline, on the other hand, may rise to the level of unreasonable, especially where the student is injured. *See, e.g., Metzger v. Osbeck, supra; Hogenson v. Willams,* 542 S.W.2d 456 (Tex. Civ. App. 1976) (summary judgment denied where student hospitalized); *P.B. v. Koch,* 96 F.2d 1298 (9th Cir. 1996) (principal not immune from § 1983 claim where principal allegedly punched, slapped, and choked students).

3. Excessive punishment may expose teachers or other officials to civil and criminal liability. As discussed above, courts focus on the reasonableness of the punishment. If the punishment is found to be reasonable, the teacher will not be held liable. *See also Williams v. Colton,* 346 So. 2d 1039 (Fla. Ct. App. 1977). In determining the reasonableness of the punishment administered, courts consider many factors. For example, the court in *LeBay v. Jenkins,* 381 So. 2d 1290 (La. Ct. App. 1980), examined the following: the age and physical condition of the student; the seriousness of the misconduct; the type and severity of the punishment; the attitude and past behavior of the student; and the availability of other, less severe means of punishment. *See also People ex rel. Hogan v. Newton,* 56 N.Y.S.2d 779 (N.Y. 1945).

Questions

1. Should school officials be allowed to administer corporal punishment? Should parental permission be required before a school official spanks a student? If the parent refuses such permission, how should the student be disciplined?

2. Assume that a school board decides that the potential liabilities are too great if school officials are allowed to physically punish students. Should a parent, notified of her child's misconduct, be permitted to come to the school and paddle the student? Could the school district be held liable if the parent administers an unreasonably severe punishment?

3. The Court in *Ingraham* worried that requiring a hearing before a child could be paddled would tie the hands of school officials and unduly interfere with the operation of schools. Contrast this with the decision in *Goss v. Lopez, supra,* in Section B, where the Court held that a pre-suspension hearing simply required that the child be told what he was accused of doing and given an opportunity "to explain his version of the facts." Would a *Goss*-style hearing before school officials paddle a child unduly interfere with the efficient operation of the school? Which case has the more persuasive reasoning? Are the two cases consistent with each other? Is a one-day suspension more of an intrusion into the student's rights than a school-administered paddling?

4. Many people believe in the biblical principal that to "spare the rod" is to "spoil the child" and that the increasing violence among our nation's youth is attributable, at least in part, to a decline in the use of corporal punishment. Do you agree? Are there other, better ways to correct children than spanking? Should spanking ever be used as a last resort?

For several divergent perspectives on this issue, see Noel M. Johnston, *The Chicago Public Schools and Its Violent Students: How Can the Law Protect Teachers?,* 48 DEPAUL L. REV. 907 (1999); Richard Garner, *Fundamentally Speaking: Application of Ohio's Domestic Violence Laws in Parental Discipline Cases—A Parental Perspective,* 30 U. TOL. L. REV. 1 (1998); Susan H. Bitensky, *The Child's Right to Humane Discipline Under the U.N. Convention on the Rights of the Child: The Mandate Against All Corporal Punishment of Children,* 4 LOY. POVERTY L.J. 47 (1998).

Problem

As the only attorney on the school board, you are often consulted by other board members regarding the legality of proposed rules. Several members of the board have recently become concerned about the district's policy allowing corporal punishment in the district's grade schools. While most members do not wish to abandon the policy, they do want to insure that school officials understand when to resort to corporal punishment and how paddling should be administered, and to insulate the school district and school officials from possible liability arising from the use of such punishment. The board members have come to you for advice on the matter.

Draft a new rule for the district that will permit corporal punishment and will, at the same time, give adequate guidance to school principals and teachers. The rule should, of course, be written to withstand constitutional challenges. In drafting the new rule, consider the following questions. Who should administer the paddling? Should the person administering the punishment be of the same sex as the child being punished? Would you recommend the presence of witnesses? Should the parents be notified before the child is paddled? Should parental permission be required in advance of administering corporal punishment? Would you permit the parents to be present, or to administer the paddling themselves?

D. Fourth Amendment: Search and Seizure

New Jersey v. T.L.O.

469 U.S. 325, 105 S. Ct. 733, 83 L. Ed. 2d 720 (1985)

Justice WHITE delivered the opinion of the Court.

We granted certiorari in this case to examine the appropriateness of the exclusionary rule as a remedy for searches carried out in violation of the Fourth Amendment by public school authorities. Our consideration of the proper application of the Fourth Amendment to the public schools, however, has led us to conclude that the search that gave rise to the case now before us did not violate the Fourth Amendment. Accordingly, we here address only the questions of the proper standard for assessing the legality of searches conducted by public school officials and the application of that standard to the facts of this case.

I

On March 7, 1980, a teacher at Piscataway High School in Middlesex County, N.J., discovered two girls smoking in a lavatory. One of the two girls was the respondent T.L.O., who at that time was a 14-year-old high school freshman. Because smoking in the lavatory was a violation of a school rule, the teacher took the two girls to the Principal's Office, where they met with Assistant Vice Principal Theodore Choplick. . . . T.L.O. denied that she had been smoking in the lavatory and claimed that she did not smoke at all.

Mr. Choplick asked T.L.O. to come into his private office and demanded to see her purse. Opening the purse, he found a pack of cigarettes. . . . As he reached into the purse for the cigarettes, Mr. Choplick also noticed a package of cigarette rolling papers. . . . Suspecting that a closer examination of the purse might yield further evidence of drug use, Mr. Choplick proceeded to search the purse thoroughly. The search revealed a small amount of marijuana, a pipe, a number of empty plastic bags, a substantial quantity of money in one-dollar bills, an index card that appeared to be a list of students who owed T.L.O. money, and two letters that implicated T.L.O. in marijuana dealing.

Mr. Choplick notified T.L.O.'s mother and the police, and turned the evidence of drug dealing over to the police. . . . On the basis of . . . the evidence seized by Mr. Choplick, the State brought delinquency charges against T.L.O. in the Juvenile and Domestic Relations Court of Middlesex County. Contending that Mr. Choplick's search of her purse violated the Fourth Amendment, T.L.O.

moved to suppress the evidence found in her purse. . . . The Juvenile Court denied the motion to suppress. Although the court concluded that the Fourth Amendment did apply to searches carried out by school officials, it held that . . . the search conducted by Mr. Choplick was a reasonable one. The initial decision to open the purse was justified by Mr. Choplick's well-founded suspicion that T.L.O. had violated the rule forbidding smoking in the lavatory. Once the purse was open, evidence of marijuana violations was in plain view, and Mr. Choplick was entitled to conduct a thorough search to determine the nature and extent of T.L.O.'s drug-related activities. Having denied the motion to suppress, the court on March 23, 1981, found T.L.O. to be a delinquent and on January 8, 1982, sentenced her to a year's probation.

On appeal from the final judgment of the Juvenile Court, a divided Appellate Division affirmed the trial court's finding that there had been no Fourth Amendment violation. . . . T.L.O. appealed the Fourth Amendment ruling, and the Supreme Court of New Jersey reversed the judgment of the Appellate Division and ordered the suppression of the evidence found in T.L.O.'s purse. *State ex rel. T.L.O.*, 94 N.J. 331, 463 A.2d 934 (1983).

The New Jersey Supreme Court agreed with the lower courts that the Fourth Amendment applies to searches conducted by school officials. The court also rejected the State of New Jersey's argument that the exclusionary rule should not be employed to prevent the use in juvenile proceedings of evidence unlawfully seized by school officials. [T]he court held . . . that the precedents of this Court establish that "if an official search violates constitutional rights, the evidence is not admissible in criminal proceedings." *Id.* at 341, 463 A.2d at 939 (footnote omitted).

With respect to the question of the legality of the search before it, the court agreed with the Juvenile Court that a warrantless search by a school official does not violate the Fourth Amendment so long as the official "has reasonable grounds to believe that a student possesses evidence of illegal activity or activity that would interfere with school discipline and order." *Id.* at 346, 463 A.2d at 941-942. However, the court, with two justices dissenting, sharply disagreed with the Juvenile Court's conclusion that the search of the purse was reasonable. According to the majority, the contents of T.L.O.'s purse had no bearing on the accusation against T.L.O., for possession of cigarettes . . . did not violate school rules, and a mere desire for evidence that would impeach T.L.O.'s claim that she did not smoke cigarettes could not justify the search. Moreover, even if a reasonable suspicion that T.L.O. had cigarettes in her purse would justify a search, Mr. Choplick had no such suspicion, as no one had furnished him with any specific information that there were cigarettes in the purse. Finally, leaving aside the question whether Mr. Choplick was justified in opening the purse, the court held that the evidence of drug use that he saw inside did not justify the extensive "rummaging" through T.L.O.'s papers and effects that followed.

* * *

Although we originally granted certiorari to decide the issue of the appropriate remedy in juvenile court proceedings for unlawful school searches, our doubts regarding the wisdom of deciding that question in isolation from the broader question of what limits, if any, the Fourth Amendment places on the activities of school authorities prompted us to order reargument on that question. Having heard argument on the legality of the search of T.L.O.'s purse, we are satisfied that the search did not violate the Fourth Amendment.[3]

II.

It is now beyond dispute that "the Federal Constitution, by virtue of the Fourteenth Amendment, prohibits unreasonable searches and seizures by state officers." *Elkins v. United States,* 364 U.S. 205, 213, (1960); *accord, Mapp v. Ohio*, 367 U.S. 643 (1961); *Wolf v. Colorado*, 338 U.S. 25 (1949). Equally indisputable is the proposition that the Fourteenth Amendment protects the rights of students against encroachment by public school officials:

> The Fourteenth Amendment, as now applied to the States, protects the citizen against the State itself and all of its creatures—Boards of Education not excepted. These have, of course, important, delicate, and highly discretionary functions, but none that they may not perform within the limits of the Bill of Rights. . . .

West Virginia State Bd. Of Ed. v. Barnette, 319 U.S. 624, 637 (1943).

* * *

Notwithstanding the general applicability of the Fourth Amendment to the activities of civil authorities, a few courts have concluded that school officials are exempt from the dictates of the Fourth Amendment by virtue of the special nature of their authority over schoolchildren. Teachers and school administrators, it is said, act *in loco parentis* in their dealings with students: their authority is that of the parent, not the State, and is therefore not subject to the limits of the Fourth Amendment.

Such reasoning is in tension with contemporary reality and the teachings of this Court. We have held school officials subject to the commands of the First Amendment, *see Tinker v. Des Moines Independent Community School District,* 393 U.S. 503 (1969), and the Due Process Clause of the Fourteenth Amendment, *see Goss v. Lopez,* 419 U.S. 565 (1975). . . . More generally, the Court has recognized that "the concept of parental delegation" as a source of school authority is not entirely "consonant with compulsory education laws." *Ingraham v. Wright,* 430 U.S. 651, 622 (1977). Today's public school officials do not merely exercise authority voluntarily conferred on them by individual parents; rather, they act in furtherance of publicly mandated educational and disciplinary policies. . . . In carrying out searches and other disciplinary functions pur-

---

[3] In holding that the search of T.L.O.'s purse did not violate the Fourth Amendment, we do not implicitly determine that the exclusionary rule applies to the fruits of unlawful searches conducted by school authorities. The question whether evidence should be excluded from a criminal proceeding involves two discrete inquiries: whether the evidence was seized in violation of the Fourth Amendment, and whether the exclusionary rule is the appropriate remedy for the violation. Neither question is logically antecedent to the other, for a negative answer to either question is sufficient to dispose of the case. Thus, our determination that the search at issue in this case did not violate the Fourth Amendment implies no particular resolution of the question of the applicability of the exclusionary rule.

suant to such policies, school officials act as representatives of the State, not merely as surrogates for the parents, and they cannot claim the parents' immunity from the strictures of the Fourth Amendment.

III

To hold that the Fourth Amendment applies to searches conducted by school authorities is only to begin the inquiry into the standards governing such searches. Although the underlying command of the Fourth Amendment is always that searches and seizures be reasonable, what is reasonable depends on the context within which a search takes place. The determination of the standard of reasonableness governing any specific class of searches requires "balancing the need to search against the invasion which the search entails." *Camara v. Municipal Court,* 387 U.S. 523, 536-537 (1967). On one side of the balance are arrayed the individual's legitimate expectations of privacy and personal security; on the other, the government's need for effective methods to deal with breaches of public order.

We have recognized that even a limited search of the person is a substantial invasion of privacy. *Terry v. Ohio,* 392 U.S. 1, 24-25 (1967). We have also recognized that searches of closed items of personal luggage are intrusions on protected privacy interests, for "the Fourth Amendment provides protection to the owner of every container that conceals its contents from plain view." *United States v. Ross,* 456 U.S. 798, 822-823 (1982). A search of a child's person or of a closed purse or other bag carried on her person, no less than a similar search carried out on an adult, is undoubtedly a severe violation of subjective expectations of privacy.

* * *

Against the child's interest in privacy must be set the substantial interest of teachers and administrators in maintaining discipline in the classroom and on school grounds. . . . [T]he preservation of order and a proper educational environment requires close supervision of schoolchildren, as well as the enforcement of rules against conduct that would be perfectly permissible if undertaken by an adult. "Events calling for discipline are frequent occurrences and sometimes require immediate, effective action." *Goss v. Lopez,* 419 U.S. at 580. Accordingly, we have recognized that maintaining security and order in the schools requires a certain degree of flexibility in school disciplinary procedures, and we have respected the value of preserving the informality of the student-teacher relationship. *See id.* at 582-583, *Ingraham v. Wright,* 430 U.S. at 680-82.

How, then, should we strike the balance between the schoolchild's legitimate expectations of privacy and the school's equally legitimate need to maintain an environment in which learning can take place? It is evident that the school setting requires some easing of the restrictions to which searches by public authorities are ordinarily subject. The warrant requirement in particular, is unsuited to the school environment. . . . [W]e hold today that school officials need not obtain a warrant before searching a student who is under their authority.

The school setting also requires some modification of the level of suspicion of illicit activity needed to justify a search. Ordinarily, a search . . . must be based upon "probable cause" to believe that a violation of the law has occurred. *See, e.g., Almeida-Sanchez v. United States*, 413 U.S. 266, 273 (1973); *Sibron v. New York,* 392 U.S. 40, 62-66 (1968). However, "probable cause" is not an irreducible requirement of a valid search. The fundamental command of the Fourth Amendment is that searches and seizures be reasonable, and although "both the concept of probable cause and the requirement of a warrant bear on the reasonableness of a search, . . . in certain limited circumstances neither is required." *Almeda-Sanchez v. United States, supra*, at 277 (Powell, J., concurring). Thus, we have in a number of cases recognized the legality of searches and seizures based on suspicions that, although "reasonable," do not rise to the level of probable cause. *See, e.g., Terry v. Ohio* , 392 U.S. 1 (1968). . . . Where a careful balancing of governmental and private interests suggests that the public interest is best served by a Fourth Amendment standard of reasonableness that stops short of probable cause, we have not hesitated to adopt such a standard.

We join the majority of courts that have examined this issue in concluding that the accommodation of the privacy interests of schoolchildren with the substantial need of teachers and administrators for freedom to maintain order in the schools does not require strict adherence to the requirement that searches be based on probable cause to believe that the subject of the search has violated or is violating the law. Rather, the legality of a search of a student should depend simply on the reasonableness, under all the circumstances, of the search. Determining the reasonableness of any search involves a twofold inquiry: first, one must consider "whether the . . . action was justified at its inception," *Terry v. Ohio*, 392 U.S. at 20; second, one must determine whether the search as actually conducted "was reasonably related in scope to the circumstances which justified the interference in the first place," *ibid.* Under ordinary circumstances, a search of a student by a teacher or other school official will be "justified at its inception" when there are reasonable grounds for suspecting that the search will turn up evidence that the student has violated or is violating either the law or the rules of the school. Such a search will be permissible in its scope when the measures adopted are reasonably related to the objectives of the search and not excessively intrusive in light of the age and sex of the student and the nature of the infraction.

This standard will, we trust, neither unduly burden the efforts of school authorities to maintain order in their schools nor authorize unrestrained intrusions upon the privacy of schoolchildren. By focusing attention on the question of reasonableness, the standard will spare teachers and school administrators the necessity of schooling themselves in the niceties of probable cause and permit them to regulate their conduct according to the dictates of reason and common sense. At the same time, the reasonableness standard should ensure that the interests of students will be invaded no more than is necessary to achieve the legitimate end of preserving order in the schools.

IV

There remains the question of the legality of the search in this case. We recognize that the "reasonable grounds" standard applied by the New Jersey Supreme Court in its consideration of this question is not substantially different from the standard that we have adopted today. Nonetheless, we believe that the New Jersey court's application of that standard to strike down the search of T.L.O.'s purse reflects a somewhat crabbed notion of reasonableness. Our review of the facts surrounding the search leads us to conclude that the search was in no sense unreasonable for Fourth Amendment purposes.

* * *

Our conclusion that Mr. Choplick's decision to open T.L.O.'s purse was reasonable brings us to the question of the further search for marijuana once the pack of cigarettes was located. The suspicion upon which the search for marijuana was founded was provided when Mr. Choplick observed a package of rolling papers in the purse as he removed the pack of cigarettes. . . . The discovery of the rolling papers . . . gave rise to a reasonable suspicion that T.L.O. was carrying marijuana as well as cigarettes in her purse. This suspicion justified further exploration of T.L.O.'s purse, which turned up more evidence of drug-related activities: a pipe, a number of plastic bags of the type commonly used to store marijuana, a small quantity of marijuana, and a fairly substantial amount of money. . . . In short, we cannot conclude that the search for marijuana was unreasonable in any respect.

Because the search resulting in the discovery of the evidence of marijuana dealing by T.L.O. was reasonable, the New Jersey Supreme Court's decision to exclude that evidence from T.L.O.'s juvenile delinquency proceedings on Fourth Amendment grounds was erroneous. Accordingly, the judgment of the Supreme Court of New Jersey is reversed.

[The concurring opinions of Justices POWELL, BLACKMUN, BRENNAN, and STEVENS are omitted.]

Isiah B. v. State
500 N.W.2d 637 (Wis. 1993)

STEINMETZ, Justice.

Isiah B. appeals contending that the random search of his school locker was unconstitutional under the Fourth Amendment to the United States Constitution and article I, Sec. 11 of the Wisconsin Constitution. At the time of the search, there was a significant risk of imminent, serious personal harm to students and staff. We conclude that under the circumstances present at Madison High School, Milwaukee, Wisconsin, on November 19, 1990, the random search of the locker was permissible under the United States and Wisconsin Constitutions. Accordingly, we affirm the judgment of the circuit court.

The problems at Madison High School began in the fall of 1990 when the school administration was confronted with a series of gun-involved complaints and/or incidents in and around the school. In total, between October 23, 1990, and November 17, 1990, the Madison High School administration investigated five or six incidents where guns were said to have been used or were present on the school's premises. . . . In addition, due to two incidents involving threats to the same student, the administration, at the urging of the student's parents, agreed to allow the student to transfer because of fear for his safety. . . . [The] circuit court concluded that "[these] incidents appeared to be escalating in terms of the immediate threat of harm to students and staff at Madison High School."

On the weekend of November 16, 1990, the weekend before the search at issue, two incidents occurred which involved gunfire on school premises. First, on Friday night students reported that they were fired at as they left the school following a basketball game. Second, on Saturday night following a school dance a near riot occurred on school grounds when the departing students and security personnel for the school heard multiple gunshots. Large numbers of students were on the school grounds at the time. The presence of guns was confirmed, not only by the sounds of gunfire and the reaction of the crowd, but also by the recovery of spent casings on school grounds.

The circuit court found that on the following Monday morning, November 19, 1990, "an atmosphere of tension and fear dominated" Madison High School. The school staff and security personnel received reports of guns present in the school, gun sightings on school buses, and rumors that a shootout at the school on that date was, in effect, inevitable. . . . Despite announcements by Principal Willie Lee Jude regarding the administration's ongoing investigation into the incidents and the administration's efforts to address the situation, some staff members and students requested to leave the school out of fear for their safety. . . . The circuit court found that the administration's efforts were met with little success.

Due to the heightened fear and tension and the significant risk of imminent, serious personal harm to students and staff, Principal Jude ordered school security personnel to begin a "random" search of student lockers as a preventative measure while he continued investigatory interviews. . . . [E]vidence was introduced, including a Milwaukee Public School Handbook, to indicate that "it is announced school policy that lockers are the property of the school system and subject to inspection as determined necessary or appropriate." Students and parents are apprised of this policy. In addition, the school administration has pass keys [sic] for the lockers, and students are prohibited from putting private locks on their lockers.

Nathan Shoate, a Madison High School security aide, conducted the individual locker searches at the direction of Principal Jude. Using the school's pass key [sic], Shoate opened the lockers and visually inspected the locker interiors, moving articles to facilitate the observation. Shoate acknowledged that he also patted down coats or inspected personal articles during the course of the locker searches. Shoate conducted between 75-100 locker searches before he opened the locker that was later identified as Isiah B.'s. The school officials had no particularized or individualized suspicion that Isiah B.'s locker would contain evidence of law or school rule violations. Isiah B. did not have a history of prior weapon violations nor did the school officials suspect his involvement in the recent gun incidents.

At Isiah B.'s locker, Shoate opened the locker, removed a coat and immediately believed it to be unusually heavy. He then patted the exterior of the coat and felt a hard object, which he believed to be a gun, in an interior pocket. Shoate immediately notified the principal. Before the principal arrived, Shoate observed the handle of a gun in the coat by pulling open the pocket. . . . [T]he coat was then brought to the principal's office, where Isiah B. was confronted with it, whereupon he admitted that cocaine was also in the coat. . . . [T]he cocaine was discovered prior to the time Isiah B. came to the office. . . . Principal Jude testified that he knew that the cocaine was in the pocket before questioning Isiah B. stating: "I could see it. I could see it in the same pocket [as the gun]."

Subsequently, a delinquency petition was filed against Isiah B. alleging possession of a dangerous weapon on school property and possession of cocaine with intent to deliver. Isiah B. moved the circuit court for an order suppressing the gun and cocaine as products of an illegal search. The circuit court denied Isiah B.'s motion to suppress the evidence gathered in the search and adjudicated Isiah B. a delinquent child upon findings that he possessed a dangerous weapon on school premises, . . . and that he possessed a controlled substance with intent to deliver. . . .

* * *

Unlike many cases involving the constitutionality of a search, the search at issue in this case was not conducted by law enforcement officials. Rather, Madison High School officials conducted the search of Isiah B.'s locker. The law concerning the legality of searches conducted by public school officials was quite unsettled until 1985. In 1985, the United States Supreme Court decided *New Jersey v. T.L.O.*, 469 U.S. 325, 105 S.Ct. 733, 83 L.Ed. 2d 720 (1985), a case addressing the proper standard for assessing the legality of searches conducted by public school officials. Although the opinion in *T.L.O.* left some unanswered questions, it provides a framework of analysis for resolving this case.

[Justice Steinmetz discussed the facts and holding of *T.L.O.*, ending with the Court's conclusion that] "In carrying out searches and other disciplinary functions pursuant to such policies, school officials act as representatives of the State, not merely as surrogates for the parents, and they cannot claim the parents' immunity from the strictures of the Fourth Amendment." *Id.*, 469 U.S. at 336-37, 105 S.Ct. at 740. . . . We are bound by the Supreme Court's conclusion that public school officials are state agents for purposes of Fourth Amendment search and seizure analysis and as such must conform their conduct to the strictures of that amendment. Thus, applying the dictates of the Fourth Amendment, the question in this case is whether the search of Isiah B.'s locker was one done subject to the Fourth Amendment.

* * *

Recognizing that before a balancing of interests can take place, a court must first conclude that a reasonable expectation of privacy exists on the student's side of the balance, the [*T.L.O.*] Court concluded that a student has a legitimate reasonable expectation of privacy in a purse. *Id.* at 337-38, 105 S.Ct. at 740-41. However, the Court specifically declined to express any opinion on whether a student has a legitimate reasonable expectation of privacy in a school locker. *See id.* at 377 n.5, 105 S.Ct. at 740 n.5. The State of Wisconsin urges this court to conclude that Isiah B. had no reasonable expectation of privacy in his locker and thus no search for Fourth Amendment purposes took place.

We agree with the State and hold that when the Milwaukee Public School System (M.P.S.), as here, has a written policy retaining ownership and possessory control of school lockers . . . and notice of the locker policy is given to student, then students have no reasonable expectation of privacy in those lockers. . . . Because Isiah B. had no reasonable expectation of privacy in his locker, there was no Fourth Amendment violation, and the circuit court properly denied Isiah B.'s motion to suppress. We affirm the judgment of the circuit court. . . .

Vernonia School District 47J v. Acton

515 U.S. 646, 115 S. Ct. 2386, 132 L. Ed. 2d 564 (1995)

Justice SCALIA delivered the opinion of the Court.

The Student Athlete Drug Policy adopted by School District 47J in the town of Vernonia, Oregon, authorizes random urinalysis drug testing of students who participate in the District's school athletics programs. We granted certiorari to decide whether this violates the Fourth and Fourteenth Amendments to the United States Constitution.

I

A

Petitioner Vernonia School District 47J (District) operates one high school and three grade schools in the logging community of Vernonia, Oregon. As elsewhere in small town America, school sports play a prominent role in the town's life, and student athletes are admired in their schools and in the community.

Drugs had not been a major problem in Vernonia schools. In the mid-to-late 1980s, however, teachers and administrators observed a sharp increase in drug use. Students began to speak out about their attraction to the drug culture and to boast that there was nothing the school could do about it. Along with more drugs came more disciplinary problems. Between 1988 and 1989, the number of disciplinary referrals in Vernonia schools rose to more than twice the number reported in the early 1980s, and several students were suspended. Students became increasingly rude during class; outbursts of profane language became common.

Not only were student athletes included among the drug users but, as the District Court found, athletes were the leaders of the drug culture. This caused the District's administrators particular concern, since drug use increases the risk of sports-related injury. . . .

Initially, the District responded to the drug problem by offering special classes, speakers, and presentations designed to deter drug use. It even brought in a specially trained dog to detect drugs, but the drug problem persisted. . . .

At that point, District officials began considering a drug-testing program. They held a parent "input night" to discuss the proposed Student Athlete Drug Policy (Policy), and the parents in attendance gave their unanimous approval. The school board approved the Policy for implementation in the Fall of 1989. Its expressed purpose is to prevent student athletes from using drugs to protect their health and safety, and to provide drug users with assistance programs.

B

The Policy applies to all students participating in interscholastic athletics. Students wishing to play sports must sign a form consenting to the testing and must obtain the written consent of their parents. Athletes are tested at the beginning of the season for their sport. In addition, once each week of the season the names of the athletes are placed in a "pool" from which a student with the supervision of two adults, blindly draws the names of 10% of the athletes for random testing. Those selected are notified and tested the same day, if possible.

The student to be tested completes a specimen control form which bears an assigned number. Prescription medications that the student is taking must be identified. . . . The student then enters an empty locker room accompanied by an adult monitor of the same sex. Each boy selected produces a sample at a urinal, remaining fully clothed with his back to the monitor. . . . Monitors may (though do not always) watch the student while he produces the sample, and they listen for normal sounds of urination. Girls produce samples in an enclosed bathroom stall; so that they can be heard but not observed. After the sample is produced, it is given to the monitor, who checks it for temperature and tampering and then transfers it to a vial.

The samples are sent to an independent laboratory, which routinely tests them for amphetamines, cocaine, and marijuana. . . . The District follows strict procedures regarding the chain of custody and access to test results. . . . Only the superintendent, principals, vice-principals, and athletic directors have access to test results, and the results are not kept for more than one year.

If a sample tests positive, a second test is administered as soon as possible to confirm the result. If the second test is negative, no further action is taken. If the second test is positive, the athlete's parents are notified, and the school principal convenes a meeting with the student and his parents, at which the student is given the option of (1) participating for six weeks in an assistance program that includes weekly urinalysis, or (2) suffering suspension from athletics for the remainder of the current season and the next athletic season. The student is then retested prior to the start of the next athletic season for which he or she is eligible. The Policy states that a second offense results in automatic imposition of option (2); a third offense in suspension for the remainder of the current season and the next two athletic seasons.

C

In the Fall of 1991, respondent James Acton, then a seventh-grader, signed up to play football at one of the District's grade schools. He was denied participation, however, because he and his parents refused to sign the testing consent forms. The Actons filed suit, seeking declaratory and injunctive relief from enforcement of the Policy on the grounds that it violated the Fourth and Fourteenth Amendments to the United States Constitution. . . . After a bench trial, the District Court entered an order denying the claims on the merits and dismissing the action. The United States Court of Appeals for the Ninth Circuit reversed, holding that the Policy violated both the Fourth and Fourteenth Amendments. . . .

II

The Fourth Amendment to the United States Constitution provides that the Federal Government shall not violate "[t]he right of the people to be secure in their persons, houses, papers, and effects, against unreasonable searches and seizures. . . ." We have held that the Fourteenth Amendment extends this constitutional guarantee to searches and seizures by state officers, *Elkins v. United States*, 364 U.S. 206, 213 (1960), including public school officials, *New Jersey v. T.L.O.*, 469 U.S. 325, 336-337 (1985). In *Skinner v. Railway Labor Executives' Assn.*, 489 U.S. 602, 617 (1989), we held that state-compelled collection and testing of urine . . . constitutes a "search" subject to the demands of the Fourth Amendment. *See also Treasury Employees v. Von Raab*, 489 U.S. 656, 665 (1989).

As the text of the Fourth Amendment indicates, the ultimate measure of the constitutionality of a governmental search is "reasonableness. . . ." [W]hether a particular search meets the reasonableness standard "'is judged by balancing its intrusion on the individual's Fourth Amendment interests against its promotion of legitimate governmental interest.'" *Skinner, supra*, at 619 (quoting *Delaware v. Prouse,* 440 U.S. 648, 654 (1979)). . . . A search unsupported by probable cause can be constitutional, we have said, "when special needs, beyond the normal need for law enforcement, make the warrant and probable-cause requirement impracticable." *Griffin v. Wisconsin,* 483 U.S. 868, 873 (1987) (internal quotation marks omitted).

We have found such "special needs" to exist in the public-school context. . . . The school search we approved in *T.L.O.,* while not based on probable cause, *was* based on individualized *suspicion* of wrongdoing. As we explicitly acknowledged, however, "'the Fourth Amendment imposes no irreducible requirement of such suspicion,'" 469 U.S. 342, n.8 (quoting *United States v. Martinez-Fuerte,* 428 U.S. 543, 560-561 (1976)). . . .

III

The first factor to be considered is the nature of the privacy interest upon which the search here at issue intrudes. . . . Central, in our view, to the present case is the fact that the subjects of the Policy are (1) children, who (2) have been committed to the temporary custody of the State as schoolmaster.

Traditionally at common law, and still today, unemancipated minors lack some of the most fundamental rights of self-determination. . . . When parents place minor children in . . . schools for their education, the teachers and administrators of those schools stand *in loco parentis* over the children entrusted to them. . . .

* * *

Fourth Amendment rights . . . are different in public schools than elsewhere; the "reasonableness" inquiry cannot disregard the schools' custodial and tutelary responsibility for children. For their own good and that of their classmates, public school children are routinely required to submit to various physical examinations, and to be vaccinated against various diseases. . . . Particularly with regard to medical examinations and procedures, therefore, "students within the school environment have a lesser expectation of privacy than members of the population generally." *T.L.O.*, 469 U.S. at 348 (Powell, J., concurring).

Legitimate privacy expectations are even less with regard to student athletes. School sports are not for the bashful. They require "suiting up" before each practice or event, and showering and changing afterwards. Public school locker rooms, the usual sites for these activities, are not notable for the privacy they afford. . . .

There is an additional respect in which school athletes have a reduced expectation of privacy. By choosing to "go out for the team," they voluntarily subject themselves to a degree of regulation even higher than that imposed on students generally. In Vernonia's public schools, they must submit to a preseason physical exam . . . and comply with any "rules of conduct, dress, training hours and related matters as may be established for each sport by the head coach and athletic director with the principal's approval." . . . [S]tudents who voluntarily participate in school athletics have reason to expect intrusions upon normal rights and privileges, including privacy.

IV

Having considered the scope of the legitimate expectation of privacy at issue here, we turn next to the character of the intrusion that is complained of. . . . Under the District's Policy, male students produce samples at a urinal along a wall. They remain fully clothed and are only observed from behind, if at all. Female students produce samples in an enclosed stall, with a female monitor standing outside listening only for sounds of tampering. These conditions are nearly identical to those typically encountered in public restrooms, which men, women, and especially school children use daily. Under such conditions, the privacy interests compromised by the process of obtaining the urine sample are in our view negligible.

The other privacy-invasive aspect of urinalysis is, of course, the information it discloses concerning the state of the subject's body and the materials he has ingested. In this regard it is significant that the tests at issue here look only for drugs, and not for whether the student is, for example, epileptic, pregnant, or diabetic. Moreover, the drugs for which the samples are screened are standard, and do not vary according to the identity of the student. And finally, the results of the tests are disclosed only to a limited class of school personnel who have a need to know; and they are not turned over to law enforcement authorities or used for any internal disciplinary function.

Respondents argue, however, that the District's Policy is in fact more intrusive than this suggests, because it requires the students, if they are to avoid sanctions for a falsely positive test, to identify *in advance* prescription medications they are taking. We agree that this raises some cause for concern. . . . On the other hand, we have never indicated that requiring advance disclosure of medications is *per se* unreasonable. . . .

[While] the practice of the District seems to have been to have a school official take medication information from the student at the time of the test, that practice is not . . . required by the Policy, which says simply: "Student athletes who . . . are or have been taking prescription medication must provide verification (either by a copy of the prescription or by doctor's authorization) prior to being tested." It may well be that, if and when James was selected for random testing at a time that he was taking medication, the School District would have permitted him to provide the requested information in a confidential manner—for example, in a sealed envelope delivered to the testing lab. Nothing in the Policy contradicts that, and when respondents choose, in effect, to challenge the Policy on its face, we will not assume the worst. Accordingly, we reach the [conclusion] that the invasion of privacy was not significant.

V

Finally, we turn to consider the nature and immediacy of the governmental concern at issue here, and the efficacy of this means for meeting it. In both *Skinner* and *Van Raab*, we characterized the government interest motivating the search as "compelling." *Skinner, supra,* 489 U.S. at 628. Relying on these cases, the District Court held that because the District's program also called for drug testing in the absence of individualized suspicion, the District "must demonstrate a 'compelling need' for the program." The Court of Appeals appears to have agreed with this view. It is a mistake, however, to think that the phrase "compelling state interest," in the Fourth Amendment context, describes a fixed, minimum quantum of governmental concern. . . . Rather, the phrase describes an interest which appears *important enough* to justify the particular search at hand, in light of other factors which show the search to be relatively intrusive upon a genuine expectation of privacy. Whether that relatively high degree of government concern is necessary in this case or not, we think it is met.

That the nature of the concern is important—indeed, perhaps compelling—can hardly be doubted. . . . School years are the time when the physical, psychological, and addictive effects of drugs are most severe. . . . And of course the effects of a drug-infested school are visited not just upon the users, but upon the entire student body and faculty, as the educational process is disrupted. In the present case, moreover, the necessity for the State to act is magnified by the fact that this evil is being visited not just upon individuals at large, but upon children for whom it has undertaken a special responsibility of care and direction. Finally, it must not be lost sight of that this program is directed more narrowly to drug use by school athletes, where the risk of immediate physical harm to the drug user or those with whom he is playing his sport is particularly high. . . .

As for the immediacy of the district's concerns: We are not inclined to question—indeed, we could not possibly find clearly erroneous—the District Court's conclusion that "a large segment of the student body, particularly those involved in interscholastic athletics, was in a state of rebellion," that "[d]isciplinary actions had reached 'epidemic proportions,'" and that "the rebellion was being fueled by alcohol and drug abuse as well as by the student's misperceptions about the drug culture. . . ."

As to the efficacy of this means for addressing the problem: It seems to us self-evident that a drug problem largely fueled by the "role model" effect of athletes' drug use, and of particular danger to athletes, is effectively addressed by making sure that athletes do not use drugs. Respondents argue that a "less intrusive means to the same end" was available, namely, "drug testing on suspicion of drug use." We have repeatedly refused to declare that only the "least intrusive" search practicable can be reasonable under the Fourth Amendment. *Skinner, supra,* at 629, n.9 (collecting cases). Respondents' alternative entails substantial difficulties—if it is indeed practicable at all. . . . Respondents' proposal brings the risk that teachers will impose testing arbitrarily upon troublesome but not drug-likely students. It generates the expense of defending lawsuits that charge such arbitrary imposition, or that simply demand greater process before accusatory drug testing is imposed. And not least of all, it adds to the ever-expanding diversionary duties of schoolteachers the new function of spotting and bringing to account drug abuse, a task for which they are ill prepared, and which is not readily compatible with their vocation. . . . In many respects, we think, testing based on "suspicion" of drug use would not be better, but worse.

VI

Taking into account all the factors we have considered above—the decreased expectation of privacy, the relative unobtrusiveness of the search, and the severity of the need met by the search—we conclude Vernonia's Policy is reasonable and hence constitutional.

We caution against the assumption that suspicionless drug testing will readily pass constitutional muster in other contexts. The most significant element in this case is the first we discussed: that the Policy was undertaken in furtherance of the government's responsibilities, under a public school system as guardian and tutor of children entrusted to its care. . . . [W]hen the government acts as guardian and tutor the relevant question is whether the search is one that a reasonable guardian and tutor might undertake. Given the findings of need made by the District Court, we conclude that in the present case it is.

We may note that the primary guardians of Vernonia's schoolchildren appear to agree. The record shows no objection to this district wide program by any parents other than the couple before us here. . . . We find insufficient basis to contradict the judgment of Vernonia's parents, its school board, and the District Court, as to what was reasonably in the interest of these children under the circumstances.

The Ninth Circuit held that Vernonia's Policy not only violated the Fourth Amendment, but also, by reason of that violation, contravened Article I, § 9 of the Oregon Constitution. Our conclusion that the former holding was in error means that the latter holding rested on a flawed premise. We therefore vacate the judgment, and remand the case to the Court of Appeals for further proceedings consistent with this opinion.

[Justice GINSBURG's concurring opinion is omitted.]

Justice O'CONNOR, with whom Justice STEVENS and Justice SOUTER join, dissenting.

The population of our Nation's public schools, grades 7 through 12, numbers about 18 million. By the reasoning of today's decision, the millions of these students who participate in interscholastic sports, an overwhelming majority of whom have given school officials no reason whatsoever to suspect they use drugs at school, are open to an intrusive bodily search.

In justifying this result, the Court dispenses with a requirement of individualized suspicion on considered policy grounds. First, it explains that precisely because *every* student athlete is being tested, there is no concern that school officials might act arbitrarily in choosing whom to test. Second, a broad-based search regime, the Court reasons, dilutes the accusatory nature of the search. In making these policy arguments, of course, the Court sidesteps powerful, countervailing privacy concerns. Blanket searches, because they can involve "thousands or millions" of searches, "pos[e] a greater threat to liberty" than do suspicion-based ones, which "affec[t] one person at a time," *Illinois v. Krull*, 480 U.S. 340, 365 (1987) (O'Connor, J., dissenting). Searches based on individualized suspicion also afford potential targets considerable control over whether they will, in fact, be searched because a person can avoid such a search by not acting in an objectively suspicious way. And given that the surest way to avoid acting suspiciously is to avoid the underlying wrongdoing, the costs of such a regime, one would think, are minimal.

But whether a blanket search is "better" than a regime based on individualized suspicion is not a debate in which we should engage. For most of our constitutional history, mass, suspicionless searches have been generally considered *per se* unreasonable within the meaning of the Fourth Amendment. And we have allowed exceptions in recent years only where it has been clear that a suspicion-based regime would be ineffectual. Because that is not the case here, I dissent.

I

A

In *Carroll v. United States*, 267 U.S. 132 (1925), the Court explained that "[t]he Fourth Amendment does not denounce all searches or seizures, but only such as are unreasonable." *Id.* at 147. The Court also held, however, that a warrantless car search *was* unreasonable unless supported by some level of individualized suspicion, namely probable cause. . . .

* * *

The view that mass, suspicionless searches, however evenhanded, are generally unreasonable remains inviolate in the criminal law enforcement context, *see Ybara v. Illinois,* 444 U.S. 85 (1979), at least where the search is more than minimally intrusive, *see Michigan Dept. of State Police v. Sitz*, 496 U.S. 444 (1980). It is worth noting in this regard that state-compelled, state-monitored collection and testing of urine . . . is . . . "particularly destructive of privacy and offensive to personal dignity." *Treasury Employees v. Von Raab,* 489 U.S. 656, 680 (1989) (Scalia, J., dissenting). . . . And certainly monitored urination combined with urine testing is more intrusive than some personal searches we have said trigger Fourth Amendment protections in the past. . . .

* * *

Outside the criminal context, however, . . . our cases have upheld several evenhanded blanket searches, including some that are more than minimally intrusive, after balancing the invasion of privacy against the government's strong need. Most of these cases, of course, are distinguishable insofar as they involved searches either not of a personally intrusive nature . . . or arising in unique contexts such as prisons. . . .

* * *

Moreover, an individualized suspicion requirement was often impractical in these cases because they involved situations in which even one undetected instance of wrongdoing could have injurious consequences for a great number of people. . . .

B

The instant case stands in marked contrast. . . . [T]he Court treats a suspicion-based regime as if it were just any run-of-the-mill, less intrusive alternative—that is, an alternative that officials may bypass if the lesser intrusion, in their reasonable estimation, is outweighed by policy concerns unrelated to practicability.

* * *

In addition to overstating its concerns with a suspicion-based program, the District seems to have *understated* the extent to which such a program is less intrusive of students' privacy. By invading the privacy of a few students rather than many . . . , and by giving potential search targets substantial control over whether they will, in fact, be searched, a suspicion-based scheme is *significantly* less intrusive.

In any event, whether the Court is right that the District reasonably weighed the lesser intrusion of a suspicion-based scheme against its policy concerns is beside the point. As stated, a suspicion-based search regime is not just any less intrusive alternative; the individualized suspicion requirement has a legal pedigree as old as the Fourth Amendment itself, and it may not be easily cast aide in the name of policy concerns. . . .

* * *

[The] great irony of this case is that most (though not all) of the evidence the District introduced to justify its suspicionless drug-testing program consisted of first- or second-hand stories of particular, identifiable students acting in ways that plainly gave rise to reasonable suspicion of in-school drug use—and thus that would have justified a drug-related search under our *T.L.O.* decision. . . .

In light of [the] evidence of drug use by particular students, there is a substantial basis for concluding that a vigorous regime of suspicion-based testing . . . would have gone a long way toward solving Vernonia's school drug problem while preserving the Fourth Amendment rights of James Acton and others like him. . . . In these circumstances, the Fourth Amendment dictates that a mass, suspicionless search regime is categorically unreasonable.

* * *

II

I do not believe that suspicionless drug testing is justified on these facts. But even if I agreed that some such testing were reasonable here, I see two other Fourth Amendment flaws in the District's program. First, and most serious, there is virtually no evidence in the record of a drug problem at the Washington Grade School, which includes the 7th and 8th grades, and which Acton attended when this litigation began. . . . The only evidence of a grade school drug problem that my review of the record uncovered is a "guarantee" by the late-arriving grade school principal that "our problems . . . didn't start at the high school level. They started in the elementary school." But I would hope that a single assertion of this sort would not serve as an adequate basis on which to uphold mass, suspicionless drug testing of two entire grades of student-athletes—in Vernonia and, by the Court's reasoning, in other school districts as well. . . .

Second, even as to the high school, I find unreasonable the school's choice of student athletes as the class to subject to suspicionless testing—a choice that appears to have been driven more by a belief in what would pass constitutional muster . . . than by a belief in what was required to meet the District's principal disciplinary concern. . . . [T]he record in this case surely demonstrates there was a drug-related discipline problem in Vernonia of "'epidemic proportions.'" The evidence of a drug-related sports injury problem at Vernonia, by contrast, was considerably weaker.

On this record, then, it seems to me that the far more reasonable choice would have been to focus on the class of students found to have violated published school rules against severe disruption in class and around campus. . . . Such a choice would share two of the virtues of a suspicion-based regime: testing dramatically fewer students, tens as against hundreds, and giving students control, through their behavior, over the likelihood that they would be tested. . . .

Notes

1. After *T.L.O.*, it was established that although students do have constitutional rights under the Fourth Amendment, the need for order and discipline necessitates an easing of search and seizure restrictions in the public school setting. The Supreme Court recognized, as have other courts, that school officials investigating infractions of school rules are not law enforcement officers and should therefore not be subject to the same restrictions as the police. The test for the reasonableness of a school search focuses on whether the school official had reasonable cause to carry out the search in the first place and whether the search, as conducted, was reasonably related to the grounds for the search. This requires consideration of the infraction of school rules or criminal law suspected, as well as of the student's age, sex, and past behavioral history.

Courts generally go a long way to uphold the reasonableness of a search (*see, e.g., Isiah B., supra*), but there are limits as to what a court will allow. For example, courts tend to disfavor strip searches of school students. *See, e.g., Kennedy v. Dexter Consolidated Schools*, 955 P.2d 693 (N.M. 1998) (strip search illegal search where school official lacked reasonable, individualized suspicion); *see also Konop v. Northwestern School District,* 26 F. Supp. 1189 (D.S.D. 1998). However, even strip searches are allowed in properly limited circumstances. *See, e.g., Jenkins v. Talladega City Board of Education*, 115 F.3d 821 (11th Cir. 1997); *Cornfield v. Consolidated High School District*, 991 F.2d 1316 (7th Cir. 1993) (school officials had reasonable suspicion that student was "crotching" drugs; search reasonable even though no drugs found).

2. Unreasonable searches in the public school setting may have different consequences than their criminal counterparts. While evidence obtained in an illegal school search like that obtained illegally by law-enforcement officers, would not be admissible in a criminal proceeding against a student, that same "poisoned fruit" may be used in school disciplinary proceedings. *See Thompson v. Carthage School District*, 87 F.2d 979 (8th Cir. 1996); *Juan C. v. Cortines*, 679 N.E.2d 1061 (N.Y. 1997); *Gordon v. Santa Ana Unified School District*, 208 Cal. Rptr. 657 (Cal. Ct. App. 1985). However, a school official who conducts or supervises an illegal search may be held liable for damages under 42 U.S.C. § 1983. *See Picha v. Wielgos*, 410 F. Supp. 1214 (N.D. Ill. 1976); *Kennedy v. Dexter Consolidated Schools, supra; Cales v. Howell Public School,* 635 F. Supp. 454 (E.D. Mich. 1985).

3. Another search issue arising with increasing frequency is the propriety of using drug dogs in the public school setting. The general rule seems to be that sniffing by drug dogs of lockers, cars, and other items on school property is not a search for Fourth Amendment purposes. Courts cite the limited expectation of privacy in items brought onto a public school campus and the minimal intrusiveness of such sniff checks to support this conclusion. Moreover, if the drug dog is shown to be reliable, an alert by the dog on a particular locker or car provides reasonable suspicion to conduct an individual search of that locker or car. *See, e.g., Horton v. Goose Creek Independent School District,* 690 F.2d 470 (5th Cir. 1982); *Commonwealth v. Cass*, 709 A.2d 350 (Pa. 1998); *Zamora v. Pomeroy,* 639 F.2d 662 (10th Cir. 1981). Using a drug dog to sniff a student or group of students, however, is a search and thus requires reasonable suspicion before the dog is used on the individual(s). *See, e.g., Horton, supra; State v. Barrett,* 683 So. 2d 331 (La. Ct. App. 1996).

4. The majority in *Isiah B.* held that the student had no reasonable expectation of privacy in his school locker. In her dissenting opinion, Justice Abrahamson stated the following:

> The majority concludes that Isiah's Fourth Amendment [sic] rights were not violated because he had no reasonable expectation of privacy in his locker. The majority bases this conclusion on the school district policy reserving the right to conduct a general search of student lockers. I disagree with this conclusion.
>
> The right to be free from unreasonable searches is constitutional in nature and dimension. While notice that a locker may be searched might diminish the reasonableness of a student's expectations that items stored there will be kept secret, numerous courts have repeatedly

> stated that a government proclamation cannot eradicate Fourth Amendment rights. . . . The school's ownership or partial control of the lockers cannot negate the students' expectation of privacy in the contents of the lockers. As the United States Supreme Court explained in *Katz v. United States*, 389 U.S. 347, 351-52, 88 S. Ct. 507, 511, 19 L. Ed. 2d 579 (1967), "[w]hat a person seeks to preserve as private, even in an area accessible to the public, may be constitutionally protected."

500 N.W. 2d at 645. Justice Abrahamson would have held that Isiah and his classmates had a reasonable expectation of privacy in their lockers, regardless of the district's stated search policy. Other courts have agreed with this view and have held that public school students have at least some expectation of privacy in the contents of their lockers. *See, e.g., State v. Michael G.,* 748 P.2d 17 (N.M. 1987); *In re S.C.,* 583 So. 2d 188 (Miss. 1991). Even where courts recognize such an expectation of privacy, however, they generally find that reasonable suspicion by school officials is sufficient to justify a locker search. *See, e.g., Commonwealth v. Cass, supra; Commonwealth v. Snyder,* 597 N.E.2d 1363 (Mass. 1992); *State v. Joseph T.,* 336 S.E.2d 728 (W. Va. 1985).

5. After *Acton*, there seems to be little doubt that school officials can require students to undergo drug testing in certain situations. Just what those situations are, however, is far from settled. *See Willis v. Anderson Community School Corporation*, 158 F.3d 415 (7th Cir. 1998), *cert. denied,* 526 U.S. 1019 (1999) (urine tests to detect alcohol or drug use by students suspended for fighting not justified by special needs of public school); *Trinidad School District No. 1 v. Lopez*, 963 P.2d 1095 (Colo. 1998) (school district cannot require random drug testing of all students involved in extracurricular activities); *Todd v. Rush County Schools,* 133 F.3d 984 (7th Cir.), *cert. denied,* 119 S. Ct. 68, 142 L. Ed. 2d 53 (1998) (school can require random urinalysis to test for drugs, alcohol, and tobacco for any student involved in any extracurricular activities or wishing to drive to school).

Questions

1. The Court in *T.L.O.* acknowledges that the "reasonable grounds" standard applied by the New Jersey Supreme Court is substantially the same as its own analysis of the "reasonableness, under all the circumstances," yet the Court goes on to claim that the state court's decision reflects a "somewhat crabbed notion of reasonableness." Which court got it right? Was the New Jersey Supreme Court too harsh in its application of the standard, or was the Supreme Court too forgiving? What reasons, besides those given in the majority opinion, might the Court have had for upholding the validity of the search at issue in this case?

2. In *Acton*, the Court views the protection of student athletes as one of the main issues in the case. Do you agree with this characterization? If so, does Justice O'Connor miss the point by requiring individualized suspicion? In Justice O'Connor's view, the "surest way to avoid acting suspiciously is to avoid the underlying wrongdoing." Is she assuming by this statement that grade school and high school students will make rational choices regarding drug use?

3. Is there merit to the dissent's assertion in *Acton* that the school district's decision to test student athletes may have been based more on a "belief in what would pass constitutional muster" than by its stated desire to protect athletes from injury? Assume that the district was motivated by the desire to create an unchallengable rule. Would this fact change the outcome in *Acton*? Why or why not?

Chapter 5

The Waiver Decision: Whether to Charge the Juvenile as an Adult

This chapter deals with what is variously known as waiver, transfer, bindover, removal, or certification. Whatever its label, the decision is the same: whether to try a child accused of committing a delinquent act in an adult criminal court. This decision can have serious consequences for the child. For example, once her case is removed to criminal court, the juvenile is no longer protected by the confidentiality requirements that may apply to juvenile adjudications. She will, in most instances, be tried in open court, and her case may be subject to the same publicity as an adult trial. Further, the child will lose access to the rehabilitative resources available in the juvenile justice system and will be punished as an adult. Finally, unlike most juvenile records, her conviction in adult court will not be sealed upon her reaching majority.

The use of waiver has gained increased popularity because of the rise in violent offenses committed by juveniles since the early 1980s. BUREAU OF JUST. ASSISTANCE, U.S. DEP'T OF JUST., JUVENILES IN ADULT PRISONS AND JAILS 1, 1-3 (2000). The arrest rate of juveniles for violent offenses rose 78% from 1984-1994. Although the rate of juveniles arrested for violent offenses decreased 19% from 1994-1998, the number of arrested juvenile violent offenders still remains at historic levels. In response to the historic level of violent offenses committed by juveniles, most states have begun to expand the use of waivers through several different means. Some states, such as Connecticut, Georgia, Illinois, Louisiana, Massachusetts, Michigan, New York, North Carolina, South Carolina, and Texas have lowered the statutory age for which juveniles can be tried in adult courts. *Id.* at 28. Other states have increased the number of offenses for which a prosecutor may charge a juvenile offender—many offenses which have traditionally not applied to juveniles. For a survey of state legislation which expands the use of waivers, *see id.* at 71-124.

The decision whether to waive a child for trial in adult court may be made in several ways. First, the juvenile court judge may have the discretion to determine whether the child should remain in the juvenile system or be transferred to the criminal court. The judge may be aided in this decision by legislation or by *stare decisis,* either of which may simply offer the judge guidance or may create a framework within which the judge must make a determination. Under the second form of waiver, the judge's discretion is replaced by statutory standards. If the child and/or the offense meet certain listed criteria, the case is automatically transferred to the criminal court. Finally, the prosecutor may be vested with the power to determine in which court to try the child's case. After a case has been transferred to an adult court, whether by judicial, prosecutorial, or automatic waiver, the child may be able to have his case sent back to the juvenile court through a process known as "reverse waiver." Each of these procedures will be discussed more fully in the following chapter.

A. Due Process and the Waiver Hearing

Kent v. United States

383 U.S. 541, 86 S. Ct. 1045, 16 L. Ed. 2d 84 (1966)

Mr. Justice FORTAS delivered the opinion of the Court.

This case is here on certiorari to the United States Court of Appeals for the District of Columbia Circuit. The facts and the contentions of counsel raise a number of disturbing questions concerning the administration by the police and the Juvenile Court authorities of the District of Columbia laws relating to juveniles. . . . Because we conclude that the Juvenile Court's order waiving jurisdiction of petitioner was entered without compliance with required procedures, we remand the case to the trial court.

Morris A. Kent, Jr., first came under the authority of the Juvenile Court of the District of Columbia in 1959. He was then aged 14. He was apprehended as a result of several housebreakings and an attempted purse snatching. He was placed on probation, in the custody of his mother who had been separated from her husband since Kent was two years old. Juvenile Court officials interviewed Kent from time to time during the probation period and accumulated a "Social Service" file.

On September 2, 1961, an intruder entered the apartment of a woman in the District of Columbia. He took her wallet. He raped her. The police found in the apartment latent fingerprints. They were developed and processed. They matched the fingerprints of Morris Kent, taken when he was 14 years old and under the jurisdiction of the Juvenile Court. At about 3 p.m. on September 5, 1961, Kent was taken into custody by the police. Kent was then 16 and therefore subject to the "exclusive jurisdiction" of the Juvenile Court. D.C. Code § 11-907 (1961), now § 11-1551 (Supp. IV, 1965). He was still on probation to that court as a result of the 1959 proceedings.

Upon being apprehended, Kent was taken to police headquarters where he was interrogated by police officers. It appears that he admitted his involvement in the offense which led to his apprehension and volunteered information as to similar offenses involving housebreaking, robbery, and rape. . . .

* * *

The record does not show when his mother became aware that the boy was in custody, but shortly after 2 p.m. on September 6, 1961, the day following petitioner's apprehension, she retained counsel. Counsel, together with petitioner's mother, promptly conferred with the Social Service Director of the Juvenile Court. In a brief interview, they discussed the possibility that the Juvenile Court might waive jurisdiction under D.C. Code § 11-914 (1961), now § 11-1553 (Supp. IV, 1965), and remit Kent to trial by the District Court. Counsel made known his intention to oppose waiver.

Petitioner was detained at the Receiving Home for almost a week. There was no arraignment during this time, no determination by a judicial officer of probable cause for petitioner's apprehension.

* * *

[P]etitioner's counsel moved that the Juvenile Court should give him access to the Social Service file relating to petitioner which had been accumulated by the staff of the Juvenile Court during petitioner's probation period, and which would be available to the Juvenile Court judge in considering the question whether it should retain or waive jurisdiction. Petitioner's counsel represented that access to this file was essential to his providing petitioner with effective assistance of counsel.

The Juvenile Court judge did not rule on [this motion]. He held no hearing. He did not confer with petitioner or petitioner's parents or petitioner's counsel. He entered an order reciting that after "full investigation, I do hereby waive" jurisdiction of petitioner and directing that he be "held for trial for [the alleged] offenses under the regular procedure of the U.S. District Court for the District of Columbia." He made no findings. He did not recite any reason for the waiver. . . .

* * *

The provision of the Juvenile Court Act governing waiver expressly provides only for "full investigation." It states the circumstances in which jurisdiction may be waived and the child held for trial under adult procedures, but it does not state standards to govern the Juvenile Court's decision as to waiver. The provision reads as follows:

> If a child sixteen years of age or older is charged with an offense which would amount to a felony in the case of an adult, or any child charged with an offense which if committed by an adult is punishable by death or life imprisonment, the judge may, after full investigation, waive jurisdiction and order such child held for trial under the regular procedure of the court which would have jurisdiction of such offense if committed by an adult; or such other court may exercise the powers conferred upon the juvenile court in this subchapter in conducting and disposing of such cases.[6]

---

6 D.C. Code § 11-914 (1961), now § 11-1553 (Supp. IV, 1965).

Petitioner appealed from the Juvenile Court's waiver order to the Municipal Court of Appeals, which affirmed, and also applied to the United States District Court for a writ of habeas corpus, which was denied. On appeal from these judgments, the United States Court of Appeals held on January 22, 1963, that neither appeal to the Municipal Court of Appeals nor habeas corpus was available. . . .

Meanwhile, on September 25, 1961, shortly after the Juvenile Court order waiving its jurisdiction, petitioner was indicted by a grand jury of the United States District Court for the District of Columbia. The indictment contained eight counts alleging two instances of housebreaking, robbery, and rape, and one of housebreaking and robbery. On November 16, 1961, petitioner moved the District Court to dismiss the indictment on the grounds that the waiver was invalid. . . .

The District Court denied the motion to dismiss the indictment. The District Court ruled that it would not "go behind" the Juvenile Court judge's recital that his order was entered "after full investigation." It held that "The only matter before me is as to whether or not the statutory provisions were complied with and the Courts have held . . . with reference to full investigation, that that does not mean a quasi judicial or judicial hearing. No hearing is required."

* * *

At trial, petitioner's defense was wholly directed toward proving that he was not criminally responsible because "his unlawful act was the product of mental disease or mental defect." *Durham v. United States*, 94 U.S. App. D.C. 228, 241, 214 F.2d 862, 875 (1954). Extensive evidence, including expert testimony, was presented to support this defense. The jury found as to the counts alleging rape that petitioner was "not guilty by reason of insanity." Under District of Columbia law, this made it mandatory that petitioner be transferred to St. Elizabeths Hospital, a mental institution, until his sanity is restored. On the six counts of housebreaking and robbery, the jury found that petitioner was guilty.[10]

Kent was sentenced to serve five to 15 years on each count as to which he was found guilty, or a total of 30 to 90 years in prison. The District Court ordered that the time to be spent at St. Elizabeths on the mandatory commitment after the insanity acquittal be counted as part of the 30- to 90-year sentence. Petitioner appealed to the United States Court of Appeals for the District of Columbia Circuit. That Court affirmed. 119 U.S. App. D. C. 378, 343 F.2d 247 (1964).

* * *

It is to petitioner's arguments as to the infirmity of the proceedings by which the Juvenile Court waived its otherwise exclusive jurisdiction that we

---

10 The basis for this distinction—that petitioner was "sane" for purposes of the housebreaking and robbery but "insane" for the purposes of rape—apparently was the hypothesis, for which there is some support in the record, that the jury might find that the robberies had anteceded the rapes, and in that event, it might conclude that the housebreakings and robberies were not the products of his mental disease or defect, while the rapes were produced thereby.

address out attention. Petitioner attacks the waiver of jurisdiction on a number of statutory and constitutional grounds. He contends that the waiver is defective because no hearing was held; because no findings were made by the Juvenile Court; because the Juvenile Court stated no reasons for waiver; and because counsel was denied access to the Social Service file which presumably was considered by the Juvenile Court in determining to waive jurisdiction.

We agree that the order of the Juvenile Court waiving its jurisdiction and transferring petitioner for trial in the United States District Court for the District of Columbia was invalid. . . . The issue is the standards to be applied upon . . . review.

[The] statute gives the Juvenile Court a substantial degree of discretion as to the factual considerations to be evaluated, the weight to be given them and the conclusion to be reached. It does not confer upon the Juvenile Court a license for arbitrary procedure. The statute does not permit the Juvenile Court to determine in isolation and without the participation or any representation of the child the "critically important" question whether a child will be deprived of the special protections and provisions of the Juvenile Court Act. It does not authorize the Juvenile Court, in total disregard of a motion for hearing filed by counsel, and without any hearing or statement or reasons, to decide—as in this case—that the child will be taken from the Receiving Home for Children and transferred to jail along with adults, and that he will be exposed to the possibility of a death sentence[17] instead of treatment for a maximum, in Kent's case, of five years, until he is 21.[18]

We do not consider whether, on the merits, Kent should have been transferred; but there is no place in our system of law for reaching a result of such tremendous consequences without ceremony—without hearing, without effective assistance of counsel, without a statement of reasons. It is inconceivable that a court of justice dealing with adults, with respect to a similar issue, would proceed in this manner. It would be extraordinary if society's special concern for children, as reflected in the District of Columbia's Juvenile Court Act, permitted this procedure. We hold that it does not.

1. The theory of the District's Juvenile Court Act, like that of other jurisdictions, is rooted in social welfare philosophy rather than in the *corpus juris*. Proceedings are designated as civil rather than criminal. The Juvenile Court is theoretically engaged in determining the needs of the child and of society rather than adjudicating criminal conduct. The objectives are to provide measures of guidance and rehabilitation for the child and protection for society, not to fix criminal responsibility, guilt and punishment. The State is *parens patriae* rather than prosecuting attorney and judge. But the admonition to function in a "parental" relationship is not an invitation to procedural arbitrariness.

2. Because the State is supposed to proceed in respect of the child as parens patriae and not as adversary, courts have relied on the premise that the

---

17 D.C. Code § 22-2801 (1961) fixes the punishment for rape at 30 years, or death if the jury so provides in its verdict.

18 The jurisdiction of the Juvenile Court over a child ceases when he becomes 21. D.C. Code § 11-907 (1961), now § 11-1551 (Supp. IV, 1965).

proceedings are "civil" in nature and not criminal, and have asserted that the child cannot complain of the deprivation of important rights available in criminal case. . . .

While there can be no doubt of the original laudable purpose of juvenile courts, studies and critiques in recent years raise serious questions as to whether actual performance measures well enough against theoretical purpose to make tolerable the immunity of the process from the reach of constitutional guaranties applicable to adults. . . . There is evidence, in fact, that there may be grounds for concern that the child receives the worst of both worlds; that he gets neither the protections accorded to adults nor the solicitous care and regenerative treatment postulated for children.

* * *

3. It is clear beyond dispute that the waiver of jurisdiction is a "critically important" action determining vitally important statutory rights of the juvenile. . . . The Juvenile Court is vested with "original and exclusive jurisdiction" of the child. This jurisdiction confers special rights and immunities. He is, as specified by the statute, shielded from publicity. He may be confined, but with rare exception he may not be jailed along with adults. He may be detained, but only until he is 21 years of age. The court is admonished by the statute to give preference to retaining the child in the custody of his parents "unless his welfare and the safety and protection of the public can not be adequately safeguarded without . . . removal." The child is protected against consequences of adult conviction such as the loss of civil rights, the use of adjudication against him in subsequent proceedings, and disqualification for public employment. D.C. Code §§ 11-907, 11-915, 11-927, 11-929 (1961).

The net, therefore, is that petitioner—then a boy of 16—was by statute entitled to certain procedures and benefits as a consequence of his statutory right to the "exclusive" jurisdiction of the Juvenile Court. In these circumstances, considering particularly that decision as to waiver of jurisdiction and transfer of the matter to the District Court was potentially as important to petitioner as the difference between five years' confinement and a death sentence, we conclude that, as a condition to a valid waiver order, petitioner was entitled to a hearing, including access by his counsel to the social records and probation or similar reports which presumably are considered by the court, and to a statement of reasons for the Juvenile Court's decision. We believe that this result is required by the statute read in the context of constitutional principles relating to due process and the assistance of counsel.

* * *

In *Black v. United States*, 355 F.2d 104 (D.C. Cir. 1965), decided by the Court of Appeals on December 8, 1965, the court held that assistance of counsel in the "critically important" determination of waiver is essential to the proper administration of juvenile proceedings. Because the juvenile was not advised of his right to retained or appointed counsel, the judgment of the District Court, following waiver of jurisdiction by the Juvenile Court, was reversed. The court relied upon its decision in *Shioutakon v. District of Columbia*, 98 U.S. App. D.C. 371, 236 F.2d 666 (1956), in which it had held that effective assistance of counsel in juvenile court proceedings is essential. In *Black*, the court referred to the Criminal Justice Act, enacted four years after *Shioutakon*, in which Congress provided for the assistance of counsel "in proceedings before the juvenile court of the District of Columbia." D.C. Code § 2-2202 (1961). The court held that "The need is even greater in the adjudication of waiver [than in a case like *Shioutakon*] since it contemplates the imposition of criminal sanctions." 355 F.2d at 106.

In *Watkins v. United States*, 119 U.S. App. D.C. 409, 343 F.2d 278 (1964), decided in November, 1964, the Juvenile Court had waived jurisdiction of appellant who was charged with housebreaking and larceny. In the District Court, appellant sought disclosure of the social record in order to attack the validity of the waiver. The Court of Appeals held that in a waiver proceeding a juvenile's attorney is entitled to access to such records. . . . The Court remanded the [case] to the District Court for a determination of the extent to which the records should be disclosed.

The Court of Appeals' decision in the present case was handed down on October 26, 1964, prior to its decisions in *Black* and *Watkins*. The Court of Appeals assumed that since petitioner had been a probationer of the Juvenile Court for two years, that court had before it sufficient evidence to make an informed judgment. It therefore concluded that the statutory requirement of a "full investigation" had been met. It noted that absence of "a specification by the Juvenile Court Judge of precisely why he concluded to waive jurisdiction," 119 U.S. App. D.C. at 384, 343 F.2d at 253, [but] it did not conclude that the absence thereof invalidated the waiver.

As to the denial of access to the social records, the Court of Appeals stated that "the statute is ambiguous. . . ." It characterized counsel's proper function as being merely that of bringing forward affirmative information which might help the court. . . . Accordingly, it held that the Juvenile Court had not abused its discretion in denying access to the social records.

We are of the opinion that the Court of Appeals misconceived the basic issue and the underlying values in this case. . . . The Juvenile Court Act confers upon the child a right to avail himself of that court's "exclusive" jurisdiction. As the Court of Appeals has said, "[I]t is implicit in [the Juvenile Court] scheme that non-criminal treatment is to be the rule—and the adult criminal treatment, the exception which must be governed by the particular factors of individual cases." *Harling v. United States,* 111 U.S. App. D.C. 174, 177-178, 295 F.2d 161, 164-65 (1961).

Meaningful review requires that the reviewing court should review. It should not be remitted to assumptions. It must have before it a statement of the reasons motivating the waiver including, of course, a statement of the relevant facts. It may not "assume" that there are adequate reasons, nor may it merely assume that "full investigation" has been made. Accordingly, we hold that it is incumbent upon the Juvenile Court to accompany its waiver order with a statement of the reasons or considerations therefor. . . . [T]he statement should be sufficient to demonstrate that the statutory requirement of "full investigation" has been met; and that the question has received the careful consideration of the Juvenile Court; and it must set forth the basis for the order with sufficient specificity to permit meaningful review.

Correspondingly, we conclude that an opportunity for a hearing which may be informal, must be given the child prior to entry of a waiver order. Under *Black*, the child is entitled to counsel in connection with a waiver proceeding, and under *Watkins*, counsel is entitled to see the child's social records. These rights are meaningless—an illusion, a mockery—unless counsel is given an opportunity to function.

The right to representation by counsel is . . . of the essence of justice. Appointment of counsel without affording an opportunity for hearing on a "critically important" decision is tantamount to denial of counsel. There is no justification for the failure of the Juvenile Court to rule on the motion for hearing filed by petitioner's counsel, and it was error to fail to grant a hearing.

We do not mean by this to indicate that the hearing to be held must conform with all of the requirements of a criminal trial or even of the usual administrative hearing; but we do hold that the hearing must measure up to the essentials of due process and fair treatment. *Pee v. United States,* 107 U.S. App. D.C. 47, 50, 274 F.2d 556, 559 (1959).

With respect to access by the child's counsel to the social records of the child, we deem it obvious that since these are to be considered by the Juvenile Court in making its decision to waive, they must be made available to the child's counsel. . . . The Court of Appeals has held in *Black*, and we agree, that counsel must be afforded to the child in waiver proceedings. Counsel, therefore have a "legitimate interest" in the protection of the child, and must be afforded access to these records.

* * *

For the reasons stated, we conclude that the Court of Appeals and the District Court erred in sustaining the validity of the waiver by the Juvenile court. The Government urges that any error committed by the Juvenile Court was cured by the proceedings before the District Court. . . . But we agree with the Court of Appeals in *Black*, that "the waiver question was primarily and initially one for the Juvenile Court to decide and its failure to do so in a valid manner cannot be said to be harmless error. It is the Juvenile Court, not the District Court, which has the facilities, personnel and expertise for a proper determination of the waiver issue." 122 U.S. App. D.C. at 396, 355 F.2d at 107.

[W]e vacate the order of the Court of Appeals and the judgment of the District Court and remand the case to the District Court for a hearing *de novo* on waiver, consistent with this opinion. If that court finds that waiver was inappropriate, petitioner's conviction must be vacated. If, however, it finds that the waiver order was proper when originally made, the District Court may proceed, after consideration of such motions as counsel may make and such further proceedings, if any, as may be warranted, to enter an appropriate judgment.

Reversed and remanded.

[Justice STEWART, joined by Justices BLACK, HARLAN, and WHITE, filed a dissenting opinion. Justice Stewart would have vacated the judgment and "remanded the case . . . for reconsideration in light of . . . *Watkins v. United States* and *Black v. United States*" (citations omitted).]

Notes

1. In recent years the American criminal justice system has been criticized for its failure to control crime. Many critics of the system advocate a change in the focus of the laws from rehabilitation and treatment to deterrence and retribution. The move away from rehabilitation and treatment has an impact on the criminal justice system, but also impacts the juvenile justice system. Since the turn of the century, the juvenile justice system has been kept separate from the adult criminal justice system. The recent trend jeopardizes this division as it advocates treating certain juvenile offenders the same as adult offenders. *See* Eric Fritsch & Craig Hemmens, J.D., *Juvenile Waiver in the United States 1979-1995: A Comparison and Analysis of State Waiver Statutes,* 46 JUV. & FAM. CT. J. 17, 17-23 (1995).

2. The Supreme Court in *Kent* held that a juvenile subject to waiver to an adult court for prosecution was entitled to a "full investigation" under "basic requirements of due process and fairness." To the Court, this meant the juvenile was, at a minimum, entitled to: (1) a judicial hearing; (2) the aid of counsel at the hearing; (3) access by counsel to the juvenile's records and social services files; and (4) a written report by the court outlining the judge's reasons for granting or denying the waiver. The Court left unanswered the question of whether this was a constitutional issue, applicable to sate courts, or was limited to courts of federal jurisdiction. This question was answered the following year by *In re Gault,* 387 U.S. 1 (1967), which held for the first time that procedural due process extended to the juvenile setting in all courts (*see, infra,* Chapter 6).

3. After the Supreme Court decided *Kent*, many observers believed that a juvenile was entitled to a waiver hearing anytime her case could be transferred to an adult criminal court. It was not uncommon, however, for state law to allow certain cases to be transferred to an adult court automatically, without a hearing. As discussed in the following note, such statutes generally provided for the automatic transfer of cases involving recidivistic offenders or those accused of specifically enumerated crimes. Not surprisingly, the constitutionality of these statutes was brought into question in the wake of the *Kent* decision.

Six years after *Kent*, the Court of Appeals for the District of Columbia Circuit upheld a provision of the District's revised juvenile code mandating the transfer of certain juvenile offenders to adult court without a hearing. *United States v. Bland,* 472 F.2d 1329 (D.C. Cir. 1972), *cert. denied,* 412 U.S. 909 (1973). The provision excepted any juvenile sixteen years old or older charged with certain serious offenses from the statutory definition of a "child," and thereby excluded such a juvenile from the jurisdiction of the juvenile court. In upholding the provision, the majority found that Congress had the power to change the statutory definition of "child." *Id.* at 1335. The court further found that "[u]ntil it is determined whether a person is a 'child' within the statutory definition, there is no jurisdiction; therefore, a *fortiori* there can be no waiver of jurisdiction." *Id.*

Judge J. Skelly Wright dissented in *Bland*. In his view, *Kent* mandates a hearing whenever a juvenile court contemplates a waiver. He classified the statute at issue in *Bland* as a "blatant attempt to evade the force of the *Kent* decision," an attempt he felt "should not be permitted to succeed." *Id.* at 1341. While he did not question the constitutionality of shifting the waiver decision from the juvenile court judge to the prosecutor, Judge Wright disagreed with the majority that this shift eliminates the need for a *Kent*-style waiver hearing. *Id.* at 1342. In Judge Wright's view, "[t]he transfer of the waiver decision from the neutral judge to the partisan prosecutor increases rather than diminishes the need for due process protection for the child." *Id.* at 1343. Notwithstanding Judge Wright's misgivings, courts routinely uphold automatic waiver statutes. *See, e.g., State v. Behl,* 564 N.W.2d 560 (Minn. 1997); *People v. Thorpe,* 641 P.2d 935 (Colo. 1982); *State v. Bell,* 785 P.2d 390 (Utah 1989); *Morrow v. United States,* 592 A.2d 1042 (D.C. 1991); *Jackson v. State*, 311 So. 2d 658 (Miss. 1975).

4. There are three methods by which a juvenile may be transferred to an adult criminal court for trial: judicial waiver, automatic (or statutory) waiver, and prosecutorial waiver (or direct file). State law determines which method or methods can be used for "transferring" juveniles from the juvenile to the criminal system. *See generally* OFF. OF JUV. JUST. & DELINQ. PREVENTION, U.S. DEP'T OF JUSTICE, DELINQUENCY CASES WAIVED TO CRIMINAL COURT, 1987-1996 (April 1999). The majority of transfers are accomplished through judicial waiver. *See* Barry C. Feld, *The Juvenile Court Meets the Principle of the Offense: Legislative Changes in Juvenile Waiver Statutes,* 78 J. CRIM. L. & CRIMINOLOGY 471, 488 (1987). Under this type of waiver, the juvenile court judge holds a hearing and will ordinarily grant a transfer upon a showing that the juvenile is not a suitable candidate for rehabilitation in the juvenile system and that it is in the best interest of the child and society to try the case in an adult court. Most states provide for judicial waiver through legislation, and courts routinely uphold judicial waiver statutes. *See, e.g.,* NEV. REV. STAT. § 62.080 (1999) (judge may waive juvenile court jurisdiction over juvenile fourteen years of age or older and charged with a felony); ALA. CODE § 12-15-34(a) (Lexis Supp. 2000) (may waive jurisdiction for child sixteen years old or older). *See also United States v. A.D.J.,* 108 F.2d 851 (8th Cir. 1997) (upholding judicial waiver decision).

In recent years, a growing number of states have implemented statutory waivers and prosecutorial waivers. The second waiver method, statutory or automatic waiver, has become more prevalent in the past two decades, largely as a reaction to what many perceive as juvenile courts' leniency toward violent juvenile offenders. *See* Eric K. Klein, Note, *Dennis the Menace or Billy the Kid: An Analysis of the Role of Transfer to Criminal Court in Juvenile Justice,* 35 AM. CRIM. L. REV. 371, 384 (1998). All states now have laws providing for the automatic transfer of juveniles to criminal courts under certain conditions. *Id.; see, e.g.,* UTAH CODE ANN. § 78-3a-602 (Lexis 1996) (mandatory waiver for juveniles sixteen or older charged with enumerated offense); N.C. GEN. STAT. ANN. § 7A-608 (Lexis 1999) (thirteen or older charged with Class A felony). As discussed in the previous note, state courts routinely uphold automatic waiver statutes.

Automatic transfers generally affect juveniles who are accused of committing specific offenses (generally murder, kidnapping, rape, or armed robbery), or who have previously been adjudicated delinquent for the offense now charged. *See* Feld, *The Juvenile Court Meets the Principle of the Offense: Legislative Changes in Juvenile Waiver Statutes, supra* at 494. A statutory transfer is generally effected in one of two ways. The juvenile may automatically be transferred when certain conditions are shown to exist (e.g., the juvenile is of a certain age and is accused of a statutorily enumerated offense). Alternatively, the law may remove the juvenile court's jurisdiction over any juvenile accused of an offense listed in the statute. *See, e.g., United States v. Bland, supra.*

The third method by which a juvenile may be waived for trial in an adult criminal court is through direct file, also known as prosecutorial waiver. This method is found in the few states in which the juvenile and criminal courts have concurrent jurisdiction over certain juvenile offenders. *See, e.g.*, NEB. REV. STAT. § 43-247 (1998); ARK. CODE ANN. § 9-27-318(b) (Michie Supp. 2001). In these states, a juvenile accused of an enumerated offense falls within the jurisdiction of both the juvenile and criminal courts, and the prosecutor determines what charges to file (and, therefore, which court will hear the case). Prosecutor discretion provisions are limited by age and offense criteria. *See generally* Eric Fritsch & Craig Hemmens, J.D., *Juvenile Waiver in the United States 1979-1995: A Comparison and Analysis of State Waiver Statutes,* 46 JUV. & FAM. CT. J. 17 (1995).

Most states now rely on a combination of transfer provisions. The most common combination is judicial waiver with statutory exclusion. Eighteen states now use this combination of transfer provisions. *See* OFF. OF JUV. JUST. & DELINQ. PREVENTION, U.S. DEP'T OF JUST., JUVENILE TRANSFERS TO CRIMINAL COURT IN THE 1990S: LESSONS LEARNED FROM FOUR STUDIES xi (Aug. 2000).

Another change in this area of the law is that states are making it easier for juveniles to be transferred to adult court. In the 1970s and 1980s most states amended their statutory provisions for transferring juveniles. Then, between 1992 and 1997, every state but six expanded their statutory provisions yet again. *See* Eric Fritsch & Craig Hemmens, J.D., *Juvenile Waiver in the United States 1979-1995: A Comparison and Analysis of State Waiver Statutes,* 46 JUV. & FAM. CT. J. 17, 23-32 (1995), for the changes made in the statutory provisions during these periods.

5. Most courts have found that a juvenile is entitled to protection against self-incrimination under the Fifth Amendment during a juvenile transfer hearing. *See, e.g., State v. Gullings,* 416 P.2d 311 (Or. 1966); *In re C.R.M.*, 552 N.W.2d 324 (N.D. 1996); *In re Mark E.P.,* 363 S.E.2d 729 (W. Va. 1987); *People v. Hana,* 504 N.W.2d 166 (Mich. 1993). A few courts, by contrast, have held that, because the juvenile's guilt or innocence is not at issue during a transfer, the Fifth Amendment does not apply. *See, e.g., Martin v. State,* 603 P.2d 1056 (Nev. 1979); *Clemons v. State,* 317 N.E.2d 859 (Ind. Ct. App. 1974). Some courts have gone so far as to allow illegally obtained confessions to be admitted for the purpose of determining whether waiver to an adult court is appropriate. *See, e.g., Clemons v. State, supra; In re J.G.,* 350 N.W.2d 668 (Wis. 1984).

A similar issue arises in relation to a child's right under the Sixth Amendment to confrontation at a waiver hearing. Some courts hold that this right is only applicable to criminal proceedings and is therefore unavailable during a transfer hearing. *See, e.g., United States v. Parker*, 956 F.2d 169 (8th Cir. 1992); *In re Dinson,* 574 P.2d 119 (Haw. 1978). These courts allow hearsay evidence under the theory that the juvenile may present witnesses to rebut the hearsay testimony. *See, e.g., Wolf v. State,* 583 P.2d 1011 (Idaho 1978). Other courts take the opposite view, finding that a waiver hearing is a "critical stage" of the juvenile process, and, therefore, the Sixth Amendment applies and excludes hearsay testimony. *See, e.g., D.D.A. v. State*, 650 So. 2d 571 (Ala. Crim. App. 1994); *In re Keijam T.,* 602 A.2d 967 (Conn. 1992).

6. In *In re A.M.*, No. 74983, 2000 Ohio App. LEXIS 3811 (Aug. 24, 2000), the Ohio Court of Appeals held that a juvenile facing a transfer hearing that could result in his mandatory transfer to adult court is entitled to the protection of the Fourteenth Amendment's Due Process Clause. A juvenile, therefore, has a right to discovery in a transfer hearing. This protection is limited to the issues that will be determinative of the transfer question. The *A.M.* court relied on *Kent*'s finding that a juvenile facing a transfer hearing is entitled to access information considered by the juvenile court in its determination whether to transfer the case to adult criminal court. In his dissent, Judge Patton expressed several concerns regarding the majority's holding. Judge Patton feared that the state would be unfairly burdened because the state would have to prepare their case far in advance of the actual adjudication. Also, Judge Patton argued that a right to discovery should not exist in a hearing because there is no determination of guilt or innocence.

Questions

1. The Juvenile Court judge in *Kent* claimed to make the waiver decision after a "full investigation," a claim to which Justice Fortas gave little credence. Would the result in *Kent* have been different if there had been some indication on the record that the Juvenile Court judge had conducted an investigation before making his decision? Would your answer depend on whether there had been a waiver hearing, regardless of any investigation? Do you think the case would have reached the Supreme Court if the record showed that the Juvenile Court judge had conducted a thorough investigation but had still denied Kent a hearing?

2. Why do you think the judge did not rule on counsel's motion to gain access to the child's Social Service file? Could the seriousness of the offense have affected the judge's decision regarding the file and the need for a hearing?

3. Would the result in the case have been the same under the District of Columbia's juvenile code as amended after *Kent*? *See United States v. Bland*, 472 F.2d 1329 (D.C. Cir. 1972) (discussed in Note 3, *supra*).

IJA-ABA Standards Relating to Transfer Between Courts

Juvenile Justice Standards Annotated 285-92
(Robert E. Sheperd, Jr., ed., 1996)*

PART I: JURISDICTION

1.1 Age limits.

A. The juvenile court should have jurisdiction in any proceeding against any person whose alleged conduct would constitute an offense on which a juvenile court adjudication could be based if at the time the offense is alleged to have occurred such person was not more than seventeen years of age.

---

* Reprinted with permission.

B. No criminal court should have jurisdiction in any proceeding against any person whose alleged conduct would constitute an offense on which a juvenile court adjudication could be based if at the time the offense is alleged to have occurred such person was not more than fourteen years of age.

C. No criminal court should have jurisdiction in any proceeding against any person whose alleged conduct would constitute an offense on which a juvenile court adjudication could be based if at the time the offense is alleged to have occurred such person was fifteen, sixteen, or seventeen years of age, unless the juvenile court has waived its jurisdiction over that person.

* * *

PART II: WAIVER

2.1 Time requirements.

A. Within [two] court days of the filing of any petition alleging conduct which constitutes a class one or class two juvenile offense against a person who was fifteen, sixteen, or seventeen years of age when the alleged offense occurred, the clerk of the juvenile court should give the prosecuting attorney written notice of the possibility of waiver.

B. Within [three] court days of the filing of [the] petition . . . , the prosecuting attorney should give such [juvenile] written notice, multilingual if appropriate, of the possibility of waiver.

C. Within [seven] court days of the filing of [the] petition . . . , the prosecuting attorney may request by written motion that the juvenile court waive its jurisdiction over the juvenile. The prosecuting attorney should deliver a signed, acknowledged copy of the waiver motion to the juvenile and counsel for the juvenile within [twenty-four] hours after the filing of such motion in the juvenile court.

D. The juvenile court should initiate a hearing on waiver within [ten] court days of the filing of the waiver motion or, if the juvenile seeks to suspend this requirement, within a reasonable time thereafter.

E. The juvenile court should issue a written decision setting forth its findings and the reasons therefor, including a statement of the evidence relied on in reaching the decision, within [ten] court days after conclusion of the waiver hearing.

F. No waiver notice should be given, no waiver motion should be accepted for filing, no waiver hearing should be initiated, and no waiver decision should be issued relating to any juvenile court petition after commencement of any adjudicatory hearing relating to any transaction or episode alleged in that petition.

2.2 Necessary findings.

A. The juvenile court should waive its jurisdiction only upon finding:

1. that probable cause exists to believe that the juvenile has committed the class one or class two juvenile offense alleged in the petition; and

2. that by clear and convincing evidence, the juvenile is not a proper person to be handled by the juvenile court.

B. A finding of probable cause to believe that a juvenile has committed a class one or class two juvenile offense should be base solely on evidence admissible in an adjudicatory hearing of the juvenile court.

C. A finding that a juvenile is not a proper person to be handled by the juvenile court must include determinations, by clear and convincing evidence, of:

1. the seriousness of the alleged class one or class two juvenile offense;

2. a prior record of adjudicated delinquency involving the infliction or threat of significant bodily injury, if the juvenile is alleged to have committed a class two juvenile offense;

3. the likely inefficacy of the dispositions available to the juvenile court as demonstrated by previous dispositions of the juvenile; and

4. the appropriateness of the services and dispositional alternatives available in the criminal justice system for dealing with the juvenile's problems and whether they are, in fact, available. . . .

* * *

2.3. The hearing.

A. The juvenile should be represented by counsel at the waiver hearing. . . .

B. The juvenile court should appoint counsel to represent any juvenile unable to afford representation by counsel at the waiver hearing. . . .

* * *

E. The prosecuting attorney should bear the burden of proving that probable cause exists to believe that the juvenile has committed a class one or class two juvenile offense and that the juvenile is not a proper person to be handled by the juvenile court.

F. The juvenile may contest the waiver motion by challenging, or producing evidence tending to challenge, the evidence of the prosecuting attorney.

G. The juvenile may examine any person who prepared any report concerning the juvenile which is presented at the waiver hearing.

H. All evidence presented at the waiver hearing should be under oath and subject to cross-examination.

I. The juvenile may remain silent at the waiver hearing. No admission by the juvenile during the waiver hearing should be admissible to establish guilt or to impeach testimony in any subsequent proceeding, except a perjury proceeding.

* * *

2.4 Appeal.

A. The juvenile or the prosecuting attorney may file an appeal of the waiver decision with the court authorized to hear appeals from final judgments of the juvenile court within [seven] court days of the decision of the juvenile court. . . .

Questions

1. According to § 1.1 of the IJA-ABA Standards, can a criminal court ever obtain jurisdiction over a thirteen-year-old juvenile? Under what circumstances would the juvenile court have jurisdiction over a fourteen-year-old child? A seventeen-year-old? How does this compare to the statutes discussed in Note 4 following *Kent*?

2. Of the three types of waiver discussed in the notes following *Kent*, which is the most appropriate under the IJA-ABA Standards? Would the others be acceptable in a jurisdiction adopting these standards? Why or why not?

B. Criteria for Waiver of Juvenile Court Jurisdiction

Connecticut General Statutes Annotated

§ 46b-127 (West Supp. 2001)

§ 46b-127. Transfer of child charged with a felony to regular criminal docket.

(a) The court shall automatically transfer from the docket for juvenile matters to the regular criminal docket of the Superior Court the case of any child charged with the commission of a capital felony [or] a class A or B felony . . . , provided such offense was committed after such child attained the age of fourteen years and counsel has been appointed for such child if such child is indigent. Such counsel may appear with the child but shall not be permitted to make any argument or file any motion in opposition to the transfer. . . . A state's attorney may, not later than ten working days after such arraignment, file a motion to transfer the case of any child charged with the commission of a class B felony to the docket for juvenile matters. . . .

(b) Upon motion of a juvenile prosecutor and order of the court, the case of any child charged with the commission of a class C or D felony or an unclassified felony shall be transferred from the docket for juvenile matters to the regular criminal docket of the Superior Court, provided such offense was committed after such child attained the age of fourteen years and the court finds *ex parte* that there is probable cause to believe the child has committed the act for which he is charged. . . . The court sitting for the regular criminal docket may return any such case to the docket for juvenile matters. . . .

(c) Upon the effectuation of the transfer, such child shall stand trial and be sentenced, if convicted, as if he were sixteen years of age [the age of majority in Connecticut].

United States v. K.J.C.

976 F. Supp. 1219 (N.D. Iowa 1997)

BENNETT, District Judge

* * *

I. INTRODUCTION AND BACKGROUND

Defendant juvenile K.J.C. is currently charged with the commission of three offenses: aiding and abetting a bank robbery; possessing LSD with intent to distribute; and aiding and abetting in the distribution of LSD. [T]he government filed motions to transfer the proceedings against K.J.C. to adult criminal prosecution pursuant to 18 U.S.C. § 5032.

The government also filed a certification stating that K.J.C. is charged with a violent felony and that there is a substantial federal interest in this case which warrants the exercise of federal jurisdiction. An evidentiary hearing . . . was held. . . . Defendant K.J.C. offered no testimony. Defendant K.J.C. was present at the evidentiary hearing with his parents. . . .

The court turns first to a brief review of the history of the Federal Juvenile Justice and Delinquency Prevention Act, 18 U.S.C. §§ 5031-5042 ("the Act"). The court will then review the standards applicable to motions to transfer juveniles to adult prosecution, and finally the court will conduct a legal analysis of the six statutorily mandated factors to determine whether the transfer of K.J.C. for adult prosecution is appropriate in this case.

II. LEGAL ANALYSIS

A. The Federal Juvenile Justice and Delinquency Prevention Act

The Act was enacted on September 7, 1974. The Act amended the Federal Juvenile Delinquency Act ("FJDA") which had remained virtually unchanged since Congressional enactment in 1938. The FJDA granted the Attorney General unlimited discretion in deciding whether to offer prosecution as a juvenile to any defendant under the age of eighteen not surrendered to state officials or charged with offenses punishable by life imprisonment or death. . . .

The Act made four substantive changes to the FJDA: (1) the Act altered the definition of a juvenile, (2) the Act added the requirement for judicial approval before prosecuting a juvenile as an adult, (3) it placed limits on the number of offenses for which a juvenile could be tried as an adult, and (4) it provided for federal prosecution of juveniles when no state would exercise jurisdiction over the offender. *See* 18 U.S.C. §§ 5031-5032. Congress subsequently amended the Act by its enactment of the Comprehensive Crime Control Act of 1984, Pub. L. No. 98-473, tit. II, 98 Stat. 1976 (1984). Congress expanded the federal role in juvenile justice by authorizing the prosecution of juveniles as adults for additional offenses and mandating adult trial of juveniles in certain cases. 18 U.S.C. § 5032. Congressional passage of the Violent Crime Control and Law Enforcement Act of 1994, Pub. L. No. 103-323, 108 Stat. 1796, further amended the Act. The Violent Crime Control and Law Enforcement Act authorizes the criminal prosecution of juveniles as young as thirteen years of age for certain serious felonies, including first and second degree murder, attempted murder, and bank robbery. 18 U.S.C. § 5032.

B. The Act's Framework

The Act provides a special framework for the prosecution of persons who are juveniles at the time a federal crime is committed. The Act's purpose is to "'remove juveniles from the ordinary criminal process in order to avoid the stigma of a prior criminal conviction and to encourage treatment and rehabilitation.'" *United States v. Doe*, 94 F.3d 532, 536 (9th Cir. 1996); *United States v. T.F.F.*, 55 F.3d 118, 1120 (6th Cir. 1995). The Act's purpose, however, must be weighed against "the need to protect the public from 'violent and dangerous individuals and provid[e] sanctions for anti-social acts. And that balance must be struck by the district court in the context of a transfer hearing.'" *Doe*, 94 F.3d at 536.

In order to proceed against a juvenile in federal court, the Attorney General must certify to the appropriate district court, after investigation,

> that (1) the juvenile court or other appropriate court of a State does not have jurisdiction or refuses to assume jurisdiction over said juvenile with respect to such alleged act of juvenile delinquency, (2) the States does not have available programs and services adequate for the needs of juveniles, or (3) the offense charged is a crime of violence that is a felony . . . and that there is a substantial Federal interest in the case or the offense to warrant the exercise of Federal jurisdiction. If the Attorney General does not so certify, such juvenile shall be surrendered to the appropriate legal authorities of such State.

18 U.S.C. § 5032.

Here, the government has certified defendant K.J.C. for prosecution in federal court pursuant to the third clause.[7] Once federal jurisdiction is obtained over the juvenile, the juvenile is generally subject to be proceeded against in juvenile delinquency proceedings unless the juvenile requests to be proceeded against as an adult or the district court, upon motion by the United States Attorney General and after a hearing, determines that transfer for adult criminal prosecution would be "in the interest of justice." 18 U.S.C. § 5032.

The "substantial Federal interest" category was added to the Act as part of the Comprehensive Crime Control Act of 1984 in order to permit federal authorities to proceed against juveniles charged with particularly serious, violent offenses in criminal prosecutions. The government has made such a motion to transfer defendant K.J.C. for adult criminal prosecution. Therefore, the court must address the appropriate standards for making the "interest of justice" determination under § 5032.

C. Interest of Justice Determination

In determining whether transfer would be in the "interests of justice," the Eighth Circuit Court of Appeals has held that a district court must consider the six statutory factors identified in § 5032. *United States v. A.D.J.*, 108 F.3d 851, 852 (8th Cir. 1997). As explained in § 5032, those six factors are:

> [1] the age and social background of the juvenile, [2] the nature of the alleged offense, [3] the extent and nature of the juvenile's prior delinquency records, [4] the juvenile's present intellectual development and psychological maturity, [5] the nature of past treatment efforts

---

7 The majority of the circuits to consider the issue have determined that the Attorney General's certification based on a "substantial Federal interest" is not subject to judicial review. *See United States v. Juvenile No. 1*, 118 F.3d 298, 300 (5th Cir. 1997); *Impounded (Juvenile R.G.),* 117 F.3d 730, 737 (3d Cir. 1997); *United States v. I.D.P.*, 102 F.3d 507 (11th Cir. 1996), *petition for cert. filed* (U.S. July 28, 1997) (No. 97-5383). *But see United States v. Juvenile Male No. 1,* 86 F.2d 1314 (4th Cir. 1996) (holding certification is reviewable).

> and the juvenile's response to such efforts, [and, 6] the availability of programs designed to treat the juvenile's behavioral problems.

18 U.S.C. § 5032.

For purposes of the transfer hearing, a court may assume the juvenile committed the alleged offenses. . . . The government bears the burden of rebutting the statutory presumption of juvenile treatment. . . . However, the government need only persuade the court by a preponderance of the evidence. . . .

It is clear that "'[t]he decision whether to transfer a juvenile to trial as an adult under 18 U.S.C. § 5032 is within the sound discretion of the trial court, provided the court employs and makes findings as to the six criteria outlined in the Code.'" *Juvenile No. 1*, 118 F.3d at 307. . . . In conducting the requisite six-factor analysis, the court is not required to give each factor equal weight. *Juvenile No. 1*, 118 F.3d at 307. Instead, "[a] court may weigh the statutory factors as it deems appropriate and 'is free to determine how much weight to give each factor.'" *United States v. Wellington*, 102 F.3d 499, 506 (11th Cir. 1996). . . . Indeed, the Eleventh Circuit has held that "the procedure established by section 5032 does not require that a district court or magistrate judge provide any explanation as to why it treated any particular finding as weighing in favor of or against transfer." *Wellington,* 102 F.3d at 505.

D. Application of the Section 5032 Factors to This Case

As noted above, the court must consider each of the six factors enumerated in section 5032 when determining whether to transfer the juvenile for adult prosecution. The court will now consider each of the six § 5032 factors seriatim.

1. Age and Social Background

The first of the six statutorily required factors the court must consider in the transfer calculus is the age and social background of the juvenile. The court should focus on the age of the juvenile at the time of the alleged offense. The court may also focus on the age of the juvenile at the time of the transfer hearing.

K.J.C. . . . was seventeen years old at the time of each of the charged offenses, as well as at the time of the transfer hearings. K.J.C.'s age at the time of the offenses weighs in favor of transfer. . . . Although the court believes that the closer a juvenile is to age eighteen the more appropriate it is to consider this factor as weighing in favor of transfer, the juvenile's age alone is not dispositive, and it must be viewed in the context of the other § 5032 factors.

The other portion of this factor requires the court to examine the social background of K.J.C. K.J.C. resides with his parents in Cedar Rapids, Iowa and has just begun his senior year of high school at Washington High School. . . . K.J.C. has a good relationship with his family members, and they are all supportive of K.J.C. K.J.C.'s home environment is positive and suggests that it would support rehabilitative efforts directed toward K.J.C. . . .

* * *

K.J.C. has been employed the past two years by the Elm Crest Country Club as a counselor in its summer youth activities club. . . . He is described by his supervisor, Leslie Nelson, as being a "fantastic" worker. . . . The court finds that K.J.C.'s social background would be a major factor in his ability to be rehabilitated. The court reaches this conclusion based on K.J.C.'s supportive family environment, K.J.C.'s positive family relationship with his parents and siblings, his excellent work ethic, and his conduciveness to supervision. Thus, the court concludes that K.J.C.'s social background, taken as a whole, must be considered to weigh against transfer.

Because K.J.C.'s age weighs in favor of transfer while his social background weighs against it, the court concludes that this first factor is neutral in the transfer analysis.

2. Nature of the Alleged Offense

The second factor the court must consider is the nature of the alleged offenses. For purposes of the transfer hearing, the court has assumed that K.J.C. committed the alleged offenses. Concerning this particular factor, section 5032 states:

> In considering the nature of the offense, as required by this paragraph, the court shall consider the extent to which the juvenile played a leadership role in an organization, or otherwise influenced other persons to take part in criminal activities, involving the use or distribution of controlled substances or firearms. . . .

18 U.S.C. § 5032.

* * *

In examining the bank robbery offense, the court observes that there is no evidence in the record that K.J.C. was involved in its planning, or took a leadership role in its commission. Indeed, the court finds that his actual involvement can best be described as minimal. He only offered the "would be" bank robber, Washburn, a means of transport to the bank. . . . Thus, the court concludes that K.J.C.'s minor involvement in the commission of the bank robbery militates against transfer.

K.J.C.'s involvement in the sale of LSD to classmates is more compelling. Section 5032 specifically provides that where a juvenile influenced other persons to take part in criminal activities involving the use of controlled substances, such action weighs in favor of a transfer to adult status. K.J.C.'s sale of LSD to classmates meets such a classification. However, the mere fact that K.J.C. was involved in LSD drug sales does not necessarily require the court to weigh this factor heavily in favor of transfer. While K.J.C. profited from theses sales, some of the sales can be characterized as accommodation sales. K.J.C. can best be described as a low-level dealer. Although the offenses alleged, namely the sale of LSD near a school, are quite serious, K.J.C. did not commit an act of violence in the commission of those offenses, nor are the circumstances of these offenses particularly heinous or striking. The court further notes that the government has not come forward with evidence that K.J.C. possessed weapons or firearms in the furtherance of his drug sales, a factor several courts have deemed to be significant. Accordingly, the court concludes that while the nature of the alleged controlled substance offenses here weighs in favor of transfer, the nature of the offenses does not weigh heavily in favor of transfer. . . .

3. Prior Delinquency Record

The next factor the court is required to examine in determining whether or not to transfer K.J.C. is his prior delinquency record. Here, K.J.C. has only one instance of delinquency in his record, a charge of criminal mischief. On August 7, 1995, K.J.C. and three other juveniles spray painted graffiti on the side of a Jack's store in Cedar Rapids. K.J.C. was fifteen at the time of the offense. . . . The court takes specific note of the fact that K.J.C.'s sole juvenile offense did not involve violence. The court concludes that K.J.C.'s limited delinquency record weighs against transfer because such a limited record of juvenile criminal involvement supports the notion that he can be rehabilitated by the time he reaches age twenty-one. . . .

4. Intellectual Development and Psychological Maturity

K.J.C. has long been afflicted with ADD which has required him to take medication. Despite this affliction, K.J.C. has progressed through high school and has begun his senior year of high school. His teachers view him as having average maturity. . . . The court has not been provided with any results from intelligence tests or psychological examinations. Nonetheless, the court views K.J.C. as having at least average intelligence and age appropriate psychological maturity. Analysis of this factor does not reflect the existence of any condition which would hinder K.J.C.'s potential for rehabilitation. Indeed, each witness who was questioned about K.J.C.'s possible likelihood for rehabilitation testified that they [sic] were of the opinion that K.J.C. was a good candidate for rehabilitation.

* * *

5. Past Treatment Efforts

The fifth statutory factor is past treatment efforts and their success or lack of effectiveness. As far as the court is aware, K.J.C. has not been the subject of any prior treatment efforts. The complete absence of any treatment efforts suggests that an attempt at rehabilitation should be undertaken. Such an attempt at treatment is entirely in keeping with the Act's statutory policy of favoring treatment and rehabilitation. . . . Moreover, the government has not come forward with any evidence that would indicate that K.J.C. is unamenable to treatment or is otherwise ill-suited to treatment. Thus, the court concludes that the complete absence of any prior attempts at treatment causes this factor to weigh in favor of not transferring K.J.C. for adult prosecution. . . .

6. The Availability Of Programs For Treatment

The final factor the court must consider is the availability of programs for treatment. The government bears the burden to show that there is a lack of available programs designed to treat defendant's problems. . . .

* * *

Because the government presented evidence of possible juvenile treatment programs available for K.J.C. in the Federal Bureau of Prisons, the court concludes that appropriate programs are available for the treatment of K.J.C.

... The existence of juvenile programs that are available for the treatment of K.J.C. is particularly significant in this case since K.J.C. has never undergone prior juvenile treatment. The significance of this factor is increased by the fact that each witness who was questioned about K.J.C.'s possible likelihood for rehabilitation testified that they [sic] believed K.J.C. was a good candidate for rehabilitation. Thus, there appears to be a good chance K.J.C. can be rehabilitated to become a useful member of society.

III. CONCLUSION

The court concludes, upon balancing the six § 5032 factors, that the interests of justice do not warrant transferring K.J.C. for adult prosecution. . . . The court concludes that K.J.C. is a promising prospect for rehabilitation. . . . For these reasons, . . . the court denies the government's motions to transfer K.J.C. to adult status.

Notes

1. *K.J.C.* addresses two separate waiver issues. It is important to distinguish between waiver to a federal court and waiver for adult criminal prosecution. This note will address each in turn.

a. *Waiver to Federal Court*

The District Court judge in *K.J.C.* did not review the government's certification of the juvenile for prosecution in federal court. This certification was made pursuant to 18 U.S.C. § 5032. Section 5032 lists three factors, one of which the Attorney General must assert in order to transfer the juvenile to federal court for prosecution. The factors, reprinted in pertinent part in *K.J.C.*, are (1) that no state court has or is willing to assume jurisdiction over the juvenile in relation to the alleged act; (2) that the state does not have programs or services to meet the juvenile's needs; and (3) that the offense alleged is a violent felony and there is a substantial federal interest that warrants the exercise of federal jurisdiction. The third factor, which includes the "substantial Federal interest," is the one most often invoked in the transfer of juveniles to federal court. In addition to *K.J.C.*, *see United States v. Juvenile Male J.A.J.*, 134 F.3d 905 (8th Cir. 1998); *United States v. I.D.P.*, 102 F.3d 507 (11th Cir. 1996). Although the language of the statute does not specify whether a showing of a substantial federal interest is necessary in every case, one court has recently held that such an interest is not required if the government moves to transfer under either of the first two factors. *See United States v. White*, 139 F.3d 998 (4th Cir. 1998).

Transfer to federal court is also distinguishable from transfer to adult criminal court in that certification of federal court jurisdiction is considered an act of prosecutorial discretion, which is generally not subject to judicial review. *See, e.g., United States v. J.A.J., supra; United States v. I.D.P., supra; United States v. Doe*, 49 F.3d 859 (2d Cir. 1995); *but see United States v. Juvenile Male No. I*, 86 F.3d 1314 (4th Cir. 1996). The Fourth Circuit stands alone in holding that a court may review the Attorney General's certification of federal interest. *See Juvenile Male No. I, supra; K.J.C.*, 976 F. Supp. 1219, 1223 n.7.

b. *Waiver for Adult Criminal Prosecution*

As discussed above, the issue of transfer to adult criminal court is distinct from transfer to federal court. This second issue often arises in federal prosecutions of juveniles, but unlike transfer to federal court, it is also an issue in state courts. Federal transfers are regulated by the six criteria set forth in the Juvenile Justice and Delinquency Prevention Act (J.J.D.P.A.), as discussed in *K.J.C.* When considering a motion to transfer a juvenile for adult prosecution in federal court, the judge must consider each of the six J.J.D.P.A. criteria and enter findings regarding each in the record. *See* 18 U.S.C. § 5032; *see also United States v. I.D.P., supra; United States v. Doe, supra; United States v. A.D.J.,* 108 F.3d 851 (8th Cir. 1997); *United States v. T.F.F.,* 55 F.3d 1118 (6th Cir. 1995). However, as discussed in *K.J.C.*, the court has considerable discretion in weighing the factors and determining their relevance to the transfer motion. *See also United States v. T.F.F., supra; United States v. Wellington*, 102 F.2d 499 (11th Cir. 1996); *United States v. Juvenile No. 1*, 118 F.3d 298 (5th Cir. 1997).

In an appendix to *Kent v. United States,* 383 U.S. 541 (1966) (*see supra*, Part A), the Supreme Court recommended criteria for analyzing a waiver motion. The Court said:

> The determinative factors which will be considered by the Judge in deciding whether the Juvenile Court's jurisdiction over such offenses will be waived are the following:
>
> 1. The seriousness of the alleged offense to the community and whether the protection of the community requires waiver.
>
> 2. Whether the alleged offense was committed in an aggressive, violent, premeditated or willful manner.
>
> 3. Whether the alleged offense was against persons or against property, greater weight being given to offenses against persons especially if personal injury resulted.
>
> 4. The prosecutive merit of the complaint, i.e., whether there is evidence upon which a Grand Jury may be expected to return an indictment. . . .
>
> 5. The desirability of trial and disposition of the entire offense in one court when the juvenile's associates in the alleged offense are adults . . . .
>
> 6. The sophistication and maturity of the juvenile as determined by consideration of his home, environmental situation, emotional attitude and pattern of living.
>
> 7. The record and previous history of the juvenile . . . .
>
> 8. The prospects for adequate protection of the public and the likelihood of reasonable rehabilitation of the juvenile . . . by the use of procedures, services and facilities currently available to the Juvenile Court. [Although] not all such factors will be involved in an individual case, the Judge will consider the relevant factors in a specific case before reaching a conclusion to waive juvenile jurisdiction and transfer the case . . . for trial under . . . adult procedures. . . .

Id. at 566-68. Although federal courts are governed by the J.J.D.P.A. criteria, some state courts have embraced the criteria listed in *Kent*, either in whole or with some modification. For example, the District of Columbia, where Morris Kent's case originated, statutorily adopted the analysis recommended in the *Kent* appendix following the Supreme Court's decision. *See* D.C. CODE ANN. § 16-2307(e) (Lexis Supp. 2001). Other states have also enacted the *Kent* criteria through legislation. *See, e.g.,* FLA. STAT. ANN. § 985.226(3)(c) (West 2001); 705 ILL. COMP. STAT. ANN. 405/5-805(2)(b) (West Supp. 2001); TEX. FAM. CODE ANN. § 54.02(f) (West Supp. 2001). The legislatures of other states have adopted criteria similar to those listed in the *Kent* appendix. *See, e.g.,* ALASKA STAT. § 47.12.100(b) (Lexis 2000); MICH. COMP. LAWS ANN. § 712A.4(4) (West Supp. 2001).

Most states, however, have not established specific waiver criteria. The relevant statutes in these jurisdictions generally require only a showing that the child is not amenable to rehabilitation in the juvenile justice system. *See, e.g.,* MINN. STAT. ANN. § 260B.125(2)(6) (West Supp. 2001); N.J. STAT. ANN. § 2A:4A-26(a)(3) (West Supp. 2001); OHIO REV. CODE ANN. § 2151.26(C)(1)(c) (Anderson Supp. 2000). Although they do not establish specific criteria that the judge must consider when analyzing a waiver motion, these statutes have withstood constitutional challenges for overbreadth. *See, e.g., In re Wefare of I.Q.S.,* 224 N.W.2d 30 (Minn. 1976); *State v. Green,* 544 P.2d 356 (Kan. 1975). Where the relevant legislation lacks specific criteria, standards that are more precise may be judicially adopted. *See, e.g., Summers v. State*, 230 N.E.2d 320 (Ind. 1967); *State v. Gibbs,* 500 P.2d 209 (Idaho 1972); *Davis v. State,* 297 So. 2d 289 (Fla. 1974); *State v. Smagula*, 377 A.2d 608 (N.H. 1977). In a few states, these judicially-adopted standards have subsequently been incorporated into legislation. *See, e.g.,* FLA. STAT., *supra*; IND. CODE §§ 31-30-3-2 & -3 (Michie 1997). *See* OFF. OF JUV. JUST. & DELINQ. PREVENTION, U.S DEP'T OF JUST., JUVENILE TRANSFERS TO CRIMINAL COURT IN THE 1990'S: LESSONS LEARNED FROM FOUR STUDIES (Aug. 2000), for the results of four studies designed to identify the factors considered in the decision whether to transfer a case from juvenile to criminal court.

As noted above, the prosecutor's decision to invoke federal jurisdiction over a juvenile is generally not subject to judicial review. Waiver for adult criminal prosecution, on the other hand, is reviewable on appeal. The standard of review is for abuse of discretion in both federal and state courts. *See, e.g., United States v. J.A.J., supra*; *United States v. I.D.P., supra; United States v. Doe, supra; Gerrick v. State,* 451 N.E.2d 327 (Ind. 1983); *Commonwealth v. Spencer,* 695 N.E.2d 677 (Mass. App. Ct. 1998); *State v. Jensen,* 579 N.W.2d 613 (S.D. 1998).

2. The prosecutor bears the burden of proving that a juvenile is not amendable to treatment by the juvenile justice system. Every federal court to consider the issue has held that the state must prove the propriety of a transfer motion by a preponderance of the evidence. In addition to *K.J.C., see United States v. I.D.P., supra; United States v. Doe, supra; United States v. T.F.F., supra.* The United States Supreme Court has not ruled on the matter and has recently refused to hear a case raising the issue. *See Rosado v. Corrections,* 109 F.3d 62 (1st Cir. 1997). Most state courts have also adopted a preponderance of the evidence standard, either judicially or through legislation. *See, e.g., In re F.S.,* 586 P.2d 607 (Alaska 1978); *In re Randolph T.,* 437 A.2d 230 (Md. 1981); *Imel v. State,* 342 N.E. 2d 897 (Ind. Ct. App. 1976); ME. REV. STAT. ANN. tit. 15, § 3101.4.E-2 (West Supp. 2000). A few jurisdictions, however, require a clear and convincing showing before a transfer will be approved. *See, e.g.,* MINN. STAT. ANN. § 260B.125(2)(6), *supra;* WIS. STAT. § 938.18(6) (West 2000); *Brooks v. State,* 929 S.W.2d 160 (Ark. 1996).

Questions

1. Which of the factors outlined in the Juvenile Justice and Delinquency Prevention Act and the appendix to *Kent v. United States* most closely approach the goals of the juvenile justice system as you understand them? Which of the factors should be required in an analysis of a transfer petition? Are there any other criteria you would add? Can a court realistically be expected to make an analysis employing the listed factors in every case? Does the judge always have enough information? Does the discretion given to judges employing the J.J.D.P.A. criteria render theses standards useless?

2. Do the state laws, discussed in the Notes section above, which require only a showing of unamenability to rehabilitation in the juvenile system, offer sufficient protection to a child facing waiver to adult court? If not, what would you add to these statutes to adequately protect juveniles facing waiver to adult courts?

3. What burden of proof should be required in a transfer hearing? Does a preponderance of the evidence standard sufficiently protect juveniles? How do courts and legislatures justify a preponderance standard? (*See* Note 4 following *Kent v. United States, supra,* Part A.)

Problem

Arnold Lax recently turned seventeen years of age. He quit school when he was sixteen. His mother works during the day. Arnold is unemployed and spends much of his time "hanging out" at the bus station, the Seven-Eleven and the apartment complex where he lives. The mother of Tanya, a twelve-year-old girl, reported to the police that Tanya met Arnold at the bus station and that Arnold had called Tanya on the telephone. Also, Arnold persuaded Tanya to skip school and spend the day at his apartment, while his mother was at work. Tanya told her mother and the police that she and Arnold watched the video "Deep Throat" and after the movie Arnold removed her clothes. Tanya described how Arnold kissed her breasts and fondled her vaginal area, but he stopped in his attempt to have intercourse when she screamed that it hurt. Tanya stated that she didn't want Arnold to touch her, but she was afraid that he would become angry and make her go home and she would get into trouble for skipping school. The police took photographs of fresh bruises on Tanya's neck which she described as "hickies" caused by Arnold. Tanya's mother stated that Tanya came home at the usual time and seemed fine. Later in the evening, the mother noticed that Tanya was unusually quiet and asked her if something was wrong. Tanya then described to her mother what happened. Tanya was examined at the hospital and no trauma was evident. Arnold agreed to make a statement to the police. He admitted that Tanya skipped school at his suggestion and they watched "Deep Throat" but that it was Tanya's idea to take off her clothes. Arnold admitted that he and Tanya experimented sexually but that Tanya was a willing participant. Arnold said he stopped when Tanya asked him to.

Should the prosecuting attorney file a waiver petition in the juvenile court under the following statutes:

> Section 1. Waiver Of Jurisdiction Defined.
>
> Waiver of jurisdiction refers to an order of the juvenile court that waives the case to a court that would have jurisdiction had the act been committed by an adult. Waiver is for the offense charged and all included offenses.
>
> Section 2. Heinous or Aggravated Act or Act as Part of Repetitive Pattern of Delinquent Acts.,
>
> Upon motion of the prosecuting attorney and after full investigation and hearing, the juvenile court may waive jurisdiction if it finds that:
>
> 1. the child is charged with an act:
>   1) that is heinous or aggravated, with greater weight given to acts against the person than to acts against property; or
>   2) that is part of a repetitive pattern of delinquent acts, even though less serious;
> 2. the child was at least (14) years of age when the act charged was allegedly committed;
> 3. there is probable cause to believe that the child committed the act;
> 4. the child is beyond rehabilitation under the juvenile justice system; and
> 5. it is in the best interests of the safety and welfare of the community that the childstand trial as an adult.

If a petition for waiver is filed, should the court find by a preponderance of evidence that jurisdiction of Arnold's case should be waived to adult court? Why or why not?

C. Reverse Waiver

State v. Verhagen

542 N.W.2d 189 (Wis. Ct. App. 1995)

NETTESHIEM, Judge

This appeal concerns the "reverse waiver" proceedings contemplated by § 970.032, [WIS.] STATS. That statute authorizes the adult criminal court, which otherwise has exclusive original jurisdiction pursuant to § 48.183, STATS., over a child alleged to have committed a battery under special circumstances to transfer jurisdiction to the juvenile court.

[On] appeal, Verhagen contends that: (1) the statutory scheme violates his equal protection rights, (2) the adult court improperly assigned a portion of the burden of proof to him in the "reverse waiver" proceeding, and (3) the adult court erred by retaining adult court jurisdiction.

Based on existing precedent, we conclude that the statutory scheme does not violate Verhagen's right to equal protection of the Law. We further conclude that a juvenile defendant has the burden of proof in a reverse waiver proceeding. Finally, we conclude that the adult court properly exercised its discretion when it decided to retain jurisdiction over Verhagen. We therefore affirm the nonfinal order.

BACKGROUND

The State charged Verhagen with the February 3, 1994, battery of a youth counselor at the Ethan Allen School for Boys where Verhagen was committed as a juvenile offender. The complaint alleged that Verhagen's conduct violated § 940.20(1) STATS., which is punishable by the penalties delineated in § 939.635, STATS.

On February 4, 1994, Verhagen made an initial appearance in adult court before the Honorable Kathryn W. Foster pursuant to § 48.183, STATS. This statute presumptively grants the adult criminal court "exclusive original jurisdiction" over a child alleged to have violated § 940.20(1), STATS., unless the adult court transfers jurisdiction to the juvenile court in a "reverse waiver" proceeding pursuant to § 970.032, STATS. Verhagen challenged the adult court's jurisdiction on constitutional and statutory grounds. In due course, Judge Foster denied these challenges.

Thereafter, Verhagen filed a timely request for substitution of judge against Judge Foster and the matter was assigned to the Honorable Marianne E. Becker, who presided over the preliminary hearing and the concurrent reverse waiver hearing. . . . Following a probable cause determination, Judge Becker addressed the reverse waiver question. The judge allocated the burden of proof to both parties, requiring the state to make a prima facie showing for retention of jurisdiction and requiring Verhagen to demonstrate that a transfer to the juvenile court was warranted.

At the conclusion of the reverse waiver hearing, Judge Becker ruled that the State had carried its burden but that Verhagen had not carried his. The court therefore retained jurisdiction over Verhagen.

Verhagen petitioned this court for leave to appeal the rulings of both Judge Foster and Judge Becker. Verhagen challenged Judge Foster's ruling that the statutory scheme did not violate his constitutional equal protection rights, and he challenged Judge Becker's allocation of the burden of proof. We accepted Verhagen's petition because the burden of proof question presented an issue of first impression. Verhagen's constitutional issues are governed by *State v. Martin*, 191 Wis. 2d 646, 650, 530 N.W.2d 420, 421 (Ct. App. 1995), in which the court of appeals rejected the arguments made by Verhagen here. We do not discuss them further in this opinion. We will recite additional facts as we address the appellate issues.

DISCUSSION

Burden of Proof

On appeal, both parties dispute Judge Becker's "shared allocation" of the burden of proof on the reverse waiver issue. The State contends that the burden was fully Verhagen's; Verhagen contends that the burden was fully the State's. The dispute requires that we construe § 970.032, STATS. The interpretation of a statute presents a question of law which we review independently. *State v. Skamfer,* 176 Wis. 2d 304, 307, 500 N.W.2d 369, 370 (Ct. App. 1993).

Section 48.183, STATS., vests the adult criminal court with "exclusive original jurisdiction over a child who is alleged to have violated § 940.20(1)." Section 970.032(2), STATS. provides that if at the preliminary hearing the adult court finds probable cause to believe that a juvenile has violated § 940.20, STATS., the court must then determine whether to retain jurisdiction or to transfer jurisdiction to children's court. Section 970.032(2) further mandates that the court "shall retain jurisdiction" unless the court finds that all of the following considerations are satisfied:

> (a) That, if convicted, the child could not receive adequate treatment in the criminal justice system.
> (b) That transferring jurisdiction . . . would not depreciate the seriousness of the offense.
> (c) That retaining jurisdiction is not necessary to deter the child or other children from committing violations of § 940.20(1) . . . while placed in a secured correctional facility. . . .

This statute does not specify which party carries the burden of proof as to reverse waiver. Nor, if the burden is shared, does the statute specify which party bears the burden as to a particular question. Given this silence, we conclude that reasonable minds could differ on this question. Thus, the statute is ambiguous.

The State cites cases from several jurisdictions which have held that the burden rests with a juvenile to prove that transfer from adult court to the juvenile court is warranted. Although these cases provide some guidance, we observe that the particular statutory language under scrutiny in those cases more clearly signals that the burden rests with the juvenile because the statutes require the juvenile to bring a motion or to seek application for a transfer. *See, e.g., State v. Anderson,* 385 A.2d 738, 739 n.2 (Del. Super. Ct. 1978) (the court may transfer the case to family court upon application of the defendant); *Carter v. State,* 382 So.2d 871, 872 (Fla. Dist. Ct. App. 1980) (juvenile defendant treated as an adult unless he or she files a motion requesting transfer to juvenile division); *State v. Woodward,* 737 P.2d 569, 569 (Okla. Crim. App.), *and modified,* 745 P.2d 1180 (Okla. Crim. App. 1987) (an accused person shall file a motion for certification as a child).

Unlike these statutes, § 970.032, STATS., does not expressly require the juvenile to bring a motion requesting the transfer to juvenile court. Nonetheless, we conclude that the juvenile properly bears the burden of proof on a reverse waiver question.

We begin with an examination of the law regarding the assignment of a burden of proof. Absent express legislative direction on the question, we employ a five-factor analysis in determining which party has the burden of proof. *See State v. Hanson,* 98 Wis. 2d 80, 85-90, 295 N.W.2d 209, 213-15 (Ct. App. 1980), *aff'd,* 100 Wis. 2d 549, 302 N.W. 2d 452 (1981). The five factors are: (1) special policy considerations, (2) the judicial estimate of probabilities, (3) the natural tendency to place the burdens on the party desiring change, (4) the fairness factors, and (5) convenience. *Hanson*, 98 Wis. 2d at 85-86, 295 N.W.2d at 213. We will consider each of these factors in turn.

1. Policy Considerations

Section 48.183, STATS., grants the adult court exclusive original jurisdiction over a juvenile who has committed an assault or battery while an inmate in a secured correctional facility. The adult court retains this jurisdiction unless all of the criteria set out in § 970.032(2), STATS., are satisfied. . . .

By this enactment, the legislature has clearly recognized that assaults and batteries committed by juveniles while inmates of correctional facilities are matters of serious public concern. The legislative policy presumptively favors adult court jurisdiction over juvenile court jurisdiction. These policy considerations favor placing the burden for undoing this presumption on the juvenile defendant.

2. Judicial Estimate of Probabilities

Judicial estimate of probabilities recognizes that the "risk of failure of proof may be placed upon the party who contends that the more unusual has occurred." *Hanson*, 98 Wis. 2d at 88, 295 N.W.2d at 214 . . . . Here, the usual situation is that the criminal court "shall retain jurisdiction" over a juvenile who violates § 940.20(1), STATS. The unusual situation under the statutory scheme is one in which the court orders a transfer of jurisdiction to the juvenile court. Thus, this consideration favors placing the burden regarding the statutory factors on the juvenile.

3. Natural Tendency to Place Burden on Party Seeking Change

Akin to the foregoing, the next factor recognizes the law's natural tendency to place the burden on the party seeking change in the present state of affairs. *See Hanson*, 98 Wis. 2d, at 90, 295 N.W.2d at 215. As we have already demonstrated, the statutory scheme presumptively vests the adult criminal court with exclusive original jurisdiction. A transfer to juvenile court changes that presumption. Therefore, this consideration also favors placing the burden on the juvenile.

4. Fairness Factor

The fairness factor has two components: "proof of exceptions" and "proof of negatives." *Id.* at 89, 295 N.W.2d at 214. Proof of exceptions is the rule that the one who relies on an exception to a general rule or statute has the burden of proving that the case falls within the exception. *Id.* As we have noted, § 47.183, STATS., vests the adult criminal court with exclusive original jurisdiction. In addition, § 970.032(2), STATS., provides that the adult court "shall retain jurisdiction *unless* the court finds all of the following [factors supporting transfer]." (Emphasis added.) A transfer to the juvenile court would constitute an "exception" or a "negative" to that state of affairs. This consideration also supports placing the burden on the juvenile.

5. Convenience

The convenience factor addresses which party most readily has the facts at its command to provide the court with information about whether the adult or the juvenile court should exercise jurisdiction. *See id.; Hanson,* 98 Wis. 2d at 87-88, 295 N.W.2d at 214. We acknowledge that the State might, in a given case, have relevant information about the juvenile and the State's ability to provide adequate treatment in the justice system. However, it seems obvious that the juvenile would have the best command and knowledge of information about himself or herself relative to the reverse waiver question. We conclude that this consideration also favors placing the burden on the juvenile.

We therefore hold that the juvenile bears the burden of proof to demonstrate that the statutory factors under § 970.032(2), STATS., support transferring jurisdiction to the juvenile court. Thus, Judge Becker's assignment of a portion of this burden to the State was partial error. However, since the error inured to the benefit of Verhagen, no reversible error occurred.

REVERSE WAIVER

Verhagen next challenges Judge Becker's determination that the evidence as applied to the statutory factors set out in § 970.032(2)(a)-(c), STATS., did not support a transfer of jurisdiction to the juvenile court. We conclude that the court's findings are supported by the evidence and represent a proper application of the statutory factors.

It is well established that a juvenile court's decision to waive jurisdiction to adult court is a discretionary decision for the juvenile court. *See State v. C.W.,* 142 Wis. 2d 763, 766-67, 419 N.W.2d 327, 328-29 (Ct. App. 1987). We see no reason why a decision to retain or transfer jurisdiction in a reverse waiver situation should be any different. We therefore will review Judge Becker's reverse waiver ruling as a discretionary determination.

A discretionary determination must be the product of a rational mental process by which the facts of record and law relied upon are stated and considered together for the purpose of achieving a reasoned and reasonable determination. *Breuer v. Town of Addison,* 194 Wis. 2d 617, 626, 534 N.W.2d 634, 638-39 (Ct. App. 1995). We will not reverse a trial court's discretionary act if the record reflects that discretion was in fact exercised and there was a reasonable basis for the court's determination. When reviewing a trial court's exercise of discretion, we will look for reasons to sustain the decision.

Verhagen's victim, James Woods, testified about the facts and circumstances surrounding the February 3, 1994 incident. On that day, Verhagen was a kitchen worker who had special privileges in the minimum-security unit and concurrent restrictions on his contact with the other residents. Verhagen had been warned earlier in the day to end his horseplay with other residents, but was discovered after dinner engaged in the same conduct with other residents in a bathroom. Woods ordered Verhagen out of the bathroom and to his room. Verhagen became angry and refused. Eventually, another staff member persuaded Verhagen to go to his room.

Later, as Woods was making his rounds up and down the hallway where Verhagen's room was located, Verhagen repeatedly told Woods he wanted to talk to him. Eventually, Woods went to the door but remained in the hallway to talk to Verhagen because regulations required two staff members to go into a resident's room.

As the two talked, Verhagen got angrier and louder, so Woods attempted to close the door and continue his duties. Verhagen put his foot in front of the door and yanked the door to prevent Woods from closing it. As Verhagen tugged at the door, Woods' keys fell to the floor and into Verhagen's room. As Woods looked for his keys, Verhagen used his fist to hit Woods on the head, causing Woods' glasses to fly down the hallway. Verhagen told Woods he was an "asshole" as he hit Woods on the head with his fist. Verhagen swung at Woods again, but Woods blocked the punch. Verhagen then ripped Woods' shirt over his head and threw it on the floor. Woods tried to restrain Verhagen, but he continued to swing at Woods and began kicking him.

When Woods finally restrained Verhagen in a corner by holding his arms, Verhagen used his elbow to hit Woods on the top of the head between six and eight times. Another staff member arrived to help Woods keep Verhagen against the wall. Verhagen then heaved his knee upward to hit Woods under the chin and rammed his head into the right corner of Woods' eye, knocking Woods' teeth together and giving him a raised lump on the side of his eye. When a third staff member arrived, they were able to use a compression hold to get Verhagen's hands behind his back. Verhagen was kept face down on his bed in handcuffs until the supervisors arrived, placed him in leg irons and took him to the maximum-security unit.

* * *

Judge Becker specifically considered the factors in subsec. (2)(a)-(c) of § 970.032, STATS., when deciding to retain adult court jurisdiction. The court described Verhagen's conduct as "a vicious major attack" and concluded that transferring jurisdiction to the juvenile court would depreciate the seriousness of the offense.

The trial court also concluded that Verhagen needed to spend time in jail to be deterred from committing future offenses and that retention in the criminal justice system would give him an idea of how much worse the consequences would be if he did not reform. The court further determined that retaining jurisdiction was necessary to deter other children in the Ethan Allen School because others were looking to see who "gets away with what" and whether "they can get away with pushing people around," especially the security officers.

The trial court acknowledged that Verhagen's treatment in the adult system might not be as adequate as that in the juvenile system, but the court concluded, on balance, that the other statutory factors in favor of retaining adult court jurisdiction overrode this consideration. It is thus obvious that the court engaged in a rational mental process based on the facts of record and balanced the relevant legal criteria. The court exercised its discretion and provided a reasonable basis for its decision. The law of discretion requires no more.

We affirm Judge Becker's ruling retaining adult court jurisdiction. We remand for further future proceedings.

Order affirmed and cause remanded.

Notes

1. Although reverse waivers are a relatively recent development in the law relating to juveniles, the issue can be expected to arise with increasing frequency in light of the growing number of statutory waivers. (See the Notes following *Kent v. United States, supra,* Part A.) Only a few courts have addressed the issue, and those have been universal in holding that the burden is on the juvenile to initiate reverse waiver proceedings and to show that a reverse waiver is warranted. *See, e.g., State v. Terry,* 569 N.W.2d 364 (Iowa 1997) (burden on defendant to show good cause for reverse waiver); *King v. State,* 373 A.2d 292 (Md. Ct. Spec. App. 1977) (burden on juvenile to move for reverse waiver and show good cause); *State v. Beulow*, 587 A.2d 948 (Vt. 1990); *In re N.H.B.,* 777 P.2d 487 (Utah Ct. App. 1989); *M.K.H. v. State,* 946 P.2d 677 (Okla. Crim. App. 1997) (burden on juvenile, but due process requires that juvenile be informed of right to file for reverse waiver). Most of these holdings stem from statutory waiver schemes. *See, e.g.* IOWA CODE ANN. § 232.8(1)(c) (West Supp. 2001).

Questions

1. Do you agree that the burden of proof should be on the juvenile in a reverse waiver determination? Should courts be required, as in the Oklahoma case discussed in the Note section, *supra*, to inform the juvenile of the right to seek a reverse waiver?

2. Under what circumstances should a court grant a reverse waiver? Must the juvenile show amenability to rehabilitation? A willingness to take responsibility for her actions? Remorse? Would requiring any of these force a juvenile to chose between a criminal trial and an admission of guilt? If so, is this constitutional?

3. Should statutory waivers be subject to reverse waiver consideration, or do the reasons for allowing automatic waiver of juvenile court jurisdiction preclude such review? Put differently, does a juvenile who fits the automatic waiver criteria deserve to have his case considered for reversal of jurisdiction to the juvenile court?

Chapter 6
Adjudication in Delinquency Proceedings

This chapter examines the adjudication or trial of juvenile delinquents. The juvenile justice system was separated from the criminal justice system because society believed the two systems should have different goals. Criminal proceedings attempt to punish, whereas juvenile proceedings aim to rehabilitate through treatment of the child. The juvenile court was established as a non-adversarial social welfare institution. The courts thus found the issue of whether juveniles needed due process rights irrelevant. Today, juvenile proceedings, like the adult criminal system, are increasingly focused on punishment and protection of society.

Much is at stake during the adjudication of a juvenile delinquent; not only may a juvenile's permanent record be affected, but the child may be detained for a long period of time. The courts began to re-examine the issue of whether juveniles are entitled to due process rights. The leading case is *In re Gault*, 387 U.S.1 (1967), which established the due process framework for the adjudication stage of juvenile court proceedings and will be discussed in this chapter. After *Gault* and its progeny, what is the role of *parens patriae* in juvenile court proceedings? The cases in this chapter invite comparison and contrast of the juvenile and adult criminal justice systems and analysis of factors which suggest that adjudication of children should be different.

A. Competency of Juvenile to Stand Trial

In re Carey

615 N.W.2d 742 (Mich. Ct. App. 2000)

BANDSTRA, C.J.

In this appeal we consider whether a court must determine the competency of a juvenile accused of an offense when a claim is raised that the juvenile is incompetent to stand trial in the adjudicative phase of a delinquency proceedings. We hold that the Due Process Clause requires this determination. We further hold that, in making this determination, the provisions of the Mental Health Code applicable to determinations of adult competency for criminal trials should be employed. We reverse and remand for further proceedings.

FACTS

A petition was filed in the Alpena County Probate Court, Juvenile Division . . . alleging that responded had committed second-degree criminal sexual conduct, MCL 750.520c; MSA 28.788(3). Shortly after the petition was filed, the prosecutor moved that respondent be evaluated concerning both his competency to stand trial and his criminal responsibility. The trial court granted this motion. Respondent was examined by Jason Stentoumis, a psychologist at Northeast Michigan Community Health. After this examination was performed, counsel for respondent moved for a competency hearing, claiming that respondent had a due process right to a hearing and requesting that the practice for determining competency in adult criminal cases be followed.

* * *

[T]he trial court did not allow Stentoumis to testify directly about respondent's competency to stand trial. However, it allowed Stentoumis to testify about respondent's current level of functioning. According to Stentoumis, respondent's full scale IQ was 65, which placed him in the lowest one percentile of people his age. Respondent could understand simple language, but abstract matters were difficult for him to comprehend. In addition, he had short-term memory problems. However, respondent was capable of carrying on a conversation that was goal-oriented. Stentoumis believed that respondent was aware he had done something wrong because, as Stentoumis put it, "his mother was angry with him and [respondent] stated he wouldn't do it again because his Mom was upset with him." Stentoumis was not sure whether respondent would be able to assist counsel.

[O]n May 15, 1998, the court concluded that respondent was not competent to stand trial because he could not understand the nature and object of the proceedings. . . .

Respondent contends that he has a due process right not to be subjected to the adjudicative phase of a delinquency proceeding while incompetent to stand trial and a right to have his competency determined. A claim of incompetency to stand trial, and the right to a competency determination, implicates constitutional due process protections. *People v. Newton, (After Remand)*, 179 Mich. App. 484, 487; 446 N.W.2d 487 (1989). Issues of constitutional law are reviewed de novo. *People v. Sierb,* 456 Mich. 519, 522; 581 N.W.2d 219 (1998); *People v. Walker,* 234 Mich. App. 299, 302; 593 N.W.2d 673 (1999).

QUESTIONS PRESENTED

No cases in Michigan have addressed the due process right of a juvenile to be determined competent as a prerequisite to the adjudicative phase of a delinquency proceedings. Further, Michigan has no statutory procedures expressly dealing with competency in the context of juvenile proceedings. While there are Mental Health Code procedures for determining the competency of adult criminal defendants, *see* MCL 330.2020 *et seq.;* MSA 14.800(1020) *et seq.*, proceedings held in the family division of the circuit court, which include delinquency proceedings, are not considered to be criminal proceedings. MCL 712A.1(2); MSA 27.3178(598.1)(2). Thus, the questions before this Court are (1) whether due process demands that a competency determination be made before a questionably competent juvenile is subjected to the adjudicative phase of a delinquency proceedings, and (2) if such a right exists, whether the provisions of the Mental Health Code for competency determinations apply to juvenile competency proceedings. We conclude that (1) juveniles have a due process right not to be subjected to the adjudicative phase of juvenile proceedings while incompetent, and (2) although the Mental Health Code provisions for competency determinations by their terms apply only to defendants in criminal proceedings, they can serve as a guide for juvenile competency determinations.

GENERAL LEGAL BACKGROUND

Although juvenile proceedings are not considered adversarial in nature, they are closely analogous to the adversary criminal process. *In re Wilson,* 113 Mich. App. 113, 121; 317 N.W.2d 309 (1982). Proceedings in a juvenile court need not conform with all the requirements of a criminal trial; however, essential requirements of due process and fair treatment must be met. *In re Gault,* 387 U.S. 1, 30-31; 87 S. Ct. 1428; 18 L.Ed. 2d 527 (1967); *In re Belcher,* 143 Mich. App. 68, 71: 371 N.W.2d 474 (1985). Among the essential requirements of due process and fair treatment are the requirement that the allegations in a delinquency petition be proved beyond a reasonable doubt, *In re Winship,* 397 U.S. 358, 368; 90 S. Ct. 1068; 25 L. Ed. 2d 368 (1970), the right to notice of the charges, *Gault, supra* at 34, the right to counsel, *Gault,* 387 U.S. at 41, the right to confrontation and cross-examination, *Gault,* 387 U.S. at 57, the privilege against self-incrimination, *Gault,* 387 U.S. at 55, and the right not to be placed in jeopardy twice, *see Breed v. Jones,* 421 U.S. 519, 529-531; 95 S. Ct. 1779; 44 L. Ed. 2d 346 (1975). However, not all due process rights conferred on adults accused of a crime are applied to juveniles in delinquency proceedings, primarily because of the special nature of the proceedings. *See, e.g., McKeiver v. Pennsylvania,* 403 U.S. 528, 545; 91 S. Ct. 1976; 29 L. Ed. 2d 647 (1971). (Due process does not require a trial by jury in juvenile cases.).

The conviction of an individual when legally incompetent violates due process of law. *Newton, supra* at 487; US Const Ams V, XIV; Const 1963 art 1, § 17. The protection afforded by the Due Process Clause requires that a court sua sponte hold a hearing regarding competency when any evidence raises a bona fide doubt about the competency of the defendant. *People v. Ray,* 431 Mich. 260, 270, n.5; 430 N.W.2d 626 (1988).

Competence to stand trial is rudimentary, for upon it depends the main part of those rights deemed essential to a fair trial, including the right to effective assistance of counsel, the rights to summon, to confront, and to cross-examine witnesses, and the right to testify on one's own behalf or to remain silent without penalty for doing so. [*Riggins v. Nevada,* 504 U.S. 127, 139-140; 112 S. Ct. 1810; 118 L. Ed. 2d 479 (1992) (Kennedy, J. concurring), *citing Drope v. Missouri*, 420 U.S. 162, 171-172; 95 S. Ct. 896; 43 L. Ed. 2d 103 (1975).]

DUE PROCESS AND JUVENILE COMPETENCY DETERMINATIONS

Although this state has not addressed the issue of competency determinations in juvenile proceedings, a number of other jurisdictions have concluded that competency, if properly raised, must be determined by the court. In *James H. v. Superior Court of Riverside Co.,* 77 Cal. App. 3d 169, 174; 143 Cal. Rptr. 398 (1978), the California Court of Appeals held that juveniles had a due process right to be afforded a hearing when a question arose with respect to competency. The court reasoned that an incompetent juvenile would be unable to cooperate with counsel, thus denying the juvenile the effective assistance of counsel. *Id.* The court also held that the trial court had the inherent power to conduct a competency hearing; thus, it reasoned, the lack of statutory procedures did not preclude holding a hearing. *Id.* at 175. The Supreme Court of Louisiana concluded that the right of an incompetent juvenile not to be subjected to juvenile proceedings was "fundamental" and "essential," and analogized this right to the right not to be tried in absentia. *In re Causey*, 363 So. 2d 472, 476 (La. 1978). In *In re Two Minor Children,* 95 Nev. 225, 230-231; 592 P.2d 166 (1979), the Nevada Supreme Court similarly found a due process right to a competency hearing. Its holding was based on Justice Black's concurring opinion in *Gault, supra* at 61, as well as *James H., supra.* The Minnesota Supreme Court held, as the Louisiana Supreme Court had earlier, that the right of an incompetent juvenile not to be subjected to juvenile proceedings was fundamental. *In re Welfare of SWT,* 277 N.W.2d 507, 511 (Minn. 1979). In *State ex rel Dandoy v. Superior Ct,* 127 Ariz. 184, 187; 619 P.2d 12 (1980), the Arizona Supreme Court reached a similar conclusion, relying again on the right to effective counsel as the basis for concluding that a juvenile must be able to confer with counsel. The District of Columbia Court of Appeals found that the juvenile system under review did not adequately protect the right of an incompetent juvenile not to be tried. *In re WAF,* 573 A.2d 1264, 1266 (DC App. 1990). The Georgia Court of Appeals found that "a want of competence renders [the rights recognized in *Gault* and its progeny] meaningless." *In re SH,* 220 Ga. App. 569, 571; 469 S.E.2d 810 (1996). The Washington Court of Appeals, in addressing the procedure to be followed for competency proceedings involving juveniles, recognized without discussion the right of juveniles to a competency determination. *State v. EC,* 83 Wn. App. 523, 527-528; 922 P.2d 152 (1996). The Ohio Court of Appeals found that the right not to be tried while incompetent is "as fundamental in juvenile proceedings as it is in criminal trials of adults." *In re Williams,* 116 Ohio App. 3d 237, 241; 687 N.E. 2d 507 (1997). It appears that all courts that have spoken on this issue have recognized the right of juveniles to a competency determination.

We find the reasoning presented in these cases to be persuasive. . . . Even though, as previously mentioned, juvenile proceedings are not considered adversarial, they have many of the trappings of criminal proceedings; the petition is filed by the prosecutor, notice is required, there must be a preliminary hearing, which resembles an arraignment in criminal proceedings, and the functions of the prosecutor and court are the equivalent to their functions in a criminal proceedings. *Wilson,* 113 Mich. App. at 121-122. As noted earlier, due process requires that a juvenile must be afforded the right to counsel during these proceedings. *Gault, supra* at 41. This right to counsel means little if the juvenile is unaware of the proceedings or unable to communicate with counsel because of a psychological or developmental disability. Cf. *Cooper v. Oklahoma,* 517 U.S. 348, 368; 116 S. Ct. 1373; 134 L. Ed. 2d 498 (1996); *Dusky v. United States,* 362 U.S. 402, 402; 80 S. Ct. 788; 4 L. Ed. 2d 824 (1960) (common-law standard for determining competency is whether defendant has sufficient present ability to consult with lawyer with a reasonable degree of rational understanding and whether defendant has a rational as well as factual understanding of the proceedings against him). We conclude, as have many other jurisdictions, that the right not to be tried while incompetent is a fundamental in juvenile proceedings as it is in the criminal context.

There is no rule or statute of procedure that expressly controls the procedure for making a competency determination in juvenile cases. . . .

* * *

We do not conclude that the Mental Health Code establishes the procedure that must be followed in juvenile cases. By its terms, the Mental Health Code applies to "a defendant to a criminal charge." MCL 330.2020(1); MSA 14.800 (1020)(1); *see also* MCL 330.2026; MSA 14.800(1026), MCL 330.2044; MSA 14.800(1044). Again, juvenile proceedings are not considered criminal. MCL 712A.1(2); MSA 27.3178(598.1)(2). . . .

Nonetheless, as we have already determined, there is a due process right not to be subjected to the adjudicative phase of a delinquency proceeding while not competent. It is thus incumbent on us to provide some direction to the trial courts in making this important determination. Further, the competency provisions of the Mental Health Code do not appear to conflict with any applicable court rules and, under *McDaniel, supra,* they could be applied in the juvenile context.

We believe that the Mental Health Code provisions for competency determinations can provide a useful guide for the trial courts in this context. As summarized above, they provide a standard of competency and a process by which questions of competency can be raised and determined. We hold that, in the absence of other applicable rules or statutes, these provisions should be used to assure that the due process rights of a juvenile are protected.

In reaching this conclusion, however, we further note that it is possible that a juvenile, merely because of youthfulness, would be unable to understand the proceedings with the same degree of comprehension an adult would. *Causey, supra* at 476. *See* Grisso, *The Competence of Adolescents as Trial Defendants,* 3 Psych, Pub Pol'y & L 3, 14 (1997). Accordingly we further hold that, in juvenile competency hearings, competency evaluations should be made in light of juvenile, rather than adult, norms. *Williams, supra* at 242. A juvenile need not be found incompetent just because, under adult standards, the juvenile would be found incompetent to stand trial in a criminal proceedings.

We reverse and remand for proceedings consistent with this opinion. We do not retain jurisdiction. (Footnotes omitted throughout.)

Notes

1. During the first half of this century, when modern juvenile law was in its infancy, the issue of competency to stand trial (and, indeed, other due process issues) did not arise often in juvenile courts. The rehabilitative, non-criminal nature of these courts made the issue irrelevant. As juvenile dispositions have become increasingly punitive and more like adult criminal sentences, and as juveniles are waived to adult courts with greater frequency, this view has changed. Courts and legislatures have been forced to address the question of when a juvenile is or is not competent to stand trial, even in juvenile proceedings. *See generally*, Thomas Grisso, *The Competence of Adolescents as Trial Defendants*, 3 PSYCHOL. PUB. POL'Y & L. 3 (1997) (outlining history of competency issue in juvenile adjudications). Approximately half the states have established, either judicially or through legislation, a juvenile's right to a competency determination prior to a delinquency adjudication. *See* Lynda E. Frost & Robert E. Shepherd, Jr., *Mental Health Issues in Juvenile Delinquency Proceedings,* 11 CRIM. JUST. 52 (Fall 1996); *see also In re Welfare of S.W.T.,* 277 N.W.2d 507 (Minn. 1979); *State v. Kempf,* 282 N.W.2d 704 (Iowa 1979); N.C. GEN. STAT. § 7A-628 (Lexis 1999). The only state to hold otherwise is Oklahoma. In *G.J.I. v. State*, 778 P.2d 485 (Okla. Crim. App. 1989), the court held that, because a delinquency proceeding is not a criminal trial, a juvenile is not entitled to a competency hearing prior to adjudication. *Id.* at 487.

2. As discussed in the principal case, the juvenile must have the ability to understand the nature of the charges against her, as well as the nature of the proceedings, and must be able to effectively assist in her own defense. This latter consideration becomes especially important in juvenile cases where the child may have problems communicating effectively with her counsel even absent any mental deficiency. One recent study has shown that younger juveniles, especially those under the age of fourteen, may be unable to effectively communicate with counsel because of normal developmental immaturity. *See* Grisso, *The Competence of Adolescents as Trial Defendants, supra* at 17. The ability of counsel to adequately defend a juvenile may also be hampered by the common misperception among many juveniles that the defense attorney's role includes the responsibility to report the defendant's guilt to court authorities. *See* Thomas Grisso, *Juvenile Competency to Stand Trial: Questions in an Era of Punitive Reform*, 12 CRIM. JUST. 5, 8 (Fall 1997).

3. Most courts that have addressed the issue consider competency to stand trial an essential component of due process. *See, e.g., In re T.D.W.,* 441 N.E.2d 155 (Ill. App. Ct. 1982) (constitutional right to competency determination); *State ex rel. Dandoy v. Superior Court,* 619 P.2d 12 (Ariz. 1980) (due process requires inquiry into competence); *In re S.H.,* 469 S.E.2d 810 (Ga. Ct. App. 1996) (competency is cornerstone of other due process considerations); *see also* Vance L. Cowden & Geoffrey R. McKee, *Competency to Stand Trial in Juvenile Delinquency Proceedings—Cognitive Maturity and the Attorney-Client Relationship,* 33 U. LOUISVILLE J. FAM. L. 629 (1995). The reasoning generally is: *In re Gault,* 387 U.S. 1, (1967) (*see infra,* Part B), extended the right to counsel to juveniles during adjudication; the right to counsel means the right to the effective assistance of counsel; counsel cannot be effective if the juvenile is not competent to assist in his own defense; the protections of *Gault*, therefore, require that the juvenile be competent to stand trial. *See* Cowden & McKee, *Competency to Stand Trial in Juvenile Delinquency Proceedings—Cognitive Maturity and the Attorney-Client Relationship, supra* at 641; *James H. v. Superior Court,* 143 Cal. Rptr. 398 (Ct. App. 1978); *In re Two Minor Children*, 592 P.2d 166 (Nev. 1979).

4. If a juvenile is tried in an adult criminal court, the juvenile is entitled to the same competency determination as an adult defendant. As discussed above, about half the states have determined that a juvenile is also entitled to a competency determination in a juvenile court. Many of these states apply adult competency standards to juveniles. *See, e.g., In re T.D.W., supra; State ex rel. Dandoy v. Superior Court, supra; In re Two Minor Children, supra.* These standards generally include a determination of whether the defendant or juvenile is incompetent due to mental illness or mental retardation. *See* Grisso, *The Competence of Adolescents as Trial Defendants, supra* at 6. Some courts, however, hold that a competency determination involving a juvenile must also involve the consideration of additional factors, such as the juvenile's age and level of maturity. *See, e.g., State v. Causey,* 363 So. 2d 472 (La. 1978); *In re Gladys R.,* 464 P.2d 127 (Cal. 1970).

5. As with adults, if a juvenile is found incompetent to stand trial, proceedings are suspended. If it appears that the juvenile will not regain competency within a reasonable period of time (generally one year), charges must be dismissed. *See, e.g., State v. E.C.,* 922 P.2d 152, 153 (Wash. Ct. App. 1996) (charges dismissed where juvenile not likely to become competent in "reasonably near future"). If, on the other hand, the court believes, based on psychological or psychiatric reports, that the juvenile may become competent, and therefore able to stand trial within a reasonable amount of time, the adjudication process is put on hold while attempts are made to restore the child's competence. A troubling issue in this area, and one that has only recently come to the attention of the legal community, is that, as noted above, the child's incompetence may be caused by her developmental immaturity, which she may not outgrow in the "reasonable" time allotted. The court must thus decide whether to dismiss the charges due to the child's incompetence or detain and "treat" the juvenile for longer than the statutorily prescribed period. To date, there is no clear answer to this issue. *See generally In re W.A.F.,* 573 A.2d 1264 (D.C. 1990).

Questions

1. A juvenile's lawyer must decide whether the child understands the nature of the charges and the proceedings such that the child can aid the lawyer in preparing a defense. Given that mental health professionals differ in their opinions regarding the capacity of a juvenile to comprehend such matters, can an attorney be expected to determine whether a juvenile really understands the charges or is just trying to be cooperative? How might a lawyer make such a determination? What should the lawyer do if she suspects that the child does not grasp the nature of the case or that the child is not capable of assisting in his own defense?

2. Assume the child has shown some understanding of the charges and the nature of the judicial process. What should the lawyer do if the child makes a decision that the lawyer feels is clearly not in the child's best interest? Does it matter in such a situation that the client is a juvenile? Should the child's age make any difference? What should the lawyer do who believes that, although the child has shown some understanding of the case, the child's immaturity and inexperience with the legal system are causing him to make an obviously bad decision?

3. As discussed in the Notes, juveniles often cannot aid in their own defense due to normal mental immaturity. Is it just to try such juveniles in criminal court? Should the juveniles who are most likely to be too immature to aid their counsel, e.g., those under the age of fourteen, be barred from criminal prosecution? If juveniles are entitled to the effective assistance of counsel even in juvenile court, should such immature juveniles also be precluded from an adjudication of delinquency?

4. Do you think that the threshold of competency should be the same in juvenile court as it is in adult criminal court? Or should juvenile court have a lower competency requirement? What justification could you offer for a lower threshold of competency in a juvenile court?

B. The Adjudication Hearing

1. Due Process Framework

In re Gault

387 U.S. 1, 87 S. Ct. 1428, 18 L. Ed. 2d 527 (1967)

Mr. Justice FORTAS delivered the opinion of the Court.

This is an appeal under 28 U.S.C. § 1257(2) from a judgment of the Supreme Court of Arizona affirming the dismissal of a petition for a writ of habeas corpus. The petition sought the release of Gerald Francis Gault, appellants' 15 year-old-son, who had been committed as a juvenile delinquent to the State Industrial School by the Juvenile Court of Gila County, Arizona. The Supreme Court of Arizona affirmed dismissal of the writ. . . . It concluded that the proceedings ending in commitment of Gerald Gault did not offend [due process] requirements. We do not agree, and we reverse. . . .

I

On Monday, June 8, 1964, at about 10 a.m., Gerald Francis Gault and a friend, Ronald Lewis, were taken into custody by the Sheriff of Gila County. Gerald was then still subject to a six months' probation order which had been entered on February 25, 1964, as a result of his having been in the company of another boy who had stolen a wallet from a lady's purse. The police action on June 8 was taken as the result of a verbal complaint by a neighbor of the boys, Mrs. Cook, about a telephone call made to her in which the caller or callers made lewd or indecent remarks . . . of the irritatingly offensive, adolescent, sex variety.

At the time Gerald was picked up, his mother and father were both at work. No notice that Gerald was being taken into custody was left at the home. No other steps were taken to advise them that their son had, in effect, been arrested. Gerald was taken to the Children's Detention Home. When his mother arrived home at about 6 o'clock, Gerald was not there. Gerald's older brother was sent to look for him at the trailer home of the Lewis family. He apparently learned then that Gerald was in custody. He so informed his mother. The two of them went to the Detention Home. The deputy probation officer, Flagg, who was also superintendent of the Detention Home, told Mrs. Gault "why Jerry was there" and said that a hearing would be held in Juvenile Court at 3 o'clock the following day, June 9.

Officer Flagg filed a petition with the court on the hearing day, June 9, 1964. It was not served on the Gaults. Indeed, none of them saw this petition until the habeas corpus hearing on August 17, 1964. The petition . . . recited only that "said minor is under the age of eighteen years, and . . . is a delinquent minor." It prayed for a hearing and an order regarding "the care and custody of said minor. . . ."

On June 9, Gerald, his mother, his older brother, and Probation Officers Flagg and Henderson appeared before the Juvenile Judge in chambers. . . . Mrs. Cook, the complainant, was not there. No one was sworn at this hearing. No transcript or recording was made. No memorandum or record of the substance of the proceedings was prepared. Our information about the proceedings and the subsequent hearing on June 15, derives entirely from the testimony of the Juvenile Court Judge, Mr. and Mrs. Gault and Officer Flagg at the habeas corpus proceeding conducted two months later. From this, it appears that at the June 9 hearing Gerald was questioned by the judge about the telephone call. There was conflict as to what he said. His mother recalled that Gerald said he only dialed Mrs. Cook's number and handed the telephone to his friend, Ronald. Officer Flagg recalled that Gerald had admitted making the lewd remarks. Judge McGhee testified that Gerald "admitted making one of these [lewd] statements." At the conclusion of the hearing, the judge said he would "think about it." Gerald was taken back to the Detention Home. . . . On June 11 or 12, after having been detained since June 8, Gerald was released and driven home. There is no explanation in the record as to why he was kept in the Detention Home or why he was released. At 5 p.m. on the day of Gerald's release, Mrs. Gault received a note signed by Officer Flagg. It was on plain paper, not letterhead. Its entire text was as follows:

> Mrs. Gault:
> Judge McGhee has set Monday June 15, 1964
> at 11:00 A.M. as the date and time for further
> Hearings on Gerald's delinquency.
> /s/Flagg

At the appointed time on Monday, June 15, Gerald, his father and mother, Ronald Lewis and his father, and Officers Flagg and Henderson were present before Judge McGhee. Witnesses at the habeas corpus proceeding differed in their recollections of Gerald's testimony at the June 15 hearing. Mr. and Mrs. Gault recalled that Gerald again testified that he had only dialed the number and that the other boy had made the remarks. Officer Flagg agreed that at this hearing Gerald did not admit making the lewd remarks. But Judge McGhee recalled that "there was some admission again of some of the lewd statements. . . . Again, the complainant, Mrs. Cook, was not present. Mrs. Gault asked that Mrs. Cook be present. . . . The Juvenile Judge said "she didn't have to be present at that hearing." The judge did not speak to Mrs. Cook or communicate with her at any time. Probation Officer Flagg had talked to her once—over the telephone on June 9. . . . At the conclusion of the hearing, the judge committed Gerald as a juvenile delinquent to the State Industrial School "for the period of his minority [that is, until 21], unless sooner discharged by due process of law. . . ."

No appeal is permitted by Arizona law in juvenile cases. On August 3, 1964, a petition for a writ of habeas corpus was filed with the Supreme Court of Arizona and referred by it to the Superior Court for hearing.

At the habeas corpus hearing on August 17, Judge McGhee was vigorously cross-examined as to the basis for his actions. He testified that he had taken into account the fact that Gerald was on probation. He was asked "under what section of . . . the code you found the boy delinquent?"

His answer is set forth in the margin.[5] In substance, he concluded that Gerald came within ARS § 8-201-6(a), which specifies that a "delinquent child" includes one "who has violated a law of the state or an ordinance or regulation of a political subdivision thereof." The law which Gerald was found to have violated is ARS § 13-377. This section of the Arizona Criminal Code provides that a person who "in the presence or hearing of any woman or child . . . uses vulgar, abusive or obscene language, is guilty of a misdemeanor. . . ." The penalty specified in the Criminal Code, which would apply to an adult, is $5 to $50, or imprisonment for not more than two months. The judge also testified that he acted under ARS § 8-201-6(d) which includes in the definition of a "delinquent child" one who, as the judge phrased it, is "habitually involved in immoral matters."[6]

Asked about the basis for his conclusion that Gerald was "habitually involved in immoral matters," the judge testified, somewhat vaguely, that two years earlier, on July 2, 1962, a "referral" was made concerning Gerald, "where

---

5 "Q. All right. Now, Judge, would you tell me under what section of the law or tell me under what section of—of the code you found the boy delinquent?

"A. Well there is a—I think it amounts to disturbing the peace. I can't give you the section, but I can tell you the law, that when one person uses lewd language in the presence of another person, that it can amount to—and I consider that when a person makes it over the phone, that it is considered in the presence, I might be wrong, that is one section. The other section upon which I consider the boy delinquent is Section 8-201, Subsection (d), habitually involved in immoral matters."

6 ARS § 8-201-6, the section of the Arizona Juvenile Code which defines a delinquent child, reads [in pertinent part]:

> "(a) A child who has violated a law of the state or an ordinance or regulation of a political subdivision thereof. . . .
>
> (d) A child who habitually so deports himself as to injure or endanger the morals or health of himself or others."

the boy had stolen a baseball glove from another boy and lied to the Police Department about it." The judge said there was "no hearing," and "no accusation" relating to this incident, "because of lack of material foundation." But it seems to have remained in his mind as a relevant factor. The judge also testified that Gerald had admitted making other nuisance phone calls in the past which, as the judge recalled the boy's testimony, were "silly calls, or funny calls, or something like that."

The Superior Court dismissed the writ, and appellants sought review in the Arizona Supreme Court. . . .

The Supreme Court handed down an elaborate and wide-ranging opinion affirming dismissal of the writ. . . . [A]pellants do not urge upon us all of the points passed upon by the Supreme Court of Arizona. They urge that we hold the Juvenile Code of Arizona invalid on its face or as applied in this case because, contrary to the Due Process Clause of the Fourteenth Amendment, the juvenile is taken from the custody of his parents and committed to a state institution pursuant to proceedings in which the Juvenile Court has virtually unlimited discretion, and in which the following basic rights are denied:

1. Notice of the charges;
2. Right to counsel;
3. Right to confrontation and cross-examination;
4. Privilege against self-incrimination;
5. Right to a transcript of the proceedings; and
6. Right to appellate review. . . .

II

The Supreme Court of Arizona held that due process of law is requisite to the constitutional validity of proceedings in which a court reaches the conclusion that a juvenile . . . has engaged in conduct prohibited by law . . . with the consequence that he is committed to an institution in which his freedom is curtailed. This conclusion is in accord with the decisions of a number of courts under both federal and state constitutions.

This Court has not heretofore decided the precise question. In *Kent v. United States,* 383 U.S. 541 (1966), we considered the requirements for a valid waiver of the "exclusive" jurisdiction of the Juvenile Court of the District of Columbia so that a juvenile could be tried in the adult criminal court of the District. Although our decision turned upon the language of the statute, we emphasized the necessity that "the basic requirements of due process and fairness" be satisfied in such proceedings. 383 U.S. at 501. *Haley v. Ohio,* 332 U.S. 596 (1948), involved the admissibility, in a state criminal court of general jurisdiction, of a confession by a 15-year-old boy. The Court held that the Fourteenth Amendment applied to prohibit the use of the coerced confession. . . . [T]hese cases . . . indicate that . . . neither the Fourteenth Amendment nor the Bill of Rights is for adults alone.

We do not in this opinion consider the impact of these constitutional provisions upon the totality of the relationship of the juvenile and the state. . . . For example, we are not here concerned with the procedures or constitutional rights applicable to the pre-judicial stages of the juvenile process, nor do we direct our attention to the post-adjudicative or dispositional process. We consider only the problems presented to us by this case. These relate to the proceedings by which a determination is made as to whether a juvenile is a "delinquent" as a result of alleged misconduct on his part, with the consequence that he may be committed to a state institution. As to these proceedings, there appears to be little current dissent from the proposition that the Due Process Clause has a role to play. The problem is to ascertain the precise impact of the due process requirement upon such proceedings.

From the inception of the juvenile court system, wide differences have been tolerated—indeed insisted upon—between the procedural rights accorded to adults and those of juveniles. In practically all jurisdictions, there are rights granted to adults which are withheld from juveniles. . . .

* * *

. . . Due process of law is the primary and indispensable foundation of individual freedom. It is the basic and essential term in the social compact which defines the rights of the individual and delimits the powers which the state may exercise.[26] As Mr. Justice Frankfurter has said: "The history of American freedom is, in no small measure, the history of procedure. . . .[27] [D]ue process . . . enhance[s] the possibility that truth will emerge from the confrontation of opposing versions and conflicting data. . . .

It is claimed that juveniles obtain benefits from the special procedures applicable to them which more than offset the disadvantages of denial of the substance of normal due process. As we shall discuss, the observation of due process standards, intelligently and not ruthlessly administered, will not compel the States to abandon or displace any of the substantive benefits of the juvenile process. But it is important, we think, that the claimed benefits of the juvenile process should be candidly appraised. . . .

Certainly . . . the high crime rates among juveniles . . . could not lead us to conclude that the absence of constitutional protections reduces crime, or that the juvenile system, functioning free of constitutional inhibitions as it has largely done, is effective to reduce crime or rehabilitate offenders. We do not mean by this to denigrate the juvenile court process or to suggest that there are not aspects of the juvenile system relating to offenders which are valuable. But

---

[26] The impact of denying fundamental procedural due process to juveniles involved in "delinquency" charges is dramatized by the following considerations: (1) In 1965, persons under 18 accounted for about one-fifth of all arrests for serious crimes and over half of all arrests for serious property offenses, and in the same year some 601,000 children under 18, or 2% of all children between 10 and 17, came before juvenile courts. About one out of nine youths will be referred to juvenile court in connection with a delinquent act (excluding traffic offenses) before he is 18. . . . (3) In about one-half of the States, a juvenile may be transferred to an adult penal institution after a juvenile court has found him "delinquent" (4) In some jurisdictions a juvenile may be subjected to criminal prosecution for the same offense for which he has served under a juvenile court commitment. However, the Texas procedure to this effect has recently been held unconstitutional by a federal district court judge, in a habeas corpus action. *Sawyer v. Hauch,* 245 F. Supp 55 (D.C. W.D. Tex. 1965). (5) In most of the States the juvenile may end in criminal court through waiver (citations omitted).

[27] *Malinski v. New York,* 324 U.S. 401, 414 (1945) (separate opinion).

the features of the juvenile system which its proponents have asserted are of unique benefit will not be impaired by constitutional domestication. For example, the commendable principles relating to the processing and treatment of juveniles separately from adults are in no way involved or affected by the procedural issues under discussion. Further, we are told that one of the important benefits of the special juvenile court procedures is that they avoid classifying the juvenile as a "criminal." The juvenile offender is now classed as a "delinquent." There is, of course, no reason why this should not continue. It is disconcerting, however, that this term has come to involve only slightly less stigma than the term "criminal" applied to adults. . . .

Beyond this, it is frequently said that juveniles are protected by the process from disclosure of their deviational behavior. As the Supreme Court of Arizona phrased it in the present case, the summary procedures of Juvenile Courts are sometimes defended by a statement that it is the law's policy "to hide youthful errors from the full gaze of the public and bury them in the graveyard of the forgotten past." This claim of secrecy, however, is more rhetoric than reality. Disclosure of court records is discretionary with the judge in most jurisdictions. . . . Of more importance are police records. In most States the police keep a complete file of juvenile "police contacts" and have complete discretion as to disclosure of juvenile records. Police departments receive requests for information from the FBI and other law-enforcement agencies, the Armed Forces, and social service agencies, and most of them generally comply. . . .

In any event, there is no reason why, consistently with due process, a State cannot continue, if it deems it appropriate, to provide and to improve provision for the confidentiality of records of police contacts and court action relating to juveniles. . . .

Further, it is urged that the juvenile benefits from informal proceedings in the court. The early conception of the Juvenile Court proceeding was one in which a fatherly judge touched the heart and conscience of the erring youth . . . by paternal advice and admonition, and in which, in extreme situations, benevolent and wise institutions of the State provided guidance and help "to save him from a downward career". . . .[36] But recent studies have, with surprising unanimity, entered sharp dissent as to the validity of this gentle conception. . . . For example, in a recent study, the sociologists Wheeler and Cottrell observe that when the procedural laxness of the "*parens patriae*" attitude is followed by stern disciplining, the contrast may have an adverse effect upon the child, who feels that he has been deceived or enticed. They conclude as follows: "Unless appropriate due process of law is followed, even the juvenile who has violated the law may not feel that he is being fairly treated and may therefore resist the rehabilitative efforts of court personnel". . . .[37]

Ultimately, however, we confront the reality of that portion of the Juvenile Court process with which we deal in this case. A boy is charged with miscon-

---

[36] Mack, *The Juvenile Court*, 23 HARV. L. REV. 104, 120 (1909).

[37] JUVENILE DELINQUENCY—ITS PREVENTION AND CONTROL (Russell Sage Foundation, 1966), p. 33. . . .

duct. The boy is committed to an institution where he may be restrained of liberty for years. . . . Instead of mother and father and sisters and brothers and friends and classmates, his world is peopled by guards, custodians, state employees, and "delinquents" confined with him for anything from waywardness to rape and homicide.

In view of this, it would be extraordinary if our Constitution did not require the procedural regularity and the exercise of care implied in the phrase "due process." Under our Constitution, the condition of being a boy does not justify a kangaroo court. The traditional ideas of Juvenile Court procedure, indeed, contemplated that time would be available and care would be used to establish precisely what the juvenile did and why he did it. . . . Under traditional notions, one would assume that in a case like that of Gerald Gault, where the juvenile appears to have a home, a working mother and father, and an older brother, the Juvenile Judge would have made a careful inquiry and judgment as to the possibility that the boy could be disciplined and dealt with at home, despite his previous transgressions. Indeed, so far as appears in the record before us, . . . the points to which the judge directed his attention were little different from those that would be involved in determining any charge of violation of a penal statute. The essential difference between Gerald's case and a normal criminal case is that safeguards available to adults were discarded in Gerald's case. The summary procedure as well as the long commitment was possible because Gerald was 15 years of age instead of over 18.

If Gerald had been over 18, . . . the maximum punishment would have been a fine of $5 to $50, or imprisonment in jail for not more than two months. Instead, he was committed to custody for a maximum of six years. If he had been over 18 and had committed an offense to which such a sentence might apply, he would have been entitled to substantial rights under the Constitution of the United States as well as under Arizona's laws and constitution. The United States Constitution would guarantee him rights and protections with respect to arrest, search and seizure, and pretrial interrogation. It would assure him of specific notice of the charges and adequate time to decide his course of action and to prepare his defense. He would be entitled to clear advice that he could be represented by counsel, and, at least if a felony were involved, the State would be required to provide counsel if his parents were unable to afford it. If the court acted on the basis of his confession, careful procedures would be required to assure its voluntariness. If the case went to trial, confrontation and opportunity for cross-examination would be guaranteed. So wide a gulf between the State's treatment of the adult and of the child requires a bridge sturdier than mere verbiage, and reasons more persuasive than cliché can provide. . . .

In *Kent v. United States, supra,* we stated that the Juvenile Court Judge's exercise of the power of the state as *parens patriae* was not unlimited. We said that "the admonition to function in a 'parental' relationship is not an invitation to procedural arbitrariness". . . . We reiterate this view, here in connection with a juvenile court adjudication of "delinquency," as a requirement which is part of the Due Process Clause of the Fourteenth Amendment of our Constitution.

We now turn to the specific issues which are presented to us in the present case.

III

NOTICE OF CHARGES

Appellants allege that the Arizona Juvenile Code is unconstitutional or alternatively that the proceedings before the Juvenile Court were constitutionally defective because of failure to provide adequate notice of the hearings. No notice was given to Gerald's parents when he was taken into custody on Monday, June 8. . . . The only written notice Gerald's parents received at any time was a note on plain paper from Officer Flagg delivered on Thursday or Friday, June 11 or 12, to the effect that the judge had set Monday, June 15, "for further hearings on Gerald's delinquency."

A "petition" was filed with the court on June 9 by Officer Flagg, reciting only that he was informed and believed that "said minor is a delinquent minor and that it is necessary that some order be made by the Honorable Court for said minor's welfare." The applicable Arizona statute provides for a petition to be filed in Juvenile Court, alleging in general terms that the child is "neglected, dependent or delinquent". . . . There is no requirement that the petition be served and it was not served upon, given to, or shown to Gerald or his parents.

The Supreme Court of Arizona rejected appellants' claim that due process was denied because of inadequate notice. . . . The court held that because "the policy of the juvenile law is to hide youthful errors from the full gaze of the public and bury them in the graveyard of the forgotten past," advance notice of the specific charges or basis for taking the juvenile into custody and for the hearing is not necessary. It held that the appropriate rule is that "the infant and his parent or guardian will receive a petition only reciting a conclusion of delinquency.[51] But no later than the initial hearing by the judge, they must be advised of the facts involved in the case. If the charges are denied, they must be given a reasonable period of time to prepare."

We cannot agree with the court's conclusion that adequate notice was given in this case. . . . The "initial hearing" in the present case was a hearing on the merits. Notice at the time is not timely; and even if there were a conceivable purpose served by the deferral proposed by the court below, it would have to yield to the requirements that the child and his parents or guardian be notified, in writing, of the specific charge or factual allegations to be considered at the hearing, and that such written notice be given at the earliest practicable time, and in any event sufficiently in advance of the hearing to permit preparation. Due process of law requires notice . . . which would be deemed constitutionally adequate in a civil or criminal proceeding. It does not allow a hearing to be held in which a youth's freedom and his parents' right to his custody are at stake without giving them timely notice, in advance of the hearing, of the specific issues that they must meet. Nor, in the circumstances of this case, can it reasonably be said that the requirement of notice was waived.[54]

---

51 No such petition was served or supplied in the present case.

54 Mrs. Gault's "knowledge" of the charge against Gerald, and/or the asserted failure to object, does not excuse the lack of adequate notice. . . . Since the Gaults had no counsel and were not told of their right to counsel, we cannot consider their failure to object to the lack of constitutionally adequate notice as a waiver of their rights. . . .

IV

RIGHT TO COUNSEL

Appellants charge that the Juvenile Court proceedings were fatally defective because the court did not advise Gerald or his parents of their right to counsel, and proceeded with the hearing, the adjudication of delinquency and the order of commitment in the absence of counsel for the child and his parents or an express waiver of the right thereto. The Supreme Court of Arizona . . . referred to a provision of the Juvenile Code which it characterized as requiring "that the probation officer shall look after the interests of neglected, delinquent and dependent children," including representing their interests in court.[56] The court argued that "The parent and the probation officer may be relied upon to protect the infant's interests." Accordingly, it rejected the proposition that "due process requires that an infant have a right to counsel. . . ." We do not agree. Probation officers, in the Arizona scheme, are also arresting officers. . . . The probation officer cannot act as counsel for the child. His role in the adjudicatory hearing, by statute and in fact, is as arresting officer and witness against the child. . . . A proceeding where the issue is whether the child will be found to be "delinquent" and subjected to the loss of his liberty for years is comparable in seriousness to a felony prosecution. The juvenile needs the assistance of counsel to cope with problems of law, to make skilled inquiry into the facts, to insist upon regularity of the proceedings, and to ascertain whether he has a defense and to prepare and submit it. The child "requires the guiding hand of counsel at every step in the proceedings against him."[59] [T]he assistance of counsel is essential. . . for the determination of delinquency, carrying with it the awesome prospect of incarceration in a state institution until the juvenile reaches the age of 21.

During the last decade, court decisions, experts, and legislatures have demonstrated increasing recognition of this view. In at least one-third of the States, statutes now provide for the right of representation by retained counsel in juvenile delinquency proceedings, notice of the right, or assignment of counsel, or a combination of these. In other States, court rules have similar provisions.

We conclude that the Due Process Clause of the Fourteenth Amendment requires that in . . . proceedings to determine delinquency which may result in commitment to an institution in which the juvenile's freedom is curtailed, the child and his parents must be notified of the child's right to be represented by

---

[56] The section cited by the court, ARS § 8-204-C, reads as follows:

The probation officer shall have the authority of a peace officer. He shall:

1. Look after the interests of neglected, delinquent and dependent children of the county.
2. Make investigations and file petitions.
3. Be present in court when cases are heard concerning children and represent their interests.
4. Furnish the court information and assistance as it may require.
5. Assist in the collection of sums ordered paid for the support of children.
6. Perform other acts ordered by the court.

[59] *Powell v. Alabama*, 287 U.S. 45, 69 (1932)

counsel retained by them, or if they are unable to afford counsel, that counsel will be appointed to represent the child.

* * *

V.

CONFRONTATION, SELF-INCRIMINATION, CROSS-EXAMINATION

Appellants urge that the writ of habeas corpus should have been granted because of the denial of the rights of confrontation and cross-examination in the Juvenile Court hearings, and because the privilege against self-incrimination was not observed. The Juvenile Court Judge testified at the habeas corpus hearing that he had proceeded on the basis of Gerald's admissions at the hearings. Appellants attack this on the ground that the admissions were obtained in disregard of the privilege against self-incrimination. If the confession is disregarded, appellants argue that the delinquency conclusion, since it was fundamentally based on a finding that Gerald had made lewd remarks during the phone call to Mrs. Cook, is fatally defective for failure to accord the rights of confrontation and cross-examination which the Due Process Clause of the Fourteenth Amendment of the Federal Constitution guarantees in state proceedings generally.

Our first question, then, is whether Gerald's admission was improperly obtained and relied on as the basis of decision, in conflict with the Federal Constitution. . . .

* * *

The Arizona Supreme Court rejected appellants' contention that Gerald had a right to be advised that he need not incriminate himself. It said: "We think the necessary flexibility for individualized treatment will be enhanced by a rule which does not require the judge to advise the infant of a privilege against self-incrimination."

* * *

This Court [however] has emphasized that admissions and confessions of juveniles require special caution. In *Haley v. Ohio*, 332 U.S. 596, where this Court reversed the conviction of a 15-year-old boy for murder, Mr. Justice Douglas said:

> What transpired would make us pause for careful inquiry if a mature man were involved. And when, as here, a mere child—an easy victim of the law—is before us, special care in scrutinizing the record must be used. . . . A 15-year-old lad, questioned through the dead of night by relays of police, is a ready victim of the inquisition. Mature men possible might stand the ordeal from midnight to 5 a.m. But we cannot believe that a lad of tender years is a match for the police in such a contest. He needs counsel and support if he is not to become the victim first of fear, then of panic. . . . No friend stood at the side of this 15-year-old boy as the police, working in relays, questioned him hour after hour, from midnight until dawn. No lawyer stood

guard to make sure that the police went so far and no father, to see to it that they stopped short of the point where he became the victim of coercion. No counsel or friend was called during the critical hours of questioning.[76]

In *Haley*, as we have discussed, the boy was convicted in an adult court, and not a juvenile court. In notable decisions, the New York Court of Appeals and the Supreme Court of New Jersey have recently considered decisions of Juvenile Courts in which boys have been adjudged "delinquent" on the basis of confessions obtained in circumstances comparable to those in *Haley*. . . . In each case . . . the juvenile court's determination of delinquency was set aside on the grounds of inadmissibility of the confession. *In the Matters of Gregory W. and Gerald S.*, 19 N.Y.2d 55, 224 N.E.2d 102 (1966) (opinion by Keating, J.), and *In the Interests of Carlo and Stasilowicz,* 48 N.J. 224, 225 A.2d 110 (1966) (opinion by Proctor, J.).

The privilege against self-incrimination is, of course, related to the question of the safeguards necessary to assure that admissions or confessions are reasonably trustworthy, that they are not the mere fruits of fear or coercion, but are reliable expressions of the truth. . . .

* * *

It would . . . be surprising if the privilege against self-incrimination were available to hardened criminals but not to children. The language of the Fifth Amendment, applicable to the States by operation for the Fourteenth Amendment, is unequivocal and without exception. And the scope of the privilege is comprehensive. . . .

* * *

Against the application to juveniles of the right to silence, it is argued that juvenile proceedings are "civil" and not "criminal," and therefore the privilege should not apply. It is true that the statement of the privilege in the Fifth Amendment, which is applicable to the States by reason of the Fourteenth Amendment, is that no person "shall be compelled in any *criminal case* to be a witness against himself." However, it is also clear that the availability of the privilege does not turn upon the type of proceeding in which its protection is invoked, but upon the nature of the statement or admission and the exposure which it invites. . . .

It would be entirely unrealistic to carve out of the Fifth Amendment all statements by juveniles on the ground that these cannot lead to "criminal" involvement. In the first place, juvenile proceedings to determine "delinquency," which may lead to commitment to a state institution, must be regarded as "criminal" for purposes of the privilege against self-incrimination. . . . For this purpose, at least, commitment is a deprivation of liberty. It is incarceration against one's will, whether it is called "criminal" or "civil." And our Constitution guarantees that no person shall be "compelled" to be a witness against himself

---

[76] 332 U.S. at 599-600 (opinion of Mr. Justice Douglas, joined by Justices Black, Murphy and Rutledge; Justice Frankfurter concurred in a separate opinion).

when he is threatened with deprivation of his liberty. . . .

In addition, . . . the fact of the matter is that there is little or no assurance in Arizona, as in most if not all of the Sates, that a juvenile apprehended and interrogated by the police or even by the Juvenile Court itself will remain outside of the reach of adult courts as a consequence of the offense for which he has been taken into custody. In Arizona, as in other Sates, provision is made for Juvenile Courts to relinquish or waive jurisdiction to the ordinary criminal courts. In the present case, when Gerald Gault was interrogated concerning violation of a section of the Arizona Criminal Code, it could not be certain that the Juvenile Court Judge would decide to "suspend" criminal prosecution in court for adults by proceeding to an adjudication in Juvenile Court.

* * *

Further, authoritative opinion has cast formidable doubt upon the reliability and trustworthiness of "confessions" by children. . . . The recent decision of the New York Court of Appeals . . . *In the Matters of Gregory W. and Gerald S.*, deals with a dramatic and, it is to be hoped, extreme example. Two 12-year-old Negro boys were taken into custody for the brutal assault and rape of two aged domestics, one of whom died as the result of the attack. One of the boys was schizophrenic and had been locked in the security ward of a mental institution at the time of the attacks. By a process that may best be described as bizarre, his confession was obtain by the police. A psychiatrist testified that the boy would admit "whatever he thought was expected so that he could get out of the immediate situation." The other 12-year-old also "confessed." Both confessions were in specific detail, albeit they contained various inconsistencies. The Court of Appeals, in an opinion by Keating, J., concluded that the confessions were products of the will of the police instead of the boys. The confessions were therefore held involuntary. . . .

* * *

We conclude that the constitutional privilege against self-incrimination is applicable in the case of juveniles as it is with respect to adults. . . . The participation of counsel will, of course, assist the police, Juvenile Courts and appellate tribunals in administering the privilege. If counsel was not present for some permissible reason when an admission was obtained, the greatest care must be taken to assure that the admission was voluntary, in the sense not only that it was not coerced or suggested, but also that it was not the product of ignorance of rights or of adolescent fantasy, fright or despair.

The "confession" of Gerald Gault was first obtained by Officer Flagg, out of the presence of Gerald's parents, without counsel and without advising him of his right to silence, as far as appears. The judgment of the Juvenile Court was stated by the judge to be based on Gerald's admissions in court. Neither "admission" was reduced to writing, and, to say the least, the process by which the "admissions" were obtained and received must be characterized as lacking the certainty and order which are required of proceedings of such formidable consequences. Apart from the "admissions," there was nothing upon which a judgment or finding might be based. There was no sworn testimony. Mrs. Cook, the complainant, was not present. The Arizona Supreme Curt held that "sworn testimony must be required of all witnesses including police officers, probation officers and others who are part of or officially related to the juvenile court structure." We hold that this is not enough. No reason is suggested or appears for a different rule in respect of sworn testimony in juvenile courts than in adult tribunals. Absent a valid confession adequate to support the determination of the Juvenile Court, confrontation and sworn testimony by witnesses available for cross-examination were essential for a finding of "delinquency" and an order committing Gerald to a state institution for a maximum of six years.

* * *

. . . We now hold that, absent a valid confession, a determination of delinquency and an order of commitment to a state institution cannot be sustained in the absence of sworn testimony subjected to the opportunity for cross-examination in accordance with our law and constitutional requirements.

VI

APPELLATE REVIEW AND TRANSCRIPT OF PROCEEDINGS

Appellants urge that the Arizona statute is unconstitutional under the Due Process Clause because, as construed by its Supreme Court, "there is no right of appeal from a juvenile court order. . . ." The court held that there is no right to a transcript because there is no right to appeal and because the proceedings are confidential and any record must be destroyed after a prescribed period of time. Whether a transcript or other recording is made, it held, is a matter for the discretion of the juvenile court.

This Court has not held that a State is required by the Federal Constitution "to provide appellate courts or a right to appellate review at all."[101] In view of the fact that we must reverse the Supreme Court of Arizona's affirmance of the dismissal of the writ of habeas corpus for other reasons, we need not rule on this question in the present case or upon the failure to provide a transcript or recording of the hearings—or, indeed, the failure of the Juvenile Judge to state the grounds for his conclusion. . . . As the present case illustrates, the consequences of failure to provide an appeal, to record the proceedings, or to make findings or state the grounds for the juvenile court's conclusion may be to throw a burden upon the machinery for habeas corpus, to saddle the reviewing process with the burden of attempting to reconstruct a record, and to impose upon the Juvenile Judge the unseemly duty of testifying under cross-examination as to the events that transpired in the hearings before him.

For the reasons stated, the judgment of the Supreme Court of Arizona is reversed, and the cause remanded for further proceedings not inconsistent with this opinion.

Mr. Justice BLACK, concurring.

* * *

---

101 *Griffin v. Illinois*, 351 U.S. 12, 18 (1956).

The juvenile court planners envisaged a system that would practically immunize juveniles from "punishment" for "crimes" in an effort to save them from youthful indiscretions and stigmas due to criminal charges or convictions. I agree with the Court, however, that this exalted ideal has failed of achievement since the beginning of the system. . . .

Where a person, infant or adult, can be seized by the State, charged, and convicted for violating a state criminal law, and then ordered by the State to be confined for six years, I think the Constitution requires that he be tried in accordance with the guarantees of all the provisions of the Bill of Rights made applicable to the States by the Fourteenth Amendment. . . . I consequently agree with the Court that the Arizona law as applied here denied to the parents and their son the right of notice, right to counsel, right against self-incrimination, and right to confront the witnesses against young Gault. Appellants are entitled to these rights, not because "fairness, impartiality and orderliness—in short, the essentials of due process"—require them . . . , but because they are specifically and unequivocally granted by provisions of the Fifth and Sixth Amendments which the Fourteenth Amendment makes applicable to the States.

* * *

. . . I do not vote to invalidate this Arizona law on the ground that it is "unfair" but solely on the ground that it violates the Fifth and Sixth Amendments made obligatory on the States by the Fourteenth Amendment. It is enough for me that the Arizona law as here applied collides head-on with the Fifth and Sixth Amendments. . . . The only relevance to me of the Due Process Clause is that it would, of course, violate due process . . . to enforce a law that collides with the Bill of Rights.

Mr. Justice WHITE, concurring.

I join the Court's opinion except for Part V. . . . I do not . . . find an adequate basis in the record for determining whether [the] privilege [against self-incrimination] was violated in this case. . . .

* * *

Mr. Justice HARLAN, concurring in part and dissenting in part.

. . . This case brings before this Court for the first time the question of what limitations the Constitution places upon the operation of [juvenile courts]. For reasons which follow, I have concluded that the Court has gone too far in some respects, and fallen short in others, in assessing the procedural requirements demanded by the Fourteenth Amendment.

I

* * *

The proper issue here is . . . whether the proceedings in Arizona's juvenile courts include procedural guarantees which satisfy the requirements of the Fourteenth Amendment. Among the first premises of our constitutional system is the obligation to conduct any proceeding in which an individual may be deprived of liberty or property in a fashion consistent with the "traditions and conscience of our people." *Snyder v Massachusetts*, 291 U.S. 97, 105. . . . Nothing before us suggests that juvenile courts were intended as a device to escape constitutional constraints, but I entirely agree with the Court that we are nonetheless obliged to examine with circumspection the procedural guarantees the State has provided.

The central issue here, and the principal one upon which I am divided from the Court, is the method by which the procedural requirements of due process should be measured. . . .

* * *

[R]elevant judicial history suggest[s] three criteria by which the procedural requirements of due process should be measured. . . . First, no more restrictions should be imposed than are imperative to assure the proceedings' fundamental fairness; second, the restrictions which are imposed should be those which preserve, so far as possible, the essential elements of the State's purpose; and finally, restrictions should be chosen which will later permit the orderly selection of any additional protections which may ultimately prove necessary. In this way, the Court may guarantee the fundamental fairness of the proceeding, and yet permit the State to continue development of an effective response to the problems of juvenile crime.

II

Measured by these criteria, only three procedural requirements should, in my opinion, now be deemed required of state juvenile courts by the Due Process Clause of the Fourteenth Amendment: first, timely notice must be provided to parents and children of the nature and terms of any juvenile court proceeding . . . ; second, unequivocal and timely notice must be given that counsel may appear . . . on behalf of the child and its parents, and that counsel may, in circumstances of indigency, be appointed for them; and third, the court must maintain a written record, or its equivalent, adequate to permit effective review on appeal. . . .

These requirements would guarantee to juveniles the tools with which their rights could be fully vindicated, and yet permit the States to pursue without unnecessary hindrance the purposes which they believe imperative in this field . . . .

* * *

The question remains whether certain additional requirements, among them the privilege against self-incrimination, confrontation, and cross-examination, must now, as the Court holds, also be imposed. . . .

Initially, I must vouchsafe that I cannot determine with certainty the reasoning by which the Court concludes that these further requirements are now imperative. The Court begins from the premise . . . that juvenile courts need not satisfy "all of the requirements of a criminal trial." It therefore scarcely suffices . . . for the Court to declare that juvenile court proceedings are essentially criminal, and thereupon to recall that these are requisites for a criminal trial. . . .

The problem here is to determine what forms of procedural protection are necessary to guarantee the fundamental fairness of juvenile proceedings, and not which of the procedures now employed in criminal trials should be transplanted intact to proceedings in these specialized courts.

[Q]uite unlike notice, counsel, and a record, these requirements might radically alter the character of juvenile court proceedings. The evidence from which the Court reasons that they would not is inconclusive. . . . At the least, it is plain that these additional requirements would contribute materially to the creation in these proceedings of the atmosphere of an ordinary criminal trial, and would, even if they do no more, thereby largely frustrate a central purpose of these specialized courts. . . . Surely this illustrates that prudence and the principles of the Fourteenth Amendment alike require that the Court should now impose no more procedural restrictions than are imperative to assure fundamental fairness . . . .

III

Finally, I turn to assess the validity of this juvenile court proceeding under the criteria discussed in this opinion. Measured by them, the judgment below must, in my opinion, fall. Gerald Gault and his parents were not provided adequate notice of the terms and purposes of the proceedings in which he was adjudged delinquent; they were not advised of their rights to be represented by counsel; and no record in any form was maintained of the proceedings. It follows, for the reasons given in this opinion, that Gerald Gault was deprived of his liberty without due process of law, and I therefore concur in the judgment of the Court.

Mr. Justice STEWART, dissenting.

The Court today uses an obscure Arizona case as a vehicle to impose upon thousands of juvenile courts throughout the Nation restrictions that the Constitution made applicable to adversary criminal trials. I believe the Court's decision is wholly unsound as a matter of constitutional law, and sadly unwise as a matter of judicial policy.

Juvenile proceedings are not criminal trials. They are not civil trials. They are simply not adversary proceedings. . . .

* * *

I possess neither the specialized experience nor the expert knowledge to predict with any certainty where may lie the brightest hope for progress in dealing with the serious problems of juvenile delinquency. But I am certain that the answer does not lie in the Court's opinion in this case, which serves to convert a juvenile proceeding into a criminal prosecution.

The inflexible restrictions that the Constitution so wisely made applicable to adversary criminal trials have no inevitable place in the proceedings of those public social agencies known as juvenile or family courts. And to impose the Court's long catalog of requirements upon juvenile proceedings in every area of the country is to invite a long step backwards. . . .

A State in all its dealings must, of course, accord every person due process of law. And due process may require that some of the same restrictions which the Constitution has placed upon criminal trials must be imposed upon juvenile proceedings. For example, I suppose that all would agree that a brutally coerced confession could not constitutionally be considered in a juvenile court hearing. But it surely does not follow that the testimonial privilege against self-incrimination is applicable in all juvenile proceedings. Similarly, due process clearly requires timely notice of the purpose and scope of any proceedings affecting the relationship of parent and child. But it certainly does not follow that notice of a juvenile hearing must be framed with all the technical niceties of a criminal indictment.

In any event, there is no reason to deal with issues such as these in the present case. The Supreme Court of Arizona found that the parents of Gerald Gault "knew of their right to counsel, to subpoena and cross examine witnesses, of the right to confront the witnesses against Gerald and the possible consequences of a finding of delinquency." It further found that "Mrs. Gault knew the exact nature of the charge against Gerald from the day he was taken to the detention home." And, as Mr. Justice White correctly points out, no issue of compulsory self-incrimination is presented by this case.

I would dismiss the appeal.

Notes

1. *Gault* is generally regarded as the first case of the modern juvenile law era and as the Supreme Court's first major attempt at extending consititutional principles to the juvenile justice system. The Court in *Gault* recognized that juveniles were entitled to due process protections and that these safeguards were necessitated by the failures of the juvenile justice system in its attempts to act as *parens patriae.* Although it did not extend to juveniles all of the rights afforded defendants in criminal courts, the Court did acknowledge that juvenile courts were essentially like their criminal counterparts.

The *Gault* Court held that a juvenile subject to possible incarceration is entitled, at a minimum, to: (1) notice of the charges against her; (2) representation by counsel; (3) the right to confront and cross-examine adverse witnesses; and (4) the privilege against self-incrimination. The Court left several questions unanswered, and there has been much discussion regarding the scope of the case. For example, the Court held that the above-named rights are available to a juvenile during the adjudication phase of a juvenile proceeding. However, the majority declined to decide the issue of whether any or all of these protections also apply to the pre- and post-adjudicatory phases of juvenile proceedings. By specifically holding that the enumerated protections apply whenever a juvenile may be subject to incarceration, the Court also left open the issue of whether *Gault* applies where the potential disposition does not include confinement. For example, the Court's opinion does not indicate whether probation entails a sufficient "loss of liberty" to trigger due process protections. The states and lower federal courts have been left to deal with these issues largely on their own.

2. One of the due process requirements outlined in *Gault* is the right to notice of the charges against the juvenile. The notice requirement entails two issues: timeliness and specificity. To meet constitutional requirements, notice must be provided early enough that the juvenile and the juvenile's counsel, if the child is represented, have time to prepare a defense. Although state laws on the issue of timeliness vary, they typically require notice of a hearing at least twenty-four hours in advance if the notice is personally served, or at least five days if it is mailed. *See, e.g.,* N.D. CENT. CODE § 27-20-23 (Lexis 1991); *In re Steven G.,* 556 A.2d 131 (Conn. 1989) (juvenile entitled to notice sufficiently in advance of hearing to prepare defense). The applicable statute may also limit the time between notice and the hearing if the juvenile is in custody. *See, e.g.,* TEX. FAM. CODE ANN. § 53.05 (West 1996) (no more than ten days if juvenile is detained).

The notice given to the juvenile must also be sufficiently definite so as to apprise the juvenile of the specific issues to be considered at the hearing. *See, e.g.,* IOWA CODE ANN. § 232.28(6) (West Supp. 1998); *In re Wilson,* 264 A.2d 614 (Pa. 1970) (adequate and timely notice of specific issues). Some states have determined that the notice must contain the same level of specificity as that required in a criminal information or indictment. *See, e.g.,* TEX. FAM. CODE ANN. § 53.04(d)(1) (West 1996); *In re Dennis,* 291 So. 2d 731 (Miss. 1974).

Another issue related to the notice requirement that arises in juvenile cases is whether notice must be given to the juvenile's parents. Although the Juvenile Justice and Delinquency Prevention Act contains a parental notice provision (*see* 18 U.S.C. § 5033), several federal courts have held that this is not a strict requirement, and that as long as the juvenile has adequate notice of the charges in time to prepare a defense, defective parental notice is harmless. *See, e.g., United States v. Watts,* 513 F.2d 5 (10th Cir. 1975); *United States v. White Bear,* 668 F.2d 409 (8th Cir. 1982); *but see United States v. Doe,* 862 F.2d 776 (9th Cir. 1988) (§ 5033 requires reasonable effort be made to notify parents). A few states have upheld delinquency adjudications absent parental notification. *See, e.g., O.M. v. State,* 595 So. 2d 514 (Ala. Crim. App. 1991). Most states, however, require parental notification of a pending delinquency hearing, either judicially or through legislation. *See, e.g.,* MICH. COMP. LAWS ANN. § 712A.12 (West 1993); MINN. STAT. ANN. § 260B.143 & 260C.143 (West Supp. 2001); WASH. REV. CODE ANN. § 13-40-100(2) (West Supp. 2001); *In re Holmes,* 109 A.2d 523 (Pa. 1954).

3. *Kent v. United States,* 383 U.S. 541 (1966), established a juvenile's right to the assistance of counsel at a transfer hearing (*see supra* Chapter 5, Part A). *Gault* extended the right to counsel to the adjudicatory stage of juvenile proceedings. However, neither *Kent* nor *Gault* put the issue of a juvenile's right to counsel to rest. For example, both cases left open the question of whether a juvenile is entitled to the assistance of an attorney during the pre-indictment stages of an investigation. The Court answered this question in *Kirby v. Illinois,* 406 U.S. 682 (1972). Although the case did not involve juvenile defendants, it did establish that a suspect is not entitled to an attorney until the commencement of formal charges. Pre-indictment procedures (such as an informal lineup) are not considered "critical stages" for the purposes of due process protections. As noted above, however, the interpretation and application of these holdings has been left largely to the states.

Nearly all states statutorily require that counsel be available to a juvenile during delinquency proceedings. *See* Tory J. Caeti et al., *Juvenile Right to Counsel: A National Comparison of State Legal Codes,* 23 AM. J. CRIM. L. 611, 624 (1996) (forty-four states provide for counsel during juvenile delinquency proceedings);

see also 705 ILL. COMP. STAT. ANN. 405/1-5(1) (West Supp. 2001); NEB. REV. STAT. § 43-272(1) (Supp. 2000). Although *Gault* required the availability of counsel only during the adjudicatory stage of juvenile proceedings, many states provide for counsel at all stages of the juvenile process. *See, e.g.,* GA. CODE ANN. § 15-11-30(b) (Lexis Supp. 2000); N.M. STAT. ANN. § 32A-2-14(H) (Michie 1999); VA. CODE ANN. §§ 16.1-266(B) & -268 (Michie 1999); *James H. v. Superior Court,* 143 Cal. Rptr. 398 (Ct. App. 1978). Although the presence of an attorney is provided for in almost all jurisdictions, less than half of all juveniles are represented by counsel during adjudication. *See* Barry C. Feld, In re Gault *Revisited: A Cross-State Comparison of the Right to Counsel in Juvenile Court,* 34 CRIME & DELINQ. 393 (1988). This statistic may be less surprising when one remembers that juveniles often misperceive the role of defense counsel during a delinquency proceeding. Additionally, it has been determined that, as a rule, juveniles who are represented by counsel during delinquency proceedings receive harsher sentences than those who proceed *pro se. See* Caeti et al., *Juvenile Right to Counsel: A National Comparison of State Legal Codes, supra* at 612-13.

State courts and legislatures have also dealt with the issue of whether and in what circumstances a juvenile can waive the right to counsel. The Criminal Justice Section of the American Bar Association recommends an unwaivable right to counsel for juveniles at all stages of the juvenile delinquency process. *See Standards Relating to Pretrial Court Proceeding,* in JUVENILE JUSTICE STANDARDS ANNOTATED, 243, 254-55 (Richard E. Shepherd, Jr. ed., 1996). While Texas is in accord with the IJA-ABA standards (*see* TEX. FAM. CODE ANN. § 51.10(b) (West 1996)), most states allow a juvenile to waive the right to counsel. As discussed in Chapter 3, *supra*, most courts follow the "totality of the circumstances" test outlined in *Fare v. Michael C.,* 442 U.S. 707 (1979), when analyzing the voluntariness of a waiver decision. Some states allow a juvenile to waive the right to counsel only after consultation with an attorney. *See, e.g., State ex rel. J.M. v. Taylor,* 276 S.E.2d 199 (W. Va. 1981); *In re Appeal No. 544,* 332 A.2d 680 (Md. Ct. Spec. App. 1975). Others require the juvenile court judge to explain the ramifications of a waiver, including possible dispositions in the case, to both the juvenile and his parents. *See, e.g.,* ARK. CODE ANN. § 9-27-317(a) (Michie Supp. 2001); *In re B.M.H.,* 339 S.E.2d 757 (Ga. Ct. App. 1986).

Another issue that has arisen in state courts subsequent to the decision in *Gault* is whether counsel appointed to represent a juvenile may withdraw. This issue arises most often where the juvenile wishes to file an appeal that the attorney believes is without merit. In *In re D.A.S.,* 973 S.W.2d (Tex. 1998), a recent ruling on the issue, the Supreme Court of Texas held that a juvenile's appointed counsel may withdraw pursuant to the procedures outlined by the United States Supreme Court in *Anders v. California,* 386 U.S. 738 (1967). The *Anders* decision dealt with the withdrawal of counsel appointed to represent an indigent adult criminal defendant on appeal and held that counsel could withdraw only after a thorough review of the record convinced the attorney that the appeal was wholly without merit. The attorney must file a brief with the court. The court then independently reviews the record to determine if any part of the record could arguably support an appeal. If the court agrees with the attorney, and the client is unable to raise any meritorious points to the court, the request for withdrawal is granted. In *In re D.A.S.,* the Court reversed the appellate court, holding that *Anders* applies to juvenile proceedings. The *D.A.S.* Court pointed out that all states to consider the issue have found the *Anders* procedure applicable to juveniles. It appears that thirteen states currently apply *Anders* to the withdrawal of counsel in the appeal of a juvenile delinquency adjudication. *See, e.g., In re Smith,* 597 So. 2d 101 (La. Ct. App. 1992); *In re Stacey R.,* 428 S.E.2d 869 (S.C. 1993); *In re Unrue,* 682 N.E.2d 686 (Ohio Ct. App. 1996). In addition, two states have held that *Anders* applies to criminal appeals made by juveniles, indicating that these states might also apply the withdrawal procedure to delinquency appeals. *See M.E.C. v. State,* 611 So. 2d 1201 (Ala. Crim. App. 1992); *Hans v. State,* 942 P.2d 674 (Mont. 1997).

4. The Supreme Court in *Gault* held that a juvenile must be afforded the right to confront and cross-examine adverse witnesses and the right against self-incrimination. A juvenile's right to confrontation and cross-examination has been codified by many states. *See, e.g.,* CONN. GEN. STAT. ANN. § 46b-135(a) (West Supp. 2001); TENN. CODE ANN. § 37-1-127(a) (Lexis 1996); WYO. STAT. ANN. § 14-6-223(b) (Lexis 1999). Other states have judicially adopted these rights. *See, e.g., People ex rel. Lauring v. Mucci,* 355 N.Y.S.2d 786 (App. Div. 1974); *O.M. v. State,* 595 So. 2d 514 (Ala. Crim. App. 1991). The rules of evidence applicable to criminal court generally also govern juvenile delinquency proceedings. For example, hearsay evidence is generally inadmissible as violative of the right to confrontation and cross-examination, unless one of the limited exceptions applies. *See, e.g., In re Michael,* 694 N.E.2d 538 (Ohio Ct. App. 1997) (hearsay evidence admissible if is a result of an excited utterance); *C.A.J. v. State,* 195 S.E.2d 225 (Ga. Ct. App. 1973) (excited utterance); *In re L.Z.,* 396 N.W.2d 214, 219 (Minn. 1986) (hearsay evidence acceptable if "necessary and reliable").

Many states have also codified a juvenile's right against self-incrimination. *See, e.g.,* GA. CODE ANN. § 15-11-31(b) (Lexis Supp. 2000); TENN. CODE ANN. § 37-1-127(b) (Lexis 1996); WYO. STAT. ANN. § 14-6-223(a) (Lexis 1999). As with the right to confrontation, the right against self-incrimination is generally the same as that afforded to adults. *See, e.g., In re Dennis,* 291 So. 2d 731 (Miss. 1974); *Fare v. Michael C., supra,* Chapter 3, Part D, and Notes following.

Questions

1. Did the Court in *Gault* achieve its goal of extending due process rights to juveniles without equating juvenile adjudications with criminal trials? Did the Court go too far in extending constitutional principles to the juvenile justice system? Did it go far enough?

2. Are the notice requirements, as interpreted by most states, adequate? Given the informal nature of the juvenile justice system, does a juvenile require the same notice as an adult criminal defendant? Are the juvenile's parents entitled to notice of the charges against their child? Can the child's interest be adequately protected by timely and specific notice and the provision of counsel even absent parental notice?

3. Should a juvenile be entitled to the assistance of counsel only at a delinquency hearing, or is counsel appropriate for "all stages" of the juvenile process, as many states have held? Under what circumstances, if any, should a juvenile be allowed to waive the right to counsel? Should a juvenile's appointed counsel be permitted to withdraw before a delinquency adjudication? During appeal? What would you require before allowing appointed counsel to withdraw? Are the *Anders* criteria applicable to the juvenile justice system?

4. Should the rules of evidence be relaxed at a juvenile adjudicatory hearing? Does the less formal nature of the juvenile court justify a departure from the rules applicable to a criminal trial? Would the possible disposition applicable to the offense (e.g., whether the juvenile may face confinement) affect your answer?

5. Should a child be compelled to testify in juvenile court? If not, what message might this send to a child regarding the necessity to tell the truth and "own up" to her errors? What should be the parental response where a child has been instructed by an officer of the court that he does not have to answer your questions if his answers might get him into trouble?

2. Burden of Proof

In re Winship

397 U.S. 358, 90 S. Ct. 1068, 25 L. Ed. 2d 368 (1970)

Mr. Justice BRENNAN delivered the opinion of the Court.

Constitutional questions decided by this Court concerning the juvenile process have centered on the adjudicatory stage at "which a determination is made as to whether a juvenile is a delinquent . . . , with the consequence that he may be committed to a state institution." *In re Gault,* 387 U.S. 1, 13 (1967). . . .

This case presents the single, narrow question whether proof beyond a reasonable doubt is among the "essentials of due process and fair treatment," required during the adjudicatory stage when a juvenile is charged with an act which would constitute a crime if committed by an adult.

. . . During a 1967 adjudicatory hearing, . . . a judge in New York Family Court found that appellant, then a 12-year-old boy, had entered a locker and stolen $112 from a woman's pocket-book. The petition which charged appellant with delinquency alleged that his act, "if done by an adult, would constitute the crime . . . of Larceny." The judge acknowledged that the proof might not establish guilt beyond a reasonable doubt, but rejected appellant's contention that such proof was required by the Fourteenth Amendment. The judge relied instead on § 744(b) of the New York Family Court Act which provides that "[a]ny determination at the conclusion of [an adjudicatory] hearing that a [juvenile] did an act or acts must be based on a preponderance of the evidence." During a subsequent dispositional hearing, appellant was ordered placed in a training school for an initial period of 18 months, subject to annual extensions of his commitment until his 18th birthday—six years in appellant's case. The Appellate Division of the New York Supreme Court, First Judicial Department, affirmed without opinion. The New York Court of Appeals then affirmed by a four-to-three vote, expressly sustaining the constitutionality of § 744(b), 24

N.Y.2d 196, 247 N. E. 2d 253 (1969). . . .

Expressions in many opinions of this Court indicate that it has long been assumed that proof of a criminal charge beyond a reasonable doubt is constitutionally required . . . .

In *Davis v. United States,* 160 U.S. 469, 493 (1895)], . . . [t]his Court said: "No man should be deprived of his life . . . unless . . . the evidence . . . is sufficient to show beyond a reasonable doubt the existence of every fact necessary to constitute the crime charged."

The reasonable-doubt standard plays a vital role in the American scheme of criminal procedure. . . . As the dissenters in the New York Court of Appeals observed, and we agree, "a person accused of a crime . . . would be at a severe disadvantage, a disadvantage amounting to a lack of fundamental fairness, if he could be adjudged guilty and imprisoned for years on the strength of the same evidence as would suffice in a civil case." 24 N.Y.2d at 205, 247 N.E.2d at 259.

. . . The accused during a criminal prosecution has at stake interests of immense importance, both because of the possibility that he may lose his liberty upon conviction and because of the certainty that he would be stigmatized by the conviction. Accordingly, a society that values the good name and freedom of every individual should not condemn a man for commission of a crime when there is reasonable doubt about his guilt. . . .

Moreover, use of the reasonable-doubt standard is indispensable to command the respect and confidence of the community in applications of the criminal law. It is critical that the moral force of the criminal law not be diluted by a standard of proof that leaves people in doubt whether innocent men are being condemned. It is also important in our free society that every individual going about his ordinary affairs have confidence that his government cannot adjudge him guilty of a criminal offense without convinced a proper factfinder of his guilt with utmost certainty.

Lest there remain any doubt about the constitutional stature of the reasonable-doubt standard, we explicitly hold that the Due Process Clause protects the accused against conviction except upon proof beyond a reasonable doubt of every fact necessary to constitute the crime with which he is charged.

II

We turn to the question whether juveniles, like adults, are constitutionally entitled to proof beyond a reasonable doubt when they are charged with violation of a criminal law. The same considerations that demand extreme caution in factfinding to protect the innocent adult apply as well to the innocent child. We do not find convincing the contrary arguments of the New York Court of Appeals. *Gault* rendered untenable much of the reasoning relied upon by that court to sustain the constitutionality of § 744 (b). . . .

In effect the Court of Appeals distinguished the proceedings in question here from a criminal prosecution by use of what *Gault* called the "'civil' label-of-convenience which has been attached to juvenile proceedings." 387 U. S. at 50. But *Gault* expressly rejected that distinction as a reason for holding the Due Process Clause inapplicable to a juvenile proceeding. The Court of Appeals also attempted to justify the preponderance standard on the related ground that juvenile proceedings are designed "not to punish, but to save the child." 24 N.Y.2d at 197, 247 N.E.2d at 254. Again, however, *Gault* . . . made clear . . . that . . . "[a] proceeding where the issue is whether the child will be found to be 'delinquent' and subjected to the loss of his liberty for years is comparable in seriousness to a felony prosecution." *Id.* at 36.

Nor do we perceive any merit in the argument that to afford juveniles the protection of proof beyond a reasonable doubt would risk destruction of beneficial aspects of the juvenile process. Use of the reasonable-doubt standard during the adjudicatory hearing will not disturb New York's policies that a finding that a child has violated a criminal law does not constitute a criminal conviction, that such a finding does not deprive the child of his civil rights, and that juvenile proceedings are confidential. Nor will there be any effect on the informality, flexibility, or speed of the hearing at which the factfinding takes place. . . .

* * *

We conclude, as we concluded regarding the essential due process safeguards applied in *Gault*, that the observance of the standard of proof beyond a reasonable doubt "will not compel the States to abandon or displace any of the substantive benefits of the juvenile process." *Gault, supra,* at 21.

Finally, we reject the Court of Appeals' suggestion that there is, in any event, only a "tenuous difference" between the reasonable-doubt and preponderance standards. The suggestion is singularly unpersuasive. In this very case, the trial judge's ability to distinguish between the two standards enabled him to make a finding of guilt that he conceded he might not have made under the standard of proof beyond a reasonable doubt. . . .

III

In sum, the constitutional safeguard of proof beyond a reasonable doubt is as much required during the adjudicatory stage of a delinquency proceeding as are those constitutional safeguards applied in *Gault*—notice of charges, right to counsel, the rights of confrontation and examination, and the privilege against self-incrimination. We therefore hold, in agreement with Chief Judge Fuld in dissent in the Court of Appeals, "that, where a 12-year-old child is charged with an act of stealing which renders him liable to confinement for as long as six years, then, as a matter of due process . . . the case against him must be proved beyond a reasonable doubt." 24 N.Y.2d at 207, 247 N.E.2d at 260.

Reversed.

Mr. Justice HARLAN, concurring.

No one, I daresay, would contend that state juvenile court trials are subject to *no* federal constitutional limitations. Differences have existed, however, among the members of this Court as to *what* constitutional protections do apply. *See In re Gault,* 387 U.S. 1 (1967).

. . . While I am in full agreement [with the majority], I am constrained to add something to what my Brother Brennan has written for the Court, lest the true nature of the constitutional problem presented become obscured or the impact on state juvenile court systems of what the Court holds today be exaggerated.

* * *

I

. . . In a civil suit between two private parties for money damages . . . , we view it as no more serious in general for there to be an erroneous verdict in the defendant's favor than for there to be an erroneous verdict in the plaintiff's favor. A preponderance of the evidence standard therefore [is] appropriate. . . .

In a criminal case, on the other hand, we do not view the social disutility of convicting an innocent man as equivalent to the disutility of acquitting someone who is guilty. . . . [T]he requirement of proof beyond a reasonable doubt in a criminal case [is] bottomed on a fundamental value determination of our society that it is far worse to convict an innocent man than to let a guilty man go free. . . .

II

When one assesses the consequences of an erroneous factual determination in a juvenile delinquency proceeding in which a youth is accused of a crime, I think it must be concluded that, while the consequences are not identical to those in a criminal case, the differences will not support a distinction in the standard of proof. . . .

Although there are no doubt costs to society (and possibly even to the youth himself) in letting a guilty youth go free, I think here, as in a criminal case, it is far worse to declare an innocent youth a delinquent. I therefore agree that a juvenile court judge should be no less convinced of the factual conclusion that the accused committed the criminal act with which he is charged than would be required in a criminal trial.

* * *

Mr. Chief Justice BURGER, with whom Mr. Justice STEWART joins, dissenting.

The Court's opinion today rests entirely on the assumption that all juvenile proceedings are "criminal prosecutions," hence subject to constitutional limitations. This derives from earlier holdings, which, like today's holding, were steps eroding the differences between juvenile courts and traditional criminal courts. . . .

* * *

My hope is that today's decision will not spell the end of a generously conceived program of compassionate treatment intended to mitigate the rigors and trauma of exposing youthful offenders to a traditional criminal court. . . . I cannot regard it as a manifestation of progress to transform juvenile courts into criminal courts which is what we are well on the way to accomplishing. . . . (footnotes omitted throughout).

[Justice BLACK'S dissenting opinion reiterates his belief that the states are constrained in their ability to make laws only by the black letter of the

Constitution and the Bill of Rights. *See In re Gault,* 387 U.S.1 (1967) (Black, J., concurring). Because the Due Process clause does not specifically require proof beyond a reasonable doubt, Justice Black would not impose such a restriction on the States, but would instead allow State legislatures to determine the standard of proof for their courts "unless . . . otherwise unconstitutional."]

Notes

1. The Court's holding in *Winship*, like that in *Gault,* attempted to extend due process protections to juveniles involved in delinquency proceedings without equating juvenile courts with their criminal counterparts. Although it avoided labeling juvenile delinquency dispositions as criminal punishments, the opinion nonetheless echoed its predecessor in voicing the Court's skepticism of the juvenile justice system's ability to act as *parens patriae*. Rather than relying on the often punitive nature of juvenile dispositions, Justice Brennan, in his opinion for the Court, focused on accurate fact-finding in juvenile dispositions.

The Court gave two reasons for holding that juveniles are entitled to proof beyond a reasonable doubt in delinquency adjudications: the stigma of being labeled "delinquent" and the possibility of "institutional confinement" that may result from an adjudication of delinquency. Irene Rosenberg, the public defender who represented Samuel Winship in the original delinquency proceeding, surmises that the *Winship* Court, like the Court in *Gault*, realized that juvenile proceedings are essentially the same as criminal trials, although in neither opinion did the Court wish to extend all protections of the criminal law to juveniles. *See* Irene Merker Rosenberg, Winship *Redux: 1970 to 1990*, 69 TEX. L. REV. 109, 123 (1990).

Like the Court's opinion in *Gault*, the holding in *Winship* is limited to the adjudicatory stage of delinquency proceedings. The Court thereby left unanswered two questions. First, what burden of proof is necessary in the other stages of a delinquency proceeding? Second, does *Winship* mandate proof beyond a reasonable doubt in other juvenile proceedings? The first question relates to the applicable burden of proof in the pre- and post-adjudicatory stages of a delinquency hearing, the second to proceedings other than delinquency adjudications, such as those relating to status offenses.

2. When addressing the question of whether *Winship's* reasonable doubt standard applies to the other stages of a delinquency proceeding, most state courts have answered in the negative. For example, most courts have determined that a pre-adjudicatory waiver decision need be based only upon a preponderance of the evidence (*see supra,* Chapter 5, Part B, Notes following *United States v. K.J.C.*). Similarly, not all courts apply the reasonable doubt standard to probation revocation hearings (a post-adjudicatory, dispositional matter), although some do require such a showing before nullifying a juvenile's parole. *See infra,* Chapter 7, Part B.

3. State courts and legislatures have also had to determine whether the *Winship* reasonable doubt standard applies to juvenile proceedings other than delinquency adjudications, such as those relating to status offenses or CHINS proceedings. Nearly all states have codified the reasonable doubt standard of proof as it relates to delinquency adjudications, with several states amending their statutes to conform with the holding in *Winship. See, e.g.,* Cal. Welf. & Inst. Code § 701 (West 1998) (amended in 1971, replacing "by a preponderance of the evidence" with "beyond a reasonable doubt"); Md. Code Ann., Cts. & Jud. Proc. § 3-819(b) (Lexis Supp. 2000); N.M. Stat. Ann. § 32A-2-16(E) (Michie 1999); Tenn. Code Ann. § 37-1-129(b) (Lexis Supp. 2000). Approximately half of the states have gone a step further, requiring proof beyond a reasonable doubt in all juvenile adjudications. *See, e.g.,* N.Y. Fam. Ct. Act §§ 342.2(2) & 744(b) (McKinney 1999); N.D. Cent. Code § 27-20-29(2) (Lexis 1991); S.D. Codified Laws §§ 26-7A-86 & -87 (Lexis 1999); Tex. Fam. Code Ann. § 54.03(f) (West Supp. 2001). The remaining states are split on the issue of the burden of proof in non-delinquency cases. Some require proof by a preponderance of the evidence (*see, e.g.,* Cal. Welf. & Inst. Code § 701 (West 1998); 705 Ill. Comp. Stat. Ann. 405/2-18(1) & 405/3-20 (West 1999); Md. Code Ann., Cts. & Jud. Proc. § 3-819(d) (Lexis Supp. 2000)), while others require a clear and convincing showing (*see, e.g.,* N.M. Stat. Ann. §§ 32A-3B-14(b) & -4-20(H) (Michie 1999); Tenn. Code Ann. § 37-1-129(c) (Lexis Supp. 2000)).

Questions

1. Does the Court's silence on the burden of proof required in the pre- and post-adjudicatory phases of the delinquency process and in other, non-delinquency procedures give the states complete freedom in legislating the required burden on these issues? Does due process of law mandate some minimum level of proof in all juvenile justice proceedings?

2. Why does the *Winship* Court, like its predecessor in *Gault*, attempt to extend due process protections to juveniles without equating the juvenile justice system with criminal courts? If the Court has given up on the notion of the state as *parens patriae,* what justification is there for a separate juvenile justice system? Should the Court and the states, as some commentators have suggested, abandon the juvenile system as a failed experiment and simply deal with juveniles in adult criminal courts?

3. Why do you suppose most states require only a preponderance of the evidence or a clear and convincing showing in a waiver hearing, while many require proof beyond a reasonable doubt in a parole revocation hearing? Does the possible result of the hearing affect the burden of proof required? Should it?

4. Are juveniles entitled to proof beyond a reasonable doubt in a non-delinquency adjudication, such as a status offense or CHINS proceeding? Why or why not?

3. Jury Trial

McKeiver v. Pennsylvania

403 U.S. 528, 91 S. Ct. 1976, 29 L. Ed. 2d 647 (1971)

Mr. Justice BLACKMUN announced the judgments of the Court and an opinion in which THE CHIEF JUSTICE, Mr. Justice STEWART, and Mr. Justice WHITE join.

These cases present the narrow but precise issue whether the Due Process Clause of the Fourteenth Amendment assures the right to trial by jury in the adjudicative phase of a state juvenile court delinquency proceeding.

From [our previous] cases . . . it is apparent that :

1. Some of the constitutional requirements attendant upon the state criminal trial have equal application to that part of the state juvenile proceeding that is adjudicative in nature. Among these are the rights to appropriate notice, to counsel, to confrontation and to cross-examination, and the privilege against self-incrimination. Included, also, is the standard of proof beyond a reasonable doubt.

2. The Court, however, has not yet said that *all* rights constitutionally assured to an adult accused of crime also are to be enforced or made available to the juvenile in his delinquency proceeding. Indeed, the Court specifically has refrained from going that far:

> "We do not mean by this to indicate that the hearing to be held must conform with all of the requirements of a criminal trial or even of the usual administrative hearing; but we do hold that the hearing must measure up to the essentials of due process and fair treatment." *Kent v. United States,* 383 U.S. 541, 562 (1966); *In re Gault*, 387 U.S.1, 30 (1967).

3. The Court . . . has also noted the disappointments of the system's performance and experience and the resulting widespread disaffection. *Kent,* 383 U.S. at 555-556; *Gault,* 387 U.S. at 17-19. . . . There has been praise for the system and its purposes, and there has been alarm over its defects.

4. The Court has insisted that these successive decisions do not spell the doom of the juvenile court system or even deprive it of its "informality, flexibility, or speed." *In re Winship,* 397 U.S. 358, 366 (1970). . . .

With this substantial background already developed, we turn to the facts of the present cases:

No. 322. Joseph McKeiver, then age 16, in May 1968 was charged with robbery, larceny, and receiving stolen goods as acts of juvenile delinquency. At the time of the adjudication hearing he was represented by counsel. His request for a jury trial was denied and his case was heard by Judge Theodore S. Gutowicz of the Court of Common Pleas, Family Division, Juvenile Branch, of Philadelphia County, Pennsylvania. McKeiver was adjudged a delinquent upon findings that he had violated a law of the Commonwealth. He was placed on probation. On appeal, the Superior Court affirmed without opinion.

Edward Terry, then age 15, in January 1969 was charged with assault and battery on a police officer and conspiracy as acts of juvenile delinquency. His counsel's request for a jury trial was denied and his case was heard by Judge Joseph C. Bruno of the same Juvenile Branch of the Court of Common Pleas of Philadelphia County. Terry was adjudged a delinquent on the charges. . . . He was committed . . . to the Youth Development Center at Cornwells Heights. On appeal, the Superior Court affirmed without opinion.

The Supreme Court of Pennsylvania granted leave to appeal. . . . The single question considered, as phrased by the court, was "whether there is a constitutional right to a jury trial in juvenile court." The answer, one justice dissenting, was in the negative. *In re Terry,* 438 Pa. 339, 265 A.2d 350 (1970). . . .

No. 128. Barbara Burrus and approximately 45 other black children, ranging in age from 11 to 15 years, were the subjects of juvenile court summonses issued in Hyde County, North Carolina, in January 1969.

The charges arose out of a series of demonstrations in the county in late 1968 by black adults and children protesting school assignments and a school consolidation plan. Petitions were filed by North Carolina state highway patrolmen. [T]he petitions charged the respective juveniles with wilfully impeding traffic. . . .

The several cases were consolidated into groups for hearing before District Judge Hallet S. Ward, sitting as a juvenile court. The same lawyer appeared for all the juveniles. Over counsel's objection, made in all except two of the cases, the general public was excluded. A request for a jury trial in each case was denied.

* * *

In each case the court found that the juvenile had committed "an act for which an adult may be punished by law. . . ." The court . . . placed each juvenile on probation for either one or two years. . . . None of the juveniles has been confined on these charges.

On appeal, . . . [t]he North Carolina Court of Appeals affirmed. In its turn the Supreme Court of North Carolina . . . affirmed. . . .

The right to an impartial jury "[i]n all criminal prosecutions" under federal law is guaranteed by the Sixth Amendment. Through the Fourteenth Amendment that requirement has now been imposed upon the States. . . . This is because the Court has said it believes "that trial by jury in criminal cases is fundamental to the American scheme of justice." *Duncan v. Louisiana,* 391 U.S. 145, 149 (1968); *Bloom v. Illinois,* 391 U.S. 194, 210-211 (1968).

This, of course, does not automatically provide the answer to the present jury trial issue, if for no other reason than that the juvenile court proceeding has not yet been held to be a "criminal prosecution," within the meaning and reach of the Sixth Amendment, and also has not yet been regarded as devoid of criminal aspects merely because it usually has been given the civil label. *Kent,* 383 U.S. at 554; *Gault,* 387 U.S. at 17, 49-50; *Winship,* 397 U.S. at 365-366.

* * *

[A]ccepting "the proposition that the Due Process Clause has a role to play," *Gault*, 387 U.S. at 13, our task here with respect to trial by jury, as it was in *Gault* with respect to other claimed rights, "is to ascertain the precise impact of the due process requirement." *Id.* at 13-14.

The Pennsylvania juveniles' basic argument is that they were tried in proceedings "substantially similar to a criminal trial. . . ." The North Carolina juveniles . . . urge that the requirement of a jury trial would not operate to deny the supposed benefits of the juvenile court system; . . . that the jury trial provides an independent protective factor; that experience has shown that jury trials in juvenile courts are manageable; that no reason exists why protection traditionally accorded in criminal proceedings should be denied young people subject to involuntary incarceration for lengthy periods; and that the juvenile courts deserve healthy public scrutiny.

All the litigants here agree that the applicable due process standard in juvenile proceedings, as developed by *Gault* and *Winship,* is fundamental fairness. As that standard was applied in those two cases, we have an emphasis on factfinding procedures. . . . But one cannot say that in our legal system the jury is a necessary component of accurate factfinding. [W]e have been content to pursue other ways for determining facts. . . . In *Duncan* the Court stated, "We would not assert, . . . that every criminal trial . . . held before a judge alone is unfair or that a defendant may never be as fairly treated by a judge as he would be by a jury." 391 U.S. at 158. . . .

* * *

[W]e conclude that trial by jury in the juvenile court's adjudicative stage is not a constitutional requirement. We so conclude for a number of reasons.

1. The Court has refrained . . . from taking the easy way with a flat holding that all rights constitutionally assured for the adult accused are to be imposed upon the state juvenile proceeding. . . .

2. There is a possibility, at least, that the jury trial, if required as a matter of constitutional precept, will remake the juvenile proceeding into a full adversary process and will put an effective end to what has been the idealistic prospect of an intimate, informal protective proceeding.

* * *

3. The Court specifically has recognized by dictum that a jury is not a necessary part even of every criminal process that is fair and equitable. *Duncan v. Louisiana,* 391 U.S. at 149-150, n.14, and 158.

4. The imposition of the jury trial on the juvenile court system would not strengthen greatly, if at all, the factfinding function, and . . . would tend once again to place the juvenile squarely in the routine of the criminal process.

5. If, in its wisdom, any State feels the jury trial is desirable in all cases, or in certain kinds, there appears to be no impediment to its installing a system embracing that feature. That, however, is the State's privilege and not its obligation.

6. There is, of course, nothing to prevent a juvenile court judge, in a particular case where he feels the need, or when the need is demonstrated, from using an advisory jury.

7. Since *Gault* and since *Duncan* the great majority of States, in addition to Pennsylvania and North Carolina, that have faced the issue have concluded that the considerations that led to the result in those two cases do not compel trial by jury in the juvenile court. . . .

8. Stopping short of proposing the jury trial for juvenile proceedings are the Uniform Juvenile Court Act, § 24(a), approved in July 1968 by the National Conference of Commissioners on Uniform State Laws; the Standard Juvenile Court Act, Art. V, § 19, proposed by the National Council on Crime and Delinquency (*see* W. Sheridan, Standards for Juvenile and Family Courts 73, Dept. Of H.E.W., Children's Bureau Pub. No. 437-1966); and the Legislative Guide for Drafting Family and Juvenile Court Acts § 29 (a) (Dept. of H.E.W., Children's Bureau Pub. No. 472-1969).

9. If the jury trial were to be injected into the juvenile court system as a matter of right, it would bring with it into that system the traditional delay, the formality, and the clamor of the adversary system and, possibly, the public trial. . . .

10. Finally, the arguments advanced by the juveniles here . . . necessarily equate the juvenile proceeding . . . with the criminal trial. . . .

If the formalities of the criminal adjudicative process are to be superimposed upon the juvenile court system, there is little need for its separate existence. Perhaps that ultimate disillusionment will come one day, but for the moment we are disinclined to give impetus to it.

Affirmed.

Mr. Justice BRENNAN, concurring in the judgment in No. 322 and dissenting in No. 128.

[T]he question in these cases is whether jury trial is among the "essentials of due process and fair treatment," *In re Gault*, 387 U.S.1, 30 (1967), required during the adjudication of a charge of delinquency based upon acts that would constitute a crime if engaged in by an adult. . . .

[T]he States are not bound to provide jury trials on demand so long as some other aspect of the process adequately protects the interests that Sixth Amendment jury trials are intended to serve.[1]

* * *

. . . The availability of trial by jury allows an accused to protect himself against possible oppression by what is in essence an appeal to the community conscience, as embodied in the jury that hears his case. To some extent, however, a similar protection may be obtained when an accused may in essence appeal to the community at large, by focusing public attention upon the facts of

---

[1] "A criminal process which was fair and equitable but used no juries is easy to imagine. It would make use of alternative guarantees and protections which would serve the purposes that the jury serves in the English and American systems." *Duncan v. Louisiana,* 391 U.S. 145, 150 n.14 (1968). This conclusion is, of course, inescapable in light of our decisions that petty criminal offenses may be tried without a jury notwithstanding the defendant's request.

his trial, exposing improper judicial behavior to public view, and obtaining if necessary, executive redress through the medium of public indignation. . . . In the Pennsylvania cases before us, there appears to be no statutory ban upon admission of the public to juvenile trials. Appellants themselves, without contradiction, assert that "the press is generally admitted" to juvenile delinquency proceedings in Philadelphia. Most important, the record in these cases is bare of any indication that any person whom appellants sought to have admitted to the courtroom was excluded. In these circumstances, I agree that the judgment in No. 322 must be affirmed.

The North Carolina cases, however, present a different situation. North Carolina law either permits or requires exclusion of the general public from juvenile trials. In the cases before us, the trial judge "ordered the general public excluded from the hearing room," *In re Burrus,* 4 N.C. App. 523, 525, 167 S.E.2d 454, 456 (1969), notwithstanding petitioners' repeated demand for a public hearing. . . . [N]either the opinions supporting the judgment nor the respondent in No. 128 has pointed to any feature of North Carolina's juvenile proceedings that could substitute for public or jury trial in protecting the petitioners against misuse of the judicial process.

Mr. Justice DOUGLAS, with whom Mr. Justice BLACK and Mr. Justice MARSHALL concur, dissenting.

These cases from Pennsylvania and North Carolina present the issue of the right to a jury trial for offenders charged in juvenile court and facing a possible incarceration until they reach their majority. I believe the guarantees of the Bill of Rights, made applicable to the States by the Fourteenth Amendment, require a jury trial.

* * *

We held in *In re Gault,* 387 U.S. 1, 13, that "neither the Fourteenth Amendment nor the Bill of Rights is for adults alone. . . . [W]here a State uses its juvenile court proceedings to prosecute a juvenile for a criminal act and to order "confinement" until the child reaches 21 years of age . . . , then he is entitled to the same procedural protection as an adult. . . ."

* * *

In the present cases imprisonment or confinement up to 10 years was possible for one child and each faced at least a possible five-year incarceration. No adult could be denied a jury trial in those circumstances. *Duncan v. Louisiana,* 391 U.S. 145, 162. The Fourteenth Amendment which makes trial by jury provided in the Sixth Amendment applicable to the States, speaks of denial of rights to "any person," not denial of rights to "any adult person"; and we have held indeed that where a juvenile is charged with an act that would constitute a crime if committed by an adult, he is entitled to be tried under a standard of proof beyond a reasonable doubt. *In re Winship,* 397 U.S. 358.

These cases should be remanded for trial by jury on the criminal charges filed against these youngsters.

[The separate concurring opinions of Justices WHITE and HARLAN are omitted, as is the Appendix to the dissenting opinion of Justice DOUGLAS.]

Notes

1. *McKeiver* is unique among the Supreme Court's pronouncements regarding the juvenile justice system in that it is the only case in which the Court has declined to extend a specific constitutional protection to juveniles subject to delinquency adjudications. The *McKeiver* Court held that a juvenile is not entitled to a jury trial in a delinquency proceeding, even though the act charged would be a crime if committed by an adult and the adjudication could result in the juvenile's confinement. *McKeiver* is also one of the few modern juvenile cases to be decided by a plurality of the Court. As with the Court's holding in *Winship*, the *McKeiver* Court's focus was on accurate fact-finding and fundamental fairness issues rather than the due process issues at the center of its opinion in *Gault*. The Court again recognized the shortcomings of the juvenile justice system and the near equivalence of juvenile adjudications to criminal trials, but as in its earlier holdings, refused to recognize the juvenile system as a complete failure.

Some commentators believe that the Court's holding in *McKeiver* can be justified by the rehabilitative ideals of the juvenile justice system. The absence of a jury, it is held, keeps juvenile hearings from becoming full-blown trials with all their adversarial attachments, and thereby protects and promotes the use of juvenile adjudications for rehabilitative rather than punitive purposes.

2. The American Bar Association contends that a juvenile should have the right to trial by jury if the juvenile denies the allegations of the petition. *See Standards Relating to Adjudication,* in JUVENILE JUSTICE STANDARDS ANNOTATED 1, 8 (Robert E. Shepherd, Jr., ed., 1996). The Standards call for a jury of at least six members and require unanimity for an adjudication of delinquency. *Id.* This portion of the Standards, however, has not been widely adopted. *See, e.g., In re N.E.,* 361 N.W.2d 693, 698 (Wis. 1985) (juvenile's right to jury trial controlled by statue; is not a fundamental right as indicated by Standards).

3. Although the *McKeiver* Court held that the states are not compelled by the Fourteenth Amendment to provide jury trials to alleged juvenile delinquents, the Court did not forbid states from doing so as a matter of state law. Slightly less than a third of the states have established a juvenile's right to a jury in a delinquency adjudication under some circumstances. *See, e.g.,* COLO. REV. STAT. ANN. § 19-2-107 (2000); KAN. STAT. ANN. § 38-1656 (West 2000); MONT. CODE ANN. § 41-5-1502(1) (1999); W. VA. CODE § 49-5-6 (Lexis 1999); *In re S.H.,* 846 S.W.2d 103 (Tex. Ct. App. 1992); *R.L.R. v. State,* 487 P.2d 27 (Alaska 1971). The majority of states, however, statutorily deny juveniles the right to jury determinations in delinquency proceedings. *See, e.g.,* D.C. CODE ANN. § 16-2316(a) (Lexis 1997); HAW. REV. STAT. ANN. § 571-41(a) (1993); N.J. STAT. ANN. § 2A:4A-40 (West 1987); TENN. CODE ANN. § 37-1-124(a) (Lexis 1996). Moreover, many of these states had judicially decided this issue before the Supreme Court's decision in *McKeiver*. *See, e.g., In re Fucini,* N.E.2d 380 (Ill. 1970); *Dryden v. Commonwealth,* 435 S.W.2d 457 (Ky. 1968); *State v. Turner,* 453 P.2d 910 (Or. 1969).

Courts have continued to follow *McKeiver* in justifying the denial of the right to a jury trial in a juvenile hearing by emphasizing the distinction between juvenile adjudications and criminal trials. This is true despite the fact that juvenile adjudications and dispositions have increasingly come to parallel their criminal counterparts. *See, e.g., State v. Lawley*, 591 P.2d 772 (Wash. 1979); *State ex rel. Juvenile Department v. Reynolds*, 857 P.2d 842 (Or. 1993).

4. State courts have also held that juveniles have no right to a jury during the dispositional phase of a delinquency adjudication. *See, e.g., In re S.H.*, 846 S.W.2d 103 (Tex. Ct. App. 1992); *Alford v. Carter*, 504 P.2d 436 (Okla. Crim. App. 1972); *In re Miller*, 445 N.W.2d 168 (Mich. Ct. App. 1989). The right to a jury has also been denied to juveniles during status offense adjudications (*see e.g., State v. LaMunyon*, 911 P.2d 151 (Kan. 1996) (right to jury trial only for felony offense)) and in waiver hearings. *See e.g., In re E.D.M.*, 916 S.W.2d 9 (Tex. Ct. App. 1995).

5. Several commentators have joined the A.B.A. in calling for the right to a jury trial in all juvenile delinquency proceedings. *See, e.g.*, Susan E. Brooks, *Juvenile Injustice: The Ban on Jury Trials for Juveniles in the District of Columbia*, 33 U. LOUISVILLE J. FAM. L. 875 (1995); Korine L. Larsen, Comment, *With Liberty and Justice for All: Extending the Right to a Jury Trial to the Juvenile Courts*, 20 WM. MITCHELL L. REV. 835 (1994) (espousing the right to jury trial for juveniles in Minnesota courts).

Questions

1. Do the purposes and goals of the juvenile justice system warrant withholding the right to trial by jury from juveniles? Would granting juveniles the right to a jury trial amount to equating juvenile delinquency hearings with criminal trials? Are the two proceedings enough alike already to justify requiring jury trials for juveniles?

2. Are the IJA-ABA standards correct in providing that a juvenile is entitled to trial by jury? Should it make a difference if the juvenile denies the allegations of the petition? Why do you think most states follow the holding in *McKeiver* rather than adopting the IJA-ABA standards on this issue?

4. Public Trial

IJA-ABA Standards Relating to Adjudication

Juvenile Justice Standards Annotated 1, 11-12
(Robert E. Shepherd, Jr., ed., 1996)*

Public Access to Adjdication Proceedings

Right to a public trial.

Each jurisdiction should provide by law that a respondent in juvenile court adjudication proceeding has a right to a public trial.

Implementing the right to a public trial.

A. Each jurisdiction should provide by law that the respondent, after consulting with counsel, may waive the right to a public trial.

---

* Reprinted with permission.

B. Each jurisdiction should provide by law that the judge of the juvenile court has discretion to permit members of the public who have a legitimate interest in the proceedings or in the work of the court, including representatives of the news media, to view adjudication proceedings when the respondent has waived the right to a public trial.

C. The judge of the juvenile court should honor any request by the respondent, respondent's attorney, or family that specified members of the public be permitted to observe the respondent's adjudication proceeding when the respondent has waived the right to a public trial.

D. The judge of the juvenile court should use judicial power to prevent distractions from and disruptions of adjudication proceeding and should use that power to order removed from the courtroom any member of the public causing a distraction or disruption.

Prohibiting disclosure of respondent's identity.

A. Each jurisdiction should provide by law that members of the public permitted by the judge of the juvenile court to observe adjudication proceedings may not disclose to others the identity of the respondent when the respondent has waived the right to a public trial.

B. Each jurisdiction should provide by law that the judge of the juvenile court should announce to members of the public present to view an adjudication proceeding when the respondent has waived the right to a public trial that they may not disclose to others the identity of the respondent.

Alabama Code

§ 12-15-65 (Lexis Supp. 2000)

§ 12-15-65. Hearings; procedure; prehearing review.

(a) Hearings under this chapter shall be conducted by the court without a jury and separate from other proceedings. The general public shall be excluded from delinquency, in need of supervision, or dependency hearings and only the parties, their counsel, witnesses, and other persons requested by a party shall be admitted. Other persons as the court finds to have a proper interest in the case or in the work of the court may be admitted by the court on condition that the persons refrain from divulging any information which would identify the child or family involved. If the court finds that it is in the best interest of the child, the child may be temporarily excluded from the hearings, except while allegations of delinquency or in need of supervision are being heard. . . .

* * *

In re Jesse McM.

164 Cal. Rptr. 199 (Cal. Ct. App. 1980)

ROUSE, Associate Justice.

Jesse McM., a minor, appeals from an order declaring him a ward of the court and committing him to the California Youth Authority (hereafter Youth Authority).

* * *

Following a jurisdictional hearing, the court found the allegations of the [delinquency] petition to be true and ordered Jesse committed to the Youth Authority for a maximum period of five years. Since Jesse does not challenge the sufficiency of the evidence presented at the hearing, we shall . . . confine ourselves to a discussion of those facts which are necessarily involved in the resolution of issues raised in this appeal.

Jesse's . . . contention is that, because he was deprived of his right to a public trial, the court's finding of jurisdiction must be reversed. He reasons that, since the defendant in a criminal trial has the constitutional right to a public trial, the same right should exist in juvenile court proceedings. Jesse concedes that section 346 of the Welfare and Institutions Code[1] requires that the minor and his parent must affirmatively request a public trial; however, he contends that he did make such a request in a timely manner. . . .

A recent California Supreme Court pronouncement on the subject makes it clear that a minor possesses no constitutional right to a public trial in juvenile court proceedings. In *In re Mitchell P.* (1978) 22 Cal.3d 946, 950-951, 151 Cal. Rptr. 330, 587 P.2d 1144, the court reaffirmed the rule that disparate treatment may be accorded to persons charged with crimes and persons charged with juvenile misconduct. . . . In so holding, the court quoted with approval the following language from *McKeiver v. Pennsylvania* (1971) 403 U.S. 528, 550, 91 S. Ct. 1976, 1988, 29 L. Ed. 2d 647: "'If the jury trial were to be injected into the juvenile court system as a matter of right, it would bring with it into that system the traditional delay, the formality, and the clamor of the adversary system and, *possibly, the public trial.*'" (22 Cal. 3d p. 953, 151 Cal. Rptr. p. 336, 587 P.2d p. 1149; emphasis supplied.) It is evident from this language that a public trial in a juvenile court is neither constitutionally mandated nor, in most instances, even desirable.

Section 676 of the Welfare and Institutions Code provides that "Unless requested by the minor concerning whom the petition has been filed and any parent or guardian present, the public shall not be admitted to a juvenile court hearing. The judge or referee may nevertheless admit such persons as he deems to have a direct and legitimate interest in the particular case or the work of the court."

* * *

We are satisfied that in enacting section 676, the Legislature did not intend to grant the minor and his or her parent an *absolute* right to a public hearing, without any regard for the circumstances of the case. Such an interpretation would appear to be incompatible with the last sentence of section 676, which permits the judge, in the exercise of his discretion, to "admit such persons as he deems to have a direct and legitimate interest in the particular case or the work of the court."

---

[1] We think that Jesse intended to refer to section 676 of the Welfare and Institutions Code, rather than 346, since the latter section pertains to proceedings involving dependent children. However, the language of the two sections is identical. Henceforth, our reference herein will be to section 676, rather than section 346.

Even in criminal trials, the trial court has discretion to close portions of the trial to the public, without the consent of the defendant, where there is good cause based upon justice or the protection of the parties. In *Kirstowsky v. Superior Court* (1956) 143 Cal. App. 2d 745, 754, 300 P.2d 163, 169, the court quoted with approval from 156 A.L.R. 289: "'A criminal trial judge, in the exercise of a sound discretion, may exclude members of the public as it may become reasonably necessary in order to protect a witness or party from embarrassment by reason of having to testify to delicate or revolting facts, as a child, or where it is demonstrated that the one testifying cannot, without being freed from such embarrassment, testify to facts material to the case.'"

In this instance, it was necessary for two boys, aged nine and ten, to testify to delicate and revolting facts. Under such circumstances, even if Jesse's request for a public trial had been made in a more timely fashion and his mother had joined in said request, we find that the situation nevertheless was one where it was appropriate for the court to exercise its discretion by denying Jesse's request for a public trial.

Notes

1. The Supreme Court has not addressed the issue of a juvenile's right to a public trial during a delinquency proceeding. As noted in *Jesse McM.,* however, the Court in *McKeiver* strongly hinted that a juvenile is not entitled to a public trial. Most states hold that a juvenile does not have the right to open proceedings in the juvenile court. *See, e.g., In re Burrus,* 167 S.E.2d 454 (N.C. Ct. App. 1969) (one of the cases involved in the *McKeiver* decision); *State v. Eddie K.,* 460 S.E.2d 489 (W. Va. 1995) (no right to presence of public at sentencing); *United States v. Doe,* 385 F. Supp. 902 (D. Ariz. 1974); N.Y. FAM. CT. ACT § 341.1 (McKinney 1999); *but see Nieves v. United States*, 280 F. Supp. 994 (S.D.N.Y. 1968) (juvenile may be entitled to a public trial); *R.L.R. v. State,* 487 P.2d 27 (Alaska 1971) (juvenile entitled to a public trial under the state constitution).

2. The general public is ordinarily excluded from juvenile hearings. However, as evidenced by the Alabama Code section reprinted, *supra*, state law often gives the juvenile court judge the discretion to admit those with a significant interest in the case, such as the victim or the family members of the victim or juvenile. *See also* CAL. WELF. & INST. CODE § 346 (West 1998); N.Y. FAM. CT. ACT § 341.1 (McKinney 1999).

Some states allow the public to attend juvenile hearings under some circumstances. *See, e.g.,* GA. CODE ANN. § 15-11-28(c.1) (Lexis Supp. 2000) (public admitted in limited circumstances; for example, in the case of repeat delinquent or designated felony); *In re Chase,* 446 N.Y.S.2d 1000 (Fam. Ct. 1982) (juvenile has no constitutional right to a private trial). The states which grant the public a presumptive right to attend delinquency hearings weigh this right against the juvenile's rights, such as the right to confidentiality, in determining whether to admit members of the public over the juvenile's objections. *See, e.g., Ex parte Columbia Newspapers, Inc.,* 333 S.E.2d 337 (S.C. 1985); *In re Chase, supra*. However, even where the public has a presumptive right to attend delinquency adjudications, the juvenile court judge is nevertheless vested with the power to order the hearing closed where appropriate. *See, e.g., In re J.S.*, 438 A.2d 1125 (Vt. 1981) (press does not have constitutional right of access to juvenile court); *In re K.P.*, 709 A.2d 315 (N.J. Ch. 1997) (same). Moreover, although the juvenile may not have standing to oppose the admission of reporters or other members of the public to the delinquency hearing, the victim may. *Id.*

3. In *State ex rel. Plain Dealer Publishing Co. v. Geauga County Court of Common Pleas, Juvenile Division, Ohio,* 734 N.E.2d 1214 (Ohio 2000), the court held that juvenile proceedings are presumed neither open nor closed. Citing case precedent, *Plain Dealer Publishing Co.* stated that a court may restrict public access to delinquency proceedings if the court finds a reasonable and substantial basis for believing that (1) public access would endanger the fairness of the hearing, (2) the potential harm outweighs the benefit of public access, and (3) no reasonable alternatives to closure exist. Under the *Plain Dealer Publishing Co.* holding, the party seeking a delinquency proceeding without public access has the burden of proving to the court that such closure is necessary.

Questions

1. Should a juvenile have the right to demand a public trial? If so, should the juvenile court judge or the victim have any say in the matter?

2. Should a judge be authorized to admit members of the public to a juvenile hearing over the juvenile's objections? Over the objections of the victim or the victim's family? Is a juvenile entitled to confidentiality regardless of the outcome of the adjudication or the seriousness of the offense?

3. Should members of the media have the same right of access to the juvenile court as they do to criminal trials? What steps can the juvenile court judge take to protect the identity of the victim and the juvenile when reporters are admitted to the hearing?

5. Speedy Trial

In re C.T.F.

316 N.W.2d 865 (Iowa 1982)

SCHULTZ, Justice.

The sole issue presented in this appeal is whether a juvenile has a statutory or constitutional right to a speedy trial in a juvenile delinquency proceeding. The juvenile court determined that a juvenile does not have a right to a speedy trial. We hold that a juvenile has a constitutional, but not a statutory, right to a speedy trial. Since the juvenile in this appeal failed to show that he was denied his constitutional right to a speedy trial, however, we affirm the juvenile court.

On July 1, 1980, a petition was filed alleging that on June 16, 1980, C.T.F., a juvenile, committed a delinquent act. . . . On July 11, a deputy clerk of the juvenile court mailed an original notice, with an attached copy of the petition, to both the juvenile and his father. The notice stated that they would be notified at a later date of the time and place of the hearing on the petition. On July 17, the juvenile's father filed an application on behalf of the juvenile for appointment of counsel. On October 8, the juvenile court appointed the juvenile's present attorney to act as his attorney and guardian ad litem.

On October 11, the attorney filed a motion to dismiss the petition, alleging that the juvenile's right to a speedy trial under the federal and Iowa constitutions and Iowa R. Crim. P. 27(2)(b) had been abridged. On October 15, the juvenile court scheduled a hearing on the petition for November 7. Prior to the commencement of the hearing on the petition, the juvenile court orally overruled the motion to dismiss on the basis that a juvenile does not have a right to a speedy trial in a juvenile delinquency proceeding. No evidence was offered [by the juvenile] in support of the motion.

Following the hearing the juvenile court, by written order, found the evidence sufficient to establish that the juvenile had committed the delinquent act, as alleged in the petition. After a dispositional hearing, the court entered an order releasing the juvenile, subject to specified conditions of probation, into the custody of his father.

The juvenile filed a timely notice of appeal, asserting that the juvenile court erred in overruling his motion to dismiss. He contends: (1) the Sixth Amendment to the United States Constitution and article one, section ten of the Iowa Constitution provide juveniles the constitutional right to a speedy trial, and (2) Iowa R. Crim. P. 27(2)(b) . . . provide[s] juveniles a statutory right to a speedy trial.

I. *Statutory right to a speedy trial.* The juvenile maintains that the filing of a petition charging a juvenile with commission of a delinquent act . . . is tantamount to filing an indictment or trial information in a criminal prosecution. He argues that since the Juvenile Justice Act . . . does not establish a time limit for commencing the formal adjudicatory hearing . . . it would be reasonable to adopt the speedy trial provisions of Iowa R. Crim. P. 27(2)(b).[1] We disagree.

We have long recognized that a juvenile court proceeding is not a prosecution for crime, but a special proceeding that serves as an ameliorative alternative to a criminal prosecution. *States v. McGhee,* 280 N.W.2d 436, 438 (Iowa 1979), *cert. denied,* 444 U.S. 1039, 100 S. Ct. 712, 62 L. Ed. 2d 674 (1980); *In re Johnson,* 257 N.W.2d 47, 48 (Iowa 1977); *State v. White,* 223 N.W.2d 173, 175 (Iowa 1974). . . .

---

[1] Rule 27(2)(b) provides:

> It is the public policy of the state of Iowa that criminal prosecutions be concluded at the earliest possible time consistent with a fair trial to both parties. Applications for dismissals under this subsection may be made by the prosecuting attorney or the defendant or by the court on its own motion. If a defendant indicted for a public offense has not waived his right to a speedy trial he must be brought to trial within ninety days after indictment is found or the court must order the indictment to be dismissed unless good cause to the contrary be shown.

. . . The filing of a petition accusing a juvenile of committing a delinquent act is not equivalent to indictment for a public offense in a criminal prosecution. A juvenile is not amenable to prosecution for a public offense under the provisions of the Criminal Code until it is ordered that the juvenile be transferred to the district court for prosecution as an adult. *McGhee,* 280 N.W.2d at 438-39; *In re Johnson,* 257 N.W.2d at 48-49. . . . Since a delinquent act does not constitute a public offense, we hold that rule 27(2)(b) does not provide a juvenile the right to a speedy trial in a juvenile court proceeding.

* * *

II. *Constitutional right to a speedy trial.* The Sixth Amendment to the United States Constitution provides in part: "In all criminal prosecutions, the accused shall enjoy the right to a speedy . . . trial . . . ." Similarly, article one, section ten of the Iowa Constitution provides in part: "In all criminal prosecutions, and in cases involving the life, or liberty of an individual the accused shall have a right to a speedy and public trial. . . ." The juvenile contends that these provisions guarantee the right to a speedy trial in juvenile court proceedings.

Traditionally, juvenile delinquency proceedings were held to be special proceedings that were not subject to the provisions of either the state or federal constitutions; thus, juveniles did not enjoy the protection of constitutional rights applicable in criminal prosecutions of adults. In 1967, however, the United States Supreme Court decided the landmark case of *In re Gault,* 387 U.S. 1, 87 S. Ct. 1428, 18 L. Ed. 2d 527 (1967). The Court held that when delinquency proceedings may result in the detention of the child, the Due Process Clause of the Fourteenth Amendment requires states to observe certain fundamental rights. . . .

The *Gault* Court refrained from stating that all constitutional rights of an adult in a criminal prosecution are available to a juvenile in a delinquency proceeding, however. Instead, the Court prescribed a case-by-case determination of the applicability of constitutional rights available in juvenile proceedings predicated on fair treatment, tempered by the nature of the juvenile hearing. The Court stated that "[t]he problem is to ascertain the precise impact of the due process requirement upon such proceedings." *Id.* at 13-14, 87 S. Ct. at 1436, 18 L. Ed. 2d at 538.

The Supreme Court has applied its case-by-case due process test on several occasions since *Gault*. In *In re Winship*, 397 U.S. 358, 90 S. Ct. 1068, 25 L. Ed. 2d 368 (1970), . . . [t]he Court held that under the due process clause the juvenile had a constitutional right to the beyond-a-reasonable-doubt standard of proof in the adjudicatory hearing. *Id.* at 368, 90 S. Ct. at 1075, 25 L. Ed. 2d at 377-78. In *McKeiver v. Pennsylvania*, 403 U.S. 528, 545, 91 S. Ct. 1976, 1986, 29 L. Ed. 2d 647, 661 (1971), however, the Court held that a juvenile does not have a constitutional right to a jury trial in a delinquency proceeding. A plurality of the Court concluded that because of the impact a constitutionally required jury would have on juvenile proceedings, fundamental fairness did not require a jury trial. *Id.* at 543, 91 S. Ct. at 1985, 29 L. Ed. 2d at 659-60.

The United States Supreme Court has not addressed the issue whether a juvenile has a constitutional right to a speedy trial in a delinquency proceeding. Nor has this court previously addressed the issue. A juvenile delinquency proceeding has not been held to be a "criminal prosecution" within the meaning of either the Sixth Amendment to the United States Constitution or article one, section ten of the Iowa Constitution. We hold, however, that the Due Process Clauses of the Fourteenth Amendment to the Federal Constitution and article one, section nine of the Iowa Constitution provide juveniles the right to a speedy trial in delinquency proceedings.

[W]e conclude that the *Gault* due process test should be applied in determining whether the Due Process Clause of article one, section nine[3] requires a speedy trial. We therefore apply the same test under both federal and Iowa constitutional provisions. In balancing the fair treatment of juveniles against the effect that a right to a speedy trial would have on the juvenile justice system, we conclude that fundamental fairness requires that juveniles have the right to speedy trial.

Charging a juvenile with a delinquent act results in family stress and causes concern and anxiety on the part of the juvenile. It often affects the juvenile's relationships with peer groups, school officials, and other adult authorities. Also, unreasonable delay may affect the quality and quantity of evidence presented, impairing the juvenile's defense and preventing a fair hearing. Finally, in the event the juvenile is found to have committed the delinquent act, the delay may be detrimental to the youth's rehabilitation. We therefore conclude that juveniles have a constitutional right to a speedy trial.

The State maintains that even if the juvenile has a constitutional right to a speedy trial there is no evidence in the record that the right was violated in this case. The State bases its contention on the four-factor test enunciated by the United States Supreme Court in *Barker v. Wingo,* 407 U.S. 514, 92 S. Ct. 2182, 33 L. Ed. 2d 101 (1972), for determining whether an accused has been denied the right to a speedy trial under the sixth amendment. In *Barker* the Court stated that under the circumstances of each case the following factors must be considered: (1) the length of the delay; (2) the reason for the delay; (3) whether the accused asserted the right; and (4) whether the accused was prejudiced by the delay. *Id.* at 530, 92 S. Ct. at 2192, 33 L. Ed. 2d at 116-17. . . .

We believe the *Barker* test is appropriate for determining whether a juvenile has been denied the right to a speedy trial under the applicable due process provisions of both the federal and Iowa constitutions. Its application, however, should take into consideration the differences between adult criminal prosecutions and juvenile delinquency proceedings. In this case, as already noted, the juvenile did not offer any evidence to support his motion to dismiss. The record reveals only that the juvenile hearing commenced four months and one week after the petition was filed. There is no evidence concerning the reason for the delay, that the juvenile asserted and was denied the right to a speedy trial prior to the motion to dismiss, or that the juvenile was prejudiced by the delay. We therefore hold that the juvenile failed to prove that he was denied the right to a speedy trial.

---

[3] The Due Process Clause of article one, section nine, in language virtually identical to that of the Fourteenth Amendment, provides that "no person shall be deprived of life, liberty, or property, without due process of law."

Since the juvenile failed to prove that his constitutional right to a speedy trial was violated, we find no reversible error on the part of the juvenile court. Accordingly, we affirm the court's order adjudging that the juvenile committed a delinquent act.

Notes

1. As with the right to a public trial in delinquency proceedings, the Supreme Court has not addressed the issue of a juvenile's right to a speedy trial. However, whereas most states do not guarantee juveniles a public trial in delinquency proceedings, the majority of jurisdictions do extend the right to a speedy trial to juveniles. As evidenced in the *C.T.F.* opinion, most courts find that the due process requirements outlined in *In re Gault* mandate the right to a speedy trial for juveniles. In *Piland v. Clark County Juvenile Court Services,* for example, the Nevada Supreme Court held that the right to a speedy trial is "axiomatic, because of the mandates announced in *Gault.*" 457 P.2d 523, 525 (Nev. 1969). The court found that the safeguards outlined in the *Gault* opinion would be worthless if the juvenile was not brought to trial in a timely manner. *Id.*

C.T.F. outlines the reasons typically given for requiring a speedy trial for juveniles. The court pointed to the stress a pending adjudication causes to the juvenile and the child's family, to evidentiary concerns, and to the loss of rehabilitative potential where the adjudicative hearing is too far attenuated from the alleged act of delinquency. Most courts addressing the issue rely on the same or similar factors.

2. The American Bar Association would guarantee a speedy trial to all juveniles charged with delinquency. The IJA-ABA recommendations call for trial within fifteen days of arrest or the filing of charges (whichever occurs first) if the juvenile is held in detention for more than twenty-four hours or a trial within thirty days if the juvenile is not detained. *See Standards Relating to Interim Status: The Release, Control and Detention of Accused Juvenile Offenders Between Arrest and Disposition, in* JUVENILE JUSTICE STANDARDS ANNOTATED 119, 136-37 (Robert E. Shepherd, Jr., ed., 1996).

3. Most states have judicially recognized the right to a speedy trial for juveniles accused of delinquency. *See, e.g., In re Anthony P.,* 430 N.Y.S.2d 479 (Fam. Ct. 1980) (juvenile has constitutional right to speedy trial); *State v. J.H.,* 295 So. 2d 698 (Fla. Dist. Ct. App. 1974); *State v. Young,* 339 N.E.2d 668 (Ohio Ct. App. 1975). These cases often extend to juveniles the same statutory speedy trial rights mandated in criminal trials. *See, e.g., State v. Henry,* 434 P.2d 692 (N.M. 1967). Some states have codified the right to speedy trial specifically for juveniles. *See, e.g.,* ARK. CODE ANN. § 9-27-327(b) (Michie Supp. 2001) (trial must be held within fourteen days if juvenile detained); DEL. CODE ANN. tit. 10, § 1007(g) (Michie 1999) (within thirty days if juvenile detained); VA. CODE ANN. § 16.1-277.1 (Michie 1999) (within twenty-one days if detained, otherwise within 120 days).

4. In the federal system, a juvenile's right to a speedy trial is governed by the Juvenile Justice and Delinquency Prevention Act. The J.J.D.P.A. requires timely adjudication only where the juvenile is in custody. 18 U.S.C.S. § 5036 (Law. Co-op. 1990). The speedy trial provision of the Act is triggered when the juvenile has been detained for thirty days pending adjudication. Several federal circuit courts have held that the § 5036 requirement is only applicable to strict confinement and that it does not apply, for example, to restrictive bail conditions. *See United States v. Doe,* 149 F.3d 945 (9th Cir. 1998), and the cases cited therein.

5. The right to a speedy trial for juveniles is not an absolute right. For example, the juvenile may waive the right, either expressly or by requesting a continuance. *See, e.g., E.S. v. State,* 215 S.E.2d 732 (Ga. Ct. App. 1975) (juvenile has waivable right to speedy trial); *Jackson v. Commonwealth,* 499 S.E.2d 538 (Va. 1998) (juvenile waived right to speedy trial by seeking repeated continuances and joining in state's continuance motions). Moreover, a juvenile's right to a speedy trial may be overcome by other competing interests. *See, e.g., State v. Dixon*, 792 P.2d 137 (Wash. 1990) (no violation of right to speedy trial where prosecutor delayed bringing charges until trial of codefendant completed).

Questions

1. Could the court in *C.T.F.* have reached the same result relying on the Sixth Amendment to the U.S. Constitution or Article 1, Section 10 of the Iowa Constitution? If so, why did the court rely on the Fourteenth Amendment instead? Does the Fourteenth Amendment offer more support for the holding than the Sixth Amendment or should the case have been decided solely on Iowa constitutional law? Did the court reach the right result under the four factors of the *Barker* test?

2. Should the right to a speedy trial be dependent on whether the juvenile is (or was) in custody prior to adjudication? In relation to 18 U.S.C. § 5036, do you agree with the federal circuit courts that only strict confinement amounts to detention and that restrictive bail conditions do not involve so significant a loss of liberty as to trigger speedy trial protections?

6. Double Jeopardy

Breed v. Jones

421 U.S. 519, 95 S. Ct. 1779, 44 L. Ed. 2d 346 (1975)

Mr. Chief Justice BURGER delivered the opinion of the Court.

We granted certiorari to decide whether the prosecution of respondent as an adult, after Juvenile Court proceedings which resulted in a finding that respondent had violated a criminal statute and a subsequent finding that he was unfit for treatment as a juvenile, violated the Fifth and Fourteenth Amendments to the United States Constitution.

On February 9, 1971, a petition was filed in the Superior Court of California, County of Los Angeles, Juvenile Court, alleging that respondent, then 17 years of age, was a person described by Cal. Welf. & Inst'ns Code § 602 (1966),[1] in that, on or about February 8, while armed with a deadly weapon, he had committed acts which, if committed by an adult, would constitute the crime of robbery. . . .

The following day, a detention hearing was held, at the conclusion of which respondent was ordered detained pending a hearing on the petition.

The . . . adjudicatory hearing was conducted on March 1. . . . After taking testimony from two prosecution witnesses and respondent, the Juvenile Court found that the allegations in the petition were true and that respondent was a person described by § 602 and it sustained the petition. The proceedings were continued for a dispositional hearing, pending which the court ordered that respondent remain detained.

At a hearing conducted on March 15, the Juvenile Court indicated its intention to find respondent "not . . . amenable to the care, treatment and training programs available through the facilities of the juvenile court. . . ." The court continued the matter for one week, at which time, having considered the report of the probation officer assigned to the case and having heard her testimony, it declared respondent, "unfit for treatment as a juvenile," and ordered that he be prosecuted as an adult.

Thereafter, respondent filed a petition for a writ of habeas corpus in Juvenile Court, raising the same double jeopardy claim now presented. Upon the denial of that petition, respondent sought habeas corpus relief in the California Court of Appeal, Second Appellate District. [T]hat court denied the petition. *In re Gary J.*, 17 Cal. App. 3d 704, 95 Cal. Rptr. 185 (1971). The Supreme Court of California denied respondent's petition for hearing.

After a preliminary hearing respondent was ordered held for trial in Superior Court, where an information was subsequently filed accusing him of having committed robbery . . . while armed with a deadly weapon, on or about February 8, 1971. Respondent entered a plea of not guilty, and he also pleaded that he had "already been placed once in jeopardy and convicted of the offense charged, by the judgment of the Superior Court of the County of Los Angeles Juvenile Court, rendered . . . on the 1st day of March, 1971. . . ." The court found respondent guilty of robbery in the first degree . . . and ordered that he be committed to the California Youth Authority. No appeal was taken from the judgment of conviction.

On December 10, 1971, respondent, through his mother as guardian *ad litem*, filed the instant petition for a writ of habeas corpus in the United States District Court for the Central District of California. In his petition he alleged that his transfer to adult court and subsequent trial there "placed him in dou-

---

[1] As of the date of filing of the petition in this case, Cal. Welf. & Inst. Code § 602 (1966) provided:

> Any person under the age of 21 years who violates any law of this State or of the United States . . . is within the jurisdiction of the juvenile court, which may adjudge such person to be a ward of the court. . . .

ble jeopardy." The District Court denied the petition, rejecting respondent's contention that jeopardy attached at his adjudicatory hearing. . . .

The Court of Appeals reversed, concluding that applying double jeopardy protection to juvenile proceedings would not "impede the juvenile courts in carrying out their basic goal of rehabilitating the erring youth. . . ." The court . . . held that the Double Jeopardy Clause "is fully applicable to juvenile court proceedings." 497 F.2d 1160, 1165 (CA9 1974).

Turning to the question whether there had been a constitutional violation in this case, the Court of Appeals pointed to the power of the Juvenile Court to "impose severe restrictions upon the juvenile's liberty," *Ibid.,* in support of its conclusion that jeopardy attached in respondent's adjudicatory hearing. . . . The court . . . held that once jeopardy attached at the adjudicatory hearing a minor could not be retried as an adult or a juvenile. . . .

We granted certiorari because of a conflict between Courts of Appeals and the highest courts of a number of States on the issue presented in this case and similar issues and because of the importance of final resolution of the issue to the administration of the juvenile court system.

The parties agree that, following his transfer from Juvenile Court, and as a defendant to a felony information, respondent was entitled to the full protection of the Double Jeopardy Clause of the Fifth Amendment as applied to the States through the Fourteenth Amendment. In addition, they agree that respondent was put in jeopardy by the proceedings on that information which resulted in an adjudication that he was guilty of robbery in the first degree and in a sentence of commitment. Finally, there is no dispute that the petition filed in Juvenile Court and the information filed in Superior Court related to the "same offence" within the meaning of the constitutional prohibition. The point of disagreement between the parties, and the question for our decision, is whether, by reason of the proceedings in Juvenile Court, respondent was "twice put in jeopardy."

* * *

[O]ur decisions in recent years have recognized that there is a gap between the originally benign conception of the [juvenile court] system and its realities. With the exception of *McKeiver v. Pennsylvania,* 403 U.S. 528 (1971), the Court's response to that perception has been to make applicable in juvenile proceedings constitutional guarantees associated with traditional criminal prosecutions. *In re Gault*, 387 U.S. 1 (1967); *In re Winship,* 397 U.S. 358 (1970). In so doing the Court has evinced awareness of the threat which such a process represents to the efforts of the juvenile court system, functioning in a unique manner, to ameliorate the harshness of criminal justice when applied to youthful offenders. That the system has fallen short of the high expectations of its sponsors in no way detracts from the broad social benefits sought or from those benefits that can survive constitutional scrutiny.

We believe it is simply too late in the day to conclude, as did the District Court in this case, that a juvenile is not put in jeopardy at a proceeding . . . whose potential consequences include . . . the deprivation of liberty for many years. . . .

* * *

In *In re Gault, supra,* at 36, this Court concluded that, for purposes of the right to counsel, a "proceeding where the issue is whether the child will be found to be 'delinquent' and subjected to the loss of his liberty for years is comparable in seriousness to a felony prosecution." The Court stated that the term "delinquent" had "come to involve only slightly less stigma than the term 'criminal' applied to adults,' *In re Gault, supra,* at 24 and that, for purposes of the privilege against self-incrimination, "commitment is a deprivation of liberty. It is incarceration against one's will, whether it is called 'criminal' or 'civil.'" *In re Gault, supra,* at 50. *See* 387 U.S., at 27; *In re Winship, supra*, at 367.

Thus, in terms of potential consequences, there is little to distinguish an adjudicatory hearing such as was held in this case from a traditional criminal prosecution. . . .

We deal here, not with "the formalities of the criminal adjudicative process," *McKeiver v. Pennsylvania*, 403 U.S., at 551 (opinion of Blackmun. J.), but with an analysis of an aspect of the juvenile-court system in terms of the kind of risk to which jeopardy refers. [W]e can find no persuasive distinction . . . between the proceeding conducted in this case . . . and a criminal prosecution. . . . We therefore conclude that respondent was put in jeopardy at the adjudicatory hearing. Jeopardy attached when respondent was "put to trial before the trier of the facts," *United States v. Jorn,* 400 U.S. 470, 479 (1971), that is, when the Juvenile Court, as the trier of the facts, began to hear evidence.

* * *

We cannot agree with petitioner that the trial of respondent in Superior Court on an information charging the same offense as that for which he had been tried in Juvenile Court violated none of the policies of the Double Jeopardy Clause. For even accepting petitioner's premise that respondent "never faced the risk of more than one punishment," we have pointed out that "the Double Jeopardy Clause . . . is written in terms of potential or risk of *trial* and conviction, not punishment." *Price v. Georgia,* 398 U.S. 323, 329 (1979). . . .

Respondent was subjected to the burden of two trials for the same offense; he was twice put to the task of marshaling his resources against those of the State, twice subjected to the "heavy personal strain" which such an experience represents. *United States v. Jorn*, 400 U.S. at 479. We turn, therefore, to inquire whether either traditional principles or "the juvenile court's assumed ability to function in a unique manner," *McKeiver v. Pennsylvania, supra,* at 547 supports an exception to the "constitutional policy of finality" to which respondent would otherwise be entitled. *United States v. Jorn, supra,* at 479.

In denying respondent's petitions for writs of habeas corpus, the California Court of Appeal first, and the United States District Court later, concluded that no new jeopardy arose as a result of his transfer from Juvenile Court and trial in Superior Court. In the view of those courts, the jeopardy that attaches at an adjudicatory hearing continues until there is a final disposition of the case under the adult charge.

* * *

[T]he fact that the proceedings against respondent had not "run their full course," *Price v. Geogia, supra* at 326 within the contemplation of the California Welfare and Institutions Code at the time of transfer, does not satisfactorily explain why respondent should be deprived of the constitutional protection against a second trial. If there is to be an exception to that protection in the context of the juvenile-court system, it must be justified by interests of society, reflected in that unique institution, or of juveniles themselves, of sufficient substance to render tolerable the costs and burdens, noted earlier, which the exception will entail in individual cases.

The possibility of transfer from juvenile court to a court of general criminal jurisdiction is a matter of great significance to the juvenile. *See Kent v. United States,* 383 U.S. 541 (1966). At the same time, there appears to be widely shared agreement that not all juveniles can benefit from the special features and programs of the juvenile court system and that a procedure for transfer to an adult court should be available. This general agreement is reflected in the fact that an overwhelming majority of jurisdictions permits transfer in certain circumstances. . . . [S]uch transfer provisions represent an attempt to impart to the juvenile-court system the flexibility needed to deal with youthful offenders who cannot benefit from the specialized guidance and treatment contemplated by the system.

We do not agree with petitioner that giving respondent the constitutional protection against multiple trials in this context will diminish flexibility and informality to the extent that those qualities relate uniquely to the goals of the juvenile-court system. We agree that such a holding will require, in most cases, that the transfer decision be made prior to an adjudicatory hearing. To the extent that evidence concerning the alleged offense is considered relevant, it may be that, in those cases where transfer is considered and rejected, some added burden will be imposed on the juvenile courts by reason of duplicative proceedings. Finally, the nature of the evidence considered at a transfer hearing may in some States require that, if transfer is rejected, a different judge preside at the adjudicatory hearing.

We recognize that juvenile courts, perhaps even more than most courts, suffer from the problems created by spiraling caseloads unaccompanied by enlarged resources and manpower. *See* President's Commission on Law Enforcement and Administration of Justice, Task Force Report: Juvenile Delinquency and Youth Crime 7-8 (1967). And courts should be reluctant to impose on the juvenile-court system any additional requirements which could so strain its resources as to endanger its unique functions. However, the burdens that petitioner envisions appear to us neither qualitatively nor quantitatively sufficient to justify a departure in this context from the fundamental prohibition against double jeopardy.

A requirement that transfer hearings be held prior to adjudicatory hearings affects not at all the nature of the latter proceedings. More significantly, such a requirement need not affect the quality of decisionmaking at transfer hearings themselves. In *Kent v. United States,* 383 U.S. at 562, the Court held that hearings under the statute there involved "must measure up to the essentials of due process and fair treatment." However, the Court has never attempted to prescribe criteria for, or the nature and quantum of evidence that must support a decision to transfer a juvenile for trial in adult court. We require only that, whatever the relevant criteria, and whatever the evidence demanded, a State determine whether it wants to treat a juvenile within the juvenile court system before entering upon a proceeding that may result in an adjudication that he has violated a criminal law and in a substantial deprivation of liberty, rather than subject him to the expense, delay, strain, and embarrassment of two such proceedings.[18]

Moreover, we are not persuaded that the burdens petitioner envisions would pose a significant problem for the administration of the juvenile court system. The large number of jurisdictions that presently require that the transfer decision be made prior to an adjudicatory hearing, and the absence of any indication that the juvenile courts in those jurisdictions have not been able to perform their task within that framework, suggest the contrary. . . .

To the extent that transfer hearings held prior to adjudication result in some duplication of evidence if transfer is rejected, the burden on juvenile courts will tend to be offset somewhat by the cases in which, because of transfer, no further proceedings in juvenile court are required. Moreover, when transfer has previously been rejected, juveniles may well be more likely to admit the commission of the offense charged, thereby obviating the need for adjudicatory hearings, than if transfer remains a possibility. Finally, we note that those States which presently require a different judge to preside at an adjudicatory hearing if transfer is rejected also permit waiver of that requirement. . . .[21] What concerns us here is the dilemma that the possibility of transfer after an adjudicatory hearing presents for a juvenile. . . . If he appears uncooperative, he runs the risk of an adverse adjudication, as well as of an unfavorable dispositional recommendation. If, on the other hand, he is cooperative, he runs the risk of prejudicing his chances in adult court if transfer is ordered. We regard a procedure that results in such a dilemma as at odds with the goal that, to the extent fundamental fairness permits, adjudicatory hearings be informal and nonadversary. Knowledge of the risk of transfer after an adjudicatory hearing can only undermine the potential for informality and cooperation which was intended to be the hallmark of the juvenile court system. Rather than concerning themselves with the matter at hand, establishing innocence or seeking a disposition best suited to individual correctional needs, the juvenile and his attorney are pressed into a posture of adversary wariness that is conducive to neither.

---

[18] We note that nothing decided today forecloses States from requiring, as a prerequisite to the transfer of a juvenile, substantial evidence that he committed the offense charged, so long as the showing required is not made in an adjudicatory proceeding. . . .

[21] . . . "The reason for this waiver provision is clear. A juvenile will ordinarily not want to dismiss a judge who has refused to transfer him to a criminal court. There is a risk of having another judge assigned to the case who is not as sympathetic. Morever, in many cases, a rapport has been established between the judge and the juvenile, and the goal of rehabilitation is well on its way to being met." Brief for National Council of Juvenile Court Judges as *Amicus Curiae* 38.

We hold that the prosecution of respondent in Superior Court, after an adjudicatory proceeding in Juvenile Court, violated the Double Jeopardy Clause of the Fifth Amendment, as applied to the States through the Fourteenth Amendment. . . . Since respondent is no longer subject to the jurisdiction of the California Juvenile Court, we vacate the judgment and remand the case to the Court of Appeals for . . . further proceedings consistent with this opinion. . . .

Notes

1. The Supreme Court's holding in *Breed* differs from the Court's other juvenile law opinions in that it relies on the functional equivalence of criminal trials and juvenile delinquency hearings to extend a Fifth Amendment right to juveniles. Unlike the Court's other juvenile cases, *Breed* does not rely on a fundamental fairness analysis in its opinion. As with the Court's other juvenile law pronouncements, however, the *Breed* Court did not go so far as to say that the functional equivalence of criminal trials and juvenile delinquency hearings means that there is no place for the juvenile justice system in our society.

The Court held that juveniles are entitled to the Fifth Amendment protection against double jeopardy. The Court found that jeopardy attaches in a juvenile proceeding when the juvenile court begins to hear evidence, regardless of whether the court adjudicates the juvenile's guilt or innocence. The *Breed* Court thus held that the right against double jeopardy protects the juvenile from subsequent trials for the same acts, not merely against multiple punishments.

2. *Breed* held that the protection against double jeopardy precludes trying a juvenile in criminal court on the same charges for which the juvenile has already answered in juvenile court. State courts routinely apply the *Breed* holding in this manner. *See, e.g., Smith v. State,* 316 So. 2d 552 (Fla. 1975); *Lincoln v. State,* 225 S.E.2d 708 (Ga. Ct. App. 1976). State courts also apply *Breed* to preclude subsequent delinquency adjudications where the juvenile has already been tried in adult criminal court for the same acts. *See, e.g., In re R.L.K.,* 384 N.E.2d 531 (Ill. App. Ct. 1978); *In re Drakeford,* 230 S.E.2d 779 (N.C. Ct. App. 1977). Most states have incorporated the double jeopardy protection for juveniles into state law. *See, e.g.,* ARK. CODE ANN. § 9-27-319 (Michie 1993); 42 PA. CONS. STAT. ANN. § 6340(e) (West Supp. 2001); UTAH CODE ANN. § 78-3a-117(3) (Lexis Supp. 2000).

3. The juvenile laws of some states provide for the use of masters or referees who make preliminary investigations into alleged acts of delinquency. Following an inquiry into the alleged acts, the referee submits a report to the juvenile court or the prosecutor. The report may, among other things, recommend the closure of the inquiry or the filing of a formal petition against the juvenile. In the wake of the Supreme Court's decision in *Breed*, lower courts faced the issue of whether this preliminary investigation placed the juvenile in jeopardy and thereby triggered the child's Fifth Amendment protection against being twice made to answer for the same charges. The Supreme Court addressed this issue in *Swisher v. Brady,* 438 U.S. 204 (1978). The Court held that the juvenile court's review of the master's recommendations amounted to a continuation of the same hearing and therefore did not violate the Double Jeopardy Clause.

Notwithstanding the Court's holding in *Swisher*, state courts have split on the issue of whether jeopardy attaches to the juvenile master's findings. In *In re Stephens*, for example, the Pennsylvania Supreme Court found that the referee's findings were merely advisory and thus did not place the juvenile in jeopardy. 461 A.2d 1223 (Pa. 1983). Several courts, on the other hand, have held that jeopardy attaches to the master's findings; therefore, the Double Jeopardy Clause precludes the juvenile court judge from finding a minor delinquent where the master recommends dismissal of the charges. *See, e.g., Jesse W. v. Superior Court,* 603 P.2d 1296 (Cal. 1979); *R.G.S. v. District Court,* 636 P.2d 340 (Okla. Crim. App. 1981).

4. In addressing the issue of transfer motions, state courts generally find that a waiver hearing is not a delinquency proceeding for the purposes of the Double Jeopardy Clause. Because no jeopardy attaches to the waiver finding, the protections of the Clause do not apply. *See, e.g., Cruse v. State,* 489 So. 2d 694 (Ala. Crim. App. 1986); *Stokes v. Commonwealth,* 336 N.E.2d 735 (Mass. 1975); *In re L.V.A.,* 248 N.W.2d 864 (S.D. 1976).

Questions

1. Why does the Supreme Court seem to equate juvenile adjudications with criminal trials for Fifth Amendment purposes when it has refused to do so for purposes of the Sixth Amendment?

2. In making a waiver determination, a juvenile court judge must consider all relevant information, including the allegations made against the juvenile. This examination necessarily entails hearing at least limited preliminary evidence against the child. If, as the Court held in *Breed*, jeopardy attaches when the juvenile court judge begins to hear evidence in the case, why is the Double Jeopardy Clause held inapplicable to transfer hearings? Should the judge who presides over the transfer hearing be precluded from adjudicating the case if transfer is denied?

7. Sealing and Expungement of Juvenile Records

Kentucky Bar Association v. Guidugli
967 S.W.2d 587 (Ky. 1998)

This is a disciplinary matter brought by the Kentucky Bar Association against John J. Guidugli. . . . Guidugli has been a member of the Kentucky Bar Association since 1993. He is charged with having violated SCR 3.130-8.1(a) and (b) by having failed to disclose information requested in the application for character and fitness certification when he applied for the bar examination. Following a hearing before a trial commissioner, and upon vote of the board of Governors, Respondent has been found guilty of that charge. The penalty imposed by the board was a thirty day suspension from the practice of law, with reinstatement dependent upon the results of a Character and Fitness evaluation. . . . We affirm the decision of the Board of Governors.

In 1987, Respondent entered an Alford plea to a misdemeanor charge of endangering the welfare of a minor. . . . One charged with endangering a minor would be within the "exclusive jurisdiction" of the juvenile session. Respondent received a one-year sentence, conditionally discharged for two years, provided he fulfill a number of special conditions prohibiting contact with the victim of the offense and limiting the contact with other juveniles. . . .

The presiding judge ordered the record sealed as a regular record of the juvenile court, until further orders of the court or unless "requested by any court in which the Defendant may be on trial for any charge relating to sexual abuse of a minor."

[Respondent] attended law school and took the Kentucky bar exam in 1993. He then obtained employment with the Kenton County Attorney's office and was placed in charge of the Juvenile Division of that office. The 1987 criminal proceedings came to light when the victim became aware of Respondent's employment in that position and went to the local newspapers.

The specific questions which Respondent is charged with having answered falsely are as follows:

> Have you ever been charged with or convicted of or plead guilty or no contest to a felony charge, or to a misdemeanor charge, excluding traffic? Is there any other incident(s) or occurrence(s) in your life, which is not otherwise referred to in this application, which has a bearing, either directly or indirectly, upon your character and fitness for admission to the bar?

He was charged with a violation of SCR 3.130-8.1, which states:

> An applicant for admission to the bar . . . shall not: (a) Knowingly make a false statement of material fact; or (b) Fail to disclose a fact necessary to correct a misapprehension known by the person to have arisen in the matter, or knowingly fail to respond to a lawful demand for information from an admissions or disciplinary authority. . . .

The defense asserted . . . that Respondent relied upon legal advice given to him both by the lawyer who represented him at the time of the Alford plea and by his brother, who was at the time of the plea a district judge. Respondent testified that it was their advice that, because the record of his plea was sealed, it was as though the conviction had never existed and thus did not need to be revealed. Reference was made to KRS 208.27(4), since repealed, which provided as follows:

> Upon the entry of an order to seal the records, the proceedings in the case shall be deemed never to have occurred, and all index references shall be deleted and the person and the court may properly reply that no record exists with respect to such person upon any inquiry in the matter.

[Respondent] also testified, as did his brother, that a request for a record search was made to pre-trial services, which search revealed no charge. As the Trial Commissioner found, however, there was never an expungement of the record . . . nor was there a motion made for expungement. Our review of the record indicates that Respondent acted in good faith and with diligence in ascertaining whether to reveal the proceedings that took place in the juvenile court.

Our own review of the statutes involved indicates that the distinction between a sealed record and an expunged record is not immediately clear. . . . Because of this narrow distinction and the dearth of case law on the issue, Respondent's actions in seeking legal counsel on the issue of disclosure render his decision within reasonable boundaries. [Nevertheless,] we agree with the Board that the appropriate penalty . . . is a thirty (30) day suspension with a requirement that Respondent's petition for reinstatement be contingent upon approval of the Character and Fitness Committee.

It is [so] ordered. . . .

Doe v. United States

964 F. Supp. 1429 (S.D. Cal. 1997)

This is an action for equitable relief to expunge Plaintiff's criminal arrest record. . . . The defendant filed a motion to dismiss, or in the alternative for summary judgment. . . . [The] Court hereby denies Defendant's motions to dismiss and for summary judgment and orders the Defendant to show cause why an expunction should not be granted. . . .

On November 1, 1970, the plaintiff, John Doe ("Doe"), then a minor, was arrested and charged for failure to pay a special tax on imported marijuana. . . . Doe pled guilty and the court ordered him to the custody of the Attorney General as a youthful offender under the Federal Youth Corrections Act ("FYCA"). . . . Doe was sentenced to three years' probation.

Prior to the expiration of the three-year probation period, the court issued an order terminating Doe's probation. In 1973, a certification of vacation of conviction was filed and Doe's file was ordered sealed. Since that time, Doe has been neither arrested nor convicted of any crime.

Doe has worked for approximately 20 years in the auto sales industry. . . . In December of 1995, he found a position with WFS Financial Inc. as a sales manager. . . . His progress with WFS, however, came to a halt when a routine FBI background check revealed his juvenile delinquency conviction. Federal law prohibits any person convicted of a crime involving dishonesty from working for a federally insured financial institution. . . . WFS has a policy to terminate all employees with any prior criminal conviction. After discussing the conviction with his supervisor, . . . WFS told him that if he does not receive an expunction, it will terminate his employment. On April 14, 1997, WFS placed Doe on indefinite leave pending the outcome of the matter.

[On] October 1, 1996, Doe filed an ex parte motion, bearing the original criminal case number, to expunge the record of his November 1, 1970, arrest and conviction. The court declined to entertain the motion because the case had been long terminated. The court advised Doe that he should file a new civil action seeking declaratory or injunctive relief. On January 22, 1997, Doe filed the instant action naming the United States as the defendant and seeking the following relief:

(1) a declaration that Doe's arrest record and booking be expunged;

(2) the fingerprints, photographs, and palmprints taken during and following his arrest be returned to him;

(3) that the Clerk of Court destroy the records filed in his criminal case; and

(4) that his arrest on November 1, 1970 be deemed a nullity and that he be restored, in contemplation of the law, to the status he occupied before the arrest. . . .

Expunction of criminal records may be granted where there is a constitutional violation, the records are inaccurate, or other unusual or extraordinary circumstances exist. . . . [Doe] does not assert a constitutional violation or that the records are inaccurate. Therefore, the only issue is whether Doe can demonstrate that extraordinary circumstances exist which justify an order granting expunction. In determining whether extraordinary circumstances exist, the Court should weigh the interest of the government in maintaining the individual's criminal record and the harm caused to the individual by the existence of such records. . . . Where the harm outweighs the government interest, it is within the Court's discretion to find that extraordinary circumstances exist which warrant an expunction.

The government has failed to establish that it has any interest in maintaining Doe's criminal record. Doe pled guilty to a crime that he committed over twenty-five years ago in violation of a statute that has long since been repealed. Doe has had no trouble with the law in the intervening twenty-seven years. Moreover, he committed the crime as a minor and was sentenced under the FYCA. Finally, the sentencing judge vacated his conviction and ordered his record sealed, leading Doe to believe that his record would have no lasting effect on his attempt to seek future employment. Therefore, an expunction would not affect the accuracy of the government's criminal records because, for all practical purposes, the record is obsolete.

While the government has no interest in maintaining a record of Doe's crime, the potential harm to him if expunction is denied is great. . . . If his record is not expunged, he will lose his job with WFS. . . . Further, if he were to seek employment at any financial institution, . . . they would inquire about his leaving WFS. . . . At that point, Doe would be forced to disclose the fact that he has an arrest record. Moreover, Doe was a minor when he committed the crime and his conviction was vacated, making its probative value extremely low.

* * *

[Doe's] guilty plea was over twenty-five years ago, and he has had no problems with the law since. Doe has also been gainfully employed for the last twenty years. Moreover, Doe has demonstrated that his record has had an actual effect on his employment in that his employer suspended him indefinitely pending the outcome of this lawsuit. . . . Most importantly, Doe's conviction under the FYCA was "set-aside" in that it was vacated and ordered sealed by the judge. Additionally, Doe states in his declaration that the judge told him that after seven years he was not required to report his record to anyone, and led him to believe that his criminal record would have no effect on his future employment. . . .

Defendant asserts that . . . there exist no extraordinary circumstances which would justify expunction in this case. Defendant emphasizes that expunction should only be used in extreme cases. The court finds these circumstances are extreme; Doe may lose a good job and be a risk for future prolonged unemployment based on a single criminal conviction which occurred twenty-seven years ago when Doe was a minor, and which has already been vacated. . . .

[The] Court finds that the harm to Doe substantially outweighs any interest that the government might have in maintaining his criminal records, and that extraordinary circumstances exist that warrant expunction. For these reasons, the Court denies Defendant's motion for summary judgment. . . .

Notes

1. The statutes that govern the expungement of juvenile records vary between the states. There are jurisdictional differences as to which offenses will be expunged from a juvenile's record and at what age expungement is appropriate. Some commentators argue that these disparities create a system that rewards chronic offenders who have the good fortune of being tried in an expungement aggressive district. For example, an offender with a lengthy juvenile record enjoys the benefits of being a "first-time offender" at his first adult sentencing in an expungement aggressive jurisdiction. This is because the juvenile record of past offenses has been wiped clean and the lengthier sentence generally reserved for a repeat offender is thus apparently not warranted. For a discussion on the effects of aggressive expungement on sentencing judges and the resulting punishments, see T. Markus Funk & Daniel D. Polsby, *Distributional Consequences of Expunging Juvenile Delinquency Records: The Problem of Lemons,* 52 WASH. U. J. URB. & CONTEMP. L. 161 (1977).

In a similar vein, there are state statutes that limit the expungement of certain offenses in order to provide sentencing judges with what is deemed necessary information. For example, the court in *L.H. v. Arkansas*, 973 S.W.2d 477 (Ark. 1998), determined that the legislature intended to retain the delinquency records for offenses in which the juvenile could have been tried as an adult for a statutory term of 10 years. The court reiterated the purpose of this statute by stating that the "retaining of those records is to allow prosecutors to enhance the juvenile's sentence, in the event the juvenile is charged as an adult with a criminal offense." *Id.* at 480. *See also Michigan v. Smith*, 470 N.W.2d 70 (Mich. 1991), holding that a defendant's expunged juvenile record can be considered when the defendant is sentenced as an adult.

2. The philosophical origins of expungement are parallel with the rehabilitative ideals of the juvenile justice system: lessening the stigma of youthful criminal activity by wiping the slate clean at majority. However, some argue that this ideal is no longer compatible with today's violent juvenile offenders and suggest that legislatures attempt to identify and separate those offenses that deserve expungement and those that do not. The argument continues that certain offenses contain valuable information that is useful to sentencing judges, law enforcement, employers, and college admissions officers. For a discussion on this point, see T. Markus Funk, *The Dangers of Hiding Criminal Pasts,* 66 TENN. L. REV. 287 (1998).

The holding in *In re P.L.F.*, 352 N.W.2d 183 (Neb. 1984), reflects this notion by determining that the records of certain offenses should only be sealed and not expunged. The court stated that in deciding whether to expunge a juvenile's record, the interests of society and the individual must be weighed. *Id.* at 185. In so doing, the court is able to maintain access to records on the basis of societal interest.

3. Despite these criticisms, expungement of juvenile records is supported by some as a valid rehabilitative tool and a valuable aspect of the social policies that underlie the current system. They argue that a sealed or expunged record statute is an incentive for many young offenders to change their focus and "put their mistakes behind them." *See* Carie T. Hollister, *The Impossible Predicament of Gina Grant,* 44 UCLA L. REV. 913 (1997).

Questions

1. What is the difference between expungement and sealing of juvenile records? If a juvenile's records are truly "sealed," should anyone ever have access to them? If not, aren't the records, in effect, expunged?

2. Should juvenile records be expunged? After how long? Should the nature of the offense have any bearing on the issue? Does the very nature of the juvenile court, concerned as it is with assisting the child rather than merely punishing him, require that juveniles be given a chance to "start over" once they reach majority? How much difference is there between an offense committed by a seventeen year old and the same offense committed by an eighteen year old? Should the former, but not the latter, have his record sealed?

Chapter 7

Dispositions in Delinquency Proceedings

The materials in this chapter deal with dispositional hearings in juvenile delinquency proceedings. Delinquency dispositions are the juvenile justice counterpart to adult criminal sentences. The juvenile court judge has at her disposal an array of dispositional sanctions, some of which resemble adult criminal sentences, but many of which are unique to the juvenile justice system. For example, although both a juvenile delinquent and an adult criminal may be placed on probation, the conditions of the child's probation may control and restrict his actions in a manner unthinkable in the adult criminal justice system. The following recent statistics indicate that a majority of delinquents either choose probation voluntarily or are placed on probation by juvenile courts:

Probation was the most likely disposition for cases in which the youth was adjudicated delinquent

	Percent of all cases in which the juvenile was adjudicated delinquent		
Most Severe Disposition	1988	1993	1997
Total	100%	100%	100%
Probation	56	54	55
Residential placement	31	29	28
Other sanction	10	13	13
Released without additional sanction	4	4	4

Note: Detail may not add to 100% because of rounding.

Meghan C. Scahill, U.S. DEP'T OF JUST., *Juvenile Delinquency Probation Caseload, 1988-1997* (2000).

As we have already seen, the ostensible purpose of the juvenile justice system vis-à-vis delinquent children is to provide for their rehabilitation. However, nowhere has this design been more harshly criticized in recent years than in the dispositional phase of delinquency proceedings. Perceived increases in violent crimes committed by increasingly youthful offenders have led many to call for harsher sentences for juvenile delinquents. This discussion has led legislatures and courts to weigh issues such as societal protection, punishment, and deterrence more heavily in delinquency dispositions. Thus, the "best interests of the child" may now include the interests of third persons with whom the child may have (actual or potential) contact. These and other considerations facing the modern juvenile court judge in the disposition of delinquency cases will be the focus of this chapter.

A. Treatment and Rehabilitation

1. Right to Treatment

Martarella v. Kelley
349 F. Supp. 575 (S.D.N.Y. 1972)

* * *

We come to the final and most difficult legal issue in this case, which has poignantly presented questions of the rights of children in urban American society: The right to treatment.

To give the analysis focus, historic perspective is necessary. As one commentator has put it:

> Our society has increasingly divested certain groups from the traditional criminal justice court, and acting under its asserted role of *parens patriae*, substituted new therapeutic controls. The most dramatic example of this divestment has been in the treatment of offending juveniles, where the arrested juvenile is subjected not to the sanctions of the criminal tribunals, but to the disposition of the juvenile courts. The latter, at least purportedly, do not dispense criminal justice; instead their function is to offer the offending juvenile regenerative treatment.[18]

Although the concept of the right to "effective treatment" was first articulated not much more than a decade ago, it has come into nearly full flower in the intervening period, and has been applied to the mentally ill, sexual psy-

---

[18] Kittrie: "Can the Right to Treatment Remedy the Ills of the Juvenile Process?", in "A Symposium: The Right to Treatment" 57 Georgetown Law Journal, 848, 851-2 (1969)....

chopaths, defective delinquents, persons committed following acquittal by reason of insanity, drug addicts and children, whether delinquent or merely in need of supervision

* * *

There can be no doubt that the right to treatment, generally, for those held in non-criminal custody (whether based on due process, equal protection or the Eighth Amendment, or a combination of them) has by now been recognized by the Supreme Court, the lower federal courts and the courts of New York. *Robinson v. California*, 370 U.S. 660, 82 S. Ct. 1417, 8 L. Ed. 2d 758 (1962), dealt with the rights of a drug addict plaintiff. The court held California's statute, which declared addiction a crime, unconstitutional in the absence of rehabilitative treatment. This was punishment for a *status*, rather than a crime; and although the State might legally detain non-criminals for compulsory treatment or other legitimate purposes which protected society or the person in custody, detention for mere illness—without a curative program—would be impermissible. "Even one day in prison would be a cruel and unusual punishment for the 'crime' of having a common cold"—*Robinson, supra* at 667, 82 S. Ct. at 1421. Although other recent Supreme Court decisions which have dealt in depth with the rights of children, such as *In re Gault*, 387 U.S. 1, 87 S. Ct. 1428, 18 L. Ed. 2d 527 (1967), have not focused on the right to treatment, they have indicated markedly increased solicitude for the constitutional rights of children. *Gault* touches on the right to treatment *en passant*, but with great significance: (at Footnote 30)

> While we are concerned only with procedure before the juvenile court in this case, it should be noted that to the extent that the special procedures for juveniles are thought to be justified by the special consideration and treatment afforded them, there is reason to doubt that juveniles always receive the benefits of such a *quid pro quo*. . . . The high rate of juvenile recidivism casts some doubt upon the adequacy of treatment afforded juveniles. . . .
>
> In fact some courts have recently indicated that appropriate treatment is essential to the validity of juvenile custody, and therefore that a juvenile may challenge the validity of his custody on the ground that he is not in fact receiving any special treatment. (Citations omitted).

* * *

Judge Bazelon's seminal opinion in *Rouse v. Cameron*, 125 U.S. App. D.C. 366, 373 F.2d 451 (1966), dealt more directly with the issue of the right to treatment, and is generally regarded as the leading case. *Rouse* was involuntarily hospitalized in a mental hospital after having been acquitted of a misdemeanor by reason of insanity. He petitioned for a writ of habeas corpus, claiming the right to be discharged in the absence of receiving treatment. The court sustained his argument on statutory grounds but with considerable emphasis on the constitutional questions raised, observing that:

> Absent treatment, the hospital is transform[ed] . . . into a penitentiary where one could be held indefinitely for no convicted offense. . . .

* * *

Prior to *Rouse*, in *Sas v. State of Maryland*, 334 F. 2d 506, (4th Cir. 1964), the court had recognized analogous rights under Maryland's defective delinquent statute, observing that "[d]eficiencies in staff, facilities, and finances would undermine . . . the justification for the law, and ultimately the constitutionality of its application."

* * *

In *Wyatt v. Stickney*, 325 F. Supp. 781 (N.D. Ala. 1971), Chief Judge Johnson strongly affirmed the right of treatment for persons in non-criminal custody and held that hospital programs for the mentally ill in the case before him were *constitutionally* inadequate. In following *Rouse v. Cameron, supra* he declared:

> To deprive any citizen of his or her liberty upon the altruistic theory that the confinement is for humane therapeutic reasons and then fail to provide adequate treatment violates the very fundamentals of due process.

* * *

In sum, the law has developed to a point which justifies the assertion that:

> A new concept of substantive due process is evolving in the therapeutic realm. This concept is founded upon a recognition of the concurrency between the state's exercise of sanctioning powers and its assumption of the duties of social responsibility. Its implication is that effective treatment must be the *quid pro quo* for society's right to exercise its *parens patriae* controls. Whether specifically recognized by statutory enactment or implicitly derived from the constitutional requirements of due process, the right to treatment exists. . . .[23]

Whatever Happened to the Right to Treatment?: The Modern Quest for a Historical Promise

Paul Holland & Wallace J. Mlyniec
68 TEMP. L. REV. 1791 (1995)[*]

Since the creation of the first juvenile court in 1899,[1] state training schools have been the primary place of confinement for children removed from their homes. Although the rhetoric of the Progressive Reformers created an impres-

---

[23] Kittrie, *supra*. . . .

[1] In 1899, Illinois enacted the Juvenile Court Act which provided that the court was to afford the child "the care, custody and discipline" which would "approximate as nearly as may be that which should have been given by its parents." 1899 Ill. Laws 131.

sion that children placed out of their homes by juvenile court judges would reside in pleasant cottages staffed with benevolent substitute parents, most children lived in large impersonal institutions. The cause of their removal from their homes was irrelevant. Delinquent children, status offenders, and neglected children were placed together with a promise of care and rehabilitation. Notwithstanding their idyllic-sounding names and their laudatory purposes, the institutions have historically been understaffed, unhealthy, and devoid of rehabilitative programming. Many were, and some continue to be, extremely dangerous places for children. By the time the "children's rights revolution" began in the 1960s, it was clear to an observer that the promise of the juvenile court had never been fulfilled. Indeed, the United States Supreme Court stated in 1966 that "[t]here is evidence . . . that the child receives the worst of both worlds: that he gets neither the protection accorded to adults nor the solicitous care and regenerative treatment postulated for children."[5]

Between 1972 and 1982, in an effort to ameliorate wretched institutional conditions, advocates for children filed suits in state and federal courts arguing that children confined in state training schools had both a statutory and constitutional "right to treatment." Although the cases produced few court opinions, the litigation induced many state and county governments to improve the conditions in state training schools.

The proponents of a right to treatment asserted that if a state takes custody of a child for a rehabilitative purpose, it must provide treatment to effectuate that rehabilitation. This assertion had historical validity. The rehabilitation of wayward children was the goal of the Progressive Reformers who led the juvenile court movement. . . . [T]he juvenile court judge was not to adjudicate and sentence the youth, but was to identify the conditions which had led him astray and to "treat" him for those conditions. The treatment provided would be guidance and care to steer the youth away from a life of crime and immorality. Thus, the original and subsequent juvenile court statutes promised that children who were removed from their families by a judge would receive the care, custody, and discipline that their parents should have provided.

Relying on the historical promise of the juvenile court and on contemporary cases concerning mental health facilities, judges began to rule that children sent to a state training school had a right to treatment. The rulings were based on the purpose clauses of state juvenile codes, the substantive and procedural prongs of the Due Process Clause of the Fourteenth Amendment to the United States Constitution, and the Cruel and Unusual Punishment Clause of the Eighth Amendment. . . .

In 1983, the United States Supreme Court wrote its only opinion about the right to treatment in the case of *Youngberg v. Romeo.*[15] Although this case involved a challenge to the training program in a mental retardation facility, it has affected litigation in the juvenile justice context as well. Similarly, cases beginning with *Rhodes v. Chapman*[16] and continuing through *Farmer v. Bren-*

---

5 *Kent v. United States*, 383 U.S. 541, 556 (1966).

15 457 U.S. 307 (1982). . . .

16 452 U.S. 337 (1981). . . .

nan,[17] which curtailed the scope of the Eighth Amendment in prison conditions cases, have also had an effect. These opinions have drastically limited the prospects for constitutional relief for children residing in institutions.

While some of the most egregious abuses described in the pleadings and opinions of the 1970s have abated, many training schools remain ill-equipped to provide children living in them with the education, behavior modification, counseling, substance abuse treatment, and the mental and physical health care they need. The laws of most states still promise such care. In recent years, however, a wave of legislation increasing the severity with which children who break the law are treated has compromised that promise. Legislatures have introduced punishment into juvenile codes, authorized mandatory minimum commitments in the juvenile justice system, and expanded the possibilities for prosecuting children in criminal courts. Some juvenile courts now have the power to impose a criminal sentence as part of a juvenile disposition, with the criminal sentence stayed—either temporarily or permanently—depending upon the youth's performance during the course of the juvenile disposition.

[D]espite the current trend, state laws preserve their original rehabilitative goals and form the heart of delinquent children's right to receive such care and services. Simply put, states are obligated to serve as the substitute parents they promise to be. They are responsible, along with parents, for ensuring that the children in their care master the identifiable skills needed to develop into responsible and productive adult citizens. This understanding of the state's role accommodates appropriate punishment and accountability alongside care and rehabilitation. . . .

* * *

In light of *Youngberg* and recent Eighth Amendment jurisprudence, the constitutional right to treatment for confined juveniles has lost much of its doctrinal foundation. As currently understood, the Fourteenth and Eighth Amendments require only freedom from unnecessary restraint and minimally humane conditions of confinement. Food, clothing, shelter and medical care must only be adequate enough to avoid harm. In the main, treatment or training is directed at little more than preserving the peace within the training school.

Moreover, to the extent that a violation of even these minimal standards occurs, federal judges are precluded from issuing sweeping corrective injunctions by the "hands off" doctrine. As early as 1974, the United States Supreme Court began to show great deference to prison administrators and to tell trial court judges to refrain from interfering with the day-to-day operations of prisons. Both principles were spelled out forcefully in *Bell v. Wolfish.*[125] In *Bell*, the Supreme Court recognized that pre-trial detainees have constitutional rights, but stated that by virtue of their situation, they do not possess the full range of freedoms possessed by an unincarcerated person and that a mutual accommodation must exist between the constitutionally protected rights of the inmate and the legitimate needs of the institution. . . . In its concluding paragraphs, the

---

[17] 114 S. Ct. 1970 (1994).

[125] 441 U.S. 520 (1979).

Court chastised trial judges who had become "enmeshed in the minutiae of prison operations,"[129] and limited a court's inquiry into prison management to the question of whether the regimen violates the Constitution.

This deference towards institutional administrators has not been limited to prison officials. In the same year as *Bell*, the Supreme Court took the same approach to officials working in mental health facilities.[131] Later, in *Youngberg*, the Supreme Court extended both prongs of the "hands off" doctrine to conditions in mental health facilities by balancing the patient's freedom from restraint against institutional needs and conferring a presumption of correctness upon judgments made by medical professionals.[132] Thus, judicial rulings concerning both types of right to treatment cases, those involving humane conditions in corrections facilities and those involving the quasi-medical model, are now limited by the "hands off" doctrine.

* * *

As the constitutional right to treatment withered, rehabilitation lost its place as the sole purpose of juvenile justice systems in several states. Legislatures have explicitly endorsed punishment,[157] accountability,[158] and other principles besides rehabilitation[159] within the juvenile justice system. Some disposition statutes, which formerly focused almost exclusively on the needs of

---

129 *Id.* at 562.

131 *See Parham v. J.R.*, 442 U.S. 584, 620 (1979).

132 *Youngberg v. Romeo*, 457 U.S. 307, 324 (1982).

157 *See* ARK. CODE ANN. § 9-27-302(3) (Michie 1987) (authorizing sanctions based on seriousness of offense); CAL. WELF. & INST. CODE § 202(e) (West 1984) (defining punishment as either payment of fine, limitations on minor's liberty, or commitment to local detention or treatment facility); FLA. STAT. ANN. § 39.001(c) (West 1941 & Supp. 1995) (stating that purpose of statute is partially to ensure protection of society and to provide appropriate control, discipline and punishment); HAW. REV. STAT. § 571-1 (1988) (stating that statute creates policy and purpose of courts to "render appropriate punishment to offenders"); WASH. REV. CODE ANN. § 13.40.010 (West 1995) (stating that punishment, accountability and treatment are "equally important" purposes); *see also In re* J.L.A., 643 A.2d 538 (N.J. 1994) (discussing New Jersey's Juvenile Code and noting that statute recognizes needs of public safety and provides harsher penalties).

158 *See* ALA. CODE § 12-15-71 (1975 & Supp. 1994) (placing accountability for children in hands of parents or children); IDAHO CODE § 16-1801 (1979 & Supp. 1994) (stating that accountability for juvenile offenders is with case managers, families and community); MISS. CODE ANN. § 43-21-103 (1972) (providing that parents of juvenile offenders are primarily responsible for care, support, education and welfare of children); N.M. STAT. ANN. § 32A-2-2(A) (Michie 1978) (holding juvenile offenders accountable for their actions); TEX. FAM. CODE ANN. § 51.01(c) (West 1995) (stating that purpose of statute is to provide treatment, training and rehabilitation that emphasizes accountability and responsibility of parent and child for child's conduct.)

159 *See* NEB. REV. STAT. § 43-246(3) (1994) (providing that intent of statute is to reduce possibility of juvenile offenders committing future crimes); OKLA. STAT. ANN. tit. 10, § 7001-1.2 (West 1995) (calling for maintaining integrity of substantive law prohibiting certain behavior); TEX. FAM. CODE ANN. § 51.01(2) (West 1995) (stating that statute should be construed to effectuate purpose of controlling commission of unlawful acts by children). In addition, numerous statutes recognize the need to protect the public safety). *See, e.g.*, N.D. CENT. CODE § 27-20-01 (1993) (stating that public safety is of utmost concern).

the offender, now include mandatory minimum terms of commitment based solely on the instant offense or the child's record of offenses.[160]

Although these developments represent a dramatic change in the design of the juvenile justice systems of some states, they do not warrant the conclusion that the provision of rehabilitative care is no longer an essential aspect of modern juvenile justice. Most state juvenile codes contain express promises of rehabilitative care. Several state courts have recently reaffirmed the rehabilitative approach to juvenile justice. Additionally, every juvenile court in the country exercises jurisdiction as *parens patriae*. For a century, this doctrine has committed the state to providing delinquent children with substituted parental care. As it has from the beginning, this means care that will enable children to develop into adults who are capable of meeting their own need, providing for their families, and contributing positively to their communities.

* * *

The infliction of punishment has coexisted with the promise of rehabilitation for as long as delinquent children have been securely confined. The belief that confinement ever could be wholly rehabilitative and not at all punitive ignores the experience of the confined children. To them, confinement is punishment, no matter what a judge, counselor, or correctional officer calls it, and no matter how helpful or rehabilitative it actually is. Acknowledging the existence and even inevitability of punishment in juvenile justice does not render rehabilitation unattainable or dispensable. The challenge today, as ever, is to insure that meaningful rehabilitation accompanies the inevitable punishment. The problem is a practical one, not a doctrinal one. States need only take advantage of existing knowledge about what programs are effective and provide sufficient funds and facilities for their operation.

* * *

[T]his balance between discipline and support [is] consistent with accepted notions of child-rearing. As parents may lawfully impose discipline, so may the state as it seeks to guide delinquent children in their development into responsible adults. The higher profile given to punishment and accountability in recent legislation should not divert attention away from the still-present promise to provide rehabilitative care. All children must learn discipline and responsibility. . . . Just as care can co-exist with punishment in a properly functioning juvenile justice system, so must a concern for public safety be tied to a responsibility to rehabilitate delinquent children. In fact, public safety cannot likely be maintained unless children receive the care which they need and which the law promises them.

* * *

A juvenile court cannot hope to solve such a complicated problem by the application of "treatment," like a doctor prescribing pills. [T]he states have an

---

[160] *See, e.g.*, ALA. CODE § 12-15-71.1 (1975 & Supp. 1994) (setting forth sentencing guidelines based on degree of offense).

obligation to provide care for all their delinquent children, and little of the care needed would qualify as "treatment" within a medical model. All children can be taught how to handle difficult situations, relate with other people, and exercise good judgment. They all can increase their fund of knowledge, develop learning skills, and cultivate vocational aptitudes. These are the specific skills which parents are responsible for facilitating while children are in their care. . . .

* * *

The call for abandoning the term "treatment" should not be interpreted as a rejection of the traditional juvenile court mission of providing care which aids delinquent children in growing up to be more capable of controlling their own behavior, caring for others, and contributing to their community. . . . While traditional individual and peer-group counseling have not had much effect on helping children to change their behavior, several other programs have produced beneficial results. The most promising programs are those which are family-oriented and address communication and problem-solving skills of the children and other family members. . . . A second class of successful programs emphasizes cognitive and behavioral skills. These programs differ from traditional individual and group counseling in that they focus the counselor and the child on specific social skills such as self-control, moral reasoning, and problem-solving. Again, their success has been demonstrated by changed behavior patterns for those children who receive such services.

These programs are likely to be much more effective than boot camps and other programs which are based on the notion that offenders can be "shocked" into changing their behavior. If the prospect of negative consequences for failure was enough to change delinquent children's behavior, we would expect to see greatly reduced recidivism among those who have been confined. What is missing from these negative-reinforcement strategies is sufficient opportunity for youths to develop the skills that they will need in the settings where they eventually will live (i.e., family, school, community, workplace) and where they will have to make the difficult decisions that will take them away from the troubles of their past. Unless steps are taken to help youths translate the discipline and aptitudes learned at boot camp into their homes and neighborhoods, the drills will be no more than wasted sweating and shouting.

* * *

The misallocation of resources into more restrictive confinement instead of more effective institutional and community-based programs results from more than a simple misunderstanding about whether or not such programs work. In many communities, too many people have given up on the notion that offenders, both juvenile and adult, can be and should be reintegrated into the larger community. Too many people reject any connection with the young men and women involved in the juvenile justice system and see the world as divided between offenders (and potential offenders) and victims (and potential victims). The first group, it is widely thought, must be put in secure facilities to assure the safety of the second. . . . The result is an over-reliance on costly, large, secure institutions which have been proven to be no more effective in terms of public safety than less expensive, smaller, community-based programs. . . .

* * *

One recently developed juvenile justice model takes as its starting point the need to engage all community members, and especially victims, in the response to delinquent behavior. This model, called the Balanced Approach, consists of three major elements: accountability, competency development, and community protection. The designers of this model call its core principle restorative justice, which refers to the imperative of making the victim whole. The goals of the program go far beyond this, however. The model calls for a new relationship among the victim, the offender, and the community. It recognizes the offender's responsibility toward the victim and the community, but also recognizes a reciprocal responsibility on the part of the community toward the offender. This responsibility obligates the community to provide the offender with an opportunity to develop competency in important areas. The model emphasizes providing youths with skills and opportunities related to basic social interactions, educational advancement, employment training, and community service. Its proponents argue that by emphasizing competency development in specific concrete settings which are important parts of the life-course to adulthood, the Balanced Approach renders itself more accountable to the community and the children it serves. If the children do not demonstrate improved ability in the identified areas, then the programs in place are not adequate. . . .

Another important contribution of the Balanced Approach is its emphasis on the ongoing relationship between the child and the juvenile justice system. Having received assistance in developing important skills while in the state's care, the child will be expected to utilize those skills to live a crime-free, productive life. If he does not, despite having been given the opportunity to do so, it is understandable that society would demand harsher response to a subsequent offense. If, however, the child was never given a meaningful opportunity to utilize his skills, due to circumstances at home or school or in the community, it is equally understandable that an attorney or judge would demand further assistance in creating an environment in which the skills become meaningful. The more specific the discussion is, about just what should be done and by whom, the more likely some agreement can be found among the child, family, caseworker, and judge. This focus on responsibilities and relationships is likely to be more fruitful than a search for a cause or a treatment to cure it. Moreover, this specificity enables the community to assess more readily how the juvenile justice system is performing and whether the causes for its failures lie within the system or elsewhere.

In the first century of the juvenile court's existence, providing effective rehabilitative care to delinquent children has proven to be as difficult as it is important. Even in good juvenile justice systems, courts struggle with the limits of their authority and expertise, and agencies struggle to help each child amid the competing claims of other children for the same resources and the clamor of the community for protection from these very same children. In the many dysfunctional juvenile justice systems across this country, these inherent tensions spill over into chaos that deprives children of opportunities and keeps communities fearful. There are no magic words to make these problems go away. Lawyers cannot assert a "right to treatment" and expect judges to nod, administrators to cower, nightmarish conditions to vanish, and effective programs to appear. . . . On the other hand, politicians cannot simply call for "punishment" and thereby make delinquent children, their many and various needs, and the problems in their communities disappear. Communities can turn their backs and order more fences, walls, locks, and bars, but the children will still come home someday. If they come home having been uncared for and feeling unwanted, neither they nor the community will ever benefit from their abilities. As the centennial of the juvenile court approaches, we can waste our time looking for answers in constitutions, codes and courtrooms; or we can instead look closely at our children and ourselves, demand responsibility from both, apply the lessons of successful and failed programs, and have some reason to hope that tomorrow and the next century will be better.

Notes

1. The concept of the right to treatment for juveniles developed in the early 1970s. In addition to the Kittrie article cited in *Maratella, see* JUDGE JERRY L. MERSHON, JUVENILE JUSTICE: THE ADJUDICATORY AND DISPOSITIONAL PROCESS 150 (1991). Proponents of the right to treatment largely relied on two arguments. First, they believed that the State's duties as *parens patriae* included the duty, where possible, to rehabilitate the child. This meant that the juvenile justice system owed it to the child to make a bona fide attempt at rehabilitation. As noted in the Holland & Mlyniec article, failures in the attempt to rehabilitate were to be met not with harsher penalties on the child but with further efforts to assess the child's needs and provide adequate treatment. The proponents of the right to treatment also believed that children had a constitutional right to rehabilitation. This right was seen as arising under the Due Process Clause of the Fourteenth Amendment, the Cruel and Unusual Punishment Clause of the Eighth Amendment, or both.

2. The notion of the right to treatment for children gained some acceptance in the early part of the 1970s. Courts relied on the various justifications proposed by reformers in holding that children were entitled to treatment and rehabilitation. For some early cases embracing the right to treatment, see *Creek v. Stone,* 379 F.2d 106 (D.C. Cir. 1967); *In re Jeannette P.,* 310 N.Y.S.2d 125 (N.Y. App. Div. 1970); *Inmates of Boys' School v. Affleck,* 346 F. Supp. 1354 (D.R.I. 1972). This reform movement never gained full acceptance, however, and by the mid-1980s, it had fallen out of favor with most courts. *See, e.g., Santana v. Collazo,* 793 F.2d 41 (1st Cir. 1986) (state has no constitutional duty to provide rehabilitative treatment to juveniles in custody).

3. It is widely accepted today that the right to treatment, if it exists at all, does not arise under the United States Constitution. *See, e.g., Commonwealth v. Cotto,* 708 A.2d 806 (Pa. Super Ct. 1998) (juvenile does not have right to treatment under Constitution, but may have right under statutory law of State); *State v. Campbell,* 617 A.2d 889 (Conn. 1992) (state's Juvenile Act "does not create either a right to treatment . . . in lieu of incarceration or a justifiable expectation of receiving such treatment"); *Keith G. v. Bilbray,* 43 Cal. Rptr. 2d 277 (Cal. Ct. App. 1995) (no constitutional right to treatment resulting from detention). It should be noted that the U.S. Supreme Court has not ruled out a juvenile's right to treatment. BUREAU OF JUST. ASSISTANCE, U.S. DEP'T OF JUST., JUVENILES IN ADULT PRISONS AND JAILS 19 (2000). Many courts, however, continue to recognize a right to treatment under state statutory law or state constitutions. *See, e.g., Commonwealth v. Cotto, supra; State v. S.H.,* 877 P.2d 205 (Wash. Ct. App. 1994) (juvenile has statutory right to individualized care and treatment); *In re Baxley,* 328 S.E.2d 831 (N.C. Ct. App. 1985) (juvenile has right to treatment under North Carolina Constitution).

Questions

1. There is a fundamental difference between rehabilitation and punishment. While the former is concerned with the needs of the child rather than her past acts, the latter seeks to penalize the child for her behavior. Do you agree with Holland & Mlyniec that rehabilitation always includes punishment, or are the two ideas separable? If it is possible to have one without the other, which should juvenile courts seek to impose? In answering the previous question, does it matter what the juvenile is accused of having done? Are both rehabilitation and punishment necessary to teach discipline and responsibility?

2. How does one balance the needs of the child, including the need for treatment and rehabilitation, with the juvenile justice system's other concerns, such as retribution, deterrence, punishment, and the protection of society? When these objectives are in conflict, which should prevail?

2. Least Restrictive Alternative

State ex rel. R.S. v. Trent
289 S.E.2d 166 (W. Va. 1982)

MCGRAW, Justice:

The petitioner, a sixteen-year-old male currently incarcerated in the West Virginia Industrial School for Boys, seeks a writ of habeas corpus to compel his release from the institution and a writ of mandamus to compel the committing court to place him in an appropriate residential treatment facility to meet his individual rehabilitative needs. He contends that his incarceration is illegal in that . . . he was not accorded the least restrictive dispositional alternative. The petitioner also contends that he is entitled to receive individual treatment consistent with his therapeutic needs. We find merit in the petitioner's contentions and we grant the writ of mandamus prayed for. The writ of habeas corpus is conditionally awarded.

The petitioner has a history of delinquent and maladaptive behavior since the age of eight. He was expelled from school in the third grade and never returned. He has a history of severe drug and alcohol abuse since the age of eleven and may have been the subject of child abuse. He has been charged with numerous instances of breaking and entering, destruction of property, shoplifting and auto theft and has spent a good deal, if not the majority, of his youth in mental health facilities, detention centers and correctional institutions. Periodic psychological evaluations of the petitioner have led to diagnoses that he suffers from organic brain syndrome with behavioral reaction, emerging antisocial personality disturbance, borderline mental retardation and possible learning disabilities, all generally characterized as being within the mild to moderate range of impairment. Prognoses vary from below average to poor.

On April 21, 1980, the petitioner was committed to the Industrial School for Boys by the Circuit Court of Ohio County, after being adjudged delinquent on a charge of breaking and entering. He remained incarcerated there until April 7, 1981, at which time he was released from custody upon the recommendation of the Superintendent of the Industrial School, who had determined that continued incarceration of the petitioner at the school would be of no benefit to him. The petitioner was released into the custody of his mother but was placed with an aunt until his mother could move into a mobile home. On April 10, 1981, the petitioner was arrested for stealing a car and was incarcerated in the Ohio County Jail until April 12, 1981. On April 15, 1981, he was again arrested and incarcerated for the theft of a motor home. . . . On May 8, 1981, the petitioner was adjudged delinquent and was committed to the Industrial School for Boys for a term of not less than six months nor more than one year. . . .

* * *

We turn to the petitioner's contention that his commitment to the Industrial School by the circuit court on May 8, 1981, was unlawful. . . . W. Va. Code § 49-5-13(b) (1980) requires the juvenile court at the dispositional stage of delinquency proceedings to "give precedence to the least restrictive" of the enumerated dispositional alternatives "consistent with the best interests and welfare of the public and the child." Moreover, juveniles are constitutionally entitled to the least restrictive treatment that is consistent with the purpose of their custody. A juvenile against whom delinquency proceedings are brought as the result of the child's commission of an act which would be a crime if committed by an adult may be committed to an industrial home or correctional facility "[u]pon a finding that no less restrictive alternative would accomplish the requisite rehabilitation of the child. . . ." W. Va. Code § 49-5-13(b)(5).

In *State ex rel. D.D.H. v. Dostert*, W. Va., 269 S.E. 2d 401 (1980), however, we held that a court having jurisdiction of juvenile proceedings "cannot justify incarceration in a secure, prison-like facility on the grounds of rehabilitation alone." Rather the court's decision to commit the juvenile to an industrial school or correctional facility must be grounded on a number of factors indicating that incarceration is the appropriate disposition. . . . Before ordering the incarceration of the child, the juvenile court is required to set forth upon the record the facts which lead to the conclusion that no less restrictive alternative is appropriate. The record must affirmatively show

> that the child's behavioral problem is not the result of social conditions beyond the child's control, but rather of an intentional failure

> on the part of the child to conform his actions to the law, or that the child will be dangerous if any other disposition is used, or that the child will not cooperate with any rehabilitative program absent physical restraint.

Id. at 413-414.

Upon reviewing the circuit court's order committing the petitioner to the Industrial School, we find that the court made the following "specific findings":

> 1. Every reasonable alternative with regard to placement has been explored.
> 2. Due to his continuous violent and destructive behavior, [the petitioner] presents a danger to himself and to others.
> 3. There is at this time no less restrictive alternative available or appropriate for [the petitioner] than placement into the custody of the Commissioner of Institutions of West Virginia, for placement at the Industrial School for Boys.

The circuit court made no recitation of facts to support the findings. There is no mention of the alternatives explored by the court and the reasons for their rejection. There is no indication of other less restrictive disposition alternatives already tried by the court or by social service agencies. There are no factual findings with regard to the extensive psychiatric and psychological evaluations of the petitioner nor any mention of the results of the court-ordered psychological examination of the petitioner which was conducted shortly before the dispositional hearing. The circuit court did not make a sufficient record in light of the guidelines set forth in *State ex rel. D.D.H. V. Dostert, supra,* which would enable this Court to review the reasons for the circuit court's determination that the petitioner's rehabilitation could be accomplished by no less restrictive alternative than incarceration at the Industrial School.

The other exhibits presented by the petitioner and the respondents, which should have been before the circuit court at the time of the dispositional hearing, reveal facts that might support the circuit court's conclusions. The psychiatric evaluations of the petitioner over a period of three years indicated that he required a structured, secure environment where he could be taught forced acceptance of responsibility in order to conform his behavior to the law. The staff psychologists at the mental health facilities where the petitioner was hospitalized were of the opinion that hospitalization at those facilities was not conducive to the petitioner's rehabilitation. The petitioner's repeated delinquent behavior was indicative of the fact that past rehabilitative efforts had proved unsuccessful. On at least one occasion the petitioner had run away from the facility to which he had been committed and had committed a delinquent act.

The circuit court made no mention of these factors in its dispositional order, however. Moreover, it is uncontested that the petitioner had been incarcerated on a prior occasion at the Industrial School and had been released upon the assertion of the Superintendent that that facility was unable to fulfill the petitioner's rehabilitative needs. Since we have no record which would enable us to determine the factors that led to the conclusion that incarceration was the least restrictive appropriate alternative and to decide whether that conclusion was justified, we award a writ of habeas corpus in accordance with our decision in *State ex rel. D.D.H. v. Dostert, supra,* and order the petitioner discharged from the custody of the Superintendent of the Industrial School. . . .

Notes

1. As in *Trent,* other appellate courts agree that trial courts must consider the least restrictive alternative when entering a juvenile disposition. In *In re Jose P.*, 161 Cal. Rptr. 400 (Cal. Ct. App. 1980), the court ruled that judicial review of the least restrictive alternative is necessary to promote rehabilitation of the child. *Id.* at 404. In *In re Jose P.,* the prosecution argued that Jose, a Mexican juvenile, stole cars in California and then sold them in Mexico. Prior to his recent arrest, Jose was deported by United States Customs and instructed not to return to the United States. The prosecution requested that the court place Jose in juvenile confinement to prevent him from running away and stealing more automobiles. The trial court granted the prosecution's request but did not look at other alternatives for Jose. The appellate court overruled the trial court and held that the trial judge abused his discretion by not considering other dispositional alternatives.

An Illinois appellate court ruled in *In re B.S.,* 549 N.E.2d 695 (1989), that a child cannot be committed to juvenile confinement solely on the basis that there were no suitable alternatives presented by the parties. The court reversed and held that the trial court should consider all alternative dispositions for a juvenile, even when alternatives are not presented by either party. *See also In re Aline D.,* 536 P.2d 65 (Cal. 1975).

2. What is the least restrictive alternative in a delinquency proceeding? A wide range of possible dispositional alternatives emerge from the decisional law. *See P.R.J. v. State*, 787 P.2d 123 (Alaska Ct. App. 1990) (state training may be the least restrictive alternative for a juvenile with a history of running away); *In Interest of T.L.B.*, 539 N.E.2d 1340 (Ill. App. Ct. 1989) (child may be sent to training school even if other least restrictive alternatives exist where juvenile's prior dispositional history suggests confinement appropriate); *State v. Burt*, 546 So. 2d 931 (La. Ct. App. 1989) (a juvenile confined until twenty-one years of age for a sex offense is not so outrageous as to shock the conscience); *In Interest of B.M.*, 303 N.W.2d 601 (Wis. 1981) (child who poses a danger to property of others may be deemed a danger to the public).

3. That a juvenile should receive the least restrictive dispositional alternative has been codified in many states. *See* ALA. CODE § 12-15-1.1 (Lexis Supp. 2000); ALASKA STAT. § 47.10.080 (Lexis 2000); ARK. CODE ANN. § 9-27-329(d) (Michie Supp. 2001); CAL. WELF. & INST. CODE § 626 (West 1998); 705 ILL. COMP. STAT. ANN. 405/5-750 (West 1999); ME. REV. STAT. ANN. tit. 15, § 3315 (West Supp. 2000); N.J. STAT. ANN. § 30:4-123.59 (West Supp. 2001); N.Y. FAM. CT. ACT § 352.2 (McKinney Supp. 2001); S.D. CODIFIED LAWS § 26-7A-56 (Lexis 1999).

Questions

1. In CHILDREN AND THE LAW: DOCTRINE, POLICY AND PRACTICE 1169 (2000), authors Douglas E. Abrams and Sarah H. Ramsey wrote that the least restrictive alternative has been criticized as little more than a "slap on the wrists" for some juveniles. Is the least restrictive alternative too soft on repeat juvenile offenders? Is there a point when the least restrictive alternative should be punitive rather than rehabilitative?

2. Assume that a court holds that a delinquent juvenile needs mental health assistance. The court finds that the juvenile can receive the treatment and care he needs and still live with his parents. The court admits, however, that the juvenile poses a possible threat to the neighbors' property. As the juvenile's attorney, what would you ague would be the least restrictive alternative for the juvenile? What arguments would you use to support your submission to the court? How should the court weigh the juvenile's best interests and the interests of the neighbors?

3. Use of Predispositional Reports

In re B.B.

647 So. 2d 268 (Fla. Dist. Ct. App. 1994)

STEVENSON, Judge.

B.B., a juvenile, pled guilty to two counts of simple battery, was adjudicated delinquent, and in this appeal, challenges the trial court's disposition order. Appellant was placed on supervised community control until her nineteenth birthday with the special conditions that she complete fifty hours of community service, apologize to the victim in writing, pay fifty dollars to the Florida Crime Compensation fund, and obtain a GED within one year. Appellant argues that the trial court erred in failing to consider a predisposition report prior to disposition. . . . [We] find merit in appellant's . . . argument, [and] we vacate the disposition order.

We agree with appellant that the trial court erred in making a disposition in this case without first considering a predisposition report. Failure to consider a predisposition report prior to disposition in a juvenile case is reversible error. *M.H. v. State*, 621 So. 2d 527 (Fla.2d DCA 1993). Although consideration of a predisposition report is necessary under the statute, we agree with *M.H. v. State* that the report may be knowingly and intelligently waived. In the present case, the trial court's order noted that appellant waived the predisposition report, but the record does not reflect the waiver. Because the record does not disclose that appellant knowingly and intelligently waived her right to a predisposition report, we must vacate the sentence and remand this case for a new disposition hearing. On remand, appellant must either waive her right to a predisposition report on the record, or the trial court must order a predisposition report prior to disposition.

* * *

We vacate the disposition and remand for further proceedings.

In re Pima County Delinquency Action No. 90101-1

744 P. 2d 20 (Ariz. Ct. App. 1987)

PER CURIAM

This appeal raises the question whether, in a delinquency proceeding, the minor's parents are "aggrieved" parties for purposes of appeal. We do not believe that they are and dismiss the appeal.

The minor had been adjudicated delinquent and placed on probation. Subsequently, the probation was revoked. A predisposition report was prepared and, based upon the recommendations of the probation officer, the court again placed the minor on probation, which included the condition that he participate in the special supervision project. The court also ordered that the minor be placed with foster parents. At the disposition proceedings, the minor's parents appeared with counsel, who insisted that they had a right to review the contents of the predisposition report "to determine if the information is accurate in there and on what basis the probation office is making their recommendation." The court denied the request, stating that no purpose would be served by allowing the minor's parents to review the predisposition report so long as they were aware of the impact or results of the recommendations. Counsel for the parents then requested permission to cross-examine the probation officer regarding the predisposition investigation. At that point, the court sustained the state's objection and ruled that the minor's parents lacked standing to review the report or to examine the probation officer. It is from that order that the minor's parents have filed their appeal. . . .

[Arizona Revised Statutes] § 8-236 provides that any "aggrieved party" may appeal from a final order of the juvenile court. Here, the parents argue that they are aggrieved parties. We disagree. The parties to a delinquency proceeding are the state and the minor child. Therefore, the parents are not "aggrieved" for purposes of the statute.

The parents next argue that they have a fundamental right to participate in the predisposition phase of a delinquency proceeding and to appeal from the court's order denying them access to the predisposition report and the opportunity to examine the probation officer. Again, we disagree. The disposition of a minor who has been adjudged delinquent is solely within the discretion of the juvenile judge. The parents do not have a fundamental right to review the predisposition report or to participate in the ultimate determination of an appropriate disposition order. All of the cases cited by the parents involve situations where the relationships between parents and minors were affected, such as dependency proceedings, terminations of parental rights, or custody proceedings. Such rights are not affected by a juvenile court's disposition order entered pursuant to A.R.S. § 8-241(A)(2) and (3).

Finally, although we believe that the parents are not aggrieved parties and do not have standing to participate in these proceedings, we find Rule 9, Rules of Procedure for the Juvenile Court, 17-A A.R.S., to be dispositive. That rule allows the juvenile court, in its discretion, to withhold the probation officer's investigations and/or reports should it determine that the material would be psychologically damaging or would be destructive of relationships among family members. Assuming for purposes of argument that the parents are properly before us on appeal, the juvenile court's order is nonetheless appropriate and within the court's discretion as allowed by Rule 9(b), Rules of Procedure for the Juvenile Court.

The appeal filed by the minor's parents in this case is dismissed.

Notes

1. The predispositional report should reflect consideration of several factors. In *Anton v. State*, 224 N.E.2d 516 (Ind. Ct. App. 1967), the court required a predispositional report to include information concerning the juvenile's living conditions and the stability of the juvenile's family, as well as an analysis of the juvenile's physical, emotional, and psychological needs.

Indiana's statutes governing predispositional reports are similar to those adopted by other states. *See* IND. CODE ANN. § 31-34-18-1(a) (Lexis 1997) (predispositional report requires an assessment of the child's needs and recommendations for the care, treatment, rehabilitation, or placement of child); IND. CODE ANN. § 31-34-18-2 (Lexis 1997) (predispositional report should include the degree of parental participation in the care, treatment, or rehabilitation of the child); IND. CODE ANN. § 31-34-18-1.1 (Lexis 1997) (probation officer who is writing the predispositional report has the option to confer with professionals unless mandated by the court); IND. CODE ANN. § 31-34-18-6.1 (Lexis 1997) (probation officer must list all options the officer considered before completing a recommendation); IND. CODE ANN. § 31-34-18-4 (Lexis 1997) (recommendation must be the least restrictive dispositional alternative); IND. CODE ANN. § 31-34-18-3 (Lexis 1997) (probation officer must include a report detailing the parents' financial ability to pay for the child's treatment). *See also* MO. REV. STAT. § 211.071(6) (West 1996).

2. The predispositional report should help the judge individualize the disposition to the child by providing a panorama of the juvenile's history for the court's consideration. *See* JUDGE JERRY L. MERSHON, JUVENILE JUSTICE: THE ADJUDICATORY AND DISPOSITIONAL PROCESS 140 (1991). When writing the predispositional report, the probation officer should have an awareness of how the child views himself, weigh the child's past in terms of the future and determine the type and quality of treatment services available. *Id.* at 140. Because of the importance of the dispositional order, the predispositional report is not the only recommendation a judge may consider before deciding questions of placement, services, etc. The judge may consider recommendations from the guardian ad litem, the parents, the prosecutor, the juvenile, and other appropriate parties. *See id.* at 141.

Questions

1. The *Pima County* court ruled that the parents were not "aggrieved" parties for the purpose of viewing the predispositional report. Suppose the court in the exercise of discretion decided that the information in the report was so sensitive that it would be harmful to the child to read the report. Who would then review the report in behalf of the child's interests to verify the accuracy of the report? Is it ever fair to exclude both the child and the parents from reading the report? Would the court violate the child's due process rights by preventing both the child and the parents from reading the report?

2. The *B.B.* court acknowledged that a juvenile may knowingly and intelligently waive his or her right to a predispositional report. Because legislatures and courts emphasize the importance of the court reading a predispositional report, why would a juvenile waive his or her right to the report? Is there any strategic value in waiving the right to a predispositional report?

B. Probation: Conditions and Challenges

1. Restitution

P.R. v. State

210 S.E.2d 839 (Ga. Ct. App. 1974)

CLARK, Judge.

Does our Juvenile Court Code empower the court to require restitution as a condition precedent for placing the offender on probation? That is the principal problem presented by this appeal.

Two brothers, then 16 and 13 years old respectively, were ruled delinquent at a joint adjudicatory hearing of theft by taking of publications valued at $15 from a self-service store. The principal witness was a female clerk who was alone in the place when these brothers and another younger lad had walked out of the establishment without paying for paper-back books and magazines, which she testified had been hidden inside their shirts. Although she had not seen the actual purloining, her accusation was based upon a bulge in their shirts and a glimpse of books. Being fearful of physical harm if she immediately accused them, she permitted their departure and then notified the police. When the youngsters were shortly thereafter returned to the store, she identified them as the culprits. No merchandise was found on them nor were the missing publications discovered during a neighborhood search. Although both brothers denied the charge, they were ruled guilty, the judge regarding the circumstantial evidence as sufficient. Thereafter, at a joint dispositional hearing both appellants were sentenced to twelve months probation on condition that each pay $7.50 as restitution to the merchant whose goods were filched.

Our 1971 Juvenile Court Code . . . begins with [t]he specific legislative directive . . . that "This code shall be liberally construed to the end that children whose well-being is threatened shall be assisted and protected and restored, if possible, as secure law-abiding members of society. . . ." Code Ann. § 24A-101.

Probation rather than penalization is one of the statutory methods provided for in § 24A-2302. There it is provided that if the result of the adjudicatory hearing is a determination that the child is found to be in need of treatment or rehabilitation, the court as one of the alternatives "best suited to his treatment, rehabilitation, and welfare" may order "(b) Placing the child on probation under the supervision of the probation officer of the court or the court of another state as provided in Section 24A-3003, or any public agency authorized by law to receive and provide care for the child, . . . *under conditions and limitations the court prescribes.*" (Emphasis supplied.)

In discussing the emphasized Codal words, counsel for the appellee has expressed views which we adopt as being applicable to this appeal:

> Certainly these "conditions and limitations" must include the right to order restitution. This right is inherent in the power of the court, in what is, in effect, the burden upon the court, to make such disposition of a delinquent child as is "best suited to his treatment, rehabilitation, and welfare," Ga. Code Ann. Section 24A-2302.
>
> The paramount duty imposed upon the Juvenile Court both philosophically and statutorily is that of rehabilitating and treating the delinquent child so as to act in is own best interest and for his protection. It is incumbent upon the Juvenile Court to make the child before it aware that he had committed a wrongful act and to teach him why that act is wrongful and to restore him, if possible, as a secure and law-abiding member of society.
>
> * * *
>
> In cases like the one at hand in which a child's wrongful act has occasioned some loss to befall another party, it is both therapeutic and rehabilitative to require the child to make such restitution as he is able to do. Restitution is beneficial both to the child and to his victim.
>
> The avenues for disposition of a delinquent child which the Juvenile Court has open to it are not unlimited. At present the Juvenile Court basically may place such a child on probation or may commit the child to the Division of Children and Youth for placement in one of the Youth Development Centers.
>
> There may be many instances in which the Juvenile Court would deem that the placing of a child on probation with the condition that restitution be made by the child is sufficient for the treatment and rehabilitation of the child and that such a probation obviates the need to commit the child to the State for treatment. . . .

These eloquent expressions establish that both the power and necessity to require restitution as a condition for probation exist under our Juvenile Court code.

Capable counsel for appellants contend that the effect of our ruling in *E.P. v. State of Ga.,* 130 Ga. App. 512, 203 S.E.2d 757 prevents a Juvenile Court from insisting upon restitution. There we held that "There is no statutory authority authorizing a juvenile court to impose a monetary fine on a minor adjudged to be delinquent." Appellants' contention would equate a fine with restitution. This would be erroneous because a fine is penal in nature with payment to the government and with no relationship to the offense. Whereas restitution is rehabilitative in nature, is related directly to the offense, and goes to the party who has been deprived of property. Restitution is indemnification rather than forfeiture.

* * *

Because of our Court's ruling in *E.P. v. State of Ga., supra,* prohibiting imposition of a fine it is obvious that the restitution computation must not be such as to permit an aggrieved individual to profit out of a sad situation. The evidence here indicates the loss to the aggrieved party to approximately $25. Restitution totaling $15 is within the limits of the evidence and is in the nature of a judicial determination of the amount.

Our review of the transcript has led us to the conclusion that the juvenile court judge did not err in failing to grant a motion to dismiss as there was competent evidence in the record that appellants had committed the alleged offense even though the pilfered publications were not found by the police.

Judgment affirmed.

Notes

1. A majority of states use restitution to rehabilitate delinquent juveniles. These jurisdictions generally have relied upon case law to determine the appropriate scope of restitution for delinquents. *See Charles S. v. Superior Court of Los Angeles*, 653 P.2d 648 (Cal. 1982) (restitution is proper and a desirable form of disposition); *In Interest of I.V.,* 326 N.W.2d 127 (Wis. Ct. App. 1982) (restitution may include unrecovered stolen property); *In Interest of Joseph Eugene M.*, 338 S.E.2d 328 (S.C. 1985) (restitution can only be ordered as part of probation not in conjunction with commitment to the state); *In Interest of Steven J.,* 497 A.2d 125 (Pa. Super. Ct. 1985) (juvenile who is able to pay for restitution).

2. The law remains unsettled on the issue of whether to impose restitution or fines as dispositions for delinquents. Jurisdictions supporting the use of restitution claim it is consistent with the juvenile law goal of rehabilitating a delinquent juvenile. Proponents of restitution argue that if a juvenile is forced to compensate the victim the juvenile will learn from the mistake and become a better person. Restitution teaches the juvenile a lesson and compensates the victim for the loss resulting from the delinquent act and society does not burden the loss of the delinquent act. *See* N.Y. FAM. CT. ACT § 353.6(1)(a) (McKinney 1999); *In Interest of Joseph Eugene M.,* 338 S.E.2d 328 (S.C. 1985). Today, however, there are a growing number of states using fines as punitive disposition. Jurisdiction that support the use of fines claim restitution sometimes amounts to a "slap on the wrist" resulting in a juvenile not "learning a lesson." *See E.E. v. E.M.*, No. CH98-07191, 1999 WL 1456948, at *13 (Del. Fam. Ct.); NEB. REV. STAT. § 43-286(1)(a) (Supp. 2000).

3. The American Bar Association maintains the following stance concerning restitution as condition of probation:

IJA-ABA Juvenile Justice Standards,
Standards Relating to Dispositions
§ 3.2(B)(1) (1980)*

a. Restitution should be directly related to the juvenile's offense, the actual harm caused, and the juvenile's ability to pay.

b. The means to carry out a restitution should be available.

c. Either full or partial restitution may be ordered.

d. Repayment may be required in a lump sum or in installments.

e. Consultation with victims may be encouraged but not required. Payments may be made directly to victims, or indirectly, through the court.

f. The juvenile's duty of repayment should be limited in duration; in no event should the time necessary for repayment exceed the maximum term permissible for the offense.

Questions

1. Debate continues on the question of whether courts may use restitution as a disposition by itself or as a condition of probation. How does this relate to the issues raised by the restitution versus the fines issue? What policy arguments can be made supporting the use of restitution as a disposition by itself or as a condition of probation?

2. Suppose a court determines that Craig and Keith should be adjudicated delinquent for the same offense. Craig's parents are corporate attorneys while Keith's parents are on welfare. If the judge orders restitution as a condition of their probation, would it serve a rehabilitative purpose? Assuming fines are a possible dispositional alternative, should the court impose an additional fine on Craig? What additional options might the court consider to impose a hardship on Craig so as to "teach him a lesson"? What additional goals or problems of juvenile law are raised in this example?

---

* Reprinted with permission.

2. Community Service

M.J.W. v. State

210 S.E.2d 842 (Ga. Ct. App. 1974)

CLARK, Judge.

Does the imposition of a requirement that a juvenile delinquent contribute free labor to the Parks and Recreation Department amount to involuntary servitude in violation of his constitutional rights? Is the imposition of such requirement similar to a monetary fine which is prohibited? These interesting questions are presented for determination.

* * *

Having found no error in the court's ruling on delinquency, we turn to a consideration of appellant's attacks upon the validity of the punishment. As a condition to the offender being placed on probation for one year, he was required to "contribute 100 hours to Parks and Recreation Department of DeKalb County." Appellant's able attorney argues this condition to be invalid for two reasons. These are: (1) the court in effect was placing a fine upon the offender contrary to the ruling of *E.P. v. State of Ga.*, 130 Ga. App. 512, 203 S.E.2d 757 that no statutory authority exists for imposing a monetary fine on a minor adjudged to be delinquent; and (2) this would constitute involuntary servitude in violation of the juvenile's constitutional rights.

We hold that neither attack has merit in the light of the provisions of our Juvenile Court Code and the nature of probation. The permeating premise of our statute is that juvenile offenders can be rehabilitated and transformed into productive citizens by a system specially designed to achieve those ends. One of the methods provided in that statute is probation. Code Ann. § 24A-2303. In *P.R. v. State of Ga.*, 133 Ga. App. 346, 210 S.E.2d 839 we made an exhaustive examination into this subject of probation conditions and concluded that a requirement of restitution was permissible because it was not in the nature of a fine. The reasoning in that case applies here in two respects. The first is that designation of work of a public purpose for destruction of public property is akin to restitution and does not resemble a monetary penalty. Secondly, useful services for the public good are in the pattern of probation, which is a specialized judicial tool and is helpful towards achieving the statute's pervading purpose of producing a good adult citizen. As the trial judge stated: "This is specific action designed to foster in him an understanding that he's got some responsibilities and what it takes to create something as opposed to going around destroying things." It is constructive rather than punitive. It comes within the statutory mandate that juvenile court judges are to make such disposition of a delinquent child as is "best suited to his treatment, rehabilitation, and welfare." Code Ann. § 24A-2302.

Nor does this condition amount to prohibited involuntary servitude. In *Loeb v. Jennings,* 133 Ga. 796, 67 S.E. 101, *aff'd* 219 U.S. 582, 31 S. Ct. 469, 55 L. Ed. 345, Justice Joseph Henry Lumpkin wrote an opinion holding that a violator of a municipal ordinance could be required to labor on the streets or other public works of a city and this would be neither involuntary servitude nor cruel or unusual punishment. His ruling was based on the constitutional exclusion of "punishment for crime." Even though juvenile court proceedings are not criminal proceedings and Code Ann. § 24A-2401 declares that an adjudication order is non-criminal, nevertheless, we must recognize "the quasi-criminal aspects of juvenile law." Additionally, the courts frequently apply criminal law procedural safeguards to juveniles. *See Kent v. United States,* 383 U.S. 541, 86 S. Ct. 1045, 15 L. Ed. 2d 84 (due process); *In re Gault*, 387 U.S. 1, 87 S. Ct. 1428, 18 L. Ed. 2d 527 (right to counsel); and *In re Winship*, 397 U.S. 358, 90 S. Ct. 1068, 25 L. Ed. 2d 368 (beyond reasonable doubt). The Juvenile Court Code defines a delinquent act as one "designated a crime by the laws of Georgia." Code Ann. § 24A-401(e)(1). Accordingly, a juvenile court order of this type would come within the constitutional exception as it is "punishment for crime," even though it is rehabilitative rather than punitive.

* * *

We reiterate that the requirement of performing public service is in accord with the theme of probation. In considering the State Wide Probation Act we pointed out in *Falkenhainer v. State*, 122 Ga. App. 478, 480, 177 S.E.2d 380 that our statute was not exclusive in its provisions and that "the court has authority to impose restrictions not specifically listed therein. This reasoning is most apropos to the letter and spirit of our enlightened Juvenile Court Code with its broad probation provisions and its curative goal of rehabilitation. The instant public-work condition conforms to today's approach which courts make in seeking alternatives to jail. . . . This innovative and imaginative approach seeks to avoid "a trauma left on the victim or the community" while aiming to give the offender a chance "for a sense of satisfaction and accomplishment that prison rarely offers." In short, to make the punishment fit the offender rather than follow The Mikado's musical mandate: "Let the punishment fit the crime."

Judgment affirmed.

Notes

1. Many states recognize community service as an acceptable condition of probation for delinquents. *See, e.g.,* CAL. WELF. & INST. CODE § 202 (West Supp. 2001); TEX. FAM. CODE ANN. § 59.005(a)(2), (6), (7) (West Supp. 2001). Community service can function as a separate disposition or as a condition of probation. SAMUEL DAVIS, RIGHTS OF JUVENILES 6-20 (1994). Juvenile courts use community service as a condition of probation to benefit the community, teach the juvenile a lesson to accept responsibility, and to afford the juvenile working experience. DONALD KRAMER, LEGAL RIGHTS OF CHILDREN 388 (2d ed. 1994).

2. When a delinquent's probation is conditioned on the performance of community service, several forms of work assignments exist. Martin Gardner, in his book UNDERSTANDING JUVENILE LAW 315 (1997), gives several service options a court may assign to a delinquent. Courts may order juveniles to work in parks, cemeteries, hospitals, or zoos. Courts may also require juveniles to help supervise recreational programs for other juveniles. *Id.* at 315. The court monitors the delinquent's work to ensure it meets the conditions of the juvenile's probation.

3. A court may not require a juvenile to perform community service as a condition of probation for a longer period of time than that the juvenile would have to serve if committed to custodial confinement. *See, e.g., M.G. v. State*, 556 So. 2d 820 (Fla. Dist. Ct. App. 1990); *H.B.E., III v. State*, 484 So. 2d 486 (Fla. Dist. Ct. App. 1986). It is interesting to note that while states like Florida place time restrictions on the length of community service for juveniles, Florida does not impose a time restriction on the length of community service for adults. Adult offenders whose probation is conditioned on performance of community service may be required to work longer than if the adult had been incarcerated. FLA. STAT. ANN. § 948.04 (West 2001).

Questions

1. The *M.J.W.* court held that, "[T]he designation of work of a public purpose for destruction of public property is akin to restitution and does not resemble a monetary penalty." *Supra,* at 843. The court left open the question as to what extent community service must relate to the offense. Would it be permissible for a court to require a juvenile to perform community service as a condition of the probation for a delinquent act unrelated to destruction of public property? Consider:

a. A juvenile is found delinquent based on the theft of his neighbor's lawnmower. The judge, realizing that the court in *M.J.W.* justified community service in part because the juvenile destroyed public property, justifies giving the juvenile community service as a condition of his probation because community service serves as a rehabilitative function.

b. A juvenile is found delinquent on the basis of assault and battery. The predispositional report indicates that the juvenile is not a member of a street gang nor has she ever before had problems with the law. The presiding judge determines that the juvenile's probation will be conditioned on her performance of fifty hours of community service. The judge justifies his decision by pointing out that the juvenile has never been in trouble with the law and that community service will teach the juvenile a valuable lesson.

In your jurisdiction, the holding in *In re M.J.W.* controls. Analyze the illustrations above and decide whether or not community service is an appropriate condition of probation.

2. The Thirteenth Amendment of the United States Constitution prohibits the imposition of "involuntary servitude *except as a punishment for a crime.*" U.S. CONST. Amend. XIII (emphasis added). If a juvenile court imposes community service as a condition of probation for rehabilitation, does this condition violate the Thirteenth Amendment? Reflecting upon the arguments and social policies by the *M.J.W.* court, prepare both sides of the argument.

3. Curfew

In re Rodriguez

687 S.W.2d 421 (Tex. App. 1985)

DRAUGHN, Justice.

This is an appeal, in a juvenile case, from an Order modifying Disposition. Under the order, Jerry R. Rodriguez was committed to the Texas Youth Commission. Rodriguez . . . argues that the trial court abused its discretion in modifying its prior disposition order. We affirm.

On January 20, 1984, Rodriguez was adjudicated a juvenile delinquent for making bomb threats to Alvin Junior High School. The trial court ordered that he be placed on probation for a period of twelve months. A list of conditions of probation was attached to the Order of Disposition. One of the conditions, entitled "Curfew," provided:

> I will be home at 1818 W. Phillips between 7:00 p.m., and 7:00 a.m., Sunday through Thursday and between 10:00 p.m., and 7:00 a.m., on Friday or Saturday. (There shall be no exception to this condition unless obtained in advance and in writing from my probation officer, unless I am with my relative or guardian.)

The conditions were signed by Rodriguez.

A petition was filed to revoke the probation. One of the grounds listed in support of the application to revoke probation was that on June 28, 1984, Rodriguez had violated his curfew. After a hearing on the mater, the trial court found that the curfew had been violated. The trial judge ordered that he be "committed to the Texas Youth Commission until his 18th birthday."

The first point of error is that "the trial court abused its discretion in modifying its prior disposition order because the evidence was legally insufficient to show that the Appellant had violated the curfew condition of his probation." Rodriguez contends that the only evidence on whether the curfew was violated was hearsay testimony which will not support the modifying of the disposition order.

The only testimony of the alleged curfew violation was supplied by Officer Jim Truelove of the Alvin Police Department. Truelove testified that he saw Rodriguez on June 28, 1984, at 11:04 p.m., outside Captain B's Gameroom, an establishment in Alvin. On cross-examination, Truelove explained that the time of 11:04 p.m. was determined from the log records at the Alvin Police Department and that he did not look at his watch to determine what time it was. Rodriguez's counsel moved to have the testimony struck because it was based on hearsay. The motion was overruled.

Even if we assume that the objected to testimony was hearsay, an issue we do not decide, we cannot agree that there is no evidence in the record showing that Rodriguez violated his curfew. An attack on the legal sufficiency of the evidence requires this court to consider only the evidence and inferences from the evidence which tend to support the judgment of the trial court and disregard all evidence and inferences to the contrary.

On redirect examination, Truelove testified that on the night in question he was on duty from 6:00 p.m. until 2:00 a.m., and that when he arrived at Captain B's Gameroom it was dark. Truelove testified that he left that area at approximately 11:30 p.m. and that time was not based upon his calling or checking the dispatcher's log. Truelove's testimony and the inferences from such testimony support the conclusion that Rodriguez violated his curfew. Point of error one is overruled.

Point of error two is that modification of the disposition order was an abuse of discretion because the alleged curfew violation was not a violation of a reasonable order of the court. The disposition of a delinquent child may be modified so as to commit the child to the Texas Youth Commission if the child has violated a reasonable and lawful order of the court. *In re D.E.P.*, 512 S.W.2d 789 (Tex.Civ.App.-Houston [14th Dist.] 1974, no writ); TEX. FAM. CODE ANN. § 54.05(f) (Vernon Supp. 1985). The conditions which caused the violations in the *D.E.P.* case were out of the control of the child involved. The basis of this court's decision in *In re D.E.P.* was that these uncontrollable circumstances made the order of the court unreasonable, not that a curfew is an unreasonable condition. *In re D.E.P.*, 512 S.W.2d at 792. Given the facts in this case, the trial court's order conditioning the child's probation on his following the curfew was a reasonable order of the court. Point of error two is overruled.

The third point of error is that the modification of the disposition order was an abuse of discretion because "there was no evidence that the Appellant had not received permission from his probation officer to be out after curfew hours, and there is no evidence that the Appellant was not with a relative or guardian."

Even if we accept the premise that the State had to disprove the exceptions to the curfew condition, there is some evidence that Rodriguez did not have permission and was not with a relative or guardian. The probation officer recommended that Rodriguez be committed to the Texas Youth Commission for the curfew violation. A logical inference from that fact is that the probation officer did not authorize, in writing, the curfew violation. Officer Truelove testified that he observed only one person outside the gameroom. That person was Rodriguez. We cannot say there was no evidence refuting the two exceptions of the curfew. Point of error three is overruled.

* * *

The judgment is affirmed.

Notes

1. A California appellate court ruled in *In re Laylah K.*, 281 Cal. Rptr. 6 (Cal. Ct. App. 1991), that a court may use curfew as a condition of probation to prevent delinquents from falling into the influence of street gangs. In *In re Laylah K.*, two sisters were found to be delinquent after beating a pedestrian. The juvenile court ruled that the sisters must observe a curfew as well as not wear particular colors worn by members of the Crips street gang as conditions of their probation. The sisters, associates of the gang, challenged the conditions of the probation as violative of their constitutional rights. The court, affirming the trial court's terms of probation, held that the trial court could impose the conditions because of the serious danger which association with street gangs poses to the juveniles as well as society. The court specifically addressed the constitutional challenge presented by the sisters by referring to its opinion in *In re Michael D.*, 264 Cal. Rptr. 475 (Cal. Ct. App. 1989) "[E]ven conditions which infringe on constitutional rights may not be invalid if tailored specifically to meet the needs of the juvenile [citation]." *In re Layla, supra*, at 1502 (citing *In re Michael D., supra*). *See also In re Jason J.*, 284 Cal. Rptr. 673 (Cal. Ct. App. 1991); Nikki Gfellers, et al., *Juvenile*, 21 CAMPBELL L. REV. 399 (1999); Ronald P. Corbett, Jr., *Juvenile Probation on the Eve of the Next Millennium*, 64 FED. PROBATION 78 (1999).

2. While some courts use curfew as a condition of probation without any statute giving the court such power, some state legislatures have passed statutes giving courts the power to use curfew as a condition of a delinquent's probation. *See* 1998 N.C. Sess. Laws 202; WYO. STAT. ANN. § 14-6-244 (Lexis 1999); CAL. WELF. & INST. CODE § 729.3(c) (West 1998).

4. Association

In re Babak S.

22 Cal. Rptr. 2d 893 (Cal. Ct. App. 1993)

MIHARA, Associate Justice.

I

Babak S., a minor, appeals from an order committing him to the California Youth Authority after the juvenile court sustained a petition filed pursuant to Welfare and Institutions Code section 777, alleging that the minor had violated the conditions of his probation by living in the United States with his parents, and by associating with a known probationer or gang member. On appeal, the minor contends the order must be reversed because (1) the former allegation was premised upon an unconstitutional probation condition banishing him to Iran; (2) he was not under order to refrain from associating with probationers or gang members; (3) assuming he was under such order, there was insufficient evidence to sustain the allegation; (4) reconsideration of the probationer/gang allegation is prohibited by principles of double jeopardy; and (5) the juvenile court was without authority to impose a suspended CYA commitment. For reasons explained below, we find the first and last contentions to be meritorious. Accordingly, we reverse the dispositional order and remand for further proceedings.

II. Background

Babak first became a ward of the juvenile court in 1989 when he admitted the commission of four misdemeanor offenses pursuant to a negotiated agreement. The court admitted Babak to probation with various conditions, and ordered the minor detained at a county ranch facility.

During the next year and a half, the court sustained three supplemental petitions. . . . At the disposition hearing on the third petition, the court ordered all previously imposed conditions of probation to remain in effect and imposed an additional condition prohibiting Babak from associating with any "known probationer, parolee, or gang member."

* * *

On January 30, 1992, a petition alleging ranch failure was filed after Babak and another ranch detainee fought over their respective gang affiliations. In a report to the court, Babak's probation officer, Christine Frederick, recommended that a Youth Authority commitment be suspended on condition that the minor move to Iran to live with his parents or relatives and that he not return to the United States without prior court approval. This recommendation was premised upon the parents' request that Babak be permitted to live with them in Iran.

On February 18, 1992, the juvenile court sustained the petition. In accordance with the recommendation of the probation officer, the court committed the minor to the Youth Authority, said commitment to be suspended on condition that the minor (1) reside with his parents in Iran for two years, (2) report to the probation officer as directed, and (3) not change his place of residence without the prior approval of the probation officer. All previous orders which were consistent with the court's disposition were to remain in effect. Babak was ordered detained at juvenile hall until such time as he could be transported to the airport for his departure to Iran.

On July 13, 1992, Frederick received information that Babak was back in the United States. The following day, Frederick went to the minor's residence where she discovered Babak and Lonnie M. asleep in Babak's bedroom. Two days later, Frederick filed a supplemental petition alleging that Babak had violated the court's previous order by "living with his parents in the United States." The petition was subsequently amended to include an allegation that Babak had been in the company of Lonnie M., a "known probationer and gang member."

At a contested hearing on the petition, Frederick testified that on June 18, 1991, Babak was placed under a probation order forbidding his association with a probationer or gang member. The court then took judicial notice of its "own order." Frederick went on to testify to her discovery of appellant and Lonnie, whom she described as a known probationer and gang member. Following his arrest on the underlying petition, appellant admitted that he had been back in the United States for over two weeks. When Frederick asked appellant why he hadn't contacted her following his return, appellant said "he was going to, but . . . hadn't done that yet."

* * *

Babak testified that he had gone to Iran with his father and had stayed there approximately two months. After his grandmother's death, he had no other relatives with whom he could stay, and his father had then decided he should return to the United States. Babak testified he "had to come back [because he] had no other choice."

Babak admitted his association and friendship with Lonnie, but testified Lonnie had told him he was no longer associated with a gang. Lonnie did not know whether he was on probation or not, but thought he was "off probation" because he was eighteen and his case had been "cleared." Babak admitted that he had not called his probation officer during the six-week period since his return from Iran.

The juvenile court sustained the petition and held that the previous disposition had not been effective. The court justified its findings as follows:

> Okay. As you know . . . before I can invoke [a] more restrictive disposition on [Babak] I'd have to find that . . . the previous disposition has not been effective in the rehabilitation of [the minor], and I'm prepared at this time to make such a finding.
>
> And I do that . . . for several reasons. First of all, he was personally aware of the law, his probation order that he was to go to Iran, come back here and then go back on probation. He came. He'd been here for three, two, three months and never reported to his probation officer. He's He's flagrantly violated a court order by doing that, and he's been on probation enough times and he's been at the ranch enough times to know he's got to stay in contact with his probation officer. And he flagrantly violated that court order, and I think that's sufficient enough to find that his previous disposition has not been effective in his rehabilitation.
>
> Now, when you take in consideration all the prior commitments that he's had, he's been given every chance. He's had every opportunity to do everything that the juvenile court has to offer, and he's . . . blown every one of 'em. He's really put handcuffs on me. I can't send him any other place but the Californa Youth Authority. And I think that's where the best place is for him.

The court then "lift[ed] the prior suspension of the California Youth Authority commitment . . ." and committed the minor to that institution for a maximum term of four years and seven months, with credit for time served.

A. The Banishment Condition

Section 730 of the Welfare and Institutions Code grants courts broad discretion in establishing conditions of probation in juvenile cases. The court may impose "any reasonable conditions that it may determine fitting and proper to the end that justice may be done and the reformation and rehabilitation of the ward enhanced." However "[a] condition of probation which (1) has no relationship to the crime of which the offender was convicted, (2) relates to conduct which is not in itself criminal, and (3) requires or forbids conduct which is not reasonably related to future criminality does not serve the statutory ends of probation and is invalid." (*Peple v. Dominguez* (1967) 256 Cal. App. 2d 623, 627, 64 Cal. Rptr. 290; *accord People v. Lent* (1975) 15 Cal. 3d 481, 486, 124 Cal. Rptr. 905, 541 P.2d 545.) Stated another way, "a condition of probation which requires or forbids conduct which is not itself criminal is valid if that conduct is reasonably related to the crime of which the defendant was convicted or to future criminality." (*People v. Lent, supra,* at p. 486, 124 Cal. Rptr. 905, 541 P.2d 545.)

... Conditions of banishment affect the probationer's basic constitutional scrutiny, such conditions not only must be reasonably related to present or future criminality, but also must be narrowly drawn and specifically tailored to the individual probationer. In the instant case, the People make no serious attempt to justify the banishment condition per se, and an analysis of relevant case law readily establishes that the condition at issue here does not pass constitutional muster.

* * *

B. The Condition Forbidding Association with a Probationer or Gang Member

As is indicated in our factual summary, the probationer/gang condition was first imposed after the court sustained a supplemental petition in June of 1991. The following month, in July of 1991, a petition was filed charging Babak with the commission of a new offense, possession of a dagger, and alleging that upon the sustaining of the petition, the court "[might] find the previous disposition has not been effective." The allegations were found to be true and Babak was continued on probation.

On appeal, Babak contends that the record does not contain sufficient evidence to establish that the probationer/gang condition was in effect at the time of the alleged violation. ... We disagree.

Babak's argument rests upon the assumption that the sustaining of a section 602/777 petition is analogous to revocation proceedings in adult court and thus results in a revocation of probation which terminates previously imposed probation conditions. It is therefore asserted that the juvenile court was required either to reimpose the probationer/gang condition or, alternatively, to decree that all previous orders were to remain in effect. The law is otherwise.

* * *

Taking into account the rehabilitative goal of juvenile proceedings (*In re Aline D.* (1975) 14 Cal. 3d 557, 567, 121 Cal. Rptr. 816, 536 P.2d 65), the fact that probation is not revoked upon the sustaining of a supplemental petition, the requirement that a juvenile court set reasonable terms and conditions when placing a minor on probation, and the lack of any indication of an intent on the part of the juvenile court in this case to terminate any of the previously imposed probation conditions, we conclude that record provides substantial evidence that the minor in this case remained subject to an order forbidding his association with known probationers or gang members.

C. Sufficiency of the Evidence

Babak contends that even if he did remain subject to the probationer/gang order, the evidence adduced below was insufficient to establish a violation of the court's order. We do not find this contention to be meritorious

* * *

On the question of Babak's knowledge of Lonnie's probationary status, the minor himself testified that Lonnie had indicated he did not know whether he was still on probation, but believed he had been released because he had attained the age of eighteen years and his case had thus been "cleared." Even if we take this testimony at face value, it established that the minor had discussed the issue with Lonnie, knew Lonnie had been on probation, and had received an equivocal answer, at best, as to the youth's current status. Based on this evidence, it could reasonably he inferred that Babak had associated with a known probationer. Accordingly, we conclude that the record contains evidence sufficient to support the court's finding that the minor had violated the probation condition forbidding his association with a known probationer.

However, even though the record supports a violation of probation on this ground, we cannot sustain the court's finding that the previous dispositional order had been ineffective. In making its finding, the court explicitly relied upon the violation of the banishment condition and Babak's failure to contact his probation officer, factors which we have determined to be invalid. Though the court might have found the previous dispositional order ineffective based only upon the minor's violation of the probationer/gang condition, we cannot conclude on this record that the court would have imposed a Youth Authority commitment based solely upon Babak's association with Lonnie. . . .

D. The Imposition of a Suspended Commitment to the Youth Authority

At the February, 1992, disposition hearing, the court indicated that it was imposing a suspended Youth Authority commitment. Later, at the August 1992 disposition hearing from which the present appeal arises, the court "lift[ed] the prior suspension" and committed Babak to the Youth Authority. Citing *In re Ronnie P.* (1992) 10 Cal. App. 4th 1079, 12 Cal. Rptr. 2d 875, Babak contends the court erred by relying on a previous dispositional order purporting to impose a suspended Youth Authority Commitment. We agree.

In re Ronnie P., supra, presents a factual situation analogous to that at issue in the present case. There, the juvenile court had previously imposed a suspended commitment to the Youth Authority under which the minor would be sent to that institution if he were to engage in any further misconduct (*In re Ronnie P., supra,* 10 Cal. App. 4th at p. 1086, 12 Cal. Rptr. 2d 875.) Upon the sustaining of a subsequent supplemental petition, the court "concluded that commitment to the Youth Authority necessarily followed. . . ." (*Id.* at pp. 1086-1087 12 Cal. Rptr. 2d 875.)

On appeal, the reviewing court found a "complete absence of authority for an order imposing a 'suspended' or 'stayed' Youth Authority commitment." (*In re Ronnie P., supra,* 10 Cal. App. 4th at P. 1087, 12 Cal. Rptr. 2d 875.) . . . The court also held that a juvenile court may not "forego a thorough review of dispositional considerations in favor of a previously 'stayed' Youth Authority commitment." (*Ibid.*) Where the court predetermines the outcome of a hearing without "a complete reassessment of dispositional issues in light of then-prevailing circumstances," it fails to exercise "a discretion conferred and compelled by law," thereby depriving the minor of a fair hearing and fundamental procedural rights. (*Id.* at pp. 1087-1091, 12 Cal. Rptr. 2d 875.)

We find the reasoning of *Ronnie P.* applicable in the instant case. While it is true the juvenile court gave some consideration to the inefficacy of the minor's "prior commitments," the court's statement also demonstrates that its dispositional order was premised, at least in part, upon improper factors (i.e., the banishment condition and the unnoticed charge of failing to report to the probation officer) as well as an unauthorized sentence. . . . For the above-stated reasons, we cannot uphold the dispositional order.

Our comments should not be read as expressing any opinion concerning the appropriate disposition on remand. We mean only to inform the trial court that its order must be based upon an independent review of the dispositional issues, including the efficacy of less restrictive dispositions, the safety and protection of the public, and the best interest of the minor.

IV. Disposition

The order is reversed and the matter remanded for further proceedings consistent with the views expressed herein.

Notes

1. An unresolved issue in juvenile dispositions is whether and to what extent the court has the power to prohibit a delinquent from associating with certain people or groups.

The American Bar Association requires a condition of probation pertaining to association to be reasonably related to rehabilitation and not unduly restrictive of the juvenile's liberty. STANDARDS FOR PROBATION § 3.2(b). However, most states give judges broad discretion to determine what conditions are appropriate for the rehabilitation of the delinquent juvenile. A further question is what degree of contact with a particular person or group violates an association condition of probation. For more information on both of these issues and related case law, see Annotation, *Propriety of Conditioning Probation on Defendant's Not Associating With Particular Person*, 99 A.L.R.3D 967 (1980).

2. A judge must be careful not to tread on a juvenile's First Amendment rights when conditioning the juvenile's probation on not associating with certain individuals or groups. As illustrated in *In re Babak S.*, *supra*, attorneys are likely to argue that the juvenile's freedom of speech and freedom to associate with others are violated by an association condition. Another First Amendment right that the condition of association may tread upon is the freedom of religion. In *In the Matter of A.H.*, 459 A.2d 1045 (D.C. 1983), the trial court conditioned the juvenile's probation on her not associating with a certain Islamic sect that promoted violence in the name of Allah. The juvenile appealed and claimed that the condition violated her religious freedom. The court disagreed and affirmed the condition.

Questions

1. The *Babak* court raises the question of what *mens rea* a juvenile must possess to violate a condition of probation that prohibits a juvenile from associating with a large group of people. Even though Babak argued that he thought Lonnie was "cleared of probation," the court held that it could be inferred that Babak had associated with a known probationer. Do you agree with the court's decision? How does the *Babak* court's decision further the goals of juvenile law?

2. States often require judges to order juvenile dispositions that relate to the crime committed. Should a judge have the power to order a disposition which relates to the crime committed, in addition to unrelated concerns the court may have about the juvenile?

Problem

A judge found Joe delinquent for his role in a non-gang related robbery. The predispositional report detailed Joe's previous arrest for possession of marijuana. The report also revealed that Joe is a member of a street gang but does not regularly associate with the gang and its members. Because of increasing gang violence among juveniles in the city, the judge expressed concern about Joe's ties with a street gang. Can the judge prohibit Joe's association with gang members as a condition of probation for the non-gang related robbery? If the report noted that the robbery was the most recent in a series of non-gang related crimes committed by Joe since becoming a gang member, can the judge use Joe's history of delinquent behavior to justify banning Joe's association with his gang? What possible constitutional arguments might Joe use to argue against such a disposition?

5. Home Supervision

In re Curtis T.

263 Cal. Rptr. 296 (Cal. Ct. App. 1989)

KREMER, Presiding Justice

Curtis T. admitted an allegation he possessed stereo equipment with obliterated serial numbers in violation of Penal Code section 537e and was declared a ward of the court. (Welf. & Inst. Code, § 602.) On appeal, Curtis contends the court erred in denying his suppression motion.

FACTS

On May 3, 1988, a petition was filed alleging Curtis had unlawfully possessed cocaine. He was placed on home supervision pursuant to a home supervision agreement signed by Curtis and his mother. On Friday, May 13, 1989, Assistant Deputy Probation Officer Charlotte Welch, who was assigned to the home supervision detail, called Curtis's home and asked to speak with him.

She spoke to his mother who told her Curtis was not at home. This violated the terms of Curtis's home supervision agreement. Welch stated she would come by the following morning to pick up Curtis and take him to juvenile hall for violating his home supervision.

At about 9 a.m. Saturday morning, Welsh and another probation officer accompanied by La Mesa Police Officer Ozeroff and his partner went to Curtis's house to arrest him for violating the conditions of his home supervision. . . .

Curtis's mother answered the door and invited the officers into the living room. The mother and Officer Ozeroff testified that once inside the house, the mother said she would be back out with Curtis in a moment. The mother testified several times she specifically asked the officers to wait in the living room for her to awaken Curtis and bring him from his bedroom into the living room. Officer Ozeroff testified he told the mother he wanted to go with her because he was afraid Curtis might flee. The mother, after opening the door to the bedroom, stepped aside, letting the officers enter first. She testified she felt she had no choice but to let the officers enter the room.

* * *

Once in the bedroom, Officer Ozerff noticed some car stereo equipment piled on the floor. It struck him as unusual to have so much equipment in one place. He also noticed the wires on an AM/FM car radio had been cut. The manner in which the wires had been cut, all to the same length, and his past experience led Officer Ozeroff to believe the stereo had been stolen from a car. Accordingly, Officer Ozeroff picked up the stereo to check the serial number and run a computer check on it. The serial number, however, had been obliterated. He then examined two other pieces of stereo equipment for serial numbers and found another obliterated serial number. The serial number on the last item was intact and the item had not been reported stolen.

Curtis moved to suppress the evidence, contending the officers had no right to enter his bedroom and no right to search the stereo equipment. He presented evidence his mother had told the officers to wait in the living room, that the stereo equipment had been covered with towels at the time the officers entered the room and that his mother had protested Officer Ozeroff's lack of a search warrant when Ozeroff picked up the car radio to examine it. Curtis also contended the condition of his home supervision stating the probation officer "shall have access to the minor and the minor's school attendance records at all times" did not justify the officers' intrusion into the bedroom.

The trial court denied the suppression motion. Immediately following the court's denial of his suppression motion, Curtis admitted the allegation of the petition.

DISCUSSION

Curtis contends the home supervision condition, stating the probation officer "shall have access to the minor . . . at all times" did not justify the officers' entry into his bedroom nor act as a waiver to his or his parents' expectation of privacy.

Home supervision is " . . . a program in which persons who would otherwise be detained in the juvenile hall are permitted to remain in their homes pending court disposition of their cases, under the supervision of a deputy probation officer, probation aid, or probation volunteer." (§ 840.) As a condition of home supervision, the minor is required to sign a written promise that he understands and will observe specific conditions of home supervision release. (§ 628.1.) If the minor violates one of the specified conditions of home supervision release contained in his written promise to obey, then he may be taken into custody and placed in secure detention, subject to court review at a detention hearing. (*Ibid.*) The minor, while on home supervision, is "entitled to the same legal protections as a minor in secure detention, including a detention hearing." (*Ibid.*) A probation officer, aide, community worker or volunteer is assigned to the minor "to assure that the minor obeys the conditions of his release and commits no public offenses pending final disposition of his case." (§ 841.)

In arguing the "access" condition of home supervision authorized the officers' entry into Curtis's bedroom, the Attorney General argues the situation here is similar to a search conducted pursuant to a condition of probation or parole. It is true, the home supervision program has some similarity to probation and parole, in the sense that the minor's release to home supervision (rather than detention in a secure facility) is conditional, but there are also some important differences. In the probation and parole cases cited by the Attorney General, the defendants expressly consented to searches of their person, cars, homes and property without a warrant. In contrast, here, the condition does not specifically authorize search of Curtis's house; instead it refers only to allowing the probation officer "access to the minor."

In construing the scope of this condition, we find instructive the [California] Supreme Court's analysis in *People v. Bravo* (1987) 43 Cal. 3d 600, 238 Cal. Rptr 282, 738 P.2d 336, *certiorari denied* 485 U.S. 904[, 108 S. Ct. 1074, 99 L. Ed. 2d 234]. In the *Bravo* case, the Supreme Court rejected an argument a probation condition waiving Fourth Amendment protections should be narrowly construed. The court noted the cases apply a strict standard to waivers of constitutional rights generally (*see, e.g.*, *Johnson v. Zerbst* (1938) 394 U.S. 458, 58 S. Ct. 1019, 82 L. Ed. 1461, rejecting implied waivers and requiring a waiver be both knowing and intelligent) but do not strictly construe waivers of Fourth Amendment protection, e.g., consent to searches. The *Bravo* court looked to the United States Supreme Court's decision in *Schneckloth v. Bustamonte* (1973) 412 U.S. 218, 93 S. Ct. 2041, 36 L. Ed. 2d 854 where the Supreme Court stated:

> There is a vast difference between those rights that protect a fair criminal trial and the rights guaranteed under the Fourth Amendment. Nothing, either in the purposes behind requiring a "knowing" and "intelligent" waiver of trial rights, or in the practical application of such a requirement suggests that it ought to be extended to the constitutional guarantee against unreasonable searches and seizures. . . .
>
> The protections of the Fourth Amendment are of a wholly different order, and have nothing whatever to do with promoting the fair ascertainment of truth at a criminal trial. . . . The guarantees of the Fourth Amendment stand "as a protection of quite different consti-

> tutional values—values reflecting the concern of our society for the right of each individual to be let alone. . . ." [Citation.] Nor can it even be said that a search, as opposed to an eventual trial, is somehow "unfair" if a person consents to a search. . . . And, like those constitutional guarantees that protect a defendant at trial, it cannot be said every reasonable presumption ought to be indulged against voluntary relinquishment."

(*Id.* at pp. 241-243, 93 S. Ct. at pp. 2055-2056.)

* * *

Like the search condition involved in the *Bravo* case, the access condition involved here implicates Fourth Amendment concerns. Accordingly, we believe the objective test delineated in the *Bravo* case applies here rather than a strict scrutiny test. We conclude a reasonable person would understand the language of the access condition to permit the entry into Curtis's bedroom.

The purpose of the access condition is to ensure the minor complies with his written promises. Since the home supervision agreement contemplates the minor will be at home (unless he is at another permitted location such as a school or place of employment), the probation officer in charge of the home supervision must necessarily have access to the minor in his home. Reasonably, this access would extend to the place in the home normally occupied by the minor, i.e., his bedroom.

Curtis contends the condition required only that he present himself upon demand to the probation officer or that his parents produce him upon request. The condition Curtis and his parents agreed to, however, does not state Curtis must "present " himself upon request, or that his mother must "produce" him on request; the condition states the probation officer "shall have access to the minor . . . at all times." Reasonably interpreted, this language means the probation officer has a right of immediate access and does not have to wait for him to present himself or for the parents to produce him. Curtis gives the condition an unduly strict interpretation.

* * *

We conclude the officers' entry into Curtis's bedroom was authorized by the access condition of his home supervision agreement.[3]

---

3 The Attorney General also argues the entry was justified by consent to enter given by the mother. The Attorney General acknowledges there was a conflict in the evidence below (i.e., whether the mother asked the officers to wait in the living room or invited them to follow her to Curtis's bedroom) and concedes the trial court did not base its ruling on this ground but argues we should reject the evidence the mother did not consent because the court disbelieved the mother on another point. In other words, the Attorney General asks us to weigh the evidence and to judge the credibility of witnesses in a way the trial court might have done but did not, in fact, do. This we may not do.

Notes

1. Even though the states remain divided as to whether a probation officer has immediate access to a juvenile even if not specified as a condition of the juvenile's probation, most jurisdictions agree that a juvenile must submit to a warrantless search if it is a specified condition of probation. If a juvenile agrees to warrantless searches as a condition of probation, then the juvenile should expect to be searched at anytime. *See* Phillip E. Hassman, Annotation, *Validity of Requirement That, As Condition of Probation, Defendant Submit to Warrantless Searches,* 79 A.L.R.3D 1083 (1977).

2. Several arguments supportive of warrantless searches of juvenile probationers can be made. For example, if the juvenile knows a search may take place at anytime, he or she is not likely to violate the conditions of probation or engage in criminal activity for fear of being caught. Another argument used by jurisdictions supportive of warrantless searches is that due to their status, juvenile probationers enjoy only conditional liberties subject to court determined restrictions. *See* Lidia Stiglich, Comment, *Fourth Amendment Protection for Juvenile Probationers in California, Slim or None?:* In re Tyrell J., 22 HASTINGS CONST. L.Q. 893, 895 n.10 (1995).

3. Some state legislatures have passed laws allowing probation officers to search the dwellings and automobiles of adult and juvenile probationers without advance notice. For example, the Ohio legislature created "Operation Nightlight" which allows probation officers to make surprise visits to the homes of delinquent juveniles. Marjorie Millman, in her note *Juveniles Staying Cool After School,* 26 OHIO N.U. L. REV. 141 (2000), stated that the Ohio legislature created "Operation Nightlight" to verify that juveniles adhere to the condition(s) of the probation. Juvenile compliance with conditions of probation imposed by courts have increased fifty percent since "Operation Nightlight" took effect. *Id.* at 141.

Questions

1. The Stiglich comment, *supra* Note 2, noted in California that the standard for a reasonable search of a probationer is much less than the normal citizen. Should other jurisdictions follow California's lead and apply a different standard for searches of juvenile probationers? What constitutional implications might exist if a probation officer has the power to search a juvenile probationer's body and residence without a search warrant? Should courts place limits on the scope of what they would consider to be an acceptable warrantless search of a juvenile on probation? If so, what limits should exist?

2. In a jurisdiction that follows the *Curtis* holding, juveniles would be subject to warrantless searches in either their own homes or in state confinement. Should juveniles be afforded more constitutional protection while under home supervision than in state confinement? Is the rehabilitative function of juvenile law served by allowing probation officers to make warrantless searches? If so, how should a judge weigh the juvenile's constitutional rights in light of rehabilitation?

6. Drug Testing

In re Kacy S.

80 Cal. Rptr. 2d 432 (Cal. Ct. App. 1998)

PUGLIA, Associate Justice.

The minor, Daren S., admitted he was within the provisions of Welfare and Institutions Code section 602 in that he challenged a person in a public place to a fight. The minor, Kacy S., the brother of Daren, admitted he was within the provisions of Welfare and Institutions Code section 602 in that, in a public place, he used offensive words which were inherently likely to provoke an immediate, violent reaction. The minors were not removed from the physical custody of their parents but were placed on six months' probation on the conditions they each "submit to urine testing to determine the presence of alcohol and illegal drugs in [their] system[s] pursuant to section 729.3 of the Welfare and Institutions Code. . . ."

The minors appeal, contending imposition of the urine testing condition was improper . . . . [W]e shall affirm the judgment as to each minor.

After school hours on October 18, 1995, Tim Gallagher, a teacher at Quincy High School, observed an argument between Wyatt O. and Jason B. Gallagher and told Daren, Kacy and Jason to leave the area. Rather than leave, Daren became involved in a physical altercation with Wyatt. When Gallagher attempted to break up the fight, Kacy stepped in front of him with arms outstretched, preventing him from intervening. Kacy was not involved in the physical altercation but continuously yelled profanities at teaching staff and students.

I

The minors contend the juvenile court abused its discretion in imposing a urine testing condition because neither their offenses nor their social histories suggest substance abuse. Moreover, they assert the condition violates their constitutional rights to privacy, protection from unreasonable searches and seizures, due process of law and equal protection.[1] None of these claims has merit.

The authority to require urine testing as a condition of probation is conferred by Welfare and Institutions Code section 729.3 which provides; "If a minor is found to be a person described in Section 601 or 602 and the court does

---

1 At the probation hearing, Daren's counsel stated her client "has no objection to the testing," but nevertheless voiced her "personal belief" that the condition lacked any basis in the record. Because counsel's remarks brought the matter to the juvenile court's attention and gave it an opportunity to change its ruling, the purpose of the rule requiring objections to probation conditions has been satisfied. . . . We thus consider Daren's argument on the merits.

not remove the minor from the physical custody of his or her parent or guardian, the court, as a condition of probation, *may require the minor to submit to urine testing* upon the request of a peace officer or probation officer for the purpose of determining the presence of alcohol or drugs." (Italics added.) By providing that the court "may" require urine testing, section 729.3 commits the decision to order testing in a particular case to the juvenile court's discretion.

The minors contend that notwithstanding section 729.3, "the decision to impose urine testing in a case which does not involve use of drugs or alcohol, or in which the social history of the juvenile indicates no drug or alcohol use, constitutes an abuse of discretion." Our task is simply to construe, not amend, the statute. We may not under the guise of construction, rewrite section 729.3 or, as the minors propose, ignore the plain meaning of its terms.

* * *

"In *People v. Lent* (1975) 15 Cal.3d 481, 124 Cal. Reptr. 905, 541 P.2d 545, the court determined [a] condition of probation will not be held invalid unless it (1) has no relationship to the crime of which the offender was convicted, (2) relates to conduct which is not in itself criminal, and (3) requires or forbids conduct which is not reasonably related to future criminality. . . ." (*In re Laylah K.* (1991) 229 Cal. App. 3d 1496, 1500, 281 Cal. Rptr. 6.)

The urine testing condition is designed to detect the presence of substances whose use by minors *is unlawful*. (Cal. Const. Art. XX, § 22 [alcohol]; Health & Saf. Code, § 11000 et seq. [drugs].) Thus, the testing "relates to conduct which is . . . in itself criminal." (*Lent, supra,* 15 Cal. 3d at p. 486, 124 Cal. Rptr. 905, 541 P.2d 545). Moreover, in enacting section 729.3, the Legislature has found that "alcohol and drug abuse" are "precursors of serious criminality. . . ." (Stats. 1989, ch. 1117, § 1, sud. (A)(2)). Thus, the testing is also "reasonably related to future criminality." (*Lent, supra,* 15 Cal. 3d at p. 486, 124 Cal. Rptr. 905, 541 P.2d 545.) Because the testing condition relates to criminal conduct and is reasonably related to future criminality, its imposition is within the juvenile court's discretion even as measured by the *Lent* formulation.

The minors contend that, by authorizing testing where alcohol and drugs are not implicated in their offenses or social histories, section 928.3 unconstitutionally invades their privacy and subjects them to unreasonable search and seizure (U.S. Const 4th Amend; Cal. Const. Art. I, § 13.)

The collection and testing of urine intrudes upon expectations of privacy that society has long recognized as reasonable; these intrusions are searches under the Fourth Amendment. (*Skinner v. Railway labor Exec. Assn.* (1989) 489 US. 602, 617, 109 S. Ct. 1402 1413, 103 L. Ed. 2d 639, 660.) Whether a particular search and seizure is unreasonable "is judged by balancing its intrusion on the individual's Fourth Amendment interests against its promotion of legitimate governmental interests." (*Id.* at 619, 109 S. Ct. at p. 1414, 103 L. Ed. 2d at p. 661; citations and internal quotations omitted.) "On one side of the balance are arrayed the individual's legitimate expectations of privacy and personal security; on the other, the government's need for effective methods to deal with breaches of public order." (*New Jersey v. T.L.O.* (1985) 469 U.S. 325, 337, 105 S. Ct. 733, 740, 83 L. Ed. 2d 720, 731-732.)

Although urine tests are not physically intrusive (*Skinner, supra,* 489 U.S. at p. 626, 109 S. Ct. at p. 1418, 103 L. Ed. 2d at p. 665), collection of the samples under the direct observation of a monitor to ensure their integrity does implicate protected privacy interests. (*Id.* at 626, 109 S. Ct. at p. 1418, 103 L. Ed. 2d at p. 666.) However, a probationer's expectations of privacy are diminished by his probation status and are subordinated to governmental activities which reasonably limit the right of privacy. (*In re Tyrell J.* (1994) 8 Cal. 4th 68, 85, 32 Cal. Rptr. 2d 33, 876 P.2d 519).

The testing condition is a reasonable intrusion upon a probationer's expectations of privacy. (*Skinner, supra,* 489 U.S. at p 628, 109 S. Ct. at p. 1419, 103 L. Ed. 2d at p. 667.) The governmental interest in testing is strong. The juvenile court's goals are to protect the public and rehabilitate the minor. Section 729.3 serves both goals. It protects the public by establishing procedures to deter or prevent use of alcohol and unlawful drugs by minors. It advances the rehabilitation of young offenders by seeking to detect alcohol or drug use as a precursor of criminal activity in order to facilitate intervention at the earliest time. Although urine testing constitutes an intrusion on privacy, the effect of the intrusion is outweighed by the government's legitimate interest in closely monitoring the rehabilitation of minors who are granted probation and returned to the custody of their parents. (*Skinner, supra,* 489 U.S. at p. 617, 109 S. Ct. at p. 1413, 103 L. Ed. 2d at pp. 659-660).

The minors contend that, by allowing testing even where there is no previous involvement with alcohol and drugs, section 729.3 is arbitrary, capricious and thus violative of substantive due process.

As noted, section 729.3 is designed to detect conduct that is a precursor of criminal activity at the earliest possible time. Early intervention has a "real and substantial relation to the object sought to be attained" (*Nebbia v. New York* (1934) 291 U.S. 502, 525, 54 S. Ct. 505, 510, 78 L. Ed. 940, 950), because "[t]he young offender who exhibits the symptoms of future delinquency presents the most significant potential for rehabilitation. . . ." (Stats. 1989, ch. 1117, § 1, subd. (A)(3).) In contrast, delaying testing until after the minor's alcohol or drug abuse has contributed to recidivist criminal conduct would diminish the prospects of rehabilitation. Section 729.3 represents a reasonable legislative response to a serious social problem and thus does not violate substantive due process.

* * *

[The dissenting opinion of Justice BLEASE is omitted.]

Notes

1. For many years, the courts viewed probation for adults or juveniles as an "act of grace." *See* WAYNE LAFAVE, SEARCH AND SEIZURE § 10.10(a) (1987). The theory that probation was an act of grace formed the basis for courts to hold that a drug test is an implied condition of probation. Courts could only imply a drug test as a condition of probation if the purposes of the probation were rehabilitation of the offender, protection of the community, and deterrence. *See United States v. Tonry*, 605 F.2d 144, 155 (5th Cir. 1979); *United States v. Consuelo-Gonzalez,* 521 F.2d 259, 265 (9th Cir. 1975). When the probationer accepted probation, the court considered it as an implied acceptance of drug testing as a condition of the probation. In *Griffin v. Wisconsin*, 483 U.S. 868 (1987), however, the U.S. Supreme Court later rejected the idea that acceptance of probation implied acceptance of drug testing as a condition of probation. The Court held that warrants and the probable cause requirement were not needed in probation because drug testing met the "special needs" exception to the Fourth Amendment. *Id.* at 873 (citing *New Jersey v. T.L.O.*, 469 U.S. 325, 251 (1985)). The special needs of probation rendered both warrants and probable cause impracticable. For a critique of *Griffin,* see Cathryn Jo Rosen, *The Fourth Amendment Implications of Urine Testing for Evidence of Drug Use in Probation,* 55 BROOK. L. REV. 1159, 1199-1201 (1990). Today, most drug tests of probationers are done without any suspicion of the probationer using drugs. *Id.* at 1205.

2. States justify the use of drug testing as a condition of probation using various rationales. Some states allow drug testing for deterrence and treatment. *See* Cathryn Jo Rosen & John S. Goldkamp, *The Constitutionality of Drug Testing at the Bail Stage,* 80 J. CRIM. L. & CRIMINOLOGY 114 (1989). Random testing serves either a rehabilitative or prevention purpose because it discourages probationers from using drugs. Other states like South Carolina use drug testing of probationers to detect possible drug use and indicate which probationers may need drug treatment in the future. Rosen, *supra*, at 1176. A state may also use urine tests to bolster its claim that probation should be revoked for non drug-related reasons. *Id.* at 1177.

3. Most jurisdictions follow the rule that using drug testing as a condition of probation does not violate the probationer's constitutional rights when the probationer was convicted of a drug-related crime or the probationer has a documented record of drug abuse. *See, e.g., State v. Fetterkoff*, 739 S.W.2d 573 (Mo. Ct. App. 1989); *Vento v. State*, 724 S.W.2d 948 (Tex. Ct. App. 1987). However, jurisdictions remain split as to the propriety of conditioning probation on drug testing when the probationer did not commit a drug-related crime and has no documented record of drug abuse. In *Carswell v. State*, 721 N.E.2d 1255 (Ind. Ct. App. 1999), a probationer was convicted of child molestation. The probationer had no history of drug abuse and the molestation was not drug-related. The court affirmed the trial court's decision to impose drug testing as a condition of probation because possession of drugs is illegal and abstinence was reasonably related to the protection of children and the probationer's rehabilitation. However, a California court in *People v. Keller*, 143 Cal. Rptr. 184 (Ct. App. 1978), held that a trial court abused its discretion to impose drug testing as a condition of probation for a probationer with no documented drug abuse history and whose crime was not drug-related.

4. Most jurisdictions recognize that courts have broad discretion to impose conditions of probation on a delinquent juvenile. In *In re Jimi A.*, 257 Cal. Rptr. 147 (Ct. App. 1989), the court affirmed the propriety of the trial court imposing drug testing as a condition of probation because the delinquent was found guilty of a drug-related crime. The court noted, however, that courts in general have broader discretion to impose drug testing as a condition of probation on a delinquent juvenile than on an adult convicted of a crime in general. The court reasoned that the courts need broader discretionary power over juvenile probation conditions because drug testing services a rehabilitative function. In *In re Jose R.,* 186 Cal. Rptr. 898 (Ct. App. 1982), the court affirmed the trial court's decision to impose drug testing as a condition of probation on a juvenile even though the juvenile had no documented history of drug abuse and the delinquent act was not drug-related. The court ruled that the trial court did not abuse its discretion because the juvenile's home surroundings were drug-infested. The court further held that imposing drug testing as a condition of probation was appropriate in light of the minor's social history and the legislature's desire to curb drug use.

Questions

The court in *Jimi A.* noted that courts have greater discretionary power in imposing conditions of probation for delinquent juveniles. The court seems to suggest that a court can impose drug testing as a condition of probation if it serves a rehabilitative function. Does this give too much power to juvenile courts, or is this discretion necessary to rehabilitate delinquent youth? If you were a judge in a delinquency case, what factors might you consider when asked to impose drug testing as a condition of a juvenile's probation? As juvenile law becomes more punitive in nature, will drug testing as a condition of probation serve more of a rehabilitative or punitive purpose in delinquency cases?

Problem

A juvenile court recently found Jessica delinquent for vandalizing public property when she spray-painted expletives on a fire station. Jessica has no recorded history of drug abuse nor did she commit the delinquent act while under the influence of drugs. All six of Jessica's older adult brothers and sisters began to abuse drugs after they moved out of their parents' home, which is in a drug-infested neighborhood. Jessica's parents are very protective of her and constantly remind Jessica not to follow her older siblings' example and abuse drugs. Jessica does not associate with any drug abusers and is the vice-president of her high school's S.A.D.D. (Students Against Drunk Driving) chapter. As a judge, which of these factors would you consider when deciding whether or not to impose drug testing as a condition of Jessica's probation? Are there factors other than those mentioned above that you would want to know more about? As a prosecutor, what conditions of probation (including other conditions you have studied in this chapter) would you recommend to the court?

7. Church Attendance

L.M. v. State
610 So. 2d 1314 (Fla. Dist. Ct. App. 1992)

ZAHMER, Judge

L. M., a child, appeals an order of disposition based on his commission of a delinquent act. He contends that the condition of community control requiring him to obey all lawful and reasonable demands of his mother, *including participation in church youth programs*, is unlawful. We do not agree and affirm.

In December, 1990, L.M., then age 13, was charged with petit theft and burglary. He entered pleas of guilty to the petit theft charge and guilty to the lesser offense of trespassing in the burglary case. The trial court ordered a predisposition investigation prior to sentencing. The resulting predisposition report included information related by L.M.'s mother to the delinquency case management counselor. She stated that she had been having problems with L.M. for several years. L.M. would not listen or do as he was told. She often has disciplined L.M., usually by placing him on restriction. She had quit her night job because L.M. would not stay at home and she felt he was too old for a baby sitter. . . . L.M. has made poor grades in school (receiving all F's during the first two grading quarters of the 7th grade), and often has been referred to the Dean's office for disciplinary problems. He has not done his homework, has used profanity toward his teachers, has been in fights, has lied, and often has been suspended. . . . The report also reflected that L.M. was previously charged with arson, retail theft, and . . . larceny; adjudication was withheld in the arson and retail theft cases. . . . He was adjudicated delinquent in the petit larceny case and placed on . . . community control. The counselor's report concluded by stating that L.M. was showing signs of ungovernable behavior, and "unless firm actions are imposed, his mother will probably lose control."

At the disposition hearing on February 20, 1991, the trial court noted that the mother was affiliated with New Friendship Baptist Church and asked her whether L.M. was affiliated or involved in any youth or other church programs. She replied that he was not. Later in the hearing, the following colloquy occurred:

> THE COURT: Is there any program at your church that is there, a youth program at your church?
>
> THE MOTHER: Yes, it is but he doesn't want to go.
>
> THE COURT: Okay. All right. I'm going to—I'm going to adjudicate him to be delinquent; I'm going to commit him to level 2; I'm going to require that he go to the JMI program and successfully complete it. And I want—I'm serious about that if he's not—if he's messing up I want him to be violated; okay? If you mess up I'm going to put you either in the Stop-Step or in training school. Do you understand that?
>
> THE CHILD: Yes, sir.
>
> THE COURT: Probably training school because I'll be pretty disappointed by that time. Also, I'm going to require that he enroll in

> and that he successfully participate in any and all youth programs they have at your church. I want you to get with the pastor.

The trial court entered written orders of adjudication and commitment, and specified as a condition of community control that L.M. "Obey all lawful and reasonable demands of guardian and assigned counselor" and "mother shall enroll child in youth programs at church."

L.M. appealed the validity of the community control condition that L.M. "Get with the pastor" of his mother's church and enroll in any and all of its youth programs. We held this condition invalid because it required a community controllee to submit to a course of religious instruction in contravention of the First Amendment. *In the Interest of L.M. v. State*, 587 So. 2d 648 (Fla. 1st DCA 1991). We explained that this condition unlawfully "delegate[d] to the pastor of a church the judicial function of determining those programs best suited to meet [L.M.'s] rehabilitation needs." *Id.* at 649. The opinion further stated, however, that on remand the trial court could impose alternate conditions of community control, including the requirement that L.M. attend youth programs of secular content.

In the meantime, L.M. had committed another act of delinquency, and a consolidated hearing was held in the remanded case with the new prosecution on a charge of loitering and prowling. L.M. pleaded guilty to this new charge. . . . At that point, the court realized that L.M.'s term of community control for the previous cases had already expired. The attorneys agreed that the court need not amend those sentences on remand, and that the court need only sentence L.M. for the new offense. The hearing continued:

> THE COURT: . . . I'm going to place him—I'm going to adjudicate him delinquent, place him on community control. Now, these are the conditions of your community control. Number one, you must perform forty-five hours—this is a second degree?
>
> MS. STEELY [L.M.'s ATTORNEY]: Yes, sir.
>
> THE COURT: Forty-five hours of community service within the next forty-five days. Number two, you must obey all reasonable rules of your mother and, your HRS counselor. Do you understand, sir?
>
> THE CHILD: Yes, sir.
>
> THE COURT: Number three, you must—you're under a curfew—how old are you?
>
> THE CHILD: Fourteen.
>
> THE COURT: You're under a curfew of 7:00 o'clock every evening. You must be back in the home by 7:00 o'clock every evening. Do you understand, sir?
>
> THE CHILD: Yes, sir.
>
> THE COURT: There's no roaming the streets and the only exception is for school or church activities or if you're somewhere with you[r] mother. Do you understand, sir?
>
> THE CHILD: Yes, sir.
>
> THE COURT: Now, also, I'm going to require—I'm going to try this a little bit different this time. I'm going to require that you obey all the reasonable demands of your parent including participating in

community or church programs to be chosen by your mother. Do you understand that, sir?

THE CHILD: Yes, sir.

THE COURT: And I'll put the exact wording in the order. Is there any other request from the State or the defense?

MR. METZGER [Co-Counsel for L.M.]: Are you referring specifically to church youth programs that are of a secular content?

THE COURT: . . .That will be up to the mother what programs he attends. Also, I would allow them to use the time that he puts into those youth programs as community service. That can count as credit for his community service hours. All right. Is [sic] there any other requests—did I say obey all the reasonable rules of your mother and your HRS counselor and obey all laws. Any other requests from the State or defense?

MR. METZGER: We're going to object at this point to the condition that he attend youth programs whether through the church or not, as directed by his mother. Frankly, I think that violates the order that the District Court of Appeals has entered in his other cases. One of the things they say in that opinion and I'll quote from it is, "The condition is also erroneous in that it delegates to the pastor of the church the judicial function of determining those programs best for the child suited to meet Appellant's Rehabilitation needs. *See Singleton v. State.*" That's error. What you did is exactly one of the things that they point out in the other case, is allowing someone else to determine what particular programs it is that he would be involved with.

The second problem with it is now that you're providing that he go to a program that his mother picks, his mother may pick a program at the church. She would therefore be supported by the Court in requiring him to attend that because he can be violated if he chooses not to attend. We have no indication that the programs that the mother may pick will have a nonreligious nature. They must be secular in nature. That's one of the things that the L.M. decision says, you can't order somebody into programs that have religious content to them. You violated what the DCA has already reversed you on.

THE COURT: Well, this is quite a different order here and what I'm saying is the parent can choose and I think there is a presumption under the Florida law that the parent does have control over their [sic] child while he is a minor. I'm not delegating to a church official. I'm delegating to the mother who already has the control over her son to begin with. So, this is the order and you all are welcome to appeal it.

The written order of disposition entered pursuant to this hearing contains the following condition: "obey all lawful and reasonable demands of the mother, including, but not limited to participation in civic, school, church and/or community youth programs, if the mother directs." The order further requires the mother to report any violations of the conditions of community control to the assigned HRS counselor.

On this appeal, L.M. challenges the validity of the quoted condition on three grounds. . . .

L.M. next argues that the questioned condition must be reversed because it amounts to an improper delegation of judicial authority to L.M.'s mother to determine what particular youth programs or activities L.M. will be required to attend. In support of this argument he cites *M.A.R. v. State*, 433 So. 2d 29, 30 (Fla. 5th DCA), *pet. for rev. denied*, 441 So. 2d 632 (Fla. 1983) (condition of probation "to make restitution for the damages to the vehicle 'under terms and conditions specified by H.R.S.' " held erroneous delegation of authority); *Singleton v. State,* 582 So. 2d 657, 658 (Fla. 1st DCA 1991) (error to delegate to probation officer authority to determine whether defendant "'will seek evaluation and treatment under the sexual offender program'"); and *L.M. v. State*, 587 So. 2d 648 (error to delegate to pastor of church authority to direct probationer to enroll in religious youth program).

We note that neither these cases nor any of the additional cases cited in L.M.'s reply brief involve an issue of unlawful delegation of judicial authority to a child's parent incident to a specific condition of community control. As the trial judge did below, and as the state now argues to us, we perceive a significant difference between, on the one hand, the matter of delegating judicial authority to a probation officer by requiring obedience to the officer's lawful demands to participate in a particular program, and on the other hand, requiring a delinquent child to obey parental directions, which may include the child's participation in church youth programs or activities. In the first case, the court must specify which programs the child is to attend. In the latter case, the court has not specified participation in any particular program, but leaves that matter to the discretion of the parents as natural guardians having custody of the child.

In this case it is readily apparent that the court, HRS, and the mother are concerned that this young boy be made to interact with society in a manner that will teach him acceptable social and moral values before his antisocial attitude and conduct mold him into a hardened criminal. The court is attempting to accomplish this by not placing the child in a secured environment void of parental love and care. Rather, the court has recognized that the mother is the natural guardian of L.M., and has left L.M. in her custody and control rather than placing him in the custody of HRS. As natural guardian, L.M.'s mother has the legal authority to direct that he participate or not participate in various youth programs or activities in accordance with her legal obligation to do those things that are in the child's best interests. Thus it is neither unreasonable nor illegal for the court to require L.M. to obey the "lawful and reasonable" demands of his mother in respect to his daily activities. None of the cases cited to us deals with the validity of a condition requiring a delinquent child to obey the reasonable and lawful directions of his parents, and we are aware of no statute or case law that would make such a condition invalid.

We hold, therefore, that the condition of community control in question does not constitute an unlawful delegation of judicial authority to the mother. Whether the mother's demand or direction to L.M. on a particular occasion is lawful and reasonable, such that it would support a violation of this condition should L.M. refuse to obey his mother, is a matter that can be determined only if and when a dispute arises between L.M. and his mother that leads to a charge of violation of this condition.

Our conclusion on the second point leads directly to L.M.'s third point—that the stated condition of probation requires L.M.'s participation in church programs chosen by his mother and thus violates L.M.'s rights under the First Amendment to the United States Constitution and article I, section 3, of the Florida Constitution relating to the free exercise of religion and precluding the state's power to require participation in any particular religion. He argues that this condition directly violates our decision in L.M.'s previous appeal. We disagree for the following reasons.

Inherent in parents' authority and control over their unemancipated child living in the parents' household is the parents' right to require that their child attend church with them as part of the child's religious and moral training. However, to what extent a court can or should have authority to enforce parental directions when the child refuses to obey presents significant issues that need not be decided on this record. It is plainly evident from our previous decision involving L.M. that the court cannot direct L.M. to attend a particular church or participate in specified religious instruction. But we also recognized in that case that the court could require L.M. to attend youth programs of secular content....

Whether youth programs where L.M. and his mother attend church will involve predominantly religious instruction and practice, or will be predominantly of secular content is an issue that can only be determined if and when a dispute over the validity of a particular direction or demand arises. . . . We conclude that it is more consistent with public policy and the law governing parental authority over their unemancipated child that a condition of community control requiring obedience to reasonable and lawful demand of a parent by an unemancipated child left in the custody of that parent be treated as presumptively valid. Determination of whether the child's refusal to obey a particular parental demand will support intervention by the court for a violation of this condition should be made only after a hearing at which all facts relevant and material to the nature of the demand and the child's conduct in response can be established and considered.

Affirmed.

Notes

1. A leading case concerning court usage of mandatory church attendance as a condition of juvenile probation is *Jones v. Commonwealth*, 38 S.E.2d 444 (Va. 1946). In *Jones,* two juveniles were found delinquent for throwing rocks at a sign hanging on the side of a woman's house. The trial judge gave the juveniles probation conditioned on the juveniles attending Sunday school and church each Sunday for one year. The appellate court held that requiring the juveniles to attend Sunday school and church violated the children's right of freedom of religion. The court quoted the Virginia Constitution:

> 16. That religion, or the duty which we owe to our Creator, and the manner of discharging it, can be directed only by the reason and conviction, not by force or violence; and therefore all men are created equally entitled to the free exercise of religion, according to the free exercise of religion, according to the dictates of conscience; and that it is the mutual duty of all to practice Christian forbearance, love, and charity towards each other.

Id. at 448 (citing VA. CONST. § 16).

The *Jones* court also reasoned that forcing religion onto a juvenile would not have the rehabilitative effect sought by a judge. The court found that a juvenile must freely pursue religious devotion in order for it to truly affect him. *Id.* at 449.

2. The second *L.M.* decision held that a court may not require a juvenile to take a course of religious instruction in contravention of the First Amendment. *See In the Interest of L.M. v. State,* 587 So. 2d 648 (Fla. Dist. Ct. App. 1991). The court also found that a court may require a juvenile on probation to follow his or her legal guardians' will which may include attending Sunday school and church on a weekly basis.

3. As previously noted in this section, probation restricts a juvenile's personal liberties and may deprive the juvenile of certain constitutional rights. The juvenile may appeal the condition of probation as a violation of the probationer's constitutional rights if it is not reasonably related to the purpose of rehabilitation. *See* Susan Schwarzenberger, Comment, *Juvenile Probation: Restrictions, Rights, and Rehabilitation,* 16 ST. LOUIS U. L.J. 276, 284 (1971) [hereinafter *Juvenile Probation*]; *see also In re Allen,* 78 Cal. Rptr. 207, 208 (Ct. App. 1969). Several tests can be used to determine whether or not a probation condition unduly restricts a juvenile's constitutional right. *See Juvenile Probation, supra*, at 284. A California appellate court held that the government must show:

> (1) that the conditions reasonably relate to the purposes sought by the legislation which confers the benefit; (2) that the value accruing to the public from imposition of those conditions manifestly outweighs any resulting impairment of constitutional rights; and (3) that there are available no alternative means less subversive of constitutional rights, narrowly drawn so as to correlate more closely with the purposes contemplated by conferring the benefit.

Juvenile Probation, *supra*, at 284 & n.43 (citing *In re Mannino,* 92 Cal. Rptr. 880, 889 (Ct. App. 1971).

Another test used to determine if a juvenile's constitutional rights are violated by a condition of probation is to balance the state's interests in preventing future delinquency and the rehabilitating juvenile's interest in preserving his First Amendment rights. *See* MODEL PENAL CODE § 301.1(2)(1).

Questions

1. If courts enforce the parent's dictate that the juvenile probationer attend a particular church, as in the second *L.M.* case, *supra*, at Note 2, do they violate the juvenile's freedom of religion? If court action would violate the juvenile's religious freedom, what other action(s) might the court take? *See also K.K.B. v. State*, 609 S.W.2d 824 (Tex. Civ. App. 1980) (probation condition that juvenile must obey the reasonable rules of the custodian is constitutional).

2. The second *L.M.* decision held that a court could give parents the responsibility to determine how best to rehabilitate a juvenile delinquent. What advantages and disadvantages does this alternative present? Does the parent's knowledge of the juvenile's nature and behavior outweigh the greater number of resources the court can use to rehabilitate the delinquent juvenile?

8. Restrictions on Travel

In re Pedro Q.

257 Cal. Rptr. 821 (Cal. Ct. App. 1989)

SONENSHINE, Associate Justice

Pedro Q. appeals his California Youth Authority (CYA) commitment. [W]e consider his contentions that probation conditions restricting his travel were improperly imposed by the probation officer and were, in any event, unconstitutional.

In March, 1986, Pedro was placed on juvenile probation for assault with a deadly weapon. The following terms were imposed: (1) commitment to Los Pinos Conservation Camp for nine months; (2) no association with members of "F-Troop," a Santa Ana gang to which the minor belonged; (3) participation in a program of therapy and counseling as directed; (4) submission to search and seizure; and (5) no use or possession of alcohol, drugs or dangerous weapons.

On May 18th, 1987, Pedro's probation officer, Robert Gates, added several conditions to his probation, including an 8 p.m. curfew and a directive not to be in an area bounded by First, Bristol, Raitt and McFadden Streets, the operating territory of F-Troop. Gates explained the new terms to Pedro, who stated he understood and, at Gates' request, placed his initials next to the conditions.

In June, 1987, a supplemental petition was filed charging Pedro with using PCP. On June 20, the minor admitted the petition and the dispositional hearing was set for August.

On July 13, Gates visited Pedro's residence at 10 p.m., but he was not at home. As a result, Gates informed other probation officers to arrest Pedro if they saw him in F-Troop territory.

* * *

On July 29, a supplemental petition alleged the minor violated his probation by missing curfew and traveling within the restricted area. In August the hearing on the supplemental petition was joined with the dispositional hearing on the PCP charges. On October 19, the court sustained the petition alleging the probation violations, committed the minor to CYA, and fixed the maximum confinement at 10 years and 8 months.

Pedro contends the condition restricting his travel cannot support a probation violation because it was unilaterally imposed by the probation officer. He argues the court alone has the power to modify probation by adding new terms. We agree.

It is well settled that courts may not delegate the exercise of their discretion to probation officers. Welfare and Institutions Code section 730, which authorizes juvenile courts to establish probation conditions, provides in part: "The *court* may impose and require any and all reasonable conditions that it may determine fitting and proper to the end that justice may be done and the reformation and rehabilitation of the ward enhanced." (Emphasis added.) . . . The probation officer may recommend probation terms but it is the court's responsibility to tailor the conditions specifically to each minor. "[I]n planning the conditions of appellant's supervision, the juvenile *court* must consider not only the circumstances of the crime but also the minor's social history." (*In re Todd L.* (1980) 113 Cal. App. 3d 14, 20, 169 Cal. Rptr. 625, emphasis added).

Here, the court never considered the modification restricting travel; in fact, it was never even informed of the change. Pedro was placed on probation in March, 1986; the "standard probation terms" were imposed in addition to a nine-month commitment to Los Pinos and a non-association order. Afterward, he was released to his parents' custody. In May, 1987, the probation officer met with Pedro to explain several new probation terms which included the travel restriction. The terms were written on a form entitled "Gang Violence Suppression Terms and Conditions of Probation." Those terms were devised by probation officers as part of a group effort to monitor suspected gang activities. The juvenile court was never informed of the additional probation terms, nor was a copy of the form forwarded to the court.

* * *

Probation officers have wide discretion to enforce court-ordered conditions, and directives to the probationer will not require prior court approval if they are reasonably related to previously imposed terms. This was not the case here. This was not a derivative order that flowed logically from a general term, such as an order to "violate no laws," but an altogether new term. . . . Pedro's mere presence in the prohibited area did not establish a violation of any *court* imposed condition.

In light of our decision, we need not discuss at length the minor's claim that probation conditions restricting his travel were unconstitutional. We note in passing, however, that conditions infringing on constitutional rights are not automatically invalid (*People v. White* (1979) 97 Cal. App. 3d 141, 149, 158 Cal. Rptr. 562); indeed, they will pass muster if tailored to fit the individual probationer. (*Id.* at p. 151, 1585 Cal. Rptr. 562.) For example, while a travel restriction may be proper for a minor who lives outside the gang's territory, it may be overbroad for one who lives, works or goes to school within the area. But the court alone is empowered to determine the propriety of the proposed conditions and their applicability to the individual offender.

Nevertheless, we do not overturn the court's order revoking probation. The evidence supported the court's conclusion Pedro violated his curfew on two occasions. Moreover, he admitted the charge of being under the influence of PCP. These incidents alone support the court's finding that Pedro violated his probation.

The eight months imposed for the weapons enhancement is ordered deleted; the minor's maximum confinement period in CYA is reduced to 10 years, and the abstract of judgment should be amended accordingly.

The judgment is affirmed as modified.

Notes

1. When a court conditions a juvenile's probation on where the juvenile can travel, the court infringes upon the juvenile's constitutional right of freedom of movement. There are situations, however, where a court may be justified in restricting a probationer's movement despite violating his or her constitutional rights. In *United States v. Lowe*, 654 F.2d 562 (9th Cir. 1981), the court held that restricting a probationer's First Amendment right of freedom of movement is acceptable if the probation is designed to rehabilitate the probationer and protect the public. The *Lowe* court stated that the purpose of the restriction, the degree of infringement, and the legitimate needs of law enforcement should all be taken into consideration by the court when restricting the probationer's movement. In *Oyoghok v. Anchorage,* 641 P.2d 1267 (Alaska 1982), the court considered additional factors—whether the probationer lived or worked in the restricted area and whether the probationer needed to travel through the area. *See also In re Miller*, 611 N.E.2d 451 (Ohio Ct. App. 1992) (area restriction must directly relate to the crime or serve some rehabilitative function); *In re Babak S.,* 22 Cal. Rptr. 893 (Ct. App. 1993) (condition restricting travel must be reasonably related to present or future criminality and narrowly drawn and specifically tailored to individual probationer); S. DAVIS, RIGHTS OF JUVENILES 583 (2000); Susan Schwarzenberger, Comment, *Juvenile Probation: Restrictions, Rights and Rehabilitation,* 16 ST. LOUIS U. L.J. 276, 282-83 (1971).

2. Juvenile courts often restrict a probationer's travel (1) through areas where a delinquent act was committed (*see Lowe, supra*, Note 1 (a court can restrict a probationer's movement through an area where a crime was committed); *State ex rel. Plotkin v. Department of Health and Social Services*, 217 N.W.2d 641 (Wis. 1974) (probationer cannot enter restricted area even if probationer does not commit illegal act upon return to area); *but see Edison v. State,* 709 P.2d 510 (Alaska 1983); (2) where the victim lives (*see People v. Myatt*, 681 N.Y.S.2d 114 (N.Y. App. Div. 1998) (juvenile on probation restricted from entering ten-mile diameter area around victim's house)); or (3) where the juvenile's street gang is located. (*see generally In re Pedro Q., supra;* JERRY L. MERSHON, JUVENILE JUSTICE: THE ADJUDICATORY AND DISPOSITIONAL PROCESS 91-95 (1991).

3. In the previous section, you learned that a judge may not permit a probation officer to determine what probation conditions a juvenile must follow. A court may, however, give a probation officer the power to determine when a juvenile may or may not enter a prohibited area. In *People v. Pickens*, 542 N.E.2d 1253 (Ill. App. Ct. 1989), the court held that a restriction not to enter an area without a probation officer's permission is reasonable because the probationer must have a good reason to enter the area. This allows the probationer to serve a rehabilitative function and still afford flexibility as the probation officer deems appropriate.

Questions

1. If a judge determines that a juvenile should be restricted from a certain area, how specific should the court make the condition? Should the judge have the power to restrict a juvenile from entering the immediate location of the victim as well as the locality? Would such a restriction be unduly vague and overbroad, or would it pass constitutional muster while protecting the victim from the probationer? For conflicting opinions on this issue, see *In re White*, 158 Cal. Rptr. 562 (Ct. App. 1979); *but see King v. State,* 574 So. 2d 1013 (Ala. Crim. App. 1990).

2. What other constitutional arguments (other than violation of the right to travel) might the juvenile raise to challenge conditions of probation which restrict movement?

Problem

Assume that Diana, a juvenile living with her mother, is restricted according to a condition of her probation not to enter the 1600 block of the city where the victim of Diana's battery lives. Under the condition, Diana will not be able to stay with her father on weekends because her father also lives in the same block as the victim. Will Diana's challenge to this probation condition be successful? What arguments should she make? What response by the state? What if Diana can only see her father at his home because he is bed-ridden due to illness? What if Diana swore she would try to hit her victim again if she ever saw her? How should the court assess Diana's need to see her father versus the danger Diana poses for the victim?

9. Implied Conditions

In re Litdell

232 So. 2d 733 (Miss. 1970)

SMITH, Justice:

This is an appeal from an order of the Youth Court of Montgomery County revoking the probation of Jon Henry Litdell, a delinquent minor.

In May of 1968, the court had adjudged Litdell to be a delinquent within the meaning of Mississippi Code 1942 Annotated Section 7185-09 (1952). He was not discharged but was placed on probation, in the custody of his mother.

In February of 1969, the District Attorney for Montgomery County petitioned the court to revoke Litdell's probation upon the grounds that . . . he had committed acts which would have constituted felonies if done by an adult. . . .

[The court first discusses Litdell's claim that he did not have adequate notice of his hearing. The court finds this claim to be without merit.]

As to the second ground urged for reversal, that no violation of a condition of the probation was shown, it is conceded that there had been no violation of any express condition. . . . Appellant's position . . . is that since there had been no violation of any express condition of his probation, and he had not actually been convicted of any criminal offense, the court was without power to revoke the probation or to change its conditions.

The State's response to this proposition, is, in effect, that the youth court's probation of any youth adjudged to be a delinquent carries with it an implied condition of good behavior.

The principle of implied conditions is well grounded in the law. For example, in Note, Legal Aspects of Probation Revocation, 59 Colum. L. Rev. 311, 315 (1959), there is a discussion of implied conditions in cases of probation:

> Further, it seems clear that some minimal restraints on a probationer's behavior may be implied in the nature and purposes of the probation system. *Thus, the courts have found implied conditions that the probationer must not commit a felony and that he must obey reasonable directions and orders of the trial judge or a probation officer. Apparently, conditions are implied only as to conduct which the probationer clearly should have realized might result in revocation.* (Emphasis added).

In *People v. Perez*, 243 Cal. App. 2d 528, 52 Cal. Rptr. 51, 517 (1966) the California court relied on implied conditions:

> Although the terms and conditions of the probation order are not disclosed by the record, *it is an implicit condition of every such order that the probationer refrain from engaging in any criminal activity or becoming "abandoned to improper associates or a vicious life."* (Emphasis added).

The proof here showed that Litdell, while on probation, had been taken into custody on numerous occasions by law officers in connection with various acts of misconduct, which included "car prowling," shop lifting, two incidents of assault and battery, and creating a public disturbance.

It is to be borne in mind that the Mississippi Youth Court Act provides that disposition of the child, *after adjudication*, is made by the court upon the basis of an investigation. . . .

Obviously, the youth court might have directed the placement of Litdell in a training school at the time of his adjudication as a delinquent. The court did not do this. But neither did the court "terminate its jurisdiction." Rather, the court imposed the least restraint and the mildest supervision upon Litdell in the hope that this would be sufficient. The youth court's jurisdiction of youth adjudged to be delinquent is a continuing one, with a continuing power to alter the terms of the probation if, in the interests of the child, the original arrangement proves inadequate or to have been ill advised. Without this flexibility the court no longer would be in such an advantageous position to give a delinquent youth "another chance" as an initial measure, at least, by granting probation upon terms of the least possible restraint and the mildest supervision as was done in this case.

We have concluded that, under the circumstances in the record, appellant was not denied due process and that the court had jurisdiction, as well as power, to alter the arrangement originally made in order to provide necessary supervision and control of appellant, the original arrangement having proven inadequate in both respects.

Affirmed.

C. Movement of Juveniles Across State Lines

Interstate Compact on Juveniles

ARTICLE I—*Findings and Purposes*

That juveniles who are not under proper supervision and control, or who have absconded, escaped or run away, are likely to endanger their own health, morals and welfare, and the health, morals and welfare of others. The cooperation of the states party to this compact is therefore necessary to provide for the welfare and protection of juveniles and of the public with respect to (1) cooperative supervision of delinquent juveniles on probation or parole; (2) the return, from one state to another, of delinquent juveniles who have escaped or absconded; (3) the return from one state to another, of non-dependent juveniles who have run away from home; and (4) additional measures for the protection of juveniles and of the public, which any two or more of the party states may find desirable to undertake cooperatively. In carrying out the provisions of this compact the party states shall be guided by the non-criminal, reformative and protective policies which guide their laws concerning delinquent, neglected or dependent juveniles generally. It shall be the policy of the states party to this compact to cooperate and observe their respective responsibilities for the prompt return and acceptance of juveniles and delinquent juveniles who become subject to the provisions of this contract. The provisions of this compact shall be reasonably and liberally construed to accomplish the foregoing purposes.

ARTICLE II—*Existing Rights and Remedies*

That all remedies and procedures provided by this compact shall be in addition to and not in substitution for other rights, remedies and procedures, and shall not be in derogation of parental rights and responsibilities.

ARTICLE III—*Definitions*

That, for the purposes of this compact, "delinquent juvenile" means any juvenile who has been adjudged delinquent and who, at the time the provisions of this compact are invoked, is still subject to the jurisdiction of the court that has made such adjudication or to the jurisdiction or supervision of an agency or institution pursuant to an order of such court; "probation or parole" means any kind of conditional release of juveniles authorized under the laws of the states party hereto; "court" means any court having jurisdiction over delinquent, neglected or dependent children; "state" means any state, territory or possession of the United States, the District of Columbia, and the Commonwealth of Puerto Rico; and "residence" or any variant thereof means a place at which a home or regular place of abode is maintained.

ARTICLE IV—*Return of Runaways*

(a) That the parent, guardian, person or agency entitled to legal custody of a juvenile who has not been adjudged delinquent but who has run away without the consent of such parent, guardian, person or agency may petition the proper court in demanding state for the issuance of a requisition for his return. The petition shall state the name and age of the juvenile, the name of the petitioner and the basis of entitlement to the juvenile's custody, the circumstances of his running away, his location, if known, at the time application is made, and such other facts as may tend to show that the juvenile who has run away is endangering his own welfare or the welfare of others and is not an emancipated minor. . . . The judge of the court to which this application is made may hold a hearing thereon to determine whether for the purposes of this compact the petitioner is entitled to the legal custody of the juvenile, whether or not it appears that the juvenile has in fact run away without consent, whether or not he is an emancipated minor, and whether or not it is in the best interest of the juvenile to compel his return to the state. If the judge determines, either with or without a hearing, that the juvenile should be returned, he shall present to the appropriate court or to the executive authority of the state where the juvenile is alleged to be located a written requisition for the return of such juvenile. . . . In the event that a proceeding for the adjudication of the juvenile as a delinquent, neglected or dependent juvenile is pending in the court at the time when such juvenile runs away, the court may issue a requisition for the return of such juvenile upon its motion, regardless of the consent of the parent, guardian, person or agency entitled to legal custody, reciting therein the nature and circumstances of the pending proceeding. . . . Upon reasonable information that a person is a juvenile who has run away from another state party to this compact without the consent of a parent, guardian, person or agency entitled to his legal custody, such juvenile may be taken into custody without a requisition and brought forthwith before a judge of the appropriate court who may appoint counsel or guardian ad litem for such juvenile and who shall determine after a hearing whether sufficient cause exists to hold the person, subject to the order of the court, for his own protection and welfare, for such a time not exceeding ninety (90) days as will enable his return to another state party to this compact pursuant to a requisition for his return from a court of that state. If, at the time that a state seeks the return of a juvenile who had run away, there is a pending in the state wherein he is found any criminal charge or any proceeding to have him adjudicated a delinquent juvenile for an act committed in such state, or if he is suspected of having committed within such a state a criminal offense or an act of juvenile delinquency, he shall not be returned without the consent of such state until discharged from prosecution or other form of proceeding, imprisonment, detention or supervision for such offense or juvenile delinquency. The duly accredited officers of any state party to this compact, upon the establishment of their authority and the identity of the juvenile being returned, shall be permitted to transport such juvenile through any and all states party to this compact, without interference. Upon his return to the state from which he ran away, the juvenile shall be subject to such further proceedings as may be appropriate under the laws of that state.

* * *

(c) That "juvenile" as used in this article means any person who is a minor under the law of the state of residence of the parent, guardian, person or agency entitled to the legal custody of such minor.

ARTICLE V—*Return of Escapees and Absconders*

(a) That the appropriate person or authority from whose probation or parole supervision a delinquent juvenile has absconded or from whose institutional custody he has escaped shall present to the appropriate court or to the executive authority of the state where the delinquent juvenile is alleged to be located a written requisition for the return of such delinquent juvenile. . . . Upon reasonable information that a person is a delinquent who has absconded while on probation or parole, or escaped from an institution or agency vested with his legal custody or supervision in any state party to this compact, such person may be taken into custody in any other state party to this compact without a requisition. But, in such event, he must be taken forthwith before a judge of the appropriate court, who may appoint counsel or guardian ad litem for such person and who shall determine, after a hearing, whether sufficient cause exists to hold the person subject to the order of the court for such time, not exceeding ninety (90) days, as will enable his detention under a detention order issued on a requisition pursuant to this article. If, at the time when a state seeks the return of a delinquent juvenile who has either absconded while on probation or parole or escaped from an institution or agency vested with his legal custody or supervision, there is pending in the state wherein he is detained any criminal charge or any proceeding to have him adjudicated a delinquent juvenile for an act committed in such state, or if he is suspected of having committed within such state a criminal offense or an act of juvenile delinquency, he shall not be returned without the consent of such state until discharged from prosecution or other form of proceeding, imprisonment, detention or supervision for such offense or juvenile delinquency. . . .

ARTICLE VI—*Voluntary Return Procedure*

That any delinquent juvenile who has absconded while on probation or parole, or escaped from an institution or agency vested with his legal custody or supervision in any state party to this compact, and any juvenile who has run away from any state party to this compact, who is taken into custody without a requisition in another state party to this compact under the provisions of Article IV(a) or of Article V(a), may consent to his immediate return to the state from which he absconded, escaped or ran away. Such consent shall be given by the juvenile or delinquent juvenile and his counsel or guardian ad litem if any, by executing or subscribing a writing, in the presence of a judge of the appropriate court, which states that the juvenile or delinquent juvenile and his counsel or guardian ad litem, if any, consent to his return to the demanding state. Before such consent shall be executed or subscribed, however, the judge, in the presence of counsel or guardian ad litem, if any, shall inform the juvenile or delinquent juvenile of his rights under this compact. . . .

ARTICLE VII—*Cooperative Supervision of Probationers and Parolees*

(a) That the duly constituted judicial and administrative authorities of a state party to this compact (herein called "sending state") may permit any delinquent juvenile within such state, placed on probation or parole, to reside in any other state party to this compact (herein called "receiving state") while on probation or parole, and the receiving state shall accept such delinquent juvenile, if the parent, guardian or person entitled to the legal custody of such delinquent juvenile is residing or undertakes to reside within the receiving state. Before granting such permission, opportunity shall be given to the receiving state to make such investigations as it deems necessary. The authorities of the sending state shall send to the authorities of the receiving state copies of pertinent court orders, social case studies and all other available information which may be of value to assist the receiving state in supervising a probationer or parolee under this compact. A receiving state, in its discretion, may agree to accept supervision of a probationer or parolee in cases where the parent, guardian or person entitled to the legal custody of the delinquent juvenile is not a resident of the receiving state, and if so accepted the sending state may transfer supervision accordingly.

(b) That each receiving state will assume the duties of visitation and of supervision over any such delinquent juvenile and in the exercise of those duties will be governed by the same standards of visitation and supervision that prevail for its own delinquent juveniles released on probation or parole.

(c) That, after consultation between the appropriate authorities of the sending state and of the receiving state as to the desirability and necessity of returning such a delinquent juvenile, the duly accredited officers of a sending state may enter a receiving state and there apprehend and retake any such delinquent juvenile on probation or parole. For that purpose, no formalities will be required, other than establishing the authority of the officer and the identity of the delinquent juvenile to be retaken and returned. The decision of the sending state to retake a delinquent juvenile on probation or parole shall be conclusive upon and not reviewable within the receiving state, but if, at the time the sending state seeks to retake a delinquent juvenile on probation or parole, there is pending against him within the receiving state any criminal charge or any proceeding to have him adjudicated a delinquent juvenile for any act committed in such state, or if he is suspected of having committed within such state a criminal offense or an act of juvenile delinquency, he shall not be returned without the consent of the receiving state until discharged from prosecution or other form of proceeding, imprisonment, detention or supervision for such offense or juvenile delinquency.

* * *

ARTICLE IX—*Detention Practices*

That, to every extent possible, it shall be the policy of states party to this compact that no juvenile or delinquent juvenile shall be placed or detained in any prison, jail or lockup nor be detained or transported in association with criminal, vicious or dissolute persons.

ARTICLE X—*Supplementary Agreements*

That the duly constituted administrative authorities of a state party to this compact may enter into supplementary agreements with any other state or states party hereto for the cooperative care, treatment and rehabilitation of delinquent juveniles whenever they shall find that such agreements will improve the facilities or programs available for such care, treatment and rehabilitation. Such care, treatment and rehabilitation may be provided in an institution located within any state entering into such supplementary agreement. Such supplementary agreements shall:

(1) provide the rates to be paid for the care, treatment and custody of such delinquent juveniles, taking into consideration the character of facilities, services and subsistence furnished;

(2) provide that the delinquent juvenile shall be given a court hearing prior to his being sent to another state for care, treatment and custody;

(3) provide that the state receiving such a delinquent juvenile in one of its institutions shall act solely as agent for the state sending such delinquent juvenile;

(4) provide that the sending state shall at all times retain jurisdiction over delinquent juveniles sent to an institution in another state;

(5) provide for reasonable inspection of such institutions by the sending state;

(6) provide that the consent of the parent, guardian, person or agency entitled to the legal custody of said delinquent juvenile shall be secured prior to his being sent to another state; and

(7) make provision for such other matters and details as shall be necessary to protect the rights and equities of such delinquent juveniles and of the cooperating states.

* * *

RUNAWAY AMENDMENT[1]

a. That this article shall provide additional remedies, and shall be binding only as among and between those party states which specifically execute the same.

b. For the purposes of this article, "child," as used herein, means any minor within the jurisdictional age limits of any court in the home state.

---

[1] The following three amendments do not appear in all state statutory language.

c. When any child is brought before a court of a state which such a child is not a resident, and such state is willing to permit such child's return to the home state of such child, such home state, upon being so advised be the state in which such proceeding is pending, shall immediately institute proceedings to determine the residence and jurisdictional facts as to such child in such home state, and upon finding that such child is in fact a resident of said state and subject to the jurisdiction of the court thereof, shall within five (5) days authorize the return of such child to the home state, and to the parent or custodial agency legally authorized to accept such custody in such home state, and at the expense of such home state, to be paid from such funds as such home state may procure, designate, or provide, prompt action being of the essence.

RENDITION AMENDMENT

a. This amendment shall provide additional remedies and shall be binding only as among and between those party states which specifically adopt the same.

b. All provisions and procedures of articles V and VI of this compact shall be construed to apply to any juvenile charged with being a delinquent by reason of a violation of any criminal law. Any juvenile, charged with being a delinquent by reason of violating any criminal law shall be returned to the requesting state where the violation of criminal law is alleged to have been committed. The petition may be filed regardless of whether the juvenile has left the state before or after the filing of the petition. The requisition described in article V of the compact shall be forwarded by the judge of the court in which the petition has been filed.

OUT-OF-STATE CONFINEMENT AMENDMENT

(1)(a) Whenever the duly constituted judicial or administrative authorities in a sending state shall determine that confinement of a probationer or reconfinement of a parolee is necessary or desirable, said officials may direct that the confinement or reconfinement be in an appropriate institution for delinquent juveniles within the territory of the receiving state, such receiving state to act in that regard solely as agent for the sending state.

b. Escapees and absconders who would otherwise be returned pursuant to article V of the compact may be confined or reconfined in the receiving state pursuant to this amendment. In any such case the information and allegations required to be made and furnished in a requisition pursuant to such article shall be made and furnished, but in place of the demand pursuant to article V, the sending state shall request confinement or reconfinement in the receiving state. Whenever applicable, detention orders as provided in article V may be empowered pursuant to this paragraph preliminary to disposition of the escapee or absconder.

c. The confinement or reconfinement of a parolee, probationer, escapee, or absconder pursuant to this amendment shall require the concurrence of the appropriate judicial or administrative authorities of the receiving state.

* * *

Notes

1. The Interstate Compact on Juveniles (ICJ) is a legal contract between all fifty states and the District of Columbia which allows jurisdictions to monitor the interstate movement of juveniles under court supervision. *See* Christopher Holloway, Dep't of Just., Interstate Compact on Juveniles (2000). The ICJ focuses on runaways, juveniles who require institutional care or specialized services in another state, juveniles absconded from probation or parole in another state, juveniles who have pending court proceedings in another state, and juveniles on probation or parole but who reside in another state. Each participating jurisdiction appoints members to the Association of Juvenile Compact Administrators (AJCA) which develops and adopts regulations concerning the administration of the ICJ. Furthermore, the ACJA also provides uniform supervision of juveniles on probation and parole, provides for prompt return of runaways, and promotes education and training for juvenile justice professionals.

2. The three amendments to the ICJ have not been adopted by all fifty states; the Runaway Amendment has been adopted by 24 states; the Out-Of-State Confinement Amendment has been adopted by 15 states; and the Rendition Amendment has been adopted by 47 states. On August 26, 2000, the ACJA enacted rules and regulations for the uniform administration of the ICJ.

D. Institutional Confinement

1. Deterrence

Scott L. v. State

760 P.2d 134 (Nev. 1988)

Springer, Justice:

Appellant Scott L., a sixteen-year-old high school student, was heavily involved in the sale of marijuana to his fellow students. Following a sale of marijuana to an undercover drug enforcement agent the minor was adjudicated a delinquent and committed by the juvenile court to the Spring Mountain Youth Camp, a "place of involuntary confinement and punitive incarceration." *See Glenda Kay S., A Minor v. State,* 103 Nev. 53, 732 P.2d 1356 (1987). The sole reason given by the presiding juvenile court judge for such disposition was the "deterrent effect" of incarcerating a youthful drug dealer. We approve of the juvenile court's decision in this case and affirm its dispositional order.

The juvenile court judge wisely and properly stated in open court his reasons for ordering this punitive disposition, namely, that "[t]here is a deterrent effect by incarcerating" a youth who engages in the sale of marijuana to other minors. Said the judge:

> When children sell [drugs] to children, the other children in the community are watching, all right. There is a deterrent effect by incarcerating....

* * *

> [B]y removal from the community, removing them from their friends, kids talk, they know who is gone, they know who is back in the community. . . .
>
> [I]t is in the public's interest to institutionalize this young man for at least the first semester of the school year, because I believe very strongly that it is "in order to deter . . . others.

The minor claims, citing *Glenda Kay*, above, that there is not in this case "sufficient reason to depart from the presumption that a child should be placed in his home" and to put him in confinement.

We deem the deterrence of others from engaging in drug sales in our schools to be "sufficient reason" to incarcerate a youth adjudged guilty of such criminal conduct, and we see the juvenile court as having acted in an eminently wise and prudent manner in deciding upon this disposition.

* * *

[T]he record . . . support[s] a conclusion by the juvenile court that the best interests of Scott would be served by this disposition. Spring has a regular high school educational program conducted by the Clark County School District and offers several treatment and rehabilitation programs likely to be of benefit to Scott. . . .

* * *

All in all the "paramount" public interest purposes of the juvenile courts appear to have been optimally served by the juvenile court judge's decision "to institutionalize this young man" for purposes of deterrence. . . . We affirm the order of commitment.

Notes

1. All jurisdictions are not in agreement with the *Scott L.* court's ruling that dispositions can be used solely to deter future delinquent behavior. States such as North Dakota and Minnesota require institutional confinement to be used for rehabilitative purposes only. In *Walter v. State*, 172 N.W.2d 603 (N.D. 1969), the court criticized the trial court's attitude and satisfaction of public indignation and its intent to set an example for purposes of deterrence. The *Walter* court ruled that the statute which requires delinquency proceedings to focus on the juvenile's own welfare should not be interpreted so broadly as to include deterrence. In *In the Welfare of C.A.W.,* 579 N.W.2d 494 (Minn. Ct. App. 1998), the court held that neither retribution nor deterrence satisfied the rehabilitation requirement imposed by Minnesota law for juvenile delinquent offenses.

2. State laws also reflect the split between states as to whether juvenile law should punish or rehabilitate delinquent juveniles. Some states have adopted purely punitive delinquency laws. *See* Bradette Jepsen, *This New Breed of Juve-*

nile Offenders, CORRECTIONS TODAY, June 1, 1997, at 68. Other states have retained laws requiring judges to decide delinquency cases with rehabilitating the juvenile as a top priority. *See* FLA. STAT. ANN. §§ 39.001-.002 (West Supp. 2001); 1 GA. CODE ANN. § 15-11-1 (Lexis Supp. 2000); MINN. STAT. ANN. § 260.012 (West Supp. 2001); N.H. REV. STAT. ANN. § 169-B:1 (Lexis Supp. 2000); N.J. STAT. ANN. § 2A:4A-21 (West Supp. 2001); OHIO REV. CODE ANN. § 2151.01 (Anderson Supp. 2000); TENN. CODE ANN. § 37-1-101 (Lexis 1996); VT. STAT. ANN. tit. 33, § 5501 (Lexis 2001); W. VA. CODE § 49-1-1 (Lexis 1999).

3. How successful is institutional confinement of juveniles as a deterrent to delinquency? Statistics indicate that recidivism among institutionalized delinquents is increasing, giving support to the argument that confinement does not deter delinquency. *See* ANNE SCHNEIDER, DETERRENCE AND JUVENILE CRIME 5 (1990). Amy Campbell in *Trying Minors as Adults in the United States and England: Balancing the Goal of Rehabilitation With the Need to Protect Society*, 19 SUFFOLK TRANSNAT'L L. REV. 345 (1995), compared with the juvenile law system in the United States, which has become increasingly punitive over the last twenty years, to England's juvenile law system. Campbell found that England's recidivism juvenile crime rate is considerably lower than in the United States. *Id.* at 357.

Questions

1. During the past century, the juvenile justice systems in the United States have kept delinquency cases confidential for rehabilitation purposes. If juvenile court judges purport to deter other juveniles from committing delinquent acts, can their decisions serve as an effective deterrent if they remain confidential? Would delinquency proceedings serve as a more effective deterrent if made public like adult criminal proceedings? If delinquency proceedings are made public, what additional constitutional safeguards, if any, should be afforded a juvenile in a delinquency hearing?

2. As the dangers associated with juvenile street gangs become more apparent, should judges have the power to commit delinquent youth to institutional confinement to deter other gang members from committing delinquent acts? Would your opinion change if the predispositional report suggested that the delinquent gang member could be rehabilitated if placed on probation with the condition of home supervision? How should a court balance the deterrent effect institutional confinement might have on juveniles versus the delinquent juvenile's best interests?

2. Protection of Society

In re Michael D.

234 Cal. Rptr. 103 (Cal. Ct. App. 1987)

Low, Presiding Justice

We hold that an order of the juvenile court committing a minor to the California Youth Authority may be validly based on punishment and public safety grounds so long as it will also provide rehabilitative benefit to the minor.

The minor, Michael D., appeals from an order of wardship (Welf. & Inst. Code, § 602) committing him to the California Youth Authority (CYA) after he admitted to one count of sexual battery. The minor contends that the juvenile court judge abused his discretion in committing him to CYA. We affirm.

On January 12, 1986, officers responded to a report that a rape was in progress in the Day Street Park playground. They found a woman being raped by a minor; appellant was observed leaning over the victim near her head and appeared to be holding her down. The minor was leaning over the neck of the victim with his hands out in front, but there was no conclusive evidence he was choking the victim. However, it was clear from the medical evidence that the victim had lacerations and bruises consistent with attempted strangulation. After the incident, the minor showed little remorse for the incident nor any concern for the victim. The minor eventually admitted to one count of sexual battery.

* * *

The probation report concluded that "[t]he magnitude and outrageousness of the conduct alone warrants a commitment to the CYA." The report concluded that an out-of-home placement would not be suitable and, "[w]eighing all the factors objectively, . . . in order to afford adequate [sic] protection of the community and to have this minor atone for his participation in this most 'vicious crime,'" recommended CYA placement.

The juvenile court found the minor "guilty" of a "very brutal, heinous and vicious crime, and the conduct in this matter [was] outrageous." The judge also stated that the minor's history of drug and alcohol abuse was a significant factor, and found him "to be a threat and danger to society. . . . [H]is own interests and the interest of society would be best served by his being at this time in the California Youth Authority." He also stated that the minor would benefit from the reformatory educational discipline provided by the CYA.

I.

The minor contends that his commitment to CYA was an abuse of discretion by the juvenile court in that (1) the minor was improperly committed to CYA for purposes of retribution rather than rehabilitation; (2) the juvenile court did not properly consider less restrictive alternatives; and (3) the minor could not be benefitted by commitment to CYA.

The decision of the juvenile court may be reversed on appeal only upon a showing that the court abused its discretion in committing a minor to CYA. . . . We must indulge all reasonable inferences to support the decision of the juvenile court and will not disturb its findings when there is substantial evidence to support them. In determining whether there was substantial evidence to support the commitment, we must examine the record presented at the disposition hearing in light of the purposes of the Juvenile Court Law.

At the core of the dispute before us is a fundamental disagreement over the purposes of the Juvenile Court Law. Prior to the amending of section 202, California courts have consistently held that "[j]uvenile commitment proceedings are designed for the purposes of rehabilitation and treatment, not punishment," (*In re Aline D.* (1975) 14 Cal. 3d 557, 567, 121 Cal. Rptr. 816, 536 P. 2d 65.) The *Aline* court derived its conclusion from the terms of former section 502 (now § 202): "to secure for each minor . . . such care and guidance, preferably in the minor's own home, as will serve the spiritual, emotional, mental, and physical welfare of the minor. . . ." (*Id.* at p. 562, 121 Cal. Rptr. 816, 526 P.2d 65.) . . .

In 1984, the Legislature replaced the provisions of section 202 with new language which emphasized different priorities for the juvenile justice system. The new provisions recognized punishment as a rehabilitative tool. Section 202 also shifted its emphasis from a primarily less restrictive alternative approach oriented towards the benefit of the minor to the express "protection and safety of the public," where care, treatment, and guidance shall conform to the interests of public safety and protection.

Thus, it is clear that the Legislature intended to place greater emphasis on punishment for rehabilitative purposes and on a restrictive commitment as a means of protecting the public safety. This interpretation by no means loses sight of the "rehabilitative objectives" of the Juvenile Court Law. (§ 202, subd. (b)). Because commitment to CYA cannot be based solely on retribution grounds, there must continue to be evidence demonstrating (1) probable benefit to the minor and (2) that less restrictive alternatives are ineffective or inappropriate. However, these must be taken together with the Legislature's purposes in amending the Juvenile Court Law. . . .

II

* * *

[T]he court-appointed psychologist concluded that the minor was "beyond parental control" and the psychologist retained by the minor also seriously questioned whether his parents could place the strict limits on his behavior necessary for rehabilitation. The minor had poor social and moral judgment that required firm guidance. The minor also admitted that he has a problem with drugs and alcohol, which the psychologists agree requires substantial help. From all these facts, the trial court could have inferred (1) that the minor's best interests required an environment providing firm, strict discipline for his "out of control" behavior, evidenced by his participation in a violent crime, (2) without such discipline and realignment of his social and moral structure he poses a demonstrated threat to public safety, and (3) that the minor required intensive rehabilitative treatment for his substance abuse, and (4) the minor's parents were demonstrably incapable of caring for the minor consistent with the minor's best interests in treatment and guidance and the objective of the protection of the public. . . . In its discretion, the juvenile court chose commitment to CYA over the obviously unsuitable alternative of release to parental custody. There was substantial evidence supporting the trial court's exercise of discretion.

The order of wardship is affirmed.

Notes

1. As teen violence continues to alarm the public (*see, e.g.,* Glen Martin, *Youth Sentenced in Girl's Horrific Slaying,* S.F. CHRON., Mar. 8, 1997, at A15), and the media sensationalizes the delinquent acts of juveniles (*see, e.g.,* Martin Strassburg, *Justice for Juveniles? The Second Circuit Declares Juvenile Prevention Detention Statute Unconstitutional,* 50 BROOK. L. REV. 517 (1984)), the general public has become concerned that the current system of rehabilitating delinquent juveniles is ineffective and does not protect society from the threat posed by modern teen violence. *See* Kimberly A. Tolhurst, *A Search for Solutions: Evaluating the Latest Anti-Stalking Developments and the National Institute of Justice Model Stalking Code,* 1 WM. & MARY J. WOMEN & L. 269 (1994). Some legislatures, in response to growing concern that society needs to be protected from teen violence, have passed laws that allow judges to take into consideration the danger a delinquent juvenile poses to society when deciding on a proper disposition. The following New York statute is an example of a state legislature's effort to require judges to take into consideration both the juvenile's best interests and the security interests of society as a whole:

> In determining an appropriate order the court shall consider the needs and best interests of the respondent as well as the need for protection of the community. If the respondent has committed a designated felony act the court shall determine the appropriate disposition in accord with section 353.5. In all other cases the court shall order the least restrictive available alternative enumerated in subdivision one which is consistent with the needs and best interests of the respondent and the need for protection of the community.

N.Y. JUD. LAW § 352.2(2)(a) (McKinney 2001).

2. The trend in juvenile law toward locking up kids to protect society has had a negative impact on juvenile confinement centers. The laws designed to protect society and "get tough" with delinquent juveniles have caused conditions in juvenile confinement facilities to deteriorate. *See* Frank Green, *Efforts in Prisons Defended,* RICHMOND TIMES-DISPATCH, Feb. 17, 1996, at B1, *available in* 1996 WL 2290939. Overcrowding has proven to be the biggest problem leading to unsanitary conditions and rendering the facility unable to properly protect and rehabilitate juveniles. Overcrowding has also led to increased institutional violence and suicidal behavior. *See* Amy E. Webbink, *Access Denied: Incarcerated Juveniles and Their Right of Access to Courts*, 7 WM. & MARY BILL RTS. J. 613, 627 (1999). As overcrowding becomes more prevalent in juvenile confinement centers, juveniles are increasingly exposed to more gang activity and drug abuse.

Questions

1. Several legislatures like New York, *supra*, Note 1, allow judges to take into consideration the safety of society as well as the delinquent juvenile's best interests when determining a proper disposition. Is the safety of society necessarily compatible with the delinquent juvenile's best interests? How should a judge weigh the two interests? Because an adult criminal court allows judges to consider the threat a criminal poses towards society, should a juvenile also be allowed the same constitutional rights as an adult in a criminal trial if a judge is allowed to consider public safety in the juvenile's disposition? What impact would this have on the rehabilitative ideals of the juvenile justice system?

2. Does placing a juvenile in crowded institutional confinement actually protect society? How can society protect itself from delinquent juveniles and yet not expose the juveniles to additional delinquent and criminal behavior in a confinement setting? As a legislator, what proposals would you make that would satisfy the general public's desire to be protected from violent offenders and yet alleviate the current facility overcrowding problem? Would your proposed legislation have the capacity to protect society and rehabilitate the delinquent juvenile?

3. Punishment

Scott L. v. State

760 P.2d 134 (Nev. 1988)

SPRINGER, Justice:

[For the factual background of this case, see subsection 1, *supra*.]

Factors other than deterrence present themselves in justification of the juvenile court's removal of Scott from the community and his commitment to Spring Mountain. In *Glenda Kay* we noted that the integrity of the criminal law is maintained by seeing to it that those who commit crimes are punished. We noted also that punitive incarceration may be justified in juvenile cases for serious criminal violations because the youthful offender deserves to be punished.

To permit Scott to remain at home and escape any appreciable punitive sanction for so serious a crime would tend to be destructive of the integrity of the criminal law. When the law is broken something must be done about it. The law must be vindicated; otherwise, it loses its meaning and effect as law. Scott is described in the record as a "middleman in drug sales" among high school students. If such a person can be adjudged guilty of drug sales in the schools and escape any punitive sanction, the law and its moral force are indeed in jeopardy. To maintain the integrity of our drug laws some punishment must follow, as it did here, from the violation of these laws.

We also mentioned in *Glenda Kay* that a criminal offender may be punished because he *deserves* it. Retribution or just desserts as a response to criminal law violation is thought by many jurists and social theorists to be archaic and inappropriate. We disagree. Although the juvenile court judge has in the present case eschewed the use of punishment *as punishment* in a juvenile court case, reason tells us that the juvenile court's decision to incarcerate could well have been grounded on the fact that Scott deserved to be punished. He has a previous juvenile record (carrying an illegal weapon). He was deeply involved in drug trafficking to minors. He was a disciplinary problem in school. It is hard to argue that Scott did not deserve to be removed from his home and school environment and confined in a youth camp. This is little enough punishment for a crime calling for a life sentence.

. . . [W]e must not ignore the value of punishment itself as a rehabilitative tool. Using punishment as a means for changing youthful behavior is not exactly a new phenomenon; and, punishment must be recognized as a valid and useful rehabilitative tool. This court has recognized that "punishment has in many cases a rehabilitative effect on the child and . . . will serve the child's best interests a well as the state's." *In the Matter of Seven Minors*, 99 Nev. 427, 664 P.2d 947 (1983). . . .

In *Seven Minors* we recognized the beneficence and utility of "educative and rehabilitative measures properly taken by the juvenile court," but noted firmly that "the court's duty to the public is paramount." The juvenile court judge in the present case was correct in declaring that it was "in the public's interest to institutionalize this young man." . . .

We affirm the order of commitment.

Notes

1. The general public's perception of the juvenile justice system is that the juvenile courts are too lenient with delinquent juveniles. *See* Ralph A. Rossum, *Holding Juveniles Accountable: Reforming America's "Juvenile Justice System"*, 22 PEPP. L. REV. 907 (1997). According to a 1989 poll, 70% of those polled said they believed that juvenile courts were too lenient on delinquent juveniles while 79% said that juvenile courts need to impose tougher criminal penalties for juvenile offenders. *Id.* at 908. Moreover, a 1990 poll indicated that 73% of persons polled believed that the juvenile court system should focus on punishment as well as on treatment and rehabilitation. *See* Beth Wilbourn, Note, *Waiver of Juvenile Court Jurisdiction: National Trends and the Inadequacy of the Texas Response,* 23 AM. J. CRIM. L. 633, 636-37 (1996) (citing Ira M. Schwartz, *Public Attitudes Toward Juvenile Crime and Juvenile Justice Implications for Public Policy,* 13 HAMLINE J. PUB. L. & POL'Y 241, 249 (1992)). The same article revealed that 76% of persons polled favored trying juvenile offenders in adult courts for serious violent crimes. *Id.* at 637 (citing IRA M. SCHWARTZ ET AL., THE PERCEPTION AND REALITY OF JUVENILE CRIME IN MICHIGAN at i (1990)).

2. In his article *The Juvenile Court Meets the Principle of the Offense: Punishment, Treatment, and the Difference It Makes,* 68 B.U. L. REV. 821, 833-34 (1988), Professor Barry C. Feld argues that punishment and rehabilitation are mutually exclusive goals. Punishment and rehabilitation are based on two distinctly different presumptions. Punishment assumes that the individual has a free-will, knows what is right or wrong, and should be punished accordingly for any offense committed. Rehabilitation, however, assumes that a degree of determinism exists. *Id.* at 833 (citing DAVID MATZA, DELINQUENCY AND DRIFT 5 (1964)). While punishment imposes unpleasant consequences for unlawful acts, rehabilitation focuses on certain antecedent factors which caused the person to commit the unlawful act and tries to correct them. Punishment focuses on the commission of a past offense and determines the proper penalty according to the severity of the offense committed. Rehabilitation, on the other hand, addresses the need to prevent the future commission of an unlawful offense and determines the proper remedy according to the individual's needs.

3. States place different degrees of emphasis on the need for punitive sanctions. For a survey of how individual states view the need for punitive sanctions in the juvenile courts, *see id.* at 850-79; Martin L. Forst & Martha-Elin Bloomquist, *Cracking Down on Juveniles: The Changing Ideology of Youth Corrections*, 4 NOTRE DAME J. L. ETHICS & PUB. POL'Y 323 (1991).

4. Punitive sanctions in juvenile courts have proven to be fairly ineffective. The crime rate of violent delinquent offenders has not decreased. Juveniles waived to adult courts usually receive lenient sanctions because adult courts generally classify juveniles as first-time offenders. When juvenile courts send delinquents to adult prisons for serious violent crimes, the juveniles are surrounded by adult criminals who victimize the juveniles. *See* Shari Del Carlo, *Oregon Voters Get Tough on Juvenile Crime: One Strike and You Are Out!*, 75 OR. L. REV. 1223, 1244 (1996).

Questions

1. Can a juvenile court order a juvenile a disposition that is in the youth's best interests and is both punitive and rehabilitative? If so, give an example. Would the disposition be more effective if it was punitive or rehabilitative? How does your answer affect the discretionary power of a juvenile court judge? How does you answer affect the need for either indefinite or definite sentences in juvenile law?

2. One proposal to reform juvenile law is to eliminate the juvenile court system, try juveniles in adult criminal courts, and allow the juvenile to use youth as a mitigating factor when the judge sentences the delinquent juvenile. How does this proposal address the "deficiencies" of the current juvenile court system? Does this reform proposal reflect punitive or rehabilitative ideals or both? For further insight into this proposal, see Barry C. Feld, *Abolish the Juvenile Court: Youthfulness, Criminal Responsibility, and Sentencing Policy,* 88 J. CRIM. L. & CRIMINOLOGY 68 (1997).

4. No Confinement for Status Offenders

In re Ellery C.

300 N.E.2d 424 (N.Y. 1973)

FULD, Chief Judge

The appellant, Ellery C., now 16 years old, was adjudged a person in need of supervision (PINS) on the application of his mother in March of 1971. About a year later, the Family Court (Kings County), on recommendation of the Probation Department, sent him to the New York State Training School at Otisville. The Appellate Division, by a closely divided vote, affirmed that disposition (40 A.D. 2d 862, 337 N.Y.S. 2d 936).

Until 1962, a child who committed acts which now warrant his adjudication as a person in need of supervision was treated as a juvenile delinquent. The new PINS statute "represents enlightened legislative recognition of the difference between youngsters [juvenile delinquents] who commit criminal acts and those who merely misbehave in ways which, frequently, would not be objectionable save for the fact that the actor is a minor (e.g., running away from home, keeping late hours, truancy, etc.)." (*Matter of Jeanette P.,* 34 A.D.2d 661, 310 N.Y.S.2d 125.) There is a vital distinction between a finding of delinquency and a determination of a need for supervision. The Family Court Act provides that a "dispositional hearing" in a case involving delinquency is one to determine whether the juvenile requires supervision, treatment or confinement, while such a hearing in a need-for-supervision case is to ascertain whether the youngster requires supervision or treatment. The omission of the word "confinement" is no mere oversight. Children in need of supervision should not be placed in institutions in which juvenile delinquents are confined and, as might be expected, the practice has been severely condemned.[2]

The conclusion is clear. Proper facilities must be made available to provide adequate supervision and treatment for children found to be persons in need of supervision. We thoroughly agree, therefore, with the view, expressed by Justice Shapiro in the course of his dissenting opinion [below] (40 A.D.2d, at p. 864, 337 N.Y.S. 2d, at p. 940), that the appellant's confinement in the training school, along with juveniles convicted of committing criminal acts, "can hardly, in any realistic sense, serve as 'supervision' and 'treatment' for him. On the contrary, it may well result in his emerging from his incarceration well tutored in the ways of crime. . . ."

Nor may the appellant's commitment to the State training school be justified by the respondent's claim that, "while not ideal, [it] is the only facility available which could possibly help this boy become a constructive member of society." In the first place, the record before us does not support that claim and,

---

[2] It has been well said that the distinction between the two types of children—juvenile delinquents and those in need of supervision—"becomes useless where, as here, the treatment accorded the one must be identical to that accorded the other because no other adequate alternative has been provided." (*Matter of Jeanette P.*, 34 A.D.2d at p. 661, 310 N.Y.S.2d, at p. 127).

in the second place, to cull from the dissenting opinion below (40 A.D. 2d, at pp. 864-865, 337 N.Y.S.2d at p. 940), even if it did, "it would hardly justify . . . [appellant's] confinement . . . with adjudicated juvenile delinquents in a prison environment." It follows, therefore, that persons in need of supervision may not validly be placed in a State training school.

* * *

The order appealed from should be reversed and the proceeding remitted to the Family Court for the purpose of placing the appellant in a suitable environment.

Notes

1. Some states have not ruled out incarceration for status offenders who enter the juvenile justice system. In *State ex rel. Harris v. Calendine,* 233 S.E.2d 318 (W. Va. 1977), the court ruled that a status offender may be incarcerated as an initial disposition only if no other reasonable alternative is available or the juvenile is not amenable to treatment provided outside of a secure facility. Some states do not allow status offenders to be placed in confinement, but do allow these juveniles to be locked up if they violate their probation. *See, e.g., In re C.H.*, 683 P.2d 931 (Mont. 1984). Furthermore, while some states allow a court to use its contempt power to incarcerate a status offender, a few states prohibit incarcerating status offenders regardless of the circumstances. *See, e.g., W.M. v. State*, 437 N.E.2d 1028 (Ind. Ct. App. 1982).

2. The United States Congress passed the Juvenile Justice and Delinquency Prevention Act of 1974, 42 U.S.C. § 5601, which enabled states to secure federal funds for programs related to juvenile justice. The Act was in part concerned with the exposure of status offenders to delinquent juveniles while incarcerated in the same facility. Senator Birch Bayh, Chairman of the United States Senate Judiciary Committee, said, ". . . I have heard testimony from countless juveniles who have been incarcerated for acts which would not be crimes as adults, and who have emerged from institutions embittered and highly sophisticated in the ways of crime." Honorable Birch Bayh, *Juveniles and the Law: An Introduction*, 12 CRIM. L. REV. 1 (1974). The original Act's "deinstitutionalized" mandate required states to prohibit placing any juvenile status offender in a secure detention center. Because states could not lock up a juvenile status offender, states were powerless in trying to keep runaway juveniles from leaving the secure detention facilities. Congress amended the Act in 1980, allowing courts to temporarily lockup juvenile status offenders for criminal contempt. 42 U.S.C. § 5633 (a)(12)(A). Despite the financial incentive from Congress, some jurisdictions still allow status offenders to be incarcerated alongside delinquent juveniles. *See* SAMUEL M. DAVIS, RIGHTS OF JUVENILES, 6-21 (1996).

3. Alternatives to incarceration for status offenders include non-secure but supervised residential care centers; residential treatment for status offenders in need of psychiatric and emotional assistance; specialized foster care arranged through the child welfare agency; and a group home surrounding with a necessary medical and psychiatric staff available for assistance.

Questions

What is the purpose of status offense jurisdiction in the juvenile court? How does this differ from the juvenile court's purpose with respect to delinquent juveniles? What are the arguments for and against taking status offense jurisdiction away from the juvenile court and conferring it upon an administrative agency?

Problem

A juvenile court finds Aaron, age seventeen, to be incorrigible. According to state law, a juvenile court judge may rule that a juvenile is incorrigible if "wayward" or "morally depraved" and incarcerate the child. (For a discussion of a similar statute, see *People v. Allen*, 239 N.E.2d 879 (N.Y. 1968)). Instead of confinement, the judge sends Aaron to a forest camp where he and other incorrigible juveniles participate in work projects. As Aaron's counsel, what constitutional argument(s) would you present to challenge the statute? How should the prosecution argue in support of the state's interest in sending Aaron to the forest camp?

5. Education Rights of Incarcerated Juveniles

Tunstall ex rel. Tunstall v. Bergeson

5 P.3d 691 (Wash. 2000)

Inmates brought this class action suit against the State and those school districts where DOC facilities are located. Inmates' class was certified to include: All individuals who are now, or who will in the future be, committed to the custody of the Washington Department of Corrections, who are allegedly denied access to *basic or special education during that custody, and who are, during that custody, under the age of 21, or disabled and under the age of 22.* CP at 203-04 (emphasis added).

The inmates alleged that the State's failure to provide them with basic and special education services violated article IX of the Washington Constitution . . . the federal Individuals with Disabilities Education Act (IDEA), 20 U.S.C. §§ 1400-1436, and § 504 of the Rehabilitation Act of 1973, 29 U.S.C. § 794(a); and constitutional due process and equal protection. . . .

INMATES' STATE CONSTITUTIONAL RIGHT TO BASIC AND SPECIAL EDUCATION UNDER ARTICLE IX

In resolving the issue of whether article IX requires the State to provide basic and special education to persons up to age 21 or 22 who are incarcerated in adult DOC prisons, we must first define the term "children" for purposes of article IX. We hold that "children" under article IX includes individuals up to age 18, including those children incarcerated in adult DOC facilities. . . .

Regarding the definition of "children" under article IX, our constitution provides little guidance, leaving the term undefined. Consequently, we must look elsewhere for guidance.

* * *

Under current law, only individuals under age 18 are required to attend school. RCW 28A.225.010 (children up to age 18 required to attend school, subject to certain exceptions). This statute supports the idea that individuals are treated like adults once they hit age 18, as choice is commonly recognized as a hallmark of adulthood. Furthermore, . . . chapter 28A.193 RCW's "definition" of children counteracts any argument that the Legislature intended to establish a child age-limit regarding education above age 18. RCW 28A.193.030(3)-(4); RCW 72.09.460(2) (act mandates that DOC inmates receive education until age 18). Finally, although not within the education context, individuals over age 18 are generally emancipated and are able to marry without parental consent, to execute a will, to vote, to enter into a legally binding contract, to make medical decisions about their own care and those of their issue, and to sue and be sued . . . These statutes demonstrate that the common understanding of the definition of "children" for most purposes in Washington, including education, includes individuals up to age 18. Consequently, we hold that the term "children" under article IX includes individuals up to age 18.

The State raises the alternative argument that whatever statutory or constitutional rights to an education the inmates may have had, they disqualified themselves through their own criminal conduct. Specifically, the State contends that by engaging in conduct which compels their removal from the school system, the inmates have, by their own conduct and not through any failing of the State, disqualified themselves from the educational opportunities provided them. We find the State's arguments unpersuasive and find it unnecessary to deal with this issue further since the Legislature has seen fit to provide an educational program to DOC inmates.

Having determined that the State is constitutionally required to provide educational services to children incarcerated in DOC facilities up to age 18, we need to determine whether the State is meeting its obligation. . . .

It is a well-established general rule that where the constitutionality of a statute is challenged, that statute is presumed constitutional and the burden is on the party challenging the statute to prove its unconstitutionality beyond a reasonable doubt. E.g., *Island County v. State*, 135 Wash.2d 141, 146-47, 955 P.2d 377 (1998) (citing cases). . . .

Article IX, section 2 clearly requires the State to create and "provide for a *general and uniform* system of public schools." (Emphasis added.) We have long held that this provision imposes upon the State a fundamental duty to create a common school system. In *Seattle Sch. Dist. No. 1*, we held that all children in Washington "have a 'right' to be amply provided with an education[; that] 'right' is constitutionally paramount and must be achieved through a 'general and uniform system of public schools.'" 90 Wash.2d at 513, 537-38, 585 P.2d 71; *see also Newman v. Schlarb*, 184 Wash. 147, 153, 50 P.2d 36 (1935) (duty imposed upon Legislature to provide "'a general and uniform system of public schools.'") (quoting *School Dist. v. Bryan*, 51 Wash. 498, 502, 99 P. 28 (1909)). The Legislature satisfied part of its general obligation under article IX through Title 28A RCW's "Common School Provisions," which includes the basic education act.

However, as we stated earlier, the State's constitutional duty to provide educational services does not end with the creation of a "general and uniform" school system. In addition to the requirements under article IX, section 2, the State has a "paramount duty . . . to make ample provision for the education of all children residing within its borders. . . ." Wash. Const. art. IX, section 1 . . .; *see also Seattle Sch. Dist. No. 1*, 90 Wash.2d at 499, 585 P.2d 71. Nothing in this provision, however, mandates that the education must be identical. We recognized as much in *Tommy P.* when we held that a different education program in juvenile detention centers might be necessary to "reasonably address special needs of juvenile offenders." 97 Wash.2d at 398, 645 P.2d 697.

Having outlined the general requirements of article IX, the question remains whether we are convinced beyond a reasonable doubt that there is no set of circumstances in which chapter 28A.193 RCW could meet the constitutional minimum due under article IX. Here, the educational program outlined in chapter 28A.193 RCW must provide each offender a choice of curriculum that will assist the inmate in achieving a high school diploma or general equivalency diploma. The program of education may include but not be limited to basic education, prevocational training, work ethic skills, conflict resolution counseling, substance abuse intervention, and anger management counseling. The curriculum may balance these and other rehabilitation, work and training components. RCW 72.09.460(2). The statute also outlines the infrastructure and support services required, and the proper allocation of money received from the Legislature's biennial appropriations. RCW 28A.193.005, .050, .080.

The inmates have failed to prove beyond a reasonable doubt that chapter 28A.193 RCW violates article IX. This statute makes ample provision for educational programs designed to address the special educational and rehabilitative needs of children incarcerated in adult prisons. As we have often held, it is not this court's role to micromanage education in Washington. *See Tommy P.*, 97 Wash.2d at 398, 645 P.2d 697 (Legislature's need to customize education programs recognized); *Seattle Sch. Dist. No. 1*, 90 Wash.2d at 520, 585 P.2d 71 ("While the Legislature must act pursuant to the constitutional mandate to discharge its duty, the general authority to select the means of discharging that duty should be left to the Legislature."). Consequently, we exercise judicial restraint and hold that under article IX's broad constitutional guidelines, chapter 28A.193 RCW is constitutional on its face. *See Seattle Sch. Dist. No. 1*, 90 Wash. 2d at 518, 585 P.2d 71 (judiciary required to provide broad constitutional guidelines regarding education within which Legislature may work).

The inmate class also argues that chapter 28A.193 RCW violates Washington's equal protection clause, article I, section 12. The inmates reiterate their argument that RCW 28A.193 infringes on a fundamental or absolute right, and thus is presumptively invalid. Under the inmates' theory, the State violates Washington's equal protection clause because it treats incarcerated youths differently from nonincarcerated youths while failing to justify the disparate treatment through a compelling state interest. We disagree and hold that under the proper equal protection analysis, chapter 28A.193 RCW does not violate Washington's equal protection clause.

The first step in conducting any equal protection analysis is determining the appropriate standard of review. *Foley v. Department of Fisheries*, 119 Wash.2d 783, 789, 837 P.2d 14 (1992) (citing case). Contrary to the dissent's assertions, to apply strict scrutiny, we must first find that a fundamental right is being infringed or a suspect class is involved. *See O'Day v. King County*, 109 Wash.2d 796, 814, 749 P.2d 142 (1988); *City of Seattle v. State*, 103 Wash.2d 663, 670-71, 694 P.2d 641 (1985).

* * *

As we previously held, however, chapter 28A.193 RCW does not infringe upon an inmate's fundamental right to education under article IX. Consequently, the only alternative for applying strict scrutiny if the statute targeted a suspect class. . . . In the absence of infringement of a fundamental right or involvement of a suspect class, rational basis review applies.

Under rational basis review, there is a presumption of constitutionality and a statute is upheld "unless it rests on grounds wholly irrelevant to achievement of legitimate state objectives." *Shawn P.*, 122 Wash.2d at 561, 859 P.2d 1220. In other words, the rational basis test provides that "a statutory classification will be upheld if any conceivable state of facts reasonably justifies the classification." *Shawn P.*, 122 Wash.2d at 563-64, 859 P.2d 1220. The party challenging the legislation has the burden of proving that the classification is "purely arbitrary." *State v. Coria*, 120 Wash.2d 156, 172, 839 P.2d 890 (1992).

Under these standards, we find the Legislature's decision to treat individuals under age 18 in prison different with respect to education from individuals under age 18 who are in the normal school system completely justified. Incarcerated and nonincarcerated youths are not similarly situated for the purpose of education. As we have previously recognized, incarcerated children may have different educational needs and may require different training programs more appropriate to their circumstances. *See Tommy P.*, 97 Wash.2d at 398, 645 P.2d 697 (educational program offered in juvenile detention facilities "should reasonably address the special needs of juvenile offenders"). Chapter 28A.193 RCW, in conjunction with RCW 72.09.460(2), allows the State to properly tailor its educational programs for members of the inmate class. We find that the State's provision of education for incarcerated children through chapter 28A.193 RCW is rationally related to the legitimate state objective of meeting the unique education needs of the inmates.

We similarly find the different treatment of individuals over age 18 who are in prison justified under the rational basis test. As detailed in our discussion of inmate rights under article IX, inmates over age 18 are not children, and thus have no fundamental right to education. While we may agree with the dissent that the Legislature should dedicate resources toward educating members of the inmates' class, it is not our choice and the State is within its prerogative under the rational basis standard to prioritize its resources regarding the education of individuals over age 18.

THE STATE'S DUTY UNDER THE IDEA

. . . The inmates argue that the State has a duty under the IDEA to provide special education to disabled persons under age 22 who are incarcerated in Washington State prisons and that this duty existed under the IDEA both before and after the 1997 amendments to the act. We disagree and hold that the IDEA does not require the State to provide special education services to persons over age 18 who are incarcerated in adult prisons.

The IDEA was enacted to address the special educational needs of disabled children. The act's purpose is "to assure that all children with disabilities have available to them . . . a free appropriate public education which emphasizes special education and related services designed to meet their unique needs. . . ." 20 U.S.C. § 1400(c). One goal of the IDEA is to provide comparable education to disabled students as that provided to nondisabled students. States that comply with the IDEA are entitled to federal funding to assist in the provision of a free appropriate public education to disabled children residing within the state. 20 U.S.C. § 1412. In 1997, Congress amended the IDEA to expressly require states receiving funds under the act to provide a free appropriate public education (FAPE) to children with disabilities who are expelled or suspended from school. IDEA Amendments for 1997, Pub.L. No. 105-17, § 612, 111 Stat. 37, 60.

Contrary to the inmates' assertions, the pre-1997 amendments version of the IDEA did not require the State to provide special education to persons who have been incarcerated in adult correctional facilities for conduct wholly unrelated to their disability. *See Commonwealth of Virginia Department of Educ. v. Riley*, 106 F.3d 559, 561 (4th Cir.1997) (IDEA did not apply to disabled children expelled or suspended from school). . . .

Having determined that the pre-1997 amendment version of the IDEA did not apply to members of the inmate class, we examine the IDEA after the 1997 amendments. In addition to explicitly including disabled children who are expelled or suspended from school, the 1997 amendments contain an exception to a state's duty to provide special educational services to disabled children. Under the exception, a state's duty to provide a FAPE to children with disabilities does not apply to (1) children aged 3 through 5 and 18 through 21 in a state where its application would be inconsistent with state law or practice; and (2) children aged 18 through 21 where state law does not require that special education related services under 20 U.S.C. § 1412(a)(1)(B) be provided to children with disabilities who, prior to their incarceration in an adult prison, (a) were not actually identified as being a child with a disability under § 1401(3) or (b) did not have an individualized education program under § 1412(a)(1)(B). 34 C.F.R. § 300.122 (citing 20 U.S.C. § 1412(a)(1)(B)).

* * *

Here, the clear language of the educational provider contracts requires that the provider of educational services at the DOC facilities "[p]rovide special education, consistent with Chapter 392-172 WAC." CP at 1697; *see also* Ex. 2, at 2 (agreement between DOC and special education services), Mot. to Supplement the R., *Tunstall v. Bergeson,* No. 67448-5 (Wash. Supreme Ct. Sept. 13, 1999). Consequently, the State is currently in full compliance with its duty under the IDEA to provide special education to disabled inmates who are under age 18. Therefore, we hold that the trial court properly dismissed the inmates' IDEA claims.

THE STATE'S DUTY UNDER § 504 OF THE REHABILITATION ACT OF 1973

The inmates also argue that the State has a duty under § 504 of the Rehabilitation Act of 1973 to ensure that disabled children in prison receive a FAPE. It has been held that a state's duty under the IDEA and § 504 may be different. However, "It is well-settled that . . . where the IDEA claims are subject to dismissal the § 504 claims based upon the same allegations, [§ 504 claims] must also be dismissed." *Doe v. Arlington County Sch. Bd.*, 41 F.Supp.2d 599, 608 (E.D.Va.1999) (citing, inter alia, *Independent Sch. Dist. No. 283 v. S.D.*, 88 F.3d 556, 562 (8th Cir. 1996). . . . Consequently, we hold that compliance in this case with the IDEA constitutes compliance with § 504 of the Rehabilitation Act of 1973, and thus the trial court properly dismissed the inmates' § 504 claims.

* * *

In sum, we hold that: . . . the term "children" as used in article IX of the Washington Constitution includes individuals up to age 18, including individuals incarcerated in DOC facilities; chapter 28A.193 RCW satisfies the requirements of article IX and does not violate equal protection; [and] neither the IDEA nor § 504 of the Rehabilitation Act of 1973 is violated by the lack of special education services to DOC inmates up to age 22. . . .

Notes

1. Regardless of educational background, a child is at serious risk of falling further behind educationally once he or she is incarcerated. *See* Sacha M.Coupet, *What to Do With the Sheep in Wolf's Clothing: The Role of Rhetoric and Reality About Youth Offenders in the Constructive Dismantling of the Juvenile Justice System*, 148 U. PA. L. REV. 1303, 1334 (2000). Furthermore, transferred juveniles rarely receive the education they would typically have received in the juvenile justice system. *See* Amy M. Thorsen, *From Parens Patriae to Crime Control: A Comparison of the History and Effectiveness of the Juvenile Justice Systems in the United States and Canada*, 16 ARIZ. J. INT'L & COMP. L. 845, 862 (1999). According to a 1989 study, 70% of juveniles who enter incarceration facilities experience considerable difficulty reading or are completely illiterate. Pamela J. Smith, *Looking Beyond Traditional Educational Paradigms: When Old Victims Become New Victimizers,* 23 HAMLINE L. REV. 101 (1999).

In response to an incarcerated juvenile's need for an education, several courts have found that incarcerated juveniles have a due process right to education for as long as they remain incarcerated. *See, e.g., Alexander S. by and Through Bowers v. Boyd,* 876 F. Supp. 773 (D.S.C. 1995) (a "minimally adequate level of programming is required in order to provide juveniles with a reasonable opportunity to accomplish the purpose of their confinement, to protect the safety of the juveniles and the staff, and to ensure the safety of the community once the juveniles are ultimately released."); *Morgan v. Sproat,* 432 F. Supp. 1130 (S.D. Miss. 1977) (states must provide reasonable educational programs for an incarcerated juvenile if the purpose of the incarceration is to rehabilitate the juvenile).

Most states have enacted legislation to educate incarcerated juveniles, thereby protecting their due process rights. The following statute is an example of how a state may provide educational instructional for an incarcerated juvenile:

Georgia Code Annotated

§ 42-2-5.1 (Lexis 1997)

> § 42-2-5.1 Special school district for school age youth; education programs for adult offenders.
>
> (a) In order to provide education for any school age youths incarcerated within any facility of the Department of Corrections, the department shall be considered a special school district which shall be given the same funding consideration for federal funds that school districts within the state are given. The special school district under the department shall have the powers, privileges, and authority exercised or capable of exercise by any other school district. . . . The Board of Corrections shall serve as the board of education for such district. The board, acting alone or in cooperation with the State Board of Education, shall establish education standards for the district. A far as is practicable, such standards shall adhere to the standards adopted by the State Board of Education for the education of school age youth, while taking into account:
>
> (1) The overriding security needs of correctional institutions and other restrictions inherent to the nature of correctional facilities;
>
> (2) The effect of limited funding on the capability of the Department of Corrections to meet certain school standards; and
>
> (3) Existing juvenile education standards of the Correctional Education Association and the American Correctional Association, which shall be given primary consideration where any conflicts arise.

* * *

2. The Individuals with Disabilities Act of 1975 (IDEA) requires states to provide "free and appropriate education" (FAPE) to all children with disabilities. For a detailed discussion of the function and purpose of the IDEA, see Joseph B. Tulman & Mary G. Hynes, *Enforcing Special Education Law on Behalf of Incarcerated Children: A Blueprint for Deconstruction,* 18 CHILDREN'S LEGAL RTS. J. 48, 50-51 (1998). The United States Supreme Court stated in *Board of Education v. Rowley,* 438 U.S. 176 (1982), that FAPE is satisfied:

> when the state provides personalized instruction with sufficient support services that permits the disabled child to benefit educationally from

> that instruction. Such instruction and services must be provided at public expense, must meet the state's educational standards, must approximate grade levels used in the state's regular education program and must comport with the child's IEP as formulated in accordance with the Act's requirements.

Ronald D. Wenkart, *Juvenile Offenders, Residential Placement, and Special Education,* 144 ED. LAW REP. 1, 2 (2000). The IDEA serves an important function in incarceration facilities because 30-50% of all incarcerated juveniles have some form of learning disability. Smith, *supra*, in Note 1.

The 1997 IDEA Amendments mentioned in *Tunstall* apply only to incarcerated juveniles in adult facilities and not to juvenile detention centers. For a discussion of how the 1997 IDEA Amendments affect the current administration of education to disabled incarcerated juveniles, see Melisa C. George, *A New IDEA: The Individuals With Disabilities Education Act After the 1997 Amendments*, 23 LAW & PSYCHOL. REV. 91, 95-96 (1999); Wenkhart at 51-52.

E. Community Based Programs

State v. J.D.G.

No. 38758-8-I, 1997 WL 731963, at *1
(Wash. Ct. App. Nov. 24, 1997)

KENNEDY, A.J.C.

J.D.G., a juvenile, contends that he was wrongfully denied credit for time spent at a sex offender treatment facility upon the revocation of his special sex offender disposition alternative and execution of his suspended sentence. Because we cannot determine from the record that the juvenile was in "confinement" at the treatment facility, or that the treatment facility was "operated by or pursuant to a contract with the state," we affirm.

J.D.G. pleaded guilty to rape of a child in the first degree in King County Superior Court, Juvenile Division, on October 27, 1994, and was sentenced under the Special Sex Offender Disposition Alternative (SSODA). The court imposed the standard range of commitment for 21 to 28 weeks but suspended the commitment on the condition that J.D.G. successfully comply with the conditions of probation. The SSODA conditions included, among other things, "successful progress and participation in comprehensive individual and family therapy" for 2 years.

J.D.G. was placed under community supervision for a period of 24 months. The Department of Social and Health Services (DSHS) placed J.D.G. at the Ruth Dykeman Children's Center to receive the SSODA treatment. Among the conditions of probation were that J.D.G. maintain his placement at the Children's Center, that he regularly attend school with no unexcused absences, and that he not use or possess any drugs unless prescribed by a physician.

* * *

On May 2, 1996, after J.D.G. repeatedly violated various SSODA conditions, the juvenile court revoked the SSODA and imposed the suspended standard range sentence. The court credited J.D.G. with 49 days previously served in detention but denied the juvenile's motion for approximately 18 months of credit for time spent at the Children's Center. J.D.G. appeals.

* * *

Under the Juvenile Justice Act of 1977 (JJA), the juvenile court may, in appropriate cases involving first time sex offenders, suspend execution of the juvenile's disposition of confinement, place him or her on community supervision for up to 2 years, require outpatient sex offender treatment for up to 2 years or inpatient sex offender treatment not to exceed the standard range of confinement for that offense, and impose various educational, employment, geographical, reporting, and restitution conditions. If the juvenile violates a condition of the SSODA, the court may, after a hearing, modify the SSODA and impose a penalty of up to 30 days in confinement, or revoke the SSODA and order execution of the suspended disposition.

Upon revocation of a SSODA and execution of the suspended dispostion, the "court shall give credit for any confinement time previously served if that confinement was for the offense for which the suspension is being revoked." RCW 13.40.160(5). The JJA defines "confinement" as "physical custody by the department of social and health services in a facility operated by or pursuant to a contract with the state, or physical custody in a detention facility operated by or pursuant to a contract with any county." RCW 13.40.020(7).

* * *

The record provides few details concerning the conditions under which J.D.G. resided at the Children's Center. According to J.D.G., he was "pretty much under secured conditions for the last 18 months." However, the record indicates that J.D.G. was allowed to leave the Center in order to attend school. The record also indicates that among the SSODA conditions that J.D.G. violated were possession of non-prescribed drugs, failure to have his guardian's permission regarding his whereabouts, hours and activities, failure to attend school on a regular basis, running away from his DSHS placement at the Children's Center and shoplifting. These violations indicate that J.D.G., although required to reside at the Children's Center and not free to change his place of residence, was not confined to the Center 24 hours a day. Indeed, it would appear that J.D.G.'s violations occurred while he was physically away from the Center and not while he was physically on the premises of the Center.

It is also clear from the record that J.D.G. was on community supervision. The JJA defines community supervision as "an order of disposition by the court of an adjudicated youth not committed to the department or an order granting a deferred adjudication pursuant to RCW 13.40.125." RCW 13.40.020(3). That same section also provides that community supervision is an individualized program comprised of one or more listed requirements, one of which is "community-based rehabilitation." RCW 13.40.020(30(b). "Community-based rehabilitation" is defined as one or more of the following: "Attendance of information classes; counseling, outpatient substance abuse treatment programs, outpatient mental health programs, anger management classes, education or outpatient treatment programs to prevent animal cruelty, or other services; or attendance at school or other educational programs appropriate for the juvenile as determined by the school district." RCW 13.40.040(5). . . . J.D.G. was ordered to undergo treatment for a period of 2 years, whereas the standard range sentence was 21 to 28 weeks. All of this suggests that the treatment J.D.G. was receiving at the Children's Center was outpatient treatment, not inpatient treatment, regardless of the fact that J.D.G. was required to reside at the Center.

The Legislature has expressed a clear preference that when sexual offenses against children occur in the home, the offender and not the child victim shall be removed from the home. . . . Here, the victim of the child rape was J.D.G.'s sister, who was less than 12 years of age at the time of the offense. . . . [J.D.G.] was likely placed in residence at the Children's Center at least in part because he could no longer live in the family home in the company of his sister. . . . J.D.G. . . . has not sustained his burden of persuading this court that he was actually confined for inpatient treatment as a condition of his SSODA, rather than receiving outpatient, community-based treatment as reflected by the order of disposition. Although J.D.G. was not "free to leave" his residential placement at the treatment facility, the inadequacy of the evidence in the record precludes this court from drawing a definitive conclusion that he was in "confinement" within the meaning of RCW 13.40.020(7). . . .

In sum, based upon the record before this court, J.D.G. has failed to present sufficient evidence that he was in "confinement." . . . Specifically, the record fails to establish that J.D.G. was in "physical custody" or that the Children's Center "was operated by or pursuant to a contract with the state." . . . We conclude that, based on the evidence before it, the trial court did not err by denying J.D.G. credit for time spent at the Children's Center.

* * *

In re Groves

376 S.E.2d 481 (N.C. App. 1989)

This is an appeal from a juvenile delinquency dispositional hearing. The question presented is whether community-based alternatives to commitment were sufficiently explored before the juvenile was committed to training school. We conclude they were not, vacate the order, and remand the cause.

Juvenile petitions were filed 6 November 1987, alleging that Randy Ray Groves, age 15, was a delinquent juvenile. Randy, who was on probation for one charge of shoplifting, conspiracy to commit shoplifting, and receiving stolen goods, failed to appear at the first scheduled hearing. At a second hearing . . . Randy admitted the allegations of his petitions, namely, that he was intoxicated and disruptive in public, and that he stole five cartons of cigarettes. Randy also admitted that he had a substance abuse problem with Dilaudid (a highly addictive narcotic pain reliever) and cocaine. . . .

At the dispositional phase of the hearing, Randy's attorney asked that the court counselor look into programs appropriate to Randy's situation. The counselor responded, "[W]e don't have a Drug Rehabilitation Program. His mother has tried to get him into treatment. She does not have any insurance." The judge then suggested training school as a dispositional alternative, since Randy could receive treatment for drug abuse there. . . .

Randy's attorney argued that Randy's offenses were not so serious as to warrant commitment to training school, that training school was not designed to be a drug treatment facility, and that less restrictive dispositional alternatives existed and should be tried before resorting to commitment to training school. The attorney offered several suggestions, including . . . a group home, . . . a private substance abuse facility, . . . placing Randy in the custody of the Department of Social Services through which drug treatment could be arranged or hospitalization.

* * *

The judge . . . made several findings of fact. . . .

> [T]he alternatives to commitment have been attempted unsuccessfully or are inappropriate and . . . the juvenile's behavior constitutes a threat to property . . . and . . . to his own well being.

The judge ordered Randy to be committed to training school "for an indeterminate period of time not to exceed two years," and further ordered the training school to ". . . provide the necessary treatment for any condition they may find, including but not limited to controlled substance abuse."

* * *

The focus of the juvenile justice system is not on punishing the juvenile offender but on achieving an individualized disposition that meets the juvenile's needs and promotes his best interests. . . . The best interest of the State and safety of the public are also factors to be weighed in arriving at the appropriate disposition. . . .

Section 7A-649 lists ten dispositional alternatives for delinquent juveniles, the most severe of which is commitment to training school; the other nine are various "community-level" alternatives. . . . Among these alternatives are: . . . ordering participation in a supervised day program . . . ; intermittent confinement in a detention facility; placement in a community-based educational program; and placement in a professional residential or nonresidential treatment program. . . .

The judge may also allow the parent to arrange for necessary care or treatment, and if the parent is unwilling or unable to do so, the judge may order it himself. . . . In that case, "the judge may order the parent to pay the cost of such care . . . [or] [i]f the judge finds the parent is unable to pay the cost of care, the judge may charge the cost to the county.". . .

The legislative preference for a community-based solution to the juvenile offender problem is reflected throughout the Juvenile Code. . . . Section 7A-646 mandates that "appropriate community resources" be considered, and if possible, employed, before resorting to . . . commitment to a training school. N.C. Gen. St. Sec. 7A-646 (1986). . . . thus, commitment to training school is an option to be reserved only for those extraordinary situations. . . .

Before a delinquent juvenile may be committed to training school, the judge must find that two tests have been met: first, "that alternatives to commitment . . . have been attempted unsuccessfully or are inappropriate," and second, "that the juvenile's behavior constitutes a threat to persons or property in the community." N.C. Gen. St. Sec.7a-6552(a) (1986). . . . Randy assigns error to the judge's finding regarding the first test.

Randy contends that the evidence in the record does not support the finding that alternatives to commitment (1) were tried unsuccessfully or (2) were inappropriate. We agree.

* * *

First, there was inadequate exploration of what alternatives . . . existed. . . . [It] appears that the judge did not consider any of the broad range of community-level alternatives. . . . Moreover, although Randy's attorney offered several examples of appropriate alternative programs, the judge apparently failed to entertain these. . . . We hold that the judge had an affirmative obligation to inquire into and to seriously consider the merits of alternative dispositions, and that his failure to do so was error.

Second, the only statutory alternative actually attempted was probation. None of the remaining alternatives . . . were attempted. . . . The inability of Randy 's mother to pay for drug treatment does not amount to an "attempt," let alone an "unsuccessful attempt" at drug rehabilitation. In our view, the determination of what disposition is appropriate . . . cannot be predicated on the parent's ability . . . to pay. . . . Thus, there is no evidence in the record to support the finding that alternatives to commitment were attempted unsuccessfully.

Randy also challenges the finding that alternatives to commitment "were inappropriate.". . . Here, no alternatives to training school were presented by the court counselor, and therefore none were considered by the judge. There is thus no basis in the evidence for the judge's finding that the alternatives were inappropriate. [We] find no evidence that medical or psychological evaluations were performed to assist the judge in assessing the extent of, or fashioning an appropriate response to, Randy' asserted drug problem. . . .

While it may not be necessary to seek medical or psychiatric input in every juvenile case in which drug use is implicated, the case before us provides a compelling example of when such an inquiry is merited. The emphasis throughout the hearing was on Randy's drug use: its role in the offenses he committed; Randy's withdrawal reaction while in custody; his mother's unsuccessful attempt to have him admitted to a treatment program; and the judge's firm belief that Randy needed to overcome his drug dependency.

The superficial inquiry into the nature of Randy's needs and the range of programs that might meet those needs leads us to conclude that there is no support in the record for the finding that the remaining alternatives . . . were "inappropriate." . . .

[The] evidence and findings did not support the appropriateness of incarceration in this case. . . . The judge was required by statute to select the least restrictive dispositional alternative in light of the circumstances. . . . This he failed to do.

Arguably, Randy's current and previous offenses were not so serious as to justify commitment to training school. However, since no community-based alternatives, short of probation, were first attempted, or for that matter, even considered, we hold that imposing the harshest alternative, commitment to training school, was inappropriate. . . .

[We] hold that it was error to commit Randy Groves to training school without first examining the appropriateness of community-based dispositional alternatives. We conclude that the judge's finding . . . was not supported by the evidence. Accordingly, we vacate the commitment order and remand the cause for a new dispositional hearing.

On remand, the judge should carefully assess Randy's needs. The judge should also instruct the court counselor to inform him of alternative programs that might meet these needs. We offer some examples of dispositional alternatives the court might consider . . . admission to a State, charitable, or for-profit residential or out-patient drug treatment program; enrollment in a substance abuse program . . . ; placement in a group home, supervised day care, or specialized foster care where the opportunity for drug use is curtailed and drug treatment can be arranged; or placing custody in the Department of Social Services through which appropriate drug treatment will be secured.

Affirmed.

Notes

1. Courts that have the option to send a delinquent juvenile to either a community based program or a state institution are very reluctant to confine the juvenile in an institution. *See, e.g., In re John H.*, 369 N.Y.S.2d 196 (App. Div. 1995). In *In re Aline D.*, 536 P.2d 65 (Cal. 1975), the court held that a juvenile cannot be committed to an institution solely on the basis that no other suitable alternatives exist. The *Aline D.* court held that the state must show that the child will benefit from treatment offered at the state institution before the juvenile can be sent there.

2. Massachusetts completely overhauled its juvenile justice system in 1980 in favor of smaller, private, non-profit organizations. *The Massachusetts Juvenile Justice System of the 1990s: Re-Thinking a National Model,* 21 NEW ENG. J. ON CRIM. & CIV. CONFINEMENT 339 (1995). Massachusetts abolished juvenile detention centers and created a system in which delinquent juveniles are either placed under the power of the court through probation or under the power of the Department of Youth Services (DYS). *Id.* at 349. If a delinquent juvenile is placed under the care of the DYS, then a small DYS staff evaluates the juvenile on an individual basis to determine what treatment the juvenile requires for rehabilitation. *Id.* at 348. Less serious offenders under the care of DYS may be placed in foster care or in a training camp. For the more serious offenders, the DYS staff weigh the danger of the juvenile toward society against the ability of the juvenile to control his or her delinquent behavior. *Id.* Massachusetts' focus on community-based programs as the main component of rehabilitation has received national recognition for its success in reducing delinquent recidivism. Samuel Davis wrote in RIGHTS OF JUVENILES § 6.3, 6-15 (2000) that other community-based programs like Massachusetts' have also met with considerable success in lowering the recidivism rate among juvenile delinquents.

Questions

The court in *In re Groves* held that a juvenile court should consider community based alternatives before placing the child in state detention facilities. What policy considerations that you have studied thus far does this requirement reflect? Is a court in a better position to determine what treatment a juvenile requires than an administrative board, such as in the Massachusetts' plan, *supra,* Note 2?

Problem

Assume that Jason, a juvenile with no history of delinquency, is charged with an act of delinquency, i.e. possession of methydrine, a controlled substance. Jason's father has an extensive background in drug rehabilitation, having worked in a drug-rehabilitation facility for twenty years. Four years ago, Jason's father refused to cooperate with the court when Jason's older sister was placed on probation. At Jason's dispositional hearing, the judge must determine whether probation or a community based program is the least restrictive alternative. Given Jason's drug problem, his father's background knowledge of drug rehabilitation, and the father's prior uncooperative attitude toward probation, should the court order that probation or a community based program is the appropriate disposition for Jason? If the predispositional report and the social workers all recommend that Jason be placed on probation as the least restrictive alternative, can the judge choose to place Jason in a community based program? What factors should be the basis for placement in a community based program? *See In the Interest of A.J.D.,* 515 N.E.2d 1277 (Ill. App. Ct. 1987); *In re Andrew M.M.,* 589 N.Y.S.2d 1008 (App. Div. 1992). For the importance of imposing the least restrictive alternative for drug or alcohol abuse among juvenile delinquents, see *Commonwealth v. Ramos,* 573 A.2d 1027 (Pa. Super. Ct. 1990); *In re J.F.,* 787 P.2d 364 (Mont. 1990).

F. Blended Sentencing

Blended sentencing utilizes a combination of adult and juvenile sanctions that are statutorily determined based on the age of the offender and the offense at issue. The juvenile court retains jurisdiction of the young offender, yet has the authority to sentence the juvenile with adult sanctions. Two models of blended sentencing include the contiguous structure and inclusive sanctioning.

With contiguous sentencing, the juvenile court imposes a juvenile correctional sanction that may remain in place beyond the age that terminates the juvenile court's jurisdiction, at which point various procedures are implemented to transfer the case to the adult correctional system. Under an inclusive sentencing regime, the juvenile court imposes both a juvenile and an adult correctional sanction, with the adult sanction suspended pending a violation of the juvenile disposition.

In re L.J.S.

539 N.W.2d 408 (Minn. Ct. App. 1995)

LANSING, Judge.

The consolidated certified questions raise constitutional challenges to the new extended jurisdiction juvenile statute and to the new presumption of certification applied in certain juvenile delinquency proceedings. . . . The trial court in each case denied defense challenges to the constitutionality of the statute, but certified the question as important and doubtful. We conclude that the statutes are constitutional and answer the consolidated certified questions in the negative.

[The] legislature amended the laws pertaining to juveniles to provide extended jurisdiction that allows the juvenile court to retain jurisdiction until age twenty-one and to impose a juvenile disposition subject to a stayed adult penalty that can be imposed if the juvenile violates the conditions of his disposition or commits a new offense. . . . Presumptive certification may be rebutted by clear and convincing evidence that retaining the proceeding in juvenile court serves the public interest. . . .

* * *

The following issues are certified as important and doubtful:

I. Is the provision in Minn. Stat. Section 260.126, subd. 1(2) for prosecutor-designated extended jurisdiction proceedings unconstitutionally vague?

II. Does the prosecutor-designated extended jurisdiction juvenile provision violate the separation of powers?

III. Does the presumptive certification statute, Minn. Stat. Section 260.125, subd. 2a, violate equal protection?

IV. Does the presumptive certification statute violate due process by creating a mandatory irrebuttable presumption of certification?

V. Does the presumptive certification statute violate due process by placing on the juvenile the burden of persuasion?

I.

The section of Minn. Stat. Section 260.126 at issue provides that a proceeding involving a child alleged to have committed a felony offense is an extended jurisdiction juvenile prosecution if:

* * *

2. the child was 16 or 17 years old at the time of the alleged offense; the child is alleged to have committed an offense for which the sentencing guidelines and applicable statutes presume a commitment to

> prison or to have committed any felony in which the child allegedly used a firearm; and the prosecutor designated in the delinquency petition that the proceeding is an extended jurisdiction juvenile prosecution. . . .

[J.T.K.] asserts that this language is unconstitutionally vague and violates due process by creating the potential for arbitrary and discriminatory enforcement. . . .

* * *

A prosecutor can designate an extended jurisdiction juvenile proceeding only if the juvenile is sixteen or seventeen years old and only if the petition alleges an offense with a presumptively executed guidelines sentence or an offense involving the use of a firearm. . . . The criteria in the current statute for prosecutor-designated extended jurisdiction juvenile prosecutions are . . . specific. The statute does not lack minimal guidelines for extended jurisdiction juvenile designation or give too much discretion to prosecutors. . . . We reject J.T.K.'s suggestion that a higher standard or definiteness should apply because the designation is made by the prosecutor rather than the court. . . . [We] conclude that Minn.Stat. Section 260.126, subd 1(2) is not unconstitutionally vague. . . .

II.

J.T.K. argues that the prosecutor's exclusive role in designating the extended jurisdiction juvenile proceedings . . . violates the separation of powers. He maintains that only the court can constitutionally designate a juvenile case as an extended jurisdiction juvenile proceedings because the designation sharply restricts the court's sentencing powers. . . . J.T.K. characterizes the prosecutor's designation . . . as essentially a sentencing determination because it prevents the court from imposing a purely juvenile disposition. The state counters that the decision is merely a charging decision. . . .

[The] U.S. Supreme Court in recent years has emphasized a "flexible understanding of separation of powers" that does not require a "hermetic division among the Branches." *Mistretta v. United States,* 488 U.S. 361, 381 (1989). Even if the prosecutor's extended jurisdiction juvenile designation restricts to some degree the court's ultimate sentencing options, some interplay between the responsibilities of the executive and judicial branches is permitted. . . . [We] conclude that the prosecutor-designated extended jurisdiction juvenile provision does not violate the separation of powers.

III.

L.J.S. argues that the presumptive certification provision . . . violates equal protection because there is no rational basis for distinguishing those juveniles subject to the provision from those not within its definition. The presumptive certification provision states:

> It is presumed that a proceeding involving an offense committed by a child will be certified to district court if:

> (1) the child was 16 or 17 years old at the time of the offense; and
> (2) the delinquency petition alleges that the child committed an offense that would result in a presumptive commitment to prison under the sentencing guidelines and applicable statutes, or that the child committed any felony offense while using . . . a firearm. Minn. Stat. Section 260.125, subd. 2a (1994).

If the presumption applies, then the juvenile bears the burden of rebutting it by clear and convincing evidence. L.J.S. concedes that . . . the "rational basis" test is the appropriate standard for determining whether the statute violates equal protection.

L.J.S. is claiming only a violation of the Minnesota Constitution. Under Minnesota's "rational basis" test, there must be a genuine and substantial distinction between those included in the classification and those excluded, the classification must be relevant to the purpose of the statute. The purpose of the juvenile certification statute has been narrowed to protecting public safety. . . . The juvenile's age is highly relevant to whether the juvenile jurisdiction serves public safety. . . . If a juvenile's age curtails the length of time available for juvenile treatment, and if the offense indicates danger to the public, the public safety is not served.

The offense criteria are also directly related to the danger to public safety. Offenses carrying a presumptively executed sentence are generally crimes against the person, representing a greater threat to public safety. . . . Crimes involving the use of firearms also pose a greater threat to public safety. [We] conclude that the presumptive certification statute does not violate equal protection.

IV.

L.J.S. argues that the presumptive certification statute violates due process because it creates a mandatory, irrebuttable presumption. . . . The presumptive certification statute does not affect the state's burden of proving an element of the offense, and so does not conflict with the presumption of innocence. . . . Neither does the presumptive certification statute create an irrebuttable presumption. The juvenile may rebut . . . "by demonstrating by clear and convincing evidence that retaining the proceeding in juvenile court serves public safety." Minn. Stat. Section 260.125, subd. 2a. The juvenile may present relevant evidence on several listed factors. . . . L.J.S. cites no authority to support his claim that a presumption is irrebuttable. . . .

V.

Finally, L.J.S. argues that the presumptive certification statute violates due process by shifting the burden of persuasion to the juvenile. Shifts in the burden of persuasion on any element in a criminal offense violate due process. . . . The certification presumption applies only to a pretrial procedure, although one that determines which court will try the juvenile. But criminal defendants routinely bear the burden of persuasion on some pretrial motions, such as constitutional challenges to statutes. . . .

The state concedes that some presumptions, at least irrebuttable ones, may violate due process even though they occur in civil context which does not implicate the presumption of innocence. . . . But, the presumption of certification that applies to L.J.S. is not irrebuttable. Moreover, the presumption does not shift the burden of persuasion on any element of offense. The presumption merely determines which court will try the case and evaluate the elements of the offense.

The statutory provision for a prosecutor-designated extended jurisdiction juvenile proceeding is not unconstitutionally vague and does not violate the separation-of-powers doctrine. The presumptive certification statute does not violate equal protection of due process.

Certified questions answered in the negative.

Notes

1. The punitive trend in sentencing juvenile offenders has created various methods for addressing juvenile crime, including mandatory minimum sentencing, sentence enhancements, and extended transfer provisions. Blended sentencing represents the latest legislative attempt to answer the public outcry against violent juvenile crime. This model is unique in that it allows a juvenile court judge to access the benefits of both the juvenile court and the adult criminal system. With inclusive sentencing, the judge is able to simultaneously impose a juvenile disposition and an adult correctional sentence, with the latter being suspended pending a violation of the juvenile's disposition or the commission of another offense. With contiguous sentencing, the juvenile court can impose a sanction that goes beyond the court's extended jurisdiction and which is transferred to the adult correctional system once the juvenile reaches the age of majority.

Accessing both systems enables the judge to employ the benefits of both systems. First, the young offender is given a "last chance" to benefit from the unique advantages of the juvenile system, which focuses primarily on rehabilitation. The pending adult sentence is seen as a deterrent for the young offender, a form of motivation encouraging compliance with the juvenile disposition. In the event the juvenile is unable or unwilling to satisfy the conditions of her juvenile disposition, she faces additional time in the adult correctional system.

Mary E. Spring, in her article *Extended Jurisdiction Prosecution: A New Approach to the Problem of Juvenile Delinquency in Illinois,* 31 J. MARSHALL L. REV. 1351 (1998), argues that neither the juvenile nor adult correctional systems alone can effectively address chronic and potentially violent juvenile offenders. Spring suggests that the rehabilitative focus of the juvenile system does not promote accountability, and thereby fosters recidivism. The criminal system, with its focus on punishment, does not provide many of the services needed by these young offenders, such as training classes, educational advancement, and psychological counseling. However, overlapping the jurisdiction of these systems effectively provides the flexibility required to successfully handle these cases. She suggests that extended jurisdiction juvenile prosecution provides the necessary accountability with the imposition of a stayed adult sentence, which has the effect of encouraging the youth to accept offered rehabilitation.

2. Blended sentencing, or "last chance" legislation, is seen by some as the most effective way to address violent youth offenders. *See, e.g.,* Cathi J. Hunt, Note, *Juvenile Sentencing: Effects of Recent Punitive Sentencing Legislation on Juvenile Offenders and a Proposal for Sentencing in the Juvenile Court,* 19 B.C. THIRD WORLD L.J. 621 (1999). While blended sentencing is promising, some commentators warn judges and prosecutors to use caution in the implementation of these statutes. They suggest that there are specific due process and equal protection considerations unique to this approach, due to the fundamental differences between the adult and juvenile systems. Juvenile court proceedings do not guarantee the same rights enjoyed by adults in criminal proceedings. Yet juveniles are exposed to adult sanctions through blended sentencing and are without defenses available to their adult counterparts when these sanctions are imposed in a juvenile disposition. For an interesting discussion on this point, see Sarah M. Cotton, Comment, *When the Punishment Cannot Fit the Crime: The Case for Reforming the Juvenile Justice System,* 52 ARK. L. REV. 563 (1999).

Questions

1. One of the primary concerns of juvenile courts prior to the 1970s was the ability of the juvenile to comprehend the nature and consequences of his or her delinquent act. If a juvenile commits a serious delinquent act and the prosecutor seeks a blended sentence, should the juvenile be tried as a reasonable juvenile of similar age and ability or as a reasonable adult? Why would this distinction be significant during the delinquency hearing? If a judge in the same case determines that the juvenile is incompetent because of youth and immaturity, what should the judge do with the juvenile?

2. What additional due process safeguards should courts afford juveniles when a prosecutor seeks a blended sentence? What would be the most effective vehicle for making sure that juveniles who face a blended sentence can utilize the protections of the law afforded to adults?

G. Death Penalty for Children

Thompson v. Oklahoma

487 U.S. 815, 108 S. Ct. 2687, 101 L. Ed. 2d 702 (1988)

Justice STEVENS announced the judgment of the Court and delivered an opinion in which Justice BRENNAN, Justice MARSHALL, and Justice BLACKMUN join.

Petitioner was convicted of first-degree murder and sentenced to death. The principal question presented is whether the execution of that sentence would violate the constitutional prohibition against the infliction of "cruel and unusual punishments" because petitioner was only 15 years old at the time of his offense.

I

Because there is no claim that the punishment would be excessive if the crime had been committed by an adult, only a brief statement of facts is necessary. In concert with three older persons, petitioner actively participated in the brutal murder of his former brother-in-law in the early morning hours of January 23, 1983. The evidence disclosed that the victim had been shot twice, and that his throat, chest, and abdomen had been cut. He also had multiple bruises and a broken leg. His body had been chained to a concrete block and thrown into a river where it remained for almost four weeks. Each of the four participants was tried separately and each was sentenced to death.

Because petitioner was a "child" as a matter of Oklahoma law, the District Attorney filed a statutory petition . . . seeking an order finding "that said child is competent and had the mental capacity to know and appreciate the wrongfulness of his [conduct]." After a hearing, the trial court concluded "that there are virtually no *reasonable* prospects for rehabilitation of William Wayne Thompson within the juvenile system and William Wayne Thompson should be held accountable for his acts as if he were an adult and should be certified to stand trial as an adult."

* * *

At the penalty phase of the trial, the prosecutor asked the jury to find two aggravating circumstances: that the murder was especially heinous, atrocious, or cruel; and that there was a probability that the defendant would commit criminal acts of violence that would constitute a continuing threat to society. The jury found the first, but not the second, and fixed petitioner's punishment at death.

The Court of Criminal Appeals affirmed the conviction and sentence, 724 P.2d 780 (1986), *citing its earlier opinion in Eddings v. State*, 616 P.2d 1159 (1980), *rev'd on other grounds*, 455 U.S. 104 (1982), for the proposition that "once a minor is certified to stand trial as an adult, he may also, without violating the Constitution, be punished as an adult." 724 P.2d at 784. We granted certiorari to consider whether a sentence of death is cruel and unusual punishment for a crime committed by a 15-year-old child. . . .

II

The authors of the Eighth Amendment drafted a categorical prohibition against the infliction of cruel and unusual punishments, but they made no attempt to define the contours of that category. They delegated that task to future generations of judges who have been guided by the "evolving standards of decency that mark the progress of a maturing society." *Trop v. Dulles*, 356 U.S. 86, 101 (1958) (plurality opinion) (Warren, C.J.). . . . Thus, in confronting the question whether the youth of the defendant—more specifically, the fact that he was less than 16 years old at the time of his offense—is a sufficient reason for denying the State the power to sentence him to death, we first review relevant legislative enactments, then refer to jury determinations,[7] and finally explain why these indicators of contemporary standards of decency confirm our judgment that such a young person is not capable of acting with the degree of culpability that can justify the ultimate penalty.

III

Justice Powell has repeatedly reminded us of the importance of "the experience of mankind, as well as the long history of our law, recognizing that there *are* differences which must be accommodated in determining the rights and duties of children as compared with those of adults. . . ." *Goss v. Lopez*, 419 U.S. 565, 590-91 (1975) (dissenting opinion). Oklahoma recognizes this basic distinction in a number of its statutes. Thus, a minor is not eligible to vote, to sit on a jury, to marry without parental consent, or to purchase alcohol or cigarettes. Like all other States, Oklahoma has developed a juvenile justice system in which most offenders under the age of 18 are not held criminally responsible. Its statutes do provide, however, that a 16- or 17-year-old charged with murder and other serious felonies shall be considered an adult. . . .

The line between childhood and adulthood is drawn in different ways by various States. There is, however, complete or near unanimity among all 50 States and the District of Columbia in treating a person under 15 as a minor for several important purposes. . . . Most relevant . . . is the fact that all States have enacted legislation designating the maximum age for juvenile court jurisdiction at no less than 16.[22] All of this legislation is consistent with the experience of mankind, as well as the long history of our law, that the normal 15-year-old is not prepared to assume the full responsibilities of an adult.[23]

Most state legislatures have not expressly confronted the question of establishing a minimum age for imposition of the death penalty. In 14 States, capital punishment is not authorized at all, and in 19 others capital punishment is authorized but no minimum age is expressly stated in the death penalty statute. One might argue on the basis of this body of legislation that there is no

---

[7] Our capital punishment jurisprudence has consistently recognized that contemporary standard, as reflected by the actions of legislatures and juries, provide an important measure of whether the death penalty is "cruel and unusual." Part of the rationale for this index of constitutional value lies in the very language of the construed clause: whether an action is "unusual" depends, in common usage, upon the frequency of its occurrence or the magnitude of its acceptance. . . .

[22] S. DAVIS, RIGHTS OF JUVENILES: THE JUVENILE JUSTICE SYSTEM, Appendix B (1987). Thus, every State has adopted "a rebuttable presumption" that a person under 16 "is not mature and responsible enough to be punished as an adult," no matter how minor the offense may be.

[23] The law must often adjust the manner in which it affords rights to those whose status renders them unable to exercise choice freely and rationally. . . . [S]tatutes . . . from both Oklahoma and other states, reflect this basic assumption that our society makes about children as a class; we assume that they do not yet act as adults do, and thus we act in their interest by restricting certain choices that we feel they are not yet ready to make. . . . It would be ironic if these assumptions that we so readily make about children as a class—about their inherent difference from adults in their capacity as agents, as choosers, as shapers of their own lives—were suddenly unavailable in determining whether it is cruel and unusual to treat children the same as adults for purposes of inflicting capital punishment. . . .

chronological age at which the imposition of the death penalty is unconstitutional. . . . We think it self-evident that such an argument is unacceptable; indeed, no such argument has been advanced in this case. If, therefore, we accept the premise that some offenders are simply too young to be put to death, it is reasonable to put this group of statutes to one side because they do not focus on the question of where the chronological age line should be drawn. When we confine our attention to the 18 States that have expressly established a minimum age in their death penalty statutes, we find that all of them require that the defendant have attained at least the age of 16 at the time of the capital offense.

The conclusion that it would offend civilized standards of decency to execute a person who was less than 16 years old at the time of his or her offense is consistent with the views that have been expressed by respected professional organizations, by other nations that share our Anglo-American heritage, and by the leading members of the Western European community. Thus the American Bar Association and the American Law Institute have formally expressed their opposition to the death penalty for juveniles. Although the death penalty has not been entirely abolished in the United Kingdom or New Zealand . . . , in neither of those countries may a juvenile be executed. The death penalty has been abolished in West Germany, France, Portugal, The Netherlands, and all of the Scandinavian countries, and is available only for exceptional crimes such as treason in Canada, Italy, Spain, and Switzerland. Juvenile executions are also prohibited in the Soviet Union.

IV

The second societal factor the Court has examined in determining the acceptability of capital punishment to the American sensibility is the behavior of juries. In fact, the infrequent and haphazard handing out of death sentences by capital juries was a prime factor underlying our judgment in *Furman v. Georgia*, 408 U.S. 238 (1972), that the death penalty, as then administered in unguided fashion, was unconstitutional.

While it is not known precisely how many persons have been executed during the 20th century for crimes committed under the age of 16, a scholar has recently complied a table revealing this number to be between 18 and 20.[36] All of these occurred during the first half of the century, with the last such execution taking place . . . in 1948. . . . The road we have traveled during the past four decades . . . leads to the unambiguous conclusion that the imposition of the death penalty on a 15-year-old offender is now generally abhorrent to the conscience of the community.

Department of Justice statistics indicate that during the years 1982 through 1986 an average of over 16,000 persons were arrested for willful criminal homicide . . . each year. Of that group of 82,094 persons, 1,393 were sentenced to death. Only 5 of them, including the petitioner in this case, were less than 16 years old at the time of the offense. Statistics of this kind . . . suggest

---

[36] V. STREIB, DEATH PENALTY FOR JUVENILES 190-208 (1987).

that these five young offenders have received sentences that are "cruel and unusual in the same way that being struck by lightning is cruel and unusual." *Furman v. Georgia,* 408 U.S. at 309 (Stewart J., concurring).

V

"Although the judgments of legislatures, juries, and prosecutors weigh heavily in the balance, it is for us ultimately to judge whether the Eighth Amendment permits imposition of the death penalty" on one such as petitioner who committed a heinous murder when he was only 15 years old. *Enmund v. Florida*, 458 U.S. 782, 797 (1982). In making that judgment, we first ask whether the juvenile's culpability should be measured by the same standard as that of an adult and then consider whether the application of the death penalty to this class of offenders "measurably contributes" to the social purposes that are served by the death penalty. *Id.* at 798.

It is generally agreed "that punishment should be directly related to the personal culpability of the criminal defendant." *California v. Brown*, 479 U.S. 538 (1987) (O'Connor, J., concurring). There is also broad agreement on the proposition that adolescents as a class are less mature and responsible than adults. We stressed this difference in explaining the importance of treating the defendant's youth as a mitigating factor in capital cases:

> "But youth is more than a chronological fact. It is a time and condition of life when a person may be most susceptible to influence and to psychological damages. Our history is replete with laws and judicial recognition that minors, especially in their earlier years, generally are less mature and responsible than adults. Particularly 'during the formative years of childhood and adolescence, minors often lack the experience, perspective, and judgment' expected of adults. *Bellotti v. Baird,* 443 U.S. 622, 635 (1979)." *Eddings v. Oklahoma,* 455 U.S. 104, 115-116 (1982) (footnotes omitted).

To add further emphasis to the special mitigating force of youth, Justice Powell quoted the following passage from the 1978 Report of the Twentieth Century Fund Task Force on Sentencing Policy Toward Young Offenders:

> "[A]dolescents, particularly in the early and middle teen years, are more vulnerable, more impulsive, and less self-disciplined than adults. Crimes committed by youths may be just as harmful to victims as those committed by older persons, but they deserve less punishment because adolescents may have less capacity to control their conduct and to think in long-range terms than adults. Moreover, youth crime as such is not exclusively the offender's fault; offenses by the young also represent a failure of family, school, and the social system, which share responsibility for the development of America's youth."

455 U.S. at 115 n.11.

Thus, the Court has already endorsed the proposition that less culpability should attach to a crime committed by a juvenile than to a comparable crime committed by an adult. . . . The reasons why juveniles are not trusted with the privileges and responsibilities of an adult also explain why their irresponsible conduct is not as morally reprehensible as that of an adult.

"The death penalty is said to serve two principal social purposes: retribution and deterrence of capital crimes by prospective offenders." *Gregg v. Georgia,* 428 U.S. 153, 183 (1976) (joint opinion of Stewart, Powell, and Stevens, JJ.). In *Gregg* we concluded that as "an expression of society's moral outrage at particularly offensive conduct," retribution was not "inconsistent with our respect for the dignity of men." *Ibid.* Given the lesser culpability of the juvenile offender, the teenager's capacity for growth, and society's fiduciary obligations to its children, this conclusion is simply inapplicable to the execution of a 15-year-old offender.

For such a young offender, the deterrence rationale is equally unacceptable. The Department of Justice statistics indicate that about 98% of the arrests for willful homicide involved persons who were over 16 at the time of the offense. Thus, excluding younger persons from the class that is eligible for the death penalty will not diminish the deterrent value of capital punishment for the vast majority of potential offenders. And even with respect to those under 16 years of age, . . . the potential deterrent value of the death sentence is insignificant. . . . The likelihood that the teenage offender has made the kind of cost-benefit analysis that attaches any weight to the possibility of execution is so remote as to be virtually nonexistent. And . . . it is fanciful to believe that he would be deterred by the knowledge that a small number of persons his age have been executed during the 20th century. In short we are not persuaded that the imposition of the death penalty for offenses committed by persons under 16 years of age has made, or can be expected to make, any measurable contribution to the goals that capital punishment is intended to achieve. It is, therefore, "nothing more than the purposeless and needless imposition of pain and suffering," *Coker v. Georgia,* 433 U.S. 584, 592 (1977), and thus an unconstitutional punishment.

Petitioner's counsel and various *amici curiae* have asked us to "draw a line" that would prohibit the execution of any person who was under the age of 18 at the time of the offense. Our task today, however, is to decide the case before us; we do so by concluding that the Eighth and Fourteenth Amendments prohibit the execution of a person who was under 16 years of age at the time of his or her offense.

The judgment of the Court of Criminal Appeals is vacated, and the case is remanded with instructions to enter an appropriate order vacating petitioner's death sentence.

Justice KENNEDY took no part in the consideration or decision of this case.

Justice O'CONNOR, concurring in the judgment.

. . . Although I believe that a national consensus forbidding the execution of any person for a crime committed before the age of 16 very likely does exist, I am reluctant to adopt this conclusion as a matter of constitutional law without better evidence than we now possess. Because I conclude that the sentence in this case can and should be set aside on narrower grounds than those adopted by the plurality, . . . I concur only in the judgment of the Court.

I

Both the plurality and the dissent look initially to the decisions of American legislatures for signs of a national consensus about the minimum age at which a juvenile's crimes may lead to capital punishment. Although I agree with the dissent's contention that these decisions should provide the most reliable signs of a society-wide consensus on this issue, I cannot agree with the dissent's interpretation of the evidence.

The most salient statistic that bears on this case is that every single American legislature that has expressly set a minimum age for capital punishment has set that age at 16 or above. When one adds these 18 States to the 14 that have rejected capital punishment completely, it appears that almost two-thirds of the state legislatures have definitely concluded that no 15-year-old should be exposed to the threat of execution. . . . Where such a large majority of the state legislatures have unambiguously outlawed capital punishment for 15-year-olds, and where no legislature in this country has affirmatively and unequivocally endorsed such a practice, strong counterevidence would be required to persuade me that a national consensus against this practice does not exist.

The dissent argues that it has found such counterevidence in the laws of the 19 States that authorize capital punishment without setting any statutory minimum age. If we could be sure that each of these 19 state legislatures had deliberately chosen to authorize capital punishment for crimes committed at the age of 15, one could hardly suppose that there is a settled national consensus opposing such a practice. In fact, however, the statistics relied on by the dissent may be quite misleading. When a legislature provides for some 15-year-olds to be processed through the adult criminal justice system, and capital punishment is available for adults in that jurisdiction, the death penalty becomes at least theoretically applicable to such defendants. . . . As the plurality points out, however, it does not necessarily follow that the legislatures in those jurisdictions have deliberately concluded that it would be appropriate to impose capital punishment on 15-year-olds (or on even younger defendants who may be tried as adults in some jurisdictions).

* * *

. . . The day may come when we must decide whether a legislature may deliberately and unequivocally resolve upon a policy authorizing capital punishment for crimes committed at the age of 15. In that event, we shall have to decide the Eighth Amendment issue that divides the plurality and the dissent in this case, and we shall have to evaluate the evidence of societal standards of decency that is available to us at that time. In my view, however, we need not and should not decide the question today.

II

* * *

The case before us today raises some of the same concerns that have led us to erect barriers to the imposition of capital punishment in other contexts. Oklahoma has enacted a statute that authorizes capital punishment for murder, without setting any minimum age at which the commission of murder may lead to the imposition of that penalty. The State has also, but quite separately, provided that 15-year-old murder defendants may be treated as adults in some circumstances. Because it proceeded in this manner, there is a considerable risk that the Oklahoma legislature either did not realize that its actions would have the effect of rendering 15-year-old defendants death eligible or did not give the question the serious consideration that would have been reflected in the explicit choice of some minimum age for death eligibility. . . . [T]he Oklahoma statutes have presented this court with a result that is of very dubious constitutionality, and they have done so without the earmarks of careful consideration that we have required for other kinds of decisions leading to the death penalty. In this unique situation, I am prepared to conclude that petitioner and others who were below the age of 16 at the time of their offense may not be executed under the authority of a capital punishment statute that specifies no minimum age at which the commission of a capital crime can lead to the offender's execution.

. . . By leaving open for now the broader Eighth Amendment question that both the plurality and the dissent would resolve, the approach I take allows the ultimate moral issue at stake in the constitutional question to be addressed in the first instance by those best suited to do so, the people's elected representatives.

For the reasons stated in this position, I agree that petitioner's death sentence should be vacated, and I therefore concur in the judgment of the Court.

Justice SCALIA with whom THE CHIEF JUSTICE and Justice WHITE join, dissenting.

. . . In upsetting this particularized judgment on the basis of a constitutional absolute, the plurality pronounces it to be a fundamental principle of our society that no one who is as little as one day short of his 16th birthday can have sufficient maturity and moral responsibility to be subjected to capital punishment for any crime. As a sociological and moral conclusion that is implausible; and it is doubly implausible as an interpretation of the United States Constitution.

* * *

[T]he plurality seeks to rest its holding on the conclusion that Thompson's punishment as an adult is contrary to the "evolving standards of decency that mark the progress of a maturing society." *Trop v. Dulles,* 356 U.S. 86, 101 (1958) (plurality opinion) (Warren, C.J.). . . . It will rarely if ever be the case that the Members of this Court will have a better sense of the evolution in views of the American people than do their elected representatives.

It is thus significant that, only four years ago in the Comprehensive Crime Control Act of 1984, Pub. L. 98-473, 98 Stat. 2149, Congress expressly addressed the effect of youth upon the imposition of criminal punishment, and changed the law in precisely the opposite direction from that which the plurality's perceived evolution in social attitudes would suggest: It lowered from 16 to 15 the age at which a juvenile's case can, "in the interest of justice," be transferred from juvenile court to Federal District court, enabling him to be tried and punished as an adult. 18 U.S.C. § 5032 (1982 ed., Supp. IV). . . . Since there are federal death penalty statutes which have not been determined to be unconstitutional, adoption of this new legislation could at least theoretically result in the imposition of the death penalty upon a 15-year-old. There is, to be sure, no reason to believe that the Members of Congress had the death penalty specifically in mind; but that does not alter the reality of what federal law now on its face permits. . . .

* * *

When the Federal Government, and almost 40% of the States, including a majority of the States that include capital punishment as a permissible sanction, allow for the imposition of the death penalty on any juvenile who has been tried as an adult, . . . it is obviously impossible for the plurality to rely upon any evolved societal consensus discernible in legislation. . . .

* * *

If one believes that the data the plurality relies upon are effective to establish, with the requisite degree of certainty, a constitutional consensus in this society that no person can ever be executed for a crime committed under the age of 16, it is difficult to see why the same judgment should not extend to crimes committed under the age of 17, or of 18. . . . It seems plain to me . . . that there is no clear line here, which suggests that the plurality is inappropriately acting in a legislative rather than a judicial capacity. Doubtless at some age a line does exist . . . below which a juvenile can *never* be considered fully responsible for murder. The evidence that the views of our society . . . regard that absolute age to be 16 is nonexistent.

B

Having avoided any attempt to justify its holding on the basis of the original understanding of what was "cruel and unusual punishment," and having utterly failed in justifying its holding on the basis of "evolving standards of decency" evidenced by "the work product of state legislatures and sentencing juries," the plurality proceeds, in Part V of the opinion, to set forth its views regarding the desirability of ever imposing capital punishment for a murder committed by a 15-year-old. That discussion . . . to the conclusion that "[g]iven the lesser culpability of the juvenile offender, the teenager's capacity for growth, and society's fiduciary obligations to its children," none of the rationales for the death penalty can apply to the execution of a 15-year-old criminal, so that it is "nothing more than the purposeless and needless imposition of pain and suffering." . . .

* * *

. . . [T]here is another point of view [however] suggested in the following passage written by our esteemed former colleague Justice Powell, whose views the plurality several times invokes for support:

> "Minors who become embroiled with the law range from the very young up to those on the brink of majority. Some of the older minors become fully 'street-wise,' hardened criminals, deserving no greater consideration than that properly accorded all persons suspected of

crime." *Fare v. Michael C.*, 442 U.S. 707, 734, n.4 (1979) (dissenting opinion)

The view that it is possible for a 15-year-old to come within this category uncontestably prevailed when the Eighth and Fourteenth Amendments were adopted, and, judging from the actions of the society's democratically elected representatives, still persuades a substantial segment of the people whose "evolving standards of decency" we have been appointed to discern rather than decree. It is not necessary, as the plurality's opinion suggests, that "we [be] persuaded" of the correctness of the people's views.

* * *

For the foregoing reasons, I respectfully dissent from the judgment of the Court.

Stanford v. Kentucky

492 U.S. 361, 109 S. Ct. 2969, 106 L. Ed. 2d 306 (1989)

Justice SCALIA announced the judgment of the Court and delivered the opinion of the Court with respect to Parts I, II, III, and IV-A, and an opinion with respect to Parts IV-B and V, in which THE CHIEF JUSTICE, Justice WHITE and Justice KENNEDY join.

These two consolidated cases require us to decide whether the imposition of capital punishment on an individual for a crime committed at 16 or 17 years of age constitutes cruel and unusual punishment under the Eighth Amendment.

I

The first case, . . . involves the shooting death of 20-year-old Barbel Poore in Jefferson County, Kentucky. Petitioner Kevin Stanford committed the murder on January 7, 1981, when he was approximately 17 years and 4 months of age. Stanford and his accomplice repeatedly raped and sodomized Poore during and after their commission of a robbery at a gas station, where Stanford shot her pointblank in the face and then in the back of her head. . . .

After Stanford's arrest, a Kentucky juvenile court conducted hearings to determine whether he should be transferred for trial as an adult under Ky. Rev. Stat. Ann. § 208.170 (Michie 1982). That statute provided that juvenile court jurisdiction could be waived and an offender tried as an adult if he was either charged with a Class A felony or capital crime, or was over 16 years of age and charged with a felony. Stressing the seriousness of petitioner's offenses and the unsuccessful attempts of the juvenile system to treat him for numerous instances of past delinquency, the juvenile court found certification for trial as an adult to be in the best interest of petitioner and the community.

Stanford was convicted of murder, first-degree sodomy, first-degree robbery and receiving stolen property, and was sentenced to death. . . . The Kentucky Supreme Court affirmed the death sentence. . . . 734 S.W.2d 781 (Ky. 1997). Finding that the record clearly demonstrated that "there was no program or treatment appropriate for the appellant in the juvenile justice system," the court held that the juvenile court did not err in certifying petitioner for trial as an adult. The court also stated that petitioner's "age and the possibility that he might be rehabilitated were mitigating factors appropriately left to the consideration of the jury that tried him." *Id.* at 792.

The second case . . . involves the stabbing death of Nancy Allen, a 26-year-old mother of two who was working behind the sales counter of the convenience store she and David Allen owned and operated in Avondale, Missouri. Petitioner Heath Wilkins committed the murder on July 27, 1985, when he was approximately 16 years and 6 months of age. The record reflects that Wilkins' plan was to rob the store and murder "whoever was behind the counter" because "a dead person can't talk." While Wilkins' accomplice, Patrick Stevens, held Allen, Wilkins stabbed her, causing her to fall to the floor. When Stevens had trouble operating the cash register, Allen spoke up to assist him, leading Wilkins to stab her three more times in her chest. Two of these wounds penetrated the victim's heart. When Allen began to beg for her life, Wilkins stabbed her four more times in the neck, opening her carotid artery. After helping themselves to liquor, cigarettes, rolling papers, and approximately $450 in cash and checks, Wilkins and Stevens left Allen to die on the floor.

Because he was roughly six months short of the age of majority for purposes of criminal prosecution, Mo. Rev. Stat. § 211.021 (1) (1986), Wilkins could not automatically be tried as an adult under Missouri law. Before that could happen, the juvenile court was required to terminate juvenile court jurisdiction and certify Wilkins for trial as an adult under § 211.071, which permits individuals between 14 and 17 years of age who have committed felonies to be tried as adults. Relying on the "viciousness, force and violence" of the alleged crime, petitioner's maturity, and the failure of the juvenile justice system to rehabilitate him after previous delinquent acts, the juvenile court made the necessary certification.

Wilkins was charged with first-degree murder, armed criminal action, and carrying a concealed weapon. After the court found him competent, petitioner entered guilty pleas to all charges. A punishment hearing was held, at which both the State and petitioner himself urged imposition of the death sentence. Evidence at the hearing revealed that petitioner had been in and out of juvenile facilities since the age of eight for various acts of burglary, theft, and arson, had attempted to kill his mother by putting insecticide into Tylenol capsules, and had killed several animals in his neighborhood. Although psychiatric testimony indicated that Wilkins had "personality disorders," the witnesses agreed that Wilkins was aware of his actions and could distinguish right from wrong.

Determining that the death penalty was appropriate the trial court entered the following order:

> [T]he court finds beyond reasonable doubt that the following aggravating circumstances exist:
>
> 1. The murder in the first degree was committed while the defendant was engaged in the perpetration of the felony of robbery, and

> 2. The murder in the first degree involved depravity of mind and that as a result thereof, it was outrageously or wantonly vile, horrible or inhuman.

On mandatory review of Wilkins' death sentence, the Supreme Court of Missouri affirmed, rejecting the argument that the punishment violated the Eighth Amendment. 736 S.W.2d 409 (1987).

We granted certiorari in these cases to decide whether the Eighth Amendment precludes the death penalty for individuals who commit crimes at 16 or 17 years of age.

II

The thrust of both Wilkins' and Stanford's arguments is that imposition of the death penalty on those who were juveniles when they committed their crimes falls within the Eighth Amendment's prohibition against "cruel and unusual punishments". . . .

* * *

[P]etitioners . . . argue that their punishment is contrary to the "evolving standards of decency that mark the progress of a maturing society," *Trop v. Dulles*, 356 U.S. 896, 101 (1958) (plurality opinion). They are correct in asserting that this Court has "not confined the prohibition embodied in the Eighth Amendment to 'barbarous' methods that were generally outlawed in the 18th century," but instead has interpreted the Amendment "in a flexible and dynamic manner." *Gregg v. Georgia*, 428 U.S. 153, 171 (1976) (opinion of Stewart, Powell, and Stevens, JJ.). In determining what standards have "evolved," however, we have looked not to our own conceptions of decency, but to those of modern American society as a whole. As we have said, "Eighth Amendment judgments should not be or appear to be, merely the subjective views of individual Justices; judgment should be informed by objective factors to the maximum possible extent." *Coker v. Georgia*, 433 U.S. 584, 592 (1977) (plurality opinion). . . .

III

"[F]irst" among the "objective indicia that reflect the public attitude toward a given sanction" are statutes passed by society's elected representatives. *McCleskey v. Kemp*, 481 U.S. 279, 300 (1987), *quoting Gregg v. Georgia, supra,* at 173. Of the 37 States whose laws permit capital punishment, 15 decline to impose it upon 16-year-old offenders and 12 decline to impose it on 17-year-old offenders.[2] This does not establish the degree of national consensus

---

[2] . . . .

The dissent takes issue with our failure to include, among those States evidencing a consensus against executing 16- to 17-year old offenders, the District of Columbia and the 14 States that do not authorize capital punishment. It seems to us, however, that while the number of those jurisdictions bears upon the question whether there is a consensus against capital punishment altogether, it is quite irrelevant to the specific inquiry in this case: whether there is a settled consensus in favor of punishing offenders under 18 differently from those over 18 insofar as capital punishment is concerned. . . . The issue in the present case is not whether capital punishment is thought to be desirable but whether persons under 18 are thought to be specially exempt from it. . . .

this Court has previously thought sufficient to label a particular punishment cruel and unusual. . . .

Since a majority of the States that permit capital punishment authorize it for crimes committed at age 16 or above, petitioners' cases are . . . analogous to *Tison v. Arizona*, 481 U.S. 137 (1987). . . . In *Tison*, which upheld Arizona's imposition of the death penalty for major participation in a felony with reckless indifference to human life, we noted that only 11 of those jurisdictions imposing capital punishment rejected its use in such circumstances. *Id.* at 154. As we noted earlier, here the number is 15 for offenders under 17, and 12 for offenders under 18. We think the same conclusion as in *Tison* is required in these cases.

. . . It is not the burden of Kentucky and Missouri . . . to establish a national consensus approving what their citizens have voted to do; rather, it is the "heavy burden" of petitioners, *Gregg v. Georgia*, 428 U.S. at 175, to establish a national consensus *against* it. As far as the primary and most reliable indication of consensus is concerned—the pattern of enacted laws—petitioners have therefore failed to carry that burden.

IV

A

Wilkins and Stanford argue, however, that even if the laws themselves do not establish a settled consensus, the application of the laws does. . . . Petitioners are quite correct that a far smaller number of offenders under 18 than over 18 have been sentenced to death in this country. From 1982 through 1988, for example, out of 2,106 total death sentences, only 15 were imposed on individuals who were 16 or under when they committed their crimes, and only 30 on individuals who were 17 at the time of the crime. *See* Streib, Imposition of Death Sentences For Juvenile Offenses, January 1, 1982, Through April 1, 1989, p. 2 (paper for Cleveland-Marshall College of Law, April 5, 1989). And it appears that actual executions for crimes committed under age 18 accounted for only about two percent of the total number of executions that occurred between 1982 and 1986. *See* STREIB, DEATH PENALTY FOR JUVENILES 55, 57 (1987). . . . These statistics, however carry little significance. Given the undisputed fact that a far smaller percentage of capital crimes are committed by persons under 18 than over 18, the discrepancy in treatment is much less than might seem. Granted, however, that a substantial discrepancy exists, that does not establish the requisite proposition that the death sentence for offenders under 18 is categorically unacceptable to prosecutors and juries. To the contrary, it is not only possible, but overwhelmingly probable, that the very considerations which induce petitioners and their supporters to believe that death should *never* be imposed on offenders under 18 cause prosecutors and juries to believe that it should *rarely* be imposed.

B

[T]here is also no relevance to the laws cited by petitioners . . . which set 18 or more as the legal age for engaging in various activities, ranging from driving to drinking alcoholic beverages to voting. . . . [T]he age statutes . . . do not represent a social judgment that all persons under the designated ages are not responsible enough to drive, to drink, or to vote, but at most a judgment that the vast majority are not. These laws set the appropriate ages for the operation of a system that makes its determination in gross, and that does not conduct individualized maturity tests for each driver, drinker, or voter. The criminal justice system, however, does provide individualized testing. In the realm of capital punishment in particular, "individualized consideration [is] a constitutional requirement," *Lockett v. Ohio*, 438 U.S. 586, 605 (1978) (opinion of Burger, C.J.) (Footnote omitted); *see also Zant v. Stephens,* 462 U.S. 862, 879 (1983) (collecting cases), and one of the individualized mitigating factors that sentencers must be permitted to consider is the defendant's age, *see Eddings v. Oklahoma*, 455 U.S. 104, 115-116 (1982). Twenty-nine States, including both Kentucky and Missouri, have codified this constitutional requirement in laws specifically designating the defendant's age as a mitigating factor in capital cases. . . . What displays society's views . . . are not the ages set forth in the generalized system of driving, drinking, and voting laws cited by petitioners . . . but the ages at which the States permit their particularized capital punishment systems to be applied.[7]

V

Having failed to establish a consensus against capital punishment for 16- and17-year old offenders through state and federal statutes and the behavior of prosecutors and juries, petitioners seek to demonstrate it through other indicia, including public opinion polls, the views of interest groups, and the positions adopted by various professional associations. We decline the invitation to rest constitutional law upon such uncertain foundations. . . .

We also reject petitioners' argument that we should invalidate capital punishment of 16- and 17-year old offenders on the ground that it fails to serve the legitimate goals of penology. According to petitioners, it fails to deter because juveniles, possessing less developed cognitive skills than adults, are less likely to fear death; and it fails to exact just retribution because juveniles, being less mature and responsible, are also less morally blameworthy. In support of these claims, petitioners and their supporting *amici* marshall an array of socioscientific evidence concerning the psychological and emotional development of 16- and 17-year-olds.

. . . The punishment is either "cruel *and* unusual" . . . or it is not. The audience for these arguments . . . is not this Court but the citizenry of the United States. It is they, not we, who must be persuaded. For as we stated earlier, our job is to *identify* the "evolving standards of decency"; to determine, not what

---

7 The dissent believes that individualized consideration is no solution, because "the Eighth Amendment requires that a person who lacks that full degree of responsibility for his or her actions associated with adulthood not be sentenced to death," and this absolute cannot be assured if "a juvenile offender's level of responsibility [is] taken into account only along with a host of other factors that the court or jury may decide outweigh that want of responsibility." But it is equally true that individualized consideration will not absolutely assure immunity from the death penalty to the *non*-juvenile who happens to be immature. If individualized consideration is constitutionally inadequate, then the only logical conclusion is that *everyone* is exempt from the death penalty.

they *should* be, but what they *are*. We have no power under the Eighth Amendment to substitute our belief in the scientific evidence for the society's apparent skepticism. . . .

* * *

We discern neither a historical nor a modern societal consensus forbidding the imposition of capital punishment on any person who murders at 16 or 17 years of age. Accordingly, we conclude that such punishment does not offend the Eighth Amendment's prohibition against cruel and unusual punishment.

The judgments of the Supreme Court of Kentucky and the Supreme Court of Missouri are therefore affirmed.

Justice O'CONNOR, concurring in part and concurring in the judgment.

. . . [T]he death sentences for capital murder imposed by Missouri and Kentucky on petitioners Wilkins and Stanford . . . should not be set aside because it is sufficiently clear that no national consensus forbids the imposition of capital punishment on 16- or 17-year-old capital murderers.

In *Thompson v. Oklahoma,* 487 U.S. 815, 840 (1988) (opinion concurring in judgment), I noted that "[t]he most salient statistic that bears on this case is that every single American legislature that has expressly set a minimum age for capital punishment has set that age at 16 or above." It is this difference between *Thompson* and these cases, more than any other, that convinces me there is no national consensus forbidding the imposition of capital punishment for crimes committed at the age of 16 or older. . . . The day may come when there is such general legislative rejection of the execution of 16- or 17-year-old capital murderers that a clear national consensus can be said to have developed. Because I do not believe that day has yet arrived, I concur in Parts I, II III, and IV-A of the Court's opinion, and I concur in its judgment.

I am unable, however, to join the remainder of the plurality's opinion. . . . [A]lthough I do not believe that these particular cases can be resolved through proportionality analysis, see *Thompson, supra,* at 853-854, I reject the suggestion that the use of such analysis is improper as a matter of Eighth Amendment jurisprudence. Accordingly, I join all but Parts IV-B and V of Justice SCALIA's opinion.

Justice BRENNAN, with whom Justice MARSHALL, Justice BLACKMUN, and Justice STEVENS join, dissenting.

I believe that to take the life of a person as punishment for a crime committed when below the age of 18 is cruel and unusual and hence is prohibited by the Eighth Amendment.

The method by which this Court assesses a claim that a punishment is unconstitutional because it is cruel and unusual is established by our precedents, and it bears little resemblance to the method four Members of the Court apply in this case. To be sure, we *begin* the task of deciding whether a punishment is unconstitutional by reviewing legislative enactments and the work of sentencing juries . . . to determine whether our Nation has set its face against a punishment to an extent that it can be concluded that the punishment offends our "evolving standards of decency." *Trop v. Dulles,* 356 U.S. 86, 101 (1958) (plurality opinion). . . . In my view, [however], inquiry must in these cases go beyond age-based statutory classifications relating to matters other than capital punishment. . . . Only then can we be in a position to judge, as our cases require, whether a punishment is unconstitutionally excessive, either because it is disproportionate given the culpability of the offender, or because it serves no legitimate penal goal.

I

Our judgment about the constitutionality of a punishment under the Eighth Amendment is informed, though not determined, by an examination of contemporary attitudes toward the punishment, as evidenced in the actions of legislatures and of juries. *McCleskey v. Kemp*, 481 U.S. 279 300 (1987); *Coker v. Georgia*, 433 U.S. 584, 592 (1977) (plurality opinion). The views of organizations with expertise in relevant fields and the choices of governments elsewhere in the world also merit our attention as indicators whether a punishment is acceptable in a civilized society.

A

The Court's discussion of state laws concerning capital sentencing gives a distorted view of the evidence of contemporary standards that these legislative determinations provide. Currently, 12 of the States whose statutes permit capital punishment specifically mandate that offenders under age 18 not be sentenced to death. When one adds to these 12 States the 15 (including the District of Columbia) in which capital punishment is not authorized at all, it appears that the governments in fully 27 of the States have concluded that no one under 18 should face the death penalty. A further three States explicitly refuse to authorize sentences of death for those who committed their offense when under 17, making a total of 30 States that would not tolerate the execution of petitioner Wilkins. . . .

* * *

B

The application of these laws is another indicator the Court agrees to be relevant. The fact that juries have on occasion sentenced a minor to death shows, the Court says, that the death penalty for adolescents is not categorically unacceptable to juries. This, of course, it true; but it is not a conclusion that takes Eighth Amendment analysis very far. Just as we have never insisted that a punishment have been rejected unanimously by the States before we may judge it cruel and unusual, so we have never adopted the extraordinary view that a punishment is beyond Eighth Amendment challenge if it is sometimes handed down by a jury. . . . .

The Court speculates that this very small number of capital sentences imposed on adolescents indicates that juries have considered the youth of the offender when determining sentence, and have reserved the punishment for rare cases in which it is nevertheless appropriate. . . . It is certainly true that in the vast majority of cases, juries have not sentenced juveniles to death, and it seems to me perfectly proper to conclude that a sentence so rarely imposed is "unusual."

Further indicators of contemporary standards of decency that should inform our consideration of the Eighth Amendment question are the opinions of respected organizations. *Thompson v. United States*, 487 U.S. 815, 930 (1989) (plurality opinion).... There is no dearth of opinion from such groups that the state-sanctioned killing of minors is unjustified.... The American Bar Association has adopted a resolution opposing the imposition of capital punishment upon any person for an offense committed while under age 18, as has the National Council of Juvenile and Family Court Judges. The American Law Institute's Model Penal Code similarly includes a lower age limit of 18 for the death sentence. And the National Commission on Reform of the Federal Criminal Laws also recommended that 18 be the minimum age.

Our cases recognize that objective indicators of contemporary standards of decency in the form of legislation in other countries is also of relevance to Eighth Amendment analysis.... Many countries, of course—over 50, including nearly all in Western Europe—have formally abolished the death penalty, or have limited its use to exceptional crimes. . . . Twenty-seven others do not in practice impose the penalty. Of the nations that retain capital punishment, a majority—65—prohibit the execution of juveniles. . . . Within the world community, the imposition of the death penalty for juvenile crimes appears to be overwhelmingly disapproved.

D

Together, the rejection of the death penalty for juveniles by a majority of the States, the rarity of the sentence for juveniles, . . . the decisions of respected organizations in relevant fields that this punishment is unacceptable, and its rejection generally throughout the world, provide to my mind a strong grounding for the view that it is not constitutionally tolerable that certain States persist in authorizing the execution of adolescent offenders. It is unnecessary, however, to resist a view that the Eighth Amendment prohibits the execution of minors solely upon a judgment as to the meaning to be attached to the evidence of contemporary values outlined above, for the execution of juveniles fails to satisfy two well-established and independent Eighth Amendment requirements—that a punishment not be disproportionate, and that it make a contribution to acceptable goals of punishment.

* * *

III

There can be no doubt at this point in our constitutional history that the Eighth Amendment forbids punishment that is wholly disproportionate to the blameworthiness of the offender. "The constitutional principle of proportionality has been recognized explicitly in this Court for almost a century." *Solem v. Helm,* 463 U.S. 277, 286 (1983). . . .

Proportionality analysis requires that we compare "the gravity of the offense," understood to include not only the injury caused, but also the defendant's culpability, with "the harshness of the penalty." *Solem, supra,* at 292. In my view, juveniles so generally lack the degree of responsibility for their crimes that is a predicate for the constitutional imposition of the death penalty that the Eighth Amendment forbids that they receive that punishment.

* * *

IV

Under a second strand of Eighth Amendment inquiry into whether a particular sentence is excessive and hence unconstitutional, we ask whether the sentence makes a measurable contribution to acceptable goals of punishment. *Thompson, supra,* at 833, *Enmund v. Florida,* 458 U.S. 782, 798, (1982), *Coker v. Georgia,* 433 U.S. at 592; *Gregg v. Georgia,* 428 U.S. 153, 173 (1976). The two "principal social purposes" of capital punishment are said to be "retribution and the deterrence of capital crimes by prospective offenders." *Gregg, supra,* at 183; *see Enmund,* 458 U.S. at 798. Unless the death penalty applied to persons for offenses committed under 18 measurably contributes to one of these goals, the Eighth Amendment prohibits it.

"[R]etribution as a justification for executing [offenders] very much depends on the degree of [their] culpability." *Id.* at 800. . . . I believe juveniles lack the culpability that makes a crime so extreme that it may warrant, according to this Court's cases, the death penalty. . . . These same considerations persuade me that executing juveniles "does not measurably contribute to the retributive end of ensuring that the criminal gets his just deserts." *Id.* at 801.

Nor does the execution of juvenile offenders measurably contribute to the goal of deterrence. Excluding juveniles from the class of persons eligible to receive the death penalty will have little effect on any deterrent value capital punishment may have for potential offenders who are over 18. . . . As the plurality noted in *Thompson, supra,* at 837, "[t]he likelihood that the teenage offender has made the kind of cost-benefit analysis that attaches any weight to the possibility of execution is so remote as to be virtually nonexistent. . . ." Because imposition of the death penalty on persons for offenses committed under the age of 18 makes no measurable contribution to the goals of either retribution or deterrence, it is "nothing more than the purposeless and needless imposition of pain and suffering," *Coker, supra,* at 592, and is thus excessive and unconstitutional.

V

There are strong indications that the execution of juvenile offenders violates contemporary standards of decency: a majority of States decline to permit juveniles to be sentenced to death; imposition of the sentence upon minors is very unusual even in those States that permit it; and respected organizations with expertise in relevant areas regard the execution of juveniles as unacceptable, as does international opinion. These indicators serve to confirm in my view my conclusion that the Eighth Amendment prohibits the execution of persons for offenses they committed while below the age of 18, because the death penalty is disproportionate when applied to such young offenders and fails measurably to serve the goals of capital punishment. I dissent.

Notes

1. Several professional organizations oppose capital punishment for delinquent juveniles. According to the Model Penal Code, juveniles should not be given the death penalty: "(1) Death Sentence Excluded. When a defendant is found guilty of murder, the Court shall impose sentence for a felony of the first degree if it is satisfied that . . . (d) the defendant was under 18 years of age at the time of the commission of the crime. . . ." MODEL PENAL CODE § 210.6 (1980). The American Bar Association is another organization opposed to juveniles receiving the death penalty for a delinquent act.

IJA-ABA Juvenile Justice Standards,
Standard Relating to Juvenile Delinquency and Sanctions
§§ 5.2 & 6.2 (1980)*

* * *

5.2 Classes of juvenile offense

* * *

B. Where, under a criminal statute or ordinance made applicable to juveniles pursuant to Standard 2.2, the maximum sentence authorized upon conviction for such offense is

1. death or imprisonment for life . . . it is a class one juvenile offense;

* * *

6.2 Limitations on type and duration of sanctions

A. The juvenile court should not impose a sanction more severe than,

1. where the juvenile is found to have committed a class one juvenile offense,

a) confinement in a secure facility or placement in a nonsecure facility or residence for a period of twenty-four months, or

b) conditional freedom for a period of thirty-six months;

* * *

2. The United States is one of the few countries which allow juveniles to receive capital punishment. Since 1985, only Nigeria, Iran, Iraq, Bangladesh, Pakistan, Saudi Arabia, Yemen, and the United States have executed a juvenile as punishment for a crime committed. *See* Victor L. Streib, *Moratorium on the Death Penalty for Juveniles*, 61 LAW & CONTEMP. PROBS. 55, 65 (1998). The United States has executed nine juveniles in the past decade, which accounts for half of all juveniles killed by capital punishment in the world since 1990. *See* Human Rights Watch, WORLD REPORT 1999, *available at* <www.hrw.org/hrw/worldreport99/usa/

---

* Reprinted with permission.

index.html>. The United States is a signatory to several human rights conventions which consider giving juveniles the death penalty to be a human rights violation. *See* INTERNATIONAL COVENANT ON CIVIL AND POLITICAL RIGHTS art. 6(5), Annex to G.A. Res. 220, 21 U.N. GAOR Res. Supp. (No. 16) 53, U.N. Doc. A/6316 (1966); AMERICAN CONVENTION ON HUMAN RIGHTS, art. 4(5), O.A.S. Official Records, OES/Ser.K/XVI/1.1, Doc. 65, Rev. 1, Corr. 2 (1970); GENEVA CONVENTION RELATIVE TO THE PROTECTION OF CIVILIAN PERSONS IN TIME OF WAR, August 22-23, 1949, Art. 68, 6 U.S.T. 3516, 3560, T.I.A.S. No. 3365.75 U.N.T.S. 287. For additional information concerning the United States' stand on capital punishment for juveniles, as compared to the rest of the international community, see V.P. Nanda, *The United States Reservation to the Ban of the Death Penalty For Juvenile Offenders: An Appraisal Under the International Convention on Civil and Political Rights,* 42 DEPAUL L. REV. 1311 (1993).

3. For a history of the death penalty for juveniles in the United States as well as charts and graphs explaining the profiles (race, sex, age) of juveniles on death row and the number of juveniles on death row per state, see LYNN COTHERN, U.S. DEP'T OF JUST., JUVENILES AND THE DEATH PENALTY (2000). For additional information addressing the constitutional and moral aspects of juveniles being given the death penalty, see Suzanne D. Strater, *The Juvenile Death Penalty: In the Best Interests of the Child?,* 26 LOY. U. CHI. L.J. (1995); Rodger A. Maynes, Note, *The Death Penalty for Juveniles—A Constitutional Alternative*, 7 J. JUV. L. 54 (1983); Maria M. Homan, Note, *The Juvenile Death Penalty: Counsel's Role in the Development of a Mitigating Defense*, 53 BROOK. L. REV. 767 (1987); Victor Streib, *The Eighth Amendment and Capital Punishment of Juveniles,* 34 CLEV. ST. L. REV. 363 (1989); AMNESTY INT'L U.S.A., THE DEATH PENALTY AND JUVENILE OFFENDERS (Oct. 1991); Victor Strieb & Lynn Sametz, *Executing Female Juveniles*, 22 CONN. L. REV. 3 (1989); James P. Fischer, Comment, *Capital Punishment for Juveniles—A Constitutional Minimum Set by Elastic Principles,* 16 CAP. U. L. REV. 655 (1987); Elisabeth Gasparini, *Juvenile Capital Punishment: A Spectacle of a Child's Injustice*, 49 S.C. L. REV. 1073 (1998).

Questions

1. The majority in *Stanford* questions whether giving a juvenile the death penalty violates the Eighth Amendment as cruel and unusual punishment. If a juvenile under 16 years of age has the mental capacity to understand the seriousness of an offense and the possible consequences, should courts be allowed to give the juvenile the death penalty? Or, is the *Thompson* bright-line rule that giving a juvenile under 16 years of age the death penalty is cruel and unusual a better policy? Should legislatures, and not the courts, be allowed to determine on a state-by-state basis whether or not state courts may give juveniles the death penalty as advocated by the *Thompson* dissent?

2. The Court in *Thompson* and *Stanford* wrestled with the problem of where to draw the line for a minimum age at which a juvenile could face the death penalty. From what you have read about the goals of juvenile law and the courts' views on a juvenile's ability to comprehend the seriousness of a delinquent act, where should the line be drawn? Should the Supreme Court set a minimum age requirement for the death penalty? Should courts evaluate each juvenile and his or her capacity to understand the wrongfulness of the act committed on an individual basis and then determine whether the death penalty is appropriate? Are children mentally capable of understanding the death penalty as a deterrent or are there traits unique to youth which impede their understanding the possible consequences of their delinquent acts?

Chapter 8

Dependency, Abuse, and Neglect: The Child as Victim

Juvenile delinquency and child protection proceedings share the same goal—both seek to do what is in the best interests of the child. In both types of proceedings, the state aims to protect and treat juveniles in need. In delinquency cases the child is the respondent, who has committed a wrongful act (often a crime), whereas in child welfare proceedings the child is the victim, who has usually done nothing wrong. Since the *Gault* decision, delinquency proceedings have become heavily constitutionalized and, in reality, a mini-criminal court. Child welfare proceedings are civil and less adversary in nature with the focus on the child's safety and reunification of the family, if feasible.

In child welfare proceedings, the child can be found to be dependent, abused, or neglected. The states rely on the same fundamental concept—protection of the child—when defining these categories, but there may be slight variations from state to state. California, for example, includes all maltreated children under the statutory label of dependency. A specific definition of dependency may cover a child who is without the proper care or family support through no fault of the parent or guardian. A child may be found to be abused where there is excessive corporal punishment, sex abuse, serious mental injury, or fetal abuse such as alcohol or drug use during pregnancy. A child may be deemed neglected if the parent refuses or is unable to provide for the child's nutrition, housing, medical needs or education. If there is a lack of supervision or domestic violence, the court may also find the child to be neglected.

These three categories are used to determine whether the state needs to intervene in the privacy of family life to protect a particular child. If the court determines that a child is dependent, abused or neglected, the court may react in a variety of ways depending on the circumstances. The court may allow the child to remain in the home under a court order of protection or the child may be removed from the parent's custody. While reading this chapter, analyze the definitions of dependency, abuse, and neglect. Do these statutory definitions allow the State to protect all children who are victims? Do the categories go too far and infringe upon family privacy when a child does not need protection? Are any groups unfairly affected? Are the poor unfairly impacted? What about single mothers, members of certain religious groups or racial or ethnic minorities?

A. Jurisdiction—General

Idaho Code
§ 16-1603 (Michie 2001)

§ 16-1603 Jurisdiction of the courts

Except as otherwise provided herein, the court shall have exclusive original jurisdiction in all proceedings under this chapter concerning any child living or found within the state:

(a) who is neglected, abused or abandoned by his parents, guardian or other legal custodian, or who is homeless; or
(b) whose parents or other legal custodian fails or is unable to provide a stable home environment.

Note

Some states limit the scope of a juvenile court's jurisdiction by distinguishing a dependent child from a neglected child. The distinction is based upon the degree of willfulness exhibited by the parent, guardian, or custodian toward the needs of the juvenile. In these jurisdictions, "neglected" children are deprived of physical, mental, or emotional health by a parent who has the means to care for the child's needs. "Dependent" children, on the other hand, are children who are deprived of physical, mental, or emotional health by a parent who is unable to provide and care for the child's needs. An example of a statute that distinguishes between a neglected child and a dependent child is the New York Family Court Act. The New York Family Court Act limits the juvenile court's jurisdiction by giving the court jurisdiction over "neglected" children but allowing "dependent" children to be dealt with under the separate social welfare law.

N.Y. Family Court Act
§ 1012(f) (McKinney Supp. 2001)

§ 1012—Definitions

(f) "Neglected child" means a child less than eighteen years of age

(i) whose physical, mental or emotional condition has been impaired or is in imminent danger of becoming impaired as a result of the failure of his parent or other person legally responsible for his care to exercise a minimum degree of care

(A) in supplying the child with adequate food, clothing, shelter or education . . . or mental, dental, optometrical, or surgical care, though financially able to so or offered financial or other reasonable means to do so; . . .

* * *

It should be noted that not every state distinguishes between a "neglected" and a "dependent" child. States such as California, for example, place abused and neglected children under the "dependent child" umbrella. *See, e.g.*, CAL. WELF. & INST. CODE § 213.5(a) (West Supp. 2001).

B. Duty to Report

Florida Statutes Annotated

§ 39.201 (West Supp. 2001)

§ 39.201. Mandatory reports of child abuse, abandonment, or neglect; mandatory reports of death; central abuse hotline

(1) Any person, including, but not limited to, any:

(a) Physician, osteopathic physician, medical examiner, chiropractic physician, nurse, or hospital personnel engaged in the admission, examination, care, or treatment of persons;

(b) Health or mental health professional other than one listed in paragraph (a);

(c) Practitioner who relies solely on spiritual means for healing;

(d) School teacher or other school official or personnel;

(e) Social worker, day care center worker, or other professional child care, foster care, residential, or institutional worker;

(f) Law enforcement officer; or

(g) Judge, who knows, or has reasonable cause to suspect, that a child is abused, abandoned, or neglected by a parent, legal custodian, caregiver, or other person responsible for the child's welfare shall report such knowledge or suspicion to the department in the manner prescribed in subsection (2).

(2) (a) Each report of known or suspected child abuse, abandonment, or neglect pursuant to this section, . . . shall be made immediately to the department's central abuse hotline on the single statewide toll-free telephone number, and, if the report is of an instance of known or suspected child abuse by a noncaretaker, the call shall be immediately electronically transferred to the appropriate county sheriff's office by the central abuse hotline. . . .

* * *

(c) Reporters in occupation categories designated in subsection (1) are required to provide their names to the hotline staff. The names of reporters shall be entered into the record of the report, but shall be held confidential as provided in § 39.202.

(d) Reports involving known or suspected institutional child abuse or neglect shall be made and received in the same manner as all other reports made pursuant to this section.

* * *

(g) Hotline counselors shall receive periodic training in encouraging reporters to provide their names when reporting abuse, abandonment, or neglect. Callers shall be advised of the confidentiality provisions of § 39.202. The department shall secure and install electronic equipment that automatically provides to the hotline the number from which the call is placed. This number shall be entered into the report of abuse, abandonment, or neglect and become a part of the record of the report, but shall enjoy the same confidentiality as provided to the identity of the caller pursuant to § 39.202.

* * *

(3) Any person required to report or investigate cases of suspected child abuse, abandonment, or neglect who has reasonable cause to suspect that a child died as a result of child abuse, abandonment, or neglect shall report his or her suspicion to the appropriate medical examiner. The medical examiner shall accept the report for investigation and shall report his or her findings, in writing, to the local law enforcement agency, the appropriate state attorney, and the department. Autopsy reports maintained by the medical examiner are not subject to the confidentiality requirements provided for in § 39.202.

State v. Snell

714 A.2d 977 (N.J. Super. Ct. App. Div. 1998)

KIMMELMAN, J.A.D.

At issue is whether the privilege against disclosure of confidential communications made with respect to the relationship of patient and physician and psychologist and client must yield to the obligation imposed upon "any person" to report evidence of child abuse to the Division of Youth and Family Services (DYFS). N.J.S.A. 9:6-8.10 The trial court held that the psychiatrist consulted by defendant John Snell for treatment: (1) properly reported to DYFS the evidence of child abuse disclosed to him by defendant, and (2) could furnish testimony at defendant's trial.

As a result of the doctor's report, DYFS notified the Trenton police. Defendant was arrested and ultimately indicted. Following the trial court's ruling that defendant's statements to the psychiatrist were properly reportable to DYFS and also admissible at trial, defendant, pled guilty to aggravated sexual assault, a first-degree offense. . . . As a part of the plea agreement, defendant reserved the right to lodge this appeal contesting the trial court's evidentiary ruling.

On this appeal, defendant argues that his admission of acts of child abuse during his consultation with Dr. Philip Torrance, a psychiatrist whom defendant characterizes in his brief as a psychotherapist, was privileged, and that alternatively, he should not have been committed to the Adult Diagnostic and Treatment Center at Avenel.

The facts are not in dispute. Defendant, fifty-nine years old, was engaged in a long-term relationship with a woman, whom we refer to as his paramour. She had two granddaughters, eleven-year-old K.M. and ten-year-old S.M., who were sisters. Safety concerns had led DYFS to remove S.M. from her mother's home and place her with her grandmother, but K.M. lived nearby in Trenton and would occasionally visit. The children regarded defendant as a substitute grandfather. It appears that, over a period of more than a year, defendant repeatedly performed cunnilingus on them. On at least one occasion, S.M. was present and witnessed the act being performed on her sister. Defendant claimed that it was his intent to instruct or educate the minors so that they would not become sexually involved with boys.

For some reason not apparent in the record, defendant told his paramuor what had been taking place with her granddaughters. She demanded that defendant see a psychiatrist for help. Defendant made an appointment and, accompanied by S.M., professionally consulted with Dr. Torrance at his office. During the consultation, defendant admitted to the doctor that he had performed one act of cunnilingus on each of the two girls. At the conclusion of the session, Dr. Torrance felt it incumbent upon himself, pursuant to N.J.S.A. 9:6-8.10, to report to DYFS the evidence of child abuse that defendant had disclosed to him.

N.J.S.A. 9:6-8.10 provides in pertinent part, that

> Any person having reasonable cause to believe that a child has been subjected to child abuse or acts of child abuse shall report the same immediately to the Division of Youth and Family Services by telephone or otherwise.

Undoubtedly, this statute is expressive of the Legislature's paramount consideration of protecting children from injury or abuse "by other than accidental means." N.J.S.A. 9:6-8.8. To that end, "any person" having reasonable grounds is required to report evidence of child abuse, under pain of prosecution as a disorderly person for failure to do so. As a means of persuasion, and by way of protection, it is provided that anyone making a report pursuant to the statute shall have immunity from any civil or criminal liability that might otherwise be incurred or imposed as a result of the making of the report.

There is no mechanism built into the statute to relieve persons who may be privy to confidential communications from the duty to report child abuse to DYFS. By mandating that "any person" having reasonable grounds to suspect child abuse report those suspicions to DYFS, the Legislature simply meant *any person*, without limitation. Where the language of a statute is clear, as we find N.J.S.A. 9:6-8.10 to be, we are obliged to apply that statute as written.

* * *

Under the physician-patient privilege, "information which the physician or the patient is required to report to a public official" is not privileged. N.J.S.A. 2A:84A-22.5 and N.J.R.E. 506(e). We find this language to be sufficiently circumscribed to waive the privilege only as to the requirement of making an initial report to a public official. The physician-patient privilege may not be regarded as being waived *in toto*. . . .

Although Dr. Torrance is a physician, defendant seeks to avoid the foregoing exception to the physician-patient privilege by relying instead upon the psychologist privilege, [which] contain(s) no exception where reporting to a public official is required. It is claimed by defendant that he, accompanied by S.M., went to Dr. Torrance not for medical treatment, but for help in the form of psychotherapy and, therefore, the psychologist rather than physician privilege applies. Such claim does not seem to have been rejected by the trial court.

As argued by defendant, the precise wording of neither the statute nor the rule establishing the psychologist privilege contains an exception which applies when State law requires the making of a report to a public agency. The relevant text of the statute and rule is as follows:

> The confidential relations and communications between and among a licensed practicing psychologist and individuals, couples, families or groups in the course of the practice of psychology are placed on the same basis as those provided between attorney and client, and *nothing in this act shall be construed to require any such privileged communications to be disclosed by any such person.*

[N.J.S.A. 45;14B-28 and N.J.R.E. 505 (emphasis added).]

Defendant urges us not to countenance any deviation from the language built into the psychologist privilege. . . . On the other hand, the State argues that, by placing the psychologist privilege "on the same basis as . . . provided between attorney and client," the Legislature intended that Dr. Torrance's report to DYFS be free of psychologist-confidentiality privilege because under analogous circumstances the lawyer-client privilege does "not extend to a communication made in the course of legal services sought or obtained in aid of the commission of a crime or a fraud." *See* N.J.S.A. 2A:84A-20(2) and N.J.R.E. 504(2)(a). Dr. Torrance opined that the nature of the familial relationship which existed between defendant and the children made it highly probable that the defendant would continue to commit acts of abuse. Thus, the State argues that Dr. Torrance, being subject to a limited privilege on the same basis as that of an attorney, was bound to make the report to DYFS under the crime or fraud exception.

While we agree with the State's conclusion that the doctor had the duty to report, we are unable to accept the State's entire reasoning, because we find that defendant's consultation with Dr. Torrance was not akin to a client seeking an attorney's aid in the commission of a crime or fraud. Defendant ostensibly consulted Dr. Torrance to seek treatment so that he might refrain from committing further acts of child abuse; not to seek aid in the commission of further such acts. Hence, under the factual scenario of this case, the State may not rely upon the crime or fraud exception to the attorney-client privilege to justify Dr. Torrance's deviation from the psychologist-patient privilege.

State v. L.J.P., 270 N.J. Super 429, 438-39, 637 A.2d 532 (Ch. Div. 1994) clearly summarizes the psychologist privilege:

> The psychologist-patient privilege was created by the New Jersey legislature as a part of a comprehensive statutory scheme designed to license and regulate practicing psychologists. The privilege was

> created two years before the codification of the common law physician-patient privilege in 1968. Those two privileges are not treated alike by the courts and are not subject to the same exceptions. Rather, the psychologist-patient privilege is akin to the attorney-client privilege. The privilege belongs to the patient and any waiver to the privilege must be made by the patient.
>
> * * *
>
> However, the privilege, like the attorney-client privilege, is not absolute. Although the psychologist-patient privilege affords even greater confidentiality than the physician-patient privilege, it still may be defeated where common notions of fairness clearly compel at least limited disclosure of otherwise confidential communications. Like other privileges, it must in some circumstances yield to the higher demands of order. (citations omitted).

Privileges are justified in order to encourage candid and frank communication between attorney and client, physician and patient, and psychotherapist and patient, because of the primary concern that the client or patient should receive informed legal advice or proper diagnosis and treatment. However, we do recognize that not all such privileges must be strictly construed, because they may come in conflict with the promotion and preservation of justice, truth, and fair dealing. Accordingly, we must effect a balance between the reporting directive contained in N.J.S.A. 9:6-8.10 and the privilege against disclosure contained in N.J.S.A. 45:14B-28 and N.J.R.E. 505.

As a matter of statutory construction, it is well established that, where two statutes conflict, the more specific statute must prevail over the more general. *New Jersey Transit Corp. v. Borough of Somerville,* 139 N.J. 582, 591, 661 A.2d 778 (1995). To be sure, the statute mandating the reporting of suspected child abuse is more particularized and specific than are the statute and rule pertaining to confidential relations and communications. . . . The protection of children from injury, harm, or abuse by means of the statutory reporting requirement may not be blocked or hindered by the assertion of a blanket testimonial privilege. For these reasons, the general provisions of the psychologist-patient privilege must yield to the specific mandate of N.J.S.A. 9:6-8.10. We stress that the statute requires only a report to DYFS in order to protect the child in danger; the privilege remains otherwise intact.

Consequently, the trial court's order of August 2, 1994, is modified. We conclude that Dr. Torrance's report to DYFS was proper, but that he may not be compelled by the State to testify to the content of privileged communications at defendant's criminal trial. We make no ruling as to whether our decision furnished grounds for defendant to withdraw his guilty plea. That is a matter which must be addressed by the trial court. Finally, we find no fault with the trial court's finding that, under the facts, defendant was a repetitive and compulsive sex offender, justifying his commitment to Avenel for concurrent terms of eighteen years.

Affirmed as modified.

Notes

1. States require adults to report child abuse so that the abused child can be protected, treated appropriately and to prevent future abuse. The report sets in motion a complaint-response investigation by the child welfare agency. New York, for example, follows a statutory framework to determine whether or not child abuse actually occurs. *See Valmonte v. Bane*, 18 F.2d 992 (2d Cir. 1994). In New York, the hotline operator screens all child abuse calls to determine whether or not the call should be transferred to the county Department of Social Services (DSS). After DSS completes an investigation of the reported abuse, it prepares a report of its findings. If DSS finds credible evidence of abuse, the adult's name is given to the Central Registry. The Central Registry then places the adult's name on a list of child abusers. Some state agencies, private businesses, and all licensing agencies in the child care field are then required by law to check whether a potential employee is on the Registry. The adult whose name is placed on the list may petition the DSS to expunge his or her name from the list. If the state DSS refuses to expunge the record, an administrative hearing is held where the local DSS must provide evidence of the abuse. *See Valmonte, supra,* regarding the Second Circuit's consideration of constitutional challenges and issues facing central registries.

2. A majority of states provide criminal sanctions for adults who do not report child abuse. *See, e.g.,* CAL. PENAL CODE §§ 11161.8, 11166 (West Supp. 2001); R.I. GEN. LAWS § 40-11-6.1 (Lexis 1997). In *Landeros v. Flood*, 551 P.2d 389 (Cal. 1976), the court held that conviction for failure to report child abuse charges did not necessarily result in civil tort liability. Some states also provide civil causes of action against adults who do not report child abuse. In *Williams v. Coleman*, 488 N.W.2d 464 (Mich. Ct. App. 1992), a plaintiff was awarded $900,000 for the defendant's failure to report child abuse, which was a proximate cause of a child's death.

3. Does a school psychologist have a duty to divulge information of abuse given by a student? In *Pesce v. J. Sterling Morton High School District 302*, 651 F. Supp. 152 (N.D. Ill. 1986), the court supported the local school board which "found that the suspension of plaintiff [psychologist] was necessary in order to ensure that school personnel reported incidents of abuse. . . ." In *Pesce*, a student told the psychotherapist that another student (the victim) had a homosexual encounter with a male teacher. The psychotherapist also discovered that the victim was contemplating suicide. The psychotherapist, however, felt it was in the victim's best interest for him not to breach confidentiality without the victim's consent. The victim finally reported the abuse to the psychotherapist, and, with the victim's permission, the psychotherapist reported the abuse to the school. The school suspended the psychotherapist five days for not immediately revealing the abuse. The psychotherapist filed suit, arguing that his failure to report was constitutionally protected and the suspension violated his right to free speech. The court used a two-prong test introduced by the United States Supreme Court in *Connick v. Myers*, 461 U.S. 138 (1983), to determine if the school's disciplining of a public employee violated the First Amendment. The court determined that (1) the speech was a private matter not protected by the Constitution, and (2) the psychotherapist was required to disclose the sensitive information because of the "compelling nature of the school's own interest in the health, safety, and welfare of its students relative to any asserted interest in confidentiality."

Questions

1. The *Pesce* and *Snell* courts attempted to clarify who is required by law to report child abuse. A problem demonstrated by both cases is the conflict between the reporting statute and certain types of privileged communications. If a psychotherapist or a doctor must report child abuse, is it likely to deter parents of abused children from seeking treatment for themselves as well as for their children? If children do not receive the treatment they need, because parents refuse to take them to psychotherapists or doctors, should the law permit these professionals to treat parents and abused children without making a report?

Members of the clergy are also covered by privileged communication laws. Should clergy members also be required to report abuse? Could this infringe upon a family's freedom of religion or other rights protected by the Constitution? *See generally* Raymond O'Brien & Michael Flannery, *The Pending Gauntlet to Free Exercise: Mandating That Clergy Report Child Abuse,* 25 LOY. L.A. L. REV. 1 (1991).

2. A future employer, the local police, a judge, or other state agencies which have access to the central registry can deny those labeled child abusers future employment and the chance to become a foster parent. Jill D. Moore, Comment, *Charting A Course Between Scylla and Charybdis: Child Abuse Registries and Procedural Due Process*, 73 N.C. L. REV. 2063, 2081 (1995). Because of the implications of being listed on the child abuse registry, who should be allowed access to a central registry's information? What burden of proof should be required to list an individual on the central registry? After a person's name is placed on the list, should it become a part of the individual's permanent record?

C. Substantive Requirements

1. Dependency

General Statutes of North Carolina
§ 7B-101(9) (Lexis 1999)

§ 7B-101(9). Dependent juvenile.

A juvenile in need of assistance or placement because the juvenile has no parent, guardian, or custodian responsible for the juvenile's care or supervision or whose parent, guardian, or custodian is unable to provide for the care or supervision and lacks an appropriate alternative child care arrangement.

In re Tikyra A.

659 N.E.2d 867 (Ohio Ct. App. 1995)

SHERCK, Judge

This consolidated appeal comes to us from judgments issued by the Huron County Court of Common Pleas, Juvenile Division. That court found dependent two children who were abandoned by their teenage mother to the care of their grandmother. Because we have determined that the trial court judgments were not supported by the evidence, we reverse.

Appellant is the mother of Quionna B. and Tikyra A. At the time when the incident which provoked the dependency complaints occurred, Quionna was two years old and Tikyra was eights months old.

On or about June 26, 1994, appellant, herself only seventeen years old at the time, became involved in an argument with her mother, with whom she and the two children lived. As a result of this argument, appellant left her mother's Norwalk home without her mother's permission. This violated a condition of appellant's probation, which was the result of a prior delinquency adjudication. Appellant left behind her oldest child and took with her the youngest. At the time appellant left, she had not reached an understanding with her mother concerning the care to be given either child.

Appellant went to the city of Sandusky. The Sandusky house in which she resided was later characterized in testimony by at least one witness as a place where drugs were used. After a week, appellant sent her youngest daughter back to Norwalk where both children were cared for by her mother. Appellant remained in the Sandusky house for another two weeks until police, in response to a report by appellant's mother that appellant was a runaway, arrested her.

Following appellant's arrest, appellee, Huron County Department of Human Services, initiated complaints alleging that both children were dependent pursuant to R.C. 2151.04(A). Following an adjudicatory hearing, the trial court found the children to be dependent and awarded their legal custody to appellant's mother. . . .

Appellant challenges the weight of the evidence by which the trial court adjudicated these children as dependent. The decision of a trier of fact relating to the adjudication of a child as dependent will not be overturned as against the manifest weight of the evidence, so long as the record contains clear and convincing evidence of dependency. Clear and convincing evidence of dependency is that evidence by which the trial court could have formed a firm belief or conviction that the essential statutory elements for dependency have been established.

R.C. 2151.04 provides:

> As used in this chapter, "dependent child" includes any child:
>
> (A) Who is homeless or destitute or without proper care or support, through no fault of his parents, guardian, or custodian. . . .

Appellant argues that at no time were these children without a home, food or necessaries. At all times they were in the care of their grandmother. Therefore, according to appellant, these children did not fall within the statutory definition of a dependent child and any finding that they were dependent is against the manifest weight of the evidence.

It is common practice that dependency complaints are coupled with neglect complaints. Indeed, in this matter, the evidence establishes that the children are better described in the language of neglect than dependency. For example, a neglected child is one who is abandoned by his or her parent, R.C. 2151.03(A)(1), or who lacks proper parental care due to the fault of his or her parent, R C. 2151.03(A)(2).

In the instant case for whatever reason, appellee chose to charge only under R.C. 2151.04(A). The curiosity here is that while appellee may have proved that the children were neglected (generally considered to be the more serious allegation), it failed to prove any of the elements which define dependency. These children were not homeless, destitute, without proper care or without support. It is undisputed that their needs for shelter, food and other necessaries were satisfied.

By the plain language of R.C. 2151.04(A), it must be demonstrated that a child is "homeless or destitute or without proper care or support" before he or she can be deemed a dependent child. As appellee failed to demonstrate that these children suffered from any of these conditions, an adjudication that they are dependent is against the manifest weight of the evidence. Accordingly, appellant's sole assignment of error is found well taken.

The judgment of the Huron County Court of Common Pleas, Juvenile Division, is reversed. It is ordered that appellee pay the court costs of this appeal.

Notes

1. In *In re Christopher B.,* 147 Cal. Rptr. 390 (Ct. App. 1978), the court held that two different standards of proof are required to show either that a child is dependent or that the child should be removed from a parent's home. The *Christopher B.* court explained that not all children who are declared dependent should or could be removed from the parent's home. The court ruled that preponderance of evidence is required to prove a child is dependent while clear and convincing evidence is required to remove a child from his or her home.

2. Some states lump all types of abuse and neglect under the dependency label. A good example is the following California statute:

California Welfare and Institutions Code
§ 300 (West Supp. 2001)

§ 300. Children subject to jurisdiction; legislative intent and declarations; guardian defined

Any child who comes within any of the following descriptions is within the jurisdiction of the juvenile court which may adjudge that person to be a dependent child of the court:

(a) The child has suffered, or there is a substantial risk that the child will suffer, serious physical harm inflicted nonaccidentally upon the child by the child's parent or guardian. . . .

(b) The child has suffered, or there is a substantial risk that the child will suffer, serious physical harm or illness, as a result of the failure or inability of his or her parent or guardian to adequately supervise or protect the child, or the willful or negligent failure of the child's parent or guardian to adequately supervise or protect the child from the conduct of the custodian with whom the child has been left, or by the willful or negligent failure of the parent or guardian to provide the child adequate food, clothing, shelter, or medical treatment, or by the inability of the parent or guardian to provide regular care for the child due to the parent's or guardian's mental illness, developmental disability, or substance abuse. . . .

(c) The child is suffering serious emotional damage, or is at substantial risk of suffering serious emotional damage, evidenced by severe anxiety, depression, withdrawal, or untoward aggressive behavior toward self or others, as a result of the conduct of the parent or guardian or who has no parent or guardian capable of providing appropriate care. . . .

(d) The child has been sexually abused, or there is a substantial risk that the child will be sexually abused . . . by his or her parent or guardian or a member of his or her household. . . .

(e) The child is under the age of five and has suffered severe physical abuse by a parent, or by any person known by the parent, if the parent knew or reasonably should have known that the person was physically abusing the child. . . .

(f) The child's parent or guardian caused the death of another child through abuse or neglect.

* * *

(h) The child has been freed for adoption by one or both parents for 12 months by either relinquishment or termination of parental rights or an adoption petition has been granted.

(i) The child has been subjected to an act or acts of cruelty by the parent or guardian or a member of his or her household. . . .

(j) The child's sibling has been abused or neglected . . . and there is substantial risk that the child will be abused or neglected. . . .

* * *

Question

As illustrated by North Carolina General Statute § 7B-101(9), *supra*, and California Welfare and Institutions Code § 300, *supra,* in Note 2, the approaches to defining dependency vary among the states. What interests would be served by more uniform statutory definitions of the various types of maltreatment that children suffer?

Problem

Zoe is a precocious fourteen-year-old girl. She and her parents have recently had heated arguments over the parents' rules on dating and Zoe's weekend curfew. The parents have threatened to lock Zoe out of the home if she comes home late again. Last Saturday, Zoe came home several hours late and another argument ensued. Zoe's father drove Zoe to Safe Center and told the staff, "You take her. She refuses to abide by the rules of our home." Should Zoe be detained by child welfare officials? Is Zoe a dependent child under North Carolina or California law?

2. Abuse—Generally

General Statutes of North Carolina
§ 7B-101(1) (Lexis 1999)

7B-101. Definitions

As used in this Subchapter, unless the context clearly requires otherwise, the following words have the listed meanings:

1. Abused juveniles.—Any juvenile less than 18 years of age whose parent, guardian, custodian, or caretaker:

a. Inflicts or allows to be inflicted upon the juvenile a serious physical injury by other than accidental means;

b. Creates or allows to be created a substantial risk of serious physical injury to the juvenile by other than accidental means;

c. Uses or allows to be used upon the juvenile cruel or grossly inappropriate procedures or cruel or grossly inappropriate devices to modify behavior;

d. Commits, permits, or encourages the commission of a violation of the following laws by, with, or upon the juvenile: first-degree rape, . . . second degree rape, . . . first-degree sexual offense, . . . second degree sexual offense, . . . sexual act by custodian, . . . preparation of obscene photographs, slides, or motion pictures of the juvenile, . . . employing or permitting the juvenile to assist in a violation of the obscenity laws . . ., dissemination of obscene material to the juvenile . . ., displaying or disseminating material harmful to the juvenile . . ., first and second degree sexual exploitation of the juvenile . . ., promoting the prostitution of the juvenile . . . and taking indecent liberties with the juvenile . . . regardless of the age of the parties;

e. Creates or allows to be created serious emotional damage to the juvenile; serious emotional damage is evidenced by a juvenile's severe anxiety, depression, withdrawal, or aggressive behavior toward himself or others; or

f. Encourages, directs, or approves of delinquent acts involving moral turpitude committed by the juvenile.

a. Physical Abuse

Utah Code Annotated
§ 76-5-109 (Lexis Supp. 2000)

§ 76-5-109 Child Abuse.

(1) As used in this section:

(a) "Child" means a human being who is 18 years of age.

* * *

(c) "Physical injury" means an injury to or condition of a child which impairs the physical condition of the child, including:

(i) a bruise or other contusion of the skin;

(ii) a minor laceration or abrasion;

(iii) failure to thrive or malnutrition; or

(iv) any other condition which imperils the child's health or welfare and which is not a serious physical injury. . . .

(d) "Serious physical injury" means any physical injury or set of injuries which seriously impairs the child's health, or which involves physical torture or causes serious emotional harm to the child, or which involves a substantial risk of death to the child, including:

(i) fracture of any bone or bones;

(ii) intracranial bleeding, swelling or contusion of the brain, whether caused by blows, shaking or causing the child's head to impact with an object or surface;

(iii) any burn, including burns inflicted by hot water, or those caused by placing a hot object upon the skin or body of the child;

(iv) any injury caused by use of a dangerous weapon . . .;

(v) any combination of two or more physical injuries inflicted by the same person, either at the same time or on different occasions;

(vi) any damage to internal organs of the body;

(vii) any conduct toward a child which results in severe emotional harm, severe developmental delay or retardation, or severe impairment of the child's ability to function;

(viii) any injury which creates a permanent disfigurement or protracted loss or impairment of the function of a bodily member, limb, or organ;

(ix) any conduct which causes a child to cease breathing, even if resuscitation is successful following the conduct; or

(x) any conduct which results in starvation or failure to thrive or malnutrition that jeopardizes the child's life.

(2) Any person who inflicts upon a child serious physical injury or, having the care or custody of such child, causes or permits another to inflict serious physical injury upon a child is guilty of an offense as follows:

(a) if done intentionally or knowingly, the offense is a felony of the second degree;

(b) if done recklessly, the offense is a felony of the third degree; or

(c) if done with criminal negligence, the offense is a class A misdemeanor.

(3) Any person who inflicts upon a child physical injury or, having the care or custody of such child, causes or permits another to inflict physical injury upon a child is guilty of an offense as follows:

(a) if done intentionally or knowingly, the offense is a class A misdemeanor;

(b) if done recklessly, the offense is a class B misdemeanor; or

(c) if done with criminal negligence, the offense is a class C misdemeanor.

* * *

In re Ethan H.

609 A.2d 1222 (N.H. 1992)

OPINION:

The respondent, a physician, is the mother of four children. On May 1, 1988, she observed her seven-year-old son, Ethan, throwing food at the diner table. When she commanded Ethan to behave, he allegedly ignored her. In response, she took Ethan to a bedroom and struck his bare buttocks approximately six times with an imitation leather belt.

The next day, the local elementary school reported to the New Hampshire Division for Children and Youth Services (DCYS) that it had received an anonymous phone call that Ethan may have been struck by his mother. The DCYS immediately began to investigate the matter. On May 3, a social worker entered the respondent's home pursuant to a court order. She interviewed Ethan and observed several bruises on his lower back. Ethan admitted that his mother had struck him and that he had additional bruises on his buttocks.

Based on the social worker's observations, the District Court (*Gauthier,* J.) ordered on May 5 that Ethan be placed in protective supervision of the DCYS and "be immediately medically examined to document the physical injuries." Accordingly, the social worker took Ethan to the Nashua Memorial Hospital where he was examined by Dr. David Walker. . . . Dr. Walker also recalls telling the social worker that, based on Ethan's condition, he "would have never thought that Ethan was abused." He later told the State's attorney that he "would *not* have suspected abuse nor filed a report as mandatory by law." (Emphasis added.)

The DCYS nonetheless proceeded with its investigation. On June 8, 1988, the District Court (*Howarth,* J.) conducted a hearing to determine whether Ethan was an "abused child" under the Child Protection Act. RSA 169-C:3, II defines an "abused child" as:

> Any child who has been:
>
> (a) Sexually abused, or
>
> (b) Intentionally physically injured; or
>
> (c) Psychologically injured so that said child exhibits symptoms of emotional problems generally recognized to result from consistent mistreatment or neglect; or

(d) *Physically injured by other than accidental means.*

(Emphasis added.) The district court found that "[Ethan] has incurred physical injury by other than accidental means within the meaning of RSA 169-C:3[,] II(d)."

The respondent appealed to the superior court for a *de novo* review pursuant to RSA 169-C:28. On December 20, 1988, the superior court conducted a hearing in which the DCYS called the respondent, the social worker, and Dr. Rantan Dandekar to testify.

* * *

The superior court upheld the district court's finding that Ethan was an "abused child." The respondent then appealed to this court. We remanded for reconsideration in light of our then-recent decision in *Petition of Doe,* 132 N.H. 270, 564 A.2d 433 (1989), and the superior court conducted a second hearing on October 5, 1990.

The DCYS presented no witnesses at the second hearing. The respondent, however, called three witnesses, including her father, a retired physician. His testimony concerned the relationship between pain, injury, and bruising. He opined that "[n]either bruising nor pain is a valid criteria [of determining injury]" and that "approximately 80 percent of the bruises that present at a doctor's office the patient has no idea how the bruises came [about]." He also explained that the buttocks is perhaps the safest area of the body upon which to administer corporal punishment. During an extremely short cross-examination covering only three pages in the trial transcript, the DCYS attorney did not significantly challenge the credibility of the father's testimony. Moreover, the attorney presented no evidence rebutting his testimony.

As noted earlier, RSA 169-C:3, II(d) defines an "abused child" as "any child who has been . . . [p]hysically injured by other than accidental means." In *Petition of Doe*, we addressed the proper scope of RSA 160-C:3, II(d). We noted that the provision, if interpreted literally, "is overly broad and could encompass reasonable forms of corporal punishment that do not threaten the well-being of the child." *Petition of Doe*, 132 N.H. at 277, 564 A.1d at 438. We concluded that

> a proper finding of child abuse under RSA 169-C:3, II(d) (Supp. 1988) must include a determination of whether the alleged abusive act was committed under circumstances *indicating harm or threatened harm to the child's life, health, or welfare.* Such harm may be demonstrated by, for example, the severity of the intentionally inflicted injuries; *recurring or a threat of recurring injury:* or injury when a profile of the child's caretaker indicates a history of, or a propensity for, abuse. These examples are in no way intended to be limiting, as we recognize the myriad situations in which harm or threatened harm may exist.

Id. at 277-78, 564 A.2d at 439-39 (emphasis added).

In its decision of October 15, 1990, the superior court applied the above standards to the evidence presented at both the 1988 and 1990 hearings and found that Ethan was an "abused child" under RSA 169-C:3, II(d). The court first looked to the dictionary meaning of the term "bruise" and concluded that "[a] bruise is most certainly, by its plain meaning, an injury." The court then reasoned that

> [t]he decision in *Petition of Jane Doe* acknowledges that conduct causing minor injuries may constitute abuse if recurring injury or threat of recurring injury is demonstrated. This is exactly the case here. [The respondent] intentionally struck her 6 year-old son with a belt across his bare buttocks about 6 times, causing linear bruises which were still visible after 5 days. Such "strappings" had been occasioned to Ethan in the past as deemed required by his misbehavior. . . . [The respondent] also demonstrated her intent to continue to discipline her son in this manner in the future. . . . Upon reviewing the evidence presented at both the 1988 and 1990 hearings, we conclude that the superior court's finding that Ethan's bruises "indicat[ed] harm or threatened harm to [his] health and welfare" was unsupported by the evidence.

The respondent presented substantial evidence that Ethan, although bruised, was not harmed. First, her friend and sister both indicated that Ethan tended to bruise easily. Second, the sister indicated that Ethan was actively playing outside after the corporal punishment was administered. Third, the respondent's father testified regarding the tenuous relationship between bruising and harm. As noted earlier, the father's testimony went uncontroverted by any other professional witness. Indeed, the DCYS failed to present *any* testimony of its own indicating that Ethan was harmed or injured. This failure is stunning in light of the fact that the 1990 hearing occurred after this court remanded the matter for further consideration in light of *Petition of Doe*, the very case requiring "harm or threatened harm" for a finding of child abuse.

Additionally, the DCYS failed to present the testimony of Dr. Walker, *who examined Ethan on behalf of the DCYS*, at either hearing. In the absence of any showing to the contrary, we are left to presume that Dr. Walker was not called by the DCYS due to his opinion that he "would not have suspected abuse" based on Ethan's bruises.

Lastly, we note that neither in this case nor in *Petition of Doe* has this court been called upon to either condone or condemn the use of corporal punishment as a means of disciplining one's children. The legislature has already established as policy that *reasonable* corporal punishment is allowable. . . . Today, we hold only that the DCYS, by failing to establish that Ethan's bruises were indicative of harm or injury, has not established child abuse under the standards set forth in *Petition of Doe*. We recognize that in future cases a child's bruises may be of such a nature as to establish *prima facie* evidence of "harm or threatened harm."

Because we conclude that no child abuse exists in this case, it is not necessary for us to address whether the responded was justified in "strapping" Ethan under RSA 627:6, I, which provides that "[a] parent, guardian or other person responsible for the general care and welfare of a minor is justified in using force against such minor when and to the extent that he reasonably believes is necessary to prevent or punish such minor's misconduct." This statute merely codified the well-recognized precept of Anglo-American jurisprudence that the parent of a minor child or one standing *in loco parentis* was justified in using a reasonable amount of force upon a child for the purpose of safe-guarding or promoting the child's welfare. (Citations omitted.)

* * *

Reversed.

Hawaii v. Kaimimoku

841 P.2d 1076 (Haw. Ct. App. 1992)

FACTS

According to the State's witnesses, the facts are as follows: On February 13, 1991, Father was home alone with his three-month-old grandson (Grandson) from 7:30 a.m. until early afternoon. When Father's wife (Mother) and their Daughter, who is Grandson's mother, returned home, Father began yelling and using profanity at Mother because she had been gone for a long time and he had had a difficult time with Grandson. Mother tried to explain why she was delayed, but Father continued to yell at her. Daughter came to Mother's defense, using profanity at Father and yelling at him to stop picking on Mother. Father responded by yelling and using profanity at Daughter, telling her to stop yelling and using profanity at him because his communications with Mother were none of Daughter's business. Father and Daughter were nose to nose while communicating with each other. . . .

Father was "holding" Daughter. Mother tried to separate them and Daughter ran outside. On her way out, she yelled to Mother, "Ma, call the cops. Call the cops." Mother did so. Father followed Daughter down the road about a hundred feet. Daughter testified that Father, while standing about five feet away from her, with an "open fist slapped [her] on [her] face" and "whacked" her on her face "with an open fist straight on and on the right side of her face." Daughter also testified that Father punched her on her shoulders with a "closed fist," but she could not remember how many times.

* * *

Daughter then returned to the house and told Mother that Father had beat up on her. Mother therefore summoned the police again, requesting that assault charges be filed against Father. Officer Paiva arrived at the scene a second time and this time spoke to Daughter who did not show him any injuries but complained of pain to the back and chest area. Father was arrested later that day, without incident, for the offense of abuse of a family or household member.

* * *

Following a bench trial at which Father raised the defense of parental discipline justification under HRS § 703-309(1), the family court orally stated, "I don't find that this was a disciplinary action. . . . This is one more chaotic incident in a chaotic family life. . . . And even if I would get to measuring force, I think the case law is pretty ample that this would fall outside of the reasonable force."

* * *

The court thereupon convicted Father of abuse of a family or household member and sentenced him to 60 days' incarceration, with 30 days suspended for one year, provided Father remain arrest- and conviction-free. The court also ordered Father to attend individual and anger management counseling at the Waianae Mental Health Center.

HRS § 709-906(1) (1985) states in relevant part as follows: "It shall be unlawful for any person, singly or in concert, to physically abuse a family or household member[.]" Father concedes that Daughter is a family member and that he struck her. He maintains, however, that he struck her to discipline her and that his conduct was justified under HRS § 703-309 (1985).

Father's contentions require us to examine the parameters of appropriate parental discipline under the Hawaii Penal Code.

HRS § 703-309 states in relevant part as follows:

> Use of force by persons with special responsibility for care, discipline, or safety of others. The use of force upon or toward the person of another is justifiable under the following circumstances:
>
> (1) The actor is the parent or guardian or other person similarly responsible for the general care and supervision of a minor, or a person acting at the request of such parent, guardian, or other responsible person; and
>
> (a) The force is used for the purpose of safeguarding or promoting the welfare of the minor, including the prevention or punishment of his misconduct; and
>
> (b) The force used is not designed to cause or known to create a substantial risk of causing death, serious bodily injury, disfigurement, extreme pain or mental distress, or gross degradation.

In order to invoke the justification defense of HRS § 703-309(1), a defendant must meet a four-part test. First, the defendant must be a parent, guardian, or other person described in subsection (1). Second, the defendant must have used force against a minor for whose care and supervision the defendant is responsible. Third, the defendant must have used the force for the purpose of safeguarding or promoting the welfare of the minor. Finally, the force used by the defendant must not have been designed to cause or known to create a substantial risk of the results listed in subsection (1)(b).

According to the Commentary to HRS § 703-309, subsection (1) "sets a fairly simple and unexceptionable standard; the right of parents to use force to discipline their children is recognized, subject to clear requirements not to cause permanent injury."

* * *

Subsection (1) deals with the parent or guardian of a minor or a person similarly responsible for his general care and supervision. As the justification is defined, its scope has two determinants: (a) that force is used for the purpose of safeguarding or promoting the welfare of the minor, including the prevention or punishment of his misconduct; and (b) that the force is not designed to cause or known to create a substantial risk of causing death, serious bodily injury, disfigurement, extreme pain or mental distress or gross degradation.

* * *

HRS § 703-309(1) thus grants to parents considerable autonomy to discipline their children, and as long as parents use moderate force for permissible purposes in disciplining their children and do not create a substantial risk of the excessive injuries specified in subsection (1)(b), they will not be criminally liable.

With the foregoing background and historical perspective in mind, we review the evidence in the instant case.

The record is clear that Father is the parent of Daughter, that Daughter is Father's child, and that Daughter was a minor on February 13, 1991, the date of the offense. Father also concedes that he struck Daughter. Therefore, the first two parts of the four part test to invoke the parental discipline defense have been met.

We next consider whether there is substantial evidence on the record that the force used by Father on Daughter was not used by Father for the purpose of punishment of Daughter's misconduct. Father testified that he used force on Daughter to punish her for yelling profanities at him, disobeying him, and being disrespectful. Daughter admitted that she yelled profanities at Father and that she did not obey him when he told her not to yell profanities at him. There is no evidence on the record that Father struck Daughter for any purpose other than for punishment. Therefore, the third part of Father's justification defense has been met.

Finally, we determine whether there is substantial evidence on the record that the force Father used was "not designed to cause or known to create a substantial risk of causing death, serious bodily injury, disfigurement, extreme pain or mental distress, or gross degradation." HRS § 703-309(1)(b).

In *State v. DeLeon*, 72 Haw. 241, 813 P.3d 1382 (1991), the Hawaii Supreme Court considered a situation involving a father who hit his 14-year-old daughter "from six to ten times, with a crisscross motion, on her stretch pants, above the knees, with a 36-inch long belt, folded in two. The belt was one and one-half inches wide. [The daughter] testified that she felt a little pain, that the spanking stung her, and that the pain lasted an hour and a half. She had bruises for about a week." *Id.* at 242, 813 P.2d at 1383. The Hawaii Supreme Court concluded that this evidence was insufficient to support a finding that the force used by Father exceeded the protection provided by HRS § 703-309(1)(b).

In the light of *DeLeon*, we conclude that the fourth part of Father's justification defense has been met.

* * *

holding

Accordingly, we reverse the family court's May 13, 1991 judgement convicting defendant Henry A. K. Kaimimoku of abuse of family and household members, HRS § 709-906.

Notes

1. In child abuse proceedings, state law determines what presumptions exist and what burdens of proof each party must satisfy to make a prima facie case. The following are examples of statutory presumptions in abuse proceedings:

Utah Code Annotated

§ 78-3a-305.1 (Lexis Supp. 2000)

§ 78-3a-305.1. Presumption of responsibility

> In determining whether a minor is an abused child or neglected child it may be presumed that the person having the minor under his direct and exclusive care and control at the time of the abuse is responsible for the abuse or neglect.

The state typically has the initial burden of proof in a dependency adjudication. *See Matter of Perkins*, 352 N.E.2d 502 (Ind. Ct. App. 1976). The following is an example of a statute creating a rebuttable presumption of abuse once the state satisfies its initial burden of proof:

Indiana Code Annotated

§ 31-34-12-4 (Lexis 1997)

§ 31-34-12-4. Rebuttable presumption that child is in need of services.

> A rebuttable presumption is raised that the child is a child in need of services because of an act or omission of the child's parent, guardian, or custodian if the state introduces competent evidence of probative value that:
>
> (1) the child has been injured;
>
> (2) at the time the child was injured, the parent, guardian, or custodian:
>
> (A) had the care, custody, or control of the child; or
>
> (B) had legal responsibility for the care, custody, or control of the child; and
>
> (3) the injury would not ordinarily be sustained except for the act or omission of a parent, guardian, or custodian.

2. Most jurisdictions as a general rule allow parents to inflict corporal punishment that is reasonable under the circumstances. *See, e.g., State v. West,* 515 N.W.2d 484 (Wis. Ct. App. 1994); *Singleton v. State*, 200 S.E.2d 507 (Ga. Ct. App. 1973); *State v. Bell*, 223 N.W.2d 181 (Iowa 1974); *Moore v. State*, 291 A.2d 74 (Md. Ct. Spec. App. 1972).

The RESTATEMENT (SECOND) OF TORTS and the Model Penal Code, although distinctive in their supportive rationale, also allow parents to use punishment on their children.

Restatement (Second) of Torts

§§ 147, 150 (1965)

§ 147. General Principle.

> (1) A parent is privileged to apply such reasonable force or to impose such reasonable confinement upon his child as he reasonably believes to be necessary for its proper control, training, or education. . . .

§ 150. Factors Involved in Determining Reasonableness of Punishment

In determining whether force or confinement is reasonable for control, training, or education of a child, the following factors are to be considered:

(a) whether the actor is a parent;

(b) the age, sex, and physical and mental condition of the child;

(c) the nature of his offense and his apparent motive;

(d) the influence of his example upon other children of the same family or group;

(e) whether the force or confinement is reasonably necessary and appropriate to compel obedience to a proper command;

(f) whether it is disproportionate to the offense, unnecessarily degrading, or likely to cause serious or permanent harm.

Model Penal Code

§ 3.08 (1985)

§ 3.08. Use of Force by Persons with Special Responsibility for Care, Discipline or Safety of Others

The use of force upon or toward the person of another is justifiable if:

(1) the actor is the parent or guardian or other person similarly responsible for the general care and supervision of a minor or a person acting at the request of such parent, guardian, or other responsible person and;

(a) the force is used for the purpose of safeguarding or promoting the welfare of the minor, including the prevention or punishment of his misconduct; and

(b) the force used is not designed to cause or known to create a substantial risk of causing death, serious bodily harm, disfigurement, extreme pain or mental distress or gross degradation. . . .

3. Courts have also held that school teachers may inflict reasonable punishment on a child at school. *See, e.g., People v. Ball*, 317 N.E.2d 54 (Ill. 1974). School teachers may also inflict reasonable punishment on a child away from school grounds. *See generally* Daniel E. Feld, *Right To Discipline Pupil For Conduct Away From School Grounds or Not Immediately Connected With School Activities*, 55 A.L.R.3D 1124 (1973).

Questions

1. Suppose a family's religious beliefs permit the parents to physically punish their children. Should the family's religious beliefs be given precedence over state laws which prohibit physical abuse? What arguments would you expect the social service agency and the parents to raise on this question?

2. In *Stanley v. Illinois*, 405 U.S. 645 (1972), the United States Supreme Court stated "Procedure by presumption is always cheaper and easier than individualized determination. But when, as here, the procedure forecloses the determinative issues of competence and care, when it explicitly disdains present realities in deference to past formalities, it needlessly risks running roughshod over the important interests of both parent and child." For the complete opinion, see Chapter 14, Section B.1.a. In light of the Utah and Indiana statutes, *supra*, in Note 1, what risks exist in creating the presumptions of child abuse against parents? What arguments support codification of the presumptions? What constitutional issues may arise?

b. Sexual Abuse

West Virginia Code

§ 49-1-3 (Lexis 1999)

§ 49-1-3. Definitions relating to abuse and neglect.

(a) "Abused child" means a child whose health or welfare is harmed or threatened by:

* * *

(2) Sexual abuse or sexual exploitation. . . .

* * *

(c) "Child abuse and neglect" or "child abuse or neglect" means . . . sexual abuse [or] sexual exploitation . . . by a parent, guardian or custodian who is responsible for the child's welfare, under circumstances which harm or threaten the health and welfare of the child.

* * *

(j) "Sexual abuse" means:

(A) As to a child who is less than sixteen years of age, any of the following acts which a parent, guardian or custodian shall engage in, attempt to engage in, or knowingly procure another person to engage in, with such child, notwithstanding the fact that the child may have willingly participated in such conduct or the fact that the child may have suffered no apparent physical injury or mental or emotional injury as a result of such conduct:

(i) Sexual intercourse;
(ii) Sexual intrusion; or
(iii) Sexual contact;

(B) As to a child who is sixteen years of age or older, any of the following acts which a parent, guardian or custodian shall engage in, attempt to engage in, or knowingly procure another person to engage in, with such child, notwithstanding the fact that the child may have consented to such conduct or the fact that the child may have suffered no apparent physical injury or mental or emotional injury as a result of such conduct:

(i) Sexual intercourse;
(ii) Sexual intrusion; or
(iii) Sexual contact;

(C) Any conduct whereby a parent, guardian or custodian displays his or her sex organs to a child, or procures another person to display his or her sex organs to a child, for the purpose of gratifying the sexual desire of the parent, guardian or custodian, of the person making such display, or of the child, or for the purpose of affronting or alarming the child.

* * *

(l) "Sexual exploitation" means an act whereby:

(1) A parent, guardian or custodian, whether for financial gain or not, persuades, induces, entices or coerces a child to engage in sexually explicit conduct . . . ;

(2) A parent, guardian or custodian persuades, induces, entices or coerces a child to display his or her sex organs for the sexual gratification of the parent, guardian, custodian or a third person, or to display his or her sex organs under circumstances in which the parent, guardian or custodian knows such display is likely to be observed by others who would be affronted or alarmed.

* * *

Alaska v. Jackson

776 P.2d 320 (Alaska Ct. App. 1989)

In the summer of 1987, Matthew Jackson [twenty-seven years of age] became romantically involved with thirteen-year-old M.S. Jackson was a teacher at a private gymnastics school. M.S. was one of his students. The relationship between Jackson and M.S. progressed during the fall of 1987, and, in December or January, approximately the time M.S. turned fourteen, Jackson engaged in sexual intercourse with her for the first time. . . .

From December of 1987 until March of 1988, Jackson had sexual intercourse with M.S. on five or six additional occasions. Jackson and M.S. also engaged in oral sex on several other occasions. One of these occasions occurred in March, 1988, while Jackson and M.S. were in Seattle, Washington, attending a gymnastics meet.

Sexual relations between Jackson and M.S. ended sometime in March, 1988; they were apparently stopped by Jackson. During the summer of 1988, M.S. reported her sexual involvement with Jackson. Jackson encouraged her to report their relationship, and, once it was reported, he admitted his involvement and acknowledged responsibility.

None of the incidents of sexual intercourse between Jackson and M.S. involved any force or coercion. Jackson and M.S. were mutually attracted to each other. After reporting the relationship, M.S. felt guilty and suffered some emotional difficulty. She indicated that she was still in love with Jackson and expressed a desire to marry him when she turned eighteen. Disclosure of the relationship also had a significant impact on the relationship between M.S. and her parents. As a result of the disclosure, M.S. and her parents found it necessary to undergo regular family counseling sessions.

* * *

Jackson was charged with one count of sexual abuse of a minor in the second degree. The statute governing the offense, AS 11.41.436, proscribes several distinct forms of sexual contact between adults and minors. Jackson was charged under AS 11.41.436(a)(1), which covers conduct formerly called statutory rape. The relevant portion of AS 11.41.436(a)(1) provides that the offense of sexual abuse of a minor in the second degree occurs when an offender who is sixteen years of age or older "engages in sexual penetration with a person who is 13, 14, or 15 years of age and at least three years younger than the offender."

Sexual abuse of a minor in the second degree is a class B felony, AS 11.41.436(b), and is punishable by a maximum term of ten years' imprisonment. Presumptive terms for second and subsequent felony offenders are four and six years. No presumptive term is prescribed for individuals who, like Jackson, have not previously been convicted of a felony. See AS 12.55.125(d).

* * *

At the conclusion of the hearing, Judge Johnstone found that Jackson's conduct toward M.S. had resulted from genuine and reciprocal affection between Jackson and M.S. The judge also found Jackson to be sincerely remorseful and contrite and noted that there was no evidence to indicate that Jackson had engaged in similarly inappropriate behavior toward other minors. Judge Johnstone concluded that Jackson was not a person who had an abnormal affinity toward children or who was prone to deviant sexual behavior. The judge believed that, instead, Jackson's offense was situational and that it was consequently unlikely to recur.

* * *

Accordingly, the judge sentenced Jackson to a term of three years, suspended the entire term, and ordered Jackson to complete a three-year period of probation. As special conditions of probation, the judge required Jackson to complete a course of outpatient counseling for sexual offenders and to perform 1,000 hours of community service.

On appeal, the state argues that the sentence imposed below is clearly mistaken, *McClain v. State,* 519 P.2d 811, 813-14 (Alaska 1974), in that it gives insufficient attention to the seriousness of Jackson's criminal misconduct and fails to make adequate provision for the sentencing goal of community condemnation. We find that the state's argument has merit. In our view, a probationary sentence was clearly mistaken under the circumstances of Jackson's case.

A. Relevant Case Law

Our analysis must begin with *State v. Coats,* 699 P.2d 1329 (Alaska App. 1983). In *Coats*, we had occasion to discuss the seriousness of the harm that results from sexual abuse of minors and the consequent need for emphasis on the sentencing goal of community condemnation, or reaffirmation of societal norms:

> [T]his court has consistently expressed the view that sexual abuse of children cannot be condoned. There is a compelling need in such cases to express community condemnation of those who sexually abuse children and to make clear to offenders that conduct is abhorrent to contemporary social norms.

In most sexual abuse cases, the young victims are particularly vulnerable to abuse and are as a practical matter incapable of effectively defending themselves. Innocent children who have been the victims of sexual abuse may suffer serious, long-term emotional and psychological injuries; the nature and scope of the injuries is often difficult to predict with accuracy. In almost all cases, a sexual abuse victim must have tremendous courage and determination simply to cope with the emotional trauma involved as the primary witness in the adversary process of a formal prosecution. And often the disruption of normal family life occasioned by a prosecution will lead a youthful victim to feel confused and guilty.

Coats involved a conviction under Alaska's former sexual abuse of children statute, AS 11.41.440, which ranked the offense as a class C felony—the lowest category of felony offenses. Nevertheless, given the seriousness of the harm in child sexual abuse cases, we specifically concluded in *Coats* that, even for first offenders, probationary sentences are appropriate only under limited circumstances. . . .

Coats thus makes it clear that, to justify a probationary sentence, the sentencing court must find not only that the offender has an unusually strong potential for rehabilitation, but also that the circumstances surrounding the commission of the offense are mitigated.

* * *

In *State v. Woods*, 680 P.2d 1195 (Alaska App. 1983), the defendant was convicted of a single episode of sexually abusing his five-year-old daughter. The sentencing court found Woods' conduct to be comparable to the conduct involved in *State v. Coats*, and found that Woods' prospects for rehabilitation were comparable to Coats'. Accordingly, the court imposed an unsuspended sentence of six months' imprisonment—the sentence that this court had indicated as minimally appropriate for Coats. *See State v. Coats*, 629 P.2d at 1334. We disapproved Woods' six-month sentence as too lenient, noting that Woods' offense involved a child younger that the child involved in the *Coats* case and emphasizing that Woods had been convicted of a class B felony instead of a class C felony. We concluded that an unsuspended term of at least eighteen months to serve should have been imposed. *Id.* at 1197-98.

In *Foster v. State*, 751 P.2d 1383 (Alaska App. 1988), a statutory rape case like Jackson's, the defendant, a twenty-five-year old first offender, was convicted of a single incident of sexual intercourse with a fourteen-year-old girl. Foster was sentenced to serve four years with two and one-half years suspended. The superior court thereafter declined Foster's motion to reduce the sentence. We upheld the superior court's decision, noting that the sentencing record supported the court's apparent conclusion that Foster's conduct was not particularly mitigated and that his prospects for rehabilitation were not particularly favorable.

When significant aggravating circumstances have been established or when an offender's potential for rehabilitation has been shown to be particularly bad, we have not hesitated to approve first offense child sexual abuse sentences substantially exceeding eighteen months of unsuspended incarceration.

. . .

B. Application of Case Law to Jackson's Case

. . . The sentencing court's primary focus was on Jackson's potential for rehabilitation. Given the court's findings there seems little doubt concerning Jackson's unusually favorable prospects for rehabilitation. Jackson's strong family and community ties, his solid educational and employment history, his lack of any prior criminal record, the situational nature of his offense, and his genuine remorse and contrition all support the conclusion that incarceration is unnecessary to further the sentencing goals of rehabilitation, personal deterrence, or isolation.

In contrast to the attention it gave to Jackson's background and prospects for rehabilitation, the sentencing court made comparatively few specific findings concerning the seriousness of Jacksons' conduct. We see little if anything in this case to justify the conclusion that Jackson's conduct was significantly less serious than the norm for the offense.

M.S. was thirteen and fourteen years of age at the time of the offense. Her age falls within the lower range of the statutorily specified limits for the offense. Conversely, while Jackson was not particularly advanced in age, neither was he a youthful offender. At age 27, Jackson was a full thirteen years older than M.S.

It is also significant that Jackson was not convicted for an isolated instance of misconduct. His offense involved multiple incidents occurring over a lengthy period of time. *See, e.g, Smith v. State,* 745 P.2d 1375, 1377 n. 2 (Alaska App. 1987); *Higgs v. State,* 676 P.2d 610 (Alaska App. 1984). *See also State v. Karnos*, 696 P.2d at 687.

It is even more significant that, in sexually abusing M.S., who was one of his gymnastics students, Jackson violated the trust placed in him by M.S. and her parents. *See Goulden v. State,* 656 P.2d at 1221; *State v. Andrews,* 707 P.2d 900, 911 (Alaska App. 1985); *Depp v. State*, 686 P.2d 712, 721 (Alaska App. 1984). While this breach of trust might not have been as significant as it would have been had Jackson been M.S.'s teacher at school, or her parent or guardian, the breach nonetheless contributes markedly to the seriousness of the offense and, in our view, precludes the conclusion that Jackson's conduct was significantly less serious than the norm for the offense. *See Skrepich v. State,* 740 P.2d at 954.

It is true, as Jackson points out, that his conduct toward M.S. was motivated by genuine reciprocal affection and involved no coercion or force. However, while the sincerity of Jackson's feelings toward M.S. may to a limited extent be viewed as an extenuating circumstance, the absence of force or coercion cannot. Neither force nor lack of consent is an element of sexual abuse of a minor in the second degree. In cases of statutory rape, the typical offense involves mutually consensual conduct. It is precisely because the law deems children to be incapable of rendering meaningful consent in such situations that the offense has been defined to make consent irrelevant. Thus, had Jackson used force or coercion in committing his offense, his conduct would have been significantly aggravated. The absence of such conduct, however, does not mitigate the offense.

* * *

In summary, Jackson's actual conduct in committing the offense for which he was convicted was at best only slightly mitigated. Thus, while Jackson's favorable prospects for rehabilitation would have justified a sentence below the one-year to four-year range of typical first offenses, the absence of significantly mitigated conduct calls for imposition of a nonprobationary term—one equivalent to at least ninety days of incarceration.

Notes

1. The following Model Penal Code provision defines sexual abuse:

Model Penal Code
§ 213.4 (1980)

A person who has sexual contact with another not his spouse, or causes such other to have sexual contact with him, is guilty of sexual assault, a misdemeanor, if:

(1) he knows that the contact is offensive to the other person; or

(2) he knows that the other person suffers from a mental disease or defect which renders him or her incapable of appraising the nature of his or her conduct; or

(3) he knows that the other person is unaware that a sexual act is being committed; or

(4) the other person is less than 10 years old; or

(5) he has substantially impaired the other person's power to appraise or control his or her conduct, by administering or employing without the other's knowledge drugs, intoxicants or other means for the purpose of preventing resistance; or

(6) the other person is less than [16] years old and the actor is at least [four] years older than the other person; or

(7) the other person is less than 21 years old and the actor is his guardian or otherwise responsible for general supervision of his welfare; or

(8) the other person is in custody of law or detained in a hospital or other institution and the actor has supervisory or disciplinary authority over him.

2. Some states have created a hearsay exception to permit the use of a child's out-of-court statement in a sexual abuse case. *See, e.g.,* 735 ILL. COMP. STAT. ANN. 5/8-2601 (West 1992). For a contrast of a sexually abused child's out-of- court statement in a criminal trial, see ARIZ. REV. STAT. ANN. § 13-1416 (West 2001); WASH. REV. CODE ANN. § 9A-44.120 (West 2000). *See generally* Lynn M. Matshall, Note, Hutton v. State: *Whose Rights are Paramount, the Dependent's or the*

Child Victim's?, 27 U. BALT. L. REV. 291 (1997); Dara Loren Steele, Note, *Expert Testimony: Seeking an Appropriate Admissibility Standard for Behavioral Science in Child Sexual Abuse Prosecutions,* 48 DUKE L.J. 932 (1999).

3. The behavior of sexually abused children is often explained by evidence of various traits common to victims. The evidence is often described as the child sexual abuse accommodation syndrome (CSAAS), which was presented by Dr. Roland Summit. *See* Roland C. Summit, *The Child Sexual Abuse Accommodation Syndrome,* 7 CHILD ABUSE & NEGLECT 133 (1983). The New Jersey Supreme Court in *State v. J.Q.*, 617 A.2d 1196, 1204-05 (1993), reviewed the following traits which comprise CSAAS:

1. secrecy—often the child is either threatened by the aggressor to keep quiet or is scared to tell anyone in fear of retaliation by the aggressor;
2. helplessness—children who are sexually abused often feel a sense of total dependence on the abusing adult's authority;
3. entrapment—sexually abused children may feel that the only way to survive the pain is to accept things as they are;
4. delayed disclosure—often strife in the family will trigger disclosure of an adult's sexual abuse of a child; and
5. retraction—a sexually abused child may retract his or her claim that abuse occurred once the accusation causes strife in the family, and the child believes the problems are his or her fault.

The full text of the opinion in *State v. J.Q.* is located in Chapter 13, Part B.1.

4. In *John D. v. Department of Social Services*, 744 N.E.2d 659 (Mass. 2001), the court held that a stepfather's conversations with his stepdaughter, replete with sexual themes, constituted "verbal sexual contact" and that the stepfather was properly charged with having sexual contact with his stepdaughter. The *John D.* court noted that the proper focus of sexual abuse is not only the nature of the interaction, but also the potential effect upon the child. According to the court, the stepfather's conversations about oral sexual acts created a risk of harm to the stepdaughter's well-being, and, therefore, the stepfather's conversations fell within the ambit of the sexual abuse statute.

Questions

1. When should the state through its child welfare agency or court intervene in a parent's teaching a child about sexual matters? For example, what is the state's interest where a father rents a sexually explicit video for his twelve-year-old daughter? What if the father encourages her to "discover the pleasure" of masturbation in his presence? What if the father encourages the child to masturbate in the privacy of her bedroom? *See, e.g., Ginsberg v. New York*, 390 U.S. 629 (1968).

2. Children occasionally sexually experiment by kissing, fondling, rubbing, or even exposing themselves to other children. Researchers remain undecided as to when a child sexually abuses another child. What factors should a court consider when determining if sexual abuse occurs between two children? *See generally* VERNON WIEHE, PERILOUS RIVALRY: WHEN SIBLINGS BECOME ABUSIVE (1991); *see also State v. J.D.*, 701 N.E.2d 908 (Ind. Ct. App. 1998); *K.B.S. v. State*, 725 So. 2d 448 (Fla. Dist. Ct. App. 1999).

3. Recent statistics indicate a decline in the incidents of child sexual abuse in the 1990s after increases in the 1980s. *See* LISA JONES & DAVID FINKELHOR, U.S. DEP'T OF JUST., THE DECLINE IN CHILD SEXUAL ABUSE CASES (2001). The number of child sex abuse cases dropped 31% from 1992 (149,800 cases) to 1998 (103,600). Furthermore, 36 of 47 states reported "a decline of more than 30 percent since their peak year." The U.S. Department of Justice Report suggests that a number of reasons may explain the decrease in child sexual abuse cases, including increased public awareness, successful prevention programs, incarceration of child sexual abuse offenders, treatment programs that successfully treat offenders, and laws that "improve monitoring of sex offenders in the community." The report also indicates the decline in child sexual abuse may also be a result of a general decline in reporting such incidents. For an illustration of how these factors may contribute to the decline in child sexual abuse, see *id.* at 5.

c. Mental Abuse

23 Pennsylvania Consolidated Statutes Annotated
§ 6303 (West Supp. 2001)

Section 6303. Definitions

(a) General rule.—The following words and phrases when used in this chapter shall have the meanings given to them in this section unless the context clearly indicates otherwise:

* * *

"Serious mental injury." A psychological condition, as diagnosed by a physician or licensed psychologist, including the refusal of appropriate treatment, that:

(1) renders a child chronically and severely anxious, agitated, depressed, socially withdrawn, psychotic or in reasonable fear that the child's life or safety is threatened; or

(2) seriously interferes with a child's ability to accomplish age-appropriate developmental and social tasks.

* * *

(b) Child abuse.—

(1) The term "child abuse" shall mean any of the following:

* * *

(ii) An act or failure to act by a perpetrator which causes nonaccidental serious mental injury . . . of a child under 18 years of age.

* * *

T.S. v. Department of Health and Rehabilitative Services

654 So. 2d 1028 (Fla. Dist. Ct. App. 1995)

BOOTH, Judge.

This cause is before us on appeal from a final order of the Department of Health and Rehabilitative Services (HRS) denying appellant's request to expunge a proposed confirmed report that he perpetrated "mental abuse," "other mental injury-abuse" or "other threatened harm" on his son, J.S. § 415.504(4), Fla. Stat. (1993). We must reverse and remand.

HRS presented testimony of expert and lay witnesses to establish mental abuse. T.S. presented no evidence. He acknowledged that the events occurred as charged by HRS, but defended on the ground that there was no resulting mental injury, or at least none that could be proved.

In the recommended order, the hearing officer noted that the term "mental abuse" is not defined under section 415.503 and held that other statutory terms such as "abused or neglected child," "child abuse or neglect," "harm" and "mental injury" would have to be considered. The hearing officer then concluded that the following test should be applied:

> If one reads and applies the foregoing statutory definitions in sequential order, which clearly is the way in which the legislature intended these definitions to be read, it would appear the HRS' report can only remain as it is presently classified if there is a preponderance of evidence that T.S. *harmed or threatened harm to J.S.' mental health or welfare by the infliction of mental injury.* [Emphasis original]

The hearing officer then determined that the evidence failed to show that T.S. "inflicted a discernible or substantial impairment, i.e., mental injury, upon J.S." and recommended that the report be expunged. HRS accepted the hearing officer's findings of fact as set forth in the recommended order. HRS also adopted the hearing officer's conclusions of law, except for the ultimate determination that the facts found did not constitute mental injury as defined in section 415.503(11), Florida Statutes (1993).[8] Accordingly, HRS denied expunction, and T.S. appealed.

The pertinent definition sections of section 415.503, Florida Statutes (1993), are as follows:

> (1) "Abused or neglected child" means a child whose physical or mental health or welfare is harmed, or threatened with harm, by the acts or omissions of the parent or other person responsible for the child's welfare. . . .

* * *

---

[8] § 415.503(11), Fla. Stat. (1993), provides:

> (11) "Mental injury" means an injury to the intellectual or psychological capacity of a child as evidenced by a discernible and substantial impairment in his ability to function within his normal range of performance and behavior, with due regard to his culture.

(3) "Child abuse or neglect" means harm or threatened harm to a child's physical or mental health or welfare by the acts or omissions of a parent, adult household member, or other person responsible for the child's welfare, or, for purposes of reporting requirements, by any person.

* * *

(9) "Harm" to a child's health or welfare can occur when the parent or other person responsible for the child's welfare:

(a) Inflicts, or allows to be inflicted, upon the child physical or mental injury.

We hold that the hearing officer and HRS erred in combining the statutory provisions to produce one standard which requires proof of mental injury. The conduct of the perpetrator may constitute mental abuse or neglect even though the child has not, as yet, suffered mental injury. . . . The statute includes the terms "threatened with harm" (section 415.503(1)) and "threatened harm" (section 415.503(3)). Thus, mental abuse may be proved by evidence that the child's mental health or welfare is *threatened* with harm by the acts or omissions of the abuser, as well as by evidence that the child has been harmed, which we equate with mental injury. In the instant case, there is evidence, if believed by the factfinder, that will support a finding of mental abuse or neglect under the law as stated above.

In addition to the error in interpretation of section 415.504, HRS erred in accepting the factual findings below, which are insufficient. The order merely summarizes the testimony of the witnesses without accepting or rejecting the testimony.

On remand, the hearing officer shall accept or reject the evidence offered and make definitive findings. Accordingly, this case must be reversed and remanded for the hearing officer to apply the law as stated herein.

Notes

1. General patterns of behavior have been identified in adults who mentally abuse their children. In THE PSYCHOLOGICALLY BATTERED CHILD 25-29 (1986), Garbino, Guttman and Seeley explain that abusive adults may exhibit the following characteristics leading to the mental abuse of children:

1. rejection—an abusive adult may not recognize the child's worth or fail to notice the child's needs. As a result, the child may feel worthless and expendable.
2. isolation—an abusive adult may cut the child off from the rest of the world leaving the child in isolation. The abused child, as a result, will not form friendships necessary for the child's growth, and the child will not participate in social events.
3. terrorizing—an abusive adult may verbally abuse a child to the extent that the adult frightens and bullies the child into doing what

the adult wants. An abused child who is terrified of his or her abusive parent may take on the view that the world is a very cold and bitter place.

4. ignoring—an abusive adult may deprive the growing child of any emotional stimulation by not responding to the successes or accomplishments of the child. As a result, the child's mental growth may be stifled.
5. reinforcing deviance—an abusive adult may by his or her own violent or deviant behavior reinforce the idea that deviance is acceptable. The child, as a result, may develop a deviant and destructive attitude towards society.

2. Physical and sexual abuse and neglect frequently have components of mental abuse. For example, a child who suffers from a parent's physical or sexual abuse may be afraid to tell anyone for fear of parental retaliation. Moreover, a child may believe he or she is "dirty" and worthless because the one person the child trusts—the parent—is abusing the child. In *In re J.M.*, 479 So. 2d 826 (Fla. Dist. Ct. App. 1985), a child was physically abused and had numerous bruises and scars all over the child's body. Because of the mental trauma and shame that accompanied the physical abuse, the child became a recluse and rarely associated with anyone other than the child's parents.

Although cases of mental abuse arising from physical and sexual maltreatment of children are more common, mental abuse can also be the result of parental neglect. In *In the Interest of B.B.,* 500 N.W.2d 9 (Iowa 1993), a mother was so obsessed with her child being free of illness that she refused to send her child to school and wouldn't allow the child to interact with children of the same age. As a result, the child grew up without a proper education, which led to the child's retardation.

Questions

1. Precise, acceptable definition of mental abuse is elusive. If a father refers to his homosexual son as a "fag" and calls him a "queer" to his face, is this mental abuse? *See In re Shane T.,* 453 N.Y.S.2d 590 (Fam. Ct. 1982). If a stepmother tells her stepson that she does not like him and that his guitar playing sounds like a "dead cow," is this mental abuse? What if the stepmother tells him that he is not welcome to visit his father in the stepmother's house? *See In re Leif Z.*, 431 N.Y.S.2d 290 (Fam. Ct. 1980).

2. Mentally abused children may become violent towards their abusers after months or even years of abuse. In some extreme cases, an abused child may become so violent that he or she murders the abuser. *See, e.g., State v. Jane*, 850 P.2d 495 (Wash. 1993). Should the law allow a child to use his or her mental abuse as a defense to murder or should mental abuse be considered as a mitigating factor at sentencing? For a discussion of mental abuse as a possible defense to murder, see Jamie Heather Sacks, Comment, *A New Age of Understanding: Allowing Self-Defense Claims For Battered Children Who Kill Their Abusers,* 10 J. CONTEMP. HEALTH L. & POL'Y 349 (1993).

d. Fetal Abuse

State ex rel. Angela M.W. v. Kruzicki
561 N.W.2d 729 (Wis. 1997)

Ann Walsh BRADLEY, Justice

The petitioner, Angela M.W., seeks review of a court of appeals' decision denying her request for either a writ of habeas corpus or a supervisory writ to prohibit the Waukesha County Circuit Court, Kathryn W. Foster, Judge, from continuing to exercise jurisdiction in a CHIPS (child alleged to be in need of protection or services) proceeding. She maintains that the CHIPS statute does not confer jurisdiction over her or her viable fetus. In the alternative, if the CHIPS statute does confer such jurisdiction, the petitioner contends that as applied to her, it violates her equal protection and due process rights. Because we determine that the legislature did not intend to include a fetus within the Children's Code definition of "child," we reverse the decision of the court of appeals.

* * *

The petitioner was an adult carrying a viable fetus with a projected delivery date of October 4, 1995. Based upon observations made while providing the petitioner with prenatal care, her obstetrician suspected that she was using cocaine or other drugs. Blood tests performed on May 31, June 26, and July 21, 1995, confirmed the obstetrician's suspicion that the petitioner was using cocaine or other drugs.

On July 21, 1995, the obstetrician confronted the petitioner about her drug use and its effect on her viable fetus. The petitioner expressed remorse, but declined the obstetrician's advice to seek treatment. On August 15, 1995, a blood test again confirmed that the petitioner was ingesting cocaine or other drugs. Afterward, the petitioner canceled a scheduled August 28, 1995, appointment, and rescheduled the appointment for September 1, 1995. When she failed to keep the September 1 appointment, her obstetrician reported his concerns to Waukesha County authorities.

On September 5, 1995, the Waukesha County Department of Health and Human Services (the County) filed a "MOTION TO TAKE AN UNBORN CHILD INTO CUSTODY," pursuant to Wis. Stat. § 48.19(1)(c) (1993-94). . . . In its motion, the County requested an order "removing the above-named unborn child from his or her present custody, and placing the unborn child" in protective custody. The motion was supported by the affidavit of the petitioner's obstetrician, which set out the obstetrician's observations and medical opinion that "without intervention forcing [the petitioner] to cease her drug use," her fetus would suffer serious physical harm.

In an order filed on September 6, 1995, the juvenile court directed that:

> the [petitioner's] unborn child . . . be detained under Section 48.207(1)(g), Wis. Stats., by the Waukesha County Sheriff's Department and transported to Waukesha Memorial Hospital for inpatient treatment and protection. Such detention will by necessity result in the detention of the unborn child's mother. . . .

* * *

Also on September 6, 1995, the County filed a CHIPS petition in the juvenile court, alleging that the petitioner's viable fetus was in need of protection or services because the petitioner "neglect[ed], refuse[ed] or [was] unable for reasons other than poverty to provide necessary care, food, clothing, medical or dental care or shelter so as to seriously endanger the physical health of the child, pursuant to Section 48.13(10) of the Wisconsin Statutes." The County alleged that the petitioner's 36-week-old viable fetus had been exposed to drugs prenatally through the mother's drug use. . . .

* * *

On September 13, 1995, the petitioner commenced an original action in the court of appeals, seeking a writ of habeas corpus, or, in the alternative, a supervisory writ staying all proceedings in the juvenile court and dismissing the CHIPS petition. In support of her request, the petitioner asserted that Chapter 48 does not vest the juvenile court with jurisdiction over her or her viable fetus. Alternatively, if the statute does grant such authority, the petitioner argued that it violates the constitutional guarantees of procedural and substantive due process, as well as equal protection of the laws.

The court of appeals declined to stay the juvenile court proceedings, and issued an order on September 21, 1995, denying both writ petitions. The petitioner gave birth to a baby boy on September 28, 1995. Subsequently, the court of appeals issued an opinion supplementing its earlier order.

A divided court of appeals determined that the juvenile court did not exceed its jurisdiction in this case. The court reasoned that the United States Supreme Court, the Wisconsin legislature, and this court have each articulated public policy considerations supporting the conclusion that a viable fetus is a "person" within the meaning of the CHIPS statute's definition of "child." The court also held that application of the CHIPS statute to the petitioner did not deprive her of equal protection or due process, since the statute was a properly tailored means of vindicating the State's compelling interest in the health, safety, and welfare of a viable fetus. The petitioner then sought review in this court, raising substantially the same arguments she raised before the court of appeals.[6]

We stress at the outset of our analysis that this case is not about the propriety or morality of the petitioner's conduct. . . . Rather, this case is one of statutory construction. The issue presented is whether a viable fetus is included in the definition of "child" provided in Wis. Stat. § 48.02(2).

---

[6] Because the petitioner has given birth and is no longer being detained, this action is moot. However, we will retain an otherwise moot case for determination in certain circumstances. For example, we have recognized an exception to the general rule of dismissal for mootness when the issues presented are of great public importance, or the question is capable and likely of repetition and yet evades appellate review because the appellate process usually cannot be completed in time to have a practical effect on the parties. Because this case satisfies both of the cited mootness exceptions, we proceed to a consideration of the issues presented.

The interpretation of a statute presents a question of law which this court reviews under a *de novo* standard. *Stockbridge School Dist. v. DPI,* 202 Wis. 2d 214, 219, 550 N.W.2d 96 (1996). Our primary purpose when interpreting a statute is to give effect to the legislature's intent. We first look to the language of the statute, and if the language is clear and unambiguous, we define the language of the statute in accordance with its ordinary meaning. If the language of the statute is ambiguous and does not clearly set forth the legislative intent, we will construe the statute so as to ascertain and carry out the legislative intent. In construing an ambiguous statute, we examine the history, content, subject matter, scope, and object of the statute. *Id.* at 220, 550 N.W.2d 96 (citing *Jungbluth v. Hometown, Inc.,* 201 Wis. 3d 320, 327, 548 N.W.2d 519 (1996)).

The statutory language at issue confers on the juvenile court "exclusive original jurisdiction over a child alleged to be in need of protection or services which can be ordered by the court. . . ." § 48.13. A "child" is defined in Chapter 48 as "a person who is less than 18 years of age." § 48.02(2). The petitioner contends that the Chapter 48 definition of "child" is clear on its face, and mandates the conclusion that Chapter 48 uses the term "child" to mean a person born alive. . . . In contrast, the County asserts that courts in this State and other jurisdictions have determined that "child" and "person" are ambiguous terms. As such, the County contends that we are required to look beyond the language of the statute for the meaning of "child."

Statutory language is ambiguous if reasonable minds could differ as to its meaning. While the parties' differing interpretations of a statute do not alone create ambiguity, equally sensible interpretations of a term by different authorities are indicative of the term's ability to support more than one meaning.

Case law reveals that different courts have given different meanings to the term "person" and "child." This court has previously held that a viable fetus is a "person" for purposes of Wisconsin's wrongful death statute. *Kwaterski v. State Farm Mut. Automobile Ins. Co.,* 34 Wis. 2d 14, 22, 148 N.W.2d 107 (1967). On the other hand, the United States Supreme Court has concluded that a fetus is not a "person" under the Fourteenth Amendment to the United States Constitution. *Roe v. Wade,* 410 U.S. 113, 158, 93 S. Ct. 705, 729, 35 L. Ed. 2d 147 (1973). Perhaps most compelling, courts in other states have arrived at different interpretations of statutory language nearly identical to that in § 48.02(2). *Compare State v. Gray*, 62 Ohio St. 2d 514, 584 N.E.2d 710, 713 (1992) (holding that a third trimester fetus is not "a child under eighteen years of age," as provided in Ohio's child endangerment statute), with *Whitner v. State,* 328 S.C. 1, 492 S.E.2d 777 (S.C. July 15, 1996) (concluding that a viable fetus is a "person under the age of eighteen," pursuant to South Carolina's child abuse and endangerment statute). Against this backdrop of conflicting authority, we conclude that the term "child" is ambiguous.

* * *

In examining the legislative history, we find the drafting files of the more recent amendments to the Code devoid of information which might illuminate our search. We also find no news accounts of debate, dialogue, or even consideration of whether fetus should be included in the definition of "child" in Chapter 48. Furthermore, the parties offer no specific historical references to support their respective positions. The issue of whether the Chapter 48 definition of "child" includes a fetus is one of a controversial and complex nature. One would expect heated dialogue and intense debate if the legislature intended to include fetus within the definition of "child." Yet, we are met with legislative silence.

The dissent maintains that the legislature has impliedly ratified the court of appeals' interpretation of § 48.02(2), because amendments to the Code in the months since the court of appeals' decision have left undisturbed the language at issue. However, the very cases relied upon by the dissent demonstrate the fundamental error of applying the doctrine of legislative acquiescence to the present case.

The application of the doctrine of legislative acquiescence is justified when the legislature can be "presumed to know that in absence of its changing the law, the construction put upon it by the courts will remain unchanged." *Reiter v. Dyken,* 95 Wis. 2d 461, 471, 290 N.W.2d 510 (1980) (quoting *Zimmerman v. Wisconsin Elec. Power Co.,* 38 Wis. 2d 626, 633-34, 157 N.W.2d 648 (1968)). Of course, if this court has accepted review of a court of appeals' decision construing a statute, the legislature cannot be presumed to know that the court of appeals' interpretation "will remain unchanged. . . ." Thus, the doctrine presupposes the existence of a decision which, unlike the instant court of appeals' decision, is not subject to further appellate review.

* * *

In this case, the petitioner filed a timely petition for review of the court of appeals' decision, and we granted review on January 23, 1996. The purported acts of legislative acquiescence occurred after that date. The dissent fails to explain how the legislature can be presumed to possess advance knowledge that the court of appeals' construction of § 48.02(2) would "remain unchanged" upon review by this court. . . .

We turn next to a consideration of context, examining the § 48.02(2) definition of "child" in conjunction with other relevant sections of the Code. When attempting to ascertain the meaning of statutory language, we are obligated to avoid a construction which would result in an absurdity. With this in mind, we note that certain relevant sections of the Code would be rendered absurd if "child" is understood to include a viable fetus. For example, in this case, the initial order taking the fetus into custody was issued pursuant to § 48.19(1)(c). That statute allows a child to be taken into custody by judicial order "upon a showing satisfactory to the judge that the welfare of the child demands that the child be immediately *removed from his or her present custody* [emphasis added]. It is obviously inappropriate to apply this language to a viable fetus in utero.

* * *

Section 48.20(2) requires a person taking a child into custody to make every effort to immediately release the child to its parent. This language assumes that the child is at some point removed from the parent. Again, it is axiomatic that a viable fetus in utero cannot be removed from a pregnant woman in the sense conveyed by the statute.

why Statute does not apply to fetus

By reading the definition of "child" in context with other relevant sections of Chapter 48, we find a compelling basis for concluding that the legislature intended a "child" to mean a human being born alive. . . . It is manifest that the separation envisioned by the statute cannot be achieved in the context of a pregnant woman and her fetus.[10]

The court of appeals determined, and the County asserts, that some prior decisions of this court support the proposition that a fetus is a child under the Children's Code. For example, the court of appeals analogized the present case to those in which this court has recognized a degree of fetal personhood under tort law. In support of its analogy, the court of appeals cited our holding in *Kwaterski* that "an eighth-month, viable unborn child, whose later stillbirth is caused by the wrongful act of another, is 'a person' within the meaning of [the wrongful death statute] so as to give rise to a wrongful-death action by the parents of the stillborn infant." *Kwaterski*, 34 Wis. 2d at 15, 148 N.W.2d 107.

* * *

Initially, we note that this court has historically been wary of expanding the scope of the Children's Code by reading into it language not expressly mentioned within the text of Chapter 48. While Chapter 48 is to be liberally construed, we will not discern from the statute a legislative intent that is not evident. . . . The directive is to liberally construe the statute to effectuate its purpose of providing for the care, protection, and development of children. . . . Finally, our decisions placing limited legal duties upon a third person should not be read to confer full legal status upon a fetus. Each must be examined to identify the particular rights and policies underlying the law that is being addressed.

We find the tort law analogy unpersuasive in this context. Instead, we agree with the United States Supreme Court that declaring a fetus a person for purposes of the wrongful death statute does no more than vindicate the interest of parents in the potential life that a fetus represents. *See Roe,* 410 U.S. at 162, 93 S. Ct. at 731. Indeed, we have recognized that until born, a fetus has no cause of action for fetal injury:

> Injuries suffered before birth impose a conditional liability on the tort-feasor. This liability becomes unconditional, or complete, upon the birth of the injured separated entity as a legal person. If such personality is not achieved, there would be no liability [to the fetus] because of no damage to a legal person.

Puhl, 8 Wis. 2d at 356, 99 N.W.2d 163. For these reasons, we agree with the court of appeals' dissent that our tort law jurisprudence dealing with fetal injury has limited applicability to the present case.

---

[10] The dissent asserts that interpreting "child" to not include a fetus is to work an absurd result, "by rendering the state's power to protect a child dependent upon whether the child is inside or outside of the womb." This argument employs a circular method of reasoning, which may be summarized as follows: the legislature intended the term "child" to include a viable fetus because the State must have the power to protect children. We decline to consider an argument that assumes the result.

Similarly, we reject the County's argument that the protections accorded fetuses by property law have a bearing on the Children's Code definition of "child." As the dissent below noted, "[P]roperty law does not confer the full rights of personhood upon the fetus. Instead, it creates a means of fulfilling the intentions of testators by protecting the right of a fetus to inherit property upon live birth." When there is no live birth, there is no inheritance right.

We also find unpersuasive the court of appeals' citation to *State v. Black,* 188 Wis.2d, 639, 526 N.W.2d 132 (1994). In *Black*, we held that the defendant was properly charged with feticide, "intentionally destroy[ing] the life of an unborn quick child." Wis. Stat. § 940.04(2)(a). As we noted in that case, "the words of the statute could hardly be clearer." *Black,* 188 Wis. 2d at 642, 526 N.W.2d 132. . . .

Black demonstrates the ease and clarity with which the legislature may, if it so chooses, apply a statute to the unborn. In its several amendments to the Children's Code, the legislature has had ample opportunity to state in similarly clear and unambiguous terms that a fetus is a child. Yet, the legislature has failed to take such action.

* * *

The court of appeals' reliance on *Roe, Kwaterski, Puhl,* and *Black* evidences the fundamental error in its analysis. While positing the correct question—whether the legislature intended to include a fetus within the § 48.02(2) definition of "child"—the court of appeals answered a distinctly different one—whether the legislature could, consistent with the United States and Wisconsin Constitutions, have included a fetus within the term "child." Because we conclude that the legislature did not intend to equate a fetus with a child, we do not reach the question answered by the court of appeals.

Finally, the confinement of a pregnant woman for the benefit of her fetus is a decision bristling with important social policy issues. We determine that the legislature is in a better position than the courts to gather, weigh, and reconcile the competing policy proposals addressed to this sensitive area of the law. . . .

* * *

This court in no way condones the conduct of the petitioner. Yet, we are not free to register moral disapproval by rewriting the Children's Code under the guise of statutory construction.

Our search to ascertain and carry out the legislature's intent results in the conclusion that the legislature did not intend to include fetus within the definition of "child." The legislative history sounds in silence. Although the issue of whether to include a fetus within the definition of "child" in Chapter 48 is one of great social, medical, religious, and ethical significance, there is no record of any dialogue or consideration of the issue. A reading of § 48.02(2) in context with other relevant provisions of the Children's Code, supports the conclusion that the legislature intended "child" to mean one born alive. Despite ample opportunity, the legislature has not expressly provided that a fetus is a "child" under the Code. . . . Moreover, the sensitive social policy issues raised in this case weigh strongly in favor of refraining from exercising CHIPS jurisdiction over a fetus until the legislature has spoken definitively on the matter.

holding

For the above reasons, we hold that the definition of "child" in § 48.02(2) does not include a viable fetus. Because the court of appeals erroneously held that the § 48.02(2) definition of "child" includes a fetus, we reverse the decision of that court.

The decision of the court of appeals is reversed.

N. Patrick CROOKS, Justice (dissenting); [joined by Justices STEINMATZ and WILCOX.]

I do not join the majority opinion because the majority has not interpreted Wis. Stat. § 48.02(2) (1993-94) in conformity with the express legislative purpose of the Children's Code. I also am not persuaded by the majority's attempt to distinguish the present case from past cases in which this court has indicated that the definitions of "child" and "person" include a viable fetus. Furthermore, I find it significant that although the legislature amended the Children's Code last session, it did not act to alter the court of appeals' interpretation of § 48.02(2). . . .

* * *

The initial issue before the court is whether the definition of "child" in Wis. Stat. § 48.02(2) includes a viable fetus. Section 48.02(2) defines "child" as "a person who is less than 18 years of age." § 48.02(2). Accordingly, resolution of this issue depends upon whether the legislature intended the words "child" and "person" to include a viable fetus.

As determined by the majority, reasonable minds could differ as to whether the definition of "child" in Wis. Stat. § 48.02(2) includes a viable fetus; therefore, the statute is ambiguous. Accordingly, the court must examine extrinsic matters such as the history, context, subject matter, scope, and object of the statute in order to ascertain the legislative intent. *See, e.g., Stockbridge School Dist. v. DPI,* 202 Wis. 2d 214, 220, 550 N.W.2d 96 (1996) (quoting *Jungbluth v. Hometown, Inc.,* 201 Wis. 2d 320, 327, 548 N.W.2d 519 (1996)). After considering these extrinsic matters, I conclude that the legislature intended the word "child" in § 48.02(2) to include a viable fetus for three reasons: (1) the ordinary and accepted meaning of the words "child" and "person;" (2) the express legislative purpose of ch. 48; and, (3) legislative inaction to the recent court of appeals' decision in *State ex rel. Angela M.W.*

A.

First, in construing a statute, a court must give effect to the ordinary and accepted meaning of the language. In light of medical knowledge concerning fetal development, several sources, including precedent of this court, indicate that the ordinary and accepted meaning of the words "child" and "persons" include a viable fetus.[3]

---

[3] *See In re Baby Girl K.*, 113 Wis. 2d 429, 335 N.W.2d 846 (1983) (holding that the word "child" as used in Wis. Stat. § 48.415(6)(b) includes a fetus), *appeal dismissed, Buhse v. Krueger,* 465 U.S. 10-16, 104 S. Ct. 1262, 79 L. Ed. 2d 670 (1984); *Kwaterski v. State Farm Mut. Auto. Inc. Co.,* 34 Wis.2d 14, 148 N.W.2d 107 (1967) (concluding that the word "person" includes a viable fetus for purposes of wrongful death statute); *Puhl v. Milwaukee Auto. Ins. Co.,* 8 Wis. 2d 343, 355-56 99

* * *

This court relied heavily on *Puhl* in *Kwaterski v. State Farm Mut. Auto. Ins. Co.,* 34 Wis.2d 14, 148 N.W.2d 107 (1967). The *Kwaterski* court was asked to determine whether the term "person" in Wis.Stat. § 331.03 (1963) includes a viable fetus. . . . After considering *Puhl* in great detail, the *Kwaterski* court determined: "[T]he weight of authority continues the trend noticed in *Puhl,* favoring recognition of an unborn child as a person for purposes of recovery under a wrongful-death statute." *Id.* at 19, 148 N.W.2d 107. The court therefore held that a viable fetus is a "person" within the meaning of § 331.03. *Id.* at 22, 148 N.W.2d 107.

Kwaterski has significant precedential value in the present case because the legislature has defined "child" as a "person" in Wis. Stat. § 48.02(2). *Kwaterski* therefore supports the proposition that the definition of "person," and hence "child," includes a viable fetus.

* * *

B.

Second, the legislative objectives enunciated in the Children's Code support a conclusion that "child" in Wis. Stat. § 48.02(2) includes a viable fetus. The preamble to the Children's Code expressly directs that the chapter "shall be liberally construed to effect the objectives" set forth by the legislature. Wis. Stat. § 48.01(2). One of the objectives set forth by the legislature is "[t]o provide for the care, protection, and wholesome mental and physical development of children. . . ." § 48.01(1)(b). Section 48.01(2) also mandates that "[t]he best interests of the child shall always be of paramount consideration."

This court has stated that "a 'cardinal rule in interpreting statutes' is to favor a construction which will fulfill the purpose of the statute over a construction which defeats the manifest object of the act." *In re Estate of Halsted,* 116 Wis. 2d 23, 29, 341 N.W.2d 389 (1983). We likewise have indicated that "the intent of a section of a statute must be derived from the act as a whole." *Standard Theatres, Inc. v. State, Dept. of Transp., Div. Of Highways,* 118 Wis. 2d 740, 750, 349 N.W.2d 661 (1984).

Accordingly, the canons of statutory construction require the court to interpret the word "child" in Wis. Stat. § 48.02(2) consistently with the purpose of the Children's Code, which is clearly to protect children at risk from harm. There can be no dispute that a mother's ingestion of cocaine after her fetus becomes viable has a substantial impact on the physical development of her child in utero and ultimately after birth. Certainly, a mother's ingestion of cocaine is not in the best interests of her child, born or unborn. . . . Thus, interpreting the word "child" to include a viable fetus fulfills the express legislative

---

N.W.2d 163 (1959) (referring to a viable fetus as a "child"), *overruled on other grounds by In re Estate of Stromsted,* 99 Wis. 2d 136, 299 N.W.2d 226 (1980); *Whitner v. State,* 328 S.C. 1, 492 S.E.2d 777 (S.C. July 15, 1996) (in an analogous case, the court interpreted a provision of South Carolina's Children's Code that defined "child" as "person under the age of eighteen." The court held that the word "person," and therefore "child," includes a viable fetus.); *American Heritage Dictionary* 332 (3d ed 1992) (defining "child" as "[a]n unborn infant; a fetus"); *Black's Law Dictionary* 239 (6th ed. 1990) (defining "child" as "unborn or recently born human being").

objectives of the Children's Code, by allowing the state to intervene to protect and care for the physical development of an unborn child. Conversely, the majority's interpretation of "child" fails to liberally construe the Children's Code in order to carry out its intentions, fails to consider adequately the best interests of the child, and, in fact, defeats the manifest objectives of Ch. 48.[13]

C.

Third, legislative inaction after the decision by the court of appeals . . . indicates that the court correctly interpreted Wis. Stat. § 48.02(2). "Legislative inaction following judicial construction of a statute, while not conclusive, evinces legislative approval of the interpretation." *State v. Johnson,* 207 Wis. 2d 240, 247, 558 N.W.2d 375 (1997). . . .

In the current case, the court of appeals' holding . . . that the definition of "child" under Wis. Stat. § 48.02(2) includes a viable fetus was released on October 6, 1995. This was a published decision of the court of appeals, which therefore had "statewide precedential effect." Wis. Stat. § 752.41(2); *Wolf v. F & M Banks,* 193 Wis.2d 439, 455-56, 534 N.W.2d 877 (Ct. App.). After October 6, 1995, the legislature revised the definition of "child," and made substantial changes to the Children's Code in general. . . . However, the legislature did not alter the court of appeals' interpretation of "child" in either of these amendments. This legislative inaction following the court of appeals' decision demonstrates legislative approval of the court's interpretation of § 48.02(2).

Despite this overwhelming support to the contrary, the majority has reached the conclusion that the legislature did not intend to include viable fetus within the definition of "child". The majority states: "Despite ample opportunity, the legislature has not expressly provided that a fetus is a 'child' under the Code. We decline the . . . invitation to 'take on this burden' to fill the legislative void." However, interpreting the term "child" in Wis. Stat. § 48.02(2) to include a viable fetus does not constitute a "rewriting [of] the Children's Code under the guise of statutory construction," as the majority suggests. Instead, interpreting the word "child" to include a viable fetus fulfills the express purpose of the legislature in ch. 48, and is in conformity with precedent of this court. It simply is not within the spirit of the children's Code or in accordance with past case law to exclude a viable fetus, capable of life outside the womb, from the same protection afforded a born child under the Children's Code.

* * *

For these reasons, I respectfully dissent.

---

[13] The majority claims: "The logical extension of the dissent's argument regarding liberal construction would expand the definition of 'child' to the moment after conception." I stress that this case deals only with the issue of whether the words "child" and "person" include a viable fetus. In addition, I emphasize that the United States Supreme Court and this court have drawn the line a viability. *See Planned Parenthood v. Casey*, 505 U.S. 833, 112 S. Ct. 2791, 120 L. Ed. 2d 674 (1992); *Roe v. Wade,* 410 U.S. 113, 93 S. Ct. 705, 35 L. Ed. 2d 147 (1973); *Kwaterski v. State Farm Mut. Auto. Ins. Co.*, 34 Wis. 2d 14, 148 N.W.2d 107 (1967).

Notes

1. Most recent criminal prosecutions of mothers ingesting drugs or alcohol during pregnancy have failed because courts are reluctant to label the fetus a "child" unless the legislature mandates such an interpretation. *See generally* Doretta Massardo McGinnis, *Prosecution of Mother's Drug-Exposed Babies: Constitutional and Criminal Theory, in* CHILD, PARENT, AND STATE 84 (1994). Many courts hold that they do not have jurisdiction over a fetus. *See, e.g., Cox v. Court of Common Pleas of Franklin County*, 537 N.E.2d 721 (Ohio Ct. App. 1988); *In re Steven S.*, 178 Cal. Rptr. 525 (Ct. App. 1981); *Taft v. Taft*, 446 N.E.2d 395 (Mass. 1983). *But see Jefferson v. Griffin Spaulding County Hospital Authority*, 274 S.E.2d 457 (Ga. 1981).

2. Scientists are currently seeking to determine the full range of effect on a fetus of being exposed to drugs or alcohol. Possible side effects of an expectant mother exposing a fetus to drugs or alcohol include the following: drug or alcohol addiction at birth, a premature birth, a low birth rate, slower mental development at puberty, or behavioral disturbances as the child grows. *See generally* Fried & Watkinson, *36- and 48-Month Neurobehavioral Follow-Up of Children Prenatally Exposed to Marijuana, Cigarettes, and Alcohol,* 11 J. DEV. & BEHAV. PEDIATRICS 49 (1990).

3. In *Kia P. v. McIntyre*, 235 F.3d 749 (2d Cir. 2000), the court held that a hospital did not violate a mother and her baby's rights under the United States Constitution when the hospital detained the baby after an initial drug test, the results of which were later determined to be in error, revealed the presence of methadone in the baby's urine. In *Kia P.*, the hospital performed a drug test on the mother when the mother informed the hospital of her past cocaine use, history of tuberculosis, and HIV-positive condition. When the initial drug test revealed the presence of methadone in the baby, the hospital detained the baby. A later drug test, however, revealed that the initial test results were in error. Upon clearing the child for discharge, the hospital then detained the baby for two more days until the child welfare authorities approved the hospital's release of the baby to the mother. The *Kia P.* court affirmed the trial court's holding that the hospital did not violate the due process and Fourth Amendment rights of the mother and the baby by detaining the baby an additional two days. The court concluded that the hospital's decision to detain the child while it conferred with the child welfare authorities was reasonable and furthered the state's compelling interest in protecting children from abuse. The *Kia P.* court also determined that the hospital's seizure of the baby was reasonable under the Fourth Amendment because the hospital detained the baby with the intent to give the child welfare authorities additional time to decide what further action needed to be taken.

Questions

1. In some states that prohibit criminal prosecutions of pregnant women for drug and alcohol fetal abuse, prosecutors have attempted to civilly confine in treatment centers pregnant women who are drug or alcohol addicts. *See, e.g.,* S.D.

CODIFIED LAWS § 34-20A-63(3) (Lexis Supp. 2001); *People v. Pointer*, 199 Cal. Rptr. 357 (Ct. App. 1984). What constitutional challenges to such involuntary confinement should a pregnant mother raise? How might this confinement affect the mother's right to an abortion?

2. In an attempt to criminally prosecute a pregnant woman for drug or alcohol fetal abuse, some prosecutors have filed criminal charges against mothers immediately after the mother gives birth, claiming that a mother gives drugs or alcohol to a "child" during the short time period when the baby is outside the other's body but is still attached by the umbilical cord. *See, e.g., Johnson v. State*, 602 So. 2d 1288, 1290 (Fla. 1992). Should courts agree with this view and rule that mothers can be criminally prosecuted for giving illegal substances to a child through the umbilical cord after the child is out of the mother's body? Should the courts take into consideration whether or not the baby's urine contains illegal substances given to it by the mother? What social policies should legislatures consider before enacting a law to either allow or disallow prosecution under these circumstances?

3. Neglect

General Statutes of North Carolina
§ 7B-101(15) (Lexis 1999)

§ 7B-101. Definitions

(15) Neglected juvenile.—A juvenile who does not receive proper care, supervision, or discipline from the juvenile's parent, guardian, custodian, or caretaker; or who has been abandoned; or who is not provided necessary medical care; or who is not provided necessary remedial care; or who lives in an environment injurious to the juvenile's welfare; or who has been placed for care or adoption in violation of law. In determining whether a juvenile is a neglected juvenile, it is relevant whether that juvenile lives in a home where another juvenile has died as a result of suspected abuse or neglect or lives in a home where another juvenile has been subjected to abuse or neglect by an adult who regularly lives in the home.

a. Nutritional Neglect

In re Mendez
986 P.2d 670 (Or. Ct. App. 1999)

The state appeals the trial court's dismissal of its petition to terminate the parental rights of mother and father to three of their minor children. . . . We conclude that the state established a prima facie case and . . . reverse and remand for further proceedings.

In December, 1997, the State Office of Services for Children and Families (SCF) filed petitions to terminate the parental rights of mother and father to their two-year-old triplets. SCF alleged . . . [t]hat the parents were unfit to parent . . . due . . . to "[p]hysical and emotional neglect of the children," and "[l]ack of effort to adjust the . . . circumstances, conduct or conditions to make return of the children . . . possible, or failure to effect a lasting adjustment after reasonable efforts by available social agencies . . . that it appears reasonable that no lasting adjustment can be effected."

Mother and father have seven children. The children subject to these proceedings are the three youngest children of the mother. . . . The children at issue here, the triplets, were born in June, 1995.

Concern for the well-being of the triplets began in March 1996, when their pediatrician, Dr. Dunbrasky, noted a marked decline in the triplets' growth. Dunbrasky . . . noticed that each of the triplets' weight was below what was to be expected, based on their own prior performance. . . . Dunbrasky could identify no medical reason for the decline in growth at nine months but learned that the mother and father no longer participated in the Women, Infant, and Children (WIC) program that provides free nutritional information, as well as food vouchers. Dunbrasky encouraged the parents to return to the WIC program. She began to monitor carefully the children's weight, height, and head circumference.

Dunbrasky was concerned enough in March to refer county health nurses to mother and father's home to take monthly weights of the triplets. By June, 1996, the growth rate of all three children had declined further. Most disconcerting was the fact that the growth rate of each triplet's head circumference had also declined. Dunbrasky explained that the lack of expected increase in head circumference . . . demonstrated that the triplets were not receiving adequate nutrition to grow. Further medical testimony explained that the human body places a priority on brain growth. . . . [It] is only when nutritional deficiency is severe that changes in brain growth and head circumference become evident.

In June, 1996, Dunbrasky formally diagnosed the triplets with nonorganic "failure to thrive," a generic term meaning that a child is failing to grow at a normal pace. Causes may be either organic or nonorganic. Organic causes are chronic diseases or other problems prohibiting the absorption of food and calories. The nonorganic cause is lack of adequate nutrition. Consistent with Dunbrasky's diagnosis, evidence showed that when the triplets were placed in an environment where they received adequate nutrition, their bodies were able to absorb that nutrition, and they were able to gain weight. Dunbransky notified SCF, who became involved in August 1996. SCF provided a wealth of services, including in-home instruction on nutrition and feeding techniques. . . .

At the termination hearing, the medical experts agreed that the triplets failed to grow at a healthy rate and that their decreased rate of growth in head circumference indicated developmental failure that put them at risk for permanent developmental delay. . . . In October, 1997, . . . a specialist in children of small stature and in the failure to thrive medical condition, confirmed Dunbrasky's diagnosis of nonorganic failure to thrive. . . . Dunbrasky concurred and stated that if the triplets' failure to thrive continued, the children might not be able to live independently as adults. . . .

Dunbrasky . . . primarily measured the triplets' decline in growth against a standardized growth curve chart. . . . The evidence showed that when the triplets were born, they were below all the percentages in the growth chart. . . .

After over a year of intensive support from social agencies, Dunbrasky explained that the children have thrived only "intermittently" with that support in the home. . . . While the record indicates that the triplets were often ill, it also indicates that mother and father had difficulty providing adequate nutrition to the triplets. Testimony revealed that the parents did not follow instructions on nutrition and feeding or follow instructions to place the triplets on a regular feeding schedule and to offer them a variety of food. . . . Social service workers were concerned about how the triplets could be surviving on the little food they observed the triplets eat.

Dr. Starr, a psychologist, . . . diagnosed mother with a personality disorder exhibiting passive aggressive, narcissistic, and antisocial features. Her intelligence testing indicated borderline intellectual functioning. . . . Starr explained that mother was capable of understanding information given her concerning homemaking or parenting skills but would have difficulty using that information. . . . Starr stated that the father was borderline intellectual functioning and diagnosed him with a personality disorder exhibiting passive aggressive and paranoid features. Starr explained that father would have difficulty understanding cognitive-based therapy or training and that he would be resistant to assistance because his profile suggested that he may not recognize his problems as a parent. . . . Starr . . . believed that neither were able to parent five young children.

The trial court dismissed the case at the close of the state's evidence, finding that the state had not presented sufficient evidence to establish a prima facie case for termination of mother and father's parental rights. . . . [T]he trial court did not find the evidence of the triplets' weight, height, and head circumference development as indicating anything other than that they were small in stature like their parents. The trial court explained that the state could not "tie" all the pieces of developmental evidence together to establish grounds for termination.

On appeal, the state argues that the growth curve chart was competent evidence to measure the triplets' normal rate of growth and that the curve indicated that the triplets were failing to maintain healthy development. . . . [T]he state argues that the testimony . . . established that the faltering development was due to inadequate nutrition and that developmental delay would be permanent if the triplets continued depressed growth. Mother and father . . . argue that the state failed to prove "failure to thrive" due to nonorganic causes. They argue that the triplets were often ill and that the state . . . did not rule out organic causes for failure to thrive. Father further argues that, even if the evidence was sufficient to establish a prima facie case for termination of mother's rights, it was not sufficient to establish a prima facie case for termination of father's rights arguing that SCF has not met its statutory duty to provide reasonable efforts to father.

We examine whether the state established a prima facie case that mother and father were presently unfit to parent the triplets and that the present inability was unlikely to change. . . . Once that is established, we examine whether the state has similarly established a prima facie case that the children's best interests will be served by terminating mother and father's rights. . . .

We have previously recognized the diagnosis of "failure to thrive" as evidence supporting parental termination. . . . The state provided sufficient evidence to establish a prima facie case for termination. The evidence established that the growth curve was applicable as a measure for the triplets' rate of growth and that the triplets did not follow a normal rate of growth and development. The medical experts attributed that condition to lack of nutrition and their opinions were corroborated circumstantially when the children gained weight in environments where they received adequate nutrition. It was further corroborated by testimony illustrating the parents' difficulty with feeding the triplets. While the triplets were often ill, none of the medical experts identified that as a cause of depressed development. . . . The experts also took into account the small stature of the parents and the triplets when making their diagnoses. Thus, with a sound benchmark for the rate of development, the genetic factors taken into account, the apparent severity of the failure to develop, and the circumstantial evidence in the record corroborating the diagnosis, the state presented sufficient evidence to show that the triplets had failed to thrive due to inadequate nutrition.

Further, the state presented sufficient evidence to show that the condition was due to the parent's inability to provide for the basic physical needs of the triplets despite the reasonable efforts of social services agencies to assist parents. Those services were equally available and intended to reach both parents. Father's choice not to participate does not change our conclusion that the social agencies made reasonable efforts to assist him. . . . Thus, the state's evidence also presented a prima facie case that both parents have failed to make a lasting adjustment sufficient to warrant return of the triplets after reasonable efforts by the agencies in question. The state has likewise presented sufficient evidence to establish a prima facie case that both mother and father were unlikely to be able to parent in the foreseeable future. . . . Last, given the severity of the development delays and the likelihood that they will be permanent unless corrected, the state has established a prima facie case that termination of mother and father's parental rights will be in each of the triplets' best interests.

We reverse the trial court's judgement of dismissal and remand for continuation of the termination proceedings.

Notes

1. "Failure to thrive" (F.T.T.) is the "impaired growth and development associated with malnutrition" which "has been found to have both biological and psychosocial causes." Jeffery M. Daly & Sandra L. Fritsch, *Case Study: Maternal Residual Attention Deficit Disorder Associated With Failure to Thrive In a Two-Month Old Infant*, 34 J. AM. ACAD. CHILD & ADOLESCENT PSYCHIATRY 55 (1995). Symptoms of failure to thrive include a loss of weight, poor muscle tone, and lack of growth. As the *Mendez* court suggests, if a child suffering from failure to thrive is not cared for properly over an extended period of time, the symptoms may become permanent. To determine if a child is suffering from F.T.T., the child is usually placed in another home or in a hospital to measure the difference between the growth experienced in the out-of-home placement versus the child's growth while in the care of the parent, custodian or guardian. *See generally* Rose & Meezan, *Defining Child Neglect: Evolution, Influences, and Issues*, 67 SOC. SERV. REV. 279 (1993).

2. The Special Supplemental Nutrition Program for Women, Infants, and Children (WIC program), 42 U.S.C. § 1786, is a federally funded program providing food, formula, and the like to qualifying women, infants, and children. *In re Mendez*, 986 P.2d at 673 n.5. The program also provides information and demonstrations on how to properly provide nutrition for a growing baby. The following are pertinent excerpts of the statute:

42 U.S.C.A.

§ 1786 (West 1994)

1786. Special supplemental nutrition program for women, infants, and children

(a) Congressional findings and declaration of purpose.

Congress finds that substantial numbers of pregnant, postpartum, and breastfeeding women, infants, and young children from families with inadequate income are at a special risk with respect to their physical and mental health by reason of inadequate nutrition. . . . It is . . . the purpose of the program . . . to provide . . . supplemental foods and nutritional education through any eligible local agency. . . . The program shall serve as an adjunct to good health care, during critical times of growth and development . . . and [to] improve the health status of these persons.

(b) Definitions

As used in this section—

* * *

(2) "Children" means persons who have had their first birthday but have not yet attained their fifth birthday.

* * *

(7) "Nutrition education" means individual or group sessions and the provision of materials designed to improve health status . . . and emphasize relationships between nutrition and health . . . .

* * *

(d) Eligible participants

(1) Participation in the program . . . shall be limited to pregnant, postpartum, and breastfeeding women, infants, and children from low-income families who are . . . at nutritional risk.

* * *

Questions

1. Is the state's interest greater than the parents' interest in deciding how to nourish their children? Would the state's interest, for example, be more compelling than the parents' religious beliefs to provide certain food to children?

2. The WIC program focuses on children between the ages of one and five years. Should the court also have the power to order removal of other children (over age five) from home to ensure they receive proper nutrition? Should the court have the power to remove the future children of the same family to make sure the children receive proper nutrition?

b. Housing Neglect

In re E.R.

432 N.W.2d 834 (Neb. 1988)

This is an appeal from two juvenile court orders terminating parental rights to three small children because of substantial, continuous, or repeated neglect or refusal by the parents to give the children necessary care and protection as required by Nebraska Revised Statutes § 43-292(2) (Reissue 1984).

The termination orders were entered only after extensive attempts at rehabilitation of the parents by the Department of Social Services (DSS).

We affirm the juvenile court's orders.

The children, E.R., J.R., and A.R., originally came under the jurisdiction of the juvenile court because they lacked proper parental care by reason of the fault or habits of their parents, who neglected or refused to provide proper care necessary for the children's health, morals, and well-being. . . .

E.R. . . . and J.R. . . . were first removed from their parents' home on June 2, 1986. On that date, two Child Protective Services workers responding to a complaint "found the house to be in a very filthy condition." Large quantities of dirt and garbage were found in every room. Dog feces were found on the floor in various parts of the house, along with used feminine sanitary pads dragged from the bathroom by one of the parents' three dogs. Assorted kittens and a large number of flies also occupied the home. Dirty pots and pans cluttered the kitchen, including the floor, and there was virtually no food in the home.

At a hearing on June 24, 1986 the parents admitted that their home was not suitable when E.R. and J.R. were removed. Evidence at the hearing showed that the condition of the home had substantially improved. . . . The children were returned to their parents, with DSS retaining legal custody.

Conditions in the home deteriorated, and the children were again removed, in August of 1986. A report prepared by the DSS family support provider in September of 1986 reflects that both parents exhibited poor hygiene. Both wore dirty clothing, at times for several days. The worker found the children dirty. They were wearing soiled diapers, which appeared to have not been changed for several hours. In the home, dried food was on the stove, sink, counters, table, and high chair. Liquid was found oozing from a box of rotting vegetables on the floor. The children were sitting near the vegetables.

Between August of 1986 and September of 1987, the parents received services from an independent living specialist, vocational rehabilitation services, marital counseling, and parenting classes. In addition, the parents received the services of a caseworker and family support worker as part of a rehabilitation agreement with DSS. The parents substantially complied with the terms of the agreement.

On September 17, 1987, A.R. was born. The condition of the home improved substantially, and E.R. and J.R. were returned to their parents on October 29, 1987. At this time, the caseworker offered additional services to ease the transition. This offer was refused. . . .

The caseworker again went to the home. . . . The caseworker described the condition of the house as "deplorable.". . . Soiled underwear lay over a toothbrush in the bathroom sink, and tools littered the bathroom floor.

The children's beds had food on them, and an open bottle of aspirin lay on their bedroom floor. E.R. was on the floor eating the aspirin. When the caseworker pointed to this dangerous situation, the mother's response was inaction. . . .

A court order was obtained, and all three children were removed on December 30, 1987.

Subsequently, a motion was filed requesting the termination of the parents' rights in E.R. and J.R. A supplemental petition was filed at the same time, seeking termination of parental rights in A.R. . . .

The juvenile court found that "the conditions [of the home] at the time of each removal were so substantial as to endanger the health and safety of each of the minors, as well as the health of any person resident on the premises." The parents' rights to their three children were terminated.

* * *

An order terminating parental rights must be based on clear and convincing evidence. (citation omitted) Past decisions of this court make it clear that poor housekeeping, alone, is not a sufficient basis for terminating parental rights (*In re Interest of M.W.M., supra; In re Interest of D.*, 209 Neb. 529, 308 N.W.2d 729 (1981)). However, a primary consideration in a case involving termination of parental rights is the best interests of the children (*In re Interest of M.W.M., supra*) Where, as here, "poor housekeeping" degenerates into a continuing health hazard, the best interest of the children require termination of parental rights.

. . . As stated earlier, testimony showed that when the children were removed for the second time, the house had deteriorated to prior conditions. The uncleanliness of the house was discussed with the mother. It was the caseworker's testimony that the condition of the house, along with the father's threats, was the basis for removal. . . . The unsanitary conditions of the house and the health hazard to the children by themselves justified the removal.

The testimony and exhibits presented provide clear and convincing evidence that the best interests of these children require termination of their parents' rights. The photographs of the house taken on December 29, 1987, are particularly graphic evidence of the unhealthy condition in which these children were forced to live. By that date, DSS had provided extensive training to the parents. The lessons were learned, and, from time to time, the skills were exhibited by the parents. The condition of the home . . . shows the parents' total lack of motivation to change their living patterns in order to protect the health and safety of their children.

We find that the State has proved by clear and convincing evidence that the parents have substantially, continually, or repeatedly neglected all three children and refused to provide them with necessary parental care and protection. The orders of the trial court are affirmed. . . .

Notes

1. Critics of removing children from filthy homes claim that splitting a family for this reason may be a drastic solution. Theses critics argue that other alternatives such as home based services should be preferred by the court rather than removing children from the home. The house-based services would have to be sufficiently funded and staffed. "The worker, foster grandparent, case aide, or home maker will have to be present in the home three or four times a week. They will have to help clean, help transport, help apply for benefits, and do whatever it takes to help the family rehabilitate." Ana M. Novoa, *Count the Brown Faces: Where is the "Family" in the Family Law of Child Protective Services*, 1 THE SCHOLAR: ST. MARY'S L. REV. ON MINORITY ISSUES 5, 40 (1999). For an interesting discussion supportive of action taken by the state to help families keep houses habitable, see *In re M.N.W.*, 461 N.W. 2d 478, 483 (Iowa Ct. App. 1990) (Sackett, J., dissenting). For further discussion that state-sponsored house maintenance assistance will not prevent house neglect, see *Leal v. Texas Dept. of Protective and Regulatory Services*, 25 S.W.3d 315 (Tex. App. 2000); *In Interest of S.S.*, 501 S.E.2d 618 (Ga. Ct. App. 1998); *Howard v. Howard*, 1995 WL 595369 (Neb. App. 1995); *L. v. A.S.*, 649 So. 2d 1183 (La. Ct. App. 1995); *People v. Heitzman*, 886 P.2d 1229 (Cal. 1994).

2. For further discussion of housing neglect, see *In the Interest of Tibbs*, 248 N.W.2d 330 (Neb. 1976) (children lived in dirty, disorderly, and unsanitary house despite father's good income); *Rejda v. Rejda*, 253 N.W.2d 295 (Neb. 1977) (home littered with food, beer cans, and ash trays); *In re Susan Lynn M.,* 125 Cal. Rptr. 707 (Ct. App. 1975) (mother unable to keep house clean); *In re Johnson*, 198 N.W.2d 466 (Neb. 1972) (home inadequately furnished due to parental indifference); *In Interest of Norwood*, 234 N.W.2d 601 (Neb.1975) (parents refuse to spend welfare check to clean house); *In re Hartman*, 1999 N.W.2d 26 (Neb. 1972) (house filthy, and firearms and ammunition within the reach of children); *Germaine v. State*, 718 N.E.2d 1125 (Ind. App. Ct. 1999) (house full of rotting garbage and vermin); *Matter of M.L.M.*, 682 P.2d 982 (Wyo. 1984) (house not heated); *In the Interest of A.B.*, 839 P.2d 386 (Wyo. 1992) (dog feces throughout); *State In Interest of L.A.V.*, 516 So. 2d 1315 (La. Ct. App. 1987) (no bathtub or hot water in home and roaches in refrigerator).

Questions

In *In re E.R.,* if the bottle of aspirin had not been open and on the floor for E.R. to eat, would the household conditions have endangered the children requiring their removal? If both parents suffer from physical ailments and find it difficult to clean the house, should the court remove the children even though the filthy condition is not the result of the parents' laziness? What interests should be balanced in this situation?

Problem

Judy Brown is the single mother of Melissa, age seven. Melissa is a first-grader in school. A neighbor, George Crone, called child welfare authorities and reported that Melissa was at risk from living in "the dirtiest house I've ever seen." A caseworker made a surprise visit to the Brown home and described the home in her report as follows, ". . . most cluttered house I've seen in five years as a caseworker. Closets nearly empty. All but two items of clothing in the home are piled on the floor or on the household furniture, along with soiled towels, bed sheets, etc. (photographs in the file). Otherwise, the house is reasonably clean." The caseworker determined there was probable cause that Melissa was a neglected child, removed her from home and placed Melissa in foster care. You represent Judy Brown at the detention hearing two days later. What arguments should be put forward in the mother's behalf? What is the agency's position? Should the court adjudicate Melissa a neglected child? Assume that the court dismisses the action after Judy brings to the detention hearing pictures showing the home in perfect order. What result if within thirty days the caseworker reports that the home has returned to the same cluttered condition?

c. Medical Neglect

In re E.G.

549 N.E.2d 322 (Ill. 1989)

RYAN, Justice.

* * *

In February of 1987, E.G. was diagnosed as having acute nonlymphatic leukemia, a malignant disease of the white blood cells. When E.G. and her mother, Rosie Denton, were informed that treatment of the disease would involve blood transfusions, they refused to consent to this medical procedure on the basis of their religious beliefs. As Jehovah's Witnesses, both E.G. and her mother desired to observe their religion's prohibition against the "eating" of blood. Mrs. Denton did authorize any other treatment and signed a waiver absolving the medical providers of liability for failure to administer transfusions.

As a result of Denton's and E.G.'s refusal to assent to blood transfusions, the State filed a neglect petition in juvenile court. . . .

Dr. Yachnin stated that he discussed the proposed course of treatment with E.G. He testified that E.G. was competent to understand the consequences of accepting or rejecting treatment, and he was impressed with her maturity and the sincerity of her beliefs. . . .

On April 8, 1987, further hearings were held on this matter. E.G., having received several blood transfusions, was strong enough to take the stand. She testified that the decision to refuse blood transfusions was her own and that she fully understood the nature of her disease and the consequences of her decision. She indicated that her decision was not based on any wish to die, but instead was grounded in her religious convictions. E.G. further stated that when informed that she would undergo transfusions, she asked to be sedated prior to the administration of the blood. She testified that the court's decision upset her, and said: "[I]t seems as if everything that I wanted or believed in was just being disregarded."

* * *

The trial court ruled that E.G. was medically neglected, and appointed a guardian to consent to medical treatment. . . . The court felt that the State's interest in this case was greater than the interest E.G. and her mother had in refusing to consent to treatment. . . .

* * *

The appellate court noted that E.G., at the time of trial, was only six months shy of her eighteenth birthday, and that the trial court believed E.G. to be a mature individual. Based on these facts, the appellate court declared that E.G. was partially emancipated and therefore had the right to refuse transfusions. The court, however, affirmed the finding of neglect against Denton, E.G.'s mother.

We granted the State's petition for leave to appeal. . . . This case presents several issues for our consideration. . . . Whether a minor has a right to refuse medical treatment and if so, how this right may be exercised . . . and . . . whether the trial court's finding of neglect against Denton should stand.

* * *

The paramount issue raised by this appeal is whether a minor like E.G. has a right to refuse medical treatment. . . . An adult has a common law right to refuse medical treatment, even if it is of a life-sustaining nature. . . . This court has also held that an adult may refuse life-saving blood transfusions on first amendment free exercise of religion grounds. . . . In the matter before us, E.G. was a minor, but one who was just months shy of her eighteenth birthday, and an individual that the record indicates was mature for her age. Although the age of majority in Illinois is 18, that age is not an impenetrable barrier that magically precludes a minor from possessing and exercising certain rights normally associated with adulthood. Numerous exceptions are found in this jurisdiction and others which threat minors as adults under specific circumstances.

* * *

In an analogous area of law, no "bright line" age restriction of 18 exists either. . . . To be convicted of many of the offenses in the Criminal Code, a trier of fact would have to find that a minor had a certain mental state at the time the alleged crime was committed. Implied in finding this mental state would be an acknowledgment that a minor was mature enough to have formulated this *mens rea.* Consequently, the Juvenile Court Act presupposes a "sliding scale of maturity" in which young minors can be deemed mature enough to possess certain mental states and be tried and convicted as adults. This act reflects the common law, which allowed infancy to be a defense to criminal acts. The infancy defense at common law was "based upon an unwillingness to punish those thought to be *incapable of forming criminal intent* and not of an age where the threat of punishment could serve as a deterrent." (Emphasis added.) (W. LAFAVE & A. SCOTT, CRIMINAL LAW § 46 (1972)). When a minor is mature enough to have the capacity to formulate criminal intent, both the common law and our Juvenile Court Act treat the minor as an adult.

Another area of the law where minors are treated as adults is constitutional law, including the constitutional right of abortion. The United States Supreme Court has adopted a mature minor doctrine, which allows women under the age of majority to undergo abortions without parental consent. . . . In the abortion rights context, the Court has noted: "Constitutional rights do not mature and come into being magically only when one attains the state-defined age of majority. Minors, as well as adults, are protected by the Constitution and possess constitutional rights." (*Planned Parenthood of Central Missouri v. Danforth* (1976) 428 U.S. 52, 74, 49 L. Ed. 2d 788, 808, 96 S. Ct. 2831, 2843.) Moreover, children enjoy the protection of other constitutional rights, including the right of privacy (*Carey v. Population Services International* (1977), 431 U.S. 678, 52 L.Ed. 2d 675, 97 S. Ct. 2010), freedom of expression *(Tinker v. Des Moines Independent Community School District* (1969), 393 U.S. 503, 21 L. Ed. 2d 731, 89 S. Ct. 733), freedom from unreasonable searches and seizures *(New Jersey v. T.L.O.* (1985), 469 U.S. 325, 83 L. Ed. 2d 720, 105 S.Ct. 733), and procedural due process *(In re Application of Gault* (1967), 387 U.S. 1, 18 L. Ed. 2d 527, 87 S. Ct. 1428). Nevertheless, the Supreme Court has not held that a constitutionally based right to refuse medical treatment exists, either for adults or minors. While we find the language from the cases cited above instructive, we do not feel, as the appellate court did, that an extension of the constitutional mature minor doctrine to the case at bar is "inevitable." These cases do show, however that no "bright line" age restriction of 18 is tenable in restricting the rights of mature minors, whether the rights be based on constitutional or other grounds. Accordingly, we hold that in addition to these constitutionally based rights expressly delineated by the Supreme Court, mature minors may possess and exercise rights regarding medical care that are rooted in this State's common law.

The common law right to control one's health care was also the basis for the right of an incompetent patient to refuse life-sustaining treatment through a surrogate in *In re Estate of Longeway*, 133 Ill. 2d. at 45-46. While the issue before us in this case is not exactly the same as in *Longeway*, the foundation of the common law right . . . is the same. We see no reason why this right of dominion over one's own person should not extend to mature minors. . . .

. . . Here, E.G. contends she was mature enough to have controlled her own health care. We find that she may have done so if indeed she would have been adjudged mature.

The trial judge must determine whether a minor is mature enough to make health care choices on her own. An exception to this, of course, is if the legislature has provided otherwise. . . .

First, Illinois public policy values the sanctity of life (citation omitted). When a minor's health and life are at stake, this policy becomes a critical consideration. A minor may have a long and fruitful life ahead that an immature, foolish decision could jeopardize. Consequently, when the trial judge weighs the evidence in making a determination of whether a minor is mature enough to handle a health care decision, he must find proof of this maturity by clear and convincing evidence.

Second, the State has a *parens patriae* power to protect those incompetent to protect themselves (*Longeway*, 133 Ill. 2d at 52; 27 AM JUR. 2D *Equity* § 69 (1966). . . . The State's *parens patriae* power pertaining to minors is strongest when the minor is immature and thus incompetent (lacking in capacity) to make these decisions on her own. The *parens patriae* authority fades, however, as the minor gets older and disappears upon her reaching adulthood. The State interest in protecting a mature minor in these situations will vary depending upon the nature of the medical treatment involved. Where the health care issues are potentially life threatening, the State's *parens patriae* interest is greater than if the health care matter is less consequential.

Therefore, the trial judge must weigh these two principles against the evidence he receives of a minor's maturity. If the evidence is clear and convincing that the minor is mature enough to appreciate the consequences of her actions, and that the minor is mature enough to exercise the judgment of an adult, then the mature minor doctrine affords her the common law right to consent to or refuse medical treatment. . . . This common law right is not absolute. The right must be balanced against four State interests: (1) the preservation of life; (2) protecting the interests of third parties; (3) prevention of suicide; and (4) maintaining the ethical integrity of the medical profession (citation omitted). Of these four concerns, protecting the interests of third parties is clearly the most significant here. The principal third parties in these cases would be parents, guardians, adult siblings, and other relatives. If a parent or guardian opposes an unemancipated mature minor's refusal to consent to treatment for a life-threatening health problem, this opposition would weigh heavily against the minor's right to refuse. In this case, for example, had E.G. refused the transfusions *against* her mother, then the court would have given serious consideration to her mother's desire. . . .

Because we find that a mature minor may exercise a common law right to consent to or refuse medical are, we decline to address the constitutional issue.

. . .

The final issue we must address is whether the finding of neglect entered against Rosie Denton, E.G.'s mother, should stand. If the trial judge had ruled that E.G. was a mature minor, then no finding of neglect would be proper.

Although the trial judge was impressed with E.G.'s maturity and sincerity, the judge did not explicitly hold that E.G. was a mature minor. . . . Since the trial judge did not have any clear guidance on the mature minor doctrine, we believe that the finding of neglect should not stand. Accordingly, we affirm the appellate court in part and reverse in part, and remand this case to the circuit court of Cook County for the sole purpose of expunging the finding of neglect against Denton. . . . (dissent omitted)

Notes

1. Several states have laws that provide spiritual treatment exemptions to certain medical procedures. The following Delaware spiritual treatment exemption law is an example:

> . . . No child who in good faith is under treatment solely by spiritual means through prayer in accordance with the tenets and practices of a recognized church or religious denomination by a duly accredited practitioner thereof shall for that reason alone be considered a neglected child for purposes of this chapter.

DEL. CODE ANN. tit. 10, § 901(11) (Michie 1999). In *State v. Norman*, 808 P.2d 1159 (Wash. Ct. App. 1991), the court held that without a spiritual treatment exemption clause, parents can't use freedom of religion as an excuse for refusing treatment. For further discussion, see Ann MacLean Massie, *The Religion Clauses and Parental Health Care Decision-Making for Children: Suggestions for a New Approach*, 21 HASTINGS CONST. L.Q. 724 (1994); Eric W. Treene, Note, *Prayer-Treatment Exemptions to Child Abuse and Neglect Statutes, Manslaughter Prosecutions and Due Process of Law*, 30 HARV. J. ON LEGIS. 135 (1993).

2. For additional discussion of religion and medical neglect, see Ann MacLean Massie, *The Religion Clauses and Parental Health Care Decision Making for Children: Suggestions for a New Approach,* 21 HASTINGS CONST. L.Q. 724 (1994); James G. Dwyer, *Parents' Religion and Children's Welfare: Debunking the Doctrine of Parents' Rights,* 82 CAL. L. REV. 1371, 1447 (1995); Timothy J. Aspinwall, *Religious Exemptions to Childhood Immunization Statutes: Reaching For a More Optimal Balance Between Religious Freedom and Public Health,* 29 LOY. U. CHI. L.J. 11 (1997); Lauren A. Greenberg, Comment, *In God We Trust: Faith Healing Subject to Liability,* 14 J. CONTEMP. HEALTH L. & POL'Y 451 (1998).

3. For a discussion of the child's input in health care decision-making, see Cynthia Price Cohen, *The Developing Jurisprudence of the Rights of the Child,* 6 ST. THOMAS L. REV. 1 (1993); Wallace J. Mlyniec, *A Judge's Ethical Dilemma: Assessing a Child's Capacity to Choose,* 64 FORDHAM L. REV. 1873 (1996); Elizabeth S. Scott et al., *Evaluating Adolescent Decision Making In Legal Contexts*, 19 LAW & HUM. BEHAV. 221 (1995).

4. Some treatments such as chemotherapy may involve several years of outpatient treatment. If the parents are unwilling to administer the treatment at their home the treatment will not be successful. In such a case, the court may have to remove the child from the parents and either hospitalize the child or place him or her in a foster home until the treatment is complete. Separation of the child from the parent(s) may have harmful psychological consequences for both the parents and the child. *See* Angela R. Holder, *Circumstances Warranting Court-Ordered Medical Treatment of Minors*, 24 AM. JUR. 2D *Proof of Facts* § 169 (1980). As you review the law and literature on medical neglect, consider the consequences of the juvenile court's decision and how the parties involved may be affected.

Questions

1. How serious should the threat of the child's death be before the state's interest in seeking medical treatment for the child is greater than the parents' interest in the child not receiving the treatment?

2. Is it medical neglect when a parent for religious reasons refuses a child's blood transfusion under life-threatening circumstances? *See In re McCauley*, 565 N.E.2d 411 (Mass. 1991); *Hoener v. Bertinato*, 171 A.2d 140 (N.J. Super. Ct. App. Div. 1961); *In re Cabrera,* 552 A.2d 1114 (Pa. Super. Ct. 1989). What if a parent refuses to consent to a treatment that has a 40% chance of curing the ailing child? *See Mitchell v. Davis,* 205 S.W.2d 812 (Tex. Civ. App. 1947); *but see In re Frank*, 248 P.2d 553 (Wash. 1952). What if a parent refuses to consent to a medical procedure that is not necessary to save the child's life or prevent permanent disfigurement but is highly desirable? *See In re Karwath*, 199 N.W.2d 147 (Iowa 1977). Is a mother neglecting a child if she refuses to consent to a medical procedure that will cause minimum disfigurement of her child's face and benefit the child's psychological well-being? *See In re Sampson*, 317 N.Y.S.2d 641 (Fam. Ct. 1970); *but see In re Green*, 292 A.2d 387 (Pa. 1972). Is a parent neglecting a child if the parent refuses for religious reasons to vaccinate the child for diseases as required by the local school district? *See Berg v. Glen Cove City School District,* 853 F. Supp. 651 (E.D.N.Y. 1994).

3. Most doctors treat leukemia with chemotherapy rather than laetrile therapy, because laetrile therapy doesn't have a proven success record in treating leukemia. If a licensed doctor recommends to a parent that a child with leukemia should be treated with chemotherapy but the parent chooses laetrile therapy instead, should a juvenile court find the parent has medically neglected the child? Does it matter if the parent chooses a treatment endorsed by the parent's religion and not by a licensed professional? *See generally In re Custody of Minor*, 393 N.E.2d 836 (Mass. 1979).

4. As mentioned in Note 1, *supra*, several states have enacted laws containing spiritual treatment exemptions. What constitutional challenges to the exemption might the state raise? What response by the parents?

d. Educational Neglect

In re B.A.B.

572 N.W.2d 776 (Minn. Ct. App. 1998)

LANSING, Judge.

A parent challenges the district court's determination that her child is in need of protective services (CHIPS) as lacking necessary education under Minn. Stat. § 260.015, subd. 2a(3) (1996) . . . when the child's absences do not meet the statutory definition of habitual truancy. We affirm.

* * *

The evidence at the hearing demonstrated B.A.B. began the 1996-97 school year as a first-grade student, but was returned to kindergarten in November 1996 because of poor academic performance. She continues to struggle academically and receives special services in reading and math. By mid-September 1996 B.A.B. already had several absences. The family services coordinator made multiple visits to B.A.B.'s home to discuss school attendance. Various explanations were provided for B.A.B.'s absences, including illness and oversleeping. The meetings with B.A.B.'s parent did not result in any improvement in B.A.B.'s attendance. The coordinator testified that on at least five occasions during the current school year, she had personally gone to B.A.B.'s home to pick her up when B.A.B. did not arrive at school. A parenting aide who works with the family through a county human services program also stated that she had often given B.A.B. a ride to school because she had missed the bus. . . .

* * *

B.A.B.'s parent testified that health problems, including earaches, asthma, and head lice, were the primary reason for B.A.B.'s absences from school. On some days B.A.B.'s parent contacted the school to explain why B.A.B. was absent, but on other days the family just overslept.

* * *

The district court adjudicated B.A.B. to be in need of protection or services on the ground that B.A.B. is without necessary education because her parent is unable or unwilling to provide that care. . . . The court directed B.A.B.'s parent to ensure that B.A.B. attends school, specifying that the only valid excuse for missing school would be illness, verified by a physician's statement. The order also provided that absent an emergency, B.A.B.'s doctor appointments must be made after school hours.

Does clear and convincing evidence support the district court's determination that B.A.B. is in need of protection or services because she is without necessary education due to appellant's neglect?

* * *

In juvenile protection proceedings, this court determines whether the record contains substantial evidence to support the district court's decision, taking into account that the burden of proof in the district court is "clear and convincing" evidence (citation omitted). . . .

The CHIPS petition alleged both educational neglect under Minn. Stat. § 260.015, subd. 2a(3) and that B.A.B. is an "habitual truant" under . . . the same statute. The district court determined that there was educational neglect . . . but did not address the allegation that B.A.B. is an habitual truant.

A child is in need of protection or services when the child is without necessary food, clothing, shelter, education, or other required care for the child's physical or mental health or morals because the child's parent, guardian or custodian is unable or unwilling to provide that care.

* * *

An "habitual truant". . . is a child under the age of 16 years who is absent from attendance at school without lawful excuse for seven school days if the child is in elementary school or for one or more class periods of seven school days if the child is in middle school, junior high school, or high school.

. . . B.A.B.'s parent contends that the record does not show more than seven unexcused absences which is necessary to sustain a finding of habitual truancy, and therefore the evidence is insufficient to support a finding of educational neglect. We disagree.

Statutes "in pari materia" are those "relating to the same person or thing or having a common purpose." *Apple Valley Red-E-Mix, Inc. v. State*, 352 N.W.2d 402, 404 (Minn. 1984) (citing *Black's Law Dictionary* (Rev. 5th ed. 1979)). Statutes in pari materia should be construed in light of one another. *Id*. But the educational neglect and habitual truancy provisions are not in pari materia because the statutes address different child protection issues. . . . Because habitual truancy focuses on the behavior of the child, whereas educational neglect focuses on the behavior of the parent, the threshold requirement for a finding of habitual truancy that an elementary school child be absent from school for seven school days without lawful excuse does not apply to an educational neglect determination.

* * *

Our review of the record convinces us that some of B.A.B.'s absences were due to illness and that B.A.B.'s parent has not demonstrated an indifferent attitude towards B.A.B.'s welfare. But the record amply supports the district court's findings with respect to B.A.B.'s unexcused absences and the finding that on other occasions the family services coordinator and county parenting aide assumed the responsibility of insuring B.A.B.'s attendance at school. We note also the evidence that regular school attendance is particularly critical for B.A.B. because of her academic problems. Under these circumstances, the parent's persistent failure to ensure B.A.B.'s regular attendance at school warranted the CHIPS adjudication. . . .

Notes

1. Compulsory school attendance laws sometimes clash directly with a family's or community's religious beliefs. In the landmark case of *Wisconsin v. Yoder*, 406 U.S. 205 (1972), two Amish parents took their children out of the public schools after they completed the eighth grade. The children then were kept at home to work and learn a craft or trade. The Court held that where state enforcement of compulsory school attendance law would endanger or possibly destroy the free exercise of religion, the parents' exercise of religious freedom circumvented the state's compulsory attendance law. According to the majority:

> A way of life, however virtuous and admirable, may not be interposed as a barrier to reasonable state regulation of education if it is based on purely secular considerations; to have the protection of the Religion Clauses, the claims must be rooted in religious belief. Although a determination of what is "religious" belief or practice entitled to constitutional protection may present a most delicate question, the very concept of ordered liberty precludes allowing every person to make his own standards on matters of conduct in which society as a whole has important interests.

406 U.S. at 215.

Other parents who have violated compulsory school attendance laws have not fared well. *See Hill v. State,* 410 So. 2d 431 (Ala. Crim. App. 1981) (parents were convicted for violation of compulsory school attendance laws where the statutes did not violate the free exercise of religion). *See also Madyun v. Franzen,* 704 F.2d 954 (7th Cir. 1983); *Jeffs v. Stubbs,* 970 P.2d 1234 (Utah 1998); *Francis v. Keane,* 888 F. Supp. 568 (S.D.N.Y. 1995). *See generally* C.S. Patrinelis, Annotation, *Religious Beliefs of Parents as Defense to Prosecution For Failure to Comply With Compulsory Education Laws*, 3 A.L.R.2D 1401 (1949).

2. Courts have created other exceptions to compulsory education laws. *See In re Richards,* 2 N.Y.S.2d 608 (Fam. Ct. 1938) (child does not have to attend school when the path to school is dangerous); *In re Skipwith,* 180 N.Y.S.2d 852 (Fam. Ct. 1958) (children do not have to attend school if the school is inferior because of racial discrimination).

3. Home schooling raises special issues, as illustrated by the following statute:

W. Va. Code
§ 18-8-1 (Lexis Supp. 2000)

> § 18-8-1. Commencement and termination of compulsory school attendance; exemptions.
>
> * * *
>
> Exemption B, Instruction in home or other approved place.—(a) Such instruction shall be in the home of such child or children or at some other place approved by the county board of education and for a time equal to the school term of the county. . . . The instruction in such cases shall be conducted by a person or persons who, in the judg-

ment of the county superintendent and county board of education, are qualified to give instruction in subject required to be taught in the free elementary schools of the state. It shall be the duty of the person or persons providing the instruction, upon request of the county superintendent, to furnish to the county board of education such information and records as may be required from time to time with respect to attendance, instruction and progress of pupils enrolled between the entrance age and sixteen years receiving such instruction. . . .

* * *

For further discussion about in-home schooling and educational neglect, see *Mazanec v. North Judson-San Pierre School Corp.,* 614 F. Supp. 1152 (N.D. Ind. 1985), *judgment aff'd*, 798 F.2d 230 (7th Cir. 1986); *State v. Schmidt*, 505 N.E.2d 627 (Ohio 1987); *State v. Riddle,* 285 S.E.2d 359 (W. Va. 1981).

Questions

1. Is a child being educationally neglected if she is an intelligent child, but is falling asleep at school on a regular basis and failing most of her classes? If a parent does not allow a child to go to school one day a week in observance of a religious day, is the child being neglected? *See In re Currence,* 248 N.Y.S.2d 251 (Fam. Ct. 1963). If parents have to move frequently for work purposes, should the parents be charged with educational neglect if their children of average intelligence do very poorly in school? *See generally* Len Biernat & Dr. Christine Jax, *Limiting Mobility And Improving Student Achievement*, 23 HAMLINE L. REV. 1 (1999).

2. If a father because of religious reasons refuses to allow his daughter to receive the vaccinations for attendance at a public school, where she has excelled in sports, thus preventing her from attending the school, should the father be charged with educational neglect? What is meant by education in this situation?

3. Is it educational neglect for a single mother with five children to alternate keeping her two oldest children out of school to babysit for the three pre-school children while the mother works part-time to support her family? How should courts handle this common situation?

e. Lack of Supervision

In re Zeiser

728 N.E.2d 10 (Ohio Ct. App. 1999)

CHRISTLEY, Judge.

In these consolidated cases, a visiting judge in the Lake County Court of Common Pleas, Juvenile Division, found that appellant, Corrine Walsh, was guilty of neglect of her two sons, Douglas, age eight, and Keith Zeiser, age six. Appellant has appealed separate judgments as to each boy asserting one assignment of error: "The trial court's finding that the children in controversy were neglected children was not supported by sufficient evidence." We find that there was sufficient evidence.

* * *

We do not quarrel with the idea that all parents have a fundamental right to control the raising of their children. *Zivich v. Mentor Soccer Club, Inc.* (Apr. 21, 1997), Lake App. No. 95-L-183, unreported, at 3, 1997 WL 203646 (Ford, P.J., concurring in judgment only). While the instant matter was not a situation where the state sought to remove the children, the rights of a parent to be free from unnecessary state interference are no less important. To ensure that the state does not lightly interfere with this right, it is required that a charge of neglect must be proven by clear and convincing evidence. R.C. 2151.35(A).

* * *

As will be seen, some of the evidence presented created a credibility issue that the juvenile court had to resolve. The county's case focused on the testimony of a social worker who testified that on March 28, 1997, she paid appellant an unannounced visit in response to a confidential complaint about the lack of supervision for the children. The subsequent testimony of all witnesses regarding these unsupervised incidents, which were the basis of the charges, can be grouped into three categories.

First, the social worker testified that appellant admitted to her on this first visit that both boys were "latchkey" kids, that they were home alone every day for about two hours, from the time they got off the school bus at 3:15 p.m. to the time she came home from work at 5:15 p.m. to 5:30 p.m. The older boy, Douglas, who was eight at the times specified in the neglect complaint, was left in charge of the younger boy, Keith, who was six.

Second, appellant allegedly admitted to the social worker that six-year-old Keith was left by himself on Wednesdays and Fridays from 7:00 a.m. when appellant went to work, until 3:15 p.m., when Douglas came home from school. Wednesday and Friday were the two full days when Keith did not have kindergarten. The social worker emphatically claimed that appellant admitted to her that Keith was left this way essentially every week since the beginning of the school year on September 1, 1996 until the March visit.

* * *

There was testimony by the social worker that the Lake County Department of Human Services has enacted an internal policy of "supervision guidelines," according to which a child under the age of nine years should never be left home alone, regardless of the individual child's maturity level. In defense of the policy the social worker argued that one can imagine a whole host of dangers that may befall an unattended youngster, such as a fire, strangers coming to the door and ingesting toxic or poisonous chemical or medicines.

The social worker and appellant both testified that during the March visit the social worker discussed two possible options for care: latchkey services and protective care paid for by Children's Services. The social worker said she would investigate the availability of these two possibilities and get back to appellant.

* * *

On April 4 and April 16, the social worker contacted appellant by phone to inform her of her eligibility, but appellant responded that she had no need for those services, and she wanted the boys to remain at home.

The evidence submitted by appellant at the hearing showed that she was a single mother trying her best to make ends meet and to provide a good home for her two sons. She worked as a "pricing specialist" and made about $8 an hour. The natural father paid child support, but had no contact with the boys for three years before the hearing, so appellant received no supervision help from that quarter.

Appellant stated she had been receiving government assistance for her child care expenses in the summer of 1996. With that assistance, she had been able to place Douglas and Keith in a daycare center while she was at work. When school started that September, she claimed, her government assistance was eliminated, and she could not afford to keep her children in the daycare center.

In appellant's opinion, the boys were very mature and responsible for their ages. She testified that Douglas and Keith were both very intelligent, capable, and responsible. . . . Appellant considered leaving them home alone after school every day because she felt her budget would not accommodate any other solution. She claimed she called the Willoughby police department and asked if there was any age at which it was illegal to leave children alone, and she was told there was not. Appellant also said she called the director of the daycare center and asked her if she thought it would be appropriate to leave them home alone and said she was told it would be appropriate to leave them home alone. At the adjudicatory hearing, the director, in fact, testified that the boys were mature and responsible enough to be left by themselves for a few hours occasionally.

* * *

Appellant also testified extensively as to how she gave each of the children a key and provided them with a very detailed list of instructions. They were not allowed to use the stove. They could only use the microwave if they called appellant so that she could walk them through its operation step by step. They were not allowed to answer the phone if they did not recognize the phone number displayed on the Caller I.D. They were not allowed to leave the yard if they went outside. They were not allowed to answer the door.

* * *

Appellant provided the boys with a series of telephone numbers, including her 1-800 work number, her cellular phone number, and Nichols's number at the bowling alley. The older child had memorized all these numbers.

The testimony was that they also were instructed to call 911 if there was an emergency. They were to call appellant at work when they arrived home. While they were home alone, appellant and Nichols claimed, they would each frequently call to check on the boys. Also, appellant said the boys often called her for various reasons, for example, to get permission to eat a certain snack or to play a certain game.

* * *

We do not believe that the only type of situation that would justify immediate state intervention is one in which the parent decides to leave children alone in a house with an undue danger or dangerous condition, such as a gun. *See, e.g., In re Leftwich* (Apr. 22, 1997), Franklin App. No. 96APF09-1263, unreported, 1997 WL 202247; *In re Skeen* (June 23, 1994), Franklin App. Nos. 93APF12-1633, 93APF12-1634, 93APF12-1635, unreported, 1994 WL 283659.

Appellant and the guardian ad litem appear to argue that if children, regardless of age, are found to be highly intelligent and very mature for their ages, then they are presumptively capable of caring for themselves on a regular basis, either for a few hours or an entire day.

To the contrary, we believe that, regardless of maturity or intelligence, the ages alone of unsupervised children could constitute some clear and convincing evidence that showed that children of that age who were regularly left alone for extended periods of time, separately or together, were put at undue risk to their health and safety.

There were three facts that we believe were determinative of the issue of neglect: (1) the ages of the children, (2) the pattern, regularity, and length of the incidents of no supervision,[1] and (3) the likelihood that the lack of supervision would continue because of the inability or unwillingness of appellant to acknowledge the implicit and immediate danger of such a situation.

First, let us say that we would agree that allowing an eight-year-old child such as Douglas to fend for himself for two hours after school would raise a debatable question as to whether that constituted neglect. If it is, then thousands of children in this district are neglected. However, our situation is not that simple. Not only was Douglas left without supervision, he was required to babysit and interact with the six-year-old. We are apparently being asked to believe that there was never any horseplay, roughhousing, anger, resentment, jealousy, daredevil behavior, or poor judgment displayed between the two brothers during these unsupervised intervals. The guardian ad litem testified that Keith told her sometimes they fought when they were home alone, that his brother picked on him, but that it was no big deal.

Common sense tells us that no matter how good, how mature, or how intelligent a six or an eight-year-old child might be, he is not good, mature, or intelligent all the time. To assert that such children will never put themselves in harm's way by doing something stupid or by panicking during a crisis is the height of self-deception on the part of a parent.

As previously indicated, there was, in fact, testimony that Keith was very athletic, that he does not get into much trouble, that he was very energetic, and that he and his older brother accepted discipline very well. Another way of summarizing those comments would be to say that six-year-old Keith is a very active child who occasionally gets into trouble, and sometimes he and his older brother need to be disciplined.

---

1 The juvenile court specifically found appellant's testimony to be less than credible because he found the children were "left home on a regular basis without adequate supervision between from September 1, 1996 to April 9, 1997."

That is the point of providing adequate supervision—to provide for the times when those aberrations in the behavior of good children occur.

Thus, we find absolutely no impediment whatsoever to determining that it constitutes neglect per se to allow a six-year-old child to be left alone for two entire days per week on a regular basis and to be regularly left at other times under the supervision of his eight-year-old sibling. As for Douglas we determine minimally that he was too young to be the babysitter for the younger child on a regular daily basis for intervals of two hours plus.

The second factor was the pattern and regularity of the lack of supervision. As previously acknowledged, there would be vary few parents who could testify that they have never left their children unattended. As a result, the media regularly records tragedies that occur during those few moments of neglect, regardless of whether it was regular or occasional in nature. However, it is not the occasional lack of supervision that occurs on an irregular basis that is the issue here.

* * *

While appellant testified that she saw no problem with the supervision of the six-year-old by the eight-year-old, the social worker testified that she told appellant on the March visit that such behavior was not fair to Douglas and was not a good situation. Frankly, expert testimony is not needed to reach the conclusion that the regular supervision of a six-year-old by an eight-year-old is an invitation to disaster.

This brings us to the third critical fact, namely the self-serving rationalization of appellant and her failure to acknowledge the inherent dangers of the situation, such that it was apparent that the situation would continue. It was obvious from the record that, for all intents and purposes, appellant had simply stopped using babysitters or caregivers, except for the Monday preschool program.[8] That is unacceptable.

Of necessity, the juvenile court is given a substantially greater amount of discretion than the rest of the court system. We sympathize and commiserate with the attorney who has to defend his or her client on neglect allegations in what is admittedly somewhat of a never-never land of both substantive and procedural law. There is, however, no legislation that is capable of defining every conceivable instance of child neglect. Thus, there must be a certain amount of common sense left for the juvenile court judge to exercise in interpreting the scope and intent of the phrase "adequate parental care," particularly when viewed in light of the definition of shelter as discussed earlier.

Like the juvenile court, we agree that there was clear and convincing evidence of neglect. We find that, in light of the ages of the children, the regularity, pattern, and extended lengths of the unsupervised incidents, and the likelihood of continuance without intervention, there was clear and convincing evidence of inadequate parental care constitution neglect. Further, such behavior unreasonably exposed the children to undue risk to their health and safety.

---

8 Nichols's testimony of his last specific recollection of using a babysitter was when he and appellant vacationed for a week in the spring of 1997 and left the boys with an adult sitter.

It was behavior in which a reasonable and responsible parent would not engage because of the risk.

We do not believe that the juvenile court was required to wait until a tragedy actually occurred in order to determine that it was very probable that a tragedy could and would occur if this pattern of behavior were allowed to continue uncorrected.

* * *

For the reasons stated, the judgment of the juvenile court is affirmed. Judgment affirmed.

[Dissenting opinion omitted.]

Notes

1. Poverty significantly increases the likelihood of neglect by lack of supervision. Bruce A. Boyer, *Ethical Issues In the Representation of Parents in Child Welfare Cases*, 64 FORDHAM L. REV. 1621, 1646 (1996). *In re Zieser, supra,* is a good example of a single parent who tried to financially support the children but, while at work, left the children unsupervised. *See also* Howard Davidson, *Symposium: Violence in America: How Can We Save Our Children? No Consequences—Reexamining Parental Responsibility Laws,* 7 STAN. L. & POL'Y REV. 23 (1995-96) (lack of supervision while parent working can lead to violent behavior); Jason Emilios Dimitris, Comment, *Parental Responsibility Statutes—And The Programs That Must Accompany Them*, 27 STETSON L. REV. 655 n.121 (1997) (negative effect of lack of supervision on "good kids" when parents must work full time).

2. Parents may also neglect their children through lack of supervision by their inability or unwillingness to provide continual supervision. In *In the Interest of A.C., M.C., and J.C.,* 1999 WL 1255793, 4 (Iowa Ct. App. 1999), the court admonished the parents of three neglected children by holding that parenting and supervision "cannot be turned on and off like a spigot; it must be constant, responsible, and reliable" (citing *In re L.L.*, 459 N.W.2d 489, 495 Iowa)). In *A.C.,* the parents of the three children were either unable or unwilling to supervise or discipline their children. As a result, the older children often assumed the duty of disciplining which led to severe violence. The children came and went as they pleased without the parents knowing the children's whereabouts. When asked to terminate parental rights based on lack of supervision, many courts like the *A.C.* court also take into account other forms of neglect and abuse. *See, e.g., In re Denice F.*, 658 A.2d 1070 (Me. 1995); *In re Interest of Steven A.,* 1994 WL 697696 (Neb. Ct. App. Dec. 13, 1994); *In re Meyer*, 648 N.E.2d 52 (Ohio Ct. App. 1994).

3. State laws frequently define lack of supervision by either providing a laundry list of examples or by allowing courts to use a reasonableness standard to define what constitutes lack of supervision. For further discussion of these two ways states define lack of supervision, see A. Dale Ihrie III, Comment, *Parental Delinquency: Should Parents Be Criminally Liable For Failing to Supervise Their Children?*, 74 DET. MERCY L. REV. 93 (1996).

Questions

1. What are the public policy implications of lack of supervision being specifically defined by state law versus a reasonableness standard? What constitutional issues may arise?

2. To what degree may the state require a parent to supervise his or her child? How should the court balance the interests of the state versus the interests of the parent in deciding how to rear a child?

f. Domestic Violence

Delaware Code Annotated

Tit. 13, § 705A (Michie Supp. 2000)

§ 705A. Rebuttable presumption against custody or residence of minor child to perpetrator of domestic violence.

(a) Notwithstanding other provisions of this title, there shall be a rebuttable presumption that no perpetrator of domestic violence shall be awarded sole or joint custody of any child.

(b) Notwithstanding other provisions of this title, there shall be a rebuttable presumption that no child shall primarily reside with a perpetrator of domestic violence.

(c) The above presumptions shall be overcome if there have been no further acts of domestic violence and the perpetrator of domestic violence has: (1) successfully completed a program of evaluation and counselling designed specifically for perpetrators of family violence and conducted by a public or private agency or a certified mental health professional; and (2) successfully completed a program of alcohol or drug abuse counselling if the Court determines that such counselling is appropriate; and (3) demonstrated that giving custodial or residential responsibilities to the perpetrator of domestic violence is in the best interests of the child. The presumption may otherwise be overcome only if a judicial officer finds extraordinary circumstances that warrant the rejection of the presumption, such as evidence demonstrating that there exists no significant risk of future violence any adult or minor child living in the home or any other family member, including any ex-spouse.

(d) In those cases in which both parents are perpetrators of domestic violence, the case shall be referred to the Division of Family Services of the Department of Services for Children, Youth and their Families for investigation and presentation of findings. Upon consideration of such presentation, and all other relevant evidence, including but not limited to, evidence about the history of abuse between the parents and evidence regarding whether 1 parent has been the primary aggressor in the household, the Court shall decide custody and residence pursuant to the best interests of the child.

In re Lonell J.

673 N.Y.S.2d 116 (N.Y. App. Div. 1998)

ROSENBERGER, J.

issue

The issue in this case is whether a pattern of domestic violence between respondent parents in the presence of their children may be sufficient to establish neglect under Family Court Act § 1012, absent expert testimony that the parents' strife has caused specific harm to the children.

Respondents Lonell J. (the father) and Nicole B. (the mother) are the parents of Latisha . . . and Lonell, Jr. . . . When the incidents giving rise to this action took place, the family lived in a Tier 2 Shelter in the Bronx. The Administration for Children's Services (ACS) removed the children from the parents' home on January 11, 1996, and they have been in foster care since then. Neglect petitions were filed against the parents on January 16, 1996, based on alleged instances of medical neglect and of domestic violence in which the father beat the mother in front of the children. The petitions also alleged that the parents had failed to attend the counseling prescribed by the Child Welfare Administration.

A fact-finding hearing was held over four days in December 1996. Two ACS caseworkers presented evidence that the father habitually abused the mother and also testified to their observations of the children's poor health and unsanitary conditions. . . .

* * *

Other evidence at the hearing indicated that the police had been called on several occasions over a one-month period due to the parents' fights. . . . The January visit resulted in the father's arrest. An order of protection was issued against him on January 6. The father denied that these events had occurred, but the mother admitted it, though she tried to minimize the extent of the violence.

The parents offered alternate explanations for the children's allegedly sickly and unkept condition. Lonell, Jr. was said to be suffering from an illness that made it hard for him to keep food down. The parents stated that they had taken him to the doctor several times for this condition. As for Latisha's diaper, they said that the caseworker had come early in the morning, before the parents had a chance to change the diaper from the night before.

The hearing court concluded that the petitioner had failed to prove medical neglect. While the court believed that the parents were not credible as to the extent of the fighting, it refused to find emotional neglect on this basis. The court's position was that until the Legislature amended Family Court Act § 1012 to make domestic violence between parents a per se act of neglect, expert testimony was necessary to establish that these children had been traumatized by witnessing their parent's fights. Accordingly, it dismissed the petitions. We find that this was error.

The hearing court's interpretation of Family Court Act § 1012 was unnecessarily narrow. . . . Family Court Act § 1012(f)(i) defines a "neglected child" as one "whose physical, mental or emotional condition has been impaired or is in imminent danger of becoming impaired by the parent's failure to exercise minimal care. The statute enumerates various examples of neglectful behavior (e.g., parental drug abuse, failure to provide food or medical treatment), but also states that in addition to these examples, a finding of neglect can be based on "any other acts of a similarly serious nature requiring the aid of the court" (Family Ct. Act § 1012[f][i][B]).

It appears that the hearing court mistakenly read Family Court Act § 1012 according to the principle of *inclusio unius est exclusio alterius,* ignoring the plain language of section 1012(f)(i)(B), whose catch-all provision (quoted, *supra*) clearly contemplates that the instances of neglectful behavior mentioned therein are not an exclusive list. The statute's goal of protecting children from all types of dangerous parental misconduct would not be well served by an interpretation requiring a higher burden of proof as to any type of neglect not so enumerated.

Moreover, nothing in section 1012 itself requires expert testimony, as opposed to other convincing evidence of neglect. In fact, Family Court Act § 1036(a)(viii) which directly addresses this issue, does not support the hearing court's reasoning. That provision states that "proof of the 'impairment of emotional health' or 'impairment of mental or emotional condition' as a result of the unwillingness or inability of the respondent to exercise a minimum degree of care toward a child *may include* competent opinion or expert testimony" (emphasis added). Such inclusive language undermines any conclusion that expert testimony is required. . . .

* * *

In its supplemental opinion, which urges the Legislature to amend section 1012 to define domestic violence in the child's presence as neglect, the hearing court quoted legislative history taking notice of the physical and mental effects of spousal abuse on children. In enacting the Family Protection and Domestic Violence Intervention Act of 1994 (1994, ch 222), the Legislature cited several studies proving that children in violent homes experience delayed development, psychosomatic illness and feelings of fear and depression, and often become the victims of abuse themselves (citation omitted). . . . It seems only logical that parents' spousal abuse, no less than their drug and alcohol abuse (specifically mentioned in section 1012), should be considered "other acts of a similarly serious nature" under section 1012(f)(i)(B). To hold otherwise would be to find that spousal abuse, in which the immediate physical harm is to the nonabusing parent of the child, is necessarily less serious than substance abuse, in which the immediate physical harm is to the abuser himself.

Studies show that infants exposed to domestic violence often experience poor health and eating problems (citation omitted). Based on a review of the record, we find that the subject children were neglected within the meaning of Family Court Act § 1012.

* * *

Notes

1. Children can suffer physically, emotionally, and mentally as a result of witnessing domestic violence. *See* Amy Haddix, *Unseen Victims: Acknowledging the Effects of Domestic Violence Through Statutory Termination of Parental Rights,* 84 CAL. L. REV. 757, 789-90 (1996). An infant can suffer from poor health resulting from losing weight and eating problems. When battered mothers are hospitalized, they are separated from their babies preventing their babies from getting the nourishment they need. Mothers who are battered may also struggle to feed their babies on a regular basis because of the domestic violence. The children, even if not directly involved in the domestic violence, may accidentally get caught in between the fighting parents and suffer from physical abuse. As the children grow up, they may suffer from low self-esteem because of family instability, resort to violence to solve problems, and beat their own spouses in the future. *Id.* at 790. For further discussion on how children who witness domestic violence are affected, see Alan Rosenbaum & Daniel O'Leary, *Children: The Unintended Victims of Marital Violence,* 51 AM. J. ORTHOPSYCHIATRY 692, 698 (1991).

2. Advocates of labeling domestic violence as a form of neglect argue that presumptions against a parent who commits domestic violence will result in fewer children being abused. *See generally* Linda R. Keenen, Note, *Domestic Violence and Custody Litigation: The Need For Statutory Reform,* 13 HOFSTRA L. REV. 407 (1985). Still, critics claim separating a child from a parent may be counterproductive. Even though the child may be protected for the moment, the threat the parent poses to society may be less likely to recede because family contact helps reduce recidivism rates. *See* Stephanie J. Millet, Note, *The Age of Criminal Responsibility in an Era of Violence: Has Great Britain Set a New International Standard?*, 28 VAND. J. TRANSNAT'L L. 295, 232 n. 241 (1995). For a discussion of the effect of domestic violence on a child and how states have responded to this type of neglect, see Deborah Ahrens, Note, *Not in Front of the Children: Prohibition on Child Custody as Civil Branding for Criminal Activity,* 75 N.Y.U. L. REV. 737 (2000).

3. For further discussion of courts removing from home children who witness domestic violence, see *In re Athena M.*, 678 N.Y.S.2d 11 (N.Y. App. Div. 1998); *In re Deborah T.,* 676 N.Y.S.2d 666 (N.Y. App. Div. 1998); *In re B.J.B.,* 546 S.W.2d 674 (Tex. Civ. App. 1977); *G.W.H. v. D.A.H.,* 650 S.W.2d 480 (Tex. Civ. App. 1983). *See generally* Kym L. Kilpatrick & Leanne M. Williams, *Potential Mediators of Post-Traumatic Stress Disorder in Child Witnesses to Domestic Violence,* 22(4) CHILD ABUSE & NEGLECT 319 (1998). For a discussion in favor of giving greater emphasis to the interests of the child and victim, see Kim Susser, *Weighing the Domestic Violence Factor In Custody Cases: Tipping the Scales in Favor of Protecting Victims and Their Children,* 27 FORDHAM URB. L.J. 875 (2000).

Questions

If there is domestic violence in a home, are the children of the family necessarily in "imminent harm"? Should a judge rule that a child is neglected even though there is no proof that the domestic violence has had a negative impact on the child?

Problem

When Joni was five years of age, she saw her intoxicated father beat her mother unconscious in the living room. The juvenile court determined that removing Joni from her father's custody was in her best interests. Joni, now fourteen years of age, lives with her mother and her live-in boyfriend. The boyfriend routinely beats Joni's mother after drinking and using drugs. Based upon the father's report, child welfare authorities file a neglect petition against the mother and the boyfriend. The father claims that he has been sober for two years and wants sole physical custody of Joni. What factors should the court consider before deciding what is in Joni's best interests?

Chapter 9

The Child's Right to State Protection

The Fourteenth Amendment has been used to insure that the state does not go too far in its effort to improve the quality of society. The Fourteenth Amendment insures that "[n]o State shall . . . deprive any person of life, liberty, or property, without due process of law." The courts have determined that liberty includes not only freedom from bodily restraint, but also all rights that have been recognized at common law as essential to the orderly pursuit of happiness by free men and women. One such fundamental right is the right to family privacy. The Fourteenth Amendment has been used to protect the private realm of family life from state interference. The family, however, is not beyond regulation. *Meyer v. Nebraska*, 262 U.S. 390 (1923), held that fundamental rights can be interfered with if the state is protecting the public interest and the legislative action is not arbitrary or without reasonable relation to any end within the competency of the state. In its role as *parens patriae*, the state has a compelling interest in protecting the welfare of the child. Hence, when there is parental neglect, abuse or abandonment, the state may interfere in family life. *DeShaney v. Winnebago Department of Social Services,* 489 U.S. 189 (1989), holds, however, that the State does not have an affirmative constitutional duty to protect a child, who is not in state care, from harm caused by a parent or custodian, absent a "special relationship" between the state and the child. This chapter explores various contexts in which the state's duty of child protection is analyzed, including the child in a foster care situation.

A. Constitutional Protections: Parental Authority and Family Privacy

Meyer v. Nebraska

262 U.S. 390, 43 S. Ct. 625, 67 L. Ed. 1042 (1923)

Mr. Justice McREYNOLDS delivered the opinion of the Court.

Plaintiff in error was tried and convicted in the District Court for Hamilton County, Nebraska, under an information which charged that on May 25, 1920, while an instructor in Zion Parochial School, he unlawfully taught the subject of reading in the German language to Raymond Parpart, a child of ten years who had not attained and successfully passed the eighth grade. The information is based upon "An act relating to the teaching of foreign languages in the State of Nebraska," approved April 9, 1919, which follows [Laws 1919, c. 249.]:

> Section 1. No person, individually or as a teacher, shall, in any private, denominational parochial or public school, teach any subject to any person in any language other than the English language.
> Sec. 2. Languages, other than the English language, may be taught as languages only after a pupil shall have attained and successfully passed the eighth grade. . . .
>
> * * *
>
> Sec. 4. Whereas, an emergency exists, this act shall be in force from and after its passage and approval.

The Supreme Court of the State affirmed the judgment of conviction. . . . And it held that the statute . . . did not conflict with the Fourteenth Amendment, but was a valid exercise of the police power. The following excerpts from the opinion sufficiently indicate the reasons advanced to support the conclusion.

> The salutary purpose of the statute is clear. The legislature had seen the baneful effects of permitting foreigners, who had taken residence in this country, to rear and educate their children in the language of their native land. . . . To allow the children of foreigners, who had emigrated here, to be taught from early childhood the language of the country of their parents was to rear them with that language as their mother tongue. It was to educate them so that they must always think in that language, and, as a consequence, naturally inculcate in them the ideas and sentiments foreign to the best interests of this country. The statute, therefore, was intended not only to require that the education of all children be conducted in the English language, but that, until they had grown into that language and until it had become a part of them, they should not in the schools be taught any other language. The obvious purpose of this statute was that the English language should be and become the mother tongue

of all children reared in this state. The enactment of such a statute comes reasonably within the police power of the state.

Phol v. State, 132 N.E. (Ohio) 20; *State v. Bartels*, 181 N.W. (Ia.) 508.

* * *

The problem for our determination is whether the statute as construed and applied unreasonably infringes the liberty guaranteed to the plaintiff in error by the Fourteenth Amendment. "No State shall . . . deprive any person of life, liberty, or property, without due process of law."

While this court has not attempted to define with exactness the liberty thus guaranteed, the term has received much consideration and some of the included things have been definitely stated. Without doubt, it denotes not merely freedom from bodily restraint but also the right of the individual to contract, to engage in any of the common occupations of life, to acquire useful knowledge, to marry, establish a home and bring up children, to worship God according to the dictates of his own conscience, and generally to enjoy those privileges long recognized at common law as essential to the orderly pursuit of happiness by free men. The established doctrine is that this liberty may not be interfered with, under the guise of protecting the public interest, by legislative action which is arbitrary or without reasonable relation to some purpose within the competency of the State to effect. Determination by the legislature of what constitutes proper exercise of police power is not final or conclusive but is subject to supervision by the courts.

* * *

It is said the purpose of the legislation was to promote civic development by inhibiting training and education of the immature in foreign tongues and ideals before they could learn English and acquire American ideals; and "that the English language should be and become the mother tongue of all children reared in this State." It is also affirmed that the foreign born population is very large, that certain communities commonly use foreign words, follow foreign leaders, move in a foreign atmosphere, and that the children are thereby hindered from becoming citizens of the most useful type and the public safety is imperiled.

That the State may do much, go very far, indeed, in order to improve the quality of its citizens, physically, mentally and morally, is clear; but the individual has certain fundamental rights which must be respected. The protection of the Constitution extends to all, to those who speak other languages as well as to those born with English on the tongue. Perhaps it would be highly advantageous if all had ready understanding of our ordinary speech, but this cannot be coerced by methods which conflict with the Constitution—a desirable end cannot be promoted by prohibited means.

* * *

The desire of the legislature to foster a homogeneous people with American ideals prepared readily to understand current discussions of civic matters is easy to appreciate. . . . But the means adopted, we think, exceed the limitations upon the power of the State and conflict with rights assured to plaintiff in error. The interference is plain enough and no adequate reason therefor in time of peace and domestic tranquility has been shown.

. . . *Adams v. Tanner,* 244 U.S. 590, 594, pointed out that mere abuse incident to an occupation ordinarily useful is not enough to justify its abolition, although regulation may be entirely proper. No emergency has arisen which renders knowledge by a child of some language other than English so clearly harmful as to justify its inhibition with the consequent infringement of rights long freely enjoyed. We are constrained to conclude that the statute as applied is arbitrary and without reasonable relation to any end within the competency of the State.

* * *

The judgment of the court below must be reversed and the cause remanded for further proceedings not inconsistent with this opinion.

[The dissenting opinion of Justice HOLMES is omitted.]

Pierce v. Society of Sisters

268 U.S. 510, 45 S. Ct. 571, 69 L. Ed. 1070 (1925)

Mr. Justice MCREYNOLDS delivered the opinion of the Court.

These appeals are from decrees, based upon undenied allegations, which granted preliminary orders restraining appellants from threatening or attempting to enforce the Compulsory Education Act adopted November 7, 1922. . . . Rights said to be guaranteed by the federal Constitution were specially set up, and appropriate prayers asked for their protection.

The challenged Act, effective September 1, 1926, requires every parent, guardian or other person having control or charge or custody of a child between eight and sixteen years to send him "to a public school for the period of time a public school shall be held during the current year" in the district where the child resides; and failure so to do is declared a misdemeanor. . . . The manifest purpose is to compel general attendance at public schools by . . . children, between eight and sixteen, who have not completed the eighth grade. And without doubt enforcement of the statute would seriously impair, perhaps destroy the profitable features of appellees' business and greatly diminish the value of their property.

Appellee, the Society of Sisters, is an Oregon corporation, organized in 1880, with power to care for orphans, educate and instruct the youth, establish and maintain academies or schools, and acquire necessary real and personal property. It has long devoted its property and effort to the secular and religious education and care of children, and has acquired the valuable good will of many parents and guardians. It conducts interdependent primary and high schools and junior colleges, and maintains orphanages for the custody and control of children between eight and sixteen. In its primary schools many children between those ages are taught the subjects usually pursued in Oregon public schools during the first eight years. . . . All courses of study, both temporal and religious, contemplate continuity of training under appellee's charge; the primary schools are essential to the system and the most profitable. . . . The Compulsory Education Act of 1922 has already caused the withdrawal from its schools of children who would otherwise continue, and their income has steadily declined. The appellants, public officers, have proclaimed their purpose strictly to enforce the statute.

* * *

The [D]istrict Court ruled that the Fourteenth Amendment guaranteed appellees against the deprivation of their property without due process of law consequent upon the unlawful interference by appellants with the free choice of patrons, present and prospective. It declared the right to conduct schools was property and that parents and guardians, as a part of their liberty, might direct the education of children by selecting reputable teachers and places. Also, that appellee's schools were not unfit or harmful to the public, and that enforcement of the challenged statute would unlawfully deprive them of patronage and thereby destroy their owners' business and property. Finally, that the threats to enforce the Act would continue to cause irreparable injury; and the suits were not premature.

No question is raised concerning the power of the State reasonably to regulate all schools, to inspect, supervise and examine them, their teachers and pupils; to require that all children of proper age attend some school, that teachers shall be of good moral character and patriotic disposition, that certain studies plainly essential to good citizenship must be taught, and that nothing be taught which is manifestly inimical to the public welfare.

The inevitable practical result of enforcing the Act under consideration would be destruction of appellees' primary schools, and perhaps all other private primary schools. . . within the State of Oregon. These parties are engaged in a kind of undertaking not inherently harmful, but long regarded as useful and meritorious. Certainly there is nothing in the present records to indicate that they have failed to discharge their obligations to patrons, students or the State. And there are no peculiar circumstances or present emergencies which demand extraordinary measures relative to primary education.

Under the doctrine of *Meyer v. Nebraska*, 262 U.S. 390, we think it entirely plain that the Act of 1922 unreasonably interferes with the liberty of parents and guardians to direct the upbringing and education of children under their control. As often heretofore pointed out, rights guaranteed by the Constitution may not be abridged by legislation which has no reasonable relation to some purpose within the competency of the State. The fundamental theory of liberty upon which all governments in this Union repose excludes any general power of the State to standardize its children by forcing them to accept instruction from public teachers only. The child is not the mere creature of the State; those who nurture him and direct his destiny have the right, coupled with the high duty, to recognize and prepare him for additional obligations.

Appellees are corporations and therefore, it is said, they cannot claim for themselves the liberty which the Fourteenth Amendment guarantees. Accepted in the proper sense, this is true. But they have business and property for which they claim protection. These are threatened with destruction through the unwarranted compulsion which appellants are exercising over present and prospective patrons of their schools. And this court has gone very far to protect against loss threatened by such action. *Truax v. Raich*, 239 U.S. 33; *Traux v. Corrigan*, 257 U.S. 312; *Terrace v. Thompson*, 263 U.S. 197.

* * *

Generally it is entirely true, as urged by counsel, that no person in any business has such an interest in possible customers as to enable him to restrain exercise of proper power of the State upon the ground that he will be deprived of patronage. But the injunctions here sought are not against the exercise of any *proper* power. Plaintiffs asked protection against arbitrary, unreasonable and unlawful interference with their patrons and the consequent destruction of their business and property. Their interest is clear and immediate, within the rule approved in *Traux v. Raich, Truax v. Corrigan* and *Terrace v. Thompson, supra,* and many other cases where injunctions have issued to protect business enterprises against interference with the freedom of patrons or customers.

The suits were not premature. The injury to appellees was present and very real, not a mere possibility in the remote future. If no relief had been possible prior to the effective date of the Act, the injury would have become irreparable. Prevention of impending injury by unlawful action is a well recognized function of courts of equity.

holding

The decrees below are affirmed.

B. Compelling State Interest of Child Protection

1. Intervention in Family Life

Prince v. Massachusetts

321 U.S. 158, 64 S. Ct. 438, 88 L. Ed. 645 (1944)

Mr. Justice RUTLEDGE delivered the opinion of the Court.

issue

. . . Sarah Prince appeals from convictions for violating Massachusetts' child labor laws, by acts said to be a rightful exercise of her religious convictions.

When the offenses were committed she was the aunt and custodian of Betty Simmons, a girl nine years of age. Originally there were three separate complaints. They were, shortly, for (1) refusal to disclose Betty's identity and age to a public officer . . . ; (2) furnishing her with magazines, knowing she was to sell them unlawfully, that is, on the street; and (3) as Betty's custodian, permitting her to work contrary to law. The complaints were made, respectively, pursuant to §§ 79, 80 and 81 of Chapter 149, Gen. Laws of Mass. (Ter. Ed.). The Supreme Judicial Court reversed the conviction under the first complaint on state grounds, but sustained the judgments founded on the other two. [T]he only questions for our decision . . . are whether §§ 80 and 81, as applied, contravene the Fourteenth Amendment by denying or abridging appellant's freedom of religion and by denying to her the equal protection of the laws.

procedure

Sections 80 and 81 form parts of Massachusetts' comprehensive child labor law. They provide methods for enforcing the prohibitions of § 69 which is as follows:

> "No boy under twelve and no girl under eighteen shall sell, expose or offer for sale any newspapers, magazines, periodicals or any other articles of merchandise of any description . . . in any street or public place."
>
> Sections 80 and 81, so far as pertinent, read:
>
> "Whoever furnishes or sells to any minor any article of any description with the knowledge that the minor intends to sell such article in violation of any provision of sections sixty-nine to seventy-three, inclusive, or after having received written notice to this effect from any officer charged with the enforcement thereof, or knowingly procures or encourages any minor to violate any provisions of said sections, shall be punished by a fine of not less than ten or more than two hundred dollars or by imprisonment for not more than two months, or both." § 80.
>
> "Any parent, guardian or custodian having a minor under his control who compels or permits such minor to work in violation of any provision of sections sixty to seventy-four, inclusive, . . . shall for a first offense be punished by a fine of not less than two nor more than ten dollars or by imprisonment for not more than five days, or both. . . ." § 81.

. . . Mrs. Prince, living in Brockton, is the mother of two young sons. She also has legal custody of Betty Simmons, who lives with them. The children too are Jehovah's Witnesses and both Mrs. Prince and Betty testified they were ordained ministers. The former was accustomed to go each week on the streets of Brockton to distribute "Watchtower" and "Consolation. . . ." She had permitted the children to engage in this activity previously, and had been warned against doing so by the school attendance officer, Mr. Perkins. But, until December 18, 1941, she generally did not take them with her at night.

That evening, as Mrs. Prince was preparing to leave her home, the children asked to go. She at first refused. Childlike, they resorted to tears; and, motherlike, she yielded. Arriving downtown, Mrs. Prince permitted the children "to engage in the preaching work with her upon the sidewalks." That is, with specific reference to Betty, she and Mrs. Prince took positions about twenty feet apart near a street intersection. Betty held up in her hand, for passers-by to see, copies of "Watchtower" and "Consolation." From her shoulder hung the usual canvas magazine bag, on which was printed: "Watchtower and Consolation 5¢ per copy." No one accepted a copy from Betty that evening and she received no money. Nor did her aunt. But on other occasions, Betty had received funds and given out copies.

Mrs. Prince and Betty remained until 8:45 p.m. A few minutes before this, Mr. Perkins approached Mrs. Prince. . . . He inquired and she refused to give Betty's name. . . . Mr. Perkins referred to his previous warnings and said he would allow five minutes for them to get off the street. Mrs. Prince admitted she supplied Betty with the magazines and said, "[N]either you nor anybody else can stop me. . . . This child is exercising her God-given right and her constitutional right to preach the gospel, and no creature has a right to interfere with God's commands." However, Mrs. Prince and Betty departed. . . .

As the case reaches us, the . . . only question remaining . . . is whether, as construed and applied, the statute is valid. Upon this the [State] court said: "We think that freedom of the press and of religion is subject to incidental regulation to the slight degree involved in the prohibition of the selling of religious literature in streets and public places by boys under twelve and girls under eighteen. . . ."

Appellant does not stand on freedom of the press. . . . Hence, she rests squarely on freedom of religion under the First Amendment, applied by the Fourteenth to the states. She buttresses this foundation, however, with a claim of parental right as secured by the due process clause of the latter Amendment. Cf. *Meyer v. Nebraska*, 262 U.S. 390. These guarantees, she thinks, guard alike herself and the child in what they have done. Thus, two claimed liberties are at stake. One is the parent's, to bring up the child in the way he should go, which for appellant means to teach him the tenets and the practices of their faith. The other freedom is the child's, to observe these; and among them is "to preach the gospel. . . by public distribution" of "Watchtower" and "Consolation," in conformity with the scripture: "A little child shall lead them."

* * *

To make accommodation between these freedoms and an exercise of state authority always is delicate. It hardly could be more so than in such a clash as this case presents. . . . The parent's conflict with the state over control of the child and his training is serious enough when only secular matters are concerned. It becomes the more so when an element of religious conviction enters. Against these sacred private interests, basic in a democracy, stand the interests of society to protect the welfare of children, and the state's assertion of authority to that end. . . .

The rights of children to exercise their religion, and of parents to give them religious training . . . as against . . . assertion of state power . . . have had recognition here, most recently in *West Virginia State Board of Education v. Barnette*, 319 U.S. 624. Previously in *Pierce v. Society of Sisters*, 268 U.S. 510, this Court had sustained the parent's authority to provide religious with secular schooling, and the child's right to receive it, as against the state's requirement of attendance at public schools. And in *Meyer v. Nebraska*, 262 U.S. 390, children's rights to receive teaching in languages other than the nation's common tongue were guarded against the state's encroachment. It is cardinal with us that the custody, care and nurture of the child reside first in the parents, whose primary function and freedom include preparation for obligations the state can neither supply nor hinder. And it is in recognition of this that these decisions have respected the private realm of family life which the state cannot enter.

But the family itself is not beyond regulation in the public interest, as against a claim of religious liberty. And neither rights of religion nor rights of parenthood are beyond limitation. Acting to guard the general interest in youth's well being, the state as *parens patriae* may restrict the parent's control by requiring school attendance,[9] regulating or prohibiting the child's labor,[10] and in many other ways. Its authority is not nullified merely because the parent grounds his claim to control the child's course of conduct on religion or conscience.... [T]he state has a wide range of power for limiting parental freedom and authority in things affecting the child's welfare; and this includes, to some extent, matters of conscience and religious conviction.

* * *

The state's authority over children's activities is broader than overt like actions of adults.... Among evils most appropriate for [state regulation] are the crippling effects of child employment, more especially in public places.... It is too late now to doubt that legislation appropriately designed to reach such evils is within the state's police power, whether against the parent's claim to control of the child or one that religious scruples dictate contrary action.

* * *

... The zealous though lawful exercise of the right to engage in propagandizing the community, whether in religious, political or other matters, may and at times does create situations difficult enough for adults to cope with and wholly inappropriate for children, especially of tender years, to face.... Parents may be free to become martyrs themselves. But it does not follow they are free, in identical circumstances, to make martyrs of their children before they have reached the age of full and legal discretion when they can make that choice for themselves.... We think that with reference to the public proclaiming of religion, ... the power of the state to control the conduct of children reaches beyond the scope of its authority over adults, as is true in the case of other freedoms, and the rightful boundary of its power has not been crossed in this case.

In so ruling we dispose also of appellant's argument founded upon denial of equal protection.... However Jehovah's Witnesses may conceive them, the public highways have not become their religious property merely by their assertion. And there is no denial of equal protection in excluding their children from doing there what no other children may do.

Our ruling does not extend beyond the facts the case presents.... The religious training and indoctrination of children may be accomplished in many ways, some of which, as we have noted, have received constitutional protection through decisions of this Court. These and all others except the public proclaiming of religion on the streets ... remain unaffected by the decision.

The judgment is affirmed.

---

9 *State v. Bailey*, 157 Ind. 324, 61 N.E. 730; compare *Meyer v. Nebraska*, 262 U.S. 390; *Pierce v. Society of Sisters*, 268 U.S. 510; *West Virginia State Board of Education v. Barnette*, 319 U.S. 624.

10 *Sturgis & Burn Mfg. Co. v. Beauchamp*, 231 U.S. 320; compare *Muller v. Oregon*, 208 U.S. 412.

Mr. Justice MURPHY, dissenting.

This attempt by the state of Massachusetts to prohibit a child from exercising her constitutional right to practice her religion on the public streets cannot, in my opinion, be sustained.

* * *

The state, in my opinion, has completely failed to sustain its burden of proving the existence of any grave or immediate danger to any interest which it may lawfully protect. There is no proof that Betty Simmons' mode of worship constituted a serious menace to the public. It was carried on in an orderly, lawful manner at a public street corner. . . . The sidewalk, no less than the cathedral or the evangelist's tent, is a proper place, under the Constitution, for the orderly worship of God. Such use of the streets is as necessary to the Jehovah's Witnesses, the Salvation Army and others who practice religion without benefit of conventional shelters as is the use of the streets for purposes of passage. . . .

[Justice JACKSON's dissenting opinion is omitted.]

2. Removal of Child from Home

[See, *infra*, Chapter 10, Parts A.1-3.]

In the Matter of the Appeal in Cochise County Juvenile Action No. 5666-J

650 P.2d 459 (Ariz. 1982)

The issue we must decide is if there was sufficient evidence to warrant state interference with the fundamental right of a parent to the custody and control of his or her child, particularly to "monitor" the health of the child when there is no known medical danger and when providing medical care is contrary to the parent's religious beliefs.

On March 20, 1981, Mrs. Drew took her six-year old son, Therial, to the emergency room of the Copper Queen Community Hospital in Bisbee, Arizona. Therial was pronounced "dead on arrival," and an autopsy revealed that the cause of death was "septicemia and peritonitis secondary to perforation of a strangulated inguinal hernia." This condition occurs when a part of the intestine protrudes out through a defective part of the abdominal wall. The intestine may and often does slip back into place. If the intestine gets caught, however, the blood supply to the area will be cut off, the tissue will die, and the bowel will become obstructed, eventually causing a rupture. Upon rupture the materials in the digestive tract spill into the abdominal cavity causing infection and possibly leading to cardiac arrest and death.

Because of the circumstances of Therial's death the physician who performed the autopsy contacted the Arizona Department of Economic Security [D.E.S.]. Two D.E.S. caseworkers visited the Drew residence on March 31, 1981 and interviewed Mrs. Drew for twenty minutes. In response to questioning, Mrs. Drew explained that she had faith that miracles would safeguard her children and she would not seek medical help if any of the remaining children became ill. D.E.S. subsequently filed a petition requesting that the seven Drew children be adjudged dependent.

A dependency hearing was held on July 23, 1981. After hearing testimony from two physicians, a superintendent of schools, and the two D.E.S. caseworkers, the court declined to adjudge the children dependent as defined in A.R.S. § 8-201(10) . . . . The Court of Appeals reversed the juvenile court and found there was sufficient evidence upon which to declare the seven Drew children dependent.

* * *

Using the formula of the Supreme Court, the risk of error and the weighing of the private and public interests convinces us that the preponderance of the evidence standard is the proper standard of proof in dependency proceedings. *See* Ariz.R.P.Juv.Ct. 17(a)(2). Therefore, we must decide if the state has proved by a preponderance of the evidence that interference with the Drew family was warranted.

* * *

It is not disputed that parents owe certain duties to their children. It is incumbent on a parent to provide "necessaries" for a child. The definition of necessaries is not a fixed term. What is necessary for the well-being of a child may be defined differently in different cultures or economic and social groups, and may change with the times.

Although we recognize the term "necessary" is flexible, the state may impose a minimum threshold of care a parent must provide any child. In general, a parent must provide a child with a place to live, clothing, an education, attention, and medical care as may be required. By necessity these are fluid terms and may depend on the financial wherewithal of the parents, cultural mores, etc. *See Branham v. State*, 33 Ariz. 170, 263 P. 1 (1928).

Accordingly, when we discuss the rights of the parent, the state, and the child, we must weigh and balance the interests of each. Hard and fast judicial rules are sometimes desirable because they increase predictability. But an inelastic rule would not further justice when, as here, we are concerned with a right so important and sensitive as that of parenting a child. Not only must these rights be balanced, but it must also be recognized that a great deal of discretion is vested in the trial court and in the administrative body, here the D.E.S., which feeds information to the court. Just as "what is necessary" is not a rigid definition, neither is the definition of "neglect," *see In re Pima County Juvenile Action No. J-31853*, 18 Ariz.App. 219, 501 P.2d 395 (1972), nor of "abuse."

The United States Supreme Court has consistently declared the significance of the family unit in American society. The right to raise one's family is essential, *see Meyer v. Nebraska*, 262 U.S. 390, 43 S.Ct. 625, 67 L.Ed. 1042 (1925), and the right to procreate is one of the "basic rights" of all persons. *Skinner v. Oklahoma*, 316 U.S. 535, 62 S.Ct. 1110, 86 L.Ed. 1655 (1942). "It is cardinal with us that the custody, care and nurture of the child reside first in the parents, whose primary function and freedom include preparation for obligations the state can neither supply nor hinder." *Prince v. Massachusetts*, 321 U.S. 158, 166, 64 S.Ct. 438, 442, 88 L.Ed. 645, 652 (1944).

The Supreme Court has adopted the concept of family privacy acknowledging that there are certain aspects of our lives into which the government cannot intrude. *See Moore v. City of East Cleveland, Ohio*, 431 U.S. 494, 97 S.Ct. 1932, 52 L.Ed.2d 531 (1977) (government cannot intrude on choices concerning family living arrangements); *Roe v. Wade,* 410 U.S. 113, 93 S.Ct. 705, 35 L.Ed.2d 147 (1973) (state law proscribing abortion infringes on an individual's right of personal privacy); *Stanley v. Illinois,* 405 U.S. 645, 92 S.Ct. 1208, 31 L.Ed.2d 551 (1972) (state law presuming unmarried fathers unsuitable parents violated the natural father's interest in his children); *Griswold v. Connecticut*, 381 U.S. 479, 85 S.Ct. 1678, 14 L.Ed.2d 510 (1965) (state law proscribing the use of contraceptives unconstitutionally intrudes upon a person's right to marital privacy). The Court recently reaffirmed the parents' fundamental liberty interest "in the care, custody, and management of their child." *Santosky*, 102 S.Ct. at 1394, 71 L.Ed.2d at 606.

We have stated that "[b]ecause the child has attained a favored beneficient status in our social and legal systems does not detract from the well-settled rule that the right of parents to the custody of minor children is both a natural and legal right." *Arizona State Dept. of Public Welfare v. Barlow,* 80 Ariz. 249, 252, 296 P.2d 298, 300 (1956) . . . . Arizona recognizes that the right to control and custody of one's children is fundamental. *In re Pima County Juvenile Action No. S-111*, 25 Ariz.App. 380, 543 P.2d 809 (1975).

The rights of parents to the custody of their children, however, is not absolute. *Barlow, supra.* The state has an interest in the welfare and health of children. *See Roe v. Wade*, 410 U.S. 113, 93 S.Ct. 705, 35 L.Ed.2d 147 (1973). If the interest of the state is great enough—that is, if the welfare of the child is seriously jeopardized—the state may act and invade the rights of the parent and the family. Of no little concern in this balancing process are the rights of the child. The bundle of rights a child may have does not lend itself to a comprehensive list. But the child is entitled to have his or her basic needs cared for. If the parent fails to furnish these needs, the state may and should act on behalf of the child. In a case involving the custody of children, our paramount interest is always the best interest of the child. *In re Marriage of Gove*, 117 Ariz. 324, 572 P.2d 458 (App.1977).

The Court of Appeals read our juvenile statutes as demanding that "every child in Arizona is entitled to a home where the parent or guardian is willing to seek medical attention for him [or her] *should he [or she] become sick or injured.*" 650 P.2d at 468 (emphasis added).We agree with this reading of our statutes. At this juncture we depart from the analysis of the appellate court because the Drew children are not known to be sick or injured, and, therefore, there is no known need of medical attention. The evidence from the dependency hearing indicates that after Therial's death, two D.E.S. caseworkers went to the Drew home. The caseworkers identified themselves and Mrs. Drew invited them into her home. They discussed Therial's death and Mrs. Drew explained to the caseworkers that the other seven children were in good health. . . .

We emphasize that the state is not without remedy in this matter. D.E.S. has broad supervisory powers. As this case demonstrates, D.E.S. may investigate a family if there is reason to believe a child may be endangered. In this instance, D.E.S. was alerted by Therial's death to a possible problem concerning the welfare of the other children. D.E.S. properly visited the Drew residence to assess the situation and determine whether the other children were fed, clothed, and adequately supervised. D.E.S. retains this supervisory power. It may continue to keep a close eye on the progress of the Drew children. Because of the special circumstances of this case, D.E.S. may be prompted to investigate by something less than would be necessary in a typical situation. An absence from school, a teacher's notification, or a report from a neighbor or other source may permit D.E.S. to inquire further into protecting the welfare of the children. If D.E.S. does compile more information warranting state intrusion into the Drew family, it may again institute dependency proceedings.

We agree with Judge Hathaway's dissent in the Court of Appeals' opinion, 133 Ariz. 165, 650 P.2d 471 (Hathaway, J., dissenting), that the holding of the majority would have been subject to possible misuse.

We find that the evidence is not sufficient for a finding of dependency. We vacate the opinion of the Court of Appeals and affirm the juvenile court's dismissal of the state's petition.

Notes

1. As discussed in *Cochise County Juvenile Action No. 5666-J,* in dependency cases that involve removal of a child from a parent, custodian, or guardian there is at the outset a constitutional collision between the parent's fundamental right of privacy and the state's compelling interest in child protection. This balance between substantive due process, which recognizes the caregiver's autonomy in making decisions concerning the child and the state's obligation to safeguard the child's welfare, is addressed by the court throughout the proceedings. At the time of removal or detention of the child, the court must conclude that child protection trumps the parent's substantive due process rights and reasonable efforts were made to avoid removal of the child. The obligation to reunify the family continues through adjudication, where the court determines that coercive intervention is necessary and that the child's at-risk condition requires the child to remain in care outside the home.

Another good illustration of the state's role in protecting the welfare of the child is *Parker v. Monroe County Department of Public Welfare,* 533 N.E.2d 177 (Ind. Ct. App. 1989). In *Parker,* a mother forgot she left her children at a friend's house after she abused valium and speed and later reported she lost her children at a local shopping mall. The mother suffered from depression, agoraphobia, nightmares, suicidal thoughts, insomnia, and temper problems. The mother appealed a CHINS adjudication, claiming there was insufficient evidence to support the judgment. The court affirmed the decision stating, "[f]undamental rights to family integrity protect the relationship between the parent and child from state action; however, in the event of parental neglect, abuse, or abandonment, the State has a compelling interest in protecting the welfare of the child." Citing Indiana Code Annotated § 31-6-4-3 (repealed), the court stated that the welfare department "need not wait until a tragedy occurs or the children are irretrievably ruined by a parent who is out of control in order to take action." For further discussion of cases that have addressed a parent's right to rear a child and the state's compelling interest in protecting the child, see Carroll J. Miller, Annotation, *Validity and Application of Statute Allowing Endangered Child to be Temporarily Removed From Parental Custody*, 38 A.L.R.4TH 756 (1985).

2. If state officials unreasonably remove a child from his home, they may be successfully sued for constitutional violations under 42 U.S.C. § 1983. In *Brokaw v. Mercer County*, 235 F.3d 1000 (7th Cir. 2000), a deputy sheriff and a probation officer forcibly removed without a court order two children, C.A. and his sister, from their home based on "baseless and scurrilous" claims of child neglect made by the children's relatives. When C.A. reached the age of majority, he filed a *pro se* complaint under 42 U.S.C. § 1983 against several defendants, including Mercer County, the deputy sheriff, and the probation officer. According to the court, C.A. claimed the state officials "violated his Fourth Amendment rights by forcibly removing him from his home without cause. . . ." The court first stated that C.A.'s claim against the state officials, including the deputy sheriff and the probation officer, was not barred by the Eleventh Amendment because the state defendants treated C.A.'s claim as an individual capacity suit and not as an official capacity suit. Citing *Tenenbaum v. Williams*, 193 F.3d 581 (2d Cir. 1999), *infra* Chapter 10, Part A, the court then noted that the removal or seizure of a child is reasonable for purposes of the Fourth Amendment if it is pursuant to a court order, supported by probable cause, or justified by exigent circumstances. The court stated that the three *Tenenbaum* conditions of reasonableness were not satisfied and held that the deputy sheriff and probation officer violated C.A.'s Fourth Amendment rights.

C. Duty of State to Protect Child

DeShaney v. Winnebago Department of Social Services

489 U.S. 189, 109 S. Ct. 998, 103 L. Ed. 2d 249 (1989)

Chief Justice REHNQUIST delivered the opinion of the Court.

Petitioner is a boy who was beaten and permanently injured by his father, with whom he lived. Respondents are social workers and other local officials who received complaints that petitioner was being abused by his father and had reason to believe that this was the case, but nonetheless did not act to remove petitioner from his father's custody. Petitioner sued respondents claiming that their failure to act deprived him of his liberty in violation of the Due Process Clause of the Fourteenth Amendment to the United States Constitution. We hold that it did not.

I

The facts of this case are undeniably tragic. Petitioner Joshua DeShaney was born in 1979. In 1980, a Wyoming court granted his parents a divorce and awarded custody of Joshua to his father, Randy DeShaney. The father shortly thereafter moved to Winnebago County, Wisconsin, taking the infant Joshua with him. There he entered into a second marriage, which also ended in divorce.

The Winnebago County authorities first learned that Joshua DeShney might be a victim of child abuse in January 1982 when his father's second wife complained to the police, at the time of their divorce, that he had previously "hit the boy causing marks and [was] a prime case for child abuse." The Winnebago County Department of Social Services (DSS) interviewed the father, but he denied the accusations, and DSS did not pursue them further. In January 1983, Joshua was admitted to a local hospital with multiple bruises and abrasions. The examining physician suspected child abuse and notified DSS, which immediately obtained an order from a Wisconsin juvenile court placing Joshua in the temporary custody of the hospital. Three days later, the county convened an ad hoc "Child Protection Team" [which] decided that there was insufficient evidence of child abuse to retain Joshua in the custody of the court. The Team did, however, decide to recommend several measures to protect Joshua, including enrolling him in a preschool program, providing his father with certain counseling services, and encouraging his father's girlfriend to move out of the home. Randy DeShaney entered into a voluntary agreement with DSS in which he promised to cooperate with them in accomplishing these goals.

[T]he juvenile court dismissed the child protection case and returned Joshua to the custody of his father. A month later, emergency room personnel called the DSS caseworker handling Joshua's case to report that he had once again been treated for suspicious injuries. The caseworker concluded that there was no basis for action. For the next six months, the caseworker made monthly visits to the DeShaney home, during which she observed a number of suspicious injuries on Joshua's head; she also noticed that he had not been enrolled in school, and that the girlfriend had not moved out. The caseworker dutifully recorded these incidents in her files, along with her continuing suspicions that someone in the DeShaney household was physically abusing Joshua, but she did nothing more. In November 1983, the emergency room notified DSS that Joshua had been treated once again for injuries that they believed to be caused by child abuse. On the caseworker's next two visits to the DeShaney home, she was told that Joshua was too ill to see her. Still DSS took no action.

In March 1983 Randy DeShaney beat 4-year-old Joshua so severely that he fell into a life-threatening coma. Emergency brain surgery revealed a series of hemorrhages caused by traumatic injuries to the head inflicted over a long period of time. Joshua did not die, but he suffered brain damage so severe that he is expected to spend the rest of his life confined to an institution for the profoundly retarded. Randy DeShaney was subsequently tried and convicted of child abuse.

Joshua and his mother brought this action under 42 U.S.C. § 1983 in the United States District Court for the Eastern District of Wisconsin against respondents Winnebago County, DSS, and various individual employees of DSS.

The complaint alleged that respondents had deprived Joshua of his liberty without due process of law, in violation of his rights under the Fourteenth Amendment by failing to intervene to protect him against a risk of violence at his father's hand of which they knew or should have known. The District Court granted summary judgment for respondents.

The Court of Appeals for the Seventh Circuit affirmed, holding that petitioners had not made out an actionable § 1983 claim for two alternative reasons. First, the court held that the Due Process Clause of the Fourteenth Amendment does not require a state or local governmental entity to protect its citizens from "private violence, or other mishaps not attributable to the conduct of its employees." In so holding, the court specifically rejected the position endorsed by [courts in other circuits] that once the State learns that a particular child is in danger of abuse from third parties and actually undertakes to protect him from that danger, a "special relationship" arises between it and the child which imposes an affirmative constitutional duty to provide adequate protection. Second, the court held, in reliance on our decision in *Martinez v. California,* 444 U.S. 277, 285 (1980), that the causal connection between respondents' conduct and Joshua's injuries was too attenuated to establish a deprivation of constitutional rights actionable under § 1983. . . .

Because of the inconsistent approaches taken by the lower courts in determining when, if ever, the failure of a state or local governmental entity or its agents to provide an individual with adequate protective services constitutes a violation of the individual's due process rights, and the importance of the issue to the administration of state and local governments, we granted certiorari. We now affirm.

II

The Due Process Clause of the Fourteenth Amendment provides that "[n]o State shall . . . deprive any person of life, liberty, or property, without due process of law." Petitioners contend that the State deprived Joshua of his liberty interest in "free[dom] from . . . unjustified intrusions on personal security," *see Ingraham v. Wright*, 430 U.S. 651, 673 (1977), by failing to provide him with adequate protection against his father's violence. The claim is one invoking the substantive rather than the procedural component of the Due Process Clause; petitioners do not claim that the State denied Joshua protection without according him appropriate procedural safeguards, *see Morrissey v. Brewer,* 408 U.S. 471, 481 (1972), but that it was categorically obligated to protect him in these circumstances, *see Youngberg v. Romeo,* 457 U.S. 307, 309 (1982).

But nothing in the language of the Due Process Clause itself requires the State to protect the life, liberty, and property of its citizens against invasion by private actors. The Clause is phrased as a limitation on the State's power to act, not as a guarantee of certain minimal levels of safety and security. It forbids the State itself to deprive individuals of life, liberty, or property without "due process of law," but its language cannot fairly be extended to impose an affirmative obligation on the State to ensure that those interests do not come to harm through other means. . . . Its purpose [is] to protect the people from the State, not to ensure that the State protect[s] them from each other. . . .

Consistent with these principles, our cases have recognized that the Due Process Clauses generally confer no affirmative right to governmental aid, even where such aid may be necessary to secure life, liberty, or property interests of which the government itself may not deprive the individual. . . . If the Due Process Clause does not require the State to provide its citizens with particular protective services, it follows that the State cannot be held liable under the Clause for injuries that could have been averted had it chosen to provide them. As a general matter, then, we conclude that a State's failure to protect an individual against private violence simply does not constitute a violation of the Due Process Clause.

Petitioners contend, however, that even if the Due Process Clause imposes no affirmative obligation on the State to provide the general public with adequate protective services, such a duty may arise out of certain "special relationships" created or assumed by the State with respect to particular individuals. Petitioners argue that such a "special relationship" existed here because the State knew that Joshua faced a special danger of abuse at his father's hands and specifically proclaimed, by word and by deed, its intention to protect him against that danger. Having actually undertaken to protect Joshua from this danger . . . , the State acquired an affirmative "duty," enforceable through the Due Process Clause, to do so in a reasonably competent fashion. Its failure to discharge that duty, so the argument goes, was an abuse of governmental power [which] constitute[s] a substantive due process violation.

We reject this argument. It is true that in certain limited circumstances the Constitution imposes upon the State affirmative duties of care and protection with respect to particular individuals. In *Estelle v. Gamble,* 429 U.S. 97 (1976), we recognized that the Eighth Amendment's prohibition against cruel and unusual punishment, made applicable to the States through the Fourteenth Amendment's Due Process Clause, *Robinson v. California*, 370 U.S. 660 (1962), requires the State to provide adequate medical care to incarcerated prisoners. We reasoned that because the prisoner is unable "by reasons of the deprivation of his liberty [to] care for himself," it is only "just" that the State be required to care for him. *Id.* at 103-104, *quoting Spicer v. Williamson*, 191 N.C. 487, 490, 132 S.E. 291, 293 (1926).

In *Youngberg v. Romeo,* 457 U.S. 307 (1982), we extended this analysis beyond the Eighth Amendment setting, holding that the substantive component of the Fourteenth Amendment's Due Process Clause requires the State to provide involuntarily committed mental patients with such services as are necessary to ensure their "reasonable safety" from themselves and others. *Id.* at 314-325.

But these cases afford petitioners no help. Taken together, they stand only for the proposition that when the State takes a person into its custody and holds him there against his will, the Constitution imposes upon it a corresponding duty to assume some responsibility for his safety and general well-being. . . . In the substantive due process analysis, it is the State's affirmative act of restraining the individual's freedom to act on his own behalf—through incarceration, institutionalization, or other similar restraint of personal liberty—which is the "deprivation of liberty" triggering the protections of the Due

Process Clause, not its failure to act to protect his liberty interests against harms inflicted by other means.

The *Estelle-Youngberg* analysis simply has no applicability in the present case. Petitioners concede that the harms Joshua suffered occurred not while he was in the State's custody, but while he was in the custody of his natural father, who was in no sense a state actor.[9] While the State may have been aware of the dangers that Joshua faced in the free world, it played no part in their creation, nor did it do anything to render him any more vulnerable to them. That the State once took temporary custody of Joshua does not alter the analysis, for when it returned him to his father's custody, it placed him in no worse position than that in which he would have been had it not acted at all; the State does not become the permanent guarantor of an individual's safety by having once offered him shelter. Under these circumstances the State had no constitutional duty to protect Joshua.

It may well be that, by voluntarily undertaking to protect Joshua against a danger it concedely played no part in creating, the State acquired a duty under state tort law to provide him with adequate protection against that danger. But the claim here is based on the Due Process Clause of the Fourteenth Amendment, which, as we have said many times, does not transform every tort committed by a state actor into a constitutional violation. . . . Because . . . the State had no constitutional duty to protect Joshua against his father's violence, its failure to do so—though calamitous in hindsight—simply does not constitute a violation of the Due Process Clause.

. . . The most that can be said of the state functionaries in this case is that they stood by and did nothing when suspicious circumstances dictated a more active role for them. In defense of them it must also be said that had they moved too soon to take custody of the son away from the father, they would likely have been met with charges of improperly intruding into the parent-child relationship, charges based on the same Due Process Clause that forms the basis for the present charge of failure to provide adequate protection.

The people of Wisconsin may well prefer a system of liability which would place upon the State and its officials the responsibility for failure to act in situations such as the present one. They may create such a system, if they do not have it already, by changing the tort law of the state in accordance with the regular lawmaking process. But they should not have it thrust upon them by this Court's expansion of the Due Process Clause of the Fourteenth Amendment.

Affirmed.

---

[9] . . . Had the State by the affirmative exercise of its power removed Joshua from free society and placed him in a foster home operated by its agents, we might have a situation sufficiently analogous to incarceration or institutionalization to give rise to an affirmative duty to protect. Indeed, several Courts of Appeals have held, by analogy to *Estelle* and *Youngberg*, that the State may be held liable under the Due Process Clause for failing to protect children in foster homes from mistreatment at the hands of their foster parents. *See Doe v. New York City Dept. of Social Services,* 649 F.2d 134, 141-142 (CA2 1981), *after remand*, 709 F.2d 782, *cert. denied sub nom. Catholic Home Bureau v. Doe,* 646 U.S. 864 (1983); *Taylor ex rel. Walker v. Ledbetter,* 818 F.2d 791, 794-797 (CA11 1987) (en banc), *cert. pending Ledbetter v. Taylor,* No. 87-521. We express no view on the validity of this analogy, however, as it is not before us in the present case.

Justice BRENNAN, with whom Justice MARSHALL and Justice BLACKMUN join, dissenting.

"The most that can be said of the state functionaries in this case," the Court today concludes, "is that they stood by and did nothing when suspicious circumstances dictated a more active role for them." Because I believe that this description of respondents' conduct tells only part of the story and that, accordingly, the Constitution itself "dictated a more active role" for respondents in the circumstances presented here, I cannot agree that respondents had no constitutional duty to help Joshua DeShaney.

* * *

Wisconsin has established a chid-welfare system specifically designed to help children like Joshua. Wisconsin law places upon the local departments of social services such as respondent . . . a duty to investigate reported instances of child abuse. *See* Wis. Stat. § 48.981(3) (1987-1988). While other governmental bodies and private persons are largely responsible for the reporting of possible cases of child abuse, *see* § 48.981(2), Wisconsin law channels all such reports to the local departments of social services for evaluation and, if necessary, further action. § 48.981(3). Even when it is the sheriff's office or police department that receives a report of suspected child abuse, that report is referred to local social services departments for action, *see* § 48.981(3)(a). . . . In this way, Wisconsin law invites—indeed, directs—citizens and other governmental entities to depend on local departments of social services such as respondent to protect children from abuse.

The specific facts before us bear out this view of Wisconsin's system of protecting children. Each time someone voiced a suspicion that Joshua was being abused, that information was relayed to the Department for investigation and possible action. When Randy DeShaney's second wife told the police that he had "hit the boy causing marks and [was] a prime case for child abuse," the police referred her complaint to DSS. When, on three separate occasions, emergency room personnel noticed suspicious injuries on Joshua's body, they went to DSS with this information. When neighbors informed the police that they had seen or heard Joshua's father or his father's lover beating or otherwise abusing Joshua, the police brought these reports to the attention of DSS. And when [Joshua's social worker] through these reports and through her own observations in the course of nearly 20 visits to the DeShaney home, compiled growing evidence that Joshua was being abused, that information stayed within the Department—chronicled by the social worker in detail that seems almost eerie in light of her failure to act upon it. . . .

* * *

In these circumstances, a private citizen, or even a person working in a government agency other that DSS, would doubtless feel that her job was done as soon as she had reported her suspicions of child abuse to DSS. Through its child-welfare program, in other words, the State of Wisconsin has relieved ordinary citizens and governmental bodies other than the Department of any sense of obligation to do anything more than report their suspicions of child abuse to DSS. If DSS ignores or dismisses these suspicions, no one will step in to fill the gap. Wisconsin's child-protection program thus effectively confined Joshua DeShaney within the walls of Randy DeShaney's violent home until such time as DSS took action to remove him. Conceivably then, children like Joshua are made worse off by the existence of this program when the persons and entities charged with carrying it out fail to do their jobs.

It simply belies reality, therefore, to contend that the State "stood by and did nothing" with respect to Joshua. Through its child-protection program, the State actively intervened in Joshua's life and, by virtue of this intervention, acquired ever more certain knowledge that Joshua was in grave danger. . . .

* * *

As the Court today reminds us, "the Due Process Clause of the Fourteenth Amendment was intended to prevent government 'from abusing [its] power, or employing it as an instrument of oppression.'" My disagreement with the Court arises from its failure to see that inaction can be every bit as abusive of power as action, that oppression can result when a State undertakes a vital duty and then ignores it. Today's opinion construes the Due Process Clause to permit a State to displace private sources of protection and then, at the critical moment, to shrug its shoulders and turn away from the harm that it had promised to try to prevent. Because I cannot agree that our Constitution is indifferent to such indifference, I respectfully dissent.

[Justice BLACKMUN'S dissenting opinion is omitted.]

Nicini v. Morra

212 F.3d 798 (3d Cir. 2000)

SLOVITER, Circuit Judge.

I

FACTS

In February 1990, fifteen-year-old Anthony Nicini, Jr., was admitted to the John F. Kennedy Hospital's Crisis Center (JFK) after an apparent suicide attempt. DYFS became involved when JFK notified it of Nicini's allegations that his father had physically abused him. . . . DYFS also assigned caseworker Frank Cyrus to Nicini's case . . . . Nicini . . . left home after an argument with his mother. . . . DYFS received a call from the police . . . that Nicini had been located. . . . A DYFS case worker contacted Nicini's mother, who said she did not want Nicini to return home, and his father, who could not identify any relatives with whom Nicini could stay. Nicini's father came to DYFS to sign a foster care placement agreement.

* * *

Nicini ran to the home of Edward and Dolores Morra in Cherry Hill, New Jersey. Nicnini's older brother Danny had gone to school with their children and had stayed with them while experiencing similar family problems. On February

9, 1991, the police notified DYFS that they had located Nicini at the Morra home. . . .

* * *

Between February 9, 1991, and February 28, 1991, Cyrus visited Nicini twice at the Morra home. He also had telephone contacts with Nicini and the Morras. App. at 226. Cyrus's first visit was apparently on Monday, February 11, 1991. App. at 250 (expert report). It was Cyrus's overall impression that "everything was positive," App. at 226-27, and that everything "pointed toward Nicini doing well there and becoming stabilized and progressing . . .," App. at 228. Additionally, a counselor from an outreach center visited Nicini once a week at the Morra home. During that same time period, Cyrus performed a perpetrator ("PERP") check on the Morras, which would have revealed any criminal record of sexual abuse in the State of New Jersey, including any reports of such abuse to DYFS. The PERP check revealed nothing.

Cyrus interviewed the Morras during a home visit. He did not remember asking whether they had ever had any contact with any law enforcement agency but he recalled asking Edward Morra if anything would prevent him from becoming a foster parent, and Morra replied in the negative. On February 28, 1991, Nicini appeared at a hearing before the Honorable Vincent D. Segal in the Family Part of the Chancery Division of the Superior Court of New Jersey. . . . As a result of the hearing, Judge Segal sentenced Nicini to two years probation and also concluded that Nicini should remain with the Morras. . . .

* * *

When Judge Segal asked Nicini's mother for her comments, she stated as to the Morras:

> They have harbored my oldest son on several occasions when he had taken off . . . I don't know them personally, only—only what I had heard. My oldest daughter knows—goes to school with kids that are friends with Eric Morra, their son, which I believe is 16 of 17, and I've been told that he's into drugs. I don't know if it's true or not, but it's just what I've heard. I don't know, something just seems strange about these people, why they would—if they don't know Tony, why they would even take him in. App. at 158. Nicini's attorney suggested to the court, in light of these concerns, that Nicini "should also be monitored for drugs periodically and—and maybe something should be looked in with this Morra family, in light of what Mrs. Nicini had said. I think maybe a closer investigation on whether or not that's an appropriate placement. . . .

App. at 163.

* * *

Judge Segal ruled that Nicini would "come[] under the care and supervision" of DYFS, that he would remain with the Morras "for as long as [DYFS] thinks that's an appropriate placement," App. at 167, and that "under no circumstances is DYFS to return the boy to the home of his parents without the authority of the Court," App. at 169. Judge Segal specifically declined to order drug monitoring despite the request of Nicini's attorney because there was no indication that drugs were involved in the matter.

* * *

On March 15, 1991, four days after Cyrus sent the application to the Morras, Nicini fled the Morra home. He later told investigators that since the second or third day of his arrival there, Edward Morra had been providing him with drugs and alcohol and assaulting him sexually. Further investigation revealed that Edward Morra had been convicted in New York in 1975 for corrupting the morals of a minor and for distribution of controlled substances to minors. . . .

On May 19, 1995, Nicini filed suit in the United States District Court for the District of New Jersey against Edward Morra, the New Jersey Department of Human Services ("DHS"), DYFS, and Cyrus. Nicini alleged a substantive due process violation pursuant to 42 U.S.C. § 1983 and various state tort law violations. In particular, Nicini alleged that Cyrus "had actual and/or constructive knowledge" of objections by Nicini's parents that "awarding custody to defendant, Edward Morra, was inappropriate in that . . . [he] permitted illicit narcotic and alcoholic use by minors at this residence." App. at 136, 137. Nicini also alleged that Cyrus "failed to fully and properly investigate the background of Morra before [placing him] . . . in Morra's care"; and that Cyrus "had access to or could have requested an authorization from Morra to conduct a criminal record background check." App. at 137. Nicini further alleged that DHS and DYFS had a policy and practice that "no criminal background check would be conducted of voluntary guardians of children in the custody of defendants if the guardian was a resident of the State of New Jersey." App. at 140.

By order dated May 29, 1996, the District Court dismissed all claims against DHS, DYFS, and Cyrus in his official capacity based on Eleventh Amendment immunity. . . .

Nicini's claims against Edward Morra proceeded and, on February 11, 1998, the court granted Nicini's motion for a default judgment against Morra. The case was then referred to a Magistrate Judge to conduct a hearing to determine the amount of Nicini's damages. In an order dated March 6, 1998, the Magistrate Judge entered judgment by default against Morra and awarded Nicini $500,000 in compensatory and $500,00 in punitive damages. . . .

Nicini appealed from the order of March 6, 1998. . . .

To establish a claim under 42 U.S.C § 1983, a plaintiff must demonstrate a violation of a right protected by the Constitution or laws of the United States that was committed by a person acting under the color of state law. *See Kneipp v. Tedder*, 95 F. 2d 1199, 1204 (3d Cir. 1996). . . .

Nicini's section 1983 claim rests on the Due Process Clause of the Fourteenth Amendment. He invokes the substantive component of due process, which "protects individual liberty against 'certain government actions regardless of the fairness of the procedures used to implement them.'" *Collins v. City of Harker Heights, Tex.,* 503 U.S. 115, 125, 117 L. Ed. 2d 261, 112 S. Ct. 1061 (1992) (*Daniels v. Williams*, 474 U.S. 327, 331, 88 L. Ed. 2d 662, 106 S. Ct. 662 (1986)). Specifically, Nicini alleges that Cyrus, acting under color of state law, deprived him of "the right to be free from the infliction of unnecessary pain or abuse . . . and the fundamental right to physical safety." App. at 52 (Nicini's brief in opposition to summary judgment).

As a general proposition, a state's failure to protect an individual against private violence does not constitute a violation of due process. *DeShaney*, 489 U.S. at 202. Thus, in *Deshaney* the Court held that a child who was beaten so severely by his father that he suffered permanent brain damage did not have a claim against the state agency for violation of his substantive due process rights by failing to remove him from his father's custody although agency personnel had reason to know of the abuse. However, the Court recognized that "in certain limited circumstances the Constitution imposes upon the State affirmative duties of care and protection with respect to particular individuals." 489 U.S. at 198. As examples of situations in which the state has such a duty, the Court cited its decision in *Estelle v. Gamble*, 429 U.S. 97, 50 L. Ed. 2d 251, 97 S. Ct. 285 (1976), which held that the Eighth Amendment's prohibition against cruel and unusual punishment required the state "to provide adequate medical care to incarcerated prisoners" *DeShaney*, 489 U.S. at198, and *Youngberg v. Romeo*, 457 U.S. 307, 73 L. Ed. 2d 28, 102 S. Ct. 2452 (1982), which held that substantive due process "requires the State to provide involuntarily committed mental patients with such services as are necessary to ensure their 'reasonable safety' from themselves and others," *DeShaney*, 489 U.S. at 199 (citation omitted).

The state's affirmative "duty of care and protection," *id.* at 198, in those cases stemmed "not from the State's knowledge of the individual's predicament or from its expressions of intent to help him, but from the limitation which it has imposed on his freedom to act on his own behalf." *Id.* at 200. In holding that the state did not have such a "special relationship" with Joshua DeShaney, the Court explained that "while the state may have been aware of the dangers that Joshua faced in the free world, it played no part in their creation, nor did it do anything to render him any more vulnerable to them." *Id.* at 201. (footnote omitted)

Of particular significance to the matter before us, the Court also suggested that "had the State by the affirmative exercise of its power removed Joshua from free society and placed him in a foster home operated by its agents, we might have a situation sufficiently analogous to incarceration or institutionalization to give rise to an affirmative duty to protect." 489 U.S. at 201 n.9. The Court noted that several courts of appeals had already found such a duty in the foster care context but declined to comment on the merit of those decisions. *See id.* (citing *Doe v. New York City Dep't of Social Servs.,* 649 F.2d 134 (2d Cir. 1981); *Taylor v. Ledbetter,* 818 F.2d 791 (11th Cir. 1987) (en banc)).

After *DeShaney*, many of our sister Courts of Appeals held that foster children have a substantive due process right to be free from harm at the hands of state-regulated foster parents. *See, e.g., Lintz v. Skipski,* 25 F.3d 304. 305 (6th Cir. 1994); *Norfleet v. Arkansas Dep't of Human Servs.* 989 F. 2d 89, 293 (8th Cir. 1993); *Yvonne L. v. New Mexico Dep't of Human Servs.*, 959 F.2d 883, 891-93 (10th Cir. 1992); *K.H. v. Morgan,* 914 F.2d 846, 848-49 (7th Cir. 1990). These courts have accepted the analogy between persons the state places in foster care and those it incarcerates or institutionalizes. *See, e.g., K.H.*, 914 F.2d at 849 ("Once the state assumes custody of a person, it owes him a rudimentary duty of safekeeping. . . ."); *Yvonne L.*, 959 F.2d at 891-93 (discussing and approving cases imposing liability in foster care context).

We have suggested, although never directly held, that state actors owe a duty to children placed in foster care. In *D.R.*, 972 F.2d at 1368-73, we held that a public high school student who was allegedly sexually molested by other students during school hours could not maintain a claim against school officials based on a "special relationship" theory. We held that public high school students were not comparable to prisoners or the involuntarily committed because "parents remain the [students'] primary caretakers," *id.* at 1371, and because students "may turn to persons unrelated to the state for help on a daily basis," *id.* at 1372. We also noted that this court has principally read *DeShaney* as "setting out a test of physical custody." *Id.* at 1370. . . .

* * *

We find our discussion in *D.R.* and the numerous decisions of the other courts of appeals on this issue persuasive. Foster children, like the incarcerated or the involuntarily committed, are "placed . . . in a custodial environment . . . [and are] unable to seek alternative living arrangements." *Taylor v. Ledbetter,* 818 F.2d 791, 795 (11th Cir. 1987) (en banc). We now hold that when the state places a child in a state-reguated foster care, the state has entered into a special relationship with that child which imposes upon it certain affirmative duties. The failure to perform such duties can give rise, under sufficiently culpable circumstances, to liability under section 1983.

We recognize that the analogy between foster children on the one hand and prisoners and institutionalized persons on the other is incomplete. For example, foster children, especially older ones, enjoy a greater degree of freedom and are more likely to be able to take steps to ensure their own safety. Nonetheless, any distinctions between children placed in foster care and the prisoners at issue in *Estelle* or the institutionalized mentally retarded persons at issue in *Youngberg* are matters of degree rather than of kind. *See Norflet,* 989 F.2d at 292. . . .

We are aware that Nicini came to stay with the Morras on his own initiative and that the Morras were not officially approved by the state as either foster or para-foster parents. (footnote omitted)

However, Cyrus does not contest that Nicini was in DYFS custody throughout the relevant period. Furthermore, the record is replete with evidence that Nicini was substantially dependent upon DYFS and that DYFS acquiesced in Nicini's stay at the Morra home. At last by October 10, 1990, when Nicini's father signed a foster care placement agreement, DYFS was able to arrange for his foster placement. At some point, the Superior Court of New Jersey awarded custody of Nicini to DYFS and DHS. App. At 136. Nicini was thereafter placed on several occasions with DYFS-approved foster parents and with relatives. It also appears that after the police located Nicini at the Morra home and took him to JFK, DYFS returned him to their home over the objections of his aunt and his father. Under these facts, we believe Nicini's situation is sufficiently analogous to a foster care placement to fall within the "special relationship" exception to *DeShaney*.

* * *

Having established that Nicini has alleged a protected interest and a sufficient relationship with the sate to state a cause of action under section 1983, we turn to the District Court's determination that summary judgment was appropriate because Cyrus's actions did not amount to a violation of Nicini's constitutional rights. We must first determine what level of conduct is egregious enough to amount to a constitutional violation and, then, whether there is sufficient evidence that Cyrus's conduct rose to that level.

We begin with the decision in *Country of Sacramento v. Lewis,* 523 U.S. 833, 140 L. Ed. 2d 1043, 118 S. Ct. 1708 (1998), where the Supreme Court granted certiorari "to resolve a conflict among the Circuits over the standard of culpability on the part of a law enforcement officer for violating substantive due process in a pursuit case." *Id.* at 839. In *Lewis* , the Court emphasized that "'the touchstone of due process is protection of the individual against arbitrary action of government.'" *Lewis*, 523 U.S. at 845 (quoting *Wolff v. McDonnel,* 418 U.S. 539, 588, 41 L.Ed. 2d 935, 94 S. Ct. 2963 (1974)). It then noted that where the challenge is to executive rather than legislative action, "only the most egregious official conduct can be said to be 'arbitrary in the constitutional sense'" 523 U.S. at 846 (quoting *Collins v. Harker Heights*, 503 U.S. 115, 129, 117 L. Ed. 2d 261, 112 S. Ct. 1061 (1992)). . . . Under *Lewis*, substantive due process liability attaches only to executive action that is "so ill-conceived or malicious that it 'shocks the conscience.'" *Miller v. City of Philadelphia,* 174 F.3d 368,375 (3d Cir. 1999) (quoting *Lewis*, 523 U.S. at 846).

The "exact degree of wrongfulness necessary to reach the 'conscience-shocking level depends upon the circumstances of a particular case.'" *Id.* at 375. . . .

Lewis therefore makes clear that a plaintiff seeking to establish a constitutional violation must demonstrate that the official's conduct "shocks the conscience" in the particular setting in which that conduct occurred. In some circumstances, conduct that is deliberately indifferent will shock the conscience. Indeed, in the foster care context, most of the courts of appeals have applied the deliberate indifference standard, although they have defined that standard in slightly different ways. *See, e.g., White v. Chambliss*, 112 F.2d 731, 737 (4th Cir. 1997) (liability if defendant was "plainly placed on notice of a danger and chose to ignore the danger"); *Tayor*, 818 F.2d at 796 (foster child must show "actual knowledge of abuse or that agency personnel deliberately failed to learn what was occurring in the foster home"); *Doe v. New York City Dept. of Soc. Servs.*, 649 F.2d 134,145 (2d Cir. 1981) (deliberate indifference "cannot exist absent some knowledge triggering an affirmative duty to act. . . . Defendants may be held liable [for] . . . deliberate indifference to a known injury, a known risk, or a specific duty").

In *Miller,* we evaluated the actions of a social worker who after receiving allegations of abuse separated a child from her natural parent under a standard that "exceeded . . . deliberate indifference." *Miller*, 174 F.3d at 375. We held that the worker would be liable only if his conduct reached "a level of gross negligence or arbitrariness that indeed shocks the conscience." *Id.* at 375-76. (Quotation omitted). . . . .

In *Farmer v. Brennan,* 511 U.S. 825, 128 L. Ed. 2d 811, 114 S. Ct. 1970 (1994), the Court clarified the deliberate indifference standard applicable in suits challenging prison conditions under the Eighth Amendment. It adopted a subjective standard of liability consistent with recklessness as that term is defined in criminal law. . . .

This case does not require us to determine whether an official's failure to act in light of a risk of which the official should have known, as opposed to failure to act in light of an actually known risk, constitutes deliberately indifferent conduct in this setting. We will assume arguendo that Nicini's proposed standard of "should have known" is applicable. Nevertheless, as *Lewis* makes clear, the relevant inquiry is whether the defendant's conduct "shocks the conscience."

Under the circumstances of this case, we cannot agree that Cyrus's conduct meets that standard. To the contrary, we conclude that Cyrus's conduct in investigating the Morras amounted, at most, to negligence. For the same reason, we need not consider whether failure to perform a specific duty can ever amount to deliberate indifference, *see Taylor*, 818 F.2d at 797; *Doe,* 659 F.2d at 145, as there is no evidence that Cyrus failed to perform any required duty.

* * *

Notes

1. *DeShaney* left open the question of under what limited circumstances the Constitution imposes upon the state an affirmative duty of care and protection with respect to particular individuals. *Nicini* at 807 (quoting *DeShaney* at 1998). *Nicini* joined other federal circuits by holding that when the state places a child in state-regulated foster care, the state enters into a special relationship with the juvenile in which the state assumes an affirmative duty of care and protection. *Nicini* also held that for the state to be liable for placing a child in a potentially dangerous environment the state's actions must "shock the conscience" of the court. The *Nicini* court found that the state's actions did not shock the conscience of the court because the state did not act with deliberate indifference. *See County of Sacramento v. Lewis*, 523 U.S. 833 (1998).

2. One possible interpretation of the *DeShaney* holding is that the state is liable when it physically restrains a child. Accordingly, the state is not liable for injuries suffered by a child when someone independent of the government, such as the father in *DeShaney*, physically restrains a child. For further discussion of this interpretation, see Catherine S. Crosby-Currie & N. Dickon Reppucci, *The Missing Child in Child Protection: The Constitutional Context of Child Maltreatment From* Meyer *to* DeShaney, 21 LAW & POL'Y 129 (1999); Kristen L. Davenport, Note, *Due Process—Claims of Abused Children Against State Protective Agencies—The State's Responsibility After* DeShaney v. Winnebago County Department of Social Services, *489 U.S. 189 (1989),* 19 FLA. ST. U. L. REV. 243 (1991); Laura Oren, *The State's Failure to Protect Children and Substantive Due Process:* DeShaney *in Context*, 68 N.C. L. REV. 659 (1990); Kevin M. Ryan, *Stemming the Tide of Foster Care Runaways: A Due Process Perspective,* 42 CATH. U. L. REV. 271 (1993).

3. Professors Akhil Reed Amar and Daniel Widawsky argue that the Thirteenth Amendment (involuntary servitude) is an appropriate constitutional challenge in *DeShaney*-type situations. For a discussion, see Akil Reed Amar & Daniel Widawsky, *Child Abuse As Slavery: A Thirteenth Amendment Response to* DeShaney, 105 HARV. L. REV. 1359 (1992).

4. For further discussion of *DeShaney* and its progency, see Kristen L. Davenport, *Due Process—Claims of Abused children Against State Protective Agencies—The State's Responsiblity after* DeShaney v. Winnebago County Department of Social Services, *489 U.S. 189 (1989),* 19 FLA. ST. U. L. REV. 243 (1991); Breadan Marshall Douthett, *The Death of Constitutional Duty: The Court Reacts to the Expansion of Section 1983 Liability in* DeShaney v. Winnebago County Department of Social Services, 52 OHIO ST. L.J. 643 (1992); Roger J.R. Levesque & Alan J. Thomkins, *Revisioning Juvenile Justice: Implications of the New Child Protection Movement,* 48 WASH. U. J. URB. & CONTEMP. L. 87 (1995); Laura Oren, *The State's Failure to Protect Children and Substantive Due Process:* DeShaney *in Context,* 68; N.C .L. REV. 659 (1990); Amy Sinden, *In Search of Affirmative Duties Toward Children Under a Post-*DeShaney *Constitution,* 139 U. PA. L. REV. 227 (1990); Garret Smith, DeShaney v. Winnebago County, *The Narrowing Scope of Constitutional Torts,* 49 MD. L. REV. 484 (1990).

Questions

1. In *DeShaney*, the Court states that the Constitution protects children from state action rather than state inaction. What did the Court mean by this statement? Should states have an affirmative constitutional duty to protect children who are suspected victims of abuse or neglect but left in the care and custody of the alleged perpetrator?

2. Why is a child like Joshua DeShaney not treated like a mental health patient or a prisoner in terms of his deprivation of liberty?

Problem

Responding to a call of suspected neglect, a social worker for the State of Tennessee arrived at a home to find four children being "supervised" by a five-year-old boy. The social worker immediately took custody of all five children, including two-year-old Adrian. Upon investigation, the social worker discovered that Adrian's mother, who had legal custody of the child, was living in California and could not immediately return to Tennessee. The state took legal and physical custody of Adrian while attempting to find a suitable placement for him. After a hearing, the judge granted custody of Adrian to his father. Shortly thereafter, Adrian's mother returned from California and alerted social services that Adrian's father was abusive to her and the child, and accused the father of physically abusing Adrian while the child was in his care.

A few months later, the state took temporary custody of Adrian when the child was found to have numerous bruises on his body. However, no charges were filed, and Adrian was returned to his father three days later. The state received several reports that Adrian was being abused by his father over the next several months, but no action was taken. Finally, Adrian's father brought the child to the emergency room of the local hospital. The child had severe burns over much of his body and died the next day. Adrian's father is now serving a life sentence for killing Adrian by pouring boiling water on him.

Adrian's mother and Adrian's estate have filed suit against the state and its agents, claiming Adrian's rights (under 42 U.S.C. § 1983) had been violated and that Adrian was denied due process. The state has filed a motion for summary judgment, citing *DeShaney* for the proposition that, because Adrian was in his father's care at the time of his death, the state and its agents are relieved from any liability as a matter of law.

The plaintiffs claim that this case falls under an exception to *DeShaney,* the so-called danger-creation exception. They maintain that because state agents knew or should have known that the child would be in danger if placed in the custody of his father, the state is liable for the child's death. Further, the plaintiffs claim that this case differs from *DeShaney* in that the state had custody of Adrian before placing the child with his father, whereas in *DeShaney* the child was in his father's custody at all relevant times. This fact, they argue, supports liability on the part of the state for "creating a dangerous situation" by placing the child with someone they know or should have known might harm him. In their brief, the plaintiffs cite two Pennsylvania cases, both of which held that, where the state created danger to the child by placing him with a known abuser, the danger-creation exception applies and the protection of *DeShaney* is not available to the state.

You are a clerk for the judge who must rule on the summary judgement motion. She tells you that the cases cited by the plaintiffs were from different federal district courts in Pennsylvania and that the facts in those cases were nearly identical to the facts in this case. However, she also tells you that other jurisdictions have not been uniform in their response to similar situations. In fact, several courts have held that whenever a parent or other family member has physical custody of the child, the state can never be held liable for civil rights abuses if that parent abuses the child.

The judge tells you that she is inclined to rule against the state on the summary judgment motion, but she is not yet certain which way she will rule. She asks for your opinion on the validity of the plaintiff's argument and the defendants' counter argument. She also asks you to prepare a first draft of the court's order, pointing out the strengths and weaknesses of the positions taken by both sides and the reasons the motion should be granted or denied. (*See Currier v. Doran,* 23 F. Supp. 2d 1277 (D.N.M. 1998).)

Chapter 10

The Child Welfare Process

When there are allegations of dependency, abuse or neglect of a child, a family enters the child welfare process. The Fourteenth Amendment protects the parents during this process by the various guarantees of substantive and procedural process. In terms of procedural due process, parents are entitled to notice and an opportunity to be heard in a fundamentally fair proceeding. Parents continue to be entitled to due process as they encounter the various hearings in the child welfare system. *See Santosky v. Kramer*, 455 U.S. 745 (1982). Substantively, parents receive heightened protection against government interference when fundamental rights are involved. *See Washington v. Glucksberg*, 521 U.S. 702 (1997). The interest of parents in the care, custody, and control of their children may be the oldest fundamental liberty interest recognized by the Court; hence, it is guarded closely. The state, however, may interfere with this fundamental liberty interest due to its strong interest in the welfare of the child. The law attempts to balance the rights and interests of parents, children and the state. The two-part test that is used with fundamental rights demonstrates this balance. First, the state can regulate these fundamental rights only when there is a "compelling state interest," e.g., child protection. Second, the legislative enactments must be narrowly drawn to achieve the objective.

After an allegation of abuse or neglect is made, a state child welfare officer determines whether the child should be taken into protective custody. The intake official may remove a child from the custody of the parents when it is objectively reasonable to believe there is an imminent threat to the child's safety and there is insufficient time to obtain a court order. If an emergency situation does not exist, the state may not remove the child without judicial authorization, which may be ex parte or following a detention hearing, or by parental consent.

An initial hearing, and subsequently a factfinding hearing, occur before the court. At the initial hearing, the parent, custodian or guardian is informed of the allegations in the petition and is asked to admit or deny them. If necessary, a factfinding hearing follows. A court may choose one of three courses of action after hearing the facts of the case. First, a court may take protective custody of a child. A court will not take protective custody, however, unless there is an immediate risk of danger to the child. Many argue that it is in the best interests of a child to remain in the care of her biological family even when the parental care is minimal, because of a child's need for stability. Is this a proper justification for leaving a child in the home? A court's second option is to reunite the family on the condition that the parents follow the restrictions established by the court. These restrictions must be in accordance with due process and be limited to the means necessary for family reunification. The final option is to find the charges unfounded and reunite the family with no restrictions.

If the child is adjudicated to be in need of services, state law requires a permanency plan be prepared. The case plan must state what factors are used to determine the child's placement and what actions are necessary prior to the submission of the plan. The case plan must also account for the future. If the child is returned home, the plan must state the measures necessary to prevent the child from being harmed. If the child is not returned home, the plan must set out what services are to be completed in order for the child to return home.

Where is the child welfare process successful in protecting the best interests of the child? Where can the process be improved? Should the child welfare system have a role in prevention of abuse and neglect? Legislatures continue to make adjustments in their attempt to balance the parties interests and rights. In 1980, the Adoption Assistance and Child Welfare Act (AACWA) was passed, with the main goal of reunification of families. Recently, the Adoption and Safe Families Act of 1997 shifted the primary focus from reunification to the health and safety of the child. Under ASFA, the states were given financial incentives for successful adoptions, hence encouraging the termination of parental rights. While reading this chapter, please consider the arguments to support these respective priorities.

A. Emergency Removal of Children

1. Due Process

Tenenbaum v. Williams
193 F.3d 581 (2d Cir. 1999)

SACK, Circuit Judge:

The facts underlying this appeal are largely undisputed. Five-year-old Sarah Tenenbaum . . . slept while her class was being told a story and attendance was being taken. When she awoke, she was crying. Murphy asked Sarah why; Sarah did not respond. . . . When Murphy asked whether someone at home had hurt her, Sarah nodded "yes." . . . "When [Murphy] asked [Sarah] if her father was hurting her, her eyes welled up in tears and she shook her head, yes, and she started to really cry."

Later that day, Murphy talked to Sarah again and asked Sarah to indicate on a doll she was holding where Sarah was being hurt. Sarah pointed to the groin area of the doll. In order to make sure she was not misunderstanding Sarah, Murphy asked Sarah to indicate again where she was being hurt and Sarah again pointed to the doll's groin area. Murphy did not report the incident that day.

During the following day, Friday, January 5, according to Murphy, Sarah drew a picture of two figures. Murphy asked Sarah what was happening in the picture and Sarah said "Sarah and . . . Daddy kneeling, hurt," and then fell silent.

* * *

The department (Department of Social Services' Central Register of Child Abuse and Maltreatment) telecopied the Form 2221 to defendant Nat Williams, a supervisor in the child protective unit of the CWA in Brooklyn. . . .

Williams then met with a recently hired provisional caseworker, defendant Veronica James, and assigned her to the Sarah Tenenbaum case. . . . Williams issued explicit instructions to James not to raise the issue of sexual abuse.

That evening, James, accompanied by colleague Thomas O'Connell, who was sent along by Williams in case any male children might be involved, arrived unannounced at the Tenenbaum's home. James told the Tenenbaums that she and O'Connell were investigating a report that Sarah was developmentally delayed and was sleeping in school. In accordance with Williams' instructions, they did not mention the real reason they were there—the reports of possible sexual abuse.

* * *

James returned to her office and reported to Williams on her visit. Williams testified that after being told by James that Murphy had confirmed the information contained on the Form 2221 received Friday, he decided to wait for the call he expected from Mr. or Mrs. Tenenbaum. The call never came. The Tenenbaums, as already noted, deny that they had ever received any request to contact Williams. Neither did Williams call the Tenenbaums even though he knew how to reach them. . . .

Although CWA lawyers were on staff at Williams' and James' office, neither sought legal advice before removing Sarah from school and subjecting her to the examination. Neither Williams nor James made an attempt—indeed, no one considered making an attempt—to obtain parental consent for a physical examination of Sarah as provided by § 1021 of the New York Family Court Act,[5] and no one considered seeking a court order for her removal and examination under § 1022 of that Act[6] even though Williams understood that such an order could be obtained within a day.

* * *

Following Williams' instruction, James went to P.S. 230 on Tuesday, January 9 at about noon, without court or parental consent, and effected an "emergency" removal of Sarah for the purpose of determining whether she had been sexually abused. . . . James, by herself, took Sarah to the emergency room at Coney Island Hospital where, after several hours' delay, Sarah was examined by both a pediatrician and a gynecologist. The gynecological examination included the insertion of a cotton swab in Sarah's vagina and anus. No evidence of sexual abuse was discovered, although the hospital report stated that it could not be ruled out.

While James and Sarah were at the hospital, Williams contacted Mrs. Tenenbaum and told her that Sarah had been taken from school. Mrs. Tenenbaum telephoned her husband and both parents went to Williams' office. When they arrived, Williams confronted Mr. Tenenbaum for the first time with the sexual abuse charge. He heatedly denied it.

* * *

In January 1991, the Tenenbaums filed a complaint. The complaint alleged various constitutional and state-law violations by the defendants against the Tenenbaums in both their individual capacities and on behalf of Sarah.

The defendants moved for summary judgment and the Tenenbaums cross-moved for partial summary judgment. On September 30, 1994, the district court granted defendants' motion in part and denied it in part. . . .

---

5 Section 1021 of the New York Family Court Act provides that an authorized official may temporarily remove a child who is abused or neglected under the Act with the written consent of the child's parents or other person legally responsible for his or her care. *See* N.Y. Fam. Ct. Act § 1021.

6 Section 1022 provides that under certain circumstances the family court may enter an order directing the temporary removal of a child from the place where he or she is residing *See* N.Y. Fam. Ct. Act § 1022.

I. Procedural Due-Process Claims

The Due Process Clause of the Fourteenth Amendment provides that no State shall "deprive any person of life, liberty, or property, without due process of law." The Tenenbaums claim that they have a liberty interest in the care, management and custody of their daughter Sarah, and that her removal from school without their consent and without court authorization deprived them of that interest without due process of law. The district court disagreed, finding that reasonable grounds existed for Sarah's emergency removal. *Tenenbaum I,* 862 F. Supp. at 969-72. The court also found that even had the individual defendants violated plaintiffs' due-process rights, those defendants were entitled to qualified immunity because officials "of reasonable competence could disagree on whether [there was] probable cause" for Sarah's removal. *Id.* at 972 (internal quotation marks and citation omitted).

The Tenenbaums claim a similar liberty interest with respect to their daughter's subjection to a medical examination. The district court agreed. In contrast to its conclusion as to Sarah's removal, the court held that [the] defendants' actions violated the Tenenbaums' and Sarah's procedural due-process rights as a matter of law. It reasoned that whatever emergency may have existed at the time of Sarah's removal from school, it had abated by the time Sarah was at the hospital. Because there was no emergency, absent parental consent judicial authorization was required by the Due Process Clause. It had not been obtained. *Id.* at 972-73. The court nevertheless found that the individual defendants were entitled to qualified immunity on this claim too, and granted summary judgment to them on that basis. *Id.* at 973. The City, to which the qualified immunity defense does not apply, was held potentially liable on this claim and the court denied summary judgment as to it. *See id.* After the district court denied its motion for reargument, the City conceded that the actions of the CWA caseworkers were taken pursuant to City policy. *See Tenenbaum III,* at 2-3. A damage trial followed and the court awarded the plaintiffs and Sarah damages on this claim. *See Tenenbaum III,* at 7-12.

On appeal, the Tenenbaums contend that the district court erred when it granted summary judgment for the defendants on the Tenenbaums' claim that, aside from the medical examination, Sarah's removal from school violated their and Sarah's due-process rights. They also challenge the district court's finding that qualified immunity shields the individual defendants from liability. For its part, the City asserts that the district court erred in holding that the medical examination violated the plaintiffs' due-process rights. The Tenenbaums argue that this aspect of the court's decision was correct, but insist that the individual defendants are not entitled to qualified immunity as to this claim.

This Court reviews the district court's grant of summary judgment de novo, *see Marguitre v. Citicorp Retail Servs., Inc.,* 147 F.3d 232, 235 (2d Cir. 1998), and we construe the evidence in the light most favorable to the non-moving party. *See Anderson v. Liberty Lobby, Inc.*, 477 U.S. 242, 255, 91 L. Ed. 2d 202, 106 S. Ct. 2505 (1986). We well affirm the decision only if the record indicates that "there is no genuine issue as to any material fact and that the moving party is entitled to a judgment as a matter of law." Fed. R. Civ. P. 56(c). "A dispute regarding a material fact is genuine 'if the evidence is such that a reasonable jury could return a verdict for the nonmoving party.'" *Stuart v. American Cyanamid Co.,* 158 F.2d 622, 626 (2d Cir. 1998) (quoting Anderson, 477 U.S. at 258), *cert. denied,* 153 L. Ed. 2d 543, 119 S. Ct. 1456 (1999).

"Choices about marriage, family life, and the upbringing of children are among associational rights [the Supreme] Court has ranked as 'of basic importance in our society,' . . . rights sheltered by the Fourteenth Amendment against the State's unwarranted usurpation, disregard, or disrespect." *M.L.B. v. S.L.J.,* 519 U.S. 102, 116, 117 S. Ct. 555, 136 L. Ed 2d 473 (1996).

At the same time, however, the state has a profound interest in the welfare of the child, particularly his or her being sheltered from abuse. In "'emergency' circumstances," *Hurlman,* 927 F.2d at 80 (citing *Robison,* 821 F.2d at 921), a child may be taken into custody by a responsible state official without court authorization or parental consent. "Emergency circumstances mean circumstances in which the child is immediately threatened with harm." *Id.* (citing *Robison,* 821 F.2d at 922). "The mere 'possibility' of danger" is not enough. 927 F.2d at 81. . . . The law thus seeks to strike a balance among the rights and interest of parents, children, and the State. *See Hollingsworth v. Hill,* 110 F.2d 733, 739 (10th Cir. 1997); *Robison,* 821 F.2d at 920.

. . . The district court found that Williams, who ordered Sarah's removal, had probable cause, i.e., an objectively reasonable basis, to believe emergency circumstances existed because "the substance of what the child communicated to Murphy . . . is essentially uncontroverted, viz. that Sarah's father hurt her through contact with her vaginal area at night." *Id.* This was enough to satisfy the district court that as a mater of law there were emergency circumstances that permitted Sarah's removal from school for a physical examination without a court order. *See id.* at 971. We disagree.

While "there is a sufficient emergency to warrant officials' taking [a child into] custody without a prior hearing if [he or she] is immediately threatened with harm," *Robison,* 821 F.2d at 922 (citation omitted), the converse is also true. If the danger to the child is not so imminent that there is reasonably sufficient time to seek prior judicial authorization, . . . then the circumstances are not emergent; there is no reason to excuse the absence of the judiciary's participation in depriving the parents of the care, custody and management of their child. If, irrespective of whether there is time to obtain a court order, all interventions are effected on an "emergency" basis without judicial process, pre-seizure procedural due process for the parents and their child evaporates.

. . . The evidence suggests that the purpose of removing Sarah from school was not to sweep Sarah out of harm's way but rather "to rule out [the possibility that Sarah had been] sexually abused." Based on those facts and the others recited in detail above, a properly instructed jury could conclude that at the time the caseworkers decided to remove Sarah, there was reasonably sufficient time, entirely consistent with Sarah's safety, to seek a court order. If there was reasonably sufficient time, there was no emergency. A jury could find that use of emergency, extra-judicial procedures was an infringement of the Tenenbaums' and Sarah's procedural due-process rights.

Because we now hold that it is unconstitutional for state officials to effect a child's removal on an "emergency" basis where there is reasonable time safely to obtain judicial authorization consistent with the child's safety, caseworkers can no longer claim, as did the defendants here, that they are immune from liability for such actions because the law is not "clearly established." But there remains substantial protection for caseworkers under the second prong of the qualified immunity test, so long as it is "objectively reasonable [for them] to believe that [their] acts [do] not violate these clearly established rights." *Young,* 160 F.2d at 903. "The objective reasonableness test is met—and the defendant is entitled to immunity—'if officers of reasonable competence could disagree' on the legality of the defendant's actions." *Lennon v. Miller,* 66 F.2d 416, 410 (2d Cir. 1995)(quoting *Malley v. Briggs,* 475 U.S. 336, 341, 89 L. Ed. 2d 271, 106 S. Ct. 1092 (1986)). We continue to recognize such protection to be essential.

* * *

II. Substantive Due-Process Claims

The Tenenbaums also contend that Sarah's temporary removal for the purpose of subjecting her to a medical examination violated their and Sarah's substantive due-process rights. The district court granted the defendants' motion for summary judgment on this claim, finding that "defendants' deprivation of the Tenenbaums of their child for a single afternoon for a medical examination did not significantly infringe their fundamental right to live together without interference from the state." *Tenenbaum I,* 862 F. Supp. at 969. We agree with the district court's conclusion, although we affirm its grant of summary judgment as to the claim brought on Sarah's behalf on different grounds.

The Tenenbaums and their family have, in general terms, a substantive right under the Due Process Clause "to remain together without the coercive interference of the awesome power of the state." *Duchesne,* 566 F. 2d at 825. We could agree with the Tenenbaums that this right was violated by the defendants in this case only if we were to conclude that the removal of Sarah for several hours under these circumstances would have been prohibited by the Constitution even had the Tenenbaums been given all the procedural protections to which they were entitled. *See Daniels v. Williams,* 474 U.S. 327, 331, 88 L. Ed. 2d 662, 106 S. Ct. 662 (1986)(substantive due-process rights bar "certain government actions regardless of the fairness of the procedures used to implement them."). The substantive rights arising out of the Due Process Clause are not so broad.

* * *

. . . It does not follow from the principle that brief seizures of people may be unreasonable and therefore violate the Fourth Amendment that brief removals of children from their parents to protect them from abuse are "without any reasonable justification in the service of a legitimate governmental objective," *County of Sacramento,* 523 U.S. at 846, under the Due Process clause. The district court properly granted summary judgment for all the defendants on this claim.

III. Fourth Amendment Claims

* * *

Sarah was taken by a government official from her school to a hospital where she was required to remain for several hours before being examined and returned to her parents. We agree with the district court that this constituted a "seizure" under the Fourth Amendment. *Cf. Graham,* 490 U.S. at 395 n.10 ("A 'seizure', triggering the Fourth Amendment 's protections occurs . . . when government actors have, 'by means of physical force or show of authority . . . in some way restrained the liberty of a citizen.'"); *Gardiner,* 50 F.2d at 155 (an individual is seized if, under the circumstances presented, "a reasonable person would have believed he was not free to leave.")(internal quotation marks and citations omitted).

* * *

There is a threshold issue, as the district court recognized. Does the ordinary probable-cause standard applicable to, among others, law enforcement officials making warrantless arrests also apply to caseworkers seizing children without prior court authorization? Although all agencies of government are governed by the unreasonable searches and seizures provision of the Fourth Amendment, there are some agencies outside the realm of criminal law enforcement where government officials have "special needs beyond the normal need for law enforcement [that] make the warrant and probable-cause requirement impracticable." *O'Connor v. Ortega,* 480 U.S. 709, 720, 94 L. Ed. 2d 714, 107 S. Ct. 1492 (1987) (plurality opinion) (internal quotation marks and citation omitted); *see also id.* at 732 (Scalia, J., concurring). If forcing a non law-enforcement government officer to follow ordinary law-enforcement requirements under the Fourth Amendment would impose intolerable burdens on the officer or the courts, would prevent the officer from taking necessary action or tend to render action ineffective, the government officer may be relieved of those requirements and subjected to less stringent reasonableness requirements instead. *See O'Connor,* 480 U.S. at 720; *see also, e.g., T.L.O.,* 469 U.S. at 340-43 (school administrator's search of a student's purse was not subject to the warrant and probable cause requirements).

Case law in other circuits indicates that emergency removal of a child by caseworkers is not such a "special needs" situation.

But we refrain from deciding categorically, as did the district court, that the removal of a child of whom abuse is suspected is not a "special needs" situation. There may be circumstances in which the law of warrant and probable cause established in the criminal setting does not work effectively in the child removal or child examination context. This is not such a case.

* * *

Whatever Fourth Amendment analysis is employed, then, it results in a test for present purposes similar to the procedural due-process standard. If information possessed by Williams or James warranted a person of reasonable caution in the belief that Sarah was subject to the danger of abuse if not removed from school before court authorization reasonably could be obtained, Sarah's removal complied with Fourth Amendment requirements despite the absence of a warrant equivalent because probable cause, reasonable cause, and exigent circumstances sufficient to justify it existed. A jury could reasonably conclude that the case here was otherwise. We reverse the district court's grant of summary judgment against Sarah on her Fourth Amendment removal claim.

* * *

In sum we, find that, with respect to Sarah's removal from school by the CWA, the district court erred in concluding as a matter of law that the Tenenbaums' and Sarah's procedural due-process rights and Sarah's Fourth Amendment rights were not infringed as a matter of law, and remand those claims to the district court for further proceedings. We conclude, however, that (1) the district court was correct in deciding that the defendants did not violate the Tenenbaums' or Sarah's substantive due-process rights as a matter of law; (2) with respect to Sarah's physical examination, the district court was correct in deciding that the Tenenbaums' and Sarah's procedural due-process rights and Sarah's Fourth Amendment rights were infringed; and (3) with respect to all the assertions of constitutional violations, the district court was correct in deciding that the individual defendants are entitled to qualified immunity. We also affirm the district court's assessment of damages with respect to Sarah's physical examinations and its dismissal of the Tenenbaums' state-law claims.

[The concurring and dissenting opinions are omitted]

Notes

1. Recognizing the importance of family privacy and a parent's liberty interest in the parent-child relationship, the *Tenenbaum* court ruled that a child can be temporarily removed from his or her parents without parental consent or without a court order only in an emergency situation. An emergency can be defined as an imminent threat of safety (*see Hurlman v. Rice*, 927 F.2d 74 (2d Cir. 1991); *Sims v. State Department of Public Welfare,* 438 F. Supp. 1179, 1192 (S.D. Tex. 1977)), or where there is evidence of continual abuse and an official fears imminent recurrence (*see Lossman v. Pekarski*, 707 F.2d 288 (7th Cir. 1983)). While emergency circumstances may lead to acceptable deprivation of the parents' and children's due process rights, the emergency does not eliminate the need for notice to the court or appropriate agency. *See Boddie v. Connecticut,* 401 U.S. 371, 379 (1971).

2. Because of the emphasis courts have placed on family privacy and parental control of children, it should come as no surprise that laws allowing the temporary removal of children in an emergency situation without parental consent must be reasonably specific to avoid vagueness problems. The American Bar Association Standard § 4.1 is a model statute for the temporary removal of children in an emergency situation without parental consent.

IJA-ABA Juvenile Justice Standards
Authorized Emergency Custody of Endangered Child
§ 4.1 (1980)*

Any physician, police or law enforcement official, or agent or employee of an agency designated pursuant to Standard 4.1C should be authorized to take physical custody of a child, not-withstanding the

* Reprinted with permission.

wishes of the child's parents or other such caretakers, if the physician, official, or agent or employee has probable cause to believe such custody is necessary to prevent the child's imminent death or serious bodily injury and that the child's parents or other such caretakers are unable or unwilling to protect the child from such imminent death or injury; . . .

Commentary:

* * *

Standard 4.1A sets four important limitations on taking of emergency custody of an endangered child:

1. Removal or retentive action is authorized only by specific personnel.
2. Emergency removal is limited to situations of imminent danger of death or serious injury where there is no time to take steps seeking a court order.
3. An individual taking emergency custody is required to immediately contact and turn custody over to an agency authorized to handle such cases.
4. Where the child's danger is the result solely of his/her being unattended, removal is not to be effected until the alternative course of sending an agency caretaker into the home has been tried, and the parent has not returned and the time lapse indicates that he/she does not intend to return.

For state statutes that allow designated personnel to take temporary custody of a child in an emergency situation without parental consent, see TEX. FAM. CODE ANN. § 39.401(1)(3) (West 1996); KY. REV. STAT. ANN. § 620.060 (West 2000). For further discussion of vagueness attacks on such laws, see *Los Angeles County Department of Children's Services v. Superior Court,* 246 Cal. Rptr. 150 (Ct. App. 1988); *E.P. v. District Court of Garfield County*, 696 P.2d 254 (Colo. 1985); *In re Juvenile Appeal (83-CD),* 455 A.2d 1313 (Conn. 1983); *In re J.M.,* 524 N.E.2d 1241 (Ill. App. Ct. 1998); *In re Jordan,* 616 N.E.2d 920 (Ind. Ct. App. 1993); *Stremski v. Owens*, 734 P.2d 1152 (Kan. 1987); *In re Vanessa C.,* 656 A.2d 795 (Md. Ct. Spec. App. 1995); *Peery v. Hanley,* 897 P.2d 1189 (Or. Ct. App. 1995); *Laramire v. Hysong,* 808 P.2d 199 (Wyo. 1991).

3. In *P.K. v. Polk County*, 2000 WL 1593391, *1 (Iowa Ct. App. Oct 25, 2000), the court held that a state worker must swear or affirm abuse or neglect allegations as required by the Fourth Amendment when making an ex parte court application to remove a child from home. Noting that the United States Supreme Court has held that the Fourth Amendment does apply to searches in civil cases, *P.K.* stated that the Fourth Amendment must be satisfied when state officials temporarily remove a child for purposes such as examining the child for suspected abuse or neglect. According to *P.K.*, state officials must meet the Fourth Amendment's probably cause standard for warrants when none of the amendments exceptions exist.

4. The Vienna Convention on Consular Relations (VCCR) requires an agency that removes a foreign national (any child who is not a U.S. citizen) to notify the consular post that represents the child's home country. According to Article 37(b) of the VCCR, "[i]f the relevant information is available," authorities have a duty to "inform the competent consular post without delay of any case where the appointment appears to be in the interest of the minor . . . who is a national of the sending state." If the foreign national is taken into custody for abuse, neglect, or abandonment, the child protection service agency or agency attorney has the primary responsibility for giving notice to the appropriate consular officer. For cases involving the application of Article 37(b), see *In re L.A.M.*, 996 P.2d 839 (Kan. 2000) (notice from the minor's aunt's attorney to the Mexican consulate is sufficient); *E.R. v. Marion County Office of Family and Children*, 729 N.E.2d 1052 (Ind. Ct. App. 2000) (purpose of treaty fulfilled and technical violation of notice provision warrants no relief where father of removed children contacted Mexican consulate); *Arteaga v. Texas Dep't of Protective and Regulatory Services*, 924 S.W.2d 756 (Tex. App. Ct. 1996) (claim that termination of parental rights was void for failure to notify the Mexican consulate rejected where state contacted consulate); *In re Stephanie M.*, 867 P.2d 706 (Cal. 1994) (failure to notify Mexican consulate neither deprives a court of jurisdiction nor supports a due process claim). For further discussion of Article 37(b), see Pamela Kemp Parker, *When a Foreign Child Comes into Care, Ask: Has the Consul Been Notified?*, 19 CHILD L. PRAC. 177 (Feb. 2001).

Questions

1. What problems may arise when relying on a statement given by a child to establish probable cause?

2. In light of *Tenenbaum*, what are the due process implications of an intake officer removing a minor child from class at school to conduct a ten-minute interview? What if the child were taken to the school nurse and examined for physical signs of sexual abuse?

2. Detention Hearing

Washington Revised Code Annotated

§ 13.40.050 (West Supp. 2001)

§ 13.40.050. Detention procedures—Notice of hearing—Conditions of release—Consultation with parent, guardian, or custodian

(1) When a juvenile taken into custody is held in detention:

(a) An information, a community supervision modification or termination of diversion petition, or a parole modification petition shall be filed within seventy-two hours, Saturdays, Sundays, and holidays excluded, or the juvenile shall be released; and

(b) A detention hearing, a community supervision modification or termination of diversion petition, or a parole modification petition shall be held within seventy-two hours, Saturdays, Sundays, and holidays excluded, from the time of filing the information or petition, to determine whether continued detention is necessary under RCW 13.40.040.

(2) Notice of the detention hearing, stating the time, place, and purpose of the hearing, stating the right to counsel, and requiring attendance shall be given to the parent, guardian, or custodian if such person can be found and shall also be given to the juvenile if over twelve years of age.

(3) At the commencement of the detention hearing, the court shall advise the parties of their rights under this chapter and shall appoint counsel as specified in this chapter.

(4) The court shall, based upon the allegations in the information, determine whether the case is properly before it or whether the case should be treated as a diversion case under RCW 13.40.080. If the case is not properly before the court the juvenile shall be ordered released.

(5) Notwithstanding a determination that the case is properly before the court and that probable cause exists, a juvenile shall at the detention hearing be ordered released on the juvenile's personal recognizance pending further hearing unless the court finds detention is necessary under RCW 13.40.040.

(6) If detention is not necessary under RCW 13.40.040, the court shall impose the most appropriate of the following conditions or, if necessary, any combination of the following conditions:

(a) Place the juvenile in the custody of a designated person agreeing to supervise such juvenile;

(b) Place restrictions on the travel of the juvenile during the period of release;

(c) Require the juvenile to report regularly to and remain under the supervision of the juvenile court;

(d) Impose any condition other than detention deemed reasonably necessary to assure appearance as required;

(e) Require that the juvenile return to detention during specified hours; or

(f) Require the juvenile to post a probation bond set by the court under terms and conditions as provided in RCW 13.40.040(4).

(7) A juvenile may be released only to a responsible adult or the department.

(8) If the parent, guardian, or custodian of the juvenile in detention is available, the court shall consult with them prior to a determination to further detain or release the juvenile or treat the case as a diversion case under RCW 13.40.080.

* * *

3. Reasonable Efforts to Reunify

The Adoption Assistance and Child Welfare Act of 1980, Pub. L. No. 96 272, 94 Stat. 500 (codified in scattered sections of 42 U.S.C.), established a reasonable efforts requirement regarding the removal of children from their homes. Section 471(a)(15) of the Act (42 U.S.C. § 671(a)(15)) reads as follows:

> (a) In order for the State to be eligible for payments [for foster care and adoption assistance from the Federal government], it shall have a plan approved by the Secretary which—
>
> * * *
>
> (15) . . . provides that, in each case, reasonable efforts will be made (A) prior to the placement of a child in foster care to prevent or eliminate the need for removal of the child from his home, and (B) to make it possible for the child to return to his home. . . .

These reasonable efforts requirements were clarified and expanded under the Adoption and Safe Families Act of 1997, Pub. L. No. 105-89, 111 Stat. 2116, the relevant portions of which are reprinted below.

Title I—Reasonable Efforts and Safety Requirements for Foster Care and Adoption Placements

Sec. 101. Clarification of the Reasonable Efforts Requirement.

(A) In General.—Section 471(a)(15) of the Social Security Act (42 U.S.C. § 671(a)(15)) is amended to read as follows:

(15) provides that—

(A) in determining reasonable efforts to be made with respect to a child, as described in this paragraph, and in making such reasonable efforts, the child's health and safety shall be the paramount concern;

(B) except as provided in subparagraph (D), reasonable efforts shall be made to preserve and reunify families—

(i) prior to the placement of a child in foster care, to prevent or eliminate the need for removing the child from the child's home; and

(ii) to make it possible for a child to safely return to the child's home;

(C) if continuation of reasonable efforts of the type described in subparagraph (B) is determined to be inconsistent with the permanency plan for the child, reasonable efforts shall be made to place the child in a timely manner in accordance with the permanency plan, and to complete whatever steps are necessary to finalize the permanent placement of the child;

(D) reasonable efforts of the type described in subparagraph (B) shall not be required to be made with respect to a parent of a child if a court of competent jurisdiction has determined that—

(i) the parent has subjected the child to aggravated circumstances (as defined in State law, which definition may include but need not be limited to abandonment, torture, chronic abuse, and sexual abuse);

(ii) the parent has—

(I) committed murder (which would have been an offense under section 1111(a) of Title 18, if the offense had occurred in the special maritime or territorial jurisdiction of the United States) of another child of the parent;

(II) committed voluntary manslaughter (which would have been an offense under section 1112(a) of Title 18, if the offense had occurred in the special maritime or territorial jurisdiction of the United States) of another child of the parent;

(III) aided or abetted, attempted, conspired, or solicited to commit such a murder or such a voluntary manslaughter; or

(IV) committed a felony assault that results in serious bodily injury to the child or another child of the parent; or

(iii) the parental rights of the parent to a sibling have been terminated involuntarily;

(E) if reasonable efforts of the type described in subparagraph (B) are not made with respect to a child as a result of a determination made by a court of competent jurisdiction in accordance with subparagraph (D)—

(i) a permanency hearing (as described in section 675(5)(C)) shall be held for the child within 30 days after the determination; and

(ii) reasonable efforts shall be made to place the child in a timely manner in accordance with the permanency plan, and to complete whatever steps are necessary to finalize the permanent placement of the child; and

(F) reasonable efforts to place a child for adoption or with a legal guardian may be made concurrently with reasonable efforts of the type described in subparagraph (B).

Notes

1. The number of children placed in foster care increased from 8,000 in 1970 to over 100,000 in 1980, an increase of 1200%. Staff of House Comm. on Ways and Means, 103d Cong., Overview of Entitlement Programs: 1994 Green Book, H.R. DOC. No. 103-27, at 639 (1994). The Adoption Assistance and Child Welfare Act of 1980 (AACWA) was passed by Congress in response to a growing national concern that states focused too much on placing children with foster parents. AACWA created the "reasonable efforts" standard in an effort to curb the number of foster care placements. In order for states to receive federal matching funds, states were required to use "reasonable efforts" to keep families together.

As the number of children placed in foster care decreased, the number of children returned to at risk environments increased, resulting in an increase in child abuse and neglect deaths. In 1995, 1248 children died as a result of abuse or neglect. National Committee to Prevent Child Abuse, Statistical Abstract 55 (1996). In an effort to follow the mandate of keeping families together, states often went too far in avoiding removal, even when removal was necessary to preserve the child's well-being.

In response to national criticism about children not being removed from dangerous homes when necessary, Congress passed the Adoption and Safe Families Act of 1997 (ASFA). ASFA attempted to define reasonable efforts to encourage the removal of children from at risk homes. On January 25, 2000, the U.S. Department of Health and Human Services (HHS) published final regulations of ASFA. Those regulations clarify and expand on the federal statute. *See* Debra Ratterman Baker, *The New Federal Regulations on ASFA*, 19 CHILD L. PRAC. 53 (2000), for a summary of the HHS regulations. For further discussion of the policy goals and shortcomings of AACWA and ASFA, see David J. Herring, *The Adoption and Safe Families Act—Hope and Its Subversion*, 34 FAM. L.Q. 329 (2000).

2. One criticism of ASFA is that it lists exceptions where a determination of reasonable efforts to keep a family together are not required. The fear is that ASFA goes too far in its efforts to protect the chldren and infringes on the parents' rights. If reasonable efforts are no longer necessary, then reunification is not possible in these cases. The question is whether this is always in the best interests of the child. *See generally* Shawn L. Raymond, Note, *Where Are the Reasonable Efforts to Enforce the Reasonable Efforts Requirement?: Monitoring State Compliance Under the Adoption Assistance and Child Welfare Act of 1980,* 77 TEX. L. REV. 1235 (1999); Christine H. Kim, Note, *Putting the Reason Back Into the Reasonable Efforts Requirement In Child Abuse and Neglect Cases,* 1999 U. ILL. L. REV. 287 (1999); Ernestine Steward Gray, *The Adoption and Safe Families Act of 1997*, 46 LA. B.J. 477 (1999).

3. For a review of various state laws concerning reasonable efforts in child welfare cases, see ALA. CODE § 12-15-65 (Lexis Supp. 2000); ALASKA STAT. § 47.10.086 (Lexis 2000); ARIZ. REV. STAT. ANN. § 8-871 (West Supp. 2000); ARK. CODE ANN. § 9-9-201 (Michie Supp. 2001); CAL. WELF. & INST. CODE § 361 (West 1998); COLO. REV. STAT. § 19-3-604 (2000); FLA. STAT. ANN. § 39.704 (West Supp. 2001); 705 ILL. COMP. STAT. ANN. 405/2-13.1 (West 1999); IND. CODE ANN. § 31-34-21-5.6 (Lexis Supp. 2000); IOWA CODE ANN. § 232.116 (West 2000); KAN. STAT. ANN. § 59-2136 (West 1994); LA. REV. STAT. ANN. Ch. C. § 682 (West Supp. 2001); MASS. GEN. LAWS ANN. ch. 119, § 29C (Lexis Supp. 2001); MICH. COMP. LAWS ANN. § 712A.18f (West Supp. 2001); MINN. STAT. ANN. § 260.012 (West Supp. 2001); NEB. REV. STAT. § 43-283.01 (1998); NEV. REV. STAT. § 432B.393 (1999); N.H. REV. STAT. ANN. § 169-C:24-a (Lexis Supp. 2000); N.J. STAT. ANN. § 30:4C-11.3 (West Supp. 2001); N.C. GEN. STAT. § 7B-507 (Lexis 1999); N.D. CENT. CODE § 27-20-32.2 (Lexis Supp. 1999); OHIO REV. CODE ANN. § 2151.419 (Anderson Supp. 2000); 42 PA. CONS. STAT. ANN. § 6351 (West 2000); S.C. CODE ANN. § 20-7-763 (West Supp. 2000); S.D. CODIFIED LAWS § 26-8A-26 (Lexis Supp. 2001); TEX. FAM. CODE ANN. § 262.201 (West Supp. 2001).

Questions

1. Should states make reasonable efforts to provide reunification services to parents with serious physical disabilities which may hamper their ability to care for their children? What about for mentally ill parents? *See* Krista Gallager, Note, *Parents in Distress: A State's Duty to Provide Reunification Services to Mentally Ill Parents*, 38 FAM. & CONCILIATION CTS. REV. 234 (2000).

2. According to ASFA, states may not have to use reasonable efforts to reunite a family if "aggravating circumstances" exist. What are the problems with this standard?

Problem

Child welfare intake officials receive a mid-November report from the police concerning the Bowman home. The caseworker arrives at 814 North Main Street at 6:30 p.m. to find the police officer and two minor children, ages nine and seven, alone in the home. The children are huddled next to an electric space heater in the living room. The home is heated by gas which has been turned off. The home is otherwise in reasonable living condition. The children report that their grandmother lives "down the street," their mother has been gone for several hours and they are hungry. The caseworker removes the children from the home and places them in foster care. At the detention hearing, counsel for the mother submits a motion to return the children to the home, stating that the state failed to fulfill its statutory duty to make reasonable efforts to avoid removal and violated the mother's constitutional rights. How should the state respond to the mother's arguments?

B. Initial Hearing

1. Superseding Public Law Jurisdiction

Alexander v. Cole

697 N.E.2d 80 (Ind. Ct. App. 1998)

STATON, Judge

Daryl Alexander appeals the denial of his motion for relief from an order transferring legal custody of his two minor children to their mother, Kimberly D. (Alexander) Cole. Daryl raises two related issues which we consolidate and restate as: whether the custody modification order is void.

We reverse.

On November 25, 1987, in a dissolution proceeding between the parties, a special judge awarded Daryl custody of the couple's two oldest children and awarded Kimberly custody of their youngest child. Approximately ten years later, on September 25, 1997, Kimberly filed a *pro se* petition seeking legal custody of the two oldest children who had allegedly been living with her since April 21, 1997. On the same day, without notice to Daryl and without an evidentiary hearing, the regular circuit court judge assumed jurisdiction of the case and issued an *ex parte* order granting custody to Kimberly. Daryl learned of the change of custody that night.

Thereafter, Daryl filed a motion for relief from judgment which the trial court denied. At a subsequent hearing to set child support, Kimberly testified that the children had been placed in her care pursuant to a Children in Need of

Services (CHINS) petition. Kimberly placed in evidence a "Petition for Approval of Program of Informal Adjustment" which had been filed in juvenile court on August 12, 1997, some six weeks before the date Kimberly filed her request for modification of custody in the circuit court. Apparently, the trial court had no prior knowledge of the CHINS petition, but, nevertheless, declined to vacate its order. Daryl now appeals.

At the outset we observe that Kimberly has not filed an appellee's brief. In this situation, we do not undertake the burden of developing arguments for the appellee. Instead we apply a less stringent standard of review with respect to showings of reversible error, and we may reverse the trial court if the appellant can establish *prima facie* error. . . .

Daryl first argues the modification order is void because the special judge rather than the circuit court judge had jurisdiction over Kimberly's petition. We agree that the special judge had not relinquished his continuing jurisdiction. However, we need not further examine this argument because the record clearly shows a Child in Need of Services (CHINS) proceeding was filed prior to the filing of Kimberly's petition.

This is significant because the juvenile court has exclusive original jurisdiction in proceedings in which a child, including a child of divorced parents, is alleged to be a child in need of services. IND. CODE § 31-30-1-1 (Supp. 1997). The juvenile court retains that jurisdiction until:

1. the child becomes twenty-one (21) years of age, unless the court discharges the child and the child's parent, guardian, or custodian at an earlier time; or
2. guardianship of the child is awarded to the department of correction.

IND. CODE § 31-30-2-1 (Supp. 1997). Custody determinations are collateral to the juvenile court's jurisdiction. Consequently, in this case, the juvenile court had jurisdiction over custody decisions until that court discharged the parties or transferred the cause.

We have acknowledged that a judgment may be void for a court's lack of authority to render the particular judgment even though the court may have had jurisdiction over the subject matter and the parties. Here, the trial court was without authority to make a custody determination, and the order purporting to do so is void. Daryl has shown *prima facie* error in this regard.

* * *

We conclude that the . . . order transferring legal custody of the chldren to Kimberly is void due to the court's lack of authority to make a custody determination during the pending CHINS action. We reverse and remand with instructions to vacate the . . . order and for future proceedings consistent with this opinion.

Reversed.

Notes

1. States remain split as to whether a juvenile court's jurisdiction supersedes the jurisdiction of another civil court when the civil court already has jurisdiction over the child. In *State ex rel. Dubinsky v. Weinstein*, 413 S.W.2d 178 (Mo. 1967), the court held that a juvenile court retains exclusive original jurisdiction over a child to declare him or her dependent, delinquent, or neglected regardless of whether another court currently retains jurisdiction over the child's custody. In *Weinstein*, a civil court gave the mother custody of her child in a divorce proceeding. The father immediately filed a petition in a juvenile court alleging the child was being neglected by the mother and asked the state to take custody of the child. The court stated that the Missouri legislature, in creating the juvenile court, intended to give the court paramount jurisdiction over other state courts in matters of child custody. *But see Cleveland Protestant Orphan Asylum v. Soule,* 5 Ohio App. 67 (1915), where the court held that a juvenile court does not have superseding jurisdiction over other state courts. The court stated:

> It would be doing violence to all known rules of procedure to assume that the general assembly intended by the passage of a juvenile law to confer authority on the juvenile court to relitigate matters already determined in another court, particularly in view of the fact that the orders as to the custody of children are continuing orders.

Id. at 2.

2. For further discussion on the superseding jurisdiction of juvenile courts over divorce and other civil court jurisdiction, see *Fox v. Arthur,* 714 N.E.2d 305 (Ind. Ct. App. 1999); *In re B.W.,* 714 N.E.2d 370 (Ind. Ct. App. 1999); *Mafnas v. Owen County Office of Family and Children,* 699 N.E.2d 1210 (Ind. Ct. App. 1998); *Anderson v. Anderson,* 416 P.2d 308 (Utah 1966); Doris Freed & Henry Foster *Family Law in the Fifty States 1998-99: Cases Digests,* 33 FAM. L.Q. 919, 953 (2000); 24A AM. JUR. 2D, *Divorce and Separation* § 947 (1998); 47 AM. JUR. 2D, *Juvenile Courts and Delinquent and Dependent Children* § 39 (1995). *See also* IND. CODE § 31-30-2-1 (Lexis 1997).

Questions

1. The dissent in *Weinstein, supra,* in Note 1 suggested that a parent could use a child as a "pawn" by initiating a dependency petition with the juvenile court immediately after losing custody of the child to the other parent in a divorce proceeding. Should it matter if the state or a parent initiates juvenile court proceedings? What role should the child's best interests play in this situation? If a parent initiates a juvenile court action without proof of neglect or abuse, should the law provide a civil remedy for the other parent?

2. There are usually several courts that may determine a child's custody status. In the State of Missouri, for example, a child's custody status may be determined in habeas corpus proceedings, divorce proceedings, the juvenile court, and guardianship proceedings in a probate court. *See Weinstein* at 180. It is inevitable that jurisdictional conflicts arise when several courts have the power to adjudicate rights of children and parents. As a legislator, what proposal(s) would you make to address this problem? How do the *Alexander, Weinstein,* and *Cleveland Protestant Orphan Asylum* decisions affect your reasoning?

2. Due Process Framework

Arizona Revised Statutes Annotated

§ 8-843 (West Supp. 2000)

§ 8-843. Initial dependency hearing; rights; determinations

A. At the initial dependency hearing, the court shall ensure that the parent or guardian has been advised of the following rights:

1. The right to counsel, including appointed counsel if the parent or guardian is indigent.

2. The right to trial by the court on the allegations in the petition.

3. The right to cross-examine all witnesses that are called to testify against the parent or guardian.

4. The right to use the process of the court to compel the attendance of witnesses.

B. If the parent or guardian admits or does not contest the allegations in the petition, the court shall determine that the parent or guardian understands the rights described in subsection A of this section and that the parent or guardian knowingly, intelligently and voluntarily waives these rights.

C. If the parent or guardian denies the allegations in the petition, the court shall set the settlement conference, pretrial conference or mediation prescribed in § 8-844.

D. The court shall also determine if reasonable efforts were made to prevent or eliminate the need for removal of a child from the child's home and if services are available that would eliminate the need for continued removal. If the child is:

1. In the custody of the department, the court shall order the department to make reasonable efforts to provide services to the child and parent to facilitate the reunification of the family, except as provided in subsection E of this section.

2. Not in the custody of the department and the department is not a party, the court may direct the parties to participate in reasonable services that will facilitate reunification of the family or another permanent plan for the child. The court shall not require the department to provide services pursuant to this paragraph.

* * *

In re E.P.

653 N.E.2d 1026 (Ind. Ct. App. 1995)

RUCKER, Judge.

In this interlocutory appeal we address two issues: 1) whether a parent in a Child In Need of Services (CHINS) proceeding is entitled to a jury trial; and 2) whether a parent in a Child In Need of Services (CHINS) proceeding is entitled to court-appointed counsel.

On August 10, 1992, the Marion County Office of Family and Children (Welfare Department) filed a petition in the Marion Superior Court, Juvenile Division, alleging that the children of Tonya Dunn, J.P. and E.P., were in need of services. The petition followed allegations that J.P. had been sexually molested by Dunn's boyfriend. Dunn appeared for an initial hearing on August 19, 1992, at which time the court advised her that she had a right to an attorney and also the right to a continuance in order to obtain an attorney. After explaining that the CHINS proceeding was not a criminal matter the trial court continued, "[t]hat also means though, the Court is not responsible to appoint an attorney for you. If you want a lawyer and can't afford one, there are several organizations available in Marion County to represent you. They include Legal Aid Society, Legal Services Organization and a program through the Indianapolis Bar Association called the Pro Bono Panel." Dunn then requested a continuance for the purpose of obtaining counsel.

At the continued hearing on September 2, 1992, Dunn again advised the court that she had been unable to obtain counsel. Dunn also denied the allegations in the CHINS petition. . . . The case was set for a factfinding hearing on January 6, 1993. . . . The factfinding hearing ultimately began March 3, 1993, and again Dunn appeared without counsel. The Welfare Department called as a witness Kelly Verbeck, a social worker with Child Protective Services. Ms. Verbeck recounted the contents of a medical report concerning J.P., her conversations with the physician who treated J.P., and testified as to what the physician told her that J.P. said to him. Ms. Verbeck also testified concerning what she had been told by a police detective investigating the child molesting allegations. The Welfare Department then rested. Dunn took the stand in her own defense. However, because related criminal charges were pending against her, the trial court first admonished Dunn concerning the possibilities of self incrimination, and then decided to continue the hearing so that Dunn could consult with an attorney. The continued hearing began June 23, 1993, at which time counsel appeared for Dunn for the limited purpose of requesting court-appointed counsel on Dunn's behalf and demanding a jury trial. The court denied both motions and this interlocutory appeal ensued in due course.

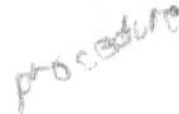

I.

Dunn contends the trial court erroneously refused her demand for a jury trial. According to Dunn her entitlement to a jury arises from three sources; Article I. § 20 of the Indiana Constitution, the Seventh Amendment to the United States Constitution, and Ind. Trial Rule 38.

We first observe that IND. CODE § 31-6-7-10(c) specifically provides *"[a]ll matters in juvenile court shall be tried to the court,* except that a trial of an adult charged with a crime, unless he requests a bench trial, shall be tried to a jury."

(Emphasis added.) Dunn does not challenge the foregoing statute as unconstitutional. Rather, she asserts it is not sufficiently specific to deny parents in CHINS proceedings the right to trial by jury. We disagree. The statute makes clear that except in those instances where an adult is charged with a crime "all matters" within the jurisdiction of the juvenile court shall be tried by the court rather than a jury. . . . Contrary to Dunn's assertion, the statute here is specific and precludes any entitlement to trial by jury.

As for the Indiana Constitutional right[2] to a jury trial the law is settled. The right has been construed to apply only to actions triable by jury at common law. Because no special judicial system for juveniles existed at common law, juvenile matters obviously were not triable by jury. Thus, we have consistently held that Art. I § 20 does not give a party a right to a jury in juvenile court proceedings. *Shupe v. Bell* (1957), 127 Ind. App. 292, 141 N.E.2d 351.

* * *

Dunn's argument that the Seventh Amendment to the United States Constitution[3] guarantees her a right to trial by jury is contrary to existing case authority. The Amendment's guarantee of a jury trial is a limitation on the federal government and does not prohibit states from restricting the right in state courts. *State Line Elevator, Inc. v. Board of Tax Comm'rs* (1988), Ind. Tax, 526 N.E.2d 753, *reconsideration granted* 528 N.E.2d 501. Indeed individual states may even abolish the right to jury trials. *New Jersey Chiropractic Ass'n v. State Bd. Of Medical Examiners,* 79 F. Supp. 327 (D.N.J.1948). Although Indiana has not abolished the right to trial by jury, our courts have long held that the Seventh Amendment to the United States Constitution is not applicable to trials in this state's courts. *Hayworth v. Bromwell* (1959), 239 Ind. 430, 158 N.E.2d 285. Accordingly, Dunn's reliance on the Seventh Amendment is misplaced.

Without elaboration or citation to authority Dunn asserts "Trial Rule 38 provides for the right to trial by jury." Dunn is mistaken. Section (b) of the rule provides in pertinent part:

> *Any party may demand a trial by jury of any issue triable by right of a jury* by filing with the court and serving upon the other parties a demand therefor in writing at any time after the commencement of the action and not later than ten [10] days after the first responsive pleading to the complaint, or to a counterclaim, cross-claim or other claim if one properly is pleaded; and if no responsive pleading is filed or required, within ten [10] days after the time such pleading otherwise would have been required.

(Emphasis added.) Setting aside the fact that Dunn did not satisfy the ten-day requirement for requesting a jury trial, her argument nonetheless fails. Trial

---

2 Article I § 20 of the Indiana Constitution provides: "In all civil cases, the right of trial by jury shall remain inviolate."

3 The Seventh Amendment provides; "In suits at common law, where the value in controversy shall exceed twenty dollars, the right of trial by jury shall be preserved, and no fact tried by a jury, shall be otherwise reexamined in any court of the United States, than according to the rules of the common law."

Rule 38(B) does not provide a right to a jury trial; rather, it merely sets forth the procedure for exercising the right where the right already exists. As previously discussed, CHINS proceedings are not triable to a jury as a matter of right. . . . The trial court properly denied Dunn's request for a jury trial. We find no error here.

II.

Dunn next contends the trial court erred in denying her request for court-appointed counsel. According to Dunn, she is entitled to counsel by reason of the Due Process Clause of the Fourteenth Amendment . . . and IND. CODE § 34-1-1-3 which entitles a "poor person" to appointment of counsel where the person does not have sufficient means to prosecute or defend an action.

Due Process Clause

The Fourteenth Amendment to the United States Constitution requires that no person shall be deprived of life, liberty, or property without due process of law. Although due process has never been precisely defined, the phrase expresses the requirement of "fundamental fairness." *Lassiter v. Department of Social Servs.,* 452 U.S. 18, 26, 101 S. Ct. 2153, 2159, 68 L. Ed. 2d 640 (1981), *reh'g denied.* In the context of representation of counsel, the fundamental fairness requirement does not mandate that counsel shall be appointed in all cases. To the contrary there is a presumption against appointment of counsel where the litigant's physical liberty is not at stake. "[A]n indigent litigant has a [Fourteenth Amendment due process] right to appointed counsel *only when,* if he loses, he may be deprived of his physical liberty." *Lassiter,* 452 U.S. at 26-27, 101 S. Ct. at 2159 (emphasis added). This presumption may be overcome, however, where other elements of due process so require. In determining whether an indigent litigant may be entitled to court appointed counsel we must first evaluate (1) the private interests at stake, (2) the government's interest, and (3) the risk that the procedures used will lead to an erroneous decision. *Lassiter,* 452 U.S. at 25-27, 101 S. Ct. at 2159.

There is no question that the private interests implicated here are substantial. The United States Supreme Court has recognized that the relationship between parent and child is constitutionally protected. *Quilloin v. Walcott,* 434 U.S. 246, 98 S. Ct. 549, 43 L. Ed. 2d 511 (1978), *reh'g denied.* . . . Indeed, the courts of this state have long and consistently held that the right to raise one's children is essential, basic, more precious than property rights, and within the protection of the Fourteenth Amendment to the United States Constitution. *See, e.g., Duckworth v. Duckworth* (1932), 203 Ind. 276, 179 N.E. 773.

On the other hand, . . . the state has a compelling interest in protecting the welfare of the child by intervening in the parent-child relationship when parental neglect, abuse, or abandonment are at issue. *See Matter of Joseph* (1981), Ind. App., 416 N.E.2d 857. Also, "[i]t is the policy of this state . . . [t]o strengthen family life by assisting parents to fulfill their parental obligations; and [t]o remove children from their families only when it is in the child's best interest or in the best interest of public safety." IND. CODE § 31-6-1-1. Thus, it is clear that a parent's constitutionally protected right to raise his or her child is not without limitation. The right must at all times yield to the child's best interest as determined by the courts of this state. . . .

Finally, we must consider the risk that the procedure used will lead to an erroneous result. There is no question that CHINS proceedings are a complex legal matter potentially involving several court hearings. We also acknowledge that litigating any case, including a CHINS matter, without the benefit of counsel may increase the risk of an erroneous decision. Here, for example, unchallenged hearsay testimony provided the basis for the court to determine that Dunn's children were in need of services.... However, unlike a termination proceeding, ... an erroneous CHINS adjudication has a far less disastrous impact on the parent-child relationship.... Even where the juvenile court adjudges a child as a CHINS, the court's ultimate disposition, consistent with the child's welfare and the safety of the community, must be one that: (1) is in the best interest of the child; (2) least interferes with family autonomy; (3) is least disruptive of family life; (4) imposes the least restraint on the freedom of the child and his parent, guardian, or custodian; and (5) provides a reasonable opportunity for participation by the child's parent, guardian, or custodian. IND. CODE § 31-6-4-15.3(3). Thus even assuming without deciding that the risk of an erroneous CHINS adjudication is great when an indigent parent has no counsel to assist her through the various stages of the proceedings or to conduct vigorous cross-examination of the petitioner's key witness, we do not view the risk as outweighing the presumption against court-appointed counsel.

Balancing the private interests at stake, the government's interest, and the risk that the procedure used will lead to an erroneous decision, and weighing them against the presumption that there is no right to appointed counsel unless the litigant's physical liberty is at stake, we conclude that the due process guarantee of the Fourteenth Amendment does not require court-appointed counsel in this case.

* * *

Dunn also contends that she is entitled to counsel under the provisions of IND. CODE § 34-1-1-3 which provides in relevant part:

> *Attorney for poor person.*—Any poor person not having sufficient means to prosecute or defend an action may apply to the court in which the action is intended to be brought, or is pending, for leave to prosecute or defend as a poor person. The court, if satisfied that such person has not sufficient means to prosecute or defend the action, shall admit the applicant to prosecute or defend as a poor person, and shall assign him an attorney....

In order to invoke this statute, the litigant must request appointment of counsel based on his or her economic status. The trial court must then satisfy itself that the litigant does not have "sufficient means to prosecute or defend the action." IND. CODE § 34-1-1-3; *see also Offutt v. Sheehan* (1976), 168 Ind. App. 491, 344 N.E.2d 92, 101. Although our research reveals no case authority so declaring, the statute makes clear that once the trial court is satisfied that the applicant has insufficient financial resources to proceed in an action the court "shall assign him an attorney." The trial court's determination of whether a litigant has sufficient means to prosecute or defend an action is reviewed for an abuse of discretion.

The Welfare Department counters that appointment of counsel in a CHINS proceeding is specifically governed by IND. CODE § 31-6-7-2(b) and therefore IND. CODE § 34-1-1-3 is not applicable. We disagree. Where two statutes address the same subject matter, we construe them consistently and harmoniously if possible. *Decatur Township of Marion County v. Marion County Home Bd.* (1991), Ind. App., 578 N.E.2d 390, 393, *trans. denied.* If the statutes cannot be harmonized or reconciled, then the more specific or detailed statute will prevail over the more general statute as to the subject it covers. *Id.* The statutes here address the same subject matter, namely, appointment of counsel. However we need not debate whether one is specific and the other more detailed because the statutes can be harmonized. Under the provisions of IND. CODE § 34-1-1-3 all persons in any civil action are entitled to court-appointed counsel, provided counsel is requested and the evidence reveals the person does not have sufficient means to prosecute or defend the action. On the other hand IND. CODE § 31-6-7-2(b) affords the court discretion to appoint counsel for parents in a juvenile court proceeding regardless of financial status. Thus an indigent parent may qualify for court-appointed counsel under one statute but no the other. In essence we see no irreconcilable conflict between the two statutes.

The record shows that at the continued hearing on June 23, 1993, counsel appeared on Dunn's behalf for the limited purpose of requesting court-appointed counsel and demanding a trial by jury. As to the request for court-appointed counsel, a written motion was filed on Dunn's behalf and attached thereto was Dunn's affidavit asserting in part "I do not have the funds with which to hire counsel. . . ." The trial court entertained argument on the motion. However the record is absent any indication that an inquiry was made or a hearing conducted to determine whether Dunn in fact had "sufficient means to prosecute or defend the action." IND. CODE § 34-1-1-3. Therefore we must remand this case to the trial court for an appropriate proceeding concerning Dunn's financial and economic resources. If the trial court determines that Dunn does not have the resources to hire private counsel, then counsel must be appointed for her and paid at public expense. On the other hand should the trial court determine that Dunn has sufficient means to hire her own attorney, then the court's decision may be reviewed for abuse of discretion. This case is remanded for proceedings consistent with this opinion. In all other respects the judgment of the trial court is affirmed. . . .

New Mexico v. Lili L.

911 P.2d 884 (N.M. Ct. App. 1995)

In the spring of 1991, Mother, aged fifteen, a non-citizen and an indigent, was living in Socorro, New Mexico, with her two minor sons, Jesus L., born September 3, 1988, and Michael L., born May 7, 1990. On April 2, 1991, the Department filed suit against Mother in Socorro County . . . alleging that her two children were "neglected and/or abused."

The neglect and abuse action sought to have the custody of the two children placed in the Department. The Department was granted custody of Jesus by ex parte order on April 2, 1991. A guardian ad litem was appointed to represent Mother's two children on April 8, 1991. On April 10, 1991, the Department was granted custody of Michael. Mother was unrepresented by counsel at the hearing on April 10, 1991. At the custody hearing, the children's court heard testimony from a social worker, Mother, and Mother's boyfriend. At the conclusion of the hearing, the children's court granted temporary custody of Mother's two sons to the Department pending a subsequent adjudicatory hearing.

On June 12, 1991, the date set for an adjudicatory hearing, Mother was still without counsel. The children's court continued the hearing and appointed Neil P. Mertz, a Socorro attorney, to represent Mother, and rescheduled the adjudicatory hearing for July 8, 1991. Mother was not present at this hearing because she had been deported on June 28, 1991, by immigration authorities. Mother's court-appointed counsel requested that he be permitted to withdraw. In response to this motion, the children's court appointed John Lawit, an Albuquerque attorney who practiced primarily in immigration law, to represent Mother, and again rescheduled the adjudicatory hearing set for August 15, 1991. This hearing date was also subsequently continued. Shortly thereafter Mother re-entered the United States and filed an application with federal authorities for resident status.

On July 31, 1992, Mother personally appeared before the children's court. Her court-appointed attorney was not physically present, but communicated with the court at the hearing by telephone. At this hearing, the children's court attorney presented a stipulated judgment and disposition to the court, stated that it had been approved by Mother's counsel, and requested that it be signed by the children's court.

Mother's court-appointed counsel advised the children's court over the telephone that Mother agreed to enter a consent decree, admit the allegations of neglect, and to consent to the entry of the stipulated judgment and disposition. The children's court did not question Mother to determine whether she understood the nature of the proceedings or whether she concurred in the representations of her court-appointed attorney. At the conclusion of the hearing, the children's court approved the stipulated judgment and disposition.

Under the provisions of the stipulated judgment, Mother purportedly admitted the allegations of the petition, and the parties agreed to the implementation of a treatment plan to assist Mother in developing her parenting skills, with a view to reuniting Mother and her two sons. After working with Mother for approximately one year, on June 12, 1993, the Department filed a second suit . . . seeking to terminate Mother's parental rights. The petition alleged . . .

The children were placed in the Department's custody in April, 1991, due to physical abuse and physical neglect. . . . [Mother] was 15 years old. The father of [Jesus] (then 1 year old) is Luis L. who was [Mother's] stepfather. Despite efforts by the Department . . . [Mother] has not made progress. . . . Although she has acknowledged to the Department that her live-in boyfriend, who was the abuser, will not allow her children to live in his home, she has made no effort to change her living arrangements.

Thereafter, the children's court appointed the law firm of Rodey, Dickason, Sloan, Akin and Robb to represent Mother in the second case.

. . . Trial on the merits began on November 22, 1993, was suspended until September 15, 1994, was thereafter continued to November 29, 1994, and was concluded on January 3, 1995. At trial on the merits, over Mother's objection, the Department relied on the provisions of the stipulated order and disposition . . . to establish that the children had been neglected. At the conclusion of the trial, the children's court adopted findings of fact and conclusions of law, and, on February 17, 1995, entered a judgment terminating Mother's parental rights to her two sons.

I. Failure to Appoint Guardian Ad Litem

Mother argues that because she was a minor and only fifteen years of age at the time the children's court approved her consent to the entry of a stipulated judgment, the court should have appointed both a guardian ad litem and an attorney to represent her. Mother argues that this omission deprived the children's court of jurisdiction, thus invalidating any subsequent proceedings.

As a general rule, the court, upon being apprised that a minor is unrepresented by counsel, has a duty to appoint a guardian ad litem or an attorney to protect the interests of such child. . . . [W]hen an infant defendant is without representation, it is the duty of the court to "appoint a guardian ad litem for [such] infant or incompetent person not otherwise represented in [the] action or shall make such other order as it deems proper for the protection of the infant or incompetent person." . . .

* * *

Although, as noted by our Supreme Court in *Collins ex rel. Collins v. Tabet*, 111 N.M. 391, 400, 806 P.2d 40, 49 (1991), while it is a general practice . . . for a guardian ad litem to be appointed to represent a minor who is a defendant in a civil case, it is clear the court is not required to appoint a guardian ad litem where the child is represented by counsel in such action. Here, despite the initial delay in appointing an attorney to represent Mother in the neglect and abuse case, such delay did not deprive the children's court of jurisdiction. . . .

Mother correctly observes that a failure to appoint either counsel or a guardian ad litem to protect the interests of a minor may constitute a denial of due process, thereby invalidating such proceedings. . . . However, the failure to appoint a guardian ad litem for Mother was not fatal. Upon learning that Mother was without legal representation, the children's court duly appointed counsel to represent her . . . ; thus, we agree with the Department that the children's court was not deprived of jurisdiction in the proceedings below.

II. Validity of the Stipulated Judgment and Disposition

Next, Mother argues that the children's court's failure to personally address her in open court . . . concerning her understanding and consent to the stipulated judgment and disposition voided her purported admission that her children were neglected. She also argues that the children's court's decision to terminate her parental rights . . . is invalid because the children's court premised its finding that the children were neglected on Mother's invalid admission in the first case.

The children's court in the termination case found that "[t]he children have been adjudicated as neglected children . . . as shown by the Stipulated Judgment and disposition entered on July 31, 1992 [and] . . . [t]he Department met its burden of proof by clear and convincing evidence."

At the July 31, 1992, hearing in the neglect proceedings, although Mother appeared personally in court, her court-appointed attorney was not present. He, instead, communicated with the court by telephone. The Department presented a proposed stipulated judgment and disposition. The children's court inquired of Mother's attorney as to whether he had approved the proposed judgment and he informed the court that he did. The children's court, however, did not personally question Mother's attorney concerning the extent to which he had explained the nature of the proceedings to her, whether she consented to the allegations of the petition, or whether she fully understood the import of the stipulated judgment, the proposed disposition, or the consequences of the entry of the stipulated agreement.

... We conclude that the failure to make personal inquiry of Mother of the matters . . . under the circumstances existing here, precludes the use of Mother's purported admission of neglect in the proceedings for the termination of Mother's parental rights. SCRA 10-307, states in applicable part:

> C. Inquiry of respondent. The court shall not accept an admission or approve a consent decree without first, by addressing the respondent personally in open court, determining that:
>
> (1) he understands the allegations of the petition;
>
> (2) he understands the dispositions that the court may make if the allegations of the petition are found to be true;
>
> (3) he understands that he has the right to deny the allegations in the petition and to have a trial on the allegations;
>
> (4) he understands that if he makes an admission or agrees to the entry of the consent decree, he is waiving the right to a trial; and
>
> (5) the admission or provisions of the consent decree are voluntary and not the result of force or threats or of promises other than any consent decree agreement reached.
>
> D. Basis for admission or consent decree. The court shall not enter judgment upon an admission or approve a consent decree without making such inquiry as shall satisfy the court that there is a factual basis for the admission or consent decree.

The language directing that "[t]he court shall not accept an admission or approve a consent decree without first, by addressing the respondent personally in open court," is mandatory. . . .

... SCRA 5-303(E) specifies, in pertinent part, that "[t]he court shall not accept a plea of guilty, no contest or guilty but mentally ill without first, by addressing the defendant personally in open court, informing the defendant of [certain rights] and determining that]the defendant] understands [the consequences of such plea]." Similarly, SCRA 5-303(F) directs, in pertinent part, that "[t]he court shall not accept a plea of guilty, no contest or guilty but mentally ill without first, by addressing the defendant personally in open court, determining that the plea is voluntary and not the result of force or threats or of promises apart from a plea agreement."

. . . [I]t is undisputed that Mother was a fifteen-year-old foreign national, that her counsel was not personally present before the children's court, and that no inquiries as required by SCRA 10-307 were directed to Mother at the hearing. . . . Under this record, we conclude that due process and fundamental fairness preclude the use of Mother's purported admission of child neglect as a basis for terminating her parental rights. . . .

The Department asserts that since Mother has not moved to withdraw her admission of neglect . . . her admission of neglect was properly admitted in the termination case. The Department also argues that Mother should have moved to set aside the stipulated judgment in the first case. . . . We find these arguments unpersuasive. Because the children's court consolidated the neglect proceedings with the action to terminate Mother's parental rights, and the order terminating her parental rights in the consolidated cases is before us on appeal, Mother's challenge to the validity of her consent to the entry of the stipulated judgment was properly preserved below and constitutes a proper issue on appeal.

At the time of the entry of the consent decree . . . [m]other was a minor and a foreign national, she was indigent, had no guardian ad litem or parents present, her court-appointed attorney admitted that he had a lack of familiarity with children's court proceedings and requested that co-counsel be appointed, and that there were not inquiries made of Mother in open court. Under this state of the record, we conclude that due process precludes the use of Mother's purported admissions. . . . Here, there was a failure to determine Mother's understanding of the stipulated judgment and whether there was a factual basis for her admissions as required by SCRA 10-307(C) and (D). Therefore, it was error to permit the Department to use Mother's alleged admission of neglect in the earlier case as evidence in the termination proceeding.

* * *

. . . Manifestly, considerations of fundamental fairness preclude the use of Mother's purported admissions in the 1992 stipulated judgment and disposition as a basis to establish neglect and terminate her parental rights. . . .

CONCLUSION

The children's court's finding of neglect was based on Mother's admissions in the consent decree. Because we conclude that it was improper to use this admission to establish neglect, the use of this admission violated Mother's due process rights, and the record does not contain other sufficient evidence to establish neglect on the part of Mother, the order terminating Mother's parental rights is reversed. . . .

The cause is reversed and remanded to the children's court to conduct further proceedings . . . or to reinstate termination proceedings, excluding any evidence of Mother's admissions. . . .

It Is So Ordered.

Notes

1. *In re E.P.* stated that the trial court's failure to provide counsel for the mother did not violate the mother's Fourteenth Amendment rights but may have violated a state statute giving her the right to court-appointed counsel. Not all jurisdictions are in agreement with the reasoning in *In re E.P.* For jurisdictions which hold that due process requires an indigent parent to be provided an attorney in dependency hearings, see *K.P.B. v. D.C.A.,* 685 So. 2d 750 (Ala. Civ. App. 1996); *In the Matter of K.L.J.,* 813 P.2d 276 (Alaska 1991); *In re Kristin H.,* 54 Cal. Rptr. 2d 722 (Ct. App. 1996); *McKenzie v. Department of Health and Rehabilitative Services,* 663 So. 2d 682 (Fla. Dist. Ct. App. 1995); *Ostrum v. Department of Health and Rehabilitative Services,* 663 So. 2d 139 (Fla. Dist. Ct. App. 1995); *In Interest of Robertson,* 359 N.E.2d 491 (Ill. App. Ct. 1977); *Matter of Trowbridge,* 401 N.W.2d 65 (Mich. Ct. App. 1986); *In re J.S.P.L.,* 532 N.W.2d 653 (N.D. 1995); *In re Lindsey C.,* 473 S.E.2d 110 (W. Va. 1995). For jurisdictions which hold that an indigent parent should be provided counsel as required by state law, see *K.P.B. v. D.C.A., supra; In re Kirstin H., supra; State v. Doe,* 850 P.2d 211 (Idaho Ct. App. 1993); *In re W.L.W. III,* 702 N.E.2d 606 (Ill. App. Ct. 1998); *State in the Interest of S.C. v. D.N.C.,* 639 So. 2d 426 (La. Ct. App. 1994); *In re Brodbeck,* 647 N.E.2d 240 (Ohio Ct. App. 1994); *In re S.M.,* 614 A.2d 312 (Pa. Super. Ct. 1992); *Ybarra v. Texas Dept. of Human Servs.,* 869 S.W.2d 574 (Tex. Civ. App. 1993).

2. For further discussion concerning the due process rights of parents in child welfare proceedings, see Kathleen A. Bailie, *The Other "Neglected" Parties In Child Protective Proceedings: Parents In Poverty and the Role of the Lawyers Who Represent Them,* 66 FORDHAM L. REV. 2285 (1998); Note, *Child Neglect: Due Process for the Parent,* 70 COLUM. L. REV. 465 (1970); Amy Sinden, *"Why Won't Mom Cooperate?": A Critique of Informalities In Child Proceedings*, 11 YALE. J.L. & FEMINISM 339 (1999); Kathy M. Devito, *Proceedings From Petition to Adjudicatory Hearing in Dependency Cases,* JUVL FL-CLE 13-1 (1997); *Family, Custody, Elderly Issues,* 23 MENTAL & PHYSICAL DISABILITY L. REP. 239 (1999); Richard J. Gelles & Ira Schwartz, *Children and the Child Welfare System,* 2 U. PA. J. CONST. L. 95 (1999); Bruce A. Boyer & Steven Lubet, *The Kidnapping of Edgar Mortar: Contemporary Lessons In the Child Welfare Wars,* 45 VILL. L. REV. 245 (2000); William Wesley, *It Matters Not What Is But What Might Have Been: The Standard of Appellate Review for Denial of Counsel in Child Dependency and Parental Severance Trials,* 12 WHITTIER L. REV. 537 (1991); George Dorsett, *The Right To Counsel in Child Dependency Proceedings: Conflict Between Florida and the Fifth Circuit*, 35 U. MIAMI L. REV. 384 (1991).

Questions

1. What is the purpose of the initial hearing? How is this hearing like the arraignment in criminal cases?

2. Why is the right to court-appointed counsel for parents in dependency proceedings significant?

C. Factfinding Hearing

Wisconsin Statutes Annotated
§ 48.31 (West Supp. 2000)

§ 48.31. Fact-finding hearing

(1) In this section, "fact-finding hearing" means a hearing to determine if the allegations in a petition under § 48.13 or 48.133 or a petition to terminate parental rights are proved by clear and convincing evidence.

(2) The hearing shall be to the court unless the child, the child's parent, guardian or legal custodian, the unborn child by the unborn child's guardian ad litem or the expectant mother of the unborn child exercises the right to a jury trial by demanding a jury trial at any time before or during the plea hearing. If a jury trial is demanded in a proceeding under § 48.13 or 48.133, the jury shall consist of 6 persons. If a jury trial is demanded in a proceeding under § 48.42, the jury shall consist of 12 persons unless the parties agree to a lesser number. . . . At the conclusion of the hearing, the court or jury shall make a determination of the facts, except that in a case alleging a child or an unborn child to be in need of protection or services under § 48.13 or 48.133, the court shall make the determination under § 48.13 (intro.) or 48.133 (intro.) relating to whether the child or unborn child is in need of protection or services which can be ordered by the court. If the court finds that the child or unborn child is not within the jurisdiction of the court or, in a case alleging a child or an unborn child to be in need of protection or services under § 48.13 or 48.133, that the child or unborn child is not in need of protection or services which can be ordered by the court or if the court or jury finds that the facts alleged in the petition have not been proved, the court shall dismiss the petition with prejudice.

(4) The court or jury shall make findings of fact and the court shall make conclusions of law relating to the allegations of a petition filed. . . . In cases alleging a child to be in need of protection or services under § 48.13(11), the court may not find that the child is suffering emotional damage unless a licensed physician specializing in psychiatry or a licensed psychologist appointed by the court to examine the child has testified at the hearing that in his or her opinion the condition exists, and adequate opportunity for the cross-examination of the physician or psychologist has been afforded. The judge may use the written reports if the right to have testimony presented is voluntarily, knowingly and intelligently waived by the guardian ad litem or legal counsel for the child and the parent or guardian. In cases alleging a child to be in need of protection or services . . . the court may not find that the child or the expectant mother of the unborn child is in need of treatment and education for needs and problems related to the use or abuse of alcohol beverages, controlled substances or controlled substance analogs and its medical, personal, family or social effects unless an assessment for alcohol and other drug abuse that conforms to the criteria specified under § 48.547(4) has been conducted by an approved treatment facility.

(7)(a) At the close of the fact-finding hearing, the court shall set a date for the dispositional hearing which allows a reasonable time for the parties to prepare but is no more than 10 days after the fact-finding hearing for a child in secure custody and no more than 30 days after the fact-finding hearing for a child or expectant mother who is not held in secure custody. If all parties consent, the court may immediately proceed with a dispositional hearing.

(b) If it appears to the court that disposition of the case may include placement of the child outside the child's home, the court shall order the child's parent to provide a statement of income, assets, debts and living expenses to the court or the designated agency under § 48.33(1) at least 5 days before the scheduled date of the dispositional hearing or as otherwise ordered by the court. The clerk of court shall provide, without charge, to any parent ordered to provide a statement of income, assets, debts and living expenses a document setting forth the percentage standard established by the department of workforce development under § 49.22(9) and the manner of its application established by the department of health and family services under § 46.247 and listing the factors that a court may consider under § 46.10(14)(c). . . .

* * *

1. Burden of Proof

In re N.H.

569 A.2d 1179 (D.C. 1990)

ROGERS, Chief Judge:

Appellant, T.H., appeals from the determination that her child was a neglected child pursuant to D.C. Code § 16-230(9)(B) and (C) (1989 Repl.) on the ground that the statutory scheme violated her constitutional right to due process. Specifically, she maintains that D.C. Code § 16-2317 (1989 Repl.) is unconstitutional because it fails to require proof of neglect by clear and convincing evidence. . . .

T.H. gave birth to N.H. on December 22, 1985, at D.C. General Hospital. At the time she had no plans for a home for the child. For that reason and because of the child's medical problems, N.H. remained in the hospital until February 3, 1986. When the child was released from the hospital, the mother then requested that the D.C. Department of Human Services (DHS) provide emergency care for the child which was available for a maximum of 90 days. During the 90 days that N.H. was under the protective care of the DHS, the mother was admitted to St. Elizabeth's Hospital on an emergency basis when she was found drunk lying in the street. The child was not returned to her mother after the 90 day period was over.

On November 21, 1986, the District of Columbia filed a petition alleging that N.H. was a neglected child under D.C. Code §§ 16-2301(9)(B)(C) because "her mother is unable to discharge her responsibility to and for the child because of mental illness." On December 10, 1986, Judge Huhn ordered that the child be placed in shelter care, with the provision that "the mother shall be entitled to reasonable rights of *supervised* visits." (Emphasis in original) . . .

The mother filed a motion to end shelter care for N.H., asserting that the child's maternal grandmother was now willing to have the child live in her home and other siblings of the mother—a 30 year old brother and a 20 year old sister—were also living at the home and could assist in caring for the child. This motion, filed on May 29, 1987, when N.H. was 17 months old, was opposed by the government on the grounds that the mother had a history of mental disorders, having been hospitalized at St. Elizabeth's Hospital at least three times, and had been admitted to emergency care at St. Elizabeth's Hospital as recently as May 21, 1986, after being found drunk and lying in the street, and had left the hospital on July 10, 1986 against medical advice and then failed to continue outpatient psychiatric treatment. The government also asserted that all of the relatives were not living in the grandmother's home and that Dr. Spevak, the doctor who had examined the mother on March 23, 1987, recommended the mother not be given custody of the child because of her mental incapacity. The mother thereafter filed affidavits of three relatives who had volunteered to take custody of the child. The mother also filed a motion to dismiss the neglect petition or to change the burden of proof to require proof by clear and convincing evidence that a child was neglected under the §§ 16-2301(9)(B)(C). The child, for whom counsel had been appointed, opposed the motion to end shelter care and the motion to dismiss the neglect petition. Judge Levie denied the mother's motion.

A hearing was held on the neglect petition on January 29, 1988, more than a year after the neglect petition had been filed. A social worker testified that the mother did not act like a normal mother toward N.H. and frequently had missed scheduled visits with her daughter. Dr. Vivienne Isaacson, a staff psychiatrist at St. Elizabeth's Hospital, testified that the mother was suffering from "a[n] organic affected disorder, which is a mood disorder associated with organic brain disorder, mixed substance abuse and a history of seizure disorders since childhood." Dr. Spevak, a psychiatrist employed by the DHS, testified that the mother "was a woman with an impaired memory," "effectively unstable," and "was suffering from an organic brain syndrome that significantly impaired her ability to take care of herself, much less anyone who would be primarily dependent upon her." Judge Wertheim found that the mother "suffers from an organic brain syndrome and did so at the time of the petition," that the mother's "mental incapacity effected [sic] her ability to care for a child" and that the mother's "conduct with the child indicates an inability to accurately perceive the child's needs and to respond appropriately even in the most elementary way." Judge Wertheim ruled that the government had met its burden of proof by a preponderance of the evidence to show that N.H. was a neglected child within the meaning of D.C. Code § 16-2301(9)(B) and (C).

On appeal the mother contends that the statutory scheme, and specifically § 16-2317(c)(2), violates due process because it only requires that a finding of neglect be based on a preponderance of the evidence. She argues that this standard fails to strike a fair balance between her interest as the mother in regaining custody of her daughter, the child's interest in an accurate judgment at trial, and the government's administrative interest in maintaining the preponderance standard as well as its *parens patriae* obligation to reunite the mother and the child if possible. She maintains that the effect of the neglect determination means it is likely she will never be able to regain custody of her child and, therefore, the standard of proof should be higher than a preponderance of the evidence. She relies principally on *Santosky v. Kramer,* 455 U.S. 745, 102 S. Ct. 1388, 671 L.Ed. 2d 599 (1982).

Unquestionably, "the fundamental liberty interest of natural parents in the care, custody and management of their children does not evaporate simply because they have not been model parents or have lost temporary custody of their child to the state." *Santosky v. Kramer, supra,* 455 U.S. at 753, 102 S. Ct. at 1395. The right of a natural parent to raise one's child is a fundamental and essential precept which is constitutionally protected. *Stanley v. Illinois,* 405 U.S. 645, 92 S. Ct. 1208, 31 L. Ed.2d 551 (1972). At the same time, however, the Supreme Court has recognized that this right is not absolute and that the state has both the right and the duty to protect minor children through judicial determinations of their interests. *Id.*

* * *

Whether the "preponderance of the evidence" burden of proof is constitutionally sufficient depends on the magnitude of the interest in the right which is being infringed. *See Santosky v. Kramer, supra,* 455 U.S. at 744, 102 S.Ct. At 1395. As the Supreme Court stated in *Addington v. Texas*, 441 U.S. 418, 99 S.Ct. 1804, 60 L.Ed.2d 323 (1979), "the function of a standard of proof, as the concept is embodied in the Due Process Clause and in the realm of factfinding, is to instruct the factfinder concerning the degree of confidence our society thinks he [or she] should have in the correctness of factual conclusions for a particular type of adjudication." *Id.* at 423, 99 S.Ct. at 18081 (quoting *In re Winship*, 397 U.S. 358, 370, 90 S.Ct. 1068, 1076, 25 L.Ed.2d 368 (1970) (Harlan, J., concurring)). [2]

In re L.E.J., 465 A.2d 374 (D.C. 1983), this court distinguished *Santosky v. Kramer:*

> In *Santosky v. Kramer*, 455 U.S. 745 [102 S.Ct. 1388, 71 L.Ed.2d 599] (1982), the Supreme Court held that a state must present "clear and convincing" evidence of neglect or abuse before terminating a parent's right to the custody of a child. The higher standard of proof imposed by *Santosky*, however, need not be met here because this case involves only a temporary suspension, not a permanent deprivation, of parental rights.

465 A.2d at 377 n.5. Because the statutory scheme for child neglect involves temporary, third party placement or supervised placement of a child with the

---

2 Commenting on *Addington* in *Santosky v. Kramer*, the Supreme Court stated that "[i]n any given proceeding, the minimum standard of proof tolerated by the due process requirement reflects not only the weight of the public and private interest affected, but also a societal judgment about how the risk of error should be distributed between the litigants." 455 U.S. at 755, 102 S.Ct. at 1395. The Court has mandated an intermediate standard of proof—"clear and convincing evidence"—when the individual interests at stake in a state proceeding are both "particularly important" and "more substantial than mere loss of money." *Santosky v. Kramer, supra,* 455 U.S. at 755, 102 S.Ct. at 1395 (parental termination); *Addington v. Texas, supra,* 441 U.S. at 424, 99 S.Ct. at 1809 (civil commitment); *Woodby v. INS*, 385 U.S. 275, 87 S. Ct. 483, 17 L.Ed.2d 362 (1966) (deportation).

parent for a two-year period, followed by annual reviews after notice and hearing and a new determination that the child is neglected, we conclude that these procedures accord procedural due process to the parent and the child.

* * *

Accordingly, the judgment is affirmed.

Notes

1. Most states require the state agency to prove by a preponderance of evidence that a child is dependent. *See, e.g.*, ARIZ. REV. STAT. ANN. § 8-844 (West Supp. 2000); COLO. REV. STAT. § 19-3-505 (2000); 705 ILL. COMP. STAT. ANN. 405/2-21 (West 1999); KY. REV. STAT. ANN. § 620.100 (West 2000). Some states, however, require the agency to prove dependency by clear and convincing evidence. *See, e.g.*, ALA. CODE § 12-15-65 (Lexis Supp. 2000); OHIO REV. CODE ANN. § 2151.35 (Anderson Supp. 2000); TENN. CODE ANN. § 37-1-129 (Lexis Supp. 2000).

2. California, like most other states, requires the state to prove dependency and termination of parental rights by two different standards of proof. In *In re Christopher B.,* 147 Cal. Rptr. 390 (Ct. App. 1978), the court held that the state must prove by a preponderance of the evidence that a child is dependent. The preponderance of the evidence standard is used because an erroneous judgment against one party is no more harmful than an erroneous judgment against the other party. *See* Michael Freeman White, Comment, *Dependency Proceedings: What Standard of Proof? An Argument Against the Standard of "Clear and Convincing"*, 14 SAN DIEGO L. REV. 1155 (1977). *Christopher B.* also held that once a child is adjudicated dependent by a preponderance of the evidence, the state cannot sever the parent-child relationship unless the state then proves that separation of the child from the parents is necessary by clear and convincing evidence.

A few jurisdictions, such as Pennsylvania, require the state to use the clear and convincing standard to prove that the child is dependent or that the child should be removed from his or her family. *See Interest of Jones*, 429 A.2d 671 (Pa. Super. Ct. 1981). After a juvenile court declares the child to be dependent, the state must prove by clear and convincing evidence that "aggravating factors" exist making it necessary to remove the child from the home permanently. 42 PA. CONS. STAT. ANN. § 6341 (West Supp. 2001).

Questions

1. State statutes require the state to meet different standards of proof for adjudication of status offenders, delinquents, and dependents. What purposes of the juvenile justice system and public policies are served by these different burdens of proof?

2. Given the rules concerning family preservation and the rights of the parties in a dependency proceeding, what is the appropriate burden of proof at the factfinding hearing?

2. Need for Coercive Court Intervention

Indiana Code Annotated
§ 31-34-1-1 (Lexis 1997)

§ 31-34-1-1 Impairment or serious endangerment of physical or mental condition.—

A child is a child in need of services if before the child becomes eighteen (18) years of age:

(1) the child's physical or mental condition is seriously impaired or seriously endangered as a result of the inability, refusal, or neglect of the child's parent, guardian, or custodian to supply the child with necessary food, clothing, shelter, medical care, education, or supervision; and

(2) the child needs care, treatment, or rehabilitation that the child:

(A) is not receiving; and

(B) is unlikely to be provided or accepted without the coercive intervention of the court.

In re Juvenile Appeal (83-CD)
455 A.2d 1313 (Conn. 1983)

This is an appeal by the defendant, mother . . . from the order of the Superior Court for juvenile matters granting temporary custody of her children to the plaintiff commissioner of the department of children and youth services.

The defendant and her six children . . . had been receiving services from the Department of Children and Youth Services (DCYS) as a protective service family since 1976, and were supported by the Aid to Families with Dependent Children program. Michelle Spicknall, a DCYS caseworker, was assigned to the defendant's case in January 1979. In the next nine months she visited the defendant's home twenty-seven times. She considered the family situation "marginal," but noted that the children were not "abused [or] neglected." It was Spicknall's opinion that the children were very happy and active, and that they had a "very warm" relationship with their mother.

During the night of September 4-5, 1979, the defendant's youngest child, nine month old Christopher died. . . . No cause of death could be determined at that time, but the pediatrician noticed some unexplained superficial marks on Christopher's body.

Because of Christopher's unexplained death, the plaintiff commissioner of children and youth services seized custody of the defendant's five remaining children on September 5, 1979, under the authority of the "96-hour hold" provision of General Statutes § 17-38a(e), which permits summary seizure if the commissioner has probable cause to believe that the child is "suffering from serious physical illness or serious physical injury of is in immediate physical danger from his surroundings, and that immediate removal from such surroundings is necessary to insure the child's safety. . . ."

On September 7, 1979 . . . DCYS filed petitions of neglect . . . for each of the defendant's children. Accompanying each petition was an affidavit for orders of temporary custody asking that the court issue temporary ex parte orders to keep the five children in DCYS custody under the authority of § 46 (b)-129(b)(2). The petitions alleged, in addition to Christopher's unexplained death, that the defendant's apartment was dirty, that numerous roaches could be found there, that beer cans were to be found in the apartment, that the defendant had been observed drinking beer, that on one occasion the defendant may have been drunk, that a neighbor reported that the children had once been left alone all night, and that the two older children had occasionally come to school without having eaten breakfast. On the basis of these allegations, on September 7, 1979, the court granted, ex parte, temporary custody to the commissioner pending a noticed hearing on temporary custody set for September 14, 1979, within ten days of the ex parte order as required by § 46 (b)-129(b)(2). The court also set October 1, 1979, for a hearing on the neglect petitions.

At the September 14 temporary custody hearing, DCYS presented testimony of Spicknall confirming and elaborating on the conditions of the defendant's home and on the defendant's beer drinking. Christopher's pediatrician testified concerning Christopher's treatment and physical appearance when the child was brought to the hospital. . . . The doctor . . . testified that, although the pathologist's report on the autopsy was not complete, the external marks on Christopher's body were not a cause of death, that no internal injuries were found, and that the child had a viral lung infection. . . . At the conclusion of the state's case, the court found "probable cause" and ordered temporary custody of the children to remain with the plaintiff commissioner of children and youth services.

The defendant appealed to this court, claiming that General Statutes § 46b-129(b) violates the Due Process Clause of the Fourteenth Amendment both because it is an impermissible infringement on her right to family integrity, and because the statute is unconstitutionally vague. . . . We conclude that § 46b-129(b) is constitutional. . . .

Where fundamental rights are concerned we have a two-part test; "[1] regulations limiting these rights may be justified only by a 'compelling state interest,' and . . . [2] legislative enactments must be narrowly drawn to express only legitimate state interests at stake." *Roe v. Wade,* 410 U.S. 113, 155, 93 S.Ct. 705, 727, L.Ed.2d 147 (1973). The state has a substantial interest in protecting minor children; *Stanley v. Illinois,* 405 U.S. 645, 649, 92S.Ct. 1208, 1211; *Prince v. Massachusetts,* 321 U.S. 158, 166, 64 S.Ct. 438, 442, 88 L.Ed. 645 (1944); intervention in family matters by the state is justified, however, only when such intervention is actually "in the best interests of the child," a standard long used in this state. . . .

Studies indicate that the best interests of the child are usually served by keeping the child in the home with his or her parents. . . . The love and attention not only of parents, but also of siblings, which is available in the home environment, cannot be provided by the state. Unfortunately, an order of temporary custody often results in the children of one family being separated and scattered to different foster homes. . . . Even where the parent-child relationship is "marginal," it is usually in the best interests of the child to remain at home and still benefit from a family environment.

The defendants challenge to the temporary custody statute, § 46b-129(b), must be addressed in light of the foregoing considerations. The defendant contends that only when the child is "at risk of harm" does the state's interest become a compelling one, justifying even temporary removal of the child from the home. We agree.

In custody proceedings, any criteria used to determine when intervention is permissible must take into account the competing interest involved. The parent has only one interest, that of family integrity, . . . and the state has only one compelling interest, that of protecting minor children. . . . The child, however, has two distinct and often contradictory interests. The first is a basic interest in safety; the second is the important interest . . . in having a stable family environment. Connecticut's child welfare statutes recognize both the conflicting interests and the constitutional limitations involved in any intervention situation. Thus, under the criteria of General Statutes § 17-38a(e), summary assumption of temporary custody is authorized only when there is probable cause to believe that "the child is suffering from serious physical illness or serious physical injury or is in immediate physical danger from his surroundings, and that immediate removal from such surroundings is necessary to insure the child's safety. . . ."

The language of § 17-38a(e) clearly limits the scope of intervention to cases where the state interest is compelling, as required by the first part of the test from *Roe v. Wade, supra*. Intervention is permitted only where "serious physical illness or serious physical injury" is found or where "immediate physical danger" is present. It is at this point that the child's interest no longer coincides with that of any parent, thereby diminishing the magnitude of the parent's rights to family integrity . . . and therefore the state's intervention as *parens patriae* to protect the child becomes so necessary that it can be considered paramount. A determination that the state interest is compelling does not alone affirm the constitutionality of the statute. . . . The second part of the due process analysis . . . requires that statutes affecting fundamental rights be "narrowly drawn to express only the legitimate state interests at stake." General Statutes § 17-38a(e) meets this part of the test by requiring, in addition to the compelling need to protect the child, that the assumption of temporary custody by the commissioner be immediately "necessary to insure the child's safety." This phrase requires that various steps short of removal from the home be used when possible in preference to disturbing the integrity of the family. . . .

In the instant case, no substantial showing was made at the temporary custody hearing that the defendant's five children were suffering from either serious physical illness or serious physical injury, or that they would be in immediate physical danger if they were returned to the defendant's home. The DCYS caseworker admitted at trial, as did the state's counsel at argument before this court, that without the unexplained death of Christopher, there was no reason for DCYS to have custody of the other children. The medical evidence at the hearing indicated no connection between Christopher's death and either the defendant or the conditions in her home. . . . There was . . . no evidence before the court to indicate whether his death was from natural causes or was the result of abuse. Yet with nothing before it but subjective suspicion, the court granted the commissioner custody of the defendant's other children. It was error for the court to grant to the commissioner temporary custody when no immediate risk of danger to the children was shown. . . . [The] case is remanded with direction to set aside the orders of temporary custody.

Notes

1. The primary purpose of a fact-finding hearing "is to allow courts to order remedial measures to preserve and mend family ties, and alleviate the problems which prompted the State's initial intervention" if warranted. *In re Dependency of A.W.,* 765 P.2d 307 (Wash. Ct. App. 1988). *See also In re A.M.D.,* 648 P.2d 625 (Colo. 1982). When a court declares a child dependent or neglected, the court must also determine whether or not the child should be returned to his or her parents based on the fault of the parents and the lack of parental care. *See, e.g., In re Joshua S.,* 252 Cal. Rptr. 106 (Ct. App. 1988); *Custody of Minor,* 289 N.E.2d 68 (Mass. 1979). Because the best interest of a child is thought to be in a stable, continuous environment of his or her own family, most courts will only allow state intervention when the parents are unable to provide a stable environment for the child's protection and care. *See Custody of Minor, supra. See also Roe v. Conn,* 417 F. Supp. 769, 779 (M.D. Ala. 1976); Robert A. Burt, *Developing Constitutional Rights Of, In, and For Children,* 39 LAW & CONTEMP. PROBS. 118, 128 (Summer 1975). If a court decides to reunite a child with his or her parents, the court may place restrictions on the parents that are in accordance with due process and limited to the means necessary for family reunification. *See* 43 C.J.S. *Infant* § 71 (1978).

2. Courts may impose on parents conditions under which they may retain custody of their neglected or dependent child. In *In re Alpha J.,* 2000 WL 192962, at *1, *2 (Conn. Super. Ct. Feb. 3, 2000), the court imposed on a mother and an abusive father the following conditions:

1. Cooperate with visits by the child's attorney and provide access to the child to talk with his attorney alone. The child's attorney is ordered to meet with the child a minimum of two times during the period of protective supervision.
2. Keep the child's whereabouts and your whereabouts known to DCF, your attorney, and the attorney of the child.
3. Participate in counseling and make progress toward the identified treatment goal of eradicating domestic violence in the home. The counseling service can be chosen by the parents but must be approved by the court. . . .
4. Alpha is to be evaluated by a counselor . . . and is to attend sessions with his counselor as often as the counselor deems appropriate during the period of the supervision.

5. The respondents are to consistently and timely meet and address the child's physical, educational, medical, or emotional needs, including, but not limited to, keeping the child's appointments with his medical, psychological, psychiatric or educational providers.

* * *

7. Maintain the child within the State of Connecticut during the duration of this order.

Problem

Sally was removed from her home on September 1 following a substantiated allegation of physical abuse by her father. After initial denial by Sally's father and mother that the father beat Sally with a belt, the parents admitted the father's abuse. Both parents have started counseling at the suggestion of their minister. The father has also enrolled in rage management counseling. At the fact-finding hearing, the family minister tells the court that the father is truly repentant and has initiated services to address his problems. Counsel for the parents urges the court to dismiss the CHINS petition because coercive intervention of the court is not necessary. What factors should the court consider in ruling on the parents' motion?

D. Permanency Hearings

1. Permanency Plan

Iowa Code Annotated

§ 232.104 (West Supp. 2001)

§ 232.104. Permanency hearing

1. . . .

c. . . . During the hearing, the court shall consider the child's need for a secure and permanent placement in light of any permanency plan or evidence submitted to the court. Upon completion of the hearing the court shall enter written findings and make a determination identifying a primary permanency goal for the child. If a permanency plan is in effect at the time of the hearing, the court shall also make a determination as to whether reasonable progress is being made in achieving the permanency goal and other provisions of that permanency plan.

2. After a permanency hearing the court shall do one of the following:

a. Enter an order pursuant to section 232.102 to return the child to the child's home.

b. Enter an order pursuant to section 232.102 to continue placement of the child for an additional six months at which time the court shall hold a hearing to consider modification of its permanency order. . . .

c. Direct the county attorney or the attorney for the child to institute proceedings to terminate the parent-child relationship.

d. Enter an order, pursuant to findings required by subsection 3, to do one of the following:

(1) Transfer guardianship and custody of the child to a suitable person.

(2) Transfer sole custody of the child from one parent to another parent.

(3) Transfer custody of the child to a suitable person for the purpose of long-term care.

(4) Order long-term foster care placement for the child in a licensed foster care home or facility.

3. Prior to entering a permanency order pursuant to subsection 2, paragraph "d", convincing evidence must exist showing that all of the following apply:

a. A termination of the parent-child relationship would not be in the best interest of the child.

b. Services were offered to the child's family to correct the situation which led to the child's removal from the home.

c. The child cannot be returned to the child's home.

4. Any permanency order may provide restrictions upon the contact between the child and the child's parent or parents, consistent with the best interest of the child.

5. Subsequent to the entry of a permanency order pursuant to this section, the child shall not be returned to the care, custody, or control of the child's parent or parents, over a formal objection filed by the child's attorney or guardian ad litem, unless the court finds by a preponderance of the evidence, that returning the child to such custody would be in the best interest of the child.

6. Following an initial permanency hearing and the entry of a permanency order which places a child in the custody or guardianship of another person or agency, the court shall retain jurisdiction and annually review the order to ascertain whether the best interest of the child is being served. . . .

Adoption and Safe Families Act (1997)

42 U.S.C. § 675(5)(C) (West Supp. 2001)

§ 675. Definitions

(5) The term "case review system" means a procedure for assuring that—

* * *

(C) with respect to each . . . child, procedural safeguards will be applied, among other things, to assure each child in foster care under the supervision of the State of a permanency hearing to be held, in a family or juvenile court or another court . . . of competent jurisdiction, . . . no later than 12 months after the date the child is considered to have entered foster care . . . (and not less frequently than every 12 months thereafter during the continuation of foster care), which hearing shall determine the permanency plan for the child that includes whether, and if applicable when, the child will be returned to the parent, placed for adoption . . . , or referred for legal guardianship, or . . . placed in another planned permanent living arrangement. . . .

In re Scott Y.

499 N.W.2d 218 (Wis. Ct. App. 1993)

CANE, Presiding Judge.

Thomas Y. appeals the orders placing two of his sons, Scott Y. and Ryan Y., in foster care following a consolidated CHIPS proceeding. Thomas argues that the trial court lost its jurisdiction to proceed on the petition because the St. Croix County Department of Human Services (the county) failed to file a permanency plan with the court within sixty days after Scott and Ryan were placed outside of Thomas' home, as required by sec. 48.38(3), Stats . . . . Because we conclude that the sixty-day filing requirement in sec. 48.38(3) is nonjurisdictional . . . the orders are affirmed.

Scott and Ryan were taken into custody under sec. 48.19(1)(d)5, Stats., on March 18, 1991, after the county received reports that the children were victims of physical abuse in Thomas' home. Both children affirmed that they had been physically abused on several occasions by their stepmother, Janet Y. The county filed a petition for determination of the children's need for protection services under sec. 48.13(3) the next day, and the county was granted temporary physical custody. Although Thomas continually opposed placement of his children outside his home, he stipulated that the children had been victims of physical abuse in his home and were in need of protective services. The court held numerous hearings reviewing the county's temporary physical custody of the children.

In August 1991, the county filed a permanency plan and predispositional report with the court and the court held a dispositional hearing. At the hearing, the county caseworker testified that she continually informed Thomas and Janet of the requirements for the children's return to Thomas' home. She also testified that the county's records reflected extensive and continuous physical abuse of the children. She further testified that Thomas and Janet failed to comply with those requirements, cooperate with the county and recognize the problems and the need to rectify the conditions that necessitated the children's removal from their home.

* * *

The court made the following findings, among others: (1) The county failed to hold a timely permanency planning meeting or to file a permanency plan with the court as required by sec. 48.38(3), Stats; (2) the dispositional hearing was delayed several times at Thomas' request; and (3) the best interests of the children lie in continuing placement in a family foster home under the county's supervision. The court adopted the recommendations in the predispositional report and the conditions for the children's return to Thomas' home. The court concluded that the county's failure to comply with the time constraints in sec. 48.38(3) did not deprive it of jurisdiction. The court ordered, in part, that the children remain in foster care under the county's supervision, the children receive therapy and that Thomas and Janet enter and successfully complete various counseling programs and psychological assessments.

Section 48.38(3), Stats., provides, in part, "The agency shall file the permanency plan with the court within 60 days after the date on which the child was first held in physical custody or placed outside of his or her home under a court order. . . ." It is undisputed that the county failed to file a permanency plan with the court within sixty days of March 13, 1991, the date the county took physical custody of Scott and Ryan. Thomas argues that this failure deprived the court of subject-matter jurisdiction. . . . We are not persuaded.

This issue involves construction and application of a statute to undisputed facts, which is a question of law that we review independently of the trial court's determination. We note that the plain language of the statute requires filing of the permanency plan "within 60 days after the date on which the child was first held in physical custody *or* placed outside of his or her home under a court order. . . ." (Emphasis added.) Here, the permanency plan was filed *before* the court ordered placement of the children outside of Thomas' home. Arguably, as long as a permanency plan was filed within sixty days of whichever event occurs later, the statutory time limit has been complied with.

However, we need not address that issue because even if we concluded that the county failed to comply with sec. 48.43(3) Stats., by failing to file a permanency plan within sixty days of the date it first took custody of Scott and Ryan, the failure is nonjurisdictional for several reasons. First, we note that sec. 48.43 does not deal with subject-matter jurisdiction and sec. 48.13 does not list the timely filing of a permanency plan as a prerequisite for jurisdiction over children alleged to be in need of protection or services. Second, as the county notes, preparing a permanency plan is an administrative requirement that does not involve the court, is not part of the court procedures governed by Subchaper V and does not arise out of the court's jurisdiction. . . . We therefore conclude that the time limits in sec. 48.38(3), Stats., are not prerequisites to trial court subject matter jurisdiction or competency over proceedings.

* * *

Orders affirmed.

Notes

1. State laws require permanency plans to document the factors used to determine where to place the child and what actions were taken prior to the submission of the permanency plan. State laws may also require documentation of the following: a concise statement of why the child is in the custody of the state; if the child is to remain at home, what measures are necessary to prevent the child from being harmed (*see* KY. REV. STAT. ANN. § 620.230(1) (West 2000)); if the child is to be placed outside of the home because of dangerous conditions at home, what would need to occur in order for the child to be returned home safely (*id.* at § 620.230(2)(e) (West 2000)); possible placements for the child; or whether the child should be permanently separated from his or her parents, placed for adoption, or placed in the care of a guardian (*see* MD. CODE ANN., CTS. & JUD. PROC. § 3-286.1(d)(2)-(3) (Lexis Supp. 2000)). For further information on required documentation in a permanency plan, see 42 U.S.C.A. § 675(1); MD. CODE ANN., CTS. & JUD. PROC. § 3-826 (Lexis Supp. 2000); KY. REV. STAT. ANN. § 620.230 (West 2000). For further discussion of the importance of the permanency plan in the permanency hearing, see ARK. CODE ANN. § 9-27-338 (Michie Supp. 2001); COLO. REV. STAT. ANN. § 19-3-702 (2000); 20 ILL. COMP. STAT. ANN. 505/7 (West Supp. 2001).

2. According to some critics, the Adoption and Safe Families Act of 1997 (ASFA) has a negative impact on a state's ability to create a permanency plan that would sufficiently include the child's best interests. For example, AFSA requires that the permanency hearing be held twelve months after the child is placed in foster care. The state sometimes needs longer than twelve months to put together a permanency plan which meets the child's best interests (*see* ASFA § 675(5)(c)). *See* Madelyn Freundlich, *Expediting Termination of Parental Rights: Solving a Problem or Sowing the Seeds of a New Predicament?*, 28 CAP. U. L. REV. 97, 106 (2000). If the state is rushed to put together a permanency plan, the state may make a decision which doesn't properly reflect the child's best interests, leaving the child in an at-risk environment or being permanently removed from his or her parents. A second problem is that AFSA "may foreclose opportunities for parents to consider voluntary relinquishment and cooperative adoption arrangements that allow some level of ongoing relationship with their children." *Id.* (citing Jeanne Etter, *Levels of Cooperation and Satisfaction in 56 Open Adoptions*, 72 CHILD WELFARE 257, 257-64 (1993)). *See also* Megan M. O'Laughlin, *A Theory of Relativity: Kinship Foster Care May Be the Key to Stopping the Pendulum of Terminations vs. Reunification,* 51 VAND. L. REV. 1427 (1998); Harriette Gross, *Open Adoption: A Research Based Literature Review and New Data*, 72 CHILD WELFARE 269 (1993); Claire Sandt, *ASFA: From Policy to Practice*, 19 CHILD L. PRAC. 58 (2000).

Questions

1. What is the purpose of the permanency plan? How should a permanency plan balance the interests of the child, the state, and the parents? What factors should the state take into consideration when creating a permanency plan?

2. What are the policy and due process arguments for and against the imposition of a time limit for a permanency plan?

2. Reunification Services

In re Angel N.

679 A.2d 1136 (N.H. 1996)

BRODERICK, Justice.

The Hillsborough County Probate Court granted the petition of the State Division for Children, Youth, and Families (DCYF) to terminate the parental rights of Kathleen B. and Richard N. over their daughter, Angel N. The parents appeal independently. We affirm.

Angel was born on March 11, 1989. Because of previous history involving Kathleen and DCYF and concerns expressed by hospital personnel about the parents' conduct, DCYF provided a visiting nurse and a social worker as daily support to the family once Angel was brought home from the hospital. Despite the early assistance, when Angel was two weeks old, her mother reported to DCYF that she and Richard had been fighting and that Richard had dropped Angel into her bassinet.

As a result, DCYF filed neglect petitions against both parents in the Nashua District Court. Both parents consented to the neglect petitions. DCYF obtained legal custody of Angel and placed her in temporary foster care.

After five days, Angel was returned to her mother, who was then separated from Richard and sharing an apartment with another man. Thereafter, DCYF provided both parents with outpatient counseling, parenting classes, and transportation.

In apparent disregard of a restraining order allowing Richard and Kathleen to have "peaceful contact" outside Angel's presence, Kathleen and Richard had yet another altercation in Angel's presence in downtown Manchester on July 25, 1989. After Richard ran from the scene, several witnesses observed Kathleen strike Angel on her head and back, causing red welts. The police officer dispatched to the scene reported that Kathleen asked him to "find someone to take the baby" because she could not properly care for her. DCYF, which still retained legal custody, once again placed Angel in foster care.

During this separation, DCYF continued to provide support services to both Kathleen and Richard. Reports to the district court during this period revealed that Kathleen displayed "[u]ncontrollable outbursts and mood shifts"; that "[w]hile she may comply with [court-ordered therapy], it appears she would be 'going through the motions,' resisting change and cognitively unable to benefit much from therapy"; that although she had "made some gains," she had "much further to go before the prospect of reuniting her with Angel occurs"; and that she needed "further help in dealing with increased or unpredictable stress." Similarly, reports on Richard's progress noted that he had not consistently exercised good judgment during visitations with Angel, that he "resumed drinking and stopped keeping his appointments and fulfilling his responsibilities in general," and that "[o]verall, Richard does not at this time appear a realistic candidate for ind[e]pendent care of his daughter."

* * *

Angel was reunited with Kathleen on August 26, 1991, after more than two years of separation. The reunion was short-lived. On September 23, 1991, following a physical assault on Kathleen by her male roommate in Angel's presence, Kathleen agreed that her daughter should return to foster care. On October 16, 1991, after Kathleen secured a "stable and appropriate residence," DCYF returned Angel to her care once again.

One month later, Kathleen and Richard were involved in yet another violent altercation in Angel's presence. The argument culminated in Kathleen stabbing Richard in the arm with a steak knife. For the fourth and final time, Angel was placed in foster care.

DCYF continued to provide parenting classes and counseling; progress was slow. The underlying theme in reports to the district court was that it was "too soon" to consider reunification, even though DCYF had been working with the parents for more than three years with no demonstrable improvement.

In early 1992, Kathleen was counseled to "stay away from" her abusive relationships with Richard and her male roommate; nevertheless, she lived twice with Richard and twice with the male roommate, notwithstanding the assaults that resulted in Angel's third and fourth foster care placements.

The district court continued to review their progress. It noted that both Richard and Kathleen were awaiting the outcome of felony proceedings for theft in the superior court, for which Richard was later sentenced to six months in the house of correction. The court also acknowledged the concern of Angel's counsel that Richard and Kathleen "have a long history of short-term improvement which deteriorates into long-term problems," and his fear that their past pattern of behavior would be repeated. Reports to the district court noted once again that Richard and Kathleen needed "continued services to learn parenting skills and anger management," and "additional time to reach their goals."

In July 1993, Richard and Kathleen had three altercations. The first was an incident of kicking; two additional fights involved hitting, punching, and choking. The district court responded that these events "raise continued concerns about the wisdom of having Angel returned home to her parents." The court continued:

> The parties['] . . . progress is unavoidably slow, which operates to the detriment of Angel since the court is unable to reach the statutory and regulatory objective of providing a permanency plan within a time frame which is appropriate for Angel's welfare. The court has no specific calendar date on which it intends to make a final decision. However, the passage of time is alone becoming an issue, and the progress of the parties will be watched very closely in the ensuing months. If sufficient progress is not achieved, the court would expect [DCYF] to pursue its sometime objective of termination of parental rights.

In early 1994, DCYF petitioned the probate court to terminate Kathleen's and Richard's parental rights. Following four days of hearings, the probate court found beyond a reasonable doubt that Richard and Kathleen had failed to correct the conditions leading to the neglect finding within eighteen months and terminated their parental rights.

* * *

Kathleen . . . argues that the probate court erroneously terminated her parental rights for failing to correct her unstable housing. [L]ess than ideal parenting, particularly when it is caused by poverty, is an insufficient basis for terminating parental rights. Rather, the State must prove that the parent has "failed for as long as eighteen months to rectify the conditions of neglect, despite the court's attempts to promote their correction." *In re Tricia H.*, 126 N.H. 418, 425, 493 A.2d 1146, 1151 (1985). Here, the probate court relied on more than Kathleen's unstable housing in ordering termination. The neglect found and not corrected in this case was not due to economics. It related largely to a fundamental lack of parenting skills and concern for Angel's neglect merely because the people responsible for her welfare and safety were burdened with many of life's disadvantages.

Kathleen lastly argues that the evidence was insufficient to support termination. The probate court was required to assess Kathleen's efforts to rectify the conditions leading to the neglect finding during the eighteen months following that finding. Here, as in a termination of parental rights premised on abandonment, the court also considered events that occurred beyond the eighteen-month period to determine whether DCYF had proven the statutory grounds for termination beyond a reasonable doubt.

Even though no documented violence between Kathleen and Richard occurred for several months after the November 16, 1991, stabbing, during this time frame Kathleen "trashed" Richard's room at his mother's home; got so upset at being asked to leave Richard's mother's home that she scratched her face, leaving red welts; and associated with a "known sex offender." This "violence-free" period was then followed by the three incidents in July 1993—involving kicking, hitting, punching and choking.

Although Kathleen was benefitting from the therapy provided by the district court, improvement alone is not sufficient. "[W]hile parental improvement is a factor to consider, the real test is whether there is a reasonable possibility of reuniting parent and child within a reasonable period of time." *In re J.J.*, 143 Vt. 1, 458 A.2d 1129, 1131 (1983).

* * *

Although the law should not attempt to micromanage families, society does have a right to insist that children not be neglected. When neglect is due to a parent's unwillingness or reluctance to assume basic responsibilities, then society has a right to interfere to protect the innocent child. In an effort to save and nurture the unique bond between parent and child, the State, in the first instance, should take reasonable and appropriate steps whenever possible to assist in maintaining the legal link between parent and offspring. In the case at hand, the State took such steps over a period of approximately five years. The parents failed to respond as required. Regrettably, they acted or failed to act at their peril. Neglect cannot and will not be tolerated.

Affirmed.

In re Joshua H.

17 Cal. Rptr. 2d 282 (Cal. Ct. App. 1993)

DIBIASO, Associate Justice.

Linda H. challenges a disposition order in a juvenile dependency matter involving her young son Joshua H. Infant Joshua suffered severe physical abuse at the hands of his mother's boyfriend; the mother knew her boyfriend was abusing her son. (Welf. & Inst. Code,[1] § 300, subd. (e)). Based on these circumstances and pursuant to section 361.5, subdivision (b)(5) and (c), the juvenile court declined to order any reunification services for the mother and set the matter for a permanency planning hearing under section 366.26. This court stayed the section 366.26 proceedings pending review. We . . . deny the mother's writ petition and dismiss her appeal.

* * *

Linda H. was a 17-year-old who until mid-January of 1992 lived in Texas with her son and her grandparents. She had had nothing to do with the baby's father since before Joshua was born. In the fall of 1991 she met Ryan G., a 16-year-old from Fresno, who was staying with a relative in Texas at the request of his mother.

In January 1992, Ryan received his mother's permission to not only return to Fresno but to bring Linda and the baby with him. The three arrived in Fresno in mid-January. Linda and Ryan settled in Clovis.

Almost immediately the baby began "getting on Ryan's nerves" and the teenager was unable to control his emotions. Ryan would pick on the baby and become angry when Linda gave Joshua more attention. Eventually, Ryan started injuring the child. The situation became increasingly worse when Linda commenced school around the first of February.

On two occasions, Linda witnessed Ryan using his open hand against the baby's forehead and pushing him, causing Joshua to fall. Another time she attempted to stop Ryan from hitting Joshua with a closed fist; the baby was nevertheless struck, which caused him to fall against the headboard of the bed. She further witnessed her boyfriend repeatedly push a walker, while Joshua was seated in it, with such force that the baby's neck snapped backwards.

On February 3rd, Linda took Joshua to a day-care center located on the campus of the high school she attended. A nurse at the center questioned Linda about bruises on Joshua's forehead. The mother claimed Joshua had bumped his head against his crib or a wall. In fact, Ryan had caused the bruising by head-butting the baby. For the next several days the mother kept Joshua out of the day-care center and paid a sitter to watch him in an attempt to keep the center from reporting her to the authorities.

Around the 3rd of February, Linda left Joshua with Ryan while she went out to play basketball. During this baby-sitting episode, Ryan placed Joshua on his back and used his closed fists to repeatedly punch the baby in the chest.

---

[1] All statutory references are to the Welfare and Institutions Code unless otherwise indicated.

Ryan admitted to the police that on or about February 4th he slapped Joshua 9 to 10 times on the left side of the face, causing the baby to suffer a black eye.

On February 11, the day-care center apparently contacted Child Protective Services. That day, according to social worker and police reports, Joshua had multiple bruises on his face and abdomen. Doctors at Valley Medical Center examined the minor and reported that, in addition to the bruising, Joshua had sustained eight rib fractures. They diagnosed Joshua as suffering from battered child syndrome.

Both Linda and Ryan were arrested and detained at juvenile hall.

* * *

At the dispositional hearing in May, the department recommended, pursuant to section 361.5, subdivisions (b)(5) and (c), that the juvenile court deny the mother reunification services and set the case for a permanency planning hearing under section 366.26. To this end, the department introduced evidence intended to establish: (1) the provision of reunification services would not prevent Joshua's reabuse and (2) the absence of reunification services would not be detrimental because the child was not closely and positively attached to his mother.[3]

Gordon Cappelletty, a clinical psychologist, interviewed the mother in early April to determine the feasibility of reuniting her with Joshua. He reported Linda had suffered a number of emotional traumas as a child, which made her very vulnerable emotionally and produced strong needs for attention and affection from others. "These needs manifested themselves in a clinging dependency on the male figures in her life."

> When these needs are not met, which is likely to be much of the time, she will develop a great deal of anger, and resentment. . . . With or without the use of drugs, Ms. [H.]'s relationships are likely to be quite volatile and unstable. . . . Though she claimed in a very sincere manner that she was no longer interested in her former boyfriend, her sincerity at terminating the relationship with him is very questionable. At the least, she will probably enter into another relationship which is as violent as her previous relationship.
>
> . . . Ms. [H.]'s fear of being abandoned by her boyfriend over-rode her desire to protect her child.

Nevertheless, the psychologist wrote in his report:

> . . . Ms. [H.]'s chances to benefit from treatment are fair to good. She appears to be highly motivated, has good verbal skills, and is adequately able to reflect on herself and her behavior. The treatment plan that would best meet Ms. [H.]'s needs would involve a combination of psychotherapy, parenting classes, anger management, and

---

[3] The mother does not contend Joshua was closely and positively attached to her. Thus, the evidence on this issue has not been summarized.

> assertiveness training. The assertiveness training is very important in order to break the cycle of dependency on others. . . .

At the disposition hearing, Cappelletty testified about the importance of the mother's motivation to change the circumstances of her life. If she lacked such motivation, no amount of treatment would be successful in helping her overcome the psychological problems which led her to allow Joshua's abuse. If she were using drugs, it would greatly reduce the effect of counseling and call into question the degree of her motivation. It would also cause the psychologist to question her sincerity, since she had denied to him that she had used any drugs after becoming pregnant with Joshua. If the mother were using drugs, then Cappelletty believed it would be unlikely Joshua could return to her custody within a year's time and not suffer further abuse.

The department introduced evidence that the mother was at least a chronic abuser of alcohol, marijuana and KJ (apparently an acronym for "killer joint" or a marijuana cigarette laced with phencyclidine [PCP]). There was also evidence that around the time the mother was interviewed by Dr. Cappelletty she had twice ingested PCP. Further, there was evidence the mother had told a counselor she was going to continue her relationship with Ryan.

At the conclusion of the hearing, the court announced it would not order reunification services for the mother. It determined the evidence was insufficient to establish either a close relationship between Joshua and his mother or a likelihood that she could sufficiently reunify with Joshua so as to protect him from future abuse. The court then ordered that a section 366.26 hearing be set for 120 days from the disposition hearing.

* * *

Next, the mother complains the juvenile court erroneously refused her the benefit of reunification services. She offers a variety of arguments to support her claim. We find no error.

The juvenile court denied the mother reunification services based on the language of section 361.5, subdivision (b)(5) and subdivision (c); these subdivisions provide:

> (b) Reunification services need not be provided to a parent described in this subdivision when the court finds, by clear and convincing evidence, any of the following:
>
> * * *
>
> (5) That the minor was brought within the jurisdiction of the court under subdivision (e) of Section 300 because of the conduct of that parent.
> (c) In deciding whether to order reunification in any case in which this section applies, the court shall hold a dispositional hearing. The probation officer shall prepare a report which discusses whether reunification services shall be provided. . . .
> When paragraph (3), (4), or (5), inclusive, of subdivision (b) is applicable, the court shall not order reunification unless it finds that, based on competent testimony, those services are likely to prevent

> reabuse or continued neglect of the child or that failure to try reunification will be detrimental to the child because the child is closely and positively attached to that parent. . . .
>
> The failure of the parent to respond to previous services, the fact that the child was abused while the parent was under the influence of drugs or alcohol, a past history of violent behavior, or testimony by a competent professional that the parent's behavior is unlikely to be changed by services are among the factors indicating that reunification services are unlikely to be successful. The fact that a parent or guardian is no longer living with an individual who severely abused the minor may be considered in deciding that reunification services are likely to be successful, provided that the court shall consider any pattern of behavior on the part of the parent that has exposed the child to repeated abuse.

The mother contends section 361.5, subdivision (b)(5) was inapplicable in her case and should not have been relied upon by the juvenile court, since the subdivision (e) finding was based not on her conduct but rather on the conduct of her boyfriend. According to the mother, the phrase "because of the conduct of that parent" in subdivision (b)(5) of section 361.5 limits the applicability of the subdivision to those situations where the parent is the person who actually inflicts the severe physical abuse on the child. Since this was indisputably not the case here, the mother asserts she was entitled to, and should have been afforded, reunification services. Alternatively, she claims the language of section 361.5, subdivision (b)(5) is impermissibly vague.

Construing section 361.5 in its entirety, as we must, we do not find subdivision (b)(5) of the statute to be vague. Rather, we find it was properly applied to the mother in the circumstances disclosed by the record before the juvenile court.

Subdivision (c) of section 361.5 explains how the court should proceed if it makes an affirmative finding under subdivision (b)(5). In such a case, the court may not order the provision of reunification services *unless* it finds:

> Those services are likely to prevent reabuse or continued neglect of the child or that failure to try reunification will be detrimental to the child because the child is closely and positively attached to that parent.

Subdivision (c) also provides explicit guidance for the juvenile court in determining whether reunification is likely to prevent reabuse. In this connection, it says:

> The fact that a parent or guardian is no longer living with an individual who severely abused the minor may be considered in deciding that reunification services are likely to be successful. . . .

This provision in section 361.5, subdivision (c) confirms that the Legislature intended subdivision (b)(5) of section 361.5 to apply to the parent who, knowing the actual abuser, knows or reasonably should have known that the other person was physically mistreating the child, as well as to the parent who personally abuses his or her child. Were it otherwise, as the mother proposes, this particular statutory language would be meaningless, for there would be no reason for the court to consider whether the parent was currently living with a third person if the parent was the abuser.

* * *

We believe our construction of section 361.5, subdivision (b)(5) gives effect to, and harmonizes, all parts of section 361.5, and carries out our obligation to interpret a statute, when reasonably possible, in such a manner as to render the enactment valid and constitutional rather than invalid and unconstitutional.

For reasons expressed, we find no basis for the mother's assertion the juvenile court improperly applied section 361, subdivision (b)(5) to her or that the statute is unlawfully vague.

The petition for writ of mandate is denied. The appeal from the disposition order is dismissed. The order granting a stay of the section 366.26 hearing is vacated; the stay of such hearing is dissolved.

Notes

1. Most state agencies use reunification services to satisfy the reasonable efforts to reunify requirements of AACWA and ASFA. If a state agency fails to make reasonable efforts to reunify a family, the federal government may demand reimbursement of funds granted to the state for foster care placement. *See* Michael J. Bufkin, Note, *The "Reasonable Efforts" Requirement: Does it Place Children at Risk of Abuse or Neglect?*, 35 U. LOUISVILLE J. FAM. L. 355, 361 (1996-1997); John Haney & Lisa Kay, *Making Reasonable Efforts in Iowa Foster Care Cases: An Empirical Analysis,* 81 IOWA L. REV. 1629 (1996); David J. Herring, *Inclusion of the Reasonable Efforts Requirement in Termination of Parental Rights Statutes: Punishing the Child for the Failures of the State Child Welfare System,* 54 U. PITT. L. REV. 139, 154 (1992). Some states individually place a duty on state agencies to use reasonable efforts to avoid the termination of parental rights. *See, e.g., In re Dino E.*, 8 Cal. Rptr. 2d 416 (Ct. App. 1992) (the reunification plan must be specifically tailored to the needs of the family).

2. Time is an important factor when reunifying a family. The longer a child spends in foster care away from his or her parents, the more the bond between the parents and the child becomes strained. Some states have attempted to limit the length a child stays in foster care by limiting how long a family may receive reunification services. In California, a family is permitted to receive reunification services for a maximum of six months. *See* MARIANNE BARRY, KEEPING FAMILIES TOGETHER 4 (1994). In fact, the average duration of reunification services per family in California is three months. *Id.*

3. In *In re A.A.*, 20 P.3d 492 (Wash. App. Ct. 2001), the court held that "all reasonable services" as required by a TPR statute does not obligate a state to try to place children with their relatives. In *A.A.*, the parents appealed the termination of their parental rights because Washington authorities failed to comply with a judge's order to investigate the child's out-of-state grandparents as a replacement option. In reaching its holding, the *A.A.* court distinguished "services" from an "outcome" of a dependency proceeding. According to the court, the TPR statute obligated the state to provide reasonable services such as parenting classes and drug abuse counseling which are aimed at enabling parents to resume custody of their children. The placement of children with relatives, however, is an outcome of the dependency proceedings and is therefore not a service that a state must provide during the dependency.

4. In *In re Ashley M.*, 754 A.2d 341 (Me. 2000), the court held that shaking a baby with the degree of force necessary to cause shaken baby syndrome was sufficient for a trial court to order to order reunification services be discontinued. In *Ashley M.*, a five-month-old baby was admitted to the hospital on two different occasions for injuries sustained when her father shook her with sufficient force to cause severe injury. Upon the second admission, the child welfare department took the baby into custody. The trial court found that violent shaking by the father constituted aggravating circumstances under ASFA. The court, therefore, relieved the child welfare department of its duty to provide reunifications services to the father. The *Ashley M.* court affirmed the trial court and found that all of the statutory elements of aggravated assault were present. The court noted that ASFA explicitly provides aggravating assault as an exception to the requirement that the reunification services be provided to parents of abused or neglected children.

Questions

1. Does the state have a duty to provide reunification services to parents if the services are not likely to create better conditions for the child's safe return? Should the state provide in addition to reunification services extra resources to help the family create a favorable environment for the child's return? What social concerns are present when the state takes a child away from poor parents who are "neglecting" the child?

2. Should the state require parents to admit abuse or neglect in order to receive reunification services? What impact would parents' denial of abuse and neglect have on the state's attempt to reunify the family through reunification services? What ethical implications might arise if parents must admit the abuse or neglect in order to receive reunification services?

3. Reunification Versus Child Protection

In re Edward C.

178 Cal. Rptr. 694 (Cal. Ct. App. 1981)

BARRY-DEAL, Associate Justice.

Appellants, Edmond and Deborah C., appeal from judgments of the juvenile court declaring their children, Eric and Edward, dependent children of the juvenile court under section 300, subdivision (a), of the Welfare and Institutions Code[1] and removing the children from their custody and control pursuant to sections 361 and 362 of the code.

Appellants assert . . . that . . . the disposition orders must be set aside because they do not contain a reunification plan. . . .

We affirm the judgments.

Facts

As an appellate court, we must review the record in the light most favorable to the judgment below, and we must indulge in all reasonable inferences to support the findings of the juvenile court. With this basic rule in mind, we set out the facts from the evidence adduced at the combined jurisdiction and disposition hearing.

Appellants have three children: Eric (born January 21, 1971), Marlee (born May 31, 1972), and Edward (born November 7, 1973).

In 1973 the family was living in Idaho, as was Mrs. R., the maternal grandmother. Dependency proceedings were instituted there for Marlee, 11 months old at the time, because she was malnourished and had suffered a probable concussion of questionable origin. She was adjudged a dependent child and placed in the home of Mrs. R., who adopted Marlee through formal proceedings in Idaho in 1977. . . .

Appellants, with Eric and Edward, returned to California to live. In 1975, in Santa Clara County, the two boys were placed in protective custody because there was no food in the home, the home was in a disheveled condition, and because Eric, then four, had received numerous marks and welts as a result of excessive discipline by the father throughout the night. A petition requesting that the boys be adjudged dependents and placed in a foster home was sustained. In July 1977 the foster family moved away, and the boys were allowed

---

[1] Unless otherwise specified, all references hereafter will be to the Welfare and Institutions Code. As relevant, section 300 provides; "Any person under the age of 18 years who comes within any of the following descriptions is within the jurisdiction of the juvenile court which may adjudge such person to be a dependent child of the court:

"(a) Who is in need of proper and effective parental care of control and has no parent or guardian, or has no parent or guardian willing to exercise or capable of exercising such care or control, or has no parent or guardian actually exercising such care or control. . . .

* * *

"(d) Whose home is an unfit place for him by reason of neglect, cruelty, depravity, or physical abuse of either of this parents, or of his guardian or other person in whose custody or care he is."

to return to appellants on a 60-day trial basis. Appellants refused counseling, offered minimal cooperation, and failed to maintain regular contact with the probation department. Nevertheless, dependency proceedings for the boys were terminated on December 28, 1978. . . .

In August 1979 the maternal grandmother, believing that the father had permanently left the home and hoping that the children could be reacquainted, allowed Marlee an extended visit with her mother and two brothers in California. . . .

During her two-week visit in March 1980, the grandmother observed the father disciplining the three children by hitting them with a leather strap, looped over. Although the boys were spanked a few times with clothing on, Marlee was beaten at least a dozen times, usually on her bare flesh. The boys witnessed Marlee's whippings, heard her cry, and listened to their father, while administering the beating, explain to the children that he was doing it because God wanted him to and that it was Biblically ordained. The grandmother was not allowed near the children except at mealtime, so she was unable to see whether Marlee was severely injured.

The grandmother testified that one night Marlee was strapped three times during the night for wetting the bed, and she could hear Marlee screaming. This incident was corroborated by a neighbor whose call to the police for investigation was ineffectual.

* * *

After one severe beating of Marlee prompted by her inability to recall what she had learned in church, the grandmother observed blood on Marlee's underpants. This incident firmed the grandmother's resolve to remove Marlee from appellants' household. She called the police for assistance and requested that they look at all three children for signs of abuse. A visual check of Marlee revealed numerous abrasions, bruises, and lacerations on her buttocks, legs, and arms; she was taken into protective custody. (Apparently, there were no significant bruises on the boys.) A petition was filed concerning Marlee on March 26, and she was detained in the Children's Shelter pending a jurisdictional hearing.[2]

Petitions were filed for Eric and Edward after an incident on March 27. . . .

The father, admitting that he had "spanked" the children since his return home, denied that he had caused any bruises on them or that he had even noticed any injuries other than insect bites. He proclaimed that he loved and treated his children equally and that God directed his discipline of them. Counseling would be useless since he had given his heart to the Lord. The mother did not testify, but she informed the investigating officer that she supported her husband's manner of discipline. . . .

---

[2] The petition for Marlee was dismissed and she was returned to the custody of her grandmother after the Idaho adoption decree had been confirmed.

At the conclusion of the dependency hearing on April 18, 1980, the court found (1) that Marlee's injuries reflected infliction upon a child of unjustifiable physical pain and suffering . . . ; (2) that those injuries established the imposition of cruel and inhuman corporal punishment . . . ; (3) that there had been presented competent professional evidence that the injuries were of such a nature as would ordinarily not be sustained except as a result of unreasonable or neglectful acts or omissions of either parent or guardian . . . ; and (4) that there was clear and convincing evidence as it related to each of the petitions on behalf of the minors; the allegations of the petitions filed April 14, 1980, were found to be true and the minors to come within the provisions of Welfare and Institutions Code section 300, subdivision (a), and adjudged dependents of the court. The court found that the return of the minors to the physical custody of the parents would be detrimental to the welfare of the minors, and they were committed to the care, custody, and control of the probation officer for suitable foster or relative home placement. The parents were ordered to be involved in a program of counseling for as long as deemed necessary by the supervising probation officer, such program to include a psychological evaluation.

II. *Plan for Reunification of Family*

Rule 1376, California Rules of Court, provides in pertinent part: "(b) . . . If a recommendation is made to remove the minor from the home, the . . . social worker shall also include in the social study a recommended plan for reuniting the minor with the family. . . ."

In the case before us, the probation report contained the following:

. . . "Until [appellants] alone can show some cooperation in working towards proper care and discipline of the children, it is felt the boys would be more effectively cared for in a foster home, due to the excessive discipline administered to them by their father."

The report also recommended "[t]hat the parents be involved in a counseling program for as long as deemed necessary by the supervising Probation Officer."

Appellants contend that the above provisions do not comply with the requirements of rule 1376(b). . . and, therefore, that the order removing the children from their parents must be reversed. . . . They urge that "seeking ways of becoming effective parents" is a vague recommendation and does not tell them what they must do to regain custody of their children.

We are cognizant of the legislative and judicial concern for family relationships and for the need to strengthen family ties. We do not think, however, that the Legislature has mandated . . . a mechanical approach to a reunification plan for a family. Such a plan must be appropriate for each family and be based on the unique facts relating to that family.

Appellants have been through dependency proceedings three times. Because of the father's brutality, Marlee has been removed from the home twice, and Eric was removed from the home in 1975. Now both Eric and Edward are being removed to avert their further victimization. Three proceedings must surely have alerted the father to the inappropriateness of his disciplining techniques. Yet the father has shown no remorse, has persistently denied physical abuse of the children, has denied seeing bruises on Marlee, has declared his equal treatment of the children according to the tenets of his beliefs, and has disclaimed any need for counseling other than with the Lord. The mother has supported the father in his beliefs. After the first two proceedings, appellants showed no willingness to cooperate with the probation department and, indeed, failed even to apprise the department of their whereabouts for the most part.

In the face of the appellants' massive denial of any wrongdoing and refusal to participate in any plan for counseling, a detailed plan for reunification would have been a futile gesture to mechanically satisfy the provisions of rule 1376. The recommendation for counseling and the court order for counseling were sufficient to apprise appellants of the steps needed for reunification of the family. We find no error.

* * *

The judgments are affirmed.

Notes

1. Reunification of children and families often involves balancing the child's best interests versus the parents' interest in keeping the family together. One test to consider when balancing these competing interests was discussed in *New Jersey Division of Youth and Family Services v. A.W.,* 512 A.2d 438, 445-48 (N.J. 1986). The court created the following four-prong test to determine whether a court should reunify a family or terminate a parent's rights: (1) whether the child's health and development has been or will be seriously impaired by the parental relationship; (2) whether the parents are unable or unwilling to eliminate the harm or that a delay in permanent placement will add to the harm suffered by the child; (3) whether the alternatives to terminate parental rights have been thoroughly explored and exhausted and whether sufficient efforts have been made to help the parents cure the problems that led to the placement; and (4) whether all considerations must confirm that termination of parental rights will not do more harm than good.

2. The Uniform Juvenile Court Act defines what are proper dispositions for "deprived" children and provides for the termination of parental rights if the child would be in danger upon returning to his or her parents.

Uniform Juvenile Court Act

§ 30(a) (2000)

§ 30(a). Disposition of Deprived Child.

If the child is found to be a deprived child the court may make any of the following orders of disposition best suited to the protection and physical, mental, and moral welfare of the child:

1. permit the child to remain with his parents, guardian, or other custodian, subject to the conditions and limitations as the court prescribes, including supervision as directed by the court prescribes,

including supervision as described by the court for the protection of the child;

2. subject to conditions and limitations as the court prescribes transfer temporary legal custody. . . .

Uniform Juvenile Court Act

§ 47(a) (2000)

§ 47(a). Termination of Parental Rights.

The court by order may terminate the parental rights of a parent with respect to his child if:

* * *

2. the child is a deprived child and the court finds that the conditions and causes of the deprivation are likely to continue or will not be remedied and that by reason thereof the child is suffering or will probably suffer serious physical, mental, moral, or emotional harm;

* * *

3. Another problem created by ASFA's imposition of a time limit on the permanency hearing (*see* ASFA § 675(C)) is the frequent inability of parents attempting to recover from a drug or alcohol addiction to recover in time to reunite with their children. Many experts believe that the extraordinary increase in foster care populations is directly related to parental substance abuse. *See* Dorothy Roberts, *The Challenge of Substance Abuse for Family Preservation Policy,* 3 J. HEALTH CARE L. & POL'Y 72 (1999) (citing NAT'L CENTER ON ADDICTION AND SUBSTANCE ABUSE AT COLUM. U., NO SAFE HAVEN: CHILDREN OF SUBSTANCE ABUSING PARENTS 13 (1999)). Drug addiction treatment often lasts twenty-four months or longer while the permanency planning time limit requires a hearing within twelve months. *Id.* at 77. As a result, parents may leave their rehabilitation program before completion in order to regain placement of their child at the permanency hearing. If the parent does not complete the program, the parent is likely to relapse into the addiction, resulting in the child being removed again. However, if the parent is still in rehab when the permanency hearing takes place, the judge may sever the child's ties with the parent in order to meet the time limit imposed by law.

Questions

1. What should the state do when a parent makes a good faith attempt to meet the requirements of the permanency plan but "falls short" of some of its requirements?

2. Whose interest—those of the parent or child—should the juvenile court consider paramount? If the foster parents teach the child values and religious beliefs different than the natural parents' values and beliefs, how should the court balance the child's interests in a safe, healthy environment versus the parents' interests in teaching the child their own values and religious beliefs?

3. What are some concerns for children of parents who are mentally ill? *See In Interest of T.O.*, 470 N.W.2d 8 (Iowa 1991); *Egly v. Blackford County Dept. of Public Welfare,* 575 N.E.2d 312 (Ind. Ct. App. 1991).

E. Dispositional Orders

1. Child Placement—Interstate Dimension

Interstate Compact on the Placement of Children (1961)

Council of State Governments,
Suggested State Legislature 49 (1961)

Article I—Purpose and Policy

It is the purpose and policy of the party states to cooperate with each other in the interstate placement of children to the end that:

a. Each child requiring placement shall receive the maximum opportunity to be placed in a suitable environment and with persons or institutions having appropriate qualifications and facilities to provide a necessary and desirable degree and type of care.

b. The appropriate authorities in a state where a child is to be placed may have full opportunity to ascertain the circumstances of the proposed placement, thereby promoting full compliance with applicable requirements for the protection of the child.

c. The proper authorities of the state from which the placement is made may obtain the most complete information on the basis of which to evaluate a projected placement before it is made.

d. Appropriate jurisdictional arrangements for the care of children will be promoted.

Article II—Definitions

As used in this compact:

a. "Child" means a person who, by reason of minority, is legally subject to parental, guardianship, or similar control.

b. "Sending agency" means a party state, or officer or employee thereof, a subdivision of a party state, or officer or employee thereof; a court of a party state; a person, corporation, association, charitable agency, or other entity which sends, brings, or causes to be sent or brought any child to another party state.

c. "Receiving state" means the state to which a child is sent, brought, or caused to be sent or brought, whether by public authorities or private persons or agencies, and whether for placement with state or local public authorities or for placement with private agencies or persons.

d. "Placement" means the arrangement for the care of a child in a family free or boarding home or in a child-caring agency or institution but does not include any institution caring for the mentally ill, mentally defective, or epileptic or any institution primarily educational in character, and any hospital or other medical facility.

Article III—Conditions for Placements

1. No sending agency shall send, bring, or cause to be sent or brought into any other party state any child for placement in foster care or as a preliminary to a possible adoption unless the sending agency shall comply with each and every requirement set forth in this article and with the applicable laws of the receiving state governing the placement of the children therein.

2. Prior to sending, bringing, or causing any child to be sent or brought into a receiving state for placement in foster care or as a preliminary to a possible adoption, the sending agency shall furnish the appropriate public authorities in the receiving state written notice of the intention to send, bring, or place the child in the receiving state. The notice shall contain:

a. The name, date, and place of birth of the child.

b. The identity and address or addresses of the parents or legal guardian.

c. The name and address of the person, agency, or institution to or with which the sending agency proposes to send, bring, or place the child.

d. A full statement of the reasons for such proposed action and evidence of the authority pursuant to which the placement is proposed to be made.

3. Any public officer or agency in a receiving state which is in receipt of a notice pursuant to subsection 92 of this article may request of the sending agency, or any other appropriate officer or agency of or in the sending agency's state, and shall be entitled to receive therefrom, such supporting or additional information as it may deem necessary under the circumstances to carry out the purpose and policy of this compact.

4. The child shall not be sent, brought, or caused to be sent or brought into the receiving state until the appropriate public authorities in the receiving state shall notify the sending agency, in writing, to the effect that the proposed placement does not appear to be contrary to the interests of the child.

Article IV—Penalty for Illegal Placement

The sending, bringing, or causing to be sent or brought into any receiving state of a child in violation of the terms of this compact shall constitute a violation of the laws respecting the placement of children of both the state in which the sending agency is located or from which it sends or brings the child and of the receiving state. Such violation may be punished or subjected to penalty in either jurisdiction in accordance with its laws. In addition to liability for any such punishment or penalty, any such violation shall constitute full and sufficient grounds for the suspension or revocation of any license, permit, or other legal authorization held by the sending agency which empowers or allows it to place, or care for the children.

Article V—Retention of Jurisdiction

1. The sending agency shall retain jurisdiction over the child sufficient to determine all matters in relation to the custody, supervision, care, treatment, and the disposition of the child which it would have had if the child had remained in the sending agency's state, until the child is adopted, reaches

majority, becomes self-supporting, or is discharged with the concurrence of the appropriate authority in the receiving state. Such jurisdiction shall also include the power to effect or cause the return of the child or its transfer to another location and custody pursuant to law. The sending agency shall continue to have financial responsibility for support and maintenance of the child during the period of the placement. Nothing contained herein shall defeat a claim of jurisdiction by a receiving state sufficient to deal with an act of delinquency or crime committed therein.

2. When the sending agency is a public agency, it may enter into an agreement with an authorized public or private agency in the receiving state providing for the performance of 1 or more services in respect of such case by the latter as agent for the sending agency.

3. Nothing in this compact shall be construed to prevent a private charitable agency authorized to place children in the receiving state from performing services or acting as agent in that state for a private charitable agency of the sending state; nor to prevent the agency in the receiving state from discharging financial responsibility for the support and maintenance of a child who has been placed on behalf of the sending agency without relieving the responsibility set forth in subsection (1) of this article.

Article VI—Institutional Care of Delinquent Children

A child adjudicated delinquent may be placed in an institution in another party jurisdiction pursuant to this compact but no such placement shall be made unless the child is given a court hearing on notice to the parent or guardian with opportunity to be heard, prior to his or her being sent to such other party jurisdiction for institutional care and the court finds that:

a. Equivalent facilities for the child are not available in the sending agency's jurisdiction; and

b. Institutional care in the other jurisdiction is in the best interest of the child and will not produce undue hardship.

Article VII—Compact Administrator

The executive head of each jurisdiction party to this compact shall designate an officer who shall be general coordinator of activities under this compact in the officer's jurisdiction and who, acting jointly with like officers of other party jurisdictions, shall have power to promulgate rules and regulations to carry out more effectively the terms and provisions of this compact.

Article VIII—Limitations

This compact shall not apply to:

a. The sending or bringing of a child into a receiving state by the child's parent, stepparent, grandparent, adult brother or sister, adult uncle or aunt, or the child's guardian and leaving the child with any such relative or nonagency guardian in the receiving state.

b. Any placement, sending, or bringing of a child into a receiving state pursuant to any other interstate compact to which both the state from which the child is sent or brought and the receiving state are party, or to any other agreement between said states which has the force of law.

* * *

Article X—Construction and Severability

The provisions of this compact shall be liberally construed to effectuate the purposes thereof. The provisions of this compact shall be severable and if any phrase, clause, sentence or provision of this compact is declared to be contrary to the constitution of any party state or of the United States or the applicability thereof to any government, agency, person or circumstance is held invalid, the validity of the remainder of this compact and the applicability thereof to any government, agency, person or circumstance shall not be affected thereby. If this compact shall be held contrary to the constitution of any state party thereto, the compact shall remain in full force and effect as to the remaining states and in full force and effect as to the state affected as to all severable matters.

In re Adoption of A.M.M.

949 P.2d 1155 (Kan. Ct. App. 1997)

ROGG, Judge:

C.P. and J.P., the prospective adoptive parents, appeal the district court's order granting the natural mother's motion to revoke her consent and dismiss the adoption petition based on failure to comply with the Interstate Compact on the Placement of Children (ICPC), K.S.A. 38-1201 *et seq.*

On May 20, 1996, E.P. gave birth to twins, A.M.M. and A.N.M. At the time of their births, E.P. resided in Kansas City, Kansas. On May 24, 1996, E.P. moved to Kansas City, Missouri. Prior to the birth of the twins, E.P. had asked appellants, her former foster parents, if they would consider adopting the twins.

* * *

While E.P. lived in Missouri, her two older children attended Missouri schools. She acquired Missouri telephone service and a Missouri bank account. She applied for and received Missouri public assistance. E.P. testified that at the time she moved to Missouri in May 1996, she intended to stay in Missouri, and during the period she was there, she considered herself a Missouri resident.

E.P. had several conversations with appellants about adopting the twins, and on January 17, 1997, E.P. attended a meeting with her former foster father, C.P., and his attorney to get some general adoption information. E.P.'s residence was discussed and it was noted that if she were a resident of Missouri and if she proceeded with the adoption, the issue of the ICPC would have to be addressed, but if she were a Kansas resident, the ICPC would not apply.

C.P. testified that the parties discussed what steps could be taken in order for E.P. to establish residency in Kansas because the Kansas adoption procedure was less complicated. C.P. claimed that E.P. was going to move into a trailer he owned in Kansas and get a job in Lawrence.

E.P. testified that on January 19, 1997, she called appellants in Kansas and asked whether they would take care of the twins because she was under a lot of stress. They agreed and picked up the twins in Missouri and brought them back to their home in Kansas. The parties agreed that on that date, the placement with appellants was not for the purpose of an adoption.

On January 21, 1997, E.P. went to appellants' attorney's office in Kansas and signed consents to adoption for A.M.M. and A.N.M. On the forms, she listed her residence as Missouri, and she returned to Missouri after signing the forms. Then on January 22, 1997, E.P. went back to Kansas to sign power of attorney documents to allow appellants to give medical care to the twins.

On February 12, 1997, E.P. entered into a lease agreement with her former foster father to rent a trailer home in Kansas. She enrolled her children in school and applied for Kansas welfare benefits. By February 20, 1997, R.W., a potential father of the twins, had indicated his willingness to sign a consent for A.M.M.'s and A.N.M.'s adoption. The actual consent was not signed until February 28, 1997, however, because R.W. was involved in an accident. P.S., another potential father, signed a consent on February 25, 1997.

Between February 23 and February 25, E.P. communicated to appellants that she did not want to go through with the adoption. Appellants, however, proceeded to file a petition for adoption on February 26, 1997.

On February 27, 1997, E.P. filed a written revocation of consent and a petition for declaratory judgment seeking a declaration that her consent be revoked. On March 25, 1997, E.P. filed a motion to dismiss, claiming that the ICPC had not been complied with and, therefore, the petition should be dismissed.

On April 10, 1997, the district court held a hearing on the limited issue of noncompliance with the ICPC. After the hearing, the district court granted E.P.'s motion to dismiss. The court found that, at the time the twins were transferred to appellants, E.P. was a resident of Missouri and, therefore, the ICPC applied. The court further found the parties did not comply with the ICPC, and it revoked E.P.'s consent and dismissed the petition for adoption.

A pivotal issue concerns which date should be used to determine the natural mother's residency at the "time of placement for adoption" and, thus, whether the ICPC applies. The district court made the following finding regarding E.P.'s residency: "On January 21, 1997, [E.P.], still a resident of Missouri, came to Kansas and signed consents to the adoptions." The district court used January 21, 1997, as the date to determine residency under the ICPC.

Appellants claim that the district court looked at the wrong date to determine E.P.'s residency. They claim that the consent date was not the proper date to consider but, rather, February 25, 1997, should have been used because that was the date the "conditional" consent was satisfied, and on that date E.P. was a resident of Kansas. Appellants claim that until the conditions for the use of E.P.'s consents were satisfied, those being the date when both fathers indicated their support of the adoption and the uncertainty about E.P.'s residency had been resolved, it was not possible to determine the relationship of the parties or properly determine the residence of the birth mother.

K.S.A. 38-1202, art. III(a) states:

> "No sending agency shall send, bring, or cause to be sent or brought into any other party state any child for *placement in foster care or as a preliminary to a possible adoption* unless the sending agency shall comply with each and every requirement set forth in this article and

with the applicable laws of the receiving state governing the placement of children therein." (Emphasis added.)

On January 19, 1997, appellants took physical custody of A.M.M. and A.N.M. At that point, all parties conceded and the district court found that the placement of the twins with appellants was *not* for the purpose of adoption. On January 21, 1997, E.P. signed consents to adoption in which she relinquished custody of A.M.M. and A.N.M. The consents specifically stated that she consented and agreed to the adoption of A.M.M. and A.N.M. by appellants. The consents further waived notice of any future hearings concerning the adoption. There is nothing in the ICPC requiring that a placement be unconditional before the ICPC comes into effect, and appellants cite no authority for such proposition. Courts in other jurisdictions have found the ICPC came into effect prior to the adoption petition being filed. *See In re Adoption No. 10087*, 324 Md. 394, 597 A.2d 456 (1991) (ICPC came into effect when the child was transported across state lines for the purpose of adoption); *In the Matter of T.M.M.*, 186 Mont. 460, 461-62, 608 P.2d 130 (1980).

* * *

Once E.P. signed consents for adoption of the twins, the status of appellants changed from that of providing respite care to that of placement preliminary to a possible adoption, and the ICPC came into effect.

* * *

It is the placement of a child as preliminary to a possible adoption which triggers the ICPC. The district court properly considered January 21, 1997, as the date on which to determine E.P's state of residency, because that is the date the purpose of the placement of A.M.M. and A.N.M. became clear.

* * *

The district court allowed E.P. to revoke her consent and dismissed the adoption petition based on the parties' noncompliance with the ICPC. Appellants contend that if the ICPC applied, the district court imposed an improper remedy.

The ICPC does not define the penalties that should apply when a person, rather than an agency, fails to comply with the ICPC's notice requirements. The issue of the proper remedy for failure to comply with the ICPC is an issue of first impression in Kansas. For guidance on how to handle this issue, it is helpful to review how other states have handled such an issue and their rationale.

In *T.M.M.*, 186 Mont. 460, 608 P.2d 130, the natural mother, a resident of Mississippi, executed a parent's consent relinquishing her rights in her child and allowing for adoption by the prospective adoptive parents, residents of Montana. The prospective adoptive parents picked up the child in Mississippi and, after a brief stay, returned to Montana. The prospective adoptive parents then filed a petition for adoption in Montana. The district court in Montana entered an order terminating the natural mother's rights.

The natural mother filed an action in Montana to withdraw her consent. The district court dismissed her challenge for lack of standing. The natural mother appealed, contending that the prospective adoptive parents did not follow the provisions of the ICPC. The Montana Supreme Court found that pursuant to the ICPC, the prospective adoptive parents were required to furnish SRS with written notice of their intention to bring the child to Montana. The court stated: "By virtue of the failure of the prospective adoptive parents to comply with the Compact, the placement of the child with the prospective adoptive parents in Montana constituted an illegal placement under the provisions of the Compact." 186 Mont. at 466, 608 P.2d 130. It went on to find that the "parent's consent" was the "legal authorization" held by the prospective adoptive parents and, therefore, their failure to comply with the terms and provisions of the Compact constituted sufficient grounds for revocation of the "parent's consent."

In *In re Adoption/Guardianship No. 3598*, 109 Md.App. 475, 499, 675 A.2d 170, *cert. granted* 342 Md. 582, 678 A.2d 1047 (1996), the court was faced with the issue of how to remedy a situation in which the adoptive parents removed a child from the state in violation of the ICPC and held the child for a sufficient period of time that the best interests of the child appeared to dictate adoption, but a natural parent had contested the adoption. It held:

> "Allowing violations to continue under the best interests of the child exception is problematic; the exception swallows up the rule. Every time there is a violation of the ICPC, the adoptive parents will have bonded with the child, making adoption the most attractive course. . . . In this case, unlike other cases that have ignored the violations of the ICPC for the sake of the child's best interests, there is a willing and able natural father who wants custody of the child. We cannot conclude that such placement is contrary to the child's best interests. In cases in which a child can be returned to a natural parent, a circuit court should enforce the spirit of the [ICPC]."

109 Md.App. at 510, 675 A.2d 170.

In *Matter of Jon K.*, 141 Misc.2d 949, 950, 535 N.Y.S.2d 660 (1988), petitioners sought to adopt an infant who had been brought into New York in violation of the ICPC. The court held that the best interests of the child test did not preclude dismissing a petition for adoption where the ICPC was violated.

* * *

In *In re C.M.A.*, 447 N.W.2d 353, 358 (Minn. App. 1996) *rev. denied* April 15, 1997, the court held that a violation of the ICPC did not warrant vacation of the adoption decree where the violation was not knowingly done.

In *In re Baby Girl*, 850 S.W.2d 64 (Mo. 1993), the natural mother signed a consent to adoption shortly after the birth of the child. The child was then taken from Missouri to Arkansas, and the adoptive parents filed a petition for adoption in Arkansas. The natural mother then sought to revoke her consent. Although the court spoke favorably of the holding in *T.M.M.*, it went on to hold:

> "[T]he statute provides that 'any such violation shall constitute full and sufficient grounds for the suspension or revocation of any license, or permit, or other legal authorization held by the sending

> agency which empowers or allows it to place, or care for children.' We believe this language allows the trial court discretion to enter an order as to the continuing validity of a consent and the custody of the child that it finds just in light of the facts and circumstances of the case before it. Again, at the pinnacle of the court's decision must be the child's best interests, not the interests of the other parties or even 'public policy.' These matters must be determined on a case-by-case basis. Revocation of consent based merely on Compact noncompliance could produce a potentially harsh result that may be contrary to the child's best interest."

850 S.W.2d at 71.

* * *

In the present case, the district court expressly found E.P. to be a "sending agency," but it went on to find that both parties violated the ICPC's provisions. Appellants argue that because E.P. was the "sending agency" and because she violated the ICPC, the district court wrongfully rewarded her by allowing her to withdraw her consent.

E.P. counters by arguing that appellants should also be considered a "sending agency" because they "brought or caused the children to be brought into the state for purposes of adoption." She argues that appellants also had a duty to comply with the ICPC but failed to do so. In their brief, appellants claimed they "did not knowingly or intentionally violate the provisions of the ICPC."

> "'Sending agency' means a party state, officer or employee thereof; a subdivision of a party state, or officer or employee thereof; a court of a party state, *a person*, corporation, association, charitable agency or other entity which sends, brings, or causes to be sent or brought any child to another party state." (Emphasis added.)

K.S.A. 38-1201, art. II(b).

Appellant C.P. knew that on January 17, 1997, when he and E.P. went to meet with his attorney, E.P. was a Missouri resident. C.P. testified that the parties discussed what steps would need to be taken in order for E.P. to establish residency in Kansas because the Kansas adoption procedure was less complicated, and they could avoid the requirements of the ICPC by doing so. C.P. claimed that they discussed that E.P. could move into a trailer he owned in Kansas in order to establish her residency in Kansas. Appellants were aware of the ICPC, and it appears that they were trying to avoid its application by having E.P. become a Kansas resident prior to the adoption.

Appellants erred in believing that the ICPC would not go into effect until an adoption petition was filed on the theory that the consents were conditional until that date. To allow appellants to claim that they had no duty to comply with the ICPC, when they knew of its existence at the time they were holding the twins preliminary to a prospective adoption, would go against the purpose of the ICPC. Their mistaken belief as to its application date is no excuse when they knew that it would apply in an interstate adoption. Based on the unique fact situation, appellants also violated the ICPC.

Applicants urge us to adopt a best interests of the child exception to counter any noncompliance with the ICPC. We decline to do so. As the Maryland Court of Appeals stated:

> "[I]t needs to be asked whether it is really good to make 'an exception' of each case on the pleas of the 'best interests of the chid.' It would not take many dismissals of adoption petitions and removal of children from homes in violation of placement laws to stop these efforts at evasion. They continue because failure to enforce the law encourages others to do likewise." *In re Adoption / Guardianship No. 3598,* 109 Md.App. At 506, 675 A.2d 170 (quoting American Public Welfare Association, *The Interstate Compact on the Placement of Children: Compact Administrator's Manual,* 3.157-3.158 [1993]).

Such rationale is persuasive and should be followed by this court. Strict compliance with the ICPC should be enforced. Furthermore, Kansas recognizes a parental preference in custody disputes between a parent not found to be unfit and a third-party nonparent. *In re Guardianship of Williams,* 254 Kan. 814, 825, 869 P.12d 661 (1994).

Therefore, based on the specific factual situation in this case, the district court did not err in revoking the consent of E.P. based on a violation of the ICPC.

* * *

Affirmed.

Notes

1. The Interstate Compact on the Placement of Children (ICPC) (1961) was created because of three major concerns with interstate child placement: (1) state importation and exportation statutes did not protect children being placed in another state; (2) receiving states were not required to provide any assistance in the placement of the child even if the placement of the child was to his or her detriment; and (3) the sending state lacked any kind of jurisdiction over the child once the child was placed in another state. *See* THE SECRETARIAT TO THE ASS'N OF ADMINISTRATORS OF THE INTERSTATE COMPACT ON THE PLACEMENT OF CHILDREN, GUIDE TO THE INTERSTATE COMPACT ON THE PLACEMENT OF CHILDREN 3 (1985). Before the ICPC was adopted, children placed in another state might have received no protection or support because the receiving state owed no duty to the child and the sending state lost jurisdiction over the child. Today, all fifty states have ratified the ICPC. *See* Connie E. Eiseman, *Recent Decisions: The Maryland Court of Appeals,* 58 MD. L. REV. 920, 931 (1999). For further discussion of the purpose, policy and possible weaknesses of the ICPC, see Bernadette W. Hartfield, *The Role of the Interstate Compact On the Placement of Children in Interstate Adoption*, 58 NEB. L. REV. 292 (1989); Eiseman, *supra.*

2. In *In Adoption of Calynn*, 523 N.Y.S.2d 729, 730 (Fam. Ct. 1987), the court noted that parties frequently violate the ICPC. Critics of the ICPC blame the Compact's unclear enforcement and penalty mechanisms for frequent violations. The ICPC provides two forms of punishment for violations. First, courts may deny petitions for interstate placement. Several courts, however, make the argument that denying a petition for interstate placement might not be in the best interests of the child. *See, e.g., In re Adoption/Guardianship No. A91-71A,* 640 A.2d 1085 (Md. 1994); *Dietrich v. Anderson*, 43 A.2d 186 (Md. 1945). Therefore, the ICPC provides courts with little guidance in a case involving an ICPC violation whether to rule in the best interests of the child or to punish the child for the mistakes of the parents. This uncertainty often produces inconsistent sanctions among the states in ICPC violation situations. The ICPC also allows courts to punish statutory violations by using sanctions created by the laws of the sending or receiving states. While the ICPC does not provide for such a remedy, the court in *Calynn* penalized the attorneys who violated the ICPC by reducing the fees they could charge the parents for the adoption service. Some critics advocate penalizing attorneys for intentionally violating the ICPC as the best method for preventing violations of the ICPC. *See* Hartfield, *supra.*

Questions

1. What factors should the court consider when providing a remedy for violation of the ICPC?

2. The *Calynn* court punished the attorneys for intentionally trying to circumvent the ICPC. What if an attorney unintentionally violates the ICPC?

2. Visitation

Troxel v. Granville

530 U.S. 57, 120 S. Ct. 2054, 147 L. Ed. 2d 49 (2000)

* * *

Opinion:

Justice O'CONNOR announced the judgment of the Court and delivered an opinion, in which the CHIEF JUSTICE, Justice GINSBURG, and Justice BREYER join.

Section 26.10.160(3) of the Revised Code of Washington permits "any person" to petition a superior court for visitation rights "at any time," and authorizes that court to grant such visitation rights whenever "visitation may serve the best interest of the child." Petitioners Jenifer and Gary Troxel petitioned a Washington Superior Court for the right to visit their grandchildren, Isabelle and Natalie Troxel. Respondent Tommie Granville, the mother of Isabelle and Natalie, opposed the petition. The case ultimately reached the Washington

Supreme Court, which held that § 26.10.160(3) unconstitutionally interferes with the fundamental right of parents to rear their children.

I

Tommie Granville and Brad Troxel shared a relationship that ended in June 1991. The two never married, but they had two daughters, Isabelle and Natalie. Jenifer and Gary Troxel are Brad's parents, and thus the paternal grandparents of Isabelle and Natalie. After Tommie and Brad separated in 1991, Brad lived with his parents and regularly brought his daughters to his parents' home for weekend visitation. Brad committed suicide in May 1993. Although the Troxels at first continued to see Isabelle and Natalie on a regular basis after their son's death, Tommie Granville informed the Troxels in October 1993 that she wished to limit their visitation with her daughters to one short visit per month. *In re Smith*, 137 Wn.2d 1, 6, 969 P.2d 21, 23-24 (1998); *In re Troxel*, 87 Wn. App. 131, 133, 940 P.2d 698, 698-699 (1997).

In December 1993, the Troxels commenced the present action by filing, in the Washington Superior Court for Skagit County, a petition to obtain visitation rights with Isabelle and Natalie. The Troxels filed their petition under two Washington statutes, Wash. Rev. Code §§ 26.09.240 and 26.10.160(3) (1994). Only the latter statute is at issue in this case. Section 26.10.160(3) provides: "Any person may petition the court for visitation rights at any time including, but not limited to, custody proceedings. The court may order visitation rights for any person when visitation may serve the best interest of the child whether or not there has been any change of circumstances." At trial, the Troxels requested two weekends of overnight visitation per month and two weeks of visitation each summer. Granville did not oppose visitation altogether, but instead asked the court to order one day of visitation per month with no overnight stay. 87 Wn. App. at 133-134, 940 P.2d at 699. In 1995, the Superior Court issued an oral ruling and entered a visitation decree ordering visitation one weekend per month, one week during the summer, and four hours on both of the petitioning grandparents' birthdays. 137 Wn.2d at 6, 969 P.2d at 12; App. to Pet. For Cert. 76a-78a.

Granville appealed, during which time she married Kelly Wynn. Before addressing the merits of Granville's appeal, the Washington Court of Appeals remanded the case to the Superior Court for entry of written findings of fact and conclusions of law. 137 Wn.2d at 6, 969 P.2d at 23. On remand, the Superior Court found that visitation was in Isabelle and Natalie's best interests:

> "The Petitioners [the Troxels] are part of a large, central, loving family, all located in this area, and the Petitioners can provide opportunities for the children in the areas of cousins and music.
>
> ". . . The children would be benefitted from spending quality time with the Petitioners, provided that that time is balanced with time with the childrens' [*sic*] nuclear family. The court finds that the childrens' [*sic*] best interests are served by spending time with their mother and stepfather's other six children."

App. 70a.

Approximately nine months after the Superior Court entered its order on remand, Granville's husband formally adopted Isabelle and Natalie. *Id.* at 60a-67a.

The Washington Court of Appeals reversed the lower court's visitation order and dismissed the Troxels' petition for visitation, holding that nonparents lack standing to seek visitation under § 26.10.160(3) unless a custody action is pending. In the Court of Appeals' view, that limitation on nonparental visitation actions was "consistent with the constitutional restrictions on state interference with parents' fundamental liberty interest in the care, custody, and management of their children." 87 Wn. App. at 135, 940 P.2d at 700 (internal quotations marks omitted). Having resolved the case on the statutory ground, however, the Court of Appeals did not expressly pass on Granville's constitutional challenge to the visitation statute. *Id.* at 138, 940 P.2d at 701.

The Washington Supreme Court granted the Troxels petition for review and, after consolidating their case with two other visitation cases, affirmed. The court disagreed with the Court of Appeals' decision on the statutory issue and found that the plain language of § 2610.160(3) gave the Troxels standing to seek visitation, irrespective of whether a custody action was pending. 137 Wn.2d at 12, 969 P.2d at 26-27. The Washington Supreme Court nevertheless agreed with the Court of Appeals' ultimate conclusion that the Troxels could not obtain visitation of Isabelle and Natalie pursuant to § 26.10.160(3). The court rested its decision on the Federal Constitution, holding that § 26.10.160(3) unconstitutionally infringes on the fundamental right of parents to rear their children. In the court's view, there were at least two problems with the non-parental visitation statute. First, according to the Washington Supreme Court, the Constitution permits a State to interfere with the right of parents to rear their children only to prevent harm or potential harm to a child. Section 26.10.160(3) fails that standard because it requires no threshold showing of harm. *Id.* at 15-20, 969 P.2d at 28-30. Second, by allowing "'any person' to petition for forced visitation of a child at 'any time' with the only requirement being that the visitation serve the best interest of the child," the Washington visitation statute sweeps too broadly. *Id.* at 20, 969 P.2d at 30. . . . The Washington Supreme Court held that "parents have a right to limit visitation of their children with third persons," and that between parents and judges, "the parents should be the ones to choose whether to expose their children to certain people or ideas." *Id.* at 21, 9069 P.2d at 31. . . .

We granted certiorari, 517 U.S. 1069 (1999), and now affirm the judgment.

II

The demographic changes of the past century make it difficult to speak of an average American family. The composition of families varies greatly from household to household. . . . In 1996, children living with only one parent accounted for 28 percent of all children under age 18 in the United States. U.S. Dept. of Commerce, Bureau of Census, Current Population Reports, 1997 Population Profile of the United States 27 (1998). Understandably, in these single-parent households, persons outside the nuclear family are called upon with increasing frequency to assist in the everyday tasks of child rearing. In many cases, grandparents play an important role. For example, in 1998, approximately 4 million children—or 5.6 percent of all children under age 18—lived in the household of their grandparents. U.S. Dept. of Commerce, Bureau of Census, Current Population Reports, Marital Status and Living Arrangements: March 1998 (Update), p. *i* (1998).

The nationwide enactment of nonparental visitation statutes is assuredly due, in some part, to the States' recognition of these changing realities of the American family. Because grandparents and other relatives undertake duties of a parental nature in many households, States have sought to ensure the welfare of the children therein by protecting the relationships those children form with such third parties. The States' nonparental visitation statutes are further supported by a recognition, which varies from State to State, that children should have the opportunity to benefit from relationships with statutorily specified persons—for example, their grandparents. The extension of statutory rights in this area to persons other than a child's parents, however, comes with an obvious cost. For example, the State's recognition of an independent third-party interest in a child can place a substantial burden on the traditional parent-child relationship. . . . [T]hese statutes can present questions of constitutional import. In this case, we are presented with just such a question. Specifically, we are asked to decide whether § 26.10.160(3), as applied to Tommie Granville and her family, violates the Federal Constitution.

The Fourteenth Amendment provides that no State shall "deprive any person of life, liberty, or property, without due process of law." We have long recognized that the Amendment's Due Process Clause, like its Fifth Amendment counterpart, "guarantees more than fair process." *Washington v. Glucksberg*, 521 U.S. 702, 719, 138 L. Ed. 2d 772, 117 S. Ct. 228 (1997). The Clause also includes a substantive component that "provides heightened protection against government interference with certain fundamental rights and liberty interests." 521 U.S. at 720, *see also Reno v. Flores*, 507 U.S. 292, 301-302, 123 L. Ed. 2d 1, 113 S. Ct. 1439 (1993).

The liberty interest at issue in this case—the interest of parents in the care, custody, and control of their children—is perhaps the oldest of the fundamental liberty interests recognized by this Court. More than 75 years ago, in *Meyer v. Nebraska*, 262 U.S. 390, 399, 401 67 L. Ed. 1042, 43 S. Ct. 625 (1923), we held that the "liberty" protected by the Due Process Clause includes the right of parents to "establish a home and bring up children" and "to control the education of their own." Two years later, in *Pierce v. Society of Sisters*, 268 U.S. 510, 534-535, 69 L. Ed. 1070, 45 S. Ct. 571 (1925), we again held that the "liberty of parents and guardians" includes the right "to direct the upbringing and education of children under their control." We explained in *Pierce* that "the child is not the mere creature of the State; those who nurture him and direct his destiny have the right, coupled with the high duty, to recognize and prepare him for additional obligations." 268 U.S. at 535. . . .

In subsequent cases also, we have recognized the fundamental right of parents to make decisions concerning the care, custody, and control of their children. *See, e.g., Stanley v. Illinois,* 405 U.S. 645, 651, 31 L. Ed. 2d 551, 92 S. Ct. 1208 (1972) ("It is plain that the interest of a parent in the companionship, care, custody, and management of his or her children 'comes to this Court with a momentum for respect lacking when appeal is made to liberties which derive merely from shifting economis arrangements'" (citation omitted)); *Wisconsin v. Yoder*, 406 U.S. 205, 232, 32 L. Ed. 2d 15, 92 S. Ct. 1526 (1972) ("The history and culture of Western civilization reflect a strong tradition of parental concern for the nurture and upbringing of their children. This primary role of the parents in the upbringing of their children is now established beyond debate as an enduring American tradition"); *Quilloin v. Walcott,* 434 U.S. 246, 255, 54 L. Ed. 2d 511, 98 S. Ct. 549 (1978) ("We have recognized on numerous occasions that the relationship between parent and child is constitutionally protected"); *Parham v. J.R.*, 442 U.S. 584, 602, 61 L. Ed. 2d 101, 99 S. Ct. 2493 (1979) ("Our jurisprudence historically has reflected Western civilization concepts of the family as a unit with broad parental authority over minor children. Our cases have consistently followed that course"); *Santosky v. Kramer*, 455 U.S. 745, 753, 71 L. Ed. 2d 599, 102 S. Ct. 1388 (1982) (discussing "the fundamental liberty interest of natural parents in the care, custody, and management of their child:); *Glucksberg, supra*, at 720. ("In a long line of cases, we have held that, in addition to the specific freedoms protected by the Bill of Rights, the 'liberty' specially protected by the Due Process Clause includes the right . . . to direct the education and upbringing of one's children" (citing *Meyer* and *Pierce*)). In light of this extensive precedent, it cannot now be doubted that the Due Process Clause of the Fourteenth Amendment protects the fundamental rights of parents to make decisions concerning the care, custody, and control of their children.

Section 26.10.160(3), as applied to Granville and her family in this case, unconstitutionally infringes on that fundamental parental right. The Washington nonparental visitation statute is breathtakingly broad. According to the statute's text, *any person* may petition the court for visitation rights *at any time*," and the court may grant such visitation rights whenever "visitation may serve *the best interest of the child*." § 26.10.160(3) (emphases added). That language effectively permits any third party seeking visitation to subject any decision by a parent concerning visitation of the parent's children to state-court review. Once the visitation petition has been filed in court and the matter is placed before a judge, a parent's decision that visitation would not be in the child's best interest is accorded no deference. Section 26.10.160(3) contains no requirement that a court accord the parent's decision any presumption of validity or any weight whatsoever. Instead, the Washington statute places the best-interest determination solely in the hands of the judge. Should the judge disagree with the parent's estimation of the child's best interests, the judge's view necessarily prevails. Thus, in practical effect, in the State of Washington a court can disregard and overturn *any* decision by a fit custodial parent concerning visitation whenever a third party affected by the decision files a visitation petition, based solely on the judge's determination of the child's best interests. . . .

Turning to the facts of this case, the record reveals that the Superior Court's order was based on precisely the type of mere disagreement we have just described and nothing more. . . . To be sure, this case involves a visitation petition filed by grandparents soon after the death of their son—the father of Isabelle and Natalie—but the combination of several factors here compels our conclusion that § 26.10.160(3), as applied, exceeded the bounds of the Due Process Clause.

First, the Troxels did not allege, and no court has found, that Granville was an unfit parent. That aspect of the case is important, for there is a presumption that fit parents act in the best interests of their children. As this Court explained in *Parham:*

> "Our constitutional system long ago rejected any notion that a child is the mere creature of the State and, on the contrary, asserted that parents generally have the right, coupled with the high duty, to recognize and prepare [their children] for additional obligations. . . . The law's concept of the family rests on a presumption that parents possess what a child lacks in maturity, experience, and capacity for judgment required for making life's difficult decisions. More important, historically it has recognized that natural bonds of affection lead parents to act in the best interests of their children."

442 U.S. at 602 (alteration in original) (Internal quotation marks and citations omitted).

Accordingly, so long as a parent adequately cares for his or her children, (*i.e.*, is fit), there will normally be no reason for the state to inject itself into the private realm of the family to further question the ability of that parent to make the best decisions concerning the rearing of that parent's children. *See, e.g, Flores*, 507 U.S. at 304.

The problem here is not that the Washington Superior Court intervened, but that when it did so, it gave no special weight at all to Granville's determination of her daughters' best interests. . . . In reciting its oral ruling after the conclusion of closing arguments, the Superior Court judge explained:

> "The burden is to show that it is in the best interest of the children to have some visitation and some quality time with their grandparents. I think in most situations a commonsensical approach [is that] it is normally in the best interest of the children to spend quality time with the grandparent, unless the grandparent [*sic*] there are some issues or problems involved wherein the grandparents, their lifestyles are going to impact adversely upon the children. That certainly isn't the case here from what I can tell."

Verbatim Report of Proceedings in *In re Troxel,* No. 93-3-00650-7 (Wash. Super. Ct., Dec. 14, 19, 1994), p. 213 (hereinafter Verbatim Report).

The judge's comments suggest that he presumed the grandparents' request should be granted unless the children would be "impacted adversely." In effect, the judge placed on Granville, the fit custodial parent, the burden of *disproving* that visitation would be in the best interest of her daughters. . . .

The decisional framework employed by the Superior Court directly contravened the traditional presumption that a fit parent will act in the best interest of his or her child. *See Parham, supra*, at 602. In that respect, the court's presumption failed to provide any protection for Granville's fundamental constitutional right to make decision concerning the rearing of her own daughters. Cf., *e.g.*, Cal. Fam. Code Ann. § 3104(e) (West 1994) (rebuttable presumption that grandparent visitation is not in child's best interest if parents agree that visitation should not be granted); Me. Rev. Stat. Ann., Tit. 19A, § 1803(3) (1998)(court may award grandparent visitation if in best interest of child and "would not significantly interfere with any parent-child relationship or with the parent's rightful authority over the child"); Minn. Stat. § 257.022(2)(a)(2) (1998) (court may award grandparent visitation if in best interest of child and "such visitation would not interfere with the parent-child relationship"); Neb. Rev. Stat. § 43-1802(2) (1998) (court must find "by clear and convincing evidence" that grandparent visitation "will not adversely interfere with the parent-child relationship"); R.I. Gen. Laws § 15-5-24.3(a)(2)(v) (Supp. 1999) (grandparent must rebut, by clear and convincing evidence, presumption that parent's decision to refuse grandparent visitation was reasonable); Utah Code Ann. § 30-5-2(2)(3) (1998) (same); *Hoff v. Berg,* 1999 ND 115, 595 N.W.2d 285, 291-292 (N.D. 1999) (holding North Dakota grandparent visitation statute unconstitutional because State has no "compelling interest in presuming visitation rights of grandparents to an unmarried minor are in the child's best interests and forcing parents to accede to court-ordered grandparental visitation unless the parents are first able to prove such visitation is not in the best interests of their minor child"). In an ideal world, parents might always seek to cultivate the bonds between grandparents and their grandchildren. Needless to say, however, our world is far from perfect, and in it the decision whether such an intergenerational relationship would be beneficial in any specific case is for the parent to make in the first instance. And, if a fit parent's decision of the kind at issue here becomes subject to judicial review, the court must accord at least some special weight to the parent's own determination.

Finally, we note that there is no allegation that Granville ever sought to cut off visitation entirely. Rather, the present dispute originated when Granville informed the Troxels that she would prefer to restrict their visitation with Isabelle and Natalie to one short visit per month and special holidays. *See* 87 Wn. App. at 133, 940 P.2d at 699; Verbatim Report 12. In the Superior Court proceedings Granville did not oppose visitation but instead asked that the duration of any visitation order be shorter than that requested by the Troxels. . . . The Superior Court gave no weight to Granville's having assented to visitation even before the filing of any visitation petition or subsequent court intervention. The court instead rejected Granville's proposal and settled on a middle ground, ordering one weekend of visitation per month, one week in the summer, and time on both of the petitioning grandparents' birthdays. *See* 87 Wn. App. at 133-134, 940 P.2d at 699; Verbatim Report 216-221. Significantly, many other States expressly provide by statute that courts may not award visitation unless a parent has denied (or unreasonably denied) visitation to the concerned third party. *See, e.g.,* Miss. Code Ann. § 93-16-3(2)(a) (1994) (court must find that "the parent or custodian of the child unreasonably denied the grandparent visitation rights with the child"); Ore. Rev. Stat. § 109-121(1)(a)(B) (1997) (court may award visitation if the "custodian of the child has denied the grandparent reasonable opportunity to visit the child"); R.I. Gen. Laws § 15-5-24.3(a)(2)(iii)-(iv) (Supp. 1999) (court must find that parents prevented grandparent from visiting grandchild and that "there is no other way the petitioner is able to visit his or her grandchild without court intervention").

Considered together with the Superior Court's reasons for awarding visitation to the Troxels, the combination of these factors demonstrates that the visitation order in this case was an unconstitutional infringement on Granville's fundamental right to make decisions concerning the care, custody, and control of her two daughters. The Washington Superior Court failed to accord the determination of Granville, a fit custodial parent, any material weight. In fact, the Superior Court made only two formal findings in support of its visitation order. First, the Troxels "are part of a large, central, loving family, all located in this area, and the [Troxels] can provide opportunities for the chldren in the areas of cousins and music." App. 70a. Second, "the children would be benefitted from spending quality time with the [Troxels], provided that that time is balanced with time with the childrens' [*sic*] nuclear family." *Ibid.* These slender findings, in combination with the court's announced presumption in favor of grandparent visitation and its failure to accord significant weight to Granville's already having offered meaningful visitation to the Troxels, show that this case involves nothing more than a simple disagreement between the Washington Superior Court and Granville concerning her children's best interests. . . . As we have explained, the Due Process Clause does not permit a State to infringe on the fundamental right of parents to make childrearing decisions simply because a state judge believes a "better" decision could be made. Neither the Washington nonparental visitation statute generally—which places no limits on either the persons who may petition for visitation or the circumstances in which such a petition may be granted—nor the Superior Court in this specific case require anything more. Accordingly, we hold that § 26.10.160(3), as applied in this case, is unconstitutional.

Because we rest our decision on the sweeping breadth of § 26.10.160(3) and the application of that broad, unlimited power in this case, we do not consider the primary constitutional question passed on by the Washington Supreme Court—whether the Due Process Clause requires all no parental visitation statutes to include a showing of harm or potential harm to the child as a condition precedent to granting visitation. . . . Because much state-court adjudication in this context occurs on a case-by-case basis, we would be hesitant to hold that specific nonparental visitation statutes violate the Due Process Clause as a *per se* matter. *See, e.g. Fairbanks v. McCarter*, 330 Md. 29, 39-50, 622 A.2d 121, 126-127 (1993) (interpreting best-interest standard in grandparent visitation statute normally to require court's consideration of certain factors); *Williams v. Williams*, 256 Va. 19, 501 S.E.2d 417, 418 (1998) (interpreting Virginia nonparental visitation statute to require finding of harm as condition precedent to awarding visitation).

* * *

As we have explained, it is apparent that the entry of the visitation order in this case violated the Constitution. We should say so now, without forcing the parties into additional litigation that would further burden Granville's parental right. We therefore hold that the application of § 26.10.160(3) to Granville and her family violated her due process right to make decisions concerning the care, custody, and control of her daughters.

Accordingly, the judgment of the Washington Supreme Court is affirmed.

It is so ordered.

* * *

Justice STEVENS, dissenting:

* * *

In my view, the State Supreme Court erred in its federal constitutional analysis because neither the provision granting "any person" the right to petition the court for visitation, 137 Wn. 2d at 20, 969 P.2d at 30, nor the absence of a provision requiring a "threshold . . . finding of harm to the child," *ibid*., provides a sufficient basis for holding that the statute is invalid in all its applications. I believe that a facial challenge should fail whenever a statute has "a 'plainly legitimate sweep,'" *Washington v. Glucksberg,* 521 U.S. 702, 739-740, 138 L. Ed. 2d 772, 117 S. Ct. 2258 and n.7 (1997) (Stevens, J., concurring in judgment). Under the Washington statute, there are plainly any number of cases—indeed, one suspects, the most common to arise—in which the "person" among "any" seeking visitation is a once-custodial caregiver, an intimate relation, or even a genetic parent. Even the Court would seem to agree that in many circumstances, it would be constitutionally permissible for a court to award some visitation of a child to a parent or previous caregiver in cases of parental separation or divorce, cases of disputed custody, cases involving temporary foster care or guardianship, and so forth. As the statute plainly sweeps in a great deal of the permissible, the State Supreme Court majority incorrectly concluded that a statute authorizing "any person" to file a petition seeking visitation privileges would invariably run afoul of the Fourteenth Amendment.

* * *

Despite this Court's repeated recognition of these significant parental liberty interests, these interests have never been seen to be without limits. In *Lehr v. Robertson,* 463 U.S. 248, 77 L. Ed. 2d 614, 103 S. Ct. 2985 (1983), for example, this Court held that a putative biological father who had never established an actual relationship with his child did not have a constitutional right to notice of his child's adoption by the man who had married the child's mother. As this Court had recognized in an earlier case, a parent's liberty interests "'do not spring full-blown from the biological connection between parent and child. They require relationships more enduring.'" 463 U.S. at 250 (quoting *Caban v. Mohammed,* 441 U.S. 380, 397, 60 L. Ed. 2d 297, 99 S. Ct. 1760 (1979)).

Conversely, in *Michal H. v. Gerald D.,* 491 U.S. 110, 105 L. Ed. 2d 91, 109 S. Ct. 2333 (1989), this Court concluded that despite both biological parenthood and an established relationship with a young child, a father's due process liberty interest in maintaining some connection with that child was not sufficiently powerful to overcome a state statutory presumption that the husband of the child's mother was the child's parent. As a result of the presumption, the biological father could be denied even visitation with the child because, as a matter of state law, he was not a "parent." A plurality of this Court then recognized that the parental liberty interest was a function, not simply of "isolated factors" such as biology and intimate connection, but of the broader and apparently independent interest in family. *See, e.g.,* 491 U.S. at 123; *see also Lehr*, 463 U.S. at 251; *Smith v. Organization of Foster Families For Equality & Reform,* 431 U.S. 816, 842-847, 53 L. Ed. 2d 14, 97 S. Ct. 2094 (1977); *Moore v. East Cleveland,* 431 U.S. 494, 498-504, 52 L. Ed. 2d 531, 97 S. Ct. 1932 (1977).

A parent's rights with respect to her child have thus never been regarded as absolute, but rather are limited by the existence of an actual, developed relationship with a child, and are tied to the presence or absence of some embodiment of family. These limitations have arisen, not simply out of the definition of parenthood itself, but because of this Court's assumption that a parent's interests in a child must be balanced against the State's long-recognized interests as *parens patriae, see, e.g., Reno. V. Flores*, 507 U.S. 292, 303-304, 123 L. Ed. 2d 1, 113 S. Ct. 1439 (1993); *Santosky v. Kramer,* 455 U.S. at 766, *Parham,* 442 U.S. at 605; *Prince v. Massachusetts,* 321 U.S. 1598, 166, 98 L. Ed. 645, 64 S. Ct. 438 (1944), and, critically, the child's own complementary interest in preserving relationships that serve her welfare and protection, *Santosky*, 455 U.S. at 760.

While this Court has not yet had occasion to elucidate the nature of a child's liberty interests in preserving established familial or family-like bonds, 491 U.S. at 130 (reserving the question), it seems to me extremely likely that, to the extent parents and families have fundamental liberty interests in preserving such intimate relations, so, too, do children have these interests, and so, too, must their interests be balanced in the equation. . . . The constitutional protection against arbitrary state interference with parental rights should not be extended to prevent the States from protecting children against the arbitrary exercise of parental authority that is not in fact motivated by an interest in the welfare of the child.

* * *

This is not, of course, to suggest that a child's liberty interest in maintaining contact with a particular individual is to be treated invariably as on a par with that child's parents' contrary interests. Because our substantive due process case law includes a strong presumption that a parent will act in the best interest of her child, it would be necessary, were the state appellate courts actually to confront a challenge to the statute as applied, to consider whether the trial court's assessment of the "best interest of the child" incorporated that presumption.

* * *

Justice SCALIA, dissenting.

* * *

Judicial vindication of "parental rights" under a Constitution that does not even mention them requires . . . not only a judicially crafted definition of parents, but also—unless, as no one believes, the parental rights are to be absolute—judicially approved assessments of "harm to the child" and judicially defined gradations of other persons (grandparents, extended family, adoptive family in an adoption later found to be invalid, long-term guardians, etc.) who may have some claim against the wishes of the parents. If we embrace this unenumerated right, I think it obvious—whether we affirm or reverse the judgment here, . . . that we will be ushering in a new regime of judicially prescribed, and federally prescribed, family law. I have no reason to believe that federal judges will be better at this than state legislatures; and state legislatures have the great advantages of doing harm in a more circumscribed area, of being able to correct their mistakes in a flash, and of being removable by the people.

For these reasons, I would reverse the judgment below.

* * *

Justice KENNEDY, dissenting.

My principle concern is that the holding seems to proceed from the assumption that the parent or parents who resist visitation have always been the child's primary caregivers and that the third parties who seek visitation have no legitimate and established relationship with the child. That idea, in turn, appears influenced by the concept that the visitation standard for every domestic relations case. As we all know, this is simply not the structure or prevailing condition in many households.

* * *

Indeed, contemporary practice should give us some pause before rejecting the best interests of the child standard in all third-party visitation cases, as the Washington court has done. The standard has been recognized for many years as a basic tool of domestic relations law in visitation proceedings. Since 1965 all 50 states have enacted a third-party visitation statute of some sort. [*See ante*, plurality opinion.] Each of these statutes, save one, permits a court order to issue in certain cases if visitation is found to be in the best interests of the child . . . it can be noted that the statutes also include a variety of methods for limiting parents' exposure to third-party visitation petitions and for ensuring parental decisions are given respect. Many States limit the identity of permissible petitioners by restricting visitation petitions to grandparents, or by requiring petitioners to show a substantial relationship with a child, or both. *See, e.g.,* Kan. Stat. Ann. § 38-129 (1993 and Supp. 1998) (grandparent visitation authorized under certain circumstances if a substantial relationship exists); N.C. Gen. Stat. §§ 50-13.2, 50-13. 1A. 50-13.5 (1999) (same); Iowa Code § 598.35 (Supp. 1999) (same; visitation also authorized for great-grandparents); Wis. Stat. § 767.245 (Supp. 1999) (visitation authorized under certain circumstances for "a grandparent, greatgrandparent, stepparent, or person who has maintained a relationship similar to a parent-child relationship with the child"). The statutes vary in other respects—for instance, some permit visitation petitions when there has been a change in circumstances such as divorce or death of a parent, *see, e.g.,* N.H. Rev. Stat. Ann. § 458:17-d (1992), and some apply a presumption that parental decisions should control, *see, e.g.,* Cal. Fam. Code Ann. §§ 3104(e), (f) (West 1994): R.I. Gen. Laws § 15-4-24.3(a)(2)(v) (Supp.1999). Georgia's is the sole State Legislature to have adopted a general harm to the child standard, *see* Ga. Code Ann. § 19-7-3(c) (1999), and it did so only after the Georgia Supreme Court held the State's prior visitation statute invalid under the Federal and Georgia Constitutions, *see Brooks v. Parkerson*, 265 Ha. 189, 454 S.E.2d 769, *cert. denied*, 516 U.S. 942, 133 L. Ed. 2d 301, 116 S. Ct. 377 (1995).

* * *

In my view, it would be more appropriate to conclude that the constitutionality of the application of the best interests standard depends on more specific factors. In short, a fit parent's right vis-a-vis a complete stranger is one thing; her right vis-a-vis another parent or a *de facto* parent may be another.

* * *

It should suffice in this case to reverse the holding of the State Supreme Court that the application of the best interests of the child standard is always unconstitutional in third-party visitation cases.

* * *

In my view the judgment under review should be vacated and the case remanded for further proceedings.

Notes

1. In *In re Tamara R.*, 764 A.2d 844 (Md. Ct. App. 2000), the court held that a child's need for visitation with her siblings may outweigh the constitutional rights of the parent who opposes the visitation. The child, who was adjudicated as in need of assistance after being sexually abused by her father, petitioned the court to overrule a juvenile court's decision that granting visitation would unduly interfere with the father's constitutional right to rear his other children. The appellate court reversed the juvenile court and applied the *Troxel* holding to the child's petition to visit with her siblings. The court stated that *Troxel* did not create an irrebuttable presumption that a parent's opposition to visitation rights were in the child's best interests. Instead, *Tamara R.* read *Troxel* as holding that non-parent visitation statutes may be constitutional if courts have sufficient standards to apply in evaluating a non-parent's visitation claim and the standards include sufficient deference to the parent's determination of what is best for the child. *Tamara R.* also held that the state's interest in protecting a child in need of services was sufficient to override the parent's objection to the child's visitation with her siblings.

Questions

1. The majority in *Troxel* describes the Washington visitation statute as "breathtakingly broad." What statutory language may satisfy the Constitution after this decision?

2. How important was the fact that Tommie Granville did not prevent the Troxels from ever visiting their grandchildren? If parenting is a fundamental right could Ms. Granville have constitutionally done so?

3. What does Justice Stevens mean when he says that parental rights "do not spring full blown from the biological connection between parent and child. They require something more enduring." Do you agree?

F. Post-Disposition Proceedings

1. Court's Use of Contempt Power

Baltimore Department of Social Services v. Bouknight
493 U.S. 549, 110 S. Ct. 900, 107 L. Ed. 2d 992 (1990)

Justice O'CONNOR delivered the opinion of the Court.

In this action, we must decide whether a mother, the custodian of a child pursuant to a court order, may invoke the Fifth Amendment privilege against self-incrimination to resist an order of the juvenile court to produce the child. We hold that she may not.

I

. . . Maurice M. is an abused child. When he was three months old, he was hospitalized with a fractured left femur, and examination revealed several partially healed bone fractures and other indications of severe physical abuse. In the hospital, respondent Bouknight, Maurice's mother, was observed shaking Maurice, dropping him in his crib . . . , and otherwise handling him in a manner inconsistent with his recovery and continued health. Hospital personnel notified the Balitmore City Department of Social Services (BCDSS) . . . of suspected child abuse. In February 1987, BCDSS secured a court order removing Maurice from Bouknight's control and placing him in shelter care. . . . [T]he juvenile court declared Maurice to be a "child in need of assistance," thus asserting jurisdiction over Maurice and placing him under BCDSS' continuing oversight. BCDSS agreed that Bouknight could [act] as custodian of the child, but only pursuant to extensive conditions set forth in a court-approved protective supervision order. The order required Bouknight to "cooperate with BCDSS," "continue in therapy," participate in parental aid and training programs, and "refrain from physically punishing [Maurice]." The order's terms were "all subject to the further Order of the Court." Bouknight's attorney signed the order, and Bouknight in a separate form set forth her agreement to each term.

Eight months later, fearing for Maurice's safety, BCDSS returned to juvenile court. BCDSS caseworkers related that Bouknight would not cooperate with them and had in nearly every respect violated the terms of the protective order. . . . On April 20, 1988, the court granted BCDSS' petition to remove Maurice from Bouknight's control for placement in foster care. BCDSS officials also petitioned for judicial relief from Bouknight's failure to produce Maurice or reveal where he could be found. The petition recounted that on two recent visits by BCDSS officials to Bouknight's home, she had refused to reveal the location of the child or had indicated that the child was with an aunt whom she would not identify. The petition further asserted that inquiries of Bouknight's known relatives had revealed that none of them had recently seen Maurice and that BCDSS had prompted the police to issue a missing persons report and referred the case for investigation by the police homicide division. . . . The court issued an order to show cause why Bouknight should not be held in civil contempt for failure to produce the child. Expressing concern that Maurice was endangered or perhaps dead, the court issued a bench warrant for Bouknight's appearance.

Maurice was not produced at subsequent hearings. . . . [T]he juvenile court found Bouknight in contempt for failure to produce the child as ordered. There was and has been no indication that she was unable to comply with the order. The court directed that Bouknight be imprisoned until she "purge[d] herself of contempt by either producing [Maurice] before the court or revealing to the court his exact whereabouts."

The juvenile court rejected Bouknight's subsequent claim that the contempt order violated the Fifth Amendment's guarantee against self-incrimination. The court stated that the production of Maurice would purge the contempt and that "[t]he contempt is issued not because she refuse[d] to testify in any proceeding . . . [but] because she has failed to abide by the Order of this Court, mainly [for] the production of Maurice M. . . ." The Court of Appeals of Maryland vacated the juvenile court's judgment upholding the contempt order. *In re Maurice M.,* 314 Md. 391, 550 A.2d 1135 (1988). The Court of Appeals found that the contempt order unconstitutionally compelled Bouknight to admit through the act of production "a measure of continuing control and dominion over Maurice's person" in circumstances in which "Bouknight has a reasonable apprehension that she will be prosecuted. . . ." We granted certiorari, and we now reverse.

II

The Fifth Amendment provides that "No person . . . shall be compelled in any criminal case to be a witness against himself." The Fifth Amendment's protection "applies only when the accused is compelled to make a *testimonial* communication that is incriminating." *Fisher v. United States,* 425 U.S. 391, 308 (1976). The juvenile court concluded that Bouknight could comply with the order through the unadorned act of producing the child. . . . When the government demands that an item be produced, "the only thing compelled is the act of producing the [item]." *Fisher, supra,* at 410, n.11. The Fifth Amendment's protection may nonetheless be implicated because the act of complying with the government's demand testifies to the existence, possession, or authenticity of the things produced. . . . Bouknight claims the benefit of the privilege because the act of production would amount to testimony regarding her control over, and possession of, Maurice. Although the State could readily introduce evidence of Bouknight's continuing control over the child . . . her implicit communication of control over Maurice at the moment of production might aid the State in prosecuting Bouknight.

The possibility that a production order will compel testimonial assertions that may prove incriminating does not, in all contexts, justify invoking the privilege to resist production. Even assuming that this limited testimonial assertion is sufficiently incriminating and "sufficiently testimonial for purposes of the privilege," *Fisher, supra,* at 411, Bouknight may not invoke the privilege to resist the production order because she has assumed custodial duties related to production and because production is required as part of a noncriminal regulatory regime.

The Court has on several occasions recognized that the Fifth Amendment privilege may not be invoked to resist compliance with a regulatory regime constructed to effect the State's public purposes unrelated to the enforcement of its criminal laws. . . .

* * *

When a person assumes control over items that are the legitimate object of the government's noncriminal regulatory powers, the ability to invoke the privilege is reduced. In *Wilson v. United States,* 221 U.S. 361 (1911), the Court surveyed a range of cases involving the custody of public documents and records required by law to be kept because they related to "the appropriate subjects of governmental regulation and the enforcement of restrictions validly established." *Id.* at 380. The principle the Court drew from these cases is:

> "[W]here, by virtue of their character and the rules of law applicable to them, the books and papers are held subject to examination by the demanding authority, the custodian has no privilege to refuse production although their contents tend to criminate him. In assuming their custody he has accepted the incident obligation to permit inspection."

Id. at 382. . . .

These principles readily apply to this case. Once Maurice was adjudicated a child in need of assistance, his care and safety became the particular object of the State's regulatory interests. Maryland first placed Maurice in shelter care, authorized placement in foster care, and then entrusted responsibility for Maurice's care to Bouknight. By accepting care of Maurice subject to the custodial order's conditions (including requirements that she cooperate with BCDSS, follow a prescribed training regime, and be subject to further court orders), Bouknight submitted to the routine operation of the regulatory system and agreed to hold Maurice in a manner consonant with the State's regulatory interests and subject to inspection by BCDSS. . . . The juvenile court may place a child within its jurisdiction with social service officials or "under supervision in his own home or in the custody or under the guardianship of a relative or other fit person, upon terms the court deems appropriate." Md. Cts. & Jud. Proc. Code Ann. § 3-820(c)(1)(i) (Supp. 1989). . . . Even when the court allows a parent to retain control of a child within the court's jurisdiction, that parent is not one singled out for criminal conduct, but rather has been deemed to be, without the State's assistance, simply "unable or unwilling to give proper care and attention to the child and his problems." Md. Cts. & Jud. Proc. Code Ann. § 3-801(e) (Supp. 1989). The provision that authorized the juvenile court's efforts to gain production of Maurice reflects this broad applicability. *See* Md. Cts. & Jud. Proc. Code Ann. § 3-814(c) (1983) ("If a parent, guardian, or custodian fails to bring the child before the court when requested, the court may issue a writ of attachment directing that the child be taken into custody and brought before the court. The court may proceed against the parent, guardian, or custodian for contempt"). This provision "fairly may be said to be directed at . . . parents, guardians, and custodians who accept placement of juveniles in custody." 314 Md. at 418, 550 A.2d at 1148 (McAuliffe, J., dissenting).

. . . Even when criminal conduct may exist, the court may properly request production and return of the child, and enforce that request through exercise of the contempt power, for reasons related entirely to the child's well-being and through measures unrelated to criminal law enforcement or investigation. This case provides an illustration: concern for the child's safety underlay the efforts to gain access to and then compel production of Maurice. . . . Th[e]se orde[r]s to produce [Maurice] cannot be characterized as [an] effor[t] to gain some testimonial component of the act of production. . . . In these circumstances, Bouknight cannot invoke the privilege to resist the order to produce Maurice.

We are not called upon to define the precise limitations that may exist upon the State's ability to use the testimonial aspects of Bouknight's act of production in subsequent criminal proceedings. But we note that imposition of such limitations is not foreclosed. The same custodial role that limited the ability to resist the production order may give rise to corresponding limitations upon the direct and indirect use of that testimony. . . .

III

The judgment of the Court of Appeals of Maryland is reversed, and the cases are remanded to that court for further proceedings not inconsistent with this opinion.

Justice MARSHALL, with whom Justice BRENNAN joins, dissenting.

Although the Court assumes that respondent's act of producing her child would be testimonial and could be incriminating, it nonetheless concludes that she cannot invoke her privilege against self-incrimination and refuse to reveal her son's current location. [None] of the reasons the Court articulates to support its refusal to permit respondent to invoke her constitutional privilege justifies its decision. I therefore dissent.

I

The Court correctly assumes that Bouknight's production of her son to the Maryland court would be testimonial because it would amount to an admission of Bouknight's physical control over her son. The Court also assumes that Bouknight's act of production would be self-incriminating. I would not hesitate to hold explicitly that Bouknight's admission of possession or control presents a "'real and appreciable'" threat of self-incrimination. *Marchetti v. United*

States, 390 U.S. 39, 48 (1968). Bouknight's ability to produce the child would conclusively establish her actual and present physical control over him, and thus might "prove a significant 'link in a chain' of evidence tending to establish [her] guilt." *Ibid.*

Indeed, the stakes for Bouknight are much greater than the Court suggests. Not only could she face criminal abuse and neglect charges for her alleged mistreatment of Maurice, but she could also be charged with causing his death. The State acknowledges that it suspects that Maurice is dead, and the police are investigating his case as a possible homicide. In these circumstances, the potentially incriminating aspects to Bouknight's act of production are undoubtedly significant.

II

Notwithstanding the real threat of self-incrimination, the Court holds that "Bouknight may not invoke the privilege to resist the production order because she has assumed custodial duties related to production and because production is required as part of a noncriminal regulatory regime. . . ."

* * *

The Court's . . . reasoning turns on its view that Bouknight has agreed to exercise on behalf of the State certain custodial obligations with respect to her son, obligations that the Court analogizes to those of a custodian of the records of a collective entity. This characterization is baffling, both because it is contrary to the facts of this case and because this Court has never relied on such a characterization to override the privilege against self-incrimination except in the context of a claim of privilege by an agent of a collective entity.

Jacqueline Bouknight is Maurice's mother; she is not, and in fact could not be, his "custodian" whose rights and duties are determined solely by the Maryland juvenile protection law. *See* Md. Cts. & Jud. Proc. Code Ann. § 3-801(j) (Supp. 1989) (defining "custodian" as "person or agency to whom legal custody of a child has been given by order of the court, other than the child's parent or legal guardian"). Although Bouknight surrendered physical custody of her child during the pendency of the proceedings to determine whether Maurice was a "child in need of assistance" (CINA) within the meaning of the Maryland Code, § 3-801(e), Maurice's placement in shelter care was only temporary and did not extinguish her legal right to custody of her son. When the CINA proceedings were settled, Bouknight regained physical custody of Maurice and entered into an agreement with the Baltimore City Department of Social Services (BCDSS). In that agreement, which was approved by the juvenile court, Bouknight promised, among other things, to "cooperate with BCDSS," but she retained legal custody of Maurice.

A finding that a child is in need of assistance does not by itself divest a parent of legal or physical custody, nor does it transform such custody to something conferred by the State. Thus, the parent of a CINA continues to exercise custody because she is the child's parent, not because the State has delegated that responsibility to her. . . .

. . . Bouknight is not acting as a custodian in the traditional sense of that word because she is not acting *on behalf of the State.* In reality, she continues to exercise her parental duties, constrained by an agreement between her and the State....

Moreover, the rationale for denying a corporate custodian Fifth Amendment protection for acts done in her representative capacity does not apply to this case. The rule for a custodian of corporate records rests on the well-established principle that a collective entity, unlike a natural person, has no Fifth Amendment privilege against self-incrimination. Because an artificial entity can act only through its agents, a custodian of such an entity's documents may not invoke her personal privilege to resist producing documents that may incriminate the entity, even if the documents may also incriminate the custodian. *Wilson v. United States,* 221 U.S. 361, 384-385 (1911)....

Jacqueline Bouknight is not the agent for an artificial entity that possesses no Fifth Amendment privilege. Her role as Maurice's parent is very different from the role of a corporate custodian who is merely the instrumentality through whom the corporation acts. I am unwilling to extend the collective entity doctrine into a context where it denies individuals, acting in their personal rather than representative capacities, their constitutional privilege against self-incrimination....

Notes

1. The elements of contempt are as follows: (1) the existence of a valid order directing the contemnor to do or refrain from doing something; (2) the contemnor must receive notice of the order in time to comply with the order; (3) the contemnor must be able to comply with the order; and (4) the contemnor must be able to understand that failure to follow the order could lead to the contemnor's incarceration. *In re Darlene C.,* 301 S.E.2d 136, 138 (S.C. 1983). For a discussion of the elements of contempt in civil and criminal trials, see Floyd Abrams, *Prior Restraints*, 580 PLI/ 429, 458-59 (1999); David M. Zlotnick, *Battered Women and Justice Scalia*, 41 ARIZ. L. REV. 847, 888 (1999); Merle H. Weiner, *Domestic Violence and Custody: Importing the American Law Institute's Principles of the Law of Family Dissolution Into Oregon Law*, 35 WILLAMETTE L. REV. 643, 696 (1999); Lawrence N. Gray, *Criminal and Civil Contempt: Some Sense of a Hodgepodge*, 13 J. SUFFOLK ACAD. L. 1 (1999).

2. A juvenile court, like other courts, has the inherent authority to exercise the contempt power to seek compliance with its orders. The following is an example of a statute that gives a juvenile court the contempt power:

Arizona Revised Statutes
§ 8-247 (West Supp. 2000)

§ 8-247. Contempt Powers.

The juvenile court may punish a person for contempt of court for willfully violating, neglecting or refusing to obey or perform any lawful order of the juvenile court of for obstructing or interfering with the proceedings of the juvenile court or the enforcement of its orders subject to the laws relating to the procedures therefor and limitations thereon.

States may place limitations on the contempt power of juvenile courts. The following statute is an example of a statute that limits the contempt power of a court over a child:

Louisiana Children's Code

§ 1509.1(C) (West Supp. 2001)

§ 1509.1. Penalties for contempt; children

(c.) In families in need of services proceedings, when the child is adjudged guilty of . . . constructive contempt of court for repeated disobedience of the court's judgment of disposition, the court may:

(1) Commit the child to a shelter care facility for not more than fifteen days, including time spent there for the contempt prior to the contempt hearing,

(2) Commit the child to a secure detention facility for not more than fifteen days, including time spent there for the contempt prior to the contempt hearing, if the court finds that all of the following have occurred:

a. A judgment of disposition was entered pursuant to Article 782.

b. The child willfully violated the judgment of disposition.

c. All sanctions other than secure confinement have been exhausted or are clearly inappropriate.

3. A juvenile court uses the contempt power to coerce a party who disobeys an order of the court or obstructs and interferes with the proceedings of the juvenile court to do what the court wants. Uniform Juvenile Court Act § 58, 9A U.L.A. 95 (1998). The purpose of a juvenile court's contempt power establishes yet another significant difference between the juvenile justice system and the criminal justice system. In a criminal court, the judge's contempt power is used to punish a party for not cooperating with the judge. *See New York State National Organization for Women v. Terry*, 886 F.2d 1339, 1351 (2d Cir. 1989). *See also In re M.B.,* 3 P.3d 780 (Wash. Ct. App. 2000) (detention of a status offender in contempt of a court order satisfies due process and serves a remedial purpose as long as the juvenile can terminate the detention by complying with the court order.)

4. As in *Bouknight*, there are several reported cases where a parent was found in contempt and incarcerated for refusing the court access to a child. *See, e.g., King v. Department of Social Services,* 738 P.2d 289 (Wash. Ct. App. 1987); *Young v. Young*, 514 N.Y.S.2d 785 (App. Div. 1987). The juvenile court's power to incarcerate a party for contempt raises difficult issues of policy and pragmatism. For example, a juvenile judge may incarcerate a party indefinitely until the party agrees to follow the court's mandate, if no law limits the duration of incarceration for contempt. *See* David J. Harmer, *Limiting Incarceration for Civil Contempt in Child Custody Cases,* 4 BYU J. PUB. L. 239 (1990).

5. Some states also allow juvenile courts to find adults in contempt and impose alternative sanctions on the contemnor. The following Georgia statute is an example:

Georgia Code Annotated
§ 15-11-5(b) (Lexis Supp. 2000)

§ 15-11-5. Contempt powers of juvenile court.

(b) . . . [T]he court may impose any or all of the following sanctions when a parent, guardian, or other custodian willfully violates any order issued by the court directed to that parent, guardian, or other custodian:

(1) Require the parent, guardian, or other custodian of any child to make restitution in an amount not to exceed $2,500.00 for any damage or loss caused by the child's wrongful act;

(2) Impose a fine not to exceed $1,000.00;

(3) Reimburse the state for the costs of detention, treatment, or rehabilitation of the child;

(4) Require the parent, guardian, or other custodian of the child to perform court approved community service designed to contribute to the ability of the parent, guardian, or other custodian to provide proper prenatal care and supervision of the child; or

(5) Require the parent, guardian, or other custodian of the child to enter into a contract or plan as a part of the disposition of any charges against the child, so as to provide for the supervision and control of the child by the parent, guardian, or custodian and reunification of the child with the parent, guardian, or custodian.

Questions

1. What constitutional arguments may be raised to challenge the juvenile court's finding of contempt and order of incarceration to seek compliance with the order?

2. Under what circumstances should the child's welfare be considered by the court in a contempt proceeding (*see Bouknight, supra*)?

2. Protective Orders

California Welfare and Institutions Code
§ 213.5(a) (West Supp. 2000)

§ 213.5. Proceedings to declare a minor child a dependent child; ex parte orders

(a) After a petition has been filed pursuant to Section 311 to declare a child a dependent child of the juvenile court, and until the time that the petition is dismissed or dependency is terminated . . . , the juvenile court may issue ex parte orders (1) enjoining any parent, guardian, or current or former member of the child's household from molesting, attacking, striking, sexually assaulting, stalking, or battering the child or any other child in the household; (2) excluding any parent, guardian, or current or former member of the child's household from the dwelling of the person who has care, custody, and control of the child; and (3) enjoining a parent, guardian, or current or former member of the child's household from behavior, including contacting, threatening, or disturbing the peace of the child, that the court determines is necessary to effectuate orders under paragraph (1) or (2).

3. Administrative Review Process

Ohio Revised Code Annotated

§ 2151.416 (Anderson Supp. 2000)

§ 2151.416. Administrative reviews of case plan; annual report.

(A) Each agency that is required by section 2151.412 of the Revised Code to prepare a case plan for a child shall complete a semiannual administrative review of the case plan no later than six months after the earlier of the date on which the complaint in the case was filed or the child was first placed in shelter care. After the first administrative review, the agency shall complete semiannual administrative reviews no later than every six months. . . . When conducting a review, the child's health and safety shall be the paramount concern.

(B) Each administrative review required by division (A) of this section shall be conducted by a review panel of at least three persons, including, but not limited to, both of the following:

(1) A caseworker with day-to-day responsibility for, or familiarity with, the management of the child's case plan;

(2) A person who is not responsible for the management of the child's case plan or for the delivery of services to the child or the parents, guardian, or custodian of the child.

(C) Each semiannual administrative review shall include, but not be limited to, a joint meeting by the review panel with the parents, guardian, or custodian of the child, the guardian ad litem of the child, and the child's foster care provider and shall include an opportunity for those persons to submit any written materials to be included in the case record of the child. If a parent, guardian, custodian, guardian ad litem, or foster care provider of the child cannot be located after reasonable efforts to do so or declines to participate in the administrative review after being contacted, the agency does not have to include them in the joint meeting.

(D) The agency shall prepare a written summary of the semiannual administrative review that shall include, but not be limited to, all of the following:

(1) A conclusion regarding the safety and appropriateness of the child's foster care placement;

(2) The extent of the compliance with the case plan of all parties;

(3) The extent of progress that has been made toward alleviating the circumstances that required the agency to assume temporary custody of the child;

(4) An estimated date by which the child may be returned to and safely maintained in the child's home or placed for adoption or legal custody;

(5) An updated case plan that includes any changes that the agency is proposing in the case plan;

(6) The recommendation of the agency as to which agency or person should be given custodial rights over the child for the six-month period after the administrative review;

(7) The names of all persons who participated in the administrative review.

(E) The agency shall file the summary with the court no later than seven days after the completion of the administrative review. If the agency proposes a change to the case plan as a result of the administrative review, the agency shall file the proposed change with the court at the time it files the summary. The agency shall give notice of the summary and proposed change in writing before the end of the next day after filing them to all parties and the child's guardian ad litem. All parties and the guardian ad litem shall have seven days after the date the notice is sent to object to and request a hearing on the proposed change.

(1) If the court receives a timely request for a hearing, the court shall schedule a hearing pursuant to section 2151.417 of the Revised Code to be held not later than thirty days after the court receives the request. The court shall give notice of the date, time, and location of the hearing to all parties and the guardian ad litem. The agency may implement the proposed change after the hearing, if the court approves it. The agency shall not implement the proposed change unless it is approved by the court.

(2) If the court does not receive a timely request for a hearing, the court may approve the proposed change without a hearing. . . .

* * *

(G) The juvenile court that receives the written summary of the administrative review, upon determining, either from the written summary, case plan, or otherwise, that the custody or care arrangement is not in the best interest of the child, may terminate the custody of an agency and place the child in the custody of another institution or association certified by the department of human services under section 5103.03 of the Revised Code.

* * *

Notes

1. The administrative review process is required by the Adoption Assistance and Child Welfare Act of 1980 (AACWA), 42 U.S.C.A. §§ 620-628, 670-679 (West 2000) (*see* Section A.3 of this chapter), through which the federal government provides funding to help states pay for foster care contingent on requirements. In addition to the requirement of "reasonable efforts," states must also create a review system for children in foster care with the goal of swift permanent placement of children. The goal of the review system is to make sure the child's needs are met, to track the progress of the child, and to shorten the time necessary for permanent placement. *See* AACWA § 622. *See generally* Christina A. Zawsiya, *Protecting the Ties That Bind: Kinship Relative Care in Florida*, 23 NOVA L. REV. 455 (1998). The review system required by the AACWA consists of three main components. First, the state must create a "case plan" for the child. A case plan focuses on a placement for the child with the child's best interests and needs in mind. *See* 42 U.S.C.A. § 675 (West 2000). The second requirement is that states must keep a "written case plan" in which the state maintains accurate records of the child's placement history and current status in the foster care system. *Id.* Finally, AACWA requires that a state conduct administrative reviews every six months. The reviews focus on the child's current condition and determine what the state must do to eventually reach the goal of permanent placement.

2. Once a juvenile court places a child in the care of a child welfare agency, the court retains jurisdiction while the administrative agency simultaneously exercises authority over the child. Because the court and the agency have shared responsibilities, conflicts may arise. For a detailed discussion of the overlapping responsibilities of the court and the agency and the conflicts that result, see Bruce A. Boyer, *Jurisdiction Conflicts Between Juvenile Courts and Child Welfare Agencies: The Uneasy Relationship Between Institutional Co-Parents*, 54 MD. L. REV. 377 (1995).

G. Native American Children: The Indian Child Welfare Act

The following excerpt is from the report of the Committee on Interior and Insular Affairs. The Committee was appointed the task of reviewing the House bill that would become the Indian Child Welfare Act of 1978. The bill's purposes, as stated in the report, were "to establish standards for the placement of Indian children in foster or adoptive homes, [and] to prevent the breakup of Indian families. . . ."

House of Representatives Report No. 95-1386
(1978 U.S.C.C.A.N. 7530)

* * *

The purpose of the bill . . . is to protect the best interests of Indian children and to promote the stability and security of Indian tribes and families by establishing minimum Federal standards for the removal of Indian children from their families and the placement of such children in foster or adoptive homes or institutions which will reflect the unique values of Indian culture and by providing for assistance to Indian tribes and organizations in the operation of child and family service programs.

* * *

The wholesale separation of Indian children from their families is perhaps the most tragic and destructive aspect of American Indian life today.

Surveys of States with large Indian populations conducted by the Association of American Indian Affairs (AAIA) in 1969 and again in 1974 indicate that approximately 25-35 percent of all Indian children are separated from their families and placed in foster homes, adoptive homes, or institutions. In some States the problem is getting worse: in Minnesota, one in every eight Indian children under 18 years of age is living in an adoptive home; and, in 1971-72, nearly one in every four Indian children under 1 year of age was adopted.

The disparity in placement rates for Indians and non-Indians is shocking. In Minnesota, Indian children are placed in foster care or in adoptive homes at a per capita rate five times greater than non-Indian children. In Montana, the ratio of Indian foster-care placement is at least 13 times greater. . . . The number of South Dakota Indian children living in foster homes is per capita, nearly 16 times greater than the non-Indian rate. In the State of Washington, the Indian adoption rate is 19 times greater and the foster care rate 10 times greater. In Wisconsin, the risk run by Indian children of being separated from their parents is nearly 1,600 percent greater than it is for non-Indian children. Just as Indian children are exposed to these great hazards, their parents are too.

The Federal boarding school and dormitory programs also contribute to the destruction of Indian family and community life. The Bureau of Indian Affairs (BIA), in its school census for 1971, indicates that 34,538 children live in its institutional facilities rather than at home. This represents more than 17 percent of the Indian school age population of federally-recognized reservations and 60 percent of the children enrolled in BIA schools. On the Navajo Reservation, about 20,000 children or 90 percent of the BIA school population in grades K-12, live at boarding schools. A number of Indian children are also institutionalized in mission schools, training schools, etc.

In addition to the trauma of separation from their families, most Indian children in placement or in institutions have to cope with the problems of adjusting to a social and cultural environment much different than their own. In 16 States surveyed in 1969, approximately 85 percent of all Indian children in foster care were living in non-Indian homes. In Minnesota today, according to State figures, more than 90 percent of nonrelated adoptions of Indian children are made by non-Indian couples. . . . In most Federal and mission boarding schools, a majority of the personnel is non-Indian.

It is clear then that the Indian child welfare crisis is of massive proportions and that Indian families face vastly greater risks of involuntary separation than are typical of our society as a whole.

Standards

The Indian child welfare crisis will continue until the standards for defining mistreatment are revised. Very few Indian children are removed from their families on the grounds of physical abuse. One study of a North Dakota reservation showed that these grounds were advanced in only 1 percent of the cases.

Another study of a tribe in the Northwest showed the same incidence. The remaining 99 percent of the cases were argued on such vague grounds as "neglect" or "social deprivation" and on allegations of the emotional damage the children were subjected to by living with their parents. Indian communities are often shocked to learn that parents they regard as excellent caregivers have been judged unfit by non-Indian social workers.

In judging the fitness of a particular family, many social workers, ignorant of Indian cultural values and social norms, make decision that are wholly inappropriate in the context of Indian family life and so they frequently discover neglect or abandonment where none exists.

For example, the dynamics of Indian extended families are largely misunderstood. An Indian child may have scores of, perhaps more than a hundred, relatives who are counted as close, responsible members of the family. Many social workers, untutored in the ways of Indian family life or assuming them to be socially irresponsible, consider leaving the child with persons outside the nuclear family as neglect and thus as grounds for terminating parental rights.

* * *

The courts tend to rely on the testimony of social workers who often lack the training and insights necessary to measure the emotional risk the child is running at home. In a number of cases, the AAIA has obtained evidence from competent psychiatrists who, after examining the defendants, have been able to contradict the allegations offered by the social workers. Rejecting the notion that poverty and cultural differences constitute social deprivation and psychological abuse, the Association argues that the State must prove that there is actual physical or emotional harm resulting from the acts of the parents. . . .

Due Process

The decision to take Indian children from their natural homes is, in most cases, carried out without due process of law. For example, it is rare for either Indian children or their parents to be represented by counsel to or have the supporting testimony of expert witnesses.

Many cases do not go through an adjudicatory process at all, since the voluntary waiver of parental rights is a device widely employed by social workers to gain custody of children. Because of the availability of the waivers and because a great number of Indian parents depend on welfare payments for survival, they are exposed to the sometimes coercive arguments of welfare departments. . . . It is an unfortunate fact of life for many Indian parents that the primary service agency to which they must turn for financial help also exercises police powers over their family life and is, most frequently, the agency that initiates custody proceedings.

The conflict between Indian and non-Indian social systems operates to defeat due process. The extended family provides an example. By sharing the responsibility of child rearing, the extended family tends to strengthen the community's commitment to the child. At the same time, however, it diminishes the possibility that the nuclear family will be able to mobilize itself quickly enough when an outside agency acts to assume custody. Because it is not unusual for Indian children to spend considerable time away with other relatives, there is no immediate realization of what is happening—possibly not until the opportunity for due process has slipped away.

* * *

Social Conditions

Low-income, joblessness, poor health, substandard housing, and low educational attainment—these are the reasons most often cited for the disintegration of Indian family life. It is not that clear-cut. Not all impoverished societies, whether Indian or non-Indian, suffer from catastrophically high rates of family breakdown.

Cultural disorientation, a person's sense of powerlessness, his loss of self-esteem—these may be the most potent forces at work. They arise, in large measure, from our national attitudes as reflected in long-established Federal policy and from arbitrary acts of Government.

One of the effects of our national paternalism has been to so alienate some Indian patents [sic] from their society that they abandon their children at hospitals or to welfare departments rather than entrust them to the care of relatives in the extended family. Another expression of it is the involuntary, arbitrary, and unwarranted separation of families.

It has already been noted that the harsh living conditions in many Indian communities may prompt a welfare department to make unwarranted placements and that they make it difficult for Indian people to qualify as foster or adoptive parents. Additionally, because these conditions are often viewed as the primary cause of family breakdown and because generally there is no end to Indian poverty in sight, agencies of government often fail to recognize immediate, practical means to reduce the incidence of neglect or separation.

As surely as poverty imposes severe strains on the ability of families to function—sometimes the extra burden that is too much to bear—so too family breakdown contributes to the cycle of poverty. . . .

The Indian Child Welfare Act
Subchapter I—Child Custody Proceedings

25 U.S.C.A. §§ 1911 et seq. (West Supp. 2000)

Section 1911. Indian Tribe Jurisdiction over Indian Child Custody Proceedings.

(a) *Exclusive jurisdiction.* An Indian tribe shall have jurisdiction exclusive as to any state over any child custody proceeding involving an Indian child who resides or is domiciled within the reservation of such tribe, except where such jurisdiction is otherwise vested in the State by existing Federal law. Where an Indian child is a ward of a tribal court, the Indian tribe shall retain exclusive jurisdiction, notwithstanding the residence or domicile of the child.

(b) *Transfer of proceedings; declination by tribal court.* In any State court proceeding for the foster care placement of, or termination of parental rights to, an Indian child not domiciled or residing within the reservation of the Indian child's tribe, the court, in the absence of good cause to the contrary, shall transfer such proceeding to the jurisdiction of the tribe, absent objection by either parent, upon the petition of either parent or the Indian custodian or the Indian child's tribe: Provided, That such transfer shall be subject to declination by the tribal court of such tribe.

(c) *State court proceedings; intervention.* In any state court proceeding for the foster care placement of, or termination of parental rights to, an Indian child, the Indian custodian of the child and the Indian child's tribe shall have a right to intervene at any point in the proceeding.

(d) *Full faith and credit to public acts, records, and judicial proceedings of Indian tribes.* The United States, every State, every territory or possession of the United States, and every Indian tribe shall give full faith and credit to the public acts, records, and judicial proceedings of any Indian tribe applicable to Indian child custody proceedings to the same extent that such entities give full faith and credit to the public acts, records, and judicial proceedings of any other entity.

Section 1912. Pending Court Proceedings.

(a) *Notice, time for commencement of proceedings; additional time for preparation.* In any involuntary proceedings in a State court, where the court knows or has reason to know that an Indian child is involved, the party seeking the foster care placement of, or termination of parental rights to, an Indian child shall notify the parent or Indian custodian and the Indian child's tribe, by registered mail with return receipt requested, of the pending proceedings and of their right of intervention. If the identity or location of parent or Indian custodian and the tribe cannot be determined, such notice shall be given to the Secretary in like manner, who shall have fifteen days after receipt to provide the requisite notice to the parent or Indian custodian and the tribe. No foster care placement or termination of parental rights proceeding shall be held until at least ten days after receipt of notice by the parent or Indian custodian and the tribe or the Secretary: Provided, That the parent or Indian custodian or the tribe shall, upon request, be granted up to twenty additional days to prepare for such proceedings.

(b) *Appointment of counsel.* In any case in which the court determines indigence, the parent or Indian custodian shall have the right to court-appointed counsel in any removal, placement, or termination proceeding. The court may, in its discretion, appoint counsel for the child upon a finding that such appointment is in the best interests of the child. Where State law makes no provision for appointment of counsel in such proceedings, the court shall promptly notify the Secretary upon appointment of counsel, and the Secretary, upon certification of the presiding judge, shall pay reasonable fees and expenses out of funds which may be appropriated pursuant to section 13 of this title.

(c) *Examination of reports or other documents.* Each party to a foster care placement or termination of parental rights proceeding under State law involving an Indian child shall have the right to examine all reports or other documents filed with the court upon which any decision with respect to such action may be based.

(d) *Remedial services and rehabilitative programs; preventive measures.* Any party seeking to effect a foster care placement of, or termination of parental right to, an Indian child under State law shall satisfy the court that active efforts have been made to provide remedial services and rehabilitative programs designed to prevent the breakup of the Indian family and that these efforts have proved unsuccessful.

(e) *Foster care placement orders; evidence; determination of damage to child.* No foster care placement may be ordered in such proceeding in the absence of a determination, supported by clear and convincing evidence, including testimony of qualified expert witnesses, that the continued custody of the child by the parent or Indian custodian is likely to result in serious emotional or physical damage to the child.

(f) *Parental rights termination orders; evidence; determination of damage to child.* No termination of parental rights may be ordered in such proceeding in the absence of a determination, supported by evidence beyond a reasonable doubt, including testimony of qualified expert witnesses, that the continued custody of the child by the parent or Indian custodian is likely to result in serious emotional or physical damage to the child.

Section 1913. Parental Rights, Voluntary Termination.

(a) *Consent; record; certification matters; invalid consents.* Where any parent or Indian custodian voluntarily consents to a foster care placement or to termination of parental rights, such consent shall not be valid unless executed in writing and recorded before a judge of a court of competent jurisdiction and accompanied by the presiding judge's certificate that the terms and consequences of the consent were fully explained in detail and were fully understood by the parent or Indian custodian. The court shall also certify that either the parent or Indian custodian fully understood the explanation in English or that it was interpreted into a language that the parent or Indian custodian understood. Any consent given prior to, or within ten days after birth of the Indian child shall not be valid.

(b) *Foster care placement, withdrawal of consent.* Any parent or Indian custodian may withdraw consent to a foster care placement under State law at any time and, upon such withdrawal, the child shall be returned to the parent or Indian custodian.

(c) *Voluntary termination of parental rights or adoptive placement; withdrawal of consent; return of custody.* In any voluntary proceeding for termination of parental rights to, or adoptive placement of, an Indian child, the consent of the parent may be withdrawn for any reason at any time prior to the entry of a final decree of termination or adoption, as the case may be, and the child shall be returned to the parent.

(d) *Collateral attack; vacation of decree and return of custody; limitations.* After the entry of a final decree of adoption of an Indian child in any State court, the parent may withdraw consent thereto upon the grounds that consent was obtained through fraud or duress and may petition the court to vacate such decree. Upon a finding that such consent was obtained through fraud or duress, the court shall vacate such decree and return the child to the parent. No adoption which has been effective for at least two years may be invalidated under the provisions of this subsection unless otherwise permitted under State law.

Section 1914. Petition to Court of Competent Jurisdiction to Invalidate Action Upon Showing of Certain Violations.

Any Indian child who is the subject of any action for foster care placement or termination of parental rights under State law, any parent or Indian custodian from whose custody such child was removed, and the Indian child's tribe may petition any court of competent jurisdiction to invalidate such action upon a showing that such action violated any provision of sections 1911, 1912, and 1913 of this title.

Section 1915. Placement of Indian Children.

(a) *Adoptive placements; preferences.* In any adoptive placement of an Indian child under State law, a preference shall be given, in absence of good cause to the contrary, to a placement with (1) a member of the child's extended family; (2) other members of the Indian child's tribe; or (3) other Indian families.

(b) *Foster care of preadoptive placements, criteria; preferences.* Any child accepted for foster care of preadoptive placement shall be placed in the least restrictive setting which most approximates a family and in which his special needs, if any, may be met. The child shall also be placed within reasonable proximity to his or her home, taking into account any account any special needs of the child. In any foster care or preadoptive placement, a preference shall be given, in the absence of good cause to the contrary, to a placement with—

(i) a member of the Indian child's extended family;

(ii) a foster home licensed, approved, or specified by the Indian child's tribe;

(iii) an Indian foster home licensed or approved by an authorized non-Indian licensing authority; or

(iv) an institution for children approved by an Indian tribe or operated by an Indian organization which has a program suitable to meet the Indian child's needs.

(c) *Tribal resolution for different order of preference; personal preference considered; anonymity in application of preferences.* In the case of a placement under subsection (a) or (b) of this section, if the Indian child's tribe shall establish a different order of preference by resolution, the agency or court effecting the placement shall follow such order so long as the placement is the least restrictive setting appropriate to the particular needs of the child, as provided in subsection (b) of this section. Where appropriate, the preference of the Indian child or parent shall be considered: Provided, That where a consenting parent evidences a desire for anonymity, the court or agency shall give weight to such desire in applying the preferences.

(d) *Social and cultural standards applicable.* The standards to be applied in meeting the preference requirements of this section shall be the prevailing social and cultural standards of the Indian community in which the parent or extended family resides or with which the parent or extended family members maintain social and cultural ties.

(e) *Record of placement; availability.* A record of each such placement, under State law, of an Indian child shall be maintained by the State in which the placement was made, evidencing the efforts to comply with the order of preference specified in this section. Such record shall be made available at any time upon the request of the Secretary or the Indian child's tribe.

Section 1916. Return of Custody.

(a) *Petition; best interest of child.* Notwithstanding State law to the contrary, whenever a final decree of adoption of an Indian child has been vacated or set aside or the adoptive parents voluntarily consent to the termination of their parental rights to the child, a biological parent or prior Indian custodian may petition for return of custody and the court shall grant such petition unless there is a showing, in a proceeding subject to the provisions of section 1912 of this title, that such return of custody is not in the best interests of the child.

(b) *Removal from foster care home; placement procedure.* Whenever an Indian child is removed from a foster care home or institution for the purpose of further foster care, preadoptive, or adoptive placement, such placement shall be in accordance with the provisions of this chapter, except in the case where an Indian child is being returned to the parent or Indian custodian from whose custody the child was originally removed.

Section 1920. Improper Removal of Child from Custody; Declination of Jurisdiction; Forthwith Return of Child: Danger Exception.

Where any petitioner in an Indian child custody proceeding before a State court has improperly removed the child from custody of the parent or Indian custodian or has improperly retained custody after a visit or other temporary relinquishment of custody, the court shall decline jurisdiction over such petition and shall forthwith return the child to his parent or Indian custodian unless returning the child to his parent or custodian would subject the child to a substantial and immediate danger of threat of such danger.

Section 1922. Emergency Removal or Placement of Child; Termination Appropriate Action.

Nothing in this subchapter shall be construed to prevent the emergency removal of an Indian child who is a resident of or is domiciled on a reservation, but temporarily located off the reservation, from his parent or Indian custodian or the emergency placement of such child in a foster home or institution, under applicable State law, in order to prevent imminent physical damage or harm to the child. The State authority, official, or agency involved shall insure that the emergency removal or placement terminates immediately when such removal or placement is no longer necessary to prevent imminent physical damage or harm to the child and shall expeditiously initiate a child custody proceeding subject to the provisions of this subchapter, transfer the child to the jurisdiction of the appropriate Indian tribe, or restore the child to the parent or Indian custodian, as may be appropriate. . . .

Mississippi Band of Choctaw Indians v. Holyfield

490 U.S. 30, 109 S. Ct. 1597 104 L. Ed. 2d 29 (1989)

BRENNAN, J., delivered the opinion of the Court, in which WHITE, MARSHALL, BLACKMUN, O'CONNOR, and SCALIA, JJ., joined.

I

A

The Indian Child Welfare Act of 1978 (ICWA), 92 Stat. 3069, 25 U.S.C. §§ 1901-1963, was the product of rising concern in the mid-1970s over the consequences to Indian children, Indian families, and Indian tribes of abusive child welfare practices that resulted in the separation of large numbers of Indian children from their families and tribes through adoption or foster care placement, usually in non-Indian homes. Senate oversight hearings in 1974 yielded numerous examples, statistical data, and expert testimony documenting what one witness called "[t]he wholesale removal of Indian children from their homes, . . . the most tragic aspect of Indian life today." Indian Child Welfare Program, Hearings before the Subcommittee on Indian Affairs of the Senate Committee on Interior and Insular Affairs, 93d Cong., 2d Sess., 3 (statement of William Byler) (hereinafter 1974 Hearings). Studies undertaken by the Association on American Indian Affairs in 1969 and 1974, and presented in the Senate hearings, showed that 25 to 35% of all Indian children had been separated from their families and placed in adoptive families, foster care, or institutions. *Id.*, at 15; *see also* H.R. Rep. No. 95-1386, p. 9 (1978) (hereinafter House Report). Adoptive placements counted significantly in this total. . . . The adoption rate of Indian children was eight times that of non-Indian children. Approximately 90% of the Indian placements were in non-Indian homes. 1974 Hearings, at 75-83. A number of witnesses also testified to the serious adjustment problems encountered by such children during adolescence,[1] as well as the impact of the adoptions on Indian parents and the tribes themselves.

---

1 For example, Dr. Joseph Westermeyer, a University of Minnesota social psychiatrist, testified about his research with Indian adolescents who experienced difficulty coping in white society, despite the fact that they had been raised in a purely white environment:

> "[T]hey were raised with a white cultural and social identity. They were raised in a white home. They attended, predominantly white schools, and in almost all cases, attended a church that was predominantly white, and really came to understand very little about Indian culture, Indian behavior, and had virtually no viable Indian identity. They can recall such things as seeing cowboys and Indians on TV and feeling that Indians were a historical figure but were not a viable contemporary social group.
>
> "Then during adolescence, they found that society was not to grant them the white identity that they had. They began to find this out in a number of ways. For example, a universal experience was that when they began to date white children, the parents of the white youngsters were against this, and there were pressures among white children from the parents not to date these Indian children. . . .
>
> "The other experience was derogatory name calling in relation to their racial identity. . . .
>
> "[T]hey were finding that society was putting on them an identity which they didn't possess and taking from them an identity that they did possess."

1974 Hearings, at 46.

Further hearings, covering much the same ground, were held during 1977 and 1978 on the bill that became the ICWA.[2] While much of the testimony again focused on the harm to Indian parents and their children who were involuntarily separated by decisions of local welfare authorities, there was also considerable emphasis on the impact on the tribes themselves of the massive removal of their children. For example, Mr. Calvin Isaac, Tribal Chief of the Mississippi Band of Choctaw Indians and representative of the National Tribal Chairmen's Association, testified as follows:

> "Culturally, the chances of Indian survival are significantly reduced if our children, the only real means for the transmission of the tribal heritage, are to be raised in non-Indian homes and denied exposure to the ways of their People. Furthermore, these practices seriously undercut the tribes' ability to continue as self governing communities. Probably in no area is it more important that tribal sovereignty be respected than in an area as socially and culturally determinative as family relationships." 1978 Hearings, at 193.

Chief Isaac also summarized succinctly what numerous witnesses saw as the principal reason for the high rates of removal of Indian children:

> "One of the most serious failings of the present system is that Indian children are removed from the custody of their natural parents by nontribal government authorities who have no basis for intelligently evaluating the cultural and social premises underlying Indian home life and childrearing. Many of the individuals who decide the fate of our children are at best ignorant of our cultural values, and at worst contemptful of the Indian way and convinced that removal, usually to a non-Indian household or institution, can only benefit an Indian child."

Id. at 191-192.

The congressional findings that were incorporated into the ICWA reflect these sentiments. The Congress found:

> "(3) that there is no resource that is more vital to the continued existence and integrity of Indian tribes than their children . . . ;
> "(4) that an alarmingly high percentage of Indian families are broken up by the removal, often unwarranted, of their children from them by nontribal public and private agencies and that an alarmingly high percentage of such children are placed in non-Indian foster and adoptive homes and institutions; and
> "(5) that the states, exercising their recognized jurisdiction over Indian child custody proceedings through administrative and judicial bodies, have often failed to recognize the essential tribal relations of

---

[2] Hearing on S. 1214 before the Senate Select Committee on Indian Affairs, 95th Cong., 1st Sess. (1977) (hereinafter 1977 Hearings); Hearings on S.1214 before the Subcommittee on Indian Affairs and Public Lands of the House Committee on Interior and Insular Affairs, 95th Cong., 2d Sess. (1978) (hereinafter 1978 Hearings).

Indian people and the cultural and social standards prevailing in Indian communities and families."

25 U.S.C. § 1901.

At the heart of the ICWA are its provisions concerning jurisdiction over Indian child custody proceedings. Section 1911 lays out a dual jurisdictional scheme. Section 1911(a) established exclusive jurisdiction in the tribal courts for proceedings concerning an Indian child "who resides or is domiciled within the reservation of such tribe, "as well as for wards of tribal courts regardless of domicile. . . .

* * *

The ICWA thus, in the words of the House Report accompanying it, "seeks to protect the rights of the Indian child as an Indian and the rights of the Indian community and tribe in retaining its children in its society." House Report, at 22. It does so by establishing "a Federal policy that, where possible, an Indian child should remain in the Indian community," *ibid.*, and by making sure that Indian child welfare determinations are not based on "a white, middle-class standard which, in many cases, forecloses placement with [an] Indian family." *Id.* at 24.

B

This case involves the status of twin babies, known for our purposes as B.B. and G.B., who were born out of wedlock on December 29, 1985. Their mother, J.B., and father, W.J., were both enrolled members of appellant Mississippi Band of Choctaw Indians (Tribe), and were residents and domiciliaries of the Choctaw Reservation in Neshoba County, Mississippi. J.B. gave birth to the twins in Gulfport, Harrison County, Mississippi, some 200 miles from the reservation. On January 10, 1986, J.B. executed a consent-to-adoption form before the Chancery Court of Harrison County. W.J. signed a similar form. On January 16, appellees Orrey and Vivian Holyfield filed a petition for adoption in the same court, and the chancellor issued a Final Decree of Adoption on January 28. Despite the court's apparent awareness of the ICWA,[11] the adoption decree contained no reference to it, nor to the infants' Indian background.

Two months later the Tribe moved in the Chancery Court to vacate the adoption decree on the ground that under the ICWA exclusive jurisdiction was vested in the tribal court.[12] On July 14, 1986, the court overruled the motion, holding that the Tribe "never obtained exclusive jurisdiction over the children

---

11 The chancellor's certificates that the parents had appeared before him to consent to the adoption recited that "the Consent and Waiver was given in full compliance with Section 103(a) of Public Law 95-608" (*i.e.*, 25 U.S.C. § 1913(a)).

12 The ICWA specifically confers standing on the Indian child's tribe to participate in child custody adjudications. Title 25 U.S.C. § 1914 authorizes the tribe (as well as the child and its parents) to petition a court to invalidate any foster care placement or termination of parental rights under state law "upon a showing that such action violated any provision of sections 101, 102, and 103" of the ICWA. 92 Stat. 3072. *See also* § 1911(c) (Indian child's tribe may intervene at any point in state-court proceedings for foster care placement or termination of parental rights). "Termination of parental rights" is defined in § 1903(1)(ii) as "any action resulting in the termination of the parent-child relationship."

involved herein. . . ." The court's one-page opinion relied on two facts in reaching that conclusion. The court noted first that the twins' mother "went to some efforts to see that they were born outside the confines of the Choctaw Indian Reservation and that the parents had promptly arranged for the adoption by the Holyfields. Second, the court stated "At no time from the birth of these children to the present date have either of them resided on or physically been on the Choctaw Indiana Reservation."

The Supreme Court of Mississippi affirmed. 511 So. 2d 918 (1987). It rejected the Tribe's arguments that the state court lacked jurisdiction and that it, in any event, had not applied the standards laid out in the ICWA. The court recognized that the jurisdictional question turned on whether the twins were domiciled on the Choctaw Reservation. It answered that question as follows:

> "At no point in time can it be said the twins resided on or were domiciled within the territory set aside for the reservation. Appellant's argument that living within the womb of their mother qualifies the children's residency on the reservation may be lauded for its creativity; however, apparently it is unsupported by any law within this state, and will not be addressed at this time due to the far-reaching legal ramifications that would occur were we to follow such a complicated tangential course."

Id. at 921.

The court distinguished Mississippi cases that appeared to establish the principle that "the domicile of minor children follows that of the parents," *ibid.; see Boyle v. Griffin,* 84 Miss. 41, 36 So. 141 (1904); *Stubbs v. Stubbs,* 211 So. 2d 821 (Miss. 1968); *see also In re Guardianship of Watson,* 317 So. 2d 30 (Miss. 1975). It noted that "the Indian twins . . . were voluntarily surrendered and legally abandoned by the natural parents to the adoptive parents, and it is undisputed that the parents went to some efforts to prevent the children from being placed on the reservation as the mother arranged for their birth and adoption in Gulfport Memorial Hospital, Harrison County, Mississippi." 511 So. 2d at 921. Therefore, the court said, the twins' domicile was in Harrison County and the State court properly exercised jurisdiction over the adoption proceedings. Indeed, the court appears to have concluded that, for this reason, *none* of the provisions of the ICWA was applicable. In any case, it rejected the Tribe's contention that the requirements of the ICWA applicable in state courts had not been followed: "[T]he judge did confirm and strictly adhere to the minimum federal standards governing adoption of Indian children with respect to parental consent, notice, service of process, etc." *Ibid.*[13]

---

[13] The lower court may well have fulfilled the applicable ICWA procedural requirements. It clearly did not, however, comply with or even take cognizance of the substantive mandate of §1915(a): "In any adoptive placement of an Indian child *under State law,* a preference shall be given, in the absence of good cause to the contrary, to a placement with (1) a member of the child's extended family; (2) other members of the Indian child's tribe; or (3) other Indian families." (Emphasis added.) Section 1915(e), moreover, requires the court to maintain records "evidencing the efforts to comply with the order of preference specified in this section." Notwithstanding the Tribe's argument below that § 1915 had been violated, the Mississippi Supreme Court made no reference to it, merely stating in conclusory fashion that the "minimum federal standards" had been met. 511 So. 2d at 921.

Because of the centrality of the exclusive tribal jurisdiction provision to the overall scheme of the ICWA, as well as the conflict between this decision of the Mississippi Supreme Court and those of several other state courts, we granted plenary review. We now reverse.

II

Tribal jurisdiction over Indian child custody proceedings is not a novelty of the ICWA. Indeed, some of the ICWA's jurisdictional provisions have a strong basis in pre-ICWA case law in the federal and state courts. *See, e.g. Fisher v. District Court, Sixth Judicial District of Montana,* 424 U.S. 382 (1976) (*per curiam*) (tribal court had exclusive jurisdiction over adoption proceeding where all parties were tribal members and reservation residents); *Wisconsin Potowatomies of Hannahville Indian Community v. Houston,* 393 F. Supp. 719 (WD Mich. 1973) (tribal court had exclusive jurisdiction over custody of Indian children found to have been domiciled on reservation). In enacting the ICWA Congress confirmed that, in child custody proceedings involving Indian children domiciled on the reservation, tribal jurisdiction was exclusive as to the States.

The state-court proceeding at issue here was a "child custody proceeding." That term is defined to include any "'adoptive placement' which shall mean the permanent placement of an Indian child for adoption, including any action resulting in a final decree of adoption." 25 U.S.C. § 1902(1)(iv). Moreover, the twins were "Indian children." *See* 25 U.S.C. § 1902(4). The sole issue in this case is, as the Supreme Court of Mississippi recognized, whether the twins were "domiciled" on the reservation.

A

The meaning of "domicile" in the ICWA is, of course, a matter of Congress' intent. The ICWA itself does not define it. The initial question we must confront is whether there is any reason to believe that Congress intended the ICWA definition of "domicile" to be a matter of state law. . . . We start . . . with the general assumption that "in the absence of a plain indication to the contrary, . . . Congress when it enacts a statute is not making the application of the federal act dependent on state law." *Jerome v. United States,* 318 U.S. 101, 104 (1943). One reason for this rule of construction is that federal statutes are generally intended to have uniform nationwide application. . . . A second reason for the presumption against the application of state law is the danger that "the federal program would be impaired if state law were to control." *Jerome, supra,* at 104. For this reason, we look to the purpose of the statute to ascertain what is intended.

* * *

First, and most fundamentally, the purpose of the ICWA gives no reason to believe that Congress intended to rely on state law for the definition of a critical term; quite the contrary. It is clear from the very text of the ICWA, not to mention its legislative history and the hearings that led to its enactment, that Congress was concerned with the rights of Indian families and Indian communities vis-a-vis state authorities. More specifically, its purpose was, in part, to make clear that in certain situations the state courts did *not* have jurisdiction over child custody proceedings. Indeed, the congressional findings that are a part of the statute demonstrate that Congress perceived the States and their courts as partly responsible for the problem it intended to correct. *See* 25 U.S.C. § 1901(5) (state "judicial bodies . . . have often failed to recognize the essential tribal relations of Indian people and the cultural and social standards prevailing in Indian communities and families"). Under these circumstances it is most improbable that Congress would have intended to leave the scope of the statute's key jurisdictional provision subject to definition by state courts as a matter of state law.

Second, Congress could hardly have intended the lack of nationwide uniformity that would result from state–law definitions of domicile. An example will illustrate. In a case quite similar to this one, the New Mexico state courts found exclusive jurisdiction in the tribal court pursuant to § 1911(a), because the illegitimate child took the reservation domicile of its mother at birth—notwithstanding that the child was placed in the custody of adoptive parents 2 days after its off-reservation birth and the mother executed a consent to adoption 10 days later. *In re Adoption of Baby Child,* 102 N.M. 735, 737-738, 700 P.2d 198, 200-201 (App. 1985). Had that mother traveled to Mississippi to give birth, rather than to Albuquerque, a different result would have obtained if state-law definitions of domicile applied. . . . While the child's custody proceeding would have been subject to exclusive tribal jurisdiction in her home State, her mother, prospective adoptive parents, or an adoption intermediary could have obtained an adoption decree in state court merely by transporting her across state lines. Even if we could conceive of a federal statute under which the rules of domicile (and thus of jurisdiction) applied differently to different Indian children, a statute under which different rules apply from time to time to the same child, simply as a result of his or her transport from one State to another, cannot be what Congress had in mind.

We therefore think it beyond dispute that Congress intended a uniform federal law of domicile for the ICWA.[22]

B

It remains to give content to the term "domicile" in the circumstances of the present case. The holding of the Supreme Court of Mississippi that the twin babies were not domiciled on the Choctaw Reservation appears to have rested on two findings of fact by the trial court: (1) that they had never been physically present there, and (2) that they were "voluntarily surrendered" by their parents. 511 So. 2d at 921. The question before us, therefore, is whether under the ICWA definition of "domicile" such facts suffice to render the twins nondomiciliaries of the reservation.

* * *

---

[22] We note also the likelihood that, had Congress intended a state-law definition of domicile, it would have said so. Where Congress did intend that ICWA terms be defined by reference to other than federal law, it stated this explicitly. *See* § 1903(2) ("extended family member" defined by reference to tribal law or custom); § 1903(6) ("Indian custodian" defined by reference to tribal law or custom and to state law).

"Domicile" is, of course, a concept widely used in both federal and state courts for jurisdiction and conflict-of-laws purposes, and its meaning is generally uncontroverted. "Domicile" is not necessarily synonymous with "residence," *Perri v. Kisselbach,* 34 N.J. 84, 987, 167 A.2d 377, 379 (1961), and one can reside in one place but be domiciled in another, *In re Estate of Jones,* 192 Iowa 78, 80, 182 N.W. 227, 228 (1921). For adults, domicile is established by physical presence in a place in connection with a certain state of mind concerning one's intent to remain there. One acquires a "domicile of origin" at birth, and that domicile continues until a new one (a "domicile of choice") is acquired. *Jones, supra,* at 81, 182 N.W. at 228; *In re Estate of Moore*, 68 Wash. 2d 792, 796, 415 P.2d 653, 656 (1966). Since most minors are legally incapable of forming the requisite intent to establish a domicile, their domicile is determined by that of their parents. *Yarborough v. Yarborough,* 290 U.S. 202, 211 (1933). In the case of an illegitimate child, that has traditionally meant the domicile of its mother. *Kowalski v. Wojtkowski,* 19 N.J. 247, 258, 116 A.2d 6, 12 (1955); *Moore, supra,* at 796, 415 P. 2d at 656; Restatement § 14(2), § 22, Comment c; 25 Am. Jur. 2d, Domicil § 69 (1966). Under these principles, it is entirely logical that "[o]n occasion, a child's domicil of origin will be in a place where the child has never been." Restatement § 14, Comment b.

It is undisputed in this case that the domicile of the mother (as well as the father) has been, at all relevant times, on the Choctaw Reservation. Thus, it is clear that at their birth the twin babies were also domiciled on the reservation, even though they themselves had never been there. The statement of the Supreme Court of Mississippi that "[a]t no point in time can it be said the twins ... were domiciled within the territory set aside for the reservation," 511 So. 2d at 921, may be a correct statement of that State's law of domicile, but it is inconsistent with generally accepted doctrine in this country and cannot be what Congress had in mind when it used the term in the ICWA.

Nor can the result be any different simply because the twins were "voluntarily surrendered" by their mother. Tribal jurisdiction under § 1911(a) was not meant to be defeated by the actions of individual members of the tribe, for Congress was concerned not solely about the interest of Indian children and families, but also about the impact on the tribes themselves of the large numbers of Indian children adopted by non-Indians. The numerous perogatives accorded the tribes through the ICWA's substantive provisions, must, accordingly, be seen as a means of protecting not only the interests of individual Indian children and families, but also of the tribes themselves.

In addition, it is clear that Congress' concern over the placement of Indian children in non-Indian homes was based in part on evidence of the detrimental impact on the children themselves of such placements outside their culture. Congress determined to subject such placements to the ICWA's jurisdictional and other provisions, even in cases where the parents consented to an adoption, because of concerns going beyond the wishes of individual parents. As the 1977 Final Report of the congressionally established American Indian Policy Review Commission stated, in summarizing these two concerns, "[r]emoval of Indian children from their cultural setting seriously impacts a long-term tribal survival and has damaging social and psychological impact on many individual Indian children." Senate Report, at 52.

These congressional objectives make clear that a rule of domicile that would permit individual Indian parents to defeat the ICWA's jurisdictional scheme is inconsistent with what Congress intended. The appellees in this case argue strenuously that the twins' mother went to great lengths to give birth off the reservation so that her children could be adopted by the Holyfields. But that was precisely part of Congress' concern. Permitting individual members of the tribe to avoid tribal exclusive jurisdiction by the simple expedient of giving birth off the reservation would, to a large extent, nullify the purpose the ICWA was intended to accomplish. . . .

[T]he law of domicile Congress used in the ICWA cannot be one that permits individual reservation-domiciled tribal members to defeat the tribe's exclusive jurisdiction by the simple expedient of giving birth and placing the child for adoption off the reservation. Since, for purposes of the ICWA, the twin babies in this case were domiciled on the reservation when adoption proceedings were begun, the Choctaw tribal court possessed exclusive jurisdiction pursuant to 25 U.S.C. § 1911(a). The Chancery Court of Harrison County was, accordingly, without jurisdiction to enter a decree of adoption; under ICWA § 104, 25 U.S.C. § 1914, its decree of January 28, 1986, must be vacated.

III

We are not unaware that over three years have passed since the twin babies were born and placed in the Holyfield home, and that a court deciding their fate today is not writing on a blank slate in the same way it would have in January 1986. Three years' development of family ties cannot be undone, and a separation at this point would doubtless cause considerable pain.

Whatever feelings we might have as to where the twins should live, however, it is not for us to decide that question. We have been asked to decide the legal question of *who* should make the custody determination concerning these children—not what the outcome of that determination should be. The law places that decision in the hands of the Choctaw tribal court. Had the mandate of the ICWA been followed in 1986, of course, much potential anguish might have been avoided. . . . It is not ours to say whether the trauma that might result from removing these children from their adoptive family should outweigh the interest of the Tribe—and perhaps the children themselves—in having them raised as part of the Choctaw community. . . .

The judgment of the Supreme Court of Mississippi is reversed, and the case is remanded for further proceedings not inconsistent with this opinion.

[The dissenting opinion of Justice Stevens is omitted.]

Notes

1. Section 1911(a) of ICWA grants tribal courts exclusive jurisdiction over children who reside on a reservation, are domiciliaries of a reservation, or are wards of the court. *See* Charmel L. Cross, *The Existing Indian Family Exception: Is It Appropriate to Use a Judicially Created Exception to Render the Indian Child Welfare Act of 1978 Inapplicable?*, 26 CAP. U. L. REV. 847, 859-60 (1998) (citing 25

U.S.C.A. § 1911(a) (West 1978)). According to *Holyfield, supra,* a parent cannot defeat the exclusive jurisdiction of the tribal court as granted by the ICWA. ICWA Section 1911(b) gives tribal courts transfer jurisdiction over children who are neither residents nor domiciliaries of a reservation nor are wards of the tribal court. To block the transfer of jurisdiction from a state court to the tribal court, either parent, a custodian, or the Indian child's tribe may object by petition or otherwise. The transfer of jurisdiction to a tribal court shall be ordered unless the state court finds "good cause" not to transfer. ICWA Section 1911(b). *See also* Denise C. Stiffarm, *The Indian Child Welfare Act: Guiding the Determination of Good Cause to Depart From the Statutory Placement Preferences*, 70 WASH. L. REV. 1151 (1995).

For additional discussion of what is "good cause" under ICWA Section 1911(b), *see Matter of Guardianship of Ashley Elizabeth R.*, 863 P.2d 451 (N.M. Ct. App. 1993) (Indian Children not registered with tribe cannot be considered good cause not to transfer proceedings); *People In Interest of J.L.P.*, 870 P.2d 1252 (Colo. Ct. App. 1994) (whether good cause exists to retain jurisdiction is within juvenile court's discretion). For further discussion of the ICWA's expansion of the tribal court's jurisdiction, see John Robert Renner, *The Indian Child Welfare Act and Equal Protection Limitations on Federal Power Over Indian Affairs*, 17 AM. INDIAN L. REV. 129, 156-68 (1992); Cross, *supra*, at 1253-63; Michael J. Dale, *State Court Jurisdiction Under the Indian Child Welfare Act and the Best Unstated Best Interest of the Child Test*, 27 GONZ. L. REV. 353 (1992).

2. In *In re Baby Boy L.*, 643 P.2d 169 (Kan. 1982), the court created an exception to ICWA called the "Existing Indian Family Exception." The Existing Indian Family Exception interprets ICWA "not to apply to custody proceedings otherwise falling within the purview of the Act where the Indian child who is the subject of the proceeding does not belong to an existing Indian family unit. . . ." Sandra C. Ruffin, *Postmodernism, Spirit Healing, and the Proposed Amendments to the Indian Child Welfare Act*, 30 MCGEORGE L. REV. 1221, 1249 (1999). The courts in *In re Adoption of Crews,* 825 P.2d 305 (Wash. 1992), and *In re Bridget,* 49 Cal. Rptr. 2d 507 (Ct. App. 1996), developed the exception further by creating a minimum contacts rule for both the child and the parents. If the child's or the parents' contacts with a reservation are not sufficient to meet the minimum contact standard, then the tribal court may not exercise jurisdiction over the child's custody case. The court in *Crystal R. v. Superior Court of Santa Cruz County*, 69 Cal. Rptr. 2d 414 (Ct. App. 1997), held that the Existing Indian Family Exception was necessary for the constitutional application of the ICWA. Although the *Holyfield* court, *supra*, substantially undermined this exception by making a strict interpretation of the ICWA, the "Existing Indian Family Exception" is still followed in many jurisdictions. *See* Christine M. Metteer, *A Law Unto Itself: The Indian Child Welfare Act as Inapplicable and Inappropriate to the Transracial/Race-Matching Adoption Controversy,* 38 BRANDEIS L.J. 47 (1999).

3. For additional background information about ICWA, see Lorie M. Graham, *"The Past Never Vanishes": A Contextual Critique of the Existing Indian Family Doctrine,* 23 AM. INDIAN L. REV. 1, 1-34 (1998); Renner, *supra*, at 132-45; Sloan Philips, *The Indian Child Welfare Act in the Face of Extinction,* 21 AM. INDIAN L. REV. 351 (1997); Cross, *supra,* at 852-54. For a survey of the proposals to amend ICWA, see Metter, *supra;* Jose Monsivais, *A Glimmer of Hope: A Proposal to Keep the*

Indian Child Welfare Act of 1978 Intact, 29 AM. INDIAN L. REV. 1 (1997). For critiques of the successes and failures of ICWA, see Philips, *supra,* at 355-61; Graham, *supra,* at 34-53.

Questions

1. What parts of the ICWA might a critic attack as unconstitutional? How might an advocate of the statute respond to those attacks?

2. According to the ICWA, states may refuse to relinquish jurisdiction over the action if the state shows "good cause to the contrary." (25 U.S.C.A. § 1911(d) (West 1978).) ICWA, however, fails to define what is "good cause." In light of the intentions of the Act, how should "good cause" be defined? For a discussion of what might be meant by "good cause," see Cross, *supra*, at 859.

3. How does ICWA address the historical problems and concerns that led to its passage in 1978? How has ICWA met the expectations of the authors of the Act? How has it failed?

Chapter 11

Special Advocacy for Children

Courts have traditionally held that children lack the capacity to sue or defend an action in court. As a rule, however, children have standing as parties in delinquency, child welfare, dissolution of marriage, child custody, and termination of parental right proceedings. The court typically appoints an adult representative, a guardian ad litem (GAL) or court appointed special advocate (CASA) to represent the best interests of the child in these proceedings. The states use special advocates for children in various ways. The special advocate may be a relative or someone with an interest in the child's welfare. The child's advocate may be law trained or a lay volunteer. A child may also be represented by legal counsel. Some jurisdictions combine the roles of attorney and special advocate for the child. As the child's attorney, a GAL, for example, must advocate his client's position. As the child's special advocate, the GAL must investigate and report to the court what placement, services, etc. are in the child's best interests.

In this chapter, consider how the child's interests will best be protected. What specific measure may a special advocate take in behalf of a child? What problems may arise when a GAL has a personal interest in the welfare of the child? Does appointing both a CASA and an attorney for the child best serve the child's welfare? What problems may arise where both the attorney and CASA are involved? Is merging the roles of lawyer and special advocate preferable? What should happen when the two roles conflict?

A. The Child's Legal Status in Child Protection Proceedings

1. Party Status

Indiana Code Annotated

§ 31-34-9-7 (Lexis 1997)

§ 31-34-9-7 Right of parties.—The:

1. child;
2. child's parents, guardian, or custodian;
3. county office of family and children; and
4. guardian ad litem or court appointed special advocate;

are parties to the proceedings described in the juvenile law and have all rights of parties under the Indiana Rules of Trial Procedure.

2. Standing

Kingsley v. Kingsley

623 So. 2d 780 (Fla. Dist. Ct. App. 1993)

Rachel Kingsley, the natural mother of Gregory, a minor child, appeals the trial court's final orders terminating her parental rights based upon findings of abandonment and neglect, and granting the petition for adoption filed by Gregory's foster parents, George and Elizabeth Russ. George Russ, on behalf of Gregory, appeals the trial court's order denying his motion for summary judgment regarding the applicable burden of proof. We affirm the trial court's orders terminating Rachel's parental rights and denying the motion for summary judgment; however, we reverse the trial court's order granting the adoption petition.

On June 25, 1992, Gregory, then 11 years of age, filed in the juvenile division of the circuit court a petition for termination of the parental rights of his natural parents. He separately filed, in the civil division of the circuit court, a complaint for declaration of rights and adoption by his foster parents. . . . [T]he trial court ruled that Gregory, as a natural person who had knowledge of the facts alleged, had standing to initiate the action for termination of parental rights. . . . On September 17, 1992, Gregory filed an amended petition for termination of parental rights, and on September 18, 1992, Gregory's foster family filed a notice that its members were joining in, and adopting, Gregory's amended petition for termination of parental rights.

This matter proceeded to trial on September 24 and September 25, 1992. The court, over Rachel's objection, tried the termination of parental rights proceeding and the adoption proceeding at the same time pursuant to its earlier order allowing the two cases to travel together. After the various parties had presented their positions, the trial court, orally on the record, terminated

Rachel's parental rights. Rachel immediately filed her notice of appeal in open court, contending that the appeal suspends and supersedes the adoption proceeding. The trial court, however, proceeded orally to grant the adoption petition filed by Gregory's foster parents. Subsequently, on October 13, 1992, nunc pro tunc to September 25, 1992, the trial court entered a written judgment which terminated Rachel's parental rights and a separate written judgment which granted the adoption.

Rachel contends that the trial court erred in holding that Gregory has the capacity to bring a termination of parental rights proceeding in his own right. Specifically, Rachel argues that the disability of nonage prevents a minor from initiating or maintaining an action for termination of parental rights. We agree.

Capacity to sue means the absence of a legal disability which would deprive a party of the right to come into court. *Keehn v. Joseph C. Mackey & Co.*, 420 So. 2d 398, 399 n.1 (Fla. 4th DCA 1982); *Argonaut Insurance Co. v. Commercial Standard Insurance Co.,* 380 So. 2d 1066, 1067 (Fla. 2d DCA), *rev. denied,* 389 So. 2d 1108 (Fla. 1980); *General Development Corp. v. Kirk,* 251 So. 2d 284, 286 (Fla. 2d DCA 1971); *Earls v. King*, 785 S.W.2d 741, 743 (Mo. Ct. App. 1990); *Parker v. Bowron,* 40 Cal. 2d 344, 254 P.2d 6, 9 (Cal. 1953); 59 Am. Jur. 2d *Parties* §§ 24, 30 (1987). *See also Moorhouse A. Ambassador Insurance Co.,* 147 Mich. App. 412, 383 N.W.2d 219 (Mich. Ct. App. 1985).

In *Earls v. King,* 785 S.W.2d 742 (Mo. Ct. App. 1990), the court succinctly set forth the legal effect of the concept of capacity to sue:

> Capacity to sue is the right to come into court which exists if one is free of general disability, such as infancy or insanity. Nearly all adults have capacity to sue.

Earls, 785 S.W.2d at 743.

The necessity of a guardian ad litem or next friend, the alter ego of a guardian ad litem, to represent a minor is required by the orderly administration of justice and the procedural protection of a minor's welfare and interest by the court and, in this regard, the fact that a minor is represented by counsel, in and of itself, is not sufficient. *Brown v. Ripley*, 119 So. 2d 712 (Fla. 1st DCA 1960). *See also Roberts v. Ohio Casualty Insurance Co.,* 256 F.2d 35, 39 (5th Cir. 19598); *Zaro v. Strauss*, 167 F.2d 218 (5th Cir. 1948). Unless a child has a guardian or other like fiduciary, a child must sue by his next friend; however, the next friend does not become a party to the suit. *Brown v. Caldwell,* 389 So. 2d 287, 288 (Fla. 1st DCA 1980). Where the next friend brings the suit, the minor is the real party in interest. *Youngblood v. Taylor,* 89 So. 2d 503, 50 (Fla. 1956).

This disability of nonage has been described as procedural, rather than jurisdictional, in character because if a minor mistakenly brings an action in his own name such defect can be cured by the subsequent appointment of a next friend or guardian ad litem. *Smith v. Langford,* 255 So. 294, 297 (Fla. 1st DCA 1971). *See also Brown v. Ripley,* 119 So. 2d 712, 714-15 (Fla. 1st DCA 1960).

Thus, the concept of capacity determines the procedure which a minor must invoke in order to pursue a cause of action.

Section 39461(1), Florida Statutes (Supp. 1992), provides that petitions for termination of parental rights may be initiated either by an attorney for [HRS], or by any other person who has knowledge of the facts alleged or is informed of them and believes that they are true.

This court has construed the term "any other person who has knowledge" to mean someone who is in a peculiar position so that such knowledge can be reasonably inferred; for example, the judge familiar with the file, the guardian or attorney for the children, or neighbors or friends of the parties who, because of their proximity, would be expected to have such knowledge.

As a general rule, states "may require a minor to wait until the age of majority before being permitted to exercise legal rights independently." *Bellotti v. Baird,* 443 U.S. 622, 650, 99 S. Ct. 3035, 61 L. Ed. 2d 797 (1979). Objective criteria, such as age limits although inevitably arbitrary, are not unconstitutional unless they unduly burden the minor's pursuit of a fundamental right. *Bellotti,* 433 U.S. at 640, 643 n.23. Gregory's lack of capacity due to nonage is a procedural, not substantive, impediment which minimally restricts his right to participate as a party in proceedings brought to terminate the parental rights of his natural parents; therefore, we conclude that this procedural requirement does not unduly burden a child's fundamental liberty interest to be "free of physical and emotional violence at the hands of his . . . most trusted caretaker."

Although we conclude that the trial court erred in allowing Gregory to file the petition in his own name because Gregory lacked the requisite legal capacity, this error was rendered harmless by the fact that separate petitions for termination of parental rights were filed on behalf of Gregory by the foster father, the guardian ad litem, HRS, and the foster mother.

* * *

Affirmed in part, reversed in part; remanded for further proceedings.

[Concurring and dissenting opinions omitted.]

In re Pima County Juvenile Severance Action No. S-113432

872 P.2d 1240 (Ariz. Ct. App. 1993)

ESPINOSA, Presiding Judge.

The natural father of four children, A., born May 3, 1978, B., born September 28, 1979, C., born December 29, 1986, and D., born May 13, 1988, appeals from the juvenile court's September 1, 1992 order severing his parental rights on the grounds of physical and emotional abuse under A.R.S. § 8-533(B)(2). We affirm for the reasons stated below.

The relationship between the father and the children's mother began during the late 1970s and was marked by turbulence and violence until it ended in February 1989. The couple never married. Shortly after they separated, the mother and the four children born during the relationship began living with the mother's husband, whom she married in May 1989. About two months earlier, in March, the father filed a petition in superior court seeking a determination of custody, visitation and support. Pursuant to a stipulation between the mother and father, the court entered an order in January 1990 granting custody of the children to the mother, giving the father visitation rights and requiring that the father pay child support. In February they agreed to allow the conciliation court to prepare a report regarding visitation. The report was completed in December 1990. Visitation became a problem, particularly after an incident in March 1990. While in their respective vehicles, the father chased the stepfather around a parking area, while daughters A. and B. were passengers in the stepfather's vehicle, for which the father was later convicted of misdemeanor endangerment.

On October 15, 1990, after receiving a letter from the conciliation court, the domestic relations court appointed counsel "to investigate and report to the court and take whatever steps may be necessary to protect the interests of the children." In December 1991, the children's attorney filed a petition in juvenile court to terminate the father's parental rights on behalf of the children, then ages 14, 12, 6 and 4; in April 1992 the mother filed a notice of joinder in the petition. . . .

The father moved to dismiss the petition on the ground that neither the children's attorney nor the children had standing to file it. The court denied the motion, finding that a child may properly file a petition pursuant to A.R.S. § 8-533. . . . Following a three-day hearing, the court granted the petition, severing the father's rights under § 8-533(B)(20). The father has appealed. . . .

* * *

1. *Children as petitioner.*

Section 8-533(A) provides in pertinent part as follows:

> Any person or agency that has a legitimate interest in the welfare of a child, including, but not limited to, a relative, a foster parent, a physician, the department of economic security, or a private licensed child welfare agency, may file a petition for the termination of the parent-child relationship alleging grounds contained in subsection B.

The father argues that separate references to the child and the petitioner reflect a legislative intent that the two not be the same person. As further support for this contention, the father cites § 8-534, which sets forth the information that must be contained in a petition, and § 8-531(12), which defines "parties."

Although section 8-534 requires that the severance petition state the name, residence of the petitioner and additional information regarding the child, including the petitioner's relationship to the child, this does not necessarily mean they cannot be the same person. We also find unpersuasive the fact that § 8-531(12) defines "parties" as including the child and the petitioner. The import of this definition is that the child is always considered a party because the child is necessarily the focus of the proceedings, and the petitioner, by having commenced the proceeding, is likewise, by definition, a party. Moreover, the list of persons or agencies in § 8-533 who may file a severance petition is not, by its terms, all-inclusive. A child clearly is a person with a legitimate interest in his or her own welfare. We hold, therefore, that a child may be the petitioner in an action to sever the parental rights of that child's parents. . . .

The father's argument that such a construction is contrary to provisions reflecting minority as a legal disability, is not well taken. Children may not marry, drive a car, join the armed services or consent to surgery without the consent of a parent or guardian because the legislature has determined these acts require a certain level of maturity and capacity. The same cannot be said of a severance proceeding. Maturity has nothing to do with a child's interest in the substance of such a proceeding. Indeed, as previously noted, the child is already considered a party in such a proceeding. We see no distinction between a child's capacity to be party when the petition is brought by someone else and when the child has commenced it.

In any event, the mother joined in the petition and she is without question a person who may file a severance petition. We conclude, therefore, that the court had jurisdiction over the termination proceeding and correctly denied the motion to dismiss.

2. *Need for separate representation of the children.*

The father next argues that the trial court should have appointed independent counsel or guardians *ad litem* "for any minor where, as here the interests of the minors may differ from the interests of other minors, and where each child's best interests are not fully explored." First, the father has no standing to assert such conflicts here. If there were conflicts, it was for the children to assert them. Moreover, based on the record before us, we do not believe separate counsel or guardians *ad litem* were required. The father's rights were severed because of his abusive conduct and explosive personality, factors which had an impact on all the children. Their interests were the same. We do not believe the court was required to appoint for the children, as a guardian *ad litem*, an individual different from their counsel. . . .

* * *

The juvenile court's order severing the father's parental rights to the children is affirmed. . . .

Notes

1. Children have traditionally enjoyed fewer rights than adults. For a discussion of how courts have historically viewed the rights of children, see Chapter 1. For example, courts have traditionally held that children lack the capacity to sue or defend an action in court. *See* 42 AM. JUR. 2d *Infants* § 150 (2000); Claudio DeBellis & Marta B. Soja, Note, Gregory K.*: Child Standing in Parental Termination Proceedings and the Implications of the Foster Parent-Foster Child Relationship on the Best Interest Standard,* 8 ST. JOHN'S J. LEGAL COMMENT. 501, 508 (1993). Despite these limitations, children are granted party status in the following proceedings: delinquency (*see L.B. v. State,* 675 N.E.2d 1104 (Ind. Ct. App. 1996)); child welfare (*see In re Hirenia C.,* 22 Cal. Rptr. 2d 443 (Ct. App. 1993)); dissolution of marriage (*see Newman v. Newman*, 663 A.2d 980 (Conn. 1995); *Miller v. Miller*, 677 A.2d 64 (Me. 1996)); child custody (*see Clements v. Phillips*, 510 S.E.2d 311 (Ga. Ct. App. 1998)); and termination of parental rights proceedings (*see In re G.K.J.,* 370 S.E.2d 490 (Ga. Ct. App. 1998)). For further discussion of a child's standing to initiate termination proceedings, see Bart L. Greenwald, Note, *Irreconcilable Differences: When Children Sue Their Parents for "Divorce,"* 32 U. LOUISVILLE J. FAM. L. 67 (1993-1994); George H. Russ, *Through the Eyes of a Child, "Gregory K.": A Child's Right to Be Heard,* 27 FAM. L.Q. 365 (1993). For a general discussion of a child's standing in legal proceedings, see Leonard P. Edwards, *A Comprehensive Approach to the Representation of Children: The Child Advocacy Coordinating Council,* 27 FAM. L.Q. 417 (1993).

Because children have standing in the proceedings mentioned above but lack the capacity to sue or defend in court, children have traditionally had to initiate legal action or otherwise litigate through an adult representative. *See* Jay C. Laubscher, Note, *A Minor of "Sufficient Age and Understanding" Should Have the Right to Petition for the Termination of the Parental Relationship,* 40 N.Y.L. SCH. L. REV. 565, 576 (1996). The following excerpt from the Federal Rules of Civil Procedure explains how a child may sue or defend a cause of action:

> Whenever an infant . . . has a representative, such as a general guardian, committee, conservator, or other like fiduciary, the representative may sue or defend on behalf of the infant. . . . An infant . . . who does not have a duly appointed representative may sue by a next friend or by a guardian ad litem. The court shall appoint a guardian ad litem for an infant . . . not otherwise represented in an action or shall make such other orders as it deems proper for the protection of the infant or incompetent person.

FED. R. CIV. PRO. 17(c).

Even though a child must sue through an adult, the child still remains an interested party to the litigation. *See* Laubscher, *supra,* at 576. The special advocate, as a guardian ad litem (GAL) or court appointed special advocate (CASA), also has standing in these proceedings. *See* Mary H. Trainer, Note, *Expanding the Role of Court Appointed Special Advocate Volunteers: The Connecticut Probate Courts,* 13 QUINNIPIAC PROB. L.J. 71, 107 (1998); *In re Christina D.,* 525 A.2d 1306 (R.I. 1987). *See also State ex rel. A.D.,* 6 P.3d 1137 (Utah Ct. App. 2000) (GAL may file a petition for termination of parental rights); *In Interest of Brandon S.S.,* 507 N.W.2d 94 (Wis. Ct. App. 1993) (in termination proceedings, "petitioner must serve summons and petition on, among others, the child's guardian ad litem"); *People in Interest of G.S.,* 820 P.2d 1178 (Colo. Ct. App.1991) (once appointed by a court, the GAL is responsible in participating in the proceedings so as to adequately represent the child's needs and interests); *In Interest of R.T.,* 592 A.2d 55 (Pa. Super. Ct. 1991) (GAL may petition for "appropriate protective services" for the child or for the termination of the parent's rights).

Questions

1. What is the significance of a child having party status and standing in child welfare proceedings? How is this consistent (or inconsistent) with the history and current goals of the juvenile justice system?

2. How does the child's special advocate affect the capacity of the child to be heard in court?

B. Nature of Special Advocacy for Children

1. Role of Special Advocate

Alaska Code
§ 25.24.310 (Lexis 2000)

§ 25.24.310 Representation of Minor.

a. In an action involving a question of the custody . . .

* * *

c. Instead of, or in addition to, appointment of an attorney under (a) of this section, the court may, upon the motion of either party or upon its own motion, appoint an attorney or other person or the office of public advocacy to provide guardian ad litem services to a child in any legal proceedings involving the child's welfare. The court shall require a guardian ad litem when, in the opinion of the court, representation of the child's best interests, to be distinguished from preferences, would serve the welfare of the child. The court in its order appointing a guardian ad litem shall limit the duration of the appointment of the guardian ad litem to the pendency of the legal proceedings affecting the child's interest, and shall outline the guardian ad litem's responsibilities and limit the authority to those matters related to the guardian's effective representation of the child's best interests in the pending legal proceeding. The court shall make every reasonable effort to appoint a guardian ad litem from among persons in the community where the child's parents or the person having legal custody or guardianship of the child's person reside. . . .

New Mexico ex rel. Children, Youth and Families Department v. George F
964 P.2d 158 (N.M. Ct. App. 1998)

George F. and his younger brother, Frank, were taken into custody by the State of New Mexico on December 16, 1988. Both children had been physically and sexually abused, and they both suffered psychological injuries and behavior problems resulting from the abuse. George's emotional problems are compounded by physical problems. He is deaf and legally blind and communicates only by sign language. Both children were freed for adoption on February 23, 1991, but by December 1996, George had endured over fourteen foster placements and Frank seven. Consequently, both George and Frank are still in the custody of the State.

On May 8, 1996, the children's court ordered the Department to secure an unconditional, long-term placement for George. Upon learning of the Department's intended institutional placement, the GAL became concerned about the lack of staff at the facility who had any experience dealing with George's problems. . . . [T]he GAL was concerned that there would be no one on the staff at night who could communicate with George and no other residents with similar problems to George's. . . . After three days of unsuccessfully attempting to contact the social worker, the GAL was officially informed of the placement plan. The GAL requested and was granted a restraining order to prevent an inappropriate placement. Subsequently, the GAL and the Department came to an agreement about George's placement, and the children's court entered a stipulated order adopting that agreement. However, according to the GAL, George was never given a placement in accordance with that order.

On August 13, 1996, the children's court attorney, who is an attorney with the Department charged by law with bringing abuse and neglect cases, left a voice-mail message for the GAL telling her that she should not contact the Department employees responsible for the case without his consent. This included the social workers assigned to George's case because the children's court attorney considered them to be his clients, and he considered the GAL to be in an adversarial relationship. Over the following two months, the GAL was unable to discover any substantive information regarding the status of the case. She was informed by a social worker that he had been instructed not to speak with her, and was informed by an attorney for the Department that speaking with the social worker outside the presence of the children's court attorney would violate the ethical rule prohibiting attorneys from communicating with a party they know to be represented by counsel about the subject of the representations. . . . Speaking directly with the children's court attorney appears to have been less than satisfactory because the attorney was unfamiliar with the facts which the GAL needed to represent the child's interests to the court. On September 23, 1996, the GAL provided the children's court with written notice that she had retained separate counsel to represent George and Frank in a federal civil rights lawsuit against the State of New Mexico. . . . [O]n October 1, 1996, the Department's counsel left another voice-mail message for the GAL, referring to the civil rights lawsuit and reiterating that she should not contact the social worker outside the presence of the children's court attorney.

On October 16, 1996, the GAL petitioned the children's court for an order declaring that ex parte contact was not prohibited between the GAL and the Department social workers for the purpose of securing information bearing on the children's well-being. The children's court entered an order declaring that social workers are not clients of the Department and that no statute, rule, or ethical canon prohibited the GAL from contacting social workers in efforts to discover information relevant to representing the child. The children's court denied injunctive relief, stating that this would place the social workers at great risk to have to divulge information that the Department policies prohibit. The Department now appeals the children's court order and raises on appeal the issue of whether an attorney-client relationship exists between the children's court attorney and the social worker. . . . [W]e resolve this appeal on other grounds which do not involve the relationship between the children's court attorney and the social worker. Instead, we look at the relationship between the GAL and the child and resolve this appeal based on the difference between the role of a GAL and that of an ordinary attorney representing a client, within the spirit of Rule 16-402 of the Rules of Professional Conduct and the statutory sections of the Children's Code pertaining to the duties of the GAL.

Rule 16-402 states: In representing client, a lawyer shall not communicate about the subject of the representation with a party the lawyer knows to be represented by another lawyer in the matter, unless the lawyer has the consent of the other lawyer or is authorized by law to do so. . . .

The prohibition against ex parte communication only applies if three conditions are present: one party must be represented by counsel, another person must be an attorney representing a client, and the communication between the two must be about the subject of the representation. If any one requirement is not satisfied, the prohibition does not apply. The Department argues that all three conditions are present. On the other hand, it is argued that in New Mexico the role of a GAL is unlike that of an ordinary attorney representing a client, and thus, Rule 16-402 does not apply.

* * *

[The purpose of the Children's Code] is "first to provide for the care, protection and wholesome mental and physical development of children[,]" . . . and also "to provide for the cooperation and coordination of the civil and criminal systems for investigation, intervention and disposition of cases, to minimize interagency conflicts and to enhance the coordinated response of all agencies to achieve the best interests of the child victim. . . . In furthering the central purpose of achieving the child's best interests, the statute provides for the appointment of a GAL in abuse and neglect cases who has the duty to "zealously represent the child's best interests[.] The Children's Code also establishes the "office of children's court attorney," and provides that "[i]n cases involving civil abuse or civil neglect and the periodic review of their dispositions, the attorney . . . representing the department is the children's court attorney". . . .

. . . [I]t is argued that Rule 16-402 applies to both the GAL and the children's court attorney in the context of an abuse and neglect proceeding. We do not agree that the Department and the GAL are adversaries. Because the Department and the GAL are both acting in the child's best interests, they are not structural adversaries in any traditional legal sense, anymore than two social workers who disagree over the best course of action for a child. Such a claim is particularly inconsistent with the Children's Code, given its purpose "to provide for the cooperation and coordination . . . for investigation, intervention and disposition of cases[.]" Section 32A-1-3(E)

The Role of the GAL in Abuse and Neglect Proceedings

New Mexico requires a GAL to be "an attorney appointed by the children's court to represent and protect the best interests of the child in a court proceeding[.]" . . . The children's court found in this case that "[z]ealous representation requires full access to all information regarding or affecting the child so that the [GAL] can fulfill requirements imposed by statute, rule, and ethics." This statutory authorization is required because . . . the Children's Code exempts the child's records from the public's right to inspect public records. The legislature has determined that while it is in the child's interest to keep such records confidential, it is also in the child's best interest to allow the GAL full access to this information. Because of the young age of many of the children, the social worker may be in a unique position to learn important information about the child and communicate it to the GAL and from there to the court.

. . . [T]he qualifications of GALs vary throughout the states. If some states do not require GALs to be attorneys, there is a reasonable basis for inferring that GALs and attorneys need not be treated the same in all respects. Indeed, in the Standards of Practice for Lawyers Representing a Child in Abuse and Neglect Cases, the American Bar Association draws such a distinction by commenting that "[w]here the local law permits, the lawyer is expected to act in the dual role of [GAL] and lawyer of record." . . .

The New Mexico Supreme Court appears to agree that GALs have dual roles and, thus, do not function in the same manner as traditional attorneys. The Court has observed that a GAL can serve two distinct roles: (1) "'acting as an extension of the court by performing the quasi-judicial functions of investigating the facts and reporting to the court what placement was in [the child's] best interest[s]'" and (2) "acting as an advocate for his client's position . . . in the same way as does any other attorney for a client—advancing the interests of the client, not discharging (or assisting in the discharge of) the duties of the court." *Collins ex rel. Collins v. Tabel*, 111 N.M. 391, 398-99, 806 P.2d 40, 47-48 (1991) (quoting *Ward v. Department of Soc. Servs.*, 691 F. Supp. 238 240 (S.D. Cal. 1988)).

In an abuse and neglect case a GAL is required by statute to "report to the court on the child's adjustment to placement, the department's and respondent's compliance with prior court orders and treatment plans and the child's degree of participation during visitations[.]" In fulfilling this statutorily imposed duty, the GAL is required to "communicate with health care, mental health care and other professionals involved with the child's case[.]" . . . As noted in the comments to the ABA Standards of Practice, . . . when a GAL is "required by statute . . . to perform specific tasks, such as submitting a report or testifying as a fact or expert witness[,] [t]hese tasks are not part of functioning as a 'lawyer.'" Similarly, attorney-client privilege has been held not to apply to a GAL's communications with the child when the GAL is not functioning in the customary role of a lawyer. . . . Accordingly, we believe that when a court-appointed GAL performs factual investigations about the child's case to inform the court on the child's circumstances, the GAL is functioning less as an advocate for the child's personal interests, and more as an arm of the court. . . .

. . . [A] part of the GAL's role in abuse and neglect cases is as a fact finder assisting the court and not as an adversary to the Department. . . . The Department regulations appear to acknowledge this distinction. Whereas a "[d]irect contact between social workers and respondent's counsel is limited to exchange of routine information," the "Department routinely informs the Guardian ad Litem about all significant events relating to the child". . . .

* * *

Accordingly, we are persuaded that a GAL, when investigating the facts affecting the child in order to report to the court as required . . . is acting to "assist the court in carrying out its duty" and is not functioning solely as an attorney advocating the child's wishes, nor in the traditional manner of an attorney who represents a client with a single-minded duty solely to that client. The "dual role" of the GAL is more complex, and the rules of Professional Conduct that are designed strictly for the traditional role of attorneys do not fit this circumstance. Thus, the GAL is not prohibited by Rule 16-402 from contacting social workers outside the presence of the Department attorneys. We affirm the children's court ruling that no statute, rule, or ethical canon prohibits a GAL from contacting a social worker to discover factual information relevant to the representation of the child.

Notes

1. A guardian ad litem (GAL) is a court appointed officer who is charged with representing the best interests of the child. *See* 42 AM. JUR. 2d, *Infants* § 173 (1999). The GAL may be an attorney (*see* Marvin Ventrell, *Foster Care & Adoption Reform Legislation: Implementing the Adoption and Safe Families Act of 1997,* 14 ST. JOHN'S J. LEGAL COMMENT. 433, 436 (2000); Dana E. Prescott, *The Liability of Lawyers as Guardians Ad Litem: The Best Defense Is a Good Offense,* 11 J. AM. ACAD. MATRIM. LAW. 65 (1993); Debra H. Lahrmann, *Who Are We Protecting? An Analysis of the Law Regarding the Duties of Attorneys and Guardians Ad Litem,* 63 TEX. B.J. 123 (February 2000); *Proposed Standards of Practice For Lawyers Who Represent Children in Abuse and Neglect Cases*, 29 FAM. L.Q. 375 (1995)) or a trained lay volunteer who is often called a court appointed special advocate (CASA). *See In re A.D.R.,* No. 05-98-00629-CV, 2000 Tex. App. LEXIS 4835, at *8 n.4 (July 25, 2000); *Child v. Beame,* 412 F. Supp. 593 (S.D.N.Y. 1976) (a close relative or someone with interest in child's welfare can be a GAL); Nancy S. Erickson, *The Role of the Law Guardian in a Custody Case Involving Domestic Violence,* 27 FORDHAM URB. L.J. 817, n.5 (2000). Some states, such as Michigan, have three separate special advocates in child protection proceedings—a lawyer-GAL, an attorney, and a lay GAL. *See* Frank E. Vandervort, *Representing Children in Protective Proceedings: Learning From Michigan's Experience*, 19 CHILD L. PRACTICE 153 (2000). A GAL or CASA may also be represented by legal counsel. *See* Raven C. Lidman & Betsy R. Hollingsworth, *The Guardian Ad Litem in Child Custody Cases: The Contours of Our Judicial System Stretched Beyond Recognition,* 6 GEO. MASON L. REV. 255, 303 (1998). The responsibilities of the GAL or CASA should be distinguished from the role of the child's attorney in those cases where counsel has been appointed. *See* Dana E. Prescott, *The Guardian Ad Litem In Custody and Conflict Cases: Investigator, Champion, and Referee?*, 22 U. ARK. LITTLE ROCK L.J. 529, n.117 (2000); Lahrmann, *supra;* Carla J. Stovall, *Justice and Juveniles in Kansas: Where We Have Been and Where We Are Headed,* 47 U. KAN. L. REV. 101, 107 (1999). For further discussion of the different roles served by a child's special advocate and appointed counsel in child protection proceedings, see Donald N. Duquette, *Legal Representation for Children in Protection Proceedings: Two Distinct Lawyer Roles Are Required,* 34 FAM. L.Q. 441 (2000). Most states grant the GAL or CASA party status (*see* Lindman & Hollingsworth, *supra*, at 287; Arlene C. Huszer, *Termination of Parental Rights*, 1997 FLA. JUV. L. & PRAC. Ch. 16,15 (1997). *But see In re D.D.P., Jr.,* 819 P.2d 1212 (Kan. 1991) (CASA is not an interested party and therefore lacks standing). The special advocate receives notice of all proceedings (*see* Stewart W. Gagnon & Howard G. Baldwin, *Laws Regarding the Family, Terminations and Adoptions and Protective Orders,* 60 TEX. B.J. 794, 796 (Sept. 1997)), may file a petition with the court (*see* 705 ILL. COMP. STAT. 405/2-13.1(1)(a) (West 1999); *Joiner ex rel. Rivas v. Rivas*, 536 S.E.2d 372 (S.C. 2000); *Family Law in the Fifty States 1997-98: Case Digests*, 32 FAM. L.Q. 719, 723 (1999); Michael J. Dale, *Juvenile Law: 1996 Survey of Florida Law,* 21 NOVA L. REV. 189, 228 (1996)), and file an appeal. *See In re K.R.C.*, 510 S.E.2d 547 (Ga. Ct. App. 1998). *See generally Sosa By and through Grant v. Koshy,* 961 S.W.2d 420 (Tex. Ct. App. 1997); Karen Tapp, *The Guardian Ad Litem or Special Advocate Appointment Pursuant to KRS 26A.140,* 5 KY. CHILDREN'S RT. J. 19 (1997). Once appointed by the court, the GAL or CASA may only be removed by court order. If not removed by the court, the GAL or CASA's appointment will continue until the child reaches the age of majority or the court proceedings are finalized. *See* WIS. STAT. ANN. § 767.045(5) (West Supp. 2000); DEL. CODE ANN. tit. 31, § 3605(d) (Michie Supp. 2000).

2. The issue of whether GALs or CASAs provide proper representation in abuse and neglect cases has been the subject of several studies. In *In re Jeffrey R.L.,* 435 S.E.2d 1623 (W. Va. 1993), two studies were cited as examples of how a GAL, without proper training, probably will not adequately represent the child's best interests. One of these studies, conducted in New York, revealed that most GALs were not considered specialists in juvenile law, most of them had little interest in juvenile law, and a majority had little to no updated training in representing the welfare of children. JANE KNITZER & MERRIL SOBIE, LAW GUARDIANS IN NEW YORK STATE—A STUDY OF THE LEGAL REPRESENTATION OF CHILDREN (1984). The other study cited in *In re Jeffrey R.L.* was conducted in North Carolina. The study found that both courts and GALs often do not understand the proper advocacy role of the GAL. Robert Kelly & Sarah Ramsey, *Do Attorneys for Children In Protection Proceedings Make a Difference?—A Study of the Impact of Representation Under Conditions of High Judicial Intervention,* 21 J. FAM. L. 405 (1983). Furthermore, the North Carolina study indicated that attorneys who serve as GALs work on average five hours per case, in addition to not following up on the court's decisions as the child's best interests may require. *See generally* Donald C. Bross, *The Evolution of Independent Legal Representations for Children,* 1 J. CENTER FOR CHILDREN & CTS. 7 (1999).

3. Many states and courts have established guidelines for GALs and CASAs and promote standards of special advocacy for children in abuse and neglect cases. The *Jeffrey R.L.* court established twenty-six steps every GAL must follow in an abuse and neglect case. *Id.* at 178-80. The guidelines established by the court require GALs to fulfill the steps in three stages: 1) initial stages of representation; 2) preparation for and representation at adjudicatory and dispositional hearing; and 3) post-dispositional representation. In addition to the guidelines established by the court, West Virginia also requires GALs to complete three hours per year of continuing legal education on the representation of children in child abuse and neglect cases. W. VA. CODE § 49-6-2(a) (Lexis 1999). For additional rules and guidelines, see ABA Center on Children and the Law, *Standards of Practice for Lawyers Representing a Child in Abuse and Neglect Cases* (visited Nov. 28, 2000) <www.abanet.org/child/childrep.html>; THE COUNCIL FOR COURT EXCELLENCE, PRACTICE MANUAL FOR CHILD ABUSE AND NEGLECT CASES IN THE DISTRICT OF COLUMBIA (1988). It should be noted that while some states have statutes that provide guidelines for a guardian ad litem (*see, e.g.,* COLO. REV. STAT. ANN. § 19-3-203(3) (2000); CAL. WELF. & INST. CODE § 317 (West Supp. 2001)), other states allow case law to define the guidelines for a guardian ad litem. *See, e.g.,* WASH. REV. CODE ANN. § 26.44.053 (West Supp. 2001).

Questions

1. How does the GAL or CASA's role in an abuse or neglect proceeding differ from the role of the child's attorney?

2. What, if any, differences are there between the special advocate's role in child welfare cases and delinquency proceedings?

2. Child Protection Proceedings

In re Esperanza M.

955 P.2d 204 (N.M. Ct. App. 1998)

WECHSLER, Judge.

As a result of an investigation, the Children, Youth and Families Division (CYFD) filed an ex parte custody petition in children's court, alleging that Esperanza M. (E.M.) was abused and neglected. Specifically, the petition alleged that Jesus M., E.M.'s adoptive father, sexually abused his daughter and that Marian M., E.M.'s mother, knew or should have known of the sexual abuse but failed to protect her daughter. The children's court entered judgment that E.M. was abused and neglected as defined by NMSA 1978, Section 32A-4-2(B)(1), (B)(2), and (C)(3) (1993). Marian M. and Jesus M. (Parents) appeal raising three issues: (1) whether the children's court erred in admitting the hearsay testimony . . . ; (2) whether the case should be reassigned to a different judge on remand because of an improper comment by the children's court judge; and (3) whether Parents' motion to strike the appellate guardian ad litem's answer brief should be granted. We reverse and remand for further proceedings consistent with this opinion. We decline to order the reassignment of the case to a different judge, and we deny Parents' motion to strike the appellate guardian ad litem's answer brief.

At the adjudicatory hearing, Janis Hildebrand, a school counselor, testified that on or about December 1, 1995, E.M. and three other female students came to her office and alleged that their fathers had sexually abused them. Ms. Hildebrand then contacted the Human Services Department, the child's mother, and the police. When Robin Yoder, a social worker with CYFD, arrived at the school, Ms. Hildebrand told her what E.M. had reported to her. Ms. Yoder spoke with E.M. and her mother, and told Marian M. that CYFD would give E.M. an interview at the Albuquerque Safe House (Safe House) and a physical examination. Ms. Yoder called Dr. Renee Ornelas, a pediatrician who operates the Para Los Ninos Program at the University of New Mexico Hospital (UNM Hospital) and performs medical evaluations on sexually abused children, to arrange the interview at the Safe House. Ms. Yoder told Dr. Ornelas what E.M. had reported to Ms. Hildebrand.

Detective Mark Laws of the Crimes Against Children Unit of the Albuquerque Police Department arrived at the school, and he transported E.M. to the interview at the Safe House. At the completion of the interview, Ms. Yoder took E.M. to UNM Hospital to be examined by Dr. Orenlas. E.M. was . . . thirteen years of age at the time she reported the incident.

After Dr. Ornelas' physical examination, E.M. told Dr. Ornelas that she was there because her father had improperly touched and abused her. . . . Dr. Ornelas' findings from the physical examination were normal. There was no physical evidence of acute or old trauma. The findings of the examination were indistinguishable between a child who had been penetrated and one who had not. Based on the physical examination alone, Dr. Ornelas could not determine if E.M. had been sexually penetrated. However, relying upon E.M.'s ability to give a clear statement about the type of contact that occurred and her ability to describe graphic details such as ejaculation and sexual positions, Dr. Ornelas concluded that E.M. had been sexually abused. . . .

CYFD contacted Dr. Sandra Montoya, a clinical psychologist and neuropsychologist to testity. . . . E.M. told Dr. Montoya that her father began touching her inappropriately in a way that made her feel uncomfortable. After E.M. told her mother about the touching, it stopped, yet after the passage of time began again and eventually progressed to the point where they were having sexual intercourse. Dr. Montoya testified that E.M. felt extreme pressure to protect the family. According to Dr. Montoya, it was extremely important to E.M. that she be able to testify so that she could lie and convince the judge that the abuse never occurred. However, Dr. Montoya felt that allowing E.M. to testify would be psychologically damaging. As a result, E.M. did not testify.

Parents also did not testify. The only witness they called was Dr. Robert Gathings, an obstetrician and gynecologist. Dr. Gathings examined E.M. several weeks after the alleged abuse. He asked E.M. if she had had sex at any time, and she told him no. Dr. Gathings' physical examination of E.M. revealed her to be a normal thirteen-year-old virginal female.

* * *

In announcing his ruling at the close of the hearing, the children's court judge stated:

> I think it's interesting to note that, and disappointing in my view, that parents who insist that E.M., after all she's been through, be placed on the stand to be further subjected to disruption, but not, based on self-interest, take the same stand and subject themselves to scrutiny.

Parents argue that they had a constitutional right under both the New Mexico and United States Constitutions not to testify since the conduct they were alleged to have committed constituted a crime. Parents contend that the children's court impermissibly considered their decision not to testify in deciding whether there was clear and convincing evidence that E.M. had been sexually abused in violation of their constitutional rights. As a consequence, Parents ask that this case be reassigned to a different judge on remand.

The Fifth Amendment "privileges a defendant not to answer questions put to him in any proceeding, civil or criminal, formal or informal, where the answers might tend to incriminate him in future criminal proceedings." *Rainbo Baking Co. v. Apodaca*, 88 N.M. 501, 504, 542 P.2d 1191, 1194 (Ct. App. 1975); *see* N.M. Const. Art. II, § 15. But it does not appear that Parents reserved this issue for appeal by alerting the children's court's attention to what they perceived to be an objectionable comment. Therefore, we need not review the merits of Parents' argument on appeal.

Nevertheless, we do not believe that the comment requires our intervention. We have confidence in the trial judge's ability to afford a fair hearing to all parties on remand. We do note, however, our disapproval of the trial judge's remarks insofar as they put the parents in the untenable position of a conflict between their daughter's welfare and their own self-defense.

At the conclusion of the proceedings in the children's court, the children's court allowed the guardian ad litem who represented the child during the trial to withdraw and appointed a new guardian ad litem to represent the child incident to this appeal. Parents filed a motion to strike the appellate guardian ad litem's answer brief on grounds that the brief directly contradicts the position taken by E.M. Thereafter, the appellate guardian ad litem filed with the children's court a motion for clarification of the role of the guardian ad litem or, in the alternative, for appointment of separate counsel for E.M. The children's court did not rule on these motions because this Court had jurisdiction once Parents took their appeal. These motions raise the question of a guardian ad litem's proper role in an abuse and neglect proceeding when the guardian ad litem's professional opinion as to the best interests of the child differs from the position that the child would like to advance. At appellate oral argument, this Court did not rule on Parents' motion to strike, but heard oral argument from all the parties, including the appellate guardian ad litem.

The Children's Code provides that "[a] guardian ad litem shall zealously represent the child's best interests with respect to matters arising pursuant to the provisions of the Children's Code." NMSA 1978, § 32A-1-7(A) (1995). Subsection D provides that the guardian ad litem shall present the child's declared position to the court when a child's circumstances render it reasonable and appropriate. Section 32A-1-7(D)(2). This statute signifies a guardian ad litem's dual role of representing the child's best interests, while also presenting the child's position to the court when reasonable and appropriate, even if the child's position conflicts with what the guardian ad litem thinks should be done. The statute does not indicate which one of the two roles should be the guardian ad litem's primary function. The committee commentary to Children's Court Rule 10-108 NMRA 1998, which requires the children's court to appoint a guardian ad litem when a petition of abuse and neglect is filed, emphasizes the guardian ad litem's role in representing the child's best interests.

The major difference between the role of the guardian ad litem in a neglect or abuse case and the role of the accused's attorney in a delinquency or need of supervision proceeding is that in the former, the guardian ad litem does what he considers to be in the best interests of the child, while in the latter the attorney, although he may advise differently, follows the instructions of his client, even though he may not consider those instructions to be in the client's best interests. The guardian ad litem has much greater freedom.

The guardian ad litem is required to advocate the child's expressed position only to the extent that the child's desires are, in the guardian ad litem's professional opinion, in the child's best interests. The guardian ad litem may properly present the child's wishes to the court, and at the same time advise the court of those facts and matters which the guardian believes bear upon and affect the child's best interests.

We believe that this dual role conforms to the Rules of Professional Conduct, specifically Rule 16-102(A) NMRA 1998, which requires a lawyer to abide by a client's decision concerning the objectives of representation, and Rule 16-114(A) NMRA 1998, which requires that a lawyer, as far as reasonably possible, "maintain a normal client-lawyer relationship with the client" even when the "client's ability to make adequately considered decision in connection with the representation is impaired" because of minority or some other reason.

We commend the appellate guardian ad litem for representing in the answer brief what she perceived to be the position that was in the best interests of E.M., while still advancing the child's contrary position. The appellate guardian ad litem's answer brief clearly indicates that E.M. is in accord with Parents' brief-in-chief, and that she disagrees with the position taken by the appellate guardian ad litem on appeal. Thus the appellate guardian ad litem fulfilled the dual role established in Section 32A-1-7.

We do not believe that a conflict between a guardian ad litem's perception of the best interests of the child and the child's expressed position necessarily requires that the guardian ad litem withdraw as counsel for the child. By imposing a dual role on the guardian ad litem appointed in an abuse and neglect proceeding, the Children's Code recognizes that these dual roles may not always be compatible. Unless the guardian ad litem's perception of the child's best interests is so incongruous with the child's position that the guardian ad litem absolutely refuses to present the child's position, we see no need for the guardian ad litem to withdraw as counsel. Moreover, in this case, the appellate guardian ad litem more than adequately fulfilled her dual role of representing the child's best interest while also advocating the child's position. Consequently, we deny Parents' motion to strike the guardian ad litem's answer brief.

Although none of the parties has raised the issue of the adequacy of the guardian ad litem's representation of E.M. at trial as a basis for reversal, our review of the record indicates the trial guardian ad litem's representation was materially deficient. The trial guardian ad litem failed to actively participate in the proceedings below, did not present to the children's court her findings or position concerning the child's best interest, or the position of the child. The trial guardian ad litem did not make any pretrial motions, make an opening statement, call witnesses, adequately examine witnesses called, make proper objections, or take a position on a majority of the objections made by opposing counsel. The trial guardian ad litem's passive representation of E.M. in this case failed to meet the standards prescribed by Section 32A-1-7.

* * *

In this case, when specifically requested to make closing remarks on behalf of E.M., the trial guardian ad litem expressed some confusion about her role at trial. She indicated that as a friend of the court, she was ready to address the child's best interests, insofar as she had been able to look into the matter. The children's court judge replied that she was not acting as friend of the court, but as guardian ad litem for E.M. The guardian ad litem apologized and indicated she had that understanding. The children's court judge asked the guardian ad item if she had any remarks, to which she responded: "No, your honor, thank you." Under these circumstances, the court should have attempted to clarify the guardian ad litem's role and again requested a statement concerning the child's best interests, particularly since the guardian ad litem's participation in the proceeding had been minimal up to that point. If, at that time, the guardian ad litem again indicated that she had no remarks, the court could have considered whether the best interests of E.M. mandated that different counsel be appointed for the child. Indeed, the children's court had a duty to elicit the guardian ad litem's position on substantive issues throughout the course of the abuse and neglect proceeding in fulfilling its affirmative duty of protecting the best interest of the child.

The failure of duty on the part of the trial guardian ad litem had additional consequences. At trial, the child apparently wanted to testify; she wanted to give her position on the allegations regarding her parents. When she was not allowed to testify, due to the court's understandable concern for her welfare, there was no other way for the child's position to be effectively communicated to the court. The guardian ad litem should have assumed that responsibility.

Notes

1. Congress passed the Child Abuse Prevention and Treatment Act (CAPTA), 42 U.S.C. §§ 5101-5107, in 1974, requiring states to appoint a special advocate in every case where a neglected or abused child faces judicial proceedings. CAPTA requires states to follow the statute's mandate in order to receive federal funding designated to prevent and treat child abuse and neglect. DONALD T. KRAMER, LEGAL RIGHTS OF CHILDREN § 12.01-12.05 (2d ed. 1994). CAPTA, however, provides little guidance as to who is eligible to be a GAL or CASA or the duties of the special advocate. Therefore, states have considerable latitude in defining who may represent the best interests of abused or neglected children and the duties of the GAL or CASA.

2. As the following American Bar Association Model Standards explains, a child's attorney in an abuse or neglect proceeding may request the court to appoint a guardian *ad litem* when (1) the child cannot express his or her wishes or (2) the child's expressed preferences would be "seriously injurious" to the child:

ABA Standards of Practice for Lawyers Who Represent Children in Abuse and Neglect Cases
Section B-4 (1996)*

> 1. To the extent that a child cannot express a preference, the child's attorney shall make a good faith effort to determine the child's wishes and advocate . . . accordingly or request the appointment of a guardian *ad litem.*
>
> 2. If the child's attorney determines that the child's express preferences would be seriously injurious to this child (as opposed to merely being contrary to the lawyer's opinion of what would be in the child's best interests), the lawyer may request appointment of a separate guardian *ad litem* . . . . The child's attorney shall not reveal the basis of the request for appointment of a guardian *ad litem* which would compromise the child's position . . . .

For a discussion of the different representation by a guardian *ad litem* and an attorney representing the same child, see ANN M. HARALAMBIE, THE CHILD'S ATTORNEY—A GUIDE TO REPRESENTING CHILDREN IN CUSTODY, ADOPTION, AND PROTECTION CASES 2-5 (1993).

3. For additional discussion of the duties and roles served by GALs, see Rebecca H. Heartz, *Guardians Ad Litem in Child Abuse and Neglect Proceedings: Clarifying the Rules to Improve Effectiveness,* 27 FAM. L.Q. 327 (1993); Ann M. Haralambie, *supra*, Note 2; Kerin S. Bischoff, *The Voice of a Child: Independent Legal Representation of Children in Private Custody Disputes When Sexual Abuse Is Alleged,* 138 U. PA. L. REV. 1383 (1990); Shannon L. Wilbur, *Independent Counsel for Children,* 27 FAM. L.Q. 349 (1993).

Questions

1. What is the significance of party status for the GAL or CASA?

2. How does the role of the GAL or CASA reflect the goals and ideals of the juvenile justice system?

---

* Reprinted by permission.

3. Termination of Parental Rights Proceedings

Mississippi Code Annotated
§ 93-15-107(1) (Lexis Supp. 2000)

§ 93-15-107. Proceedings to terminate parental rights; parties; initiation of proceedings; payment of costs

(1) In an action to terminate parental rights, the mother of the child, the legal father of the child, and the putative father of the child, when known, shall be parties defendant. A guardian ad litem shall be appointed to protect the interest of the child in the termination of parental rights. A child may be made party plaintiff, and any agency holding custody of a minor shall act as party plaintiff.

Stanley v. Fairfax County Department of Social Services
405 S.E.2d 621 (Va. 1991)

WHITING, Justice.

In this appeal we decide whether a guardian ad litem of children has standing to petition for termination of the residual rights of parents.

On May 13, 1985, the Juvenile and Domestic Relations District Court of Fairfax County (the J & DR Court) found that Melvin and Donna M. Stanley had neglected and abused their three children. The J & DR Court also awarded the custody of the children to the Fairfax County Department of Social Services (the department).

On December 1, 1987, after the department's extensive efforts to counsel the parents had failed, the department filed foster care plans recommending adoption as the ultimate goal for the Stanley children. These plans further stated that the department intended to petition the court for termination of the Stanleys' residual parental rights.

For reasons not disclosed in the record, the department did not file such petitions. However, on January 21, 1988, Jeanne B. Lynch, the guardian ad litem appointed to represent the three children, filed petitions to terminate both parents' residual rights to the children. On September 22, 1988, the department amended its foster care plan for one of the children to vest his maternal grandmother with his physical custody.

On November 15, 1988, the J & DR Court terminated both parents' residual rights with respect to the three children as provided in Code § 16.1-283(A).[1]

---

[1] Code § 16.1-283(a) provides in pertinent part:

The residual parental rights of a parent or parents may be terminated by the court as hereinafter provided in a separate proceeding if the petition specifically requests such relief. No petition seeking termination of residual parental rights shall be accepted by the court prior to the filing of a foster care plan, pursuant to § 16.1-281, which documents termination of residual parental rights as being in the best interests of the child.

Donna, but not Melvin, appealed to the circuit court. On February 24, 1989, the circuit court terminated Donna's parental rights. Donna appealed to the Court of Appeals which, on July 17, 1990, affirmed the circuit court's ruling as to two of the children but reversed its ruling as to the child who was in the maternal grandmother's physical custody.[2] Deeming the question of the guardian ad litem's standing to petition for termination of parental rights to be one of significant precedential value, we awarded Donna an appeal limited to that issue.

Donna argues that a guardian ad litem can take no affirmative action to deprive his ward of any substantive right the ward already enjoys. Donna claims that a guardian ad litem has only an "advisory role." However, we have not regarded that role as merely advisory; instead, we have recognized that a guardian ad litem can appeal an adverse ruling, *see Givens v. Clem*, 107 Va. 435, 437, 59 S.E. 413, 414 (1907), and can consent to a transfer to another jurisdiction of a case involving an infant's rights. *Lemmon v. Herbert,* 92 Va. 653, 659, 24 S.E. 249, 251 (1896). Accordingly, we conclude that a guardian ad litem may file affirmative pleadings necessary to protect the ward's interest.

* * *

. . . Code § 16.1-283 . . . is intended to provide for the protection of abused and neglected children. In describing the purpose and intent of the "Juvenile and Domestic Relations District Court Law," Code § 16.1-227 provides that such law "shall be construed liberally and as remedial in character. . . . It is the intention of this law that in all proceedings the welfare of the child and the family is the paramount concern of the Commonwealth. . . ." And the best interest of a the child must be the primary concern of the court.

Even though Code § 16.1-283 says nothing about *who* may file a petition for termination of parental rights, Code § 16.1-241(A) (1990 Supp.) provided that "[t]he authority of the juvenile court to adjudicate matters involving the . . . disposition of a child shall not be limited to the consideration of petitions filed by a mother, father, or legal guardian but shall include petitions filed at any time by any party with a legitimate interest therein." A guardian ad litem certainly has a legitimate interest in whether his ward is to be subjected to continued abuse and neglect.

Further, Code § 16.1-266(A) requires the J & DR Court to "appoint a discreet and competent attorney-at-law as guardian ad litem to represent the child" in abuse and neglect proceedings as well as in proceedings involving the termination of residual parental rights. And, Code § 8.01-9 requires that "[e]very guardian ad litem shall faithfully represent the . . . interest of the person under a disability for whom he is appointed." Therefore, if a guardian ad litem feels that the best interests of his ward compel termination of the parents' residual rights, he can and should file an appropriate termination petition.

---

2 The Court of Appeals' reversal as to the one child was on the ground that the last-filed foster care plan did not recommend termination of Donna's rights to that child, as implicitly required by Code § 16.1-283, but instead recommended his continued physical custody with his maternal grandmother.

For all these reasons, we conclude that a guardian ad litem has standing to file a petition for termination of residual parental rights. Accordingly, we will affirm the judgment of the Court of Appeals.

CARRICO, Chief Justice with whom STEPHENSON, Justice joins, dissenting.

I would reverse. A guardian ad litem is "a special guardian appointed by the court in which a particular litigation is pending to represent an infant, ward or unborn person in that particular litigation, and *the status of guardian ad litem exists only in that specific litigation in which the appointment occurs.*" BLACK'S LAW DICTIONARY 706 (6th ed. 1990) (citation omitted)(emphasis added).

In this case, the guardian ad litem was appointed in the initial proceeding brought by the Department of Social Services to have the children declared wards of the court. In my opinion, the guardian ad litem's authority extended only to that particular litigation. Accordingly, I would hold that the guardian ad litem did not have authority to institute the "separate proceeding" required by Code § 16.1283(A) for termination of the residual rights of the children's parents.

Neither *Lemmon v. Herbert*, 92 Va. 653, 24 S.E. 259 (1896), nor *Givens v. Clem,* 107 Va. 435, 59 S.E. 413 (1907), cited by the majority, is contrary to my view of the matter. Each case involved action taken by a guardian ad litem in the specific litigation in which the appointment occurred and did not consist of anything remotely resembling the institution of a separate proceeding for the termination of residual parental rights.

Notes

1. The responsibilities of the GAL or CASA in a termination hearing are similar to the duties of the GAL or CASA in other child welfare proceedings. The following is an excerpt from the Florida Family Handbook that details the responsibilities of a guardian *ad litem* in termination proceedings:

> (b) The guardian *ad litem* has the following responsibilities:
>
> 1. To investigate the allegations of the petition and any subsequent matters arising in the case and, unless excused by the court, to file a written report. This report must include a statement of the wishes of the child and the recommendations of the guardian ad litem and must be provided to all parties and the court at least 48 hours before the deposition hearing.
> 2. To be present at all court hearings unless excused by the court.
> 3. To represent the interests of the child until the jurisdiction of the court over the child terminates or until excused by the court.

FLORIDA FAMILY LAW HANDBOOK PART I: FLORIDA STATUTES CHAPTER 39 PROCEEDINGS RELATED TO CHILDREN (1988). The state's interest in family stability is furthered by the special advocate facilitating necessary terminations. *See* H. Lila Hubert, *In the Child's Best Interests: The Role of the Guardian Ad Litem In Termination of Parental Rights Proceedings,* 49 U. MIAMI L. REV. 531, 563 (1994).

2. Some states differentiate between the GAL's legal status in a termination proceeding and a child welfare hearing. For example, in Florida the GAL is granted party status in termination proceedings. FLA. STAT. ANN. § 39.01(70) (West Supp. 2001). As a party to the proceedings, the GAL receives service of process (FLA. STAT. ANN. § 39.807(2)(d) (West Supp. 2001)) and is represented by a pro-bono attorney.

3. Several states require the court to appoint a GAL or CASA for a child in termination of parental rights proceedings. *See* ARIZ. REV. STAT. ANN. § 8-535 (West Supp. 2000); COLO. REV. STAT. § 19-3-602 (2000); D.C. CODE ANN. § 16-2354 (Lexis Supp. 2001); FLA. STAT. ANN. § 39.807 (West Supp. 2001); KY. REV. STAT. ANN. § 625.041 (West 2000); MONT. CODE ANN. § 41-3-607 (1999); N.M. STAT. ANN. § 32A-4-29(G) (Michie 1999); S.C. CODE ANN. § 20-7-1570 (West Supp. 2000); TEX. FAM. CODE ANN. § 107.001 (West Supp. 2001).

4. A court may appoint an attorney retained by a parent in a termination of parental rights proceeding to also serve as the parent's guardian *ad litem*. In *In re C.D.*, 27 S.W.2d 826 (Mo. Ct. App. 2000), a mother claimed that the lower court was in error by requiring an attorney to "wear two hats: one as attorney, and one as guardian *ad litem*." The court recognized the different roles served by an attorney and a guardian *ad litem*. The court held, however, that no inherent conflict existed in a retained attorney assuming both roles and that a litigant has the burden of proving that such a conflict does, in fact, exist. According to the court, "[i]f . . . an attorney can show that these two goals are inconsistent, because the litigant's legal interests and best interests diverge, then it would be a reversible error to appoint the litigant's attorney to also act as guardian *ad litem*."

Problem

The three Barnett children, ages 10, 8 and 6, were detained by child welfare officials on April 11, YR-1, and placed in foster care. A court appointed special advocate (CASA) was appointed by the court to represent the best interests of the children. On June 1, YR-1, the children were adjudicated children in need of services (CHINS) by the court. The CASA included in her report information provided by the Division of Family and Children (DFC) caseworker, which was damaging to Melinda, the children's mother. The CASA testified that her recommendation (that the children be adjudicated CHINS) was based upon information provided by the caseworker. The caseworker has openly expressed her hostility and contempt for Melinda. On November 21, YR-1, the DFC and the CASA filed with the court a joint petition for termination of Melinda's parental rights. Melinda files with the court a motion for appointment of a guardian ad litem (GAL) for her children during the termination proceedings (TPR), alleging that the CASA cannot properly represent the best interests of the children because the CASA is a petitioner in the TPR action and the CASA's investigation is tainted by the DFC caseworker. What arguments should Melinda, the CASA, and the DFC present to the court? How should the court rule on Melinda's motion? *See Joiner ex rel. Rivas v. Rivas,* 536 S.E.2d 372 (S.C. 2000).

C. Immunity and Liability of Special Advocates

CASAs are lay volunteers who represent the best interests of children in child welfare cases and termination proceedings. As officers of the court, CASAs are often granted party status. The guidelines for CASA programs are established by statute. The following provision is an example:

Kansas Supreme Court Rules

Rule 110 (1999)

Court appointed special advocate (CASA) volunteer programs shall embrace the following:

(a) It shall be the primary duty of a court-appointed special advocate to personally investigate and become acquainted with the facts, conditions, and circumstances affecting the welfare of the child for whom appointed, to advocate the best interests of the child and assist the court in obtaining for the child the most permanent, safe, and homelike placement possible. A CASA volunteer, additionally should:

(1) Visit the child as often as necessary to monitor the child's essential needs are being met;

(2) Attend court hearings pertaining to the child or, if not excused by the judge, arrange for attendance of a qualified substitute approved by the judge;

(3) Participate in staffings and, to the extent possible, other meetings pertaining to the child's welfare;

(4) Participate in the development of the written plan for reintegration and/or modification of a plan already in place;

(5) Submit a written report to the court prior to each regularly scheduled court hearing involving the child; and

(6) Do all such other things on behalf of the child as are directed by the program director and the standards relating to CASA volunteer programs.

* * *

See In Interest of D.D.P., Jr., T.P., and B.J.P., 819 P.2d 1212 at 1219 (Kan. 1991). Even though a CASA is directly involved in the proceedings as the advocate for the child's welfare, the CASA is not always granted party status. *Id.* In *Foster v. Washoe County*, 964 P.2d 788, 793 (Nev. 1998), the court held that if a CASA volunteer was an interested party, the volunteer could be held liable either in a civil or criminal case. The court ruled that exposure to civil or criminal liability would likely deter other CASAs from accepting court appointments. In *Gardner v. Parson*, 874 F.2d 131, 144 (3d Cir. 1989), the court held that CASAs should be granted some form of immunity from civil and criminal liability so that they can perform their duties without the risk or worry of being sued later.

Courts and legislatures have defined CASA immunity differently. The *Gardner* court held that CASAs should be afforded absolute immunity if their actions are an "integral part of the judicial process." (*Id.* at 146) (citing *Briscoe v. Lathe*, 460 U.S. 325 (1983). The following is an example of a statute that defines a CASA's liability:

Louisiana Revised Statutes Annotated Children's Code

§ 424.10 (West Supp. 2001)

§ 424.10 CASA; immunity

No cause of action shall exist against any CASA volunteer, director, employee, staff, or volunteer who in good faith makes a report, cooperates in an investigation by an agency, or participates in judicial proceedings. Each such person shall have immunity from civil or criminal liability that might otherwise be incurred or imposed. This immunity from liability shall not extend to:

(1) An alleged principal, conspirator, or accessory to an offense involving the abuse or neglect or sexual exploitation of a child.

(2) A person who makes a report known to be false or with reckless disregard for the truth of the report.

(3) The unauthorized divulging of confidential information occasioned by the CASA volunteer's gross fault or gross neglect.

For additional statutes that define the limits of a CASA's immunity from civil and criminal liability, see ARIZ. REV. STAT. ANN. § 8-523(C) (West 1999) (not liable for actions done in good faith in connection with the CASA's responsibilities); ARK. CODE ANN. §§ 9-27-316, 16-6-105 (Michie Supp. 2001) (not liable unless actions are in bad faith or grossly negligent); D.C. CODE ANN. § 16-2372 (Lexis 1997) (not liable for omissions unless omission is reckless, willful, or wanton misconduct or intentionally tortious); 705 ILL. COMP. STAT. 405/2-17.1(8) (West Supp. 2001) (good faith is to be assumed and CASA not liable except willful and wanton recklessness); IND. CODE ANN. § 31-15-6-9 (Lexis 1997) (not liable except for gross misconduct); KAN. STAT. ANN. § 38-1505a (West 2000) (presumed prima facie in good faith and immune from all liability incurred); 42 PA. CONS. STAT. ANN. § 6342(b) (West 2000) (immune for good faith actions except gross negligence, intentional misconduct, or recklessness, willful, and wanton misconduct); R.I. GEN. LAWS § 9-1-27.2

(Lexis 1997) (liable for wanton or malicious behavior or gross negligence).

Tara M. v. City of Philadelphia

145 F.3d 625 (3d Cir. 1998)

Tara was born on April 10, 1987. Her 18-year-old mother was in the custody of the Pennsylvania child welfare system at the time, and Tara was consequently committed to the care of the child welfare system as well. . . . Authorities eventually discovered that Tara had been abused by her mother, and they determined that her mother lacked the ability properly to care for her. Therefore, in November 1990, Tara was separated from her mother and placed in another foster home. In January 1991, the Pennsylvania Court of Common Pleas appointed Nancy Kanter as guardian ad litem for Tara. In June 1995, Tara was placed in yet another foster home where she suffered sexual abuse. Tara's nightmare continued in her next foster home, where she endured a variety of physical tortures. After several months of recovery in various institutions, Tara returned to another private foster home.

In February 1997, Tara, by and through her guardian ad litem, Kanter, filed a civil action in federal district court against the City of Philadelphia, the Pennsylvania Department of Public Welfare, several other social welfare organizations, and several individuals associated with all of these organizations. Her Complaint sought recovery under both federal and state law. Counts I and II of the Complaint assert violations of substantive due process and claim a remedy under 42 U.S.C. § 1983, while Counts III to VI contain general allegations of breach of a state imposed duty of care in failing to protect Tara; failure to exercise ordinary skill, care, knowledge, and judgment in rendering care, protection, and services to her; and deviation from standards governing professional supervision, practice, and behavior in caring for and servicing dependent minors like Tara. Count VII alleges a civil conspiracy to commit unlawful acts that resulted in harm to Tara.

The city defendants filed a third-party complaint against Kanter. They claimed that if they were liable for the harm suffered by Tara, then the guardian ad litem, Kanter, must also have breached her state-law duties to protect Tara. The third-party plaintiffs alleged that Kanter's neglect was a "substantial factor" in Tara's damages, and they were therefore entitled to "contribution and/or indemnity" from Kanter as a joint tortfeasor under Pennsylvania's version of the Uniform Contribution Among Tortfeasors Act, 42 Pa. Cons. Stat. Ann. § 8324 (West 1982).

Kanter moved to dismiss the third-party complaint. She argued that section 1983 does not provide for contribution, neither federal nor state law authorized contribution for liability under section 1983, and in any event she, as a court appointed guardian ad litem, was entitled to absolute immunity under section 1983. The district court denied the motion, observing only that the third-party plaintiffs had not asserted a claim for contribution under section 1983. Kanter now appeals.

* * *

II. Discussion

. . . We need not decide whether guardians ad litem should be cloaked with immunity from liability under section 1983 . . . because any federal immunity that she may enjoy is not implicated here.

In any situation in which contribution is being sought, it is helpful to recognize that three distinct liabilities are involved that may arise from different sources. The first is the liability to the injured party of the party seeking contribution. Here, if the city defendants are liable to Tara, that liability may be based on federal law (§ 1983), state law (negligence or conspiracy), or both. The second is the liability for contribution. Here, the city defendants assert a state law basis for the duty to pay contribution (the Uniform Contribution Among Tortfeasors Act). Finally, since contribution requires a common obligation to the injured party, there is the liability to the injured party of the party from whom contribution is sought. Here, the city defendants allege that Kanter owed a state law duty to Tara . . . which was breached by her.

In a suit where the party seeking contribution alleges that a joint tortfeasor has liability to the injured party based on the federal Civil Rights Act, contribution may well be barred if the tortfeasor would have absolute immunity in a Civil Rights Act suit brought by the injured party. In such a situation, awarding contribution would impose upon the tortfeasor indirectly a liability against which she is absolutely immune under federal law.

This is not, however, the situation currently before us. Here, the party seeking contribution has alleged that Kanter is liable to Tara on the basis of a state-imposed duty of care. A state that imposes such a duty is free to determine for itself who, if anyone, will be immune from suits to enforce that duty. . . . Accordingly, in these circumstances, a grant of contribution can impose upon Kanter no liability from which she is protected under federal law. It is state law that determines the availability and extent of contribution here and, even though imposition of liability upon the city defendants is a matter of federal concern, the duty of contribution involves no potential conflict with federal law or policy.

In *Poleto v. Consolidated Rail Corp.*, 826 F.2d 1270 (3d Cir. 1987), . . . [w]e acknowledged that federal law ordinarily controls issues of contribution when the tortfeasors are alleged to share a federal liability. We held, however, that the law of Pennsylvania governed the contribution issue before us because "there was no federal interest at stake". . . .

Just as in *Poleto*, the controversy between the city defendants and Kanter sounds exclusively in state law, and we therefore hold that Kanter is not entitled to federal immunity from the contribution claim of the city defendants. Having resolved the immunity issue that brings the case before us at this time, we decline to express any view on the unrelated issue of whether the third-party complaint states a claim on which contribution can be granted under

Pennsylvania law. The district court's order denying Kanter's motion to dismiss will be affirmed.

Notes

1. Some states use the "functional approach" to determine the limits of a GAL's immunity. *See* Jennifer Paige Hanft, *Attorney for Child Versus Guardian Ad Litem: Wyoming Creates a Hybrid, But Is It a Formula for Malpractice?,* 34 LAND & WATER L. REV. 381, 394 (1999). The functional approach grants immunity to individuals whose actions are quasi-judicial in nature. *McKay v. Owens*, 937 P.2d 1222, 1232 (Idaho 1997). In *Gardner v. Parson*, 874 F.2d 131, 145-46 (3d Cir. 1989), the court explained the functional approach as follows:

> Supreme Court precedent in analogous cases . . . counsels the adoption of a functional approach to determining whether a guardian *ad litem* is absolutely immune. Under this approach, a guardian *ad litem* would be absolutely immune in exercising functions such as testifying in court, prosecuting custody or neglect petitions, and making reports and recommendations to the court in which the guardian acts as an actual functionary arm of the court. This does not exhaust the list of functions which would be immune, and each function would have to be analyzed on a case-by-case basis.

Many states grant absolute immunity to GALs and CASAs for actions that are quasi-judicial. In *Delcourt v. Silverman,* 919 S.W.2d 777, 785 (Tex. App. 1996), the court held that if guardians did not have absolute immunity, the pool of qualified GALs would shrink and make the guardian's job of giving an impartial recommendation more difficult. Furthermore, in *Short v. Short*, 730 F. Supp. 1037, 1039 (D. Colo. 1990), the court held that procedural safeguards make the threat of civil or criminal liability unnecessary. The *Short* court listed the following as procedural safeguards for the court to control the actions of GALs: (1) a guardian *ad litem* must act within the scope of his or her duties; (2) the court has the power to remove a guardian *ad litem* if necessary; (3) parents can move the court to terminate the guardian *ad litem's* appointment.

2. Some states, such as Wyoming, have merged the roles of attorney for the child and guardian *ad litem* into a hybrid function as follows:

> (a) The court shall appoint counsel to represent any child in a court proceeding in which the child is alleged to be abused or neglected. Any attorney representing a child under this section shall also serve as the child's guardian ad litem unless a guardian ad litem has been appointed by the court. The attorney or guardian ad litem shall be charged with representation of the child's best interest.

WYO. STAT. ANN. § 14-3-211(a) (Lexis 1999)

In *Clark v. Alexander*, 953 P.2d 145, 153-54 (Wyo. 1998), the court stated that an attorney/guardian *ad litem* should conduct all necessary pretrial preparation, offer evidence at trial, examine witnesses, make opening and closing statements, and make sure proceedings are expeditious. *Clark* held that if an attorney/guardian *ad litem* had less immunity, children would receive better representation. For further discussion of a lawyer's liability as a guardian *ad litem*, see Dana E. Prescott, *The Liability of Lawyers as Guardians Ad Litem: The Best Defense Is a Good Offense,* 11 J. AM. ACAD. MARTRIM. LAW. 65 (1993).

Chapter 12

The Special Role of Foster Parents

Foster parents enter into a written agreement with the state to assume temporary parental responsibility and to aid in the discharge of the government's obligation to care for and supervise children who are wards of the state. State law requires foster parents to be trained and licensed; also, they must follow the case plan determined to be in the best interests of the child. Foster parents receive a per diem to cover expenses for necessary care of the child.

Foster parent rights may vary from state to state, depending on various factors. First, courts consider the similarities and differences between foster families and biological families. In *Smith v. Organization of Foster Families*, 431 U.S. 816 (1977), the U.S. Supreme Court noted that foster parents can become a child's psychological parents. When a child lives in a foster home for a year or more, a psychological bond may develop between the child and the foster family, which constitutes a "psychological family" for the child. The Court, however, observed that important differences exist between a foster family and a biological family. A foster family's origins are in state law and contractual arrangements. The parties agree that the relationship is temporary; hence, fewer rights are afforded to the foster family. The Supreme Court declined to decide whether foster parents have a protected liberty interest in the integrity of the family unit under the Fourteenth Amendment. Since *Smith*, most lower courts have held that there is no protected interest in the foster child-parent relationship due to the differences in the nature of the foster and biological family. Second, courts want to resolve cases expeditiously so that a child attains permanency quickly. Hence, most states restrict the role of foster parents in court proceedings to providing the court with information relevant to the child's welfare. This approach is followed by the Adoption and Safe Families Act of 1997 (ASFA), which stops short of making foster parents parties in proceedings involving children in their care, but grants them the right to notice and an opportunity to be heard.

As you read this chapter, consider whether the shift in focus from family reunification in the Adoption Assistance and Child Welfare Act of 1980 (AACWA) to the child's health and safety as the paramount concern in ASFA alters the role of foster parents in the child welfare system. Does the role of foster parents change under ASFA's sytem of concurrent planning—where the state may simultaneously pursue family reunification and a different permanency plan for the child? What is the impact—both legal and practical—on the relationship between biological parents and foster parents of the front-loading of permanency decisions under ASFA? As a result of ASFA, is the foster parents' liberty interest in their relationship with the child greater?

A. Standing

Maine Revised Statutes Annotated

Title 22, § 4005-A (West Supp. 2000)

§ 4005-A. Foster parents' right to standing and intervenor status in child protection proceedings

1. Definition. As used in this section, unless the context indicates otherwise, the following terms have the following meanings.

A. "Foster parent" means a person who has had a child in the person's home for at least 120 days and who has received a license for a family foster home . . . or who is a relative.

* * *

2. Petition. A foster parent may petition for standing and intervenor status in any child protection proceeding under this chapter regarding a foster child that lives or has lived in the foster parent's home. The standing and intervenor status is limited to that proceeding unless otherwise ordered by the court.

3. Criteria. The court shall make a determination whether to grant standing based on the strength and duration of the relationship between the foster parents and the child and in the best interests of the child.

Rhode Island General Laws

§ 14-1-30.2 (Lexis 2000)

§ 14-1-30.2 Foster Parents—Notice of court proceedings.

The department of children, youth, and families shall provide notice to foster parents, pre-adoptive parents, or relatives providing care for a child of any review or hearing to be held with respect to a child in the care of the department. The foster parents, pre-adoptive parents, or relatives providing care for a child may attend the hearing and file with the court a report, either written or oral, for the purpose of conveying to the family court information relating to the best interest of the child. Nothing in this section gives the foster parents, pre-adoptive parents, or relatives providing care for a child legal standing as a party to the petition.

Worrell v. Elkhart County Office of Family and Children

704 N.E.2d 1027 (Ind. 1998)

SHEPARD, Chief Justice.

The sole issue in this case is whether Michael and Jacintha Worrell have standing to petition a trial court for visitation with their former foster children. We hold that they do not.

In 1995, R.D., S.D., and B.D., brothers sharing the same natural mother, were placed in the Worrells' home as foster children. They remained in that home for seventeen months, until the Worrells discovered that twelve-year-old B.D. kissed and held hands with their twelve-year-old natural daughter. Jacintha Worrell reported the incident to the proper authorities, and they placed B.D. in another foster home that same day. The other two brothers remained with the Worrells for two months, at which time they were placed elsewhere so that all three brothers could be reunited.

The Worrells subsequently filed petitions for visitation with each of the three boys. After a hearing, the trial court held that the Worrells lacked standing to request visitation and dismissed the petitions.

The Worrells appealed, and the Court of Appeals reversed. It held that the Worrells did have standing because they "met their initial burden of establishing the threshold requisite of a custodial and parental relationship with their former foster children. . . ." *Worrell v. Elkhart County Office of Family and Children*, 692 N.E.2d 929, 931 (Ind. Ct. App. 1998). It remanded this case to the trial court for a hearing on the merits. We grant transfer and affirm the trial court's dismissal of the petition.

* * *

The Worrells argue that their foster relationship with the children constituted a custodial and parental relationship sufficient to confer standing to request visitation. While we agree that a foster parent acts by definition in a custodial capacity, we do not agree that the foster relationship justifies standing to petition for visitation.

When the Court of Appeals established the two-prong test for third party visitation in *Collins v. Gilbreath*, it expressly limited the breadth of its application. 403 N.E.2d 921, 923-23 (Ind. Ct. App. 1980). ("In so holding we do not intend . . . to open the door and permit the granting of visitation rights to a myriad of unrelated third persons . . . who happen to feel affection for a child. Our decision is explicitly limited to the type of factual situation presented by this case. . . ."). That case involved a visitation request from a step-father who was married to the custodial natural mother of the children and who lived with the children prior to the death of the mother. *Id.* at 922. *Accord In re Custody of*

Banning, 541 N.E.2d 283 (Ind. Ct. App. 1989) (upon death of child's natural father, court upheld custody of natural mother and visitation of step-mother who knew the child through visitation with child's natural father when he was alive).

Subsequent cases extended visitation to former step-parents following divorce. *See, e.g., Cabin v. Healey*, 634 N.E. 2d 540 (Ind. Ct. App. 1994) (upon divorce of child's natural father and step-mother, court upheld custody of natural father and visitation of step-mother who raised child from infancy) cf. *Francis,* 654 N.E.2d 4 (upon divorce of children's natural mother and her ex-husband, court upheld custody of natural father and visitation of natural mother's ex-husband who raised children born during their marriage, and who did not discover that he was not the natural father until he and mother divorced).

In other cases, courts have declined to extend visitation rights to third parties who are not step-parents. *See Wolgamott v. Lanham*, 654 N.E. 23 890 (Ind. Ct. App. 1995) (court denied visitation to ex-boyfriend of mother because he was an "unrelated stranger"); *Tinsley*, 519 N.E.2d at 752-55 (upon death of mother, court denied visitation to child's great-aunt and -uncle because the relatives saw the child only five times a year at family gatherings).

We agree with the prior holdings limiting standing to step-parents, and we now hold that the test does not extend to foster parents. As the Court of Appals noted in the context of grandparent visitation, an expansion of the class of petitioners with standing to request visitation to include foster parents "should occur in a legislative, not judicial, forum." *Collins*, 403 N.E.2d 921 at 923 n.1.

Unlike parent and step-parent relationships, foster relationships are designed to be temporary, providing a "safe, nurturing environment" until the child can either be returned to the natural parents or adopted by new ones. INDIANA FOSTER FAMILY Handbook 46 (1995). Furthermore, the foster relationship is contractual; the parents are reimbursed by the State for their care of the children. *See id.* at 101-05. Finally, as Judge Garrard noted in his dissent, the foster relationship may be one in a series of temporary arrangements. *Worrell,* 692 N.E.2d at 932 (Garrad, J., dissenting). In the midst of changing family relationships, constancy of contact and support is vital, but if each of the potential profusion of foster parents had standing because he or she had custody of the child at some point, the natural or adoptive parents might be forced to defend visitation claims against a legion of petitioners. *Id.* We hold, therefore, that foster parents do not have standing to petition for visitation with their former foster children.

* * *

In re Michael Ray T.

525 S.E.2d 315 (W. Va. 1999)

DAVIS, Justice:

The appellants herein, and plaintiffs below, Paul and Virginia Williams [hereinafter collectively referred to as "the Williamses"], appeal from an order entered May 11, 1999, by the Circuit Court of Mercer County. By that order, the court denied the Wiliamses' motion to intervene in the abuse and neglect proceedings concerning their former foster children, Michael Ray T. [hereinafter referred to as "Michael"], Scottie Lee T. [hereinafter referred to as "Scottie"], and Tonya Lynn T. [hereinafter referred to as "Tonya"]. The court further refused to consider the Williamses' motion for custody, wherein they sought the return of these children to their care following the youngsters' removal from their foster care by the West Virginia Department of Health and Human Resources [hereinafter referred to as "DHHR"]. Upon a review of the parties' arguments, the appellate record, and the pertinent authorities, we conclude that the circuit court did not abuse its discretion by refusing the requested intervention. . . .

I.

FACTUAL AND PROCEDURAL HISTORY

The facts underlying the instant appeal are as follows. On April 8, 1998, the DHHR filed a petition in the Circuit Court of Mercer County requesting the immediate and temporary transfer of custody of Michael, Scottie and Tonya to the DHHR as a result of the perceived imminent danger the children would face if they remained in the home of their biological parents, Frank T. and Lizzie T. The incidents leading to this petition centered around the life-threatening injuries sustained by then six-week-old Michael when he was repeatedly and viciously attacked by rodents in his parents' home on April 4, 1998. Additionally, the DHHR remained concerned that Lizzie would again return to the family home with Michael's siblings despite the persistence of the rodent infestation and warnings by DHHR officials that the home was not safe for children. The circuit court found that "[t]he danger presented by the child(ren)'s present circumstances creates an emergency situation which has made efforts to avoid removing the child(ren) from the home unreasonable or impossible," and transferred their temporary custody to the DHHR.

As a result of the critical injuries he sustained, Michael was hospitalized for an extended period of time at Women and Children's Hospital, in Charleston, West Virginia. His siblings, Tonya and Scottie, were placed with a foster family following their removal from their parents' home. After Michael's partial recovery and release from the hospital, he was placed into foster care with the Williamses. . . .

From the time of her placement into the Williamses' home, Tonya exhibited various behavioral and disciplinary problems, believed to be the result of parentification.[9] Although Tonya and Scottie had been having regular supervised visitation with their biological parents since their removal in April, 1998, following one such supervised visit on October 14, 1998, Tonya's conduct worsened dramatically. In an attempt to protect Scottie and Michael from their sis-

[9] When she resided with her biological parents, Tonya reportedly enjoyed a great deal of control over her circumstances and assumed the care of and responsibility for her younger siblings. One of Tonya's counselors explained her behavior thusly: the term parentified child or parentification is widely accepted in the field of psychology and counseling to refer to the process in which a child is routinely permitted to assume responsibilities which appropriately belong to parents. . . .

ter, Mrs. Williams requested respite care for Tonya. Around the same time, Tonya confided in her foster parents that, during the recent supervised visit, she had been sexually abused by her biological mother. The Williamses reported this incident to the Child Protective Services [hereinafter referred to as "CPS"] caseworker who formerly had handled the children's case. Nevertheless, Mr. and Mrs. Williams received the impression that the allegation would not be investigated and that no further action would be taken with regard thereto, due in large part to Tonya's failure to cooperate with DHHR officials by telling them her story.

Following this incident, Tonya's weekly counseling sessions increased in number, and the guardian ad litem and the state jointly moved to temporarily suspend Tonya's visits with Frank and Lizzie. By order entered December 15, 1998, the circuit court suspended, for sixty days, supervised visitation between Tonya and her biological parents. In late December, 1998, the Williamses again requested respite care for Tonya because of her continued defiance of family rules. Upon Tonya's return to the Williamses' home, her demeanor improved.

Thereafter, the DHHR alleges that, as a result of their continuing difficulties with Tonya, the Williamses were admonished and instructed as to acceptable forms of discipline during a multidisciplinary treatment team [hereinafter referred to as "MDT"] meeting on January 12, 1999. Because of the persistent "power struggle" between Tonya and Mrs. Williams, arising from Tonya's defiance and attempt to obtain and retain control, and concerns that the Williamses had inappropriately and negatively discussed Frank and Lizzie in the child's presence, the team also discussed the possibility of removing the children from the Williamses' care.

* * *

In February, 1999, the circuit court ordered the gradual resumption of visits between Tonya and her biological parents. On March 26, 1999, the circuit court ordered the extension of the biological parents' improvement period to coincide with the expiration of their period of probation in October, 2002. The circuit court also allegedly ordered the commencement of in-home visitation, whereby the children would visit Frank and Lizzie in their home. The Williamses submit that, upon explaining these visits to Tonya, she revealed that she had sustained numerous additional instances of sexual abuse, involving both of her biological parents and other relatives, before she had been removed from her parents' home. . . .

. . . [T]he DHHR removed the [children] from the Williamses' home on April 5, 1999, believing such removal to be in the children's best interests. The children subsequently were placed with another foster family. . . .

* * *

As a result of the children's removal from their home, the Williamses filed a Motion to Intervene in the children's abuse and neglect proceedings and a motion requesting the circuit court to return the children to their foster care. By order entered May 11, 1999, the circuit court denied intervention and declined to consider whether the children should be returned to the Williamses' care. In so ruling the circuit court noted that

> a court has the discretion to allow foster parents who have physical custody of a child to intervene in abuse and neglect proceedings. *See In re Jonathan G.,* 198 W. Va. 716, 482 S.E.2d 983 (1996). However, in the present case, the Williams [sic] no longer have physical custody of the children. In their Motion, the Williams [sic] allege that the DHHR "improperly and unlawfully removed" the children from their home. This alleged improper removal, and the request to file a motion to have the three children returned to their foster care would be more appropriately addressed through an extraordinary remedy such as a writ of mandamus. Therefore, this Court will not address whether the DHHR should return the children to the foster care of the Williams [sic] at this time.

III

DISCUSSION

On appeal to this Court, the Williamses raise two assignments of error: (1) the circuit court erred in denying their motion to intervene and (2) the circuit court improperly refused to consider their motion for custody. The DHHR, joined by the children's guardian ad litem, rejects the Williamses' contentions and urges this Court to uphold the circuit court's rulings.

A. Motion to Intervene

The Williamses first assign as error the circuit court's denial of their motion to intervene. . . . It is apparent that our review of the circuit court's decision regarding the Williamses' intervention motion is for an abuse of discretion. . . .

Reviewing the circuit court's decision, we note, at the outset, that the Williamses were not actually the foster parents of Michael, Scottie, and Tonya at the time they sought intervention. Rather, they stood in the position of the children's former foster parents. Under a strict application of our holding in *Jonathan G.*, which dealt exclusively with the child's then current foster parents, the Williamses are not entitled to intervene in the children's abuse and neglect proceedings. *See* Syl. Pt. 1, 198 W. Va. 716, 482 S.E. 2d 893. Nevertheless, we must consider the matter further. As this emerging new body of law has dealt previously only with the intervention rights of current foster parents, the question of whether a former foster parent has standing to intervene in the abuse and neglect proceeding concerning their former foster child(ren) is a matter of first impression in this Court. . . .

The intervention rights we previously have afforded to current foster parents are limited, both by the circuit court's discretion to grant or deny such intervention and by the primary purpose for such intervention, that is to "provid[e] the circuit court with all pertinent information regarding the child." Syl. Pt. 1, in part, *Jonathan G.*, 198 W. Va. 716, 482 S.E.2d 893. When assessing the right of individuals to participate in abuse and neglect proceedings, we necessarily must be guided by our oft-repeated mantra that child abuse and neglect proceedings are, without fail, to be resolved as expeditiously as possible in order to safeguard the welfare and best interests of the fragile infant parties to such proceedings. . . .

This need for rapid finality in abuse and neglect proceedings is attributable to the overriding concern for the subject child's welfare. "'[A] child deserves resolution and permanency in his or her life. . . .'" *Johnathan G.,* 198 W. Va. at 726, 482 S.E.2d at 902 (quoting *State ex rel. Many M. v. Kaufman,* 196 W. Va. 251, 260, 470 S.E.2d 205, 214 (1996)). Moreover, "the best interests of the child is the polar star by which decisions must be made which affect children." *Michael K.T. v. Tina L.T.,* 182 W. Va. 399, 405, 387 S.E.2d 866, 872 (1989. Accordingly, in the interest of expediting the resolution and conclusion of abuse and neglect proceedings, we are hesitant to expand the realm of intervenors to individuals who are no longer guardians or custodians of the children at issue for fear that "'[u]njustified procedural delays'" undoubtedly would attend the ever-increasing roster of interest participants. *See* Syl. Pt. 3, in part, *Jonathan G.,* 198 W. Va. 716, 482 S.E.2d 893, Syl., pt. 1, in part, *Carlita B.*, 185 W Va. 613, 408 S.E.2d 365.

Furthermore, while it is true that former foster parents may have an interest in participating in cases involving children who once were entrusted to their care, we must not forget that, in the present context, the rights of adults are subordinate to those of the involved children. "Although parents have substantial rights that must be protected, the primary goal in cases involving abuse and neglect, as in all family law matters, must be the health and welfare of the children." Syl. pt. 3, *In re Katie S.*, 198 W. Va. 79, 479 S.E.2d 589 (1996). Sylabus Point 3, *Matter of Taylor B.,* 201 W. Va. 60, 491 S.E.2d 607 (1997). Syl. Pt. 3, *In re Harley C.,* 203 W. Va. 594, 509 S.E.2d 875. In other words, "[c]ases involving children must be decided not just in the context of competing sets of adults' rights, but also with a regard for the rights of the child(ren)." Syl. Pt. 7, *In re Brian D.,* 194 W. Va. 623, 461 S.E.2d 129 (1995). It is for these reasons, then, that we hold that former foster parents do not have standing to intervene in abuse and neglect proceedings involving their former foster child(ren). Based upon our decision, we further conclude that the circuit court did not abuse its discretion by refusing the Williamses' intervention motion.

In addition to our recognition of the preeminent rights of the infant child(ren) subject to abuse and neglect proceedings and our acknowledgment of the detrimental delays that would result from the extension of intervention to former foster parents, we wish to identify the very limited role that former foster parents may have in assisting a circuit court in determining the child(ren)'s best interests. . . . Former foster parents, as the former guardians, custodians, and/or caretakers of the subject child(ren), similarly have knowledge of the child(ren) that could be beneficial to a court considering the child(ren)'s best interests and ultimate fate. While complete intervention is not the proper role for former foster parents to participate in abuse and neglect proceedings, we do believe their input would, in many cases, be instructive and facilitate the court's decision. . . .

* * *

IV.

CONCLUSION

In conclusion, we find that the circuit court did not abuse its discretion in denying the Williamses' motion to intervene in the underlying abuse and neglect proceedings, as they were not the current foster parents but rather the former foster parents of the infant children involved in such proceedings. Accordingly, we hereby affirm the May 11, 1999, order of the Circuit Court of Mercer County.

Affirmed.

Notes

1. The following section of AFSA gives foster parents the right to notice and the opportunity to be heard in proceedings involving children in their care:

Adoption and Safe Families Act of 1997
42 U.S.C.A. § 675(5)(G) (West Supp. 2001)

> [T]he foster parents (if any) of a child and any preadoptive parent or relative providing care for the child are provided with notice of, and an opportunity to be heard in, any review or hearing to be held with respect to the child, except that this subparagraph shall not be construed to require that any foster parent, preadoptive parent, or relative providing care for the child be made party to such a review or hearing solely on the basis of such notice and opportunity to be heard.

2. Whether foster parents should have standing to petition the court for visitation rights remains an unsettled issue. Some courts hold that foster parents lack standing if the foster child no longer lives with the foster parents. *See, e.g., In re Jennifer P.,* 553 A.2d 196 (Conn. App. Ct. 1989); *Worrell v. Elkhart County Office of Family and Children, supra.* In *Bessette v. Saratoga*, 619 N.Y.S.2d 359 (App. Div. 1994), the court held that foster parents do not have standing to petition for visitation rights because it would diminish the natural parents' right to choose the child's associates. The *Bessette* court also stated that the foster parents lacked standing because no statute created such a right. *But see* OR. REV. STAT. § 109.119 (1999). Oregon grants foster parents and anyone else "who has established emotional ties creating a child-parent relationship or an ongoing personal relationship with a child" to petition the court for visitation rights. The impact on this type of statute by *Troxel v. Granville*, 530 U.S. 57 (2000) (*see also* Chapter 10, Part E.2), which held that a statute providing that person may petition for visitation when it may serve the best interests of the child violated the substantive due process rights of the custodial parent, remains unclear.

3. Many jurisdictions hold that foster parents lack standing to petition the court to terminate the biological parents' rights. *See* Chapter 12, Part B, Note 2, *infra*. In *In re Michael W.,* 508 N.Y.S.2d 124 (App. Div. 1986), the court stated that the foster parents were necessary parties to proceedings involving a child who lived with them for twelve months. However, the court held that the foster parents had no standing to file a termination of parental petition against the biological father. *See generally* Thomas B. Anderson, Recent Decisions, *Family Law—Adoption—Foster Parent Standing in Adoption Proceedings—The Pennsylvania Supreme Court Held That Foster Parents Lack Standing to Initiate Adoption Proceedings Absent Consent From Welfare Agency,* 34 DUQ. L. REV. 777 (1996).

Questions

In light of *In re Michael Ray T., supra,* what legal options do foster parents have to protect the welfare of a former foster child? How might these options protect the child's welfare?

Problem

Mr. and Mrs. James, foster parents, receive notice of a hearing to determine whether their foster child, Mary, should be returned to her natural parents. In the court petition, the agency claims that following successful completion of an anger management course, the father is now able to control his temper and Mary is no longer at risk of physical abuse. The foster parents appear at the hearing to make a statement and argue that the child should not be returned to the natural parents. The foster parents express their concern that the home environment might not be in the child's best interests, and that the child usually acts out after visiting the natural parents. After the statement, the judge orders the foster parents to leave the courtroom. Mr. and Mrs. James claim that the court's order violates their due process rights and the rights granted to foster parents under AFSA. The foster parents, with leave of court, file an interlocutory appeal. How should the appellate court rule?

B. Rights of Foster Parents

20 Illinois Compiled Statutes Annotated

§ 520/1-15 (West Supp. 2001)

§ 521/1-15. Foster parent rights

§ 1-15. Foster parent rights. A foster parent's rights include, but are not limited to, the following:

(1) The right to be treated with dignity, respect, and consideration as a professional member of the child welfare team.

(2) The right to be given standardized pre-service training and appropriate ongoing training to meet mutually assessed needs and improve the foster parent's skills.

(3) The right to be informed as to how to contact the appropriate child placement agency in order to receive information and assistance to access supportive services for children in the foster parent's care.

(4) The right to receive timely financial reimbursement commensurate with the care needs of the child as specified in the service plan.

(5) The right to be provided a clear, written understanding of a placement agency's plan concerning the placement of a child in the foster parent's home. Inherent in this right is the foster parent's responsibility to support activities that will promote the child's right to relationships with his or her own family and cultural heritage.

(6) The right to be provided a fair, timely, and impartial investigation of complaints concerning the foster parent's licensure, to be provided the opportunity to have a person of the foster parent's choosing present during the investigation, and to be provided due process during the investigation; the right to be provided the opportunity to request and receive mediation or an administrative review of decisions that affect licensing parameters or both mediation and an administrative review; and the right to have decisions concerning a licensing corrective action plan specifically explained and tied to the licensing standards violated.

(7) The right, at any time during which a child is placed with the foster parent, to receive additional or necessary information that is relevant to the care of the child.

(8) The right to be notified of scheduled meetings and staffings concerning the foster child in order to actively participate in the case planning and decision-making process regarding the child, including individual service planning meetings, administrative case reviews, interdisciplinary staffings, and individual educational planning meetings; the right to be informed of decisions made by the courts or the child welfare agency concerning the child; the right to provide input concerning the plan of services for the child and to have that input given full consideration in the same manner as information presented by any other professional on the team; and the right to communicate with other professionals who work with the foster child within the context of the team, including therapists, physicians, and teachers.

(9) The right to be given, in a timely and consistent manner, any information a case worker has regarding the child and the child's family which is pertinent to the care and needs of the child and to the making of a permanency plan for the child. Disclosure of information concerning the child's family shall be limited to that information that is essential for understanding the needs of and providing care to the child in order to protect the rights of the child's family. When a positive relationship exists between the foster parent and the child's family, the child's family may consent to disclosure of additional information.

(10) The right to be given reasonable written notice of (i) any change in a child's case plan, (ii) plans to terminate the placement of the child with the foster parent, and (iii) the reasons for the change or termination in placement. The notice shall be waived only in cases of a court order or when the child is determined to be at imminent risk of harm.

(11) The right to be notified in a timely and complete manner of all court hearings . . . and the right to intervene in court proceedings. . . .

(12) The right to be considered as a placement option when a foster child who was formerly placed with the foster parent is to be re-entered into foster care, if that placement is consistent with the best interest of the child and other children in the foster parent's home.

(13) The right to have timely access to the child placement agency's existing appeals process and the right to be free from acts of harassment and retaliation by any other party when exercising the right to appeal.

(14) The right to be informed of the Foster Parent Hotline established under Section 35.6 of the Children and Family Services Act and all of the rights accorded to foster parents concerning reports of misconduct by Department employees, service providers, or contractors, confidential handling of those reports, and investigation by the Inspector General appointed under Section 35.5 of the Children and Family Services Act.

Smith v. Organization of Foster Families

431 U.S. 816, 907 S. Ct. 2094, 53 L. Ed. 2d 14 (1977)

Mr. Justice BRENNAN delivered the opinion of the Court.

Appellees, individual foster parents and an organization of foster parents, brought this civil rights class action pursuant to 42 U.S.C. § 1983 in the United States District Court for the Southern District of New York, on their own behalf and on behalf of children for whom they have provided homes for a year or more. They sought declaratory and injunctive relief against New York State and New York City officials, alleging that the procedures governing the removal of foster children from foster homes provided in N.Y. Soc. Serv. Law §§ 383(2) and 400 (McKinney 1976), and in 18 N.Y.C.R.R. § 450.14 (1974) violated the Due Process and Equal Protection Clauses of the Fourteenth Amendment. . . .

A divided three-judge District Court concluded that "the pre-removal procedures presently employed by the State are constitutionally defective," holding that "before a foster child can be peremptorily transferred from the foster home in which he has been living, be it to another foster home or to the natural parents who initially placed him in foster care, he is entitled to a hearing at which all concerned parties may present any relevant information to the administrative decision maker charged with determing the future placement of the child," *Organization of Foster Families v. Dumpson*, 418 F. Supp. 277, 282 (1976). Four appeals to this Court were taken from the ensuing judgment declaring the challenged statutes unconstitutional and permanently enjoining their enforcement. . . . We reverse.

* * *

A

The expressed central policy of the New York system is that "it is generally desirable for the child to remain with or be returned to the natural parent because the child's need for a normal family life will usually best be met in the natural home, and . . . parents are entitled to bring up their own children unless the best interests of the child would be thereby endangered," Soc. Serv. Law § 384-b(1)(a)(ii) (McKinney Supp. 1976-1977). But the State has opted for foster care as one response to those situations where the natural parents are unable to provide the "positive, nurturing family relationships" and "normal family life in a permanent home" that offer "the best opportunity for children to develop and thrive." §§ 384-b(1)(b), (1)(a)(i).

* * *

Under the New York scheme children may be placed in foster care either by voluntary placement or by court order. Most foster-care placements are voluntary. They occur when physical or mental illness, economic problems, or other family crises make it impossible for natural parents, particularly single parents, to provide a stable home life for their children for some limited period. . . .

Voluntary placement requires the signing of a written agreement by the natural parent or guardian, transferring the care and custody of the child to an authorized child welfare agency. . . . The agreement may provide for return of the child to the natural parent at a specified date or upon occurrence of a particular event, and if it does not, the child must be returned by the agency, in the absence of a court order, within 20 days of notice from the parent.

. . . Foster parents . . . provide care under a contractual arrangement with the agency, and are compensated for their services. The typical contract expressly reserves the right of the agency to remove the child on request. Conversely, the foster parent may cancel the agreement at will.

The New York system divides parental functions among agency, foster parents, and natural parents. . . . The law transfers "care and custody" to the agency; but day-to-day supervision of the child and his activities, and most of the functions ordinarily associated with legal custody, are the responsibility of the foster parent. Nevertheless . . . the foster parent does not have the full authority of a legal custodian. Moreover, the natural parent's placement of the child with the agency does not surrender legal guardianship; the parent retains authority to act with respect to the child in certain circumstances. . . .

Children may also enter foster care by court order. The Family Court may order that a child be placed in the custody of an authorized child-care agency after a full adversary judicial hearing under Art. 10 of the New York Family Court Act, if it is found that the child has been abused or neglected by his natural parents. In addition, a minor adjudicated a juvenile delinquent, or "person in need of supervision" may be placed by the court with an agency. . . .

B

The provisions of the scheme specifically at issue in this litigation come into play when the agency having legal custody determines to remove the foster child from the foster home. . . . Most children are removed in order to be transferred to another foster home. The procedures by which foster parents may challenge a removal made for that purpose differ somewhat from those where the removal is made to return the child to his natural parent.

Section 383 (2) provides that the "authorized agency placing out or boarding [a foster] child . . . may in its discretion remove such child from the home where placed or boarded. . . . The agency is required, except in emergencies, to notify the foster parents in writing 10 days in advance of any removal. 18 N.Y.C.R.R. § 450.10(a) (1976). [T]he foster parents . . . may request a "conference" with the Social Services Department. . . . The foster parent may appear with counsel at the conference, where he will "be advised of the reasons [for the removal of the child] and be afforded an opportunity to submit reasons why the child should not be removed." *Ibid.* The official must render a decision in writing within five days after the close of the conference, and send notice of his decision to the foster parents and the agency. The proposed removal is stayed pending the outcome of the conference.

If the child is removed after the conference, the foster parent may appeal to the Department of Social Services for a . . . full adversary administrative hearing, under Soc. Serv. Law § 400, the determination of which is subject to judicial review . . . , however, the removal is not automatically stayed pending the hearing and judicial review.

This statutory and regulatory scheme applies statewide. In addition, regulations promulgated by the New York City Human Resources Administration, Department of Social Services—Special Services for Children (SSC) provide even greater procedural safeguards there. Under SSC Procedure No. 5 (Aug. 5, 1974), in place of or in addition to the conference provided by the state regulations, the foster parents may request a full trial-type hearing *before* the child is removed from their home. This procedure applies, however, only if the child is being transferred to another foster home, and not if the child is being returned to his natural parents.

One further preremoval procedural safeguard is available. Under Soc. Serv. Law § 392, the Family Court has jurisdiction to review, on petition of the foster parent or the agency, the status of any child who has been in foster care for 18 months or longer. . . . After hearing, the court may order that foster care be continued, or that the child be returned to his natural parents, or that the agency take steps to free the child for adoption. . . . Thus, the court may order not only that foster care be continued, but additionally, "in assistance or as a condition of" that order, that the agency leave the child with the present foster parent. . . .

* * *

II

A

Our first inquiry is whether appellees have asserted interests within the Fourteenth Amendment's protection of "liberty. . . ." *Board of Regents v. Roth*, 408 U.S. 564, 571 (1972).

* * *

. . . The appellees' basic contention is that when a child has lived in a foster home for a year or more, a psychological tie is created between the child and the foster parents which constitutes the foster family the true "psychological family" of the child. That family, they argue, has a "liberty interest" in its survival as a family protected by the Fourteenth Amendment. Upon this premise they conclude that the foster child cannot be removed without a prior hearing satisfying due process. . . .

The District Court did not reach appellees' contention "that the foster home is entitled to the same constitutional deference as that long granted to the more traditional biological family." 418 F. Supp. at 281. [T]he court based its holding that "the pre-removal procedures presently employed by the state are constitutionally defective," not on the recognized liberty interest in family privacy, but on an independent right of the foster child "to be heard before being 'condemned to suffer grievous loss,' *Joint Anti-Fascist Committee v. McGrath,* 341 U.S. 123, 168 . . . (1951) (Frankfurther, J., concurring)." *Id.* at 282.

The court apparently reached this conclusion by weighing the "harmful consequences of a precipitous and perhaps improvident decision to remove a child from his foster family," *id.* at 283, and concluding that this disruption of the stable relationships needed by the child might constitute "grievous loss." But if this was the reasoning applied by the District Court, it must be rejected. . . . What was said in *Board of Regents v. Roth, supra*, at 570-571, applies equally well here.

> "The District Court decided that procedural due process guarantees apply in this case by assessing and balancing the weights of the particular interests involved. . . . [A] weighing process has long been a part of any determination of the *form* of hearing required in particular situations by procedural due process. But, to determine whether due process requirements apply in the first place, we must look not to the 'weight' but to the *nature* of the interest at stake. . . . We must look to see if the interest is within the Fourteenth Amendment's protection of liberty and property."

We therefore turn to appellees' assertion that they have a constitutionally protected liberty interest—in the words of the District Court, a "right to familial privacy," 418 F. Supp. at 279—in the integrity of their family unit. This assertion clearly presents difficulties.

B

* * *

[T]he usual understanding of "family" implies biological relationship, and most decisions treating the relation between parent and child have stressed this element. . . . A biological relationship is not present in the case of the usual foster family. But biological relationships are not exclusive determination of the existence of a family. . . .

[T]he importance of the familial relationship, to the individuals involved and to the society, stems from the emotional attachments that derive from the intimacy of daily association, and from the role it plays in "promot[ing] a way of life" through the instruction of children, *Wisconsin v. Yoder,* 406 U.S. 205, 231-233 (1972), as well as from the fact of blood relationship. . . . At least where a child has been placed in foster care as an infant, has never known his natural parents, and has remained continuously for several years in the care of the same foster parents, it is natural that the foster family should hold the same place in the emotional life of the foster child, and fulfill the same socializing functions, as a natural family. For this reason, we cannot dismiss the foster family as a mere collection of unrelated individuals.

But there are also important distinctions between the foster family and the natural family. First, . . . the State here seeks to interfere . . . with a foster family which has its source in state law and contractual arrangements. . . . [W]hatever emotional ties may develop between foster parent and foster child have their origins in an arrangement in which the State has been a partner from the outset. While the Court has recognized that liberty interests may in some cases arise from positive-law sources, in such a case, and particularly where, as here, the claimed interest derives from a knowingly assumed contractual relation with the State, it is appropriate to ascertain from state law the expectations and entitlements of the parties. In this case, the limited recognition accorded to the foster family by the New York statutes and the contracts executed by the foster parents argue against any but the most limited constitutional "liberty" in the foster family.

* * *

As this discussion suggests, appellees' claim to a constitutionally protected liberty interest raises complex and novel questions. It is unnecessary for us to resolve those questions definitively in this case, however, for, like the District Court, we conclude that "narrower grounds exist to support" our reversal. We are persuaded that, even on the assumption that appellees have a protected "liberty interest," the District Court erred in holding that the preremoval procedures presently employed by the State are constitutionally defective.

III

* * *

It is true that "[b]efore a person is deprived of a protected interest, he must be afforded opportunity for some kind of a hearing, 'except for extraordinary situations where some valid governmental interest is at stake that justifies postponing the hearing until after the event.'" *Board of Regents v. Roth,* 408 U.S. at 570 n.7, quoting *Boddie v. Connecticut,* 401 U.S. 371, 379 (1971) . But the hearing required is only one "appropriate to the nature of the case." *Mullane v. Central Hanover Bank & Trust Co.,* 339 U.S. 306, 313 (1950). "[D]ue process is flexible and calls for such procedural protections as the particular situation demands." *Morrissey v. Brewer,* 408 U.S. 471, 481 (1972). Only last Term, the Court held that "identification of the specific dictates of due process generally requires consideration of three distinct factors: First, the private interest that will be affected by the official action; second, the risk of an erroneous deprivation of such interest through the procedures used, and the probable value, if any, of additional or substitute procedural safeguards; and finally, the Government's interest, including the function involved and the fiscal and administrative burdens that the additional or substitute procedural requirement would entail." *Mathews v. Eldridge,* 424 U.S. 319, 335 (1976). Consideration of the procedures employed by the State and New York City in light of these three factors requires the conclusion that those procedures satisfy constitutional standards.

Turning first to the procedure applicable in New York City, SSC Procedure No. 5 provides that before a child is removed from a foster home for transfer to another foster home, the foster parents may request an "independent review. . . ." Such a procedure would appear to give a more elaborate trial-type hearing to foster families than this Court has found required in other contexts of administrative determinations. *Cf. Goldberg v. Kelley,* 397 U.S. 254, 266-172 (1970). The District Court found the procedure inadequate on four grounds, none of which we find sufficient to justify the holding that the procedure violates due process.

First, the court held that the "independent review" administrative proceeding was insufficient because it was only available on the request of the foster parents. In the view of the District Court, the proceeding should be provided as a matter of course, because . . . it could not be assumed that the foster parents would invoke the hearing procedure in every case in which it was in the child's interest to have a hearing. . . . We disagree. As previously noted, the constitutional liberty, if any sought to be protected by the New York procedures is a right of *family* privacy or autonomy, and the basis for recognition of any such interest in the foster family must be that close emotional ties analogous to those between parent and child are established when a child resides for a lengthy period with a foster family. . . . Thus, consideration of the interest to be protected and the likelihood of erroneous deprivations, the first two factors identified in *Mathews v. Eldridge, supra,* as appropriate in determining the sufficiency of procedural protections, do not support the District Court's imposition of this additional requirement. . . .

Second, the District Court faulted the city procedure on the ground that participation is limited to the foster parents and the agency, and the natural parent and the child are not made parties to the hearing. . . . When the child's transfer from one foster home to another is pending, the interest arguably requiring protection is that of the foster family, not that of the natural parents. Moreover, the natural parent can generally add little to the accuracy of factfinding concerning the wisdom of such a transfer. . . .

[T]he District Court [also said]:

> "[I]t may be advisable, under certain circumstances, for the agency to appoint an adult representative better to articulate the interests of the child. . . ."

418 F. Supp. at 285-286.

. . . We assume . . . that some . . . consultation would be among the first steps that a rational factfinder, inquiring into the child's best interests, would pursue. Such consultation, however, does not require that the child or an appointed representative must be a party with full adversary powers in all preremoval hearings.

The other two defects in the city procedure found by the District Court must also be rejected. One is that the procedure does not extend to the removal of a child from foster care to be returned to his natural parent. But as we have already held, whatever liberty interest may be argued to exist in the foster family is significantly weaker in the case of removals preceding return to the natural parent, and the balance of due process interests must accordingly be different. If the city procedure is adequate where it is applicable, it is no criticism of the procedure that it does not apply in other situations where different interests are at stake. Similarly, the District Court pointed out that the New York City procedure coincided with the informal "conference" and post-removal hearings provided as a matter of state law. This overlap in procedures may be unnecessary or even to some degree unwise, but a State does not violate the Due Process Clause by providing alternative or additional procedures beyond what the Constitution requires.

Outside New York City, where only the statewide procedures apply, foster parents are provided not only with the procedures of a preremoval conference and postremoval hearing provided by 18 N.Y.C.R.R. § 450.10 (1976) and Soc. Serv. Law § 400 (McKinney 1976), but also with the preremoval *judicial* hearing available on request to foster parents who have in their care children who have been in foster care for 18 months or more, Soc. Serv. Law § 392. . . .

The District Court found three defects in this full judicial process. First, a § 392 proceeding is available only to those foster children who have been in foster care for 18 months or more. . . . We do not think that the 18-month limitation on § 392 actions renders the New York scheme constitutionally inadequate. The assumed liberty interest to be protected in this case is one rooted in the emotional attachments that develop over time between a child and the adults who care for him. But there is no reason to assume that those attachments ripen at less than 18 months or indeed at any precise point. . . .

The District Court's other two findings of infirmity in the § 392 procedure have already been considered and held to be without merit. The District Court disputed defendants' reading of § 392 as permitting an order requiring the leaving of the foster child in the same foster home. The plain words of the statute and the weight of New York judicial interpretation do not support the court. The District Court also faulted § 392, as it did the New York City procedure, in not providing an automatic hearing in every case even in cases where foster parents chose not to seek one. Our holding sustaining the adequacy of the city procedure, applies in this context as well.

Finally, the § 392 hearing is available to foster parents, both in and outside New York City, even where the removal sought is for the purpose of returning the child to his natural parents. Since this remedy provides a sufficient constitutional preremoval hearing to protect whatever liberty interest might exist in the continued existence of the foster family when the State seeks to transfer the child to another foster home, *a fortiori* the procedure is adequate to protect the lesser interest of the foster family in remaining together at the expense of the disruption of the natural family.

We deal here with issues of unusual delicacy, in an area where professional judgments regarding desirable procedures are constantly and rapidly changing. In such a context, restraint is appropriate on the part of courts called upon to adjudicate whether a particular procedural scheme is adequate under the Constitution. Since we hold that the procedures provided by New York State in § 392 and by New York City's SSC Procedure No. 5 are adequate to protect whatever liberty interests appellees may have, the judgment of the District Court is reversed.

[Justice STEWART, joined by CHIEF JUSTICE BURGER and Justice REHNQUIST, concurred in the judgment.]

Notes

1. *Smith* did not determine if foster parents have a constitutionally-protected liberty interest in the foster child-parent relationship. Since *Smith*, most lower courts have found that foster parents do not have a protected liberty interest in the relationship. *See, e.g., Rodriquez v. McLoughlin*, 214 F.3d 328 (2d Cir. 2000); *Bates v. Wells*, 508 N.W.2d 497 (Mich. 1993); *In re Dependency of H.J.*, 815 P.2d 1380 (Wash. 1991); *Gibson v. Merced County Department of Human Resources*, 799 F.2d 582 (9th Cir. 1986); *Rivera v. Marcus*, 696 F.2d 1016 (2d Cir. 1982); *Sherrard v. Owens*, 484 F. Supp. 728 (W.D. Mich. 1980), *aff'd*, 644 F.2d 542 (6th Cir.) (per curiam), *cert. denied*, 454 U.S. 828 (1981); *Keyes v. County Department of Public Welfare*, 600 F.2d 693 (7th Cir. 1979). *But see Brown v. County of San Joaquin*, 601 F. Supp. 653 (E.D. Cal. 1985).

2. Some state statutes give foster parents the right to bring an action to terminate the parental rights of the foster child's natural parents. *See* Chapter 12, Part A, Note 3, *supra*. In *Rodarte v. Cox*, 828 S.W.2d 65 (Tex. Ct. App. 1991), the court held that Texas Family Code Annotated § 11.03 (d)(4) (Vernon 1975) allowed the foster parents of a child to file a petition to terminate the parental rights of the natural parents. The court further held that the statute did not conflict with the Adoption Assistance and Child Welfare Act in regards to foster care. For further discussion of foster parents' right to petition for the termination of the natural parent's rights, see Jennifer Burns, Note, *Should Marriage Matter?: Evaluating the Rights of Legal Absentee Fathers*, 68 FORDHAM L. REV. 2299 (2000); Joseph R. Carrieri, *Termination of Parents' Rights and Proceedings*, 173 PLI/CRIM 9, 44 (1996).

3. The psychological parent theory is frequently raised by foster parents in disputes between them and a child's biological parents. For a general discussion of the psychological parent theory and its application to custody disputes, see Stacy A. Warman, Note, *There's Nothing Psychological About It: Defining a New Role for the Other Mother in a State That Treats Her as Legally Invisible*, 24 NOVA L. REV. 907 (2000); Natelie Loder Clark, *Parens Patriae and a Modest Proposal for the Twenty-First Century: Legal Philosophy and a New Look at Children's Welfare*, 6 MICH. J. GENDER & L. 381 (2000); Lawrence Schlam, *Third-Party Standing in Child Custody Disputes: Will Kentucky's New "De Facto Guardian" Provision Help?*, 27 N. KY. L. REV. 368 (2000); Lawrence Schlam, *Children in the Law Issue: Contributors Third Party Custody Disputes in Minnesota: Overcoming the "Natural Rights" of Parents or Pursuing the "Best Interests" of Children?*, 26 WM. MITCHELL L. REV. 733 (2000); Stephen Hellman, *The Child, the Step Parent, and the State: Step Parent Visitation and the Voice of the Child*, 16 TOURO L. REV. 45 (1999).

Questions

1. What factors should a court consider when weighing the rights of the foster parents, the natural parents, and the child in a dispute over the child's placement?

2. In light of the Illinois statute, *supra*, at Chapter 12, Part B, what additional rights should foster parents be granted?

C. Authority of Foster Parents

J.M.A. v. State

542 P.2d 170 (Alaska 1975)

BOOCHEVER, Justice.

On this appeal, we are presented with the novel question of whether foster parents are to be considered agents of the state for purposes of the constitutional proscription against unreasonable searches and seizures. . . .

In May 1974, appellant J.M.A. was placed in the home of Mr. And Mrs. Blankenship as a foster child. The Blankenships were licensed by the State of Alaska to operate a foster home for as many as five children. . . .

In early August 1974, Mrs. Blankenship became concerned with the fact that children who were strangers to her were coming into her home, staying briefly and departing. She suspected that these visits were related to trafficking in drugs. As a result of these suspicions, Mrs. Blankenship began periodically searching J.M.A.'s room during the first week of August. On August 8, 1974, Mrs. Blankenship listened on another extension to one of J.M.A.'s telephone calls without his knowledge or permission. During the course of this conversation, she heard J.M.A. tell the other party he had only a little pot left and needed to pick up some more plus some pills. Mrs. Blankenship again searched J.M.A.'s room and discovered no drugs, although earlier that day she had found and confiscated a pipe. During the evening of August 8, Mrs. Blankenship returned to J.M.A.'s room and searched a jacket she saw lying on the bed. Discovering a plastic bag of marijuana in one of the pockets, she removed the bag and placed it in her purse. No mention of the discovery was made to J.M.A. that day.

The next day Mrs. Blankenship called Jerry Shriner, the social worker assigned to J.M.A., seeking advice on how to deal with the problem. Mr. Shriner advised Mrs. Blankenship to place the marijuana in an envelope for safekeeping and assured her that he would visit her home in the afternoon. Mr. Shriner then called the Alaska State Troopers, and later on the same day, Mr. Shriner and a plainclothesman went to the Blankenship residence. J.M.A., who had been asked to stay home, was called into the living room where he was confronted by Mr. Shriner, Officer Fullerton and Mrs. Blankenship. Mrs. Blankenship then handed the marijuana to Office Fullerton, who identified it as such and began questioning J.M.A. about it. The officer asked J.M.A. whether the jacket in which the marijuana was found was his jacket. J.M.A. admitted that the jacket was his but denied any knowledge of the marijuana. During the course of the meeting, J.M.A. was never advised of his rights.

J.M.A. was removed from the Blankenship home by Mr. Shriner and Officer Fullerton immediately after this meeting and placed in detention pending consideration of his case by the juvenile court. Counsel for J.M.A. filed a motion to suppress all evidence obtained as a result of the overheard telephone conversation and the searches of J.M.A.'s room. On October 8, 1974, a hearing on the motion to suppress was held, and on October 29, 1974, Judge Occhipinti issued his decision denying J.M.A.'s motion to suppress the evidence gathered against him. The adjudication hearing was held on October 31, 1974, resulting in a finding of delinquency. The superior court ordered that J.M.A. be committed to the Department of Health and Social Services for an indeterminate period not to extend beyond his nineteenth birthday, and that he be placed in a correctional or detention facility.

J.M.A. now appeals both from the ruling on the motion to suppress and from the adjudication of delinquency. J.M.A. alleges that the trial court erred in failing to suppress evidence obtained by the foster mother's eavesdropping on J.M.A.'s phone call [and] in failing to suppress evidence obtained through her searches of J.M.A.'s room. . . .

With regard to J.M.A.'s allegation that the lower court erred in failing to suppress the evidence obtained by Mrs. Blankenship through her eavesdropping on J.M.A.'s telephone conversation and her searches of his room, we must determine whether the state and federal constitutional prohibitions against unreasonable searches and seizures apply to a foster parent, licensed and paid by the state, and if so, whether the exclusionary rule, whereby evidence obtained in violation of the constitution is held inadmissible, should apply. Our analysis must initially focus on the question of whether the foster parent stands in such a relationship to the state as to be subject to the constitutional prohibitions against unreasonable searches and seizures. J.M.A. contends that the evidence gathered by Mrs. Blankenship should be suppressed since these warrantless searches were executed while Mrs. Blankenship was acting as an agent of the state, and thus did not comport with constitutional requirements concerning such actions. The state, to the contrary, argues that Mrs. Blankenship, as a foster parent, is not an agent of the state for purposes of the fourth amendment.

Although the constitutional prohibitions against unreasonable searches and seizures have not been specifically limited to state action, there is little doubt but that that was the original intent. We stated in *Bell v. State:*[6]

> A search by a private citizen not acting in conjunction with or at the direction of the police does not violate the constitutional prohibitions against unreasonable search and seizure.

There is a further limitation on the scope of the Fourth Amendment in that it does not apply to searches engaged in by governmental officials when such officials act for a private purpose or outside the scope of duties related to

6 519 P.2d 804, 807 (Alaska 1974).

law enforcement. Such a limitation involves a question of the capacity in which the state agent acts during the course of the search. . . .

Considering the question of when official involvement may be said to exist for purposes of the Fourth Amendment, the Oregon Court of Appeals in *State v. Pearson,* 15 Or. App. 1, 514 P.2d 884, 886 (1973), stated:

> . . . [O]fficial involvement is not measured by the primary occupation of the actor, but by the *capacity* in which he acts at the time in question.

Similarly, in *People v. Wolder,* 4 Cal. App. 3d 984, 84 Cal. Rptr. 788 (1970), the action of an off-duty police officer in searching his daughter's apartment was found not subject to the Fourth Amendment, since, at the time, the police officer was acting in a private capacity as a concerned parent.

Applying these principles to the instant case, it is apparent that, in some respects, Mrs. Blankenship is an agent of the state. Her home is licensed and regulated by the state, and she is paid by the state for caring for foster children. But she also acts in a private capacity in managing the home for her family and herself. . . .

* * *

A foster parent is required both to assume temporarily the role of a natural parent to the child committed to his custody and to aid in the discharge of the government's obligation to care for and supervise those juveniles who have become the responsibility of the state. In substituting for a natural parent, the foster parent is no more an agent of the police than would be any natural parent. The actions of Mrs. Blankenship were in no manner instigated by the police. She testified that she did not want her children to get into trouble with the police and that she sought to work out such problems without police involvement. In fact, even after discovering the marijuana, she contacted J.M.A.'s social worker rather than the police. There is no reason for regarding Mrs. Blankenship's actions undertaken while fulfilling this parental role, which did not involve collaboration with the police, as being any different from the actions of a private parent, and, therefore, not subject to fourth amendment constitutional restraints.

* * *

. . . In this instance, the operator of a foster home is in the extremely difficult position of endeavoring to fulfill the role of parent, and, at the same time, perform the task of supervising the activities of a minor found to be a delinquent. Under the circumstances of such a relationship, a search of the room can hardly be regarded as the type of unreasonable activity constitutionally prohibited. Nevertheless, we believe that the privacy of both natural and foster children should be respected to the fullest extent consistent with parental responsibilities.

Quite obviously, the duties of foster parents do not encompass responsibilities of a law enforcement officer similar to those discussed in *Bell*. Foster parents are not charged with the enforcement of penal statutes or regulations, nor are they entrusted with ensuring the physical security of the public. They are no more responsible for the detection of criminal activity or the apprehension of those participating in such activity that would be any other private citizen. They merely supervise on behalf of the state those children committed to their care. Such responsibilities are not of the same nature as those discussed in *Bell*, and, accordingly, we hold that foster parents are not agents of the state of purposes of the Fourth Amendment.

Our conclusion that the trial court did not err in denying the motion to suppress is bolstered by application of the policies underlying the exclusionary rule to the facts of this case. . . . In the instant case, a principal motivating factor of Mrs. Blankenship's actions must have been a desire to aid her foster child as well as to have her home free of illegal drugs and criminal activity. Excluding the evidence seized herein would do nothing to deter similar future conduct by the Blankenships and other foster parents as that interest is entirely separate from a desire to have a person convicted of a crime or adjudged a delinquent. Put another way, the incentive to make a search under the circumstances here involved would not be lessened because of the likelihood that the evidence would be suppressed. In short, the primary purpose to be served by the exclusionary rule would not be served by its application in this case or ones similar to it.

* * *

In summary, in view of our holding that foster parents are not agents of the state for purposes of the Fourth Amendment, we conclude that the evidence secured by Mrs. Blankenship's efforts, both the testimony regarding the telephone conversation and the marijuana, was properly admitted.

* * *

Affirmed.

Notes

1. Foster parents are required to enter into a written agreement with the state. *See, e.g., Country Mut. Ins. Co. v. Peoples Bank*, 675 N.E.2d 1031 (Ill. App. Ct. 1997). The state reimburses foster parents for educational, medical, dental, and clothing expenses they incur caring for the foster child. The state also trains and licenses the foster parents. The state develops a case plan for each child. It is then the foster parent's responsibility to follow the state's guidelines and contribute to the implementation of the case plan for the child.

2. Despite the nature of the foster parent-child relationship, jurisdictions remain divided as to whether foster parents are state employees and, therefore, have sovereign immunity for negligent acts. In *Hunte v. Blumenthal,* 680 A.2d 1231

(Conn. 1996), the court held that foster parents are employees of the state because of the state's extensive control over the foster care system. *Hunte* further held that foster parents have sovereign immunity from negligence occurring within the scope of their employment. Some states have enacted statutes granting foster parents state employee status. *See, e.g.,* ALASKA STAT. § 34.50.020 (Lexis 2000) (referenced in ALASKA ADMIN. CODE tit. 7, § 53.100) (will indemnify and defend foster parents for their negligent acts resulting in injuries); 5 ILL. COMP. STAT. ANN. 350/1 (West Supp. 2000) ("individuals who serve as foster parents . . . when caring for a Department ward" are employees under the Illinois Employee Indemnification Act).

Other jurisdictions, however, do not classify foster parents as state employees. In *DeWater v. Washington*, 921 P.2d 1059 (Wash. 1996), the court decided that since the state does not directly control the foster home, foster parents are not employees of the state. *DeWater* held that the state cannot be held vicariously liable for the foster parents' negligent or intentional acts.

For further discussion of whether foster parents should have sovereign immunity from their acts, see Todd R. Smyth, *Foster Parent's Right to Immunity From Foster Child's Negligence Claims,* 55 A.L.R.4TH 778 (1987); Terrance J. Dee, Note, *Foster Parent Liability Under Section 1983: Foster Parents' Liability as State Actors for Abuse to Foster Children,* 69 WASH. U. L.Q. 1201 (1991). For a discussion of a state's liability after placing a child in foster care, see Sonja A. Soehnel, *Governmental Tort Liability for Social Service Agency's Negligence in Placement, or Supervision After Placement, of Children,* 90 A.L.R.3D 1214 (1979).

D. Adoption By Foster Parents

C.S. v. S.H.

671 So. 2d 260 (Fla. Dist. Ct. App. 1996)

PARIENTE, Judge.

C.S. and J.S., biological relatives (the biological relatives) of S.D.V-H., a minor, appeal from a final judgment of adoption in favor of S.H. and K.H., foster parents (the foster parents) of S.D.V-H. We reserve the final judgment of adoption because the trial court had no authority to interfere with HRS's decision to select the biological relatives as prospective adoptive parents of S.D.V-H., a child committed to the custody of HRS, where HRS's selection was appropriate, consonant with its policies and made in an expeditious manner.

We first review the background facts and complicated procedural history of this case. S.D.V-H., a baby girl, was born on August 13, 1992. At the time of her birth, she was premature, afflicted with bacterial venereal disease, addicted to crack cocaine and had four hernias. HRS filed a dependency action after S.D.V-H.'s birth. On September 22, 1992, HRS placed S.D.V-H. in temporary foster care with the foster parents. To qualify as foster parents, S.H. and K.H. were required to execute an agreement with HRS entitled "Agreement to Provide Substitute Care for Dependent Children." The agreement, as signed by the foster parents, provided:

> As substitute care parent(s) for the Department of Health and Rehabilitative Services, we agree to the following conditions considered essential for the welfare of this dependent child placed in our home:
>
> 1. This child is placed in our home on a temporary basis and is at all times under the supervision and control of [HRS].
>
> * * *
>
> 3. We will take no action to acquire legal custody or guardianship of the child.
>
> * * *
>
> 7. We will cooperate in arrangements made by [HRS] for visits with the child by his parent(s) or other relatives(s).
> 8. We will participate with [HRS] in planning for the child, which may include adoption placement, transfer to another foster home, or return to parent(s), or relatives(s).
>
> * * *
>
> 13. [HRS] may remove the child from our home at any time but will, whenever possible, give us at least two weeks [sic] notice.

C.S., the child's biological aunt who resided in upstate New York, first learned of S.D.V-H.'s birth from her sister in December of 1992. She did not give immediate credence to this representation due to prior false statements by her sister. When, in April of 1993, the birth of S.D.V-H. was confirmed, C.S. and her husband, J.S., immediately began to take steps to qualify as adoptive parents.

On April 12, 1993, HRS filed a Petition for Termination of Parental Rights seeking to terminate the natural mother's parental rights. The father of S.D.V-H. was unknown. With the natural mother's consent, her parental rights were terminated by an order entered on June 30, 1993. Pursuant to that order, S.D.V-H. was placed in the permanent custody of HRS for adoptive placement

HRS immediately arranged for a home study of the biological relatives who resided in upstate New York. After a favorable home study, on November 8, 1993, HRS advised the foster parents of its decision to approve the biological relatives as adoptive parents.

In late November 1993 the relatives, with HRS's approval, travelled from New York to Florida to visit with S.D.V-H. and return with her to New York. The foster parents refused to surrender S.D.V-H. to HRS or the biological relatives. The foster parents' refusal was in clear violation of their agreement with HRS. Further, in December 1993, the foster parents filed a complaint for injunctive relief alleging that HRS should be equitably estopped from withholding its consent to the foster parents as adoptive parents. The foster parents alleged that HRS had promised them approval as adoptive parents. A temporary injunction was entered on December 6, 1993, enjoining HRS from removing S.D.V-H. from the custody of the foster parents.

At about the same time as the foster parents' claim for injunctive relief, both the biological relatives and the foster parents separately petitioned for adoption of S.D.V-H. HRS and the biological relatives moved to dismiss the foster parents' adoption petition on the basis that they lacked standing to adopt because they did not have HRS's consent; they had not been selected by HRS as adoptive parents; and no required home study had been performed by HRS. This motion was denied. The trial court, however, granted the foster parents' motion to dismiss the biological relatives' adoption petition on the ground that the biological relatives were not Florida residents, a statutory prerequisite. The trial court, nonetheless, allowed the biological relatives to intervene in the injunction proceedings and adoption proceedings in light of the [relatives'] designation and formal approval by HRS as adoptive parents and in light of their pending adoption petition filed in New York.

On April 7, 1995, Judge Richard Oftedal entered a detailed twelve-page order denying the foster parents' request for a permanent injunction and request for equitable relief. Judge Oftedal found untenable S.H.'s position that HRS promised her that the foster parents would be the adoptive parents. The order contained the further findings that at no time did HRS "promise the [foster parents] that they would be either approved or recommended as adoptive parents." Rather, Judge Oftedal found that HRS had cautioned S.H. that it was HRS's policy at that time to accord relatives priority in adopting children in its custody.

* * *

A trial on the adoption petition was held in October 1995 before Judge Jack Cook. . . . Two psychologists testified in connection with S.D.V-H.'s bonding and potential for damage if removed from the foster parents' home. Dr. Lori Waserman testified on the foster parents' behalf. . . . She testified that to sever S.D.V-H. from her foster parents at this age (three years old at the time of the hearing) would be extremely detrimental as she had bonded with the foster parents. Dr. Wasserman did acknowledge that it would be possible to transfer S.D.V-H. from one loving home to another if the adults cooperated fully and worked toward that goal.

Dr. McGraw, the chief psychologist for the juvenile court, was appointed by the trial court to evaluate the effects of a transition from the foster home to the biological relatives. He concluded that S.D.V-H. would experience stress from the transition, but that such stress would be at acceptable levels. He concluded that S.D.V-H. would "do fine" and that he did not anticipate any permanent psychological dysfunction or impairment.

* * *

The trial court's order contains no finding that HRS's selection of the biological relatives as adoptive parents was inappropriate. According to the home study, the biological relatives live in upstate New York in a 200-year-old family farmhouse that is located on 22 acres of their land. They have two boys, aged 13 and 15, and an extended family nearby. C.S., age 38, has a degree in occupational education and works as a teacher/trainer for the New York Child Care Council. J.S., age 40, has a degree in religion/youth counseling and occupational education and is a carpenter by trade.

There is less information in the record on the foster parents. This is the foster parents' second marriage. They do not have children together, but they are both grandparents and all their children are adults. K.H., who is 61 years of age, is a retiree and works as a maintenance supervisor. They reside in one of the apartment complexes which K.H. maintains.

The trial court found both couples to "possess outstanding parenting skills" and to be "motivated by what they believe to be [S.D.V-H.'s] best interests." The trial court concluded, however, that to remove the child from her loving, caring and nurturing environment would result in psychological stress to the child. The trial court determined it had authority to grant the foster parents' adoption petition notwithstanding HRS's selection of the biological relatives as the adoptive parents because HRS unreasonably withheld its consent to adopt from the foster parents. The trial court reasoned that HRS had acted unreasonably because it was in the child's best interests for the foster parents to adopt the child given the length of time that the child had remained with the foster parents and the bonding which had occurred.

No mention is made in the trial court's decision of the fact that, as of December 1993, HRS had approved the biological relatives as adoptive parents and the biological relatives were ready, willing and able to adopt S.D.V-H. At that point, the biological relatives could have proceeded with the adoption in New York State pursuant to the Interstate Compact on the Placement of Children, with the blessing of HRS, but for the actions of the foster parents in refusing to abide by HRS's decision and their written agreement with HRS. Because the injunction remained in effect until October 1995, the time of the final hearing, the trial court effectively set in motion the sole justification for its final decision—the three-year bonding of the foster parents and S.D.V-H.

As a preliminary matter the foster parents contest the biological relatives' standing to bring this appeal. The biological relatives were permitted to intervene in both the injunction action and the adoption proceedings below. They are blood relatives approved as adoptive parents by HRS. Their interests would be directly and adversely affected if we were to approve the final judgment of adoption. The biological relatives have a direct interest in the outcome of this appeal and thus, have standing to bring this appeal.

The biological relatives and Children First, amicus curiae, contend that the provisions of Chapter 39 unambiguously vest exclusive authority in HRS to select adoptive homes for children who are committed to HRS's custody. They further argue that the trial court's actions in approving the foster parents' petition for adoption exceeded its statutory authority and violated the doctrine of separation of powers as set forth in Article II, § 3 of the Florida Constitution, between the judiciary and the executive branches.

* * *

Subsection 39.469(2) empowers the judiciary to place children whose parents' rights have been terminated in the "custody of [HRS] for purpose of adoption" or in the custody of a licensed child-placing agency. When HRS is granted custody of a child pursuant to Chapter 39, as occurred in this case, HRS has "the right to determine where and with whom the child shall live. . . ." *See* § 39.41(5), Fla.Stat. After a child is placed in the custody of HRS following the termination of parental rights, section 39.47, provides as follows:

> (1) A licensed child-placing agency or the department which is given custody of a child for subsequent adoption in accordance with this chapter may place the child in a family home for prospective subsequent adoption and may thereafter become a party to any proceeding for the legal adoption of the child and appear in any court where the adoption proceedings is pending and consent to the adoption; and that consent alone shall in all cases be sufficient.

. . . Subsection 39.47(4) provides that the court retains jurisdiction over the child subject to specific limitations:

> The court shall retain jurisdiction over any child for whom custody is given to a licensed child-placing agency or to the department until the child is placed for adoption. After custody of a child for subsequent adoption has been given to an agency or the department, the court has jurisdiction for the purpose of reviewing the status of the child and the progress being made toward permanent adoptive placement, . . . but this jurisdiction does not include the exercise of any power or influence by the court over the selection of an adoptive parent.

* * *

In *Department of Health and Rehabilitation Services v. Doe*, 643 So. 2d 1100 (Fla. 1st DCA 1994), a couple had obtained custody of an infant through a private adoption. Two months later, the infant's older sibling was permanently committed to HRS when parental rights were terminated. HRS intended to place the sibling permanently with the foster parents, not the couple who had adopted the infant. The trial court ordered HRS to consider the couple, and not the foster parents, as prospective parents.

The first district quashed the trial court's order finding that it contradicted the plain language of subsection 39.47(4), which restricts the court's jurisdiction in adoptive placement. The first district noted that the circuit court's jurisdiction "specifically 'does not include the exercise of any power or influence by the court over the selection of an adoptive parent.'" *Doe*, 643 So. 2d at 1101 (quoting § 39.47(4), Fla. Stat.).

Under the 1994 statutory amendment, the jurisdiction has been expanded to allow courts to review "the appropriateness of the adoptive placement." § 39.453(1)(c), Fla. Stat. Even prior to the 1994 amendment, we construed subsection 39.4552(7)(g), which requires the trial court to consider "the appropriateness of the child's current placement," to be applicable to post-termination jurisdiction of the courts. This judicial review, however, does not extend to authorize the trial court to make a different selection from HRS or determine that another set of parents would be more appropriate.

At the heart of the separation of powers issue between the judiciary and HRS in this case is the extent to which the trial court was statutorily authorized to scrutinize HRS's selection decision. . . . [W]hile trial courts have authorization to oversee the status of the child and the progress toward permanent adoptive placement, they are not vested with unlimited authority over children permanently committed to HRS after termination of parental rights.

The trial court agreed that it could not interfere with HRS's selection of adoptive parents, acknowledging that selection is "an administrative function which the legislature has placed in its sole discretion." It did not construe its decision to approve an adoption petition of a couple other than one selected by HRS as an exercise of the court's continuing supervisory jurisdiction under Chapter 39 to monitor the progress of HRS to make a permanent placement. Instead, the trial court distinguished *Doe*, reasoning that it was not selecting the adoptive parents, but merely ruling on the merits of a petition for adoption.

The trial court determined it had authority under subsection 63.072(4) to waive HRS's consent if it concluded that such consent had been unreasonably withheld. Section 63.072 is entitled "persons whose consent may be waived." Subsection 63.072(4) provides:

> The court may excuse the consent of the following individuals to an adoption . . . A legal guardian or lawful custodian of the person to be adopted, other than a parent, who has failed to respond in writing to a request for consent for a period of 60 days or who, after examination of his or her written reasons for withholding consent, is found by the court to [be withholding his or her consent unreasonably].

* * *

Chapter 39 specifically controls the placement for adoption of children where parental rights have been previously terminated. While Chapter 63 authorized the trial court to finalize the adoption, its provisions are triggered only after HRS places and approves a child for adoption as provided in Chapter 39. Thus, we conclude that the general grant of authority over all adoption proceedings does not supersede HRS's specific authority to select the adoptive parents.

Moreover, even if we focus on the provisions of chapter 63 relied on by the trial court, these provisions did not permit the trial court to waive HRS's consent to adoption as it did in this case. Section 63.062 addressees the consents required before a child may be legally adopted. Regarding children committed to HRS custody, subsection (4) specifically provides:

> If parental rights to the minor have previously been terminated, a licensed child placing agency or the department with whom the child has been placed for subsequent adoption may provide consent to the adoption. In that case no other consent is required.

* * *

While the trial court may have authority in its continuing supervisory jurisdiction under subsection 39.47(4) to compel HRS to make a selection of an adoptive parent if HRS has not acted expeditiously or to disapprove an inappropriate selection, we hold that subsection 63.072(4) does not authorize a trial court to waive HRS's consent and, thus, override Chapter 39. While Chapter 63 sets forth the procedures to be followed in all cases of adoption, it applies in cases involving children in the custody of HRS only after HRS, pursuant to the authority granted to it in Chapter 39, has selected an adoptive placement.

* * *

To the extent that subsection 63.072(4) could be interpreted to apply to HRS, we further hold that consent could not be considered unreasonably withheld within the context of that subsection where, as in this case, HRS has expeditiously selected an appropriate adoptive family and the delay has not been occasioned by HRS. The subsection empowers the trial court to excuse the consent of a legal guardian where there has been no written response to a request for consent or the written reasons given are found to be unreasonable. Neither proviso applies here.

It was only because the trial court entered a temporary injunction in December 1993 that HRS was prevented from removing S.D.V-H. from the custody of the foster parents and placing her in the custody of the biological relatives. Presumably at that point in time the decision of HRS to select the biological relatives as adoptive parents and thus withhold its consent from the foster parents would have been reasonable.

The only reason cited by the trial court for its decision to grant the foster parents' adoption petition was the stress to the child which would occur if the child was now transferred to the custody of the biological relatives. To approve this decision would be to legally endorse the notion that he who gets the child first, gets the child. It would also encourage individuals having temporary custody of a child to delay the adoption proceedings as long as possible so that the argument could be raised, as it was here, that separation would now cause harm.

As the supreme court noted under different circumstances in *In re Adoption of Doe*, 543 So. 2d 741, 744 (Fla. 1984), *cert. denied,* 493 U.S. 964, 110 S. Ct. 405, 107 L. Ed. 2d 371 (1989), we must be careful not to adopt a rule that "physical custody, because of substantial bonding, is determinative in contested adoptions." *Id.* at 744. The danger in measuring the child's "best interests" by the degree of bonding would make a tentative placement "effectively unreviewable." *Id.*

* * *

Of course, the trial court must act in the child's best interests in adoption proceedings. But that general statement of policy cannot supersede the specific statutory limitations on the trial court's authority to interfere with HRS's selection. The trial court does not have discretion to make a different selection simply because the foster parents filed an adoption petition. The trial court was not vested in this case with authority to make a *de novo* selection.

The courts are charged with monitoring the progress toward permanent adoptive placement to make sure that such placement occurs as expeditiously as possible. The longer the parties and the courts wait before finalizing an adoption decision, the more difficult the separation.

As recognized by the fifth district, "the passage of time required by these proceedings is harmful to everyone. As children grow older, bonding occurs and new directions are difficult." *Rivera-Berrios v. Stefanos,* 649 So. 2d 881, 882 (Fla. 5th DCA 1994), *quashed on other grounds* 674 So. 2d 12 (Fla. 1996). We urge the adoption of strict time standards for expedited hearings and appeals in these matters at both the trial and appellate levels.

Although we have expedited review of this matter . . . we nevertheless are now deciding the fate of a child who is over three years old. We recognize that our reversal will result in S.D.V-H.'s separation from the only family she has known since birth—her foster parents. We understand that the foster parents love this young child very much and have provided her with loving and nurturing care. We also recognize, however, that both psychologists who testified agreed that the transition from one loving home to another could be made with a minimum of harm if both families cooperate fully and work together. We urge the foster parents and the biological relatives to do this.

The result in this case comports with common sense as well as public policy. The foster parents should be encouraged to comply with the terms of their agreement with HRS. HRS must be able to rely on these written agreements when it places children in foster care on a temporary basis. Foster parents should not resort to the courts to interfere with HRS's selection process and circumvent the administrative procedures available to them.

In accordance with our decision, we reverse the final judgment of adoption and remand for proceedings consistent with his opinion which will allow the biological relatives to proceed to finalize their adoption in New York State. We direct the trial court to dissolve the temporary injunction which has been in effect since December 1993, and we further direct all parties to cooperate with one another so that the best interests of this young child are truly served forthwith and without further delay. . . .

Notes

1. Foster parents and a state welfare agency may enter into an agreement which prevents the foster parents from taking action to adopt the foster child. *See* 2 AM. JUR. 2d, *Adoption* § 45 (1994). Only a few reported cases have dealt with the enforceability of such foster parent-agency agreements. *See* Kristine Cordier Kamezis, Annotation, *Validity and Enforcement of Agreement by Foster Parents That They Will Not Attempt to Adopt Foster Child,* 78 A.L.R.3D 770 (1977). Courts, however, remain undecided whether to enforce the agreement in all circumstances. In *Oxendine v. Catawba Department of Social Services*, 281 S.E.2d 370 (N.C. 1982), the foster parents signed an agreement with the state agency in which the foster parents could not file for adoption unless the agency approved the action. When the agency informed the foster parents that another family intended to adopt the foster child, the foster parents filed a petition for adoption despite the agency's rejection of the petition. The court held that "[s]ince the welfare of the child is the controlling factor in an adoption proceeding, any agreement between the plaintiffs and defendant concerning the child's adoption is subject to the court's independent judgment as to what is in the best interests of the child." *Id.* at 376. Other courts have also held that agreements which prevent foster parents from initiating adoption proceedings may or may not be enforced depending on what is in the child's best interests. *See, e.g., Knight v. Deavers,* 531 S.W.2d 252 (Ark. 1976) (specific performance clause in contract subject to best interests of child); *In re Adoption of Alexander,* 206 So. 2d 452 (Fla. Dist. Ct. App. 1968) (foster parents' devotion and care for child's well-being outweighs their contractual obligation not to initiate adoption proceedings). *See also* DONALD T. KRAMER, LEGAL RIGHTS OF CHILDREN § 29.06 (2d ed. 1994); Claudio DeBellis & Marta B. Soja, Note, *Gregory K.: Child Standing in Parental Termination Proceedings and the Implications of the Foster Parent-Foster Child Relationship on the Best Interest Standard,* 8 ST. JOHN'S J. LEGAL COMMENT. 501 (1993).

2. Most courts will not allow foster parents to petition for adoption when the biological parents voluntarily place the child in foster care. *See, e.g., In re Michael B.,* 604 N.E.2d 122 (N.Y. 1992) (using emotional ties and the amount of time spent with a foster family to determine custody of a child undermines the objective of voluntary foster care as a resource for parents in temporary crisis); *Huey v. Lente,* 514 P.2d 1081 (N.M. Ct. App. 1973) (foster parents initiating adoption proceedings violated both a fiduciary duty owed to the mother and the written agreement).

3. Some states purposefully limit the legal status of foster parents to petition for adoption of a foster child. In *Little Flower Children's Services v. Andrew C.,* 545 N.Y.S.2d 444 (Fam. Ct. 1989), the court held that since the foster parent-child relationship is governed by statute, the rights of foster parents should not interfere with the court's ultimate goal of family reunification. In *Andrew C.,* the placement agency filed a habeas corpus petition to regain physical custody of the child from the foster parents. The court required the agency to bear the initial burden of proving that the biological parent was fit and that the best interests of the child were furthered by a return to the natural parent. The foster parents then had to clearly show that return of the child to the natural parent will operate to the child's "grave detriment." *But see In re Baby Girl D.,* 257 Cal. Rptr. 1 (Ct. App. 1989) (when reunification with biological parents is not possible, then foster parent with whom child has substantial emotional and psychological ties should have preference for purposes of placement).

Questions

1. If foster parents are allowed to petition for adoption, how does this affect the nature of the foster care system? What policy arguments could be made for and against permitting foster parents to petition for adoption of a foster child?

2. In an adoption proceeding initiated by foster parents, what factors should a court consider when determining whether a foster child's best interests outweigh enforcement of the agreement? If a court is willing to entertain a foster parent petition, despite the existence of the foster parent-state agency agreement, what purpose does the contract serve?

E. Foster Parent Liability

1. Liability to the Foster Child

Washington Revised Code Annotated

§ 4.24.590 (West Supp. 2001)

§ 4.24.590. Liability of foster parents

In actions for personal injury or property damage commenced by foster children or their parents against foster parents licensed pursuant to chapter 74.15 RCW, the liability of foster parents for the care and supervision of foster children shall be the same as the liability of biological and adoptive parents for the care and supervision of their children.

Mayberry v. Pryor

374 N.W.2d 683 (Mich. 1985)

CAVANAGH, Justice.

* * *

I

Defendants Alfred and Carol Pryor were properly licensed by the Department of Social Services as foster family home parents. Justin Mayberry was placed in their home in October, 1977, after the Bay County Probate Court temporarily removed him from the custody of his natural mother, plaintiff Kay Mayberry. At the time of the initial placement, Justin was twenty-two months old and deaf. Justin was briefly returned to Ms. Mayberry's custody twice, but was removed to the Pryors' home after appropriate hearings.

On November 18, 1979, Justin, then about four years old, was allegedly attacked by a German shepherd dog while sitting alone on the front porch of the Pryors' home. Because of his deafness and inability to communicate, Justin was unable to cry out for help. As a result of the attack, he suffered serious injuries and permanent brain damage. Justin apparently has been placed in a state residential facility because of his physical and mental disabilities.

Ms. Mayberry filed a complaint in June, 1980, against the Pryors for negligent supervision, and against defendants Ralph and Susan Day, the owners of the dog. The Pryors moved for summary judgment on the ground that their foster parent status entitled them to invoke the defense of parental immunity. In March, 1982, the Saginaw Circuit Court granted the Pryors' motion . . . and certified . . . that its decision was in conflict with *Grodin v. Grodin,* 102 Mich. App. 396, 301 N.W.2d 869 (1980), *lv. den* 412 Mich. 867 (1981). We granted plaintiff's application for leave to appeal. We directed the parties to brief whether *Plumley v. Klein,* 388 Mich. 1, 199 N.W.2d 169 (1972), was properly applied to the instant case and whether foster parents may invoke parental immunity.

II

In *Plumley*, this Court joined a growing number of jurisdictions which have abolished the common-law rule that children cannot bring a tort cause of action against their parents. We retained the defense of parental immunity in only two limited situations:

> "A child may maintain a lawsuit against his parent for injuries suffered as a result of the alleged ordinary negligence of the parent. Like our sister states, however, we note two exceptions to this new rule of law: (1) where the alleged negligent act involves an exercise of reasonable parental authority over the child; and (2) where the alleged negligent act involves an exercise of reasonable parental discretion with respect to the provision of food, clothing, housing, medical and dental services, and other care."

388 Mich. 8, 199 N.W.2d 169.

Although *Plumley* addressed only the tort liability of a natural parent, the circuit court and Court of Appeals concluded here that persons acting *in loco parentis* to a child could also invoke the defense of parental immunity. Citing *Hush v. Devilbiss Co.*, 77 Mich. App. 639, 259 N.W.2d 170 (1977), the circuit court reasoned that licensed foster care homes provide children, whose natural parents are unwilling or unable to provide proper care and supervision, with a healthy and supervised environment. Since by definition foster parents replace the function of natural parents, the circuit court concluded that the Pryors stood *in loco parentis* to Justin. The Court of Appeals similarly held, as a matter of law, that persons who provide temporary foster care to a child pursuant to a probate court order stand *in loco parentis* to the foster child.

Both lower courts then held that an action for negligent parental supervision is barred because it involves the exercise of parental authority over a child, which falls within the first *Plumley* exception. Finally, they concluded that the reasonableness of the exercise of parental authority is a question of law which can be disposed of by motion for summary judgment. The Court of Appeals at first distinguished, then rejected, the seemingly contrary holding in *Grodin*.

III

The tort liability of a foster parent is an issue of first impression in this state. Similar cases from other jurisdictions are conflicting. The vast majority of cases which have discussed the tort liability of persons standing *in loco parentis* to a child generally involved the child's stepparents, adoptive parents, grandparents, or other persons related by consanguinity, marriage, or adoption. In addition, the child was generally visiting with or being cared for by these persons with the natural parents' consent when the injury occurred.

The situation is markedly different when a foster care arrangement is involved. Foster parents and foster children are not related by consanguinity, marriage, or adoption. They are brought together by means of a preexisting contractual arrangement between the DSS and the foster parents in which the latter are compensated for expenses incurred in caring for the child. The foster parents and home must conform to specific statutory and regulatory guidelines and the DSS is required to monitor them.

In addition, placement of the child in a foster family home generally is not voluntary. It often occurs after the child has been physically removed from the custody of the natural parent or other caretaker by order of the probate court after an adversary hearing due to neglect, mistreatment, or abandonment. Even a "voluntary" relinquishment of a child for foster care placement may be induced by threats of court proceedings or the product of uninformed consent. *Smith v. Organization of Foster Families,* 431 U.S. 816, 834, 97 S. Ct. 2094, 2104, 53 L. Ed. 2d 14 (1977).

Finally, the goal of foster care is not to create a new "family" unit or encourage permanent emotional ties between the child and foster parents. Foster care is designed to provide a stable, nurturing, noninstitutionalized environment for the child while the natural parent or caretaker attempts to remedy the problems which precipitated the child's removal or, if parental rights have been terminated, until suitable adoptive parents are found. *Smith,* 431 U.S. 861-862 (Stewart, J., *concurring*).

There are few cases from other jurisdictions involving suits by foster children against foster parents. We are aware of only two cases in which a foster parent has been determined to stand *in loco parentis* to a foster child. In *Miller v. Pelzer*, 159 Minn. 375, 199 N.W. 97 (1924), the child was placed with the foster parents shortly after birth and lived with them for twenty-five years. When she discovered that she was not their natural child, she filed suit alleging fraud and deceit and sought compensation for farm work she had performed. In dismissing the child's suit, the Minnesota Supreme Court initially noted that the family relation which had existed "for all practical purposes was just as sacred as if plaintiff had been the natural daughter." *Id.* at 377, 199 N.W. 97. The true holding of the case, however, was that the foster parents were under no legal duty to inform the child of her true parentage and therefore plaintiff had failed to state a cause of action. Although *Miller* was cited with approval in *London Guarantee & Accident Co. v. Smith,* 242 Minn. 211, 217 n.13, 64 N.W.2d 781 (1954), the liability of a stepfather was involved in the latter case.

In *Goller v. White,* 20 Wis. 2d 402, 122 N.W.2d 193 (1963), the Wisconsin Supreme Court accepted the trial court's conclusion that the foster father stood *in loco parentis* to the foster child. It then proceeded to abolish the defense of parental immunity, except in two limited situations. Since the child's complaint sufficiently alleged negligent parental supervision, a cause of action which did not fall within either exception, the *Goller* Court concluded that the foster father could be held liable. *Id.* at 409-413, 122 N.W.2d 193. The concurring opinion would have allowed the suit on the ground that parental immunity should not be extended to foster parents. *Id.* at 413, 122 N.W.2d 193.

Several courts have permitted foster children to sue their foster parents without discussing the issue of parental immunity. Some cases are distinguishable because the foster parents allegedly engaged in intentional misconduct. *See, e.g., Blanca v. Nassau County,* 103 A.D.2d 524, 480 N.Y.S.2d 747 (1984); *Vonner v. Dep't of Public Welfare,* 273 So. 2d 252 (La. 1973); *Hanson v. Rowe,* 18 Ariz. App. 131, 500 P.2d 916 (1972). Actions alleging intentional torts were one of the first exceptions carved out from the parental immunity doctrine.

Other courts, while expressing sympathy for the plight of foster parents, have nevertheless permitted suits alleging negligent supervision. *Headrick v. Parker,* unpublished opinion of the Tennessee Court of Appeals, decided August 31, 1984 (Docket No. CA 954) (Available on LEXIS); *New Jersey Property-Liability Ins. Guaranty Ass'n v. State,* 184 N.J. Super. 348, 354-355, 446 A.2d 189 (1982), *rev'd on other grounds* 195 N.J. Super. 4, 477 A.2d 826 (1984). *See also Kern v. Steele County*, 322 N.W.2d 187 (Minn. 1982); *cf. Pickett v. Washington County*, 31 Or. App. 1263, 572 P.2d 1070 (1977).

The only jurisdiction which has thoroughly addressed the problem and concluded that foster parents are not entitled to parental immunity is New York [in] *Andrews v. Otsego County*, 112 Misc. 2d 37, 446 N.Y.S.2d 169, 172-174 (1982). . . .

. . . [Foster] parents and children are brought together solely through a contractual arrangement between the DSS and the foster parents. Foster parents are compensated by the state. The natural parents or other caretakers are required to reimburse the state or county for the cost of foster care if and to the extent they are financially capable. Placement of a child in a foster home is generally designed to be temporary and is monitored by the DSS.

We are not persuaded that the traditional rationales for the parental immunity doctrine—preservation of the family unit and domestic tranquility, protection of family resources, and a reluctance to interfere with parenting decisions—requires or justifies extending the defense to foster parents. Licensing and monitoring procedures already exist, which to some degree limit the foster parent's parenting decisions. As the *Andrews* Court noted, it would be incongruous to suspend a foster parent's license because of negligent supervision, but not allow the foster child to sue for injuries incurred because of that negligence.

We recognize that the vast majority of foster parents execute their duties conscientiously and provide quality care to their foster children. Foster parents provide a greatly needed and appreciated service to children who would otherwise have to be institutionalized. The question presented today involves a balancing of equally compelling interests—the foster child's interest in receiving proper care and being compensated for his injuries versus the foster parents' interest in providing foster care without fear of litigation. The clear judicial trend is to abolish or limit the availability of the parental immunity defense to both parents and other caretakers alike. We are similarly persuaded that the interests of the child outweigh those of the foster parents and that the parental immunity doctrine should not be further extended. We note, however, that parental immunity from tort liability can be statutorily extended to foster parents if the Legislature so desires.

IV

The decision of the Court of Appeals is reversed. The case is remanded to the Saginaw Circuit Court for further proceedings consistent with this opinion.

Notes

1. As suggested by *Mayberry*, jurisdictions remain split as to whether a foster parent may be held liable for negligence against a foster child. In *Andrews v. County of Ostego,* 446 N.Y.S.2d 169 (N.Y. Sup. Ct. 1982), the infant plaintiff alleged that he suffered an eye injury as a result of the negligent supervision of the foster parents and the County of Ostego. The court found the foster parents liable for the foster child's injury. The court held that foster parents do not stand *in loco parentis* and, as a result, are not granted parental immunity from negligent actions brought by the foster child. Also, the foster parents do not stand *in loco parentis* because they do not assume financial responsibility for the foster child (since the state reimburses them). *See also Wallace v. Smyth*, 703 N.E.2d 416 (Ill. App. Ct. 1998) (foster parents held liable for negligent act resulting in foster child's death); *Spikes v. Banks*, 586 N.W.2d 106 (Mich. Ct. App. 1998) (child neglect by foster parents is not protected by foster parent immunity statute); *Nichol v. Stass*, 735 N.E.2d 582 (Ill. 2000) (foster parents are not entitled to sovereign immunity arising from harm to foster children in their care). *But see Mitchell v. Davis*, 598 So. 2d 801 (Ala. 1992). In *Mitchell*, six foster children were killed and two were injured when the foster home burned down. The administrator of the deceased children's estate brought suite against the foster parents, alleging that the fire was caused by the foster parents' "negligence, wantonness, [and] breach of contract." The court stated that foster parents stand *in loco parentis*, and the foster family unit is functionally no different from a biological unit. The court held that foster parents have immunity only from claims of simple negligence because some differences do exist between biological and foster parents. *See also Brown v. Phillips*, 342 S.E.2d 786 (Ga. Ct. App. 1986) (absent willful or malicious action by a foster parent, a foster parent is immune from tort liability by the fact that they stand *in loco parentis).* For further discussion of a foster parent's tort liability, see Karen Cavanaugh & Daniel Pollack, *Liability Protections for Foster Parents*, 6 KAN. J.L. & PUB. POL'Y 78 (1997); Vincent S. Nadile, Note, *Promoting the Integrity of Foster Family Relationships: Needed Statutory Protections for Foster Parents,* 62 NOTRE DAME L. REV. 221 (1987).

2. Courts have generally held that foster parents cannot be held liable under 42 U.S.C. § 1983. In *Milburn v. Anne Arundel County Department of Social Services*, 871 F.2d 474 (4th Cir. 1989), *cert. denied*, 110 S. Ct. 148 (1989), the court stated that foster parents are not state actors. Therefore, the court held that a child repeatedly abused by a foster parent did not have a private cause of action under § 1983. *See also K.H. v. Morgan,* 914 F.2d 846 (7th Cir. 1990) (holding that foster parents are state actors would "undo *DeShaney").* For further analysis supporting foster parents' immunity from § 1983 actions, see Michael B. Mushlinm, *Unsafe Havens: The Case for Consitutional Protection of Foster Children From Abuse and Neglect,* 23 HARV. C.R.-C.L. L. REV. 1999 (1988). *But see* Terrence J. Dee, Note, *Foster Parent Liability Under Section 1983: Foster Parents' Liability As State Actors for Abuse to Foster Children,* 69 WASH. U. L.Q. 1201 (1991).

Questions

1. How might exposing foster parents to tort liability affect the foster care system? What degree of immunity, if any, should foster parents be given? How should a court weigh the foster child's interest in receiving proper care versus the foster parents' interest of providing care without fear of litigation?

2. What reasoning did *Mayberry* use to determine that foster parents can be held liable for negligent acts? What role did *in loco parentis* serve in the holding of the court? What policy arguments can be made for and against foster parents having *in loco parentis* status?

2. Liability to Third Parties

Missouri Annotated Statutes
§ 537.045 (West 2000)

537.045 Parent or guardian liable for damages by minor....

1. The parent or guardian, excluding foster parents, of any unemancipated minor, under eighteen years of age, in their care and custody, against whom judgment has been rendered for purposely marking upon, defacing or in any way damaging any property, shall be liable for the payment of that judgment up to an amount not to exceed two thousand dollars, provided that the parent or guardian has been joined as a party defendant in the original action. The judgment provided in this subsection to be paid shall be paid to the owner of the property damaged, but such payment shall not be a bar to any criminal action or any proceeding against the unemancipated minor for such damage for the balance of the judgment not paid by the parent or guardian.

2. The parent or guardian, excluding foster parents, of any unemancipated minor, under eighteen years of age, in their care and custody, against whom judgement has been rendered for purposely causing personal injury to any individual, shall be liable for the payment for that judgment up to an amount not to exceed two thousand dollars , provided that the parent or guardian has been joined as a party defendant in the original action. The judgment provided in this subsection to be paid shall be paid to the person injured, but such payment shall not be a bar to any criminal action or any proceeding against the unemancipated minor for such damage for the balance of the judgment not paid by the parent or guardian.

* * *

Kerins v. Lima
680 N.E.2d 32 (Mass. 1997)

GREANLEY, Justice.
General Laws c. 231, § 85G, reads as follows:

> "Parents of an unemancipated child under the age of eighteen and over the age of seven years shall be liable in a civil action for any willful act committed by said child which results in injury or death to another person or damage to the property of another, which shall include any damages resulting from a larceny or attempted larceny of property as set forth in [G.L. c. 266 § 30A], damage to cemetery property or damage to any state, county or municipal property or damage as set forth in [G.L. c.266, §§ 126A and 126B]. This section shall not apply to a parent who, as a result of a decree of any court of competent jurisdiction, does not have custody of such child at the time of the commission of the tort. Recovery under this section shall be limited to the amount of proved loss or damage but in no event shall it exceed five thousand dollars."

The plaintiff brought an action under the statute in the District Court against the defendants, alleging that the defendants, as the "parents" of Christopher Rule, a juvenile, were responsible for damages because of Rule's participation with two other juveniles in an arson that destroyed a building owned by the plaintiff. At the time of the incident, the defendants were the foster parents of Rule, who resided with them under the foster care program administered by the Department of Social Services (department). The defendants filed a "Motion to Dismiss and/or for Summary Judgment," on the ground the G.L. c. 231, § 85G, did not apply to foster parents. A judge in the District Court allowed the motion. The Appellate Division of the District Court affirmed the judge's decision and ordered the plaintiff's appeal dismissed. The plaintiff then took an appeal to the Appeals Court, and we transferred her appeal to this court on our own motion. We affirm the order of the Appellate Division.

It is undisputed that, at the time of the arson, the defendants were foster parents of Rule under a contractual agreement with the department. The dispositive question is whether the word "parents" in G.L. c. 231, § 85G, includes foster parents. In deciding that question, we keep certain principles in mind. Since G.L. c. 231, § 85G, derogates from the common law, it therefore is to be strictly construed, *Falmouth Ob-Gyn Assocs., Inc. v. Abisla,* 417 Mass. 176, 179, 629 N.E.2d 291 (1994), and a court "will not presume that the Legislature intended . . . a radical change in the common law without a clear expression of such intent." *Commercial Wharf E. Condominium Ass'n v. Waterfront Parking Corp.,* 407 Mass. 123, 129, 5521 N.E.2d 66 (1990), S.C., 412 Mass. 309, 588 N.E.2d 675 (1992). We consider such a statute in the light of the common law that it superceded, in an attempt to discern the meaning of the term "parents."

At common law, in the absence of an agency relationship, a parent was not vicariously liable for the tort of a child unless the parent directed, encouraged, or ratified the child's conduct. W.P. PROSSER & R.E. KEETON, TORTS § 123, at 913-914 (5th ed. 1984). In the Commonwealth, parents also were held liable for a child's intentional acts when the parent knew or should have known of the child's propensity for the type of harmful conduct with which the child was charged but failed to take reasonable corrective measures. *See DePasquale v. Dello Russo*, 349 Mass. 655, 658, 212 N.E.2d 237 (1965), and cases cited. Absent evidence of such a "dangerous tendency," however, liability was not imposed. *Id.* at 659, 212 N.E.2d 237, and cases cited (declining to "expose[] parents to liability for the torts of their children solely because of their parenthood"). *See Smith v. Jordan,* 211 Mass. 269, 270, 97 N.E. 761 (1912) ("A father is not liable for the torts of his minor son, simply because of paternity"). Thus, under the common law before the enactment of G.L. c 231, § 85G, a parent could not be held vicariously liable for the intentional acts of his child solely on the basis of his or her status as a parent.

In enacting G.L. c. 231, § 85G, however, the Legislature changed this common law rule and imposed strict liability on the parent for the intentional acts of his or her child. This was a radical change in the common law. We therefore construe the term "Parent" narrowly, and apply its ordinary meaning, "unless there is something in the statute indicating [it] should have a different significance." *Meunier's Case,* 319 Mas. 421, 423, 66 N.E.2d 198 (1946)

The ordinary meaning of the word parent is "[t]he lawful father or the mother of a person." BLACK'S LAW DICTIONARY 1269 (4th ed. 1951).[4] There is nothing in G.L.c. 231, § 85G, to indicate that the word should have a different or supplemental meaning. The ordinary meaning of the term "parent" does not include individuals, such as foster parents, who are not the lawful parents of the child, but merely act in a parental capacity because of a temporary contractual agreement with the State; the relationship between parent and child is not contractual, it is familial. . . .

. . . The [statute] requires both parentage and custody as prerequisites for the imposition of strict liability. The evolution of the statute, from one that established relatively broad liability to one that imposed liability only on the "[p]arents of an unemancipated child," suggests a legislative intent not to include within the ambit of the statute caretakers of children who may have responsibility for, or may stand in some way in loco parentis to, a minor.

We also note additional evidence of the Legislature's intent that the statute apply exclusively to a child's parents, as that term is commonly used. First, the bill that became the statute was entitled "An Act providing that parents shall be liable for damages resulting from certain acts of wilful misconduct by *their* minor children" (emphasis added). The title suggests that parents would be held liable for the wilful acts of their own children and not the children of others for whom they might be providing care. Second, the exemption from liability in the statute for a parent who does not have "custody" of the child

---

[4] The plaintiff argues for a more expansive definition of this term, citing BLACK'S LAW DICTIONARY 1114 (6th ed. 1990). Although the definition preferred by the plaintiff could be read to include individuals other than the mother and father of a child, nonetheless, the edition of BLACK'S LAW DICTIONARY cited in the text is the edition that would have been available to the Legislature at the time that the original statute was enacted. We conclude that the definition we apply above is the one intended by the Legislature.

"as a result of a decree of any court of competent jurisdiction" appears to address the issue of the possible liability of a noncustodial parent under a divorce judgment, a situation that has no relevance to foster parents. Third, in statutes enacted prior to the adoption of G.L. c. 231, § 85G, continue to reflect the Legislature's understanding that the ordinary meaning of "parent" is mother and father and that, when the word is intended to have a broader meaning it is usually appropriate to provide a definition. Thus, the term "parent" appears to have "'acquired a peculiar and appropriate meaning in law' [and] we are bound to give the word that meaning." *Levin v. Wall*, 290 Mass. 423, 425, 195 N.E. 790 (1935), quoting G.L. c. 4, § 6, Third.

Finally, we note that it does not seem proper to import into the responsibilities of foster parents an obligation of liability for wilful misconduct by foster children given over to their care. There exists a chronic shortage of families willing to provide foster care. Holding foster parents liable under G.L. c. 231, § 85G, would have a chilling effect on the willingness of families to open their homes to children in need of care and would make it considerably more difficult for the department to provide appropriate, non-institutionalized care for children whose natural parents cannot provide adequately for them. We doubt that the legislature intended a result that is so clearly contrary to the public policy supporting the needs of children. Further, if G.L. c. 231, § 85G, seeks to hold parents responsible if they fail adequately to supervise their children, the statute's interests would not be substantially advanced by extending liability to foster parents.[10]

---

[10] In an opinion to the State Secretary of Employment and Social Services, the Attorney General of Maryland concluded that foster parents should not be liable for the wrongful acts of foster children. In the course of the opinion, the Attorney General stated the following, which has pertinence to the interpretation we place on G.L. c. 231, § 85G:

> [W]hile it may be that, as against innocent third parties, persons who bear and raise a child should carry the financial burden of that child's wrongdoing, it is exceedingly more difficult to reach the same result when weighing the relative innocence of injured third parties against that of persons who, at the request of their government and without profit, are temporarily providing a home for an unrelated child. Under such circumstances the relative equities do not necessarily weigh in favor of the injured party. Moreover, because foster parents may not share the relatively unfettered freedom which natural and adoptive parents enjoy over their own children, and since a foster child's tortious behavior may well stem from the very problems which caused him to be placed in foster care in the first instance, the deterrent effect of such legislation is arguably misdirected at foster parents (footnote omitted).

59 Annual Report and Official Opinions of the Attorney General of Maryland 356, 361-362) (Mar. 5, 1974).

Chapter 13
Medical and Psychological Issues

This chapter deals with the intersection of law, medicine and psychology. Courts have traditionally felt comfortable putting medical evidence in front of a jury. The courts have been uneasy, however, with the aura of infallibility of evidence derived from a new or novel scientific technique. To assure the reliability of scientific evidence, the courts traditionally have turned to the rule of *Frye v. United States,* 293 F. 1013 (D.C. Cir. 1923), which requires the process, system or theory upon which evidence is based to be generally accepted in the field in which it belongs. Most of the subjects of expert witness testimony (because they are not considered "scientific evidence") are unaffected by the foundation requirements of *Frye*. With the enactment of the Federal Rules of Evidence in 1975 and the state codification of evidence law, many courts began to apply the more flexible test of the Federal Rules to what the courts labeled scientific evidence. Instead of general acceptance in the scientific community, established by a nose-counting of experts, courts determined reliability by analyzing (1) whether the expert witness is qualified under Rule 702; (2) whether the evidence is relevant under Rule 401; (3) whether the expert's opinion will assist the fact-finder, a "helpfulness" test under Rule 702; (4) whether the expert's opinion is properly based under Rule 703; and (5) whether the probative value of the evidence is substantially outweighed by the trial concerns of Rule 403, e.g., undue prejudice, confusion of the issues or misleading the jury. This departure from the *Frye* test by some courts meant that there was no separate rule for scientific evidence; rather the trial court, in the exercise of discretion, would analyze all expert testimony under the same set of evidence rules.

With the proliferation of non-traditional, "soft," psychological evidence came confusion for the courts, which were accustomed to applying the *Frye* test to theories and techniques derived from "hard science." Some courts which encountered psychological profile or syndrome evidence required a foundation for scientific evidence while other courts did not. In *Daubert v. Merrell Dow Pharmaceuticals, Inc.*, 509 U.S. 579

(1993), the Court held that the Federal Rules of Evidence, not *Frye*, provide the standard for admitting scientific testimony in a federal trial. Under *Daubert,* when faced with a proffer of expert testimony under Rule 702 of the Federal Rules of Evidence, the trial court, pursuant to Rule 104(a), must make a preliminary assessment of whether the testimony's underlying reasoning or methodology is scientifically valid and properly can be applied to the facts at issue. The court's preliminary considerations include whether the theory or technique (1) can be (and has been) tested; (2) is subject to peer review and publication; (3) has a known or potential error rate; (4) is subject to existing and maintained standards controlling operation; and (5) has attracted widespread acceptance within the relevant scientific community. The inquiry under *Daubert* is flexible, focusing solely on the scientific principles and methodology, not the conclusions generated, and the court should be mindful of other evidence rules. On remand in *Daubert v. Merrell Dow Pharmaceuticals, Inc.,* 43 F.3d 1311 (9th Cir. 1995), the court held that to determine whether the expert's proposed testimony reflects scientific knowledge, there must be a showing that the expert will testify about research conducted independently of the litigation or that the research has been subjected to peer review. In *Kumho Tire Co. v. Carmichael*, 526 U.S. 137 (1999), the Court held that the federal trial court's gatekeeper role under Role 702, as interpreted by *Daubert*, to ensure that expert testimony is both relevant and reliable, applies not just to testimony based on scientific knowledge, but also to testimony based on "technical" and "other specialized knowledge." Many states have adopted the *Daubert-Kumho* approach to expert evidence while some jurisdictions have retained the *Frye* general acceptance test. As you read the cases in this chapter, consider the standard applied by the court to the medical and psychological evidence presented. How would the evidence fare if another test for admissibility were applied?

A. Medical Issues

1. Maternal Deprivation Syndrome (Failure to Thrive)

In re Riffe

382 N.W.2d 842 (Mich. Ct. App. 1985)

CYNAR, Judge.

Respondent Shirley Riffe appeals as of right from the probate court's order terminating her parental rights in her two minor sons. . . . Respondent Charles L. Riffe has not appealed the order terminating his parental rights. We affirm.

Respondents are the parents of two boys, David Allan Riffe, born in 1983, and Charles L. Riffe, Jr., born in 1982. . . . On August 24, 1984, a petition was filed alleging that the probate court should exercise jurisdiction over both of the minor children of the parties, Charles, Jr., and David, for the following reasons:

> "A. On 05-18-84 David Alan Riffe was diagnosed a 'failure to thrive' child.
> "B. Said parents failed to bring David in for his scheduled doctor's appointment on 06-04-84 thereby jeopardizing his health and well-being and also failed to reschedule another appointment with the doctor.
> "C. David's present height and weight measurements are below the chart for normal development.
> "D. David's weight has severely dropped.
> "E. On 08-24-84 Charles had a severe urine burn in which both the penis and testicles were red.
> "F. On 05-25-80, a petition was filed in Saginaw County Probate Court by Kathryn Morley, alleging that Rosalie Marie McKinnon, said child of Shirley Riffe, was the victim of neglect and on 7-16-80 Rosalie Marie McKinnon was adjudicated a temporary ward of the Court under neglect jurisdiction and not returned to the care of the mother."

A temporary order of care was entered for David on September 5, 1984, and he was placed in foster care. . . . An order of temporary care was entered on October 8, 1984, placing Charles, Jr., in the care and custody of the Saginaw Child Receiving Home and he too was eventually placed in foster care.

* * *

The hearing [took place on] January 22, 1985. . . . As a preliminary matter, counsel for respondent Shirley Riffe moved to strike allegation (F) . . . which alleged that a daughter of Shirley Riffe, Rosalie Marie McKinnon, had been made a temporary ward of the court on July 16, 1980, under neglect jurisdiction and had not been returned to the care of her mother. The trial court ruled that allegations of prior neglect of other children of a parent are properly considered by a trial court in neglect cases. The court then proceeded with the adjudicative phase of the juvenile hearing.

Respondent Charles Riffe admitted allegations (A) through (F). . . . However, as respondent Shirley Riffe continued to contest the truth of the allegations, several witnesses were called.

Dr. David Booth testified that David, diagnosed as a failure-to-thrive child, had been scheduled for an office visit with him on June 4, 1984, but the appointment had not been kept. When he finally saw 10-month-old David on August 13, 1984, his height and weight were below the 5th percentile and he had received none of the appropriate immunizations normally administered to children. From August 13 to September 19, 1984, David was resident of the child receiving home. Dr. Booth saw David again on September 19, 1984. During the intervening period, David had gained two pounds, 10 ounces, and his weight was at or slightly above the 5th percentile and his height slightly below that percentile. When last seen by Dr. Booth on January 17, 1985, David's weight had increased to the 10th percentile and his height to the 25th percentile. The increases indicated to Dr. Booth that originally David's growth was not within the normal growth range for David, and that since his placement in a more nurturing environment of a foster home he had done extraordinarily well. Dr. Booth concluded that David's failure to thrive was the result of a poor home situation and that a combination of emotional and physical neglect had been responsible for David's failure to thrive.

* * *

Marilyn Schreiner, an employee at Mid-Michigan Child Care Center at the First Congregational Church, testified that David came to the center on July 23, 1984. At that time he was 14 months of age. He attended the center for less than a month, only once or twice each week. However, he was so dirty when he first arrived that she bathed him. On July 23, she sent a new bottle home for him since the one he had brought was "black" and the nipple was wrapped with hair, and "there was green slime all over the nipple." She occasionally saw Charles, Jr., who was kept cleaner than David. On August 24, 1984, she observed that David's genital area was covered with a urine burn "like he had been in a Pamper maybe all weekend because he was so raw."

Respondent Shirley Riffe testified that she regularly fed David three meals a day and that she never beat him. However, she objected to the way respondent Charles Riffe disciplined Charles, Jr., although she was afraid to do anything about it for fear he would hit her and place her in the hospital as he had done in the past. Neither of the parties worked, and their daily routine was to split up the care of the children, respondent Charles Riffe being primarily responsible for the care of Charles, Jr., and respondent Shirley Riffe being primarily responsible for the care of David. Respondent Shirley Riffe testified that the responsibility was split up so that respondent Charles Riffe had more responsibility for the care of Charles, Jr., because taking care of two children was too much for her to handle and because she was trying to learn how to care for the younger child.

* * *

Respondent Charles Riffe . . . testified that . . . [h]e and respondent Shirley Riffe had decided to divide the responsibility of the children between themselves because they might get divorced. He claimed that respondent Shirley Riffe did not regularly feed David three meals a day. He also indicated that the children would be better off if they were adopted.

After reviewing the testimony, the probate judge determined that the DSS had met its burden of proving each allegation, as amended, by a preponderance of the evidence, and that the allegations were sufficient to bring both David and Charles, Jr., within the jurisdiction of the probate court.

The dispositional phase of the proceeding was conducted February 5, 1985, approximately two weeks after the adjudicative phase. Laura Patterson, a psychologist with Saginaw Psychological Services, testified that respondent Shirley Riffe refused to submit to psychological testing although it had been scheduled on two separate occasions. . . . .

John Szott, a protective services case worker for the DSS, testified that he initiated the investigation of the Riffe children after being informed by Dr. Booth's office that David Riffe had been diagnosed as a failure-to-thrive child. He recommended that both children be made permanent wards of the court and be placed for adoption. . . . He stated six reasons for recommending that the children be made permanent wards of the probate court: (1) Over the course of his involvement with both Charles and Shirley Riffe, there was little effort on either parent's part to improve their situation or to make an attempt to regain custody of the children. (2) Visitations by the parents were very irregular since August; visitations were scheduled, but not kept, and there were long periods of time with no visitation. (3) Both parents have limited mental functioning. (4) The parents have failed to cooperate in submitting to a psychological evaluation so as to better assist the DSS. (5) The general level of both parents' parenting skills is poor. (6) Respondent father has indicated that he intends to terminate his rights in both children and place them for adoption. . . .

Szott indicated he had changed his recommendation from temporary to permanent wardship because of the long pattern of neglect, because Shirley Riffe had made very little effort to improve her situation in spite of her recent signing up for parenting classes, and because Shirley Riffe's visitation with the children was very irregular. He also indicated that the children were young and at an easily-adoptable age and that he felt that adoption was in the children's best interest. . . . The department had attempted to have both respondents evaluated and had attempted to get both parents to attend parenting classes, but to no avail. The home respondents lived in at the time the children were made temporary wards was dirty, cluttered, and disorganized. . . .

* * *

The court concluded in a lengthy opinion that there was a sufficient basis by clear and convincing evidence to support the termination of the respondents' parental rights and that the best interests of the children warrant and mandate termination.

* * *

The respondent . . . contends that the petitioner did not prove by clear and convincing evidence that the termination of parental rights was warranted. We disagree.

* * *

The statute pursuant to which the trial court terminated respondent's parental rights is M.C.L. § 712A.19a(e); M.S.A. § 27.3178(598.190a)(e). Section 19a(e) reads in relevant part as follows:

> "Sec. 19a. Where a child remains in foster care in the temporary custody of the court following the initial hearing provided by section 19, the court may make a final determination and order placing the child in the permanent custody of the court, if it finds any of the following:
>
> * * *
>
> "(e) The parent or guardian is unable to provide a fit home for the child by reason of neglect."

The state bears the burden of proving by clear and convincing evidence that termination of parental rights is warranted.

Although the amount of neglect necessary to justify termination of parental rights under section 19a(e) is not capable of precise or exact definition, the entry of an order taking permanent custody due to neglect must be based upon testimony of such a nature as to establish or seriously threaten neglect of the child for the long run future. The proper standard is whether the parent has been shown by clear and convincing evidence to be unfit and unable to become fit within a reasonable period of time.

After reviewing the record of the instant proceeding, we are not left with a definite and firm conviction that the trial court made a mistake in terminating the parental rights of respondent Shirley Riffe. The minor child David was removed form the home after being diagnosed by a physician as being a failure-to-thrive child. The minor child Charles, Jr., was removed from the home as a result of a police call to the family home wherein his father and mother's boyfriend were engaged in a fistfight over the father's disciplining of the child. At that point Charles, Jr., was bruised and dirty and was removed from the home.

* * *

When difficulties arose with the care of Charles, Jr., and David, the DSS provided respondent with the opportunity to submit to psychological testing and counseling. Respondent Shirley Riffe refused to submit to psychological testing and signed up for parenting classes only a week before the final dispositional hearing was scheduled. When asked how long she felt she should attend parenting classes in order to become a fit parent, she responded it would take her "about two weeks." She also testified that the parties had split up the care of the children partially because taking care of two children was too much for her to handle.

The trial court found that the mother has a long history of neglectful behavior toward her children and that she has done very little to improve her parenting skills. We believe that the state met its burden of proving by clear and convincing evidence that the children were subjects of continuing neglect and that there is every indication that the pattern of neglectful behavior will continue and will not be remedied at any time in the foreseeable future. Therefore, the decision of the trial court that the children must be removed from the parental home and that respondent's parental rights be terminated permanently is not clearly erroneous.

Affirmed.

Notes

1. A failure-to-thrive (FTT) child is one "who has sometime in the first three years of life suffered a marked retardation or cessation of growth." Ruth C. Kempe, *The Infant with Failure-to-Thrive, in* THE BATTERED CHILD 163, 164 (C. Henry Kempe & Ray E. Helfer eds., 3d ed. 1980). This slowdown in growth is generally identified by a decline in the child's weight to the third percentile or below on a standard growth chart. *See* Donald T. Kramer, LEGAL RIGHTS OF CHILDREN § 16.29 (2d ed. 1994); *Commonwealth v. Robinson*, 565 N.E.2d 1229, 1231 n.1 (Mass. App. Ct. 1991). In finding FTT, courts often consider not only the child's actual percentile ranking but also the ranking in relation to the child's weight at birth. *See, e.g., In re M.H.*, 745 S.W.2d 424, 428 (Tex. Ct. App. 1988) (FTT found where child's weight dropped from seventy-fifth percentile at birth to fifth percentile in one month). Although a significant decline in weight or cessation of growth may signal FTT, it is especially dangerous to an infant at or below the third percentile ranking. A decline in weight to this level may indicate a life-threatening situation if left untreated. *See* Kempe, *supra*, at 164; *Commonwealth v. Robinson, supra*. While a retardation or cessation of weight gain is often the first indicator of a failure to thrive, FTT may also be diagnosed by a decline on standard growth charts of height or head circumference. These indicators are often not as readily apparent as a decline in weight gain, but they tend to indicate a more serious, longer-term growth failure. *See* Kempe, *supra*, at 164. This may point to more serious problems, especially during the child's first year of life. An infant's head should grow rapidly during the first year of life, as the brain increases in size. If the child's head circumference does not increase, brain damage and mental retardation may result. *See id.*

2. FTT may be caused by organic problems, such as genetic defects or disease, by non-organic sources, such as parental neglect, or by a combination of the two. *See* Kempe, *supra* Note 1, at 164. Parental neglect or deprivation, also referred to as "maternal deprivation syndrome," is the most common cause of FTT. *See, e.g., In re Anjelica A.*, 1997 WL 596617, at *5 (Conn. Super. Ct. Sept. 17, 1997); Kramer, *supra*, Note 1. Other causes of non-organic FTT include: lack of knowledge regarding proper parenting skills (e.g., parents who do not know how to properly prepare baby formula; parents who do not know how often to feed an infant); incapacity of one or both parents due to mental retardation, low intelligence, youth, or mental illness (*see, e.g., In re S.B.*, 724 P.2d 168, 169 (Mont. 1986)); lack of proper instruction regarding breastfeeding techniques; overfeeding, which may lead to a lack of interest in food by the child; and "feeding battles" between parent and child when the child begins to attempt to self-feed. *See* Kempe, *supra* Note 1, at 166-68.

As discussed in *Riffe,* non-organic failure-to-thrive is generally evidenced by the child's rapid growth once she has been removed from her home and either hospitalized or placed in foster care. *See also* Kramer, *supra,* Note 1. Courts generally accept an expert witness' diagnosis of FTT based on a finding that the child thrives outside of the home. This is important, as it is nearly impossible, and would be extremely expensive, time-consuming, and invasive to rule out all possible organic causes of failure-to-thrive. *See* Kempe, *supra*, Note 1, at 165.

3. There are several physical signs which, if observed by a physician, will generally lead to a diagnosis of non-organic FTT. These include a pale, weak, emaciated look, especially where the child lacks significant subcutaneous fat and has poor muscle tone. A child suffering from FTT may show retarded development of gross motor skills and social interaction. *See* Kempe, *supra,* Note 1, at 168. The child may also present evidence of an extreme lack of care and attention from the parents. For example, the child may lack age-appropriate stranger anxiety, may smile at anyone who approaches him, and may fail to react to a separation from his parents. *See id.*

If FTT is detected early in a child receiving regular medical attention, it may be possible to treat the child without resorting to removal from the home. The parents generally need to be educated regarding the proper care and feeding of the infant, and the child's development must be closely monitored. *See id*. at 169. Early detection, however, is the exception rather than the rule. Most failure-to-thrive infants are not seen by medical professionals until they are seriously malnourished and require hospitalization. The parents in these more serious cases are often encouraged to participate in the child's care. This offers the hospital staff the opportunity to observe the parents' interaction with the child, including feeding, and may, therefore, allow healthcare professionals a chance to correct the situation which led to FTT. *See id*. at 169-70.

4. According to research collected by Kempe et al., there is a high rate of recurrence of failure-to-thrive after the child is returned to the home. *See* Kempe, *supra*, Note 1, at 176. FTT infants are also often subject to other forms of abuse, including physical abuse and fatal starvation. Close monitoring of the parents of an FTT child is therefore necessary. *See id.* at 178. Failure-to-thrive is most common in children under the age of three. Older children who are neglected can often forage for food and thus do not experience the acute malnourishment seen in infants. However, a less-common form of FTT, known as "psychosocial dwarfism," has been reported in children between the ages of three and twelve and may lead to charges of parental neglect. *Id.; see also In re Pernishek*, 408 A.2d 872, 877 (Pa. Super. Ct. 1979).

Problem

Child welfare officials remove a six-month-old infant from the mother's home following a neighbor's report that the child was being bottle fed Kool-Aid instead of formula. No formula was found in the home. Upon arrival at the hospital, Sara weighed fifteen pounds, and her condition was described as flaccid and non-responsive. During her ten-day stay in the hospital, Sara's body weight increased to seventeen pounds. Sara's mother has enrolled in the WIC program and has obtained formula to feed Sara. Should Sara now be returned to her mother's care? Does the court have sufficient information to make this determination? What other factors should be considered? What is the mother's lawyer's role in this case?

2. Shaken Baby Syndrome

People v. Ripley

685 N.E.2d 362 (Ill. App. Ct. 1997)

Justice MCCUSKEY delivered the opinion of the court:

Following a jury trial, the defendant, William P. Riley, was convicted of aggravated battery of a child. The defendant was sentenced to a term of 10 years' imprisonment.

On Appeal, the defendant argues: (1) he was not proved guilty beyond a reasonable doubt; and (2) the sentence imposed was excessive. Following our careful review of the record, we affirm.

On May 30, 1995, paramedics received a call that a child was not breathing. They went to the defendant's home and found the victim, the defendant's 15-month-old foster son, in a nonresponsive state. The victim was transported to Trinity East Medical Center. He was found to be unresponsive, very pale, flaccid and had difficulty breathing on his own. He was transferred to St. Francis Hospital in Peoria by helicopter and was treated by Dr. Robert Paul Cruse, a pediatric neurologist.

Dr. Cruse testified that he examined the victim's eyes and saw hemorrhages of fresh blood in the back of both eyes. The victim underwent a computerized axial tomography (CAT) scan and magnetic resonance imaging (MRI). Both tests revealed bleeding and areas of hemorrhage in the brain. They also showed some swelling of the brain. Dr. Cruse concluded that the bleeding occurred within three to four days of the tests and that the injuries were caused by an acceleration-deceleration trauma, or shaken baby syndrome. Dr. Cruse testified that a violent force is necessary to cause the type of injuries found in the victim. He said that this type of injury requires much more violent force than the force which would cause a typical whiplash injury in a car accident. As a result of the violent force, the veins in the victim's brain tore. The doctor said that this is called a shear injury. Dr. Cruse specifically stated that bouncing or jarring a child does not cause this type of injury. Violent and rapid force of acceleration-deceleration, or shaking, is required to cause a shear injury.

Dr. Cruse testified that brain swelling caused by violent shaking usually peaks in the third or fourth day following the injury. Because this type of injury is like a "mega concussion," vomiting results and is a common symptom. Seizures are also common from this type of trauma. Dr. Cruse said that the victim had suffered damage to the motor area of the brain which controlled the right side of his body. Because of this damage, the victim has persistent paralysis to his right side and delayed language development.

The defendant initially told the police that the victim had fallen on May 27, 1995. When told by the police that the victim's injuries had been caused by a violent shaking, the defendant admitted shaking the victim in the shower on May 27. The defendant said that he shook the victim a little bit to get him to settle down.

At trial, the defendant's wife, Mary Ripley, testified that she and the defendant obtained custody of the victim in November 1994. They were in the process of adopting the victim before he was injured. She testified that neither she nor the defendant had any experience in taking care of young children. She stated that the defendant gave the victim a shower on the evening of May 27, 1995. She said she heard the defendant tell the victim to settle down. After the shower, the victim acted like he was tired and would not stand up. His eyes looked bugged out and bloodshot. The next morning, the victim went with them to church and acted normally. However, during the next few days the victim had frequent episodes of vomiting. He also had a fever the afternoon of May 29, 1995. On the morning of May 30, 1995, the victim had a seizure and appeared to stop breathing. The defendant called 911, and Mary started cardiopulmonary resuscitation (CPR).

The defendant, who was 39 years old and weighted 337 pounds, testified that the victim started to fall in the shower the evening of May 27, 1995. He grabbed the victim and yanked him back. The victim's head snapped back, and the defendant told him to settle down or he was going to get hurt. During cross-examination, the defendant admitted that he shook the victim in the shower. The defendant said he was not angry but was trying to settle the victim down. He demonstrated for the jury that he did not shake the victim very hard. The defendant testified he did not intend to hurt the victim and was not aware that shaking could cause an injury to a child.

The State presented a rebuttal witness who testified she talked to Mary on the telephone the morning of May 27, 1995. Mary stated that she and the defendant put the victim in the shower as a form of punishment when he was not behaving.

The jury found the defendant guilty of aggravated battery of a child. The presentence investigation report indicated the defendant had no prior criminal history. . . . The report also stated that the victim was now 2½ years old. The victim was, at the time of the report, just starting to be able to sit by himself and could walk with assistance. The report said the victim still suffered from paralysis of his right side and had borderline/mild mental retardation.

At the sentencing hearing the defendant presented 11 mitigation witnesses. The witnesses testified . . . that the defendant was kind, gentle, understanding and had never been a violent person. The defendant exercised his right of allocution. He said he was very sorry about the injuries to the victim and stated that he never meant for anything like that to happen.

The trial judge stated that he had considered all the evidence presented in mitigation. However, he concluded from the evidence that a sentence of probation would depreciate the seriousness of the defendant's conduct. The judge then imposed a sentence of 10 years imprisonment. The defendant filed a motion to reconsider the sentence. The trial court denied the defendant's motion. This timely appeal followed.

The defendant initially argues that the State did not prove he intentionally or knowingly caused great bodily harm to the victim. The defendant notes that he consistently said he did not intend to hurt the victim. The defendant claims the evidence failed to show he was aware that shaking the victim would cause great bodily harm.

* * *

In reaching our conclusion, we agree with the reasoning of *Rader* and *People v. Renteria*, 232 Ill. App.3d 409, 173 Ill. Dec. 740, 597 N.E.2d 714 (1992). In *Rader*, the defendant testified that he did not intend to harm the victim. In *Renteria*, the defendant testified that he shook the victim only to get him to start breathing. However, in both cases, the evidence showed that the victim's injuries were severe and permanent, were consistent with shaken baby syndrome and could only have been caused by severe and repetitive shaking. *Rader*, 272 Ill. App. 3d at 804-05, 209 Ill. Dec. at 336, 651 N.E.2d at 264; *Renteria*, 232 Ill. App. 3d at 417, 173 Ill. Dec. at 745, 597 N.E.2d at 719. In addition, the severe injuries were inconsistent with the defendant's version of what happened. Based on those facts, the court in *Rader* found that a rational trier of fact could infer that the defendant *must have known* about the substantial probability of causing injury to the victim because of the severity of the violence necessary to cause the injuries. *Rader*, 272 Ill.App.3d at 805, 209 Ill. Dec. at 336, 651 N.E.2d at 264. Both courts found the evidence was sufficient for a rational trier of fact to conclude, beyond a reasonable doubt, that the defendant acted intentionally or knowingly in causing great bodily harm to the victim.

[I]n the instant case, the evidence showed that the victim's injuries were severe and permanent, were consistent with shaken baby syndrome and could only have been caused by violent and repetitive shaking. Moreover, the severe injuries to the victim were completely inconsistent with the defendant's testimony. Under these circumstances, we hold that a rational trier of fact could properly conclude that the defendant acted intentionally or knowingly in causing great bodily harm to the victim. Accordingly, we affirm the defendant's conviction of aggravated battery of a child.

* * *

In this case, we find from the record that the trial court carefully considered the relevant mitigating and aggravating factors. The defendant claims that the trial court failed to give the mitigating factors enough weight. However, it is the province of the trial court to balance these factors and make a reasoned judgment as to the appropriate punishment to be imposed. Based on our review, we find the trial court did not abuse its discretion when it balanced the relevant factors and imposed a sentence of 10 years' imprisonment.

The defendant also claims that the trial court improperly considered the defendant's intent as an aggravating factor. We disagree. At sentencing, the defendant addressed the court and insisted that he did not mean to hurt the victim. In response, the trial judge said that, based on his review of the evidence, the defendant did intend to shake the victim and therefore intended the natural consequence of that act, severe and permanent injuries to the victim.

* * *

For the reasons indicated, the judgment of the circuit court of Rock Island County is affirmed.

Notes

1. Shaken baby syndrome (SBS) typically involves children under the age of fifteen months with a median age of three months. *See* Alan Mayor Sokobin, *Shaken Baby Syndrome: A Comparative Study: Anglo-American Law and Jewish Law—Legal, Moral, and Ethical Issues,* 29 U. TOL. L. REV. 513 (1998). A 1995 U.S. Department of Health and Human Services study states that forty-one percent of children who suffer from SBS are under twelve months of age. *See* Joseph D. Hatina, *Shaken Baby Syndrome: Who Are the True Experts?,* 46 CLEV. ST. L. REV. 557, 560 (1998). The type of force required for a diagnosis of SBS was described as follows in Jody Tabnor Thayer, *The Latest Evidence for Shaken Baby Syndrome: What Defense Lawyers and Prosecutors Need to Know*, 12 CRIM. JUST. 15 (1997):

> Many medical experts equate the force necessary to kill a child to the force of an automobile accident or a fall from an upper story window. As stated by the American Academy of Pediatrics: "[T]he act of shaking/slamming is so violent that competent individuals observing the shaking would recognize it as dangerous." Short distance falls rarely cause skull fractures . . . and differ in type from fractures seen in shaken babies. These forces require the strength of an adult; it is not plausible to explain massive intracranial injury as inflicted by another young child or as the product of normal activity such as bouncing children playfully.

The symptoms of SBS differ depending on the severity of force used. For less severe shaking episodes, a child may suffer a loss of consciousness, seizures, irritability, inability to feed, and vomiting. *See* Robert H. Kirschener, *The Pathology of Child Abuse, in* THE BATTERED CHILD 248, 273 (Mary Edna Helfer, et al. eds., 5th ed. 1997). For more serious shaking episodes, SBS children may suffer from retinal hemorrhage, brain swelling, and subdural hemorrhage. *See id.* at 272. For additional symptoms presented by a SBS child, see CAL. HEALTH AND SAFETY CODE § 24520(b) (West Supp. 2001); IND. CODE ANN. § 16-41-40-2 (Lexis Supp. 2000); Hatina, *supra,* at 561-66. For an in depth medical explanation of SBS and its consequences, see Kirschener, *supra*, at 271-75.

2. Some states have statutes that specifically address the problem of SBS. California recognizes SBS as a "medically serious, sometimes fatal, matter affecting newborns and very young children. Shaking an infant or child in anger is particularly dangerous." CAL. HEALTH & SAFETY CODE § 24520(a) (West Supp. 2001). Many adults do not understand the dangers of SBS (*see* CAL. HEALTH & SAFETY CODE § 24520(c) (West Supp. 2001) and thus several states have established programs to educate adults about SBS. *See, e.g.,* CAL. HEALTH & SAFETY CODE § 24522 (West Supp. 2001); IND. CODE ANN. § 16-41-40-5 (Lexis Supp. 2000); WASH. REV. CODE ANN. § 43.121.140 (West Supp. 2001). The following is an example of an educational program created by statute:

Tennessee Code Annotated
§ 68-143-103 (Lexis Supp. 2000)

§ 68-143-103. Duties of departments of health and human services.

(a) The departments of health and human services shall jointly develop information and instructional materials . . . for distribution, free of charge, to health care facilities, midwives, and child care agencies. The information and instructional materials provided pursuant to this section shall focus upon the serious nature of the risk to infants and young children presented by shaken baby syndrome. . . .

(b) The department of health shall provide the information and instructional materials free of charge to health care facilities and nurse midwives. Such information and instructional materials shall be provided free of charge by each health care facility to parents or guardians of each newborn, upon discharge from the health care facility. . . .

* * *

Texas requires that licensed day care centers that provide care for children under two years must receive special training to recognize and prevent SBS. *See* TEX. HUM. RES. CODE ANN. § 42-0421 (West 2001).

Questions

1. Assume that a parent is found guilty of committing battery on a child. The child's condition is diagnosed as SBS. What role should a parent's intent play in the court's placement decision? How should the court weigh a parent's ignorance of SBS?

2. How do statutes, such as those mentioned in Note 2, *supra*, address the problem of parental ignorance of SBS? What additional steps might states take to further educate the public and prevent SBS? Is there a role for courts and lawyers?

3. The Cocaine Baby

In re Valerie D.

613 A.2d 748 (Conn. 1992)

* * *

BORDEN, Associate Justice.

The dispositive issues in this appeal are whether: (1) General Statutes § 45a-717(f)(2)[1] permits the termination of the parental rights of the mother of an infant based upon the mother's prenatal conduct of injecting cocaine; and (2) General Statutes § 45a-717(f)(3), as applied to the facts of this case, permits the termination of the same parental rights upon the basis of an absence of an ongoing parent-child relationship between the mother and the infant. The respondent mother appeals, upon our grant of certification, from the judgment of the trial court that granted the petition of the commissioner of children and youth services (petitioner) for termination of the respondent's parental rights with respect to her daughter, Valerie D. (child). The trial court judgment rested on two alternative bases: (1) certain prenatal conduct of the respondent, namely, intravenous injection of cocaine, caused "serious physical injury to [the] child" that constituted "acts of parental commission or omission sufficient for the termination of parental rights," within the meaning of § 45a-717(f)(e).

* * *

The child was born to the respondent on July 26, 1989, in Bristol Hospital. On August 1, 1989, while the child was still in the hospital, the petitioner filed in the Superior Court: (1) a petition for an order of temporary care and custody of the child, pursuant to General Statutes § 46b-129(b), [defining neglect], upon the basis of an affidavit of the child's pediatrician that the respondent's use of cocaine within hours prior to beginning labor put the child "in great risk of life-threatening medical complications" and that this conduct constituted "intentional and severe parental neglect"; (2) a petition for commitment of custody of the child to the petitioner, pursuant to § 46b-129(a) upon the basis that

---

[1] General Statutes § 45a-717, formerly § 45-61f, provides as follows: "TERMINATION OF PARENTAL RIGHTS, CONDUCT OF HEARING INVESTIGATION AND REPORT. GROUNDS FOR TERMINATION.

* * *

"(f) [T]he court may approve the petition terminating the parental rights . . . if it finds, upon clear and convincing evidence that the termination is in the best interest of the child and that . . . over an extended period of time which, except as provided in subsection (g) of this section, shall not be less than one year: (1) The child has been abandoned by the parent . . . ; or (2) the child has been denied, by reason of an act or acts of parental commission or omission, the care, guidance or control necessary for his physical, educational, moral or emotional well-being . . . ; or (3) there is no ongoing parent child relationship which is defined as the relationship that ordinarily develops as a result of a parent having met on a continuing, day-to-day basis the physical, emotional, moral and educational needs of the child. . . .

"(g) The court may waive the requirement that one year expire prior to the termination of parental rights if it finds from the totality of the circumstances surrounding the child that such a waiver is necessary to promote the best interest of the child. . . ."

the child was neglected, uncared for and abused; and (3) a coterminous petition for termination of the respondent's parental rights with respect to the child . . . upon the basis that, due to the respondent's use of cocaine throughout the pregnancy resulting in the child having been born "drug addicted" and "suffering from withdrawal," the child "had been denied by reason of act or acts of commission or omission, the care, guidance or control necessary for [her][physical, educational, moral or emotional well being," and that she had "sustained a nonaccidental or inadequately explained serious injury." . . . On October 4, 1989, the petitioner amended the petition to add, as grounds for termination of parental rights, abandonment and a lack of an ongoing parent-child relationship.

[On] March 28, 1990, the court rendered an oral decision from the bench granting the coterminous petitions. With respect to the petition for termination of parental rights, the court found proven by clear and convincing evidence that: (1) by the respondent's intravenous use of cocaine in the last stages of pregnancy, the child had been denied by reason of acts of parental commission or omission the care, guidance or control necessary for her physical, educational, moral or emotional well-being; and (2) as of the adjudication date of November 8, 1989, there was no ongoing parent-child relationship between the respondent and the child, and it would be detrimental to the child's best interest to allow further time for such a relationship to be established. [T]he court found by clear and convincing evidence that it was in the child's best interest to be placed forthwith in permanent adoption. Accordingly, the court terminated the respondent's parental rights and appointed the petitioner as the child's statutory parent for the purpose of placing her in adoption. On July 24, 1990, the trial court issued a written articulation of its oral decision.

The Appellate Court affirmed the judgment of the trial court. That court held that: (1) a judgment of "termination of parental rights can be supported solely by evidence of a mother's prenatal conduct"; and (2) there was sufficient evidence to support the trial court's findings that there was no ongoing parent-child relationship between the child and the respondent, and that it would be detrimental to the child's best interest to allow further time for the establishment of such a relationship. This appeal followed.

I

The respondent claims first that § 45a-717(f)(2), properly construed, does not permit the termination of parental rights based on the prenatal conduct of the mother. We agree.

The record disclosed the following facts pertinent to this claim. The respondent who was born August 4, 1969, began using drugs at age eleven. At age fifteen she met the child's father, John M., and at age sixteen she left school and home and began living with him. Thereafter, they both began injecting cocaine intravenously in 1987, and the respondent became pregnant with her first child, Amanda. When, during the fourth month of pregnancy, she disclosed her history of drug abuse to her physician, he warned her of its impact on her unborn child and gave her literature on the subject. She was able to discontinue the use of cocaine almost completely during the pregnancy, and Amanda was born, symptom free, on May 12, 1988. Three months later, however, she resumed using cocaine, by smoking and intravenous injection, two to five times per week

In October, 1988, the respondent became pregnant with Valerie, but did not visit her physician until March, 1989, when [sic] he again warned her of the problems that her substance abuse could cause to her unborn child. By this time, however, the respondent had become addicted cocaine and was unable to stop using it. Although the respondent informed the physician that she would continue prenatal care at the Bristol Hospital clinic because she had no medical insurance, her physician learned in July, when the respondent returned to him, that she had not gone to the clinic until June 5, 1989. The court further noted that, under normal circumstances, a pregnant woman should been seen monthly for the first twenty-eight weeks, and more frequently for a high risk pregnancy posed by a drug-abusing woman.

On June 19, 1989 John M.'s probation officer visited the home, where he observed marijuana and drug paraphernalia. Both parents were arrested. Amanda was taken to Bristol Hospital, and the parents were advised to place her in foster care while they entered treatment for their admitted cocaine addiction. A hospital social worker advised the respondent of the risks to a fetus from intravenous cocaine use. After the parents refused voluntary placement of Amanda and drug treatment for themselves, the petitioner filed a neglect petition regarding Amanda and secured an order of temporary custody in order to remove her from the hospital and place her in foster care.

On July 26, 1989, when the parents were scheduled for a continued hearing on the neglect petition regarding Amanda, they telephoned and informed the court that the respondent's water had broken, that she was about to deliver and that they were on their way to the hospital. Instead, at approximately 1 p.m., the respondent intravenously injected a quarter gram of cocaine and did not arrive at the hospital until approximately 9 p.m. The child was born approximately one hour later.

During the birth process, she had passed meconium;[13] this was the result of stress to the child from a precipitous delivery that resulted, in turn, from the respondent's injection of cocaine while she was leaking amniotic fluid and expecting to go into labor. In such a case, there's a risk that the child can aspirate the meconium, causing life-threatening respiratory problems. An aggressive suctioning procedure was used to guard against that risk, and it was found that the child had not aspirated any meconium.

At birth the child was pale, had poor muscle tone and required oxygen. While the child was in the hospital, cocaine metabolites were found in her urine, and she went through cocaine withdrawal. At times, she was extraordinarily jittery and shaky, had a piercing cry, was unable to make eye contact, and required special care, such as swaddling, vertical rocking and elimination of all stimuli.

The petitioner argues that "[a]s a result of the mother's intravenous injection of cocaine when on the verge of labor, the child was born into this world

---

13 Meconium is the stool of an unborn child.

under life-threatening circumstances." This argument is based on the testimony of the pediatrician that the passage of meconium prior to delivery posed a *risk* of aspiration that, had it occurred, would have caused life-threatening respiratory problems.

The petitioner also argues that "the child *was* seriously affected at birth by her mother's cocaine use." (Emphasis in original.) The following evidence forms the basis of this argument. The presence of the meconium, the child's respiratory distress, and the precipitous delivery were caused by the respondent's cocaine use. The child's heart rate had fallen just prior to delivery, and she was born cyanotic, required oxygen, and had depressed Apgar scores, an "evaluation of a newborn infant's physical status by assigning numerical values (0 to 2) to each of five criteria: heart rate, respiratory effort, muscle tone, response to stimulation, and skin color; a score of 20 indicates the best possible condition." Stedman's Medical Dictionary (24th Ed.). The child's urine indicated the presence of cocaine metabolities, and she went through withdrawal. Furthermore, there was evidence that cocaine restricts the blood vessels, and may interfere with mental development. There was also evidence that prenatal drug abuse may ultimately result in learning disability, central nervous system damage, lens deformities, hyperactivity, and an increased risk of sudden infant death syndrome.

* * *

Based upon this evidence, the trial court rendered an adjudication, as of November 8, 1989 . . . that the child had been denied "by acts of parental commission or omission the are, guidance or control necessary for physical, educational and emotional well-being." The court specifically found that there had been "'[n]onaccidental . . . serious physical injury to [the] child . . . constitut[ing] . . . acts of parental commission or omission sufficient for the termination of parental rights.'" *See* General Statutes § 45(a)-717(f)(2).

In support of this conclusion, the trial court reasoned: "Valerie suffered serious, life-threatening, physical injury at the instant of her birth because of her mother's intravenous injection of cocaine after beginning labor. This ground would apply without question to parents who, an instant after birth, injected cocaine into the bloodstream of a newborn. The injection of the drug into the bloodstream of a baby about to be born should have no different consequences." . . . (Emphasis in original.)

. . . Our statutes and caselaw make it crystal clear that the determination of the child's best interests comes into play only *after* statutory grounds for termination of parental rights have been established by clear and convincing evidence. . . .

. . . The question posed by the facts of this case is whether the legislature intended this language to contemplate termination of parental rights based upon prenatal conduct—even prenatal conduct committed shortly before the onset of labor—that results in harm to the child upon its birth.

Although the severance of the parent-child relationship may be required under some circumstances, the United States Supreme Court has repeatedly held that the interest of parents in their children is a fundamental constitutional right that undeniably warrants deference and, absent a powerful countervailing interest, protection. *Stanley v. Illinois,* 405 U.S. 645, 651, 92 S. Ct. 1208, 31 L. Ed. 2d 551 (1972); *see also, In re Juvenile Appeal (83-CD),* [*supra,* 295] (noting that it is both a fundamental right and the policy of this state to maintain the integrity of the family). Termination of parental rights does not follow automatically from parental conduct justifying the removal of custody. The fundamental liberty interest of natural parents in the care, custody, and management of their child does not evaporate simply because they have not been model parents or have lost temporary custody of their child to the State.

Thus, in construing § 45(a)-717(f)(3), which operates "in the delicate realm of parent-child relationships, courts should prefer that construction which minimizes state intervention. . . ." (Internal quotation marks omitted). *In re Juvenile Appeal (Anonymous) v. Commissioner of Children & Youth Services,* 177 Conn. 648, 662, 420 A.2d 875 (1979). In this realm, therefore, § 45a-707(f)(2) should be read with a "preference for nonintrusion" by the state. *Id.* Because of their "fundamental nature," statutes "authorizing state intrusion into the area of parental rights" require "the strictest level of judicial scrutiny." *In re Juvenile Appeal (84-BC),* 194 Conn. 252, 257 n.9, 479 A.2d 1204 (1984); *see also In re Juvenile Appeal (83-CD), supra,* 284 (courts must keep in mind constitutional limitations imposed on state when it undertakes coercive intervention in family affairs).

* * *

With this background in mind, we turn first to the language of the statute in order to determine whether the legislature intended it to encompass prenatal conduct. For purposes of § 48a-707 "'[p]arent' means a natural or adoptive parent." General Statutes § 46b-12. The ordinary usage of the term "parent," insofar as it applies to the female, suggests that, unless the context requires otherwise, it means "one [who] . . . brings forth offspring." Webster's Third New International Dictionary. Thus, in ordinary parlance, until the child in this case was born, or was "brought forth," the respondent was not her "parent" and the conduct of the respondent with respect to her was not "parental" conduct. Similarly, the definition of "child" as a person "under sixteen years of age" suggests a limitation on the applicability of that definition to a person who has been born, since that is the ordinary beginning point of one's "age." Thus, until the moment of birth, Valerie was not a "child" within the meaning of § 45a-717(f)(2) and, therefore, the "act . . . of parental commission" that took place before that moment cannot be considered to be parental conduct that "denied [her] . . . the care . . . necessary for [her] physical . . . well-being." *Cf. Burns v. Alcala,* 420 U.S. 575, 95 S. Ct. 1180, 43 L. Ed. 2d 469 (1975) (based on axiom that statutory words are to be given ordinary meaning absent persuasive reasons to contrary, "child" as used in § 406(a) of federal Social Security Act means individual already born, with existence separate from mother).

* * *

The established principles that govern construction of § 45a-717, however, require that it be read narrowly and strictly, and require further that, absent clear indication to the contrary from the legislature, it be read so as to apply only to postnatal parental conduct.

* * *

The petitioner argues, as did the trial court, that pursuant to § 45a-717(f)(2) "[t]he fact [that] the mother's behavior occurred prior to Valerie's birth does not relieve the mother of responsibility for the injuries her child suffered at birth. Focusing on Valerie, it is difficult to discern any distinction between administering cocaine to Valerie nine hours before her birth or nine hours after her birth. The consequences to Valerie are the same. *The precise time of the injury should not be legally significant; the real issue is the injuries that Valerie suffered. The statute requires the trial court to look back at the causes of the child's injury and, most importantly, to assess the risk of continued harm to the child."* (Emphasis added.) Although on the admittedly egregious facts of this case this argument has emotional appeal, we disagree with it as the appropriate reading of § 45a-717.

In this case, the respondent's prenatal conduct took place but several hours before the onset of labor. There is no principled way, however, to confine the language of § 45a-717(f)(2) to prenatal maternal conduct that takes place only a short time before delivery of the baby, as opposed to maternal conduct that takes place early in the pregnancy. Indeed, the petitioner's argument recognizes this, and would have us read § 45a-717(f)(2) so as to "look back" throughout the entire period of the pregnancy for the causes of the child's postnatal "injuries." Nor, for that matter, is there any principled way, under the petitioner's proposed reading of the statute, to confine its language to prenatal maternal conduct that is illegal, as opposed to conduct that is merely unwise or unhealthy. . . .

* * *

The judgment of the Appellate Court is reversed, and the case is remanded to that court with direction to remand the case to the trial court with direction to render judgment for the respondent.

In this opinion the other justices concurred.

Notes

1. Pregnant mothers addicted to cocaine and its smokeable form, crack, have become a serious problem courts must face. For a discussion of the increase in the number of pregnant women addicted to cocaine, see Julie J. Zitella, Note, *Protecting the Children: A Call to Reform State Policies to Hold Pregnant Drug Addicts Accountable,* 29 J. MARSHALL L. REV. 765, 765-70 (1996). A National Association for Perinatal Addiction Research and Education found that 375,000 babies per year face potential health damage because of drug-exposure. *See* Marcy Tench Stovall, Note, *Looking For a Solution:* In re Valerie D. *and State Intervention in Prenatal Drug Abuse*, 25 CONN. L. REV. 1265 (1993). Babies addicted to cocaine can suffer from several serious and potentially life-threatening deficiencies, e.g. "prenatal strokes, premature birth, low birth weight, seizures, and behavioral abnormalities." *Id.* at 1266 (citing Jane E. Brody, *Widespread Abuse of Drugs by Pregnant Women is Found*, N.Y. TIMES, Aug. 30, 1988, at A1; Judith Larsen et al.,

Medical Evidence in Cases of Intrauterine Drug and Alcohol Exposure, 18 PEPP. L. REV. 279, 294 (1991)). For further discussion of the effects of cocaine on a child, see Zitella, *supra;* Michelle D. Mills, Comment, *Fetal Abuse Prosecutions: The Triumph of Reaction Over Reason*, 47 DEPAUL L. REV. 989 (1998); Anastasia Toufexis, *Innocent Victims*, TIME, May 13, 1991, at 56, 60.

2. In *State v. Hardy*, 469 N.W.2d 50 (Mich. Ct. App. 1991), a mother smoked crack cocaine less than 13 hours before delivering her baby, resulting in serious injuries to the child. The prosecutor charged the mother with second-degree child abuse and delivery of less than fifty grams of cocaine. The prosecutor argued that a fetus becomes a child once the baby is removed from the mother's body. According to the prosecution, the mother delivered cocaine to the child through the umbilical cord between the time the child was removed from the mother's body and when the umbilical cord was severed. The court interpreted the statute strictly and held that a mother is not criminally liable when she delivers cocaine to a baby while the baby is still attached to the mother. *See also Johnson v. State*, 602 So. 2d 1288 (Fla. 1992); *State v. Gray,* No. L-89-239, 1990 WL 125695, (Ohio Ct. App. Aug. 31, 1990); *Herron v. State*, 729 N.E.2d 1008 (Ind. Ct. App. 2000) (an unborn child is not a "dependent" for purposes of a neglect of dependency statute). *But see In re Fathima Ashanti K.J.,* 558 N.Y.S.2d 447 (Fam. Ct. 1990). In *Fathima Ashanti K.J.,* a newborn child suffered from deficiencies similar to the baby in *Valerie D.* as a result of the mother abusing cocaine during pregnancy. The court broadly interpreted New York's Family Court Act § 1013(d) and held that interpreting the statute to include the unborn was consistent with medical and scientific advances to treat the fetus while still in the mother's womb. The court found a compelling state interest to protect the health and welfare of an unborn child. For additional analysis of *Valerie D.* and its progeny, see Jeffrey F. Gostyla, Note, *The Needle or the Baby Spoon?—Termination of Parental Rights of a Drug-Abusing Mother in Connecticut,* 7 CONN. PROB. L.J. 279 (1993); Stovall, *supra*, Note 1; David Adam Hollander, Comment, In re Valerie D.: *The New Word on the Street*, 13 BRIDGEPORT L. REV. 989, 996-1019 (1993).

3. In cocaine baby cases, courts must weigh the interests of the parents versus the best interests of the child. *See* Janet L. Dolgin, *The Law's Response to Parental Alcohol and "Crack" Abuse,* 56 BROOK. L. REV. 1213 (1991). For a discussion of weighing the biological parents' rights versus the best interests of the cocaine child or fetus, see Nova D. Janssen, Note, *Fetal Rights and the Prosecution of Women for Using Drugs During Pregnancy,* 48 DRAKE L. REV. 741 (2000); Roger Burdge, Note, *Whitner v. South Carolina: Child Abuse Laws Apply to Viable Fetuses,* 1 J.L. & FAM. STUD. 277 (1999). For a general discussion of the maternal-fetal conflict, see DEBORAH MATHIEU, PREVENTING PRENATAL HARM: SHOULD THE STATE INTERVENE? (2d ed. 1996); BONNIE STEINBOCK, LIFE BEFORE BIRTH: THE MORAL AND LEGAL STATUS OF EMBRYOS AND FETUSES 127-63 (1992).

4. Jurisdictions remain divided as to whether cocaine mothers should be criminally prosecuted. One of the most frequently cited cases supporting criminal prosecution of cocaine mothers is *Whitner v. State*, 492 S.E.2d 777 (S.C. 1997). In *Whitner*, a mother exposed her fetus to cocaine during the third trimester. The court recognized that under South Carolina law a viable fetus is often considered a person with limited legal rights. The court found that public policy required the state to protect the child's rights and assess penalties to prevent one from illegally endangering the life of another. For a critique of *Whitner*, see Alma Tolliver, *Child Abuse Statute Expanded to Protect Viable Fetus: The Abusive Effects of South Carolina's Interpretation of the Word "Child"*, 24 S. ILL. U. L.J. 383 (2000); Regina M. Coady, Comment, *Extending Child Abuse Protection to the Viable Fetus:* Whitner v. State of South Carolina, 71 ST. JOHN'S L. REV. 667 (1997). *But see Johnson v. State, supra*, Note 2; *State v. Gray, supra*, Note 2; *State v. Hardy, supra,* Note 2. For a discussion of prosecuting a cocaine mother, see Patricia A. Sexton, Note, *Imposing Criminal Sanctions on Pregnant Drug Users: Throwing the Baby Out With the Bath Water,* 32 WASHBURN L.J. 410 (1993); Stovall, *supra*, at 1267-82; Page Mcquire Linden, *Drug Addiction During Pregnancy: A Call for Increased Social Responsibility,* 4 AM. U. J. GENDER & L. 105, 118-21 (1995). For a critique of current statutes imposing criminal sanctions on cocaine mothers, see Christine Hunt, Casenotes & Comments, *Criminalizing Prenatal Substance Abuse: A Preventive Means of Ensuring the Birth of a Drug-Free Child,* 33 IDAHO L. REV. 451 (1997).

Questions

1. The *Valerie D.* and *Whitner* courts take different approaches as to whether or not the fetus is a child with rights that should be protected. Which is the more reasoned argument? Should public policy control in the debate over what a "child" is?

2. How should courts weigh the interests of a parent versus the best interests of the child in cocaine baby case? What effect does *parens patriae* have, if any, on the court in balancing these interests?

3. How might imposing criminal penalties advance the policy goals of the state? What constitutional issues may arise in such a prosecution?

4. Fetal Alcohol Syndrome

Adoption of Oliver

554 N.E.2d 40 (Mass. App. Ct. 1990)

ARMSTRONG, Justice.

The mother of Oliver appeals from a decree of the Probate and Family Court entered March 15, 1988, dispensing with the mother's consent to Oliver's adoption. . . . The decree provided that it should be reviewed one year from its date unless within that time a decree of adoption should have been entered. . . . We assume no such review took place while the case was on appeal.

* * *

[T]he mother is afflicted by alcoholism and Oliver in turn by the symptoms of fetal alcohol syndrome. . . . The focus of the trial, properly, was not on placing blame for what happened in the past but, rather, on the mother's current success (or lack thereof) in coping with her alcoholism, on Oliver's particular needs arising out of his impaired condition, and on the mother's potential for success in responding to those needs.

The mother's focus at trial was in showing that she had come to grips with her alcoholism in late spring, 1984, when she participated in a twenty-eight day alcohol treatment program at the Mattapan Hospital; that from that time she had attended Alcoholics Anonymous meetings on a fairly regular basis; that, following several years of trying to cope with her problems and those of her four children as a widow, the mother remarried in 1985 and now had an established home; that she worked on a regular basis; and that since losing custody she had shown up often for scheduled visitations with Oliver and his next older brother.[6]

The petitioner, in seeking to dispense with the mother's consent to Oliver's adoption, was less sanguine about the mother's success in dealing with her alcoholism. It adduced evidence, which the judge believed, that its social workers had thought the mother to be under the influence of alcohol at least twice during the previous year and a half; that the mother's interaction with the children at the visitations was minimal (for the most part the two brothers played with each other, largely ignoring the mother's presence); that, while she had attended many of the bi-weekly meetings scheduled with Oliver and his older brother, she had generally failed to attend the meetings scheduled with a social worker to review the children's progress in their foster homes[7]; that the mother showed no initiative in inquiring as to the children's situations and progress, merely listening passively to what the social worker would bring up; and that the mother could realistically expect little support from her husband in caring for Oliver should custody be returned to her.

The decisive factor, as we read the judge's findings, was Oliver's special needs. Oliver was born six weeks premature. He was discharged from the hospital after a month but returned five months later due to inability to gain weight. The Department of Social Services was given temporary custody when Oliver was nine months old, but his mother was soon thereafter awarded physical custody. He remained with the mother for the next two years, assisted by social workers and regular clinic visits. At that time the Department was again awarded custody, and Oliver was placed in a foster home. There he showed immediate improvement; his hyperactivity decreased, he began taking naps, he began sleeping through the night, and he no longer required close supervision that had been necessary in the past. He gained three and a quarter pounds in his first month in foster care.

The last was important. As noted, Oliver has been diagnosed as a fetal alcohol syndrome child, having some of the particular facial features of such

---

6 Of the bi-weekly meetings scheduled from May 15, 1985, to the time of trial in November, 1986, the mother had attended thirty-one and either cancelled or failed to show up for eighteen. . . .

7 Of nineteen scheduled meetings, six were kept. (The mother cancelled six and failed to cancel or show up for seven.)

children, retarded growth, and some neurological dysfunction. He is developmentally and mentally delayed. His psychological testing places him in the borderline to retarded range. He is described as showing depression in his lack of social interaction with his peers. In the opinion of a pediatrician and child psychiatrist who had evaluated Oliver and testified as an expert witness, it will be pivotal to Oliver's development that he live in an enriched environment with constant stimulation, by which the doctor meant that he must have sustained contact with persons willing to take an active interest in his everyday life and willing to encourage him to take responsibility for himself. In such an environment Oliver could reasonably hope to achieve a functioning, independent status as an adult. Without it, Oliver could regress to the point of comprehensive dependence on societal support. The judge adopted this view. It was fully supported by the evidence.

Oliver's mother, in the judge's view, could not furnish the necessary environment. She regards Oliver as normal except for being small. She does not understand that he has special needs. She has shown no comprehension of his problems and does not acknowledge that he has problems. She plainly regards herself as having done a good job taking care of him in his earliest month[s], when, in the doctor's view, Oliver acquired problems of an emotional nature due more to his environment than to his being a fetal alcohol syndrome child. The mother has historically resisted counseling directed at assisting her in her problems and responsibilities. Oliver's foster parents—also evaluated by the doctor—provide, in his view, the right environment for Oliver, one of stimulation, support, and stability. There was evidence supporting the judge's finding that "[Oliver] showed more than one year's gain in psychological testing over the year preceding trial."

The judge's findings place this case within the line of authority holding that, although a parent's shortcomings, viewed in isolation, would not preclude his or her meeting the law's somewhat undemanding standard of parental fitness, they nevertheless do so when viewed against the more complex and attention-consuming needs of a child who has been impaired in his development by early neglect. . . .

In cases of this type, where the finding of parental unfitness is grounded less in continuing incidents of neglect and more in the inability of the parent, however well intentioned, to provide for the child's special needs, it would be somewhat unusual for the passage of time—even a long period like two years—to alter the balance of considerations significantly. Nevertheless, the review called for by the decree is desirable, even if only to reevaluate Oliver's progress in his pre-adoptive placement, to confirm that it continues to work out as hoped, and, if not, to reassess the potential impact of separation from the pre-adoption home at this time and return to the mother. Without in any way prejudging the outcome of that review, we emphasize that much time has been lost already and that the continuing uncertainty caused by this litigation undermines the familial security and stability widely thought conducive to child development. It is imperative, therefore, that priority be given to scheduling and completing the review called for by the decree.

Decree affirmed.

Notes

1. Fetal alcohol syndrome (FAS) is a national problem on the rise. It is estimated that from 2,000 to 12,000 FAS babies are born each year. *See* Caroline S. Palmer, *The Risks of State Intervention in Preventing Prenatal Alcohol Abuse and the Viability of an Inclusive Approach: Arguments for Limiting Punitive and Coercive Prenatal Alcohol Abuse Legislation in Minnesota,* 10 HASTINGS WOMEN'S L.J. 287, 296 (1999). *See also* S.N. Mattson & E. P. Riley, *A Review of the Neurobehavioral Deficits in Children With Fetal Alcohol Syndrome or Prenatal Exposure to Alcohol,* 22 ALCOHOLISM: CLINICAL & EXPERIMENTAL RESEARCH 279-92 (1998) (estimates 1,200 FAS babies born annually); Alison M. Leonard, Note, *Fetal Personhood, Legal Substance Abuse, and Marital Prosecutions: Child Protection or "Gestational Gestapo?",* 32 NEW ENG. L. REV. 615, 626 (1998) (estimates as high as 40,000 FAS babies born annually). Children born with FAS exhibit physical deformities and mental deficiencies, such as mental and physical growth retardation, impairment of intellectual and behavioral development skills. *See* Tom Richoff & Curtis Cukjati, *Protecting the Fetus From Maternal Drug and Alcohol Abuse: A Proposal for Texas,* 21 ST. MARY'S L.J. 259, 267-68 (1988). FAS children also present hyperactivity, wakefulness, language dysfunction, and attention deficit syndrome. *See* Sana Loue, *Legal and Epidemiological Aspects of Child Maltreatment,* 19 J. LEGAL MED. 471, 493 (1998) (citing Chasnoff, *Drug Use In Pregnancy; Parameters of Risk*, 35 PEDIATRIC CLINICS OF N.A. 1043 (1998)) (hyperactivity, wakefulness, language dysfunction, and attention deficit syndrome); Coleman & Kay, *Biological Addictions*, 25 OBSTETRICS & GYNECOLOGY CLINICS OF N.A. 1-109 (1999). *See also* Stacey L. Best, Comment, *Fetal Equality?: The State's Response to the Challenge of Protecting the Unborn*, 32 LAND & WATER L. REV. 193 (1997); Leonard, *supra*, at 625; Palmer, *supra*, at 297. The effects of FAS can last through adulthood. *See* Palmer, *supra*, at 297-98. Furthermore, providing proper care for FAS children is expensive. The United States spends $2.7 billion annually caring for FAS babies, and it is estimated that lifetime care for a FAS child costs $1.4 million. *See* Leonard, *supra*, at 626.

It should be noted, however, that not all children exposed to alcohol in utero will suffer from FAS. *See* GARY E. MCCUEN, BORN HOOKED (1991). A recent study suggests that ten to forty percent of newborns born to alcoholic mothers suffer from FAS. *See* S.N. Mattson et al., *Heavy Prenatal Alcohol Exposure With or Without Physical Features of Fetal Alcohol Syndrome Leads to I.Q. Deficits*, 131 J. OF PEDIATRICS 718-71 (1997). Some studies indicate that fetal exposure to low levels of alcohol will have no effect on the fetus. Mattson & Riley, *supra*, at 285. Because researchers are unsure how much alcohol is necessary for a fetus to be born with FAS, "it may be difficult, if not impossible to establish a clearly defined threshold beyond which the risk to the resulting child will justify, as a matter of standing policy, coercive intervention or criminal prosecution." Kenneth A. Deville & Loretta M. Kopelman, *Fetal Protection in Wisconsin's Revised Child Abuse Law: Right Goal, Wrong Remedy,* 27 J.L. MED. & ETHICS 332, 336 (1999). For a discussion of prosecuting mothers of FAS children, see Michelle D. Mills, Comment, *Fetal Abuse Prosecutions: The Triumph of Reaction Over Reason,* 47 DEPAUL L. REV. 989 (1998); Leonard, *supra*. For an examination of policies supporting mandatory reporting laws for FAS or civil commitments and prosecutions for mothers of FAS children, see Palmer, *supra,* at 320-39. For additional general information on fetal alcohol syndrome, see the National Organization on Fetal Abuse Syndrome's website <http://www.nofas.org/index2.htm>.

2. Several legislatures have addressed the FAS problem. South Carolina Statutes Annotated § 20-7-736(G) (West Supp. 2000), for example, presumes that a newborn who is diagnosed as having FAS is abused or neglected and "cannot be protected from further harm without being removed from the custody of the mother. . . ." *See also* 705 ILL. COMP. STAT. ANN. 405/2-18 (West 1999) (proof that minor has FAS is prima facie evidence of neglect); IND. CODE ANN. § 31-34-10-10 (Lexis Supp. 2000) (FAS child is a CHINS). Some states require that doctors and nurses who attend the birth of a child report an FAS child to the appropriate state agency. *See, e.g.,* UTAH CODE ANN. § 62A-4a-404 (Lexis 2000).

States have also taken measures to warn and educate the public about FAS. Most states require warning signs about FAS to be placed in plain view in establishments that sell alcohol. *See, e.g.,* 235 ILL. COMP. STAT. ANN. 5/6-24a(b) (West Supp. 2001) (requires signs state "Government Warning: According to the Surgeon General, Women Should Not Drink Alcoholic Beverages During Pregnancy Because of the Risk of Birth Defects"). *See also* TENN. CODE ANN. § 57-1-211 (Lexis Supp. 2000); WASH. REV. CODE ANN. § 66.16.110 (West 2001). Many states try to educate the public about FAS by giving couples who register for a marriage license a pamphlet describing FAS. *See* OR. REV. STAT. § 106.081 (1999); 750 ILL. COMP. STAT. ANN. 5/203(3) (West Supp. 2001); R.I. GEN. LAWS § 15-2-3.1 (Lexis 2000); WIS. STAT. ANN. § 765.12(1) (West 1993). A few states have established FAS clinics, provide training for health care and social service providers, and state grants for research. The following is an example of such a statute:

Minnesota Statutes Annotated
§ 145.9266 (West Supp. 2001)

§ 145.9266. Fetal alcohol syndrome campaign and education

Subd. 1. Public awareness and education. The commissioner of health shall design and implement an ongoing statewide campaign to raise public awareness and educate the public about fetal alcohol syndrome. . . .

Subd.2. Statewide network of fetal alcohol syndrome diagnostic clinics. A statewide network of regional fetal alcohol syndrome diagnostic clinics shall be developed between the department of health and University of Minnesota. This collaboration shall be based on a statewide needs assessment and shall include involvement from consumers, providers, and payors. . . .

Subd. 3. Professional training and education about fetal alcohol syndrome.

(a) The commissioner of health . . . shall develop curricula and materials about fetal alcohol syndrome for professional training of health care providers, social service providers, educators. . . .

(b) Training for health care providers shall focus on skill building for screening, counseling, referral, and follow-up for women using or at risk of using alcohol while pregnant. . . .

(c) Training and education for social service providers shall focus on resources for assessing, referring, and treating at-risk women . . .

Subd. 5. School pilot programs.

(a) The commissioner of children, family and learning shall award up to four grants to school for pilot programs to identify and implement effective educational strategies for individuals with fetal alcohol syndrome . . . defects.

* * *

See also MINN. STAT. ANN. § 145.9265 (West 1998); N.D. CEN. CODE §§ 15-11-35, 15-11-36 (Lexis Supp. 1999); WASH. REV. CODE ANN. §§ 70.83C.020, 70.96A.500 (West Supp. 2001).

3. In response to the growing attention given FAS and fetal alcohol effects (FAE), the United States Senate recently approved a $25 million competitive grant program that focuses on FAS and FAE prevention and treatment. *See Senate Approves $25M Grant on Fetal Alcohol Exposure,* 28 CHILD PROTECTION REPORT 115, 188 (July 20, 2000). Senator Tom Daschle stated that the program provides assistance to "families, who in many cases, have been bearing the burden . . . unaided and alone." According to a study cited by Daschle, 42% of those with FAS have trouble with the law and 94% have mental health problems. Among listing other problems associated with the children and adults with FAS, the study also found that only 11% of those in the study were diagnosed as having FAS by six years of age.

Questions

1. Medical experts are unsure of how to predict if a fetus will develop FAS or how much alcohol is necessary for a diagnosis of FAS. What types of medical and social service interventions are available to screen mothers? What is the role of the child welfare system in these kinds of preventive measure? What are the relevant public policy considerations and potential legal (constitutional) issues?

2. What factors should a court consider when addressing the question of placement of a newborn child diagnosed with FAS?

5. Battered Child Syndrome

State v. Tanner

675 P.2d 539 (Utah 1983)

DURHAM, Justice:

The defendant and appellant, Kathy Tanner, appeals from her conviction for manslaughter in the death of her three-year-old daughter. The defendant was tried before the court and sentenced to an indeterminate term of not less than one or more than fifteen years in prison. The defendant here argues that there was insufficient evidence to support the verdict, that some evidence was erroneously admitted, and that some evidence was erroneously excluded.

The key evidence in this case is the mute testimony of the body of three-year-old Tawnya Tanner. There is no question that she died on March 21, 1980, of "subdural hematoma associated with multiple contusions of the body," as stated in the autopsy report. That report, the contents of which were stipulated to by the defendant, enumerated the many contusions scattered over the child's body literally from head to foot. The contusions are clearly visible in the photographs admitted in evidence, as are the bulges of the scalp where the severely bruised brain protruded through the craniotomy sites. At trial the court permitted the prosecution's medical experts to testify regarding the condition of the child's body, the nature of the injuries and the cause of death. This testimony included the witnesses' observations regarding the "battered child syndrome." The defendant claims error in the admission of this battered child syndrome testimony and the admission of instances of prior bad acts that she alleges were presented "to establish that Tawnya was a victim of the Battered Child Syndrome."

The issue of the admissibility of "battered child syndrome" testimony has not previously been presented to this Court. The development of the medical-social concept of the battered child syndrome is traced in McCoid, "The Battered Child & Other Assaults Upon the Family: Part One" 50 Minn.L.Rev. 1 (1965). The author points out that the "development of the concept of the battered child syndrome has moved from an initial identification of physical phenomenon [sic] to concern with the causative factors outside of the body of the child." *Id.* at 19. Early publications concentrated on the identification of the pattern of injuries observed, but in the 1950s, articles began to address the origins of the trauma, including the role of the parents. . . .

McCoid summarizes:

> [I]t appears that by early 1965, there had come a recognition of a distinctive phenomenon called "the battered child syndrome" which, though it begins with a pattern of injuries to the child, is really descriptive of a pattern of conduct on the part of the parents or others who are to guard the welfare of the child. The medical description can perhaps best be summarized as multiple injuries in various stages of healing, primarily to the long bones and soft tissues and frequently coupled with poor hygiene and malnutrition, but peculiarly identified by the marked discrepancy between the clinical or physi-

> cal findings and the historical data provided by the parents. Described in terms of the conduct of the parents or their characteristics, the studies seem to confirm that the abuser is likely to be an emotionally immature individual from almost any walk or stratum of society, a person who probably suffers from the pressures of marital difficulties or economic circumstances or other emotional pressures not directly related to the child himself, so that the child becomes merely a focus for generalized frustration or anger and an outlet for the poorly controlled aggressiveness of the parent.

Id. at 18-19.

Over the past fifteen years, cases discussing the use of battered child syndrome evidence have appeared with increasing frequency in the state reporters. The battered child syndrome has become a well-recognized medical diagnosis, which must be testified to by an expert witness. . . . In *People v. Jackson,* 18 Cal.App.3d 504, 95 Cal.Rptr. 919 (1971), the court pointed out that "[a]n expert medical witness may give his opinion as to the means used to inflict a particular injury, based on his deduction from the appearance of the injury itself." *Id.* at 507, 95 Cal.Rptr. at 921. Such testimony is not accusatory, but only indicates the cause of death. Similarly, when an expert testifies as to the existence of the "battered child syndrome," he expresses no opinion regarding a defendant's culpability, but rather testifies that, as the witness in *Jackson* stated:

> "[I]t would take thousands of children to have the severity and number and degree of injuries that this child had over the span of time that we had" by accidental means. In other words, the "battered child syndrome" simply indicates that a child found with the type of injuries outlined above has not suffered those injuries by accidental means. This conclusion is based upon an extensive study of the subject by medical science.

Id.

In *Bludsworth v. State*, Nev., 646 P.2d 558 (1982), the defendants argued that evidence of bruises and a bite mark on the body of the child was incompetent because there was no prior establishment that either defendant was responsible for the injuries. The court affirmed the admission of the evidence, stating:

> Admissibility of the bite mark and other bruise evidence does not depend on connecting either defendant to the infliction of the injury. It is independent, relevant circumstantial evidence tending to show that the child was intentionally, rather than accidentally, injured on the day in question.

Id. at 559.

In *People v. DeJesus,* 71 Ill. App.3d 235, 27 Ill.Dec. 448, 389 N.E.2d 260 (1979), the defendant claimed error in the use of battered child syndrome evidence, arguing that it suggested to the jury that the defendant was guilty of prior offenses. The court held that the expert's diagnosis and explanation of medical terms of art do not indicate wrongdoing on the part of a particular defendant, but merely describe the nature of the injuries. *See also State v. Wilkerson,* 295 N.C. 559, 247 S.E.2d 905 (1978).

The defendants in these cases frequently argue that evidence of injuries other than that which is the immediate cause of death, i.e., any evidence of the battered child syndrome, is incompetent or is more prejudicial than probative. Again, we emphasize that evidence regarding the child's physical condition does not directly indicate the culpability of any particular defendant. In *Ashford v. State,* Okl.Crim., 603 P.2d 1162 (1979), an 8-month-old baby was found to have injuries from five days to two weeks old and partially healed fractures from four to eight weeks old, in addition to a fatal subdural hemorrhage. The court held that "[i]n a case of this nature, the past injuries are admissible to counter any claim that the latest injury happened through accident or simple negligence. *The pattern of abuse* is relevant to show the intent of the act." *Id.* at 1164 (emphasis added). In other words, the pattern of abuse is relevant to show that *someone* injured the child intentionally, rather than accidentally.

Battered child syndrome evidence is most frequently cited as admissible to show absence of accident. It is relevant to claims of accidents by the child, *e.g.,* "She was clumsy and fell a lot," as well as accidents by the adult, "I tripped while I was carrying him." Expert testimony as to types of injuries, their size, location and severity, together with evidence of their varying age and progress in healing, allows the lifeless or preverbal victim to testify in the only way possible. We are satisfied that the concept of the battered child syndrome is grounded in scientific research and is widely accepted in the medical community. Our research shows that all courts which have addressed the question have affirmed the admission of expert medical testimony regarding the presence of the battered child syndrome. We therefore conclude that in appropriate factual circumstances, testimony regarding the battered child syndrome is admissible when given by a properly qualified expert witness. We caution trial courts to weigh carefully the probative value against the potential for undue prejudice that may be created by the use of the term "battered child syndrome." The term should not be applied broadly or as a generalization. The expert should be able to testify in detail regarding the nature of the child's injuries and whether the explanation given for the injuries is reasonable. . . . The weight and credibility to be given an expert's testimony are matters to be decided by the factfinder. Defense counsel may of course challenge the testimony on cross-examination, but such challenge goes to the weight to be given the testimony, not to its admissibility.

In the instant case, the testimony of four medical experts was presented by the State. The doctor on duty in the emergency room described Tawnya's condition as "moribund," in other words, a dying condition. He testified that the defendant told him that Tawnya fell, but that the explanation did not seem consistent with the severity of the child's condition. A neurosurgeon was the next to examine Tawnya. He testified that he found no spontaneous respiration, that Tawnya had dilated pupils with hemorrhages in the right eye indicating intercranial pressure, and that he observed one acute "relative fresh" bruise just ahead of the right ear, several new and old bruises on the face and an old bruise on the inner thigh. He further testified that he performed a bilateral craniotomy to relieve the pressure on the brain and that he found a very large subdural hematoma or blood clot with bruised brain tissue. He stated that the severity of the swelling and the hematoma indicated that a significant amount of force had been applied. Tawnya died the next morning, never having regained consciousness.

As already mentioned, the autopsy report stating that Tawnya died of "subdural hematoma associated with multiple contusions of the body" was stipulated to at trial. The medical examiner's expert opinion was that the multiple bruises on Tawnya's chin were not consistent with a single fall. The State's fourth expert, Dr. Palmer, based his opinion on his review of the police records, the autopsy report, the neurosurgeon's report, and his extensive experience as a pediatrician specializing in the study of child abuse. Dr. Palmer testified regarding the phenomena that alert a physician to the possibility of the battered child syndrome, such as: too many bruises and bruises in atypical locations considering the child's age; fractures, such as spiral fractures, of a type and severity not otherwise explained; severe head injuries not otherwise explained; and in general, a history of the trauma given by a caretaker that is inconsistent with the child's injuries. The doctor also testified that abusive disciplinary methods are frequently part of the battered child syndrome, that the parents of such children are typically very young or inexperienced and that they are likely to have a history of prior abusive conduct. Dr. Palmer went on to identify in Tawnya the characteristics of the battered child, emphasizing in particular the inadequate explanation given by the defendant for Tawnya's injuries. Counsel for the defendant took full advantage of the opportunity to challenge Dr. Palmer's opinions and the bases for his conclusions.

All four of the State's experts were properly qualified and testified within their areas of expertise. The term "battered child syndrome" was not used broadly, but was defined and applied to Tawnya with particularity. We therefore find that the trial court did not err by admitting testimony regarding the battered child syndrome.

The defendant also alleges error in the admission of testimony regarding specific instances of prior bad acts. . . . She alleges that evidence of prior bad acts was offered to establish the existence of the battered child syndrome. In this she is mistaken. The testimony regarding the battered child syndrome was based on the experts' observations of Tawnya's damaged body and was independent of evidence of the defendant's conduct.

* * *

In cases of child abuse, such as one before us, evidence of specific instances of the defendant's treatment of the child is relevant to establish not merely a general disposition for violence or ill-will towards all children, but to establish a specific pattern of behavior by the defendant toward one particular child, the victim. We distinguish this evidence of the defendant's conduct, relevant to establishing a pattern of behavior by the defendant, from evidence of the battered child syndrome given by experts that is relevant to establishing the nature of the injuries to the child and that is nonaccusatory and independently admissible. . . . The two categories of evidence should, of course, be corroborative in order to support a conviction. This pattern of behavior by the defendant is relevant to establishing absence of accident or mistake . . . , opportunity, knowledge or the identity of the defendant as the person responsible for the crime charged.

* * *

Where there is a child abuse, there will invariably be secrecy. The great disparity of power and control between the abuser and the child assures that there will be little, if any, direct evidence. Even in cases where the victim survives, the child's age and vulnerability make it unlikely that he or she could be expected to testify competently. In these cases, it is probable that evidence of prior abusive conduct by a caretaker may be the only available link between the specific nature of the child's injuries and the caretaker who has offered either no explanation or an inadequate explanation for those injuries. However, we emphasize that the "reception of such evidence is justified by necessity and, if other evidence has substantially established the element of the crime involved (motive, intent, identity, absence of mistake, etc.), the probative value of showing another offense is diminished, and the trial court should rule it inadmissible even though relevant." *Tucker v. State,* 82 Nev. 127, 412 P.2d 970, 971 (1966).

In the instant case, the defendant told the doctors who treated Tawnya that the three-year-old had fallen off a slide at the park. . . . Leland Foote, with whom the defendant was living, . . . testified against the defendant, relating that she disciplined Tawnya harshly, especially when Tawnya wet herself. He stated that on March 20, he and the defendant's two small children walked to the defendant's place of work to meet her and walk home with her, that Tawnya was lively and well, that after returning to their apartment, he went into the bathroom where he heard two loud thumps as if something heavy had been thrown against the wall in the next room and that when he left the bathroom, he saw the defendant watching TV and he saw Tawnya lying unconscious on the floor. Foote related specific instances of the defendant's treatment of Tawnya, such as throwing her against a wall or the floor, kicking her, making her sit in a tub of cold water until the child could not stand, whipping her with a belt and rubbing the child's face in her messy pants. Additional witnesses—Foote's relatives, the defendant's relatives and the defendant's co-workers—corroborated this testimony by relating instances in which they personally saw the defendant abuse Tawnya or heard the defendant talk about disciplining Tawnya in ways they considered harsh. All of the incidents were personally observed by the witnesses, who were extensively cross-examined. The testimony was relevant not only to the absence of accident or mistake, as we noted above, but also to the defendant's pattern of behavior toward the victim. Where the presence of the battered child syndrome is shown in the child and the defendant is the child's caretaker, logic and the interests of justice demand as complete a story as possible concerning the crime and the surrounding circumstances. Medical testimony indicated that Tawnya's fatal injury was part of a pattern of abusive injuries. Evidence of the defendant's conduct during substantially all of Tawnya's life establishes an explanation for the many non-fatal injuries found on Tawnya's body. . . . This evidence, together with the defendant's lack of reasonable explanation for the injuries, is relevant to establish the identity of the one responsible for the fatal injury.

The defendant also objected to the admission of expert testimony regarding Tawnya's physical condition as an infant. Dr. Palmer's testimony was based on a report made by a physician who treated Tawnya at the Oregon Medical Center when Tawnya was three months old. Tawnya was admitted because of "failure to thrive," a condition that may be caused by a variety of physiological problems or by neglect or abuse. After her admission, a routine x-ray revealed that Tawnya had sustained fractures of the right clavical, the right eleventh rib, the right tibia, and that she had an abnormality of the left humerus. He observed that two of the fractures were spiral fractures and stated that a self-inflected spiral or tortion fracture is inconsistent with the degree of mobility possible for a three-month-old infant. He also noted that the parents' explanation of a fall from a couch was not sufficient to account for the injuries. Separate and apart from any evidence pertaining to the defendant's conduct, he testified that these physical symptoms were all indicators that would alert a physician to the possibility of the battered child syndrome. [T]his evidence is not relevant to Tawnya's condition at the time of her death, but rather is relevant to establishing a pattern of conduct by the defendant. . . . Where expert testimony has established the presence of the battered child syndrome in the victim, the pattern of conduct exhibited by the defendant-caretaker toward the child-victim is within the scope of the issues before the court. Specific instances of the defendant's prior acts were not admissible to show a generalized bad character, but to show the defendant's pattern of conduct toward Tawnya, specifically. . . .

Medical records of the child's current or past condition that indicate either the presence or absence of abusive injuries must always be relevant to the issues at trial where, as here, expert testimony has established the presence of the battered child syndrome in the victim.

* * *

Finally, the defendant argues that there was insufficient evidence to support the verdict. In reviewing a claim of insufficient evidence, this Court must view the evidence in the light most favorable to the verdict and will interfere only when the evidence is so lacking and insubstantial that a reasonable person could not possibly have reached a verdict beyond a reasonable doubt. This standard of review is the same where the court, rather than a jury, acts as the finder of fact. The defendant claims that the circumstantial nature of the evidence, together with the evidence of a favorable polygraph test, is sufficient to show that a reasonable person could not possibly have reached a verdict beyond a reasonable doubt.

We have frequently stated that circumstantial evidence alone may be competent to establish the guilt of the accused. The defendant emphasizes that in order to warrant conviction, circumstantial evidence must exclude every reasonable hypothesis other than the defendant's guilt. . . . In *Huerta v. State*, Tex. App. 635 S.W.2d 847 (1982), the court stated that "[t]he rules of circumstantial evidence do not require that the circumstances should to a moral certainty actually exclude every hypothesis that the act may have been committed by another person, but the hypothesis intended is a *reasonable* one consistent with the circumstances and facts proved." *Id.* at 851 (quoting from *Flores v. State*, Tex.Cr.App., 551 S.W.2d 364, 367 (1977)) (emphasis in original). In

Aldridge v. State, Miss., 398 So.2d 1308 (1981), the court addressed the same objection to circumstantial evidence:

> To sustain a verdict based on circumstantial evidence, it is not necessary that such evidence exclude every possible doubt or theoretical supposition in no way related to the facts or circumstances of the case. It is enough that such evidence exclude every reasonable hypothesis of innocence.

Id. at 1311. These statements, taken from cases involving similar fact situations, are in accord with our existing law and our view of the evidence in this case.

* * *

The defendant's conviction is affirmed.

[Justice Stewart's dissent is omitted.]

Notes

1. Battered Child Syndrome (BCS) is a medical diagnosis that describes a pattern of unexplained manifestations of physical abuse. *See* Michael S. Orfinger, *Battered Child Syndrome: Evidence of Prior Acts in Disguise,* 41 FLA. L. REV. 345, 347 (1989) (citing H. Raffelli, *The Battered Child—An Overview of a Medical, Legal, and Social Problem,* 16 CRIME & DELINQ. 139, 140 (1970)). BCS children may suffer from skin bruising, signs of neglect, unexplained fractures, subdural hematoma, and internal organ damage. *See* Allan H. McCoid, *The Battered Child and Other Assaults Upon the Family: Part One,* 50 MINN. L. REV. 1, 24 (1965).

In the landmark decision of *Estelle v. McGuire,* 502 U.S. 62 (1991), the U.S. Supreme Court addressed the question of whether to allow prior injuries of the child into evidence to prove BCS, even if the injuries were not caused by the defendant. In *McGuire*, a father brought his six-month-old daughter into an emergency room because the child was not breathing. After the child died, an autopsy revealed brain swelling, bruises covering the body, rib fractures, heart damage, and other internal injuries. During the father's trial for second-degree murder, the prosecutor offered evidence of the child's prior injuries to establish BCS. The father was convicted and the appellate court reversed. The Supreme Court reversed and held that evidence of prior injuries was relevant to prove the child's injuries were inflicted by an adult intentionally. The Court noted that BCS narrowed the "group of perpetrators to McGuire and his wife." The Court concluded that there was sufficient evidence for a jury to convict McGuire. For further discussion of *McGuire*, see Darin Michael Colucci, Case Comment, *Evidence—The Admissibility of Battered Child Syndrome: Giving a Voice to the Silenced*—Estelle v. McGuire, *112 S. Ct. 475 (1991)*, 26 SUFFOLK U. L. REV. 1213 (1992).

Many jurisdictions permit the admission of expert testimony in the court's discretion to describe the traits of BCS and explain the syndrome. *See, e.g., State v. Elliot*, 475 S.E.2d 202 (N.C. 1996); *Eslava v. State*, 473 So. 2d 1143 (Ala. Crim. App. 1985); *Commonwealth v. Rodgers*, 528 A.2d 610 (Pa. Super. Ct. 1987), *appeal denied*, 542 A.2d 1368 (Pa. 1988); *State v. Toennis*, 758 P.2d 539 (Wash. Ct. App. 1988); *State v. Dumlao*, 491 A.2d 404 (Conn. App. Ct. 1985); *State v. Moyer*, 727 P.2d 31 (Ariz. Ct. App. 1986). Experts can verify that the force used to create the injuries was significant and that the child would most likely be unable to cause such injury during ordinary activity. *See* Orfinger, *supra*, at 355. Furthermore, expert witnesses can demonstrate how the bruises and other injuries were inflicted over a long period of time. In order for the factfinder to form an inference of guilt, the expert must demonstrate a causal connection between the injuries suffered and the time period in which they occurred. *See, e.g., State v. Durfee,* 322 N.W.2d 778 (Minn. 1982). For further discussion of the admissibility of expert testimony in BCS cases, see Milton Roberts, Annotation, *Admissibility of Expert Medical Testimony on Battered Child Syndrome,* 98 A.L.R.3D 306 (1980); Orfinger, *supra*, at 357-63; Russell C. Prince, Case Note, *Evidence—Child Abuse—Expert Medical Testimony Concerning "Battered Children Syndrome" Held Admissible,* 42 FORDHAM L. REV. 935 (1974).

2. A growing number of children seek to use BCS as a defense for murdering an abusive parent. Annotation, *Admissibility of Evidence of Battered Children Syndrome on Issue of Self-Defense*, 22 A.L.R.5TH 787, 793 (1994). "Usually, a child commits parricide after enduring a lifetime of severe abuse that he can no longer tolerate either psychologically or physically." Elizabeth Turk, *Abuses and Syndromes: Excuses or Justifications?,* 18 WHITTIER L. REV. 901, 924 (1997) (citing Jamie Heather Sacks, *A New Age of Understanding: Allowing Self-Defense Claims for Battered Children Who Kill Their Abusers,* 10 J. CONTEMP. HEALTH L. & POL'Y 349, 365 (1993)). Courts remain divided as to whether evidence of BCS should be admissible in self-defense. *See, e.g., State v. James*, 850 P.2d 495 (Wash. 1993) (admission of evidence of BCS to prove self-defense is proper when such a defense is relevant); *State v. Young*, Ct. App. No. H-89-7, 1991 Ohio App. Lexis 6332 (Dec. 31, 1991) (expert testimony explaining BCS is helpful to the trier of fact to determine the defendant's state of mind). *But see State v. Crabtree*, 805 P.2d 1 (Kan. 1991) (evidence of BCS not admissible where insufficient evidence was given for self-defense). For further discussion concerning the use of BCS as evidence of self-defense, see Susan C. Smith, *Abused Children Who Kill Abusive Parents: Moving Toward an Appropriate Legal Response,* 42 CATH. U. L. REV. 141 (1992); Turk, *supra*; Joelle Anne Moreno, *Killing Daddy: Developing a Self-Defense Strategy for the Abused Child,* 137 U. PA. L. REV. 1281 (1989).

Questions

1. The holding in *McGuire, supra,* Note 1, permits experts to describe evidence of a child's prior abuse even if the abuse may not have been committed by the defendant. What are the implications of this rule on child welfare factfinding proceedings?

2. Suppose you are in a jurisdiction that has not addressed the issue as to whether children who kill their parents should be allowed to present evidence of BCS. Your client, a seven-year old, who has been severely abused all of his life, shot and killed his father one evening after his father whipped him with a belt, which drew blood. What arguments would you use to convince the judge that evidence of prior child abuse should be admitted to prove self-defense?

B. Psychological Evidence

1. Child Sexual Abuse Accommodation Syndrome

State v. J.Q.

617 A.2d 1196 (N.J. 1993)

O'HERN, J.

This appeal concerns the use of expert opinion testimony to aid jurors in the criminal trial of a child-sexual-abuse case. The specific issue concerns expert-opinion evidence premised on the Child Sexual Abuse Accommodation Syndrome (CSAAS), and whether there is a reliable scientific explanation for certain exhibited characteristics of an abused child, such as acceptance of the abuse or delayed reporting, that would help jurors understand why a child victim would not complain to a parent or other authority figure about the abuse. We hold that CSAAS had a sufficiently reliable scientific basis to allow an expert witness to describe traits found in victims of such abuse to aid jurors in evaluating specific defenses. In this case, the expert's opinion went beyond that limited scope and included opinions on commonplace issues, such as credibility assessments derived from conflicting versions of an event and not-yet scientifically established opinions on the ultimate issues that are for jury resolution. . . . [W]e agree with the Appellate Division that the introduction of such evidence was clearly capable of producing an unjust result and we thus affirm the Appellate Division's judgment ordering a new trial.

I

The background to the case is regrettably familiar, a story of childhoods unhinged by events so traumatic that even the participants cannot contemplate them. When first confronted with the possibility that defendant might have sexually abused his daughters, their mother was incredulous. After the girls first told their mother of the alleged abuse, she cautioned them that it was important to tell the truth about their father. The girls said that they were telling the truth. Their mother testified that she had warned her daughters never to let a stranger touch them but had never told them about sexual abuse from a father, because she never thought it could happen to her children. . . .

. . . The parents appear to be of different cultures—Karen is from the midwest and John is a recent arrival to the continental United States. They met in Indiana in 1973 or 1974 and started their life together there when Karen was thirteen and John was nineteen or twenty. John already had a child at that time. They soon moved to Brooklyn and later settled in Newark. Connie and Norma were born in 1977 and 1979, respectively. John and Karen never married. . . .

After the breakup, John customarily picked up the children and took them to Brooklyn for weekend visits. John was then living in a one-room apartment with another woman, whom he married in 1987. About two years after the separation, Karen learned that Norma, during play, had attempted to pull down her younger sister's underwear and touch her buttocks. Karen asked Norma where she had ever learned of such things and Norma reluctantly identified the person who had initiated her into such conduct by spelling out the word "D-A-D".

Although at first disbelieving, Karen consulted a family counsellor and eventually reported the incident to the police. Both Connie and Norma reported that they had been the victims of repeated acts of sexual abuse by their father in the Newark apartment in 1984 as well as during their visits to Brooklyn. An Essex County grand jury returned an indictment charging John with acts of criminal sexual abuse in New Jersey on his children between January 1, 1984, and December 31, 1984.

At trial, both Connie and Norma described, in graphic detail, the abuses committed on them involving sexual penetration and oral sexual contact. . . . A pediatric resident who conducted a genital examination of Norma testified that she found that the child had a stretched hymenal opening, an abnormal condition for a seven-year-old girl. The medical evidence relating to Connie, entered by way of stipulation, also revealed a stretched hymen. Karen described discharges that she had observed on Norma's underwear but said that she had attributed them to Norma's not changing her underwear.

Dr. [Madeline] Milchman [a child psychologist] was called to the stand . . . at trial and qualified, without objection, as an expert witness on child sexual abuse. She identified the child sexual abuse accommodation syndrome "as a pattern of behavior that is found to occur again and again in children who are victims of incest." She described the various aspects of CSAAS and related them to behavior she had observed in Connie and Norma. Dr. Milchman also testified about how she assesses the veracity of an alleged victim of child sexual abuse. At the conclusion of her direct testimony, Dr. Milchman stated that in her expert opinion, Connie and Norma had been sexually abused.

The theory of the defense was that Karen had put the children up to this story to avenge her loss of John. Defendant offered evidence that the Newark apartment housed eight people and that there was no isolated occasion during which such abuse could have occurred.

The jury convicted defendant of multiple counts of first-degree aggravated sexual assault on Connie and Norma for various acts of penetration and oral sex, and of two counts of endangering the welfare of a child. The court sentenced defendant to thirty years' imprisonment, with ten years of parole ineligibility. The Appellate Division reversed the convictions, finding that the trial court had committed plain error in permitting the use of the CSAAS testimony to establish the credibility of the witnesses rather than for other limited purposes for which it is generally reliable, i.e., to explain secrecy, belated disclosure, and recantation by a child-sexual-abuse victim. . . .

II

A.

At the outset, we must carefully distinguish the issues presented in this case from those that are not presented. There are various categories of expert testimony on child sexual abuse. For purposes of this analysis, we draw on the survey of issues by John E. B. Myers et al., *Expert Testimony in Child Sexual Abuse Litigation*, 68 NEB.L.REV. 1 (1989) [hereinafter Myers].

The authors point out that some expert testimony is routinely accepted and presents no genuine evidentiary problem. For example, expert medical testimony plays an important role in child-sexual-abuse litigation. Such testimony is based on a physician's clinical diagnostic examination and the child's medical history. Courts have permitted expert medical witnesses to describe the results of the examination and to offer opinions as to the cause of any injuries, to establish penetration, and to answer questions whether injuries could have been inflicted in a particular way or whether a caretaker's explanation for an injury is reasonable. *Myers, supra*, 68 NEB. L. REV. at 48-49.

In the behavioral-science field, the authors identify one type of expert testimony that describes behaviors commonly observed in sexually-abused children. *Id.* at 51-69. . . . Nevertheless, some behaviors, such as age-inappropriate sexualized responses, are more associated with sexual abuse than others. Thus, the authors assert that situations in which sexual abuse is likely can be identified. . . . Despite the considerable basis for this behavioral-science evidence, "most courts do not approve such testimony as substantive evidence of abuse." *Myers, supra,* 68 NEB.L.REV. at 65, 68. However, this type of testimony has an important nonsubstantive purpose of which the majority of courts approve. It can be used on rebuttal "to rehabilitate" the victim's testimony when the defense asserts that the child's delay in reporting the abuse and recanting of the story indicate that the child is unworthy of belief. *Myers, supra,* 68 NEB.L.REV. at 51, 86-92.

Another area of behavioral-science testimony seeks to address the ultimate question of whether a child was in fact sexually abused. *Myers, supra*, 68 NEB. L. REV. at 69-86. Such testimony would be based on the clinical observations of a professional "trained in the patterns, effects, and dynamics of child sexual abuse." *Id.* at 73. The authors say that many experts now believe that the study of child sexual abuse has advanced to such a point as to enable "qualified professionals" to "determine whether a child's symptoms and behavior are consistent with sexual abuse." *Id.* at 73-75. . . .

The scientific community does not yet exhibit a consensus that the requisite degree of scientific reliability has been shown. Although some argue that "under no circumstances should a court admit the opinion of an expert about whether a particular child has been abused. . . . The majority of professionals believe qualified mental health professionals can determine whether abuse occurred; not in all cases, but in some." John E. B. Myers, EVIDENCE IN CHILD ABUSE AND NEGLECT CASES § 4.31, at 283-84 (2d ed. 1992) [hereinafter Myers, EVIDENCE IN CHILD ABUSE AND NEGLECT CASES]. In evaluating the qualifications of a witness who seeks to offer substantive evidence of sexual abuse, the trial court may wish to consider the criteria suggested in Myers, *supra*, EVIDENCE IN CHILD ABUSE, AND NEGLECT CASES § 4.31, at 284-85.

> Assessing children for possible sexual abuse is a complex task requiring skill and experience. The expert must possess specialized knowledge of child development, individual and family dynamics, patterns of child sexual abuse, the disclosure process, signs and symptoms of abuse, and the use and limits of psychological tests. The expert is familiar with the literature on child abuse and understands the significance of developmentally inappropriate sexual knowledge. The expert is able to interpret medical reports and laboratory tests. The expert also is trained in the art of interviewing children, and is aware of the literature on coached and fabricated allegations of abuse. Of tremendous importance is the expert's clinical experience with sexually abused children. [*Ibid.*]

Obviously, the more limited the purpose for which the evidence is to be used, e.g., were it not for a substantive but for rehabilitative purpose, the less demanding need be the qualifications of the witness.

* * *

B.

. . . Roland C. Summit, M.D., has authored the most concise and seemingly most authoritative statement of CSAAS. Roland C. Summit, *The Child Sexual Abuse Accommodation Syndrome*, 7 CHILD ABUSE & NEGLECT 177 (1983) [hereinafter Summit]. Dr. Summit explained in 1983 that although "[c]hild sexual abuse has exploded into public awareness during a span of less than five years," the awakening of interest creates new hazards for the child victim because it increases the likelihood of discovery "but fails to protect the victim against the secondary assaults of an inconsistent intervention system." *Id.* at 178 (emphasis omitted). Dr. Summit believed that most adults who hear a distraught child accuse a "respectable" adult of sexual abuse will fault the child. *Ibid.* The "[d]isbelief and rejection by potential adult caretakers," which in Dr. Summit's view were the too-frequent responses to reports of child sexual abuse, "increase the helplessness, hopelessness, isolation and self-blame that make up the most damaging aspects of child sexual victimization."[4] *Ibid.*

To remedy the systemic injury to the child that results from disbelief, Dr. Summit undertook a scientific study of child-sexual-abuse victims. In publishing his results, Dr. Summit hoped "to provide a vehicle for a more sensitive, more therapeutic response to legitimate victims of child sexual abuse and to invite more active, more effective clinical advocacy for the child within the fam-

---

[4] Although scholars report the existence of some fabricated allegations of child sexual abuse, the highest incidence of fabrication tends to occur in custody cases. Myers, *supra,* EVIDENCE IN CHILD ABUSE AND NEGLECT CASES § 4,4., at 225. Furthermore, when fabrication does occur, an adult, not the child, is usually responsible. "[F]alse complaints made by children are very rare." *Id.* at 229 (quoting J. Spencer & R. Flin, THE EVIDENCE OF CHILDREN: THE LAW AND THE PSYCHOLOGY 269 (1990)).

ily and within the systems of child protection and criminal justice." Summit, *supra,* 7 CHILD ABUSE & NEGLECT at 179-80. . . .

. . . The child sexual abuse accommodation syndrom, or CSAAS, "represents a common denominator of the most frequently observed victim behaviors," *Ibid.* CSAAS includes five categories of behavior, each of which contradicts "the most common assumptions of adults." Summit, *supra,* 7 CHILD ABUSE & NEGLECT at 181. Of the five categories, he described two as "preconditions" to the occurrence of sexual abuse and the remaining three as "sequential contingencies" to the abuse "which take on increasing variability and complexity." *Ibid.* Obviously, the "preconditions" continue into and characterize the period of abuse.

The first of the preconditions is secrecy: child abuse happens only when the child is alone with the offending adult, and the experience must never be disclosed. That secrecy is frequently accompanied by threats: "This is our secret; nobody else will understand." "Don't tell anybody." "Nobody will believe." "Don't tell your mother; (a) she will hate you. . . . (c) she will kill you," and the like. Summit, *supra*, 7 CHILD ABUSE & NEGLECT at 181. From the secrecy, the child gets the impression of danger and fearful outcome. *Ibid.* In this case, Norma and Connie testified that they had not reported the alleged abuse because defendant had told them that if they did, he would hit them and they would get into more trouble than him.

The second precondition is helplessness. Dr. Summit explains that the abused child's sense of helplessness is an outgrowth of the child's subordinate role in an authoritarian relationship in which the adult is entrusted with the child's care, such as the parent-child relationship. Summit, *supra*, 7 CHILD ABUSE & NEGLECT at 182. The prevailing reality for the most frequent victim of child sexual abuse is a sense of total dependence on this powerful adult in the face of which the child's normal reaction is to "play possum." *Id.* at 182-83.

The third aspect of the syndrome, also the first of what Dr. Summit identifies as a sequential contingency, is a combination: the child feels trapped by the situation (entrapment), and that perception results in the behavior of accommodating the abuse (accommodation). Because of the child's helplessness, the only healthy option left is to survive by accepting the situation. "There is no way out, no place to run." Summit, *supra,* 7 CHILD ABUSE & NEGLECT at 184. Adults find that hard to believe because they lack the child's perspective, but "[t]he child cannot safely conceptualize that a parent might be ruthless and self-serving; such a conclusion is tantamount to abandonment and annihilation." *Ibid.* The roles of parent and child become reversed; it is the child who must protect the family. The abuser warns, "If you ever tell, they could send me to jail and put all you kids in an orphanage." Summit, *supra*, 7 CHILD ABUSE & NEGLECT at 185.

The fourth aspect, then, is delayed, conflicted and unconvincing disclosure. *Id.* at 186. Most victims never disclose the sexual abuse—at least not outside the immediate family. Dr. Summit found that family conflict triggers disclosure, if ever, "only after some years of continuing sexual abuse and an eventual breakdown of accommodation mechanisms." *Ibid.*

Allegations of sexual abuse seem so unbelievable to most that the natural reaction is to assume the claim is false, especially because the victim did not complain years ago when the alleged abuse was ongoing. *Ibid.* . . . There are very few clues to such abuse. Most women (indeed, even this mother) do not believe it possible that a man whom she loved would ever be capable of molesting his or her own children. Summit, *supra*, 7 Child Abuse & Neglect at 187.

The fifth and final aspect is retraction. Although this case does not involve retraction, that "[w]hatever a child says about sexual abuse, she is likely to reverse it" appears to be a fact. Summit, *supra*, 7 Child Abuse & Neglect at 188 (emphasis omitted). The post-disclosure family situation tends to confirm the victim's worst fears, which encouraged her secrecy in the first place, i.e., her mother is disbelieving or hysterical, her father threatened with removal from the home, and the blame for this state of affairs placed squarely on the victim. Once again, because of the reversed roles, the child feels obligated to preserve the family, even at the expense of his or her own well being. The only "good" choice, then, is to "capitulate" and restore a lie for the family's sake. *Ibid.*

* * *

III

. . . In a long series of cases, we have outlined the general standards that govern the admissibility of (expert opinion) evidence. . . . A summary may be found in *State in R.W.*, *supra*, describing the accepted grounds for admitting expert testimony:

> As provided in the Rules of Evidence, Evid.R. 56, and reiterated by many cases, the testimony of an expert is allowed when it relates to a subject-matter beyond the understanding of persons of ordinary experience, intelligence, and knowledge. This applies as well to the field of child sex-abuse offenses. As we have seen, such testimony may be allowed to explain generally the behavior, feelings, and attitudes of such victims when it is shown that their condition is not readily understood by persons of average intelligence and ordinary experience; and expert or scientific explanation of their condition, one accepted as reliable by the scientific community that is involved in the diagnosis, treatment, and care of such individuals, can assist a jury in understanding the evidence. [104 N.J. at 30-31, 514 A.2d 1287.]

* * *

There does not appear to be a dispute about acceptance within the scientific community of the clinical theory that CSAAS identifies or describes behavioral traits commonly found in child-abuse victims. The most pointed criticism of the theory is that the same traits may equally appear as the result of other disorders. Even extreme poverty or psychological abuse can produce the sense of entrapment or accommodation. In other words, the existence of the symptoms does not invariably prove abuse.

That would be a valid criticism if the CSAAS evidence were offered for a purpose beyond the scope of the scientific theory. An analogy may be drawn from *State v. Cavallo*, 88 N.J. 508, 443 A.2d 1020 (1982). In that case, defense counsel offered to prove that the defendant did not have the characteristics common to all or most rapists and thus to disprove the fact of rape. After reviewing the literature and cases in other jurisdictions, the Court was convinced that the medical or legal communities do not generally accept the view that psychiatrists possess the knowledge or capability to state the likelihood that an individual behaved in a particular manner on a specific occasion.

In contrast, *State v. Kelly*, 97 N.J. 178, 478 A.2d 36 explained that expert scientific evidence concerning "battered-woman's syndrome" does not aid a jury in determining whether a defendant had or had not behaved in a given manner on a particular occasion; rather, the evidence enables the jury to overcome common myths or misconceptions that a woman who had been the victim of battering would have surely left the batterer. Thus, the evidence helps the jury to understand the battered woman's state of mind. *Id.* at 190-97, 204-05, 478 A.2d 364. Because the State in *Kelly* had reinforced those myths by repeatedly asking the victim why she had taken her husband back after the battering, the Court ruled such evidence admissible to counter the myths if reliability of the evidence of a counter-intuitive behavioral pattern were established within the scientific community. *Id.* at 205-06, 211-14, 478 A.2d 364.

IV

Turning then to the application of the standards to that record of this trial, we find that the CSAAS evidence was not presented to the jury in accordance with its scientific theory, i.e., the evidence was not offered to explain the conflicting behavioral traits in this case either of accommodation or delayed disclosure. Rather, the evidence was presented to the jury as though it were to prove directly and substantially that sexual abuse had occurred. Dr. Milchman, the prosecution's expert witness on child sexual abuse, described CSAAS as a pattern of behavior found to occur consistently in children who are victims of incest, and she outlined Dr. Summit's five-part syndrome: secrecy, helplessness, entrapment and accommodation, delayed disclosure, and retraction.

The prosecutor asked whether she had examined Connie and Norma and whether, in the course of examination, Dr. Milchman had found the children to "suffer symptoms of the child sexual abuse accommodation syndrome." . . . Dr. Milchman said that Norma had exhibited four of the symptoms: secrecy, helplessness, accommodation, and delayed disclosure. . . . Dr. Milchman pointed out that Norma had revealed the abuse only after questioning initiated by her mother. She also explained that Norma had stuck to her story, instead of recanting it, because nobody was pressuring or threatening her. Connie, on the other hand, had presented herself differently as a "very brassy, very assertive, very outgoing child on the surface" but "[u]nderneath there was a lot of fear and anxiety." Dr. Milchman described Connie as being entrapped and accommodating to the abuse—she complied and accepted the abuse for a long time. She also believed Connie had given a delayed disclosure. Dr. Milchman believed that Connie had kept the abuse a secret for a long time because John had threatened her and her mother with physical violence, a threat she believed because she had seen her father be violent with her mother.

* * *

However, Dr. Milchman then proceeded to describe how one could "tell whether a child is lying." For example, a child's speaking in a mechanical way, "like it was by rote memory rather than by their own feelings," could raise the suspicion that the child was trying to remember what someone else had told him or her, thereby undermining the child's credibility. Or a child's perfectly consistent narration of all details of the story would be inconsistent, she said, with a child's natural tendency to forget minor detail. Certainly the prefatory basis of CSAAS has nothing to do with those areas of opinion.

* * *

Yet, in this case Dr. Milchman was asked, "How can you tell when a child or a victim is telling the truth about the fact that they have been sexually abused?" Although the court cautioned the jurors that it was up to them ultimately to determine that, the expert proffered a theory—again unrelated to CSAAS:

> Okay. I look for—look for many different things. I look for whether the child appears to be sincere. I look for whether or not the feeling that they have at the time goes with what they are saying or whether it contradicts what they are saying. I go for whether there are a lot of different behaviors that all point to the same conclusion. For example, is what the child [sic] saying, does that match the demonstrations that they give when they try to explain it with their hands or with dolls, does it match the pictures that they draw for me? Does it match what they told the mother; does it match what they told the DYFS worker; does it match what they told the Prosecutor or investigator; or does it match what they told me? I look for consistency across a lot of different kinds of behaviors. . . .

The final question to the witness was: "Doctor, based on your examinations of the girls can you give this jury your expert opinion as to whether or not both [Connie] and [Norma] were sexually abused?" Answer: "I believe that they were sexually abused."

At this point, whether Dr. Milchman had reached that opinion on the basis of her credibility assessments or on the basis of her understanding of CSAAS evidence is not clear to us and could not have been clear to the jury. If it were the former, it would be improper opinion evidence because it would introduce an unwarranted aura of scientific reliability to the analysis of credibility issues. If it were the latter, it would be improper opinion evidence because CSAAS is not relied on in the scientific community to detect abuse.

There has not been a showing in the record in this case, nor seemingly in other scientific literature or decisional law, of a general acceptance that would allow the use of CSAAS testimony to establish guilt or innocence. . . . As Myers noted:

> Summit did not intend the accommodation syndrome as diagnostic device. The syndrome does not detect sexual abuse. Rather, it assumes the presence of abuse, and explains the child's reactions to it. Thus, child sexual abuse accommodation syndrome is not the sex-

ual abuse analogue of battered child syndrome, which is diagnostic of physical abuse. With battered child syndrome, one reasons from type of injury to cause of injury. Thus, battered child syndrome is probative of physical abuse. With child sexual abuse accommodation syndrome, by contrast, one reasons from presence of sexual abuse to reactions to sexual abuse. Thus, the accommodation syndrome is not probative of abuse.

* * *

. . . The accommodation syndrome has a place in the courtroom. The syndrome helps explain why many sexually abused children delay reporting their abuse, and why many children recant allegations of abuse and deny that anything occurred. If use of the syndrome is confined to these rehabilitative functions, . . . the accommodation syndrome serves a useful forensic function. [Myers, *supra*, 68 NEB.L.REV. at 67-68.]

* * *

Such use accords with the use now generally afforded to rape trauma syndrome (RTS) evidence most often in the context of adult rape. RTS describes symptoms frequently experienced by rape victims, e.g., phobic reactions and sexual fears. Because RTS was developed as a therapeutic tool, not as a test to determine the existence of a past event, the California Supreme Court in *People v. Bledsoe*, 36 Cal.3d 236, 203 Cal.Rptr. 450, 681 P.2d 291 (1984), questioned the reliability of RTS in determining whether a rape has occurred. Thus, the court held that, given the history, purpose and nature of RTS, testimony on the concept was inadmissible to prove that a rape occurred, but recognized that RTS testimony has been admitted in cases in which the alleged rapist suggests that the victim's conduct after the incident was inconsistent with her claim of rape. In the latter context, expert testimony of RTS may play a particularly useful role by disabusing the jury of widely-held myths and misconceptions about rape and rape victims. *Id.* at 457, 681 P.2d at 289.

* * *

The State has argued before us that it is appropriate to admit Dr. Milchman's testimony describing CSAAS and concluding that Norma's and Connie's symptoms were consistent with sexual abuse and rendering an expert opinion that they had been sexually abused. Obviously, scientific evidence exists to aid a jury in determining whether sexual abuse has occurred. As we understand CSAAS, however, it does not purport to establish sexual abuse but helps to explain traits often found in children who have been abused. Hence we believe that in this case the "accommodation syndrome was being asked [by the State] to perform a task it could not accomplish." Myers *supra*, 68 NEB. L. REV. at 68.

In this case the theory of the defense was that the children had been put up to their stories by a vengeful scorned lover. The CSAAS evidence would have served well to counter the mythology that if the abuse had occurred, the children surely would have complained sooner and would not have put up with repeated visits to the apartment in Brooklyn. However, when the expert, without a reliable foundation, went on to offer opinions with respect to the basic factual issues, including truth-telling, she transgressed the purpose for which CSAAS testimony is admissible.

* * *

In setting forth these requirements, we do not intend in any sense to mystify the trial of child-sexual-abuse cases. All that is required is close attention to existing precedent: (1) are the factual matters "beyond the ken" of the jurors, and will expert testimony aid the jury in resolution of the matter?; (2) is the proposed expert witness qualified by education, training, experience, and knowledge to express an opinion on the factual matter in dispute?; (3) is there general acceptance of the scientific theory or even the methodology used to establish the factual proposition?; and (4) will the jury be given proper instructions limiting the evidence to the purpose for which it is offered? The study of child sexual abuse is rapidly evolving, and we may expect that behavioral scientists will continue their efforts to develop reliable criteria to detect child sexual abuse.

* * *

The judgment of the Appellate Division is affirmed.

Notes

1. For a brief discussion of the traits that make up child sexual abuse accommodation syndrome (CSAAS), see Chapter 8, Part C.2.b. The use of expert testimony to describe CSAAS introduces considerable difficulty to a trial where often the only evidence comes from a child victim. *See* Rosemary L. Flint, Note, *Child Sexual Abuse Accommodation Syndrome: Admissibility Requirements,* 23 AM. J. CRIM. L. 171, 172 (1995). Furthermore, children may wait a long period of time before reporting sexual abuse or they may retract allegations of abuse. As a result, physical or medical evidence of abuse may be difficult to obtain. Finally, children often must testify at the trial. Jurors may find it difficult to believe a child whose memory is impeded by trauma or who may be perceived as not knowing fact from fantasy. *Id.; see also* Elaine R. Cacciola, *The Admissibility of Expert Testimony in Intrafamily Child Sexual Abuse Cases,* 34 UCLA L. REV. 175, 175-76 (1986). Proponents of allowing expert testimony argue that it is for these reasons that experts should be permitted to explain CSAAS to the factfinder. Several jurisdictions have held that expert testimony of CSAAS should not be admitted into evidence. *See Lantrip v. Kentucky*, 713 S.W.2d 816 (Ky. 1986) (CSAAS rejected where no evidence was presented to demonstrate acceptance among psychologists); *Commonwealth v. Garcia*, 588 A.2d 951 (Pa. Super. Ct. 1997) (expert testimony makes child seem more credible than is necessary). For a survey of how other jurisdictions have decided the question of admission of CSAAS, see Cacciola, *supra*, at 194-205; *see also* Lisa R. Askowitz, *Restricting the Admissibility of Expert Testimony in Child Sexual Abuse Prosecutions: Pennsylvania Takes It to the Extreme,* 47 U. MIAMI L. REV. 201, 208-13 (1996); David McCord, *Expert Psychological Testimony About Child Complainants in Sexual Abuse Prosecutions: A Foray Into the Admissibility of Novel Psychological Evidence,* 77 J. CRIM. L. & CRIM-

INOLOGY 1 (1986); Monique K. Cirelli, *Expert Testimony in Child Abuse Cases: Helpful or Prejudicial?* People v. Beckley, 8 T.M. COOLEY L. REV. 425 (1991); Mary Ann Mason, *The Child Sex Abuse Syndrome: The Other Major Issue in* State of New Jersey v. Margaret Kelly Michaels, 1 PSYCHOL. PUB. POL'Y & L. 399 (1995); Linda Anderson, Note, United States v. Azure: *Admissibility of Expert Testimony in Child Sexual Abuse Cases,* 15 J. CONTEMP. L. 285 (1989); John E.B. Myers et al., *Expert Testimony in Child Sexual Abuse Litigation,* 68 NEB. L. REV. 1 (1989); Andrew Cohen, Note, *The Unreliability of Expert Testimony on the Typical Characteristics of Sexual Abuse Victims,* 74 GEO. L.J. 429 (1985); Elizabeth Vaughan Baker, *Psychological Expert Testimony on a Child's Veracity in Child Abuse Prosecutions,* 50 LA. L. REV. 1039 (1990). For further discussion of *State v. J.Q, supra*, see Gail Ezra Cary, Casenote, *Evidence—Expert Testimony—The Admissibility of Child Sexual Abuse Accommodation Syndrome in Child Sexual Abuse Prosecutions.* State v. J.Q., *130 N.J. 554, 617 A.2d 1196 (1993)*, 26 RUTGERS L.J. 251 (1994).

Questions

1. What factors should a court consider in determining whether to admit CSAAS evidence? Does it matter if the case is tried to the court or a jury?

2. How effective is the following limiting instruction by the court in a termination of parental rights trial: "Ladies and gentlemen of the jury, you may not consider Dr. Bloggs' testimony that Sara exhibited the traits of CSAA as proof that she was sexually abused by her father; however, you may consider evidence of CSAAS to explain why Sara recanted her allegation of sexual abuse by her father."

2. Anatomically Correct Dolls

In re Amber B.

236 Cal. Rptr. 623 (Cal. Ct. App. 1987)

KING, Associate Justice.

In this case we hold that the psychological technique of detecting child sexual abuse by observing the child's behavior with anatomically correct dolls and analyzing the child's report of abuse constitutes a new scientific method of proof, and therefore is admissible in court only upon a showing that the technique has been generally accepted as reliable in the scientific community in which it was developed.

* * *

A petition filed by the Solano County Department of Social Services alleged that Ron had sexually molested three-year-old Amber and that one-year-old Teela was at risk of sexual abuse. At the hearing on the petition the Department presented testimony by a psychologist, Dr. Henry Raming, who had examined Amber on three occasions. Over Ron's objection, the court permitted Dr. Raming to testify that, in his opinion, Amber had been sexually molested and she believed she had been molested by her father.

Dr. Raming's opinion was based on two factors. The first was the nature of Amber's reports of abuse, in which she described instances of abuse in varying ways. According to Dr. Raming, it is "fairly well documented in the literature . . . that children who have been molested will talk about being abused, but they will do this by consistently giving the . . . same facts or the essence in different words such that they have an event or an experience in their minds and are not merely repeating . . . rote by rote, someone else's words. . . ."

The second factor was the nature of Amber's behavior with an anatomically correct female doll in Dr. Raming's office. During two of Dr. Raming's examinations Amber placed her index finger in the vaginal anal openings of the doll and pushed and twisted her finger vigorously. According to Dr. Raming, Amber's behavior with the doll "is fairly consistent with molested children. This is not the usual type of behavior one would see in children who are in a stage of age appropriate sex exploration. . . . [W]hen children this age describe or graphically demonstrate anal or vaginal penetration, it's pretty much assumed that the child learned that from experience and not from . . . sex exploration with other children."

The only other witnesses presented by the Department, a police detective and a social worker, also testified regarding the nature of Amber's reports of abuse and her behavior with an anatomically correct doll. Amber did not testify. Ron testified in his own behalf and denied the abuse.

The court ruled that Amber had been molested while in the custody of her parents, that Amber believed she had been molested by her father, and that Teela was at risk of sexual abuse because of the sexual abuse of Amber. The court did not sustain the allegation identifying Ron as the perpetrator of the abuse. In its dispositional order the court declared both children to be dependent children of the juvenile court, placed them in the custody of their mother, afforded Ron supervised visitation, and required counseling for Amber and both parents.

Ron challenges the admission of Dr. Raming's opinion testimony that Amber had been molested and she believed she had been molested by her father. He contends the opinion was based on a new scientific method of proof—the analysis of Amber's reports of abuse and behavior with anatomically correct dolls—that had not been shown to satisfy the *Kelly-Frye* test of admissibility.

Under the *Kelly-Frye* rule, evidence based on a new scientific method of proof is admissible only upon a showing that the procedure has been generally accepted as reliable in the scientific community in which it was developed. (*People v. Kelly* (1976) 17 Cal.3d 24, [130 CAL. RPTR. 144, 549 P.2d 1240]; *Frye v. United States* (D. C. Cir. 1923) 293 F. 1013 [34 A.L.R. 145].) The test is usually applied to novel devices or processes involving the manipulation of physical evidence, such as lie detectors, experimental systems of blood typing, voiceprints, identification by human bite marks, and microscopic analysis of gunshot residue. (*See People v. McDonald* (1984) 37 Cal.3d 351, 373, 208 Cal.Rptr. 236, 690 P.2d 709.)

The *Kelly-Frye* test is not, however, limited to techniques involving the manipulation of physical evidence. In a recent decision applying the test to hypnosis, the California Supreme Court said, "[W]e do not doubt that if testimony based on a new scientific process operating on purely psychological evidence were to be offered in our courts, it would likewise be subjected to the *Frye* standard of admissibility." (*People v. Shirley* (1982) 31 Cal.3d 18, 53, 181 Cal.Rptr. 243, 723 P.2d 1354.)

The purpose of the *Kelly-Frye* test is to prevent factfinders from being misled by the "aura of infallibility" that may surround unproven scientific methods. (*People v. McDonald, supra,* 37 Cal.3d at pp. 372-373, 208 Cal.Rptr. 2690 P.2d 709.) "[L]ike many laypersons, jurors tend to ascribe an inordinately high degree of certainty to proof derived from an apparently 'scientific' mechanism, instrument, or procedure." (*Id.* at p. 372, 208 Cal.Rptr. 236, 690 P.2d 709.)

The test does not apply to mere expert testimony as distinguished from scientific evidence. "When a witness gives his personal opinion on the stand–even if he qualified as an expert–the jurors may temper their acceptance of his testimony with a healthy skepticism born of their knowledge that all human beings are fallible." (*Ibid.*) In contrast, factfinders may not view scientific evidence with such skepticism, and indeed will "tend to ascribe an inordinately high degree of certainty" to such evidence. (*Ibid.*)

The fundamental issue presented here is whether the technique employed by Dr. Raming for detecting child sexual abuse is a new scientific method of proof which must satisfy the *Kelly-Frye* test of admissibility, or whether Dr. Raming simply gave expert testimony to which the test does not apply.

In admitting Dr. Raming's testimony the trial court adhered strictly to *In re Cheryl H.* (1984) 153 Cal.App.3d 1098, 200 Cal.Rptr. 789. In that case a psychiatrist testified that in her opinion three-year-old Cheryl had been sexually abused by her father. This opinion was based upon psychological tests and Cheryl's behavior at personal interviews, including Cheryl's sexual play with anatomically correct dolls and her invention of new names for genitalia. (*Id.* at pp. 1109-1110, 200 Cal.Rptr. 789.) The appellate court held it was proper to admit the opinion that Cheryl had been abused, because Cheryl's postinjury behavior "appears to be unique to children subjected to child abuse. . . . The child played with male and female dolls in a way only children who have been sexually abused ordinarily do. She also used words and demonstrated anxiety symptoms characteristic of those who have been sexually abused." (*Id.* at p. 1117, 200 Cal.Rptr. 789.)

The *Cheryl H.* court held it was error, however, to admit the opinion that Cheryl's father was the person who committed the abuse, because this testimony impermissibly drew inferences about conduct by a third party based primarily on hearsay. (*Id.* at pp. 1118-1120, 200 Cal.Rptr. 789.) The court said the psychiatrist should only have been permitted to express an opinion that Cheryl believed her father was the one who abused her. (*Id.* at p. 1119, 200 Cal. Rptr. 780.) Accordingly, in the present case the trial court permitted Dr. Raming to testify only that Amber had been abused and she believed her father was the one who abused her.

The *Cheryl H.* opinion did not discuss the potential applicability of the *Kelly-Frye* rule. The court simply accepted the psychiatrist's analysis of Cheryl's behavior as demonstrating prior sexual abuse. The court drew an analogy to *People v. Jackson* (1971) 18 Cal.App.3d 5 Cal.Rptr. 919, which characterized as admissible expert testimony a diagnosis of "battered child syndrome" based on the presence of certain types of physical injuries. (153 Cal. App.3d at pp. 116-117, 200 Cal.Rptr. 789.)

Shortly after *Cheryl H.* the California Supreme Court decided *People v. Bledsoe* (1984) 36 Cal.3d 236, 203 Cal.Rptr. 450, 681 P.2d 291, which applied *Kelly-Frye* to testimony pertaining to the closely analogous concept of "rape trauma syndrome" and found the evidence inadmissible. The decision in *Bledsoe* calls for careful consideration of whether evidence of the sort admitted in *Cheryl H.* and the present case should be subject to the *Kelly-Frye* test.

The concept of rape trauma syndrome is based on the theory that after a rape the victim will follow a set pattern of reaction to the trauma of the rape. The court in *Bledsoe*, applying the *Kelly-Frye* test, disapproved the admission of a counselor's opinion testimony that the victim was suffering from rape trauma syndrome, because the theory was not relied upon in the relevant scientific community for the purpose employed by the prosecutor. The theory was developed as a therapeutic tool, not as a scientifically reliable means of determining whether a rape occurred. . . . The court did not discuss *why* the *Kelly-Frye* rule applied, but simply quoted the prior statement in *Shirley* that *Kelly-Frye* would apply to "testimony based on a new scientific process operating on purely psychological evidence." (36 Cal.3d at p. 247, fn. 7, 203 Cal. Rptr. 450, 681 P.2d 291, quoting *People v. Shirley, supra*, 31 Cal.3d at p. 53, 181 Cal.Rptr. 243, 723 P.2d 1354.)

The method of proof relied upon by Dr. Raming is closely analogous to that in *Bledsoe*, because in both cases the expert witnesses relied upon a psychological analysis of a subject's behavior to determine whether sexual abuse had previously occurred. Thus the decision in *Bledsoe* strongly suggests evidence of the sort admitted here and in *Cheryl H.* should be subject to *Kelly-Frye*.

* * *

Three preliminary questions must be addressed before reaching the heart of the *Kelly-Frye* issue. The first is whether . . . less strict rules of admissibility apply in dependency proceedings under Welfare and Institutions Code section 300 than in criminal cases. . . . Welfare and Institutions Code section 355 states that a finding of dependency must be supported by evidence that is "legally admissible in the trial of civil cases." The *Kelly-Frye* rule has been applied in civil cases in California. The rule therefore applies in dependency proceedings.

The second preliminary question is whether the objection to Dr. Raming's testimony was adequate to preserve the *Kelly-Frye* question for appellate review. This question is easily answered: counsel expressly sought exclusion of the testimony on the ground "there's . . . no really established scientific evidence that the type of opinion they're [sic] giving meets the *Frye* standard for admissibility. . . ."

The third preliminary question is whether Dr. Raming's testimony suffered from the same deficiency as in *Bledsoe*, that of being based on a method of therapy rather than a means of determining whether sexual abuse had occurred. In this respect the present case appears to differ from *Bledsoe*. Counsel below pointed out that Dr. Raming was appointed by the court not to perform therapy but to conduct a psychological evaluation. Dr. Raming's testimony indicates he had sought to determine whether Amber had been sexually abused. (Cf. Comment, *The Admissibility of "Child Sexual Abuse Accommodation Syndrome" in California Criminal Courts* (1986) 17 Pacific L.J.1361, 1381 [stating that theory of "child sexual abuse accommodation syndrome" is "used in the mental health field to determine if sexual abuse has occurred"].)[3]

This brings us to the heart of the *Kelly-Frye* issue: is the technique employed by Dr. Raming for detecting child sexual abuse a new scientific method of proof which must satisfy *Kelly-Frye*, or did Dr. Raming simply provide expert testimony? The answer to this question is elusive. *Kelly-Frye* is clearly applicable where evidence is produced by a machine such as a lie detector, or by a physical testing procedure such as blood typing. The cases have provided little guidance, however, for determining at what point evidence based upon a psychological analysis of behavior transcends expert testimony and becomes scientific evidence. Indeed, one of the recognized weaknesses of the *Kelly-Frye* test is the difficulty in defining what types of evidence should be classified as scientific.

* * *

Rather than attempting to determine the presence of a "new scientific method of proof" based upon factors pertaining to the nature of the challenged procedure–a difficult task in cases involving psychological analysis of behavior–it makes more sense to decide this issue by reference to the purpose of the *Kelly-Frye* rule. That purpose is to prevent factfinders from being misled by the "aura of infallibility" that may surround unproven scientific methods. (*People v. McDonald, supra*, 37 Cal.3d at pp. 372-373, 208 Cal.Rptr. 236, 690 P.2d 709.) Accordingly, a scientific procedure, technique or theory should be characterized as a "new scientific method of proof," subject to *Kelly-Frye*, if factfinders would "tend to ascribe an inordinately high degree of certainty" to it. (*See id.* at 372, 208 Cal.Rptr. 236, 690 P.2d 709.)

The determinative question in the present case thus becomes: would a trier of fact ascribe an inordinately high degree of certainty to the technique employed by Dr. Raming for determining the occurrence of child sexual abuse?

We consider that the practice of detecting child sexual abuse by (1) observing a child's behavior with anatomically correct dolls, and (2) analyzing the

---

3 "Child sexual abuse accommodation syndrome" describes the purportedly typical behavior of children who have been victims of repeated sexual abuse by a family member or an adult with whom the child has a trusting relationship. It is comprised of one or more of five elements: secrecy, helplessness, entrapment and accommodation, delayed disclosure, and retraction. Dr. Raming did not mention child sexual abuse accommodation syndrome or its elements. He confined his testimony to Amber's behavior with anatomically correct dolls and her reports of abuse. This case, therefore, does not present the issue whether the theory of child sexual abuse accommodation syndrome is subject to *Kelly-Frye*. The theory, however, seems quite similar to that of rape trauma syndrome, suggesting that, as in *Bledsoe,* the *Kelly-Frye* test would apply.

child's reports of abuse, is what *Shirley* characterizes as "a new scientific process operating on purely psychological evidence" (31 Cal.3d at p. 53, 181 Cal.Rptr. 243, 723 P.2d 1354) and is subject to the *Kelly-Frye* test. The specific causes of age-inappropriate child sexual behavior, and indeed the entire field of child sexuality since the theories of Sigmund Freud, are beyond the scope of critical analysis by the average lay person. Thus a psychologist's examination and analysis employing the technique used by Dr. Raming may be surrounded by an "aura of infallibility," and a trier of fact would tend to ascribe "an ordinately [sic] high degree of certainty" to the technique (*People v. McDonald, supra,* 37 Cal.3d at p. 372, 208 Cal.Rptr. 236, 690 P.2d 709.) Unlike with expert testimony where a witness gives a personal opinion, triers of fact are in no position to temper their acceptance of the psychological evidence "with a healthy skepticism born of their knowledge that all human beings are fallible." (*Ibid.*).

The trial court therefore erred when it failed to require a showing of general acceptance in the relevant scientific community in accordance with *Kelly-Frye*.

For this reason the dependency order must be reversed. Because of the court's ruling that Dr. Raming could testify pursuant to *Cheryl H.*, the Department made no attempt to establish general acceptance in the relevant scientific community. In cross-examining Dr. Raming, Ron's counsel briefly explored the question whether there was any disagreement among the authorities upon which Dr. Raming relied, but Dr. Raming's general responses were far from sufficient to satisfy *Kelly-Frye*. The error cannot be characterized as harmless, because the Department's entire case was based upon Dr. Raming's analysis of Amber's reports of abuse and her behavior with anatomically correct dolls. Any retrial must proceed in accordance with the requirements of *Kelly-Frye*.

We recognize that unique problems of proof are presented whenever it is claimed that a young child was the victim of sexual abuse by a parent. The child may be incompetent to testify, the act of testifying could be as traumatic as the abuse itself, and the child may be subjected to strong parental influences. The trial judge, the parties, and society in general would greatly benefit from *reliable* expert testimony addressing the question whether the child was abused, either in lieu of or in addition to testimony by the child. However, we cannot approve such expert testimony until its reliability is shown pursuant to *Kelly-Frye*.

The order is reversed.

Judgment affirmed.

Notes

1. According to the American Professional Society on the Abuse of Children, anatomically correct dolls can serve as a memory stimulus, a demonstration aid, a screening tool, and as an anatomical model. *See* JOHN E.B. MYERS, LEGAL ISSUES IN CHILD ABUSE AND NEGLECT PRACTICE 339-51 (2d ed. 1998). Anatomical dolls can be used for appropriate (*id.* at 343-46) and inappropriate uses (*id.* at 346). The court should look for the child (1) placing the dolls in sexual positions, (2) giving "oral sex" to the doll, (3) manual exploration of the genitals and visible signs of distress, aggressiveness, or fear, or (4) detailed knowledge of sexual activity.

Use of anatomically correct dolls in child sex abuse cases is widespread. *See* Dianna Younts, Note, *Evaluating and Admitting Expert Opinion Testimony in Child Sexual Abuse Prosecutions,* 41 DUKE L.J. 691, 708 (1991) (94% of child protection workers and 46% of law enforcement use dolls); Celia B. Fisher & Katherine A. Whiting, *How Valid Are Child Sexual Abuse Validations?, in* EXPERT WITNESSES IN CHILD ABUSE CASES: WHAT CAN AND SHOULD BE SAID IN COURT 159, 173 (Stephen J. Ceci & Helene Hembrooke eds.,1998) (68% to 92% of those recognized as experts in the field of sex abuse use anatomically correct dolls). However, there is considerable skepticism concerning the use of anatomically correct dolls for court-related purposes. Some argue that the dolls should be excluded from legal proceedings because of the lack of scientific knowledge to support the doll's use and the high risk of undue prejudice. Younts, *supra*, at 706 (citing *In re Amber B., supra*). *See also* Ceci at 173; Jeffrey P. Bloom, *Post-Schumpert Era Independent Interviews and Psychological Evaluations of Children,* S.C. LAW. July/Aug. 1988, at 40, 44 (1998) (dolls are inherently suggestive which leads to corrupted memory and testimony). An anatomically correct doll may corrupt a child's memory and lead to falsification. *See* John R. Christiansen, *The Testimony of Child Witnesses: Fact, Fantasy, and the Influences of Pretrial Interviews,* 62 WASH. L. REV. 705 (1987).

Furthermore, skeptics argue that anatomically correct dolls should not be used with children of certain ages. For example, toddlers who are being "potty-trained" might be more fascinated with the genitalia as a result of the constant emphasis of using the restroom on their own. *See* JAMES SELKIN, THE CHILD SEXUAL ABUSE CASE IN THE COURTROOM 217 (2d ed. 1991). For further discussion of the controversy that surrounds the use of anatomically correct dolls, see Younts, *supra,* at 708-20. For additional discussion of the admissibility and reliability of evidence obtained by using anatomically correct dolls, see L. Jampole & M.K. Weber, *An Assessment of the Behavior of Sexually Abused and Non-Sexually Abused Children With Anatomically Correct Dolls*, 11 CHILD ABUSE & NEGLECT 187-92 (1987); R.L. August & B.D. Foreman, *A Comparison of Sexually and Non-Sexually Abused Children's Behavioral Responses to Anatomically Correct Dolls,* 20 CHILD PSYCHIATRY & HUM. DEV. 39-478 (1989); G.P. Koocher et al., *Psychological Science and the Use of Anatomically Detailed Dolls in Child Sexual Abuse Assessments: Final Report of the American Psychological Association Anatomical Doll Task Force,* 138 PSYCHOL. BULL. 2 (1995); B.W. Boat & M.D. Everson, *Anatomical Doll Exploration Among Non-Referred Children: Comparison by Age, Gender, Race, and Socioeconomic Status,* 18 CHILD & NEGLECT 139-153 (1994); G.M. Realmuto et al., *Specificity and Sensitivity of Sexually Anatomically Correct Dolls in Substantiating Abuse: A Pilot Study,* 19 J. AM. ACADEMIC OF CHILD & ADOLESCENT PSYCHIATRY 743-46 (1990).

2. The National Center of Prosecution of Child Abuse recommends that prosecutors should approach the use of anatomically correct dolls with caution. *See* INVESTIGATION AND PROSECUTION OF CHILD ABUSE 80 (2d ed. 1993). Prosecutors are advised that the use of anatomically correct dolls should take place only after the child relates that sexual abuse occurred. Furthermore, prosecutors are encouraged to take a hands-off approach when the child has the doll. The prosecutor should allow the child to take off the doll's clothes without prompting or leading questions. Then the prosecutor may ask the child to identify the doll's body parts and show what happened between the child and the alleged perpetrator. Finally, prosecutors are urged to never encourage children to "imagine" or to "play" with the doll.

3. Despite the controversy surrounding the use of anatomically correct dolls, many states have codified their use. Some states allow attorneys to use anatomically correct dolls in the courtroom. *See, e.g.,* 42 PA. CONS. STAT. ANN. § 5987 (West 2000) (court shall permit use of anatomically correct dolls to assist alleged victim); N.Y. CRIM. PROC. LAW § 60.44 (McKinney 1992) (in court's discretion, any person under sixteen may use doll when testifying in incest cases); N.Y. EXEC. LAW § 642-a (McKinney Supp. 2001) (in court's discretion, child witness should be allowed to use anatomically correct doll); W. VA. CODE § 61-8-13 (Lexis 2000) (in court's discretion, child under eleven years of age may use anatomically correct doll in incest cases); 1997 N.H. LAWS 93-A (court may use anatomically correct doll in any sex-related offense in which a child is the victim). *See also* W. VA. Code §§ 61-8B-11(d), 61-8C-5(b) (Lexis 2000). Other states allow attorneys to videotape a child using anatomically correct dolls which is then admitted as evidence at trial. *See, e.g.*, WYO. STAT. ANN. § 7-11-408(f) (Lexis 1999) (videotape shall be admissible as demonstrative evidence); CONN. GEN. STAT. § 54-86g(b) (West 1994). Alabama gives the court the option of videotaping the child using the anatomically correct doll or allowing the child to use the doll in court. *See* ALA. CODE § 15-25-5 (Lexis 1995). *See generally* MICH. COMP. LAWS ANN. §§ 600.2163a, 24.275a (West 2000).

Questions

1. What objections should be made to evidence of a child's handling of anatomically correct dolls?

2. Assume that a caseworker asks a child to "show her what happened" by using anatomically correct dolls. Is the child's manipulation of the dolls assertive conduct and therefore inadmissible hearsay evidence? What policy arguments are relevant on the issue of admissibility?

3. Battering Parent Syndrome

Sanders v. State
303 S.E.2d 13 (Ga. 1983)

Lillian Sanders appeals her conviction and life sentence for the murder of her infant daughter, Cassandra Denise Sanders. There was evidence at trial showing that Cassandra was born September 11, 1981. She was twelve weeks premature and had a low birth weight, a hernia, and anemia. She was hospitalized for treatment of these ailments and was discharged November 6. On November 17 she was treated at a pediatric clinic for fussiness stemming from a suspected allergy, and on November 30 for a cold and a fungus infection. The clinic's record of the November 30 examination had a notation that Cassandra had gained weight, but did not indicate that bruises or other injuries had been found.

At about three p.m. on December 3, 1981 appellant used a neighbor's phone to call the police. She told the police dispatcher her baby was sick, and asked for an ambulance. The dispatcher later said appellant was not sobbing, and her voice seemed normal; appellant's neighbor testified she seemed worried. After making the call Sander's returned to her own home, from which the neighbor then heard crying and hollering. When the county emergency medical service arrived at appellant's residence a few minutes later, the technicians found her holding Cassandra in her arms. One technician asked what the trouble was and she replied the baby had been crying and had just stopped. She also repeatedly told them, "Please don't let my baby die." The technicians gave Cassandra a quick examination and found multiple bruises on her face, neck, chest and abdomen. A patch of skin was missing from her neck, and one side of her head was mushy due to blood and fluid under the skin. The child was gasping for breath, had a high pulse and low respiration, and appeared unconscious. The technicians then took Cassandra and her mother to the emergency room of Archbold Hospital, arriving about 3:20 p.m. At the emergency room Dr. Randolph Malone examined the infant, who had stopped breathing and was being given artificial respiration. At that point she was unconscious and appeared dead. Because she had suffered a severe head injury and had unusual bruise marks around the neck he had the police notified, and he questioned Lillian about what had happened. She told him she didn't know, even though she had been with the baby right until she left to call the ambulance.

Forest Roberts, a child protective services worker with the Thomas County Department of Family and Children Services, was summoned to the hospital and was told that Sanders was suspected of child abuse. She questioned appellant, who first told her that she didn't know what had happened to the baby, that there had been nothing wrong with her earlier, and that she had gone in to check on her and found her like that. She said she might have "popped" her to make her stop crying, but insisted she hadn't hurt her. . . . Roberts left the room, then returned and told her the child was seriously ill, that it didn't appear she'd gotten that way by herself, and appellant needed to tell her what happened. Lillian said she may have dropped the baby but didn't remember. . . . In the course of their interrogation she told them that the child had fallen out of her hands when she reached for something on a table or chest of drawers in the bedroom. She was asked if the child had struck anything except the floor, and she said she hadn't. Her demeanor during this inquiry was confused but otherwise normal, except that a few minutes later she cried.

The baby was pronounced dead at 5:30 that afternoon. Appellant was taken to the police station where shortly after seven that evening she was again questioned after being given Miranda warnings .... When queried about Cassandra's head injury, she said she may have mashed her head while picking her up.

Dr. Larry Howard, forensic pathologist and Director of the State Crime Labatory, performed the autopsy. He testified that the primary cause of death was a severe crushing type head injury which consisted of a circular skull fracture on the right side of the head. There was severe damage to the brain, including much bleeding in the brain tissue and laceration of the brain by the edges of the skull fracture. There were numerous bruises on the face, chest, and abdomen. The neck had considerable bruising and abrasions which were possible fingernail marks, indicating pressure may have been applied to the neck with a hand. Similar possible fingernail abrasions were found on the chest and the back of the right hand. The upper right arm was broken, probably by someone placing tension on it until it snapped. The liver had been split, which was an injury consistent with a blow to the front of the chest. This injury was at least four and possibly twelve hours older than many of the others, which appeared fresh. Some of the bruises were lined up as if caused by a blunt instrument with several projections, which would have been consistent with the child having been struck by the knuckles of a hand. In his opinion these injuries were not consistent with the child having been dropped on a floor, and he described them as evidencing a typical battered child syndrome. Moreover, he testified they would have been impossible for another young child to inflict.

1) Although appellant has not raised the general grounds we have nevertheless reviewed the evidence in a light most favorable to the jury's verdict. *See Payne v. State*, 249 Ga. 354(1), 291 S.E.2d 226 (1982). We conclude that a rational trier of fact could reasonably have found Sanders guilty of murder beyond a doubt, *Jackson v. Virginia*, 443 U.S. 307, 99 S. Ct. 2781, 61 L. Ed. 2d 560 (1979).

2) In her first enumeration of error appellant complains that the trial court should not have admitted into evidence the state's thirteenth exhibit, which was an autopsy photograph of the victim with her scalp reflected to show the fractured skull, lacerated brain, and blood from hemorrhaging, on the ground that it was an intentional distortion of the original evidence and was gruesome and inflammatory. Although the photograph is gruesome, we find its admission was necessary to show the cause of death, which had become apparent only because of the autopsy. *Brown v. State,* 250 Ga. 862(5), 302 S.E.2d 347 (1983).

3) In her second enumeration Sanders claims the state impermissibly placed her character in issue. The record shows that three employees of the Department of Family and Children Services ("the Department") testified for the prosecution. Their combined testimony established certain aspects of appellant's personal history and the fact that appellant had sought the Department's

help on several occasions. Specifically, they testified that during the period 1976-81 Sanders had moved several times and had asked the Department for help in locating housing; that she had sought food stamps; that both her children had been problem pregnancies; that appellant's mother had contacted the Department and complained about the quality of care Chrishenbo was receiving and about appellant's attitude toward the child; that Lillian was counseled about child care and a stable living environment; and that appellant's mother's own family had been supervised by the Department for several years. Following this testimony about appellant's background, Dr. Wallace Kennedy, a clinical psychologist, took the stand to testify about the "battering parent syndrome." . . . Dr. Kennedy constructed a profile of the typical abusive parent. . . . He testified that the characteristics of an adult who abuses a child in a life threatening fashion almost always are, first, that the parent herself is the product of a violent, abusive environment and usually commits violent acts with growing frequency; second, that the parent is under some kind of chronic environmental stress, caused by, for example, money or housing problems, and is frequently a single parent; third, that the parent has a history of poor social judgment, in that she tends to be impulsive or explosive under stress; fourth, that the child she abuses is the product of an unplanned, difficult, and unpleasant pregnancy and is prematurely born; fifth, that the abused child is a chronically difficult child, either sickly or frequently crying. . . .

We have held that under appropriate circumstances a woman who kills her husband or boyfriend and raises the defense of self-defense may, as evidence of whether she acted in fear of her life, have an expert witness describe the "battered woman syndrome," apply that model to the facts, and conclude that the woman falls within the profile. *Smith v. State,* 247 Ga. 612, 277 S.E.2d 678 (1981). We also observed in *Smith* that it is accepted practice for the state to offer expert opinion testimony that a child is a victim of "battered child syndrome" and that its injuries are not accidental. *Id.* at 617, 277 S.E.2d 678. In addition, we cited the case of *State v. Baker*, 120 N.H. 773, 424 A.2d 171 (N.H. 1980). *Smith, supra,* at 617, 277 S.E.2d 678. In *Baker* the defendant husband claimed his attempt to kill his wife as the result of insanity, but the state contended it was but a single episode in a recurring pattern of domestic violence. Baker called two psychiatrists who testified that in their opinion he was insane at the time of the crime, and the New Hampshire Supreme Court held that the state then could properly call an expert on domestic violence to testify regarding the battered wife syndrome and to give his opinion that mental illness is not an important cause of wife beating. It was also proper, the court ruled, for the state's expert to state his opinion that, based on prior testimony by Baker's wife and daughter that he had physically abused them, Baker's marriage probably fell within the contours of the battered woman syndrome. We have not previously been faced with a case wherein the state has seized the initiative and attempted to use a profile in its case-in-chief as an affirmative weapon against the defendant; however, this question has been confronted by another appellate court, *Loebach v. State*, 310 N.W.2d 58 (Minn. 1981). In that case Loebach appealed his conviction for murdering his infant son. At trial the state had called an expert on child abuse, Dr. Robert ten Bensel, to testify that, based on the child's injuries, in his opinion the child had suffered from nonaccidental physical abuse over a period of time and accordingly was a victim of battered child syndrome. Ten Bensel also testified over objection that battering parents tend to have similar personality traits and personal histories; he described those characteristics but did not suggest Loebach possessed any of them. However, evidence about Loebach's past was introduced through other witnesses. On appeal the Minnesota Supreme Court found that the testimony about Leobach's personal history and personality was nothing more than character evidence, introduced for the purpose of showing Loebach fit within ten Bensel's battering parent profile, and it held that since Loebach had not placed his character in issue, admission of the testimony was error. The court then announced a prospective rule that the prosecution would not be permitted to introduce evidence of the battering parent syndrome or establish a defendant's character as a battering parent unless the defendant first raised that issue. However, the court went on to rule that there was overwhelming evidence of Loebach's guilt without the battering parent testimony, which was only a small percentage of the evidence, and held the error was not prejudicial.

Turning to the instant case, we find that the disputed portion of Dr. Kennedy's testimony clearly implicated Sanders's character. It matters little that, as the state points out, Kennedy never expressly drew the conclusion that appellant fit his profile of battering parents; his construction of the profile, coupled with the previous testimony that appellant possessed many characteristics which Kennedy's profile identified as being shared by the typical battering parent, could lead a reasonable juror to no other inference than that the state was implying that this parent had a history of violent behavior, and, more important, that this parent fit within the syndrome, and had in fact murdered her baby. We hold that unless a defendant has placed her character in issue or had raised some defense which the battering parent syndrome is relevant to rebut, the state may not introduce evidence of the syndrome, nor may the state introduce character evidence showing a defendant's personality traits and personal history as its foundation for demonstrating the defendant has the characteristics of a typical battering parent. Accordingly, the trial court in the instant case erred in admitting the portion of Dr. Kennedy's testimony which was challenged. However, we find that it is highly probable that the error did not contribute to the verdict, since the evidence of guilt was otherwise overwhelming. . . .

Judgment affirmed.

* * *

Notes

1. Battering parent syndrome (BPS) is defined as "a set of concurrent characteristics typically or reportedly shared by parents prone to commit child abuse." 31A AM. JUR. 2d, *Expert and Opinion Evidence* § 196 (1989). In *State v. Loebach,* 310 N.W.2d 58 (Minn. 1981), the prosecution presented an expert in its case-in-chief who described characteristics of BPS. Even though the expert did not give an opinion as to whether or not the parent shared the traits identified with BPS, the prosecution called as witnesses two other acquaintances of the parent who linked the parent to the traits of BPS. The court rejected the expert's testimony as violative of the rule against allowing substantive character to prove conduct (where character is not an issue). Several other courts have followed the *Loebach* holding, stating that admission of BPS expert testimony violates Rule 404(a) of the Federal Rules of Evidence. *See* Thomas N. Bulleit, Note, *The Battering Parent Syndrome: Inexpert Testimony as Character Evidence*, 17 U. MICH. J. L. REF. 653, 660 (1984).

Another criticism of BPS is that it lacks the support of experts in the relevant scientific community. This is particularly significant in states which follow the rule of *Frye v. United States*, 293 F. 1013 (D.C. Cir. 1923) (evidence from new or novel scientific process or technique admissible if generally accepted in scientific community). Courts have been reluctant "to accept social science evidence to identify those who have committed crimes in the past." Karla Ogrodnik Boresi, *Syndrome Testimony in Child Abuse Prosecutions: The Wave of the Future?,* 8 ST. LOUIS U. PUB. L. REV. 207, 223 (1989). For further discussion about BPS and its admission at trial, see Gregory G. Sarno, Annotation, *Admissibility at Criminal Prosecution of Expert Testimony on Battering Parent Syndrome,* 43 A.L.R.4TH 1203 (1986); *State v. Conlogue,* 474 A.2d 167 (Me. 1984); *Duley v. State*, 467 A.2d 776 (Md. Ct. Spec. App. 1983).

Questions

How should a court resolve the evidentiary dilemma of BPS, which is considered reliable scientific evidence, but raises an inference of the respondent's bad character?

4. Munchausen Syndrome by Proxy

In re Jessica Z.

515 N.Y.S.2d 370 (N.Y. Fam. Ct. 1987)

Sandra MILLER, Judge.

In this child abuse proceeding, the Commissioner of Social Services (CSS) alleged that Respondent, Lori Z intentionally inflicted physical injury upon her infant daughter, Jessica (b. 11/10/85) creating a substantial risk of death, disfigurement or impairment of her physical and emotional health, by repeatedly causing her to ingest a quantity of laxative sufficient to cause severe diarrhea, infection of the blood, dehydration and hospitalization from March, 1986 to July 19, 1986.

In support of these allegations, CSS presented evidence that Respondent suffers from Munchausen Syndrome by Proxy (MSP), a psychiatric disorder in which a parent causes or fabricates a child's illness. The syndrome was first described by Dr. Ray Meadow, an English physician, in 1977. . . . MSP is a variant of Munchausen's Syndrome, a related psychiatric condition causing patients to fabricate illness and subject themselves to unpleasant and potentially harmful procedures. The eponym was taken from 16th Century Baron von Munchausen, who was famous for his remarkable tales as a soldier and sportsman.

Factors commonly found in the case histories of MSP which are reported in the medical literature and also found in the case before this court include:

1. The child's prolonged illness which presents confusing symptoms defying diagnosis and is unresponsive to medical treatment.
2. The child's recurring hospitalizations, surgery and other invasive procedures.
3. The child's dramatic improvement after removal from mother's access and care.
4. The mother's training as a nurse or in medically related fields.
5. The mother's unusual degree of attentiveness to child's needs in hospital.
6. The mother's unusually supportive and cooperative attitude toward doctors and hospital staff.
7. The mother's symbiotic relationship to the child.

Prominent American and English pediatricians and psychologists who have reported their experience with cases of MSP since 1977, indicate that the syndrome may be far commoner than previously supposed but that its true incidence is unknown because detection is so inherently difficult.

A study published in the Journal of the American Academy of Child Psychiatry in 1983, analyzing 23 cases of non-accidental poisoning of children (from 1974-80), which were attributed to MSP, indicated some of the children's presenting symptoms and the drugs or foreign materials which they had been caused to ingest. Presenting symptoms included, diarrhea, vomiting, seizures, bleeding, anorexia, pain. The ingested substances included laxatives, salt, blood, codeine, oral and fecal matter, barbiturates, pebbles. Dr. Waller, the author of the study, noted the following obstacles to appropriate diagnosis and management of MSP cases: (1) failure to appreciate fully the relationships of MSP to non-accidental poisoning of children; (2) the striking symbiotic tie between mother and child; (3) the highly persuasive denial typical of the parent/perpetrator; (4) skepticism of the legal authorities presented with the paradox of a parent who appears to be seeking the best medical care for the child, and to love and dote on the child, while at the same time causing the child's illness, suffering and even death.

* * *

Jessica was 9 months old at the commencement of this proceeding to determine whether her mother, Lori, caused her to ingest laxatives for four months, resulting in her diarrhea, surgery, and near death. The trial consumed 14 days. Twenty-one witnesses testified, including 12 doctors, 1 psychologist, respondent and her husband, Jessica's father.

After studying the medical evidence and considering all the evidence and the credibility of the witnesses, this court finds the petition is sustained by the required preponderance of the credible evidence.

The factors noted above, which are typically found in reported MSP cases, have been found to exist in the history of Jessica's illness, and in respondent characteristics.

Jessica's pediatrician referred her to the care of Dr. Leonard Newman, Chief of Pediatric Gastroenterology, at Westchester County Medical Center (WCMC) due to dehydration caused by diarrhea and vomiting. After receiving intravenous (IV) feeding, she improved and returned home, only to be readmitted shortly thereafter with the same symptoms. When exhaustive tests revealed no explanation for her condition, she underwent her first major surgical procedure, which revealed unexpected congenital abnormalities, including a "Mechals Diverticulum"[11], an "adhesive band"[12] and "gastroesophogeal reflux." The surgeon who removed the Mechals and band, testified that he was hopeful those conditions had caused Jessica's GI problems and that they would not recur. However, shortly thereafter, both the vomiting and diarrhea returned. Reluctantly, a second major surgical procedure was undertaken to determine whether Jessica's continuing diarrhea was due to adhesions from the first surgery. Neither obstruction nor adhesions that would have caused obstruction were revealed. In the course of this second surgery, Jessica's gastroesophogeal reflux was repaired, and a gastrointestinal tube and broviac catheter were inserted.

After the second surgery, Jessica's vomiting stopped but her diarrhea continued. More tests were done. Experts were contacted from other institutions—but consultation produced no answers. Every conceivable possibility, from AIDS to Cystic Fibrosis, was considered and rejected—except for one. The possibility of Jessica being poisoned never occurred to Dr. Newman or anyone else. In retrospect, Dr. Newman testified, "I just never thought of it." Everyone was so trusting—so helpful—so satisfied with the efforts of the doctors and staff.

After 55 days of hospitalization, Jessica returned home, with diarrhea, attached to two tubes, which were attached to two pumps to regulate the speed of her tubal feeding. One week later, she was re-admitted to WCMC, this time in critical condition, in shock, with a 106 degree fever having developed bacteremia. She responded to antibiotic treatment given in the intensive care (IC) unit of the hospital and rapidly improved. During her stay in the IC unit, the nursing staff provided her care. However, when she was transferred to a private room, and her parents assisted in her care, her diarrhea returned. At this juncture, Dr. Newman's suspicions were aroused. He ordered a chemical test on Jessica's stool—which revealed the presence of phenolphthalein (a chemical found in Ex-lax and other laxatives). The test was repeated the next day, on other stool samples and again found positive.

When Dr. Newman confronted respondent and her husband with the discovery that Jessica had ingested phenolphthalein, he was met with surprisingly calm denials from both, and the mother's tears. Dr. Newman notified Child Protective Services of suspected child abuse, and Jessica was placed in the care of the Department of Social Services.

---

11 Mechals Diverticulum is a congenital condition, an outpouching of the intestine.

12 Adhesive Band is a congenital condition, tissue which should have disappeared in utero.

The next day, an incident occurred at WCMC which is relevant to respondent's credibility. The incident was reported by two nurses, who were on duty that day. They testified that respondent requested they accompany her to the pantry (an unlocked room on the pediatric floor where babies' formulas and other equipment are kept.) She wanted to check the formula because she suspected someone was poisoning Jessica. The nurses testified that respondent urged them to accompany her, saying "just humor me." When the refrigerator door was opened, respondent spotted something dark in one of the partially opaque plastic formula containers. Upon examination, a large bar of Ex-Lax was found in the formula of another hospitalized child. The nurses described respondent's reaction as "elated." She said, "this should prove that Mom didn't do it", but "please don't tell Dr. Newman it was my idea to check the formula." Respondent denied making these statements.

Laboratory analysis of the stool of the baby whose formula was contaminated revealed no phenolphthalein. There were no reports of any babies, other than Jessica, suffering from suspicious diarrhea, or of any findings of phenolphthalein in any adult or infant stools. . . .

Prior to discovery of phenolphthalein in the child's stool, respondent had provided day-to-day care for Jessica, even in the hospital. After discovery of the chemical in the child's stool, when respondent's contact with Jessica was strictly supervised, Jessica's condition markedly improved. All feeding tubes were eventually removed, and Jessica started to thrive and gained weight.

In every reported case of MSP, the perpetrator has been found to be the child's natural mother who was almost invariably trained in the nursing or medically related area and was "medically sophisticated." Respondent has been employed as a dental assistant and most recently, as a medical secretary. Her command of medical terminology and ability to articulate Jessica's complicated medical history is impressive.

The MSP mother is characterized by her extraordinary dedication to her child's care in the hospital, virtually never leaving his bedside, and appearing to thrive in the hospital, making friends of nurses and staff. Of 19 MSP mothers studied in England, over half remained in the hospital with their children.

The testimony of Dr. Newman and the hospital nurses confirmed respondent's description of the exhausting attention she devoted to Jessica in the hospital. She not only assisted the nursing staff, but apparently took charge of many of the child's needs and complicated medical care, spending many days and nights at the bedside of the sick child, and even offering assistance and comfort to other mothers in the hospital.

The MSP mother's attitude toward doctors is described as unusually supportive and trusting, "virtually lifting the nursing and medical staff's spirits after each unsuccessful attempt to diagnose the child's illness." One such "caring and home-minded mother" who caused her infant son to ingest large quantities of salt, eventually causing his death, thanked the doctors for their care, after having been accused of poisoning the child, and then attempted suicide. Another MSP mother was described as "concerned and loving" but "sometimes not quite as worried about the possible cause of the (child's) illness as were the doctors." This woman had contaminated her child's urine with her own urine and menstrual blood, causing the child to exhibit baffling symptoms, which resulted in twelve hospitalizations, seven x-ray procedures, five cystoscopies, toxic drug treatment and numerous other unpleasant investigative procedures. After the mother was confronted with her falsification of the child's symptoms, she entered outpatient psychiatric treatment and the child's urinary symptoms disappeared and did not recur.

Doctors described respondent as "surprisingly trusting" when anticipating Jessica's first exploratory surgery. Her attitude differed markedly from that of other parents who appeared more "worried" and "challenging," when surgery was resorted to, in seeking a diagnosis of the child's puzzling illness. Respondent's response to the anticipated exploratory surgery, "whatever you say" was unusual. Doctors noted respondent's "trusting, helpful, supportive" attitude. The only "abnormal feature" of her reaction to Jessica was her "unusual ability to roll with the punches." She would describe a "horrible" series of medical events, without complaint.

The symbiotic nature of the relationship between MSP mother and child, noted in the literature is characterized by a "failure of differentiation of the two individuals. Hence, if the parent experiences conflicting emotions, the child, felt as part of her, may become the subject of mother's love and hate . . . resulting in an alternating feeling of blame and attack, with overprotective care. The result is the paradox of the parent administering the drugs, yet being concerned at the child's subsequent symptoms."

The MSP mother is described as almost always "doting" on the child. "Special anxiety and overprotectiveness are probably the last thing one would expect to find in conjunction with a form of child abuse. . . . The child's fabricated illness seems to express the parent's sense of being sick and need for attention and help. Inherent in the syndrome is the ultimate contradiction between love for the child and the need to make the child ill."

* * *

Significantly, the term "symbiotic," commonly applied to MSP mothers, was used to describe respondent's relationship with Jessica by Respondent's expert witness, Dr. Eileen Bloomingdale, a clinical psychologist who interviewed respondent several times. She observed respondent with Jessica in the hospital and with her 2½ year old son, Joshua at home. In addition, she administered various psychological tests to respondent. Among her observations, the doctor noted "respondent's difficulty in separating" from Jessica, remarking that she had "great identification" with the child. Dr. Bloomingdale referred to respondent's remarkably close care of the baby and her apparent "need to be needed." On the thematic aperception test (TAT), three times respondent made two different people into one, "two people who did not even look alike." Dr. Bloomingdale observed that "she ignores reality." On the Rorschach Test, respondent mingled two figures, unable to separate "me" from "thee." Dr. Bloomingdale indicated that although this behavior did not signify mental illness, it connoted a "symbiotic" intermingling of personalities between mother and child, and that she would prefer to see more of a "boundary" between them.

Dr. Newman's diagnosis of Jessica's condition as diarrhea caused by laxative ingestion was based upon his treatment and observations of her condition from March, 1986 to July, 1986, the discovery of the phenolphthalein in her stool, her recovery after removal from her mother's care, and his recognition of similarities between certain characteristics of Respondent and the typical MSP perpetrator.

Dr. Newman was the only witness who had had prior experience with MSP cases. He had encountered the syndrome twice at WCMC, and twice at other hospitals and was familiar with the literature on the subject prior to this proceeding.

Dr. Frederick Daum, Chief of Pediatric Gastroenterology at Northshore University Hospital, who testified as an expert for Respondent, disagreed with Dr. Newman's diagnosis. Basing his opinion solely upon his review of Jessica's hospital records and an examination of Jessica prior to his testimony, he found other explanations for Jessica's persistent diarrhea. Initially, the Mechals diverticulum and band could have caused diarrhea. After removal of the Mechals and band, adhesions developed with could have caused obstruction and resulting diarrhea. After removal of the adhesions, infection or other reactions could have caused diarrhea. Dr. Daum further testified that in his opinion, chronic laxative ingestion would have caused Jessica to become even more ill than she was.

Both physicians are highly qualified pediatric gastroenterologists. However, Dr. Newman's testimony is by far the more persuasive. In his role as treating physician, he had the experience of personally observing the child and frequent contact with her other physicians and hospital staff during the period in question. No motive can be ascribed to his initial diagnosis and immediate report to Child Protective Services other than his concern for the child's safety. In contrast, Dr. Daum's testimony was based solely on his review of hospital records and examination of Jessica prior to trial. He had no prior professional experience with MSP.

* * *

Dr. Milton Viderman, the Court's independent witness, found "a high probability" that respondent caused Jessica to ingest laxatives, basing his opinion on interviews with respondent and her husband, Jessica's medical history as reported by Dr. Newman, and the medical literature on the subject of MSP. He noted respondent's only unusual observable quality was her "extraordinary calm, apparent self-assurance, lack of concern and apparent confidence with the interview process."

Neither he, nor any other expert found evidence of psychosis or psychopathology. The opinion of Dr. Abraham Halpern, respondent's expert, that respondent did not suffer from MSP was based solely upon interviews. His confidence that his psychiatric training enabled him to determine the respondent's veracity ignores the frequent admonition in MSP literature regarding the remarkable ability of MSP perpetrators to deceive the medical profession. "The medical sophistication of an MSP perpetrator cannot be underestimated," was noted in a case where the MSP mother manipulated a child's broviac catheter causing him to appear to be bleeding, and subjected the child to emergency surgery.

Dr. Eileen Bloomingdale, respondent's witness, found no "one-to-one" tie between respondent and MSP, but reported that psychological testing revealed respondent as a "hysterical" personality, a characteristic common to MSP mothers (a hysterical personality, was characterized by "detachment, disassociation, isolation, dependence and passivity (floating with responsibility for what's happening))." Psychological testing also revealed respondent's symbiotic relationship with Jessica. . . .

The motivation of MSP perpetrators has yet to be fully explained. However, several authors have presented theories regarding the motivation and psychodynamics involved.

"The child's fabricated illness seems to express the parent's sense of being sick and in need of attention and help." Loneliness is noted as a possible motivation. . . . "In this symbiotic situation, the child's fabricated illness seems to expressed the parent's sense of being sick and in need of help." In one case a doctor commented the mother appeared to be "bleeding through her child's kidneys." Ambivalence toward the medical profession and feelings of inadequacy are also noted.

* * *

Laboratory reports indicating the presence of phenolphthalein in Jessica's stool in July, 1986, established the fact that she had been caused to ingest laxatives at that time. All other evidence heading to this court's finding that respondent caused Jessica to ingest laxatives from March to July, 1986, is circumstantial. However, the chain of evidence in this case establishes by more than the required preponderance the allegations of the petition. . . .

Where a child is found to sustain injury or suffer from a condition that would not ordinarily exist except for the acts or omissions of the person legally responsible for his care, there is prima facie evidence of abuse. This doctrine of *res ipsa loquitur* has been applied to explain specific injuries of children by strong inferences of abuse (or neglect). *Matter of Charmine W.*, 61 A.D.2d 769, 402 N.Y.S.2d 19 (1st Dept.1978), *Matter of Tashyne L.*, 53 A.D.2d 629, 384 N.Y.S.2d 472 (2nd Dept.1976). The application of this rule has not been limited to cases where the child is never out of the parent's control, but applied where the parent has primary custody during the critical period when injury was sustained. *Matter of Tara H.*, 129 Misc.2d 508, 494 N.Y.S.2d 953 (Fam.Ct., Westchester Cty. 1985).

No other explanation was offered as to Jessica's diarrhea from March to July other than respondent's role in causing her to ingest laxatives. Even Dr. Daum's attempt to explain Jessica's diarrhea prior to July did not explain the presence of phenolphthalein in July, or Jessica's recovery after removal from respondent's care. Who, (other than respondent, suffering from MSP), was motivated to cause Jessica's illness? The fact that Jessica's diarrhea persisted at home and in the hospital, and that no phenolphthalein was found in the stool of other children (or persons) at WCMC, discourages suspicion of a nurse/perpetrator. The child's father has not been accused, and is apparently not suspect. As no other explanation has been offered, res ipsa clearly applies.

* * *

A dispositional hearing was waived by all parties. Therefore, pursuant to FCA 1047, a combined fact finding and dispositional order is entered.

Any disposition of this matter poses serious risks to the child. Dr. Ray Meadow, who first recognized MSP, notes that more than half of the child victims of MSP have eventually been removed from parents and placed in foster care. The risks entailed in leaving the child at home include: (1) illness produced by the perpetrator; (2) illness simulated by the perpetrator; and (3) real illness not treated, due to the family's feeling of being threatened as a result of legal proceedings.

Removal of the child to the unknown circumstances of foster care poses other risks. Such an order would result in the child's separation not only from respondent/mother, but from her father, her sibling, and her grandparents. This further disruption of Jessica, who, at 13 months of age has been subjected to such great physical and emotional suffering, would cause her further trauma, and possibly permanent damage.

Neither the expert witness, nor Jessica's law guardian advocated her removal from her parents' home. Dr. Newman recommended that she be returned home with safeguards, testifying that in his experience with other MSP cases, confrontation of the mother resulted in her cessation of the abusive conduct. Dr. Bloomingdale testified that even if respondent had caused Jessica to ingest laxatives, she did not believe she was likely to do it again, once having been confronted.

The most prudent course appears to this court to be one which permits Jessica to remain at home, while providing maximum safeguards, such as have been advocated by the professionals who have had experience with MSP cases, subject to review in six months. Recommendations of others include a plan whereby communication between respondent's psychiatrist and the child's primary physician is assured. This contact is obviously necessary since the child's illness is the only reliable symptom of the mother's disorder. The necessity for psychiatric intervention is not challenged, notwithstanding its failure to be effective in all cases.

Now, therefore, it is hereby ordered:

Jessica is found to be an abused child, pursuant to FAC 1012(3)(i) in that respondent has caused her to ingest sufficient quantity of laxatives from March, 1986–July 19, 1986, so as to cause her serious illness, hospitalization and surgery.

Jessica is placed in the care and custody of her father, under the strict supervision of the Westchester County Department of Social Services, to reside in Westchester County and not be removed therefrom for a period of 18 months, the term of this order.

DSS shall structure and monitor a plan to coordinate efforts and communication between respondent's psychiatrist, Jessica's pediatrician, her father's therapist, Dr. Newman, and the DSS caseworkers.

DSS shall arrange for psychiatric treatment for respondent with a board certified psychiatrist on no less than a once a week schedule.

DSS shall arrange for therapy for Jessica's father, on a schedule convenient to his employment, to assist him in coping with the special needs of the family and Jessica.

* * *

In the event DSS finds that this order has been violated, or if, in the opinion of any one of the . . . physicians or therapists, Jessica appears to be at risk, DSS shall remove her from her parents' home without necessity of first obtaining a court order. In the event of such removal, DSS shall immediately calendar the matter for review before this court.

Schedule this order for review on July 27, 1987. Reports from all of the above noted physicians and therapists shall be submitted to the court and made available by DSS to all counsel (including the Law Guardian). The court shall then determine whether Nursing Care shall be discontinued and whether any other modification of this order is required.

Notes

1. There are approximately 250 confirmed Munchausen Syndrome by Proxy (MSP) cases reported worldwide annually. *See* Brenda Burton, *Where Murdering Hands Rock the Cradle: An Overview of America's Incoherent Treatment of Infanticidal Mothers,* 51 SMU L. REV. 519, 603 (1998). Some of the most common symptoms of MSP are blood-borne infection, vomiting, seizures, irritable bowel syndrome, and diarrhea. *See In Matter of Aaron S.,* 615 N.Y.S.2d 786, 788 (Fam. Ct. 1993). The typical MSP parent is a mother (in 98% of the cases) who "is articulate and bright, and possesses a high degree of medical knowledge and/or fascination with medical details and hospital gossip, and seems to enjoy the hospital environment." *Id.; see also* Michael T. Flannery, *Munchausen Syndrome By Proxy: Broadening the Scope of Child Abuse*, 28 U. RICH. L. REV. 1175 (1994). For further general information on MSP, see Marie M. Brady, *Munchausen Syndrome By Proxy: How Should We Weigh Our Options?,* 18 LAW & PSYCHOL. REV. 361, 362-66 (1994); Corey M. Perman, Note, *Diagnosing the Truth: Determining Physician Liability in Cases Involving Munchausen Syndrome By Proxy,* 54 WASH. U. J. URB. & CONTEMP. L. 267, 271-76 (1998); Flannery, *supra*, at 1182-89; Michael T. Flannery, *First, Do No Harm: The Use of Covert Video Surveillance to Detect Munchausen Syndrome By Proxy—An Unethical Means of "Preventing" Child Abuse*, 32 U. MICH. J. L. REF. 105 (1998); Robert Kinscherff & Richard Famularo, *Extreme Munchausen Syndrome by Proxy: The Case for Termination of Parental Rights,* 40 JUV. & FAM. CT. J. 41-53 (1991); Beatrice Crofts Yorker & Bernard B. Kahan, *The Munchausen Syndrome by Proxy Varient of Child Abuse in the Family Courts*, 42 JUV. & FAM. CT. J. 51-58 (1991).

Some jurisdictions recognize MSP as generally accepted in the scientific community. *See, e.g., Reid v. Texas*, 964 S.W.2d 723 (Tex. Ct. App. 1998). Other courts hold that expert testimony concerning MSP may be admissible only if first established at a *Frye* hearing. *See, e.g., New York v. Coulter,* 697 N.Y.S.2d 498 (N.Y. Dist. Ct. 1999). Expert testimony on MSP helps the factfinder understand the nature of the crime, provides circumstantial evidence to help the factfinder determine the parent's guilt beyond a reasonable doubt, and preserves the record for future appeals. Lynn Goldman & Beatrice Crofts Yorker, *Mommie Dearest? Prosecuting Cases of Munchausen Syndrome By Proxy,* 13 CRIM. JUST. 25, 30 (Winter 1999). For further discussion of evidentiary issues concerning MSP, see Tracy Vollaro, Note, *Munchausen Syndrome By Proxy and Its Evidentiary Problems*, 22 HOFSTRA L. REV. 495, 500-15 (1993).

2. Some hospitals use surveillance to detect MSP abuse in hospital rooms. *See Munchausern Syndrome By Proxy, supra* at 1210-12; *First, Do No Harm, supra,* at 144-46. Videotaped incidents of child abuse may assist a prosecutor in convicting the MSP parent. Dr. David Southall, a leading proponent of using video surveillance to detect MSP, believes some doctors allow non-life-threatening abuse to occur so as to later obtain sufficient evidence of life-threatening abuse by the parent. These doctors may allow "incidents like kicking and slapping the child, disconnecting monitors, forcing ingestion of disinfectant and other objects, cruelly waking the child from sleep, and roughly pushing the child away as the child reached out to the parent for comfort or affection" in order to wait for "something more abusive to occur." *Id.* at 17. According to Dr. Southall, such practice is tolerable because "the end justifies the means." *Id.*

3. Proper placement of the child in a MSP case is a difficult decision for the court. Some courts, such as in *Jessica Z.,* allow the child to remain with his or her family. *See also In the Interest of M.A.V.,* 425 S.E.2d 377 (Ga. Ct. App. 1992); *In re Colin*, 493 A.2d 1083 (Md. Ct. Spec. App. 1985); *but see In the Interest of B.B.*, 500 N.W.2d 9 (Iowa 1993) (minor placed in foster care to receive proper care and schooling). The court in *In re S.R.,* 599 A.2d 364, 366-67 (Vt. 1991), listed the following guidelines for courts to consider when determining placement of the child where MSP has been presented:

1. The interaction and interrelationship of the child with his natural parents, his foster parents if any, his siblings, and any other person who may significantly affect the child's best interests;
2. The child's adjustment to his home, school, and community;
3. The likelihood that the natural parents will be able to resume their parental duties within a reasonable period of time; and
4. Whether the natural parents have played and continue to play a constructive role, including personal contact and demonstrated love and affection, in the child's welfare.

For further discussion of factors for courts to consider when placing a child in an MSP case, see *Munchausen Syndrome By Proxy, supra*, at 1220-24.

Question

What issues of law and policy arise where a hospital suspects a parent of MSP and decides to secretly videotape the parent with the child?

5. Parent Alienation Syndrome

Karen B. v. Clyde M.

574 N.Y.S.2d 267 (N.Y. Fam. Ct. 1991)

David F. JUNG, Judge.

* * *

The subject child, Mandi M., was born September 7th, 1986. Mandi's parents, the Petitioner and Respondent herein, were never married, but an Order of Filiation was made by this Court and paternity has never been an issue. The parties lived together in the home of Respondent for one year before Mandi was born and continued together until August 15th, 1990 when they separated.

By consent, the parties entered into a joint and split custodial arrangement on July 23, 1990. . . . The agreement resulted in an Order of this Court dated July 23rd, 1990 and entered September 5th, 1990. The parties abided by the terms of the agreement and Order until September 1990 when the mother filed her Petition to modify requesting that she "retain all custody and visitation to be supervised, if at all." The mother alleged a change of circumstances in that: "Mandi had disclosed sexual advances and behavior problems. . . . Social Services is currently investigating." As a result of her allegations and upon the recommendation of the Law Guardian, the Court entered a temporary Order requiring the father's visitations with Mandi to be supervised.

According to the mother, in September 1990 Mandi disclosed to her certain sexual abuse perpetrated on Mandi by her father. He allegedly put his finger in her "peer." When she said that it hurt, he told her that he could do what he wanted. She also claimed that her Daddy's "dinkie" got bigger and "stuff came out." The mother reported this to Jan Carter, a friend of hers, employed by Community Maternity Services, and on September 9th 1990 Jan Carter went to the home of Mandi and spoke to her. Jan Carter testified that Mandi told her that Daddy put his "peer" on her "peer." She also told Ms. Carter that Daddy put his finger in her "peer" and that she told him to stop and it hurt and she cried. Ms. Carter placed a call to the New York State Central Register for Child Abuse and Maltreatment a/k/a "HOT-LINE" and reported the incident.

Sally Conkling, a caseworker with the Fulton County Department of Social Services, conducted the investigation. She testified that the child told her that the Respondent had put his finger in her vagina. . . . Mandi was interviewed by Bette Malachowski to determine whether the allegation of sexual abuse could be validated. Ms. Malachowski saw Mandi on September 10th, 13th and 14th, 1990. The witness identified herself as a child sexual abuse therapist specializing in $2\frac{1}{2}$ to 18-year old victims. She has a Masters Degree in Psychology and a Bachelor's Degree in Sociology, and in addition thereto has completed 150 hours of post-graduate work in her field. She testified that she has interviewed approximately two hundred children concerning allegations of sexual abuse and has validated seventy-five percent of them and found the remainder to be fabricated.

The mother repeated all of the allegations to Ms. Malachowski and additionally stated that on September 9th Mandi had told her that the Respondent has put his "peer" on her "peer" and that he had put his hand under the covers of the bed and touched her buns stating, "You know, like you take your temperature."

The expert observed no outward signs of emotion when the mother spoke to her and also found that the mother seemed to be repeating the story by rote. When asked what the witness meant by the expression "rote," she stated that the Petitioner had to start from the beginning and repeat the whole story. She couldn't respond to questions without starting from the beginning and completing the entire story.

At the first interview with the expert, Mandi could not identify the genital parts of the male and female. . . . At the second interview, Mandi could name the breasts as "boobies," the vagina as a "peer" and the buttocks as "butt." She stated to the expert that she had no touching troubles with her boobies, peer or butt. The witness observed no sexual play with the anatomically-correct doll nor did Mandi ever use the word "dink" when describing the male penis. At the last interview the child again stated that she had no touching troubles and responded as follows to questions by the therapist:

> Therapist: Q. "Mandi, did any kind of touching troubles happen with your pepe, boobies or your butt? Or, are you making believe?"
> Mandi: A. "Making believe. He didn't do it."
> Therapist: Q. "He didn't do it?"
> Mandi: A. "No."
> Therapist: A. "Who didn't do it?"
> Mandi: A. "My father; I was just joking about it."
> Therapist: Q. "You were just joking about it. So Daddy really didn't do anything. You were only making believe about it?"
> Mandi: A. "Yes."
> Therapist: Q. "How come you were only making believe about it?"
> Mandi: A. "I was joking."
> Therapist: Q. "How come you were just joking about it?"
> Mandi: A. "I don't know."
> Therapist: Q. "Did anybody tell you to make a joke about it?"
> Mandi: A. "Yes."
> Therapist: Q. "Who told you to make a joke about it?"
> Mandi: A. "I don't know."
> Therapist: Q. "You don't know. Alright, I think then we are done talking, okay? Is there anything else you want to talk about?"
> Mandi: A. "No."

* * *

Lawrence Horowitz, D.O., the child's pediatrician, testified that the mother brought Mandi to him for an examination on September 13th, 1990. The doctor's physical examination of the child revealed nothing and the child denied to him that anything had happened.

The Department of Social Services concluded that the allegations of sexual abuse were unfounded and so notified the parties.

In February 1991, the mother once again contacted the Department of Social Services claiming that Mandi revealed to her additional sexual abuse that had occurred at the father's home during visitation. When interviewed by Loren Dybas, a D.F.S. caseworker, on February 4th, 1991 the child claimed that "secret touch made her uncomfortable"; that Mandi placed her hand on her Dad's "dinkie" and she touched Dad's "electric dinkie" to her "dinkie." She claimed that her underpants were on and her Dad's clothes were off. During the same 45-minute interview, she stated that her panties were off when her Dad touched her with the "electric dinkie." She told the interviewer that she didn't want to see her Dad again. Ms. Dybas reported this interview through the "HOTLINE" on February 7th, 1991.

M. Frank Sack, Ph.D. also appeared as an expert witness. . . . He is a Master Expert Polygraphist and admitted that he had never attempted a validation process with a young child. . . .

Dr. Sacks interviewed Mandi once on April 25th, 1991. The expert testified that Mandi told him that she played "secret touch" with the Respondent; that while playing, the Respondent, her father, put her on a bed with her clothes off and touched her "peer" with his hands. She stated that Daddy told her not to tell anybody what had happened. The interviewer additionally stated that when Mandi told him to stop touching her, her father said, "I'll do what I want." Dr. Sack concluded that Mandi was sexually abused by her father. On cross examination, Dr. Sack stated that he was familiar with the S.A.I.D[1] Syndrome symptomized by a recent separation or divorce, hostility between the separating parents, and disclosure by the child of sex abuse to one parent. The expert was aware that many false allegations have been made and they are most common when the above factors are present.

The Court is faced with a dilemma that often confronts a jury or judge, i.e. experts have rendered diametrically opposed opinions. The consequences of this Court's decision to Mandi are potentially enormous. If she is placed with her mother, and the father limited or excluded from having contact with her, when in fact he has done her no harm, then a tremendous injustice results. If custody is placed with the father, and he has sexually abused her, an equal injustice with a potential for future harm ensues.

In coming to its conclusion, the Court found the following factors to be significant:

Shortly after the alleged abuse was disclosed to the mother, Bette Malachowski, a trained therapist familiar with the validation technique, conducted three separate interviews with the child and concluded that no abuse had taken place. She furthermore was suspicious of the mother's motivation and stated that in her report. When Ms. Malachowski testified many months later, she reiterated those concerns, and after having read Dr. Sack's report while on the witness stand, recalled that the mother had made an almost exact verbatim statement to her that was attributed to the child in Dr. Sack's report. While Dr. Sack impressed the Court with his knowledge of verification techniques and syndromes extant when sex abuse is alleged, less weight was given to his report

[1] Sex Abuse In Divorce.

and testimony since he only had one interview with the child which occurred many months after the alleged incident or incidents.

"Children who have experienced bona fide sexual abuse generally have a fairly clear visual image of the experience and recall it fairly clearly when asked to do so. The lack of such an internal visual—mental image clearly differentiates the fabricator from the child who has been genuinely abused. And this difference results in the fabricator's difficulty in providing specific details of the event(s) when asked to do so. . . . When asked to provide details, the youngster is either unable to do so or creates a scenario for the purposes of the interview. However, in subsequent interviews a different scenario may be presented. . . . [T]he child who has suffered bona fide sexual abuse will usually provide specific details, and they will be consistently the same on subsequent interviews." Richard A. Gardner, M.D., *The Parental Alienation Syndrom and the Differentiation Between Fabricated and Genuine Child Sex Abuse*, Creative Therapeutics, Cresskill, N.J., 1987, p. 110.

Mandi's descriptions of sexual activity between herself and her father vary considerably depending upon whether she was talking to Social Services caseworkers and Jan Carter, all of whom were perceived to be friends and former working associates of her mother, and professionals such as Bette Malachowski, Dr. Larry Horowitz and Dr. Sack. The closest thing to consistency was the child's statement to Dr. Sack which was almost a verbatim recitation of what the mother had told Bette Malachowski seven months earlier. It was Dr. Sack, on cross examination, who stated that the child may identify with and parrot the parent she is most bonded to.

"The child who is fabricating sexual abuse generally does not describe fear of the perpetrator and is usually free from tension in the perpetrator's presence." Gardner, *Parental Alienation*, p. 115. There was no credible testimony to suggest that the child was afraid of her father and in fact the testimony suggested a relaxed and warm relationship.

Sexually abused children may talk frequently about sex, to the point of obsession. They may be preoccupied with the desire to play sexual games with other children (especially exhibitionistic and voyeuristic) and/or may become compulsive masturbators (privately and publicly). They may become preoccupied with doll play in which sexual encounters (especially their own) are portrayed. In contrast, children who are fabricating sex abuse generally exhibit no such preoccupation with sex–other than at those times when they are asked to describe the scenarios related to the sexual encounters with the alleged perpetrator." Gardner, *Parental Alienation,* p. 116. There was no testimony to suggest that Mandi had any awareness of her sexuality nor had become involved in any sexual activity.

Dr. Gardner also suggests that children who have been genuinely sexually abused are often depressed, withdrawn, compliant, are regressive and may suffer from psychosomatic disorders together with other factors that he considers important in differentiating the fabricator from the bona fide victim. Gardner, *Parental Alienation*, pp. 118-124. . . .

In addition to the above factors, the Court had the unique opportunity of observing the demeanor of all witnesses who appeared before it and concludes that the testimony of the father is more credible than that of the mother. The mother remained stoic through six days of trial including the time that she was on the witness stand.

The Court also concludes as did Bette Malachowski and the Law Guardian that it is likely that the mother programmed her daughter to accuse the father of sexually abusing the child so that she could obtain sole custody and control or even preclude any contact that the father might have with his daughter.

In the opinion of this Court, any parent that would denigrate the other by casting the false aspersion of child sex abuse and involving the child as an instrument to achieve his or her selfish purpose is not fit to continue in the role of the parent.

In the case before the Court, Karen B. has sought to destroy the reputation of her former friend and lover by accusing him of one of the most heinous crimes known to man. The aura of the allegation, irrespective of its falsehood, may stand over him and affect him for the rest of his life. Likewise, by involving her own daughter in her nefarious scheme, she may have inflicted irreparable psychological damage on her. . . .

Considering the totality of circumstances surrounding these parties and their daughter, the Court finds that it is in the best interests of Mandi that her custody be placed with her father.

As the Court has no assurance that the mother will not continue to "brainwash" or "program" Mandi, Petitioner shall have no visitation nor contact with her daughter. That prohibition is to continue until the Court is satisfied that the parties comprehend the magnitude of what has happened and that no further danger is presented to the child. . . [T]he Probation Department of Fulton County is directed to formulate a program including, if necessary, psychological or psychiatric consultation and treatment for all members of the family. . . . If the Probation Department determines that visitation between the child and mother should commence, it shall so notify the Court with its proposal. . . .

Judgment affirmed.

Notes

1. Dr. Richard Gardner first identified the parent alienation syndrome (PAS). See the following publications on PAS by Dr. Gardner, *Recommendations For Dealing With Parents Who Induce a Parental Alienation Syndrome in Their Children,* 28 J. DIVORCE & REMARRIAGE 1-23 (1998); THE PARENTAL ALIENATION SYNDROME: SECOND ADDITION (1998); FAMILY EVALUTION IN CHILD CUSTODY MEDIATION, ARBITRATION, AND LITIGATION (1989); THE PARENTAL ALIENATION SYNDROME AND THE DIFFERENTIATION BETWEEN FABRICATED AND GENUINE CHILD SEX ABUSE (1987). PAS can be defined as a disturbance in which a child is preoccupied with viewing one parent as all "good" and the other as all "bad." *See* Anita Vestal, *Mediation and Parental Alienation Syndrome: Considerations for an Intervention Model*, 37 FAM. & CONCILIATION CTS. REV. 487 (1999). Often, the child will exhibit love and affection towards one parent while demonstrating contempt and disgust for the other. *See* Michael R. Walsh & J. Michael Bone, *Parental Alienation Syndrome: An Age-Old Custody Problem,* 71 FLA. B.J. 93 (1997). For in depth descriptions of how a child may act towards a targeted parent and how the child may justify his or her negative attitude towards the parents, see Vestal, *supra*, at 489. PAS is often identified when the child's parents separate, and one or both parents try to "win over" the child. Because of a child's need for parental guidance, parents can manipulate a child's emotions until the child, in essence, reflects the feelings of the loved parent and becomes an active participant in the dispute. *See* Douglas Darnell, *Parental Alienation: Not in the Best Interest of the Children,* 75 N.D. L. REV. 323, 325-26 (1999); Leona M. Kopetski, *Identifying Cases of Parent Alienation Syndrome—Part I,* 27 COLO. LAW. 65, 66 (1998). Children who manifest a role in PAS may become physically ill when in the presence of the disliked parent, feel isolated, depressed, and have a sense of self-hatred. Walsh, *supra*, at 93. Children may also have trouble learning at school, concentrating on daily activities, relaxing, or getting along with peers. Darnell, *supra*, at 325.

PAS can be difficult to diagnose. This presents proof problems in court. Kopetski, *supra*, at 68. Therefore, a court must look at the step-by-step process often associated with PAS development. First, the child becomes physically isolated from the targeted parent. The manipulative parent may prevent the child from seeing the targeted parent because vaguely "it would not be in the child's best interests." J. Michael Bone & Michale R. Walsh, *Parental Alienation Syndrome: How to Detect It and What to Do About It,* 73 FLA. B.J. 44 (1999). Second, the child makes unfounded allegations of abuse or neglect by the targeted parent. *See, e.g.,* Vestal, *supra,* at 489. Next, there is a noticeable deterioration in the relationship between the child and the targeted parent. The manipulative parent continues to foster contempt for the target parent, and the child believes what he or she is told regardless of the truth. Finally, the child will display a strong attachment to the manipulative parent. The child may be fearful that if he or she does not support the manipulative parent, the parent will leave the child. For detailed analysis of these four steps, see Bone, *supra*, at 44-47.

2. Even though some courts, such as *Karen B. v. Clyde M., supra*, allow the admission of PAS expert testimony, PAS evidence is controversial and not widely accepted by the psychological community. *See In the Interest of T.M.W.,* 553 So. 2d 260 (Fla. Dist. Ct. App. 1989). Critics argue that Dr. Gardner's PAS theory is flawed. For example, a majority of experts believes that the interviewing techniques Dr. Gardner used to establish PAS theory are flawed. *See* Cheri L. Wood, Note, *The Parental Alienation Syndrome: A Dangerous Aura of Reliability*, 27 LOY. L.A. L. REV. 1367 (1994). The main evidentiary problem with PAS is whether or not it is reliable. Critics argue that the characteristics of PAS can be caused by factors other than a vengeful parent. Some other reasons a child might express contempt towards a parent include: 1) that the child may feel as if he or she should take sides in the divorce to prevent losing the love and affection of both parents; 2) the child may be openly hostile towards the parent who, in the child's mind, perpetrated the divorce; 3) the child may feel betrayed by the parent who first begins to date other people. *See id.* Because these factors could also explain the child's strong dislike for a parent, proving a manipulative parent caused a child to participate in parent alienation becomes more difficult. For an additional critical assessment of PAS, see *id.* at 1369-77; Kathleen Niggmyer, *Parental Alienation Is Open Heart Surgery: It Needs More Than a Band-Aid to Fix It,* 34 CAL. W. L. REV. 567, 576-81 (1998).

Questions

1. What are the main evidentiary obstacles to admissibility of expert witness opinion that a parent exhibits the traits identified with PAS?

2. In a custody dispute, if the court finds that PAS has been proved, what is the appropriate remedy?

Chapter 14

Termination of Parental Rights

Termination of parental rights (TPR) represents the ultimate impact on the parent's substantive due process—the permanent severance of the parent-child relationship. To deprive the parent of this liberty interest, the law provides a hearing with substantial due process protections. Some courts have labeled TPR proceedings as "civil," which has resulted in limitations on certain procedural guarantees. For example, where the parent is incarcerated, the right to be physically present at the TPR hearing is balanced against whether a meaningful opportunity to be heard can otherwise be arranged, together with the cost, inconvenience and security risk of transporting the parent to court. Many courts have also held that denial of confrontation does not violate due process, based upon the "civil label of convenience" and the need to protect the emotional and psychological welfare of children.

There is disagreement among the states on who may file a TPR petition. These materials explore, in particular, whether a child may initiate an action to terminate parental rights and, if so, whether a special advocate for the child is required. The statutes vary widely on what constitutes grounds for TPR, but in general the state must prove by clear and convincing evidence that the child has been out of the home for a statutory time period; that the conditions which led to the child's removal won't be remedied; that the parent is unfit; that the parent-child relationship poses a risk of harm to the child; that TPR is in the best interests of the child; and that there is a permanent plan for the care and treatment of the child. Under the Adoption and Safe Families Act of 1997 (ASFA), the state must initiate a TPR petition (or join any existing petition) and concurrently identify and approve an adoptive family for the following groups of children:

1. children in foster care for fifteen of the most recent twenty-two months;

2. children the court has determined to be abandoned infants (as defined in state law); or
3. children for whom there has been a court determination.

ASFA provides three exceptions to TPR in these cases—(1) if the child is cared for by a relative; (2) where there is a compelling reason that filing a TPR petition is not in the best interests of the child; and (3) if the state hasn't provided the child's family timely reunification services. The courts recognize various specific grounds for TPR—pre-birth conduct of the parents (e.g., the mother's use of cocaine immediately before birth and the father's failure to support the mother during pregnancy as abandonment); post-birth abandonment; Munchausen Syndrome by Proxy (MSP); conviction of various crimes; incestuous parenthood; and failure to comply with a treatment plan. Incarceration or mental illness of a parent may be considered by the court but may not be the sole factor to support TPR.

The courts have generally held that the federal law requirement under the Americans With Disabilities Act (ADA) that a public entity make reasonable accommodations to allow disabled persons to receive services or to participate in the public entity's program does not preempt state law. Most courts have therefore held that the state's non-compliance with the ADA is not a defense to a TPR action. Another federal law, the Indian Child Welfare Act (ICWA), however, requires strict compliance in TPR cases. For example, ICWA mandates that if an Indian child is removed from his or her Indian family, then "active efforts" to reunify the family must be attempted and proven unsuccessful before TPR may occur. ICWA also requires proof beyond a reasonable doubt that continued custody of the child by the parent or Indian custodian is likely to result in serious emotional or physical harm to the child. State grounds, proved by clear and convincing evidence (*see Santosky v. Kramer*, 455 U.S. 745 (1982)), are unaffected by ICWA and provide a supplemental degree of protection for parents.

TPR may also take place at the time of adoption. The courts have held that the law may treat an unwed father of a child subject to adoption differently. The unwed father must first take steps to establish the parent-child relationship before he may receive constitutional protection of his parental rights.

A. Substantive Due Process Rights—Parents

Meyer v. Nebraska

[*See, supra,* Chapter 9, Part A.]

Pierce v. Society of Sisters

[*See, supra,* Chapter 9, Part A.]

Prince v. Massachusetts

[*See, supra,* Chapter 9, Part B.1.]

Stanley v. Illinois

405 U.S. 645, 92 S. Ct. 1208, 31 L. Ed. 2d 551 (1972)

Mr. Justice WHITE delivered the opinion of the Court.

Joan Stanley lived with Peter Stanley intermittently for 18 years, during which time they had three children. When Joan Stanley died, Peter Stanley lost not only her but also his children. Under Illinois law, the children of unwed fathers become wards of the State upon the death of the mother. Accordingly, upon Joan Stanley's death, in a dependency proceeding instituted by the State of Illinois, Stanley's children were declared wards of the State and placed with court-appointed guardians. Stanley appealed, claiming that he had never been shown to be an unfit parent and that since married fathers and unwed mothers could not be deprived of their children without such a showing, he had been deprived of the equal protection of the laws guaranteed him by the Fourteenth Amendment. The Illinois Supreme Court accepted the fact that Stanley's own unfitness had not been established but rejected the equal protection claim, holding that Stanley could properly be separated from his children upon proof of the single fact that he and the dead mother had not been married. Stanley's actual fitness as a father was irrelevant.

Stanley presses his equal protection claim here. The State continues to respond that unwed fathers are presumed unfit to raise their children and that it is unnecessary to hold individualized hearings to determine whether particular fathers are in fact unfit parents before they are separated from their children. We granted certiorari to determine whether this method of procedure by presumption could be allowed to stand in light of the fact that Illinois allows married fathers—whether divorced, widowed, or separated—and mothers—even if unwed—the benefit of the presumption that they are fit to raise their children.

I

At the outset we reject any suggestion that we need not consider the propriety of the dependency proceeding that separated the Stanleys because Stanley might be able to regain custody of his children as a guardian or through adoption proceedings. The suggestion is that if Stanley has been treated differently from other parents, the difference is immaterial and not legally cognizable for the purposes of the Fourteenth Amendment. This Court has not, however, embraced the general proposition that a wrong may be done if it can be undone. . . .

It is clear, moreover, that Stanley does not have the means at hand promptly to erase the adverse consequences of the proceeding in the course of which his children were declared wards of the State. It is first urged that Stanley could act to adopt his children. But under Illinois law, Stanley is treated not as a parent but as a stranger to his children, and the dependency proceeding has gone forward on the presumption that he is unfit to exercise parental rights. . . . It would be his burden to establish not only that he would be a suitable parent but also that he would be the most suitable of all who might want custody of the children. . . .

Before us, the State focuses on Stanley's failure to petition for "custody and control"—the second route by which, it is urged, he might regain authority for his children. Passing the obvious issue whether it would be futile or burdensome for an unmarried father—without funds and already once presumed unfit—to petition for custody, this suggestion overlooks the fact that legal custody is not parenthood or adoption. A person appointed guardian in an action for custody and control is subject to removal at any time without such cause as must be shown in a neglect proceeding against a parent. He may not take the children out of the jurisdiction without the court's approval. He may be required to report to the court as to his disposition of the children's affairs. Obviously then, even if Stanley were a mere step away from 'custody and control', to give an unwed father only 'custody and control' would still be to leave him seriously prejudiced by reason of his status.

We must therefore examine the question that Illinois would have us avoid: Is a presumption that distinguishes and burdens all unwed fathers constitutionally repugnant? We conclude that, as a matter of due process of law, Stanley was entitled to a hearing on his fitness as a parent before his children were taken from him and that, by denying him a hearing and extending it to all other parents whose custody of their children is challenged, the State denied Stanley the equal protection of the laws guaranteed by the Fourteenth Amendment.

II

Illinois has two principal methods of removing non-delinquent children from the homes of their parents. In a dependency proceeding it may demonstrate that the children are wards of the State because they have no surviving parent or guardian. In a neglect proceeding it may show that children should be wards of the State because the present parent(s) or guardian does not provide suitable care.

[W]e are faced with a dependency statute that empowers state officials to circumvent neglect proceedings on the theory that an unwed father is not a "parent" whose existing relationship with his children must be considered. "Parents," says the State, "means the father and mother of a legitimate child, or the survivor of them, or the natural mother of an illegitimate child, and include any adoptive parent," Ill. Rev. Stat., c. 37, § 701-14, but the term does not include unwed fathers.

Under Illinois law, therefore, while the children of all parents can be taken from them in neglect proceedings, that is only after notice, hearing, and proof of such unfitness as a parent as amounts to neglect, an unwed father is uniquely subject to the more simplistic dependency proceeding. By use of this proceeding, the State, on showing that the father was not married to the mother, need not prove unfitness in fact, because it is presumed at law. Thus, the unwed father's claim of parental qualification is avoided as "irrelevant."

* * *

The private interest here, that of a man in the children he has sired and raised, undeniably warrants deference [and], absent a powerful countervailing interest, protection. It is plain that the interest of a parent in the companionship, care, custody, and management of his or her children "come[s] to this Court with a momentum for respect lacking when appeal is made to liberties which derive merely from shifting economic arrangements." *Kovacs v. Cooper*, 336 U.S. 77, 95 (1949) (Frankfurter, J., concurring).

The Court has frequently emphasized the importance of the family. The rights to conceive and to raise one's children have been deemed "essential," *Meyer v. Nebraska*, 262 U.S. 390, 399 (1923), "basic civil rights of man," *Skinner v. Oklahoma*, 316 U.S. 535, 541 (1942), and "(r)ights far more precious . . . than property rights," *May v. Anderson*, 345 U.S. 528, 533 (1953). "It is cardinal with us that the custody, care and nurture of the child reside first in the parents, whose primary function and freedom include preparation for obligations the state can neither supply nor hinder." *Prince v. Massachusetts,* 321 U.S. 158, 166 (1944). The integrity of the family unit has found protection in the Due Process Clause of the Fourteenth Amendment, *Meyer v. Nebraska, supra*, at 399, the Equal Protection Clause of the Fourteenth Amendment, *Skinner v. Oklahoma, supra*, at 541, and the Ninth Amendment, *Griswold v. Connecticut,* 381 U.S. 479, 496 (1965) (Goldbert, J., concurring).

Nor has the law refused to recognize those family relationships unlegitimized by a marriage ceremony. The Court has declared unconstitutional a state statute denying natural, but illegitimate, children a wrongful-death action for the death of their mother, emphasizing that such children cannot be denied the right of other children because familial bonds in such cases were often as warm, enduring, and important as those arising within a more formally organized family unit. *Levy v. Louisiana,* 391 U.S. 68, 71-72 (1968). "To say that the test of equal protection should be the 'legal' rather than the biological relationship is to avoid the issue. For the Equal protection Clause necessarily limits the authority of a State to draw such 'legal' lines as it chooses." *Glona v. American Guarantee Co.,* 391 U.S. 73, 75-76 (1968).

These authorities make it clear that, at the least, Stanley's interest in retaining custody of his children is cognizable and substantial.

For its part, the State has made its interest quite plain: Illinois has declared that the aim of the Juvenile court Act is to protect "the moral, emotional, mental, and physical welfare of the minor and the best interests of the community" and to "strengthen the minor's family ties whenever possible, removing him from the custody of his parents only when his welfare or safety or the protection of the public cannot be adequately safeguarded without removal . . . ." Ill. Rev. Stat., c. 37, § 701-2. These are legitimate interests, well within the power of the State to implement. . . .

But we are here not asked to evaluate the legitimacy of the state ends, rather, to determine whether the means used to achieve these ends are constitutionally defensible. What is the state interest in separating children from fathers without a hearing designed to determine whether the father is unfit in a particular disputed case? We observe that the State registers no gain towards its declared goals when it separates children from the custody of fit parents. Indeed, if Stanley is a fit father, the State spites its own articulated goals when it needlessly separates him from his family.

* * *

It may be, as the State insists, that most unmarried fathers are unsuitable and neglectful parents. It may also be that Stanley is such a parent and that his children should be placed in other hands. But all unmarried fathers are not in this category; some are wholly suited to have custody of their children. This much the State readily concedes, and nothing in this record indicates that Stanley is or has been a neglectful father who has not cared for his children. Given the opportunity to make his case, Stanley may have been seen to be deserving of custody of his offspring. Had this been so, the State's statutory policy would have been furthered by leaving custody in him.

* * *

[I]t may be argued that unmarried fathers are so seldom fit that Illinois need not undergo the administrative inconvenience of inquiry in any case, including Stanley's. The establishment of prompt efficacious procedures to achieve legitimate state ends is a proper state interest worthy of cognizance in constitutional adjudication. But the Constitution recognizes higher values than speed and efficiency. Indeed, one might fairly say of the Bill of Rights in general, and the Due Process Clause in particular, that they were designed to protect the fragile values of a vulnerable citizenry from the overbearing concern for efficiency and efficacy that may characterize praiseworthy government officials no less, and perhaps more, than mediocre ones.

Procedure by presumption is always cheaper and easier than individualized determination. But when, as here, the procedure forecloses the determinative issues of competence and care, when it explicitly disdains present realities in deference to past formalities, it needlessly risks running roughshod over the important interests of both parent and child. It therefore cannot stand.

* * *

III

The State of Illinois assumes custody of the children of married parents, divorced parents, and unmarried mothers only after a hearing and proof of neglect. The children of unmarried fathers, however, are declared dependent children without a hearing on parental fitness and without proof of neglect. Stanley's claim . . . is that failure to afford him a hearing on his parental qualifications while extending it to other parents denied equal protection of the laws. We have concluded that all Illinois parents are constitutionally entitled to a hearing on their fitness before their children are removed from their custody.

It follows that denying such a hearing to Stanley and those like him while granting it to other Illinois parents is inescapably contrary to the Equal Protection Clause.

The judgment of the Supreme Court of Illinois is reversed and the case is remanded to that court for proceedings not inconsistent with this opinion.

[Mr. Chief Justice BURGER's dissenting opinion is omitted.]

Notes

1. In a long line of cases, the United States Supreme Court has held that the Due Process Clause of the Fourteenth Amendment ensures parental autonomy and privacy in matters of family life. *See Meyer v. Nebraska*, 262 U.S. 390 (1923) (liberty interest guaranteed by Fourteenth Amendment includes right to marry, to bring up children, and establish a home); *Pierce v. Society of Sisters,* 268 U.S. 510, (1925) (parents have protected right to direct their children's upbringing and education); *Skinner v. Oklahoma*, 316 U.S. 535 (1942) (Fourteenth Amendment protects right to bear children); *Griswold v. Connecticut,* 381 U.S. 479 (1965) (prohibiting contraceptives violates right of marital privacy); *Roe v. Wade*, 410 U.S. 113 (1973) (Due Process Clause protects right of privacy in woman's decision to terminate her pregnancy); *Planned Parenthood v. Casey,* 505 U.S. 833, 851 (1992) (constitutional protection extends to "marriage, procreation, contraception, family relationships, child rearing, and education."). Even though the Fourteenth Amendment protects a parent's rights over a child, these rights are not absolute. *See In re Baby Boy N.,* 874 P.2d 680 (Kan. Ct. App. 1994).

When seeking to terminate parental rights, the state must adhere to the heightened substantive standard of "family integrity." *See M.H.J. v. State Dept. of Human Resources*, No. 2990715, 2990716, 2000 WL 1300441 (Ala. Civ. App. Sept. 15, 2000) ("The right to maintain family integrity is a fundamental right protected by the due process requirements of the Constitution."); *In re B.L.S.,* No. 94306, 2000 WL 1140756 (Okla. Civ. App. Div. 1 July 7, 2000) ("interest of child in a wholesome environment has a constitutional dimension no less compelling than a parent has in the preservation of family integrity"); *Callender v. Skiles,* 591 N.W.2d 182 (Iowa 1999) (family integrity best protected by due process for purposes of termination of parental rights); *Roe v. Conn,* 417 F. Supp. 769 (M.D. Ala. 1976) (Fourteenth Amendment affords protection of family integrity from state interference); *Duchesne v. Sugarman*, 566 F.2d 817 (2d Cir. 1977) (family integrity includes constitutional rights of parents as well as children). Because the substantive due process right of family privacy is deemed fundamental, the state must demonstrate a compelling state interest to terminate parental rights. *See* Susan B. Hershkowitz, *Due Process and the Termination of Parental Rights,* 19 FAM. L.Q. 245, 254-55 (1985); *In re E.A.T.,* 989 P.2d 860 (Mont. 1999) (although family integrity is constitutionally protected, family unity should not come at "the expense of the child's best interest.").

2. Because of the significance of family privacy, the state is required to prove its case by clear and convincing evidence. *See Santosky v. Kramer*, 455 U.S.

745 (1982). *See also In the Interest of J.A.T.*, 590 So. 2d 524 (Fla. Dist. Ct. App. 1991) (a showing of a preponderance of the evidence is insufficient to terminate parental rights).

For further discussion of the substantive due process rights of parents that are impacted by TPR proceedings, see Cheryl M. Browing & Michael L. Weiner, Note, *The Right to Family Integrity: A Substantive Due Process Approach to State Removal and Termination Proceedings*, 68 GEO. L.J. 213 (1979); Wanda Ellen Wakefield, Annotation, *Validity of State Statute Providing for Termination of Parental Rights*, 22 A.L.R.4TH 774 (1983); Timothy J. Cassidy, *Termination of Parental Rights: The Substantive Due Process Issues*, 26 ST. LOUIS U. L.J. 915 (1982).

B. Procedural Due Process

1. Notice and Hearing

a. Basic Requirements

Delaware Code Annotated

Tit. 13, § 1107 (Michie Supp. 2000)

§ 1107. Hearing procedures; notice of hearing; report

(a) When a petition for the termination of parental rights is filed in which the Department or licensed agency is a party to the proceedings, the Court shall set a date for hearing thereon, and shall cause notice of the time, place and purpose of the hearing to be served upon the parent or parents, person or persons or organization holding parental rights at the respondent's last known address or to the address recited in the petition.

(b) No such notice of hearing shall be necessary if:

(1) A waiver executed by the parent or parents, person or persons or organization holding parental rights has been filed with the petition, in accordance with § 1106(d) of this title. The Court may require notice to be served upon any other person or organization.

(2) Prior to the filing of the petition for termination of parental rights, the parent or parents, person or persons or organization holding parental rights has failed to respond to the petitioning agency within 20 days after receiving notice of the intention to file the petition. Such notice shall contain information regarding the child's name and date of birth, grounds for the petition, the right to file with the Court or the petitioning agency opposition to the termination of parental rights or to deny paternity, and shall be mailed by registered or certified mail. Proof of receipt shall be attached to the petition as an exhibit.

(c) If the Court shall find that personal service within the State cannot be accomplished upon the parent or parents, person or persons or organization holding parental rights, the Court shall then cause notice of the time, place and purpose of the hearing to be published once a week, for 3 successive weeks, in such newspaper of the county, 1 or more, as the Court may judge best for giving the parent or parents, or person or persons or organization holding parental right notice, the formal wording of said notice to be approved by the Court. Such publication shall constitute conclusive evidence of service and a hearing will then proceed at the time and date set, with or without the appearance of the parent or parents, person or persons or organization so notified. Publication shall also be made in the locality in which the parent or parents, person or persons or organization holding parental rights is believed to be located if different from the county where the publication just described has been caused.

(d) If any publication is ordered pursuant to subsection (c) of this section, the Court shall also order that the Clerk of the Court, at least 3 weeks prior to the hearing, send by regular and registered or certified mail to the parent or parents or person or persons or organization holding parental rights, at the address or addresses given in the petition, a copy of the same notice, or a similar notice of the time, place and purpose of the hearing.

(e) Personal service at any time prior to the hearing shall be sufficient to give jurisdiction.

(f) When a petition for termination of parental rights is filed and the Department or a licensed agency is not a party to the proceeding, the Court shall, before any hearing, order a social study and report on the petition, by the Department or a licensed agency, to be filed within 4 months, subject to such additional time as the Court shall determine is reasonably required. The Court shall set a date for hearing to take place after the report is to be filed and notice shall be accomplished as outlined above.

(g) All hearings shall be held before the Court privately, but for reasons appearing sufficient to the Court the hearing in any particular case may be public.

Notes

1. Parents have a due process right to notice and opportunity to be heard at a hearing to terminate parental rights (TPR). In *In re Interest of Joseph L.*, 598 N.W.2d 464 (Neb. Ct. App. 1999), the DSS determined that both parents failed to complete their counseling programs and filed a TPR petition. During a visitation motion hearing, the court advised the parents of the filed TPR petition. Thereafter, the parents separated. On the day of the TPR hearing, the mother informed her attorney that she could not attend the hearing because of her in-house alcoholism counseling. The attorney appeared in court and informed the court of the mother's counseling session and requested leave to withdraw as the mother's counsel, which the court granted. Despite the absence of the mother and her attorney, the court conducted the TPR hearing and entered an order to terminate both parents' rights (the father was also not present) over the child. On review, the court reversed the trial court and held that the absence of the mother and her counsel from the TPR hearing violated the mother's due process rights. According to the court, the trial court's conducting the TPR hearing without the mother or her counsel present rose to the level of "fundamental flaws, which never have been thought harmless." *Id.* at 548 (citing *Vasquez v. Hillary*, 474 U.S. 254, 263 (1986)). In *In re Alexander V.,* 613 A.2d 780, 785 (Conn. 1992), the court held "that due process does not require a competency hearing in all termination cases but only when (1) the parent's attorney requests such a hearing, or (2) in the absence of such a request, the conduct of the parent reasonably suggests to the court, in the exercise of its discretion, the desirability of ordering such a hearing sua sponte." *See also* GA. CODE ANN. § 15-11-100 (Lexis Supp. 2000) (court may order medical examination of parties in TPR proceedings). For further analysis of cases where courts found parents were denied due process because of an improper TPR hearing, see Wanda Ellen Wakefield, Annotation, *Validity of State Statutes Providing for Termination of Parental Rights*, 22 A.L.R.4TH 774 (1983).

The conduct and procedure of TPR hearings vary among the states. The following are examples of statutes that outline the due process parameters of TPR hearings:

District of Columbia Code Annotated

§§ 16-2358, 16-2359 (Lexis 1997)

§ 16-2358 Conduct of hearings.

a. All hearings and proceedings on a motion to terminate the parent and child relationship shall be held by the judge, without a jury.

b. All hearings and proceedings held pursuant to this subchapter shall be recorded by appropriate means.

c. Except in hearings to declare a person in contempt of court, the general public shall be excluded from hearings and proceedings arising pursuant to this subchapter. Only persons necessary to such hearings and proceedings shall be admitted, but a judge may, pursuant to rules of the Superior Court of the District of Columbia, admit such other persons as have a proper interest in the case or the work of the Division on the condition that they refrain from divulging information identifying the child involved in the proceedings or members of his or her family.

d. If a judge finds it is in the best interests of the child, he or she may temporarily exclude the child from any proceeding. Under no circumstances, however, may counsel in the case be excluded.

§ 16-2359 Adjudicatory hearing.

a. A judge shall begin the adjudicatory hearing by determining whether all parties are present and whether proper notice of the hearing has been given. If the parent has been given proper notice but has failed to appear the judge may proceed in his or her absence.

b. A judge shall hear evidence presented by the moving party and the burden of proof shall rest upon the moving party.

c. Every party shall have the right to present evidence, to be heard in his or her own behalf and to cross-examine witnesses called by another party.

d. All evidence which is relevant, material, and competent to the issues before the judge shall be admitted.

e. Notwithstanding the provisions of D.C. Code, sections 14-306 and 14-307, neither the husband/wife privilege nor the physician/client or mental health professional/client privilege shall be a ground for excluding evidence in any proceeding brought under this subchapter.

f. A judge may enter an order permanently terminating the parent and child relationship after considering all of the evidence presented and after making a determination based upon clear and convincing evidence that termination of the parent and child relationship is in the best interest of the child. If a judge does not find that sufficient grounds exist for termination, the motion for termination of the parent and child relationship may be dismissed.

See also ARIZ. REV. STAT. ANN. § 8-537 (West Supp. 2000); COLO. REV. STAT. ANN. § 19-3-602 (2000); FLA. STAT. ANN. § 39.809 (West Supp. 2001); HAW. REV. STAT. § 571-62 (1993); KY. REV. STAT. ANN. § 625.042 (West 2000); NEB. REV. STAT. ANN. § 43-291 (1993).

2. Jurisdictions have codified the notice requirement in TPR proceedings. *See, e.g.,* DEL. CODE ANN. tit. 13, § 1107 (Michie Supp. 2000), *supra* Chapter 14, Part B.1.a. *See also* CAL. WELF. & INST. CODE § 366.23(b) (West Supp. 2001); ARK. CODE ANN. § 9-27-341 (Michie Supp. 2001) (petitioner provides parents either constructive or actual notice); FLA. STAT. ANN. § 39.801 (West Supp. 2001) (notice personally served); IOWA CODE ANN. § 600A.6 (West Supp. 2001) (notice by publication if certified mail or personal service fails); 705 ILL. COMP. STAT. ANN. 405/2-16 (West Supp. 2001); N.H. REV. STAT. ANN. § 170-C:7 (Lexis Supp. 2000). According to some state statutes, if the parents fail to appear for TPR proceedings and the court determines that notice has been properly served, the court may find that the failure to appear constitutes admission of the allegations in the TPR petition. *See, e.g.,* ARIZ. REV. STAT. ANN. § 8-863 (West Supp. 2000); FLA. STAT. ANN. § 39.801 (West Supp. 2001). The following is a statute which details the information a TPR notice must include:

Kentucky Rules of Jefferson Family Court

§ 403 (Banks-Baldwin, WESTLAW through 1999 Sess.)

§ 403. Contents of Notice

The summons in the action shall include the following information:

1. A statement that termination of parental rights means loss of all rights to custody, visitation, and communication with the child, and that if termination is granted, the parent will receive no notice of future legal proceedings concerning the child;

2. An explanation of the need to respond immediately to the notice, both to prepare for trial and because important hearings may take place prior to trial;

3. An explanation of how to find out the time and place of future hearings in the cases;

4. An explanation of the right to counsel and the effect of indigency;

5. The pretrial date so that the parents have notice of such date when served.

When determining whether or not the served TPR notice meets constitutional muster, the test derived in *Mathews v. Eldridge,* 424 U.S. 319 (1976), must be used. *Eldridge* states that in determining whether an individual's rights have been violated, a court must weigh (1) the private individual's interest, (2) the state's interest, and (3) the risk of erroneous deprivation of the private individual's interest. For an analysis of the application of the *Eldridge* factors to notice of TPR proceedings, see Brian A. Cute, Note, *Methods of Notice in Termination of Parental Rights Hearings,* 5 CONN. PROB. L.J. 317, 325 (1991).

3. State statutes vary in terms of the notice period before an advisory or an initial hearing to terminate parental rights. In *J.B. v. Florida Dep't of Children and Family Serv.,* 768 So. 2d 1060 (Fla. 2000), the court held that a father's due process rights were violated when the state gave him 24 hours notice of an advisory hearing addressing a petition for termination of his parental rights. Although Florida statutes do not specify how much time is required, the court stated that the statute must be interpreted to require "constitutionally reasonable notice." Noting that other jurisdictions have established a minimum number of days for notice to be given, the court found no evidence was given to necessitate a 24 hour window and that such notice failed to satisfy the father's due process rights.

Questions

1. What is the significance in terms of due process of case or statutory law labeling TPR as a civil proceeding?

2. In TPR proceedings, what accommodations for a parent with limited mental capacity are necessary to satisfy due process?

3. What issues of law and policy arise when a parent, who receives proper notice, fails to appear at a TPR hearing? What factors should a court consider when determining whether to allow the hearing to proceed as scheduled?

b. The Incarcerated Parent

California Penal Code
§ 2625 (West Supp. 2001)

§ 2625. Actions affecting prisoner's parental or marital rights; dependency guardianship; notice; order for appearance

(a) For the purposes of this section only, the term "prisoner" includes any individual in custody in a state prison, the California Rehabilitation Center, or a county jail, or who is a ward of the Department of the Youth Authority or who, upon a verdict or finding that the individual was insane at the time of committing an offense, or mentally incompetent to be tried or adjudged to punishment, is confined in a state hospital for the care and treatment of the mentally disorder or in any other public or private treatment facility.

(b) In any proceeding . . . to terminate the parental rights of any prisoner, or any proceeding . . . to adjudicate the child of a prisoner a dependent child of the court, the superior court of the county in which the proceeding is pending, or a judge thereof, shall order notice of any court proceeding regarding the proceeding transmitted to the prisoner.

(c) Service of notice shall be made pursuant to . . . the Family Code or . . . the Welfare and Institutions Code, as appropriate.

(d) Upon receipt by the court of a statement from the prisoner or his or her attorney indicating the prisoner's desire to be present during the court's proceedings, the court shall issue an order for the temporary removal of the prisoner from the institution, and for the prisoner's production before the court. No proceeding may be held . . . and no petition to adjudge the child of a prisoner a dependent child of the court . . . may be adjudicated without the physical presence of the prisoner or the prisoner's attorney, unless the court has before it a knowing waiver of the right of physical presence signed by the prisoner or an affidavit signed by the warden, superintendent, or other person in charge of the institution, or his or her designated representative stating that the prisoner has, by express statement or action, indicated an intent not to appear at the proceeding.

* * *

(g) Notwithstanding any other law, a court may not order the removal and production of a prisoner sentenced to death, whether or not that sentence is being appealed, in any action or proceeding in which the prisoner's parental rights are subject to adjudication.

In re Ruth Anne E.

974 P.2d 164 (N.M. Ct. App. 1999)

Robert E. (Father) appeals from a judgment terminating his parental rights to his three minor children, Ruth Anne E., Sonya Sue E., and Blanca Alicia E., ages eight, six, and four, respectively. The dispositive issue presented on appeal is whether Father was deprived of an opportunity to appear or to meaningfully defend against the action to terminate his parental rights. Because we conclude that Father was denied due process of law, we reverse and remand for a new hearing on the motion to terminate Father's parental rights.

[T]he Children, Youth and Families Department (the Department) received a report that Lorena R. (Mother) had left her three minor children with a babysitter . . . and had failed to return for them. The children were placed in the temporary custody of the Department.

Although the police located Mother and notified her that the children had been placed in protective custody, she did not contact the Department and she subsequently disappeared. Approximately six months later . . . Mother reappeared and indicated a desire to regain custody of her children. She stated that she had been attending a drug and rehabilitation program. . . . Mother . . . began using drugs again, and failed to keep in contact with the children or the Department.

At the time the children were initially taken into protective custody, Father was incarcerated in a Texas prison serving a sentence on a felony conviction. Father was served with a copy of the petition, alleging that the children were neglected and abused. He filed an answer asserting that he was in prison in Texas, that he was indigent, and that he wished to contest "Petitioner's Original Petition For Termination." Father's answer sought the appointment of a court-appointed attorney to represent him, and requested "that he [be permitted] to be present at any proceeding affecting the custody of [his] children as a matter of due process and equal protection of the law." Father also requested that the children's court issue an order directing that he be transported to the court so that he could "present testimony concerning the future of his natural children and defend his rights." Alternatively, Father requested that the children's court grant a continuance until "such time as [he was] released from the penitentiary and . . . able to appear in Court and defend [such] suit." The children's court appointed separate counsel to represent Father and Mother, and appointed a guardian ad litem to represent the children.

The children's court issued an order directing the Bernalillo County Sheriff's Department to transport Father from the correctional facility in Texas to an adjudicatory hearing . . . ; however, the order could not be enforced.

. . . The Department filed a motion seeking to terminate both Mother's and Father's parental rights. Father filed a response contesting the motion. The children's court scheduled a hearing on the merits. . . . At the hearing on the merits, the Father's attorney informed the children's court that Father had been released from prison but had been reincarcerated on a new charge, and that he expected to be released from jail in the immediate future. His attorney requested that the children's court grant a continuance so that Father could appear and testify. The children's court denied the request and directed that the hearing proceed.

The only witnesses who testified at the hearing on the motion to terminate parental rights were witnesses called by the Department. Neither Father nor Mother were present, although the witnesses called by the Department were cross-examined by counsel who had been appointed to represent Father and Mother. At the conclusion of the hearing, the children's court found that the children were abused and neglected, that the parental bond between the parents and the children had disintegrated, and that the parental rights of Father and Mother should be terminated.

On appeal, Father asserts, among other things, that incarceration alone is insufficient to support an allegation of abandonment, that his procedural due process rights were violated because he "was never afforded an opportunity to participate in the merits of the trial involving termination of his parental rights," that he was precluded "from presenting evidence in his own defense" and that he was not given an opportunity to refute the matters presented by the Department.

* * *

We turn next to Father's challenge to the validity of the order terminating his parental rights, which is grounded upon his claim of denial of due process. Father argues that he was never afforded the opportunity to participate in the proceeding involving the termination of his parental rights. . . . [H]e asserts he was precluded from "presenting evidence" in defense of the allegations of neglect and abandonment.

The Department urges this Court not to consider Father's due process claim, arguing that he failed to preserve such contention. The Department asserts that Father failed to sufficiently alert the children's court to his claim of denial of due process at the proceedings below. We disagree.

Father's answer to the petition to terminate his parental rights alleged that he did not have "sufficient funds or assets to hire an attorney to represent [Father's] interests in this lawsuit," attached an affidavit of indigency, and requested that the children's court appoint an attorney to represent him. The answer also requested a continuance in the termination hearing because of Father's incarceration in Texas, and stated that he "desire[d] to present testimony in his own behalf." Finally, the answer asserted that Father was entitled to be present at such proceeding "affecting the custody of [his] children as a matter of due process and equal protection of the law."

. . . By filing a pleading requesting the opportunity to present testimony on his own behalf and by requesting a continuance so that father could take part in the proceedings, Father's attorney alerted the children's court to Father's desire to actively contest the charges against him.

Not every act of a parent which results in the parent's incarceration constitutes a valid basis to terminate an individual's parental rights. . . . The Department . . . concedes that, although it is preferable that a parent . . . be physically present at a hearing on a petition to terminate parental rights, there is no constitutional requirement requiring a parent's presence.

The Department is correct that due process requirements do not mandate the personal appearance of a parent in parental termination proceedings where the parent is serving a prison sentence outside the jurisdiction where the action to terminate parental rights is pending. Although the court must utilize procedures which protect the rights of parents in hearings involving the termination of parental rights, the primary consideration must be given to the best interest of the child. . . . Courts in a number of states have addressed the question. . . . None have concluded that an individual who has been incarcerated or otherwise unable to personally appear in court has an absolute right consistent with the Due Process Clause to appear at a termination of parental rights hearing. . . .

Thus, while it is clear that a parent incarcerated out of state does not have an absolute right to appear at a parental rights termination hearing, this does not end our inquiry. We next address . . . whether a parent who is prevented from attending a termination proceeding because of his or her incarceration, is entitled by due process to have the court fashion an alternative procedure to permit the parent to respond to the matters presented by the state. Procedural due process mandates that a person be accorded an "opportunity to be heard at a meaningful time and in a meaningful manner." . . . [T]he courts acknowledge that procedural due process is a flexible right and the amount of process due depends on the particular circumstances of each case. . . . A number of states have held that a parent incarcerated out of state or otherwise prevented from attending a termination hearing was afforded due process under the circumstances when the parent received notice, was represented by counsel, and was given an opportunity to appear and testify by deposition. . . .

Courts in other cases, however, have held that due process requirements necessitate more than simply providing for a parent's appearance by deposition. They required that the parent be given an opportunity to review the evidence presented by the state, to consult with his or her attorney, and then to present evidence by deposition or by telephone. . . .

* * *

In *Mathews* the United States Supreme Court adopted a three-part test detailing the criteria which govern the inquiry concerning whether due process has been satisfied in a particular case. *See id.*, 424 U.S. at 335, 96 S. Ct. 893. . . . The *Mathews* court stated that the question of whether due process has been accorded an individual necessitates resolution of the following factors: First, [consideration of] the private interest that will be affected by the official action; second, the risk of an erroneous deprivation of such interest through the procedures used, and the probable value, if any, of additional or substitute procedural safeguards; and finally, the government's interest, including the function involved and the fiscal and administrative burdens that the additional or substitute procedural requirement would entail. 424 U.S. at 335, 96 S. Ct. 893.

In reviewing proceedings wherein the children's court has ordered that the parent-child relationships be terminated, we review the evidence in the light most favorable to the prevailing party to determine if the record is sufficient to establish clearly and convincingly a basis for termination. . . . However, in passing upon claims that the procedure utilized below resulted in a denial of procedural due process, we review such issues de novo. . . .

Applying the balancing test set forth in *Mathews* to the record before us, we conclude that the procedures utilized in the children's court herein failed to satisfy due process requirements set forth in *Mathews*. Under the first factor, it is clear that Father's interest was significant. . . . Applying the second factor to the record before us, it is also evident that the risk of an erroneous deprivation of parental rights is greatly magnified unless alternative arrangements are made to permit an incarcerated parent who preserves his or her due process right to present evidence, to consult with his or her attorney, and to confront the witnesses called by the state. . . . Under the third factor, we acknowledge the state's vital interest in protecting the welfare of children. . . .

After balancing each of the factors herein, we conclude that the second factor is determinative. Here, the procedure employed by the children's court had the effect of increasing the risk of error by denying Father an opportunity to defend against the charge of neglect and abandonment.

In sum, we determine that because a fundamental liberty interest is implicated in proceedings involving the termination of parental rights, a parent who is incarcerated and is unable to attend the hearing on the state's petition to terminate parental rights is entitled to more than simply the right to cross-examine witnesses or to present argument through his attorney, or to present deposition testimony—he or she has the right to meaningful participation in the hearing. This right includes the right to review the evidence presented against him or her, present evidence on his or her behalf, and an opportunity to challenge the evidence presented.

Although procedural due process may be adapted to the particular circumstances of each case, the Nebraska Supreme Court, in *In re L.V.*, has cogently set forth the procedural due process required in proceedings seeking to terminate parental rights under factual circumstances analogous to the instant case. The court observed:

> When a person has a right to be heard, procedural due process includes notice to the person whose right is affected by a proceeding, that is, timely notice reasonably calculated to inform the person concerning the subject and issues involved in the proceeding; a reasonable opportunity to refute or defend against a change or accusation; a reasonable opportunity to confront and cross-examine adverse witnesses and present evidence on the charge or accusation; representation by counsel, when such representation is required by constitution or statute; and a hearing before an impartial decision-maker.

In re L.V., 482 N.W.2d at 257 (citations omitted). This enumeration of the requirements of procedural due process is consistent with the decision of our Supreme Court in *In re Ronald A.*, 110 N.M. at 455, 707 P.2d at 244. . . .

By refusing to continue the hearing or adopt other procedures to permit Father's meaningful participation in the hearing, Father was denied an opportunity to defend against the allegations, to confront and cross-examine witnesses, and to present evidence on his behalf. As a result of the children's court's failure to implement any mechanism to allow Father to testify on his behalf, the risk of an erroneous deprivation of Father's constitutionally protected rights was greatly increased. . . . Without Father being able to provide evidence on his behalf, the only evidence before the children's court was that presented by the Department whose stated goal was to terminate Father's parental rights. Under these circumstances, Father was prejudiced by his inability to meaningfully participate in the hearing or to consult with his attorney.

. . . Here, although it is clear that Father could not be physically present at the proceeding, other procedures were available to permit him to participate in the proceeding. Father could have given testimony at the final hearing by telephone, or after the Department's witnesses were called, Father's deposition could have been taken so that he could have an opportunity to review such evidence and he could then be accorded an opportunity to respond.

Alternatively, a second continuance could have been granted for a brief period of time . . . to see if Father was released from the Texas jail. Failing that, the children's court could have ordered that the Department present its evidence, then that the matter be briefly recessed so that Father was given an opportunity to review the evidence, discuss it with his attorney, and then the hearing be reconvened so Father could present his evidence by telephone or deposition, and an opportunity through his counsel to effectively cross-examine the Department's witnesses. We do not believe that utilization of any of these procedures utilized in other states would greatly burden the Department.

We are mindful of the fact that cases involving the termination of parental rights should be expeditiously concluded, that the need for finality in theses cases is great, and that it is important that the children involved have a sense of stability and permanence in their lives. At the same time, a court cannot ignore a parent's fundamental liberty interest in the care and custody of his or her children. Thus, before a court can irrevocably sever the parent-child bond, it must ensure that the parent is given a fair opportunity to present evidence and defend his or her fundamental parental rights. Father was deprived of that opportunity here.

The order terminating Father's parental rights is reversed and the matter is remanded to the children's court for a new hearing consistent with the matters stated herein.

Notes

1. *Santosky v. Kramer*, 455 U.S. 745 (1982), the Supreme Court found that parents have a fundamental liberty interest in the care, custody and management of their children. *Santosky* further recognized the importance of a parent's due process right in maintaining a parent-child relationship even when the parent is incarcerated:

> The fundamental liberty interest of natural parents in the care, custody, and management of their child does not evaporate simply because they have not been model parents or have lost temporary custody of their child to the State. Even when the blood relationships are strained, parents retain a vital interest in preventing the irretrievable destruction of their family life. If anything, persons faced with forced dissolution of their parental rights have a more critical need for procedural protections than do those resisting state intervention into ongoing family affairs. When the State moves to destroy weakened familial bonds, it must provide the parents with fundamentally fair procedures.

Id. at 753.

Courts have taken different approaches in defining how much process is due incarcerated parents in TPR proceedings. In *In re Custody of Abdul Kaheem Unique Mohammed Jewel Cameron C., aka David C.,* 606 N.Y.S.2d 178 (N.Y. 1994), the court found that an incarcerated parent's rights should not be terminated without his or her presence absent unusual circumstances. The right to be present, however, is not absolute. *See In re C.J.,* 650 N.E.2d 290 (Ill. App. Ct. 1995). Whether an incarcerated parent may attend TPR hearing is within the court's discretion. *See State ex rel. Jeanette H. v. Pancake*, 529 S.E.2d 865 (W. Va. 2000) (citing numerous factors for a court to consider when determining if an incarcerated parent's presence is necessary at the TPR hearing). However, courts generally agree that if an incarcerated parent does not appear for a TPR hearing, due process requires alternative measures to insure that the parent can participate meaningfully. *See In re Ruth Anne E., supra; In re C.J., supra* (incarcerated parent should be afforded a meaningful opportunity to be heard). One alternative measure courts use to ensure that a parent can participate meaningfully in a TPR hearing is telephone communication with the court. Some courts have found, however, that allowing a parent to communicate via telephone during a TPR hearing may not satisfy the parent's procedural due process rights. *See In re Baby K.*, 722 A.2d 470 (N.H. 1998) (parent's due process rights violated where telephonic procedures did not provide incarcerated parent a fair opportunity to participate because the parent could only communicate with his attorney and not the trial court); *Orville v. Division of Family Services,* 759 A.2d 595 (Del. Super. Ct. 2000) (incarcerated mother must be allowed to participate in entire TPR hearing via telephone or must be provided with transcript or tape recording of state's case to satisfy parent's due process rights).

For further discussion of the procedural due process rights of incarcerated parents in TPR proceedings, see Elise Zealand, *Protecting the Ties That Bind From Behind Bars: A Call for Equal Opportunities for Incarcerated Fathers and the Children to Maintain the Parent-Child Relationship*, 31 COLUM. J. L. & SOC. PROBS. 247, 265-66 (1998); Gregory D. Sarno, Annotation, *Parent's Involuntary Confinement, or Failure to Care for Child as Result Thereof, as Evincing Neglect, Unfitness, or the Like in Dependency or Divestiture Proceeding,* 79 A.L.R.3D 417 (1997). For a survey of the procedural due process rights of incarcerated parents, see Philip M. Gentry, *Procedural Due Process Rights of Incarcerated Parents in Termination of Parental Rights Proceedings: A Fifty State Analysis,* 30 J. FAM. L. 757 (1991-92).

Questions

1. Are TPR proceedings civil in nature? Why is this characterization important to the incarcerated parent?

2. What specific requirements are necessary to satisfy procedural process for an incarcerated parent in a TPR trial?

2. Right to Counsel

Georgia Code Annotated
§ 17-12-38.1 (Lexis 1997)

§ 7-12-38.1 Legal representation for indigents in all felony cases and in certain misdemeanor cases.

State funded local indigent defense programs and local indigent defense programs shall provide legal representation for indigents in all felony cases and in those misdemeanor cases in which indigents are guaranteed the right to counsel in the superior, state, and magistrate courts; all actions and proceedings provided for under subparagraph (e)(4)(B) and paragraph (2) of subsection (f) of Code Section 17-7-131; and all actions and proceedings within the juvenile courts of this state in which a person is entitled to legal representation under the Constitution of the United States or the Constitution and laws of the State of Georgia, including but not limited to actions involving delinquency, unruliness, incorrigibility, deprivation, and termination of parental rights. Nothing in this Code section shall be interpreted as applying to guardians ad litem.

Lassiter v. Department of Social Services of Durham County, North Carolina

452 U.S. 18, 101 S. Ct. 2153, 68 L. Ed. 2d 640 (1981)

Justice STEWART delivered the opinion of the Court.

I

In the late spring of 1975, after hearing evidence that the petitioner, Abby Gail Lassiter, had not provided her infant son William with proper medical care, the District Court of Durham County, N.C., adjudicated him a neglected child and transferred him to the custody of the Durham County Department of Social Services, the respondent here. A year later, Ms. Lassiter was charged with first-degree murder, was convicted of second-degree murder, and began a sentence of 25-40 years of imprisonment. In 1978 the Department petitioned the court to terminate Ms. Lassiter's parental rights because, the Department alleged, she "has not had any contact with the child since December of 1975" and "has willfully left the child in foster care for more than two consecutive years without showing that substantial progress has been made in correcting the conditions which led to the removal of the child, or without showing a positive response to the diligent efforts of the Department of Social Services to strengthen her relationship to the child, or to make and follow through with constructive planning for the future of the child."

Ms. Lassiter was served with the petition and with notice that a hearing on it would be held. Although her mother had retained counsel for her in connection with an effort to invalidate the murder conviction, Ms. Lassiter never mentioned the forthcoming hearing to him. . . . At the behest of the Department of Social Services' attorney, she was brought from prison to the hearing, which was held August 31, 1978. The hearing opened, apparently at the judge's instance, with a discussion of whether Ms. Lassiter should have more time in which to find legal assistance. Since the court concluded that she "has had ample opportunity to seek and obtain counsel prior to the hearing of this matter, and [that] her failure to do so is without just cause," the court did not postpone the proceedings. Ms. Lassiter did not aver that she was indigent, and the court did not appoint counsel for her.

A social worker from the respondent Department was the first witness. She testified that in 1975 the Department "received a complaint from Duke Pediatrics that William had not been followed in the pediatric clinic for medical problems and they were having difficulty in locating Ms. Lassiter. . . ." She said that in May 1975 a social worker had taken William to the hospital, where doctors asked that he stay "because of breathing difficulties [and] malnutrition and [because] there was a great deal of scarring that indicated that he had a severe infection that had gone untreated." The witness further testified that, except for one "prearranged" visit and a chance meeting on the street, Ms. Lassiter had not seen William after he had come into the State's custody, and that neither Ms. Lassiter nor her mother had "made any contact with the Department of Social Services regarding that child." When asked whether William should be placed in his grandmother's custody, the social worker said he should not, since the grandmother "has indicated to me on a number of occasions that she was not able to take responsibility for the child" and since "I have checked with people in the community and from Ms. Lassiter's church who also feel that this additional responsibility would be more than she can handle." The social worker added that William "has not seen his grandmother since the chance meeting in July of '76 and that was the only time."

* * *

Ms. Lassiter conducted a cross-examination of the social worker, who firmly reiterated her earlier testimony. The judge explained several times, with varying degrees of clarity, that Ms. Lassiter should only ask questions at this stage; many of her questions were disallowed because they were not really questions, but arguments.

Ms. Lassiter herself then testified, under the judge's questioning, that she had properly cared for William. Under cross-examination, she said that she had seen William more than five or six times after he had been taken from her custody and that, if William could not be with her, she wanted him to be with her mother since, "He knows us. Children know they family. . . . They know they people, they know they family and that child knows us anywhere. . . . I got four more other children. Three girls and a boy and they know they little brother when they see him."

* * *

The court found that Ms. Lassiter "has not contacted the Department of Social Services about her child since December, 1975, has not expressed any concern for his care and welfare, and has made no efforts to plan for his future." Because Ms. Lassiter thus had "wilfully failed to maintain concern or responsibility for the welfare of the minor," and because it was "in the best interests of the minor," the court terminated Ms. Lassiter's status as William's parent.

On appeal, Ms. Lassiter argued only that, because she was indigent, the Due Process Clause of the Fourteenth Amendment entitled her to the assistance of counsel, and that the trial court had therefore erred in not requiring the State to provide counsel for her. The North Carolina Court of Appeals decided that "[w]hile this State action does invade a protected area of individual privacy, the invasion is not so serious or unreasonable as to compel us to hold that appointment of counsel for indigent parents is constitutionally mandated." *In re Lassiter,* 43 N.C. App. 525, 527, 259 S.E.2d 336, 337. The Supreme Court of North Carolina summarily denied Ms. Lassiter's application for discretionary review, and we granted certiorari to consider the petitioner's claim under the Due Process Clause of the Fourteenth Amendment.

II

For all its consequence, "due process" has never been, and perhaps can never be, precisely defined. "[U]nlike some legal rules," this Court has said, due process "is not a technical conception with a fixed content unrelated to time, place and circumstances." *Cafeteria Workers v. McElroy*, 367 U.S. 886, 895. Rather, the phrase expresses the requirement of "fundamental fairness," a requirement whose meaning can be as opaque as its importance is lofty. Applying the Due Process Clause is therefore an uncertain enterprise which must discover what "fundamental fairness" consists of in a particular situation by first considering any relevant precedents and then by assessing the several interests that are at stake.

A

The pre-eminent generalization that emerges from this Court's precedents on an indigent's right to appointed counsel is that such a right has been recognized to exist only where the litigant may lose his physical liberty if he loses the litigation. Thus . . . *Argersinger v. Hamlin*, 407 U.S. 25, established that counsel must be provided before any indigent may be sentenced to prison, even where the crime is petty and the prison term brief.

That it is the defendant's interest in personal freedom, and not simply the special Sixth and Fourteenth Amendments right to counsel in criminal cases, which triggers the right to appointed counsel is demonstrated by the Court's announcement in *In re Gault*, 387 U.S. 1, that "the Due Process Clause of the Fourteenth Amendment requires that in respect of proceedings to determine delinquency *which may result in commitment to an institution in which the juvenile's freedom is curtailed,*" the juvenile has a right to appointed counsel even though those proceedings may be styled "civil" and not "criminal." *Id.* at 41 (emphasis added). . . .

Significantly, as a litigant's interest in personal liberty diminishes, so does his right to appointed counsel. In *Gagnon v. Scarpelli*, 411 U.S. 778, the Court gauged the due process rights of a previously sentenced probationer at a probation-revocation hearing. In *Morrissey v. Brewer,* 408 U.S. 471, 480, which involved an analogous hearing to revoke parole, the Court had said: "Revocation deprives an individual, not of the absolute liberty to which every citizen is entitled, but only of the conditional liberty properly dependent on observance of special parole restrictions." Relying on that discussion, the Court in *Scarpelli* declined to hold that indigent probationers have, *per se*, a right to counsel at revocation hearings, and instead left the decision whether counsel should be appointed to be made on a case-by-case basis.

* * *

In sum, the Court's precedents speak with one voice about what "fundamental fairness" has meant when the Court has considered the right to appointed counsel, and we thus draw from them the presumption that an indigent litigant has a right to appointed counsel only when, if he loses, he may be deprived of his physical liberty. It is against this presumption that all the other elements in the due process decision must be measured.

B

The case of *Mathews v. Eldridge,* 424 U.S. 319, 335, propounds three elements to be evaluated in deciding what due process requires, viz., the private interests at stake, the government's interest, and the risk that the procedures used will lead to erroneous decisions. We must balance these elements against each other, and then set their net weight in the scales against the presumption that there is a right to appointed counsel only where the indigent, if he is unsuccessful, may lose his personal freedom.

This Court's decisions have by now made plain beyond the need for multiple citation that a parent's desire for and right to "the companionship, care, custody, and management of his or her children" is an important interest that "undeniably warrants deference and, absent a powerful countervailing interest, protection." *Stanley v. Illinois,* 405 U.S. 645, 651. Here the State has sought not simply to infringe upon that interest, but to end it. If the State prevails, it will have worked a unique kind of deprivation. A parent's interest in the accuracy and justice of the decision to terminate his or her parental status is, therefore, a commanding one.

Since the State has an urgent interest in the welfare of the child, it shares the parent's interest in an accurate and just decision. For this reason, the State may share the indigent parent's interest in the availability of appointed counsel. If, as our adversary system presupposes, accurate and just results are most likely to be obtained through the equal contest of opposed interests, the State's interest in the child's welfare may perhaps best be served by a hearing in which both the parent and the State acting for the child are represented by counsel, without whom the contest of interests may become unwholesomely unequal. . . .

The State's interests, however, clearly diverge from the parent's insofar as the State wishes the termination decision to be made as economically as possible and thus wants to avoid both the expense of appointed counsel and the cost of the lengthened proceedings this presence may cause. But though the State's pecuniary interest is legitimate, it is hardly significant enough to overcome private interests as important as those here, particularly in light of the concession in the respondent's brief that the "potential costs of appointed counsel in termination proceedings . . . is [*sic*] admittedly *de minimis* compared to the costs in all criminal actions."

Finally, consideration must be given to the risk that a parent will be erroneously deprived of his or her child because the parent is not represented by counsel. North Carolina law now seeks to assure accurate decisions by establishing the following procedures: A petition to terminate parental rights may be filed only by a parent seeking the termination of the other parent's rights, by a county department of social services or licensed child-placing agency with custody of the child, or by a person with whom the child has lived continuously for the two years preceding the petition. A petition must describe facts sufficient to warrant a finding that one of the grounds for termination exists, and the parent must be notified of the petition and given 30 days in which to file a written answer to it. . . . If the parent files no answer, "the court shall issue an order terminating all parental and custodial rights . . . ; provided the court shall order a hearing on the petition and may examine the petitioner or others on the facts alleged in the petition." § 7A-289.28. Findings of fact are made by a court sitting without a jury and must "be based on clear, cogent, and convincing evidence." § 7A-289.30. Any party may appeal who gives notice of appeal within 10 days after the hearing.

The respondent argues that the subject of a termination hearing—the parent's relationship with her child—far from being abstruse, technical, or unfamiliar, is one as to which the parent must be uniquely well informed and to which the parent must have given prolonged thought. The respondent also contends that a termination hearing is not likely to produce difficult points of evidentiary law, or even of substantive law, since the evidentiary problems peculiar to criminal trials are not present and since the standards for termination are not complicated. In fact, the respondent reports, the North Carolina Departments of Social Services are themselves sometimes represented at termination hearings by social workers instead of by lawyers.

Yet the ultimate issues with which a termination hearing deals are not always simple, however commonplace they may be. Expert medical and psychiatric testimony, which few parents are equipped to understand and fewer still to confute, is sometimes presented. The parents are likely to be people with little education, who have had uncommon difficulty in dealing with life, and who are, at the hearing, thrust into a distressing and disorienting situation. . . . Thus, courts have generally held that the State must appoint counsel for indigent parents at termination proceedings. The respondent is able to point to no presently authoritative case, except for the North Carolina judgment now before us, holding that an indigent parent has no due process right to appointed counsel in termination proceedings.

C

The dispositive question, which must now be addressed, is whether the three *Eldridge* factors, when weighed against the presumption that there is no right to appointed counsel in the absence of at least a potential deprivation of physical liberty, suffice to rebut that presumption and thus to lead to the conclusion that the Due Process Clause requires the appointment of counsel when a State seeks to terminate an indigent's parental status. To summarize the above discussion of the *Eldridge* factors: the parent's interest is an extremely important one (and may be supplemented by the dangers of criminal liability inherent in some termination proceedings); the State shares with the parent an interest in a correct decision, has a relatively weak pecuniary interest, and, in some but not all cases, has a possibly stronger interest in informal procedures; and the complexity of the proceeding and the incapacity of the uncounseled parent could be, but would not always be, great enough to make the risk of an erroneous deprivation of the parent's rights insupportably high.

If, in a given case, the parent's interests were at their strongest, the State's interests were at their weakest, and the risks of error were at their peak, it could not be said that the *Eldridge* factors did not overcome the presumption against the right to appointed counsel, and that due process did not therefore require the appointment of counsel. But since the *Eldridge* factors will not always be so distributed, and since "due process is not so rigid as to require that the significant interests in informality, flexibility and economy must always be sacrificed," *Gagnon v. Scarpelli,* 411 U.S. at 788, neither can we say that the Constitution requires the appointment of counsel in every parental termination proceeding. We therefore adopt the standard found appropriate in *Gagnon v. Scarpelli*, and leave the decision whether due process calls for the appointment of counsel for indigent parents in termination proceedings to be answered in the first instance by the trial court, subject, of course, to appellate review.

III

Here, as in *Scarpelli,* "[i]t is neither possible nor prudent to attempt to formulate a precise and detailed set of guidelines to be followed in determining when the providing of counsel is necessary to meet the applicable due process requirements," since here, as in that case, "[t]he facts and circumstances . . . are susceptible of almost infinite variations. . . ." 411 U.S. at 790. Nevertheless, because child-custody litigation must be concluded as rapidly as is consistent with fairness, we decide today whether the trial judge denied Ms. Lassiter due process of law when he did not appoint counsel for her.

The respondent represents that the petition to terminate Ms. Lassiter's parental rights contained no allegations of neglect or abuse upon which criminal charges could be based, and hence Ms. Lassiter could not well have argued that she required counsel for that reason. The Department of Social Services was represented at the hearing by counsel, but no expert witnesses testified, and the case presented no specially troublesome points of law, either procedural or substantive. While hearsay evidence was no doubt admitted, and while Ms. Lassiter no doubt left incomplete her defense that the Department had not adequately assisted her in rekindling her interest in her son, the weight of the evidence that she had few sparks of such an interest was sufficiently great that the presence of counsel for Ms. Lassiter could not have made a determinative difference. True, a lawyer might have done more with the argument that William should live with Ms. Lassiter's mother—but that argument was quite explicitly made by both Lassiters, and the evidence that the elder Ms. Lassiter had said she could not handle another child, that the social worker's investigation had led to a similar conclusion, and that the grandmother had displayed scant interest in the child once he had been removed from her daughter's custody was, though controverted, sufficiently substantial that the absence of counsel's guidance on this point did not render the proceedings fundamentally unfair. Finally, a court deciding whether due process requires the appointment of counsel need not ignore a parent's plain demonstration that she is not interested in attending a hearing. Here, the trial court had previously found that Ms. Lassiter had expressly declined to appear at the 1975 child custody hearing, Ms. Lassiter had not even bothered to speak to her retained lawyer after being notified of the termination hearing, and the court specifically found that Ms. Lassiter's failure to make an effort to contest the termination proceeding was without cause. In view of all these circumstances, we hold that the trial court did not err in failing to appoint counsel for Ms. Lassiter.

IV

In its Fourteenth Amendment, our Constitution imposes on the States the standards necessary to ensure that judicial proceedings are fundamentally fair. A wise public policy, however, may require that higher standards be adopted than those minimally tolerable under the Constitution. Informed opinion has clearly come to hold that an indigent parent is entitled to the assistance of appointed counsel not only in parental termination proceedings, but in dependency and neglect proceedings as well. Most significantly, 33 States and the District of Columbia provide statutorily for the appointment of counsel in termination cases. The Court's opinion today in no way implies that the standards increasingly urged by informed public opinion and now widely followed by the States are other than enlightened and wise.

For the reasons stated in this opinion, the judgment is affirmed.

Justice BLACKMUN, with whom Justice BRENNAN and Justice MARSHALL join, dissenting.

The Court today denies an indigent mother the representation of counsel in a judicial proceeding initiated by the State of North Carolina to terminate her parental rights with respect to her youngest child. The Court most appropriately recognizes that the mother's interest is a "commanding one," and its finds no countervailing state interest of even remotely comparable significance. Nonetheless, the Court avoids what seems to me the obvious conclusion that due process requires the presence of counsel for a parent threatened with judicial termination of parental rights, and, instead, revives an ad hoc approach thoroughly discredited nearly 20 years ago in *Gideon v. Wainwright,* 372 U.S. 335 (1963). Because I believe that the unique importance of a parent's interest in the care and custody of his or her child cannot constitutionally be extinguished through formal judicial proceedings without the benefit of counsel, I dissent.

* * *

Notes

1. In *Lassiter v. Department of Social Services*, the United States Supreme Court established a three-part standard courts must follow when deciding whether to appoint counsel for parents in TPR proceedings. For a discussion of an indigent parent's right to counsel in TPR hearings, see Kevin W. Shaughnessy, Note, Lassiter v. Department of Social Services: *A New Interest Balancing Test for Indigent Civil Litigants,* 32 CATH. U. L. REV. 261 (1982).

Many state courts have found that not providing an indigent parent counsel in TPR hearings violates due process under the state constitution. *See, e.g., In re D.D.F.,* 801 P.2d 793 (Okla. 1990); *In re Guardianship of B.L.N.,* 593 A.2d 398 (N.J. Super. Ct. Ch. Div. 1991) (indigent parent is entitled to counsel and expert testimony necessary to assist defense in TPR hearing); *In re A.S.A.,* 852 P.2d 127 (Mont. 1993) (use of court-appointed counsel at trial protects the fundamental rights of indigent parents granted under the state constitution and prevents putting parents at an unfair disadvantage); *In the matter of K.L.J.,* 813 P.2d 276 (Alaska 1991) (state constitution's due process protects father's fundamental interest in parent-child relationship); *In re Adoption of K.A.S.,* 499 N.W.2d 558 (N.D. 1992) (state's economic considerations not compelling enough to override parent's fundamental interest in parent-child relationship); *In re J.S.P.L.*, 532 N.W.2d 653 (N.D. 1995) (citing *K.A.S.*, failure to provide counsel violates due process granted by state constitution). Some courts have also held that the right to court-appointed counsel for an indigent parent includes the right to effective assistance of counsel. *See In re M.D.S.*, 485 N.W.2d 52 (Wis. 1992); *Oregon ex rel. Juvenile Department v. Geist*, 796 P.2d 1193 (Ore. 1990); *In re James W.H.*, 849 P.2d 1079 (N.M. Ct. App. 1993).

An indigent parent may also have the right to appointed counsel in appealing a TPR judgment. *See In re Jacqueline H.*, 548, 577 P.2d 683 (Cal. 1978); *Appellate Defenders v. Cheri S.*, 42 Cal. Rptr. 2d 195 (Ct. App. 1995). *But see In re Curtis S.*, 30 Cal. Rptr. 2d 739 (Ct. App. 1994) (parents have no federal constitutional right to appointed counsel when challenging a termination order in a private action to terminate parental rights). For further discussion of an indigent parent's right to court-appointed counsel on appeal of a TPR judgment, see Joel E. Smith, Annotation, *Right of Indigent Parent to Appointed Counsel In Proceeding For Involuntary Termination of Parental Rights*, 80 A.L.R.3D 1141 (1977).

2. Many states have statutory law which provides an indigent parent in TPR hearings with the right to counsel. The following New Mexico statute is an example:

New Mexico Statutes Annotated
§ 32A-4-29(F) (Michie 1999)

§ 32A-4-29 Termination procedure.

F. After a motion for the termination of parental rights is filed, the parent shall be advised of the right to counsel unless the parent is already represented by counsel. Counsel shall be appointed, upon request, for any parent who is unable to obtain counsel due to financial reasons or, if in the court's discretion, the interests of justice require appointment of counsel.

See also ALA. CODE § 12-15-63(b) (Lexis 1995); ARIZ. REV. STAT. ANN. § 8-221 (West Supp. 2000); CAL. WELF. & INST. CODE § 317 (West Supp. 2001); COLO. REV. STAT. § 19-3-602 (2000); CONN. GEN. STAT. ANN. § 45a-716 (West Supp. 2001); NEV. REV. STAT. § 128.100 (1999); N.D. CENT. CODE § 14-15-19(6) (Lexis 1997); WASH. REV. CODE ANN. § 13.34.090 (West Supp. 2001). For cases that recognize an indigent parent's right to counsel created by statute, see *People in Interest of J.B.*, 702 P.2d 753 (Colo. Ct. App. 1985); *In Interest of J.G.*, 577 So. 2d 695 (Fla. Dist. Ct. App. 1991); *State in the Interest of S.C. v. D.N.C.*, 639 So. 2d 426 (La. Ct. App. 1994); *In re Bluebird*, 411 S.E.2d 820 (N.C. Ct. App. 1992); *Ybarra v. Texas Dep't of Human Services*, 869 S.W.2d 574 (Tex. Ct. App. 1993).

Questions

What is the nature of a parent's liberty interest which is considered by the court when a parent requests appointment of counsel in TPR proceedings? What is the state's interest in a TPR trial without the parent being legally represented? What is the risk of error in such a procedure?

3. Exclusion of Public

Arizona Revised Statutes Annotated

§ 8-537(A) (West Supp. 2000)

§ 8-537. Termination adjudication hearing

A. If a petition for terminating the parent-child relationship is contested, the court shall hold a termination adjudication hearing. The general public shall be excluded and only such persons admitted whose presence the judge finds to have a direct interest in the case or the work of the court, provided that such person so admitted shall not disclose any information secured at the hearing. The court may require the presence of any parties and witnesses it deems necessary to the disposition of the petition, except that a parent who has executed a waiver pursuant to section 8-535, or has relinquished the parent's rights to the child shall not be required to appear at the hearing.

4. Burden of Proof

Santosky v. Kramer

455 U.S. 745, 102 S. Ct. 1388, 71 L. Ed. 2d 599 (1982)

Justice BLACKMUN delivered the opinion of the Court.

Under New York law, the State may terminate, over parental objection, the rights of parents in their natural child upon a finding that the child is "permanently neglected." N.Y. Soc. Serv. Law §§ 384-b.4(d), 384b.7(a) (McKinney Supp. 1981-1982) (Soc. Serv. Law). The New York Family Court Act § 622 (McKinney 1975 and Supp. 1981-1982) (Fam. Ct. Act) requires that only a "fair preponderance of the evidence" support that finding. Thus, in New York, the factual certainty required to extinguish the parent-child relationship is no greater than that necessary to award money damages in an ordinary civil action.

Today we hold that the Due Process Clause of the Fourteenth Amendment demands more than this. Before a State may sever completely and irrevocably the rights of parents in their natural child, due process requires that the State support its allegations by at least clear and convincing evidence.

I

A

New York authorizes its officials to remove a child temporarily from his or her home if the child appears "neglected," within the meaning of Art. 10 of the Family Court Act. Once removed, a child under the age of 18 customarily is placed "in the care of an authorized agency," Soc. Serv. Law § 384-b.7(a), usually a state institution or a foster home. At that point, "the state's first obligation is to help the family with services to . . . reunite it. . . ." § 384-b.1(a)(iii). But if convinced that "positive, nurturing parent-child relationships no longer exist," § 384-b.1.(b), the State may initiate "permanent neglect" proceedings to free the child for adoption.

The State bifurcates its permanent neglect proceeding into "fact-finding" and "dispositional" hearings. At the factfinding stage, the State must prove that the child has been "permanently neglected," as defined by Fam. Ct. Act. §§ 614.1.(a) - (d). The State must further prove that during that same period, the child's natural parents failed "substantially and continuously or repeatedly to maintain contact with or plan for the future of the child although physically and financially able to do so." § 614.1.(d). Should the State support its allegations by "a fair preponderance of the evidence," § 622, the child may be declared permanently neglected. § 611. That declaration empowers the Family Court judge to terminate permanently the natural parents' rights in the child. §§ 631(c), 634. Termination denies the natural parents physical custody, as well as the rights ever to visit, communicate with, or regain custody of the child.

New York's permanent neglect statute provides natural parents with certain procedural protections.[2] But New York permits its officials to establish "permanent neglect" with less proof than most States require. Thirty-five States, the District of Columbia, and the Virgin Islands currently specify a higher standard of proof, in parental rights termination proceedings, than a "fair preponderance of the evidence." The only analogous federal statute of which we are aware permits termination of parental rights solely upon "evidence beyond a reasonable doubt." Indian Child Welfare Act of 1978, Pub. L. 95-608, § 102(f), 92 Stat. 3072, 25 U.S.C. § 1912(f) (1976 ed., Supp. IV). The question here is whether New York's "fair preponderance of the evidence" standard is constitutionally sufficient.

B

Petitioners John Santosky II and Annie Santosky are the natural parents of Tina and John III. In November 1973, after incidents reflecting parental neglect, respondent Kramer, Commissioner of the Ulster County Department of Social Services, initiated a neglect proceeding under Fam. Ct., Act § 1022d and removed Tina from her natural home. About 10 months later, he removed John III and placed him with foster parents. On the day John was taken, Annie Santosky gave birth to a third child, Jed. When Jed was only three days old, respon-

---

2 Most notably, natural parents have a statutory right to the assistance of counsel and of court-appointed counsel if they are indigent.

dent transferred him to a foster home on the ground that immediate removal was necessary to avoid imminent danger to his life or health.

In October 1978, respondent petitioned the Ulster County Family Court to terminate petitioners' parental rights in the three children.[4] Petitioners challenged the constitutionality of the "fair preponderance of the evidence" standard specified in Fam. Ct. Act § 622. The Family Court Judge rejected this constitutional challenge and weighed the evidence under the statutory standard. While acknowledging that the Santoskys had maintained contact with their children, the judge found those visits "at best superficial and devoid of any real emotional content." After deciding that the agency had made "diligent efforts to encourage and strengthen the parental relationship," he concluded that the Santoskys were incapable, even with public assistance, of planning for the future of their children. The judge later held a dispositional hearing and ruled that the best interests of the three children required permanent termination of the Santoskys' custody.[5]

Petitioners appealed, again contesting the constitutionality of § 622's standard of proof. The New York Supreme Court, Appellate Division, affirmed, holding application of the preponderance-of-the-evidence standard "proper and constitutional." *In re John AA,* 75 App. Div. 2d 910, 427 N.Y.S. 2d 319, 320 (1980). That standard, the court reasoned, "recognizes and seeks to balance rights possessed by the child . . . with those of the natural parents. . . ."

* * *

II

* * *

The fundamental liberty interest of natural parents in the care, custody, and management of their child does not evaporate simply because they have not been model parents or have lost temporary custody of their child to the State. Even when blood relationships are strained, parents retain a vital interest in preventing the irretrievable destruction of their family life. . . .

In *Lassiter v. Dep't. Of Soc. Servs.,* 452 U.S. 18 (1981), the Court and three dissenters agreed that the nature of the process due in parental rights termination proceedings turns on a balancing of the "three distinct factors" specified in *Mathews v. Eldridge,* 424 U.S. 319, 335 (1976): the private interests affected by the proceeding; the risk of error created by the State's chosen procedure; and

---

[4] Respondent had made an earlier and unsuccessful termination effort in September 1976. After a factfinding hearing, the Family Court Judge dismissed respondent's petition for failure to prove an essential element of Fam. Ct. Act. § 614.1.(d). The New York Supreme Court, Appellate Division, affirmed, finding that "the record as a whole" revealed that petitioners had "substantially planned for the future of the children." *In re John W.,* 63 App. Div. 2d 750, 404 N.Y.S. 2d 717, 719 (1978).

[5] Since respondent Kramer took custody of Tina, John III, and Jed, the Santoskys have had two other children, James and Jeremy. The State has taken no action to remove these younger children. At oral argument, counsel for respondents replied affirmatively when asked whether he was asserting that petitioners were "unfit to handle the three older ones but not unfit to handle the two younger ones."

the countervailing governmental interest supporting use of the challenged procedure. . . .

* * *

III

In parental rights termination proceedings, the private interest affected is commanding; the risk of error from using a preponderance standard is substantial; and the countervailing governmental interest favoring that standard is comparatively slight. Evaluation of the three *Eldridge* factors compels the conclusion that use of a "fair preponderance of the evidence" standard in such proceedings is inconsistent with due process.

A

"The extent to which procedural due process must be afforded the recipient is influenced by the extent to which he may be 'condemned to suffer grievous loss.'" *Goldberg v. Kelly*, 397 U.S. 254, 262-263 (1970), quoting *Joint Anti-Fascist Refugee Committee v. McGrath*, 341 U.S. 123, 168 (1951) (Frankfurter, J., concurring). Whether the loss threatened by a particular type of proceeding is sufficiently grave to warrant more than average certainty on the part of the factfinder turns on both the nature of the private interest threatened and the permanency of the threatened loss.

Lassiter declared it "plain beyond the need for multiple citation" that a natural parent's "desire for and right to 'the companionship, care, custody, and management of his or her children'" is an interest far more precious than any property right, 452 U.S. at 27, quoting *Stanley v. Illinois,* 405 U.S. 645, 651 (1972). When the State initiates a parental rights termination proceedings, it seeks not merely to infringe that fundamental liberty interest, but to end it. "If the State prevails, it will have worked a unique kind of deprivation. . . . A parent's interest in the accuracy and justice of the decision to terminate his or her parental status is, therefore, a commanding one." 452 U.S. at 27. . . . Once affirmed on appeal, a New York decision terminating parental rights is *final* and irrevocable. Few forms of state action are both so severe and so irreversible. Thus, the first *Eldridge* factor—the private interest affected—weights heavily against use of the preponderance standard at a state-initiated permanent neglect proceeding. . . .

B

Under *Mathews v. Eldridge,* we next must consider both the risk of erroneous deprivation of private interests resulting from use of a "fair preponderance" standard and the likelihood that a higher evidentiary standard would reduce that risk. Since the factfinding phase of a permanent neglect proceeding is an adversary contest between the State and the natural parents, the relevant question is whether a preponderance standard fairly allocates the risk of an erroneous factfinding between these two parties.

In New York, the factfinding stage of a state-initiated permanent neglect proceeding bears many of the indicia of a criminal trial. The commissioner of Social Services charges the parents with permanent neglect. They are served by summons. The factfinding hearing is conducted pursuant to formal rules of evidence. The State, the parents, and the child are all represented by counsel. The State seeks to establish a series of historical facts about the intensity of its agency's efforts to reunite the family, the infrequency and insubstantiality of the parents' contacts with their child, and the parents' inability or unwillingness to formulate a plan for the child's future. The attorneys submit documentary evidence, and call witnesses who are subject to cross-examination. Based on all the evidence, the judge then determines whether the State has proved the statutory elements of permanent neglect by a fair preponderance of the evidence.

At such a proceeding, numerous factors combine to magnify the risk of erroneous factfinding. Permanent neglect proceedings employ imprecise substantive standards that leave determinations unusually open to the subjective values of the judge. . . . Because parents subject to termination proceedings are often poor, uneducated, or members of minority groups, such proceedings are often vulnerable to judgments based on cultural or class bias.

The State's ability to assemble its case almost inevitably dwarfs the parents' ability to mount a defense. No predetermined limits restrict the sums an agency may spend in prosecuting a given termination proceeding. . . . Furthermore, the primary witnesses at the hearing will be the agency's own professional caseworkers whom the State has empowered both to investigate the family situation and to testify against the parents. . . .

The disparity between the adversaries' litigation resources is matched by a striking asymmetry in their litigation options. Unlike criminal defendants, natural parents have no "double jeopardy" defense against repeated state termination efforts. If the State initially fails to win termination, as New York did here, it always can try once again to cut off the parents' rights after gathering more or better evidence. Yet even when the parents have attained the level of fitness required by the State, they have no similar means by which they can forestall future termination efforts.

Coupled with a "fair preponderance of the evidence" standard, these factors create a significant prospect of erroneous termination. A standard of proof that by its very terms demands consideration of the quantity, rather than the quality, of the evidence may misdirect the factfinder in the marginal case. Given the weight of the private interests at stake, the social cost of even occasional error is sizable.

. . . An elevated standard of proof in a parental rights termination proceeding would alleviate "the possible risk that a factfinder might decide to [deprive] an individual based solely on a few isolated instances of unusual conduct [or] . . . idiosyncratic behavior." *Addington v. Texas*, 441 U.S. at 417. "Increasing the burden of proof is one way to impress the factfinder with the importance of the decision and thereby perhaps to reduce the chances that inappropriate" terminations will be ordered. *Ibid.*

* * *

C

Two state interests are at stake in parental rights termination proceedings—a *parens patriae* interest in preserving and promoting the welfare of the child and a fiscal and administrative interest in reducing the cost and burden of such proceedings. A standard of proof more strict than preponderance of the evidence is consistent with both interests.

"Since the State has an urgent interest in the welfare of the child, it shares the parent's interest in an accurate and just decision" at the *factfinding* proceeding. *Lassiter v. Department of Social Services*, 452 U.S. at 27. As *parens patriae*, the State's goal is to provide the child with a permanent home. Yet while there is still reason to believe that positive, nurturing parent-child relationships exist, the *parens patriae* interest favors preservation, not severance, of natural familial bonds. "[T]he State registers no gain towards its declared goals when it separates children from the custody of fit parents." *Stanley v. Illinois,* 405 U.S. at 652.

* * *

Unlike a constitutional requirement of hearings or court-appointed counsel, a stricter standard of proof would reduce factual error without imposing substantial fiscal burdens upon the State. As we have observed, 35 States already have adopted a higher standard by statute or court decision without apparent effect on the speed, form, or cost of their factfinding proceedings.

* * *

IV

The logical conclusion of this balancing process is that the "fair preponderance of the evidence" standard prescribed by Fam. Ct. Act. § 622 violates the Due Process Clause of the Fourteenth Amendment. The Court noted in *Addington:* "The individual should not be asked to share equally with society the risk of error when the possible injury to the individual is significantly greater than any possible harm to the state." 441 U.S. at 427. Thus, at a parental rights termination proceeding, a near-equal allocation of risk between the parents and the State is constitutionally intolerable. The next question, then, is whether a "beyond a reasonable doubt" or a "clear and convincing" standard is constitutionally mandated.

* * *

A majority of the States have concluded that a "clear and convincing evidence" standard of proof strikes a fair balance between the rights of the natural parents and the State's legitimate concerns. We hold that such a standard adequately conveys to the factfinder the level of subjective certainty about his factual conclusions necessary to satisfy due process. We further hold that determination of the precise burden equal to or greater than that standard is a matter of state law properly left to state legislatures and state courts.

We, of course, express no view on the merits of petitioners' claims. . . . Without deciding the outcome under any of the standards we have approved, we vacate the judgment of the Appellate Division and remand the case for further proceedings not inconsistent with this opinion.

Justice REHNQUIST, with whom The Chief Justice, Justice WHITE, and Justice O'CONNOR join, dissenting.

* * *

[T]he standard of proof chosen by New York clearly reflects a constitutionally permissible balance of the interests at stake in this case. . . .

* * *

On one side is the interest of parents in a continuation of the family unit and the raising of their own children. The importance of this interest cannot easily be overstated. Few consequences of judicial action are so grave as the severance of natural family ties. . . . In creating the scheme at issue in this case, the New York Legislature was expressly aware of this right of parents "to bring up their own children." SSL § 384-B.1.(a)(ii).

On the other side of the termination proceeding are the often countervailing interests of the child. A stable, loving homelife is essential to a child's physical, emotional, and spiritual well- being. . . . If the Family Court makes an incorrect factual determination resulting in a failure to terminate a parent-child relationship which rightfully should be ended, the child involved must return either to an abusive home or to the often unstable world of foster care. . . .

* * *

When, in the context of a permanent neglect termination proceeding, the interests of the child and the State in a stable, nurturing homelife are balanced against the interests of the parents in the rearing of their child, it cannot be said that either set of interests is so clearly paramount as to require that the risk of error be allocated to one side or the other. Accordingly, a State constitutionally may conclude that the risk of error should be borne in roughly equal fashion by use of the preponderance-of-the-evidence standard of proof. This is precisely the balance which has been struck by the New York Legislature: "It is the intent of the legislature in enacting this section to provide procedures not only assuring that the rights of the natural parent are protected, but also where positive, nurturing parent-child relationships no longer exist, furthering the best interest, needs, and rights of the child by terminating the parental rights and freeing the child for adoption." SSL § 384-b.1(b). . . .

Arizona Revised Statutes Annotated

§ 8-537(B) (West Supp. 2000)

§ 8-537. Termination adjudication hearing

B. The court's findings with respect to grounds for termination shall be based upon clear and convincing evidence under the rules applicable and adhering to the trial of civil causes. The court may consider any and all reports required by this article or ordered by the court pursuant to this article and such reports are admissible in evidence without objection.

The Indian Child Welfare Act
Subchapter I—Child Custody Proceedings

25 U.S.C.A. § 1912(f) (West 2000)

Section 1912. Pending Court Proceedings

* * *

(f) *Parental rights termination orders; evidence, determination of damage to child.* No termination of parental rights may be ordered . . . in the absence of a determination, supported by evidence beyond a reasonable doubt, including testimony of qualified expert witnesses, that the continued custody of the child by the parent or Indian custodian is likely to result in serious emotional or physical damage to the child.

In re D.S.P.

480 N.W.2d 234 (Wis. 1992)

CECI, Justice.

This case is before the court on petition for review of a published decision of the court of appeals. The court of appeals affirmed an order by the circuit court for Marinette County, Circuit Judge William J. Duffy, presiding. The order terminated the parental rights of I.P. and R.A.C.P. as to their child D.S.P., an enrolled member of the Sault Ste. Marie Tribe of Chippewa Indians (the tribe), on grounds of abandonment under sec. 48.415(1)(a)1 and 3, Stats. We granted both parents' petitions for review of the court of appeals' opinion.

* * *

The facts are not in dispute. R.A.C.P. is the mother of D.S.P., who was born in March, 1984. D.S.P. was R.A.C.P.'s fifth child born to her out of wedlock. R.A.C.P.'s parental rights to the prior four children were terminated for reasons of neglect. During her entire pregnancy with D.S.P., although repeatedly advised to the contrary, R.A.C.P. continued to consume alcohol and did not eat properly.

I.P. is the adjudicated father of D.S.P. Both I.P. and D.S.P., are enrolled members of the tribe. I.P. and R.A.C.P. had married and were living in Michigan by the time of the trial in this case.

Beginning before D.S.P.'s birth and throughout the next few years, the Marinette County Department of Social Services (the Department) attempted to assist R.A.C.P. with her parenting. Though D.S.P. was in his mother's custody for the first seven months of his life, R.A.C.P. often left him with babysitters for extended periods of time without explanation.

In October 1984, D.S.P. was placed in foster care. Eventually, the Department filed a CHIPS petition stating that D.S.P. was in need of protection and services. Custody of D.S.P. was transferred to the Department, and D.S.P. was formally placed in a foster home. The parents were warned that failure to visit D.S.P. could result in termination of their parental rights.

Despite the efforts of the Department to assist the parents in establishing a relationship with D.S.P., the parents visited D.S.P. only rarely. Eventually, neither parent made any contact with D.S.P. for a period of over a year. Thus, the Department filed a petition for termination of parental rights.

At the termination of parental rights trial, Martha Snyder, representing the tribe, testified that the tribe officially recommended supporting the termination of the parental rights of both I.P. and R.A.C.P. Following the jury trial, the circuit court entered an order terminating the parental rights of both parents. On appeal, the court of appeals affirmed.

* * *

The . . . issue presented by this case, the burden of proof applicable to a termination of parental rights hearing in cases involving the ICWA, is a case of first impression in this state. Under the Wisconsin children's code, the burden of proof in a petition to terminate parental rights hearing is clear and convincing evidence. Section 48.31(1), Stats. However, under the ICWA, the burden of proof is "evidence beyond a reasonable doubt, including the testimony of qualified expert witnesses. . . ." 25 U.S.C. sec. 1912(f). [T]he circuit court instructed the jury on dual burdens of proof. R.A.C.P. asserts that the dual burden of proof was improper because the Wisconsin children's code is superseded by the ICWA and because the ICWA mandates the use of the reasonable doubt standard in an involuntary termination of parental rights proceeding.

Federal legislation preempts state legislation when it is the intent of Congress to assert federal primacy in a particular field or when the state legislation conflicts with the federal legislation. We find neither an express nor an implicit intent within the ICWA to preempt the Wisconsin children's code. Rather, the ICWA expressly calls for the use of state law rather than the ICWA if the state law "provides a higher standard of protection" than that accorded by the ICWA. 25 U.S.C. sec. 1921. In addition, the ICWA is not pervasive, all-encompassing legislation, but rather sets forth minimum standards that must be followed. This is indicated by the stated congressional policy behind the ICWA.

> The Congress hereby declares that it is the policy of this Nation to protect the best interest of Indian children and to promote the stability and security of Indian tribes and families by the establishment of minimum Federal standards for the removal of Indian children from their families and the placement of such children in foster or adoptive homes. . . .

25 U.S.C. sec. 1902.

The ICWA does not preempt the Wisconsin children's code, and, therefore, the Wisconsin statutes can be read so as to harmonize them with the ICWA. The Wisconsin children's code states that the ICWA supersedes the provisions of the children's code in any child custody proceedings covered by the ICWA. However, as the ICWA requires the use of state law whenever that state law provides a higher standard of protection than is mandated by the ICWA, we find it appropriate that where the children's code provides additional safeguards beyond what is mandated by the ICWA, those additional safeguards should be followed.

R.A.C.P. urges us to find that the ICWA mandates using the beyond a reasonable doubt standard for proof of abandonment under sec. 48.415(1)(a), Stats. R.A.C.P. argues that the policy behind the ICWA is thwarted if sec. 48.415(1)(a) is proved by only clear and convincing evidence. We do not agree. The policies behind both the ICWA and the Wisconsin children's code are similar: to protect the best interests of the child and to preserve family stability, among other things. The ICWA strives to achieve this goal by requiring evidence proving beyond a reasonable doubt that the continued custody of the child by the parent is likely to result in serious emotional or physical damage to the child before parental rights may be terminated. 25 U.S.C. sec. 1912(f). The children's code strives to achieve this goal by requiring clear and convincing evidence of abandonment, or other grounds for termination, before parental rights may be terminated.

The two different means of achieving these goals can be harmonized without requiring that the burden of proof be the same for both. Absent a clear indication that the state law should be abrogated, we decline to do so. The additional state law safeguards should be applied by the burden of proof mandated by the state law. A dual burden of proof, if mandated by the ICWA and state law, is therefore appropriate. The Alaska Supreme Court has come to a similar conclusion. *See Matter of J.R.B.,* 715 P.2d 1170, 1172 (Alaska 1986).

In the proceedings at issue here, the circuit court determined that a dual burden of proof was proper. As mandated by the ICWA, the circuit court required that the jury unanimously agree beyond a reasonable doubt "that the continued custody of the child by the parent . . . is likely to result in serious emotional or physical damages to the child." 25 U.S.C. sec. 1912(f). The circuit court also required that the jury unanimously agree that there had been "active efforts . . . made to provide remedial services and rehabilitative programs designed to prevent the breakup of the Indian family and that [those] efforts [had] proved unsuccessful." 25 U.S.C. sec 1912(d). To satisfy the requirements of the Wisconsin children's code, the circuit court then required that the jury be convinced by clear and convincing evidence that R.A.C.P. had abandoned D.S.P. under sec.48.415(1)(a)3, Stats., and that each parent was unfit to be the parent of D.S.P. These jury findings fulfill the burden of proof requirements of both the ICWA and the Wisconsin children's code.

* * *

The decision of the court of appeals is affirmed.

Notes

1. Many states have codified the clear and convincing evidence standard established by *Santosky*. The following Rhode Island statute is an example:

Rhode Island General Laws
§ 15-7-7(a) (Lexis 2000)

§ 15-7-7 Termination of parental rights.

(a) The court shall . . . terminate any and all legal rights of the parent to the child . . . if the court finds as a fact by clear and convincing evidence that:

(1) The parent has willfully neglected to provide proper care and maintenance for the child for a period of at least one year where financially able to do so. . . . ;

(2) The parent is unfit by reason of conduct or conditions seriously detrimental to the child, such as, but not limited to, the following:

(i) Institutionalization of the parent, including imprisonment, of such a duration that renders it improbable for the parent to care for the child for an extended period of time;

(ii) Conduct toward any child of a cruel or abusive nature;

(iii) The child has been placed in the legal custody or care of the department for children, youth, and families and the parent has a chronic substance abuse problem and the parent's prognosis indicates that the child will not be able to return to the custody of the parent within a reasonable period of time, considering the child's age and the need for a permanent home. . . . ;

(iv) The child has been placed with the department for children, youth, and families and the court has previously involuntarily terminated parental rights to another child of the parent and the parent continues to lack the ability or willingness to respond to services . . . ;

(v) The parent has subjected the child to aggravated circumstances . . . ;

(vi) The parent has committed murder or voluntary manslaughter on another of his or her children or has aided or abetted, attempted, conspired or solicited to commit such a murder or voluntary manslaughter; or

4. The parent has abandoned or deserted the child. . . .

The following state statutes also require proof by clear and convincing evidence in TPR proceedings: ALA. CODE §§ 12-15-65, 26-18-7 (Lexis Supp. 2000); ALASKA STAT. § 47.10.080 (Lexis 2000); ARIZ. REV. STAT. ANN. §§ 8-533, 8-863 (West Supp. 2000); COLO. REV. STAT. § 19-5-105 (2000); CONN. GEN. STAT. ANN. §§ 17a-112, 45a-717 (West Supp. 2001); FLA. STAT. ANN. § 39.802 (West Supp. 2001); GA. CODE ANN. § 19-8-10 (Lexis Supp. 2000); 705 ILL. COMP. STAT. ANN. 405/2-29 (West 1999); KAN. STAT. ANN. § 38-1583 (West 2000); KY. REV. STAT. ANN. § 625.090 (West 2000); MICH. COMP. LAWS ANN. § 722.25 (West Supp. 2001); MD. CODE ANN., FAM. LAW § 5-313 (Lexis 1999); MISS. CODE ANN. § 93-15-109 (Lexis Supp. 2000); MO. ANN. STAT.

§ 211.447 (West Supp. 2001); OHIO REV. CODE ANN. § 2151.414 (Anderson Supp. 2000); R.I. GEN. LAWS § 15-7-7 (Lexis 2000); S.D. CODIFIED LAWS § 26-8A-27 (Lexis 1999); UTAH CODE ANN. § 78-3a-406 (Lexis 1996); VA. CODE ANN. § 16.1-283 (Michie Supp. 2001); W. VA. CODE § 49-6-2 (Lexis 1999); WIS. STAT. ANN. § 48.13 (West Supp. 2000). *But see State v. Robert H.,* 393 A.2d 1387 (N.H. 1978) (state must prove the key allegations of a TPR petition beyond a reasonable doubt).

In California, the preponderance of the evidence standard for TPR under the child dependency statutes comports with due process. In *Cynthia D. v. San Diego County*, 851 P.2d 1307 (Cal. 1993), the court found no due process violation with the use of a preponderance of the evidence standard in termination proceedings. In *Cynthia D.,* a child was removed from her parents and placed in a foster home after a court found an allegation of abuse was true by clear and convincing evidence. After several review hearings, the court found by a preponderance of the evidence that the mother's parental rights should be terminated. *Cynthia D.* distinguished California Welfare & Institutions Code § 366.26 from the New York statute in *Santosky* by stating:

> [T]he purpose of the section 366.26 hearing is not to accumulate further evidence of parental unfitness and danger to the child, but to begin the task of finding the child a permanent alternative family placement. By the time dependency proceedings have reached the stage of a section 366.26 hearing, there have been multiple specific findings of parental unfitness.

The court in *Cynthia D.* found that the prior findings of parental unfitness satisfied the parent's due process rights concerning termination of parental rights. This statutory framework is calculated to limit judicial discretion, reduce the risk of erroneous findings of parental inadequacy and detriment to the child and otherwise protect the legitimate interests of parents.

2. In cases of abandonment, some courts hold that once the state proves by clear and convincing evidence that a parent's rights should be terminated, the burden of proof shifts to the parent to demonstrate that the parent has not disassociated himself or herself from the child. In *Kyle S.G. v. Carolyn S.G.,* 533 N.W.2d 794 (Wis. 1995), the court found that the state proved by clear and convincing evidence that the parent abandoned the child. According to the court, the parent must then disprove the presumed fact of abandonment by a preponderance of the evidence. *Kyle S.G.* held that the parent's due process rights were not violated by shifting the burden of proof from the state to the parent. Furthermore, the court stated that *Santosky* does not address the issue of burden shifting to the parent. *See also Termination of Parental Rights of Zanica C.,* 589 N.W.2d 457 (Wis. App. Ct. 1998). For a critique of *Kyle S.G.,* see Kenneth R. Dortzbach, *Legislative History: The Philosophies of Justices Scalia and Breyer and the Use of Legislative History by the Wisconsin State Courts*, 80 MARQ. L. REV. 161, 212 (1996).

Questions

1. Are the parent's liberty interests adequately protected in TPR proceedings by the clear and convincing evidence burden of proof? Would proof beyond a reasonable doubt be more appropriate?

2. *Kyle S.G., supra*, in Note 2, requires a parent to rebut a presumed fact of abandonment by a preponderance of the evidence. Does this burden violate a parent's right to due process in a TPR trial?

5. Confrontation

In Interest of M.S. et al.

343 S.E.2d 152 (Ga. Ct. App. 1986)

This is an appeal from the juvenile court's order terminating the appellants' parental rights in regard to their three children (M.S., age 8; S.S., age 7; A.A.S., age 4) pursuant to OCGA § 15-11-51(a)(2). They enumerate as error the procedure used by the juvenile court in the taking of testimony from the oldest child, M.S., contending that the procedure violated the due-process clause and the Sixth Amendment of the United States Constitution.

The procedure utilized to elicit the testimony of M.S. is as follows: "The interview facilities for the taking of the testimony shall be provided by the Hall County Department of Family and Children Services, which consists of an interview room wired for sound and an observation room. The interview may be seen through a one-way mirror from the observation room. People in the observation room can neither be seen nor heard by the witness who does not know that she is being observed by anyone except the guardian ad litem and the guardian ad litem's attorney, both of whom shall be the only people present in the interviewing room with the witness. The only people allowed in the observation room shall be the necessary technicians for the running of the audio and video equipment, the judge, the lawyers for the parents and the Department of Family and Children Services, a court reporter and the official juvenile court reporter. The proceedings, that is, all that is said in the interview room and the observation room, shall be transcribed. The witness, guardian ad litem, attorney for the guardian ad litem shall be viodeotaped. Attorney for the guardian ad litem shall first question the witness. Objections to the questions shall be made known to the court. . . . This will assure . . . that it's being recorded. The court will immediately rule on the objection. . . . There shall be no further argument after ruling is made. The objection and ruling can be heard by the attorney for the guardian ad litem in the interview room through a small ear-mounted receiver and she shall respond accordingly. Neither the objection nor the ruling can be heard by the guardian ad litem nor the witness in the interview room. After the guardian ad litem has completed questioning the witness, questions from the other attorneys may be propounded through the microphone in the observation room. The questions can be heard by the attorney for the guardian ad litem through the ear-mounted receiver and shall be repeated verbatim to the witness. Objections to questions shall be handled in the same manner as described above." Appellants complain not only that this procedure was defective, but that the evidence presented does not support the termination of their parental rights. Held: Our review of the record convinced us that, although the evidence was sufficient to warrant the termination of the appellants' parental rights, reversal is required because the procedure utilized to question the crucial witnesses was defective.

The United States Supreme Court has held that freedom of personal choice in matters of family life is a fundamental liberty interest protected by the Fourteenth Amendment and that state intervention to terminate the relationship between a parent and child must consequently be accompanied by procedures meeting the requisites of the due-process clause. Santosky v. Kramer, 455 U.S. 734, 753, 102 S. Ct. 1238, 1394, 71 L. Ed. 2d 599, 606 (1982). . . . "[D]ue process requires that we afford this liberty interest the same protection on appellate review as we afford those constitutionally protected interest in cases where a criminal conviction is had." Blackburn v. Blackburn, 249 Ga. 689, 693, 292 S.E.2d 821 (1982). Thus, the argument that termination proceedings are "entirely civil in nature" will not support the conclusion that the appellants in this case had no due process right to confront the witnesses on whose testimony the State's case was based. . . .

While the trial court's concern for insuring that the children were able to testify free from possible intimidation by their parents is understandable, there does not appear to have been any reason for excluding the appellants from the observation room, where, though they could not have been seen or heard by the children they would have been able to assist their counsel in propounding questions to the children. The trial court's judgment is accordingly reversed, and the case is remanded for a new hearing.

Judgment reversed and case remanded.

DISSENT

As I do not agree that the special procedure adopted by the juvenile court was violative of due process, or that the Sixth Amendment is directly applicable (other than as required by due process) to proceedings in juvenile court, I respectfully dissent.

First, I would hold appellants' reliance upon the Sixth Amendment to be misplaced. Generally, the Sixth Amendment applies to criminal prosecutions. "[T]he juvenile court proceeding has not yet been held to be a 'criminal prosecution,' within the meaning and reach of the Sixth Amendment." McKeiver v. Pa., 403 U.S. 528, 541, 91 S. Ct. 1976, 29 L. Ed. 2d 647.

* * *

Our society is increasingly facing the pervasiveness of child abuse. As more cases involving child abuse, both civil and criminal, reach the courts, we are confronted with the reality that often the abused child's testimony is essential if the truth is to be presented. Thus arises a strong State interest in eliciting the abused child's testimony. At the same time, we must avoid again abusing the child in order to obtain that testimony or depriving any party of constitutional rights. Nor should we lose sight of the gravity of the underlying controversy in the case . . . , termination of parental rights.

In re E.D.

876 P.2d 397 (Utah Ct. App. 1994)

GREENWOOD, Judge:

E.J.D. and B.D. (parents) appeal an order of the Fourth District Juvenile Court terminating their parental rights to their minor children E.D., C.D., C.S.D., and W.D. We affirm.

The four minor children involved in this termination of parental rights proceedings, E.D., C.D., C.S.D., and W.D., were born on June 11, 1983; January 9, 1985; September 16, 1986; and March 5, 1988; respectively. The three older children are girls; the youngest child, W.D., is a boy. In early January 1990, Donna Crawley, a licensed social worker and investigator with the Department of Family Services (DFS), interviewed E.D. in response to reports of possible sexual abuse by her father, and arranged for a medical examination of E.D. at Primary Children's Hospital. DFS removed the three girls from their parents' house that same month and placed them with their maternal grandparents. On February 5, 1990, the girls were removed from their grandparents' home and placed in foster care. In July 1990, DFS formulated a treatment plan for the parents, including sexual abuse treatment for B.D., the father, through the Intermountain Sexual Abuse Treatment Center (ISAT), with the goal of reuniting the family by January 1991. Although the treatment plan did not require it, E.J.D., the mother, attended the therapy sessions at ISAT as well. As part of the rehabilitation of the family, DFS began a program of unsupervised weekend visits at approximately the same time.

On November 26, 1990, Kimberly Anderson, the DFS case worker for the three girls at that time, received a phone call from the three girls' foster mother, Ms. Jones. She expressed concern about the children's well-being, based on their changed behavior after returning from a visit with their parents over Thanksgiving. Ms. Jones called Ms. Anderson again the next day and said that C.D. had divulged to her some details of her experience during the Thanksgiving visit. . . . Ms. Anderson and Diane Warner Kearney, a child protection investigator with the State of Utah, visited the foster home the same day to interview the children. C.S.D. told Ms. Kearney and Ms. Anderson that her parents had both touched and penetrated her vagina "a lot of times" and that it "hurted." She also told them her parents had touched her younger brother, W.D. Ms. Kearney and Ms. Anderson also talked to E.D., who told them her parents had touched W.D.'s genitals with their hands and a spoon.

Based upon E.D.'s and C.S.D.'s description of sexual abuse involving all four children, DFS removed W.D. from his parents' home and placed him with his sisters at the Joneses. DFS developed a new treatment plan in February

1991, requiring both the mother and father to obtain therapy at ISAT. The treatment plan permitted visitation with the children, but initially only with supervision. Again, the goal of the treatment plan was to reunite the family, this time by August 1991.

In May 1991, the parents, DFS, and the guardian ad litem for the children entered into a stipulation, approved by the juvenile court, for the reunification of the family by October 12, 1991. DFS thereafter instituted a third treatment plan, beginning in August 1991, to facilitate reunification of the family.

Pursuant to the stipulation's provision for regular visitation, the children spent the Labor Day weekend with their parents and grandmother on an unsupervised basis. Ms. Jones testified that the children were unusually quiet when she retrieved them after the visit. Later that day, when Ms. Jones's daughter gave C.D. and C.S.D. a bath, she observed that C.D.'s vagina was "really red and irritated" and alerted her mother.

When Ms. Jones questioned the children individually about the weekend visit, they told her consistent stories of sexual abuse involving the parents and grandmother. Based upon this information, Ms. Jones took E.D., C.D., and C.S.D. to Dr. Gary Behrman, a pediatrician, for an examination. Dr. Behrman first examined E.D. and found . . . that the perivaginal area was extremely red and that the opening to her vagina was larger than normal for an eight-year-old girl. Dr. Behrman testified that these abnormalities were consistent with physical stimulation and abuse. With respect to C.S.D., Dr. Behrman found perivaginal irritation and a "floppy vaginal opening." Finally, Dr. Behrman's examination of C.D. also revealed an irritated, red perivaginal area and an enlarged vaginal opening. The "floppiness" of the vaginal opening, stated Dr. Behrman, was more consistent with repeated penetration than a single incident and the redness of the perivaginal area indicated recent injury or damage.

On September 4, 1991, Gayle Seal Blanchett, a therapist at ISAT, conducted corroborative interviews of C.S.D. and W.D. at the request of Michael Handley, the four children's primary therapist at the time. Both children described actions by their parents involving inappropriate sexual interaction with the children, much of it entailing the use of kitchen utensils.

On September 5, 1991, E.D. and C.D. met with Andrew Handley, a therapist at ISAT. Both girls again stated that their parents had touched them inappropriately in the presence of their grandmother. Mr. Handley contacted DFS so that visitation could be suspended.

On September 25, 1991, Ms. Jones took the four children to Primary Children's Hospital for examination by Dr. Helen Britton, a pediatrician with expertise in the diagnosis of sexual abuse. The sole abnormalities discovered in E.D.'s examination were a significant scar indicating that some object had penetrated the labia and a "rectal tag" that is consistent with some type of injury to that area. C.S.D.'s examination was, in Dr. Britton's words, much more "remarkable." Dr. Britton found extensive scarring throughout the hymen indicating chronic penetration. C.S.D. also had two circular scars near the vaginal opening "that were just unusual in nature." Dr. Britton posited that the scars were caused by trauma with a sharp object. Finally, C.S.D. also had an abnormal vascular pattern, which again suggested she had experienced significant trauma in the perivaginal area. During C.D.'s examination, Dr. Britton found scarring probably resulting from penetrating trauma to the hymen. Dr. Brittan testified that fingers could have caused the scarring, but not C.D.'s fingers. Finally, with respect to W.D.'s examination, Dr. Britton did not find any scarring of his penis. . . . The only abnormality noted during the examination was a small "W" shaped scar on his rectum; however, Dr. Britton was unable to draw any conclusions from this scar. Nevertheless, Dr. Britton concluded that all four examinations were consistent with sexual abuse.

On May 21, 1992, DFS filed a petition for termination of parental rights. A two-day trial took place beginning on August 24, 1992. The children were not present to testify at trial because their therapists stated it would be extremely detrimental to their mental health to relate at trial the stories of their sexual abuse. . . .

At trial, ten individuals—the foster mother, case workers, investigators, doctors and therapists—all testified that they believed the children had been sexually abused. There was also detailed medical testimony, as described earlier in this opinion, about the physical and psychological condition of each of the four children. On December 2, 1992, the trial court issued an order terminating E.J.D. and B.D.'s parental rights on the grounds of neglect and abusive treatment pursuant to Utah Code Ann. § 78-3f-107(2) (Supp. 1993). The trial court denied the parents' request for reconsideration on January 13, 1993, but granted a stay of the termination order pending the resolution of this appeal.

The parents raise three issues on appeal: (1) Is the constitutional right to confrontation applicable in a parental rights termination proceeding? (2) Did the trial court fail to comply with Utah Code Ann. § 76-5-411 (1990), thereby erroneously admitting unreliable hearsay? And (3) Was the evidence adduced at trial sufficient to justify the trial court's determination granting the petition for termination of parental rights?

The trial court ruled that the four children were "unavailable" to testify based upon their therapists' statements that testifying would be extremely detrimental to their mental health and might even lead to hospitalization. The parents now claim, although they did not do so at trial, that this ruling violated their right to confront the witnesses against them under both the Sixth Amendment of the United States Constitution and article I, section 12 of the Utah Constitution.[4] The parents concede that this is not a criminal case and that they have discovered no authority extending the right to confrontation to a termination of parental rights proceeding. . . .

* * *

The parents contend that the trial court's failure to comply with the requirements of Utah Code Ann. § 76-5-411 (1990) is reversible error due to the admission of prejudicial, unreliable hearsay. This statute, contained in Utah's Criminal Code, requires the trial court to initially determine whether admission of out-of-court statements of a child victim will best serve "the interest of justice." *Id.* § 76-5-411(2). In making that determination, the court must con-

---

[4] Both amendments, by their specific language, refer to "criminal prosecutions."

sider "the age and maturity of the child, the nature and duration of the abuse, the relationship of the child to the offender, and the reliability of the assertion and of the child." *Id.*

Termination of parental rights proceedings are *civil* proceedings and are governed by the Utah Rules of Civil Procedure. Utah Code Ann. § 78-3f-106(3) (Supp. 1993). In addition to the Utah Rules of Civil Procedure, the legislature has promulgated statutes specifically controlling termination of parental rights proceedings. *See id.* §§ 78-3f-101 to-114 (Supp. 1993).

In contrast to these statutory provisions governing termination of parental rights proceedings, section 76-5-411 is part of the Criminal Code and clearly applies in the context of *criminal* proceedings. The parents have not presented any authority or legal analysis supporting application of this criminal provision to this civil proceedings. Accordingly, we decline to rule upon this issue. . . . However, we note that even if section 76-5-411 applied to termination of parental rights proceedings, the trial court's alleged violation of section 76-5-411 in this case was harmless error due to the abundance of independent, objectively ascertained evidence concerning sexual abuse of the children. . . .

* * *

The trial court did not err in its decision to terminate parental rights with respect to all of the children. We affirm.

Notes

1. The courts and legislatures generally recognize that parents have the due process right to cross-examine witnesses against them in termination proceedings. *See, e.g., In the Matter of the Appeal in Maricopa County Juvenile Action No. 7499*, 786 P.2d 1004 (Ariz. Ct. App. 1989) (right exists where witness' testimony "goes to the heart of termination proof"); NEB. REV. STAT. § 43-279.01 (1998); VA. CODE ANN. § 16.1-277.02(B) (Michie Supp. 2001). However, most courts have held that a parent's right to confront witnesses in a termination proceeding is not grounded in the Sixth Amendment, because a termination trial is not a criminal proceedings. *See In Interest of M.S. et al., supra.* To determine when a parent may or may not confront and cross-examine a witness in a termination proceeding, courts weigh the three factors found in *Mathews v. Eldridge*, 424 U.S. 319 (1976) (private interest affected by the proceeding; risk of error created by the procedure; and countervailing government interest supporting the use of the procedure). *See Maricopoa County Juvenile Action No. 7499, supra*, at 1009 ("it is essential under the adversary system that parents be given the opportunity to challenge the testimony of their children. . . . Without the opportunity, . . . the adversary process is subverted and made meaningless").

In *Oklahoma v. Walker,* No. 93899, 2000 WL 1595939 (Okla. Oct. 24, 2000), the court ordered the mother to leave the courtroom during a termination trial during the abused son's testimony. The mother objected and argued that she had an absolute right to be present during his testimony and that the state must first prove that the child would be harmed by her presence in the courtroom. In concluding that the mother could be excluded from the courtroom while her son testified, the court weighed the three *Eldridge* factors. The court found (1) the mother's private interest in continuing her family connection with her son and (2) the state's interest in protecting the child from trauma while testifying were both of the utmost importance. The court then held that the risk of error in not allowing the mother to confront her son was insufficient to require the mother's presence. The court stated that the mother's ability to communicate with her attorney after the child's direct testimony and before the cross-examination were sufficient protections of the mother's interests. The courts usually require the state to prove that the child will be harmed or the child's testimony will be directly affected by the parent's physical presence in the courtroom. *See In re Danielle D.,* 595 N.W.2d 544 (Neb. 1999); *In the Matter of M.B.,* 638 N.E.2d 804 (Ind. Ct. App. 1993); *Adoption of Kimberly,* 609 N.E.2d 73 (Mass. 1993); *In re Amber D.,* 286 Cal. Rptr. 751 (Cal. Ct. App. 1991). For a discussion of the application of these factors in criminal cases, see *Coy v. Iowa*, 484 U.S. 810 (1987), and *Maryland v. Craig*, 497 U.S. 836 (1990).

Once a court decides that a child should not testify in the presence of his parents, the court must then determine how the child witness will testify. Some jurisdictions permit testimony to be taken in a room with a one-way mirror to enable the parents and other necessary persons to observe the testimony without the child seeing them. *See, e.g., In the Interest of M.S. et al., supra.* A child's testimony may also be taken in the judge's chambers. *See, e.g., In re Danielle D., supra; In re Amber D., supra.* Several jurisdictions also allow a child's testimony to be presented on videotape or closed-circuit television. *See, e.g., S.M. v. Elkhart County Office of Family and Children,* 706 N.E.2d 596 (Ind. Ct. App. 1999); *Adoption of Kimberly, supra; In The matter of M.B., supra;* Margaret Beyer & Wallace J. Mlyniec, *Lifelines to Biological Parents: Their Effect on Termination of Parental Rights and Performance,* 20 FAM. L.Q. 233 (1986). For background information concerning the use of videotape or closed-circuit television testimony of children, see Anne M. Haralambie, *The Role of the Child's Attorney in Protecting the Child Throughout the Litigation Process,* 71 N.D. L. REV. 939, 974-76 (1995).

2. Several states have codified the admission of a child's testimony on videotape or through closed-circuit television in a termination proceeding. The following statutes are examples:

Oklahoma Statutes Annotated

Tit. 10, § 7003-4.3 (West 1998)

§ 7003-4.3. Taking testimony of child age 12 or under in room other than courtroom—Recording

A. This section shall apply only to a proceeding affecting the parent-child, guardian-child or family relationship in which a child twelve (12) years of age or younger is alleged to have been abused, and shall apply only to the testimony of that child or other child witness.

B. The court may, on the motion of a party to the proceeding, order that the testimony of the child be taken in a room other than the courtroom and be televised by closed-circuit equipment in the courtroom to be viewed by the court, the finder of fact and the parties to the proceeding. Only an attorney for each party, an attorney ad litem for the child or other person whose presence would contribute to the welfare and well-being of the child and persons necessary to operate the equipment may be present in the room with the child during the testimony of the child. Only the attorneys for the parties may question the child. The persons operating the equipment shall be confined to an adjacent room or behind a screen or mirror that permits them to see and hear the child during the testimony of the child, but does not permit the child to see or hear them.

C. The court may, on the motion of a party to the proceeding, order that the testimony of the child be taken outside the courtroom and be recorded for showing in the courtroom before the court, the finder of fact and the parties to the proceeding. Only those persons permitted to be present at the taking of testimony under subsection B of this section may be present during the taking of the child's testimony. Only the attorneys for the parties may question the child, and the persons operating the equipment shall be confined from the child's sight and hearing. The court shall ensure that:

1. The recording is both visual and aural and is recorded on film or videotape or by other electronic means;
2. The recording equipment is capable of making an accurate recording, the operator of the equipment is competent and the recording is accurate and has not been altered;
3. Every voice on the recording is identified; and
4. Each party to the proceeding is afforded an opportunity to view the recording before it is shown in the courtroom, and a copy of a written transcript transcribed by a licensed or certified court reporter is provided to the parties.

D. If the testimony of a child is taken as provided by subsections B or C of this section, the child shall not be compelled to testify in court during the proceeding.

Indiana Code Annotated

§ 31-35-4-3 (Lexis 1997)

§ 31-35-4-3. Requirements for admissibility of statements or videotapes

Sec. 3. A statement or videotape described in section 2 of this chapter is admissible in evidence in an action to determine whether the parent-child relationship should be terminated if, after notice to the parties of a hearing and of their right to be present: (1) the court finds that the time, content, and circumstances of the statement or videotape and any other evidence provide sufficient indications of reliability; and (2) the child:

A. testifies at the proceeding to determine whether the parent-child relationship should be terminated;

B. was available for face-to-face cross-examination when the statement or videotape was made; or

C. is found by the court to be unavailable as a witness because:

(i) a psychiatrist, physician, or psychologist has certified that the child's participation in the proceeding creates a substantial likelihood of emotional or mental harm to the child;

(ii) a physician has certified that the child cannot participate in the proceeding for medical reasons; or

(iii) the court has determined that the child is incapable of understanding the nature and obligation of an oath.

For an additional statute that codifies the admission of a child's testimony on videotape or closed-circuit television in termination proceedings, see 42 PA. CONS. STAT. ANN. § 5984 (West 2000).

Questions

1. How can courts best protect the interests of parents in a termination proceeding where the child testifies outside of the parents' presence? In what situations might the procedure for taking such testimony infringe upon a parent's due process and confrontation rights? Does excluding a parent from being present when a child testifies but allowing the parent's attorney to be present satisfy the parent's constitutional rights?

2. How do the Oklahoma and Indiana statutes, *supra,* in Note 2, protect the interests of the parent, the state, and the child? Are there any factors not mentioned in these statutes which a court should consider before allowing a child's videotaped testimony to be admitted in a termination trial?

C. Grounds for Termination

1. Basic Requirements

Montana Code Annotated
§ 41-3-609 (1999)

41-3-609. Criteria for termination.

(1) The court may order a termination of the parent-child legal relationship upon a finding that any of the following circumstances exist:

(a) the parents have relinquished the child . . . ;

(b) the child has been abandoned by the parents;

(c) the parent is convicted of a felony in which sexual intercourse occurred or is a minor adjudicated a delinquent youth because of an act that, if committed by an adult, would be a felony in which sexual intercourse occurred and, as a result of the sexual intercourse, the child is born;

(d) the parent has subjected the child to any of the circumstances listed in 41-3-403(2)(a) through (2)(e);

(e) the putative father meets any of the criteria listed in 43-3-403(3)(a) through (3)(c); or

(f) the child is an adjudicated youth in need of care and both of the following exist:

(i) an appropriate treatment plan that has been approved by the court has not been complied with by the parents or has not been successful; and

(ii) the conduct or condition of the parents rendering them unfit is unlikely to change within a reasonable time.

(2) In determining whether the conduct or condition of the parents is unlikely to change within a reasonable time, the court shall enter a finding that continuation of the parent-child legal relationship will likely result in continued abuse or neglect or that the conduct or the condition of the parents renders the parents unfit, unable, or unwilling to give the child adequate parental care. In making the determinations, the court shall consider but is not limited to the following:

(a) emotional illness, mental illness, or mental deficiency of the parent of a duration or nature as to render the parent unlikely to care for the ongoing physical, mental, and emotional needs of the child within a reasonable time;

(b) a history of violent behavior by the parent;

(c) excessive use of intoxicating liquor or of a narcotic or dangerous drug that affects the parent's ability to care and provide for the child; and

(d) present judicially ordered long-term confinement of the parent;

(3) In considering any of the factors in subsection (2) in terminating the parent-child relationship, the court shall give primary consideration to the physical, mental, and emotional conditions and needs of the child.

(4) A treatment plan is not required under this part upon a finding by the court following hearing if:

(a) the parent meets the criteria of subsections (1)(a) through (1)(e);

(b) two medical doctors or clinical psychologists submit testimony that the parent cannot assume the role of parent;

(c) the parent is or will be incarcerated for more than 1 year and reunification of the child with the parent is not in the best interests of the child because of the child's circumstances, including placement options, age, and developmental, cognitive, and psychological needs; or

(d) the death or serious bodily injury, as defined in 45-2-101, of a child caused by abuse or neglect by the parent has occurred.

a. Best Interests of the Child

In re Justin T.

640 A.2d 737 (Me. 1994)

CLIFFORD, Justice.

The mother of Justin T. appeals from a judgment of the District Court terminating her parental rights pursuant to 22 M.R.S.A. § 4055 (1992 & Supp. 1993). On appeal, she challenges the trial court's findings that she cannot protect her son from jeopardy, that she is unable to take responsibility for him within a time that is reasonably calculated to meet his needs, and that termination is in Justin's best interests. The mother also contends that the failure of the Department of Human Services (Department) to meet its obligations to pursue family reunification requires that the termination be vacated. We affirm the judgment.

The record reflects that in January of 1991, Justin's mother was sharing a Portland apartment with her four children, another child related to her by marriage, and her boyfriend. Justin was 21 months old at the time. On January 22, the mother left Justin in the care of her boyfriend and returned home to find the child seriously injured. She rushed Justin to a local hospital, where he spent the next 17 days recovering from injuries to his liver and pancreas, as well as the permanent impairment of one of his kidneys. The boyfriend was convicted of aggravated assault and incarcerated; Justin's mother ended their relationship.

While Justin was hospitalized, the Department obtained an order from the District court granting the Department temporary custody of the child. In April, the court entered a child protective order, with the agreement of the parties, officially placing Justin in Department custody. The Department identified substance abuse as a major problem in the mother's life and referred her for psychological evaluation, counseling, and treatment. Twice in 1992, in August and again in September, the mother entered a residential treatment program but left prior to completing it.

In March of 1993, the Department filed a petition to terminate the parental rights of Justin's mother. . . . Following a hearing, the District Court found that the mother is unable to protect Justin from jeopardy, and that those circumstances are unlikely to change within a time reasonably calculated to meet his needs. The court further found that the mother is unable to take responsibility for Justin within a time that is reasonably calculated to meet his needs. In addition, the court found that termination was in Justin's best interest, 22 M.R.S.A. § 4055(1)(B)(2)(a), and entered a judgment terminating the mother's parental rights. The mother filed this direct appeal . . . contesting the court's findings.

We will affirm an order terminating parental rights if a review of the entire record shows that the District Court could have found clear and convincing evidence to support the statutory bases for termination. *In re Elijah R.*, 620 A.2d 282, 284 (Me. 1993). "When clear and convincing evidence is required, we review whether the factfinder could reasonably have been persuaded that the required factual findings were proved to be highly probable." *In re Jeffrey*

E., 557 A.2d 954, 956 (Me. 1989) (citing *In re Misty Lee H.*, 529 A.2d 331, 333 (Me. 1987)). We will vacate the judgment only if the trial court's findings are clearly erroneous. *In re Christina H.*, 618 A.2d 228, 229 (Me. 1992).

The mother contends that the Department failed to meet its evidentiary burden as to her ability to protect Justin from jeopardy because she ended her relationship with the perpetrator of Justin's injuries, because there is no evidence that her substance abuse problems have had an impact on Justin, and because she has never been homeless notwithstanding the evidence in the record of her frequent moves. But as the court noted in its extensive and thoughtful opinion, the record amply demonstrates that the jeopardy to which this child has been exposed is not merely a function of his mother's relationship with a violent perpetrator, but stems primarily from her chronic history of substance abuse beginning when she was a small child.

Although the mother's testimony was that learning of the Department's decision to terminate her parental rights motivated her to confront her substance abuse, and despite evidence suggesting that the mother may have made some progress in dealing with it, the finding that Justin's mother remains a chronic abuser of drugs and alcohol is supported by ample evidence in the record. In particular, as recently as February of 1993, the mother was still not complying with the recommendations of her therapist that she participate fully in Alcoholics Anonymous and abstain completely from intoxicating substances. The finding that Justin's mother is unwilling or unable to protect him from jeopardy, and that these circumstances are unlikely to change within a time that is reasonable calculated to meet his needs, is not clearly erroneous. Likewise, because of the mother's substance abuse problems and her inability to provide a stable home environment, the trial court's finding that she is unable to take responsibility for Justin within a time that is reasonably calculated to meet his needs is amply supported in the record.

In addition to meeting its burden of proof as to jeopardy, it is also necessary for the Department to prove independently by clear and convincing evidence that termination is in the best interest of the child. Evidence of a parent's inability to protect her child from jeopardy is also relevant to whether termination is in the child's best interests. Courts should be cautious, however, in finding that termination is in a child's best interest when, as occurred in this case, the Department restricts the parent-child contact by instituting child protective proceedings and then cites the lack of a normal parent-child relationship as evidence that the "best interests" test is satisfied. *See Santosky v. Kramer,* 455 U.S. 745, 763, 102 S. Ct. 1388, 1400, 71 L. Ed. 2d 599 (1982) (noting the dangers inherent in the state's "power to shape the historical events that form the basis for termination"). The evidence in the record as to the relationship between Justin and his mother suggests that *some* degree of parent-child bond has endured despite all that has transpired. Nevertheless, in light of the evidence of the mother's ongoing substance abuse, her inability to provide a stable home environment, and of Justin's need for such an environment, we cannot say that the trial court clearly erred in finding that termination is in Justin's best interest. *See* 22 M.R.S.A. §§ 4003, 4050 (1993) (policy and purposes of Child and Family Services and Child Protection Act, recognizing that instability and impermanence are contrary to the welfare of children, and emphasizing the permanent placement of children who cannot be reunified with their families).

Although we affirm the judgment, we share the concern expressed by the District Court that the Department, in acting unilaterally to cease efforts to reunify Justin and his mother, failed to meet its obligations pursuant to 22 M.R.S.A. § 4041 (1992) (requiring the Department to develop a family reunification plan for children in its custody, and to make a good faith effort to implement the plan). Section 4041 requires the Department to "petition for termination of parental rights at the earliest possible time that it is determined that family reunification efforts will be discontinued . . . and that termination is in the best interests of the child." 22 M.R.S.A. § 4041(A)(6). Unfortunately, and contrary to the statute, the Department in this case waited more than five months after making the decision to discontinue its efforts to reunify Justin with his mother before it filed the termination petition. As the court properly noted, however, the Department's failure to meet its reunification obligations is only one factor to be considered in a termination case. *In re David H. & Virginia H.*, 637 A.2d 1173, 1176 (Me. 1994); *Christina H.*, 618 A.2d at 230. The court considered this factor and explicitly concluded that more vigilant attention to the reunification statute by the Department would not have affected the mother's lack of progress with her substance abuse problem. Therefore, we cannot agree with the mother's contention that the Department's failure to meet its reunification obligations compels us to vacate the termination.

Judgment affirmed.

Notes

1. Some states codify what constitutes a child's best interests. The following Wisconsin statute is an example:

Wisconsin Statutes Annotated
§ 48.426 (West 1997)

§ 48.426 Standard and factors

(1) Court considerations. In making a decision about the appropriate disposition under § 48.427, the court shall consider the standard and factors enumerated in this section and any report submitted by an agency under § 48.428.

(2) Standard. The best interests of the child shall be the prevailing factor considered by the court in determining the disposition of all proceedings under this subchapter.

(3) Factors. In considering the best interests of the child under this section the court shall consider but not be limited to the following:

(a) The likelihood of the child's adoption after termination.

(b) The age and health of the child, both at the time of the disposition and, if applicable, at the time the child was removed from the home.

(c) Whether the child has substantial relationships with the parent or other family members, and whether it would be harmful to the child to sever these relationships.

(d) The wishes of the child.

(e) The duration of the separation of the parent from the child.

(f) Whether the child will be able to enter into a more stable and permanent family relationship as a result of the termination, taking into account the conditions of the child's current placement, the likelihood of future placements and the results of prior placements.

For additional statutes that codify the requirements of the best interest standard in TPR proceedings, see DEL. CODE ANN. tit. 13, § 722(a) (Michie 1999); D.C. CODE ANN. § 16-2353 (Lexis Supp. 2001); KY. REV. STAT. ANN. § 625.090 (West 2000); MD. CODE ANN., FAM. LAW § 5-313 (Lexis 1999); OHIO REV. CODE ANN. § 2151.414 (Anderson Supp. 2000); VT. STAT. ANN. tit. 33, § 5540 (Lexis 2001).

There is considerable debate concerning how much weight a court should give the best interests of the child standard in a termination proceeding. Critics of the best interests test cite several reasons a court should not use it to determine custody status, including that "it does not provide enough protection for the rights of natural parents; . . . by basing custody decisions on psychological ties between the child and nonparents, the best interest standard creates an incentive for nonparents to wrongfully gain custody of a child; . . . [and] it has the potential for misuse because the standard is based on vague or nonexistent criteria, opening the custody decision to social biases." Gary A. Kelson, *In the Best Interest of the Child: What Have We Learned from Baby Jessica and Baby Richard?*, 33 J. MARSHALL L. REV. 353, 372 (2000). Critics cite additional factors courts improperly consider, such as a party's socioeconomic status (*id.*) or the bonds between the child and a psychological parent. *See* Theresa A. Nitti, *Stepping Back From the Psychological Parenting Theory: A Comment on* In re J.C., 46 RUTGERS L. REV. 1003 (1994); Matthew B. Johnson, *Examining Risks to Children in the Context of Parental Rights Termination Proceedings,* 32 N.Y.U. REV. L. & SOC. CHANGE 397 (1996). For further critique of other applications of the best interest standard, see Melanie B. Lewis, Case Note, *Inappropriate Application of the Best Interests of the Child Standard Leads to Worst Case Scenerio:* In re C.C.R.S., 68 U. COLO. L. REV. 259 (1997).

2. Another issue is whether a child's best interests are served by legislation which accelerates permanency decisions concerning children, which inevitably means more terminations earlier in the process. ASFA, as described in Chapter 10, Section A.3., requires termination proceedings to be initiated if a child has been in foster care for fifteen of the last twenty-two months or if the parent commits a designated offense, such as killing the child's sibling. For a critique of how removing a child from his or her home because a parent commits an act listed in AFSA, see Rachel Venier, Article, *Parental Rights and the Best Interests of the Child: Implications of the Adoption and Safe Families Act of 1997 on Domestic Violence Victim's Rights,* 8 AM. U. J. GENDER SOC. POL'Y & L. 517, 533-49 (2000).

Even prior to the passage of ASFA, legislatures and courts began speeding up the process for filing termination petitions. For example, in Michigan, in 1995,

1600 children became wards of the state through termination proceedings while only 1200 were adopted. In New York, the number of wards of the state not being adopted grew from 471 in 1987 to 2,495 in 1992. *See* Martin Guggenheim, *The Effects of Recent Trends to Accelerate the Termination of Parental Rights of Children in Foster Care—An Empirical Analysis in Two States,* 29 FAM. L.Q. 121, 121-30 (1995). For further discussion of the time limits in TPR cases created by ASFA, see Thomas J. Walsh, *The Clock Is Ticking: Do Time Limits in Wisconsin's Termination of Parental Rights Serve the Best Interests of Children?,* 83 MARQ. L. REV. 743 (2000).

Question

What are the problems of law and policy with the "best interests of the child" standard as a basis for TPR?

b. Reconciling Child's Best Interests and Parents' Rights

In re Dallas M.

581 N.W.2d 596 (Wis. Ct. App. 1998)

Ramona A. GONZALEZ, Judge. Affirmed. . . .

* * *

BACKGROUND

Sara M. had two children, Dallas M., born March 5, 1987, and Kaelan R.W.S., born August 17, 1992. In June of 1993, a referral was made to the La Crosse County Department of Human Services for alleged abuse and neglect. An attempt was made to provide services to Sara at that time. Later, on March 22, 1995, the children were placed in foster care when Sara was confined to the La Crosse County Jail. On May 25, 1995, Dallas and Kaelan were adjudged to be children in need of protection and services (CHIPS) and their placement in foster care was continued. A permanency plan was attached to the 1995 order finding the children CHIPS. On January 22, 1996, the permanency plan was reviewed by an independent panel. On May 24, 1996, an extension hearing was held to determine if the foster care should be extended. On June 7, 1996, foster care was extended to May 26, 1997 because Sara had not made substantial progress on fourteen of the fifteen conditions necessary to the return of her children. A permanency plan was also attached to the 1996 order. On May 21, 1997, the Department filed a petition to terminate the parental rights of Sara. A trial was held August 18th through August 20, 1997. The jury found that the Department had made diligent efforts to provide Sara with the services that were ordered by the court; that Sara had failed to demonstrate substantial progress toward meeting the conditions established for the return of Dallas and Kaelan to her home; and that there was a substantial likelihood that Sara would not meet the conditions for the return of the children within the twelve month period following the conclusion of the factfinding trial.

At the dispositional hearing, the circuit court . . . determined that the children were likely to be adopted after the termination of Sara's parental rights; second, that both children were in good health; third, that Kaelan and Dallas had bonded with their foster mother and father; and fourth, that neither child was subject to the Federal Indian Child Welfare Act, 25 U.S. CODE § 1911 et seq.

Based upon the findings of the jury and the findings of the court, the court then concluded, as a matter of law, that the children were in continuing need of protection and services . . . that Sara was an unfit parent and that her unfitness was so egregious, by clear and convincing evidence, as to warrant the termination of her parental rights. And finally, the court concluded that based on the recommendations of the guardian ad litem, the Department and the entire proceedings to date, it was in the best interests of Dallas and Kaelan to terminate Sara's parental rights.

In reaching its conclusions, the court carefully considered the lack of effort by Sara to meet even the most minimal needs of her children. Sara had not maintained a stable home environment into which the children might be transferred; she had been given repeated warnings about the effect on her children of the violent environment in which she placed them through her association with men who continued to batter her. The court also reviewed the diligent efforts which had been made by the Department, as it attempted to facilitate the return of the children to Sara.

On appeal, Sara asserts error on four theories: (1) that the County did not comply with the statutory requirements for timely filing permanency plans; (2) that the permanency plans that were filed were insufficient; (3) that the Department did not make a diligent effort to provide services to Sara to enable her to obtain the return of her children; and (4) that Sara's First Amendment right of free association under the United States Constitution was violated by the Department's requirement that she refrain from associating with abusive men.

DISCUSSION

We will not reverse a factual determination made by a jury or by the circuit court unless it is clearly erroneous. . . . The construction and application of a statute under facts as found by the court presents a question of law which we review independently. . . . Whether the litigant's due process rights were violated in a proceeding in circuit court is a question of law, which we review de novo.

Sara contends on appeal that her due process rights were violated because the procedures required . . . were not met. She raises three contentions in this regard: (1) that the permanency plans required . . . were not timely, (2) that the permanency plans were not reviewed; and (3) that the permanency plans that were filed were insufficient. . . . The Department argues that the permanency plans were timely filed subsequent to the children being placed outside of Sara's home under a court order, and even if they were not timely filed, there has been no constitutional deprivation because the requirement is an administrative one which does not involve the process that is due in court. The Department cites *Thomas Y.* in support of its assertion that a late permanency plan, a late review, or a plan established through the use of a form are simply administrative insufficiencies and not errors with constitutional implications. The Department also alleges that the issue of whether the thirty-day time limit for a review . . . was not raised at the circuit court level and therefore, it is waived for appeal.

In *Thomas Y.* . . . we noted that the plain language of the statute did require the filing of a permanency plan within sixty days of the date on which a child was placed outside of his or her home under a court order. However, we concluded that "preparing a permanency plan is an administrative requirement that does not involve the court, is not part of the court procedures governed by Subchapter V and does not arise out of the court's jurisdiction." *Thomas Y.*, 175 Wis.2d at 228, 499 N.W.2d at 221.

Sara argues that *Thomas Y.* was a CHIPS case and therefore, it does not apply to a termination of parental rights. We do not agree. In *Thomas Y.*, we construed the statute at issue in this case. *Thomas Y.* is controlling here. Therefore, we conclude that neither the late filing of the permanency plan nor the lack of a timely review constitutes a violation of Sara's due process rights which courts are bound to afford in termination of parental rights proceedings.

Sara next argues that the permanency plans were insufficient because forms were used, rather than narrative-style reports. That argument is without merit. The forms listed, . . . those tasks toward which Sara was required to make substantial progress if she were to obtain the return of her sons. Sara does not even argue that . . . she would have been able to comply with the requirements for the return of her sons. Additionally, this issue was never raised at any of the hearings where the permanency plan was reviewed. Therefore, we do not consider it further here.

Sara also challenges the factual findings made by the jury. She alleges that the Department did not make diligent efforts to provide services to her sufficient to enable her to obtain the return of her children. The factual findings of a jury in a termination of parental rights case will not be overturned unless such findings are against the great weight and clear preponderance of the evidence. . . . However, whether the evidence warrants a termination of parental rights is within the sound discretion of the circuit court. . . .

Here, the jury heard evidence that the Department established clear conditions for the return of Sara's children and then it provided the following services: (1) a case worker who would be available on a regular basis to assist Sara; (2) parent aid services; (3) counselors and therapists to assist Sara, both in parenting and in understanding her continuing relationships with abusive men; (4) transportation services; (5) supervised visitation with Dallas and Kaelan; (6) respite care; (7) day care; (8) vocational rehabilitation; and (9) foster care.

Sara never challenged the sufficiency of the services provided to her, all of which were provided without charge. On appeal, Sara argues that she wasn't receiving the type of counseling that she needed and that she did not trust the counselor initially provided by the Department. However, at no point in the proceedings in the circuit court did she ask for a different counselor or let anyone know that she did not trust the one who had been assigned. Furthermore, the jury also heard Sara missed seventeen of the fifty appointments the Department set with the initial counselor, and when a different counselor was provided after the petition to termination her rights had been filed, Sara missed twenty-five percent of the scheduled appointments. The jury heard that Sara was given repeated warnings of the possibility of the termination of her parental rights if she did not work toward achieving those skills necessary for the return of her children. Therefore, we conclude there was an ample factual record to support the jury's findings.

* * *

CONCLUSION

Because we find no reversible error in the substance or the procedures which attended the court's termination of Sara's parental rights, we affirm the judgment of the circuit court.

Judgment affirmed.

Notes

Courts have traditionally recognized a parent's constitutional right to maintain a family relationship with his or her child. In *Meyer v. Nebraska, supra*, in Chapter 9, Part A, the Supreme Court recognized the parent's right to establish and maintain a home. In *Prince v. Massachusetts, supra,* in Chapter 9, Part B.1, the court held that a parent has the right to care for, nurture, and choose a child's educational training. In *Stanley v. Illinois, supra,* in Chapter 14, Part A, the Court found that parents have a constitutional right to rear their children and that this right can only be defeated by a showing of parental unfitness.

It is in this historical backdrop of the parents' substantive due process rights that courts today must consider the rights of the parties in termination proceedings. Some courts consider only the parent's constitutional rights, as acknowledged by *Meyer, Prince,* and *Stanley*, in maintaining the family relationship in termination proceedings. By focusing on the constitutional rights of the parents, these courts terminate the parent-child relationship when there is a showing of clear and convincing evidence of some inability of the parent to maintain the relationship. *See, e.g., In re H.J.P.,* 789 P.2d 69 (Wash. 1990); *In re Marriage of Matzen,* 600 So. 2d 487 (Fla. Dist. Ct. App. 1992); *Wade v. Green,* 743 P.2d 1070 (Okla. 1987). In *In Matter of J.C.,* 608 A.2d 1312 (N.J. 1992), the court focused on a mother's inability to maintain a parent-child relationship rather than the best interests of the child in a termination proceeding. The mother was homeless, abused by her male companions, and suffered from substance abuse. The mother also failed to complete both her inpatient and outpatient substance abuse programs. The state had the burden of proof to demonstrate the mother's inability to maintain the relationship with her three children. Because *parens patriae* "involves the State acting in the place of parents, it is limited to situations in which the state has demonstrated that the child's parent or custodian is unfit, . . . or the child has been neglected or harmed." Despite the fact that the children were very happy in their foster homes, demonstrated marked improvement, and obtained better grades in school, the court held that the state failed to demonstrate by clear and convincing evidence the mother's unfitness in rearing her children. For further discussion of parental unfitness as the sole factor considered by some courts in termination proceedings, see Toby Solomon & James B. Boskey, *In Whose Best Interests: Child v. Parent,* N.J. LAW. MAG., Nov.-Dec. 1993 at 36 (1993). *But see In re Samantha D.,* 740 P.2d 1168 (N.M. Ct. App. 1987). In *In Samatha D.,* a mother filed suit to regain legal custody over a child she voluntarily gave up for adoption. The court determined that the mother's parental rights could only be terminated if the state proved by clear and convincing evidence that the child's best interests would be properly served by terminating the relationship. In considering only the best interests of the child, the court terminated the mother's parental rights after finding that the child had lived in a foster home since birth, the parent-child relationship had disintegrated, a psychological parent-child relationship had developed between the foster family and the child, and the foster family desired to adopt the child. It should be noted that very few courts, such as *In re Samantha D.,* base termination of parental rights solely on the best interests of the child. *See* Vanessa L. Warzynski, Comment, *Termination Of Parental Rights: The "Psychological Parent" Standard*, 39 VILL. L. REV. 737, 761 (1994).

Most courts, however, utilize the best interests standard by focusing on the interests of the child and the constitutional rights of the parents. *See id.* at 763. *See, e.g., In re Higby,* 611 N.E.2d 403 (Ohio Ct. App. 1992); *In re Christina H.,* 618 A.2d 228 (Me. 1992); *In the Matter of R.H.N.,* 710 P.2d 481 (Colo. 1985). In *R.H.N.,* the stepfather of three children petitioned the court to terminate the parental rights of their biological father. The father visited his children on several occasions but refused to pay child support when his ex-wife refused to let him see their children. The father was later incarcerated and continued to not provide any type of financial support to the children. The court determined that "the best interests of the child should be considered both with respect to termination of the natural parent's rights and with respect to the adoption in a stepparent adoption proceeding." The court considered several factors to satisfy the best interests standard, including "family stability, the present and future effects of adoption, including the detrimental effects of termination of parental rights, the child's emotional ties to and interaction with the contestants, the adjustment of the child to the living situation, the child's age, and the mental and physical health of the parties." *Id.* at 486. The court terminated the biological father's parental rights because it was in the children's best interests and because the father refused to provide his children a "reasonable proportion" of his daily income while in jail.

Questions

How are the constitutional rights of both parties reconciled in a termination proceeding? How does the court's *parens patriae* role affect the rights of the parties?

2. Special Grounds

a. Mother's Prenatal Conduct

Adoption of Oliver

[*See, supra*, Chapter 13, Part A.4.]

In re Valerie D.

595 A.2d 922 (Conn. 1991)

NORCOTT, Judge.

The respondent mother appeals from the judgment of the trial court finding her daughter, Valerie, to be a neglected child and terminating her parental rights with respect to that child. She challenges, in essence, the court's (1) ruling that her conduct while she was pregnant with Valerie can support a neglect petition or a petition for termination of parental rights and (2) factual findings. We affirm the judgment of the trial court.

The trial court could reasonably have found the following facts. Valerie was born on July 26, 1989. The birth was complicated by her passage of stool, or meconium, prior to delivery. If a baby inhales and swallows the meconium, severe, life threatening respiratory problems can result. In Valerie's case, although meconium aspiration did not occur, the passage of stool was most likely caused by the respondent's ingestion of cocaine after her water had broken, some eight to ten hours before delivery.

When Valerie was born, she exhibited many classic signs of cocaine withdrawal. She was jittery, shaking, crying hard, breathing with difficulty and making no eye contact. A urine test showed that Valerie had been born with cocaine in her bloodstream.

On the basis of these facts, the Department of Children and Youth Services filed coterminous petitions for neglect and for termination of the respondent's parental rights on August 1, 1989. The petitions alleged that Valerie was abused, neglected and uncared for as a result of the respondent's prenatal drug use and sought termination of the respondent's parental rights because "the child has been denied by reason of act or acts of commission or omission, the care, guidance or control necessary for [her] physical, moral or emotional well being" in that she had sustained "nonaccidental or inadequately explained serious physical injury." The Department later amended its petitions, additionally claiming that Valerie had been abandoned and that she did not have an ongoing parent-child relationship with the respondent.

After a hearing held over the course of several days between December 13, 1989, and February 21, 1990, the trial court rendered its decision orally from the bench on March 28, 1990, finding Valerie to be a neglected child under General Statutes § 46b-120 and terminating the respondent's parental rights pursuant to General Statutes §§ 17a-112 and 45a-717. In an articulation filed on July 30, 1990, the court further found that Valerie was abused, neglected and uncared for as those terms are used in § 46b-120. The court also terminated the respondent's parental rights on the basis of its findings that Valerie had sustained "nonaccidental or inadequately explained serious physical injury" as a result of the respondent's prenatal drug use; and that no ongoing parent-child relationship existed between Valerie and the respondent. Finally, the court, relying on authority from other jurisdictions, noted that "[t]he fact that the act resulting in the detriment to the child occurred prior to birth does not require the conclusion that the child's condition *at* birth was other than that of a neglected child." (Emphasis in original.) The respondent appeals from the trial court's ruling.

The respondent first claims that the trial court improperly determined that her conduct while pregnant can support a petition for neglect or termination of parental rights. This issue has yet to be decided in this state. In order for us to answer this question, we must examine our statutes allowing petitions to be brought for neglect and termination of parental rights.

General Statutes § 46a-120 defines a neglected child as one who "(i) has been abandoned or (ii) is being denied proper care and attention, physically, educationally, emotionally or morally or (iii) is being permitted to live under conditions, circumstances or associations injurious to his well-being, or (iv) has been abused." A child may be found uncared for under that statute "who is homeless or whose home cannot provide the specialized care which his physical, emotional or mental condition requires." The statute defines "child" as "any person under sixteen years of age."

General Statutes § 17a-112(b) provides, in pertinent part, that parental rights may be terminated if "(3) the child has been denied, by reason of an act or acts of parental commission or omission, the care, guidance or control necessary for his physical, educational, moral or emotional well-being. Nonaccidental or inadequately explained serious physical injury to a child shall constitute prima facie evidence of acts of parental commission or omission sufficient for the termination of parental rights; or (4) there is no ongoing parent-child relationship, which means the relationship that ordinarily develops as a result of a parent having met on a day to day basis the physical, emotional, moral and educational needs of the child and to allow further time for the establishment or reestablishment of such parent-child relationship would be detrimental to the best interest of the child."...

Although no appellate court in this state has as of yet determined whether a petition for neglect or termination of parental rights can be predicated solely on a mother's prenatal conduct, trial courts in Connecticut and other states have addressed similar issues with respect to tort and criminal law. An infant who has sustained injuries prior to birth, whether the infant is viable or not at that time, has a cause of action in negligence against the alleged wrongdoer. Similarly, a wrongful death action can be brought on behalf of a child who dies as a result of prenatal injuries regardless of whether those injuries were sustained when the fetus was viable....

For different reasons of public policy, the Superior Court in *State v. Anonymous (1986-1)*, 40 Conn. Sup. 498, 516 A.2d 156 (1986), held that an unborn but viable fetus is not a "person" within the meaning of the Connecticut statutes defining murder. Person is defined for the purpose of the homicide statutes as a "human being." General Statutes § 53a-3(1). The court in *State v. Anonymous (1986-1)* found that "[i]n addition to the fact that the codes from which our Connecticut law was drawn limit the words 'human being' to those who have been born alive . . . Connecticut's legislature did not intend to define a 'human being' as an unborn but viable fetus." *State v. Anonymous (1986-1), supra,* at 501, 516 A.2d 156. The court noted the seemingly inconsistent developments in tort law, reasoning that "'[d]iffering objectives . . . in tort and criminal law foster the development of different principles governing the same factual situation.'" *Id.* at 505, 516 A.2d 156.

Because neglect proceedings and proceedings to terminate parental rights are neither tort nor criminal actions, we must now decide which of the above paths to follow in creating a rule of law to apply in theses cases. The Connecticut legislature has stated that the policy underlying its neglect and termination statutes is, in pertinent part, "[t]o protect children whose health and welfare may be adversely affected through injury and neglect. . . ." General Statutes § 17a-101. This rationale is akin to that of the cases allowing a child to recover for injuries sustained in utero, or, if those injuries result in death, allowing the child's representative to bring wrongful death action. We therefore hold that a petition for neglect or termination of parental rights can be based solely on a mother's prenatal conduct.

* * *

The respondent's final challenge is directed at the trial court's findings that (1) the fetus' passage of meconium was caused by her ingestion of cocaine prior to delivery, (2) Valerie suffered serious physical injury, and (3) Valerie and the respondent had not developed a parent-child relationship and it would not be in Valerie's best interest to allow time for such a relationship to develop. It is axiomatic that "[a] reviewing authority may not substitute its findings for those of the trier of facts." *Wilcox Trucking, Inc. v. Mansour Builders, Inc.* 20 Conn. App. 420, 423, 567 A.2d 1250 (1989), *cert. denied,* 214 Conn. 804, 573 A.2d 318 (1990). "On appeal, we determine only whether in light of the evidence in the whole record, the court's decision was clearly erroneous. We will not retry the facts. *Pandolphe's Auto Parts, Inc. v. Manchester,* 181 Conn. 217, 221-22, 435 A.2d 24 (1980)." *Hart, Nininger & Campbell Associates, Inc. v. Rogers,* 16 Conn. App. 619, 627, 548 A.2d 758 (1988).

The trial court found two grounds for termination. The second ground was based on the court's findings that there was no ongoing parent-child relationship. General Statutes § 45a-717(f)(3). The trial court found that after the birth of Valerie the respondent refused inpatient drug treatment and dropped out of the out-patient program after five sessions when she tested positive for cocaine, did not bond with the child, had psychological problems apart from her chronic drug problems, which resulted in chronic joblessness and homelessness, and did not adhere to the court articulated expectations of drug treatment, regular visitation and adequate housing on which Valerie's return was premised. In finding that it would be detrimental to the best interest of this child to allow further time for the reestablishment of the parent-child relationship, the trial court determined that it was highly probable, due to the drug and psychological problems of the respondent, that to wait a year for a favorable outcome would be clearly and convincingly detrimental to the well being of a fragile infant whose need for permanency is secondary only to her need for adequate physical care. There was overwhelming evidence to substantiate the trial court's finding that there was no ongoing parent-child relationship between Valerie and the respondent and that to allow further time for the establishment of the parent-child relationship would be detrimental to Valerie's best interests. General Statutes § 45a-717(f)(3). The trial court found two grounds for termination when only one ground need be found. General Statutes § 45a-717.

Our review of the record in this case reveals that the challenged findings were not clearly erroneous. We therefore decline to upset the trial court's ruling.

The judgment is affirmed.

Note

For a discussion of how courts in termination of parental rights cases analyze a mother's prenatal conduct, see Chapter 13, Parts A.3-4.

b. Mental Status of Parents

In re Welfare of P.J.K.

369 N.W.2d 286 (Minn. 1985)

YETKA, Justice.

This case comes to this court on a petition for further review of the court of appeals' decision reversing the decision of the Hennepin County Juvenile Court terminating the parental rights of the father. We reverse the court of appeals and reinstate the judgment of the juvenile court.

Minn. Stat. § 260.221 (1984) allows termination of parental rights for any one of a number of grounds. The juvenile court terminated the father's parental rights on [the following] . . . :

> That a parent is palpably unfit to be a party to the parent and child relationship because of a consistent pattern of specific conduct before the child or of specific conditions directly relating to the parent and child relationship either of which are determined by the court to be permanently detrimental to the physical or mental health of the child; . . . .

Minn.Stat. § 260.221, subds 4, 5, 7 (1984). We find that there is adequate evidence to sustain the trial court's finding . . . and we, therefore, reverse the court of appeals.

A brief summary of the facts is required. The father of the two children whose welfare is the subject of this case is mentally retarded with an IQ of 68. Throughout his life, he has shown an inability to hold a job for any length of time. He and the children's mother, who is also mentally retarded, separated in October 1974, and dissolved the marriage in September of 1975.

Their two children are also mentally and emotionally handicapped. P.J.K., who is now 11, is more handicapped than his brother J.L.K., who is now 10. P.J.K. has difficulty walking, dressing, and relieving himself. He is reluctant to talk and far behind his age group in school. J.L.K. is developmentally delayed. Although given to nervousness, facial tics, and speech problems, he is the brighter, more active, and more outgoing of the two. J.L.K. looks after P.J.K. much of the time and often answers for P.J.K. when P.J.K. is spoken to.

After the dissolution, the children were in the custody of their mother. The living conditions were so dismal that the children were removed from the mother's custody, determined dependent, and placed in a shelter. During the whole time that the children were in their mother's custody, the father never visited them or expressed any concern for their living conditions.

After the children were removed, the father petitioned for their custody. A custody study was conducted. It recommended that, as of January 8, 1979, neither parent should have custody, but that the county should retain custody under the dependency and neglect statutes. The author of the study had serious doubts about the father's fitness as a parent:

> [The father], similarly, appears a slow-learning and inadequate person who has, at best, limited knowledge of his children's problems and needs. There is ample indication that if both [P.J.K.] and [J.L.K.] are to grow into healthy, happy, reasonably well-adjusted children, they will need the very best in a home environment, adequate parenting, love, guidance, and supervision, if this is to be accomplished. . . . I am gravely concerned with regard to [the father's] temper, his seeming inability to hold jobs and more importantly, his lack of any real understanding of his children. For these reasons I cannot recommend [the father] as a custodian for his children.

The matter was resolved by a court order on May 11, 1979. The father admitted that the children were dependent. Under that disposition, the father was required to seek individual counseling, attend parenting classes, follow through on any recommendation of a psychological evaluation, meet with a social worker to inform that social worker of his address, and visit with the children under supervision.

The father has done little to follow through with the goals of the 1979 order. Some individual counseling apparently was provided. The father also attended group parenting classes under Dr. Pi Nian Chang, a pediatric psychologist with the University of Minnesota. Dr. Chang recommended that the father stop attending, however, when, early on, it became evident that the father was not benefiting because of his inability to comprehend and discuss the class topics. In a report, Dr. Chang wrote, "However, I do see the need for continuous enrollment in parent training groups so that he will develop more concrete skills." The father attended no other parenting classes.

The father's relationship with the social workers on his case has been turbulent. He believes that he has been persecuted and given the "run-around" in the social work bureaucracy. He has been verbally abusive to both the social workers and to the foster parents of his children. In short, the father blames Hennepin County for keeping his children away from him and refuses to work with them.

Visitation has also been a problem. On the rare occasions when he has visited the children, their reactions have been adverse. Both foster mothers noticed that, after the visits, the children would be hyperactive and upset for several days, rocking and wetting their beds. When the father did not visit the children, they were less agitated, the rocking and bedwetting subsided. The boys hardly ever talked about their father when he was away.

The father's visitation record has been poor. From the May 11, 1979, order until August, 1979, the father visited the boys under supervision. Barbra Jarmuzek, the boys' foster mother at the time, had a number of altercations with the father. He shook his fist at her because she had taken tinker toys with sharp ends away from the boys for fear that they might poke themselves in the eyes. Another time, late in returning the children to the foster home, the father, in an argument with Ms. Jarmuzek, cursed her and created a disturbance in the neighborhood. Because of the father's abusiveness, visitation was suspended until December of 1979.

In December of 1979, Southside Services, Inc., provided a staff member, Lynda Meador, to supervise the father's visits with the children. After about a year of providing supervision, however, Southside could not afford to continue and had to transfer the supervision to Domestic Relations Services. The father would not accept supervised visitation and would not see his children until a year later in December, 1981.

Shortly thereafter, the father disappeared. Social services looked for him, but could not find him. The father's own attorney did not know where he was. It eventually came to light that he had moved to the Iron Range to find work. The father's explanation for why he disappeared without contacting anyone about his whereabouts was that he was so frustrated with the county that he was afraid he might hit someone. No visits were made to the children until December, 1982. In 1983, the father visited his sons in February, March, and October.

Dr. Susan Lund, a clinical psychologist who specializes in "multiple problem children and families," observed the father on a visit with his sons. She found that the children did not speak much about their father and that their feelings were mixed—a combination of a desire to see and a fear of their father. She observed that the father did not understand "basic interactional and parenting principles." He expected too much out of the children and was much too directive with them, causing the boys to be frustrated and fearful of him. It was Dr. Lund's opinion that the boys would be difficult for a parent with normal intelligence and parenting skills to handle. Without a structured, stable environment, the children would be unlikely to develop intellectually and emotionally. Dr. Lund's opinion was that the father could not provide such an environment for the children and that his problems are irreversible, making it unlikely he will ever be able to parent his children. The children's guardian ad litem, Susan Stacy, who has been with the case since the dependency/neglect action began in 1978, also feels the father will never be able to care for his children.

There was some favorable evidence on the father's behalf. Lynda Meador from Southside Services testified. She supervised visitation in 1980. She believed that the father loved his children and felt that the children warmed up to their father after visitation went on for awhile. Carla Lehtinen, the director of Southside Services, also testified to the father's love for his children. He would come to their offices regularly and talk about the boys. She admitted, however, that once the supervision had stopped, the father did not have the inner ability to continue his relationship with his children.

The father himself testified. He denied his abusive behavior towards the social workers and the foster parents, blamed Hennepin County for giving him the "run-around," and claimed he could help his sons. Although currently unemployed and chronically unable to hold a job, he claimed he would find a job to support himself and the boys and that he would find someone to marry to take care of them while he was gone.

[The] children's mother has agreed to terminate her parental rights, provided that the father's rights are similarly terminated. Hennepin County petitioned for termination of the father's parental rights, presumably, to place the children for adoption into a permanent home situation.

The issue on appeal is whether there was clear and convincing evidence to support the trial court's finding that the necessary conditions existed for termination of the father's parental rights. We find that there was.

Termination of parental rights is a very troubling, but sometimes necessary, part of the law. Although parents' right to custody of their children should not be taken from them but for "grave and weighty reasons," the law secures parents' right to custody, "only so long as they shall promptly recognize and discharge their corresponding obligations." *In re HGB,* 306 N.W.2d 821, 825 (Minn.1981). In Minnesota, strict statutory factors must be met before parental rights can be terminated. The trial court must make specific findings that meet the statutory requirements. . . . Although those findings "will not be overturned in a termination case unless 'clearly erroneous,'" this court will "continue to exercise great caution in termination proceedings, finding such action proper only when the evidence clearly mandates such a result in accordance with the statutory grounds." *In re Solomon,* 291 N.W.2d 364, 367 (Minn.1980).

[Subdivision 4] provides for termination if "*specific conditions* directly relating to the parent and child relationship" are found to make the parent "palpably unfit" to parent the child and that that condition is "permanently detrimental to the physical or mental health of the child." Minn.Stat. § 260.221, subd. b(4). . . .

In the context of mental illness, which is analogous to mental retardation in this context, this court interpreted the statute:

> [M]ental illness in and of itself shall not be classified as "other conduct" which will permit termination of parental rights. Rather, in each case, the actual conduct of the parent is to be evaluated to determine his or her fitness to maintain the parental relationship with the child in question so as to not be detrimental to the child.

In re Kidd, 261 N.W.2d 833, 835 (Minn.1978). By analogy then, mental retardation alone is not considered reason enough to terminate parental rights under the old statute.

The "other conduct" language was dropped in a total rewriting and modernization of the statute. The new language appears to us to allow the court to look not just at conduct, but at the actual condition, mental illness or mental retardation, and determine if the parent is unfit. Even under this standard, however, the mere fact of mental retardation or illness alone is insufficient to show that parental rights should be terminated. Rather, the statute requires that the retardation or illness directly relate to parenting and that it be permanently detrimental to the physical or mental health of the child.

In this case, the court found that the father, because of his retardation, lacks the capacity to learn the skills needed to parent and properly care for his sons. Both children are retarded and need special attention. A family of average intelligence and parenting skills would be pressed to care for the boys' needs. The father could not grasp even the most basic parenting skills as taught in Dr. Chang's parenting class. The father had little to do with the boys' rearing, showed no concern for their condition when in their mother's care, and visited only occasionally since then. What appearances the father has made in the children's lives has produced trauma. In addition to her concerns about possible physical abuse, emotional abuse, and neglect, Dr. Lund was convinced the children would "regress or fail to develop to their full level of potential" if placed in their father's care. Since the father's retardation is permanent, Dr. Lund, Susan Stacy, and other professionals involved have little or no hope that the father can ever learn the skills necessary to care for the boys. The only contrary evidence is the father's own testimony and Southside workers who, though testifying to the father's love for the boys, admitted that, without supervision, the father did not have the inner ability to continue his relationship with his children. Thus, the vast weight of evidence seems to show that the father's mental retardation, which is permanent, renders him unable to care even minimally for the needs of his children. Clear and convincing evidence of the father's permanent unfitness detrimental to his children's mental health and development has been presented. Thus, the trial court's findings were not erroneous, and the court of appeals incorrectly reversed the trial court.

* * *

The court of appeals is reversed and the judgment of the trial court is reinstated.

Notes

1. Many jurisdictions allow courts to consider a parent's mental status as a factor in terminating a parent's rights. *See* MISS. CODE ANN. § 93-15-103 (Lexis Supp. 2000) (severe mental deficiencies cause parental behavior which would "make it impossible to return the child"); MONT. CODE ANN. § 41-3-609 (1999) (emotional and mental illnesses may be considered when determining whether the parent's conduct will change); KY. REV. STAT. ANN. § 625.090 (West 2000) (parent's mental status may be considered when determining what is in the child's best interests); *In re Interest of Michael B.,* 604 N.W.2d 405 (Neb. 2000). In *Michael B.,* a mentally deficient mother was accused of physically abusing her children and failing to provide proper care for them. In the termination trial, the state called two expert witnesses to testify that the mother was borderline retarded. The court held that mental deficiency alone is not grounds for the termination of a parent's rights.

Instead, the court stated that the state must prove that the parent's mental deficiency makes the parent unfit to raise his or her child. *See also Egly v. Blackford County Department of Public Welfare,* 592 N.E.2d 1232 (Ind. 1992) (mental status of parent may be a factor but not sole basis for terminating a parent's rights).

The following New Hampshire statute is an example of a statute that allows the state to terminate parental rights if the parent's mental illness or deficiency prevents the child from receiving proper care and protection:

New Hampshire Revised Statutes Annotated
§ 170-C:5 (Lexis 1994)

§ 170-C:5 Grounds for Termination of the Parent-Child Relationship

The petition may be granted where the court finds that one or more of the following conditions exist: . . .

IV. Because of mental deficiency or mental illness, the parent is and will continue to be incapable of giving the child proper parental care and protection for a longer period of time than would be wise or prudent to leave the child in an unstable or impermanent environment. Mental deficiency or mental illness shall be established by the testimony of either 2 licensed psychiatrists or clinical psychologists or one of each acting together.

* * *

Jurisdictions generally require that the State prove by clear and convincing evidence that a parent's mental handicap makes the parent unfit to raise his or her child in order to terminate the parent's rights. *See also* ALA. CODE § 26-18-7(a)(2) (Lexis Supp. 2000) (must prove by clear and convincing evidence that a mother's mental illness or deficiency makes her unable to properly care for children); KAN. STAT. ANN. § 38-1583 (West 2000); *In re M.M.,* 709 N.E.2d 259 (Ill. App. Ct. 1999) (expert testimony provided clear and convincing evidence that mother's mental impairment led to her inability to maintain a clean home and protect her children from her abusive boyfriend). For further discussion of how courts consider a parent's mental status in termination proceedings, see Rosemary Shaw Sackett, *Terminating Parental Rights of the Handicapped*, 25 FAM. L.Q. 235, 265-68 (1991). *See generally* Anne M. Payne, Annotation, *Parental Mental Deficiency as a Factor in Termination of Parental Rights—Modern Status,* 1 A.L.R.5TH 469 (1992); Susan Kerr, *The Application of the Americans with Disabilities Act to the Termination of the Parental Rights of Individuals With Mental Disabilities,* 16 J. CONTEMP. HEALTH L. & POL'Y 387, 402 (2000) (citing Chris Watkins, *Beyond Status: The Americans With Disabilities Act and the Parental Rights of People Labeled Developmentally Disabled or Mentally Retarded*, 83 CAL. L. REV. 1415, 1436 (1995)).

2. Jurisdictions remain unsettled as to whether a mentally deficient parent has the constitutional right to rehabilitative services before his or her parental rights are terminated. In *In re Everett S.,* 403 N.Y.S.2d 802 (App. Div. 1978), a mentally deficient mother argued that the state must prove that it made diligent efforts to "strengthen the parental relationship." The court disagreed and found that a mentally deficient parent has no right to rehabilitative services before his or her parental rights are terminated. *But see In re E.S.*, 213 Cal. Rptr. 2d 690 (Ct. App. 1985) (due process requires that services as the "least detrimental alternative" be provided before a parent's rights are terminated). In Montana, treatment plans are not required if a court finds "two medical doctors or clinical psychologists submit testimony that the parent cannot assume the role of a parent." MONT. CODE ANN. § 41-3-609(4)(b) (1999).

3. Whether a parent is entitled to reunification services also varies among states. The following Arizona statute creates a presumption that a mentally deficient parent is not entitled to reunification services when certain factors are met:

Arizona Revised Statutes Annotated
§ 8-846(C) (West 1999)

§ 8-846. Services provided to the child and family

(C) A presumption exists that reunification services should not be provided if the court finds by clear and convincing evidence that any of the following circumstances exists:

2. The parent or guardian is suffering from a mental illness or mental deficiency of such magnitude that it renders the parent or guardian incapable of benefitting from the reunification services. This finding shall be based on competent evidence from a psychologist or physician that establishes that, even with the provision of reunification services, the parent or guardian is unlikely to be capable of adequately caring for the child within twelve months after the date of the disposition order.

* * *

For a discussion of whether states have an obligation to provide mentally deficient parents with reunification services before terminating their parental rights, see Krista A. Gallager, Note, *Parents in Distress: A State's Duty to Provide Reunification Services to Mentally Ill Parents,* 38 FAM. & CONCILIATION CTS. REV. 234, 244-51 (2000).

Questions

1. How should courts weigh a mentally deficient parent's constitutional right to rear a child with the state's interest in protecting the child from harm? What constitutional issues arise when the state seeks to terminate a mentally deficient parent's rights?

2. What arguments support or refute the proposition that parents with mental deficiencies should receive rehabilitative and reunification services? What additional procedural protections might the state afford such parents in termination proceedings?

c. Incarceration of Parent

Florida Statutes Annotated
§ 39.806(1)(d) (West Supp. 2001)

§ 39.806. Grounds for termination of parental rights.—

(1) The department, the guardian ad litem, a licensed child-placing agency, or any person who has knowledge of the facts alleged or who is informed of said facts and believes that they are true, may petition for the termination of parental rights under any of the following circumstances:

(d) When the parent of a child is incarcerated in a state or federal correctional institution and either:

1. The period of time for which the parent is expected to be incarcerated will constitute a substantial portion of the period of time before the child will attain the age of 18 years;

2. The incarcerated parent has been determined by the court to be a violent career criminal as defined in § 775.084, a habitual violent felony offender as defined in § 775.084, or a sexual predator as defined in § 775.21; has been convicted of first degree or second degree murder in violation of § 782.04 or a sexual battery that constitutes a capital, life, or first degree felony violation of § 794.011; or has been convicted of an offense in another jurisdiction which is substantially similar to one of the offenses listed in this paragraph. . . . ; or

3. The court determines by clear and convincing evidence that continuing the parental relationship with the incarcerated parent would be harmful to the child and, for this reason, that termination of the parental rights of the incarcerated parent is in the best interest of the child.

In the Matter of the Adoption of C.A.W.
683 A.2d 911 (Pa. Super. Ct. 1996)

E.W. ("Father"), the appellant herein, has a long history of criminal involvement beginning in 1984. In 1986, he was sentenced to 11½ to 23 months' incarceration in the Erie County Prison for corruption of minors. In early 1988, K.B.W. ("Mother") began living with Father. Mother and Father were married on March 31, 1989. C.A.W., born January 30, 1989, and A.A.W., born January 24, 1990, (sometimes referred to herein as "the Children") are the children of Mother and Father and are the subjects of this involuntary termination proceeding.

When OCY began contact with the family in May 1993, Father was in the penitentiary, having been convicted in 1992 of kidnapping, felonious restraint, rape, statutory rape, involuntary deviate sexual intercourse, indecent assault, terroristic threats, attempted involuntary deviate sexual intercourse, and aggravated indecent assault. These convictions all related to Father's criminal conduct involving a ten-year-old girl. His aggregate sentence on these convictions, computed from May 24, 1992, is 32 to 72 years' imprisonment at the State Correctional Institution at Pittsburgh. Prior to his arrest and incarceration on May 23, 1992, Father had been in the State Correctional Institution at

Pittsburgh from August 7, 1989 to August 7, 1990 and at the State Correctional Institution at Mercer from November 1990 until August 1991. . . .

As a result of OCY's initial investigations and continuing reports of child abuse, the court of common please issued an order on December 20, 1993, requiring that all four of the children be medically evaluated. As a result of that evaluation, C.A.W. and A.A. W. were placed in foster care following a detention hearing on December 22, 1993. . . . Adjudication proceedings on the Children were held before the Master in January 1994; Father was not present but was represented by counsel. . . . On March 3, 1994, the Children were adjudicated dependent.

A dispositional hearing was held before the Juvenile Court on April 25, 1994. Again, Father was not present but was represented by counsel. . . .

At the conclusion of the dispositional hearing, the Juvenile Court found that all reasonable efforts had been made to prevent placement, and that the Children's continuation in their home would be contrary to their welfare. It thus ordered that the Children be placed under the care and supervision of OCY for an indefinite period of time. It was further ordered that the Children be placed in an OCY foster home for a period not to exceed the next six month review hearing.

* * *

. . . On March 2, 1995, an order was entered scheduling a hearing for April 3, 1995, on OCY's petition seeking the involuntary termination of Father's parental rights. The . . . [f]ather was transported to, attended, and testified at this hearing. On May 19, 1995, the Honorable John A. Bozza, P.J., made final the court's earlier order of April 11, 1995, which had granted, preliminarily, the petition for termination of Father's parental rights. Father now appeals.

Father advances a single issue for our consideration in his Statement of the Questions Involved:

A. Whether the termination of appellant's parental rights was against the weight of the evidence?

The termination decree was issued by the court of common pleas pursuant to 23 Pa. C.S. § 2511(a)(2), which provides:

> Grounds for involuntary termination
>
> (a) General rule.—The rights of a parent in regard to a child may be terminated after a petition filed on any of the following grounds:
>
> (2) The repeated and continued incapacity, abuse, neglect or refusal of the parent has caused the child to be without essential parental care, control or subsistence necessary for his physical or mental well-being and the conditions and causes of the incapacity, abuse, neglect or refusal cannot or will not be remedied by the parent.
>
> (b) Other considerations.—The court in terminating the rights of the parent shall give primary consideration to the needs and welfare of the child. The rights of a parent shall not be terminated solely on the basis of environmental factors such as inadequate housing, furnishings, income, clothing and medical care if found to be beyond the control of the parent. . . .

* * *

We turn now to the merits of Father's appeal. At the hearing on involuntary termination, the Children's caseworker testified to contacts she had with Father between December 1993 and November 1994. Father had sent numerous letters to the caseworker to be directed to Father's estranged wife, Mother. N.T., *supra,* at 32. One or two letters were directed to the caseworker regarding the Children and the upcoming hearing. Father sent the Children, in care of the caseworker, a check for $725 in May 1994 and a check for $5.00 in July 1994. *Id.* at 33. Both of these checks were sent by Father subsequent to the dispositional hearing on April 25, 1994, at which he had been represented by counsel. The checks were returned by the caseworker to Father, uncashed. The caseworker also testified to gifts sent to the Children by Father: magazines such as Sesame Street and American Girl, valentine cards in 1995, birthday cards in 1995, and one package containing a shirt and a small change purse. . [sic]

Father contends that he has done what he could for his children based upon his circumstances. He argues that his sending of gifts and letters to the Children, coupled with his attempts to send cash, demonstrates that he has never intended to relinquish his parental rights to his daughters. He submits that he has pursued the only avenues available to him. This argument, however, misses the mark. Were we called upon to consider whether Father had evidenced a settled purpose of relinquishing his parental claim to a child or had refused to perform his parental duties under Section 2511(a)(1) of the Adoption Act, his actions in sending gifts and writing letters would carry more weight. Here, however, the termination of parental rights is based upon the alleged continued incapacity of the parent that has caused the child to be without the essential parental care necessary for the child's physical or mental well-being, where that incapacity cannot or will not be remedied by the parent.

We focus, therefore, on those factors which relate to Father's alleged incapacity in determining whether the decree is supported by competent evidence. We recognize that, where the issue is not incapacity but abandonment, a parent's absence and/or failure to support due to incarceration is not conclusive. *In re Adoption of McCray*, 460 Pa. 210, 216, 331 A.2d 652, 655 (1975). Moreover, where a father, though imprisoned for life upon conviction of murder in connection with the child's mother, had made consistent efforts with the resources available to him to take and maintain a place of importance in the child's life, termination would not be warranted under Section 2511(a)(1) (abandonment). *In re Adoption of M.J.H.,* 348 Pa. Super. 65, 76, 501 A.2d 648, 651-54 (1985).

* * *

As we indicated above, the burden of proof is upon the Erie County OCY to establish by clear and convincing evidence the present and continued incapacity of Father which has caused the Children to be without the essential parental care necessary for the Children's physical or mental well-being and the condition of the incapacity cannot be remedied. *In re E.M., supra.* We conclude that this burden has been met. . . . Mother has already voluntarily relinquished her parental rights, leaving the Children without essential parental care. Since the birth of C.A.W. on January 30, 1989, Father has been out of prison only from February 1, 1989, to August 7, 1989, from August 7, 1990, to November

1990, and from August 7, 1991 to Mary 23, 1992, an aggregate period of less than nineteen months. His latest conviction has been affirmed by this Court, *Commonwealth v. [E.J.W., Jr.],* 434 Pa. Super. 670, 640 A.2d 476 (1994) (table), as has his appeal from an order denying relief under the Post Conviction Relief Act. *Commonwealth v. [E.J.W., Jr.],* 434 Pa. super. 670, 663 A.2d 256 (1995) (table). No visitation with the Children has been sought by Father and, given his criminal record, including a 1986 conviction for corruption of minors and his present incarceration on numerous sex offenses against a ten-year-old child, it is unlikely that such a petition would be granted. Father will not be eligible for parole until May 2024, when he will be fifty-six years old and the Children will be thirty-five and thirty-four, respectively. As Judge Spaeth observed in *In re Adoption of M.J.H., supra,* at 80, 501 A.2d at 656, a child's life does not come to a standstill while the child's father serves an extended term in prison. Father's minimum term of thirty-two years' incarceration, of which twenty-eight remain to be served, when coupled with the nature of the crimes for which he has been twice incarcerated and the other circumstances of this case, makes him incapable of providing the Children with what they need on a day-to-day basis. This incapacity cannot and will not be remedied. *Id.*

* * *

From the evidence established in the hearing on termination, Father has no possibility of resuming contact with his children other than in a prison setting at any time during the Children's formative years. The reasons for his incarceration relate directly to abuses visited by Father upon a ten-year-old child, and the major evidence of any attempts by Father to manifest concern for the Children occurred after the filing of a petition for termination of parental rights. Moreover, the expert testimony presented supports a finding that Father has a present and continuing incapacity to provide essential care, control or subsistence necessary for the Children's physical or mental well-being. The requirements of Section 2511(a)(2) have been met.

* * *

On the question of the best interests of the Children, OCY presented the testimony of Dr. Mary Anne Albaugh, board certified in both general and child psychiatry, with respect to the needs and status of A.A.W. Dr. Albaugh first came in contact with A.A.W. on April 5, 1994. N.T., *supra,* at 15. The Child had entered the Sarah Reed early intervention preschool program where Dr. Albaugh was a consultant, *id.* at 6. Dr. Albaugh testified to a number of difficulties which she observed in A.A.W. upon her first psychiatric evaluation. . . .

A.A.W.'s course of treatment was quite intensive. *Id.* at 10. It included numerous meetings, extensive collaborative work including treatment meetings, play therapy, and the enlistment of mobile therapy into a foster care home. It also included the Sarah Reed preschool program itself and the use of psychotropic medications. When asked by counsel for OCY as to what kind of environment A.A.W. was going to need in the future, Dr. Albaugh testified as follows:

> She's going to need a very supportive, very nurturing, very consistent, an engaged, active family that's able to provide stability. Lots of support with transitions. Even from going from schooling to home kinds of transititons, which have been difficult with just a change in a bus driver. They need to be very consistent with a sense of permanency for her. And be willing to tolerate her tremendous difficulties with her lack of trust and difficulties in attachment.

* * *

A.A.W. needs a very supportive, very consistent, engaged, and active family that is able to provide stability. She will need an environment which manifests a sense of permanency given her reactive attachment disorder of childhood. Based upon the facts established through the hearing concerning father's past conduct and present situation, father's insertion into A.A.W.'s life would cause A.A.W. to again experience regressive symptoms, become quite anxious, and have a great deal of difficulty in understanding and relating to others. The record supports the conclusion that any contact between father and A.A.W. would be traumatizing.

* * *

The neglect and abuse which the Children received led to their adjudication as dependent in early 1994. Since that adjudication, the Children have been under the custody of OCY and have been receiving care and treatment for their disorders with a guarded prognosis. Both children will require intensive nurturing and uninterrupted support and care if their best interests are to be advanced. C.A.W. is now seven years old and A.A.W. is now six. Mother has already relinquished her parental rights. We conclude that if the Children are to have any opportunity to lead a normal life in a normal environment, the order of Judge Bozza that terminated father's parental rights must be affirmed. We find no error.

Order AFFIRMED.

Notes

1. The number of incarcerated parents has grown significantly since 1991 according to a 1999 Survey of Inmates in State and Federal Correctional Facilities. CHRISTOPHER J. MUMOLA, U.S. DEP'T OF JUST., INCARCERATED PARENTS AND THEIR CHILDREN (2000). In 1999, State and Federal prisons contained approximately 721,500 parents compared to 425,000 in 1991. A significant majority (76%) of incarcerated parents are divorced, separated from a spouse, or have never been married. Of those parents incarcerated in either state or federal prisons, many were sentenced for a violent offense (44%) and/or a drug offense (67%), most on average expected to serve 80 to 103 months in prison, most reported a prior conviction (75%), and a majority were imprisoned over 100 miles from their last residence (60%). Nearly 1 in 7 incarcerated parents also reported some form of mental illness.

Approximately 1,498,800 children, or over 2% of the country's minor children, have at least one parent in prison. According to the 1999 survey, most incarcerated parents maintain some sort of contact with their children (State - 80%; Federal - 93%). For further information concerning the demographics and familial status of incarcerated parents, see Mumola, *supra.*

2. A court may terminate a parent's rights based upon his or her incarcerated status as clear and convincing evidence of abandonment. *See, e.g., In re Matthew YY,* 710 N.Y.S.2d 460 (App. Div. 2000). In *Matthew YY,* the court stated "there must be clear and convincing evidence that, for a period of six months prior to the filing of the abandonment petition, the parent failed to visit or communicate with the children and was not prevented or discouraged from doing so by the authorized agency." The court found that the incarcerated father failed to maintain direct contact with his children and "failed to articulate specific plans for obtaining employment or providing for the children's housing or education upon his release from prison." *See also In re A.B.M.*, 17 S.W.3d 912 (Mo. Ct. App. 2000) (clear and convincing evidence demonstrated that incarcerated father abandoned children by failing to provide financial support and by causing irreparable harm to the family unit by killing children's mother); *Matter of Lakeside Family and Children's Services on Behalf of Angel Takima C.,* 662 N.Y.S.2d 74 (App. Div. 1997) (where incarcerated father failed to contact child six months prior to the filing of termination petition); *In re Matter of the Adoption of Craven M.,* 915 P.2d 720 (Idaho 1996) (where incarcerated father had extensive criminal background, abused drugs, and failed to financially or emotionally support child). In New York, courts do not allow parents to use their incarcerated status as a defense against an abandonment claim. *See* Karen Rothschild Cavanaugh & Daniel Pollack, *Child Support Obligations of Incarcerated Parents,* 7 CORNELL J.L. & PUB. POL'Y 531, 534 n.14 (1998); *Matter of Ariel C.,* 669 N.Y.S.2d 1006 (App. Div. 1998), *leave to appeal denied*, 92 N.Y.2d 801 (N.Y. 1998).

A court may also terminate an incarcerated parent's rights by determining that the parent is unfit to raise his or her child. *See, e.g., In Interest of S.E.,* 695 N.E.2d 1367 (Ill. App. Ct. 1998), *appeal denied*, 705 N.E.2d 437 (Ill. 1998). In *S.E.,* the court stated that an incarcerated parent may be declared unfit and lose his or her parental rights if he or she fails to make reasonable progress in regaining custody of a neglected or abused child. The court determined that the incarcerated father's heavy drug use, gang involvement, and extensive criminal history made the father unfit to raise his child and thereby terminated his parental rights. *See also Wilson v. Georgia Dept. of Human Resources*, 318 S.E.2d 229 (Ga. Ct. App. 1984) (father deemed unfit to raise his child because of his repeated incarceration); *In re Interest of Kalie W.,* 601 N.W.2d 753 (Neb. 1999) (incarcerated father unfit because of his violent assault on his wife as well as his history of violent criminal behavior); *In Interest of K.M.H.,* 433 S.E.2d 117 (Ga. Ct. App. 1993) (where incarcerated father was unable to develop a "meaningful relationship" with his child because of his continual incarcerations). A parent's incarcerated status, however, does not necessarily make the parent unfit to raise his or her child. *See In Interest of R.A.,* 486 S.E.2d 363 (Ga. Ct. App. 1997). For a general discussion of a parent's incarcerated status as it pertains to abandonment and unfitness, see Cavanaugh, *supra*; Gregory D. Sarno, Annotation, *Parent's Involuntary Confinement, or Failure to Care for Child as Result Thereof, As Evincing Neglect, Unfitness, or the Like in Dependency or Divestiture Proceeding,* 79 A.L.R.3D 417 (1977).

3. Statutes generally permit courts to terminate an incarcerated parent's rights based on: (1) the duration of the incarceration (*see, e.g.,* FLA. STAT. ANN. § 39.809 (West Supp. 2001); IOWA CODE ANN. § 232.116 (West 2000)), (2) the nature of the crime (*see, e.g.,* NEV. REV. STAT. ANN. § 128.106 (1999); ALA. CODE 1975 § 26-18-7 (Lexis Supp. 2000); IND. CODE ANN. § 31-35-3-4 (Lexis 1997)), (3) the parent's incarcerated status (*see, e.g.,* MO. ANN. STAT. § 211.447 (West Supp. 2001)), or (4) an analysis of various aspects of the family relationship (*see In Interest of Carmen G.,* 1998 WL 46228 (Conn. Super. Ct. Jan. 26, 1998)). *See* Steven Fleischer, Note, *Termination of Parental Rights: An Additional Sentence for Incarcerated Parents,* 29 SETON HALL L. REV. 312 (1998). In *In Interest of Carmen G.,* the court took into consideration the following factors in determining whether to terminate parental rights of an incarcerated parent:

> 1) The timeliness, nature and extent of services offered. . . .
>
> 2) Whether DFC has made reasonable efforts to reunite the family pursuant to the Adoption Assistance and Child Welfare Act of 1980. . . .
>
> 3) The terms of applicable orders entered into and agreed to by any individual or agency and the extent of fulfillment of those obligations, etc. . . .
>
> 4) The feelings and emotional ties of the child with respect to the parents and foster parents, etc. . . .
>
> 5) As to the age of the child. . . . Our Supreme Court has long recognized the deleterious effect of prolonged temporary care of abused and neglected children. *In re Juvenile Appeal (84-CD)*, 189 Conn. 276, 455 A.2d 1313 (1983). . . .
>
> 6) The efforts the parents have made to adjust their circumstances or conditions. . . .
>
> 7) The court finds that there has been nothing to prevent the parents from maintaining a meaningful relationship with the child.

For a survey of how each state addresses the issue of what degree a parent's incarceration factors into a termination decision, see Philip J. Prygoski, *When a Hearing is Not a Hearing: Irrebuttable Presumptions and Termination of Parental Rights Based on Status,* 44 U. PITT. L. REV. 879 (1983).

4. A court is more likely to terminate an incarcerated parent's rights than the rights of a non-incarcerated parent. *See* Nicole S. Mauskopf, Note, *Reaching Beyond the Bars: An Analysis of Prison Nurseries,* 5 CARDOZO WOMEN'S L.J. 101, 114 (1998). For a discussion of the rights of an incarcerated mother to retain custody of her infant while still serving a sentence in prison, see Annotation, *Right of Incarcerated Mother to Retain Custody of Infant in Penal Institution,* 14 A.L.R.4TH 748 (1982). Some critics argue that incarcerated fathers receive family services inferior to those received by incarcerated mothers, and are thus more likely to have parental rights terminated than an incarcerated mother. *See generally* Elise Zealand, *Protecting the Ties That Bind From Behind Bars: A Call for Equal Oppor-*

tunities for Incarcerated Fathers and Their Children to Maintain the Parent-Child Relationship, 31 COLUM. J.L. & SOC. PROBS. 247 (1998).

Questions

1. What factors should a court consider when a TPR petition is based upon the parent's incarceration?

2. How might an attorney attack a statute that allows a parent's incarceration status to be the sole ground for termination of his or her parental rights?

d. Terminal Illness of Parent

Micah Alyn R.

504 S.E.2d 635 (W. Va. 1998)

* * *

I.

. . . [O]n July 11, 1996 . . . Ada R. placed her son in foster care by filing a voluntary placement agreement. At that time, Ada R. had been diagnosed with AIDS, and Micah, who was two and a half years old, was HIV positive. Ada R. sought foster care for Micah due to both her and her child's severe illnesses. Although Micah was placed in the care of the Department of Health and Human Resources (hereinafter "Department"), Ada R. visited her son regularly.

On September 26, 1996, the Department filed a petition for review of the voluntary placement in the Circuit Court of Raleigh County. A hearing was held on September 27, 1996, at which time appellant and the Department agreed to continue the placement and visitation. On March 25, 1997, the Department filed a supplemental petition seeking to have the parental rights of Micah's father, Hansel R., terminated. The petition indicated that Ada R. wanted Micah to be adopted. However, subsequently, Ada R. changed her mind and decided to pursue full custody.

Hansel R.['s] . . . parental rights were terminated on July 19, 1997. That same day, the Department sought termination of Ada R.'s parental rights. Kim Peck, the social services case worker, testified that she believed Ada R. was unable to physically take care of Micah because of her mental and physical condition. She stated that Ada R. was experiencing mental stress and anxiety and did not have the patience to take care of the child's needs. Mrs. Peck further testified that Ada R. had told her that she had shaken and slapped Micah and put her hands around his throat. Mrs. Peck was also concerned that Ada R. was not capable of remembering to give Micah the several different medications he was taking for his illness . . . [because] at times Ada R. had forgotten to give Micah his medication and that she once gave him the wrong dosage.

JoAnn Gibson, case manager for . . . the agency providing social services to Ada R. in connection with the voluntary placement, testified that on one occasion she observed red marks on Micah's arms and legs. . . . Micah was crying, and he told her that his mother had hit him. Ada R. later admitted that she had hit Micah on the leg with a ruler. Ms. Gibson also testified that once, she had witnessed Ada R. slamming Micah down on the bed when she was changing his diaper. However, Ms. Gibson indicated that Ada R.'s attitude towards Micah had improved dramatically within the past three weeks. . . .

Nancy Jones, a support specialist . . . testified that Ada R. was showing much more patience with Micah. . . . Micah never exhibited any actions suggesting that he was afraid of his mother. . . . [S]he only had to remind Ada R. once during the last three months to give Micah his medication.

Ada R. testified that she was feeling much stronger and was having less medical complications with her illness. She said that she loved her son very much and wanted him returned to her. Ada R.'s sister testified that she felt that Ada R. was capable of taking care of Micah and that if she needed help, her family was available.

Based on the foregoing testimony, the judge deferred making a ruling until the guardian ad litem had time to submit a recommendation. On June 25, 1997, the guardian ad litem filed a recommendation stating that it was in the best interests of the child to have any decision as to termination of parental rights held in abeyance. . . . [T]he guardian ad litem explained that he did not feel that the case was mature for a decision given the nature of Ada R.'s illness. The guardian ad litem recommended that Micah remain in foster care and that Ada R. be granted increased and liberal visitation.

In October 1997, Ada R. requested that the circuit court hold a supplemental termination hearing. In response, the Department filed a court summary. . . . The report indicated that Ada R. had become verbally aggressive and was alienating the people who were working with her. The Department was also aware that Ada R. had attended some support group meetings where she stated that Micah had been taken away from her for no reason. The report further indicated that Ada R. continues to tire easily, sleeps a lot, and complains of dizziness. The Department did not believe that Ada R. was capable of administering Micah's medication properly or providing his meals. Thus, the Department recommended that Ada R.'s parental rights be terminated, but that she be granted post-termination visitation.

The supplemental termination hearing was held on October 14, 1997. Following additional testimony by Ms. Peck and Ada R., the guardian ad litem recommended termination of Ada R.'s parental rights. As reflected in the final order, Ada R.'s parental rights were terminated, but she was afforded post-termination visitation of two hours per week.

II

* * *

As her first assignment of error, Ada R. contends that the evidence of abuse is so weak that it does not meet the definition of abuse as set forth in the statute, especially considering that Micah was never removed from her home. Ada R. does admit to striking Micah with a ruler once and shaking him, but she states that these incidents were minimal and occurred at a time when she was under a great deal of stress. She further contends that there is no evidence that she neglected her son. At the time of the termination hearings, she had been properly administering Micah's medication and had the support of her family to help with his care.

W. Va. Code 49-1-3(a)(1) (1994) defines an "abused child" as a child who is harmed or threatened by "[a] parent, guardian or custodian who knowingly or intentionally inflicts, attempts to inflict or knowingly allows another person to inflict, physical injury or mental or emotional injury, upon the child or another child in the home[.]" A "neglected child" is defined by W. Va. Code 49-1-3(g)(1)(A) as a child "[w]hose physical or mental health is harmed or threatened by a present refusal, failure or inability of the child's parent, guardian or custodian to supply the child with the necessary food, clothing, shelter, supervision, medical care or education, when such refusal, failure or inability is not due primarily to a lack of financial means on the part of the parent, guardian or custodian[.]"

The evidence in the record shows that Ada R. has experienced difficulties in properly administering Micah's medications which are crucial to his health. . . . In addition, Ada R. has admitted to striking her child with a ruler and slapping and shaking him on other occasions. These incidents clearly fit within the statutory definitions of abuse and neglect. Therefore, the circuit court did not err in finding Micah was an abused and neglected child.

Ada R. next contends that the circuit court erred in terminating her parental rights. In this regard, she argues the evidence did not support the circuit court's finding that there was no reasonable likelihood that the conditions of abuse and neglect could be corrected in the future. She asserts that even with the current knowledge about AIDS, it is difficult to project the progression of the disease on an individual basis. She further asserts that the evidence shows that she has become stronger and is under less stress indicating that any such conditions of abuse or neglect could be corrected.

W. Va. Code 49-6-5 (1996) governs the dispositional phase of abuse and neglect proceedings. Several dispositional alternatives are set forth in the statute with precedence given to the least restrictive alternative appropriate under the circumstances. With respect to these statutory provisions, we have held that:

> As a general rule the least restrictive alternative regarding parental rights to custody of a child under W. Va. Code, 49-6-5 [1977] will be employed; however, courts are not required to exhaust every speculative possibility of parental improvement before terminating parental rights where it appears that the welfare of the child will be seriously threatened, and this is particularly applicable to children under the age of three years old who are more susceptible to illness, need consistent close interaction with fully committed adults, and are likely to have emotional and physical development retarded by numerous placements.

Syl. pt. 1, *In re R.J.M.*, [164] W. Va. [496], 266 S.E.2d 114 (1980).

* * *

. . . We have further held that: Termination of parental rights, the most drastic remedy under the statutory provision covering the disposition for neglected children, W. Va. Code, 49-6-5 [1977] may be employed without the use of intervening less restrictive alternatives when it is found that there is no reasonable likelihood under W.Va.Code, 49-6-5(b) [1977] that conditions of neglect or abuse can be substantially corrected. . . . *In re R.J.M.*, 164 W. Va. 496, 266 S.E.2d 114 (1980). . . .

W. Va. Code 49-6-5(b) defines "no reasonable likelihood that the conditions of abuse and neglect can be substantially corrected" as "based upon the evidence before the court, the abusing adult or adults have demonstrated an inadequate capacity to solve the problems of abuse and neglect, on their own or with help." . . . [S]uch conditions are deemed to exist in certain circumstances. For instance, if the abusing parent willfully refused or is presently unwilling to cooperate in the development of a family case plan, a finding of no reasonable likelihood that the conditions of neglect or abuse can be substantially corrected" under the statute is warranted. Likewise, the same finding is appropriate when the abusing parent has repeatedly or seriously injured the child physically or emotionally. Arguably, both of these circumstances exist in the case sub judice. However, it appears that the principal reason that the circuit court terminated Ada R.'s parental rights is the tragic fact that she is suffering from a terminal illness.

The evidence in the record indicates that although Ada R.'s health and emotional state did improve somewhat after she initially placed Micah in foster care, by the time the supplemental termination hearing was held, her health had once again declined. She was tiring easily, sleeping a lot, complaining of dizziness, and suffering from occasional memory loss. Ms. Peck indicated that Ada R. was no longer capable of giving Micah his medication as prescribed or preparing his meals as needed. . . . Given this evidence, the circuit court did not err in finding that there was no reasonable likelihood that the conditions of abuse and neglect could be substantially corrected in the future. However, we are troubled by the circuit court's conclusion that termination of Ada R.'s parental rights was warranted.

This case illustrates the horrible crisis situation confronting many single custodial parents who are suffering from AIDS or some other terminal disease. Sadly, these parents must find someone to take care of their children once they are no longer able to do so. Unfortunately traditional guardianship law presents only two choices. In order to formally grant another person parental authority while the parent is still living, the parent must relinquish his or her own authority. Testamentary guardianship, the second option, only becomes effective upon the parent's death.

Several states have begun to offer a third alternative by adopting standby guardianship statutes. Generally, standby guardianship statutes allow parents who are at a substantial risk of becoming ill or disabled within a limited time period to select a "standby guardian" to take care of their children at the point when they become too ill or disabled to care for them. The parent does not relinquish any of his or her authority, but instead shares it with the standby guardian. Additionally, the parent may end the standby guardian's authority when he or she chooses to do so.

If the opportunity to choose a "standby guardian" had been available to Ada R., she might well have taken advantage of it. . . .

* * *

While we certainly do not condone or ignore the physical abuse that Ada R. directed toward Micah and believe that the institution of abuse and neglect proceedings was proper, we find that the circumstances in this case simply do not warrant termination of parental rights. Through no fault of her own, Ada R. has been victimized by a disease which is stealing her life and seriously threatening that of her son. Although she is no longer able to take care of her son or provide for his needs, it is quite evident that Ada R. loves her son very much. In fact, the parental bond that Ada R. shares with her son may now be her only source of comfort.

What is done in this case regarding parental right has the potential to be very far reaching. If the spread and growth of the AIDS virus remains unchecked, it will eventually touch all families, and then every family will have an Ada or a Micah. Of course, even absent AIDS, the same impossible dilemma is faced by some single parents who become profoundly disabled or who are slowly dying from cancer or other protracted terminal diseases. Would the law countenance terminating the parental rights of a parent dyng from lung cancer or breast cancer, for example? We think not.

While we believe that termination of parental rights is not appropriate in this instance, the health, safety, and welfare of the child must continue to be our primary concern. . . . As discussed previously, the evidence in this case clearly indicates that Ada R. is unable to take care of Micah. He needs a stable home to provide him the special care that is required because of his medical condition. However, the evidence also indicates that there is a close and significant emotional bond between this parent and child. We refuse to compound the tragedy in this case further by forever severing this parent-child relationship.

However, we must also consider Micah's current placement. He is presently in a good home with foster parents who are providing him with love, care, support, and a nurturing environment in addition to attending to his medical needs. The foster parents' desire to adopt Micah clearly shows that they have established a strong emotional bond with him.

* * *

Obviously, these foster parents need assurances that the adoption will be allowed to proceed in the future because they have made a substantial investment of emotional support and time.

W. Va. Code 49-1-14 (1995) does offer some protection for these foster parents. The statute provides:

> When a child has been placed in a foster care arrangement for a period in excess of eighteen consecutive months and the state department determines that the placement is a fit and proper place for the child to reside, the foster care arrangement may not be terminated unless such termination is in the best interest of the child and:

> (1) The foster care arrangement is terminated pursuant to subsection (a) of this section;
>
> (2) The foster care arrangement is terminated due to the child being returned to his or her parent or parents;
>
> (3) The foster care arrangement is terminated due to the child being united or reunited with a sibling or siblings;
>
> (4) The foster parent or parents agree to the termination in writing;
>
> (5) The foster care arrangement is terminated at the written request of a foster child who has attained the age of fourteen; or
>
> (6) A circuit court orders the termination upon a finding that the state department has developed a more suitable long-term placement for the child upon hearing evidence in a proceeding brought by the department seeking removal and transfer.

W. Va. Code 49-1-14(b). Although the record is unclear as to exactly how long Micah has been residing with the foster parents who desire to adopt him, it appears that this statute will soon provide some assurances for them. Certainly, Micah's current placement is in his best interest.

Therefore, we hold that when a parent is unable to properly care for a child due to the parent's terminal illness, so that conditions which would constitute neglect of the child occur and continue to be threatened, termination of parental rights, without consent, is contrary to public policy, even though there is no reasonable likelihood that the conditions of neglect will be substantially corrected in the future. In such circumstances, a circuit court should ordinarily postpone or defer any decision on termination of parental rights. However, such deference on the parental rights termination issue does not require a circuit court to postpone or defer decisions on custody or other issues properly before the court. In fact, efforts towards locating prospective adoptive parents shall be made so long as every measure is taken to foster and maintain the bond and ongoing relationship between the parent and child.

Accordingly, for the reasons set forth above, the final order of the circuit court is reversed and this case is remanded to the circuit court. On remand, the circuit court shall develop a visitation plan workable for all parties to permit a continued relationship between Micah and his mother. Furthermore, the circuit court shall develop a permanency plan which will provide additional protection for Micah's foster parents by ensuring that they become the adoptive parents at the appropriate time.

Reversed and remanded.

Notes

1. Whether the court should terminate the parental rights of a mother who is infected with the HIV virus or has developed AIDS is an issue of growing concern. Current statistics show that a majority of HIV-positive mothers are single parents. *See* Deborah Weimer, *Implementation of Standby Guardianship; Respect for Family Autonomy*, 100 DICK. L. REV. 65, 91 (1995). Furthermore, a greater number of healthy babies are orphaned when their mother dies from AIDS, as medication becomes available to prevent babies from becoming infected by the HIV virus. *See* Lenore M. Molee, *The Ultimate Demonstration of Love for a Child: Choosing a Standby Guardian[;] New Jersey Standby Guardianship Act*, 22 SETON HALL LEGIS. J. 475, 579 (1998). Courts must consider the constitutional rights of the infected mother and the child's best interests when determining whether to terminate the mother's rights. *See* ELIZABETH B. COOPER, AIDS AGENDA: EMERGING ISSUE IN CIVIL RIGHTS 74-81 (Nan D. Hunter & William B. Rubenstein eds., 1992). When considering the mother's rights and interests, the court is faced with several problems. First, the mother likely will experience good and bad health swings that might prevent her from providing proper care for the child only part of the time. In addition, it is often impossible for the court to determine how long a mother stricken with AIDS will live. The courts must also, however, consider the potential emotional harm the child might experience watching the mother suffer and eventually die. *See id.* at 75-76.

In determining whether to terminate the mother's rights, courts often consider the following four factors developed by the California Supreme Court in *In re Carney,* 598 P.2d 36 (1979):

1. the parent's actual and potential physical capabilities;
2. how the parent has adapted to his or her disability and manages its problems;
3. how other members of the household have adjusted;
4. any special contributions the parent makes to the family despite, or perhaps because of, his or her ability.

COOPER, *supra*, at 74.

2. Terminally ill parents may take various measures to influence who will have custody over a child upon the parents' death. *See* Kelly C. Rozmus, *Representing Families Affected by HIV/AIDS: How the Proposed Federal Standby Guardianship Act Facilitates Future Planning in the Best Interests of the Child and Family*, 6 AM. U. J. GENDER & L. 299, 303-08 (1998). Terminally ill parents may designate in their wills who shall have custody of their children. Courts, however, may decide not to honor the deceased parent's stated intention if the court determines that such intention does not serve the child's best interests. Terminally ill parents may also under guardianship law transfer their legal custody rights to another person. If a terminally ill parent chooses to do this, the parent may not be able to regain his or her parental rights in the future, should his or her health improve. Another option for terminally ill parents is placing their child in foster care. Foster care, however, is considered a short-term solution. Furthermore, when a child is placed in foster care, he or she is likely to develop emotional ties to the foster parent. If the terminally ill parent dies, the emotional bond with the foster parents may not be sufficient to overcome a relative's claim to the child. *See id.* at 308; COOPER, *supra* Note 1, at 85.

Several states have adopted standby guardianship laws to allow terminally ill parents to assure that their child is cared for when the parent becomes incompetent or dies. *See, e.g.*, CONN. GEN. STAT. ANN. § 45a-624 (West Supp. 2001); 755 ILL. COMP. STAT. ANN. 5/11-5.3 (West Supp. 2001); MASS. GEN. LAWS ANN. ch. 201, § 2D (Lexis Supp. 2001); N.J. STAT. ANN. § 3B:12-72 (West Supp. 2001); N.Y. SURR. CT. PROC. ACT LAW § 1726(3) (McKinney 1996); N.C. GEN. STAT. § 35A-1373 (Lexis 1999); VA. CODE ANN. § 16.1-349 (Michie 1999); WIS. STAT. ANN. § 880.36 (West Supp. 2000). Standby guardianship statutes, such as the Virginia statute mentioned above, prevent terminally ill parents from taking the drastic step of completely terminating their parental rights. *See* Robert E. Shepherd, Jr., *Issues Involving Children*, 32 U. RICH. L. REV. 1345, 1377 (1998). The following statute describes the creation of a standby guardianship and the powers of the standby guardian:

Florida Statutes Annotated
§ 744.304 (West Supp. 2001)

§ 744.304. Standby guardianship.—

(1) Upon petition or consent of both parents, natural or adoptive, if living, or of the surviving parent, a standby guardian of the person or property of a minor may be appointed by the court. . . .

(2) Upon petition of a currently serving guardian, a standby guardian of the person or property of an incapacitated person may be appointed by the court.

(3) The standby guardian or alternate shall be empowered to assume the duties of his or her office immediately on the death or adjudication of incapacity of the last surviving natural or adoptive parent of a minor, or upon the death, removal, or resignation of the guardian for an adult. . . .

(5) After the assumption of duties by a standby guardian, the court shall have jurisdiction over the guardian and the ward.

The standby guardian is usually designated by the parent or appointed by the court. *See* Shepherd, *supra*, at 1377. As indicated by the Florida statute a standby guardian does not exercise control over the terminally ill parent's child until a triggering event occurs, such as the parent's death or incompetence. New Jersey also considers a terminally ill parent's consent a triggering event. N.J. STAT. ANN. § 3B:12-69 (West Supp. 2001). Standby guardianships provide several advantages for terminally ill parents. If a terminally ill parent becomes incompetent but later regains competency, standby guardianship law allows the parent to regain custody over the child. *See* Weimer, *supra*, Note 1, at 71. Therefore, standby guardianships protect parental autonomy and promote keeping the terminally ill parent's family together. *See* Molee, *supra*, Note 1, at 481. The federal government has recently considered making states adopt standby guardianship laws in order to receive federal funding through ASFA. For further discussion of the proposed federal standby guardianship legislation, see Rozmus, *supra,* at 316-31.

California has adopted a variation of standby guardianship called joint guardianship. The following are relevant excerpts from the California statute:

California Probate Code
§ 2105 (West Supp. 2001)

§ 2105. Joint guardians or conservators; appointment

(a) The court, in its discretion, may appoint for a ward or conservatee:

(1) Two or more joint guardians or conservators of the person. . . .

(c) Subject to subdivisions (d) and (e):

(1) Where there are two guardians or conservators, both must concur to exercise a power.

(2) Where there are more than two guardians or conservators, a majority must concur to exercise a power.

(d) If one of the joint guardians or conservators dies or is removed or resigns, the powers and duties continue in the remaining joint guardians or conservators until further appointment is made by the court.

(e) Where joint guardians or conservators have been appointed and one or more are (1) absent from the state and unable to act, (2) otherwise unable to act, or (3) legally disqualified from serving, the court may, by order made with or without notice, authorize the remaining joint guardians or conservators to act as to all matters embraced within its order.

(f) If a custodial parent has been diagnosed as having a terminal condition, as evidenced by a declaration executed by a licensed physician, the court, in its discretion, may appoint the custodial parent and a person nominated by the custodial parent as joint guardians of the person of the minor. However, this appointment shall not be made over the objection of a noncustodial parent without a finding that the noncustodial parent's custody would be detrimental to the minor . . . .

"Terminal condition," for purposes of this subdivision, means an incurable and irreversible condition that, without the administration of life-sustaining treatment, will, within reasonable medical judgment, result in death.

* * *

Although many similarities exist between the two types of guardianships, joint guardianship is significantly different in that the terminally ill parent and the guardian jointly retain control over the child while the parent is competent. The parent and the joint guardian "must agree to the medical, educational, and living arrangements for the child." Rozmus, *supra*, at 313.

Questions

1. What problems in law and policy arise when a court is asked to remove a child from a terminally ill parent? How should courts weigh the interests of a mother who has contracted the HIV virus and the infant's best interests when deciding whether to terminate the mother's rights (to her healthy infant)? If the mother develops AIDS, how might this affect the court's decision?

2. How do the standby guardian laws, *supra*, in Note 2, and California's joint guardianship law, *supra*, in Note 2, balance the terminally ill parent's constitutional rights with the best interests of the child?

D. Application of Americans with Disabilities Act

In re B.S.

693 A.2d 716 (Vt. 1997)

DOOLEY, Justice.

The mother in this case appeals the termination of her parental rights with respect to her son, B.S., arguing that the family court . . . failed to resolve her claims under the Americans with Disabilities Act (ADA) before terminating her parental rights. We affirm.

The mother is a moderately retarded woman with a verbal I.Q. of 75 and a performance I.Q. of 87. She gave birth to her third child, B.S., on December 30, 1993. On the same day, SRS intervened because the mother and the father had been found responsible for physical abuse of their two other children and those children had been removed from their home. SRS initiated a petition alleging B.S. to be a child in need of care or supervision (CHINS) and successfully sought temporary custody of him.

On January 13, 1994, SRS and the parents entered into a written agreement which kept B.S. in SRS custody, but placed him at the Lund Family Center to reside there with the mother. Both parents agreed to accept the extensive and intensive services of the Lund Family Center. On January 31, however, the mother left the Center to be with the father, leaving B.S. at the Center with no arrangements for his care. SRS returned the child to foster care.

At a merits hearing on March 29, 1994, the parties entered into an oral agreement that: (1) the parents would not contest a merits adjudication of CHINS, (2) custody of B.S. would remain with SRS, (3) certain parts of the affidavit of the SRS worker in support of the CHINS petition would be stricken, (4) the family would be enrolled in intensive family-based services at the Baird Center, (5) the disposition hearing would be held in sixty days, and (6) SRS would not recommend termination of parental rights at the first disposition hearing. The court found CHINS "based upon the agreement of the parties and their admission," and ordered a disposition hearing to be set in sixty days.

Thereafter, the mother enrolled in the Intensive Family-Based Service Program at the Baird Center to learn parenting skills. The parents were granted, under the supervision of the Baird Program, twenty hours of visitation each week. Despite assistance from a social worker at the Baird Center, the mother made minimal progress in learning parenting skills.

The initial disposition hearing was held on August 31, 1994, substantially beyond the sixty-day time period agreed to in March, due primarily to delays in obtaining SRS's disposition report and a report from the Baird Center. SRS submitted the disposition report to the court on August 29 and, in compliance with the parties' agreement, did not recommend termination of parental rights. Instead, SRS recommended that B.S. remain in the foster home where he had been living for several months. . . .

* * *

. . . At a status conference on December 6, the SRS caseworker indicated that he would be seeking termination of the mother's parental rights. As a result, the mother sought an immediate interim placement for the child with the mother's sister. On January 15, 1995, SRS filed a supplemental disposition report, in which it recommended termination of parental rights. Combined hearings on disposition, the petition to terminate parental rights, and the mother's motion to transfer custody to the mother's sister were held on February 1, April 10, April 13, October 12 and October 13, 1995. In a written order issued March 6, 1996, the court denied the mother's motion to transfer custody. Finding that the mother's ability to care for her child had stagnated between August 1994 and October 1995, and that termination of parental rights would be in the best interests of the child, the court granted the State's petition to terminate parental rights and transferred all remaining residual rights to SRS.

* * *

The mothers second claim of error is that the court improperly terminated her parental rights without addressing her claims under Title II of the Americans with Disabilities Act (ADA), 42 U.S.C. §§ 12131-12134. She relies on the fact that she is mentally retarded and mental retardation is a disability within the meaning of the ADA. See 42 U.S.C. § 12102(2) (defining "disability"); 28 C.F.R. § 35.104(1)(ii) (mental retardation is a disabiity); *Howard v. Department of Social Welfare*, 163 Vt. 109, 115 n.1, 655 A.2d 1102, 1106 n.1 (1994) (learning disability is impairment under ADA). She argues that, with help, she has the capacity to care for her child and is therefore a qualified person eligible for accommodation under the ADA. See 42 U.S.C. § 12131(2) (defining "qualified individual with a disability") She claims that SRS has failed to accommodate her disability and, as a result, has discriminated against her in the provision of the services needed to parent her child.

For purposes of this issue, we will assume most of the mother's argument is correct. Indeed, the family court was highly critical of SRS's conduct towards the parents in this case. The court noted that the parents were treated with far less respect and compassion than this court is comfortable with. Through the actions of [the SRS caseworker] and the foster parents, the [parents] were intimidated and ignored during their visitation periods with their child. . . . [The mother] repeatedly made attempts to obtain approval from [the caseworker] to bring her mother, the child's grandmother, to visit the child. She was forced to tell her mother, a number of times, that she had to check with [the caseworker] to obtain approval. Likewise, a number of requests to take a family photograph . . . were ignored. Although these requests were apparently considered trivial by SRS, they could have been accomplished with little effort and the denial by lack of acknowledgment was demeaning to the [parents]. The issue is not, however, whether SRS properly treated the parents or treated them consistent with the requirements of the ADA. The issue instead is whether SRS's alleged violation of requirements of the ADA may be raised as a defense to a TPR petition. The family court ruled that ADA noncompliance is not a defense. We agree.

We conclude that the ADA does not directly apply to TPR proceedings. The goals of the ADA are "to assure equality of opportunity, full participation, independent living, and economic self-sufficiency" for persons with disabilities. 42 U.S.C. § 12101(a)(8). The act encompasses three areas: employment, public services, and public accommodations offered by private entities. Title II, which deals with public services provides that "no qualified individual with a disability shall, by reason of such disability, be excluded from participation in or be denied the benefits of *services, programs, or activities* of a public entity. *Id.* § 12132 (emphasis added). TPR proceedings are not "services, programs or activities" within the meaning of Title II of the ADA, 42 U.S.C. § 12132. Thus, the anti-discrimination requirement does not directly apply to TPR proceedings.

Even if the ADA applied directly to TPR proceedings, there is no specific discrimination against disabled persons in the TPR process. Mental retardation is not, by itself, a ground for terminating parental rights. In deciding whether to terminate parental rights, the court must determine the best interests of the child in accordance with four criteria set out in 33 V.S.A.§ 5540: (1) the interaction and interrelationship of the child with the child's natural parents, foster parents, siblings, and others who may significantly affect the child's best interests, (2) the child's adjustment to home and community, (3) the likelihood the natural parent will be able to resume parental duties within a reasonable period of time, and (4) whether the natural parent has played and continues to play a constructive role in the child's welfare. A mentally retarded parent is capable of meeting these criteria.

Recognizing that the TPR process is not itself discriminatory, the mother argues for an indirect method of considering her disability. The logic of her argument goes as follows: (1) SRS is responsible for providing her services that will enable her to resume her parental duties within a reasonable period of time, (2) SRS failed to do so in a manner that would be effective in light of her retardation, (3) SRS therefore discriminated against her in the extension of services in violation of the ADA, 42 U.S.C. § 12132, and (4) the TPR court cannot conclude that she cannot resume her parenting duties within a reasonable period of time because her parenting deficiencies are caused in whole or in part by SRS. We reject the fourth step in her argument.

* * *

[T]he juvenile court in this case was require to focus on the needs of the child. The Legislature has directed that the juvenile court examine whether the parents will resume parental duties within a reasonable period of time. See 33 V.S.A. § 5540(3). The period of time must be viewed from the perspective of the needs of the child. The Legislature has not called for an open-ended inquiry into how the parents might respond to the alternative SRS services and why those services have not been provided. Such an inquiry ignores the needs of the child and diverts the attention of the court to disputes between SRS and the parents.

We further note that nothing in the ADA suggests that denial of TPR is an appropriate remedy for an ADA violation. Under analogous circumstances, other courts have refused to graft ADA requirements onto unrelated statutes. See *Pact v. Arkansas Valley Correctional Facility*, 394 P.2d 34, 39 (Colo.Ct.App. 1995). This is not to say that the mother is without a remedy if SRS has violated the ADA. The ADA provides for a private right of action for Title II violations, 42 U.S.C. § 12133, and its regulations require public entities to adopt and publicize grievance procedures, 28 C.F.R. § 35.107 and outline a federal complaint procedure, *id.* § 35.170. Pursuant to these provisions, the mother could have filed a complaint or brought a civil action to obtain relief.

* * *

For the above reasons, we conclude that the mother may not raise violations of the ADA as a defense to the TPR proceeding. The two other courts that have considered the question have reached the same result. See *Stone v. Davies County Div. Of Children & Family Servics.,* 656 N.E.2d 824, 830 (Ind. Ct. App. 1995) ("any alleged noncompliance with the ADA . . . [is] a matter separate and distinct from the operation of our [parental] termination statute"); *In re Torrance P.,* 187 Wis.2d 10, 522 N.W.2d 243, 244 (App. 1994) ("alleged violation of the ADA is not a basis to attack TPR proceedings"). We are particularly persuaded by the reasoning of *Stone* because it deals with a statutory scheme similar to ours.

By this holding, we do not mean to suggest that parents lack any remedy for SRS's alleged violations of the ADA. We hope that the effect of this decision is to encourage parents and other recipients of SRS services to raise complaints about services vigorously and in a timely fashion. If that had happened in this case, the complaints could have been acted upon years ago and may have helped to bring about the reunification the parents sought, without holding the interests of the child hostage to disputes between the parents and SRS.

Affirmed.

Notes

1. The Americans With Disabilities Act (ADA) became law in 1990 in response to studies that found 43,000,000 Americans annually were discriminated against because of a disability. *See* Teri L. Mosier, Notes, *"Trying to Cure a Seven-Year Itch": The ADA Defense in Termination of Parental Rights,* 37 BRANDEIS L.J. 785, 785 (1998-99). Studies demonstrated that in 1986 three in five persons with some form of disability relied on government benefits for their financial support, and two-thirds of all people with disabilities were unemployed even though they wanted to work. *See* Robert L. Burgdorf, Jr., *The Americans With Disabilities Act: Analysis and Implications of a Second-Generation Civil Rights Statute,* 26 HARV.

C.R.-C.L. L. REV. 412, 420-25 (1991). The following is a relevant excerpt from the ADA:

42 United States Code Service
§ 12132 (Lexis 1997)

> § 12132. Discrimination
>
> Subject to the provisions of this title, no qualified individual with a disability shall, by reason of such disability, be excluded from participation in or be denied the benefits of the services, programs, or activities of a public entity, or be subjected to discrimination by any such entity.

The ADA requires that public entities make reasonable modifications of their rules and practices to accommodate individuals with disabilities. *See* Susan Kerr, *The Application of the Americans With Disabilities Act to the Termination of the Parental Rights of Individuals With Mental Disabilities,* 16 J. CONTEMP. HEALTH L. & POL'Y 387, 388 (2000). For further background information on the ADA, see Chris Watkins, *Beyond Status: The Americans With Disabilities Act and the Parental Rights of People Labeled Developmentally Disabled or Mentally Retarded,* 83 CAL. L. REV. 1415, 1428-31 (1995).

Courts have generally held that parents with disabilities may not use the ADA as a defense in termination proceedings. *See, e.g., M.C. v. Department of Children and Families,* 750 So. 2d 705 (Fla. Dist. Ct. App. 2000) (ADA defense not applicable because termination proceedings are for the benefit of children and not parents); *In re E.E.,* 736 N.E.2d 791 (Ind. Ct. App. 2000) (failure to comply with ADA does not preclude the involuntary termination of a mentally disabled mother); *J.T. v. Arkansas Dep't of Human Serv.,* 947 S.W.2d 761 (Ark. 1997) (parent's rights under ADA must be subordinated to child's best interests); *In re Anthony B.,* 735 A.2d 293, 893 (Conn. Super. Ct. 1999) (termination proceedings not a "service, program, or activity" for purposes of ADA); *In re Matthew S.,* 1999 WL 545359 (Conn. Super. Ct. July 16, 1999) (mother, who suffered from bipolar disorder, could not use ADA as defense in termination proceeding "where she did not know she had a covered disability"); *State v. Penny J.,* 890 P.2d 389 (N.M. Ct. App. 1994) (ADA does not preempt state law in termination proceeding where state required to provide services to parent "that were as effective in affording equal opportunity to the same result, to gain some benefit, or to reach the same level of achievement as that provided to others"); *Bartell v. Lohiser*, 215 F.3d 550 (6th Cir. 2000) (mother could not use ADA as a defense where she did not allege a deprivation of services or custody because of her disability). *See also Torrance P. v. Raymond C.,* 522 N.W.2d 243 (Wis. Ct. App. 1994) (ADA provides no defense in termination procedures). The *Torrance P.* court stated, however, that a parent's developmental disability is a factor in determining whether the agency used diligent efforts in providing court-ordered services. *Id.* at 245.

2. Some legal scholars, however, have suggested that a parent with a disability may use the ADA as a defense when the state has not provided "reasonable accommodations" for family reunification. *See* Mosier, *supra*, Note 1, at 788. Others argue further that the ADA applies to termination proceedings because "the termination process is administered by the courts and state agencies providing the reunification services, programs, and activities." Kerr, *supra*, Note 1, at 411 (citing *In re Welfare of A.J.R.*, 896 P.2d 1298 (Wash. Ct. App. 1995)). If the parent's ADA defense is successful, the parent might be entitled to the following remedies: "(1) the court's rejection of the TPR petition, as unsupported or made in bad faith, or appellate reversal on the same grounds; (2) additional time to investigate and propose accommodations; (3) additional time to attempt to rehabilitate and subsequent reunification after the re-provision of services with the requested accommodations." *Id.* Furthermore, parents who have disabilities might be at a considerable disadvantage in termination procedures. For example, a parent's developmental disability can lead to a presumption of parental unfitness according to some statutes. *See* Watkins, *supra* Note 1, at 1438. For further discussion supporting the use of the ADA as a defense in termination proceedings, see Mosier *supra* Note 1, at 803-05; Watkins, *supra* Note 1, at 1461-75.

Question

What are the arguments for and against allowing the ADA to be used as a defense in TPR proceedings?

E. Application of Uniform Child Custody Jurisdiction Act

In re M.C.S.

504 N.W.2d 323 (S.D. 1993)

DOBBERPUHL, Circuit Judge.

V.M.S. (husband), appeals the denial of a motion questioning the circuit court's jurisdiction, the lack of evidence to support findings of fact and conclusions of law, and the failure to provide due process to him in the matter of the termination of his parental rights to M.C.S., a minor chid, born to his wife. J.A.S. We reverse.

J.A.S., the natural mother of M.C.S., is a lifelong resident of Iowa. On June 30, 1988, J.A.S. married husband, also an Iowa resident in Doon, Iowa. The couple had two children. In November or December of 1990, the couple separated with the two children living with their mother in Rock Rapids, Iowa, while husband lived in Moville, Iowa. The couple continued to visit each other. The couple had sexual intercourse on the occasion of these visits up to and including February 14, 15, 16, 17, 1991.

In June or July 1991, J.A.S. informed husband that she was pregnant. J.A.S. told husband that the child was not his but that of J.P., a resident of Sheldon, Iowa. On October 18, 1991, J.P. stating that he was the father, signed a Consent to Termination of Parental Rights, Consent to Adoption, Waiver of Notice, and Power of Attorney pertaining to the as yet unborn child of J.A.S.

The child, M.C.S., was born on November 3, 1991, in Luverne, Minnesota, a town approximately 18 miles north of Rock Rapids, Iowa. Following the birth of M.C.S., J.A.S. traveled with the child to Sioux Falls, South Dakota, where the adoption agency, Christian Counseling Service (CCS), is located. . . . J.A.S. signed a petition seeking termination of her parental rights over M.C.S. In the petition, J.A.S. stated that J.P. was the natural father of M.C.S. It is not known what, if any, other evidence of paternity was presented since husband has been denied access to the file and consequently does not know the contents of J.P.'s statement. The director of CCS appeared as attorney in fact for J.P. The court was advised that J.A.S. was still married to husband, but he was not notified of the proceedings. Parental rights of the child were transferred to CCS on November 12, 1991.

* * *

Husband contacted CCS concerning the child prior to the finalization of the adoption. Husband filed for divorce on April 6, 1992, in Sioux City, Iowa, listing M.C.S. as one of his three children.

On May 22, 1992, husband filed a petition for writ of habeas corpus and motion for relief from order terminating parental rights. Adoption became final before the hearing. The hearing was held on June 9, 1992. The habeas petition was denied June 25, 1992, because neither CCS nor J.A.S. had custody of M.C.S. An oral motion to require CCS to identify the adoptive parents after the court ruled from the bench that the adoptive parents were a necessary party to the habeas corpus action was denied.

* * *

Husband argues that the State of South Dakota did not have subject mater jurisdiction to determine custody of M.C.S. under the Uniform Child Custody Jurisdiction Act. CCS argues that the Uniform Child Custody Jurisdiction Act does not apply because a termination is not a "custody proceeding." Instead, CCS argues that South Dakota had subject matter jurisdiction and venue in terminating the parental rights of the child based on SDCL 25-5A-5 because (1) the authorized agency, CCS, was based in Sioux Falls, (2) the child was in the physical custody of CCS at the time of the termination proceedings, (3) the child was physically present in South Dakota at the time of the termination proceeding.

The Uniform Child Custody Jurisdiction Act (UCCJA) was promulgated in 1968 by the National Conference of Commissioners on Uniform State laws in response to jurisdictional problems in interstate custody cases which were resulting in child snatchings. In these cases, the child was being denied access to one parent by the unilateral actions and efforts of the other parent. Court-shopping parents were fleeing to other states seeking to obtain more favorable decrees.

The UCCJA was enacted by the South Dakota Legislature in 1978 (S.D. Sess. L. ch. 190). *Winkelman v. Moses*, 279 N.W.2d 897, 898 n.1 (S.D. 1979). The UCCJA is intended, among other things, to assure that litigation concerning the custody of a child take place ordinarily in the state with which the child and his family have the closest connection and where significant evidence concerning the child's personal relationship is most readily available. The UCCJA's underlying policy is to eliminate forum shopping and to enable the courts to act in the best interest of the child. *Zappitello v. Moses*, 458 N.W.2d 784, 786 (S.D. 1990) (citing *Winkelman,* 279 N.W.2d at 898-99). South Dakota's UCCJA is currently codified at Chapter 26-5A.

Case law on the issue of the applicability of the UCCJA to terminations and adoptions is mixed. CCS cites *In re Johnson,* 415 N.E.2d 108 (Ind. Ct. App. 1981) in support of its argument that the UCCJA does not apply to termination proceedings. In *Johnson*, the natural father, living in Indiana, filed a petition for termination of the natural mother's parental rights seeking to open the way for a future step parent adoption without the consent of the mother. The two were parents of a child in the custody of the child's parental grandparents in Illinois pursuant to a dissolution decree entered in Indiana.

The Court of Appeals pointed out that the purpose of the UCCJA is to provide guidelines in determining a court's jurisdiction to make a custody determination. The instant action, however, was not brought for the purpose of establishing or modifying a custody decree, but rather, to terminate all parental rights of the mother. Termination of parental rights is a statutory mechanism which permits a child to be adopted without the consent of a parent. . . . As such, jurisdiction for the termination of parental rights is not encompassed by the UCCJA, but instead, is properly determined under the adoption statutes. *Id.* at 110.

The court concluded the UCCJA did not apply to termination proceedings and that it had jurisdiction under the adoption statutes.

More recent cases involving termination and adoption, however, have held otherwise as to the applicability of the UCCJA. These cases have even tended to expand the application of the UCCJA by looking to the intent of the drafters.

In *E.E.B. v. D.A.,* 899 N.J. 595, 446 A.2d 871 (1982) the Supreme Court of New Jersey applied the UCCJA to both an adoption and a habeas corpus action in the case of a child born in Ohio. . . . The Supreme Court of New Jersey pointed out that while the UCCJA focuses on custody disputes between family members, "its operative provisions are broad enough to include a dispute between a natural parent and adoptive parents." *Id.* 446 A.2d at 878. Citing *Slidell v. Valentine*, 298 N.W.2d 599, 601 (Ia. 1980), the court stated that custody proceedings include habeas corpus actions and other proceedings under state law to determine custody. *E.E.B.,* 446 A.2d at 878.

In *Souza v. Superor Court (Bristow)*, 193 Cal. App. 3d 1304, 238 Cal. Rptr. 892 (6 Dist. 1987) a case which involved a stepparent adoption brought by the natural mother and her new husband in California against the child's natural father in Hawaii, the new husband argued that the UCCJA standards do not apply in an adoption proceeding. The court found this argument to be "clearly wrong." *Id.* 238 Cal. Rptr. at 895.

> The UCCJA regulates custody of children. An adoption proceeding to determine parental custody rights is clearly a custody-determining proceeding of the most drastic kind. . . . Patently, a stepparent adoption, with its potential for completely terminating the natural father's custodial rights, is a custody-determining procedure and is equally subject to the UCCJA and the PKPA.

[The court goes on to cite cases from Georgia, Michigan and Wisconsin, all of which held that the UCCJA applies to termination proceedings.]

Based on current case law and the broad interpretation of "custody" being found by state courts which have adopted the UCCJA, the UCCJA is applicable in the case of M.C.S.

We have previously stated that a finding of any of the four grounds under SDCL 26-5A-3 is sufficient to confer jurisdiction over interstate child custody disputes in a state court. Once it is determined that jurisdiction exists under SDCL 25-5A-3, then the court must determine whether jurisdiction should be exercised in view of SDCL 26-5A-6 (simultaneous proceedings in other states), 26-5A-7 (inconvenient forum), and 26-5A-8 (reasons of conduct). *Zappitello*, 458 N.W.2d at 787.

The first ground is that the forum is the home state of the child. SDCL 26-5A-3(1). "Home state" as defined under SDCL 26-5A-2(5) includes where the child has lived for the prior six months or where the child has lived from birth with a parent. M.C.S. was only nine days old at the time of the petition so the six months cutoff is eliminated. . . . M.C.S.'s parents are her natural guardians. M.C.S.'s natural mother J.A.S., and father, whether V.M.S. or J.P., all live in Iowa.

* * *

The second ground is that "the child and his parents, or the child and at least one contestant have significant connection with this state. . . ." SDCL 26-5A-3(2)

Husband[, J.A.S.,] and the man she named as the child's father are all Iowans. None of the three work in South Dakota. Other family members, including the couple's two children, are in Iowa. The child, M.C.S., was not conceived nor born in South Dakota. Husband did not tell J.A.S. to take M.C.S. to South Dakota nor did he apparently know until after the fact that J.A.S. had taken M.C.S. to South Dakota for adoption. Husband filed for divorce in Iowa claiming parentage of M.C.S. prior to the finalization of the adoption. Only CCS, the adoption agency, is in South Dakota.

"'Physical presence' of the child alone does not suffice to confer jurisdiction." *In re Guardianship of Donaldson,* 178 Cal. App. 3d 477, 223 Cal. Rptr. 707 (5 Dist. 1986). . . . M.C.S.'s most significant connections were in Iowa prior to November 12, 1991.

The third ground is that "[t]he child is physically present in this state *and* the child has been abandoned or it is necessary in an emergency to protect the child because he has been subjected to or threatened with mistreatment or abuse or is otherwise neglected or dependent." SCL 26-5A-3(3) (emphasis added).

* * *

Clearly, at the time of the court case dealing with the petition, M.C.S. was physically present in the state of South Dakota. However, M.C.S. was not abandoned nor does the record reveal any evidence of mistreatment, child neglect, or abuse necessary to assume jurisdiction in an "emergency" situation. Both elements are necessary to meet the third ground.

The fourth ground is that no other state appears to have jurisdiction under the first three grounds. SDCL 26-5A-3(4). That is not the case here. Iowa has jurisdiction under the first two grounds.

* * *

The only proof of paternity J.P. and J.A.S. appear to have offered is their statements that J.P. is the father. Husband states that he had sexual intercourse with J.A.S. at a time when conception could reasonably have occurred. J.A.S. has not refuted that statement.

Permitting J.A.S. to change the jurisdiction of the state by merely carrying the child across the border from Iowa into South Dakota would be to abandon the very purpose of the UCCJA, that of eliminating forum shopping for the custody of children. It is vital that the underlying policy of the UCCJA remain intact enabling the court to concentrate, not on what one spouse might want over what the other spouse might want, but what is foremost in the best interest of the child.

The UCCJA applies in this termination of parental rights. Under the grounds applying the UCCJA, South Dakota does not have subject matter jurisdiction; Iowa does. The action of the court in the termination of parental rights is therefore void due to lack of subject matter jurisdiction. . . .

Uniform Child-Custody Jurisdiction and Enforcement Act

§§ 201-204, 206-207 9 U.L.A. 671 (1997)

§ 201. Initial Child-Custody Jurisdiction

a. Except as otherwise provided in Section 204, a court of this state has jurisdiction to make an initial child-custody determination only if:

1. this State is the home State of the child on the date of the commencement of the proceeding, or was the home State of the child within six months before the commencement of the proceeding and the child is absent from this state but a parent or person acting as parent continues to live in this State;

2. a court of another State does not have jurisdiction under paragraph (1), or a court of the home State of the child has declined to exercise jurisdiction on the ground that this State is the more appropriate forum under Section 207 or 208 and:

(A) the child and the child's parents, or the child and at least one parent or a person acting as a parent, have a significant connection with this State other than mere physical presence; and:

(B) substantial evidence is available in this State concerning the child's care, protection, training, and personal relationships. . . .

§ 202. Exclusive, Continuing Jurisdiction.

a. Except as otherwise provided in Section 204, a court of this State which has made a child-custody determination consistent with Section 201 or 203 has exclusive, continuing jurisdiction over the determination until:

b. a court of this State determines that neither the child, the child and one parent, nor the child and a person acting as a parent have significant connection with this State and that substantial evidence is no longer available in this State concerning the child's care, protection, training, and personal relationships; or

1. a court of this State or a court of another State determines that the child, the child's parents, and any person acting as a parent do not presently reside in this State. . . .

c. A court of this State which has made a child-custody determination and does not have exclusive, continuing jurisdiction under this section may modify that determination only if it has jurisdiction to make an initial determination under Section 201.

§ 203. Jurisdiction to Modify Determination.

Except as otherwise provided in Section 204, a court of this State may not modify a child-custody determination made by a court of another State unless a court of this State has jurisdiction to make an initial determination under Section 201(a)(1) or (2) and:

1. the court of the other State determines it no longer has exclusive, continuing jurisdiction under Section 202 or that a court of this state would be a more convenient under Section 207; or

2. a court of this State or a court of the other State determines that the child, the child's parents, and any person action as a parent do not presently reside in the other State.

§ 204. Temporary Emergency Custody.

a. A court of this State has temporary emergency jurisdiction if the child is present in this State and the child has been abandoned or it is necessary in an emergency to protect the child because the child, or a sibling or parent of the child, is subjected to or threatened with mistreatment or abuse. . . .

§ 206. Simultaneous Proceedings.

a. Except as otherwise provided in Section 204, a court of this State may not exercise its jurisdiction under this [article] if, at the time of the commencement of the proceeding, a proceeding concerning the custody of the child has been commenced in a court of another State having jurisdiction substantially in conformity with this [Act], unless the proceeding has been terminated or is stayed by the court. . . .

§ 207. Inconvenient Forum.

a. A court of this State which has jurisdiction under this [Act] to make a child-custody determination may decline to exercise jurisdiction at any time if it determines that it is an inconvenient forum or another State is a more appropriate forum. . . .

b. Before determining whether it is an inconvenient forum, a court of this State shall consider whether it is appropriate for a court of another State to exercise jurisdiction. . . .

c. If a court of this State determines that it is an inconvenient forum and that a court of another State is a more appropriate forum, it shall stay the proceedings upon condition that a child-custody proceeding be promptly commenced in another designated State. . . .

Notes

1. The Uniform Child Custody Jurisdiction Act (UCCJA) does not expressly state that either termination of parental rights or adoption constitutes a "child custody proceeding" for purposes of implementing the UCCJA. *See* Linda D. Elrod, *A Review of the Year in Family Law,* 28 FAM. L.Q. 541, 548 (1995). For a description of the UCCJA's goals and provisions, see Berndette W. Hartfield, *The Uniform Child Custody Jurisdiction Act and the Problem of Jurisdiction in Interstate Adoptions: An Easy Fix?,* 43 OKLA. L. REV. 621, 631-37 (1990). Every state has adopted the UCCJA, but some states have recently enacted the Uniform Child-Custody Jurisdiction and Enforcement Act (UCCJEA), which is consistent with the jurisdictional provisions of the federal Parental Kidnapping Protection Act (PKPA). Some states have statutory law which includes termination of parental rights. The following Montana statute is an example:

Montana Code Annotated
§ 40-7-103 (1999)

§ 40-7-103. Definitions
As used in this chapter, the following definitions apply:

* * *

(3)(a) "Child custody determination" means a judgment, decree, or other order of a court providing for the legal custody, physical custody, or visitation with respect to a child. The term includes a permanent, a temporary, an initial, and a modification order.

* * *

(4)(a) "Child custody proceeding" means a proceeding in which legal custody, physical custody, or visitation with respect to a child is an issue. The term includes a proceeding for divorce, separation, neglect, abuse, dependency, guardianship, paternity, termination of parental rights, and protection from domestic violence, in which the issue may appear.

* * *

In states that do not have a UCCJA provision for termination of parental rights, most courts have been willing to read adoption or TPR into the "child custody proceeding" provision of the UCCJA. *See* Hartfield, *supra,* at 652. *See, e.g., In re A.E.H.,* 468 N.W.2d 190 (Wis. 1991) (UCCJA applies to termination proceedings and guardianship proceedings because both are custody decrees according to state law); *Souza v. Superior Court*, 238 Cal. Rptr. 892 (Ct. App. 1987) (adoption, as a custody determination, requires application of UCCJA); *Golding v. Golding,* 667 So. 2d 404 (Fla. Dist. Ct. App. 1995) (under UCCJA, state that has jurisdiction over an adoption matter may decline to exercise the jurisdiction in favor of another state if in the best interests of the child); *Foster v. Stein,* 454 N.W.2d 244, 246 (Mich. Ct. App. 1990) (adoption proceedings are custody proceedings "because they are in the nature of a dependency proceeding"); *In the Interest of L.C.,* 857 P.2d 1375 (Kan. Ct. App. 1993) (UCCJA, as adopted and modified by state law, is applicable to termination proceedings); *Gainey v. Olivo*, 373 S.E.2d 4 (Ga. 1998) (UCCJA is applicable to adoption proceedings because they are custody determining proceedings). The *Gainey* decision also recognized that the Official Comments of the UCCJA state that "custody proceedings" should be broadly interpreted. Some jurisdictions have held that not applying UCCJA standards to adoption proceedings allows the very abuses the Act was created to prevent. *See Adoption of Zachariah K.,* 8 Cal. Rptr. 2d 423 (1992). For additional case law supporting the use of the UCCJA in interstate adoption and termination proceedings, see Danny R. Veilleux, Annotation, *What Types of Proceedings or Determinations Are Governed by the Uniform Child Custody Jurisdiction Act (UCCJA) or the Parental Kidnapping Prevention Act (PKPA)?,* 78 A.L.R.4TH 1028 (1990).

2. Some legal scholars disagree with the proposition that the UCCJA is applicable to TPR and adoption. The first argument is that the UCCJA provides nine specific examples (including divorce) of what is a "child custody proceeding" under the UCCJA. As stated in Note 1, adoption and termination proceedings are not included among the list of examples. *See* Greg Waller, *When the Rules Don't Fit the Game: Application of the Uniform Child Custody Jurisdiction Act and the Parental Kidnapping Prevention Act to Interstate Adoption Proceedings,* 33 HARV. J. LEGIS. 271, 284 (1996). For example, the custody proceedings referred to in the UCCJA, such as divorce, are considerably different from termination proceedings. Unlike TPR, divorce proceedings rarely involve the permanent termination of parental rights. Therefore termination proceedings possess an element of finality not present in the proceedings listed in the UCCJA. *See id.* at 296; Herma Hill Kay, *Adoption in the Conflict of Laws: The UAA, Not the UCCJA, Is the Answer,* 84 CAL. L. REV. 703 (1996). Furthermore, divorce proceedings take into account the best interests of the child as well as which parent is best suited to care for the child. However, TPR may focus solely on a single parent's unfitness, and such proceedings may focus to a lesser degree on the best interests of the child. *See* Waller, *supra*, at 295.

Another argument raised by some commentators is that adoption proceedings defy the goals of the UCCJA. *See id.* at 289-91. Infants who are involved in adoption rarely have "home state" jurisdiction because they often do not satisfy the residency requirements. For a state to have "home state" jurisdiction over a child, the infant must either have been born in the state or be a resident of the state for at least six months prior to filing. In an age where interstate adoptions are increasing in frequency, adopted infants often don't have a "home state." Another type of jurisdiction that satisfies the UCCJA is best interests/significant connection jurisdiction. To meet this standard, the court weighs the infant's minimum contacts with the state. It is likely that more than one state will have best interest/significant connection over the child. As a result, there may be a "race to the court house" to determine which of the two eligible states will have jurisdiction over the child's custody. *See* Kay, *supra*, at 714-15. The "race to the courthouse" directly opposes the UCCJA's goal of discouraging conflicts and competition between jurisdictions. *See* Waller, *supra*, at 291. This problem may be solved as states adopt the Uniform Child-Custody Jurisdiction and Enforcement Act (UCCJEA), which, like the Parental Kidnapping Prevention Act (PKPA), provides a statutory preference for home state jurisdiction, where two states compete for jurisdiction.

Questions

How are the UCCJA and the Interstate Compact on the Placement of Children (ICPC) consistent in their goals and procedures dealing with interstate child placement? Do we need both the UCCJA and the ICPC in interstate child placement? Why? For relevant provisions of the ICPC, see Chapter 8, Part E.1.

F. Who May File Termination Petitions

23 Pennsylvania Consolidated Statutes Annotated

§ 2512 (West Supp. 2000)

§ 2512. Petition for involuntary termination

(a) Who may file.—A petition to terminate parental rights with respect to a child under the age of 18 years may be filed by any of the following:

1. Either parent when termination is sought with respect to the other parent.
2. An agency.
3. The individual having custody or standing in loco parentis to the child and who has filed a report of intention to adopt required by section 2531 (relating to report of intention to adopt).
4. An attorney representing a child or a guardian ad litem representing a child who has been adjudicated dependent under 42 Pa. C.S. § 6341(c) (relating to adjudication).

(b) Contents.—The petition shall set forth specifically those grounds and facts alleged as the basis for terminating parental rights. The petition filed under this section shall also contain an averment that the petitioner will assume custody of the child until such time as the child is adopted. If the petitioner is an agency it shall not be required to aver that an adoption is presently contemplated nor that a person with a present intention to adopt exists.

* * *

Kingsley v. Kingsley
[*See, supra,* Chapter 11, Part A.2.]

In re Pima County Juvenile Severance, Action No. S-113432
[*See, supra,* Chapter 11, Part A.2.]

Notes

Who may bring a termination petition varies from state to state. The *Kingsley* and *Pima County* cases, for example, represent different views on whether a child should be permitted to file a termination petition. Many jurisdictions allow a child's GAL, CASA, or attorney to file a petition for the termination of a parent's rights. *See, e.g., In re L.H.,* 634 A.2d 1230 (D.C. 1993) (allowing a guardian ad litem to file a motion for the termination of parental rights does not violate the parent's due process rights); *In the Matter of Caldwell*, No. 9604-80942; CA A 105253, 2000 WL 1634992 (Or. Ct. App. Nov. 1, 2000) (child's attorney may file a termination petition where the child is authorized to file such a petition). Foster parents, in some jurisdictions, might not have the right to file a termination petition. *See, e.g., In re T.M.B.,* 641 A.2d 1118 (N.J. Super. Ct. Ch. Div. 1993) (foster parents may not file termination petition and seek adoption simultaneously, where child is not eligible for adoption). *But see* UTAH CODE ANN. § 78-3a-404 (Lexis Supp. 2000). In Utah, foster parents as well as any "interested party" may file a petition for termination of a parent-child relationship. For further discussion of standing and party status in child welfare proceedings, see Chapter 11, Part A, *supra.*

G. Termination of Parental Rights and Adoption

1. Adoption and Safe Families Act (1997)

The Adoption and Safe Families Act of 1997
[*See, supra,* Chapter 10, Part A.3.]
42 U.S.C.S. § 675(5) (Lexis 1998)

(5) The term "case review system" means a procedure for assuring that—

* * *

C. with respect to each such child, procedural safeguards will be applied, among other things, to assure each child in foster care under the supervision of the State of a permanency hearing to be held, in a family or juvenile court or another court (including a tribal court) of competent jurisdiction, or by an administrative body appointed or approved by the court, no later than 12 months after the date the child is considered to have entered foster care . . . which hearing shall determine the permanency plan for the child that includes whether, and if applicable when, the child will be returned to the parent, placed for adoption and the State will file a petition for termination of parental rights or referred for legal guardianship, or (in cases where the State agency has documented to the State court a compelling reason for determining that it would not be in the best interests of the child to return home, be referred for termination of parental rights, or be placed for adoption with a fit and willing relative, or with a legal guardian) . . . and procedural safeguards shall also be applied with respect to parental rights pertaining to the removal of the child from the home of his parents, to a change in the child's placement . . . ;

* * *

E. in the case of a child who has been in foster care under the responsibility of the State for 15 of the most recent 22 months, or, if a court of competent jurisdiction has determined a child to be an abandoned infant (as defined under State law) or has made a determination that the parent has committed murder of another child of the parent, committed voluntary manslaughter of another child of the parent, aided or abetted, attempted, conspired, or solicited to commit such a murder or such a voluntary manslaughter, or committed a felony assault that has resulted in serious bodily injury to the child or another child of the parent, the State shall file a petition to terminate the parental rights of the child's parents (or, if such a petition has been filed by another party, seek to be joined as a party to the petition), and, concurrently, to identify, recruit, process, and approve a qualified family for an adoption, unless—

i. at the option of the State, the child is being cared for by a relative;

ii. a State agency has documented in the case plan (which shall be available for court review) a compelling reason for determining that filing such a petition would not be in the best interests of the child; or

iii. the State has not provided to the family of the child, consistent with the time period in the State case plan, such services as the State deems necessary for the safe return of the child to the child's home, if reasonable efforts of the type described in section 671(a)(15)(B)(ii) of this title are required to be made with respect to the child.

* * *

The Adoption and Safe Families Act of 1997

42 U.S.C.S. § 673b (Lexis 1998)

* * *

(d) Adoption incentive payment

1. In general

[T]he adoption incentive payment payable to a State for a fiscal year under this section shall be equal to the sum of—

(A) $4,000, multiplied by the amount (if any) by which the number of foster child adoptions in the State during the fiscal year exceeds the base number of foster child adoptions for the State for the fiscal year; and

(B) $2,000, multiplied by the amount (if any) by which the number of special needs adoptions in the State during the fiscal year exceeds the base number of special needs adoption for the State for the fiscal year.

* * *

(g) Definitions

As used in this section: . . .

(3) Base number of foster child adoptions. The term "base number of foster child adoptions for a State" means—

(A) with respect to fiscal year 1998, the average number of foster child adoptions in the State in fiscal years 1995, 1996, and 1997; and

(B) with respect to any subsequent fiscal year, the number of foster child adoptions in the State in the fiscal year for which the number is the greatest in the period that begins with fiscal year 1997 and ends with the fiscal year preceding such subsequent fiscal year.

(4) Base number of special needs adoptions. The term "base number of special needs adoptions for a State" means—

(A) with respect to fiscal year 1998, the average number of special needs adoptions in the State in fiscal years 1995, 1996, and 1997; and

(B) with respect to any subsequent fiscal year, the number of special needs adoptions in the State in the fiscal year for which the number is the greatest in the period that begins with fiscal year 1997 and ends with the fiscal year preceding such subsequent fiscal year.

* * *

Notes

1. ASFA requires the court to choose from four options in determining a "permanency plan" for the child. Each of the options emphasizes permanency rather than reunification. This is consistent with the shift in focus that occurred from the Adoption Assistance and Child Welfare Act of 1980 (AACWA) to the Adoption and Safe Families Act of 1997. *See* 42 U.S.C. § 675(5)(C), *supra.*

2. ASFA attempts to decrease the problem of foster care drift. In 1995, the American Civil Liberties Union (ACLU) reported that at least 40,600 chldren were in foster care for five years or more and another 51,300 children were in care between three and five years. The ACLU revealed that system children, on average, live with three different families, but ten or more placements are not uncommon. *See* Conna Craig, *What I Need is a Mom: The Welfare State Denies Homes to Thousands of Foster Children,* 73 POL'Y REV. 42, 45 (1995). Two provisions are aimed at this goal. First, the requirement that a permanency hearing be held within twelve months of the child entering foster care shortens the time a child waits to attain permanency. *See* 42 U.S.C. § 675(5)(C), *supra*. Previously, under AACWA, the court was required to conduct a permanency hearing within eighteen months. Children will be in a permanent situation six months earlier than under AACWA. Second, the provision that states that if the child is in foster care for fifteen of the twenty-two most recent months the state shall file a petition to terminate parental rights insures that children will not remain in foster care indefinitely. *See* 42 U.S.C.S. § 673b, *supra*. This requirement presumes that termination is in the best interests of every child after the stated time period has expired. This presumption for termination can only be defeated by proof of a compelling reason that termination is not in the best interests of the child. *See* Megan O'Laughlin, *A Theory of Relativity: Kinship Foster Care May Be the Key to Stopping the Pendulum of Termination vs. Reunification,* 51 VAND. L. REV. 1427 (1998).

3. The foster care system is a financial burden on the states and the federal government. It is estimated that ten billion dollars are spent annually on the child welfare system. *See* Verne Barry, *What Will Happen to the Children? Who Will Step in When Welfare is Abolished?,* 71 POL'Y REV. 7, 9-10 (1995). In addition, ASFA offers states adoption incentive payments. These adoptive incentive payments further encourage states to complete as many adoptions as possible; adoptions that require the termination of parental rights.

4. Congress passed legislation in 1980 to provide financial assistance for the adoption of "special needs children." *See* 42 U.S.C.A. § 670. *See* Debra Ratterman Baker, *Adoption Assistance: A Legal Primer*, 19 CHILD LAW PRAC. 97 (2000). Under federal law, a state must "conclude that the child cannot be returned home and would not be adopted without the subsidy" before it provides financial assistance for an adoption. *Id.* State adoption assistance programs then provide monthly payments to adoptive parents to help offset the extra costs associated with caring for a special needs child. For purposes of adoption assistance, legislation, children who have "special needs" may include children who (1) have physical, mental, or emotional disabilities, (2) have medical conditions, or (3) belong to ethnic groups or are of a particular age that may make adoption less likely. Federal law also requires that the child be eligible for supplemental security income (SSI) or that the child would have been eligible for AFDC under the 1996 guidelines before AFDC was repealed. According to federal law, every state that participates in the federal foster care program is required to have some adoption assistance program. Most public adoptions now occur with the assistance of a subsidy. *Id.* For further discussion of the adoption assistance program for special needs children, see *id.*

Questions

Do the ASFA provisions that attempt to solve the problem of foster care drift infringe on the natural parents' constitutional rights? Do the shorter time frames give natural parents a chance to show they are able to provide for their child? For example, many of the parents whose children come into the child welfare system have drug or alcohol problems. Do these parents have enough time to demonstrate that they will succeed in a drug treatment program and, therefore, be able to provide proper care for their children? *See* Cheryl A. DeMichele, Comment, *The Illinois Adoption Act: Should a Child's Length of Time in Foster Care Measure Parental Unfitness?,* 30 LOY. U. CHI. L.J. 727 (1999). Are these provisions in the child's best interest? Do we want to terminate parental rights without guaranteeing that the child will be placed in a permanent home? *See* O'Laughlin, *supra* Note 2.

2. Constitutional Considerations

Stanley v. Illinois

[*See, supra,* at Part A.]

Lehr v. Robertson

463 U.S. 248, 103 S. Ct. 2985, 77 L. Ed. 2d 614 (1983)

Justice STEVENS delivered the opinion of the Court.

The question presented is whether New York has sufficiently protected an unmarried father's inchoate relationship with a child whom he has never supported and rarely seen in two years since her birth. The appellant, Jonathan Lehr, claims that the Due Process and Equal Protection Clauses of the Fourteenth Amendment, as interpreted in *Stanley v. Illinois*, 405 U.S. 645 (1972), and *Caban v. Mohammed*, 441 U.S. 380 (1979), give him an absolute right to notice and an opportunity to be heard before the child may be adopted. We disagree.

Jessica M. was born out of wedlock on November 9, 1976. Her mother, Lorraine Robertson, married Richard Robertson eight months after Jessica's birth. On December 21, 1978, when Jessica was over two years old, the Robertsons filed an adoption petition in the Family Court of Ulster County, New York. The court heard their testimony and received a favorable report from the Ulster County Department of Social Services. On March 7, 1979, the court entered an order of adoption. In this proceeding, appellant contends that the adoption order is invalid because he, Jessica's putative father, was not given advance notice of the adoption proceeding.

The State of New York maintains a "putative father registry." A man who files with that registry demonstrates his intent to claim paternity of a child born out of wedlock and is therefore entitled to receive notice of any proceeding to adopt that child. Before entering Jessica's adoption order, the Ulster County Family Court had the putative father registry examined. Although appellant claims to be Jessica's natural father, he had not entered his name in the registry.

In addition to the persons whose names are listed on the putative father registry, New York law requires that notice of an adoption proceeding be given to several other classes of possible fathers of children born out of wedlock—those who have been adjudicated to be the father, those who have been identified as the father on the child's birth certificate, those who live openly with the child and the child's mother and who hold themselves out to be the father, those who have been identified as the father by the mother in a sworn written statement, and those who were married to the child's mother before the child was six months old. Appellant admittedly was not a member of any of those classes. . . . Nevertheless, he contends that the following special circumstances gave him a constitutional right to notice and a hearing before Jessica was adopted.

On January 30, 1979, one month after the adoption proceeding was commenced in Ulster County, appellant filed a "visitation and paternity petition" in the Westchester County Family Court. In that petition, he asked for a determination of paternity, an order of support, and reasonable visitation privileges with Jessica. Notice of that proceeding was served on appellee on February 22, 1979. Four days later appellee's attorney informed the Ulster County Court that appellant had commenced a paternity proceeding in Westchester County; the Ulster County judge then entered an order staying appellant's paternity proceeding until he could rule on a motion to change the venue of that proceeding to Ulster County. On March 3, 1979, appellant received notice of the change of venue motion and, for the first time, learned that an adoption proceeding was pending in Ulster County.

On March 7, 1979, appellant's attorney telephoned the Ulster County judge to inform him that he planned to seek a stay of the adoption proceeding pending the determination of the paternity petition. In that telephone conversation, the judge advised the lawyer that he had already signed the adoption order earlier that day. According to appellant's attorney, the judge sated that he was aware of the pending paternity petition but did not believe he was required to give notice to appellant prior to the entry of the order of adoption.

. . . On June 22, 1979, appellant filed a petition to vacate the order of adoption on the ground that it was obtained by fraud and in violation of his constitutional rights. The Ulster County Family Court . . . denied the petition, explaining its decision in a thorough written opinion.

The Appellate Division of the Supreme Court affirmed. . . . The majority held that appellant's commencement of a paternity action did not give him any right to receive notice of the adoption proceedings, that the notice provisions of the statute were constitutional, and that *Caban v. Mohammed*, 441 U.S. 380 (1979), was not retroactive.[7] Parenthetically, the majority observed that appellant "could have insured his right to notice by signing the putative father registry."

The New York Court of Appeals also affirmed by a divided vote. The majority . . . addressed what it described as the only contention of substance advanced by appellant; that it was an abuse of discretion to enter the adoption order without requiring that notice be given to appellant. The court observed that the primary purpose of the notice provision of § 111-a was to enable the person served to provide the court with evidence concerning the best interest of the child, and that appellant had made no tender indicating any ability to provide any particular or special information relevant to Jessica's best interest. Considering the record as a whole, and acknowledging that it might have been prudent to give notice, the court concluded that the Family Court had not abused its discretion either when it entered the order without notice or when it denied appellant's petition to reopen the proceedings. The dissenting judges concluded that the Family Court had abused its discretion, both when it entered the order without notice and when it refused to reopen the proceedings.

Appellant . . . offers two alternative grounds for holding the New York statutory scheme unconstitutional. First, he contends that a putative father's

---

[7] *Caban* was decided on April 24, 1979, about two months after the entry of the order of adoption. In *Caban*, a father who had lived with his two illegitimate children and their mother for several years successfully challenged the constitutionality of the New York statute providing that children could be adopted without the father's consent even though the mother's consent was required.

actual or potential relationship with a child born out of wedlock is an interest in liberty which may not be destroyed without due process of law; he argues therefore that he had a constitutional right to prior notice and an opportunity to be heard before he was deprived of that interest. Second, he contends that the gender-based classification in the statute, which both denied him the right to consent to Jessica's adoption and accorded him fewer procedural rights than her mother, violated the Equal Protection Clause.

The Fourteenth Amendment provides that no State shall deprive any person of life, liberty, or property without due process of law. When that Clause is invoked in a novel context, it is our practice to begin the inquiry with a determination of the precise nature of the private interest that is threatened by the State. *See, e.g., Cafeteria Workers v. McElroy*, 367 U.S. 886, 895-896 (1961). Only after that interest has been identified, can we properly evaluate the adequacy of the State's process. *See Morrissey v. Brewer,* 408 U.S. 471, 483-483 (1972). We therefore first consider the nature of the interest in liberty for which appellant claims constitutional protection and then turn to a discussion of the adequacy of the procedure that New York has provided for its protection.

The intangible fibers that connect parent and child have infinite variety. They are woven throughout the fabric of our society, providing it with strength, beauty, and flexibility. It is self-evident that they are sufficiently vital to merit constitutional protection in appropriate cases. In deciding whether this is such a case, however, we must consider the broad framework that has traditionally been used to resolve the legal problems arising from the parent-child relationship.

In the vast majority of cases, state law determines the final outcome. Rules governing the inheritance of property, adoption, and child custody are generally specified in statutory enactments that vary from State to State. Moreover, equally varied state laws governing marriage and divorce affect a multitude of parent-child relationships. . . .

In some cases, however, this Court has held that the Federal Constitution supersedes state law and provides even greater protection for certain formal family relationships. In those cases, as in the state cases, the Court has emphasized the paramount interest in the welfare of children and has noted that the rights of the parents are a counterpart of the responsibilities they have assumed. Thus, the "liberty" of parents to control the education of their children that was vindicated in *Meyer v. Nebraska,* 262 U.S. 390 (1923), and *Pierce v. Society of Sisters*, 268 U.S. 510 (1925), was described as a "right, coupled with the high duty, to recognize and prepare [the child] for additional obligations." *Id.* at 535. . . . In these cases the Court has found that the relationship of love and duty in a recognized family unit is an interest in liberty entitled to constitutional protection. "[S]tate intervention to terminate [such a] relationship . . . must be accomplished by procedures meeting the requisites of the Due Process Clause." *Santosky v. Kramer*, 455 U.S. 745, 753 (1982).

There are also a few cases in which this Court has considered the extent to which the Constitution affords protection to the relationship between natural parents and children born out of wedlock. In some we have been concerned with the rights of the children, *see, e.g., Trimble v. Gordon*, 430 U.S. 762 (1977); *Jimenez v. Weinberger*, 417 U.S. 628 (1974); *Weber v. Aetna Casualty & Surety Co.,* 406 U.S. 164 (1972). In this case, however, it is a parent who claims that the State has improperly deprived him of a protected interest in liberty. This Court has examined the extent to which a natural father's biological relationship with his child receives protection under the Due Process Clause in precisely three cases: *Stanley v. Illinois*, 405 U.S. 645 (1972), *Quilloin v. Walcott* 434 U.S. 246 (1978), and *Caban v. Mohammed*, 441 U.S. 380 (1979).

Quilloin involved the constitutionality of a Georgia statute that authorized the adoption, over the objection of the natural father, of a child born out of wedlock. The father in that case had never legitimated the child. It was only after the mother had remarried and her new husband had filed an adoption petition that the natural father sought visitation rights and filed a petition for legitimation. The trial court found adoption by the new husband to be in the child's best interests, and we unanimously held that action to be consistent with the Due Process Cause.

Caban involved the conflicting claims of two natural parents who had maintained joint custody of their children from the time of their birth until they were respectively two and four years old. The father challenged the validity of an order authorizing the mother's new husband to adopt the children; he relied on both the Equal Protection Clause and the Due Process Cause. Because this Court upheld his equal protection claim, the majority did not address his due process challenge. The comments on the latter claim by the four dissenting Justices are nevertheless instructive, because they identify the clear distinction between a mere biological relationship and an actual relationship of parental responsibility.

Justice Stewart correctly observed:

> "Even if it be assumed that each married parent after divorce has some substantive due process right to maintain his or her parental relationship, it by no means follows that each unwed parent has any such right. *Parental rights do not spring full-blown from the biological connection between parent and child. They require relationships more enduring.*"

441 U.S. at 397 (emphasis added).

In a similar vein, the other three dissenters in *Caban* were prepared to "assume that, *if and when one develops*, the relationship between a father and his natural child is entitled to protection against arbitrary state action as a matter of due process." *Caban v. Mohammed, supra,* at 414 (emphasis added).

The difference between the developed parent-child relationship that was implicated in *Stanley* and *Caban*, and the potential relationship involved in *Quilloin* and this case, is both clear and significant. When an unwed father demonstrates a full commitment to the responsibilities of parenthood by "com[ing] forward to participate in the rearing of his child," *Caban*, 441 U.S. at 392, his interest in personal contact with his child acquires substantial protection under the Due Process Clause. At that point it may be said that he "act[s] as a father toward his children." *Id.* at 389, n.7. But the mere existence of a biological link does not merit equivalent constitutional protection. The actions of judges neither create nor sever genetic bonds. "[T]he importance of the familial relationship, to the individuals involved and to the society, stems from the emotional attachments that derive from the intimacy of daily association, and from the role it plays in 'promot[ing] a way of life' through the instruction of children . . . as well as from the fact of blood relationship." *Smith v. Organization of Foster Families for Equality and Reform*, 431 U.S. 816, 844 (1977) (quoting *Wisconsin v. Yoder,* 406 U.S. 205, 231-233 (1972)).

The significance of the biological connection is that it offers the natural father an opportunity that no other male possesses to develop a relationship with his offspring. If he grasps that opportunity and accepts some measure of responsibility for the child's future, he may enjoy the blessings of the parent-child relationship and make uniquely valuable contributions to the child's development.[18] If he fails to do so, the Federal Constitution will not automatically compel a State to listen to his opinion of where the child's best interests lie.

In this case, we are not assessing the constitutional adequacy of New York's procedures for terminating a developed relationship. Appellant has never had any significant relationship with Jessica, and he did not seek to establish a legal tie until after she was two years old.[19] We are concerned only with whether New York has adequately protected his opportunity to form such a relationship.

II

The most effective protection of the putative father's opportunity to develop a relationship with his child is provided by the laws that authorize formal marriage and govern its consequences. But the availability of that protection is, of course, dependent on the will of both parents of the child. Thus, New York has adopted a special statutory scheme to protect the unmarried father['s] interest in assuming a responsible role in the future of his child.

After this Court's decision in *Stanley,* the New York Legislature . . . enacted a statutory adoption scheme that automatically provides notice to seven categories of putative fathers who are likely to have assumed some responsibility for the care of their natural children. If this scheme were likely to omit many responsible fathers, and if qualification for notice were beyond the control of an interested putative father, it might be thought procedurally inadequate. Yet, as all of the New York courts that reviewed this matter observed,

---

18 Of course, we need not take sides in the ongoing debate among family psychologists over the relative weight to be accorded biological ties and psychological ties, in order to recognize that a natural father who has played a substantial role in rearing his child has a greater claim to constitutional protection than a mere biological parent. New York's statutory scheme reflects these differences, guaranteeing notice to any putative father who is living openly with the child, and providing putative fathers who have never developed a relationship with the child the opportunity to receive notice simply by mailing a postcard to the putative father registry.

19 This case happens to involve an adoption by the husband of the natural mother, but we do not believe the natural father has any greater right to object to such an adoption than to an adoption by to total strangers. If anything, the balance of equities tips the opposite way in a case such as this. In denying the putative father relief in *Quilloin v. Walcott*, 3434 U.S. 246 (1978), we made an observation equally applicable here: "Nor is this a case in which the proposed adoption would place the child with a new set of parents with whom the child had never before lived. Rather, the result of the adoption in this case is to give full recognition to a family unit already in existence, a result desired by all concerned, except appellant. Whatever might be required in other situations, we cannot say that the State was required in this situation to find anything more than that the adoption, and denial of legitimation, were in the 'best interests of the child.'" *Id.* at 255.

the right to receive notice was completely within appellant's control. By mailing a postcard to the putative father registry, he could have guaranteed that he would receive notice of any proceedings to adopt Jessica. The possibility that he may have failed to do so because of his ignorance of the law cannot be a sufficient reason for criticizing the law itself. . . .

Appellant argues, however, that even if the putative father's opportunity to establish a relationship with an illegitimate child is adequately protected by the New York statutory scheme in the normal case, he was nevertheless entitled to special notice because the court and the mother knew that he had filed an affiliation [sic] proceeding in another court. This argument amounts to nothing more than an indirect attack on the notice provisions of the New York statute. The legitimate state interests in facilitating the adoption of young children and having the adoption proceeding completed expeditiously that underlie the entire statutory scheme also justify a trial judge's determination to require all interested parties to adhere precisely to the procedural requirements of the statute. The Constitution does not require either a trial judge or a litigant to give special notice to nonparties who are presumptively capable of asserting and protecting their own rights. Since the New York statutes adequately protected appellant's inchoate interest in establishing a relationship with Jessica, we find no merit in the claim that his constitutional rights were offended because the Family Court strictly complied with the notice provisions of the statute.

* * *

The legislation at issue in this case, sections 111 and 111-a of the New York Domestic Relations Law, is intended to establish procedures for adoptions. Those procedures are designed to promote the best interests of the child, to protect the rights of interested third parties, and to ensure promptness and finality. To serve those ends, the legislation guarantees to certain people the right to veto an adoption and the right to prior notice of any adoption proceeding. The mother of an illegitimate child is always within that favored class, but only certain putative fathers are included. Appellant contends that the gender-based distinction is invidious.

As we have already explained, the existence or nonexistence of a substantial relationship between parent and child is a relevant criterion in evaluating both the rights of the parent and the best interests of the child. In *Quilloin v. Walcott,* we noted that the putative father, like appellant, "ha[d] never shouldered any significant responsibility with respect to the daily supervision, education, protection, or care of the child. Appellant does not complain of his exemption from these responsibilities. . . ." 434 U.S. at 256. We therefore found that a Georgia statute that always required a mother's consent to the adoption of a child born out of wedlock, but required the father's consent only if he had legitimated the child, did not violate the Equal Protection Clause. Because appellant, like the father in *Quillion*, has never established a substantial relationship with his daughter, the New York statutes at issue in this case did not operate to deny appellant equal protection.

. . . Whereas appellee had a continuous custodial responsibility for Jessica, appellant never established any custodial, personal, or financial relationship with her. If one parent has an established custodial relationship with the child and the other parent has either abandoned or never established a relationship the Equal Protection Clause does not prevent a State from according the two parents different legal rights.

The judgment of the New York Court of Appeals is affirmed.

Justice WHITE, with whom Justice MARSHALL and Justice BLACKMUN join, dissenting.

The question in this case is whether the State may, consistent with the Due Process Clause, deny notice and an opportunity to be heard in an adoption proceeding to a putative father when the State has actual notice of his existence, whereabouts, and interest in the child.

* * *

According to Lehr, he and Jessica's mother met in 1971 and began living together in 1974. The couple cohabited for approximately two years, until Jessica's birth in 1976. Throughout the pregnancy and after the birth, Lorraine acknowledged to friends and relatives that Lehr was Jessica's father; Lorraine told Lehr that she had reported to the New York State Department of Social Services that he was the father. Lehr visited Lorraine and Jessica in the hospital every day during Lorraine's confinement. According to Lehr, from the time Lorraine was discharged from the hospital until August 1978, she concealed her whereabouts from him. During this time Lehr never ceased his efforts to locate Lorraine and Jessica and achieved sporadic success until August 1977, after which time he was unable to locate them at all. On those occasions when he did determine Lorraine's location, he visited with her and her children to the extent she was willing to permit it. When Lehr, with the aid of a detective agency, located Lorraine and Jessica in August 1978, Lorraine was already married to Mr. Robertson. Lehr asserts that at this time he offered to provide financial assistance and to set up a trust fund for Jessica, but that Lorraine refused. Lorraine threatened Lehr with arrest unless he stayed away and refused to permit him to see Jessica. Thereafter Lehr retained counsel who wrote to Lorraine in early December 1978, requesting that she permit Lehr to visit Jessica and threatening legal action on Lehr's behalf. On December 21, 1978, perhaps as a response to Lehr's threatened legal action, appellees commenced the adoption action at issue here.

The majority posits that "[t]he intangible fibers that connect parent and child . . . are sufficiently vital to merit constitutional protection *in appropriate cases.*" It then purports to analyze the particular facts of this case to determine whether appellant has a constitutionally protected liberty interest. We have expressly rejected that approach. In *Board of Regents v. Roth*, 408 U.S. 564, 570-571 (1972), we stated that although "a weighing process has long been a part of any determination of the *form* of hearing required in particular situations . . . to determine whether due process requirements apply in the first place, we must look not to the 'weight' but to the *nature* of the interest at stake . . . to see if the interest is within the Fourteenth Amendment's protection. . . ."

The "nature of the interest" at stake here is the interest that a natural parent has in his or her child, one that has long been recognized and accorded constitutional protection. We have frequently "stressed the importance of familial bonds, whether or not legitimized by marriage, and accorded them constitutional protection." *Little v. Streater*, 452 U.S. 1, 13 (1981). If "both the child and the [putative father] in a paternity action have a compelling interest" in the accurate outcome of such a case, *ibid.*, it cannot be disputed that both the child and the putative father have a compelling interest in the outcome of a proceeding that may result in the termination of the father-child relationship. "A parent's interest in the accuracy and justice of the decision to terminate his or her parental status is . . . a commanding one." *Lassiter v. Department of Social Services*, 452 U.S. 18, 27 (1981). It is beyond dispute that a formal order of adoption, no less than a formal termination proceeding, operates to permanently terminate parent rights.

Lehr's version of the "facts" paints a far different picture than that portrayed by the majority The majority's recitation, that "[a]ppellant has never had any significant custodial, personal, or financial relationship with Jessica, and he did not seek to establish a legal tie until after she was two years old," obviously does not tell the whole story. Appellant has never been afforded an opportunity to present his case. The legitimation proceeding he instituted was first stayed, and then dismissed, on appellees' motions. Nor could appellant establish his interest during the adoption proceedings, for it is the failure to provide Lehr notice and an opportunity to be heard there that is at issue here. We cannot fairly make a judgment based on the quality or substance of a relationship without a complete and developed factual record. This case requires us to assume that Lehr's allegations are true—that but for the actions of the child's mother there would have been the kind of significant relationship that the majority concedes is entitled to the full panoply of procedural due process protections.

I reject the peculiar notion that the only significance of the biological connection between father and child is that "it offers the natural father an opportunity that no other male possesses to develop a relationship with his offspring." A "mere biological relationship" is not as unimportant in determining the nature of liberty interests as the majority suggests.

II

In this case, of course, there was no question about either the identity or the location of the putative father. The mother knew exactly who he was and both she and the court entering the order of adoption knew precisely where he was and how to give him actual notice that his parental rights were about to be terminated by an adoption order. Lehr was entitled to due process, and the right to be heard is one of the fundamentals of that right, which "has little reality or worth unless one is informed that the matter is pending and can choose for himself whether to appear or default, acquiesce or contest.'" *Schroeder v. City of New York,* 371 U.S. 208, 212 (1962), quoting *Mullane v. Central Hanover Trust Co.,* 339 U.S. 306, 314 (1950).

* * *

No state interest is substantially served by denying Lehr adequate notice and a hearing. The State no doubt has an interest in expediting adoption proceedings to prevent a child from remaining unduly long in the custody of the State or foster parents. But this is not an adoption involving a child in the custody of an authorized state agency. Here the child is in the custody of the mother and will remain in her custody. Moreover, had Lehr utilized the putative fathers' register, he wold have been granted a prompt hearing, and there was not justifiable reason, in terms of delay, to refuse him a hearing in the circumstances of this case.

The State's undoubted interest in the finality of adoption orders likewise is not well served by a procedure that will deny notice and a hearing to a father whose identity and location are known. As this case well illustrates, denying notice and a hearing to such a father may result in years of additional litigation and threaten the reopening of adoption proceedings and the vacation of the adoption. . . .

* * *

Respectfully, I dissent.

Notes

1. *Stanley v. Illinois* was the first in a line of Supreme Court decisions which "sounded a death knell for the traditional state policy of ignoring the paternal rights of putative fathers." David Line Batty, Note, Michael H. v. Gerald D.: *The Constitutional Rights of Putative Fathers and a Proposal for Reform*, 32 B.C. L. REV. 1173, 1189 (1990). In *Quilloin v. Walcott*, 434 U.S. 246 (1978), the Supreme Court faced the question of whether an unwed father, who infrequently visited his biological child and provided occasional financial support for the child, should be afforded the same constitutional rights as the custodial mother. The putative father claimed that he, as the child's biological father, should enjoy equal protection under the Constitution and have an absolute right to prevent his child's adoption. The Court disagreed and stated that for a father to enjoy parental rights under the Constitution, more than a biological connection must be present. The Court held that an unwed father did not have the right to veto an adoption unless he provided financial support as well as parental care for the child. In *Caban v. Mohammed,* 441 U.S. 380 (1979), the Court was asked to grant parental rights to a putative father who did not live with his biological children but provided financial support and regularly visited them. The mother, who had custody of the children, and the father were married to two different spouses, and both filed claims for adoption of the children. Under New York law, the mother could block the putative father from adopting the children, but he could not prevent the mother and her husband from adopting the children. The Supreme Court struck down the law as unconstitutional and found that the law was a violation of equal protection. The Court held that the unwed father was entitled to full parental rights because of his biological connection with the children and his "substantial relationship" with them. In *Lehr*, the Supreme Court held that an unwed biological father has an "opportunity interest" which he must pursue in order to have a parental right to veto his child's adoption. For further discussion of *Stanley, Quilloin, Caban,* and *Lehr,* see Lynn Kirsch, Note, *The Unwed Fathers and Their Newborn Children Placed for Adoption: Protecting the Rights of Both in Custody Disputes,* 36 ARIZ. L. REV. 1011,

1013-17 (1994); Daniel C. Zinman, Note, *Father Knows Best: The Unwed Father's Right to Raise His Infant Surrendered for Adoption,* 60 FORDHAM L. REV. 971, 974-77 (1992); Elizabeth Buchanan, *The Parent-Child Relationship and the Current Cycle of Family Law Reform: The Constitutional Rights of Unwed Fathers Before and After* Lehr v. Robertson, 45 OHIO ST. L.J. 313 (1984).

2. To address the problem of what rights to afford putative fathers, some states have excluded unwed fathers from the definition of what constitutes a parent, have established an "unfitness" characteristic that pertains only to unwed fathers, or have created no requirement for an unwed father to be notified of a pending adoption. Buchanan, *supra*, in Note 1, at 317. Other states, such as Oklahoma, have enacted laws requiring that all parents, including putative fathers, be provided notice of an adoption proceeding. *See* D. Marianna Brower Blair, *The New Oklahoma Adoption Code: A Quest to Accommodate Diverse Interests,* 33 TULSA L.J. 177, 208-11 (1997). In Oklahoma, a putative father must receive notice by mail of the pending adoption. The putative father must respond to the notice within 30 days, by either acknowledging or denying paternity. If he acknowledges paternity, the putative father must also either consent to or contest the adoption petition. If the putative father fails or refuses to respond to the notice, he waives the right to future notices concerning his parental rights, and he waives any interest in the child. For further discussion of how other states protect the constitutional rights of parents in adoption proceedings in which their rights are involuntarily terminated, see Blair, *supra*, at 215-29.

Recent case law reflects a division among the states as to when putative fathers should be granted full parental rights. Some jurisdictions have held that putative fathers have the right to receive notice of a pending adoption proceeding, as well as a hearing on the matter. *See, e.g., In re M.N.M.,* 605 A.2d 921 (D.C.), *cert. denied*, 506 U.S. 1014 (1992) (trial court's denial of statutory notice of adoption petition violated father's due process rights because he "grasped his opportunity interest"); *Adoption of Eugene,* 614 N.E.2d 645 (Mass. 1993) (unwed putative father's due process rights were violated because it is error "to remove father from the . . . proceedings on the basis of standing" where the father was not given notice that his standing would be challenged in an adoption proceeding); *Van Lue v. Collins,* 1779 P.2d 163 (Or. Ct. App. 1989), *modified,* 782 P.2d 951 (Or. Ct. app. 1989), *review denied*, 78 P.2d 888 (Or. 1989) (notice and hearing necessary where putative father repeatedly attempted to financially support his child). *But see Ivy v. Gladney Home,* 783 S.W.2d 829 (Tex. App. 1990) (procedural due process rights of putative father, who previously signed an affidavit waiving his interest in his child's welfare, were not violated when he failed to receive adequate notice of a termination proceeding); *In re A.S.B.,* 688 N.E.2d 1215 (Ill. App. Ct. 1997) (putative father's due process rights not violated when he was not served notice of pending adoption proceeding because he failed to register with Putative Father Registry and maintain a relationship with his children). For a survey of case law determining what additional factors courts consider when determining whether a putative father's consent is required for adoption, see Ardia L. Campbell, Annotation, *Rights of Unwed Father to Obstruct Adoption of His Child By Witholding Consent*, 61 A.L.R.5TH 151 (1998).

For additional discussion of the constitutional rights of putative fathers in adoption proceedings, see Tony M. Zonda, *Putative Fathers' Rights; Striking the Right Balance in Adoption Laws*, 20 WM. MITCHELL L. REV. 292 (1994); Alexandra R. Dapolito, *The Failure to Notify Putative Fathers of Adoption Proceedings Balancing the Adoption Equation,* 42 CATH. U. L. REV. 979 (1993); Karen C. Wehner, *Daddy Wants Rights Too: A Perspective on Adoption Statutes,* 31 HOUS. L. REV. 691 (1994).

Questions

Suppose a mother wants a particular family to adopt her child, and she refuses to reveal the names of the possible fathers. How should the mother's refusal to divulge this information affect the court's decision as to whether or not to enter an adoption order? What steps might a court take before ordering the adoption? If the court grants the adoption, what future legal problems might arise as a result of the mother refusing to divulge the father's identity? For an example of how the California Supreme Court decided a case where the mother actively kept the putative father from establishing a "substantial relationship" with his biological children, see *Adoption of Kelsey S.,* 823 P.2d 1216 (Cal. 1992).

Chapter 15
Mental Health Commitment of Children

The mental health professional's clinical judgment concerning children in mental health proceedings will often involve use of the AMERICAN PSYCHIATRIC ASSOCIATION'S DIAGNOSTIC AND STATISTIC MANUAL OF MENTAL DISORDERS, or DSM-IV. This manual is a classification system, which includes "physical" disorders as well as "mental" disorders. In the DSM-IV, each of the mental disorders is listed as a clinically distinct behavioral or psychological syndrome or pattern of traits, which manifest some form of dysfunction in a person. This type of grouping of behavioral traits into a pattern or syndrome was observed in some of the cases discussed in Chapter 13. There are five axes in the DSM-IV multiaxial classification:

Axis I	Clinical Disorders Other Conditions That May Be a Focus of Clinical Attention
Axis II	Personality Disorders Mental Retardation
Axis III	General Medical Conditions
Axis IV	Psychosocial and Environmental Problems
Axis V	Global Assessment of Functioning

While the use of the multiaxial system facilitates systematic clinical evaluation, there are significant risks of error or misuse when the DSM-IV categories are forced (for forensic purposes) into legal pigeon holes. The lawyer, child advocate, and judge must therefore insure that to establish "mental defect" or "mental disease," for example, evidence beyond the clinical diagnosis of a DSM-IV mental disorder is often required. There is the risk that labeling a child with a mental health classification will provide limited context for understanding how the child's mental health problems might have emerged from broader surroundings. Thus, in hearings to determine a child's competency or a mental health commitment proceeding, the court should require information beyond the psychologist's DSM-IV diagnosis.

In mental health commitment proceedings, the law allows commitment of "mentally ill" persons who present a danger to others, to self, or who are gravely disabled or unable to care for themselves. Most states also require that the person need treatment. While the clinical expert's evidence, including DSM-IV classification of the child, will assist the court, other factors (e.g., existence of a less restrictive alternative) must be considered before a legal commitment determination is made.

The Fourteenth Amendment states "[n]o State shall . . . deprive any person of life, liberty, or property, without due process of law." The mental health commitment of a child or an adult involves an infringement on the individual's liberty in two ways. First, when a person is committed, he is not free from bodily restraint. Second, a person is not free from the "emotional and psychic harm" caused by his commitment to an institution. A person thus has a constitutional right to both substantive and procedural due process before being institutionalized. The Supreme Court established the minimum requirements necessary to fulfill the due process requirement for juveniles in *Parham v. J.R.*, 422 U.S. 584 (1979) (*infra*, Part B). Do *Parham*'s minimum standards adequately protect juveniles?

While reading this chapter, please note how the courts treat juveniles who are committed for mental health reasons differently from adult commitments. Are these differences well-reasoned? For example, should both the child's and the parents' interests be weighed in juvenile cases while only the adult's interests are considered in adult commitment cases? Are there different policy or constitutional concerns when committing a juvenile than when committing an adult? Does *Parham* address these issues?

A. Mental Health Classifications

The Book of Names: DSM-IV in Context

Peter S. Jensen & Kimberly Hoagwood

9 Development and Psychopathology 231 (1997)*

While a great deal of attention has been devoted in the last two decades to the development and refinement of nosologies[1] designed to classify child and adolescent psychopathologpy, controversies continue concerning the validity of these taxonomies. . . . For good or ill, most diagnostic constructs and their

---

* Reprinted with permission.

1 Author's Note: Nosologic is defined as "relating to a classification of diseases." WEBSTER'S THIRD NEW INTERNATIONAL DICTIONARY 1542 (1986).

measures have been downwardly adapted from models of adult psychopathology. By and large, these models are descriptive, static, and unidimensional, and provide relatively little context for understanding how psychopathology emerges within the child's broader surround. The diagnostic approaches themselves do not include the category of context; they do not provide a means of viewing the child's functioning in his/her context; and perhaps most importantly, the diagnostic models and the assumptions underlying them have not been placed within a larger scientific, philosophical, cultural, and historical framework.

Concerns about these taxonomic approaches are not limited to the child psychopathology field alone. Reservations have been raised about the overly descriptive nature of the various versions of Diagnostic and Statistical Manuals (DSM) for the classification of psychiatric diseases across the entire life span, in that they fail to take into account the effects of various etiologic[2] factors, experience, and developmental history on individuals' current functioning, as well as other contextual factors more readily discerned by experienced clinicians (Cooper & Micheals, 1988; Rutter & Shaffer, 1980; Vaillant, 1984). Interviewing patients for signs and symptoms of disorders omits many portions of clinical reality, including information that pertains to the contextual, interactional, and historical factors that may have contributed to the development of the condition. Further, the more recent DSM versions give short shrift to persons' subjective attributions about their life experiences (including their DSM symptoms). Currently observable behaviors are highlighted, as if divorced from meaning and motivation, and inconvenient or difficult classes of information are eliminated or at best truncated (Trickett, 1966; Wallace, 1944). These taxonomic models of psychopathology generally do not consider the possibility that "psychopathology" in some instances may actually reflect the attempts . . . to adapt to the broader environmental context; further, these concepts of psychopathology assume a relatively stable deficit *within the individual* (American Psychiatric Association, 1944). Perhaps most importantly, these diagnostic approaches have been appropriately criticized on the grounds of both over- and underinclusiveness, the potential for misdiagnosis and misuse, and the credibility (Richters & Cicchetti, 1993; Wakefield, 1992a, 1992b). Compounding all of these difficulties is the fact that revisions have occurred before sufficient research documenting the usefulness and validity of the categories outlined in previous versions had been conducted.

Attempting to address these concerns, at least in part, the most recent changes (DSM-IV) were based upon several principles: first, developers made an explicit attempt to move beyond expert consensus and to rely on empirical documentation via extensive field trials and reanalyses of existing data sets. These data were used to determine the inclusion/exclusion of specific diagnostic criteria, diagnostic thresholds, and required levels of impairment (e.g., *see* Lahey et al., 1994). In addition, higher thresholds were established for making revisions; greater attention was paid to the needs of users within the fields of

---

[2] Author's Note: Etiology is defined as "a science or doctrine of causation or of the demonstration of causes." WEBSTER'S THIRD INTERNATIONAL DICTIONARY 782 (1986).

education, research, and clinical practice; and increased breadth and quality of the field's participation was sought in developing the revision by establishing multiple workgroups, each with 50-100 advisors and participants. Other attempts to move the DSM classification system forward included the abandonment of hierarchical assumptions (beginning first with DSM-III-R), and the explicit attempt to be "atheoretical" by avoiding clinical or etiologic inferences, relying instead on observable (or reportable) behavioral, cognitive, and emotional symptoms (Frances, Pincus, Widiger, Davis, & First, 1944)—as if empiricism were atheoretical! . . .

* * *

Clinical Approaches to Classifications

To fully consider the current classification system, it is instructive to review what experienced clinicians do when assessing patients, and to contrast that approach with current classification strategies. First, it should be noted that *all* clinicians—indeed, all human beings—bring theory-laden perspectives and conceptual filters to their assessment and diagnostic approaches with a given patient. They differ principally in the explicitness, rigidity, and awareness of their biases. A thorough clinical assessment within the medical model usually entails obtaining a history of the present illness, a careful exploration and inquiry about potential associated conditions, delineation of possible risk factors and family history of illness, a mental status exam and physical and neurologic examinations, and pertinent laboratory measures. In addition, most mental health clinicians are interested in the possibility of environmental "predisposition" or "causation," as well as the moderating effect of environmental factors on individual functioning. Consequently, most clinicians inquire about historical information concerning development milestones, formative early events, school history, and past and current contextual information, such as family and peer relations. Thus, the information obtained in a comprehensive clinical evaluation is not just a cross-sectional description of the individual's functioning. Instead, the clinician attempts to construct (hopefully, reconstruct) all biologic, psychological, and social threads from the individual's present and past to understand how they interweave into a meaningful, comprehensive, and richly patterned fabric representing the individual's current functioning.

* * *

Constraints of Current Diagnostic Systems

Given the difficulties among clinicians in coming to agreement on the nature of the difficulties of a given patient, the more recent DSM systems (DSM-III, III-R, and IV) were meant to offer a clean break from the theory-burdened, nonempirical diagnostic practices of the past. At the very least these systems were to be reliable, with the goal that over time, scientists and classifications would work towards more etiologically based systems. Indeed, the history of knowledge development in the medical sciences has often been characterized as moving from descriptive models of understanding illnesses and syndromes to a better knowledge of underlying pathophysiology (though this level of understanding has yet to be achieved in many areas of clinical medicine—Eisenberg, 1995). According to this view, just as in many areas of medicine, a symptomatic stage of classification is a necessary precursor to the development of empirically demonstrated etiologic theories (Sadler et al., 1994). However, excessive emphasis on test-retest and interrater reliability could run the risk of generating unicausal or theoretically impoverished models of psychopathology, simply because classes of information that are more important yet more difficult to operationalize and assess have been eliminated from scientific consideration.

* * *

Solutions

As a first step in reconciling some of the difficulties in our current diagnostic approaches there is a need for a more avowedly open, self-critical, developmental stance toward our diagnostic entities. Greater awareness in the research and clinical communities to avoid the reification of psychiatric labels is essential, en route to a more etiologically based process and context-elaborated nosology. In addition, some researchers have offered recommendations to address the difficulties with the current diagnostic and nosologic systems. . . .

Clinical Implications

What are the implications of these contextual and adaptational approaches to understanding of "mental disorders" and their treatment?

. . . Thinking beyond DSM-IV, clinicians and researchers must pay greater attention and give equal salience to contexts, meaning systems, and the role of adaptive versus dysfunctional processes. . . . These efforts will enable us to move beyond the current descriptive and taxonomic approaches which may run the risk of falling far too short as a simple "book of names" versus more integrative approaches that enable treatment-specific process understanding of psychopathology.

B. Substantive Requirements

New Mexico Statutes Annotated
§ 32A-6-13 (Michie 1999)

§ 32A-6-13. Involuntary residential treatment.

A. No child may receive treatment for mental disorders or habilitation for developmental disabilities on an involuntary residential basis except as provided in this section.

B. Any person who believes that a child, as a result of a mental disorder or developmental disability, is in need of residential mental health or developmental disabilities services may request that a children's court attorney file a petition with the court for the child's involuntary placement. The petition shall include a detailed description of the symptoms or behaviors of the child that support the allegations in the petition, a list of prospective witnesses for involuntary placement and a summary of matters to which they will testify. The petition should also contain a discussion of the alternatives to residential care that have been considered and the reasons for rejecting the alternatives. A copy of the petition shall be served upon the child and a copy of the petition shall be served upon a parent, guardian or legal custodian and upon the child's attorney or guardian ad litem.

C. The court shall, upon receiving the petition, appoint counsel for the child unless the child has retained an attorney or an attorney or guardian ad litem has been appointed. . . . The attorney or guardian ad litem shall represent the child at all stages of the proceedings.

D. If, after interviewing the child, the child's attorney or guardian ad litem determines that the child understands his rights and desires to waive the child's presence at the hearing on the issue of involuntary placement, the attorney or guardian ad litem shall submit a verified written statement to the court explaining the attorney's or guardian ad litem's understanding of the child's intent. If the court is satisfied that the child has voluntarily and knowingly waived his right to be present at the hearing, the child may be involuntarily placed for residential treatment or habilitation at a hearing at which the child is not present. By waiving the right to be present at the involuntary placement hearing, the child waives no other rights.

* * *

H. The court shall include in its findings either a statement of the child's parents', guardian's or custodian's opinion about whether the child should be involuntarily placed in a residential treatment or habilitation program; a statement detailing the efforts made to ascertain the parents', guardian's or custodian's opinion; or a statement of why it was not in the child's best interests to have the parent or guardian involved.

I. The court shall make an order involuntarily placing the child in residential care only if it is shown by clear and convincing evidence:

(1) that as a result of mental disorder or developmental disability the child needs the treatment or habilitation services proposed;

(2) that as a result of mental disorder or developmental disability the child is likely to benefit from the treatment or habilitation services proposed;

(3) that the proposed involuntary placement is consistent with the treatment or habilitation needs of the child; and

(4) that the proposed involuntary placement is consistent with the least drastic means principle.

J. If the court determines that the child does not meet the criteria for involuntary placement set forth in this section, it may order the child to undergo nonresidential treatment as may be appropriate and necessary or it may order no treatment. If the court determines that the child should not be involuntarily placed in residential care and if the child's family refuses to take the child back into the home, the court shall refer the case to the department for an abuse and neglect investigation. . . .

K. Every child receiving involuntary residential treatment for a mental disorder or developmental disability under this section shall have the right to periodic review of his involuntary placement at the end of every involuntary placement period. The involuntary placement period shall not exceed sixty days and any involuntary placement period commencing thereafter shall not exceed six months. At the expiration of an involuntary placement period, the child may continue in residential care only after a new involuntary placement hearing and entry of a new order of involuntary placement for one involuntary placement period.

L. If the person seeking the involuntary placement of a child to residential treatment or habilitation believes that the child is likely to cause serious bodily harm to himself or to others during the period that would be required to hold an involuntary placement hearing as provided in this section, the child may be admitted to residential care on an emergency basis. If the child is admitted on an emergency basis, appointment of counsel and other procedures shall then take place as provided elsewhere in this section.

C. Due Process Framework

New Mexico Statutes Annotated

§ 32A-6-13(E), (F) & (G) (Michie 1999)

§ 32A-6-13. Involuntary residential treatment.

E. An involuntary placement hearing shall be held within seven days of the emergency admission of the child to a residential facility under this section or within seven days from a child's declaration that he desires to terminate his voluntary admission to a residential treatment or habilitation program.

F. At the involuntary placement hearing, the child shall:

(1) at all times be represented by counsel;

(2) have the right to present evidence, including the testimony of a mental health and developmental disabilities professional of his own choosing;

(3) have the right to cross-examine witnesses;

(4) have the right to a complete record of the proceedings; and

(5) have the right to an expeditious appeal of an adverse ruling.

G. The parent, guardian or legal custodian of a child involved in an involuntary placement hearing shall have automatic standing as witnesses and shall be allowed to testify by telephone or through a written affidavit if circumstances make personal testimony too burdensome.

Kentucky Revised Statutes Annotated

§ 645.230 (West 2000)

§ 645.230. Rights of child, parent

(1) The child, parent or other person exercising custodial control or supervision of a child hospitalized under this chapter shall be entitled to confer at regular intervals with the treating or admitting physician or a member of the child's treatment team concerning the child's condition, treatment, or diagnosis.

The hospital or other proponent of certification may request that the parent or other person exercising custodial control or supervision of a child be available for consultation and cooperation in connection with the treatment process and may seek a court order to require such cooperation.

(2) A parent or other person exercising custodial control or supervision of a child who has been hospitalized pursuant to KRS 645.030 may at any time file a notice to withdraw the child from the hospital. Upon receipt of such notice, the hospital may discharge the child immediately to the custody of his parent or other person exercising custodial control or supervision, or if in the opinion of the treating physician release would be seriously detrimental to the child's health, the physician shall:

(a) Discharge the child to the custody of his parent or other person exercising custodial control or supervision against medical advice, after advising them against discharge and seeking their written acknowledgment that they have been so advised; or

(b) Refuse to discharge the child for a period of no more than seventy-two (72) hours, exclusive of weekends and holidays, after receipt of the notice to withdraw, provided that the hospital or the physician files a petition for certification within the three (3) days, exclusive of weekends and holidays, in which case the hospital may hold the child until the court's ruling following the certification hearing.

Parham v. J.R.

442 U.S. 584, 99 S. Ct. 2493, 61 L. Ed. 2d 101 (1979)

Mr. Chief Justice BURGER delivered the opinion of the Court.

The question presented in this appeal is what process is constitutionally due a minor child whose parents or guardian seek state administered institutional mental health care for the child and specifically whether an adversary proceedings is required prior to or after the commitment.

I

Appellee J.R., a child being treated in a Georgia state mental hospital, was a plaintiff in this class action based on 42 U.S.C. § 1983, in the District Court for the Middle District of Georgia. Appellants are the State's Commissioner of the Department of Human Resources, the Director of the Mental Health Division of the Department of Human Resources, and the Chief Medical Officer at the hospital where appellee was being treated. Appellee sought a declaratory judgment that Georgia's voluntary commitment procedures for children under the age of 18, Ga. Code §§ 88-503.1, 88-503.2 (1975), violated the Due Process clause of the Fourteenth Amendment and requested an injunction against their future enforcement. . . . [T]he District Court held that Georgia's statutory scheme was unconstitutional because it failed to protect adequately the appellees' due process rights.

To remedy this violation, the court enjoined future commitments based on the procedures in the Georgia statute. It also commanded Georgia to appropriate and expend whatever amount was "reasonably necessary" to provide nonhospital facilities deemed by the appellant state officials to be the most appropriate for the treatment of those members of plaintiffs' class who could be treated in a less drastic, nonhospital environment.

Appellants challenged all aspects of the District Court's judgment. . . .

* * *

Georgia Code § 88-503.1 (1975) provides for the voluntary admission to a state regional hospital of children such as [plaintiff]. Under that provision, admission begins with an application for hospitalization signed by a "parent or guardian." Upon application, the superintendent of each hospital is given the power to admit temporarily any child for "observation and diagnosis." If, after observation, the superintendent finds "evidence of mental illness" and that the child is "suitable for treatment" in the hospital, then the child may be admitted "for such period and under such conditions as may be authorized by law."

Georgia's mental health statute also provides for the discharge of voluntary patients. Any child who has been hospitalized for more than five days may be discharged at the request of a parent or guardian. § 88-503.3(a) (1975). Even without a request for discharge, however, the superintendent of each regional hospital has an affirmative duty to release any child "who has recovered from his mental illness or who has sufficiently improved that the superintendent determines that hospitalization of the patient is no longer desirable." § 88-503.2 (1975).

* * *

II

In holding unconstitutional Georgia's statutory procedure for voluntary commitment of juveniles, the District Court first determined that commitment to any of the eight regional hospitals constitutes a severe deprivation of a child's liberty. The court defined this liberty interest in terms of both freedom from bodily restraint and freedom from the "emotional and psychic harm" caused by the institutionalization. . . . It held that the process due "includes at least the right after notice to be heard before an impartial tribunal."

* * *

The District Court . . . rejected the argument that review by the superintendents of the hospitals and their staffs was sufficient to protect the child's liberty interest. The court held that the inexactness of psychiatry, coupled with the possibility that the sources of information used to make the commitment decision may not always be reliable, made the superintendent's decision too arbitrary to satisfy due process. . . .

III

* * *

The parties agree that our prior holdings have set out a general approach for testing challenged state procedures under a due process claim. Assuming the existence of a protectible property or liberty interest, the Court has required a balancing of a number of factors:

> "First, the private interest that will be affected by the official action; second, the risk of an erroneous deprivation of such interest through the procedures used, and the probable value, if any, of additional or substitute procedural safeguards; and finally, the Government's interest, including the function involved and the fiscal and administrative burdens that the additional or substitute procedural requirement would entail." *Mathews v. Eldridge*, 424 U.S. 319, 335 (1976), quoted in *Smith v. Organization of Foster Families*, 431 U.S. 816, 848-849 (1977).

In applying these criteria, we must consider first the child's interest in not being committed. Normally, however, since this interest is inextricably linked with the parents' interest in and obligation for the welfare and health of the child, the private interest at stake is a combination of the child's and parents' concerns. Next, we must examine the State's interest in the procedures it has adopted for commitment and treatment of children. Finally, we must consider how well Georgia's procedures protect against arbitrariness in the decision to commit a child to a state mental hospital.

It is not disputed that a child, in common with adults, has a substantial liberty interest in not being confined unnecessarily for medical treatment and that the State's involvement in the commitment decision constitutes state action under the Fourteenth Amendment. *See Addington v. Texas*, 441 U.S. 418, 425 (1979); *In re Gault*, 398 U.S. 1, 27 (1967); *Specht v. Patterson*, 386 U.S. 605 (1967). We also recognize that commitment sometimes produces adverse social consequences for the child because of the reaction of some to the discovery that the child has received psychiatric care.

This reaction, however, need not be equated with the community response resulting from being labeled by the state as delinquent, criminal, or mentally ill and possibly dangerous. The state through its voluntary commitment procedure does not "label" the child; it provides a diagnosis and treatment that medical specialists conclude the child requires. In terms of public reaction, the child who exhibits abnormal behavior may be seriously injured by an erroneous decision not to commit. . . . The pattern of untreated, abnormal behavior—even if nondangerous—arouses at least as much negative reaction as treatment that becomes public knowledge. A person needing, but not receiving, appropriate medical care may well face even greater social ostracism resulting from the observable symptoms of an untreated disorder.

However, we need not decide what effect these factors might have in a different case. For purposes of this decision, we assume that a child has a protectible interest not only in being free of unnecessary bodily restraints but also in not being labeled erroneously by some persons because of an improper decision by the state hospital superintendent.

We next deal with the interests of the parents who have decided, on the basis of their observations and independent professional recommendations, that their child needs institutional care. Appellees argue that the constitutional rights of the child are of such magnitude and the likelihood of parental abuse is so great that the parents' traditional interests in and responsibility for the upbringing of their child must be subordinated at least to the extent of providing a formal adversary hearing prior to a voluntary commitment.

* * *

In defining the respective rights and prerogatives of the child and parent in the voluntary commitment setting, we conclude that our precedents permit the parents to retain a substantial, if not the dominant, role in the decision, absent a finding of neglect or abuse, and that the traditional presumption that the parents act in the best interests of their child should apply. We also conclude, however, that the child's rights and the nature of the commitment decision are such that parents cannot always have absolute and unreviewable discretion to decide whether to have a child institutionalized. They, of course, retain plenary authority to seek such care for their children, subject to a physician's independent examination and medical judgment.

The State obviously has a significant interest in confining the use of its costly mental health facilities to cases of genuine need. The Georgia program seeks first to determine whether the patient seeking admission has an illness that calls for inpatient treatment. . . . In addition, the State has imposed a continuing duty on hospital superintendents to release any patient who has recovered to the point where hospitalization is no longer needed.

The State in performing its voluntarily assumed mission also has a significant interest in not imposing unnecessary procedural obstacles that may discourage the mentally ill or their families from seeking needed psychiatric assistance. The *parens patriae* interest in helping parents care for the mental health of their children cannot be fulfilled if the parents are unwilling to take advantage of the opportunities because the admission process is too onerous, too embarrassing, or too contentious. It is surely not idle to speculate as to how many parents who believe they are acting in good faith would forego state-provided hospital care if such care is contingent on participation in an adversary proceeding designed to probe their motives and other private family matters in seeking the voluntary admission.

The State also has a genuine interest in allocating priority to the diagnosis and treatment of patients as soon as they are admitted to a hospital rather than to time-consuming procedural minuets before the admission. . . . One consequence of increasing the procedures the state must provide prior to a child's voluntary admission will be that mental health professionals will be diverted even more from the treatment of patients in order to travel to and participate in—and wait for—what could be hundreds—or even thousands—of hearings each year. Obviously the cost of these procedures would come from the public moneys the legislature intended for mental health care.

We now turn to consideration of what process protects adequately the child's constitutional rights by reducing risks of error without unduly trenching on traditional parental authority and without undercutting "efforts to further the legitimate interests of both the state and the patient that are served by" voluntary commitments. *Addington v. Texas,* 441 U.S. at 430. We conclude that the risk of error inherent in the parental decision to have a child institutionalized for mental health care is sufficiently great that some kind of inquiry should be made by a "neutral factfinder" to determine whether the statutory requirements for admission are satisfied. That inquiry must carefully probe the child's background using all available sources, including, but not limited to, parents, schools, and other social agencies. Of course, the review must also include an interview with the child. It is necessary that the decisionmaker has the authority to refuse to admit any child who does not satisfy the medical standards for admission. Finally, it is necessary that the child's continuing need for commitment be reviewed periodically by a similarly independent procedure.

We are satisfied that such procedures will protect the child from an erroneous admission decision in a way that neither unduly burdens the states nor inhibits parental decisions to seek state help.

* * *

It is not necessary that the deciding physician conduct a formal or quasi-formal hearing. A state is free to require such a hearing, but due process is not violated by use of informal, traditional medical investigative techniques. Since well-established medical procedures already exist, we do not undertake to outline with specificity precisely what this investigation must involve. . . . We do no more than emphasize that the decision should represent an independent judgment of what the child requires and that all sources of information that are traditionally relied on by physicians and behavioral specialists should be consulted.

* * *

[A] formalized, factfinding hearing [includes] significant intrusion into the parent-child relationship. Pitting the parents and child as adversaries often will be at odds with the presumption that parents act in the best interests of their child. It is one thing to require a neutral physician to make a careful review of the parents' decision in order to make sure it is proper from a medical standpoint; it is a wholly different matter to employ an adversary contest to ascertain whether the parents' motivation is consistent with the child's interests.

* * *

It has been suggested that a hearing conducted by someone other than the admitting physician is necessary in order to detect instances where parents are "guilty of railroading their children into asylums" or are using "voluntary commitment procedures in order to sanction behavior of which they disapprov[e]." Ellis, Volunteering Children: Parental Commitment of Minors to Mental Institutions, 62 Calif. L. Rev. 840, 950-51 (1974). Curiously, it seems to be taken for granted that parents who seek to "dump" their children on the State will inevitably be able to conceal their motives and thus deceive the admitting psychiatrists and the other mental health professionals who make and review the admission decision. It is elementary that one early diagnostic inquiry into the cause of an emotional disturbance of a child is an examination into the environment of the child. It is unlikely, if not inconceivable, that a decision to abandon an emotionally normal, healthy child and thrust him into an institution will be a discrete act leaving no trail of circumstances. Evidence of such conflicts will emerge either in the interviews or from secondary sources. It is unrealistic to believe that trained psychiatrists, skilled in eliciting responses, sorting medically relevant facts, and sensing motivational nuances will often be deceived about the family situation surrounding a child's emotional disturbance....

By expressing some confidence in the medical decisionmaking process, we are by no means suggesting it is error free. On occasion, parents may initially mislead an admitting physician or a physician may erroneously diagnose the chid as needling institutional care either because of negligence or an overabundance of caution. That there may be risks of error in the process affords no rational predicate for holding unconstitutional an entire statutory and administrative scheme. ... In general, we are satisfied that an independent medical decisionmaking process, which includes [a] thorough psychiatric investigation ..., followed by additional periodic review of a child's condition, will protect children who should not be admitted.... The issue remains whether the Georgia practices, as described in the record before us, comport with these minimum due process requirements.

Georgia's statute envisions a careful diagnostic medical inquiry to be conducted by the admitting physician at each regional hospital. The *amicus* brief for the United States explains, at pages 7-8:

> "[I]n every instance the decision whether or not to accept the child for treatment is made by a physician employed by the State....
>
> "That decision is based on interviews and recommendations by hospital or community health center staff. The staff interviews the child and the parent or guardian who brings the child ... to the facility ... [and] attempts are made to communicate with other possible sources of information about the child...."

* * *

In the typical case, the parents of a child initially conclude from the child's behavior that there is some emotional problem—in short, that "something is wrong." They may respond to the problem in various ways, but generally the first contact with the State occurs when they bring the child to be examined by a psychologist or psychiatrist at a community mental health clinic.

Most often, the examination is followed by outpatient treatment at the community clinic. In addition, the child's parents are encouraged, and sometimes required, to participate in a family therapy program to obtain a better insight into the problem. In most instances, this is all the care a child requires. However, if , after a period of outpatient care, the child's abnormal emotional condition persists, he may be referred by the local clinic staff to an affiliated regional mental hospital.

At the regional hospital an admissions team composed of a psychiatrist and at least one other mental health professional examines and interviews the child— privately in most instances. This team then examines the medical records provided by the clinic staff and interviews the parents. Based on this information, and any additional background that can be obtained, the admissions team makes a diagnosis and determines whether the child will likely benefit from institutionalized care. If the team finds either condition not met, admission is refused.

If the team admits a child as suited for hospitalization, the child's condition and continuing need for hospital care are reviewed periodically by at least one independent, medical review group. Moreover, . . . the superintendent of each hospital is charged with an affirmative statutory duty to discharge any child who is no longer mentally ill or in need of therapy.

As with most medical procedures, Georgia's are not totally free from risk of error in the sense that they give total or absolute assurance that every child admitted to a hospital has a mental illness optimally suitable for institutionalized treatment. But it bears repeating that "procedural due process rules are shaped by the risk of error inherent in the truthfinding process as applied to the generality of cases, not the rare exception." *Matthews v. Eldridge, supra,* at 344.

* * *

We are satisfied that the . . . record . . . supports the conclusion that the admissions staffs of the hospitals have acted in a neutral and detached fashion in making medical judgments in the best interests of the children. The State, through its mental health programs, provides the authority for trained professionals to assist parents in examining, diagnosing, and treating emotionally disturbed children. . . .

* * *

IV

Our discussion in Part III was directed at the situation where a child's natural parents request his admission to a state mental hospital. Some members of appellees' class, including J.R., were wards of the state of Georgia at the time of their admission. Obviously their situation differs from those members of the class who have natural parents. While the determination of what process is due varies somewhat when the State, rather than a natural parent, makes the request for commitment, we conclude that the differences in the two situations do not justify requiring different procedures at the time of the child's initial admission to the hospital.

* * *

Since the state agency having custody and control the child *in loco parentis* has a duty to consider the best interests of the child with respect to a decision on commitment to a mental hospital, the State may constitutionally allow that custodial agency to speak for the child, subject, of course, to the restrictions governing natural parents. On this record, we cannot declare unconstitutional Georgia's admission procedures for wards of the State.

* * *

The absence of an adult who cares deeply for a child has little effect on the reliability of the initial admission decision, but it may have some effect on how long a child well remain in the hospital. . . . For a child without natural parents, we must acknowledge the risk of being "lost in the shuffle." Moreover, there is at least some indication that J.R.'s commitment was prolonged because the Department of Family and Children Services had difficulty finding a foster home for him. Whether wards of the State generally have received less protection than children with natural parents, and, if so, what should be done about it, however, are matters that must be decided in the first instance by the District Court on remand, if the court concludes the issue is still alive.

V

. . . Georgia's comprehensive mental health program . . . seeks substantively and at great cost to provide care for those who cannot afford to obtain private treatment and procedurally to screen carefully all applicants to assure that institutional care is suited to the particular patient. The State resists the complex of procedures ordered by the District Court because in its view they are unnecessary to protect the child's rights, they divert public resources from the central objective of administering health care, they risk aggravating the tensions inherent in the family situation, and they erect barriers that may discourage parents from seeking medical aid for a disturbed child.

On this record, we are satisfied that Georgia's medical factfinding processes are reasonable and consistent with constitutional guarantees. Accordingly, it was error to hold unconstitutional the State's procedures for admitting a child for treatment to a state mental hospital. The judgment is therefore reversed, and the case is remanded to the District Court for further proceedings consistent with this opinion.

[Justice STEWART's concurrence is omitted.]

Mr. Justice BRENNAN, with whom Mr. Justice MARSHALL and Mr. Justice STEVENS join, concurring in part and dissenting in part.

I agree with the Court that the commitment of juveniles to state mental hospitals by their parents or by state officials acting *in loco parentis* involves state action that impacts upon constitutionally protected interests and therefore must be accomplished through procedures consistent with the constitutional mandate of due process of law. I agree also that the District Court erred in interpreting the Due Process Clause to require preconfinement commitment hearings in all cases in which parents wish to hospitalize their children. I disagree, however, with the Court's decision . . . concerning the postadmission procedures due Georgia's institutionalized juveniles. . . . I also disagree with the Court's conclusion concerning the procedures due juvenile wards of the State of Georgia. I believe that the Georgia statute is unconstitutional in that it fails to accord preconfinement hearings to juvenile wards of the State committed by the State acting *in loco parentis*.

* * *

. . . The presumption that parents act in their children's best interests, while applicable to most child-rearing decisions, is not applicable in the commitment context. Numerous studies reveal that parental decisions to institutionalize their children often are the results of dislocation in the family unrelated to the children's mental condition. Moreover, even well-meaning parents lack the expertise necessary to evaluate the relative advantages and disadvantages of inpatient as opposed to outpatient psychiatric treatment. Parental decisions to waive hearings in which such questions could be explored, therefore, cannot be conclusively deemed either informed or intelligent. In these circumstances, I respectfully suggest, it ignores reality to assume blindly that parents act in their children's best interests when making commitment decisions and when waiving their children's due process rights. This does not mean States are obliged to treat children who are committed at the behest of their parents in precisely the same manner as other persons who are involuntarily committed. . . .

* * *

I do not believe . . . that the present Georgia juvenile commitment scheme is constitutional in its entirety. Although Georgia may postpone formal commitment hearings, when parents seek to commit their children, the State cannot dispense with such hearings altogether. . . .

* * *

The special considerations that militate against preadmission commitment hearings when parents seek to hospitalize their children do not militate against reasonably prompt postadmission commitment hearings. In the first place, postadmission hearings would not delay the commencement of needed treatment. Children could be cared for by the State pending the disposition decision.

Second, the interest in avoiding family discord would be less significant at this stage. . . . [T]he case for and against commitment would be based upon the observations of the hospital staff and the judgments of the staff psychiatrists, rather than upon parental observations and recommendations. The doctors urging commitment, and not the parents, would stand as the child's adversaries. As a consequence, postadmission commitment hearings are unlikely to involve direct challenges to parental authority, judgment, or veracity. . . .

* * *

Georgia does not accord prior hearings to juvenile wards of the State of Georgia committed by state social workers acting *in loco parentis*. The court dismisses a challenge to this practice on the grounds that state social workers are obliged by statue to act in the children's best interest.

I find this reasoning particularly unpersuasive. With equal logic, it could be argued that criminal trials are unnecessary since prosecutors are not supposed to prosecute innocent persons.

To my mind, there is no justification for denying children committed by their social workers the prior hearings that the Constitution typically requires. In the first place, such children cannot be said to have waived their rights to a prior hearing simply because their social workers wish them to be confined. The rule that parents speak for their children, even if it were applicable in the commitment context, cannot be transmuted into a rule that state social workers speak for their minor clients. . . . The social worker-child relationship is not deserving of the special protection and deference accorded to the parent-child relationship, and state officials acting *in loco parentis* cannot be equated with parents.

Second, the special considerations that justify postponement of formal commitment proceedings whenever parents seek to hospitalize their children are absent when the children are wards of the State and are being committed upon the recommendations of their social workers. The prospect of preadmission hearings is not likely to deter state social workers from discharging their duties and securing psychiatric attention for their disturbed clients. Moreover, since the children will already be in some form of state custody as wards of the State, prehospitalization hearings will not prevent needy children from receiving state care during the pendency of the commitment proceedings. Finally, hearings in which the decisions of state social workers are reviewed by other state officials are not likely to traumatize the children or to hinder their eventual recovery.

For these reasons, I believe that, in the absence of exigent circumstances, juveniles committed upon the recommendation of their social workers are entitled to preadmission commitment hearings. As a consequence, I would hold Georgia's present practice of denying these juveniles prior hearings unconstitutional. . . .

M.W. v. Davis

756 So. 2d 90 (Fla. 2000)

M.W., the petitioner in this case, is a sixteen-year-old male adolescent from Dade County. M.W. was removed from his mother's custody at the age of six due to allegations of abuse and neglect. Although M.W. was adjudicated dependent and placed in the temporary legal custody of the Department, his mother's parental rights have not been terminated. . . . The case plan goal for M.W. has been reunification with his eight siblings and his mother.

The events leading up to the issue addressed by the certified question arose from disagreement among health care professionals over the appropriate placement for M.W. In May of 1998, as a result of behavioral and psychological problems, M.W., who was fifteen at the time, was admitted to the psychiatric unit at Palmetto General Hospital for examination and treatment. . . . The two mental health professionals who evaluated M.W. at Palmetto General disagreed as to the type of placement that was appropriate for M.W. . . .

The Department then sought to place M.W. in a residential facility. M.W. contested this placement and, through his attorney, filed an emergency motion for an independent expert examination to determine whether residential psychiatric treatment was needed. The dependency court held a hearing on this motion on June 18, 1998. . . .

At this same hearing, M.W.'s counsel also advised the dependency court that M.W. had been released from Palmetto General and placed in foster care but that he had not received his prescribed psychotropic medications for two days. At a hearing held eleven days later on June 29, 1998, M.W.'s counsel advised the court that M.W. was still not receiving his medications and as a result had destabilized. M.W. thus requested that he be placed once again in the psychiatric unit at Palmetto General in order to receive his medications and stabilize. In accordance with M.W.'s request, the court ordered that M.W. be returned to Palmetto General.

* * *

Apparently, M.W.'s hospitalization dragged on because of the lack of available placements. Then, on August 10, 1998, an incident occurred in which M.W. became physically and verbally aggressive towards one of his peers at Palmetto General. . . .

On August 12, 1998, a hearing was held on M.W.'s previously filed motion to compel the Department to find him an appropriate placement. The dependency court judge ordered that M.W. be removed from Palmetto General and placed in a specialized therapeutic foster respite home, pending a search by the Department for a more appropriate home and a comprehensive assessment of his needs.

* * *

M.W.'s case came back before the dependency court judge at a status hearing on September 23, 1998. By this time, the Family Services Planning Team and the Case Review Committee had met and both recommended residential placement for M.W. Due to the conflicting recommendations from the psychologists and psychiatrists that had evaluated M.W., both the Department and M.W.'s attorney once again asked the court to schedule an evidentiary hearing to resolve the contested issue of M.W.'s placement. The Department advocated placement in a residential facility, while M.W. requested placement in a therapeutic foster care home. The dependency judge recognized the need for an evidentiary hearing, but explained that she had no time available for a hearing until November 9, 1998. Despite the protestations of M.W.'s counsel that this date was six weeks in the future and no commitment should occur without an evidentiary hearing first, the judge ordered that M.W. be placed in Lock Towns Adolescent Care Program, a locked mental health treatment facility in Broward County, "temporarily, until we have an evidentiary hearing."

In response, M.W. filed a petition for writ of habeas corpus in the Fourth District. . . .

The Fourth District concluded that it was "satisfied that the court did not abuse its discretion in concluding that this nonordinary residential placement was 'consistent with the child's best interests and special needs.'" . . .

Because M.W. asserts both a constitutional and a statutory basis for an evidentiary hearing, we first evaluate the nature and extent of the constitutional rights involved. The Fourteenth Amendment of the United States Constitution provides that no state shall "deprive any person of life, liberty, or property, without due process of law." Article I, section 9 of the Florida Constitution provides a similar guarantee that "no person shall be deprived of life, liberty or property without due process of law."

The Due Process clauses of the United States and Florida Constitutions encompass both substantive and procedural due process. *See, e.g., Department of Law Enforcement v. Real Property,* 588 So. 2d 957, 960 (Fla. 1991). As we have previously explained, "substantive due process under the Florida Constitution protects the full panoply of individual rights from unwarranted encroachment by the government." *Id.* Likewise, we have made clear that the purpose of procedural due process is to "serve[] as a vehicle to ensure fair treatment through the proper administration of justice where substantive rights are at issue." *Id.* . . .

In *Parham v. J.R.*, 442 U.S. 584, 61 L. Ed. 2d 101, 99 S. Ct. 2493 (1979), the United States Supreme Court explored the nature and extent of a child's rights when the child is committed to a state mental hospital. 442 U.S. at 606-07. The United States Supreme Court stated that "it is not disputed that a child, in common with adults, has a substantial liberty interest in not being confined unnecessarily for medical treatment and that the State's involvement in the commitment decision constitutes state action under the Fourteenth Amendment." *Parham,* 442 U.S. at 600 (emphasis supplied). Accordingly, the Court "assumed that a child has a protectible interest not only in being free of unnecessary bodily restraints but also in not being labeled erroneously by some persons because of an improper decision by the state hospital superintendent." *Id.* at 601.

* * *

Thus, the United States Supreme Court in *Parham* set forth three minimum due process requirements that must be provided when a child is committed: (1) an inquiry by a neutral factfinder, which is not required to be in the form of a judicial inquiry; (2) the inquiry must probe the child's background using all available resources; and (3) there must be periodic review by a neutral factfinder. *Id.* at 606. These minimum standards apply whether the child has been admitted by the State as the guardian of its ward or by a natural parent. *See id.* at 618-619.

Applying these constitutional principles to the present case, we note that the dependency judge's decision to place M.W. in Lock Towns was not made in a vacuum. The judge was already familiar with M.W. and had reviewed his case at several hearings in the months preceding his placement in Lock Towns. Before ordering the placement in Lock Towns, the dependency judge considered the recommendation of the citizen review panel and two psychological and psychiatric reports, which concurred that it was necessary to place M.W. in a locked residential facility. The judge expressed her view that this was the most "appropriate facility" considering the child's prior failed placements and recent hospitalization. Although the dependency judge did not hold an evidentiary hearing before placing M.W. in Lock Towns, she did recognize the need for an evidentiary hearing and scheduled one for a date six weeks in the future. Accordingly, the procedure followed in this case prior to ordering that M.W. be placed in Lock Towns satisfied minimum constitutional due process requirements as set forth in *Parham.*

Notes

1. States must follow at a constitutional minimum the due process procedures outlined in *Parham.* Only nineteen states follow the *Parham* minimum and nothing more. *See, e.g.*, ARIZ. REV. STAT. ANN. § 36-518 (West Supp. 2000); CAL. WELF. & INST. CODE § 6000 (West 1998); D.C. CODE ANN. § 21-511 (Lexis 1997); ME.

REV. STAT. ANN. tit. 34-B, § 3851 (West 1988); OR. REV. STAT. § 426.220 (1999); MO. ANN. STAT. § 632.110 (West 2000); WYO. STAT. ANN. § 25-10-106 (Lexis 1999). For a discussion of the procedures states follow in commitment proceedings, see Dennis E. Cichon, *Developing a Mental Health Code For Minors,* 13 T.M. COOLEY L. REV. 529 (1996).

2. The *Parham* court did not address the question of whether a juvenile court judge should order the least drastic alternative for a child committed to a mental hospital. In *Youngberg v. Romeo*, 457 U.S. 387 (1982), the Court refused to adopt the least drastic alternative standard for committing children and has not addressed the issue since. However, forty-seven states today have adopted least drastic alternative laws concerning the commitment of children. *See, e.g.*, ALASKA STAT. § 47.30-735(d) (Lexis 2000); DEL. CODE ANN. tit. 16, § 5010(2) (Michie 1995); FLA. STAT. ANN. § 394.467 (West Supp. 2001); IDAHO CODE § 66-329(k)(2) (Michie 2000); KY. REV. STAT. ANN. § 202A.026 (West 2000); MASS. GEN. LAWS ANN. ch. 123, § 8 (Lexis Supp. 2001); OKLA. STAT. ANN. tit. 43A, § 5-505(B)(2)(b) (West Supp. 2001); VT. STAT. ANN. tit. 18, § 7617(c) (Lexis 2000). Most juvenile courts interestingly do not cite *Youngberg* when applying state law to commitment proceedings. *See, e.g., Matter of Schauer,* 450 N.W.2d 194 (Minn. Ct. App. 1990); *In re Sharon K.,* 387 S.E.2d 804 (W. Va. 1989).

3. For additional commentary on the impact of *Parham* on commitment proceedings for children, see Ira C. Lupu, *Meditating Institution: Beyond the Public/Private Distinction: The Separation of Powers and the Protection of Children,* 61 U. CHI. L. REV. 1317 (1994); Peter O. Glaessner, *Due Process in the "Voluntary" Civil Commitment of Juvenile Wards,* 2 J. LEGAL MED. (No. 2) 169 (1981); Gary B. Melton & Gail S. Perry, *Precedential Value of Judicial Notice of Social Facts:* Parham *as an Example,* 22 J. FAM. L. 633 (1983-1984); James K. Walding, *Whatever Happened to* Parham *and Institutionalized Juveniles? Do Minors Have Procedural Rights In the Civil Commitment Area?*, 14 LAW & PSYCHOL. REV. 281 (1990); Donald P. Simet, *Power, Uncertainty, and Choice: The Voluntary Commitment of Children*—Parham v. J.R., 19 J. FAM. L. 27 (1980-1981); Susan Turner, Comment, Parham v. J.R.*: Civil Psychiatric Commitment of Minors,* 5 J. CONTEMP. HEALTH L. & POL'Y 263 (1989); Elyce H. Zenoff & Alan B. Zeints, M.D., *If Civil Commitment Is the Answer for Children, What Are the Questions?,* 51 GEO. WASH. L. REV. 171 (1983). For a discussion of the increasing admission rates for children in mental hospitals, see Lois A. Weithorn, Note, *Mental Hospitalization of Troublesome Youth: An Analysis of Skyrocketing Admission Rates,* 40 STAN. L. REV. 773 (1998).

Questions

1. In *Parham*, the Court equates the commitment of a child by his parents with voluntary commitment. What if the child disagrees with the parents' assessment? How would the *Parham* dissenters respond?

2. The *Parham* majority stated that the commitment procedures Georgia followed would prevent parents from "dumping" their unwanted or troubled children on the state. If state law did not provide voluntary admission as an option, how could the state prevent parents from "dumping" their children on the state?

3. In a commitment hearing involving a child, which should be the primary concern of the court: the physical restraint of the child or the treatment required? For weighing the interests of the committed child versus the necessary treatment, see Roy Lacoursiere, *A Footnote to* Parham*: Was J.L. a Casualty of the Mental Health Bar?*, 11 BULL. AM. ACAD. PSYCHIATRY & L. 279 (1983).

Chapter 16

The Future of the Juvenile Court

The future of the juvenile court is the subject of much debate. Some commentators argue that the success of the court hinges on its independence, emphasizing that it should remain committed to rehabilitation, with a focus on early intervention. Advocates for the court's abolition, however, point to perceived failures in the current court system and explain that there are no compelling reasons for a juvenile court to remain separate from adult criminal courts. However, a new trend toward specialization is emerging. This movement does not lose sight of the importance of rehabilitation, yet it simultaneously recognizes the necessary transformation the juvenile court must undergo to successfully address the needs of today's youth. The move toward specialization reworks the traditional juvenile court model with what these advocates suggest is an improved updated approach. So where do we go from here?

A. Maintain a Rehabilitative Approach

1. Rehabilitation Generally

Rehabilitation theory rests on the premise that a child who commits a delinquent act can be rehabilitated with treatment. Such treatment strives to change the child's thinking and value system by helping him or her cope with external influences. Those who argue that the juvenile court must maintain a rehabilitative approach emphasize the importance of intervention.

With the breakdown of the American family and the growing seriousness of problems that schools and juvenile courts are being asked to fix, what role if any should the juvenile court have in the prevention of delinquency and issues relating to abuse and neglect? Commentators suggest that delinquency can be successfully prevented through the identification of at-risk youth. Programs would target such youth by examining childhood predictors of later delinquent and criminal behavior. This school of thought focuses on early childhood intervention, complete with home visits and comprehensive observation. An example would be a program that provides home visits, pediatric services and child care to children reared in high-risk environments. For an in-depth discussion, see Jane Watson, *Crime and Juvenile Delinquency Prevention Policy: Time for Early Childhood Intervention,* 2 GEO. J. FIGHTING POVERTY 245 (1995).

An example of a program that provides intervention for previous delinquent juveniles as well as a remedial tool for delinquent children is mentoring. The Juvenile Mentoring Program (JUMP) was established by the Juvenile Justice and Delinquency Prevention Act of 1974, 42 U.S.C.A. §§ 5667e *et seq.* and was created to provide "one-on-one mentoring for youth at risk of delinquency, gang involvement, educational failure, or dropping out of school." LAURENCE C. NOVOTNEY, U.S. DEP'T OF JUST., JUVENILE MENTORING PROGRAM: A PROGRESS REVIEW 1 (2000). Current JUMP projects serve a balanced mix of boys (48.4%) and girls (51.3%), most of whom come from a single parent home and a majority of whom are African American (51.1%). *Id.* at 4. JUMP statistics indicate that a majority of JUMP participants are exposed to risk factors at school (males 74.6%/females 63.0%) or at home (males 51.7%/females 56.4%). *Id.* at 5. For further discussion of other risk factors JUMP participants face, see *id.*

Advocates for rehabilitation and intervention attack the punishment-oriented approach by citing studies which show that increased punishments do not, in fact, break the cycle of juvenile crime. In fact, those juvenile offenders sentenced to incarceration by adult courts have a higher recidivism rate than those who receive treatment in juvenile courts. For example, one commentator argues that in the treatment of juvenile sex offenders, effective rehabilitation would successfully reduce the probability of young sexual offenders becoming adult offenders. Specialized, community-based treatment centers offer the much needed counseling and treatment that is not available to juveniles in adult prison. These centers provide juvenile sex offenders with a complete, individualized assessment and treatment plan as well as access to post-treatment groups. Importantly, the author suggests that approximately 85% of juveniles enrolled in treatment programs are successfully rehabilitated. *See* Sander N. Rothchild, *Beyond Incarceration: Juvenile Sex Offender Treatment Programs Offer Youth a Second Chance*, 4 J.L. & POL'Y 719 (1996).

Rehabilitation theory rails against the transfer of juvenile offenders, through waiver, to adult courts. Proponents of rehabilitation point to studies that show juveniles transferred to adult court do not receive longer prison sentences, thereby failing to achieve what such waiver statutes hope to accomplish—criminal deterrence and the removal of juvenile offenders from the streets. Advocates of rehabilitation suggest that successful treatment programs exist for serious juvenile offenders, arguing that such rehabilitative programs are more effective at reducing recidivism than incarceration. Intervention should include consideration of the juvenile as an individual and treatment within the juvenile's own home and community. *See* Candace Zierdt, *The Little Engine That Arrived at the Wrong Station: How to Get Juvenile Justice Back on the Right Track,* 33 U.S.F. L. REV. 401 (1999). These advocates also emphasize the need for judicial discretion within the juvenile court. They argue that a system that empowers the juvenile court with authority over all cases will better serve both the juvenile and the community. The judge is equipped to analyze the individual needs of the juvenile and is in a position to determine effective rehabilitative ends. For a further description and analysis, see Rose M. Charles & Jennifer V. Zuccarelli, Note, *Serving No "Purpose": The Double-Edged Sword of New York's Juvenile Offender Law,* 12 ST. JOHN'S LEG. COMMENT. 721 (1997).

2. Restorative Justice

It has been suggested that the rehabilitative focus of the juvenile justice system be expanded to consider the victim's needs and protection of society. One such example is restorative justice. Restorative justice suggests that society must respond to a juvenile's delinquent actions by balancing the needs of the victim, the community, and the offender. In balancing the needs of these three parties, courts must determine the nature of the harm caused by the juvenile, what is needed to repair the damage, and who is responsible for repairing the harm done. Under a restorative justice model, a juvenile offender is responsible for the loss of the victim and the community. Restorative justice thus shifts the focus of the juvenile court from treatment of the offender to restoration of the victim and the community. In short, "restorative justice suggests that the most important fact about crime is that it causes harm to individuals and communities." OFFICE FOR VICTIMS OF CRIMES, DEP'T OF JUST., VICTIMS, JUDGES, AND JUVENILES: COURT REFORM THROUGH RESTORATIVE JUSTICE 4 (2000).

A recent study by the United States Department of Justice suggests restorative justice may improve the public's perception of the juvenile justice system. In this study, victims within the focus group believed the current juvenile justice system paid little attention to their status as victims, denied victims the opportunity to provide input on dispositional decisions, and suggested that more restorative justice alternatives should be available in the juvenile court process. *Id.* at 6. In the same study, many judges disagreed with the efficacy of victim input on delinquency dispositions, citing the victim's emotional involvement in the decisions. However, in general, the judges agreed that "improvements are needed in processes involving victim notification, victim participation, victim impact statements, and restitution to victims." *Id.* at 7. For a discussion of the steps states are taking to address the needs of the victims of juvenile crime, see Robert E. Shepherd, Jr., *The "Child" Grows Up: The Juvenile System Enters Its Second Century*, 33 FAM. L.Q. 589, 596 (1996).

B. Abolition of the Juvenile Court?

The arguments for abolishing the juvenile court have been expressed in various ways and, in some jurisdictions, procedurally enacted in different forms. Legislative reactions to the call for heightened responsibility of juvenile offenders have produced automatic waiver statutes, reductions in the maximum age of the juvenile court's jurisdiction, and the incorporation of adult sentencing approaches into the juvenile court system. These statutory changes have produced a system that delivers more severe sanctions to the juvenile offender, emphasizing punishment and accountability. It has thus been suggested that the juvenile justice system has begun to resemble the adult criminal justice system, absent many of the constitutional guarantees available in adult court. The focus is no longer rehabilitation, but instead responsibility.

Some commentators suggest that the punitive juvenile court cannot be distinguished from the adult criminal court, with the exception of the procedural deficiencies in the juvenile justice system. Given this, the argument contends that there are no compelling reasons to maintain an autonomous juvenile system. Instead, it is argued that the juvenile system be abolished. In its place, formal recognition of the effect of youth on culpability would be maintained through a mechanism that uses youth as a mitigating factor for younger offenders. Barry Feld, in his article *Abolish the Juvenile Court: Youthfulness, Criminal Responsibility, and Sentencing Policy,* 88 J. CRIM. L. & CRIMINOLOGY 68 (1997), argues that all offenders be tried in adult criminal court, with an age-based "youth discount" implemented in the sentencing of young offenders. Such a discount would represent a sliding scale of developmental and criminal responsibility and render a sentence that reflects the culpability of younger offenders. Feld suggests that by trying youth in criminal courts, they would enjoy full procedural parity with their adult counterparts and, with the youth discount, benefit from an additional safeguard that recognizes the social and psychological difference of youth. For further discussion, see Barry C. Feld, *The Transformation of the Juvenile Court—Part II: Race and the "Crack Down" on Youth Crime,*

84 MINN. L. REV. 327 (1999). *But see* Shannon F. McLatchey, *Juvenile Crime and Punishment: An Analysis of the "Get Tough" Approach,* 10 U. FLA. J. L. & PUB. POL'Y 401 (1999) (arguing that a unified system for adults and juveniles would lack the sufficient resources to adequately address youthful offenders and offer specialized treatment). Recent statistics, however, indicate that juveniles who are sent to the adult system are 30% more likely to be repeat offenders. *See* Donna M. Bishop, *et al., The Transfer of Juveniles to Criminal Court: Does It Make a Difference?,* 42 CRIME AND DELINQUENCY 171 (1996). *See also* U.S. DEP'T OF JUST., RECIDIVISM OF YOUNG PAROLEES (1988).

Additional statistics suggest that other support systems for juveniles need to be emphasized rather than the abolition of the juvenile court. The juvenile arrest rate for violent crimes decreased 36% from 1994 to 1999, representing the lowest arrest rate in a decade. *See* HOWARD N. SNYDER, U.S. DEP'T OF JUST., JUVENILE ARRESTS 1999, 1-7 (2000). Meanwhile, the murder arrest rate fell 68% during the same time period. The 1999 murder arrest rate was 1/3 of the 1993 rate and was the lowest since 1966. Juvenile arrests for violent offenses as well as property crimes decreased from 1994 to 1996. However, the juvenile arrest rate significantly increased from 1990 to 1999 for drug abuse offenses (132%) and for curfew violations and loitering (113%). For additional juvenile arrest rate decreases and increases from 1980 to 1999, see *id.* at 5-10; *see also* CINDY S. LEDEMAN, U.S. DEP'T OF JUST., THE JUVENILE COURT: PUTTING RESEARCH TO WORK FOR PREVENTION 22, 23 (1999). In fact, juvenile court programs actually are more effective when dealing with more serious juvenile offenders than with less serious offenders. *See* James C. Howel, *Abolish the Juvenile Court? Nonsense!,* 4 JUR. JUST. UPDATE 1 (1998). Five in six juveniles referred to juvenile courts for violent offenses do not commit subsequent violent offenses. *See* U.S. DEP'T OF JUST., AN EVOLVING JUVENILE COURT: ON THE FRONT LINES WITH JUDGE J. DEAN LEWIS (1999). What do these statistics, if at all, suggest about the juvenile justice system's ability to address the needs of today's youth? What additional steps, if any, should the juvenile justice system take to address the increase in juvenile arrest rates for non-violent offenses such as drug abuse, loitering and curfew violation? For now, it appears that the juvenile justice system is a more effective means to address the needs of juveniles. *See* Jaap Doek, *The Future of the Juvenile Court, in* THE FUTURE OF THE JUVENILE JUSTICE SYSTEM 197-210 (Josine Junger-Tas et al. eds., 1991).

C. Specialization: Different Kinds of Juvenile Courts

Many jurisdictions are finding a new, innovative answer to the complicated question of how best to address the complexities of juvenile crime. Specialization of the juvenile court has gone beyond recommending that judges be educated in the psychology of delinquency. In fact, judges and other authorities have recognized the need for specialized youth courts. This recognition has generated the development of juvenile drug courts, family drug courts in delinquency cases, and youth (or teen) courts. The underlying philosophy motivating specialization highlights the importance of individualized treatment, strict judicial oversight and community-based resources. In addition, the success of such courts depends upon frequent review hearings, family involvement, and prompt referral and availability of treatment centers.

1. Juvenile Drug Courts

One such court, the juvenile drug court, was not developed in the shadow of adult court but instead addressed the cultural and developmental issues specific to juvenile drug-related offenses. The United States Department of Justice defines juvenile drug courts as "drug courts that focus[] on juvenile delinquency (e.g., criminal) matters and status offenses (e.g., truancy) that involve substance-abusing juveniles." JUVENILE AND FAMILY DRUG COURTS: AN OVERVIEW 3 (1998). These drug courts give special consideration to the influence of peers, gangs, and families; emphasize completing thorough assessments while maintaining confidentiality; focus on motivation; and develop age-appropriate programs. To achieve these ends, the strategies employed by these juvenile drug courts include the following: more comprehensive intake assessments; greater coordination among the courts, schools, treatment providers and other agencies; active and continuous judicial supervision; and the use of sanctions with the juvenile and the family. Some jurisdictions permit moderate-to-severe juvenile drug abusers, as well as those charged with theft, domestic violence, possession of a concealed weapon, drunk driving, truancy or assault, to participate in drug court programs. *See* CAROLINE S. COOPER ET AL., U.S. DEP'T OF JUST., JUVENILE AND FAMILY DRUG COURTS: PROFILE OF PROGRAM CHARACTERISTICS AND IMPLEMENTATION ISSUES 13-15 (1998). While drug courts are still in their infancy, many states are encouraged by their initial success in reducing recidivism and successfully treating juvenile offenders.

2. Family Drug Courts

The Center for Court Innovation, located in New York City and responsible for promoting institutional change, has pioneered additional avenues of specialization within the juvenile justice arena. The Center, with the support of the U.S. Department of Justice, expands successful experimentation in New York to jurisdictions around the country. One such successful program is the Manhattan Family Treatment Court, which addresses incidents of child neglect by parents who are drug addicts. The court links parents to drug treatment, while closely monitoring their progress, which assists the judge in making timely and informed decisions regarding family reunification. This treatment court was selected by the Center for Substance Abuse as one of three model projects in the country.

3. Youth Courts

The Center for Court Innovation has also been successful in the creation of a youth court. Juveniles may be diverted to youth courts by law enforcement or prosecutor referrals, during intake, or as part of an informal disposition. JEFFREY A. BUTTS & JANEEN BUCK, U.S. DEP'T OF JUST., TEEN COURTS: A FOCUS ON RESEARCH 2 (2000). Youth courts address-low-level juvenile crime (theft, vandalism, etc.) through the enforcement and articulation of standards of behavior by a system composed of young people. In this way, peer pressure is utilized to address juvenile offenders arrested for shoplifting, vandalism and other petty crimes. For example, the Red Hook Youth Court uses positive peer pressure to ensure that justice is constructive for youth offenders and restorative for the community.

The Red Hook Youth Court is an early intervention program for young offenders, ages 10 to 15, who have committed low-level crimes in Brooklyn, New York, and are at risk for future, more serious involvement in the juvenile or adult criminal systems. The police refer cases to the Red Hook Youth Court, where offenders admit their guilt and receive sentences devised by a panel of their peers, a jury of teens. These court members, aged 14 to 18, participate in an initial training program that instructs them on criminal and delinquency law, family court operations and youth court procedures.

In creation of an individualized sentence, Red Hook Youth Court program staff conduct a clinical assessment of the offender and help to link the offender with the appropriate social services. Utilizing these services may be incorporated into the juvenile offender's sentence. The offender is further held accountable for his or her crimes by performing community service as a way to make restitution to the community. To ensure compliance, Red Hook Youth Court staff intensely supervise these offenders in the completion of their sentences. The new system has met with excellent success, as nine out of ten offenders complete their sanctions as ordered.

Red Hook Youth Court is just one of a growing number of youth courts in the United States. While some youth courts were first formed twenty years ago, 67% have been created in the last five years and are mostly operated among other courts, probation agencies, or private agencies. *Id.* at 3, 4. Most youth courts handle fewer than 100 cases per year while 5% handle 500 or more annually. *Id.* at 4. For further discussion of youth courts including the typical characteristics of a youth court, see generally *id.*; PAULA A. NESSEL, U.S. DEP'T OF JUST., TEEN COURT: A NATIONAL MOVEMENT (1998). For further discussion of the Red Hook Youth Court, see generally Alex Calabrese, *"Team Red Hook" Addresses Wide Range of Community Needs,* 72 N.Y. ST. B.J. 14, 18 (2000); Sara Bryer et al., *Materials Submitted by the Center for Court Innovation*, 183 PLI/CRIM. 49, 58-71 (1999).

Specialization of the juvenile justice system appears to be the most current response to juvenile crime and is being adopted from Santa Clara County, California, to Martin County in Florida. Authorities and commentators suggest that new methods, such as drug courts and teen courts, are essential. They argue that specialization is required to effectively and adequately address the unique causes of juvenile crime, combining individualized treatment with accountability in an age and developmentally appropriate way. For a full discussion on these new court innovations, see *Center for Court Innovation,* 183 PLI/CRIM. 49 (1999).

Index of Authorities

DOUGLAS E. ABRAMS & SARAH H. RAMSEY, CHILDREN AND THE LAW: DOCTRINE, POLICY AND PRACTICE 1169 (2000) 282

Floyd Abrams, *Prior Restraints*, 580 PLI/CRIM. 429, 458-59 (1999) 560

Akhil Reed Amar & Daniel Widawsky, *Child Abuse As Slavery: A Thirteenth Amendment Response to* DeShaney, 105 HARV. L. REV. 1359 (1992) 475

Lisa R. Askowitz, *Restricting the Admissibility of Expert Testimony in Child Sexual Abuse Prosecutions: Pennsylvania Takes It to the Extreme*, 47 U. MIAMI L. REV. 201, 208-13 (1996) 698

Timothy J. Aspinwall, *Religious Exemptions to Childhood Immunization Statutes: Reaching for a More Optimal Balance Between Religious Freedom and Public Health*, 29 LOY. U. CHI. L.J. 11 (1997) 432

R.L. August & B.D. Foreman, *A Comparison of Sexually and Non-Sexually Abused Children's Behavioral Responses to Anatomically Correct Dolls*, 20 CHILD PSYCHIATRY & HUM. DEV. 39-478 (1989) 705

Kathleen A. Bailie, *The Other "Neglected" Parties In Child Protective Proceedings: Parents In Poverty and the Role of the Lawyers Who Represent Them*, 66 FORDHAM L. REV. 2285 (1998) 505

Elizabeth Vaughan Baker, *Psychological Expert Testimony on a Child's Veracity in Child Abuse Prosecutions*, 50 LA. L. REV. 1039 (1990) 699

Debra Ratterman Baker, *Adoption Assistance: A Legal Primer*, 19 CHILD L. PRAC. 97 (2000) 830

Debra Ratterman Baker, *The New Federal Regulations on ASFA*, 19 CHILD L. PRAC. 53 (2000) 491

Verne Barry, *What Will Happen to the Children? Who Will Step in When Welfare is Abolished?*, 71 POL'Y REV. 7, 9-10 (1995) 830

MARIANNE BARY, KEEPING FAMILIES TOGETHER 4 (1994) 527

S.R. Battin et al., *The Contribution of Gang Membership to Delinquency Beyond Delinquent Friends*, 36 CRIMINOLOGY 93 (1998) 62

Honorable Birch Bayh, *Juveniles and the Law: An Introduction*, 12 CRIM. L. REV. 1 (1974) 337

Margaret Beyer & Wallace J. Mlyniec, *Lifelines to Biological Parents: Their Effect on Termination of Parental Rights and Performance*, 20 FAM. L.Q. 233 (1986) 774

Len Biernat & Dr. Christine Jax, *Limiting Mobility and Improving Student Achievement*, 23 HAMLINE L. REV. 1 (1999) 437

Kerin S. Bischoff, *The Voice of a Child: Independent Legal Representation of Children in Private Custody Disputes When Sexual Abuse Is Alleged*, 138 U. PA. L. REV. 1383 (1990) 601

Donna M. Bishop, et al., *The Transfer of Juveniles to Criminal Court: Does It Make a Difference?*, 42 CRIME AND DELINQUENCY 171 (1996) 869

Susan H. Bitensky, *The Child's Right to Humane Discipline Under the U.N. Convention on the Rights of the Child: The Mandate Against All Corporal Punishment of Children*, 4 LOY. POVERTY L.J. 47 (1998) ...152

D. Marianna Brower Blair, *The New Oklahoma Adoption Code: A Quest to Accommodate Diverse Interests*, 33 TULSA L.J. 177, 208-11 (1997) 840

Jeffrey P. Bloom, *Post* Schumpert *Era Independent Interviews and Psychological Evaluations of Children*, S.C. LAW. July/Aug. 1988, at 40, 44 (1988) 705

Arthur R. Blum, *Disclosing the Identities of Juvenile Felons: Introducing Accountability to Juvenile Justice*, 27 LOY. U. CHI. L.J. 349 (1996) 14

George L. Blum, Annotation, *Admissibility of Evidence Discovered in Search of Defendant's Property or Residence Authorized by Defendant's Adult Relative Other Than Spouse—State Cases*, 55 A.L.R.5TH 125 (1998) 76

B.W. Boat & M.D. Everson, *Anatomical Doll Exploration Among Non-Referred Children: Comparison by Age, Gender, Race, and Socioeconomic Status*, 18 CHILD & NEGLECT 139-153 (1994) 705

Carol Bombardi, *Juvenile Detention Hearings: A Proposed Model Provision to Limit Discretion During the Preadjudicatory Stage*, 12 FORDHAM URB. L.J. 285, 310 (1984) 85-86

J. Michael Bone & Michael R. Walsh, *Parental Alienation Syndrome: How to Detect It and What to Do About It*, 73 FLA. B.J. 44 (1999) 726

Karla Ogrodnik Boresi, *Syndrome Testimony in Child Abuse Prosecutions: The Wave of the Future?*, 8 ST. LOUIS U. PUB. L. REV. 207, 223 (1989) 711

Bruce A. Boyer & Steven Lubet, *The Kidnapping of Edgar Mortar: Contemporary Lessons in the Child Welfare Wars*, 45 VILL. L. REV. 245 (2000) 505

Bruce A. Boyer, *Jurisdiction Conflicts Between Juvenile Courts and Child Welfare Agencies: The Uneasy Relationship Between Institutional Co-Parents*, 54 MD. L. REV. 377 (1995) 565

Bruce A. Boyer, *Ethical Issues in the Representation of Parents in Child Welfare Cases*, 64 FORDHAM L. REV. 1621, 1646 (1996) 442

Marie M. Brady, *Munchausen Syndrome By Proxy: How Should We Weigh Our Options?*, 18 LAW & PSYCHOL. REV. 361, 362-66 (1994) 719

Jane E. Brody, *Widespread Abuse of Drugs by Pregnant Women is Found*, N.Y. TIMES, Aug. 30, 1988, at A1 673

Susan E. Brooks, *Juvenile Injustice: The Ban on Jury Trials for Juveniles in the District of Columbia*, 33 U. LOUISVILLE J. FAM. L. 875 (1995) 244

Donald C. Bross, *The Evolution of Independent Legal Representations for Children*, 1 J. CENTER FOR CHILDREN & CTS. 7 (1999) 595

Cheryl M. Browing & Michael L. Weiner, Note, *The Right to Family Integrity: A Substantive Due Process Approach to State Removal and Termination Proceedings*, 68 GEO. L.J. 213 (1979) 736

Lisa A. Brown & Christopher Gilbert, *Understanding the Constitutional Rights of School Children*, 34 HOUS. LAW. 40 (1997) 124, 151

Sara Bryer et al., *Materials Submitted by the Center for Court Innovation*, 183 PLI/CRIM. 49, 58-71 (1999) 872

Helen Bryks, *A Lesson in School Censorship:* Hazelwood v. Kuhlmeier, 55 BROOK. L. REV. 291 (1989) 124

Elizabeth Buchanan, *The Parent-Child Relationship and the Current Cycle of Family Law Reform: The Constitutional Rights of Unwed Fathers Before and After* Lehr v. Robertson, 45 OHIO ST. L.J. 313 (1984) 840

Robert L. Burgdorf, Jr., *The Americans With Disabilities Act: Analysis and Implications of a Second-Generation Civil Rights Statute*, 26 HARV. C.R.-C.L. L. REV. 412, 420-25 (1991) 817

Robert A. Burt, *Developing Constitutional Rights Of, In, and For Children*, 39 LAW & CONTEMP. PROBS. 118, 128 (Summer 1975) 514

Brenda Burton, *Where Murdering Hands Rock the Cradle: An Overview of America's Incoherent Treatment of Infanticidal Mothers*, 51 SMU L. REV. 519, 603 (1998) 719

Jeffrey A. Butts & Janeen Buck, U.S. DEP'T OF JUST., *Teen Courts: A Focus on Research* 2 (2000) 871-72

Tory J. Caeti et al., *Juvenile Right to Counsel: A National Comparison of State Legal Codes*, 23 AM. J. CRIM. L. 611, 624 (1996) 229-30

Amy Campbell, *Trying Minors as Adults in the United States and England: Balancing the Goal of Rehabilitation with the Need to Protect Society*, 19 SUFFOLK TRANSNAT'L L. REV. 345 (1995) 329

Ardia L. Campbell, Annotation, *Rights of Unwed Father to Obstruct Adoption of His Child By Withholding Consent*, 61 A.L.R.5TH 151 (1998) 840

Cynthia Price Cohen, *The Developing Jurisprudence of the Rights of the Child*, 6 ST. THOMAS L. REV. 1 (1993) 432

Caroline S. Cooper et al., U.S. DEP'T OF JUST., *Juvenile and Family Drug Courts: Profile of Program Characteristics and Implementation Issues* 13-15 (1998) 870

Ronald P. Corbett, Jr., *Juvenile Probation on the Eve of the Next Millennium*, 64 FED. PROBATION 78 (1999) 294

Lynn Cothern, U.S. DEP'T OF JUST., *Juveniles and the Death Penalty* (2000) 375

Sacha M. Coupet, *What to Do With the Sheep in Wolf's Clothing: The Role of Rhetoric and Reality About Youth Offenders in the Constructive Dismantling of the Juvenile Justice System*, 148 U. PA. L. REV. 1303, 1334 (2000) 343

Vance L. Cowden & Geoffrey R. McKee, *Competency to Stand Trial in Juvenile Delinquency Proceedings—Cognitive Maturity and the Attorney-Client Relationship*, 33 U. LOUISVILLE J. FAM. L. 629 (1995) 210-11

STEVEN M. COX & JOHN J. CONRAD, JUVENILE JUSTICE: A GUIDE TO PRACTICE AND THEORY 2-4 (1987) 1, 3, 5, 12

Catherine S. Crosby-Currie & N. Dickon Reppucci, *The Missing Child in Child Protection: The Constitutional Context of Child Maltreatment From* Meyer *to* DeShaney, 21 LAW & POL'Y 129 (1999) 474

Charmel L. Cross, *The Existing Indian Family Exception: Is It Appropriate to Use a Judicially Created Exception to Render the Indian Child Welfare Act of 1978 Inapplicable?*, 26 CAP. U. L. REV. 847, 859-60 (1998) 580-82

Alex Calabrese, *"Team Red Hook" Addresses Wide Range of Community Needs*, 72 N.Y. ST. B.J. 14, 18 (2000) 872

Timothy J. Cassidy, *Termination of Parental Rights: The Substantive Due Process Issues*, 26 ST. LOUIS U. L.J. 915 (1982) 736

Karen Cavanaugh & Daniel Pollack, *Liability Protections for Foster Parents*, 6 KAN. J.L. & PUB. POL'Y 78 (1997) 649

Karen Rothschild Cavanaugh & Daniel Pollack, *Child Support Obligations of Incarcerated Parents*, 7 CORNELL J.L. & PUB. POL'Y 531, 534 n.14 (1998) 802-03

Chasnoff, *Drug Use In Pregnancy: Parameters of Risk*, 35 PEDIATRIC CLINICS OF N.A. 1043 (1998) 678

John R. Christiansen, *The Testimony of Child Witnesses: Fact, Fantasy, and the Influences of Pretrial Interviews*, 62 WASH. L. REV. 705 (1987) 705

Dennis E. Cichon, *Developing a Mental Health Code for Minors*, 13 T.M. COOLEY L. REV. 529 (1996) 862

Monique K. Cirelli, *Expert Testimony in Child Abuse Cases: Helpful or Prejudicial?* People v. Beckley, 8 T.M. COOLEY L. REV. 425 (1991) 699

Natelie Loder Clark, *Parens Patriae and a Modest Proposal for the Twenty-First Century: Legal Philosophy and a New Look at Children's Welfare*, 6 MICH. J. GENDER & L. 381 (2000) 631

Elaine R. Cacciola, *The Admissibility of Expert Testimony in Intrafamily Child Sexual Abuse Cases*, 34 UCLA L. REV. 175, 175-76 (1986) 698

Coleman & Kay, *Biological Addictions*, 25 OBSTETRICS & GYNECOLOGY CLINICS OF N.A. 1-109 (1999) 678

ELIZABETH B. COOPER, AIDS AGENDA: EMERGING ISSUE IN CIVIL RIGHTS 74-81 (Nan D. Hunter & William B. Rubenstein eds., 1992) 810-11

Conna Craig, *What I Need is a Mom: The Welfare State Denies Homes to Thousands of Foster Children*, 73 POL'Y REV. 42, 45 (1995) 829

Michael J. Dale, *Juvenile Law: 1996 Survey of Florida Law*, 21 NOVA L. REV. 189, 228 (1996) 595

Michael J. Dale, *State Court Jurisdiction Under the Indian Child Welfare Act and the Best Unstated Best Interest of the Child Test*, 27 GONZ. L. REV. 353 (1992) 581

Jeffery M. Daly & Sandra L. Fritsch, *Case Study: Maternal Residual Attention Deficit Disorder Associated With Failure to Thrive in a Two-Month Old Infant*, 34 J. AM. ACAD. CHILD & ADOLESCENT PSYCHIATRY 55 (1995) 423

Alexandra R. Dapolito, *The Failure to Notify Putative Fathers of Adoption Proceedings Balancing the Adoption Equation*, 42 CATH. U. L. REV. 979 (1993) 841

Douglas Darnell, *Parental Alienation: Not in the Best Interest of the Children*, 75 N.D. L. REV. 323, 325-26 (1999) 726

Howard Davidson, *Symposium: Violence in America: How Can We Save Our Children? No Consequences—Reexamining Parental Responsibility Laws*, 7 STAN. L. & POL'Y REV. 23 (1995-96) 442

SAMUEL DAVIS, RIGHTS OF JUVENILES (1994) 290, 318, 337, 350

SAMUEL M. DAVIS, RIGHTS OF JUVENILES (2d ed. 1996) 75, 86

Shari Del Carlo, *Oregon Voters Get Tough on Juvenile Crime: One Strike and You Are Out!*, 75 OR. L. REV. 1223, 1244 (1996) 335

Kenneth A. Deville & Loretta M. Kopelman, *Fetal Protection in Wisconsin's Revised Child Abuse Law: Right Goal, Wrong Remedy*, 27 J.L. MED. & ETHICS 332, 336 (1999) 678

Kathy M. Devito, *Proceedings From Petition to Adjudicatory Hearing in Dependency Cases*, JUV. FL-CLE 13-1 (1997) 505

Jaap Doek, *The Future of the Juvenile Court*, *in* THE FUTURE OF THE JUVENILE JUSTICE SYSTEM 197-210 (Josine Junger Tas et al. eds., 1991) 869

Janet L. Dolgin, *The Law's Response to Parental Alcohol and "Crack" Abuse*, 56 BROOK. L. REV. 1213 (1991) 674

George Dorsett, *The Right To Counsel in Child Dependency Proceedings: Conflict Between Florida and the Fifth Circuit*, 35 U. MIAMI L. REV. 384 (1991) 505

Kenneth R. Dortzbach, *Legislative History: The Philosophies of Justices Scalia and Breyer and the Use of Legislative History by the Wisconsin State Courts*, 80 MARQ. L. REV. 161, 212 (1996) 767

Breadan Marshall Douthett, *The Death of Constitutional Duty: The Court Reacts to the Expansion of Section 1983 Liability in* DeShaney v. Winnebago County Department of Social Services, 52 OHIO ST. L.J. 643 (1992) 475

Donald N. Duquette, *Legal Representation for Children in Protection Proceedings: Two Distinct Lawyer Roles Are Required*, 34 FAM. L.Q. 441 (2000) 595

James G. Dwyer, *Parents' Religion and Children's Welfare: Debunking the Doctrine of Parents' Rights*, 82 CAL. L. REV. 1371, 1447 (1995) 432

Leonard P. Edwards, *A Comprehensive Approach to the Representation of Children: The Child Advocacy Coordinating Council*, 27 FAM. L.Q. 417 (1993) 589

Arlen Egley, U.S. DEP'T OF JUST., *Highlights of the 1999 National Youth Gang Survey* (2000) 62

Connie E. Eiseman, *Recent Decisions: The Maryland Court of Appeals*, 58 MD. L. REV. 920, 931 (1999) 542

Linda D. Elrod, *A Review of the Year in Family Law*, 28 FAM. L.Q. 541, 548 (1995) 824

Nancy S. Erickson, *The Role of the Law Guardian in a Custody Case Involving Domestic Violence*, 27 FORDHAM URB. L.J. 817 n.5 (2000) 594

Finn-Aage Esbensen, U.S. DEP'T OF JUST., *Preventing Adolescent Gang Involvement* (2000) 62

Jeanne Etter, *Levels of Cooperations and Satisfaction in 56 Open Adoptions*, 72 CHILD WELFARE 257, 257-64 (1993) 519

Barry C. Feld, *Abolish the Juvenile Court: Youthfulness, Criminal Responsibility, and Sentencing Policy*, 88 J. CRIM. L. & CRIMINOLOGY 68 (1997) 335, 868

Barry C. Feld, In re Gault *Revisited: A Cross-State Comparison of the Right to Counsel in Juvenile Court*, 34 CRIME & DELINQ. 393 (1988) 230

Barry C. Feld, *The Juvenile Court Meets the Principle of the Offense: Legislative Changes in Juvenile Waiver Statutes*, 78 J. CRIM. L. & CRIMINOLOGY 471, 488, 494 (1987) 182

Barry C. Feld, *The Juvenile Court Meets the Principle of the Offense: Punishment, Treatment, and the Difference it Makes*, 68 B.U. L. REV. 821, 833-34, 850-59 (1988) 334-35

Barry C. Feld, *The Transformation of the Juvenile Court—Part II: ace and the "Crack Down" on Youth Crime*, 84 MINN. L. REV. 327 (1999) 868-69

Daniel E. Feld, *Right to Discipline Pupil for Conduct Away from School Grounds or Not Immediately Connected With School Activities*, 55 A.L.R.3D 1124 (1973) 398

Elyce Zenoff Ferster & Thomas F. Courtless, *The Intake Process in the Affluent County Juvenile Court*, 22 HASTINGS L.J. 1127, 1128, 1133 (1971) 68-69

Celia B. Fisher & Katherine A. Whiting, *How Valid Are Child Sexual Abuse Validations?*, *in* EXPERT WITNESSES IN CHILD ABUSE CASES: WHAT CAN AND SHOULD BE SAID IN COURT 159, 173 (Stephen J. Ceci & Helene Hembrooke eds., 1998) 705

Michael T. Flannery, *First, Do No Harm: The Use of Covert Video Surveillance to Detect Munchausen Syndrome By Proxy: The Case for Termination of Parental Rights*, 40 JUV. & FAM. CT. J. 41-53 (1991) 719-20

Michael T. Flannery, *Munchausen Syndrome By Proxy: Broadening the Scope of Child Abuse*, 28 U. RICH. L. REV. 1175 (1994) 719-20

Martin L. Forst & Martha-Elin Bloomquist, *Cracking Down on Juveniles: The Changing Ideology of Youth Corrections*, 4 NOTRE DAME J. L. ETHICS & PUB. POL'Y 323 (1991) 335

Sanford J. Fox, *A Contribution to the History of the American Juvenile Court*, 49 JUV. & FAM. CT. J. 7 (1998) 3

Sanford J. Fox, *The Early History of the Court*, FUTURE OF CHILDREN 29, 30 (Winter 1996) 6

Sanford J. Fox, *Juvenile Justice Reform: An Historical Perspective*, 22 STAN. L. REV. 1187, 1190 (1970) 10

Doris Freed & Henry Foster, *Family Law in the Fifty States 1998-99: Cases Digests*, 33 FAM. L.Q. 919, 953 (2000) 494

Madelyn Freundlich, *Expediting Termination of Parental Rights: Solving a Problem or Sowing the Seeds of a New predicament?*, 28 CAP. U. L. REV. 97, 106 (2000) 519

Fried & Watkinson, *36- and 48-Month Neurobehavioral Follow-Up of Children Prenatally Exposed to Marijuana, Cigarettes, and Alcohol*, 11 J. DEV. & BEHAV. PEDIATRICS 49 (1990) 419

Eric J. Fritsch & Craig Hemmens, *An Assessment of Legislative Approaches to the Problem of Serious Juvenile Crime: A Case Study of Texas 1973-1995*, 23 AM. J. CRIM. L. 563 (1996) 64

Eric Fritsch & Craig Hemmens, J.D., *Juvenile Waiver in the United States 1979-1995: A Comparison and Analysis of State Waiver Statutes*, 46 JUV. & FAM. CT. J. 17, 17-32 (1995) 181, 183

Lynda E. Frost & Robert E. Shepherd, Jr., *Mental Health Issues in Juvenile Delinquency Proceedings*, 11 CRIM. JUST. 52 (Fall 1996) 210

T. Markus Funk, *The Dangers of Hiding Criminal Pasts*, 66 TENN. L. REV. 287 (1998) 265

T. Markus Funk & Daniel D. Polsby, *Distributional Consequences of Expunging Juvenile Delinquency Records: The Problem of Lemons*, 52 WASH. U. J. URB. & CONTEMP. L. 161 (1977) 264

Stewart W. Gagnon & Howard G. Baldwin, *Laws Regarding the Family, Terminations and Adoptions and Protective Orders*, 60 TEX. B.J. 794, 796 (Sept. 1997) 595

GARBINE, GUTTMAN & SEELEY, THE PSYCHOLOGICALLY BATTERED CHILD 25-29 (1986) 408-09

Richard Gardner, *Recommendations For Dealing With Parents Who Induce a Parental Alienation Syndrome in Their Children*, 28 J. DIVORCE & REMARRIAGE 1-23 (1998) 725

RICHARD GARDNER, THE PARENTAL ALIENATION SYNDROME AND THE DIFFERENTIATION BETWEEN FABRICATED AND GENUINE CHILD SEX ABUSE (1987) 725

RICHARD GARDNER, THE PARENTAL ALIENATION SYNDROME Second Addition (2d ed. 1998) 725

RICHARD GARDNER, FAMILY EVALUATION IN CHILD CUSTODY MEDIATION, ARBITRATION, AND LITIGATION (1989) 725

MARTIN GARDNER, UNDERSTANDING JUVENILE LAW 315 (1997) 290-91

Richard Garner, *Fundamentally Speaking: Application of Ohio's Domestic Violence Laws in Parental Discipline Cases—A Parental Perspective*, 30 U. TOL. L. REV. 1 (1998) 152

Elisabeth Gasparini, *Juvenile Capital Punishment: A Spectacle of a Child's Injustice*, 49 S.C. L. REV. 1073 (1998) 375

Richard J. Gelles & Ira Schwartz, *Children and the Child Welfare System*, 2 U. PA. J. CONST. L. 95 (1999) 505

Philip M. Gentry, *Procedural Due Process Rights of Incarcerated Parents in Termination of Parental Rights Proceedings: A Fifty State Analysis*, 30 J. FAM. L. 757 (1991-92) 747

Melisa C. George, *A New IDEA: The Individuals With Disabilities Education Act After the 1997 Amendments*, 23 LAW & PSYCHOL. REV. 91, 95-96 (1999) 345

Doni Gewirtzman, *"Make Your Own Kind of Music": Queer Student Groups and the First Amendment*, 86 CAL. L. REV. 1131 (1998) 125

Nikki Gfellers, et al., *Juvenile*, 21 CAMPBELL L. REV. 399 (1999) 294

Peter O. Glaessner, *Due Process in the "Voluntary: Civil Commitment of Juvenile Wards*, 2 J. LEGAL MED. (No. 2) 169 (1981) 862

Lynn Goldman & Beatrice Crofts Yorker, *Mommie Dearest? Prosecuting Cases of Munchausen Syndrome By Proxy*, 13 CRIM. JUST. 25, 30 (Winter 1999) 719

Lorie M. Graham, *"The Past Never Vanishes": A Contextual Critique of the Existing Indian Family Doctrine*, 23 AM. INDIAN L. REV. 1, 1-34 (1998) 581-82

Lawrence N. Gray, *Criminal and Civil Contempt: Some Sense of a Hodgepodge*, 13 J. SUFFOLK ACAD. L. 1 (1999) 560

Ernestine Steward Gray, *The Adoption and Safe Families Act of 1997*, 46 LA. B.J. 477 (1999) 491

Frank Green, *Efforts in Prisons Defended*, RICHMOND TIMES-DISPATCH, Feb. 17, 1996, at B1 332

Thomas Grisso, *The Competence of Adolescents as Trial Defendants*, 3 PSYCHOL. PUB. POL'Y & L. 3 (1997) 210

Thomas Grisso, *Juvenile Competency to Stand Trial: Questions in an Era of Punitive Reform*, 12 CRIM. JUST. 5, 8 (Fall 1997) 210

Harriette Gross, *Open Adoption: A Research Based Literature Review and New Data*, 72 CHILD WELFARE 269 (1993) 519

Martin Guggenheim, *The Effects of Recent Trends to Accelerate the Termination of Parental Rights of Children in Foster Care—An Empirical Analysis in Two States*, 29 FAM. L.Q. 121, 121-30 (1995) 782

Amy Haddix, *Unseen Victims: Acknowledging the Effects of Domestic Violence Through Statutory Termination of Parental Rights*, 84 CAL. L. REV. 757, 789-90 (1996) 446

John Haney & Lisa Kay, *Making Reasonable Efforts in Iowa Foster Care Cases: An Empirical Analysis*, 81 IOWA L. REV. 1629 (1996) 527

Jennifer Paige Hanft, *Attorney for Child Versus Guardian Ad Litem: Wyoming Creates a Hybrid, But Is It a Formula for Malpractice?*, 34 LAND & WATER L. REV. 381, 394 (1999) 610

ANN M. HARALAMBIE, THE CHILD'S ATTORNEY—A GUIDE TO REPRESENTING CHILDREN IN CUSTODY, ADOPTION, AND PROTECTION CASES 2-5 (1993) 601

Anne M. Haralambie, *The Role of the Child's Attorney in Protecting the Child Throughout the Litigation Process*, 71 N.D. L. REV. 939, 974-76 (1995) 774

David J. Harmer, *Limiting Incarceration for Civil Contempt in Child Custody Cases*, 4 BYU J. PUB. L. 239 (1990) 561

Berndette W. Hartfield, *The Uniform Child Custody Jurisdiction Act and the Problem of Jurisdiction in Interstate Adoptions: An Easy Fix?*, 43 OKLA. L. REV. 621, 631-37 (1990) 824

Bernadette W. Hartfield, *The Role of the Interstate Compact On the Placement of Children in Interstate Adoption*, 58 NEB. L. REV. 292 (1989) 542-43

Phillip E. Hassman, Annotation, *Validity of Requirement That, As Condition of Probation, Defendant Submit to Warrantless Searches*, 79 A.L.R.3D 1083 (1977) 304

Joseph D. Hatina, *Shaken Baby Syndrome: Who Are the True Experts?*, 46 CLEV. ST. L. REV. 557, 560 (1998) 666

Rebecca H. Heartz, *Guardians Ad Litem in Child Abuse and Neglect Proceedings: Clarifying the Rules to Improve Effectiveness*, 27 FAM. L.Q. 327 (1993) 601

Stephen Hellman, *The Child, the Step Parent, and the State: Step Parent Visitation and the Voice of the Child*, 16 TOURO L. REV. 45 (1999) 631

David J. Herring, *Inclusion of the Reasonable Efforts Requirement in Termination of Parental Rights Statutes: Punishing the Child for the Failures of the State Child Welfare System*, 54 U. PITT. L. REV. 139, 154 (1992) 527

David J. Herring, *The Adoption and Safe Families Act—Hope and Its Subversion*, 34 FAM. L.Q. 329 (2000) 491

Susan B. Hershkowitz, *Due Process and the Termination of Parental Rights*, 19 FAM. L.Q. 245, 254-55 (1985) 735

Angela R. Holder, *Circumstances Warranting Court-Ordered Medical Treatment of Minors*, 24 AM. JUR. 2D PROOF OF FACTS § 169 (1980) 433

Paul Holland & Wallace J. Mlyniec, *Whatever Happened to the Right to Treatment?: The Modern Quest for a Historical Promise*, 68 TEMP. L. REV. 1791 (1995) 270

Carie T. Hollister, *The Impossible Predicament of Gina Grant*, 44 UCLA L. REV. 913 (1997) 265

Christopher Holloway, DEP'T OF JUST., *Interstate Compact on Juveniles* (2000) 327

James C. Howell, U.S. DEP'T OF JUST., *Crime by Youth Gangs and Groups in the United States* (1992) 62

James C. Howell, U.S. DEP'T OF JUST., *Youth Gangs: An Overview* 1 (1988) 62

James C. Howell & James P. Lynch, U.S. DEP'T OF JUST., *Youth Gangs in Schools* (1988) 63

James C. Howel, *Abolish the Juvenile Court? Nonsense!*, 4 JUR. JUST. UPDATE 1 (1998) 869

H. Lila Hubert, *In the Child's Best Interests: The Role of the Guardian Ad Litem In Termination of Parental Rights Proceedings*, 49 U. MIAMI L. REV. 531, 563 (1994) 604

Arlene C. Huszer, *Termination of parental Rights*, 1997 FLA. JUV. L. & PRAC. Ch. 16, 15 (1997) 595

L. Jampole & M.K. Weber, *An Assessment of the Behavior of Sexually Abused and Non-Sexually Abused Children With Anatomically Correct Dolls*, 11 CHILD ABUSE & NEGLECT 187-92 (1987) 705

MARGARET C. JASPER, JUVENILE JUSTICE AND CHILDREN'S LAW 4-5 (1994) 4

Peter S. Jensen & Kimberly Hoagwood, *The Book of Names: DSM-IV in Context*, 9 DEV'T & PSYCHOPATHOLOGY 231 (1997) 844

Bradette Jepsen, *This New Breed of Juvenile Offenders*, CORRECTIONS TODAY, June 1, 1997, at 68 329

Matthew B. Johnson, *Examining Risks to Children in the Context of Parental Rights Termination Proceedings*, 32 N.Y.U. REV. L. & SOC. CHANGE 397 (1996) 781

Noel M. Johnston, *The Chicago Public Schools and Its Violent Students: How Can the Law Protect Teachers?*, 48 DEPAUL L. REV. 907 (1998) 152

Janet Boeth Jones, Annotation, *Truancy as Indicative of Delinquency or Incorrigibility, Justifying Commitment of Infant or Juvenile*, 5 A.L.R. 4TH 1211 (1981) 41

Lisa Jones & David Finkelhor, U.S. DEP'T OF JUST., *The Decline in Child Sexual Abuse Cases* (2001) 406

Kristine Cordier Kamezis, Annotation, *Validity and Enforcement of Agreement by Foster Parents that They Will Not Attempt to Adopt Foster Child*, 78 A.L.R.3D 770 (1977) 643

Herma Hill Kay, *Adoption in the Conflict of Laws: The UAA, Not the UCCJA, Is the Answer*, 84 CAL. L. REV. 703 (1996) 825-26

Robert Kelly & Sarah Ramsey, *Do Attorneys for Children In Protection Proceedings Make a Difference?—A Study of the Impact of Representation Under Conditions of High Judicial Intervention*, 21 J. FAM. L. 405 (1983) 595

Gary A. Kelson, *In the Best Interest of the Child: What Have We Learned from Baby Jessica and Baby Richard?*, 33 J. MARSHALL L. REV. 353, 372 (2000) 781

Ruth C. Kempe, *The Infant with Failure-to-Thrive*, *in* THE BATTERED CHILD 163, 164 (C. Henry Kimpe & Ray E. Helfer eds., 3d ed. 1980) 661-62

Susan Kerr, *The Application of the Americans with Disabilities Act to the Termination of the Parental Rights of People Labeled Developmentally Disabled or Mentally Retarded*, 83 CAL. L. REV. 1415, 1436 (1995) 795

Susan Kerr, *The Application of the Americans With Disabilities Act to the Termination of the Parental Rights of Individuals With Mental Disabilities*, 16 J. CONTEMP. HEALTH L. & POL'Y 387, 388 (2000) 817-18

Kym L. Kilpatrick & Leane M. Williams, *Potential Mediators of Post-Traumatic Stress Disorder in Child Witnesses to Domestic Violence*, 22(4) CHILD ABUSE & NEGLECT 319 (1998) 446

Robert H. Kirschener, *The Pathology of Child Abuse*, *in* THE BATTERED CHILD 248, 273 (Mary Edna Helfer, et al. eds., 5th ed. 1997) 666

JANE KNITZER & MERRIL SOBIE, LAW GUARDIANS IN NEW YORK STATE—A STUDY OF THE LEGAL REPRESENTATION OF CHILDREN (1984) 595

G.P. Koocher et al., *Psychological Science and the Use of Anatomically Detailed Dolls in Child Sexual Abuse Assessments: Final Report of the American Psychological Association Anatomical Doll Task Force*, 138 PSYCHOL. BULL. 2 (1995) 705

Leona M. Kopetski, *Identifying Cases of Parent Alienation Syndrome—Part I*, 27 COLO. LAW. 65-66 (1998) 726

DONALD T. KRAMER, LEGAL RIGHTS OF CHILDREN (2d ed. 1994) 290, 600, 644, 661-62

Roy Lacoursiere, *A Footnote to* Parham*: Was J.L. a Casualty of the Mental Health Bar?*, 11 BULL. AM. ACAD. PSYCHIATRY & L. 279 (1983) 863

WAYNE LAFAVE, SEARCH AND SEIZURE § 10.10(a) (1987) 307

WAYNE R. LAFAVE & JEROLD H. ISRAEL, CRIMINAL PROCEDURE § 3.10(e) (2d ed. 1992) 76

Debra H. Lahrmann, *Who Are We Protecting? An Analysis of the Law Regarding the Duties of Attorneys and Guardians Ad Litem*, 63 TEX. B.J. 123 (February 2000) 594

Judith Larsen et al., *Medical Evidence in Cases of Intrauterine Drug and Alcohol Exposure*, 18 PEPP. L. REV. 279, 294 (1991) 674

Cindy S. Ledeman, U.S. DEP'T OF JUST., *The Juvenile Court: Putting Research to Work for Prevention* 22, 23 (1999) 869

Roger J.R. Levesque & Alan J. Thomkins, *Revisioning Juvenile Justice: Implications of the New Child Protection Movement*, 48 WASH. U. J. URB. & CONTEMP. L. 87 (1995) 475

Raven C. Lidman & Betsy R. Hollingsworth, *The Guardian Ad Litem in Child Custody Cases: The Contours of Our Judicial System Stretched Beyond Recognition*, 6 GEO. MASON L. REV. 255, 303 (1998) 594-95

Page Mcquire Linden, *Drug Addiction During Pregnancy: A Call for Increased Social Responsibility*, 4 AM. U. J. GENDER & L. 105, 118-21 (1995) 675

HERBERT H. LOU, PH.D., JUVENILE COURTS IN THE UNITED STATES 13-16 (1927) 2-3, 5

Sana Loue, *Legal and Epidemiological Aspects of Child Maltreatment*, 19 J. LEGAL MED. 471, 493 (1998) 678

Ira C. Lupu, *Meditating Institution: Beyond the Public/Private Distinction: The Separation of Powers and the Protection of Children*, 61 U. CHI. L. REV. 1317 (1994) 862

Glen Martin, *Youth Sentenced in Girl's Horrific Slaying*, S.F. CHRON., Mar. 8, 1997, at A15 332

Mary Ann Mason, *The Child Sex Abuse Syndrome: The Other Major Issue in* State of New Jersey v. Margaret Kelly Michaels, 1 PSYCHOL. PUB. POL'Y & L. 399 (1995) 699

Ann MacLean Massie, *The Religion Clauses and Parental Health Care Decision-Making for Children: Suggestions for a New Approach*, 21 HASTINGS CONST. L.Q. 724 (1994) 432

DEBORAH MATHIEU, PREVENTING PRENATAL HARM: SHOULD THE STATE INTERVENE? (2d ed. 1996) 674

S.N. Mattson & E.P. Riley, *A Review of the Neurobehavioral Deficits in Children With Fetal Alcohol Syndrome or Prenatal Exposure to Alcohol*, 22 ALCOHOLISM: CLINICAL & EXPERIMENTAL RESEARCH 279-92 (1998) 678

S.N. Mattson et al., *Heavy Prenatal Alcohol Exposure With or Without Physical Features of Fetal Alcohol Syndrome Leads to I.Q. Deficits*, 131 J. OF PEDIATRICS 718-71 (1997) 678

DAVID MATZA, DELINQUENCY AND DRIFT 5 (1964) 335

Allan H. McCoid, *The Battered Child and Other Assaults Upon the Family: Part One*, 50 MINN. L. REV. 1, 24 (1965) 687

David McCord, *Expert Psychological Testimony About Child Complainants in Sexual Abuse Prosecutions: A Foray Into the Admissibility of Novel Psychological Evidence*, 77 J. CRIM. L. & CRIMINOLOGY 1 (1986) 698-99

GARY E. MCCUEN, BORN HOOKED (1991) 678

Doretta Massardo McGinnis, *Prosecution of Mother's Drug-Exposed Babies: Constitutional and Criminal Theory, in* CHILD, PARENT, AND STATE 84 (1994) 419

Shannon F. McLatchey, *Juvenile Crime and Punishment: An Analysis of the "Get Tough" Approach*, 10 U. FLA. J. L. & PUB. POL'Y 401 (1999) 869

Daniel N. McPherson, *Student-Initiated Religious Expression in the Public Schools: The Need for a Wider Opening in the Schoolhouse Gate*, 30 CREIGHTON L. REV. 393 (1997) 132-33

Marygold S. Melli, *Juvenile Justice Reform in Context*, 1996 WIS. L. REV. 375 (1996) 14, 20

Gary B. Melton & Gail S. Perry, *Precedential Value of Judicial Notice of Social Facts:* Parham *as an Example*, 22 J. FAM. L. 633 (1983-1984) 862

JERRY L. MERSHON, JUVENILE JUSTICE: THE ADJUDICATORY AND DISPOSITIONAL PROCESS 91-95, 140, 141, 150 (1991) 277, 284, 318

Christine M. Metteer, *A Law Unto Itself: The Indian Child Welfare Act as Inapplicable and Inappropriate to the Transracial/Race-Matching Adoption Controversy*, 38 BRANDEIS L.J. 47 (1999) 581

Harry Mika et al., *Mediation Interventions and Restorative Potential: A Case Study of Juvenile Restitution*, 1989 J. DISP. RESOL. 89, 90 110

Carol J. Miller, Annotation, *Validity and Application of Statute Allowing Endangered Child to be Temporarily Removed From Parental Custody*, 38 A.L.R.4TH 756 (1985) 462

W.B. Miller, U.S. DEP'T OF JUST., *Crime by Youth Gangs and Groups in the United States* (1992) 62

Marjorie Millman, *Juveniles Staying Cool After School*, 26 OHIO N.U. L. REV. 141 (2000) 304

Wallace J. Mlyniec, *A Judge's Ethical Dilemma: Assessing a Child's Capacity to Choose*, 64 FORDHAM L. REV. 1873 (1996) 432

Lenore M. Molee, *The Ultimate Demonstration of Love for a Child: Choosing a Standby Guardian[;] New Jersey Standby Guardianship Act*, 22 SETON HALL LEGIS. J. 475, 579 (1998) 810-11

Jose Monsivais, *A Glimmer of Hope: A Proposal to Keep the Indian Child Welfare Act of 1978 Intact*, 29 AM. INDIAN L. REV. 1 (1997) 581-82

J.P. Moore & C.P. Terrett, U.S. DEP'T OF JUST., *Highlights of the 1996 National Youth Gang Survey* (1997) 62

Joelle Anne Moreno, *Killing Daddy: Developing a Self-Defense Strategy for the Abused Child*, 137 U. PA. L. REV. 1281 (1989) 688

Christopher J. Mumola, U.S. DEP'T OF JUST., *Incarcerated Parents and Their Children* (2000) 801-02

Michael B. Mushlinm, *Unsafe Havens: The Case for Constitutional Protection of Foster Children From Abuse and Neglect*, 23 HARV. C.R.-C.L. L. REV. 1999 (1988) 649

John E.B. Myers, *Legal Issues in Child Abuse and Neglect Practice* 339-51 (2d ed. 1998) 704-05

John E.B. Myers et al., *Expert Testimony in Child Sexual Abuse Litigation*, 68 NEB. L. REV. 1 (1989) 699

V.P. Nanda, *The United States Reservation to the Ban of the Death Penalty for Juvenile Offenders: An Appraisal Under the International Convention on Civil and Political Rights*, 42 DEPAUL L. REV. 1311 (1993) 375

Paula A. Nessel, U.S. DEP'T OF JUST., *Teen Court: A National Movement* (1998) 872

Kathleen Niggmyer, *Parental Alienation Is Open Heart Surgery: It Needs More Than a Band-Aid to Fix It*, 34 CAL. W. L. REV. 567, 576-81 (1998) 726

Theresa A. Nitti, *Stepping Back From the Psychological Parenting Theory: A Comment on* In re J.C., 46 RUTGERS L. REV. 1003 (1994) 781

Ana M. Novoa, *Count the Brown Faces: Where is the "Family" in the Family Law of Child Protective Services?*, 1 THE SCHOLAR: ST. MARY'S L. REV. ON MINORITY ISSUES 5, 40 (1999) 427

Laurence C. Novotney, U.S. DEP'T OF JUST., *Juvenile Mentoring Program: A Progress Review* 1 (2000) 866

Raymond O'Brien & Michael Flannery, *The Pending Gauntlet to Free Exercise: Mandating that Clergy Report Child Abuse*, 25 LOY. L.A. L. REV. 1 (1991) 385

Megan M. O'Laughlin, *A Theory of Relativity: Kinship Foster Care May Be the Key to Stopping the Pendulum of Terminations vs. Reunification*, 51 VAND. L. REV. 1427 (1998) 519, 830

Laura Oren, *The State's Failure to Protect Children and Substantive Due Process:* DeShaney *in Context*, 68 N.C. L. REV. 659 (1990) 474-75

Michael S. Orfinger, *Battered Child Syndrome: Evidence of Prior Acts in Disguise*, 41 FLA. L. REV. 345, 347 (1989) 687-88

Caroline S. Palmer, *The Risks of State Intervention in Preventing Prenatal Alcohol Abuse and the Viability of an Inclusive Approach: Arguments for Limiting Punitive and Coercive Prenatal Alcohol Abuse Legislation in Minnesota*, 10 HASTINGS WOMEN'S L.J. 287, 296 (1999) 678-79

Pamela Kemp Parker, *When a Foreign Child Comes into Care, Ask: Has the Consul Been Notified?*, 19 CHILD LAW PRACTICE 177 (Feb. 2001) 487

C.S. Patrinelis, Annotation, *Religious Beliefs of Parents as Defense to Prosecution for Failure to Comply with Compulsory Education Laws*, 3 A.L.R.2D 1401 (1949) 436

Anne M. Payne, Annotation, *Parental Mental Deficiency as a Factor in Termination of Parental Rights—Modern Status*, 1 A.L.R.5TH 469 (1992) 795

Jean Koh Peters, Schall v. Martin *and the Transformation of Judicial Precedent*, 31 B.C. L. REV. 641, 644 n.12 (1990) 84

Sloan Philips, *The Indian Child Welfare Act In the Face of Extinction*, 21 AM. INDIAN L. REV. 351 (1997) 581-82

Joseph R. Carrieri, *Termination of Parents' Rights and Proceedings*, 173 PLI/CRIM 9, 44 (1996) 631

Dana E. Prescott, *The Guardian Ad Litem In Custody and Conflict Cases: Investigator, Champion, and Referee?*, 22 U. ARK. LITTLE ROCK L.J. 529, n.117 (2000) 594

Dana E. Prescott, *The Liability of Lawyers as Guardians Ad Litem: The Best Defense Is a Good Offense*, 11 J. AM. ACAD. MATRIM. L. 65 (1993) 594, 611

Philip J. Prygoski, *When a Hearing is Not a Hearing: Irrebuttable Presumptions and Termination of Parental Rights Based on Status*, 44 U. PITT. L. REV. 879 (1983) 803

H. Raffelli, *The Battered Child—An Overview of a Medical, Legal, and Social Problem*, 16 CRIME & DELINQ. 139, 140 (1970) 687

Hon. W. Don Reader, *They Grow Up So Fast: When Juveniles Commit Adult Crimes: The Laws of Unintended Results*, 29 AKRON L. REV. 477 (1996) 45

G.M. Realmuto et al., *Specificity and Sensitivity of Sexually Anatomically Correct Dolls in Substantiating Abuse: A Pilot Study*, 19 J. AM. ACADEMIC OF CHILD & ADOLESCENT PSYCHIATRY 743-46 (1990) 705

Douglas R. Rendleman, *Parens Patriae: From Chancery to the Juvenile Court*, 23 S.C. L. REV. 205, 213-23, 239-58 (1971) 4, 10, 12-13

John Robert Renner, *The Indian Child Welfare Act and Equal Protection Limitations on Federal Power Over Indian Affairs*, 17 AM. INDIAN L. REV. 129, 156-68 (1992) 581

Tom Richoff & Curtis Cukjati, *Protecting the Fetus From Maternal Drug and Alcohol Abuse: A Proposal for Texas*, 21 ST. MARY'S L.J. 259, 267-68 (1988) 678

Dorothy Roberts, *The Challenge of Substance Abuse for Family Preservation Policy*, 3 J. HEALTH CARE L. & POL'Y 72 (1999) 533

Milton Roberts, Annotation, *Admissibility of Expert Medical Testimony on Battered Child Syndrome*, 98 A.L.R.3D 306 (1980) 688

Rose & Meezan, *Defining Child Neglect: Evolution, Influences, and Issues*, 67 SOC. SERV. REV. 279 (1993) 424

Cathryn Jo Rosen & John S. Goldkamp, *The Constitutionality of Drug Testing at the Bail Stage*, 80 J. CRIM. L. & CRIMINOLOGY 114 (1989) 308

Cathryn Jo Rosen, *The Fourth Amendment Implications of Urine Testing for Evidence of Drug Use in Probation*, 55 BROOK. L. REV. 1159, 1176-77, 1199-1201, 1205 (1990) 308

Alan Rosenbaum & Daniel O'Leary, *Children: The Unintended Victims of Marital Violence*, 51 AM. J. ORTHOPSYCHIATRY 692, 698 (1991) 446

Irene Merker Rosenberg, *A Door Left Open: Applicability of the Fourth Amendment Exclusionary Rule to Juvenile Court Delinquency Hearings*, 24 AM. J. CRIM. L. 29, 31 (1996) 75-76

Irene Merker Rosenberg, Schall v. Martin*: A Child is a Child is a Child*, 12 AM. J. CRIM. L. 253 (1984) 84

Irene Merker Rosenberg, Winship *Redux: 1970 to 1990*, 69 TEX. L. REV. 109, 123 (1990) 236

Ralph A. Rossum, *Holding Juveniles Accountable: Reforming America's "Juvenile Justice System"*, 22 PEPP. L. REV. 907 (1997) 334

Sander N. Rothchild, *Beyond Incarceration: Juvenile Sex Offender Treatment Programs Offer Youth a Second Chance*, 4 J.L. & POL'Y 719 (1996) 866

Harry J. Rothgerber, Jr., *The Bootstrapping of Status Offenders: A Vicious Practice*, KY. CHILDREN'S RTS. J. 1, 3 (July 1991) 27

Kelly C. Rozmus, *Representing Families Affected by HIV/AIDS: How the Proposed Standby Guardianship Act Facilitates Future Planning in the Best Interests of the Child and Family*, 6 AM. U. J. GENDER & L. 299, 303-08 (1998) 810-12

Sandra C. Ruffin, *Postmodernism, Spirit Healing, and the Proposed Amendments to the Indian Child Welfare Act*, 30 MCGEORGE L. REV. 1221, 1249 (1999) 581

George H. Russ, *Through the Eyes of a Child,* "Gregory K."*: A Child's Right to Be Heard*, 27 FAM. L.Q. 365 (1993) 589

Kevin M. Ryan, *Stemming the Tide of Foster Care Runaways: A Due Process Perspective*, 42 CATH. U. L. REV. 271 (1993) 474

Rosemary Shaw Sackett, *Terminating Parental Rights of the Handicapped*, 25 FAM. L.Q. 235, 265-68 (1991) 795

Jamie Heather Sacks, *A New Age of Understanding: Allowing Self-Defense Claims for Battered Children Who Kill Their Abusers*, 10 J. CONTEMP. HEALTH L. & POL'Y 349, 365 (1993) 688

WILEY B. SANDERS, JUVENILE OFFENDERS FOR A THOUSAND YEARS 3-91, 96-313, 331-453 (1970) 2, 5-6

Claire Sandt, *ASFA: From Policy to Practice*, 19 CHILD L. PRAC. 58 (2000) 519

Dena M. Sarke, *Coed Naked Constitutional Law: The Benefits and Harms of Uniform Dress Regulations in American Public Schools*, 78 B.U. L. REV. 153, 167 (1998) 124

Gregory G. Sarno, Annotation, *Admissibility at Criminal Prosecution of Expert Testimony on Battering Parent Syndrome*, 43 A.L.R. 4TH 1203 (1986) 711

Gregory D. Sarno, Annotation, *Parent's Involuntary Confinement, or Failure to Care for Child as Result Thereof, as Evincing Neglect, Unfitness, or the Like in Dependency or Divestiture Proceeding*, 79 A.L.R.3D 417 (1997) 747, 803

Meghan C. Scahill, U.S. DEP'T OF JUST., *Juvenile Delinquency Probation Caseload, 1998-1997* (2000) 267

Laurie Schaffner, *Violence and Female Delinquency: Gender Transgressions and Gender Invisibility*, 14 BERKELEY WOMEN'S L.J. 40 (1999) 21

Lawrence Schlam, *Children in the Law Issue: Contributors Third Party Custody Disputes in Minnesota: Overcoming the "Natural Rights" of Parents or Pursuing the "Best Interests" of Children?*, 26 WM. MITCHELL L. REV. 733 (2000) 631

Lawrence Schalm, *Police Interrogation of Children and State Constitutions: Why Not Videotape the MTV Generation?*, 26 U. TOL. L. REV. 901, 913 (1995) 102

Lawrence Schlam, *Third-Party Standing in Child Custody Disputes: Will Kentucky's New "De Facto Guardian" Provision Help?*, 27 N. KY. L. REV. 368 (2000) 631

ANNE SCHNEIDER, DETERRENCE AND JUVENILE CRIME 5 (1990) 329

IRA M. SCHWARTZ ET AL., THE PERCEPTION AND REALITY OF JUVENILE CRIME IN MICHIGAN at i (1990) 334

Ira M. Schwartz, *Public Attitudes Toward Juvenile Crime and Juvenile Justice Implications for Public Policy*, 13 HAMLINE J. PUB. L. & POL'Y 241, 249 (1992) 334

Elizabeth S. Scott et al., *Evaluating Adolescent Decision Making in Legal Contexts*, 19 LAW & HUMAN BEHAV. 221 (1995) 432

JAMES SELKIN, THE CHILD SEXUAL ABUSE CASE IN THE COURTROOM 217 (2d ed. 1991) 705

Robert E. Shepherd, Jr., *The "Child" Grows Up: The Juvenile System Enters Its Second Century*, 33 FAM. L.Q. 589, 596 (1996) 868

Robert E. Shepherd, Jr., *Issues Involving Children*, 32 U. RICH. L. REV. 1345, 1377 (1998) 811

Robert E. Shepherd, Jr., *The Juvenile Court at 100: Birthday Cake or Funeral Pyre?*, 13 CRIM. JUST. 47 (1999) 19

Robert E. Shepherd, Jr., *The Juvenile Court Intake Process*, 5 A.B.A. SEC. CRIM. JUST. 26 (Summer 1990) 68-69

Donald P. Simet, *Power, Uncertainty, and Choice: The Voluntary Commitment of Children*—Parham v. J.R., 19 J. FAM. L. 27 (1980-1981) 862

CLIFFORD E. SIMONSEN, JUVENILE JUSTICE IN AMERICA 10-11 (1991) 2

Amy Sinden, *In Search of Affirmative Duties Toward Children Under a Post-*DeShaney *Constitution*, 139 U. PA. L. REV. 227 (1990) 475

Amy Sinden, *"Why Won't Mom Cooperate?": A Critique of Informalities in Child Proceedings*, 11 YALE J.L & FEMINISM 339 (1999) 505

Garret Smith, DeShaney v. Winnebago County, *The Narrowing Scope of Constitutional Torts*, 49 MD. L. REV. 484 (1990) 475

Joel E. Smith, Annotation, *Right of Indigent Parent to Appointed Counsel In Proceeding for Involuntary Termination of Parental Rights*, 80 A.L.R.3D 1141 (1977) 755

Pamela J. Smith, *Looking Beyond Traditional Educational Paradigms: When Old Victims Become New Victimizers*, 23 HAMLINE L. REV. 101 (1999) 343, 345

Susan C. Smith, *Abused Children Who Kill Abusive Parents: Moving Toward an Appropriate Legal Response*, 42 CATH. U. L. REV. 141 (1992) 688

Jessica Smith, *"Student-Initiated" Prayer: Assessing the Newest Initiatives to Return Prayer to the Public Schools*, 18 CAMPBELL L. REV. 303 (1996) 132

Todd R. Smyth, *Foster Parent's Right to Immunity From Foster Child's Negligence Claims*, 55 A.L.R.4TH 778 (1987) 636

Howard N. Snyder, U.S. DEP'T OF JUST., *Juvenile Arrests 1999* 1-7 (2000) 869

Sonja A. Soehnel, *Governmental Tort Liability for Social Service Agency's Negligence in Placement, or Supervision After Placement, of Children*, 90 A.L.R.3D 1214 (1979) 636

Alan Mayer Sokobin, *Shaken Baby Syndrome: A Comparative Study: Anglo-American Law and Jewish Law—Legal, Moral, and Ethical Issues*, 29 U. TOL. L. REV. 513 (1998) 666

Toby Solomon & James B. Boskey, *In Whose Best Interests: Child v. Parent*, N.J. LAW. MAG., Nov.-Dec. 1993 at 36 (1993) 786

Mary E. Spring, *Extended Jurisdiction Prosecution: A New Approach to the Problem of Juvenile Delinquency in Illinois*, 31 J. MARSHALL L. REV. 1351 (1998) 355

BONNIE STEINBOCK, LIFE BEFORE BIRTH: THE MORAL AND LEGAL STATUS OF EMBRYOS AND FETUSES 127-63 (1992) 674

David J. Steinhart, *Status Offenses*, 6 FUTURE OF CHILDREN 86 (1996) 41

Carol S. Stevenson, et al., *The Juvenile Court: Analysis and Recommendations*, 6 FUTURE OF CHILDREN 4, 13-14 (1996) 41

Denise C. Stiffarm, *The Indian Child Welfare Act: Guiding the Determination of Good Cause to Depart From the Statutory Placement Preferences*, 70 WASH. L. REV. 1151 (1995) 581

Carla J. Stovall, *Justice and Juveniles in Kansas: Where We Have Been and Where We Are Headed*, 47 U. KAN. L. REV. 101, 107 (1999) 594

Martin Strassburg, *Justice for Juveniles? The Second Circuit Declares Juvenile Prevention Detention Statute Unconstitutional*, 50 BROOK. L. REV. 517 (1984) 332

Suzanne D. Strater, *The Juvenile Death Penalty: In the Best Interests of the Child?*, 26 LOY. U. CHI. L.J. (1995) 375

Victor L. Streib, *Death Penalty for Children: The American Experience with Capital Punishment for Crimes Committed While Under Age Eighteen*, 36 OKLA. L. REV. 613, 619 (1983) 2

Victor L. Streib, *The Eighth Amendment and Capital Punishment of Juveniles*, 34 CLEV. ST. L. REV. 363 (1989) 375

Victor L. Streib, *Moratorium on the Death Penalty for Juveniles*, 61 LAW & CONTEMP. PROBS. 55, 65 (1998) 374

Victor L. Streib & Lynn Sametz, *Executing Female Juveniles*, 22 CONN. L. REV. 3 (1989) 375

Roland C. Summit, *The Child Sexual Abuse Accommodation Syndrome*, 7 CHILD ABUSE & NEGLECT 133 (1983) 405

Kim Susser, *Weighing the Domestic Violence Factor in Custody Cases: Tipping the Scales in Favor of Protecting Victims and Their Children*, 27 FORDHAM URB. L.J. 875 (2000) 446

Karen Tapp, *The Guardian Ad Litem or Special Advocate Appointment Pursuant to KRS 26A.140*, 5 KY. CHILDREN'S RTS. J. 19 (1997) 595

Jody Tabnor Thayer, *The Latest Evidence for Shaken Baby Syndrome: What Defense Lawyers and Prosecutors Need to Know*, 12 CRIM. JUST. 15 (1997) 666

Charles W. Thomas & Shay Bilchik, *Criminal Law: Prosecuting Juveniles in Criminal Courts: A Legal and Empirical Analysis*, 76 J. CRIM. L. & CRIMINOLOGY 439 (1985) 45

Tim A. Thomas, Annotation, *Defense of Infancy in Juvenile Delinquency Proceedings*, 83 A.L.R.4TH 1135 (1991) 48

T.P. Thornberry, *Membership in Youth Gangs and Involvement in Serious and Violent Offending*, *in* SERIOUS AND VIOLENT OFFENDERS: RISK FACTORS AND SUCCESSFUL INTERVENTIONS 147-66 (1998) 62

Amy M. Thorsen, *From Parens Patriae to Crime Control: A Comparison of the History and Effectiveness of the Juvenile Justice Systems in the United States and Canada*, 16 ARIZ. J. INT'L & COMP. L. 845, 862 (1999) 343

Kimberly A. Tolhurst, *A Search for Solutions: Evaluating the Latest Anti-Stalking Developments and the National Institute of Justice Model Stalking Code*, 1 WM. & MARY J. WOMEN & L. 269 (1994) 332

Alma Tolliver, *Child Abuse Statute Expanded to Protect Viable Fetus: The Abusive Effects of South Carolina's Interpretation of the Word "Child"*, 24 S. ILL. U. L.J. 383 (2000) 675

Anastasia Toufexis, *Innocent Victims*, TIME, May 13, 1991, at 56, 60 674

Joseph B. Tulman & Mary G. Hynes, *Enforcing Special Education Law on Behalf of Incarcerated Children: A Blueprint for Deconstruction*, 18 CHILDREN'S LEGAL RTS. J. 48, 50-51 (1998) 344

Elizabeth Turk, *Abuses and Syndromes: Excuses or Justifications?*, 18 WHITTIER L. REV. 901, 924 (1997) 688

Frank E. Vandervort, *Representing Children in Protective Proceedings: Learning From Michigan's Experience*, 19 CHILD L. PRACTICE 153 (2000) 594

Danny R. Veilleux, Annotation, *Validity, Construction, and Effect of Juvenile Curfew Regulations*, 83 A.L.R.4TH 1056 (1991) 37

Danny R. Veilleux, Annotation, *What Types of Proceedings or Determinations Are Governed by the Uniform Child Custody Jurisdiction Act (UCCJA) or the Parental Kidnapping Prevention Act (PKPA)?*, 78 A.L.R.4TH 1028 (1990) 825

Martin Ventrell, *Evolution of the Dependency Component of the Juvenile Court*, 19 CHILDREN'S LEGAL RTS. J. 1 (Winter 1999-2000) 2, 4, 6

Marvin Ventrell, *Foster Care and Adoption Reform Legislation: Implementing the Adoption and Safe Families Act of 1997*, 14 ST. JOHN'S LEGAL COMMENT. 433, 436 (2000) 594

Anita Vestal, *Mediation and Parental Alienation Syndrome: Considerations for an Intervention Model*, 37 FAM. & CONCILIATION CTS. REV. 487 (1999) 725-26

Wanda Ellen Wakefield, Annotation, *Validity of State Statutes Providing for Termination of Parental Rights*, 22 A.L.R.4TH 774 (1983) 736, 738

James K. Walding, *Whatever Happened to Parham and Institutionalized Juveniles? Do Minors Have Procedural Rights In the Civil Commitment Area?*, 14 LAW & PSYCHOL. REV. 281 (1990) 862

Andrew Walkover, *The Infancy Defense in the New Juvenile Court*, 31 UCLA L. REV. 503 (1984) 48

Greg Waller, *When the Rules Don't Fit the Game: Application of the Uniform Child Custody Jurisdiction Act and the Parental Kidnapping Prevention Act to Interstate Adoption Proceedings*, 33 HARV. J. LEGIS. 271, 284 (1996) 825-26

Thomas J. Walsh, *The Clock is Ticking: Do Time Limits in Wisconsin's Termination of Parental Rights Serve the Best Interests of Children?*, 83 MARQ. L. REV. 743 (2000) 782

Michael R. Walsh & J. Michael Bone, *Parental Alienation Syndrome: An Age-Old Custody Problem*, 71 FLA. B.J. 93 (1997) 725-26

Chris Watkins, *Beyond Status: The Americans With Disabilities Act and the Parental Rights of People Labeled Developmentally Disabled or Mentally Retarded*, 83 CAL. L. REV. 1415, 1428-31 (1995) 817-18

Jane Watson, *Crime and Juvenile Delinquency Prevention Policy: Time for Early Childhood Intervention*, 2 GEO. J. FIGHTING POVERTY 245 (1995) 866

Amy E. Webbink, *Access Denied: Incarcerated Juveniles and Their Right of Access to Courts*, 7 WM. & MARY BILL RTS. J. 613, 627 (1999) 332

Karen C. Wehner, *Daddy Wants Rights Too: A Perspective on Adoption Statutes*, 31 HOUS. L. REV. 691 (1994) 841

Deborah Weimer, *Implementation of Standby Guardianship: Respect for Family Autonomy*, 100 DICK. L. REV. 65, 91 (1995) 810-11

Merle H. Weiner, *Domestic Violence and Custody: Importing the American Law Institute's Principles of the Law of Family Dissolution Into Oregon Law*, 35 WILLAMETTE L. REV. 643, 696 (1999) 560

Ronald D. Wenkart, *Juvenile Offenders, Residential Placement, and Special Education*, 144 ED. LAW REP. 1, 2 (2000) 345

William Wesley, *It Matters Not What Is But What Might Have Been: The Standard of Appellate Review for Denial of Counsel in Child Dependency and Parental Severance Trials*, 12 WHITTIER L. REV. 537 (1991) 505

VERNON WIEHE, PERILOUS RIVALRY: WHEN SIBLINGS BECOME ABUSIVE (1991) 406

Shannon L. Wilbur, *Independent Counsel for Children*, 27 FAM. L.Q. 349 (1993) 601

Beatrice Crofts Yorker & Bernard B. Kahan, *The Munchausen Syndrome By Proxy Varient of Child Abuse in the Family Courts*, 42 JUV. & FAM. CT. J.51-58 (1991) 719

Christina A. Zawsiya, *Protecting the Ties That Bind: Kinship Relative Care in Florida*, 23 NOVA L. REV. 455 (1998) 565

Elise Zealand, *Protecting the Ties That Bind From Behind Bars: A Call for Equal Opportunities for Incarcerated Fathers and Their Children to Maintain the Parent-Child Relationship*, 31 COLUM. J.L. & SOC. PROBS. 247 (1998) 747, 803-04

Elyce H. Zenoff & Alan B. Zeints, M.D., *If Civil Commitment is the Answer for Children, What Are the Questions?*, 51 GEO. WASH. L. REV. 171 (1983) 862

Candace Zierdt, *The Little Engine that Arrived at the Wrong Station: How to Get Juvenile Justice Back on the Right Track*, 33 U.S.F. L. REV. 401 (1999) 4, 19, 45, 866

David M. Zlotnick, *Battered Women and Justice Scalia*, 41 ARIZ. L. REV. 847, 888 (1999) 560

Tony M. Zonda, *Putative Fathers' Rights; Striking the Right Balance in Adoption Laws*, 20 WM. MITCHELL L. REV. 292 (1994) 841

Miscellaneous Documents

ABA Standards of Practice for Lawyers Who Represent Children in Abuse and Neglect Cases, Section B-4 (1996) 601

2 AM. JUR. 2D *Adoption* § 45 (1994) 643

24A AM. JUR. 2D *Divorce and Separation* § 947 (1998) 494

31A AM. JUR. 2D *Expert and Opinion Evidence* § 196 (1989) 710

42 AM. JUR. 2D *Infants* § 150 (2000) 588

42 AM. JUR. 2D *Infants* § 173 (1999) 594

47 AM. JUR. 2D *Juvenile Courts and Delinquent and Dependant Children* § 39 (1995) 494

American Convention on Human Rights, art. 4(5), O.A.S. Official Records, OES/Ser.K/XVI/1.1, Doc. 65, Rev. 1, Corr. 2 (1970) 375

Amnesty Int'l U.S.A., The Death Penalty and Juvenile Offenders (Oct. 1991) 375

Annotation, *Admissibility of Evidence of Battered Children Syndrome on Issue of Self-Defense*, 22 A.L.R.5TH 787, 793 (1994) 688

Annotation, *Propriety of Conditioning Probation on Defendant's Not Associating With Particular Person*, 99 A.L.R.3D 967 (1980) 299

Annotation, *Right of Incarcerated Mother to Retain Custody of Infant in Penal Institution*, 14 A.L.R.4TH 748 (1982) 803

43 C.J.S. *Infant* § 71 (1978) 514

Bureau of Just. Assistance, U.S. DEP'T OF JUST., *Juveniles in Adult Prisons and Jails* 1, 1-3, 19, 28, 71-124 (2000) 173, 278

Committee on Interior and Insular Affairs, House of Representatives Report No. 95-1386 (1978 U.S.C.C.A.N. 7530) 565

Family, Custody, Elderly Issues, 23 MENTAL & PHYSICAL DISABILITY L. REP. 239 (1999) 505

FLORIDA FAMILY LAW HANDBOOK PART I: FLORIDA STATUTES CHAPTER 39 PROCEEDINGS RELATED TO CHILDREN (1998) 604

Geneva Convention Relative to the Protection of Civilian Persons in Time of War, August 22-23, 1949, Art. 68, 6 U.S.T. 3516, 3560, T.I.A.S. No. 3365.75 U.N.T.S. 287 375

IJA-ABA Standards Relating to Adjudication, in JUVENILE JUSTICE STANDARDS ANNOTATED 1, 8, 11-12 (Robert E. Shepherd, Jr., ed., 1996) 243, 244

IJA-ABA Standards Relating to Interim Status: The Release, Control and Detention of Accused Juvenile Offenders Between Arrest and Disposition, in JUVENILE JUSTICE STANDARDS ANNOTATED 119-21, 123-24, 133-34, 136-37 (Robert E. Shepherd, Jr., ed., 1996) 71, 75, 89, 91, 252

IJA-ABA Standards Relating to the Juvenile Probation Function: Intake and Predisposition Investigative Services, in JUVENILE JUSTICE STANDARDS ANNOTATED 155, 161-64 (Robert E. Shepherd, Jr., ed., 1996) 65, 68-70

IJA-ABA Standards Relating to Police Handling of Juvenile Problems, in JUVENILE JUSTICE STANDARDS ANNOTATED 233, 235-36 (Robert E. Shepherd, Jr., ed., 1996) 70

IJA-ABA Standards Relating to Pretrial Court Proceeding, in JUVENILE JUSTICE STANDARDS ANNOTATED 243, 254-55 (Robert E. Shepherd, Jr., ed., 1996) 230

IJA-ABA Standards Relating to Transfer Between Courts, in JUVENILE JUSTICE STANDARDS ANNOTATED 285-92 (Robert E. Shepherd, Jr., ed., 1996) 184, 186

IJA-ABA Standards Relating to Youth Service Agencies, in JUVENILE JUSTICE STANDARDS ANNOTATED 293-97 (Robert E. Shepherd, Jr., ed., 1996) 108

IJA-ABA Juvenile Justice Standards, Authorized Emergency Custody of Endangered Child § 4.1 (1980) 485-86

IJA-ABA Juvenile Justice Standards, Standards for Probation, § 3.2(b) (1980) 299

IJA-ABA Juvenile Justice Standards, Standards Relating to Dispositions, § 3.2(B)(1) (1980) 288

IJA-ABA Juvenile Justice Standards, Standards Relating to Juvenile Delinquency and Sanctions §§ 5.2 & 6.2 374

International Covenant on Civil and Political Rights art. 6(5), Annex to G.A. Res. 220, 21 U.N. GAOR Res. Supp. (No. 16) 53, U.N. Doc. A/6316 (1966) 375

INVESTIGATION AND PROSECUTION OF CHILD ABUSE 80 (2d ed. 1993) 705

Office of Juv. Just. & Delinq. Prevention, U.S. DEP'T OF JUST., *Delinquency Cases Waived to Criminal Court, 1987-1996* (April 1999) 182

Office of Juv. Just. & Delinq. Prevention, U.S. DEP'T OF JUST., *Juvenile Transfers to Criminal Court in the 1990s: Lessons Learned from Four Studies* xi (Aug. 2000) 183, 195

Office for Victims of Crimes, DEP'T OF JUST., *Victims, Judges, and Juveniles: Court Reform Through Restorative Justice* 4 (2000) 867-68

RESTATEMENT (SECOND) OF TORTS § 147, 150 (1965) 397-98

U.S. DEP'T OF JUST., *An Evolving Juvenile Court: On the Front Lines with Judge J. Dean Lewis* (1999) 869

U.S. DEP'T OF JUST., *National Estimates of Petitioned Status Offense Cases, in* JUVENILE COURT STATISTICS 37 (1997) 41

U.S. DEP'T OF JUST., *Recidivism of Young Parolees* (1988) 869

Notes, Comments, and Case Notes

Case Digests, *Family Law in the Fifty States 1997-98: Case Digests*, 32 FAM. L.Q. 723 (1999) 595

Comment, *The Supreme Court and Pretrial Detention of Juveniles: A Principled Solution to a Due Process Dilemma*, 132 U. PA. L. REV. 95, 95 (1983) 84-85

Leading Cases, *Leading Cases of the 1983 Term, Pretrial Detention of Juveniles*, 98 HARV. L. REV. 87, 130 (1984) 84-85, 87

Note, *Assessing the Scope of Minors' Fundamental Rights: Juvenile Curfews and the Constitution*, 97 HARV. L. REV. 1163, 1164 n.9 (1984) 35

Note, *Child Neglect: Due Process for the Parent*, 70 COLUM. L. REV. 465 (1970) 505

Note, *The Massachusetts Juvenile Justice System of the 1990s: Re-Thinking a National Model*, 21 NEW ENG. J. ON CRIM. & CIV. CONFINEMENT 339 (1995) 350

Note, *Proposed Standards of Practice For Lawyers Who Represent Children in Abuse and Neglect Cases*, 29 FAM. L.Q. 375 (1995) 594

Deborah Ahrens, Note, *Not in Front of the Children: Prohibition on Child Custody as Civil Branding for Criminal Activity*, 75 N.Y.U. L. REV. 737 (2000) 436

Linda Anderson, Note, United States v. Azure*: Admissibility of Expert Testimony in Child Sexual Abuse Cases*, 15 J. CONTEMP. L. 285 (1989) 699

Thomas B. Anderson, *Recent Decisions, Family Law—Adoption—Foster Parent Standing in Adoption Proceedings—The Pennsylvania Supreme Court Held That Foster Parents Lack Standing to Initiate Adoption Proceedings Absent Consent From Welfare Agency*, 34 DUQ. L. REV. 777 (1966) 622

David R. Barrett et al., Note, *Juvenile Delinquents: The Police, State Courts, and Individualized Justice*, 79 HARV. L. REV. 775, 775 (1966) 68-69

David Line Batty, Note, Michael H. v. Gerald D.*: The Constitutional Rights of Putative Fathers and a Proposal for Reform*, 32 B.C. L. REV. 1173, 1189 (1990) 839

Richard S. Baum, Comment, *Denial of Fourth Amendment Protections in the Pretrial Detention of Juveniles*, 35 SANTA CLARA L. REV. 689 (1995) 86

Stacey L. Best, Comment, *Fetal Equality?: The State's Response to the Challenge of Protecting the Unborn*, 32 LAND & WATER L. REV. 193 (1997) 678

Michael J. Bufkin, Note, *The "Reasonable Efforts" Requirement: Does it Place Children at Risk of Abuse or Neglect?*, 35 U. LOUISVILLE J. FAM. L. 355, 361 (1996-1997) 527

Thomas N. Bulleit, Note, *The Battering Parent Syndrome: Inexpert Testimony as Character Evidence*, 17 U. MICH. J. L. REF. 653, 660 (1984) 711

Roger Burdge, Note, Whitner v. South Carolina*: Child Abuse Laws Apply to Viable Fetuses*, 1 J.L. & FAM. STUD. 277 (1999) 674

Jennifer Burns, Note, *Should Marriage Matter?: Evaluating the Rights of Legal Absentee Fathers*, 68 FORDHAM L. REV. 2299 (2000) 631

Gail Ezra Cary, Casenote, *Evidence—Expert Testimony—The Admissibility of Child Sexual Abuse Accommodation Syndrome in Child Sexual Abuse Prosecutions:* State v. J.Q.*, 130 N.J. 554, 617 A.2d 1196 (1993)*, 26 RUTGERS L.J. 251 (1994) 699

Rose M. Charles & Jennifer V. Zuccarelli, Note, *Serving No "Purpose": The Double-Edged Sword of New York's Juvenile Offender Law*, 12 ST. JOHN'S LEG. COMMENT. 721 (1997) 867

Regina M. Coady, Comment, *Extending Child Abuse Protection to the Viable Fetus:* Whitner v. State of South Carolina, 71 ST. JOHN'S L. REV. 667 (1997) 675

Andrew Cohen, Note, *The Unreliability of Expert Testimony on the Typical Characteristics of Sexual Abuse Victims*, 74 GEO. L.J. 429 (1985) 699

Darin Michael Colucci, Case Comment, *Evidence—The Admissibility of Battered Child Syndrome: Giving a Voice to the Silenced—* Estelle v. McGuire*, 112 S. Ct. 475 (1991)*, 26 SUFFOLK U. L. REV. 1213 (1992) 687

Brian A. Cute, Note, *Methods of Notice in Termination of Parental Rights Hearings*, 5 CONN. PROB. L.J. 317, 325 (1991) 740

Kristen L. Davenport, Note, *Due Process—Claims of Abused Children Against State Protective Agencies—The State's Responsibility After* DeShaney v. Winnebago County Department of Social Services, *489 U.S. 189 (1989)*, 19 FLA. ST. U. L. REV. 243 (1991) 474-75

Claudio DeBellis & Marta B. Soja, Note, Gregory K.*: Child Standing in Parental Termination Proceedings and the Implications of the Foster Parent-Foster Child Relationship on the Best Interest Standard*, 8 ST. JOHN'S J. LEGAL COMMENT. 501 (1993) 588, 644

Terrance J. Dee, Note, *Foster Parent Liability Under Section 1983: Foster Parents' Liability as State Actors for Abuse to Foster Children*, 69 WASH. U. L.Q. 1201 (1991) 636, 649

Cheryl A. DeMichele, Comment, *The Illinois Adoption Act; Should a Child's Length of Time in Foster Care Measure Parental Unfitness?*, 30 LOY. U. CHI. L.J. 727 (1999) 830

Jason Emilios Dimitris, Comment, *Parental Responsibility Statutes—And the Programs That Must Accompany Them*, 27 STETSON L. REV. 655 n.121 (1997) 442

James P. Fisher, Comment, *Capital Punishment for Juveniles—A Constitutional Minimum Set by Elastic Principles*, 16 CAP. U. L. REV. 655 (1987) 375

Steven Fleischer, Note, *Termination of Parental Rights: An Additional Sentence for Incarcerated Parents*, 29 SETON HALL L. REV. 312 (1998) 803

Rosemary L. Flint, Note, *Child Sexual Abuse Accommodation Syndrome: Admissibility Requirements*, 23 AM. J. CRIM. L. 171, 172 (1995) 698

D. Keith Foren, Note, In re Tyvonne M. *Revisited: Criminal Defense in Connecticut*, 18 QUINNIPIAC L. REV. 733 (1999) 48

Krista Gallager, Note, *Parents in Distress: A State's Duty to Provide Reunification Services to Mentally Ill Parents*, 38 FAM. & CONCILIATION CTS. REV. 234 (2000) 491, 796

David A. Geller, Note, *Putting the "Parens" Back Into Parens Patriae: Parental Custody of Juveniles as an Alternative to Pretrial Juvenile Detention*, 21 NEW ENG. J. ON CRIM. & CIV. CONFINEMENT 509, 511 (1995) 85-87

Jeffrey F. Gostyla, Note, *The Needle or the Baby Spoon?—Termination of Parental Rights of a Drug-Abusing Mother in Connecticut*, 7 CONN. PROB. L.J. 279 (1993) 674

Lauren A. Greenberg, Comment, *In God We Trust: Faith Healing Subject to Liability*, 14 J. CONTEMP. HEALTH L. & POL'Y 451 (1998) 432

Bart L. Greenwald, Note, *Irreconcilable Differences: When Children Sue Their Parents for "Divorce,"* 32 U. LOUISVILLE J. FAM. L. 67 (1993-1994) 589

David Adam Hollander, Comment, In re Valerie D.: *The New Word on the Street*, 13 BRIDGEPORT L. REV. 989, 996-1019 (1993) 674

Maria M. Homan, Note, *The Juvenile Death Penalty: Counsel's Role in the Development of a Mitigating Defense*, 53 BROOK. L. REV. 767 (1987) 375

Christine Hunt, Casenotes and Comments, *Criminalizing Prenatal Substance Abuse: A Preventive Means of Ensuring the Birth of a Drug-Free Child*, 33 IDAHO L. REV. 451 (1997) 675

Cathi J. Hunt, Note, *Juvenile Sentencing: Effects of Recent Punitive Sentencing Legislation on Juvenile Offenders and a Proposal for Sentencing in the Juvenile Court*, 19 B.C. THIRD WORLD L.J. 621 (1999) 356

A. Dale Ihrie, III, Comment, *Parental Delinquency: Should Parents Be Criminally Liable for Failing to Supervise Their Children?*, 74 DET. MERCY L. REV. 93 (1996) 442

Nova D. Janssen, Note, *Fetal Rights and the Prosecution of Women for Using Drugs During Pregnancy*, 48 DRAKE L. REV. 741 (2000) 674

Adam D. Kamenstein, Note, *The Inner-Morality of Juvenile Justice: The Case for Consistency and Legality*, 18 CARDOZO L. REV. 2105 (1997) 44

Linda R. Keenen, Note, *Domestic Violence and Custody Litigation: The Need for Statutory Reform*, 13 HOFSTRA L. REV. 407 (1985) 446

Christine H. Kim, Note, *Putting the Reason Back Into Reasonable Efforts Requirement in child Abuse and Neglect Cases*, 1999 U. ILL. L. REV. 287 (1999) 491

Lynn Kirsch, Note, *The Unwed Fathers and Their Newborn Children Placed for Adoption: Protecting the Rights of Both in Custody Disputes*, 36 ARIZ. L. REV. 1011, 1013-17 (1994) 839-40

Eric K. Klein, Note, *Dennis the Menace or Billy the Kid: An Analysis of the Role of Transfer to Criminal Court in Juvenile Justice*, 35 AM. CRIM. L. REV. 371 (1998) 45, 182

Korine L. Larsen, Comment, *With Liberty and Justice for All: Extending the Right to a Jury Trial to the Juvenile Courts*, 20 WM. MITCHELL L. REV. 835 (1994) 244

Jay C. Laubscher, Note, *A Minor of "Sufficient Age and Understanding" Should Have the Right to Petition for the Termination of the Parental Relationship*, 40 N.Y.L. SCH. L. REV. 565, 576 (1996) 589

S'Lee Arthur Hinshaw, II, Comment, *Juvenile Diversion: An Alternative to Juvenile Court*, 1993 J. DISP. RESOL. 305, 312 110

Alison M. Leonard, Note, *Fetal Personhood, Legal Substance Abuse, and Marital Prosecutions: Child Protection or "Gestational Gestapo?"*, 32 NEW ENG. L. REV. 615, 626 (1998) 678

Melanie B. Lewis, Case Note, *Inappropriate Application of the Best Interests of the Child Standard Leads to Worst Case Scenario:* In re C.C.R.S., 68 U. COLO. L. REV. 259 (1997) 781

Lynn M. Matshall, Note, Hutton v. State*: Whose Rights are Paramount, the Dependent's or the Child Victim's?*, 27 U. BALT. L. REV. 291 (1997) 404-05

Nicole S. Mauskopf, Note, *Reaching Beyond the Bars: An Analysis of Prison Nurseries*, 5 CARDOZO WOMEN'S L.J. 101, 114 (1998) 803

Rodger A. Maynes, Note, *The Death Penalty for Juveniles—A Constitutional Alternative*, 7 J. JUV. L. 54 (1983) 375

Stephanie J. Millet, Note, *The Age of Criminal Responsibility in an Era of Violence: Has Great Britain Set a New International Standard?*, 28 VAND. J. TRANSNAT'L L. 295, 232 n.241 (1995) 446

Michelle D. Mills, Comment, *Fetal Abuse Prosecutions: the Triumph of Reaction Over Reason*, 47 DEPAUL L. REV. 989 (1998) 674, 678

Martine E. Mooney, Note, *Assessing the Constitutional Validity of Juvenile Curfew Statutes*, 52 NOTRE DAME L. REV. 858 (1977) 35

Jill D. Moore, Comment, *Charting a Course Between Scylla and Charybdis: Child Abuse Registries and Procedural Due Process*, 73 N.C. L. REV. 2063, 2081 (1995) 385

Teri L. Mosier, Notes, *"Trying to Cure a Seven-Year Itch": The ADA Defense in Termination of Parental Rights*, 37 BRANDEIS L.J. 785, 785 (1998-99) 816-17

Vincent S. Nadile, Note, *Promoting the Integrity of Foster Family Relationships: Needed Statutory Protections for Foster Parents*, 62 NOTRE DAME L. REV. 221 (1987) 649

Corey M. Perman, Note, *Diagnosing the Truth: Determining Physician Liability in Cases Involving Munchausen Syndrome By Proxy*, 54 WASH. U. J. URB. & CONTEMP. L. 267, 271-76 (1998) 719

Russell C. Prince, Case Note, *Evidence—Child Abuse—Expert Medical Testimony Concerning "Battered Children Syndrome" Held Admissible*, 42 FORDHAM L. REV. 935 (1974) 688

Shawn L. Raymond, Note, *Where Are the Reasonable Efforts to Enforce the Reasonable Efforts Requirement?: Monitoring State Compliance Under the Adoption Assistance and Child Welfare Act of 1980*, 77 TEX. L. REV. 1235 (1999) 491

Lourdes M. Rosado, Note, *Minors and the Fourth Amendment: How Juvenile Status Should Invoke Different Standards for Searcher and Seizures on the Street?*, 71 N.Y.U. L. REV. 762, 767 n.43 (1996) 76

Jamie Heather Sacks, Comment, *A New Age of Understanding: Allowing Self-Defense Claims for Battered Children Who Kill Their Abusers*, 10 J. CONTEMP. HEALTH L. & POL'Y 349 (1993) 409

Susan Schwarzenberger, Comment, *Juvenile Probation: Restrictions, Rights, and Rehabilitation*, 16 ST. LOUIS U. L.J. 276, 282-84 (1971) 315, 318

Patricia A. Sexton, Note, *Imposing Criminal Sanctions on Pregnant Drug Users: Throwing the Baby Out With the Bath Water*, 32 WASHBURN L.J. 410 (1993) 675

Kevin W. Shaughnessy, Note, Lassiter v. Department of Social Services: *A New Interest Balancing Test for Indigent Civil Litigants*, 32 CATH. U. L. REV. 261 (1982) 754

Dara Loren Steele, Note, *Expert Testimony: Seeking an Appropriate Admissibility Standard for Behavioral Science in Child Sexual Abuse Prosecutions*, 48 DUKE L.J. 932 (1999) 405

Lidia Stiglich, Comment, *Fourth Amendment Protection for Juvenile Probationeres in California, Slim or None?:* In re Tyrell J., 22 HASTINGS CONST. L.Q. 893, 895 n.10 (1995) 304

Marcy Tench Stovall, Note, *Looking for a Solution:* In re Valerie D. *and State Intervention in Prenatal Drug Abuse*, 25 CONN. L. REV. 1265 (1993) 673-75

Brian R. Suffredini, Note, *Juvenile Gunslingers: A Place for Punitive Philosophy in Rehabilitative Juvenile Justice*, 35 B.C. L. REV. 885 (1994) 21

Mary H. Trainer, Note, *Expanding the Role of Court Appointed Special Advocate Volunteers: the Connecticut Probate Courts*, 13 QUINNIPIAC PROB. L.J. 71, 107 (1998) 589

Eric W. Treene, Note *Prayer-Treatment Exemptions to Child Abuse and Neglect Statutes, Manslaughter Prosecutions and due Process of Law*, 30 HARV. J. ON LEGIS. 135 (1993) 432

Susan Turner, Comment, Parham v. J.R.: *Civil Psychiatric Commitment of Minors*, 5 J. CONTEMP. HEALTH L. & POL'Y 263 (1989) 862

Rachel Venier, Article, *Parental Rights and the Best Interest of the Child: Implications of the Adoption and Safe Families Act of 1997 on Domestic Violence Victim's Rights*, 8 AM. U. J. GENDER SOC. POL'Y & L. 517, 533-49 (2000) 781

Tracy Vollaro, Note, *Munchausen Syndrome By Proxy and Its Evidentiary Problems*, 22 HOFSTRA L. REV. 495, 500-15 (1993) 719-20

Stacy A. Warman, Note, *There's Nothing Psychological About It: Defining a New Role for the Other Mother in a State That Treats Her as Legally Invisible*, 24 NOVA L. REV. 907 (2000) 631

Vanessa L. Warzynski, Comment, *Termination of Parental Rights: The "Psychological Parent" Standard*, 39 VILL. L. REV. 737, 761 (1994) 786

Lois A. Weithorn, Note, *Mental Hospitalization of Troublesome Youth: An Analysis of Skyrocketing Admission Rates*, 40 STAN. L. REV. 773 (1998) 862

Michael Freeman White, Comment, *Dependency Proceedings: What Standard of Proof? An Argument Against the Standard of "Clear and Convincing"*, 14 SAN DIEGO L. REV. 1155 (1977) 510

Beth Wilbourn, Note, *Waiver of Juvenile Court Jurisdiction: National Trends and the Inadequacy of the Texas Response*, 23 AM. J. CRIM. L. 633, 636-37 (1996) 334

Cheri L. Wood, Note, *The Parental Alienation Syndrome: A Dangerous Aura of Reliability*, 27 LOY. L.A. L. REV. 1367 (1994) 726

Claudia Worrell, Note, *Pretrial Detention of Juveniles: Denial of Equal Protection Masked by the Parens Patriae Doctrine*, 95 YALE L.J. 174, 178-79 (1985) 84-85

Joseph F. Yeckel, Note, *Violent Juvenile Offenders: Rethinking Federal Intervention in Juvenile Justice*, 51 WASH. U. J. URB. & CONTEMP. L. 331 (1997) 21

Dianna Younts, Note, *Evaluating and Admitting Expert Opinion Testimony in Child Sexual Abuse Prosecutions*, 41 DUKE L.J. 691, 708 (1991) 705

Daniel C. Zinman, Note, *Father Knows Best: The Unwed Father's Right to Raise His Infant Surrendered for Adoption*, 60 FORDHAM L. REV. 971, 974-77 (1992) 840

Julie J. Zitella, Note, *Protecting the Children: A Call to Reform State Policies to Hold Pregnant Drug Addicts Accountable*, 29 J. MARSHALL L. REV. 765, 765-70 (1996) 673-74